Sample stanza from Einarr Skúlason, *Geisli*

16. Ok hagliga hugðisk
    hrøkkviseiðs ins døkkva
    lyngs í lopt upp ganga
    látrs stríðandi síðan.

    Lét, sás landfolks gætir,
    líknframr himinríki
    umgeypnandi opnask
    alls heims fyr gram snjǫllum.

Ok stríðandi látrs ins døkkva hrøkkviseiðs lyngs hugðisk síðan ganga hagliga upp í lopt. Líknframr umgeypnandi alls heims, sás gætir landfolks, lét himinríki opnask fyr snjǫllum gram.

And the enemy of the lair of the dark coiling fish of the heather [SNAKE > GOLD > GENEROUS MAN] thought then that he went easily up into the air. The outstandingly merciful encompasser [*lit.* holder in hand] of the whole world [= God], who watches over the people of the country, caused the kingdom of heaven to open before the clever king.

Mss: **Flat**(2ra), Bb(117rb); R(35v), T^x(37r), W(81), U(68), A(12v) (*SnE*, ll. 5-8).

Readings: [1] hagliga: *so* Bb, hverlofaðr Flat   [2] -seiðs: baugs Bb   [4] látrs: látr Bb   [5] landfolks: *so* Bb, R, T^x, W, U, A, lands folk Flat   [6] líknframr: líknsamr Bb, A, líkbjartr R, T^x, W, líknbjartr U   [7] umgeypnandi: umgeypnanda T^x; opnask: opna R, T^x, W, U, A.

Editions: *Skj* Einarr Skúlason, 6. *Geisli* 16: AI, 462, BI, 431, *Skald* I, 213; *Flat* 1860-8, I, 2, Cederschiöld 1873, 3, Chase 2005, 66, 137-8; *SnE* 1848-87, I, 450, *SnE* 1931, 159, *SnE* 1998, I, 78.

Context: Lines 5-8 occur in several mss of the *Skm* section of *SnE* among examples of kennings for Christ. Snorri comments: 'Here kennings become ambiguous, and the person interpreting the poetry has to distinguish from the context which king is being referred to. For it is normal to call the emperor of Constantinople king of the Greeks, and similarly the king that rules Palestine, to call him king of Jerusalem ... And the kenning that was quoted above, calling Christ king of men, this kenning can be applied to any king.' (Faulkes 1987, 127-8; cf. *SnE* 1998, I, 78). Snorri was aware of Einarr's use of *double entendre* to associate Óláfr with Christ. — *Notes*: [2] *hagliga* 'easily': The Bb reading is necessary for the rhyme with *hugðisk*. — [6] *líknframr* 'outstandingly merciful': The reading of the *SnE* mss R, T^x and W, *líkbjartr* 'bright in body' offers a viable alternative here, as does U's *líknbjartr* 'bright of (?shining in) mercy'. — [7, 8] *umgeypnandi alls heims* 'encompasser [*lit.* holder in hand] of the whole world': Ps. XCIV.4 (*in manu eius fines terrae* 'in his hands are all the ends of the earth') is probably the inspiration for this kenning, understood here to refer to God even though Snorri Sturluson (see Context) apparently understood it to refer to Christ. Cf. similar periphrases in Anon *Mgr* 2/5, Kálf *Kátr* 36/3, Gamlkan *Has* 29/7-8 and 64/6.

Poetry on Christian Subjects

SKALDIC POETRY OF THE SCANDINAVIAN MIDDLE AGES

Editorial Board under the auspices of the
Centre for Medieval Studies, University of Sydney

Margaret Clunies Ross (University of Sydney)
Kari Ellen Gade (Indiana University)
Guðrún Nordal (Háskóli Íslands)
Edith Marold (Universität Kiel)
Diana Whaley (University of Newcastle upon Tyne)

VOLUME VII

POETRY ON CHRISTIAN SUBJECTS
Part 1: The Twelfth and Thirteenth Centuries

Edited by

Margaret Clunies Ross

BREPOLS

British Library Cataloguing in Publication Data

Poetry on Christian subjects. - (Skaldic poetry of the
   Scandinavian Middle Ages ; v. 7)
   1. Scalds and scaldic poetry 2. Religious poetry, Old Norse
   - Iceland 3. Christian poetry
   I. Ross, Margaret Clunies
   839.6'10080382

   ISBN-13: 9782503518930

© 2007, Brepols Publishers n.v., Turnhout, Belgium

All rights reserved. No part of this publication may be reproduced,
stored in a retrieval system, or transmitted, in any form or by any means,
electronic, mechanical, photocopying, recording, or otherwise,
without the prior permission of the publisher.

D/2007/0095/105
ISBN: 978-2-503-51893-0 (in 2 vols)

Contents

Contents	v
Volume Editor's Preface	ix
Acknowledgements	xi
General Abbreviations	xiii
Sigla Used in Volume VII	xix
Technical Terms	xxxiii
The Contributors	xxxvii
Introduction	xli

Christian Skaldic Poetry: The Corpus
Part 1
The Twelfth Century

Einarr Skúlason, *Geisli* 'Light-beam' (ESk *Geisl*) edited by Martin Chase	5
Níkulás Bergsson, *Jónsdrápa* '*Drápa* about S. John' (Ník *Jóndr*) edited by Beatrice La Farge	66
Gamli kanóki, *Harmsól* 'Sun of Sorrow' (Gamlkan *Has*) edited by Katrina Attwood	70

Gamli kanóki, *Jónsdrápa* 'Drápa about S. John' (Gamlkan *Jóndr*)
  edited by Beatrice La Farge — 133

Anonymous, *Leiðarvísan* 'Way Guidance' (Anon *Leið*)
  edited by Katrina Attwood — 137

Anonymous, *Plácitusdrápa* 'Drápa about Plácitus' (Anon *Pl*)
  edited by Jonna Louis-Jensen and Tarrin Wills — 179

The Thirteenth Century

Kolbeinn Tumason, *Jónsvísur* 'Vísur about S. John' (Kolb *Jónv*)
  edited by Beatrice La Farge — 223

Anonymous, *Líknarbraut* 'Way of Grace' (Anon *Líkn*)
  edited by George Tate — 228

Anonymous, *Sólarljóð* 'Song of the Sun' (Anon *Sól*)
  edited by Carolyne Larrington and Peter Robinson — 287

Anonymous, *Hugsvinnsmál* 'Sayings of the Wise-minded One' (Anon *Hsv*)
  edited by Tarrin Wills and Stefanie Würth — 358

Anonymous, *Heilags anda drápa* 'Drápa about the Holy Spirit' (Anon *Heildr*)
  edited by Katrina Attwood — 450

PART 2

The Fourteenth Century

Anonymous, *Stanzas addressed to Fellow Ecclesiastics* 1 & 2 (Anon *Eccl* 1-2)
  edited by Jonathan Grove — 471

Anonymous, *Máríudrápa* 'Drápa about Mary' (Anon *Mdr*)
  edited by Katrina Attwood — 476

Anonymous, *Gýðingsvísur* 'Vísur about a Jew' (Anon *Gyð*)
  edited by Katrina Attwood — 515

Anonymous, *Brúðkaupsvísur* 'Vísur about a Wedding' (Anon *Brúðv*)
  edited by Valgerður Erna Þorvaldsdóttir — 527

Poetry on Christian Subjects

Anonymous, *Lilja* 'Lily' (Anon *Lil*)
    edited by Martin Chase   554

Anonymous, *Máríuvísur I* '*Vísur* about Mary I' (Anon *Mv I*)
    edited by Kari Ellen Gade   678

Anonymous, *Máríuvísur II* '*Vísur* about Mary II' (Anon *Mv II*)
    edited by Kari Ellen Gade   701

Anonymous, *Máríuvísur III* '*Vísur* about Mary III' (Anon *Mv III*)
    edited by Kari Ellen Gade   718

Anonymous, *Vitnisvísur af Máríu* 'Testimonial *Vísur* about Mary' (Anon *Vitn*)
    edited by Kari Ellen Gade   739

Anonymous, *Drápa af Máríugrát* '*Drápa* about the Lament of Mary' (Anon *Mgr*)
    edited by Kari Ellen Gade   758

Anonymous, *Pétrsdrápa* '*Drápa* about S. Peter' (Anon *Pét*)
    edited by David McDougall   796

Anonymous, *Andreasdrápa* '*Drápa* about S. Andrew' (Anon *Andr*)
    edited by Ian McDougall   845

Anonymous, *Allra postula minnisvísur* 'Celebratory *Vísur* about all the Apostles' (Anon *Alpost*)
    edited by Ian McDougall   852

Anonymous, *Heilagra manna drápa* '*Drápa* about Holy Men' (Anon *Heil*)
    edited by Kirsten Wolf   872

Anonymous, *Heilagra meyja drápa* '*Drápa* about Holy Maidens' (Anon *Mey*)
    edited by Kirsten Wolf   891

Kálfr Hallsson, *Kátrínardrápa* '*Drápa* about S. Catharine' (Kálf *Kátr*)
    edited by Kirsten Wolf   931

Anonymous, *Lausavísa* on Lawgiving (Anon *Law*)
    edited by Jonathan Grove   965

Bibliography 967

Index of First Lines 1001

Indices of Names and Terms
    Index of Ethnic Names 1029
    Index of Indigenous Terms 1030
    Index of Personal Names (incorporating Mythological and Legendary Names) 1030
    Index of Place Names 1037
    Index of Miscellaneous Names 1038

General Index
    LP Abbreviations 1039

VOLUME EDITOR'S PREFACE

In preparing Volume VII of *Skaldic Poetry of the Scandinavian Middle Ages* for publication, I have incurred many debts and the volume as it stands has benefited from the knowledge and advice of many people. It has been a pleasure to work with the fifteen Contributing Editors for this volume, whose research and editing forms the basis for each of the twenty-eight poems presented here. They have answered my many editorial questions promptly, patiently and with good humour. Aside from the presence of some of them at annual skaldic symposia and editorial meetings that the project has held since 2000, all our discussions have been conducted by email and by post. It would not have been possible to produce such a collaborative edition without the internet and, of course, the electronic version of this volume is dependent on it.

Because the edition is a collaborative one, the reader will find that individual editors have imparted their own characteristics to the individual poems presented here, even though all editors have followed the general principles outlined in the project's *Editors' Manual* (Wills *et al.* 2005). We have certainly aimed for consistency in all basic editorial procedures, but inevitably there will be some differences of general approach which will be most apparent in the Notes sections.

My greatest debt of gratitude is to my four fellow General Editors, Kari Ellen Gade, Edith Marold, Guðrún Nordal and Diana Whaley. They have been a wonderful support at all times in what has been a long-lasting and laborious enterprise. Through the process that we call 'quality control', which requires all edited poems to be checked by the remaining four General Editors after the Volume Editor has worked with the Contributing Editors on each poem or set of stanzas, each of the General Editors has been able to contribute her special skills: Kari Gade in the fields of metrics, the normalisation of texts, the treatment of foreign words, and almost everything else besides; Edith Marold particularly on the subject of kennings; Guðrún Nordal, as a native speaker of Icelandic, on acceptable Icelandic prose word order and related questions of usage; and Diana Whaley on all points grammatical and syntactic, as well as on the niceties of the English translation. I should like to give special thanks to Diana and Kari for their meticulous attention to all the finer points of skaldic poetics.

I owe a special debt to Tarrin Wills, who has been a Research Associate and, more recently, Senior Research Associate, on the skaldic editing project from 2002 to the present. Aside from his superb work in developing the project's database, web interface and data entry protocol, which allows us to generate both the hard copy text and the electronic version of the edition, Tarrin has been assiduous and consistent in his devotion to the project and its aims. He has also carried out some of the editing work himself as well as data entry and a host of other tasks. In the period 2006-7 I have also been ably assisted by two Research Assistants, Emily Baynham, who has entered a great deal of material into the skaldic database, and Melanie Heyworth, who has performed bibliographical and other checks.

In the course of preparing this edition, three Contributing Editors have found themselves unable, for personal reasons, to undertake work on some of the texts originally allocated to them, or have been unable to spend as much time as anticipated on the work of editing. I am extremely grateful to Kari Ellen Gade for taking on the editing of five poems about the Virgin Mary at short notice and to Tarrin Wills for stepping in to assist in preparing two poems for this edition, *Plácitusdrápa* and *Hugsvinnsmál*.

At various points in the course of making this volume ready for publication, I have sought specialist advice and I should like to acknowledge here the assistance provided by Anders Andrén of Stockholm University on some archaeological issues relating to *Geisli*, Gottskálk Þ. Jensson of the University of Iceland for assistance with the two Lat. poems Anon *Eccl* 1 and 2, and to Christopher Sanders, of the Dictionary of Old Norse Prose at the University of Copenhagen for advice on the meaning of several poetic words in this volume. Other debts to individuals and institutions are recorded in the Acknowledgements below and in the Notes to individual poems.

Margaret Clunies Ross,
Sydney, April 2007.

Acknowledgements

The editors wish to place on record their gratitude to the two Arnamagnæan Institutes, in Reykjavík and Copenhagen, which have been unstinting in their generosity to the skaldic project. Both Vésteinn Ólason, Director of the Stofnun Árna Magnússonar í íslenzkum fræðum, and Matthew Driscoll, Afdelingsleder, Den arnamagnæanske samling, Nordisk Forskningsinstitut, University of Copenhagen, have been instrumental in giving the project access to their manuscripts and photographic images and in allowing Tarrin Wills to scan them for use on the project's database. They and their colleagues have also been most helpful in numerous other ways, including granting access to the use of library resources. Mention should also be made of the generosity of Professor Jonna Louis-Jensen, who gave us access to the card index of skaldic verse commissioned in the 1950s by Jón Helgason. This resource, which is held by the Arnamagnæan Collection in Copenhagen, has proved very useful to the project.

We would also like to thank the staff of the Dictionary of Old Norse Prose, Nordisk Forskningsinstitut, University of Copenhagen, especially Christopher Sanders, for assistance with the meanings of words that occur in our corpus and for allowing us to link our database to their on-line resources.

It would not have been possible to carry out the skaldic editing project as a whole, and produce this volume in particular, without the support of the Australian Research Council. Margaret Clunies Ross has had a Discovery grant from the ARC during the years 2002-6, and again from 2007-9, which has enabled her to fund the position of Tarrin Wills as Research Associate, now Senior Research Associate, on the skaldic project, as well as essential travel, access to archives and other resources. In addition, the grant has allowed the employment of Research Assistants Emily Baynham and Dr Melanie Heyworth during 2006-7.

Valgerður Erna Þorvaldsdóttir has assisted in the preparation of Volume VII by undertaking transcriptions of a number of poems from manuscripts in the Stofnun Árna Magnússonar in Reykjavík. We are indebted to Professor Guðrún Nordal for making funds available for Valgerður's employment from a research grant awarded to her by the Icelandic Research Council.

Several Contributing Editors wish to acknowledge sources of funding support for their work on this edition. Martin Chase acknowledges the support of Bishop Jóhannes Gijsen, Reykjavík, the American Philosophical Society, Fordham University, the Sankt Lioba Kloster, Copenhagen, as well as the two Arnamagnæan Collections in Reykjavík and Copenhagen, together with the Dictionary of Old Norse Prose, Nordisk Forskningsinstitut, University of Copenhagen. Carolyne Larrington and Peter Robinson thank the British Academy; they also thank Matthew Driscoll and Ragnheiður Mósesdóttir for their contribution to an early stage of their *Sólarljóð* project and Antje Frotscher for her more recent assistance. Kirsten Wolf acknowledges the summer research funding support of the Graduate School at the University of Wisconsin-Madison.

The series logo, designed by Dr Peter Hupfauf of Sydney, is based upon an element in the decoration of the medieval stave church at Urnes, Norway. The editors are grateful to the Society for the Protection of Ancient Monuments (Fortidsminneforeningen) of Sogn and Fjordane, Norway, for permission to use this design element.

General Abbreviations

Note that sigla for all ON-Icel. poetry referred to in this edn are to be found in the List of sigla, with the exception of abbreviations for poems of the Elder Edda (which are listed below), while abbreviated references to ON-Icel. prose texts, journals and frequently cited books or articles are to be found listed in alphabetical order in the Bibliography. All other abbreviations are listed here.

Abbreviations are used in all parts of the edn, except at the beginnings of sentences and in the Introduction. Note that plurals of abbreviated words are written in full, e.g. 'infinitives', 'adverbs', unless pl. forms are listed below, e.g. 'll.', 'vv.'.

Grammatical and Linguistic Abbreviations

acc.	accusative
adj.	adjective
adv.	adverb
cl.	clause
comp.	comparative
conj.	conjunction
cpd	compound
dat.	dative
def. art.	definite article
e-m	*einhverjum*
e-n	*einhvern*
e-r	*einnhverr*
e-rar	*einhverrar*
e-ri	*einhverri*
e-s	*einhvers*
e-t	*eitthvat*
e-u	*einhverju*
f.	feminine
gen.	genitive
imp.	imperative
indef.	indefinite

indic.	indicative
inf.	infinitive
instr.	instrumental
interrog.	interrogative
m.	masculine
m.v.	middle voice
n.	neuter
nom.	nominative
perf.	perfect
pers. n.	personal name
pl.	plural
poss.	possessive
p. n.	place name
p.p.	past participle
prep.	preposition
pres.	present
pres. part.	present participle
pret.	preterite
pron.	pronoun
refl.	reflexive
rel.	relative (clause, pronoun)
sg.	singular
subj.	subjunctive
sup.	superlative
1st pers.	first person
2nd pers.	second person
3rd pers.	third person

Abbreviations for Languages

Goth.	Gothic
Gk	Greek
Lat.	Latin
ME	Middle English
MIcel.	Modern Icelandic
MHG	Middle High German
MLat.	Medieval Latin
MLG	Middle Low German
MNorw	Modern Norwegian
ON	Old Norse (used where differentiation between individual early Nordic [*norrænn*] languages is not necessary or possible)
OEN	Old East Norse
OWN	Old West Norse

(O)Dan.	(Old) Danish
(O)Icel.	(Old) Icelandic
(O)Norw.	(Old) Norwegian
(O)Swed.	(Old) Swedish
OE	Old English
OHG	Old High German
OS	Old Saxon
OFris.	Old Frisian
OFr.	Old French
OIr.	Old Irish

Sigla for Manuscript Collections

Adv	Advocates Library, National Library of Scotland, Edinburgh
AM	The Arnamagnæan Collection (Reykjavík, Stofnun Árna Magnússonar í íslenskum fræðum and Copenhagen, Den arnamagnæanske samling, Nordisk Forskningsinstitut, University of Copenhagen)
BL	British Library, London
BLAdd	British Library: Additional Manuscripts
Bodl Boreal	Bodleian Library Oxford, manuscripts from the collection of Finnur Magnússon
DG	Delagardieska samlingen, Uppsala Universitetsbibliotek
GKS	Den gamle kongelige samling, Det kongelige bibliotek, Copenhagen
Holm	Kungliga biblioteket, Stockholm
ÍB	Safn Hins íslenska bókmenntafélags, deildar þess í Kaupmannahöfn, Landsbókasafn Íslands, Reykjavík
ÍBR	Handritasafn Reykjavíkurdeildar Hins íslenska bókmenntafélags, Landsbókasafn Íslands, Reykjavík
JS	Safn Jóns Sigurðarsonar, Landsbókasafn Íslands, Reykjavík
Lbs	Handritasafn Landsbókasafns Íslands, Reykjavík
NKS	Den nye kongelige samling, Det kongelige bibliotek, Copenhagen & Stofnun Árna Magnússonar í íslenskum fræðum, Reykjavík
Oslo UB	Universitetsbiblioteket i Oslo
Thott	Thotts samling, Det kongelige bibliotek, Copenhagen
DKNVSB	Det Kongelige Norske Videnskabers Selskabs Bibliotek, Universitetsbiblioteket i Trondheim
UppsUB	Uppsala Universitetsbibliotek

Abbreviated references to poems of the Elder Edda in Vol. VII

Akv	*Atlakviða*
Am	*Atlamál*
Fáfn	*Fáfnismál*
Fj	*Fjǫlsvinnsmál*

Grí	*Grímnismál*
Grp	*Grípisspá*
Góg	*Gógaldr*
Grott	*Grottasǫngr*
Hávm	*Hávamál*
HHund I	*Helgakviða Hundingsbana I*
HHund II	*Helgakviða Hundingsbana II*
Hym	*Hymiskviða*
Lok	*Lokasenna*
Sigsk	*Sigurðarkviða hin skamma*
Skí	*Skírnismál*
Vafþ	*Vafþrúðismál*
Vsp	*Vǫluspá*
Þry	*Þrymskviða*

Other abbreviations

ÁM	Árni Magnússon
c.	circa
C10th	tenth century (and similarly for references to other centuries)
ch.	chapter
chs	chapters
d.	died
ed.	editor, edited (by)
edn	edition
eds	editors, editions
fol.	folio
fols	folios
hap. leg.	*hapax legomenon* (pl. *legomena*) — unique word(s)
l.	line
ll.	lines
lit.	literally (used in translations [italicised] and notes [roman])
lv.	*lausavísa*
lvv.	*lausavísur*
ms.	manuscript
mss	manuscripts
n.	note (but e.g. Anm. if notes are labelled as such in the source)
no.	number
p.	page
pp.	pages
r.	reigned (of regnal dates of kings, earls etc.)
S.	Saint
SS.	Saints

sp.	spelt/spelled
st.	stanza
sts	stanzas
v.	verse
vv.	verses
vol.	volume
w. o.	word order
*	reconstructed form, e.g. a hypothetical etymon
†	obelos symbol for textual material that is impossibly corrupt or cannot be made sense of. One † is placed immediately before the beginning of the piece of corrupt text and another immediately after it.

Sigla used in this volume

Sigla for individual stanzas are included where the numbering differs from that in *Skj*.

Alpost = Anon *Alpost*
ÁmÁrn[IV] — Vol. 4. Ámundi Árnason
   Skj: Ámundi Árnason (AII, 50-1; BII, 58-9)
ÁmÁrn Lv[IV] — Vol. 4. Ámundi Árnason, Lausavísur
   Skj: Ámundi Árnason: Lausavísur (AII, 50-1; BII, 58-9)
Andr = Anon *Andr*
Angantýr Lv 11[I] (*Heiðr* 48) — Vol. 8. *Hervarar saga ok Heiðreks* 48 (Angantýr Árngrímsson, Lausavísur, 11)
   Skj: Anonyme digte og vers [XIII]: E. 5. Vers af Fornaldarsagaer: Af Hervararsaga III 22 (AII, 249; BII, 269)
Anon 732b[III] — Vol. 3. Anonymous, Lausavísur from AM 732 b 4°
   Skj: [Anonyme digte og vers XIV]: A. 10. Løse vers (AII, 463; BII, 495-6)
Anon *Alpost* — Vol. 7. Anonymous, *Allra postula minnisvísur*
   Skj: [Anonyme digte og vers XIV]: [B. 9]. Allra postula minnisvísur (AII, 509-11; BII, 559-62)
Anon *Andr* — Vol. 7. Anonymous, *Andréasdrápa*
   Skj: [Anonyme digte og vers XIV]: [B. 8]. Af et digt om Andreas (AII, 508-9; BII, 558-9)
Anon *Bjúgvís*[III] — Vol. 3. Anonymous, *Bjúgar vísur*
   Skj: Anonyme digte og vers [XII]: G [3]. Bjúgar vísur (AI, 626; BI, 634)
Anon *Brúðv* — Vol. 7. Anonymous, *Brúðkaupsvísur*
   Not in *Skj*
Anon *Darr*[V] (*Nj*) — Vol. 5. *Njáls saga* (Anonymous, *Darraðarljóð*)
   Skj: Anonyme digte om historiske personer og begivenheder [XI]: [1]. Darraðarljóð (AI, 419-21; BI, 389-91)
Anon *Eccl* — Vol. 7. Anonymous, *Stanzas Addressed to Fellow Ecclesiastics*
   Not in *Skj*
Anon (*FoGT*) 6[III] — Vol. 3. Anonymous, Stanzas from the *Fourth Grammatical Treatise*, 6
   Skj: Anonyme digte og vers [XIII]: [C]. D. Religiøse og moraliserende vers af den 4. grammatiske afhandling 3 (AII, 163; BII, 180)

Anon (*FoGT*) 12[III] — Vol. 3. Anonymous, Stanzas from the *Fourth Grammatical Treatise*, 12
    Skj: Anonyme digte og vers [XIII]: [C]. D. Religiøse og moraliserende vers af den 4.
    grammatiske afhandling 4 (AII, 163-4; BII, 180)
Anon (*FoGT*) 35[III] — Vol. 3. Anonymous, Stanzas from the *Fourth Grammatical Treatise*, 35
    Skj: Anonyme digte og vers [XIII]: [C]. D. Religiøse og moraliserende vers af den 4.
    grammatiske afhandling 11 (AII, 165; BII, 182)
Anon *Hafg*[IV] — Vol. 4. Anonymous, *Hafgerðingadrápa*
    Skj: Anonyme digte og vers [X]: I. A. [5]. Hafgerðingadrápa (AI, 177; BI, 167)
Anon *Heildr* — Vol. 7. Anonymous, *Heilags anda drápa*
    Skj: Anonyme digte og vers [XIII]: C. [3]. Heilags anda vísur (AII, 160-3; BII, 175-80)
Anon (*Hrafn*) 8[IV] — Vol. 4. Anonymous, Stanzas from *Hrafns saga*, 8
    Skj: Anonyme digte og vers [XIII]: B. Anonyme løse vers angående bestemte historiske
    begivenheder 8 (AII, 139; BII, 148-9)
Anon *Kálfv*[III] — Vol. 3. Anonymous, *Kálfsvísa*
    Skj: Anonyme digte og vers [XII]: I. II. Þulur: Kálfsvísa (AI, 650; BI, 656-7)
Anon *Law* — Vol. 7. Anonymous, *Lausavísa on Lawgiving*
    Skj: [Anonyme digte og vers XIV]: A. 10. Løse vers 3 (AII, 463; BII, 496)
Anon *Leið* — Vol. 7. Anonymous, *Leiðarvísan*
    Skj: Anonyme digte og vers [XII]: G [2]. Leiðarvísan (AI, 618-26; BI, 622-33)
Anon *Líkn* — Vol. 7. Anonymous, *Líknarbraut*
    Skj: Anonyme digte og vers [XIII]: C. 1. Líknarbraut (AII, 150-9; BII, 160-74)
Anon *Lil* — Vol. 7. Anonymous, *Lilja*
    Skj: Eysteinn Ásgrímsson: Lilja (AII, 363-95; BII, 390-416)
Anon *Mdr* — Vol. 7. Anonymous, *Máríudrápa*
    Skj: [Anonyme digte og vers XIV]: [B. 1]. En drape om jomfru Maria (Máríudrápa)
    (AII, 464-72; BII, 496-505)
Anon *Mey* — Vol. 7. Anonymous, *Heilagra meyja drápa*
    Skj: [Anonyme digte og vers XIV]: [B. 12]. Af heilogum meyjum (AII, 526-39; BII,
    582-97)
Anon *Mfl*[III] — Vol. 3. Anonymous, *Máríuflokkr*
    Skj: Anonyme digte og vers [XII]: G [4]. Máríuflokkr (AI, 627; BI, 634)
Anon *Mgr* — Vol. 7. Anonymous, *Drápa af Máríugrát*
    Skj: [Anonyme digte og vers XIV]: [B. 2]. Máríugrátr (AII, 472-82; BII, 505-19)
Anon (*MH*) 1[II] — Vol. 2. Anonymous, Stanzas from *Magnúss saga góða ok Haralds
    harðráða*, 1
    Skj: Anonyme digte om historiske personer og begivenheder [XI]: [7]. Lausavísur 5
    (AI, 425; BI, 395)
Anon *Mhkv*[III] — Vol. 3. Anonymous, *Málsháttakvæði*
    Skj: Anonyme digte og vers [XIII]: A. [1]. Málsháttakvæði (AII, 130-6; BII, 138-45)
Anon *Morg*[III] — Vol. 3. Anonymous, *Morginsól*
    Skj: Anonyme digte og vers [XII]: A. 2. Morginsól (AI, 590; BI, 590)

Anon *Mv I* — Vol. 7. Anonymous, *Máríuvísur I*
   Skj: [Anonyme digte og vers XIV]: [B. 4]. Et digt om Marias jærtegn (AII, 487-92; BII, 526-32)
Anon *Mv II* — Vol. 7. Anonymous, *Máríuvísur II*
   Skj: [Anonyme digte og vers XIV]: [B. 5]. En digt om et andet Maria-jærtegn (AII, 492-6; BII, 532-38)
Anon *Mv III* — Vol. 7. Anonymous, *Máríuvísur III*
   Skj: [Anonyme digte og vers XIV]: [B. 6]. Et digt om et tredje Maria-jærtegn (AII, 496-500; BII, 538-45)
Anon *Níkdr*[III] — Vol. 3. Anonymous, *Níkulásdrápa*
   Skj: Anonyme digte og vers [XIII]: C. [2]. Níkulásdrápa (AII, 160; BII, 174-5)
Anon *Nkt*[II] — Vol. 2. Anonymous, *Nóregs konungatal*
   Skj: Anonyme digte og vers [XII]: [0. 2]. Nóregs konunga-tal (AI, 579-89; BI, 575-90)
Anon *Nkt* 69[II] — Vol. 2. Anonymous, *Nóregs konungatal*, 69
   Skj: Anonyme digte og vers [XII]: [0. 2]. Nóregs konunga-tal 77 (AI, 589; BI, 589)
Anon *Ól*[I] — Vol. 1. Anonymous, *Poem about Óláfr Tryggvason*
   Skj: [Anonyme digte og vers XIV]: A. 9. Af et digt om Olaf Tryggvason (AII, 462-3; BII, 494-5)
Anon *Óldr*[I] — Vol. 1. Anonymous, *Óláfs drápa Tryggvasonar*
   Skj: Anonyme digte og vers [XII]: [0. 1]. Óláfs drápa Tryggvasonar (AI, 573-8; BI, 567-74)
Anon *Pét* — Vol. 7. Anonymous, *Pétrsdrápa*
   Skj: [Anonyme digte og vers XIV]: [B. 7]. En drape om apostlen Peder (AII, 500-8; BII, 545-58)
Anon *Pl* — Vol. 7. Anonymous, *Plácitusdrápa*
   Skj: Anonyme digte og vers [XII]: G [1]. Plácítúsdrápa (AI, 607-18; BI, 606-22)
Anon *Sól* — Vol. 7. Anonymous, *Sólarljóð*
   Skj: Anonyme digte og vers [XII]: G [6]. Sólarljóð (AI, 628-40; BI, 635-48)
Anon (*Stu*) 21[IV] — Vol. 4. Anonymous, Stanzas from *Sturlunga saga*, 21
   Skj: Anonyme digte og vers [XIII]: B. Anonyme løse vers angående bestemte historiske begivenheder 17 (AII, 141; BII, 151)
Anon (*TGT*) 21[III] — Vol. 3. Anonymous, Stanzas from the *Third Grammatical Treatise*, 21
   Skj: Anonyme digte og vers [XII]: G [5]. Andre religiøse vers og herhen hørende digtbrudstykker 1 (AI, 627; BI, 634)
Anon *Vítn* — Vol. 7. Anonymous, *Vitnisvísur af Maríu*
   Skj: [Anonyme digte og vers XIV]: [B. 3]. Vitnisvísur af Maríu (AII, 483-7; BII, 520-6)
Anon *Þorgþ I*[III] — Vol. 3. Anonymous, *Þorgrímspula a*
   Skj: Anonyme digte og vers [XII]: I. I. [a]. Þulur: Þórgrímsþula (AI, 649-50; BI, 656)
Arn[II] — Vol. 2. Arnórr Þórðarson jarlaskáld
   Skj: Arnórr Þórðarson jarlaskáld (AI, 332-54; BI, 305-27)

Arn Frag^III — Vol. 3. Arnórr Þórðarson jarlaskáld, Fragments
  Skj: Arnórr Þórðarson jarlaskáld: 7. Vers af ubestemmelige digte, samt én lausavísa (AI, 353-4; BI, 326-7)
Arn Hardr^II — Vol. 2. Arnórr Þórðarson jarlaskáld, Haraldsdrápa
  Skj: Arnórr Þórðarson jarlaskáld: 6. Erfidrápa om kong Harald hårdråde (AI, 349-53; BI, 322-6)
Arn Hardr 17^II — Vol. 2. Arnórr Þórðarson jarlaskáld, Haraldsdrápa, 17
  Skj: Arnórr Þórðarson jarlaskáld: 6. Erfidrápa om kong Harald hårdråde 19 (AI, 353; BI, 326)
Arn Hryn^II — Vol. 2. Arnórr Þórðarson jarlaskáld, Hrynhenda, Magnússdrápa
  Skj: Arnórr Þórðarson jarlaskáld: 2. Hrynhenda, Magnúsdrápa (AI, 332-8; BI, 306-11)
Arn Hryn 1^II — Vol. 2. Arnórr Þórðarson jarlaskáld, Hrynhenda, Magnússdrápa, 1
  Skj: Arnórr Þórðarson jarlaskáld: 2. Hrynhenda, Magnúsdrápa 2 (AI, 333; BI, 306)
Arn Hryn 3^II — Vol. 2. Arnórr Þórðarson jarlaskáld, Hrynhenda, Magnússdrápa, 3
  Skj: Arnórr Þórðarson jarlaskáld: 2. Hrynhenda, Magnúsdrápa 1 (AI, 332-3; BI, 306)
Arn Magndr^II — Vol. 2. Arnórr Þórðarson jarlaskáld, Magnússdrápa
  Skj: Arnórr Þórðarson jarlaskáld: 3. Magnúsdrápa (AI, 338-43; BI, 311-15)
Arn Rǫgndr^III — Vol. 3. Arnórr Þórðarson jarlaskáld, Rǫgnvaldsdrápa
  Skj: Arnórr Þórðarson jarlaskáld: 1. Rǫgnvaldsdrápa (AI, 332; BI, 305-6)
Arn Þorfdr^II — Vol. 2. Arnórr Þórðarson jarlaskáld, Þorfinnsdrápa
  Skj: Arnórr Þórðarson jarlaskáld: 5. Þórfinnsdrápa (AI, 343-8; BI, 316-21)
Arngr^IV — Vol. 4. Arngrímr ábóti Brandsson
  Skj: Arngrímr ábóti Brandsson (AII, 348-63; BII, 371-90)
Arngr Gd^IV — Vol. 4. Arngrímr ábóti Brandsson, Guðmundardrápa
  Skj: Arngrímr ábóti Brandsson: 1. Guðmundar kvæði (drápa?) byskups (AII, 348-63; BII, 371-89)
Arngr Guðkv^IV — Vol. 4. Arngrímur ábóti Brandsson, Guðmundarkvæði
  Skj: Arngrímur ábóti Brandsson: 2. Af et drotkvædet digt (?) om Gudmund Arason (AII, 362-3; BII, 389-90)
Árni^IV — Vol. 4. Árni Jónsson ábóti
  Skj: Árni Jónsson ábóti (AII, 412-30; BII, 440-61)
Árni Gd^IV — Vol. 4. Árni Jónsson ábóti, Guðmundardrápa
  Skj: Árni Jónsson ábóti: 1. Guðmundar drápa (AII, 412-30; BII, 440-61)
Bjbp^I — Vol. 1. Bjarni Kolbeinsson byskup
  Skj: Bjarni Kolbeinsson (AII, 1-10; BII, 1-10)
Bjbp Jóms^I — Vol. 1. Bjarni Kolbeinsson byskup, Jómsvíkingadrápa
  Skj: Bjarni Kolbeinsson: Jómsvíkingadrápa (AII, 1-10; BII, 1-10)
Bjhit^V — (Bjǫrn hítdœlakappi)
  Skj: Bjǫrn Arngeirsson hítdœlakappi (AI, 300-5; BI, 276-83)
Bjhit Lv^V (BjH) — Vol. 5. *Bjarnar saga Hítdœlakappa* (Bjǫrn hítdœlakappi, Lausavísur)
  Skj: Bjǫrn Arngeirsson hítdœlakappi: 2. Lausavísur (AI, 300-5; BI, 277-83)

Bragi^{III} — Vol. 3. Bragi inn gamli
    Skj: Bragi enn gamli (AI, 1-5; BI, 1-5)
Bragi *Rdr*^{III} — Vol. 3. Bragi inn gamli, *Ragnarsdrápa*
    Skj: Bragi enn gamli: 1. Ragnarsdrápa (AI, 1-4; BI, 1-4)
Bragi *Þórr* 5^{III} — Vol. 3. Bragi inn gamli, *Þórr's fishing*, 5
    Skj: Bragi enn gamli: 1. Ragnarsdrápa 18 (AI, 4; BI, 4)
Brúðv = Anon *Brúðv*
Bǫlv^{II} — Vol. 2. Bǫlverkr Arnórsson
    Skj: Bǫlverkr Arnórsson (AI, 385-7; BI, 355-7)
Bǫlv *Harðr*^{II} — Vol. 2. Bǫlverkr Arnórsson, *drápa about Haraldr harðráði*
    Skj: Bǫlverkr Arnórsson: Drape om Harald hårdråde (AI, 385-387; BI, 355-357)
Egill *Arkv*^V (*Eg*) — Vol. 5. *Egils saga Skalla-Grímssonar* (Egill Skallagrímsson, *Arinbjarnarkviða*)
    Skj: Egill Skallagrímsson: 4. Arinbjarnarkviða (AI, 43-8; BI, 38-41)
Egill *Lv*^V (*Eg*) — Vol. 5. *Egils saga Skalla-Grímssonar* (Egill Skallagrímsson, Lausavísur)
    Skj: Egill Skallagrímsson: 7. Lausavísur (AI, 48-59; BI, 42-53)
Egill *Lv* 42^V (*Eg* 122) — Vol. 5. *Egils saga Skalla-Grímssonar* 122 (Egill Skallagrímsson, Lausavísur, 42)
    Skj: Egill Skallagrímsson: 7. Lausavísur 40 (AI, 58; BI, 51)
Egill *St*^V (*Eg*) — Vol. 5. *Egils saga Skalla-Grímssonar* (Egill Skallagrímsson, *Sonatorrek*)
    Skj: Egill Skallagrímsson: 3. Sonatorrek (AI, 40-3; BI, 34-7)
EGils^{IV} — Vol. 4. Einarr Gilsson
    Skj: Einarr Gilsson (AII, 397-411; BII, 418-40)
EGils *Guðv*^{IV} — Vol. 4. Einarr Gilsson, *Vísur um Guðmund biskup*
    Skj: Einarr Gilsson: 2. Et hrynhent digt om Gudmund Arason (AII, 404-8; BII, 429-34)
EGils *Guðkv*^{IV} — Vol. 4. Einarr Gilsson, *Guðmundarkvæði*
    Skj: Einarr Gilsson: 1. Et digt (drape?) om Guðmund Arason, biskop (AII, 397-404; BII, 418-29)
Eil^{III} — Vol. 3. Eilífr Goðrúnarson
    Skj: Eilífr Goðrúnarson (AI, 148-52; BI, 139-44)
Eil Frag^{III} — Vol. 3. Eilífr Goðrúnarson, Fragment
    Skj: Eilífr Goðrúnarson: 3. Af et kristeligt digt (AI, 152; BI, 144)
Eil *Þdr*^{III} — Vol. 3. Eilífr Goðrúnarson, *Þórsdrápa*
    Skj: Eilífr Goðrúnarson: 2. Þórsdrápa (AI, 148-52; BI, 139-44)
Eil *Þdr* 5^{III} — Vol. 3. Eilífr Goðrúnarson, *Þórsdrápa*, 5
    Skj: Eilífr Goðrúnarson: 2. Þórsdrápa 4 (AI, 149; BI, 140)
Ekúl^{III} — Vol. 3. Eilífr kúlnasveinn
    Skj: Eilífr kúlnasveinn (AI, 572-3; BI, 565-6)
Ekúl *Kristdr*^{III} — Vol. 3. Eilífr kúlnasveinn, *Kristsdrápa*
    Skj: Eilífr kúlnasveinn: 1. Kristsdrápa(?), el. brudstykker af digte(?). (AI, 572; BI, 565-6)
ESk^{II} — Vol. 2. Einarr Skúlason
    Skj: Einarr Skúlason (AI, 455-85; BI, 423-57)

ESk *Geisl* — Vol. 7. Einarr Skúlason, *Geisli*
    Skj: Einarr Skúlason: 6. Geisli (AI, 459-73; BI, 427-45)
Eyv[I] — Vol. 1. Eyvindr Finsson skáldaspillir
    Skj: Eyvindr Finsson skáldaspillir (AI, 64-74; BI, 57-65)
Eyv *Hák*[I] — Vol. 1. Eyvindr Finsson skáldaspillir, *Hákonarmál*
    Skj: Eyvindr Finsson skáldaspillir: 1. Hákonarmǫl (AI, 64-8; BI, 57-60)
Eyv Lv[I] — Vol. 1. Eyvindr Finsson skáldaspillir, Lausavísur
    Skj: Eyvindr Finsson skáldaspillir: 3. Lausavísur (AI, 71-4; BI, 62-5)
Gamlkan — Vol. 7. Gamli kanóki
    Skj: Gamli kanóki (AI, 561-72; BI, 547-65)
Gamlkan *Has* — Vol. 7. Gamli kanóki, *Harmsól*
    Skj: Gamli kanóki: 2. Harmsól (AI, 562-72; BI, 548-65)
Gamlkan *Jóndr* — Vol. 7. Gamli kanóki, *Jónsdrápa*
    Skj: Gamli kanóki: 1. Jóansdrápa (AI, 561; BI, 547-8)
Geisl = ESk *Geisl*
Gestr[III] — Vol. 3. Gestr Þórhallsson
    Skj: Gestr Þórhallsson (AI, 199; BI, 189-90)
Gestr Lv[III] — Vol. 3. Gestr Þórhallsson, Lausavísur
    Skj: Gestr Þórhallsson: Lausavísur (AI, 199; BI, 189-90)
Glúmr[I] — Vol. 1. Glúmr Geirason
    Skj: Glúmr Geirason (AI, 75-8; BI, 65-8)
Glúmr *Gráf*[I] — Vol. 1. Glúmr Geirason, *Gráfeldardrápa*
    Skj: Glúmr Geirason: 2. Gráfeldardrápa (AI, 75-8; BI, 66-8)
GOdds[IV] — Vol. 4. Guðmundr Oddson
    Skj: Guðmundr Oddson (AII, 79-81; BII, 90-2)
GOdds Lv[IV] — Vol. 4. Guðmundr Oddson, Lausavísur
    Skj: Guðmundr Oddson: Lausavísur (AII, 79-81; BII, 90-2)
GSvert[IV] — Vol. 4. Guðmundr Svertingsson
    Skj: Guðmundr Svertingsson (AII, 46-9; BII, 55-7)
GSvert *Hrafndr*[IV] — Vol. 4. Guðmundr Svertingsson, *Hrafnsdrápa*
    Skj: Guðmundr Svertingsson: Hrafnsdrápa (AII, 46-9; BII, 55-7)
GunnI[V] — (Gunnlaugr ormstunga Illugason)
    Skj: Gunnlaugr ormstunga Illugason (AI, 194-7; BI, 184-8)
GunnI Lv[V] (*GunnI*) — Vol. 5. *Gunnlaugs saga ormstungu* (Gunnlaugr ormstunga Illugason, Lausavísur)
    Skj: Gunnlaugr ormstunga Illugason: 3. Lausavísur (AI, 194-7; BI, 185-8)
GunnLeif[I] — (Gunnlaugr Leifsson)
    Skj: Gunnlaugr Leifsson (AII, 10-36; BII, 10-45)
GunnLeif *Merl I*[I] (*Bret*) — Vol. 8. *Breta saga* (Gunnlaugr Leifsson, *Merlínusspá I*)
    Skj: Gunnlaugr Leifsson: Merlínússpá II (AII, 22-36; BII, 24-45)
GunnLeif *Merl II*[I] (*Bret*) — Vol. 8. *Breta saga* (Gunnlaugr Leifsson, *Merlínusspá II*)
    Skj: Gunnlaugr Leifsson: Merlínússpá I (AII, 10-21; BII, 10-24)

Gyð = Anon *Gyð*
Halli XI[II] — Vol. 2. Halli stirði
    Skj: Halli stirði (AI, 401-2; BI, 370-1)
Halli XI *Fl*[I] — Vol. 2. Halli stirði, *flokkr*
    Skj: Halli stirði: Flokkr (AI, 401-2; BI, 370-1)
Hallv[III] — Vol. 3. Hallvarðr háreksblesi
    Skj: Hallvarðr háreksblesi (AI, 317-18; BI, 293-4)
Hallv *Knútdr*[III] — Vol. 3. Hallvarðr háreksblesi, *Knútsdrápa*
    Skj: Hallvarðr háreksblesi: Knútsdrápa (AI, 317-18; BI, 293-4)
Hallv *Knútdr* 5[III] — Vol. 3. Hallvarðr háreksblesi, *Knútsdrápa*, 5
    Skj: Hallvarðr háreksblesi: Knútsdrápa 4 (AI, 317; BI, 294)
Has = Gamlkan *Has*
Heil = Anon *Heil*
Hfr[I] — Vol. 1. Hallfreðr vandræðaskáld
    Skj: Hallfreðr vandræðaskáld (AI, 155-73; BI, 147-63)
Hfr *ErfÓl*[I] — Vol. 1. Hallfreðr vandræðaskáld, *Erfidrápa Óláfs Tryggvasonar*
    Skj: Hallfreðr vandræðaskáld: 3. Óláfsdrápa, erfidrápa (AI, 159-66; BI, 150-7)
Hfr *ErfÓl* 25[I] — Vol. 1. 28. Hallfreðr vandræðaskáld, *Erfidrápa Óláfs Tryggvasonar*, 25
    Skj: Hallfreðr vandræðaskáld: 3. Óláfsdrápa, erfidrápa 27 (AI, 165; BI, 156)
Hfr Lv[V] — Vol. 5. Hallfreðr vandræðaskáld, Lausavísur
    Skj: Hallfreðr vandræðaskáld: 5. Lausavísur (AI, 166-73; BI, 157-63)
Hfr *Óldr*[I] — Vol. 1. Hallfreðr vandræðaskáld, *Ólafsdrápa*
    Skj: Hallfreðr vandræðaskáld: 2. Óláfsdrápa (AI, 156-9; BI, 148-50)
Hfr *Óldr* 4[I] — Vol. 1. 28. Hallfreðr vandræðaskáld, *Óláfsdrápa*, 4
    Skj: Hallfreðr vandræðaskáld: 2. Óláfsdrápa 2, 7 (AI, 157-8; BI, 149)
HólmgB[V] — (Hólmgǫngu-Bersi Véleifsson)
    Skj: Hólmgǫngu-Bersi Véleifsson (AI, 92-5; BI, 86-9)
HólmgB Lv[V] (*Korm*) — Vol. 5. *Kormáks saga* (Hólmgǫngu-Bersi Véleifsson, Lausavísur)
    Skj: Hólmgǫngu-Bersi Véleifsson: Lausavísur (AI, 92-5; BI, 86-9)
HSt[I] — Vol. 1. Hallar-Steinn
    Skj: Hallar-Steinn (AI, 543-53; BI, 525-35)
HSt *Rst*[I] — Vol. 1. Hallar-Steinn, *Rekstefja*
    Skj: Hallar-Steinn: 1. Rekstefja (AI, 543-52; BI, 525-34)
Hsv = Anon *Hsv*
HǫrðG Lv 7[V] (*Harð* 14) — Vol. 5. *Harðar saga* 14 (Hǫrðr Grímkelsson, Lausavísur, 7)
    Skj: [Anonyme digte og vers XIV]: A. 2. Vers af sagaer: Af isl. slægtsagaer: Af Harðar saga Grímkelssonar 14 (AII, 448; BII, 480)
Ív[II] — Vol. 2. Ívarr Ingimundarson
    Skj: Ívarr Ingimundarson (AI, 495-502; BI, 467-75)
Ív *Sig*[II] — Vol. 2. Ívarr Ingimundarson, *Sigurðarbǫlkr*
    Skj: Ívarr Ingimundarson: Sigurðarbǫlkr (AI, 495-502; BI, 467-75)

Ív Sig 38^II — Vol. 2. Ívarr Ingimundarson, *Sigurðarbǫlkr*, 38
  Skj: Ívarr Ingimundarson: Sigurðarbǫlkr 39 (AI, 501; BI, 474)
Játg^II — Vol. 2. Játgeirr Torfason
  Skj: Játgeirr Torfason (AII, 81-2; BII, 93)
Játg Lv^II — Vol. 2. Játgeirr Torfason, Lausavísa
  Skj: Játgeirr Torfason: Lausavísa (AII, 81-2; BII, 93)
Jón^IV — Vol. 4. Jón Þorvaldsson
  Skj: Jón Þórvaldsson (AI, 536; BI, 517)
Jón Lv^IV — Vol. 4. Jón Þorvaldsson, Lausavísa
  Skj: Jón Þórvaldsson: Lausavísa (AI, 536; BI, 517)
Kálf — Vol. 7. Kálfr Hallsson
  Not in *Skj*
Kálf *Kátr* — Vol. 7. Kálfr Hallsson, *Kátrínardrápa*
  Skj: [Anonyme digte og vers XIV]: [B. 11]. Katrínar drápa (AII, 516-26; BII, 569-82)
Kolb^IV — Vol. 4. Kolbeinn Tumason
  Skj: Kolbeinn Tumason (AII, 37-40; BII, 45-9)
Kolb *Jónv* — Vol. 7. Kolbeinn Tumason, *Jónsvísur*
  Skj: Kolbeinn Tumason: 1. Jónsvísur (AII, 37; BII, 45-6)
Kolb Lv^IV — Vol. 4. Kolbeinn Tumason, Lausavísur
  Skj: Kolbeinn Tumason: 2. Lausavísur (AII, 38-40; BII, 47-9)
KormǪ^V — (Kormákr Ǫgmundarson)
  Skj: Kormákr Ǫgmundarson (AI, 79-91; BI, 69-70)
KormǪ Lv^V (*Korm*) — Vol. 5. *Kormáks saga* (Kormákr Ǫgmundarson, Lausavísur)
  Skj: Kormákr Ǫgmundarson: 2. Lausavísur (AI, 80-91; BI, 70-85)
KrákÁsl Lv 8^I (*Ragn* 25) — Vol. 8. *Ragnars saga loðbrókar* 25 (Kráka/Áslaug Sigurðsdóttir, Lausavísur, 8)
  Skj: Anonyme digte og vers [XIII]: E. 2. Vers af Fornaldarsagaer: Af Ragnarssaga loðbrókar VI 3 (AII, 238; BII, 257)
Leið = Anon *Leið*
Líkn = Anon *Líkn*
Lil = Anon *Lil*
Mark^II — Vol. 2. Markús Skeggjason
  Skj: Markús Skeggjason (AI, 444-53; BI, 414-21)
Mark *Eirdr*^II — Vol. 2. Markús Skeggjason, *Eiríksdrápa*
  Skj: Markús Skeggjason: 1. Eiríksdrápa (AI, 444-52; BI, 414-20)
Mark *Eirdr* 4^II — Vol. 2. Markús Skeggjason, *Eiríksdrápa*, 4
  Skj: Markús Skeggjason: 1. Eiríksdrápa 5 (AI, 445; BI, 414-5)
Mark *Eirdr* 10^II — Vol. 2. Markús Skeggjason, *Eiríksdrápa*, 10
  Skj: Markús Skeggjason: 1. Eiríksdrápa 12 (AI, 446-7; BI, 416)
Mark *Eirdr* 12^II — Vol. 2. Markús Skeggjason, *Eiríksdrápa*, 12
  Skj: Markús Skeggjason: 1. Eiríksdrápa 14 (AI, 447; BI, 416)

Mark *Eirdr* 25^{II} — Vol. 2. Markús Skeggjason, *Eiríksdrápa*, 25
    Skj: Markús Skeggjason: 1. Eiríksdrápa 27 (AI, 450; BI, 418-19)
Mark *Eirdr* 27^{II} — Vol. 2. Markús Skeggjason, *Eiríksdrápa*, 27
    Skj: Markús Skeggjason: 1. Eiríksdrápa 29 (AI, 451; BI, 419)
Mark *Eirdr* 29^{II} — Vol. 2. Markús Skeggjason, *Eiríksdrápa*, 29
    Skj: Markús Skeggjason: 1. Eiríksdrápa 31 (AI, 451; BI, 419-20)
Mark *Eirdr* 31^{II} — Vol. 2. Markús Skeggjason, *Eiríksdrápa*, 31
    Skj: Markús Skeggjason: 1. Eiríksdrápa 6 (AI, 445; BI, 415)
Mark *Frag*^{III} — Vol. 3. Markús Skeggjason, Fragments
    Skj: Markús Skeggjason: 3. Kristsdrápa(?) (AI, 452; BI, 420)
Mberf^{II} — Vol. 2. Magnús berfœttr
    Skj: Magnús berfœttr (AI, 432-3; BI, 402-3)
Mberf *Lv*^{II} — Vol. 2. Magnús berfœttr, Lausavísur
    Skj: Magnús berfœttr: Lausavísur (AI, 432-3; BI, 402-3)
Mdr = Anon *Mdr*
Mey = Anon *Mey*
Mgr = Anon *Mgr*
Mv = Anon *Mv*
Ník — Vol. 7. Níkulás Bergsson
    Skj: Níkulás Bergsson (AI, 560; BI, 546-7)
Ník *Jóndr* — Vol. 7. Níkulás Bergsson, *Jónsdrápa postula*
    Skj: Níkulás Bergsson: 1. Jóansdrápa postola (AI, 560; BI, 546-7)
Ník *Kristdr*^{III} — Vol. 3. Níkulás Bergsson, *Kristsdrápa*
    Skj: Níkulás Bergsson: 2. Kristsdrápa(?) (AI, 560; BI, 547)
Ólhv^{II} — Vol. 2. Óláfr Þórðarson hvítaskáld
    Skj: Óláfr Þórðarson hvítaskáld (AII, 92-8; BII, 104-10)
Ólhv *Hryn*^{II} — Vol. 2. Óláfr Þórðarson hvítaskáld, *Hrynhenda*
    Skj: Óláfr Þórðarson hvítaskáld: 2. Et hrynhent digt (AII, 93-7; BII, 105-8)
Ólhv *Thómdr*^{III} — Vol. 3. Óláfr Þórðarson hvítaskáld, *Thómasdrápa*
    Skj: Óláfr Þórðarson hvítaskáld: 4. Af et digt om Thomas Becket (AII, 97; BII, 109)
Ólsv^{III} — Vol. 3. Óláfr Leggsson svartaskáld
    Skj: Óláfr Leggsson, svartaskáld (AII, 84-86; BII, 96-97)
Ólsv *Kristdr*^{III} — Vol. 3. Óláfr Leggsson svartaskáld, *Kristsdrápa*
    Skj: Óláfr Leggsson, svartaskáld: 3. En drape om Kristus (?) (AII, 85; BII, 96)
Ótt^I — Vol. 1. Óttarr svarti
    Skj: Óttarr svarti (AI, 289-99; BI, 267-75)
Ótt *Hfl*^I — Vol. 1. Óttarr svarti, *Hǫfuðlausn*
    Skj: Óttarr svarti: 2. Hǫfuðlausn (AI, 290-6; BI, 268-72)
Ótt *Hfl* 17^I — Vol. 1. 38. Óttarr svarti, *Hǫfuðlausn*, 17
    Skj: Óttarr svarti: 2. Hǫfuðlausn 16 (AI, 294-5; BI, 271-2)
Pét = Anon *Pét*
Pl = Anon *Pl*

RKet[IV] — Vol. 4. Rúnólfr Ketilsson
  Skj: Rúnolfr Ketilsson (AI, 533; BI, 513-14)
RKet Lv[IV] — Vol. 4. Rúnólfr Ketilsson, Lausavísa
  Skj: Rúnolfr Ketilsson: Lausavísa (AI, 533; BI, 513-14)
RvHbreiðm *Hl*[III] — Vol. 3. Rǫgnvaldr jarl and Hallr Þórarinsson, *Háttalykill*
  Skj: Rǫgnvaldr jarl og Hallr Þórarinsson: Háttalykill (AI, 512-28; BI, 487-508)
RvHbreiðm *Hl* 5[III] — Vol. 3. Rǫgnvaldr jarl and Hallr Þórarinsson, *Háttalykill*, 5
  Skj: Rǫgnvaldr jarl og Hallr Þórarinsson: Háttalykill 3a (AI, 513; BI, 488)
RvHbreiðm *Hl* 36[III] — Vol. 3. Rǫgnvaldr jarl and Hallr Þórarinsson, *Háttalykill*, 36
  Skj: Rǫgnvaldr jarl og Hallr Þórarinsson: Háttalykill 18b (AI, 519; BI, 495-6)
RvHbreiðm *Hl* 43[III] — Vol. 3. Rǫgnvaldr jarl and Hallr Þórarinsson, *Háttalykill*, 43
  Skj: Rǫgnvaldr jarl og Hallr Þórarinsson: Háttalykill 22a (AI, 520; BI, 497)
RvHbreiðm *Hl* 57[III] — Vol. 3. Rǫgnvaldr jarl and Hallr Þórarinsson, *Háttalykill*, 57
  Skj: Rǫgnvaldr jarl og Hallr Þórarinsson: Háttalykill 29a (AI, 522; BI, 501)
RvHbreiðm *Hl* 58[III] — Vol. 3. Rǫgnvaldr jarl and Hallr Þórarinsson, *Háttalykill*, 58
  Skj: Rǫgnvaldr jarl og Hallr Þórarinsson: Háttalykill 29b (AI, 522; BI, 501)
RvHbreiðm *Hl* 65[III] — Vol. 3. Rǫgnvaldr jarl and Hallr Þórarinsson, *Háttalykill*, 65
  Skj: Rǫgnvaldr jarl og Hallr Þórarinsson: Háttalykill 33a (AI, 524-5; BI, 503)
RvHbreiðm *Hl* 66[III] — Vol. 3. Rǫgnvaldr jarl and Hallr Þórarinsson, *Háttalykill*, 66
  Skj: Rǫgnvaldr jarl og Hallr Þórarinsson: Háttalykill 33b (AI, 525; BI, 503-4)
Sigv[I] — Vol. 1. Sigvatr Þórðarson
  Skj: Sigvatr Þórðarson (AI, 223-75; BI, 213-54)
Sigv *Ást*[I] — Vol. 1. Sigvatr Þórðarson, *Poem about Queen Ástríðr*
  Skj: Sigvatr Þórðarson: 9. Et digt om dronning Astrid (AI, 248; BI, 231-2)
Sigv *Berv*[II] — Vol. 2. Sigvatr Þórðarson, *Bersǫglisvísur*
  Skj: Sigvatr Þórðarson: 11. Bersǫglisvísur (AI, 251-6; BI, 234-9)
Sigv *Knútdr*[I] — Vol. 1. Sigvatr Þórðarson, *Knútsdrápa*
  Skj: Sigvatr Þórðarson: 10. Knútsdrápa (AI, 248-51; BI, 232-4)
Sigv *Nesv*[I] — Vol. 1. Sigvatr Þórðarson, *Nesjavísur*
  Skj: Sigvatr Þórðarson: 2. Nesjavísur (AI, 228-32; BI, 217-20)
Sigv *Vestv*[I] — Vol. 1. Sigvatr Þórðarson, *Vestrfararvísur*
  Skj: Sigvatr Þórðarson: 5. Vestrfararvísur (AI, 241-3; BI, 226-8)
Sigv *Víkv*[I] — Vol. 1. Sigvatr Þórðarson, *Víkingarvísur*
  Skj: Sigvatr Þórðarson: 1. Víkingarvísur (AI, 223-8; BI, 213-16)
SkáldÞ[III] — Vol. 3. Skáld-Þórir
  Skj: Skáld-Þórir (AI, 573; BI, 567)
SkáldÞ Lv[III] — Vol. 3. Skáld-Þórir, Lausavísa
  Skj: Skáld-Þórir: Lausavísa(?) (AI, 573; BI, 567)
Skapti[III] — Vol. 3. Skapti Þóroddsson
  Skj: Skapti Þóroddsson (AI, 314; BI, 291)
Skapti Frag[III] — Vol. 3. Skapti Þóroddsson, Fragment
  Skj: Skapti Þóroddsson: Af et religiøst digt (AI, 314; BI, 291)

Skarp Lv 9^V (*Nj* 34) — Vol. 5. *Njáls saga* 34 (Skarpheðinn Njálsson, Lausavísur, 9)
  Skj: Anonyme digte og vers [XIII]: D. 1. [1]. Uægte vers af slægtsagaer: Af Njálssaga 28 (AII, 205; BII, 218)
Skarp Lv 11^V (*Nj* 44) — Vol. 5. *Njáls saga* 44 (Skarpheðinn Njálsson, Lausavísur, 11)
  Skj: Anonyme digte og vers [XII]: F b. Uægte vers i sagaer: I Njálssaga 3 (AI, 605; BI, 604)
Skúli^{III} — Vol. 3. Skúli Þorsteinsson
  Skj: Skúli Þórsteinsson (AI, 305-6; BI, 283-4)
Skúli Lv^{III} — Vol. 3. Skúli Þorsteinsson, Lausavísa
  Skj: Skúli Þórsteinsson: 2. Lausavísa (AI, 306; BI, 284)
SnSt^{III} — Vol. 3. Snorri Sturluson
  Skj: Snorri Sturluson (AII, 52-79; BII, 60-90)
SnSt *Ht*^{III} — Vol. 3. Snorri Sturluson, *Háttatal*
  Skj: Snorri Sturluson: 2. Háttatal (AII, 52-77; BII, 61-88)
Sól = Anon *Sól*
Sturl^{II} — Vol. 2. Sturla Þórðarson
  Skj: Sturla Þórðarson (AII, 101-29; BII, 112-36)
Sturl *Hákkv*^{II} — Vol. 2. Sturla Þórðarson, *Hákonarkviða*
  Skj: Sturla Þórðarson: 4. Hákonarkviða (AII, 108-19; BII, 118-26)
Sturl *Hákkv* 7^{II} — Vol. 2. Sturla Þórðarson, *Hákonarkviða*, 7
  Skj: Sturla Þórðarson: 4. Hákonarkviða 8 (AII, 110; BII, 120)
Sturl *Hákkv* 18^{II} — Vol. 2. Sturla Þórðarson, *Hákonarkviða*, 18
  Skj: Sturla Þórðarson: 4. Hákonarkviða 21 (AII, 113-14; BII, 122)
Sturl *Hákfl*^{II} — Vol. 2. Sturla Þórðarson, *Hákonarflokkr*
  Skj: Sturla Þórðarson: 6. Hákonarflokkr (AII, 124-7; BII, 132-4)
Sturl *Hrafn*^{II} — Vol. 2. Sturla Þórðarson, *Hrafnsmál*
  Skj: Sturla Þórðarson: 5. Hrafnsmál (AII, 119-24; BII, 126-31)
Sturl *Hryn*^{II} — Vol. 2. Sturla Þórðarson, *Hrynhenda*
  Skj: Sturla Þórðarson: 3. Hrynhenda (AII, 102-8; BII, 113-18)
Sturl *Hryn* 13^{II} — Vol. 2. Sturla Þórðarson, *Hrynhenda*, 13
  Skj: Sturla Þórðarson: 3. Hrynhenda 18 (AII, 107; BII, 117)
Sturl *Þverv*^{IV} — Vol. 4. Sturla Þórðarson, *Þverárvísur*
  Skj: Sturla Þórðarson: 1. Þverárvísur (AII, 101; BII, 112)
Tindr^I — Vol. 1. Tindr Hallkelsson
  Skj: Tindr Hallkelsson (AI, 144-7; BI, 136-9)
Tindr *Hákdr*^{I} — Vol. 1. Tindr Hallkelsson, *Hákonardrápa*
  Skj: Tindr Hallkelsson: 1. Drape om Hakon jarl (AI, 144-7; BI, 136-8)
ÚlfrU^{III} — Vol. 3. Úlfr Uggason
  Skj: Ulfr Uggason (AI, 136-9; BI, 128-30)
ÚlfrU *Húsdr*^{III} — Vol. 3. Úlfr Uggason, *Húsdrápa*
  Skj: Ulfr Uggason: 1. Húsdrápa (AI, 136-8; BI, 128-30)
ÚlfrU *Húsdr* 12^{III} — Vol. 3. Úlfr Uggason, *Húsdrápa*, 12
  Skj: Ulfr Uggason: 1. Húsdrápa 12 (AI, 138; BI, 130)

VGl^V — (Víga-Glúmr Eyjólfsson)
  Skj: Víga-Glúmr Eyjólfsson (AI, 118-20; BI, 112-14)
VGl Lv^V (*Glúm*) — Vol. 5. *Víga-Glúms saga* (Víga-Glúmr Eyjólfsson, Lausavísur)
  Skj: Víga-Glúmr Eyjólfsson: Lausavísur (AI, 118-20; BI, 112-14)
Vitn = Anon *Vitn*
Þdís^{III} — Vol. 3. Þorbjǫrn dísarskáld
  Skj: Þorbjǫrn dísarskáld (AI, 144; BI, 135)
Þdís *Saint*^{III} — Vol. 3. Þorbjǫrn dísarskáld, *Poem about a Saint*
  Skj: Þorbjǫrn dísarskáld: 2. Et helgendigt(?) (AI, 144; BI, 135)
Þham^{II} — Vol. 2. Þorkell hamarskáld
  Skj: Þórkell hamarskáld (AI, 438-9; BI, 407-9)
Þham *Magndr*^{II} — Vol. 2. Þorkell hamarskáld, *Magnússdrápa*
  Skj: Þórkell hamarskáld: 1. Magnúsdrápa (AI, 438-9; BI, 407-8)
ÞjóðA^{II} — Vol. 2. Þjóðólfr Arnórsson
  Skj: Þjóðólfr Arnórsson (AI, 361-83; BI, 332-53)
ÞjóðA Frag 3^{II} — Vol. 2. Þjóðólfr Arnórsson, Fragments, 3
  Skj: Þjóðólfr Arnórsson: 3. Sexstefja 31 (AI, 376; BI, 346)
ÞjóðA *Magnfl*^{II} — Vol. 2. Þjóðólfr Arnórsson, *Magnússflokkr*
  Skj: Þjóðólfr Arnórsson: 1. Magnúsflokkr (AI, 361-8; BI, 332-8)
Þjsk^I — Vol. 1. Þorleifr jarlsskáld Rauðfeldarson
  Skj: Þorleifr jarlsskáld Rauðfeldarson (Ásgeirs son rauðfeldar) (AI, 141-3; BI, 132-4)
Þjsk *Sveindr*^{I} — Vol. 1. Þorleifr jarlsskáld Rauðfeldarson, *drápa about Sveinn tjúguskegg*
  Skj: Þorleifr jarlsskáld Rauðfeldarson (Ásgeirs son rauðfeldar): 2. Drape om Sven tveskæg (AI, 141; BI, 133)
ÞKolb^I — Vol. 1. Þórðr Kolbeinsson
  Skj: Þórðr Kolbeinsson (AI, 212-19; BI, 202-9)
ÞKolb *Gunndr*^{V} (*Gunnl*) — Vol. 5. *Gunnlaugs saga ormstungu* (Þórðr Kolbeinsson, *Gunnlaugsdrápa ormstungu*)
  Skj: Þórðr Kolbeinsson: 2. Gunnlaugsdrápa ormstungu (AI, 213; BI, 203)
Þloft^I — Vol. 1. Þórarinn loftunga
  Skj: Þórarinn loftunga (AI, 322-7; BI, 298-301)
Þloft *Glækv*^{I} — Vol. 1. Þórarinn loftunga, *Glælognskviða*
  Skj: Þórarinn loftunga: 3. Glælognskviða (AI, 324-7; BI, 300-1)
Þmáhl^V — (Þórarinn svarti Þórólfsson máhlíðingr)
  Skj: Þórarinn svarti Þórólfsson máhlíðingr (AI, 111-15; BI, 105-9)
Þmáhl *Máv*^{V} (*Eb*) — Vol. 5. *Eyrbyggja saga* (Þórarinn svarti Þórólfsson máhlíðingr, *Máhlíðingavísur*)
  Skj: Þórarinn svarti Þórólfsson máhlíðingr: Máhlíðingavísur (AI, 111-15; BI, 105-9)
Þorm^V — (Þormóðr Kolbrúnarskáld)
  Skj: Þórmóðr Bersason Kolbrúnarskáld (AI, 277-88; BI, 256-66)
Þorm Lv^V (*Fbr*) — Vol. 5. *Fóstbræðra saga* (Þormóðr Kolbrúnarskáld, Lausavísur)
  Skj: Þórmóðr Bersason Kolbrúnarskáld: 2. Lausavísur (AI, 281-8; BI, 260-6)

ÞSkall^II — Vol. 2. Þorkell Skallason
    Skj: Þórkell Skallason (AI, 414; BI, 383-4)
ÞSkall *Valfl*^II — Vol. 2. Þorkell Skallason, *Valþjófsflokkr*
    Skj: Þórkell Skallason: Valþjófsflokkr (AI, 414; BI, 383-4)
Þul *Ásynja*^III — Vol. 3. Anonymous Þulur, *Ásynja heiti*
    Skj: Anonyme digte og vers [XII]: IV. h. Ásynja heiti (AI, 658-9; BI, 661)
Þul *Hesta*^III — Vol. 3. Anonymous Þulur, *Hesta heiti*
    Skj: Anonyme digte og vers [XII]: IV. rr. Hesta heiti (AI, 685-6; BI, 675-6)
Þul *Jǫtna II*^III — Vol. 3. Anonymous Þulur, *Jǫtna heiti II*
    Skj: Anonyme digte og vers [XII]: IV. f. Jǫtna heiti (II) (AI, 657-8; BI, 660)
Þul *Óðins*^III — Vol. 3. Anonymous Þulur, *Óðins nǫfn*
    Skj: Anonyme digte og vers [XII]: IV. jj. Óðins nǫfn (A; BI, 672-3)
Þul *Sea-kings*^III — Vol. 3. Anonymous Þulur, *Heiti for sea-kings*
    Skj: Anonyme digte og vers [XII]: I. III. 1. Þulur: Forskellige: Søkongenavne (AI, 651; BI, 657)
Þul *Skipa*^III — Vol. 3. Anonymous Þulur, *Skipa heiti*
    Skj: Anonyme digte og vers [XII]: IV. z. Skipa heiti (AI, 672-4; BI, 668-9)
Þul *Sækonunga*^III — Vol. 3. Anonymous Þulur, *Sækonunga heiti*
    Skj: Anonyme digte og vers [XII]: IV. a. Sækonunga heiti (AI, 653-4; BI, 658)
Þul *Valkyrja*^III — Vol. 3. Anonymous Þulur, *Heiti valkyrja*
    Skj: Anonyme digte og vers [XII]: IV. aaa. Heiti valkyrja (AI, 689; BI, 678)
Þul *Viðar*^III — Vol. 3. Anonymous Þulur, *Viðar heiti*
    Skj: Anonyme digte og vers [XII]: IV. kk. Viðar heiti (AI, 682; BI, 673)
ǪnÓf Lv 4^V (*Gr* 5) — Vol. 5. *Grettis saga Ásmundarsonar* 5 (Ǫnundr Ófeigsson, Lausavísur, 4)
    Skj: [Anonyme digte og vers XIV]: A. 1. Vers af sagaer: Af isl. slægtsagaer: Af Grettissaga 5 (AII, 431-2; BII, 463)
ǪrvOdd *Ævdr* 30^I (*Ǫrv* 102) — Vol. 8. *Ǫrvar-Odds saga* 102 (Ǫrvar-Oddr, *Ævidrápa*, 30)
    Skj: Anonyme digte og vers [XIII]: E. 10. Vers af Fornaldarsagaer: Af Ǫrvar-Oddsaga IX 30 (AII, 311; BII, 330)
ǪrvOdd *Ævdr* 36^I (*Ǫrv* 108) — Vol. 8. *Ǫrvar-Odds saga* 108 (Ǫrvar-Oddr, *Ævidrápa*, 36)
    Skj: Anonyme digte og vers [XIII]: E. 10. Vers af Fornaldarsagaer: Af Ǫrvar-Oddsaga IX 36 (AII, 312; BII, 331)

TECHNICAL TERMS USED IN THIS VOLUME

Old Norse-Icelandic technical terms

See *List of Indigenous Terms* for instances of the usage in specific poems of some of the OIcel. terms in this list.

aðalhending, combination of two syllables participating in full internal rhyme (identical vowels and postvocalic environment) within a skaldic poetic l. Normally *aðalhending* occurs in even ll. (so ll. 2, 4, 6 and 8) of a *dróttkvætt* or *hrynhent* st.

drápa, long encomiastic skaldic poem with *stef*

dróttkvætt, 'court poetry', the commonest verse-form used in skaldic poetry, comprising sts of eight six-syllable ll., regular alliteration and *hendingar* (*skothending* in odd ll. and *aðalhending* in even ones)

dunhent 'echoing rhymed', in skaldic poetics sts in which there is repetition of the last word of a l. at the beginning of the next

flokkr, long skaldic poem without *stef*

fornyrðislag, 'old story metre', ON development of the common Germanic alliterative long l.

greppaminni, 'poets' reminder', a skaldic verse-form comprising a series of short questions and answers, generally on heroic, mythological or religious lore

háttr, verse-form, metre (lit. 'mode, manner')

hálfhnept, 'half-curtailed', a skaldic verse-form in which the odd and even ll. are made up of five to seven syllables (rarely of four). Each l. ends in a heavy monosyllable preceded by another heavy monosyllable or two resolved short syllables. The odd ll. have two alliterative staves and the even ll. one stave, which falls on the first lift. The metre is characterised by internal rhymes following the patterns of *dróttkvætt*, with *skothending* in the odd and *aðalhending* in the even ll. The second *hendingr* always falls on the last syllable of the l. No traditional metrical patterns can account adequately for the rhythm of *hálfhnept*.

heiti, an alternative and often descriptive name for a frequently-occurring object or person mentioned in skaldic poetry, e.g. *skævaðr* 'high-strider' for 'horse', *Þundr*, an alternative name for the god Óðinn.

helmingr (pl. *helmingar*), a half-st. of four ll.

hending (pl. *hendingar*), lit. 'catching', a syllable participating, with one other, in full internal rhyme (*aðalhending*) or partial rhyme (*skothending*) within a verse l. of a skaldic poem

hrynhent, a skaldic verse-form, an expanded version of *dróttkvætt*, comprising eight syllables per l. and an eight-l. st.

hǫfuðstafr, 'head (main) stave', chief alliterating stave fixed in initial positions of even ll. of regular *dróttkvætt* or *hrynhent* sts.

iðurmælt 'repeatedly said', name of a skaldic verse-form employing syllabic repetition

kenning, a nominal periphrasis, consisting of a base-word and one or more determinants

kviðuháttr, skaldic verse-form in which the odd ll. consist of three syllables and the even ll. of four syllables

lausavísa (pl. *lausavísur*) 'loose verse', a separate st. or part thereof which does not belong to a long poem

liljulag, that form of *hrynhent* perfected by the poet of *Lilja* (a post-medieval term)

ljóðaháttr, 'song verse-form', a six-l. verse-form in which ll. 1-2 and 4-5 alliterate, while ll. 3 and 6 alliterate internally

nýgjǫrving, 'new creation', term applied to extending the meanings of words, usually through the use of metaphor in extended kennings

rekit, term used to refer to an extended kenning with more than two determinants

runhenda, *runhent*, skaldic metre employing end rhyme

sextánmælt, 'sixteen times spoken', a skaldic figure in which a st. consists of sixteen separate independent clauses.

skothending, combination of two syllables with different vowels and similar postvocalic environments participating in a form of internal rhyme within a skaldic poetic l. Normally *skothending* occurs in odd ll. (so ll. 1, 3, 5 and 7) of a *dróttkvætt* or *hrynhent* st.

slæmr (or *slæmr*), the concluding section of a *drápa*

stef, refrain of a skaldic *drápa*, normally occuring in the b *helmingr* of a st.

stefjabálkr, middle section of *drápa* containing one or more refrains (*stef*)

stefjamel, each of the sets of verses, ending with a refrain, within a *stefjabálkr*

stuðill, prop, support, in poetry the alliterating staves in odd ll. of sts

tvíkent, 'doubly modified', a kenning with two determinants

upphaf, beginning section of a skaldic poem, the section before the beginning of the *stefjabálkr*

vísa (pl. *vísur*), a skaldic st., in pl. often a term used of a long poem lacking a refrain (e.g. Kolbeinn Tumason, *Jónsvísur*)

Other Technical Terms

anadiplosis, reduplication of the beginning of a sentence, cl. or l. with the concluding word or words of the preceding sentence, cl. or l.

anaphora, the repetition of a word or phrase at the beginning of successive clauses for rhetorical effect

base-word, substantive member of a kenning (see above) that is modified by a genitival qualifier, called the determinant (see below)

cliticise, to add an enclitic suffix to a word (see enclitic below)

Craigie's law, a rule proposed by William A. Craigie (1900), according to which, in *dróttkvætt* poetry, no long noun, adj., inf. or part. is allowed in positions 3 and 4 of an even l., if the first two positions are occupied by two long nominal syllables; in odd ll., no noun, adj., inf. or part. is permitted in those positions if alliteration falls in positions 1 and 5 and positions 1-2 are occupied by two long nouns, adjectives, infinitives or participles.

determinant, genitival qualifier of a base-word in a skaldic kenning

epenthesis (epenthetic, adj.), a sound, usually a vowel, inserted between two others

enclitic, monosyllabic word, usually a pers. pron., added as a suffix to another word, usually a verb (see also cliticise)

hypermetrical, a poetic l. containing more syllables per l. than is normal for the metre in question

hypometrical, a poetic l. containing fewer syllables per l. than is normal for the metre in question

lectio difficilior, more difficult reading

lectio facilior, easier reading

neutralisation, a metrical situation in which two short syllables occupy one unstressed metrical position in a l.

pleonastic, syllable, word or phrase that is superfluous

polyptoton, close repetition of a word or stem but in a different grammatical form

referent, word expressing the unmentioned cognitive meaning value of a kenning, e.g. the referent of the kenning *logi fjarðar* 'flame of the fjord' is GOLD

resolution, two short syllables occupying one stressed metrical position in a l.

siglum (pl. *sigla*), abbreviation, usually a combination of alphanumeric symbols, used to designate a specific manuscript and/or the collection in which it is housed

stanza, a group of poetic ll., arranged according to a regular scheme; one of a series of such groups, which together make up a poem

svarabhakti, vowel developed between two consonants

tmesis, the separation of a word or cpd word into two parts, with another word or words between them

zeugma, a figure of speech in which a word is used to govern or modify two or more words, although appropriate to only one of them or producing a different sense with each

The Contributors

Katrina Attwood currently works in the High-Integrity Systems Engineering Group in the Department of Computer Science, University of York, where she advises Rolls-Royce on the design of computerised control systems for civil airliners. She gained a PhD from the University of Leeds in 1997 for a doctoral thesis on the poems of MS AM 757a 4°, and has published several articles on the poems in this ms. as well as writing general chapters on Christian skaldic poetry. She has translated three OIcel. sagas into English (Leifur Eiriksson 1997, one, *Gunnlaugs saga*, repr. Penguin, 2000).

Martin Chase is a Professor in the Department of English and Center for Medieval Studies, Fordham University, New York. His area of specialisation within ON-Icel. studies is Christian skaldic poetry. He has recently published an edition of Einarr Skúlason's *Geisli* (Toronto, 2005).

Margaret Clunies Ross is McCaughey Professor of English Language and Early English Literature and Director of the Centre for Medieval Studies at the University of Sydney. Among her recent publications are *The Old Norse Poetic Translations of Thomas Percy* (Turnhout, 2001), *Old Norse Myths, Literature and Society* (Odense, 2003), with Amanda J. Collins, *The Correspondence of Edward Lye* (Toronto, 2004) and *A History of Old Norse Poetry and Poetics* (Cambridge, 2005). She is one of the General Editors of *Skaldic Poetry of the Scandinavian Middle Ages* and Volume Editor of Volumes VII and VIII.

Kari Ellen Gade is Professor of Germanic Studies at Indiana University, Bloomington. She is the author of *The Structure of Old Norse* dróttkvætt *Poetry* (Ithaca and London, 1995) and, with Theodore Andersson, Morkinskinna: *the Earliest Icelandic Chronicle of the Norwegian Kings (1030-1157)* (Ithaca and London, 2000). Her research interests are in ON language, literature, culture and history, together with Germanic philology and metrics. She is one of the General Editors of *Skaldic Poetry of the Scandinavian Middle Ages* and Volume Editor of Volume II.

Jonathan Grove is a Lecturer in Scandinavian History in the Department of Anglo-Saxon, Norse and Celtic Studies, University of Cambridge, where he has taught since

2004. His doctoral work comprised a study of the competitive tradition in skaldic poetics; his research interests currently focus on aspects of Scandinavian history in the late Viking Age and the early medieval period, and constructions of the past in medieval Icelandic narrative literature.

Beatrice La Farge is a *wissenschaftliche Mitarbeiterin* for the research project *Edda-Kommentar* at the Institut für Skandinavistik, University of Frankfurt. She is one of the authors of the multi-volume *Kommentar zu den Liedern der Edda* (Heidelberg, 1996-) and, with John Tucker, author of *Glossary to the Poetic Edda* (Heidelberg, 1992).

Carolyne Larrington is a Supernumerary Teaching Fellow of St John's College, Oxford. She publishes on mythological and legendary subjects in European literature. Her works on ON-Icel. include her translation of *The Poetic Edda* (Oxford World's Classics, 1996) and *The Poetic Edda: Essays on Old Norse Mythology*, co-edited with Paul Acker (New York, 2002).

Jonna Louis-Jensen retired recently from the Chair of Icelandic at the University of Copenhagen, where she served from 1957 as a Research Assistant and later Lecturer and Professor at the Arnamagnæan Manuscript Institute. Her major publications include editions of *Trójumanna saga* (Copenhagen 1963 and 1981), a facsimile of AM 66 fol. (*Hulda*, sagas of the kings of Norway, Copenhagen, 1968), and the monograph *Kongesagastudier* (Copenhagen, 1977). Jonna Louis-Jensen was awarded an honorary doctorate by the University of Iceland in 2001. An anthology of her numerous shorter papers in the field of ON-Icel. studies appeared recently under the title *Con Amore* (Copenhagen, 2006).

David M. McDougall works at the Dictionary of Old English Project, University of Toronto. His main area of interest is in Latin sources and analogues for ON-Icel. literature.

Ian C. McDougall works at the Dictionary of Old English Project, University of Toronto. His main area of interest is in Latin sources and analogues for ON-Icel. literature.

Peter Robinson is Co-Director of the Institute for Textual Scholarship and Electronic Editing at the University of Birmingham, UK. He has published several scholarly editions, and lectured on matters relating to computing and textual editing, on text encoding, digitization, and electronic publishing, and on Geoffrey Chaucer's *The Canterbury Tales*, and he has developed computer programs used in the making and publication of scholarly editions.

George S. Tate is Professor of Humanities and Comparative Literature at Brigham Young University. His areas of interest in ON-Icel. studies are Christian skaldic poetry and the confrontation of Germanic paganism with Christianity.

Valgerður Erna Þorvaldsdóttir has been a Research Associate (from June 2002) to the project *Skaldic Poetry of the Scandinavian Middle Ages*. Her main area of interest within ON-Icel. Studies is in skaldic poetry, especially that of the thirteenth century.

Tarrin Wills is a Senior Research Associate in the Centre for Medieval Studies at the University of Sydney, where he has been working on the skaldic edition, *Skaldic Poetry of the Scandinavian Middle Ages*, since 2001. He will shortly take up a Lectureship in Scandinavian Studies at the University of Aberdeen. His other research interests include OIcel. grammatical literature and the history of the study of runes.

Kirsten Wolf is Professor and Torger Thompson Chair of Scandinavian Studies at the University of Wisconsin-Madison. She has edited a number of ON-Icel. texts, including *Saga heilagrar Önnu* (Reykjavík, 2001), *The Legend of Saint Dorothy* (Toronto, 1997) and *Gyðinga saga* (Reykjavík, 1995).

Stefanie Würth is Professor in Skandinavistik in the Deutsches Seminar of the University of Tübingen, She is the author of *Elemente des Erzählens. Die Þættir der Flateyjarbók* (Basel and Frankfurt/Main, 1991), *Isländische Antikensagas I* (Munich, 1996) and *Der 'Antikenroman' in der isländischen Literatur des Mittelalters* (Basel and Frankfurt/Main, 1998).

Introduction[1]

1. *Skaldic Poetry of the Scandinavian Middle Ages* – a New Edition

The present volume is the first to be published of the nine planned volumes of *Skaldic Poetry of the Scandinavian Middle Ages* (*SkP*), although it is volume VII in the overall sequence. There will be eight volumes of texts, and a ninth containing indices and a general bibliography of medieval Scandinavian poetry. The aim of this new edition, which is set out in more detail in Wills *et al.* 2005 (http://skaldic.arts.usyd.edu.au) and in the General Introduction to the series, to appear in Volume I, is to provide a critical edition, with accompanying English translation and notes, of the corpus of Scandinavian poetry from the Middle Ages, excluding only the Elder Edda and closely related poetry.

The edition is based on a thorough assessment of all known manuscript evidence and on a review of previous editions and commentaries, including Finnur Jónsson's *Den norsk-islandske skjaldedigtning* (*Skj* A and B), which has been the standard edition of the corpus since the early twentieth century. The interpretation of individual stanzas and the layout of the corpus differ in many instances from those of *Skj*, often reflecting a more conservative approach to the manuscript sources, and *Skj* references (titles, dates, page numbers) are provided throughout the present edition for purposes of comparison. *SkP* is available in book form and as an electronic edition. The electronic edition is fully searchable and includes both images of the base manuscript chosen by its editor for each poem or fragment and transcriptions of the base manuscript text, and, in some cases, of the text from other select manuscripts.

Whereas Finnur Jónsson was able to produce his edition single-handedly, current academic conditions make it difficult for one scholar to undertake such herculean tasks. This edition is thus the outcome of a group effort, directed by five General

---

[1] The sections of this Introduction on the treatment of foreign learned words and on the normalisation of C14th poetry were written by Kari Ellen Gade, the rest of the Introduction by Margaret Clunies Ross. We are grateful to Robert D. Fulk of Indiana University and Gottskálk Þ. Jensson, of the University of Iceland, for helpful suggestions regarding the treatment of non-Norse words.

Editors: Margaret Clunies Ross, Kari Ellen Gade, Guðrún Nordal, Edith Marold and Diana Whaley. Editorial work on individual poems and fragments has been carried out by a consortium of Contributing Editors from the community of Old Norse scholars, who have specialist expertise in the field of skaldic poetry. These editors' work is individually acknowledged in this and the other seven volumes of edited poetic texts. One of the General Editors is responsible for the overall supervision of each volume as Volume Editor. In the case of Volume VII the Volume Editor is Margaret Clunies Ross. Very occasionally, a Contributing Editor has maintained a different view on a particular editorial issue from the General Editors in concert; in such cases, both views are recorded.

Several research associates and research assistants have made a major contribution to the success of the project to date: Tarrin Wills, Emily Baynham and Melanie Heyworth in Sydney, Kate Heslop in both Sydney and Newcastle upon Tyne, Valgerður Erna Þorvaldsdóttir in Reykjavík and Lauren Goetting in Bloomington, Indiana. Tarrin Wills has been employed as a Research Associate on the project since its inception, and he has made a major, original contribution to it. He has been responsible for the design of the electronic edition, and has constructed the project's database, improving it steadily over the years. It is this database that both allows for the generation of the electronic and print editions and will make it possible for the editors to produce additional resources from the database in future years, including, it is hoped, a new dictionary of the language of Old Norse poetry and a new analysis of kennings and kenning types.

2. The Corpus of Medieval Icelandic Christian Skaldic Poetry

Volume VII comprises the bulk of Icelandic skaldic poetry with Christian devotional subject-matter composed by poets between the mid-twelfth and the beginning of the fifteenth century. Almost all this verse is of Icelandic provenance, the sole probable exception being the single stanza, *Lausavísa on Lawgiving* (Anon *Law*), preserved in a manuscript of Norwegian legal documents. One distinguishing feature of much of the present corpus is the nature of its mode of preservation, which is generally in pre-Reformation compilations of religious devotional verse, outside a prose context. This feature, and other aspects of the manuscript record, are discussed in more detail below. Some medieval Icelandic Christian poetry, of considerable significance, also appears in Volume IV, *Poetry on Icelandic History*, especially a group of hagiographical poems which are likely to have been composed to support the case for the canonisation of Bishop Guðmundr Arason (1161-1237),[2] while other Christian verse is to be found in

---

[2] These are three long poems by the lawman Einarr Gilsson: *Guðmundarkvæði* ('Poem about Bishop Guðmundr') EGils *Guðkv*[IV]; '*Vísur* about Bishop Guðmundr', EGils *Guðv*[IV] and *Selkolluvísur* ('*Vísur* about Seal Head') EGils *Selv*[IV]; Abbot Arngrímr Brandsson's *Guðmundardrápa* ('*Drápa* about Bishop Guðmundr') Arngr *Gd*[V] and his *Guðmundarkvæði*

Volume III, *Poetry from Treatises on Poetics*,³ and scattered throughout Volumes I and II, *Poetry from the Kings' Sagas* 1 and 2.

Although the majority of Norwegian and Icelandic skaldic poems were composed – and certainly recorded in writing – after the introduction of Christianity to the West Norse area from c. 1000 AD, those poems that deal squarely with the common subjects of Christian doctrine and devotion do not occur in significant numbers before the middle of the twelfth century. There are several indicative fragments and poems, which date from the late tenth (if *Hafgerðingadrápa* 'Tremendous Waves drápa' (Anon *Hafg*^IV) can be so dated),⁴ eleventh and early twelfth centuries, but the earliest skaldic poem that offers a sustained and direct treatment of a Christian subject is Einarr Skúlason's *Geisli* 'Light-beam' (ESk *Geisl*), which can be firmly dated to the year 1153. This poem breaks new ground in the skaldic art in several ways: it is a completely preserved *drápa* (long poem with refrain) belonging to one of the highest traditional skaldic genres, the encomium of a dead ruler (*erfidrápa*), and yet it also adheres to the Christian genre of hagiography, its subject being the miracle-working royal saint, King Óláfr Haraldsson.⁵ A common scholarly opinion is that *Geisl* was perceived in its own day as a model for contemporary or slightly later poets, to judge by verbal echoes in their works (Attwood 1996b).

The *terminus ad quem* for Christian skaldic poetry cannot be firmly drawn. A great deal of the poetry in this volume has been preserved in anthologies of late religious verse, made in the early sixteenth century, most likely in the north of Iceland,

---

('Poem about Bishop Guðmundr') Arngr *Guðkv*^IV; together with Abbot Árni Jónsson's *Guðmundardrápa* ('Drápa about Bishop Guðmundr') Arni *Gd*^V and his *Lausavísur* (Árni *Lv*).

³ The following poems with Christian subjects, mostly fragmentary, and from the eleventh to the thirteenth centuries, are found among the stanzas cited in treatises on poetics: Eilífr kúlnasveinn, *Kristsdrápa* ('Drápa about Christ') (Ekúl *Kristdr*^III); Markús Skeggjason, Fragments (Mark *Frag*^III); Eilífr Goðrúnarson, Fragment (Eil *Frag*^III); Skapti Þóroddsson, Fragment (Skapti *Frag*^III); Arnórr Þórðarson jarlaskáld, Fragment (Arn *Frag 1*^III); Níkulás Bergsson, *Kristsdrápa* ('Drápa about Christ') (Ník *Kristdr*^III); Óláfr Leggsson svartaskáld, *Kristsdrápa* ('Drápa about Christ') (Ólsv *Kristdr*^III); Óláfr Þórðarson hvítaskáld, *Thomasdrápa* ('Drápa about S. Thomas Becket' (Ólhv *Thómdr*^III); Þórbjǫrn dísarskáld, 'Poem about a Saint' (Þdís *Saint*^III); Anonymous, *Morginsól* ('Morning Sun') (Anon *Morg*^III); Anon (*TGT*) 24, 43, 46^III; Anonymous, *Bjúgarvísur* ('Bowing *vísur*') (Anon *Bjúgvís*^III), Anonymous, *Máríuflokkr* ('Flokkr about Mary') (Anon *Mfl*^III), Anonymous, *Níkulásdrápa* ('Drápa about S. Nicholas') (Anon *Níkdr*^III).

⁴ Jakob Benediktsson (1981) argued convincingly that a fragment of this *hrynhent* poem, quoted in versions of *Landnámabók*, and attributed there to a Hebridean Christian sailing to Greenland in an Icelandic boat, probably dates from the second half of C11th.

⁵ It is likely that Einarr was also conscious of the traditional skaldic role of critic of royal or aristocratic politics. Some of the barely veiled *ad hominem* and *ad feminam* criticism of deeds of the Norwegian royal house conveyed in *Geisli*'s miracle narratives strongly supports the impression that Einarr was continuing the tradition of plain speaking found in poems such as Sigvatr Þórðarson's *Bersǫglisvísur* 'Plain-speaking *vísur*' (Sigv *Berv*^II).

where resistance to the advent of Protestantism was strongest (Jón Helgason 1932; Stefán Karlsson 1970). These anthologies, which include AM 713 4° and AM 721 4°, contain religious poetry of varying date from the fourteenth and fifteenth centuries, possibly in one case from the thirteenth (see Introduction to *Brúðkaupsvísur* 'Vísur about a Wedding', Anon *Brúðv*). In deciding which poems to include in this volume, the editors have been guided by linguistic and metrical evidence, internal to the poems, which would place them before 1400, while acknowledging that in many cases dating remains uncertain. In large part our selection coincides with that of Finnur Jónsson in *Skj*, retained in E. A. Kock's *Den norsk-isländska skjaldediktningen* (*Skald*), though there are three additional items here, *Brúðv* and two *Stanzas addressed to Fellow Ecclesiastics* (Anon *Eccl* 1 and 2), and the chronological order of individual poems varies somewhat from theirs. In addition, we have sought to adopt a more consistent representation of the sound changes characteristic of the fourteenth century than that found in *Skj* B and *Skald* (see Section 9 below). We have also adopted a more conservative and consistent approach to the treatment of foreign words, mainly from Latin, in this poetry, compared with Finnur's tendency to Icelandicise them and disregard Latin quantity, stress and spelling (see Section 8 below).

3. Genres of Christian Skaldic Poetry

Like West Norse prose with Christian subjects (Kirby 1993), the majority of the poems in this volume fall into the common medieval categories of homiletic and hagiographical literature, the latter predominating. It is relatively easy to divide the extant corpus into these two categories, and to link poems within them to particular literary modes that express their subjects. There remain a small number of poems that fall outside these categories, but they can be accounted for in the context of either their obvious purpose or their sources of inspiration or both.

The Christian skaldic poems of homiletic or didactic kind are Gamli kanóki's *Harmsól* 'Sun of Sorrow' (Gamlkan *Has*), *Leiðarvísan* 'Way Guidance' (Anon *Leið*), *Líknarbraut* 'Way of Grace' (Anon *Líkn*) and *Lilja* 'Lily' (Anon *Lil*), the title being a reference to the Virgin Mary.[6] The first two are from the second half of the twelfth century, while *Líkn* is usually dated to the thirteenth century and *Lil* to the fourteenth. *Leið*, *Líkn* and *Lil*[7] are anonymous works, but *Has* was composed by a named author, Gamli, a canon of Þykkvabœr monastery, founded in 1168. *Has* shows many thematic and stylistic connections with sermon literature and with the liturgy. Its main didactic

---

[6] The 8-line *Lausavísa on Law-giving* (Anon *Law*) is another didactic poem with a specific agenda: it sets out the desired qualities of a Christian law-giver, with reference to those of the biblical Moses.

[7] Traditionally *Lil* has been regarded as the composition of a named author, Eysteinn Ásgrímsson, but see the Introduction to the present edition of the poem for a sceptical assessment of this claim.

purpose is to urge its hearers to repentance of their sins, citing *exempla* of famous penitents, like King David and Mary Magdalene, whom Christ forgave. However, the poet ranges over a broad sweep of Christian history, focussing on the life of Christ and his Passion, his Ascension and the Last Judgement. *Leið*, which shares many verbal and stylistic similarities with *Has*, is a versified version of the popular Christian text called the Sunday Letter, in which a letter, supposedly written by Christ, drops down from heaven to remind Christians of the religious importance of Sunday. In the central part of the *drápa*, the poet rehearses key events in Christian history that are supposed to have taken place on a Sunday. Like *Has*, *Líkn* ranges widely across Christian history, but its chief affective focus is upon Christ's Passion and the virtues of the Cross. The poet has been strongly influenced by the Good Friday liturgy but he is in no way constrained by his Latin sources, adapting them skilfully to the conventions of skaldic poetry. *Lil*, the latest of these poems, a splendid and moving poem of Christian salvation history, has often been considered as the apogee of Christian skaldic verse. As its title indicates, the poet is strongly influenced by the medieval cult of the Virgin Mary.

The majority of poems in this volume belong to the Christian genre of hagiography, or lives of the saints and apostles, as do the poems in Volume IV in honour of Guðmundr Arason. Hagiography was probably the most popular medieval European narrative genre, and these Icelandic poems are closely related to both Latin and vernacular sources, Norwegian and Icelandic, most of them in prose. In addition, they draw upon a fund of familiar Christian knowledge, expressed through the liturgy and the standard vehicles for the Christian faith that all Christians were supposed to know, such as the Creed and the Lord's Prayer. A considerable sub-group in this category comprises poems devoted to the Virgin Mary, and reflects the growing importance of her cult in Iceland in the thirteenth and fourteenth centuries.

It has been proposed (Cormack 2003) that the Church in Iceland was reluctant to use skaldic verse as a medium of devotion, on the basis of a supposed paucity of vernacular verse in honour of saints, particularly of the variety known as *opus geminatum*, 'twinned work', where both prose and more ornate poetic versions of a particular saint's life are paired. The evidence of the present edition argues against this proposition, demonstrating the close links between Christian skaldic verse and other kinds of Christian literature, both in the vernacular and in Latin. While it is true that there are few clear examples of *opus geminatum* in the Old Icelandic corpus, there are many instances of close textual connections between vernacular prose versions of saints' lives and their poetic counterparts, as can be seen from the notes to the edited texts of individual poems in this volume. A small number of poems have been preserved alongside related prose texts, but many more can be closely connected with extant prose legends of Norwegian and Icelandic provenance or to Latin sources.

There are two extant manuscripts whose contents reflect the practice of the *opus geminatum* and a third which suggests that possibility. There may once have been more. AM 649 a 4° of c. 1350-1400 contains a prose life of S. John in Icelandic (*Jón⁴*). Towards the end of the saga, the narrator quotes extracts from three skaldic poems in honour of S. John, *Jónsdrápa* 'Drápa about S. John' by Níkulás Bergsson (Ník *Jóndr*), Gamli kanóki's *Jónsdrápa* (Gamlkan *Jóndr*) and Kolbeinn Tumason's *Jónsvísur* 'Vísur about S. John' (Kolb *Jónv*).⁸ Although these poems are placed towards the end of the prose text, they do not form part of the hagiographic narrative of the apostle's life, but draw attention to the piety and poetic talents of notable Icelanders of the twelfth and early thirteenth centuries. A note on fol. 48v indicates that this manuscript belonged to the church at Hof in Vatnsdalur which was dedicated to S. John. Another manuscript that contains both prose and poetry in honour of an apostle is AM 621 4° of c. 1450-1500, where a version of *Pétrs saga postula* (*Pétr¹*) is followed by *Pétrsdrápa* 'Drápa about S. Peter' (Anon *Pét*), an anonymous verse narrative of the life of S. Peter which, as its editor in this volume, David McDougall, shows, used the prose saga as a source.

A third possible example of an originally twinned work may be the anonymous twelfth-century poem *Plácitusdrápa* 'Drápa about Plácitus' (Anon *Pl*). It has survived in a single manuscript fragment of c. 1200, AM 673 b 4°. As Jonna Louis-Jensen has shown (1998, xcii-xciii), it was once part of a larger compilation that probably included another fragment, AM 673 a II 4°, which contains the remains of an Icelandic translation of the *Physiologus* and two sermons. She has also demonstrated by detailed comparison (1998 and this volume) that *Pl* is closely related to the A and C versions of *Plácitus saga*, and that it descends from the same translation from Latin into Icelandic as A and C. Thus it is possible that, in its original context, *Pl* was intended as the poetic twin of that prose translation.

The hagiographic poems may be divided into two kinds: narrative and non-narrative. The narrative poems usually follow a known prose saint's life quite closely, though not necessarily in quite the same order as the prose sources, often embellishing the legend with plentiful and carefully worked kennings for the protagonists (see below). The narrative *vitae* include *Pl*, mentioned above, being the life of S. Eustace; *Geisl*, the life and miracles of S. Óláfr⁹; *Pét*; and *Kátrínardrápa* 'Drápa about S. Catherine' (Kálf *Kátr*), the life of S. Catherine of Alexandria by a certain Kálfr

---

⁸ On fol. 48v there is also a short Latin poem in honour of S. John; for the text, see Lehmann 1936-7 II, 118-19. The ms. is also unusual in having a faded illustration of S. John on fol. 1v.

⁹ The question of whether any written texts of Óláfr's *vita* and miracles existed at the time when Einarr composed *Geisl* is a difficult one. Certainly, liturgical texts to commemorate Óláfr were written in the decades immediately after his death in 1030, and it is likely that written texts of at least some of the miracles came into being around the same time; see further *Ordo Nidr.*, 124-5 and Chase 2005, 35-43.

Hallsson. A special narrative group comprises anonymous poems that recount miracles of the Virgin Mary. These include Brúðv, *Máríugrátr* 'Drápa about the Lament of Mary' (Anon *Mgr*), *Vitnisvísur af Máríu* 'Testimonial *Vísur* about Mary' (Anon *Vitn*), *Máríuvísur I-III* '*Vísur* about Mary *I*, *II* and *III*' (Anon *Mv I-III*) and *Gyðingsvísur* '*Vísur* about a Jew' (Anon *Gyð*). All these Marian miracles can be traced to either Latin or vernacular prose legends or to both.

It has been argued (Lindow 1982, 117) that skaldic hagiographical poetry follows a generally narrative mode, but this is not always the case. A non-narrative group is identifiable as devotional and referential rather than fully narrative, with allusion being made to saints' legends as something already known to the poets' audiences. In this group are *Allra postola minnisvísur* 'Celebratory *Vísur* about All the Apostles' (Anon *Alpost*), *Heilagra manna drápa* 'Drápa about Holy Men' (Anon *Heil*) and *Heilagra meyja drápa* 'Drápa about Holy Maidens' (Anon *Mey*). *Andréasdrápa* 'Drápa about S. Andrew' (Anon *Andr*) and the three poems in honour of S. John, Gamlkan *Jóndr*, Kolb *Jónv* and Ník *Jóndr*, are too fragmentary to allow one to decide whether they were fully narrative. The stanzas of these poems that have survived suggest a particular focus upon the apostle's virginity, his closeness to the Virgin Mary and his status as Christ's relative, in the case of S. John, and, in S. Andrew's case, his martyrdom and reception into heaven. The twenty-six remaining stanzas of *Heil* and the complete *Mey* are catalogues of male and female saints, in which the poets devote one or two stanzas to the salient events of each saint's life, a method that seems to assume the audience's prior knowledge of their *vitae*. *Alpost*, rather like the Old English *Fates of the Apostles*, also devotes one stanza to each apostle, alluding to his mode of death, and concluding with a two-line refrain in the metre *runhent* added at the end of each eight-line stanza of *dróttkvætt*. The poet welcomes each apostle in turn into a convivial company (*folk* 'people' 12/9, *sveit* 'company' 13/9) gathered at a feast (*í samkundu* 'at our feast' 12/5), where he is honoured with a *minni*, or memorial cup or toast.

Two poems in this corpus stand out on account of their devotional and affective piety and are also notable for the complexity of their composers' transformation of Latin liturgical images into Old Icelandic kennings or kenning-like circumlocutions. *Máríudrápa* 'Drápa about Mary' (Anon *Mdr*) is a hymn of praise to the Virgin Mary rather than a narrative of her life, comprising a versified catalogue of Marian epithets and prayers for her mediation and mercy. The poet succeeds in turning a good deal of the Latin or latinate vocabulary and phraseology of medieval Mariolatry, to be found particularly in the liturgy, into elaborate skaldic diction with considerable accuracy (cf. Schottmann 1973, 535-8 and see further below). In three places *Mdr* offers a direct translation of a specific liturgical text, stanzas 30-6 translating the antiphon for the Feast of the Assumption, *Ave maris stella* 'Hail star of the sea', stanzas 17-20 offering a rendition of the antiphon *Gaude virgo gratiosa* 'Rejoice, gracious virgin', sometimes attributed to Bernard of Clairvaux (1090-1153), while stanza 26 presents a version of the *Ave Maria* 'Hail Mary'. Another poem notable for its skilful rendition of Latin is *Heilags anda drápa* 'Drápa about the Holy Spirit' (Anon *Heildr*), a prayer of praise to the Holy Spirit. There are numerous kenning-like periphrases for the Holy Spirit in this poem (see below), unparalleled elsewhere in the skaldic corpus. Einar Ólafur Sveinsson (1942) demonstrated that stanzas 11-16 are a direct translation of the Latin Pentecost hymn *Veni Creator Spiritus*, usually ascribed to Hrabanus Maurus (d. 856). It is worth noting that *Heildr* and *Mdr*, perhaps the most complex poems of the Christian skaldic corpus aside from *Lilja*, occur in the same manuscript, AM 757 a 4° (B), and may have been products of the same religious community.

Further evidence of the close relationship between Christian skaldic verse and Icelandic Latinity comes from the two Latin stanzas, *Stanzas addressed to Fellow Ecclesiastics* (Anon *Eccl* 1 and 2), which, though each has been previously published, have not been included before in any edition of Icelandic skaldic verse, presumably because they are in Latin. However, as their current editor, Jonathan Grove, indicates, they have been composed in the skaldic verse-forms of *hrynhent* and *dróttkvætt* respectively and so merit inclusion in an edition of Christian skaldic poetry. These stanzas, together with two anonymous secular *lausavísur* (Anon *732b* 1-2[III]), one in coded Icelandic, the other in macaronic Latin and Icelandic, come from a learned miscellany manuscript AM 732 b 4° (c. 1300-25), and may well be the tip of an iceberg of Latin-influenced Icelandic clerical composition that has not been well preserved in the manuscript record (cf. Gottskálk Þ. Jensson 2003). This, and other evidence of the close connection between skaldic verse and Latin learning contained in this and other volumes of this edition, suggest that Guðrún Nordal's 2001 hypothesis about the coexistence of training in skaldic versifying and Latin poetics in the medieval Icelandic educational system should be taken seriously as one part of the explanation for the relatively long life of Christian skaldic verse, which continued, though in metrically attenuated form, down to the Reformation of the mid-sixteenth century.

A final category of religious poetry included in this volume shows the influence of both the Christian Church and traditional Norse poetry that is at the same time gnomic and visionary. This traditional combination is most evident in *Sólarljóð* 'Song of the Sun' (Anon *Sól*), an anonymous poem of eighty-three stanzas in which a dead Christian man describes to his son a series of sometimes grotesque visions of this world and the next. To judge by the very large number of paper manuscripts in which *Sól* has survived, this poem continued to be very popular into the modern period in Iceland, and one reason for its popularity is probably that it was based firmly on traditional eddic poetry like *Hávamál*, where we also find a mixture of visionary and gnomic literary modes. *Hugsvinnsmál* 'Sayings of the Wise-minded One' (Anon *Hsv*), on the other hand, is firmly gnomic in mode, a fairly free Icelandic rendering of the popular Latin didactic work *Disticha* (or *Dicta*) *Catonis* 'The Distichs of Cato'. Both these poems are in the *ljóðaháttr* ('song form') metre, as is usual with Old Norse didactic verse.[10]

4. Manuscripts

As has already been mentioned, a number of the poems in this volume are found in compilations that form anthologies of late medieval religious poetry. Chief among these are AM 713 4° and AM 721 4°, both dating from the first half of the sixteenth century, and both probably compiled in the north of Iceland. Besides poetry in honour of saints and apostles, these manuscripts also contain a great deal of evidence for the cult of the Virgin Mary in Iceland, and include a number of poems recounting her miracles. Devotion to the Virgin seems to have been particularly strong in the north, and may have been a consequence of the dedication of the northern cathedral at Hólar to her. Several of the Marian miracle poems in 721 and/or 713 (*Mey*, *Vitn* and *Mv I-III*) also reveal a special devotion to S. Andrew, who is mentioned in stanza 2 of each poem, in a manner that has led scholars to suppose that this group of poems may have been composed in the same religious house or for the same church community.[11] S. Andrew is also the subject of the now fragmentary *Andr* (in AM 194 8°, dated 1387) and stanza 3 of *Alpost*.

Another significant collection of Christian skaldic poetry is found in the very poorly preserved but important manuscript AM 757 a 4° (B), of c. 1400, which also contains a text of the *Third Grammatical Treatise* (*TGT*) by Óláfr Þórðarson hvítaskáld and part of the *Skáldskaparmál* section of Snorri Sturluson's *Edda*. Ms. B contains (in the following order) *Heildr*, *Leið*, *Líkn*, *Has*, *Mdr* and *Gyð*, the last-named a fragment of a Marian miracle poem in which the Virgin (as far as one can tell from the little that survives) frees a Christian from a Jew's hard bargain over money. Another interesting late medieval Icelandic miscellany, containing a collection of prose homilies and the poems *Leið* and *Hsv*, is the fifteenth-century manuscript AM 624 4°.

Mention has already been made of poems appearing in manuscripts showing the probable influence of the medieval concept of the *opus geminatum*. AM 649 a 4°, with its various contents honouring S. John in image, prose narrative and devotional verse, is among the most interesting medieval Icelandic books of hagiographical kind, while the fragment AM 673 b 4°, containing *Pl* and dated c. 1200, is the earliest extant manuscript in which a skaldic poem has been preserved.

---

[10] Comparable in terms of its collection of proverbial wisdom is the thirteenth-century Orkney poem *Málsháttakvæði* 'Proverb poem' (Anon *Mhkv*[III]) in the verse-form *runhent* and, in respect of its proverbial aspect, Gunnlaugr Leifsson's *Merlínuspá* 'Prophecies of Merlin' (GunnLeif *Merl I* and *II*[VIII]) in *fornyrðislag*.

[11] A possible contender would be a church such as Urðir in Svarfaðardalur in Eyjafjörður, which was dedicated to S. Mary and S. Andrew.

The material preservation of Einarr Skúlason's *Geisli* offers a significantly different type of manuscript environment from the other Christian skaldic poems in Volume VII. Unlike them, *Geisl* had religious and political significance of great importance in both Norway and Iceland, and indeed beyond, as an official encomium of Norway's first royal saint. This is reflected not only in the actual context of its preservation, in two major medieval compilations of historical sagas, Bergsbók, Holm perg 1 fol (Bb), and Flateyjarbók, GKS 1005 fol (Flat), both of the late fourteenth century, but also in the fact that the *drápa* is preserved entire in both manuscripts.[12] Furthermore, in Flat *Geisl* is given pride of place as the very first item in the compilation.

5. Poets and their Audiences

The majority of the twenty-eight Christian skaldic poems in this volume are anonymous, only six being by authors for whose names we have good medieval evidence.[13] This phenomenon contrasts with the situation of secular skaldic poetry, where named skalds are frequent. Chase (1993) has suggested that the anonymity of much Christian skaldic poetry may reflect the humility and self-effacement enjoined upon Christian clerics, especially those in monastic orders. Where we do know the poets' names, we also know that in four cases those poets were clerics, the exception being Kolbeinn Tumason, a leading chieftain of the late twelfth and early thirteenth century.[14] This small sample supports the inferences one can draw on grounds such as manuscript context, subject matter and style, that most of the poetry in this volume is likely to have been composed by priests or monks, either for their fellow clergy or for mixed lay and clerical audiences. Given many of the poets' attention to the minutiae of transforming liturgical phraseology into skaldic kennings, one suspects that the poets' audiences must have appreciated this kind of artistry. Such audiences, one imagines, would be most likely found in elite secular households that particularly patronised skaldic verse and were the owners of proprietary churches to which they would have contributed books and other church property (*Ordo Nidr.*, 40; cf. Guðrún

---

[12] In Flat, three stanzas (31-3) are missing, but, as the present editor, Martin Chase demonstrates (see Note to *Geisl* stanza 31), the intention was to include them, the copyist making a careless mistake.

[13] Two of the six are by the same author, Gamli kanóki.

[14] The five named poets are Einarr Skúlason, Níkulás Bergsson, Gamli kanóki, Kolbeinn Tumason and Kálfr Hallsson (for their biographies, see the Introductions to ESk *Geisl* (Einarr's biography is in Volume II), Ník *Jóndr*, Gamlkan *Has*, Kolb *Jónv* and Kálf *Kátr*). Although we do not know the name of the *Leið* poet, he is also likely to have been a cleric, because in st. 43 of his poem he thanks a certain noble priest by the name of Rúnolfr for helping him establish the foundation of his *drápa*. Rúnolfr's identity is uncertain, but the two most likely candidates both moved in ecclesiastical circles (see Note to *Leið* 43/8).

Nordal 2001, 117-43 for thirteenth-century patrons of skalds) or in religious communities or in both.

Christian skaldic poetry with didactic or homiletic intent could have been read aloud to the poets' audiences as an addition to vernacular sermons, embellishing their content in memorable and moving verse. Likewise, the poetic counterparts to prose saints' lives would have served as sophisticated reworkings of vernacular legends for the education and entertainment of elite audiences. Those poems that assume a prior knowledge of hagiography might well have been composed by clerics for specific religious houses or secular patrons devoted to particular saints. The audience of *Alpost*, for example, might well have been a religious community that possessed sculpted images of the apostles or possibly paintings or relics of them, so that, as the poem was spoken, a toast could actually have been drunk to each apostle in turn incorporating a nod to the material image. The audiences of *Heil* and *Mey* may also have been able to see images of the saints whose passions were read out to them. In the case of *Mey*, it is likely that such a large number of verses in honour of holy virgins would have been of special importance to religious communities of women. It is also quite likely, in view of its subject matter, that Kálfr Hallsson's *Kátrínardrápa* might also have been composed for religious women.[15]

One of the most likely contexts in which Christian skaldic poetry might have been read aloud would have been as an accompaniment to meals in religious, and especially monastic, communities. At meal times monks were supposed to be silent and to engage in religious contemplation. The reading of poetry in their own language, intricate though it is, would have provided appropriate substance for contemplation and reminded its audience of important Christian doctrine, especially if they were already familiar with vernacular prose lives of the saints. Sverrir Tómasson (2003) has suggested that some late skaldic verse, especially that modelled on Latin hymns, may even have been sung.

6. History of Scholarship and Reception of Christian Skaldic Poetry

Old Icelandic devotional poetry in skaldic verse-forms has been preserved for the most part in late medieval and pre-Reformation Icelandic manuscript compilations, but it did not generally become an object of study and editorial attention until the early nineteenth century. However, significant transcriptions and editions of Christian

---

[15] The number of convents in medieval Iceland was small. Poetry devoted to female saints would have been especially favoured in nunneries like Kirkjubœr in the south, founded in 1186 and dedicated to the Virgin Mary, and Staðr on Reynisnes in the north, founded in 1296. Both were Benedictine foundations. As Cormack remarks (1994, 87), the first known Katrín in Iceland was an abbess of Staðr, consecrated in 1298, and a second woman of that name was elected abbess of the same foundation in 1330. Perhaps the poet Kálfr composed his *Kátr* in honour of the saint and one or other of these two abbesses.

skaldic verse were undertaken by Icelandic scholars before 1850. From this period come several important transcripts of medieval manuscripts that had already begun to deteriorate significantly by the first half of the nineteenth century. However, much greater deterioration has taken place over the last 150 years, so that modern editors, including those preparing this volume, have found it necessary to use readings recorded by the scribes of such manuscripts as Lbs. 444 4^{ox} (444^x), a bundle of various loose paper transcriptions, and JS 399 a-b 4^{ox} (399a-b^x), a transcript of the Christian poems in B made in the mid-nineteenth century by Jón Sigurðsson (1811-79). B is now one of the most difficult of all medieval Icelandic manuscripts to read. Early editions of Christian poems are also helpful to the modern editor for their value in preserving readings that have disappeared. One of the earliest editors of Christian skaldic poetry was Sveinbjörn Egilsson (1791-1852). Notable are his editions of *Plácitusdrápa* from 1833 and his 1844 edition of four of the poems in B, *Fjøgur gømul kvæði*, which he prepared as a teaching text for the Latin school at Bessastaðir. Both these books were published by Viðey monastery.

Most of the major Icelandic scholars of the second half of the nineteenth century either edited or wrote about at least part of the corpus of Christian skaldic poetry, beginning with Sveinbjörn Egilsson and Konráð Gíslason. Non-Icelandic scholars, mainly from mainland Scandinavia and Germany, also became involved in the preparation of new editions of these poems in the last decades of the nineteenth and the first decades of the twentieth century, often as doctoral dissertations. Most of the poems in Volume VII have been previously edited by one or more scholars active in the period 1870-1920. This period of editorial activity culminated in Finnur Jónsson's *Den norsk-islandske skjaldedigtning* (*Skj*) of 1912-15, which was followed at some distance, both chronological and intellectual, by Ernst Albin Kock's *Notationes Norrœnæ* (*NN*) of 1923-44 and his *Den norsk-isländska skaldediktningen* (*Skald*) of 1946-50. Alongside these editions and studies of pre-1400 skaldic verse, one should also mention Jón Þorkelsson's seminal 1888 study of fifteenth- and sixteenth-century poetry, much of it religious, and Jón Helgason's edition of this pre-Reformation verse, published in 1936-8 in his two-volume *Íslenzk miðaldakvæði* (*ÍM*).

Studies of the literary character of Christian skaldic poetry and its sources in European Christian literature, often in Latin, began in earnest with Fredrik Paasche's *Kristendom og kvad: en studie i norrøn middelalder*, first published in 1914 and reprinted in a collection of his essays in 1948. Another, somewhat later, study of these poems' debt to Christian Latin learning was Wolfgang Lange's *Studien zur christlichen Dichtung der Nordgermanen* (1958a). A third major study, devoted specifically to poetry in honour of the Virgin Mary, was Hans Schottmann's *Die isländische Mariendichtung* of 1973. So far the literary and source study of Christian skaldic poetry had been of a general kind.

A new direction began in the 1970s, with the appearance of a group of doctoral dissertations from postgraduate students in various parts of the English-speaking world. These scholars undertook new editions of individual Christian poems which included theological and literary analysis as well as more strictly philological material. George Tate's edition of *Líknarbraut* (1974) as a Cornell University doctoral dissertation was probably the first, and this was followed by Martin Chase's University of Toronto edition and study of *Geisli* (1981) and, somewhat later, by Katrina Attwood's 1996 University of Leeds PhD thesis (Attwood 1996a), an edition of the Christian poems in B. The 1998 publication of John Tucker's edition of *Plácidus saga*, begun as an Oxford University B. Litt. thesis (1974), inspired Jonna Louis-Jensen (1998) to produce a companion edition of *Plácitusdrápa*. Alongside this new wave of editions from 1970-2000, most of them now revised for *SkP*, have appeared a relatively small number of articles exploring Christian skalds' sources or their treatment of their material.

A great deal remains to be done to bring out the merits of Christian skaldic poetry. In comparison with pre-Christian skaldic verse and with secular poetry of the twelfth and thirteenth centuries, the poems in this volume remain relatively neglected and unappreciated. Their use of kennings and kenning-like periphrases has often been dismissed either as the tired reuse of old models or as the inappropriate application of traditional frames of reference to hagiographical and liturgical subject matter. Other dimensions of their stylistic repertoires remain unappreciated, except in the case of *Lilja*, which has received much wider attention from connoisseurs of religious poetry, both inside and outside Iceland, than any of the other poems in this volume. Few scholars and critics have recognised the subtlety with which Christian skalds transformed the complexities of Latin hymns and liturgical phrases into skaldic diction, nor have there been thoroughgoing comparisons of Christian poems with their likely prose sources, whether in Latin or the vernacular. Finally, a study of the different sub-genres of Christian skaldic verse, and their stylistic and narratological characteristics, has yet to be written.

7. Verse-forms and Diction of Christian Skaldic Verse

Dróttkvætt 'court metre', was the prestige verse-form of skaldic poetry from its emergence in the late ninth century, although other verse forms were specific to particular genres, like *kviðuháttr* 'poem metre' for genealogical poetry or *fornyrðislag* 'old story metre' or *ljóðaháttr* 'song metre' for gnomic or didactic verse. Faulkes (*SnE* 1999, 75-88) gives a statistical analysis of the various metres employed in the whole poetic corpus. It is often stated (e.g. Chase 1993, 75) that Christian poets came to prefer the 8-syllable *hrynhent* ('flowing metre') verse-form over the 6-syllable *dróttkvætt*, especially in the fourteenth century, yet a reasonable number of the later poems in this volume continue to use *dróttkvætt* (e.g. *Gyð*, *Líkn*, *Mdr*, *Mv I*, *Pét* and *Vitn*). Three poems (*Brúðv*, *Mv II* and *III*) use the metre *hálfhneppt* 'half curtailed'. There is also at least one case where a skald has used a more specialised metre for particular effects; the poet of *Pét* has used *skjalfhent* 'shivering rhymed' to convey, in staccato fashion, the 'twelve strong things' that S. Peter possessed. *Hrynhent* was almost certainly a development from *dróttkvætt* under the influence of Latin hymn measures (Kuhn 1983, 337-41). As such, it must have appealed to Christian clerics creating their own vernacular devotional poetry. The earliest, securely datable example of the *hrynhent* verse-form is Árnorr Þórðarson jarlaskáld's *Hrynhenda* 'Poem in *hrynhent* verse-form' (Arn *Hryn*[II]) of c. 1045, and the earliest example in the Volume VII corpus is Gamlkan *Jóndr*, from the second half of the twelfth century. Several fourteenth-century poems, such as *Heil*, *Kátr*, *Lil* and *Mey*, are in *hrynhent*.

In a number of the probably fourteenth-century poems, the verse-forms are notably irregular in their metrical observance, and they do not keep either correct line length or correct distribution of internal rhymes and alliteration.[16] These have been regularised in cases of twelfth- and early thirteenth-century poems where scribal insertion of non-cliticised pronouns and other particles has resulted in an over-long line, but in poetry from after 1250 we have left the texts largely unmodified to reflect the growing lack of metrical consistency in these poems. It is also possible to observe that some poets' knowledge of the conventions of kenning formation (see below) was slipping. This is most obvious in *Brúðv*, whose dating this edition has placed in the fourteenth century, though its sole earlier editor, Jón Helgason (*ÍM* II, 128), thought it could be of thirteenth-century date, and in Kálf *Kátr*, where, as Kirsten Wolf explains in notes to stanzas 14/3-4, 15/8, 33/2 and 45/7, the skald understood the poetic noun *öglir* 'hawk', to mean 'snake' and consequentially produced a number of defective gold-kennings.

A majority of the Christian skaldic poems are intact *drápur* 'long poems with refrains' or fragments thereof. Even some that have traditionally been entitled *–vísur* 'verses', a term indicating a lack of refrain (*stef*), are almost certainly the remains of *drápur*. An example is *Heildr*, which has previously been entitled *Heilags anda vísur*. Conversely, some poems conventionally titled *–drápa* (e.g. *Andr*) cannot be conclusively categorised as such for lack of evidence of a refrain. The predominance of *drápur* in this corpus places the Christian long poems beside the most prestigious secular encomia of the West Norse tradition in status and dignity, and this is fitting, given their role as vectors of Christian doctrine and devotion. Several of the poets quite self-consciously refer to the various parts of their *drápur*, using the technical terms *stef*, *stefjabálkr*, *slæmr* and *upphaf* (see List of Indigenous Terms for their

---

[16] There is a full discussion of skaldic verse-forms and formal structures in the Introduction to the whole edition in Volume 1. Individual deviations and irregularities are mentioned in Notes to specific poems and stanzas.

distribution within the corpus). It is thus not surprising, given their poems' elevated form, that Christian skalds often used elaborate skaldic diction within their *drápur*.

While the kenning (see below) remains the most common form of stylistic elevation in Christian skaldic poetry, other rhetorical strategies appear, particularly in fourteenth-century verse. Where skalds strive for emotional intensity and effect, they commonly employ complex patterns of repeated but varied rhetorical formulae, which are likely to have been influenced, directly or indirectly, by the new European poetical manuals of the thirteenth and fourteenth centuries (Foote 1982). The poet of *Lil* used these techniques to great effect, and they appear in other late religious poems like *Mey*. Stanza 5 of *Mey* provides a good example of the new poetics:

Sæt María gjörði að gráta
gráti mædd í sonarins láti;
lát Júðanna fældi að fljóði;
fljóðið horfði á krossinn rjóðan.
Rjóðandi þá flaut og flóði
flóð táranna niðr um móður;
móðurbrjóstið strengt af stríði
stríðið bar sem engi síðan.

Prose order: Sæt María, mædd gráti, gjörði að gráta í láti sonarins; lát Júðanna fældi að fljóði; fljóðið horfði á rjóðan krossinn. Rjóðandi flóð táranna flaut og flóði þá niðr um móður; móðurbrjóstið, strengt af stríði, bar stríðið sem engi síðan.

Translation: Sweet Mary, overcome by weeping, cried at the death of the son; the conduct of the Jews mocked the woman; the woman looked at the red cross. The reddening stream of tears then flowed and streamed down the mother; the mother's chest, tight from grief, bore the grief like no one since.

The poet uses a variety of the echoing verse-form that Snorri Sturluson termed *iðurmæltr* 'repeatedly said' (*SnE* 1999, 22) and his purpose is to express the affective piety associated in European medieval poetry generally with the motif of the Virgin Mary weeping at the foot of Christ's cross. In combination with the native verse-form he uses repetitive word-play, a type of *adnominatio*, to suggest a rapid sequence of important events that changed the world.

Other kinds of stylistic and conceptual resources that are relatively common in medieval European devotional poetry appear quite rarely in Christian skaldic verse. It is clear from Óláfr Þórðarson's final example of poetic usage in *TGT*, a stanza by Níkulás Bergsson (Ník *Kristdr*[III]), that typological symbolism was known in Iceland at least from the mid twelfth century (Louis-Jensen 1981), but it does not seem to have been very often used by skaldic poets, except in standard circumlocutions for the

Virgin Mary modelled on Latin phrases.[17] Number symbolism and numerological structuring devices also appear relatively rarely in the Christian skaldic corpus, principally in *Lil* and *Líkn*. The poet of *Lil*, which has 100 stanzas, doubtless expressed the notion of the perfection of Christian salvation history through his choice of that round number, although another system, based on a triangular pattern within the circular structure of the poem, has also been detected (Hill 1970, 564-5). It is likely that the poet of *Líkn* chose to compose 52 stanzas in order to reflect the number of weeks in the year. George Tate, in his notes to *Líkn* in this edition, gives details of the poet's emphasis on the concept of time and the Christian year throughout the poem. *Líkn* 31-7 is also noteworthy for a series of elaborate exegetical figures comparing Christ's cross to a set of symbols (key, flower, ship, ladder, bridge, scales and altar) which can be paralleled in Latin hymns of the Middle Ages. The poet of *Sól* also seems to play on a deliberate contrast between Christian and traditional Norse number symbolism.

By far the most obvious and frequent stylistic feature of Christian skaldic poetry is the kenning, characteristically a two-part nominal periphrasis for a noun referent, comprising a base-word (MIcel. *stofnorð*, German *Grundwort*) and a determinant (MIcel. *kenniorð*, German *Bestimmung*), which is either in the genitive case or the first element of a compound. A simple example is *brjótr seima* 'breaker of gold wires' [GENEROUS MAN] (Gamlkan *Jóndr* 1/6). The referent, given here in small capitals, is not actually mentioned in the text, but must be inferred from it and from the conventional conceptual system that underpins kenning semantics and was familiar to medieval Icelandic poets and their audiences.[18] In this case, the modern reader needs to know that distributing ('breaking', 'scattering', 'wasting') gold symbolises the virtue of generosity in a ruler or other important man, the actual referent in this instance being S. John. Another example of a simple kenning, with an obviously Christian referent, is *geymir guðspjalls* 'guardian of the gospel' [HOLY MAN] (Anon *Heil* 10/5). In this instance the referent is S. Dionysus. Kennings may be simple or they may include more than one referent, what Snorri Sturluson called *tvíkent* 'twice modified', if they contained two referents, or *rekit* 'extended', if there were more than two (*SnE* 1999, 5). An example of a *rekit* kenning with three referents (the direction of interpretation

---

[17] Martin Chase (2003, 2005a, 21-7 and 124 and his edition of *Geisl* in this volume) has argued that Einarr Skúlason uses typology in *Geisl* stanzas 1-6 to identify S. Óláfr with Christ. The poet of *Pl* used a kind of typology when he compared Plácitus, who suffered many privations as tests of his Christian faith, to the Old Testament figure *Jób inn gamli* 'Job the old' (*Pl* 1/8 and 26/8). The Plácitus legend also depends on an equivalence between Christ and the hart that appeared to Plácitus while out hunting, an analogy well known to medieval Christians through the *Physiologus* tradition (see Note to *Pl* 7/7-8).

[18] For a fuller discusssion of the kenning system of skaldic poetry, see Introduction to the whole edition, *SkP*, in Volume I.

being indicated by >) is *þollar hreina nausts humra* 'fir-trees of the reindeer of the boat-house of lobsters' [SEA > SHIPS > SEAFARERS] (Gamlkan *Jóndr* 2/7-8).

This last kenning is typical of the use of such resources of diction in much Christian skaldic verse in that conventional elements of the referential system evoke the conceptual world of Scandinavian material culture, in this case seafaring, rather than the world of Christian history and legend, even though the poet is dealing with a Christian subject and the kenning here refers to Christian men in general. In some cases, indeed, Christian skalds used mythological references to supernatural beings from Old Norse paganism to ornament their Christian kennings. A simple example is Kálfr Hallsson's use of base-words for goddesses in kennings for S. Catherine, like *Þrúðr falda* 'Þrúðr <goddess> of headdresses' [WOMAN] (*Kátr* 4/8), Þrúðr being the name of the god Þórr's daughter in Norse myth, but in skaldic usage standing for any woman. Gamli, the poet of *Has*, likewise refers to Mary Magdalene as *Vǫr víns* 'Vǫr <goddess> of wine' (53/3-4), the woman-kenning in this case possibly alluding to Mary's sensual nature. Although some such skaldic kennings probably use pagan mythological references for specific contextual effect, the majority of them are quite conventional and decorative, and can be compared to the use of classical allusions in vernacular European poetry of the seventeenth and eighteenth centuries. Some modern scholars find it discordant to read kennings whose referents mean WARRIORS or SEAFARERS, when the poet is talking about the behaviour of Christian people in general, where holy women are called by the names of pagan goddesses or even valkyries, and where male saints and apostles are presented in terms appropriate to secular lords and distributors of treasure. However, there is no evidence that medieval Icelandic poets and their audiences saw any impropriety or discrepancy in these allusions. All the evidence indicates that they should be regarded as largely ornamental and in keeping with the high style of Christian skaldic *drápur* and other long poems.

There is in fact a good deal of variability among the poems in this volume in the extent to which they use kennings. In part, this reflects their age, the later poets tending to use fewer kennings, and those only of simple kind for a restricted range of referents: God, Christ, the Virgin Mary, saints and apostles, priests, Christian people and Heaven, the last-named usually embedded in a kenning for God or Christ, of the form 'lord of the heavens'. To some extent this growing simplicity of diction reflects a deliberate turn away from skaldic complexity, expressed in a well-known declaration by the poet of *Lil* that he wants to avoid obscure archaisms (*hulin fornyrðin* 98/3), on the grounds that the Christian message was most effective when it was unencumbered by abstruse and oblique language. However, as the stanza from *Mey* quoted above and the whole of *Lil* itself amply demonstrate, such manifestos cannot be taken at face value. Although poetry like that exemplified in *Mey* 5 contains not a single kenning, it is rhetorically complex in a different way.

It is observable that several of the hagiographical narratives in the collection use a great many kennings, irrespective of their age, while few of the non-narrative group do so, aside from *Heildr* and *Mdr*, which are exceptional in the extent to which their poets generate calques on Latin periphrases for the Holy Spirit and the Virgin respectively, as will be discussed below. Three narrative poems that employ a wealth of kennings for their protagonists are *Pl*, which is amongst the earliest Christian skaldic *drápur*, *Brúðv* and *Kátr*, both probably of the fourteenth century. In each case, the poet is likely to have been working closely from a vernacular prose text and one can assume that his main purpose in using a great many kennings for the protagonists of the legends the poems narrate was a desire to produce a version that was more concentrated in its effect and more highly ornamented than their prose exemplars. Jonna Louis-Jensen's detailed analysis (1998) of the skill with which the poet of *Pl* reworked the prose legend of Placitus supports this contention. It does not mean, however, that these poets, or indeed others working from the liturgy or homiletic literature, used only a poetic register. Several words and phrases that would have been neologisms in the general Icelandic vocabulary at or near the time the poems were composed appear for the first time or are among the earliest recorded usages in these poems.[19]

The corpus of kennings from poetry on Christian subjects presents a number of challenges to the editor in terms of their identification, classification and interpretation. These difficulties have been masked to a considerable extent in the standard editions to date, because of the tendency of earlier editors not to break down kennings into their component parts when interpreting and translating them. A great many Christian skaldic kennings assert qualities and activities of their referents that are demonstrably true in terms of Christian doctrine. Thus *mildingr himins* 'the king of heaven' (*Pét* 5/4) is God, while *móðir guðs* 'the mother of God' (*Pét* 37/2) can only refer to the Virgin Mary. The referents of these kennings, of which there are very many in Volume 7, are marked in the Translation by lower case nouns, rather than small capitals, and preceded by an equals sign in square brackets. So the referent of *Pét* 5/4 *mildingr himins* appears as [= God].

It is sometimes difficult to distinguish whether a particular kenning refers to the Christian deity or a human ruler, because the types of kennings most commonly employed for both are the same. Snorri Sturluson shows his awareness of the role context plays in poetry of the Christian period in determining the referents of

---

[19] There are a number of interesting examples, some from the twelfth-century *drápur*. *Leið* has *manna* 'manna' 20/7; *krisma* 'chrism' 24/6; *Has* has *paradís* 'paradise' 24/6. Of the later poems, *Alpost* has *stím* 'tumult, din' 5/6, *plagaz* 'to devote oneself' 18/8 (also *Mey* 55/7) and *frómi*, 3rd pers. sg. pres. subj, of *fróma* 'to celebrate, honour' 12/9; *Brúðv* has *fráleitr* 'ridiculous' 23/6 and *var* 'shelter' 30/3; *Lil* has *margbrugðinn*, 'often changed, shifty', 16/6 and *auðgint* 'easily beguiled' 18/1; *Mgr* has *edik* 'vinegar' 30/8.

kennings for rulers: *þar* [in *Geisl* 16/5-8, which refers to both God and S. Óláfr] *koma saman kenningar, ok verðr sá at skilja af stoð, er ræðr skáldskapinn, um hvárn kveðit er konunginn* (*SnE* 1988 I, 78) 'here kennings become ambiguous, and the person interpreting the poetry has to distinguish from the context which king is being referred to' (Faulkes 1987, 127). Similarly, it is often difficult to decide whether kennings for the deity refer to the first or the second person of the Trinity because they frequently follow the same models (specific kennings for the Holy Spirit are few, see below, and are largely confined to *Heildr*). *Meissner* notes this difficulty regarding the persons of the Christian deity (369-71).

There are two points at issue here, one theological and the second to do with the metalanguage of skaldic poetry. The fact that many, but not all, kennings for the first two persons of the Trinity follow similar models depends upon the assumption that the Christian God in his role as Father is the primary expression of the Godhead, and that the person of Christ, Son of God, is, in theological terms, secondary. Skalds seem to have expressed this dogma by using the same models for both persons in many cases. However, they were also able to distinguish God the Father and God the Son where necessary. They did this in one of two ways. First, there is a small number of kennings that can only refer to Christ, represented as the Son of God (*Meissner*, 386). In this edition, such kenning-types are represented [= Christ] in the Translations. Much more commonly, poets indicate by context alone, or by an epithet qualifying the kenning proper, that a particular kenning, which could in other contexts refer to God the Father, must in fact refer to the Son. An example is *Has* 26/5-7, where the kenning *þreknennin sættandi ýta* 'powerful reconciler of men', could refer to God but must here refer to Christ, as the immediate context includes a reference to his Passion. Such contextually-determined instances of kennings for God the Son are represented [= God (= Christ)] in the Translations, and are by far the most frequent type of kenning for Christ.

Leið 31 offers an interesting example of a skaldic poet's ability to vary standard kenning types for the Christian deity. Here the poet has carefully chosen to refer to all three persons of the Trinity in the context of his treatment of Christ's Harrowing of Hell and Resurrection on Easter Sunday. As is often the case in skaldic practice, this anonymous skald refers to, but does not produce a kenning for, the Holy Spirit (*heilagr andi* 31/6). He makes his point about the indissolubility of the Trinity by stating that *snjallastr faðir allra* 'the most valiant father of all' (31/2) rose from the dead on Easter Sunday and that *sonr hauðrs sólar* 'the son of the land of the sun' (31/3-4) comforted men. By attributing the Resurrection to the Father, the *Leið*-poet shows theological and poetic subtlety, and by deliberately introducing a rather unusual kenning for the Son (the base-word being 'son' rather than the expected 'ruler'), he underlines his awareness that it was God the Son who was resurrected and thereby made salvation possible for humanity.

A decision was made in 2005 by the General Editors of *SkP* to exclude from the count of kennings two-noun periphrases that have the form of kennings, but are actually translations into Icelandic of stereotyped Latin periphrases to be found in Christian texts (like the Bible, the liturgy, hymns, sequences and sermons), on the ground that they do not offer a model that can be varied, as the kenning proper can be.[20] In other words, form and structure are not sufficient grounds for a phrase to be classified as a kenning; variability on a conventional model or base must also be demonstrably present. In the Translations and Notes to this edition, kenning-like periphrases of this kind – and there are many of them – have not been treated as kennings, even though they fulfil some of the functions of kennings.

Some examples of kenning-like periphrases for the major referents of Christian skaldic poetry will clarify this position. Among latinate periphrases for God and Christ are: *Geisl* 4/4 *sunna réttlætis* 'sun of righteousness' (Lat. *sol justitiae*), *Mey* 3/3 *sólin riettlætis* 'the sun of justice' (used there of Christ), also Árni *Gd* 13/2[IV], used there of God; *Pét* 40/6 *lífs brunnr* 'life's well' (used of Christ), modelled on Lat. *fons vitae*; *Líkn* 7/7-8 *vísi vegs* 'king of glory', probably referring to God rather than Christ (Lat. *rex gloriae*); *Líkn* 36/1 *heims verð* 'world's price' (Lat. *pretium saeculi*); *Líkn* 37/1-2 *ljóst lamb guðs* 'the radiant Lamb of God' (Lat. *agnus Dei*), both referring to Christ. Periphrases for the Holy Spirit include *Heildr* 2/3, 4 *af mætum brunni lífsins* 'from the worthy spring of life' ; cf. Jer. II.13 *fons aquae vitae* (used in Jer. of God). The majority of kenning-like periphrases for the Holy Spirit in *Heildr* are clearly modelled on Latin phrases, especially in stanzas 11-16, which translate the hymn *Veni creator spiritus*. In all, there are no fewer than twenty-five such kenning-like periphrases for the Holy Spirit in *Heildr* but only a very small number in other skaldic poems. A possible periphrasis for Christ's Cross is *Líkn* 42/2 *sigrstoð* 'victory-post', which may be calqued on Lat. *trop(h)aeum* 'victory memorial' (see further George Tate's note to this line). This example, because its status is uncertain, has been treated as a 'normal' kenning.

There are many periphrases for the Virgin Mary modelled on Latin epithets, of which a selection are given here. *Geisl* 2/5, 8, 7 *frá bjartri stjǫrnu flæðar* '[Christ was born] from the bright star of the flood' (Lat. *stella maris* 'star of the sea'). This is the only example of such an imitation of a very popular Mary-epithet, except for *Mdr* 3/4 and 30/2 *stiarna siovar* 'star of the sea'. In *Mdr* there are many such latinate epithets for the Virgin, including, at 10/1, *ker kosta* 'vessel of virtues' (Lat. *vas honoris*). We also find periphrases like *Has* 61/1-2 *blíðr hǫfðingi snóta* 'gentle chief of women' (cf. Lat. *regina virginum* 'queen of virgins'); cf. *Mdr* 5/2 and *Pét* 5/8 *konungr vífa* 'king of women'. Also, but with significant embellishment from traditional kenning-types so that they are not simply calques on Latin phrases, there are examples like *Has* 60/2-4 *alskírt hǫfuðmusteri ens hæsta hildings himins birti* 'altogether brilliant chief temple of

---

[20] They may be repeated without change, however, by the same or different poets, as some of the examples below demonstrate.

the highest prince of the brightness of heaven' (Lat. *templum domini* 'temple of the Lord') and *enn glæsti kastali grams hauðrs glyggs* 'the beautiful fortress of the prince of the land of the wind' (*Has* 60/5, 7-8). Only the second elements of these periphrases have been treated as kennings.

The influence of Latin phrases is also perceptible in periphrases for heaven and holy men. *Geisl* 63/8 offers *friðarsýn* 'vision of peace', i.e. 'the Heavenly Jerusalem'. The compound is a direct translation of Lat. *visio pacis* 'vision of peace', which was believed to be the meaning of the name Jerusalem. This etymology was well known in the Middle Ages and appears frequently in theological writings and in hymns, the most famous being *Urbs beata Hierusalem, dicta pacis visio* (*AH* 51:119; *Ordo Nidr.*, 292-3, 335-6). The image of the martyrs and confessors living in endless heavenly bliss, ultimately derived from Scripture (Rev. VII.13-17, XXI.3-4, etc.), is a commonplace in hymns for the feasts of saints, and is probably reflected in Ník *Jóndr* 2/3 *himna sýn* 'a vision of the heavens'. The phrase *váttr dýrðar* 'witness of glory' is a periphrasis for a martyr in kenning form, which expands the sense of the Latin, ultimately Greek, noun. It occurs in *Pl* 26/3 (referring to Plácitus), while in *Geisl* 62/3 it is used of S. Óláfr. In *Andr* 2/1 *yfirpostulinn ástar* 'chief apostle of love' refers to Andrew, though the Lat. *apostolus charitatis* 'apostle of love', usually refers to either Paul or John; other periphrastic references to Andrew are *Mey* 1/7-8 *æzta lífi yfirpostulann* 'the most outstanding chief Apostle' and *Mv I* 2/1 *inn æsti ástvin guðs* 'noblest bosom friend of God'.

8. The Treatment of Foreign Learned Words and Foreign Personal Names in Skaldic Poetry

Christian skaldic poetry contains a wealth of learned foreign words and personal names, mostly Latin, or latinised Greek and Hebrew, which have been treated in a highly divergent and idiosyncratic manner by earlier editors. Whereas such words in Old English have been subject to several studies (see Sievers 1885, 492-3; Pogatscher 1888; Sievers 1893, 124-7; Pyles 1943; Campbell 1959, §§493-564, esp. §§545-64), scant attention has been paid to the spelling, stress and quantity of learned foreign words in Old Norse poetry. In an 1894 article, most likely prompted by Pogatscher's (1888) extensive study of Old English and Larsson's (1893) examination of the placement of accents in the *Icelandic Homily Book* (*HómÍsl*), Finnur Jónsson attempted to establish rules for accentuation and stress in Latin and Hebrew words in Old Norse poetry. His discussion suffers from an imperfect knowledge of Old Norse metrics and prosody, but the principles he formulated became normative in his editions of Christian poetry in *Skj* B. In *Skald*, Kock at first followed Finnur's spelling and accentuation, and only in the later stages of his editing (of *Mgr* and *Mey*) did he begin to correct Finnur's erroneous orthographic practices (see *NN* §§2680, 2970).

For the purposes of the present edition, we have reexamined the entire corpus of Latin and latinised Greek and Hebrew names in skaldic poetry from the ninth to the fourteenth century, and we have sought to establish rules for the distribution of stress and quantity that will be outlined in some detail below. The new guidelines are based on the metrical treatment of foreign words in *dróttkvætt*, *hrynhent*, *fornyrðislag* and *hálfhneppt*, while paying close attention to Old Norse prosody as well as Latin stress and quantity. Because the *dróttkvætt* and *hrynhent* metres are syllable-counting and contain internal rhymes, the metrical types are easier to identify than in Old English alliterative poetry. The placement and quality of the internal rhymes are also very helpful for establishing guidelines for the treatment of the foreign words and names (for the metrical patterns of Old Norse poetry, see Gade 1995, 73-172).

In Old Norse poetry, the stress patterns in Latin words and phrases tend to agree with the stress patterns of such words in Old English alliterative poetry (see Sievers 1885, 492-3; Pogatscher 1888; Sievers 1893, 124-7; Pyles 1943; Campbell 1959, §§545-64) while adhering to the rules that govern Old Norse metres. In other words, the words are treated as learned loanwords following native stress patterns (see Pyles 1943, 894). Full stress falls on the first syllable of a word, thus obliterating the Latin stress on the penultimate or antepenultimate in trisyllabic, tetrasyllabic and pentasyllabic words. But the syllables that received stress in Latin are usually also stressed in Old Norse (for a detailed discussion of Latin stress and quantity, see Allen 1989, 83-94).

Consider the following example (fully stressed syllables are underlined): *Heil* 11/2 *Dómiciánus* 'Domitian'. As far as fully stressed syllables are concerned, they must be metrically long (see Sievers 1885, 492; Pogatscher 1888, 21-4; Pyles 1943, 895-9). In Old Norse poetry, a syllable comprising three or more morae (a long vowel plus one or more consonants or a short vowel plus two or more consonants) is long and can occupy a metrically long, stressed position (see Kuhn 1983, 53-5; Gade 1995, 28-34): *Mey* 26/1 *Ágáða* 'Agatha', *Mgr* 29/6 *Longínus* 'Longinus'. In the present edition length is therefore assigned to a syllable occupying metrically long, stressed positions regardless of the Latin quantity (hence *Plácitus* and not *Placitus*). However, a metrically long, stressed position can also be filled by two short syllables (resolution, see Kuhn 1983, 55-6; Gade 1995, 60-6) when the metre demands this and the corresponding Latin quantity in the first of the resolved syllables is short: *Mey* 56/5 *Benedictus* 'Benedict', *Heil* 11/4 *Elutérium* 'Eleutherius'. In the excerpted corpus of Latin names and words, there are also instances in which a short syllable can resolve with a long syllable and fill a metrically long position: *Mgr* 12/6 *Pilátus* 'Pilate', *Mgr* 21/2 *korónu* 'crown', *Mgr* 7/2 *Heródes* 'Herod', *Pét* 33/5 *Saphíra* 'Sapphira' (for indigenous examples and their absence in early poetry, see Kuhn 1929, 184-214). Under reduced stress, two short syllables can occupy two metrical positions: *Pl* 6/6 *Ágápitus* 'Agapitus', *Pl* 11/6 *Plácitus* 'Placitus', and, in a metrically subordinate position, *Leið* 18/8 *pharaóni* 'Pharaoh'.

Unstressed syllables regularly occupy dips: *Mey* 26/1 *Ágáða* 'Agatha', *Mgr* 29/6 *Longínus* 'Longinus'. But a dip can also be filled by two short syllables (neutralisation; see Gade 1995, 60-6): *Mey* 52/1 *Barb<u>a</u>ra* 'Barbara', *Mey* 50/3 *Br<u>ígi</u>ða* 'Bridget'.

Latin names with hiatus (two consecutive vowels) present a special problem. In Old Norse, no syllables can consist of a sequence of two orthographic short vowels unless the two vowels are part of a diphthong. Words containing the sequence of a long vowel plus a short vowel of the type *glóa* 'glow' and *búa* 'dwell, occupy, prepare' are treated metrically like such short disyllabic words as *fara* 'go, travel' and *vita* 'know' (see Kuhn 1983, 54; Gade 1995, 29-34). In that respect, Old Norse hiatus words can occupy a lift under resolution and a dip under neutralisation, or they can be treated as disyllabic under secondary stress. The Latin names in our corpus that contain the sequence of two short vowels are treated metrically like indigenous Old Norse words with the sequence long vowel plus short vowel, and are therefore reproduced as such, that is, by assigning length to the first vowel (*Heil* 13/2 *Díonísíus* 'Dionysius'). The Latin endings *-eas, -eus, -ia, -ias, -ius* are treated uniformly as Old Norse hiatus words, regardless of Latin stress or lack thereof, and they are given as *-éas, -éus, -ía, -ías, -íus* respectively. The examples below illustrate the assignment of length and the metrical treatment of such names.

1. Resolution under full stress:
   Pl 6/8 *<u>Þe</u>opistus trú misti* 'Theopistus faith lost'
2. Non-resolution under reduced stress:
   Alpost 13/1 *heldr Matth<u>ía</u>s vildi* 'rather Matthew wanted'
3. Neutralisation under lack of stress:
   Mey 39/3 *Lúc<u>ía</u> stóð í loganum blessuð* 'Lucia stood in the flame blessed'.

As in Old English (and Gothic), the syllabic [i:] in such names as *María* 'Mary' may have developed into the glide [j] when the trisyllabic name is treated as metrically disyllabic (*Márja* rather than *María*). That is certainly the case when the name occurs in the cadence in *dróttkvætt* or *hrynhent* lines, as in *Mgr* 19/4 *sárin dróttins blessuð Már<u>ía</u>* '(the) wounds of (the) Lord blessed Mary'. Because it usually cannot be ascertained whether <ía> is treated as a resolved disyllabic ending or as [ja] (except in line-final position in the cadence), the present edition does not attempt to make a distinction between syllabic [i] and the glide [j], but retains the manuscript spellings with a syllabic vowel.

Multisyllabic names consisting of the sequence of a short vowel followed by a long vowel are not treated as hiatus words in the poetic corpus. Therefore names like *Díoclecíánus* 'Diocletian' (*Dío - cleci - ánus*, with resolution in metrical position one and neutralisation in metrical position two) and *Adríánus* 'Adrian' (*Adri - ánus*) are both tetrasyllabic from a metrical point of view: *Heil* 26/3 *Díoclecíánus dauða nýjan* 'Diocletian new death', *Pl* 58/7 *andrán Adríánus* 'life-deprivation Adrian'. In the rare event that a Latin word contains the sequence of two vowels occupying two metrical positions (fully stressed and non-stressed), length is assigned to both vowels: *Mgr* 40/2 *pátris déi formið gráti* 'of the son of God perform with weeping'. That is also the case when such names as *Síón* 'Zion' occupy two fully stressed positions: *Mv III*, 20/7 *að sönnu las hann Síóns* 'indeed read he Zion's' (*hálfhneppt* metre).

In disyllabic latinised Hebrew names it is impossible to establish the length of the second syllable unless length can be determined by metrical position or by internal rhyme. Sometimes the length assignment is straightforward, as in *Ádám* 'Adam' (*Lil* 64/4 *forn Ádám við Jésú kvámu* 'old Adam from Jesus' arrival'), *Dávíð* 'David' (*Has* 48/2 *Dávíð konungr síðan* 'David the king later') and *Ebrón* 'Hebron' (*Pét* 20/8 *Ebrón Móisi þjónar* 'Hebron Moses serves'). But the majority of such names contain a second syllable which is unstressed and occupies a dip. Following Larsson (1893), Finnur Jónsson (1894; *Skj* B) consistently assigned length to the second syllable in such names as *Tómás* 'Thomas', *Énók* 'Enoch', etc., whereas Kock (*Skald*) did not. In the present edition, length is assigned to the second syllable in disyllabic Hebrew names when warranted by internal rhyme or metre. In the absence of metrical evidence, we adhere to the Latin and Greek quantities: *Énoch, Jácob, Jósép, Símón*; but *Jónas, Júdas, Tómas*.

Some Latin and Hebrew names pose special problems for the assignment of stress and quantity because they are treated differently in different metrical environments or they are metrically ambivalent. The Hebrew name *Moyses*, for example (Latin *Mōȳsēs*, usually spelled in the Old Norse manuscripts with the diphthongs <oi> or <oy>), apparently could have length on either the first or the second element of <oi> / <oy> or on both. Consider the following examples: *Pét* 20/8 *Ebrón Móisi þjónar* 'Hebron Moses serves' (with resolution in metrical position three), *Leið* 18/2 *lagavísum Móísi* 'law-wise Moses' (treated as trisyllabic with secondary stress on *Mó-* and primary stress and internal rhyme on *-ís*). The stress patterns in such names as *Simonis* 'Simon's' and *Jacobus* 'Jacob' are also difficult to determine: *Mey* 8/8 *góðr og mildur Símonis/Símónis bróðir* 'good and generous Simon's brother', *Mey* 8/5 *mengið nefnir Jácobum/Jacóbum yngra* '(the) crowd mentions Jacob (the) younger', *Mey* 9/8 *mektar sannr og Jácobus/Jacóbus annar* 'power-true and Jacob (the) second'. In all three instances the metre allows for neutralisation in metrical position six (*-onis, -obis*) or for resolution in metrical position five (*Simón-, Jacób-*). In these cases, we observe the Latin stress pattern with stress on the penultimate syllable (*Simónis, Jacóbus, Jacóbum*).

As far as the spelling of foreign names is concerned, earlier editions (in particular *Skj* B and *Skald*) frequently icelandicise the Latin spellings found in the manuscripts (e.g. *Jóakíms* or *Jóakims* for 'ioachim', *Káfarnáum* for 'Kapharnaum', *Kéfás* or *Kéfas* for 'cephas', etc.). In the present edition we attempt to reproduce the Latin orthography in the manuscripts more faithfully, but we assign accents to show the distribution of stress and length (see the discussion above). Because the orthographic representations of Latin and latinised Greek and Hebrew words were conservative (and the pronunciation must have been conservative as well), we do not subject such words to the same rules of normalisation as we apply to the indigenous Icelandic vocabulary. For example, although <é> ([eː]) was certainly diphthongised during the fourteenth century, there is no evidence that this vowel was diphthongised in such names as *Pétrus* 'Peter' and *Andréas* 'Andrew'. Rather than subjecting these names to whole-scale normalisation (*Pietrus, Andrieas*), we retain the forms used in the manuscripts. New forms will be recorded in the texts and commented upon in the notes only when warranted by strong phonological evidence (e.g. internal rhymes).

9. Normalisation of Fourteenth-Century Poetry

The orthographic representations of fourteenth-century poems in *Skj* B and *Skald* are inconsistent and fail to reflect sound changes that are characteristic of this period. For example, even though *ǫ* and *ø* merged to *ö* in the thirteenth century, both editions consistently render the new phoneme as <ǫ> rather than as <ö>. Other changes, like the diphthongisation of *é* (*é* > *ie*; see below), are not reflected in the orthography at all. Likewise, syntactic innovations, such as the frequent omission of the relative particle *er*, are silently emended in *Skj* B and *Skald* to correspond with earlier practice. In the present edition we have adopted a series of fourteenth-century orthographic normalisations listed below (see A.), while syntactic and morphological idiosyncrasies characteristic of the fourteenth century (see B.) are left in the Text without comment.

None of the late Christian poems can be dated with any certainty, and these poems represent different stages of phonetic development. For example, progressive *v*-umlaut (*vá-* > *vó-* > *vo-*; see *ANG* §86; Björn K. Þórólfsson 1925, xi-xii; Bandle 1956, 41) is occasionally reflected in *Vitn* (8/8, 16/2), *Mv II* (8/2, 14/6), *Alpost* (8/8), and *Mey* (47/8, 54/6), but not in any other fourteenth-century poem. Likewise, the quantity of <o> in internal rhymes in such words as *dróttinn* 'lord' varies significantly from poem to poem (*dróttinn* or *drottinn*; see Björn K. Þórólfsson 1925, 6), and sometimes both [oː] and [o] are attested within the same poem (e.g. *Alpost* 4/2, 8/8). Vowel quantity was unstable during this period, and our practice is therefore conservative: progressive *v*-umlaut (*vó-*), for example, is only represented orthographically when it can be ensured by internal rhyme. The spelling of such words as *dróttinn* 'lord' (*dróttinn* or *drottinn*; see above) is left to the individual editor and justified in the Introduction or Notes. We also adhere to a conservative practice as far as desyllabification of *-r* is concerned (*-r* > *-ur*, see below), and desyllabified forms are only introduced when required by the metre.

A few observations should also be made here on the two *ljóðaháttr* poems in this volume, *Sól* and *Hsv*, as they present some special difficulties. Although it is not possible to date either poem with certainty, we have made an editorial decision to regard them as 1250+, but not post-1300. Thus, they have been normalised to later thirteenth- rather than fourteenth-century standards. However, they are mentioned here because many of the problems associated with editing them derive from the very late date of the manuscripts in which they have been preserved and from the probability that fourteenth-century and later scribes were unaware of the finer points of *ljóðaháttr* metre. Our policy with *Sól* and *Hsv* has been to leave later features of syntax and word order, such as non-cliticised pronouns and the negative adverb *eigi* 'not', unnormalised and unnoted, except where their presence is contra-indicated on metrical grounds, generally where they appear at the ends of lines. In such cases, if a metrically correct reading or word order is given in one or more of the subsidiary manuscripts, but not in the main one, the metrically correct reading has been chosen. In cases where none of the manuscripts yields a metrically correct reading, we do not emend conjecturally but point out the deficiency in the notes. Our practice thus differs greatly from that of *Skj* and *Skald*, both of which attempt to make the *ljóðaháttr* poems correspond more closely to *fornyrðislag* by deleting *eigi* and replacing it with the cliticised verbal negation *–at*, and by silently omitting pronouns, cliticised or non-cliticised, that occur in extended dips. Some of the more extreme differences between our texts and those produced by Finnur Jónsson and Kock are pointed out in the notes to individual stanzas.

When the texts of *Skj* B and *Skald* are referred to in the notes, the orthography of Finnur and Kock is retained, that is, we do not subject their texts to our principles of normalisation. Hence the notes often contain two different systems of orthographic representation (e.g. *og* and *ok* 'and', *mjög* and *mjǫk* 'much', *mier* and *mér* 'to me' etc.). This mixture of forms is unfortunate, but unavoidable.

Below is an outline of the standard normalisations (A.) adopted in the present edition and a list of fourteenth-century phonological, morphological and syntactic features (B.) which occur occasionally in the poems. Such features are retained in the texts without comment in the notes to individual stanzas.

A. **Standard Normalisations**
   I. ***Phonology***
      1. *Vowels in stressed syllables*
         i. é > ie (*ANG* §103; Björn K. Þórólfsson 1925, xiv): h*é*r > h*ie*r 'here'
         ii. e > ie | k, g, h– (*ANG* §103): k*e*till > k*ie*till 'kettle', g*e*fa > g*ie*fa 'to give', h*e*kk > h*ie*kk 'hung'
         iii. e > ei | –ng (*ANG* §102; Björn K. Þórólfsson 1925, xii): l*e*ngi > l*ei*ngi 'long' (adv.)
         iv. ö > au | –ng, nk (*ANG* §105): s*ö*ngr > s*au*ngr 'song'
      2. *Consonants*
         i. ð > d | [+short syllable] l, n, m– (*ANG* §238, 1b): tal*ð*a > tal*d*a 'counted, told'
         ii. ð > d | b, lf, lg, ng, rg– (*ANG* §238, 1b): skelf*ð*a > skelf*d*a 'trembled'
         iii. pt > ft (*ANG* §247): lo*pt* > lo*ft* 'air'

iv. t, k > ð, g | [- stress]–# (*ANG* §248; Björn K. Þórólfsson 1925, xxvii, xxxii): e*k* > eg 'I', a*t* > a*ð* 'that'
   v. rl > ll (*ANG* §272.1; Björn K. Þórólfsson 1925, xxx): ka*rl* > ka*ll* 'man'
   vi. rs > ss (*ANG* §272.3; Björn K. Þórólfsson 1925, xxx): ve*rs* > ve*ss* 'verse'
   vii. rst > st (*ANG* §272.3): ský*rst* > ský*st* 'most clear'
   viii. ts < z > > ss (*ANG* §274.2): Gi*z*urr > Gi*ss*urr 'Gissur'
   ix. gn– > n– (*ANG* §290): *gn*eisti > *n*eisti 'spark'
   II. *Morphology*
   1. Mediopassive or middle voice: –sk > –z (*ANG* §544; see also Kjartan O. Ottósson 1992): kalla*sk* > kalla*z* 'to be called'.
   2. Desyllabification (only when justified by metre): –r > –ur (*ANG* §161b; see also Jón Þorkelsson 1863; Stefán Karlsson 1964): hest*r* > hest*ur* 'horse'
B. Occasional Syntactic, Morphological, and Phonological Peculiarities
   1. Loss of the relative particle *er* in the combination demonstrative + relative particle (*NS* §261): *Vitn* 3/3 kóngr, *sá* átti unga 'king, who had a young'.
   2. Loss of *er* after *þá* 'when', *þar* 'where', *þegar* 'as soon as', *síðan* 'after' (*NS* §265, Anm. 2a): *Sól* 6/3 *þá* hann veginn vaknaði 'when he slain awoke'
   3. Loss of *að* 'that' after *svá* 'so that', *þó* 'although', *því* 'because' (*NS* §265, Anm. 2b): *Sól* 54/5 *svá* víða þótti mér 'so that widely seemed to me'
   4. 1st person sg. pret. subj. ending -a > -i (*ANG* §536.1): *Vitn* 26/1 Vær*i* eg skyldr að skýra 'should I be obliged to explain'
   5. Occasional reintroduction by analogy of v- | -o (*ANG* §235.1): *Mv II*, 4/7 *V*urðu þau; af velferð 'became they; from prosperity'
   6. 6. Devoicing of g before s: hu*x*an 'thought' as opposed to earlier hugsan (*ANG* §239.1b.): *Mv I*, 6/1 Vó*x* hræðilig huxan 'grew (a) terrible thought'.

10. How to use this Edition

SkP is intended for a variety of users: for students and scholars of Old Norse and other medieval European languages and literatures, for scholars in cognate disciplines such as history, archaeology, the history of religion, and comparative literature, and for users whose primary interest is in skaldic poetry. In view of its likely augmented readership, *SkP* contains a greater proportion of introductory and explanatory material than is to be found in most previous editions, certainly in comparison with *Skj*, where it is minimal. Most of the explanatory material is to be found in the Introductions to poems, including the skald biographies, which appear at the head of the oeuvre of named skalds whose authorship of poetry is known;[21] in the context sections, which indicate the wider prose context(s) in which a verse or set of verses has been preserved (there are few of these in Volume 7, as most Christian poems are not embedded in prose texts); and in the notes to each stanza.

Each poem, single verse (*lausavísa*) or fragment has a distinct siglum in *SkP*, which in many cases is different from that used in *Skj* and in the list at the beginning of *Lexicon Poeticum* 1931 (*LP*). A comparative table of sigla used in *SkP*, *Skj* and *LP* is included in the introductory part of each volume of *SkP*. The text of each poem, single verse or fragment has been established by its editor on the foundation of a base manuscript, judged by the editor to be the best or (in some cases) the only witness to the probable original. The text will have been normalised to the standard appropriate to its probable date of origin.[22] Below the stanza is the same text rendered in a prose order, and underneath that is an English translation. As far as possible, the translation provides a version close to the sense of the Icelandic text. Unlike most other translations of skaldic poetry, kennings are here given their full sense value, that is, both base-word and determinant are translated and the referent, not being part of the actual text but implicit in it, is given in small capitals within square brackets after each kenning. Referents of one category of kennings, which refer to specific individuals, are given within square brackets in lower case preceded by an = sign, in order to indicate that these referents are literally equivalent to the periphrasis of base-word and determinant within the text. For example, 'the son of Óðinn' is designated [= Þórr] and 'lord of the heavens' [= God]. Angle brackets within the English translation are used to provide the generic sense value of Old Norse mythological names, such as Hildr <valkyrie> or alternative poetic names for mythological beings, such as Viðurr <= Óðinn>. In the latter case, an = sign appears to the left of the 'normal' name.

The editorial apparatus allows the reader to compare the edited version of the base manuscript with the text in other manuscript witnesses. A reference is also given to the text's designation in *Skj* B, comprising the poet's name (if any) as given there, the title of the poem or fragment and equivalent stanza number. The *Mss* line lists the base manuscript first in bold type, followed by the other manuscript witnesses in assumed chronological order, each with folio or page number in round brackets immediately following. Paper manuscripts are distinguished from those of parchment or vellum by having a superscript ^{x} after the manuscript siglum. Where the poetic text is found in more than one prose source, abbreviated reference to that source is given in

---

[21] One of the biographies relevant to Volume 7 poetry, that of Einarr Skúlason, composer of *Geisli*, appears in Volume 2.

[22] A full discussion of normalisation in the edition as a whole is in the Introduction to *SkP* in Volume I. Section 9 above covers only the fourteenth century. The actual orthography of the base manuscript for each poem can be seen in the transcripts available in the electronic edition, where images of the manuscripts are also available.

italics within round brackets immediately after the group of manuscripts representing that source.

Only significant manuscript variants, not simple orthographical variants or standard normalisations are given in the *Readings* line, unless the unnormalised manuscript reading is regarded as significant for some reason or cannot be normalised, in which case it is placed within inverted commas. Where variants are given, the lemma (the reading of the base manuscript) is given first, followed by the readings of other manuscripts, separated from the lemma by a colon. In cases where the editor has not followed the base manuscript, the reading of another manuscript is in first place, followed by a colon, and the formula '*so* X', to indicate that this is not the reading of the base manuscript.

The *Editions* line lists all significant previous editions of the text, beginning with *Skj*, *Skald* and *NN*, and followed by other editions, usually in chronological order, giving their date of publication, and the page upon which the verse in question appears.

The *Notes* are intended to address significant phonological, metrical, lexicographical and above all interpretative issues as well as questions of a broader contextual nature. Although the editors do not aim to give a comprehensive history of scholarship and previous editorial practice, significant editorial interpretations and emendations are discussed and evaluated in the Notes. On the matter of emendation, this edition is more conservative than most of its predecessors. All emended text, that is, letters or words that have no manuscript attestation, are given in italics. Where editors have omitted letters or words that are present in the manuscripts, the symbol * appears in the text and prose order. Purely conjectural emendation, where the editor conjectures what might have existed in a defective text in the absence of evidence in support, is usually avoided in *SkP*, though previous editors' conjectures may be mentioned in the Notes. However, if there are metrical or other forms of evidence within the text that support a proposed emendation, this may be adopted and justified by the editor. A sample verse with graphic explanations of the main features of the edition appears in the endpapers to Volume 7.

All abbreviated references to editions are expanded in the bibliography at the end of the volume. Abbreviated references to manuscripts are explained in the Introduction to each poem, when the manuscripts are first mentioned, while abbreviated references to prose sources also appear in the bibliography, as do references to secondary literature given in the notes to each stanza. General abbreviations used in this volume, aside from those that are very common, like e.g. and cf., are listed separately, while technical terms that may be unfamiliar to the reader are also glossed.

Christian Skaldic Poetry

The Corpus

The Twelfth Century

Einarr Skúlason
Biography in Volume II

Geisli
Edited by Martin Chase

Introduction

Einarr Skúlason's *Geisli* 'Light beam' (ESk *Geisl*) was almost certainly composed in 1153. Einarr had been associated with Haraldr gilli, who ruled Norway from 1130-6, and after Haraldr's death he composed poetry for his sons Eysteinn, Sigurðr and Ingi, who reigned jointly for a time. Einarr was particularly associated with Eysteinn, who made him his *stallari* or marshall. Internal evidence (sts 8 and 71) indicates that Eysteinn commissioned *Geisl*, and that it was performed in the Trondheim cathedral, with the three kings Eysteinn, Sigurðr and Ingi, as well as Archbishop Jón Birgisson, among the assembled crowd (sts 8-11). A famous passage in *Mork* (*Mork* 1932, 446) describes the event:

> Einarr Skúlason was in the company of the brothers Sigurðr and Eysteinn, and King Eysteinn was a great friend of his. Eysteinn asked him to compose a poem in honor of Saint Óláfr, and he did so. He presented it north in Þrándheimr [Trondheim] in the very confines of Christ Church, and it was accompanied by great miracles. A sweet fragrance rose in the church, and people say that there were intimations from the king himself that he thought well of the poem (Andersson and Gade 2000, 393).

The poem refers to the see of Trondheim as an archbishopric (st. 65), which means that it was composed after the elevation of the see in the spring of 1153, and cannot have been composed later than the summer of 1155, when Ingi killed Sigurðr. The brothers were already feuding in 1154, which makes 1153 the likely date of composition. *Geisl* may have been commissioned for performance on the feast of S. Óláfr, 29 July, in that year. The establishment of an archbishopric in Norway meant more power for the church and less for the king. It also meant closer ties with Rome: Cardinal Nicholas Breakspear, the future Pope Adrian IV, travelled from Rome to Trondheim to consecrate Jón Birgisson as the first archbishop.

Geisl is the earliest skaldic *drápa* to have survived intact. It comprises an introductory section (sts 1-17), a central section in which the refrain (*stef*) appears, called the *stefjabálkr* (sts 18-45), and the conclusion or *slæmr* (sts 46-71). For an extended discussion of the poem's structure and metrics, see Chase 2005, 16-20.

Einarr Skúlason artfully demonstrates his facility with the skaldic techniques later codified by Snorri Sturluson, but he also shows his knowledge of the Lat. religious poetry of Western Europe. He celebrates the military exploits of Óláfr the Viking much as earlier skalds praised earlier kings, and at the same time celebrates the holiness of Óláfr the saint using all the conventions of Lat. hagiography. For a detailed discussion of these and the miracles attributed to Óláfr in *Geisl* and various prose sources, see Chase 2005, 21-44. *Geisl* can be viewed both as a nationalistic work celebrating the great king who unified and brought Christianity to Norway, and as a celebration of the universal church, where national boundaries fade into the background and Óláfr the saint becomes another Christ (the light beam of the Sun of Righteousness), the ruler and protector of all believers. The earliest mentions of the poem refer to it as *Óláfs drápa* (*Mork* 1932, 446; *Hkr*, *ÍF* 28, 271), but the name *Geisli* is at least as old as Flateyjarbók, in which the text is preceded by the rubric *Geisli er Einarr Skulason quad vm Olaf Haraldsson* '*Geisli* which Einarr Skúlason composed about Óláfr Haraldsson'.

Only one medieval ms., Bergsbók, Holm perg 1 fol (Bb), contains a complete text of *Geisl*, but Flateyjarbók, GKS 1005 fol (Flat), contains all but sts 31-3, which are here edited from Bb. Flat has been chosen as the base text for this edn, though readings are frequently taken from Bb, when Bb's readings are clearly superior or Flat's cannot be satisfactorily construed. While neither ms. possesses a clear advantage, the arrangement of sts in Flat is judged to be better than in Bb. Both mss are highly corrupt, but the language and orthography of Flat are more regular. Both date from the late C14th and are thus considerably later than *Geisl* itself. In addition to the texts in Flat and Bb, individual sts are quoted in three important works: *SnE*, *Hkr* and the saga of S. Óláfr known as The Great Saga (*ÓH*). The five primary mss of *SnE* (Codex Regius, GKS 2365 4° [R]; Codex Trajectinus, Traj 1374^x [T^x]; Codex Wormianus, AM 242 fol [W]; Codex Upsaliensis, DG 11 [U]; AM 748 I b 4° [A]), contain portions of sts 1 (in *TGT*: A, W), 16 (R, T^x, W, U, A) and 59 (W). St. 37 appears in various versions of *Óláfs saga helga* in Flat; Bb; AM 63 fol^x (K^x); Eirspennill, AM 47 fol (E); AM 39 fol (39); AM 73 a^x (73a^x); Tómasskinna, GKS 1008 fol (Tóm); Holm perg 2 4° (Holm2); Holm perg 4 4° (Holm4). Hulda, AM 66 fol (H), contains sts 28 and 30 in its version of *Óláfs saga helga*, and the related ms. Hrokkinskinna, GKS 1010 fol (Hr), contains sts 28, 29 and 30. *Geisl* is preserved in eleven C17th and C18th mss: AM 1009 4°^{x}; AM 72 fol^x; Thott 1498 4°^{x}; Oslo UB 262 fol^x; Trondheim DKNVSB 3 4°^{x}; Bodl Boreal 102^x; Lbs 444 4°^{x}; JS 260 4°^{x}; JS 406 4°; Edinburgh Adv 21 2 9^x; Edinburgh Adv 21 8 14^x. All these mss are transcripts of Flat and have not been used in this edn.

A full listing and description of previous eds of *Geisl* can be consulted in Chase 2005, 5-8. In the present edn, reference is made to the eds of Finnur Jónsson (*Skj* A and B) and Kock (*Skald* and *NN*), Cederschiöld 1873 and Chase 2005.

1. Eins má óð ok bænir   Gǫfugt ljós boðar geisli
— alls ráðanda ins snjalla   gunnǫflugr miskunnar
vels fróðr, sás getr góða —   — ágætan býðk ítrum
guðs þrenning mér kenna.   Óláfi brag — sólar,

Þrenning eins guðs má kenna mér óð ok bænir; vels fróðr, sás getr góða ins snjalla ráðanda alls. Gunnǫflugr geisli sólar miskunnar boðar gǫfugt ljós — býðk ágætan brag ítrum Óláfi —,

The Trinity of one God can teach me poetry and prayers; he is indeed wise who gets the goodwill of the eloquent ruler of all [= God]. The battle-strong beam of the sun of mercy [= God > = Christ/Óláfr] proclaims a splendid light — I offer the excellent poem to glorious Óláfr —,

Mss: **Flat**(2ra), Bb(117ra); A(7v), W(110) (*TGT*, ll. 1-4). — *Readings*: [1] *óð: so* Bb, A, *orð* Flat, W [2] *ráðanda: valdanda* Bb, *kjósanda* A, W; *snjalla: ljósa* A, W [3] *vels* ('vel er'): *mjǫk er* Bb, A, 'mi[...]' W; *góða: greiða* Bb.

Editions: *Skj* Einarr Skúlason, 6. *Geisli* 1: AI, 459, BI, 427, *Skald* I, 211, *NN* §924; *Flat* 1860-8, I, 1, Cederschiöld 1873, 1, Chase 2005, 51, 123-5; *TGT* 1884-6, I, 112-13, *TGT* 1998, 228-9.

Context: Lines 1-4 of st. 1 are cited by Óláfr Þórðarson in *TGT* (c. 1250) in illustration of the rhetorical figure of *parenthesis*, which Óláfr defines as 'the interruption of a sentence by an interpolated clause' and (referring to Einarr's st.) 'here a second clause is interpolated and brought to a conclusion, before the first clause is ended'. He says that this figure always occurs in the verse-type that 'we' call *stælt* 'inlaid' or *álagsháttr* 'extension form', both terms Snorri Sturluson employs in *Ht* (*SnE* 1999, 10 and 16). — *Notes*: [All]: In the reading of sts 1-2 offered here, st. 2 is syntactically in apposition to *sólar* (gen. sg.) 'of the sun' of 1/8, and the two sts (to 2/4) thus constitute a single complex sentence interspersed with intercalary clauses. — [1] *óð* 'poetry': From the point of view of meaning, *orð* 'words' is as good a reading as *óð* 'poetry', but *óð* assonates nicely with the syllables containing vowel + <ð> in ll. 2, 3, 4, 5 and 7. — [2] *ráðanda* 'ruler': Is preferable to *valdanda* 'having the power to control' and *kjósanda* 'choosing, deciding', which has fatalistic overtones, inappropriate in a Christian context (cf. *Vsp* 20/10). *Ráðanda* makes it clear that God is ruling, rather than merely asserting that God is all-powerful, and it is commonly used of God in theological texts. — [4] *þrenning* 'Trinity': An appropriate opening, given that the Trondheim cathedral, in which Einarr delivered his *drápa*, was dedicated to the Holy Trinity (see Louis-Jensen 1977, 148). — [5, 6, 8] *gunnǫflugr geisli sólar miskunnar* 'the battle-strong beam of the sun of mercy': This kenning has as its referent both Christ and Óláfr. God is the sun and Christ its sunbeam, but the poet also identifies Óláfr with Christ through a process of typology developed in sts 1-6 (see further Chase 2003 and 2005, 21-7 and 124).

2. Þeirars heims (í heimi) | Sá lét bjartr frá bjartri
(heims) myrkrum brá (þeima) | berask maðr und skýjaðri
ok (ljós meðan) var vísi | (frægr stóð af því) flœðar
veðr- (kallaðisk) -hallar. | (fǫrnuðr) rǫðull stjǫrnu.

Þeirar [sólar], [e]s brá myrkrum heims, ok var vísi veðr-hallar, meðan kallaðisk ljós heims í þeima heimi. Sá maðr, bjartr rǫðull, lét berask frá bjartri stjǫrnu flœðar und skýjaðri; frægr fǫrnuðr stóð af því.

of that [sun] which destroyed the darkness of the world, and was the prince of the wind-hall [SKY/HEAVEN > = God (= Christ)], while he called himself the light of the world in this world. That man, the bright sun, caused himself to be born from the bright star of the sea under the cloud-rim [SKY/HEAVEN]; renowned prosperity proceeded from that.

Mss: **Flat**(2ra), Bb(117ra). — *Readings*: [5] bjartr: *so* Bb, bert Flat [6] maðr: mann Bb; skýjaðri: skýranni Bb [8] stjǫrnu: stjǫrnur Bb.

Editions: *Skj* Einarr Skúlason, 6. *Geisli* 2: AI, 459, BI, 427, *Skald* I, 211, *NN* §§925, 926, 2051; *Flat* 1860-8, I, 1, Cederschiöld 1873, 1, Chase 2005, 52, 125-7.

Notes: [All]: Sts 1-2 of *Geisl* are linked as the first l. of st. 2 is dependent on the final l. of st. 1 (cf. Kuhn 1983, 210-12). — [1-4]: The theologically sophisticated reading of these ll. offered here depends on elaborate word-play, tmesis and syntactic fragmentation. By emending *veðr* (l. 4) to *veðrs*, Finnur Jónsson (*Skj* B) produces the following sense: *Þeirar [sólar], es brá heims myrkrum í þeima heimi ok kallaðisk ljós heims, meðan vas vísi veðrs hallar* 'Of that [sun], which made an end of the world's darkness in this world and is called the world's light, while he was king of the storm's hall [SKY/HEAVEN]'. — [1] *þeirar [sólar]* 'of that [sun]': The gen. pron. refers back to *sólar* (1/8). — [1-2] *heims ... heimi ... heims*: In *dróttkvætt* metre *aðalhending* is not appropriate in an odd-numbered l., hence Kock's emendation of l. 1 (*Skald*) to *þeirar húms í heimi*. But exceptions were tolerated, and the rhyming pattern here is *iðurmælt*, one of the special effects explained in *Ht* (*SnE* 1999, 22). The repetition of *heims/heimi/heims* is also an echo of the prologue to the Gospel of John: *erat lux vera quae inluminat omnem hominem venientem in mundum / in mundo erat et mundus per ipsum factus est et mundus eum non cognovit* 'That was the true light, which enlighteneth every man that cometh into this *world*. He was in the *world*: and the *world* was made by him: and the *world* knew him not' (John I.9-10). The Bb reading *bjartr frá bjartri* (l. 5) follows a similar pattern and echoes the *lumen de lumine* 'light from light' of the *Credo*; it is probably a better reading than Flat's *bert* 'clearly'. See *NN* §2051 for a discussion of the use of identical rhyme in this st. and elsewhere in skaldic poetry. — [5, 8, 7] *frá bjartri stjǫrnu flœðar* 'from the bright star of the sea': A kenning-like circumlocution for the Virgin Mary, based on the Lat. phrase *stella maris* 'star of the sea', first appearing in the C9th hymn *Ave maris stella* (*AH* 51, 140). Although this epithet has the form of a kenning, such imitations of Lat. phrases have not been treated as kennings proper in this edn; for a discussion, see Introduction to this volume. — [6] *und skýjaðri* 'under the cloud-rim': Flat's sky/heaven-kenning is the *difficilior lectio* but Bb's *und skýranni* 'beneath the cloud-hall [SKY/HEAVEN]' together with the older nom. sg. form *mannr* (over Flat's *maðr*, cf. *ANG* §§261 and 278.4b) provides *aðalhending* and is preferred by both Finnur Jónsson (*Skj* B) and Kock (*Skald*). Neither *Skj* B nor *Skald* explain how the nom. sg. can be found after *lét berask* (ll. 5, 6).

3.   Siðar heilags brá sólar   Œztr þrifnuðr réð efnask
       — setrs vas þat fyr betra   oss, þás líf á krossi
       auðfinnǫndum annars   jarðar allra fyrða
       ómjós rǫðuls — ljósi.   ónauðigr tók dauða.

Ljósi sólar heilags siðar brá; þat vas auðfinnǫndum fyr betra ómjós setrs annars rǫðuls. Œztr þrifnuðr réð efnask oss, þás tók ónauðigr líf allra fyrða jarðar dauða á krossi.

The light of the sun of holy faith [= God > = Christ] was extinguished; for finders of riches [MEN] that preceded the better [light] of the not-small abode of another sun [SKY/HEAVEN > = God (= Christ)]. The best prosperity decided to bring itself to us when he, willing, won the life of all the men of earth through death on a cross.

Mss: **Flat**(2ra), Bb(117ra). — *Readings*:   [2] setrs: setr Bb   [3] -finnǫndum ('-finnandum'): *so* Bb, '-finnendum' Flat   [4] ómjós ('o mioss'): *so* Bb, 'o míors' Flat; ljósi: *so* Bb, 'liorsi' Flat   [5] réð: nam Bb.

Editions: *Skj* Einarr Skúlason, 6. *Geisli* 3: AI, 459, BI, 427, *Skald* I, 211, *NN* §§927, 928, 2315A; *Flat* 1860-8, I, 1, Cederschiöld 1873, 1, Chase 2005, 53, 127-9.

Notes: [1] *siðar* 'faith': This edn, with Finnur Jónsson (*Skj* B) and Kock (*Skald*; *NN* §2315), reads this as the gen. sg. of the noun *siðr* 'religious practice, faith' and construes: *Ljósi sólar heilags siðar brá* 'The light of the sun of holy faith was extinguished'. Another possibility is to read the first word with a long 'i', *síðar*, the comp. form of the adv. *síð*, with the sense *Síðar brá sólar ljósi* 'Later, the light of the sun [= Christ] was destroyed'. *Síðar* is then a reference to the preceding st., and its initial position in st. 3 may suggest that it is meant as a transition between the two. For this reading, see Chase 2005, 53 and 127. The long form, *síðar*, is unmetrical, however, as resolution is required in position one to avoid a hypermetrical l. — [2] *setrs* 'of the abode': Flat's reading requires the assumption of a noun ('light') for *betra* to qualify. Kock (*NN* §927; *Skald*) adopts Bb's *setr* to give *þat vas fyr betra setr* ... 'that was for [the purpose of] a better home ...'. — [2, 4, 3] *betra ómjós setrs annars rǫðuls* 'the better [light] of the not-small abode of another sun': This kenning is likely to refer to the new and more powerful light of the resurrected Christ by contrast with the kenning *ljósi sólar heilags siðar* 'the light of the sun of holy faith' in ll. 1, 4 where the reference is to Christ's death at the Crucifixion. Alternatively, the phrase *vas fyrir* could mean 'heralded' and its object be understood simply as 'the better light of heaven' (so *Skj* B).

4. Upp rann allrar skepnu
iðvandr á dag þriðja
Kristr með krapti hæstum
kunnr réttlætis sunnu.

Veitk, at mildr frá moldu
meginfjǫlði reis hǫlða
— iflaust má þat efla
ossa vǫn — með hónum.

Iðvandr Kristr, kunnr allrar skepnu, rann upp með hæstum krapti sunnu réttlætis á þriðja dag. Veitk, at mildr meginfjǫlði hǫlða reis frá moldu með hónum; iflaust má þat efla ossa vǫn.

Carefully-acting Christ, known to all creation, rose up with the utmost strength of the sun of righteousness on the third day. I know that a worthy great assembly of men rose from earth with him; beyond doubt that can strengthen our hope.

Mss: **Flat**(2ra), Bb(117ra). — *Readings*: [1] allrar: engla Bb [2] á: of Bb [3] með: rǽðr Bb [4] kunnr: kunn Bb; sunnu: sunna Bb.

Editions: *Skj* Einarr Skúlason, 6. *Geisli* 4: AI, 459, BI, 427, *Skald* I, 211; *Flat* 1860-8, I, 1, Cederschiöld 1873, 1, Chase 2005, 54, 129.

Notes: [1-4]: Finnur Jónsson (*Skj* B) and Kock (*Skald*) adopt the five Bb readings *engla* (l. 1), *of* (l. 2), *rǽðr* (l. 3), *kunn* and *sunna* (l. 4) and construe: *Réttlætis sunna, kunn engla skepnu, rann upp of þriðja dag; iðvandr Kristr rǽðr hæstum krapti* 'The sun of righteousness, known by the host of angels (*kendt af englenes skare*), rose up on the third day; Christ, careful in his doings, possesses the greatest power'. This relies on an unlikely gen. construction and a forced understanding of *skepna* 'creation, created thing'. In the Flat version, *kunnr allrar skepnu* 'known to all creation' (ll. 1, 4), the gen. is objective. According to Scripture (e.g. Rom. XVI.25-6), the Resurrection made the hidden mystery of Christ's saving power known to all nations. — [4] *sunnu réttlætis* 'the sun of righteousness': Another kenning-like periphrasis based on Lat. *iustitiæ sol oriens* 'the rising sun of righteousness' (cf. Mal. IV.2) is a name for Christ in the sequence *Deus Pater piissime* (*AH* 15, 13), and *Jón*[4] spells out the metaphor when it speaks of *sialf rettlætis solin lukt i likam, drottinn var Jesus Cristus* 'the sun of righteousness itself, our Lord Jesus Christ, enclosed in a human body' (*Jón*[4] 1874, 466). In ON prose the image is usually associated with the Incarnation and Nativity, but the Norw. homily *Jn die sancto pasce* 'On the holy day of Easter' links it to the rising sun of Easter: *At upp-runninni solo sáo þær ængil hia grof. þvi at þa megom vér scilia himnesca luti ef ret-lætes sol skin í hiortum vaorum* 'At the rising of the sun they saw an angel by the grave, because then we may understand heavenly things if the sun of righteousness shines in our hearts' (*HómNo*, 82).

5. Sonr sté upp með yndi Lofaðr sitr englum efri
    auðar mildr frá hauðri, — ǫðlinga hnígr þingat
    jǫfra beztr, til œztrar dǫglings hirð — á dýrðar
    alls ráðanda hallar. dagbóls konungr stóli.

Sonr alls ráðanda mildr auðar, beztr jǫfra, sté upp með yndi frá hauðri til œztrar hallar. Lofaðr konungr dagbóls sitr efri englum á stóli dýrðar; hirð dǫglings ǫðlinga hnígr þingat.

The son of the ruler of all, generous with riches [= God > = Christ], the best of princes, ascended with joy from earth to the highest hall. The praised king of the day-home [SKY/HEAVEN > = God (= Christ)] sits above the angels on the throne of majesty; the cohort of the prince of princes [= God > THE BLESSED] bows down to him [*lit.* to there, to it].

Mss: Flat(2ra), Bb(117ra). — *Readings*: [5] englum: ǫllum Bb   [7] dýrðar: *so* Bb, 'dyran' Flat.

Editions: *Skj* Einarr Skúlason, 6. *Geisli* 5: AI, 460, BI, 428, *Skald* I, 211; *Flat* 1860-8, I, 1, Cederschiöld 1873, 1, Chase 2005, 55, 129-30.

Notes: [5] *sitr* 'sits': The image of Christ seated in majesty was commonly depicted on the east wall of medieval Scandinavian and Icel. churches. — [6] *hnígr* 'bows down': An allusion to the book of Revelation, where the twenty-four elders, the angels, and the blessed are said to fall down before the King of Kings (Rev. IV.10, V.8, VII.11). — [6, 7] *dǫglings ǫðlinga* 'of the prince of princes [= God]': Kennings of this type ('king of kings') signify Viking kings in earlier skaldic poetry (see *Meissner*, 371). Their use as God-kennings in *Geisl* (cf. *dróttinn harra* 25/7) and Anon *Heildr* (*hæsta konungr jǫfra* 'the highest king of kings' 12/3-4) may be either a borrowing from skaldic tradition or an imitation of the biblical variations on the theme (cf. Ezek. XXVI.7; 2 Macc. XIII.4; 1 Tim. VI.15; Rev. I.5, XVII.14, XIX.16). The figure appears frequently in Lat. and OE poetry. — [7] *dýrðar* (gen. sg.) 'of majesty': Bb's reading, *dýrðar* 'honour, majesty', followed by both *Skj* B and *Skald*, gives the construction *á stóli dýrðar* 'on the throne of majesty'. The Flat reading, 'dyran', is grammatically impossible and metrically difficult.

6. Veitti dýrðar dróttinn Þá reis upp, sús einum,
    dáðvandr gjafar anda; alþýð, guði hlýðir,
    (mǫl kynnask þau) mǫnnum — hæstr skjǫldungr býðr hauldum
    máttigs (framir vátta). himinvistar til — kristni.

Dáðvandr dróttinn dýrðar veitti mǫnnum gjafar máttigs anda; framir kynnask þau mǫl vátta. Þá reis alþýð kristni upp, sús hlýðir einum guði; hæstr skjǫldungr býðr hauldum til himinvistar.

The carefully-acting lord of glory [= God] gave to men the gifts of the mighty spirit; excellent men study those sayings of witnesses [SCRIPTURES]. Then universal Christendom rose up, that obeys one God; the highest prince invites men to heavenly hospitality.

Mss: **Flat**(2ra), **Bb**(117ra). — *Readings*: [2] gjafar: *so* Bb, gjafir Flat   [3] kynnask: sanna Bb   [4] vátta: 'vottar' Bb   [5] Þá: þaðan Bb   [8] himinvistar: himins vistar Bb.

Editions: *Skj* Einarr Skúlason, 6. *Geisli* 6: AI, 460, BI, 428, *Skald* I, 211; *Flat* 1860-8, I, 1, Cederschiöld 1873, 2, Chase 2005, 56, 130-1.

Notes: [1] *dýrðar* 'of glory': *Dýrðar* can be construed with either *dróttinn* 'Lord' (l. 1) or *váttr* 'witness' (l. 4). *Dróttinn dýrðar* 'Lord of glory' would be analogous to the Scriptural 'Lord of glory' (1 Cor. II.8) and 'king of glory' (Ps. XXIII.7-10). The syntax of the *helmingr* supports this interpretation, and is adopted here, but *dýrðar váttr* as a kenning for martyr is attested later in *Geisl* (62/3) and in Anon *Pl* 26/3. — [2, 4] *gjafar máttigs anda* 'the gifts of the mighty spirit': A theological commonplace (*dona Spiritus Sancti*). Throughout the Middle Ages and beyond the seven gifts of the Holy Spirit figure prominently in pious exercises and theological systems. — [3-4]: Both Finnur Jónsson (*Skj* B) and Kock (*Skald*) prefer Bb's equally plausible readings *sanna* and *váttar* in ll. 3-4, giving the sense *framir váttar sanna þau mál* 'excellent witnesses affirm those sayings'. — [3] *vátta* 'of witnesses': *Vátta* (nom. pl. *váttar*) refers to the Apostles, who witnessed the glory of the Holy Spirit at Pentecost, and who later earned the crown of martyrdom. — [7] *hauldum* 'noble farmers, men': Both mss give the Norw. form of the word *hǫlðr*, which is necessary to maintain *skothending*. According to Noreen the change *o*/*au* before *l* + consonant did not occur in Iceland until around 1300 (cf. *ANG* §105 and Anm.). The syntax of the *helmingr* is good, making the possibility of scribal tampering unlikely. Einarr may have chosen the form to avoid *aðalhending* in an odd-numbered l. In 4/6 he uses the forms *hǫlða* (ms. 'holda') and *meginfjǫlði* (ms. 'meginfioldi') 'multitude' to form an *aðalhending*.

7. Nú skulum gǫfgan geisla
    guðs hallar vér allir,
    ítr þanns Óláfr heitir,
    alstyrkan vel dyrka.

    Þjóð veit hann und heiða
    hríðblǫsnum sal víða
    — menn nemi mǫl, sem innik,
    mín — jartegnum skína.

Nú skulum vér allir dyrka vel gǫfgan geisla guðs hallar, alstyrkan, þanns heitir ítr Óláfr. Þjóð veit hann skína jartegnum víða und hríðblǫsnum sal heiða; menn nemi mǫl mín, sem innik.

Now we all should honour well the splendid light-beam of God's hall [HEAVEN > = Óláfr], the all-strong one, who is called glorious Óláfr. People know he shines with miracles widely beneath the storm-blown hall of heaths [SKY/HEAVEN]; may men understand my words as I tell them.

Mss: **Flat**(2ra), **Bb**(117ra).

Editions: Skj Einarr Skúlason, 6. *Geisli* 7: AI, 460, BI, 428, *Skald* I, 211-12; *Flat* 1860-8, I, 2, Cederschiöld 1873, 2, Chase 2005, 57, 131-2.

Notes: [1] *nú skulum ... geisla* 'now we should ... beam': The *skothending* depends on hearing the *s* of *skulum* together with *nu* ('*nus*-') to rhyme with *geis*-, a reminder that skaldic poetry was meant for the ear, not the eye. — [1, 2] *gofgan geisla guðs hallar* 'the splendid beam of God's hall [HEAVEN > = Óláfr]': It is a commonplace in medieval theological and devotional writing to use the symbol of the beam of light from the sun for Christ, the Son proceeding from the Father. The use of the same image for a saint takes the symbol down a notch and emphasises the saint's typological relationship to (and in theological terms his participation in) Christ. See Notes to st. 1.

8. Heyrðu til afreks orða,   Drengr berr óð fyr Inga;
    Eysteinn konungr beinna!   yðart biðk magnit styðja
    Sigurðr, hygg at því, snøggum,   mærð, þás miklu varðar,
    sóknsterkr, hvé ferk verka.   máttig hǫfuð áttar.

Heyrðu, Eysteinn konungr, til beinna orða afreks! Sóknsterkr Sigurðr, hygg at því, hvé ferk snøggum verka! Drengr berr óð fyr Inga; biðk magnit yðart styðja mærð, þás varðar miklu, máttig hǫfuð áttar.

King Eysteinn, listen to straightforward words of great deeds! Battle-strong Sigurðr, consider this, how I deliver the swift work! The man bears [I bear] poetry before Ingi; I ask that your power support the praise, which is of great importance, mighty heads of the nation [= Eysteinn, Sigurðr, Ingi].

Mss: **Flat**(2ra), Bb(117ra). — *Readings*: [4] ferk ('ek fer'): 'ek fọr' Bb [6] yðart ('yduart'): 'ydara' Bb; magnit: *om*. Bb; styðja: *so* Bb, styrkva Flat [7] þás ('þa er'): þat er Bb [8] máttig: 'maktugt' Bb.

Editions: Skj Einarr Skúlason, 6. *Geisli* 8: AI, 460, BI, 428-9, *Skald* I, 212, *NN* §2052; *Flat* 1860-8, I, 2, Cederschiöld 1873, 2, Chase 2005, 58, 132-3.

Notes: [1] *heyrðu til afreks orða* 'listen to words of great deeds': Both mss have the suffixed pron. -ðu here. Omitting the pron. (as do Finnur Jónsson and Kock) normalises the syllable count of the l. but spoils the rhyme, which is between *heyrð*- and *orð*-. On early cliticisation, of which there are three examples in this st., see *ANG* §472. — [2] *Eysteinn*: Eysteinn Haraldsson was Einarr Skúlason's principal patron and the commissioner of the poem (cf. st. 71). He was reigning jointly with his brothers Sigurðr and Ingi at the time *Geisl* was composed: see Introduction. — [6] *yðart biðk magnit styðja* 'I ask that your power support [the praise]': The l. is difficult both metrically and syntactically and the two mss diverge in several respects. Bb's reading of the final word, *styðja* 'support', is preferred here over Flat's *styrkva*, as it does not require emendation, it makes better sense and provides *aðalhending* with *yð*-. Chase 2005, 58 and 132 proposes the emendation *styrkna* 'to become strong' from Flat and reads *yðvart biðk magnit styrkna* 'I desire that your power be strengthened', assuming the scribe may have made the common error of writing *u* for *n* and arguing that *styrkna* is feasible if the l. is read as a parenthesis and *mærð* is understood to be syntactically parallel with *óð* 'poetry'. Finnur Jónsson (*Skj* B) emends Bb to *yðvarrar biðk styðja | mærð, þats miklu varðar, | máttigt hǫfuð áttar* 'I ask the mighty head of your line to strengthen the poem, which is of great importance', and Kock conflates the two texts: *yðvart biðk magn styðja | mærð, þats miklu varðar, | máttig, hǫfuð áttar!* 'I ask that your strength, mighty heads of the nation, support the poem, which is of great importance' (*NN* §2052). — [8]: The pl. form *máttig hǫfuð* in Flat makes better sense than Bb's sg. *mektugt hǫfuð* in the context of an address to three joint monarchs. In Finnur's reading, 'mighty head of your line' could refer either to Eysteinn (which would be rather insulting to Sigurðr and Ingi) or to S. Óláfr.

9. Yfirmanni býðk — unnin
upps mærð borin — lærðra
— Jóan kǫllum svá — allrar
alþýðu brag hlýða.

Hefjum hendr, en leyfa
hyggk vin rǫðuls tyggja
— stóls vex hæð, þars hvílir
heilagr konungr — fagran.

Býðk yfirmanni allrar alþýðu lærðra — svá kǫllum Jóan — hlýða brag; unnin mærð [e]s borin upp. Hefjum hendr, en hyggk leyfa fagran vin tyggja rǫðuls; hæð stóls vex, þars heilagr konungr hvílir.

I ask the superior of the whole multitude of learned men [CLERICS > BISHOP] — thus we [I] call Jón — to listen to the poetry; the finished poem is offered up. We lift up our hands, and I intend to praise the beautiful friend of the king of the sun [= God > = Óláfr]; the eminence of the [bishop's] seat increases, where the holy king rests.

Mss: **Flat**(2ra), Bb(117ra). — *Readings*: [2] borin: komin Bb; lærðra: lærðrar Bb [3] kǫllum: kalla Bb; svá: ek Bb [5] Hefjum: hófum Bb; hendr: hróðr Bb [7] vex: vegs Bb [8] heilag: *corrected from* 'heilag' Flat.

Editions: *Skj* Einarr Skúlason, 6. *Geisli* 9: AI, 460, BI, 429, *Skald* I, 212; *Flat* 1860-8, I, 2, Cederschiöld 1873, 2, Chase 2005, 59, 133.

Notes: [3] *svá kǫllum Jóan* 'thus we [I] call Jón': The *svá* refers back to the elaborate kenning for bishop in ll. 1, 2, 3, 4, a compliment to the listening and recently consecrated first archbishop of Trondheim, Jón Birgisson. — [5] *hefjum hendr* 'we lift up hands': The gesture was associated with prayer and would have been familiar from Scripture (Ps. XXVII.2, LXII.5, CXXXIII.3; Lam. III.41; 1 Tim. II.8). The psalmist's formula appears in a l. from the widely-used matins hymn *Rerum creator optime* (*AH* 51, 28; *Ordo Nidr.*, 185, 195, 198): *Mentes manusque tollimus* 'We lift up our minds and our hands'. Liturgical books commonly use the rubric *manus elevans*. The Bb reading *hróðr* is adopted in *Skj* B and *Skald*, hence *hefjum hróðr ... fagran* 'I begin my fine poem' (ll. 5, 8) — [6] *vin tyggja rǫðuls* 'friend of the king of the sun [= God > = Óláfr]': The kenning for Óláfr has associations with both the skaldic and Lat. traditions. The Scriptural *amicus Dei* 'friend of

God' (Judith VIII.22; Wisd. VII.27; Jas. II.23), translated as *guðs vinr* 'God's friend' in ON, became a commonplace in hagiography. In skaldic poetry it was customary to praise a *jarl* or lesser chieftain by calling him the close friend or confidant of a more powerful man (see *Meissner*, 362); here Einarr emphasises Óláfr's closeness to God. Cf. *spjalli lausnara* 'confidant of the Saviour' (30/2) and *vinr lausnara* 'friend of the Saviour' (62/5, 7). The God-kenning *tyggi rǫðuls* 'king of the sun' echoes the sun-imagery of the preceding sts.

10. Ǫld samir Óláfs gilda   Fannk aldri val vildra
    — orðgnóttar biðk dróttin —   — vallrjóðanda allra
    oss at óðgerð þessi   raun samir — rétt í einu
    ítrgeðs lofi kveðja.   ranni fremðarmanna.

Samir oss kveðja gilda ǫld at þessi óðgerð, lofi ítrgeðs Óláfs; biðk dróttin orðgnóttar. Fannk aldri vildra val fremðarmanna rétt í einu ranni; samir raun allra vallrjóðanda.

It is fitting for us [me] to summon able men to this poetry-making, to the praise of high-minded Óláfr; I ask the Lord for word-wealth. I never found a more agreeable selection of men of accomplishment right in one house; it befits the experience of all field-reddeners [WARRIORS].

Mss: **Flat**(2ra), Bb(117rb). — *Readings*: [1] Ǫld: Oss Bb;   Óláfs: enn at Bb;   gilda: þessu Bb [3] oss at: aldar Bb;   óðgerð: Óláfs Bb;   þessi: gilda Bb   [7] samir: dugir Bb.

Editions: *Skj* Einarr Skúlason, 6. *Geisli* 10: AI, 460-1, BI, 429, *Skald* I, 212, *NN* §§929, 930, 1204D; *Flat* 1860-8, I, 2, Cederschiöld 1873, 2, Chase 2005, 60, 133-4.

Notes: [1-4]: There is a discrepancy between the two ms. versions of the first *helmingr*. Bb reads: *Oss samir enn at þessu –,* | *orðgnóttar biðk dróttin* | *aldar – Óláfs gilda* | *ítrgeðs lofi kveðja*. This may be translated: 'It is fitting for us [me] further to summon [people] to this praise of the able, high-minded Óláfr; I ask the Lord of men [= God] for word-wealth'. There are no metrical or grammatical flaws in the Bb version, but the syntax is awkward: both the weak adj. *gilda* and the strong adj. *ítrgeðs* must be construed with *Óláfs*. In the Flat version, *ǫld* can be construed with *gilda*, providing a link with the second *helmingr* that is schematic as well as thematic: ll. 1 and 5 have the same triple-rhyme scheme (*ǫld* : *Ól-* : *gild-*; *ald* : *vál* : *vild-*). Line 2 is a complete parenthetic phrase, preferable to Bb's *biðk aldar dróttin orðgnóttar*. Flat probably represents the original text: at some point in the transmission of the Bb version ll. 1 and 3 were transposed, and then later emended by a scribe attempting to make sense of the *helmingr*. — [4] *ítrgeðs* (m. gen. sg.) 'of the high-minded': The meaning of the first element of the cpd is clear, but there is no precedent for an adj. *geðr*. *Geð*, a n. noun, is well attested, and Kock proposes a nominal compound *ítrgeð* 'high-minded one'. In his interpretation the *helmingr* reads 'it is fitting for us to summon Óláfr's able men to this poetry-making, to the praise of the high-minded one' (*NN* §929). But *ítrgeð* is unlikely as a noun, and the lexicographers allow an adj. *ítrgeðr*; cf. *LP*: *ítrgeðr* (also *CVC*; *ONP*). — [7] *samir* 'it befits': Bb has *dugir* with much the same meaning and is chosen in both *Skj* B and *Skald*, perhaps because *samir* is also used in l. 1.

11. Þreklynds skulu Þrœndir
    þegns prýðibrag hlýða
    Krists — lifir hann í hæstri
    hǫll — ok Norðmenn allir.

    Dýrð es ágæt orðin
    eljunhress í þessu
    — þjóð né þengill fœðisk
    þvílíkr — konungs ríki.

Þrœndir ok allir Norðmenn skulu hlýða prýðibrag þreklynds þegns Krists; hann lifir í hæstri hǫll. Eljunhress dýrð es orðin ágæt í þessu konungs ríki; þjóð né þvílíkr þengill fœðisk.

The Þrœndir and all Norwegians should listen to the splendid poem of the strong-minded thane of Christ [= Óláfr]; he lives in the highest hall. Energetic fame has become renowned in this king's realm; neither people nor such a prince will be born [again].

Mss: **Flat**(2ra), Bb(117rb). — *Readings*: [2] þegns prýðibrag: 'þegn prydes brag' Bb [3] Krists: Krist Bb [6] þessu: *so* Bb, þessum Flat [8] þvílíkr: *so* Bb, þvílíkr í Flat; konungs: konung Bb.

Editions: *Skj* Einarr Skúlason, 6. *Geisli* 11: AI, 461, BI, 429-30, *Skald* I, 212, *NN* §931; *Flat* 1860-8, I, 2, Cederschiöld 1873, 2, Chase 2005, 61, 134.

Notes: [All]: Flat and Bb's versions of st. 11 differ significantly, especially in ll. 2, 6 and 8. — [2] *prýðibrag þegns* 'splendid poem of the thane': Previous eds have based their texts on Bb's *þegnprýðis brag* 'poem of the thane-ornamenter [RULER = Óláfr]'. This interpretation assumes a *hap. leg. prýðir* cognate with *prýða* 'to ornament'. The *hap. leg. prýðibrag* 'splendid poem' is a more likely cpd than *þegnprýðir* (there are a variety of compounds with *prýði*-). *Þegn* (l. 2) is then construed with *Krists* (l. 3) to give a kenning for Óláfr analogous to the *miles Christi* 'soldier of Christ' familiar from Scripture (2 Tim. II.3) and hagiography (cf. *Guðs ríðari* 'God's knight' 18/6). — [3-4]: Finnur Jónsson (*Skj* B) and Kock (*Skald*) assume an intercalary cl. *hann lifir í hæstri hǫll Krists* 'he [Óláfr] lives in the highest hall of Christ', understanding 'the highest hall of Christ' as a kenning for heaven. Here, however, the sup. adj. is redundant so the phrase *í hæstri hǫll* (cf. *æztrar hallar* 5/3, 4) offers a better reading. — [5-8]: Most eds (*Skj* B, *Skald* and *NN* §931, and Wisén 1886-9, I, 55) follow Bb's *þessu* (l. 6) and omission of *í* (l. 8), which in Flat's version is both hypermetrical and unmetrical. Flat's version also requires a noun to be understood with *þessum* (l. 6). *Eljunhress* (adj.) 'energetic' may be either f. nom. sg. agreeing with *dýrð* or m. gen. sg., used substantivally, referring to Óláfr. Alternatively, it can qualify *konungs*, although this involves reading *konungs* and *ríki* in l. 8 separately rather than as comprising a single phrase. *Skj* B construes ll. 5-8 as: *dýrð eljunhress þjóðkonungs es orðin ágæt; né fœðisk þvílíkr þengill í þessu ríki* 'the fame of the energetic people-king has become renowned; there will not be born [again] such a prince in this realm'. This has the advantage of avoiding the rather awkward treatment of *þjóð* (l. 7), necessitated by Kock's solution below; instead *þjóðkonungs* is taken as a cpd with tmesis, as in a similar context in 14/3-4. Kock (*NN* §931) has *dýrð eljunhress es orðin ágæt í þessu konungsríki; þjóð né þvílíkr ðengill fæðisk* 'the fame of the hero has become renowned in this kingdom; neither people nor such a prince will be born [elsewhere]'. Kock's version, however, is the simplest, as far as word order is concerned, and metrically straightforward, and a variant of it is adopted here.

12. Sigvatr, frák, at segði   Þeir hafa þengils Mœra
    sóknbráðs konungs dáðir;   — þvís sýst — frama lýstan,
    spurt hefr ǫld, at orti   (helgum lýtk) es hétu
    Óttarr um gram dróttar.   hǫfuðskǫld (fira jǫfri).

Frák, at Sigvatr segði dáðir sóknbráðs konungs; ǫld hefr spurt, at Óttarr orti um gram dróttar. Þeir, es hétu hǫfuðskǫld, hafa lýstan frama þengils Mœra; þvís sýst; lýtk helgum jǫfri fira.

I heard that Sigvatr told the deeds of the battle-quick king; men have learnt that Óttarr composed [poetry] about the king of the court. They who were called the chief skalds have proclaimed the courage of the lord of the Mœrir [= Óláfr]; that has been done; I do homage to the holy king of men [= Óláfr].

Mss: **Flat**(2ra), Bb(117rb). — *Readings*: [2] sóknbráðs: *so* Bb, sóknbráðr Flat; konungs: jǫfurs Bb [4] um: of Bb [5] þengils: *so* Bb, þengil Flat.

Editions: *Skj* Einarr Skúlason, 6. *Geisli* 12: AI, 461, BI, 430, *Skald* I, 212; *Flat* 1860-8, I, 2, Cederschiöld 1873, 2, Chase 2005, 62, 135.

Notes: [1] *Sigvatr*: Sigvatr (or Sighvatr) Þórðarson was one of Óláfr Haraldsson's favourite and most prolific court poets, composing sts about Óláfr's battles and journeys, acting as his ambassador on several occasions, and composing an *erfidrápa* 'memorial lay' in honour of the king. He was born c. 1000 in the west of Iceland, the son of a poet, Þórðr Sigvaldaskáld, and the maternal uncle of another, Óttarr svarti (see Note to l. 4 below). Sigvatr also composed poetry for several other Scandinavian rulers. He died c. 1043 (see further Poole 1993a). Sigvatr's poetry is edited in Volume I of this edn. — [2] *sóknbráðs* (m. gen. sg.) 'battle-quick': The reading of Bb; if Flat's *sóknbráðr* were adopted, the only possible referents for it would be *Sigvatr* and *Óttarr*. 'Vehement in battle' is an unlikely epithet for a skald, and it would be a breach of protocol for the only epithet in the *helmingr* to refer to a poet rather than to the king. — [4] *Óttarr*: Óttarr svarti 'the black' was the son of Sigvatr Þórðarson's sister, and was another of S. Óláfr's favourite poets. He is cited as a skaldic authority in *FGT* (c. 1150) and is also quoted frequently by Snorri Sturluson in *Skm*. See further Guðrún Nordal 2001, 28; Poole 1993b. Óttarr's poetry is also edited in Volume I. — [5-8]: *Hétu* must be understood in its passive sense 'were called', and *jǫfurr fira* 'king of men' as an epithet for Óláfr parallel with *gram dróttar* 'the king of the court' (l. 4). For other readings see Finnur Jónsson in *Skj* B, Kock in *Skald*, where, following a suggestion of Konráð Gíslason, *fira* (l. 8) is emended to *firar*, giving *þeir es firar hétu hǫfuðskǫld* 'they whom men called chief poets'.

13. Móðr vann margar dáðir
munnrjóðr Hugins gunna;
satt vas, at siklingr bœtti
sín mein guði einum.

Leyndi lofðungr Þrœnda
liðgegn snara þegna
— fár gramr hefir fremri
fœzk — hóleitri gœzku.

Móðr munnrjóðr Hugins vann margar dáðir gunna; satt vas, at siklingr bœtti sín mein guði einum. Liðgegn lofðungr Þrœnda leyndi hóleitri gœzku snara þegna; fár gramr hefir fœzk fremri.

The brave mouth-reddener of Huginn <raven> [WARRIOR] accomplished many deeds of battles; it was true that the king made atonement for his wrongdoing to God alone. The prince of the Þrœndir, fair with men [= Óláfr], concealed sublime goodness from able thanes; not many a king has been born more distinguished.

Mss: **Flat**(2ra), Bb(117rb). — *Readings*: [1] Móðr: Móðs Bb [2] gunna: kunnan Bb [5] lofðungr: *so* Bb, 'lofdungur' *corrected from* 'lofdung' Flat [7] fár: fæstr Bb; fremri: *so* Bb, frægri Flat [8] fœzk ('fæz'): 'fest' Bb.

Editions: *Skj* Einarr Skúlason, 6. *Geisli* 13: AI, 461, BI, 430, *Skald* I, 212; *Flat* 1860-8, I, 2, Cederschiöld 1873, 2, Chase 2005, 63, 135-6.

Notes: [All]: In Bb st. 14 precedes 13. — [2] *gunna* 'of battles': Both Finnur Jónsson (*Skj* B) and Kock (*Skald*), following Cederschiöld, emend Bb's reading in l. 2 *kunnan* to *kunnar*, qualifying *dáðir*, so *kunnar einum guði* '[deeds] known to God alone'. — [7] *fremri* 'more distinguished': Completes the rhyme scheme (*skothending*) of the l. and hence is a better reading than Flat's *frægri* 'more celebrated'.

14. Réð um tolf, sás trúði,
tírbráðr, á guð, láði
(þjóð muna þegna* fœða)
þría vetr (konung betra),

áðr fullhugaðr felli
folkvaldr í dyn skjalda
(hann speni oss) fyr innan
Ǫlvishaug (frá bǫlvi).

Tírbráðr, sás trúði á guð, réð láði þría vetr um tolf — þjóð muna fœða betra konung þegna* —, áðr fullhugaðr folkvaldr felli í dyn skjalda fyr innan Ǫlvishaug; hann speni oss frá bǫlvi.

The fame-eager one, who believed in God, ruled the land for three winters beyond twelve — the people will not raise a better king of thanes —, before the very wise army-ruler [= Óláfr] fell in the din of shields [BATTLE] on the inner side of Alstahaugen; may he guide us away from evil.

Mss: **Flat**(2ra), Bb(117rb). — *Readings*: [1] um: ok Bb [3] þegna*: þegnar Flat, þengill Bb; fœða ('fæda'): 'bidia' Bb.

Editions: *Skj* Einarr Skúlason, 6. *Geisli* 14: AI, 461, BI, 430, *Skald* I, 212, *NN* §§ 932, 1853B; *Flat* 1860-8, I, 2, Cederschiöld 1873, 3, Chase 2005, 64, 136-7.

Notes: [3]: Flat's reading *þegnar* has been emended here to *þegna**, as a nom. pl. noun cannot be the subject of the sg. verb *muna* 'will not'. *Skj* B, *Skald* and *NN* §932 prefer to adopt Bb's *þengill*, thus providing a noun subject for *réð* 'ruled', and emend 'bidia' to *bíða* 'await, get' (first proposed by Cederschiöld 1873), giving *Tírbráðr þengill ... þjóð muna bíða betra konung* 'Eager for fame, the prince ... the people will not get a better king'. — [8] *Ǫlvishaug*: Lit. 'Ǫlvir's mound', Alstahaugen, Trøndelag; cf. *LP*: *Ǫlvishaugr*; Rygh 1897-1936, XV, 89 identifies it with the farmstead of Alstadhaug in Skogn, Trøndelag. Einarr doubtless knew that Óláfr fell at Stiklestad (ON Stiklastaðir; cf. sts 17 and 43). *Ǫlvishaugr* may be an allusion to a battle recorded in the sagas of S. Óláfr (*Hkr*, II, 178-81; and *ÓH* 1941, 261-9) as well as in the *Annales regii* (*s.a.* 1021), *Gottskalks Annáll* (*s.a.* 1021), and *Oddaverja Annáll* (*s.a.* 1020) (printed in Storm 1888, 106, 316 and 468 respectively). A powerful man from the Trondheim region named Ǫlvir á Eggju persisted in conducting pagan sacrifices on a grand scale long after Óláfr's imposition of Christianity, and Óláfr finally invaded the district with a large army. He interrupted the rites, killing Ǫlvir and sentencing others to imprisonment, mutilation, banishment, or execution. And thus, says Snorri, he returned all the people to the true faith, gave them teachers, and built and consecrated churches. References to these events reinforce the theme *hann speni oss frá bǫlvi* 'may he guide us away from evil'. Just as at Ǫlvishaugr Óláfr protected his people from the evil of paganism, by his martyr's death at Stiklestad (where he was killed by Kálfr Árnason, who, according to *Hkr*, II, 182, 385, married Ǫlvir's widow) he gained the power to protect Norway supernaturally. Ǫlvishaugr was just a few miles from Stiklestad, and Einarr's audience would have recognized the correspondence between the two places and events.

15. Fregit hefk satt, at sagði
    snjallri ferð, áðr berðisk
    — drótt nýtr dǫglings máttar —
    draum sinn konungr Rauma.

    Stiga sá standa fagran
    stjórnar fimr til himna
    — rausn dugir hans at hrósa —
    Hǫrða gramr af jǫrðu.

Hefk fregit satt, at konungr Rauma sagði snjallri ferð draum sinn, áðr berðisk; drótt nýtr dǫglings máttar. Gramr Hǫrða, fimr stjórnar, sá fagran stiga standa af jǫrðu til himna; dugir at hrósa rausn hans.

I have heard truly that the king of the Raumar [= Óláfr] told the clever band his dream before they fought; the court enjoys the prince's might. The king of the Hǫrðar [= Óláfr], adept at leadership, saw a beautiful ladder ascending from earth to the heavens; it is fitting to praise his greatness.

Mss: **Flat**(2ra), Bb(117rb). — *Readings*: [1] sagði: segði Bb [2] berðisk: 'bardizt' Bb [5] sá: kvað Bb [6] stjórnar: styrjar Bb.

Editions: *Skj* Einarr Skúlason, 6. *Geisli* 15: AI, 461-2, BI, 430-1, *Skald* I, 212-13; *Flat* 1860-8, I, 2, Cederschiöld 1873, 3, Chase 2005, 65, 137.

Notes: [2] *berðisk* 'they fought': Flat's form must be preferred here to give a subj. after *áðr*. — [5-6]: Óláfr's vision of the ladder ascending to heaven is said to have occurred on the eve of the battle of Stiklestad (see Chase 2005, 30-4, where there is a discussion of the typological significance of the ladder as a means of entry to heaven). On the parallel between Christ's Cross and a ladder, see also Anon *Líkn* 34 and Note. Óláfr's vision is not found in the early vernacular accounts of his miracles, and is likely to have been a learned borrowing rather than a popular addition to the legend. — [6] *fimr stjórnar* 'adept at leadership': *Skj* B and *Skald* adopt Bb's reading *fimr styrjar* 'adept at fighting'.

16. Ok hagliga hugðisk
    hrøkkviseiðs ins døkkva
    lyngs í lopt upp ganga
    látrs stríðandi síðan.

    Lét, sás landfolks gætir,
    líknframr himinríki
    umgeypnandi opnask
    alls heims fyr gram snjǫllum.

Ok stríðandi látrs ins døkkva hrøkkviseiðs lyngs hugðisk síðan ganga hagliga upp í lopt. Líknframr umgeypnandi alls heims, sás gætir landfolks, lét himinríki opnask fyr snjǫllum gram.

And the enemy of the lair of the dark coiling fish of the heather [SNAKE > GOLD > GENEROUS MAN] thought then that he went easily up into the air. The outstandingly merciful encompasser [*lit*. holder in hand] of the whole world [= God], who watches over the people of the country, caused the kingdom of heaven to open before the clever king.

Mss: **Flat**(2ra), Bb(117rb); R(35v), T^x(37r), W(81), U(68), A(12v) (*SnE*, ll. 5-8).

Readings: [1] hagliga: *so* Bb, hverlofaðr Flat [2] -seiðs: baugs Bb [4] látrs: látr Bb [5] landfolks: *so* Bb, R, T^x, W, U, A, lands folk Flat [6] líknframr: líknsamr Bb, A, líkbjartr R, T^x, W, líknbjartr U [7] umgeypnandi: umgeypnanda T^x; opnask: opna R, T^x, W, U, A.

Editions: *Skj* Einarr Skúlason, 6. *Geisli* 16: AI, 462, BI, 431, *Skald* I, 213; *Flat* 1860-8, I, 2, Cederschiöld 1873, 3, Chase 2005, 66, 137-8; *SnE* 1848-87, I, 450, *SnE* 1931, 159, *SnE* 1998, I, 78.

Context: Lines 5-8 occur in several mss of the *Skm* section of *SnE* among examples of kennings for Christ. Snorri comments: 'Here kennings become ambiguous, and the person interpreting the poetry has to distinguish from the context which king is being referred to. For it is normal to call the emperor of Constantinople king of the Greeks, and similarly the king that rules Palestine, to call him king of Jerusalem ... And the kenning that was quoted above, calling Christ king of men, this kenning can be applied to any king.' (Faulkes 1987, 127-8; cf. *SnE* 1998, I, 78). Snorri was aware of Einarr's use of *double entendre* to associate Óláfr with Christ. — *Notes*: [2] *hagliga* 'easily': The Bb reading is necessary for the rhyme with *hugðisk*. — [6] *líknframr* 'outstandingly merciful': The reading of the *SnE* mss R, T^x and W, *líkbjartr* 'bright in body' offers a viable alternative here, as does U's *líknbjartr* 'bright of (?shining in) mercy'. — [7, 8] *umgeypnandi alls heims* 'encompasser [*lit*. holder in hand] of the whole world': Ps. XCIV.4 (*in manu eius fines terrae* 'in his hands are all the ends of the earth') is probably the inspiration for this kenning, understood here to refer to

God even though Snorri Sturluson (see Context) apparently understood it to refer to Christ. Cf. similar periphrases in Anon *Mgr* 2/5, Kálf *Kátr* 36/3, Gamlkan *Has* 29/7-8 and 64/6.

17. Vakit frák víg á Stikla- Heims þessa frák hvassan
     (víðlendr) -stǫðum síðan — hvatir felldu gram skatnar —
     (Innþrœndum lét undir — þeir drýgðu bǫl — brigðu
     almreyrs lituðr dreyra). branddríf numinn lífi.

Síðan frák vakit víg á Stiklastǫðum; víðlendr lituðr almreyrs lét undir Innþrœndum dreyra. Frák hvassan branddríf numinn brigðu lífi þessa heims; hvatir skatnar felldu gram; þeir drýgðu bǫl.

Then I heard that a battle broke out at Stiklestad; the widely-landed reddener of the elm-reed [ARROW > WARRIOR] caused the wounds of the Innþrœndir to bleed. I heard that the brave sword-driver [WARRIOR] was taken from the transitory life of this world; rash men killed the king; they committed evil.

Mss: **Flat**(2ra), Bb(117rb). — *Readings*: [4] almreyrs: alm reyr Flat, 'almreys' Bb [8] brand-: baug- Bb.

Editions: Skj Einarr Skúlason, 6. *Geisli* 17: AI, 462, BI, 431, Skald I, 213; *Flat* 1860-8, I, 3, Cederschiöld 1873, 3, Chase 2005, 67, 138.

Notes: [1, 2] *Stiklastǫðum* 'Stiklestad': The battle of Stiklestad, in Verdalen, Trøndelag, at which Óláfr lost his life, took place on 29 July 1030. The p. n. occurs with tmesis every time it appears in poetry, doubtless because of the double alliteration on 'st', which would require resolution of the two short syllables (-*staðir*), impossible in position 3 in skaldic poetry before C14th. — [3] *Innþrœndum* (poss. dat. pl.): The Innþrœndir were people from the inner districts of Trøndelag. — [4] *lituðr almreyrs* 'reddener of the elm-reed [ARROW > WARRIOR]': Bb's 'almreys', presumably for *almreyrs* 'of the elm-reed', is preferred over Flat's triple cpd *almreyrlituðr* 'elm-reed-reddener', which is exceptional in skaldic usage. — [8] *branddríf* 'sword-driver': A typical warrior-kenning, but there may also be a foreshadowing of the Hneitir miracle (sts 47-50), in which the supernatural Óláfr causes his sword to move under its own power.

18. Fúss emk, þvít vann vísir, Greitt má gumnum létta
     — vas hann mestr konungr flestra — guðs ríðari stríðum;
     — drótt nemi mærð — ef mættak, rǫskr þiggr allt, sem œskir,
     manndýrðir, stef vanda. Óláfr af gram sólar.

Fúss emk vanda stef, ef mættak, þvít vísir vann manndýrðir; hann vas mestr konungr flestra; drótt nemi mærð. Guðs ríðari má greitt létta stríðum gumnum; rǫskr Óláfr þiggr allt, sem œskir, af gram sólar.

I am eager to compose a refrain, if I can, because the prince attained manly qualities; he was the greatest king among most [rulers]; may the court receive the praise poem. God's knight [SAINT = Óláfr] can easily alleviate afflictions for men; brave Óláfr gets all he desires from the king of the sun [= God].

Mss: **Flat**(2ra), Bb(117rb). — *Readings*: [1] emk ('em ek'): *so* Bb, 'er ek' Flat;   vísir: vísi Bb   [2] flestra: flestar Bb   [6] ríðari: *so* Bb, 'ridadri' Flat   [7] rǫskr: hraustr Bb;   œskir: æstir Bb.

Editions: *Skj* Einarr Skúlason, 6. *Geisli* 18: AI, 462, BI, 431, *Skald* I, 213; *Flat* 1860-8, I, 3, Cederschiöld 1873, 3, Chase 2005, 68, 138-9.

Notes: [2] *flestra* 'among most [rulers]': The Bb reading, *flestar*, allows for smoother syntax. Finnur Jónsson (*Skj* B) construes *því vísi vann flestar manndýrðir; hann vas mestr konungr* 'because the king was in possession of most splendid qualities; he was the greatest king'. — [3] *drótt nemi mærð* 'may the court receive the praise poem': This cl. may mean 'may the court receive the poem' in the sense of giving the poet a hearing, or, more actively, 'may the court learn the praise poem'. — [5-8]: These ll. constitute the *drápa*'s *stef* or refrain, and appear again at 21/5-8, 24/5-8, 27/5-8, 30/5-8, 33/5-8, 36/5-8, 39/5-8, 42/5-8 and 45/5-8. The section between sts 18-45 is the *stefjabálkr*. A small cross symbol appears in the right margin of Flat beside or above each repetition of the *stef*. — [6] *ríðari* 'knight': This is one of the earliest instances of the word in poetry, though see Mberf Lv 2/2[II], which is earlier. The kenning *Guðs ríðari* 'God's knight' also occurs in Árni *Gd* 32/1[IV]. — [8] *gram sólar* 'king of the sun': Einarr introduced this image (which has no precise analogues in Scripture or in Lat. hymns) into skaldic poetry, and it was widely imitated (cf. *Meissner*, 381-2).

19. Náðit bjartr, þás beiðir
 baugskjalda lauk aldri
 — sýndi salvǫrðr grundar
 sín tǫkn — rǫðull skína.

 Fyrr vas hitt, at harra
 hauðrtjalda brá dauða
 happ- (nýtask mér) -mætu
 (máltól) skini sólar.

Bjartr rǫðull náðit skína, þás beiðir baugskjalda lauk aldri; grundar salvǫrðr sýndi sín tǫkn. Hitt vas fyrr, at happmætu skini sólar brá dauða harra hauðrtjalda; máltól nýtask mér.

The bright sun was unable to shine when the desirer of ring-shields [WARRIOR] ended his life; the guardian of the hall of earth [(*lit.* 'hall-guardian of earth') SKY/HEAVEN > = God] showed his signs. It happened previously that the excellently fortunate shining of the sun ceased through the death of the lord of earth-tents [SKY/HEAVEN > = God (= Christ)]; speech-tools [ORGANS OF SPEECH] are of use to me.

Mss: **Flat**(2ra), Bb(117rb-va). — *Readings*: [1] Náðit: *so* Bb, 'Nædiz' Flat   [2] baugskjalda: baugs skjaldar Bb   [5] at: er Bb   [6] brá: *so* Bb, bar Flat;   dauða: aldri Bb   [7] happ-: hept Bb   [8] skini: *so* Bb, 'skinu' Flat.

Editions: *Skj* Einarr Skúlason, 6. *Geisli* 19: AI, 462, BI, 431-2, *Skald* I, 213, *NN* §933; *Flat* 1860-8, I, 3, Cederschiöld 1873, 3, Chase 2005, 69, 139-41.

Notes: [1-4]: The first *helmingr* is reminiscent of the Legendary Saga of St. Óláfr (*ÓHLeg* 1982, 196): *Nu let Olafr konongr þar lif sitt. Þar varð sva mikil ogn, at solen fal gæisla sinn oc gerði myrct, – en aðr var fagrt veðr – æftir þui sem þa var, er sialfr skaparenn for af verolldenne. Syndi Guð þa mikla ogn* 'Now king Óláfr gave up his life there. There was such great terror there that the sun concealed its rays and it grew dark – but it had been fine weather before – just as it did when the Creator himself departed from the world. God showed great terror then.' — [3] *salvǫrðr grundar* 'hall-guardian of earth': The image of God as guardian occurs frequently in OE poetry, and after Arnórr Þórðarson introduced it in Arn *Magndr* 10/6[II] and Arn *Hardr* 17/3[II] it became popular with Christian skalds (see *Meissner*, 376). — [5-8]: These ll. seem to be corrupt in both mss and there have been various suggested readings, all of which involve some emendation. The general sense of the passage is clear: it is a reference to the eclipse of the sun that is said to have occurred at Christ's Crucifixion. In an aside the poet also mentions his 'speech-tools'. In the cl. beginning *at harra hauðrtjalda*, the verb *brá* (3rd pers. sg. pret.) must be used impersonally, as *skini* 'shining' (taking Bb's reading) is dat. But it is difficult then to understand the case of *dauða* (*harra hauðrtjalda*) unless it is dat. instr., viz. 'through or by the death of the lord of earth-tents'. Thus the sense of this part of the *helmingr* must be 'that the shining of the sun ceased through the death of the lord of earth-tents [SKY/HEAVEN > = Christ]'. This then leaves unexplained the first and last words of l. 7. *Skj* B construes these two elements as part of a cpd adj. *happmætr* 'bringing good fortune', qualifying *skini*, whose two elements are separated by tmesis, as does Chase 2005, 69 and 141. Kock (*Skald* and *NN* §933) adopts Bb's reading *hept* and construes it with the intercalary *hept máltól nýtask mér*, translating *tungans band jag nu kan lossa* 'I can now undo the tongue's binding', properly 'fettered speech-tools are [now] of use to me'. — [8] *máltól* 'speech-tools [ORGANS OF SPEECH]': Kennings for the voice, tongue, and lips as the tools of the poet's trade are common in skaldic poetry; cf. *Meissner*, 132-4. Cf. st. 50/4.

20. Gerðusk brátt, þás barðisk
broddrjóðr við kyn þjóðar,
— gramr vandi*t* sá synðum
sik — jartegnir miklar.

Ljós brann líki vísa
lǫgskíðs yfir síðan,
þás ǫnd með sér sendi*s*
samdœgri*s* guð framði.

Miklar jartegnir gerðusk brátt, þás broddrjóðr barðisk við kyn þjóðar; sá gramr vandi*t* sik synðum. Síðan brann ljós yfir líki vísa, þás guð framði ǫnd sendi*s* lǫgskíðs með sér samdœgris.

Great miracles were wrought immediately, when the point-reddener [WARRIOR] had fought with the family of the people; that king did not accustom himself to sins. Then light burned over the body of the prince, when God raised the soul of the sender of the sea-ski [SHIP > SEAFARER] to himself on the same day.

Mss: **Flat**(2ra), Bb(117va). — *Readings*: [1] Gerðusk: 'Gerdiz' Flat, 'Giordizt' Bb; þás ('þá er'): þar er Bb   [3] vandi*t*: 'vandiz' Flat, 'firde' Bb   [4] miklar: so Bb, 'milar' Flat   [5] vísa: ræsis Bb

[7] *þás* ('þá er'): því at Bb;   *sendis*: 'sendiz' Flat, 'syndiz' Bb   [8] *samdœgris*: 'sam dægrs' Flat, 'samdægurs' Bb.

Editions: *Skj* Einarr Skúlason, 6. *Geisli* 20: AI, 462-3, BI, 432, *Skald* I, 213; *Flat* 1860-8, I, 3, Cederschiöld 1873, 3, Chase 2005, 70, 142.

Notes: [All]: There are numerous variant readings in this st., though in most cases the better choice is clear. However, it is necessary to emend l. 1 *Gerðusk* (following an original suggestion of Cederschiöld) to give a 3rd pers. pret. m.v. verb 'were wrought', l. 3 *vandit* '[he] did not accustom', l. 7 *sendis* 'of the sender' (where both mss have -'z', probably indicating a m.v. ending) and l. 8 *samdœgris* 'on the same day' (to give a six-syllable l.). — [1, 7] *þás, þás* 'when, when': Flat has *þás* ('þá er') 'when' in both these cases, but Bb has *þars* ('þar er') 'where' in l. 1 and *því at* 'because' in l. 7. These variants make quite a difference to the sense of the st. In the first case, Bb's version suggests that miracles were wrought on the battlefield, while Flat's indicates they occurred after the battle has taken place. In the second instance Bb suggests that the light burned over Óláfr's body because God had taken it to heaven on the same day he died (as in *ÓHLeg* 1982, 196, quoted in Chase 2005, 36-7), whereas Flat is again concerned with chronology. *Skj* B adopts Bb's readings in ll. 1, and 8, but *Skald* does so in l. 1 only.

21.   Dýrð lætr dróttins Hǫrða   Greitt má gumnum létta
      — dragisk mærð þin*ig — hrœrða   guðs ríðari stríðum;
      ítr (munat ǫðlingr betri)   rǫskr þiggr allt, sem œskir,
      alls grœðari (fœðask).   Óláfr af gram sólar.

Ítr grœðari alls lætr dýrð dróttins Hǫrða hrœrða; mærð dragisk þin*ig; betri ǫðlingr munat fœðask. Guðs ríðari má greitt létta stríðum gumnum; rǫskr Óláfr þiggr allt, sem œskir, af gram sólar.

The glorious healer of all [= God] causes the fame of the lord of the Hǫrðar [= Óláfr] to be disseminated; may the praise poem turn itself hither; a better prince will not be born. God's knight [SAINT = Óláfr] can easily alleviate afflictions for men; brave Óláfr gets all he desires from the king of the sun [= God].

Mss: **Flat**(2ra), Bb(117va). — *Readings*: [1] dróttins: dróttin Flat, dǫgling Bb   [2] dragisk mærð þin*ig hrœrða: 'dragizst mærd þannig hrærda' Flat, 'dvlezt menn vid þat gledia' Bb   [5-8]: *abbrev. as* 'Greitt' Flat, 'Greittm.' Bb.

Editions: *Skj* Einarr Skúlason, 6. *Geisli* 21: AI, 463, BI, 432, *Skald* I, 213, *NN* §3106; *Flat* 1860-8, I, 3, Cederschiöld 1873, 3-4, Chase 2005, 71, 142-3.

Notes: [1] *dróttins* 'of the lord': Sense requires a gen. sg. here, but neither ms. provides one. — [2]: This l. is obviously corrupt in Bb and is probably also some distance from the original in Flat. Flat's version makes good sense but unmetrical ms. 'þannig' 'thither' must be emended to *þinig* 'hither' to provide two short syllables; so *Skj* B and *Skald*. — [3] *grœðari alls* 'healer of all': Cf. *læknir heims* 'the healer of the world' in 57/8. The kenning may have a scriptural base (cf. Exod. XV.26 and Ps. CII.3) or be related to the hymns *Rex æterne, Domine* (*AH* 51, 5): *Tu vulnerum latentium / Bonus assistis medicus* 'You are present as the good healer of hidden wounds', and *Magnum salutis gaudium* (*AH* 51, 73): *Iesus, redemptor gentium, / sanavit orbem languidum* 'Jesus, the redeemer of the nations, healed an ailing world' (*Ordo Nidr.*, 218, 221, 368-9, 428-30). — [5-8]: The ll. of the refrain, which is abbreviated in all repeats, except for Flat's st. 30, are supplied from st. 18.

22. Drótt þó dýran sveita Satts, at Sygna dróttin*
    døglings ríks af líki   særendr guði kæran
    (vón gleðr hug) með hreinu hrings — megu heyra drengir
    (hans batnaðar) vatni.   hans brǫgð — í grǫf lǫgðu.

Drótt þó dýran sveita af líki ríks døglings með hreinu vatni; vón hans batnaðar gleðr hug. Satts, at særendr hrings lǫgðu dróttin* Sygna, kæran guði í grǫf; megu drengir heyra brǫgð hans.

The retainers washed precious blood from the body of the powerful prince with pure water; anticipation of his improvement gladdens the mind. It is true that the wounders of the ring [GENEROUS MEN] laid the lord of the Sygnir [= Óláfr], dear to God, in the grave; men can hear of his deeds.

Mss: **Flat**(2ra), Bb(117va). — *Readings*: [4] hans: hárs Bb [5] Satts ('satt er'): *so* Bb, satt var Flat; dróttin*: dróttins Flat, dróttinn Bb [7] megu: skulu Bb.

Editions: *Skj* Einarr Skúlason, 6. *Geisli* 22: AI, 463, BI, 432, *Skald* I, 213; *Flat* 1860-8, I, 3, Cederschiöld 1873, 5, Chase 2005, 72, 143-4.

Notes: [All]: Sts 22-4 relate the miracle of a blind man who regains his sight by smearing some of the bloody water used to wash Óláfr's body on his eyes; for analogues, see Chase 2005, 37-8. — [4] *hans batnaðar* 'of his improvement': Both *Skj* B and *Skald* adopt an emended form of Bb's 'hars' here instead of Flat's *hans*, viz. *hós batnaðr*, giving the sense 'hope of high improvement [salvation] gladdens the soul'. — [5] *dróttin** (acc. sg.) 'the lord': A slight emendation to Bb's reading makes better sense than Flat's *dróttins*. While it is possible to produce sense from the latter (see Chase 2005, 143 for possible readings), they are strained and involve considerable syntactic fragmentation.

23. Þar kom blindr — en byrjak Sjónbrautir þó sínar,
    blíð verk — muni síðar   seggjum kunns, í brunni
    auðar njótr, es ýtar   ǫrr, þeims Óláfs dreyra,
    jǫfurs bein þvegit hǫfðu. orms landa, vas blandinn.

Blindr njótr auðar kom þar muni síðar, es ýtar hǫfðu þvegit jǫfurs bein; en byrjak blíð verk. Ǫrr orms landa þó sjónbrautir sínar í brunni, þeims vas blandinn dreyra Óláfs, kunns seggjum.

A blind enjoyer of wealth [MAN] came there somewhat later, where men had washed the prince's bones; and I will begin the happy work. The messenger of the serpent's lands

[GOLD > MAN] washed his sight-paths [EYES] in the spring which was blended with the blood of Óláfr, known to men.

Mss: **Flat**(2ra), Bb(117va). — *Readings*: [1] Þar kom: *so* Bb, Kom þar Flat [5] þó: strauk Bb.

Editions: *Skj* Einarr Skúlason, 6. *Geisli* 23: AI, 463, BI, 432-3, *Skald* I, 213, *NN* §934; *Flat* 1860-8, I, 3, Cederschiöld 1873, 5, Chase 2005, 73, 144.

Notes: [1] *þar kom* 'there came': It is necessary to adopt Bb's word order over Flat's here in order to provide internal rhyme on a lift in position one. — [2] *blíð verk* 'happy work': This can refer either to Einarr's work of poetry or Óláfr's miraculous act of healing. — [3] *njótr auðar* 'enjoyer of wealth [MAN]': Einarr extends the sense of *njótr* in this traditional formula to signify not so much the material gifts of a chief to his retainers as the divine mercies people receive from God by way of the saint. He uses kennings of this type throughout the poem to indicate the beneficiaries of Óláfr's miracles. — [5] *þó* 'washed': *Skj* B and *Skald* adopt Bb's reading here, *strauk* < *strjúka* 'to stroke, rub, wipe'; it is the *difficilior lectio*. — [7, 8] *ǫrr orms landa* 'messenger of the serpent's lands [GOLD > MAN]': The kenning is parallel to *auðar njótr* (l. 3). *Ǫrr* 'servant' or 'messenger' as a base-word may signify that the cured man is the vehicle through which Óláfr's favour with God is made known in the world.

24. Sjón fekk seggr af hreinu
    (sú dýrð munat fyrðum)
    (fǫrnuðr mun þat) (fyrnask)
    (fjǫlgóðr) konungs blóði.
    Greitt má gumnum létta
    guðs ríðari stríðum
    rǫskr þiggr allt, sem œskir,
    Óláfr af gram sólar.

Seggr fekk sjón af hreinu blóði konungs; þat mun fjǫlgóðr fǫrnuðr; sú dýrð munat fyrnask fyrðum. Guðs ríðari má greitt létta stríðum gumnum; rǫskr Óláfr þiggr allt sem œskir af gram sólar.

The man received sight from the pure blood of the king; that will be good fortune; the fame [of it] will not be forgotten by men. God's knight [SAINT = Óláfr] can easily alleviate afflictions for men; brave Óláfr gets all he desires from the king of the sun [= God].

Mss: **Flat**(2ra), Bb(117va). — *Readings*: [2] munat: muna Bb [3] mun: var Bb [5-8]: *abbrev. as* 'Greitt' Flat, 'Greitt m.' Bb.

Editions: *Skj* Einarr Skúlason, 6. *Geisli* 24: AI, 463, BI, 433, *Skald* I, 214, *NN* §1794; *Flat* 1860-8, I, 3, Cederschiöld 1873, 5, Chase 2005, 74, 144.

Notes: [1] *seggr fekk sjón* 'the man received sight': Cf. the parallel formula *mál fekk maðr*, st. 26/1. As in biblical miracles of the restoration of sight, bodily sight is associated with intellectual or spiritual insight. — [2] *dýrð* : *fyrðum*: The rhyme, which should be *aðalhending* in an even l., is imperfect; cf. a similar rhyme *gǫfug dýrð jǫfur fyrða* 45/2. — [3] *mun* 'will be': This is retained as the *lectio difficilior*, though it may have been influenced by *muna*(*t*) in l. 2. Bb's *vas* 'was' is adopted in *Skj* B and *Skald*. — [5-8]: The ll. are supplied from st. 18.

25. Tolf mǫnuðr vas týnir   áðr an upp ór víðu
    tandrauðs huliðr sandi   ulfs nistanda kistu
    fremðar lystr ok fasta   dýrr lét dróttinn harra
    fimm nætr vala strætis,   dáðmilds koma láði.

Lystr fremðar týnir tandrauðs fasta strætis vala vas huliðr sandi tolf mǫnuðr ok fimm nætr, áðr an dýrr dróttinn harra lét kistu dáðmilds nistanda ulfs koma upp ór víðu láði.

Desirous of fame, the destroyer of the flame-red fire of the street of hawks [ARM > GOLD > GENEROUS MAN] was covered with sand for twelve months and five nights, before the dear lord of princes [= God] caused the coffin of the good-performing feeder of the wolf [WARRIOR = Óláfr] to come up out of the wide land.

Mss: **Flat**(2ra), Bb(117va). — *Readings*: [2] tandrauðs: *so* Bb, tandrauðr Flat   [6] ulfs nistanda: ulfnistanda Bb   [7] lét: *so* Bb, lætr Flat.

Editions: *Skj* Einarr Skúlason, 6. *Geisli* 25: AI, 463, BI, 433; *Skald* I, 214; *Flat* 1860-8, I, 3, Cederschiöld 1873, 5, Chase 2005, 75, 144.

Notes: [All]: St. 25 corresponds to accounts in *ÓHLeg* and *ÓH* of the translation of Óláfr's body from its original burial place to a shrine in the church of S. Clement in Trondheim (Niðaróss); see Chase 2005, 38. — [3] *lystr fremðar* 'desirous of fame': The epithet also occurs in *Pl* 9/3. Einarr may imply that Óláfr's desire for recognition is one cause of his coffin rising to the surface of the ground, though ll. 5-8 credit God with the miracle. Alternatively, and stereotypically, the epithet could refer back to Óláfr's career as a warrior and king. — [7] *lét* 'caused': Flat has *lætr* 'causes'. The use of the historic pres. tense is rare in skaldic poetry, and Bb's reading, *lét*, is probably the original.

26. Mál fekk maðr, þars hvílir   Frægð ríðr fylkis Egða
    margfríðr jǫfurr, síðan,   folksterks af því verki;
    áðr sás orða hlýru   jǫfurs snilli fremsk alla
    afskurðr farit hafði.   ungs á danska tungu.

Síðan fekk maðr mál, þars margfríðr jǫfurr hvílir, sás afskurðr hlýru orða hafði áðr farit. Frægð folksterks fylkis Egða ríðr af því verki; snilli ungs jǫfurs fremsk á alla danska tungu.

Then a man gained speech, where the very beautiful king rests, whose cut-off piece of the ship-bow of words [TONGUE] had earlier been destroyed. The fame of the army-strong leader of the Egðir [= Óláfr] travels because of that deed; the honour of the young king is advanced in the whole Norse tongue.

Mss: Flat(2ra), Bb(117va). — *Readings*: [1] þars ('þar er'): 'er' Bb   [3] hlýru: hlýðu Bb   [4] afskurðr: 'af skyfdr' Bb;   farit: 'farezt' Bb   [6] folk-: folks Bb   [7] fremsk: þreifst Bb.

Editions: *Skj* Einarr Skúlason, 6. *Geisli* 26: AI, 464, BI, 433, *Skald* I, 214, *NN* §2536; *Flat* 1860-8, I, 3, Cederschiöld 1873, 5, Chase 2005, 76, 144-5.

Notes: [1] *fekk maðr mál* 'a man gained speech': Cf. st. 24/1 *Sjón fekk seggr*. — [3-4]: There are two possible readings of these ll., one following Flat and the other Bb. Following Flat: *maðr, sás afskurðr hlýru orða hafði áðr farit* (as in translation above), the reading requires one to assume a r : ð rhyme (cf. Kuhn 1983, 79). Following Bb: *maðr, sás áðr hafði farit afskýfðr hlýðu orða* 'the man who earlier had gone deprived of the shipboard of words [TONGUE]'. The rhyme here is acceptable (*áðr* : *hlýðu*) and *hlýða* 'ship's planking' is the *difficilior lectio* (for this reading, see *Skald* and *NN* §2536). Einarr uses a similarly nautical tongue-kenning, *ǫ́r óðar* 'oar of poetry', in 40/7-8. — [8] *á alla danska tungu* 'in the whole Norse [lit. Danish] tongue': I.e. 'wherever the Norse tongue is spoken'; an idiom referring to the Scandinavian peoples whose common language was recognised to be Norse. It does not mean 'Danish' in the modern sense. Cf. also Sigv *Víkv* 15/8[I], Mark *Eirdr* 25/4[II], Anon *Lil* 4/4. The use of *tunga* is possibly a grisly pun on the theme of the first *helmingr*.

27. Fǫður skulum fultings biðja
(fremðarþjóð) ins góða
(mœðir mart á láði)
Magnúss hvatir bragnar.

Greitt má gumnum létta
guðs ríðari stríðum;
rǫskr þiggr allt, sem œskir,
Óláfr af gram sólar.

Hvatir bragnar skulum biðja fultings fǫður Magnúss ins góða; mart mœðir fremðarþjóð á láði. Guðs ríðari má greitt létta stríðum gumnum; rǫskr Óláfr þiggr allt, sem œskir, af gram sólar.

We brave men should pray for help to the father of Magnús the Good [= Óláfr]; much afflicts the valiant people in the land. God's knight [SAINT = Óláfr] can easily alleviate afflictions for men; brave Óláfr gets all he desires from the king of the sun [= God].

Mss: Flat(2ra), Bb(117va). — *Readings*: [1] Fǫður: *so* Bb, 'Faudr' Flat; skulum: 'skulu[...]' Bb [2] ins: inn Bb [5-8]: *abbrev. as* 'G.' Flat, 'Greitt ma gvmnvm.' Bb.

Editions: *Skj* Einarr Skúlason, 6. *Geisli* 27: AI, 464, BI, 433-4, *Skald* I, 214, *NN* §935; *Flat* 1860-8, I, 3, Cederschiöld 1873, 5, Chase 2005, 77, 145-6.

Notes: [1, 2, 4] *fǫður Magnúss ins góða* 'the father of Magnús the Good': The epithet for Óláfr anticipates the miracle described in sts 28-30. — [5-8]: The ll. are supplied from st. 18.

28. Gekk sínum bur søkkvir   áðr á Hlýrskógsheiði
    sólar straums í drauma,   harðgeðr konungr barðisk
    — vald lézk fylgja foldar   — góðs eldis naut gyldir
    framlyndum gram myndu —   gnótt — við heiðnar dróttir.

Søkkvir sólar straums gekk bur sínum í drauma — vald foldar lézk myndu fylgja framlyndum gram —, áðr harðgeðr konungr barðisk við heiðnar dróttir á Hlýrskógsheiði; gyldir naut gnótt góðs eldis.

The enemy of the sun of the stream [GOLD > GENEROUS MAN] appeared to his son in a dream — the strength of the land [= Óláfr] said he would help the forward-striving prince — before the hard-minded king fought against the heathen hosts at Lyrskovshede; the wolf enjoyed an abundance of good food.

Mss: **Flat**(2ra), Bb(117va); H(9r), Hr(9ra) (*H-Hr*). — *Readings*: [1] søkkvir: *so* H, Hr, 'sueckuir' Flat, 'sekir' Bb   [3] vald: valdr Bb, H, Hr; lézk: 'kuedz' Bb, Hr, 'kvadz' H   [4] -lyndum: -lundum Bb; myndu: mundu Bb, Hr   [5] Hlýr-: 'hly-' Hr   [6] -geðr: 'feingr' Bb, H, lyndr Hr; konungr: jǫfurr Bb, H, gramr Hr   [7] góðs: góð Hr; naut: fekk Bb, H, Hr.

Editions: Skj Einarr Skúlason, 6. *Geisli* 28: AI, 464, BI, 434; *Skald* I, 214; *Flat* 1860-8, I, 3-4, Cederschiöld 1873, 4-5, Chase 2005, 78, 146; *Fms* 6, 66.

Context: H and Hr quote this st. in their account of the battle of Lyrskovshede. It is introduced as follows: *Þess getr Einar Skúlason í Óláfsdrápu, at Óláfr konungr sýndisk Magnúsi konúngi í svefni fyrir þenna bardaga, ok hèt at veita honum lið. Hann segir svá* ... 'Einarr Skúlason tells of this in *Óláfsdrápa*: that King Óláfr showed himself to King Magnús in a dream before this battle, and promised to give him assistance. He says...'. — *Notes*: [All]: The miracle of Óláfr's appearance to his son Magnús in a dream the night before the battle of Hlýrskógsheiðr (Lyrskovshede) is also recounted in C12th historical writings, including Theodoricus's *Historia de Antiquitate Regum Norwagiensium* (*MHN* 48-50), Saxo Grammaticus's *Gesta Danorum* (Olrik & Ræder 1931-57, I, 302-3) and *Ágr* 1929, 37-8; for discussion see Chase 2005, 38-9. — [3] *vald foldar* 'strength of the land': Bb, H, and Hr read *valdr foldar* 'ruler of the land', a typical kenning which may be the better reading. But the Flat version is appropriate in this context. Abstract nouns were rarely used as base-words in kennings (cf. *líf* in *Geisl* 3/6), but Einarr may be imitating Scripture, where God is repeatedly called *fortitudo* 'strength' and *robur* 'power'. Cf. especially the circumlocutions in Ps. XXVII.8 (*fortitudo plebis suae* 'the strength of his people') and Joel III.16 (*fortitudo filiorum Israhel* 'the strength of the children of Israel'). — [5] *á Hlýrskógsheiði* 'at Lyrskovshede': The name of the battle, fought by Magnús the Good against the Wends on a heath in Southern Jutland between Hedeby and Ribe on 28 September 1043. The Wends were a Slavic tribe who raided and colonised along the southern coast of the Baltic. According to Adam of Bremen, the Wends attacked Denmark to avenge the killing of their chief, Ratibor, by the Danes. Magnús led an army of his own men joined with a Danish force to a great victory: 15,000 Wends were killed, according to Adam, and *Heimskringla* reports that it was the greatest carnage seen in the North in Christian times (*Gesta*, II.lxxix in Schmeidler 1917, 136-8; *Hkr*, *ÍF* 28, 43-5). Although Adam identifies Ratibor as being Christian, most Wends were not, and battles with the Wends were often regarded as campaigns against paganism. Danes and Saxons fought a series of battles with the Wends in the century following, and they were not subjugated and forcibly converted before 1169 (Helle 2003, 423). Snorri (*Hkr*, *ÍF* 28, 43-4) associates Arn *Magndr* 10[11] and ÞjóðA *Magnfl* 7[11] with this battle, although neither skald mentions the name of the place.

29. Lét jarplitan ǫtu Hrætt varð folk á flótta
     (arnar jóðs) inn góði — frón beit egg — at leggja;
     (munn rauð malmþings kennir) sorg biðu víf, en vargar,
     Magnús Hugins fagna. vinðversk, of hræ ginðu.

Magnús inn góði lét jarplitan fagna ǫtu Hugins; kennir malmþings rauð munn arnar jóðs. Hrætt folk varð at leggja á flótta; frón egg beit; vinðversk víf biðu sorg, en vargar ginðu of hræ.

Magnús the Good made the brown-coloured one rejoice with the food of Huginn <raven> [CORPSES]; the tester of the weapon-meeting [BATTLE > WARRIOR] reddened the mouth of the eagle's offspring. The frightened army had to take to flight; the sharp blade bit; Wendish women experienced sorrow, and wolves gaped over carrion.

Mss: **Flat**(2ra), Bb(117va); Hr(9ra) (*H-Hr*). — *Readings*: [1] -litan: *so* Bb, '-lidr' Flat, 'leitan' Hr [3] malmþings: mildingr Bb, Hr; kennir: innan Bb, Hr [4] Hugins: 'huginn' Bb, 'hugan' Hr [6] beit: leit Bb; at: á Hr; leggja: leggi Hr [7] biðu: hlutu Bb, Hr.

Editions: *Skj* Einarr Skúlason, 6. *Geisli* 29: AI, 464, BI, 434, *Skald* I, 214, *NN* §936; *Flat* 1860-8, I, 4, Cederschiöld 1873, 5, Chase 2005, 79, 146-7; *Fms* 6, 66-7.

Context: Immediately following st. 28 *H-Hr* reads: *Eptir fall Regbuss gerðisk Magnús konúngr svá ákafr, at hann var fremstr sinna manna, ok beið eigi merkjanna, hann hjo* [sic] *á 2 hendr, ok drap heiðingja niðr sem búfè; sá Vindr þá eingan sinn kost vænna enn flýja, þeir sem því kómu við* 'After the fall of Regbus [a Wendish king] King Magnús became so vehement that he was [fighting] at the front of his men and did not wait for the standards. He hacked to both sides, and struck the heathens down like cattle. The Wends who were able to then saw no better option than to flee'. The prose text continues in H (*Dreifðisk þá herrinn víðs vegar...* 'The army was widely scattered'), which omits st. 29, but Hr first inserts the phrase *svá segir Einarr* 'thus says Einarr' followed by the text of this st. — *Notes*: [1] *jarplitan* 'brown-coloured': The adj. does not occur elsewhere, but is a cpd of *jarpr* 'brown' and *litr* 'coloured.' The skalds often used the characteristic epithets 'black' and 'dark-coloured' in reference to the raven (see *Meissner*, 117), and Einarr sustains the metaphor by using *ǫtu Hugins* 'food of Huginn' as a kenning for the slain. St. 29 thus contains references to the three traditional beasts of battle: the raven, the eagle, and the wolf. Finnur Jónsson (*Skj* B) understands the references to the birds of battle rather differently in ll. 1-4, construing *Magnús enn góði lét hugin fagna ǫtu; malmþings kennir rauð munn jarplitaðs arnar jóðs* 'Magnús the Good let the raven enjoy food; the warrior [tester of the weapon-meeting] reddened the beak of the brown-coloured eagle [offspring of the eagle]'. Here he adopts an emendation, *jarplitaðs* (l. 1), originally suggested by Konráð Gíslason and Eiríkur Jónsson 1875-89, II, 293-5. — [8] *ginðu* 'gaped': An example of a weak pret. form of a strong verb (see *ANG* §482, Anm. 2). The vowel has been shortened to facilitate *aðalhending* with *vinðversk* (Kahle 1892, 57-9 discusses this phenomenon).

30. Rauns, at sigr gaf sínum
    snjallr lausnara spjalli
    — hrósak verkum vísa
    vígdjarfs — frǫmum arfa.
    Greitt má gumnum létta
    guðs ríðari * stríðum
    rǫskr þiggr allt, þats œskir,
    Óláfr af gram sólar.

Rauns, at snjallr spjalli lausnara gaf frǫmum arfa sínum sigr; hrósak verkum vígdjarfs vísa. Guðs ríðari má greitt létta stríðum gumnum; rǫskr Óláfr þiggr allt, þats œskir, af gram sólar.

It is a fact that the brave confidant of the Saviour [= Óláfr] gave his distinguished heir victory; I praise the deeds of the battle-bold prince. God's knight [SAINT = Óláfr] can easily alleviate the afflictions of men; brave Óláfr gets all he desires from the king of the sun [= God].

Mss: **Flat**(2ra), Bb(117va); H(9v), Hr(9va) (*H-Hr*, ll. 1-4). — *Readings*: [2] lausnara: 'lavnsara' Bb; spjalli: 'pialli' Bb [5-8]: *abbrev. as* 'Greitt ma g. l.' Bb [6] ríðari *: ríðari í Flat.

Editions: *Skj* Einarr Skúlason, 6. *Geisli* 30: AI, 464-5, BI, 434, *Skald* I, 214; *Flat* 1860-8, I, 4, Cederschiöld 1873, 5, Chase 2005, 80, 147; *Fms* 6, 70.

Context: H-Hr concludes the account of the battle with the following comment: *Þat gaf ok ǫllum vel skilja, at eigi mátti hann sigra við svá lítit lið ... nema sá sigr væri honum veittr af várum herra drottni Jesú Kristó, háleitum himnakonúngi, fyrir verðleika síns ástvinar Óláfs konúngs, sem Einar prestr Skúlason segir...* 'It was also very apparent to all, that he would not have been able to be victorious with such a small band ..., unless that victory had been given to him by our master lord Jesus Christ, the exalted king of heaven, on account of the merits of his beloved friend King Óláfr, as the priest Einarr Skúlason says ...', followed by this st. — *Notes*: [5-8]: The *stef* is written out in full in Flat, but abbreviated in Bb. The Flat scribe abbreviates it everywhere but here and in st. 18. The text differs slightly here, suggesting that the scribe wrote it out from memory: this second version has 'ridari i stridum' (l. 6) where st. 18 has 'ridadri stridum' and *þats* ('þat er', l. 7) where the first reads *sem*. The scribe's reason for writing the *stef* here has to do with the layout of the ms. When he finished copying the first *helmingr* of st. 30 he found that one ruled l. remained at the foot of column a, enough space for four ll. of *dróttkvætt*. Rather than begin a new st. and split the text between two columns of writing, he filled out the space with the *stef*.

31. Reyndi Gutthormr grundar
— gat rétt — við þrǫm sléttan,
áðr hvat Óláfs téðu
alkœns við guð bœnir.

Dag lét sinn með sigri
sóknþýðr jǫfurr prýðask,
þás í Ǫngulseyjar-
undreyr bitu -sundi.

Gutthormr reyndi við sléttan þrǫm grundar, hvat bœnir alkœns Óláfs téðu áðr við guð; gat rétt. Sóknþýðr jǫfurr lét dag sinn prýðask með sigri, þás undreyr bitu í Ǫngulseyjarsundi.

Gutthormr proved on the flat coast of the land how the prayers of much-skilled Óláfr previously prevailed with God; he guessed correctly. The battle-happy king caused his day to be adorned with victory, when wound-reeds [ARROWS] bit in the Menai Strait.

Ms.: **Bb**(117va-b).

Editions: *Skj* Einarr Skúlason, 6. *Geisli* 31: AI, 465, BI, 434-5, *Skald* I, 214, *NN* §937; Cederschiöld 1873, 5, Chase 2005, 81, 147-8.

Notes: [All]: The story of Gutthormr Gunnhildarson occupies sts 31-4. This man was S. Óláfr's nephew, son of his half-sister Gunnhildr. After a raid on the island of Angelsey, Gutthormr quarrelled with his Irish raiding partner Margaðr over the spoils and a fight ensued. Although Gutthormr's war-band was the weaker, he prayed to Óláfr on the evening before the fight (which took place on S. Óláfr's feast day, 29 July) and Óláfr helped him to win. In gratitude he donated a silver cross to the saint, which would have been visible in the cathedral at Trondheim as Einarr recited his *drápa*. The story of Gutthormr appears in numerous versions of the Óláfr-legend (Louis-Jensen 1970, 35; *ÓHLeg* 1982, 210-12; *Hkr*, *ÍF* 28, 135-7; *ÓH* 1941, 631-3; for further details, see Chase 2005, 39 and 227 n. 107; Gade 2004, 218-20). Sts 31-3 are missing from the Flat text, probably due to the scribe's carelessness. St. 30 lies at the end of a column in the ms., and the following column begins with st. 34. Both sts 30 and 33 have the *stef* as the second *helmingr*, and when the scribe shifted columns he probably mistook the conclusion of st. 33 for st. 30. The inclusion of st. 34 proves that the scribe's exemplar contained the story of Gutthormr. The missing sts are supplied from the Bb text, the only witness. — [1-4]: The syntax of the first *helmingr* is slightly awkward. Finnur Jónsson construes *Gutthormr reyndi við sléttan þrǫm grundar, hvat bænir alkœns Óláfs téðu við goð; hann gat áðr rétt* 'Gutthormr proved on the flat coast of the land how the prayers of much-skilled Óláfr prevailed with God; he had guessed correctly previously' (*Skj* B). Kock takes *gat hann rétt* 'he guessed correctly' as a parenthesis and reads *áðr hvat* as *hvat áðr*, arguing convincingly that such transposition in correlative constructions was an accepted technique (*NN* §§937 and 246D). His interpretation makes better sense: 'Gutthormr proved on the flat coast of the land how previously the prayers of much-skilled Óláfr prevailed with God; he guessed correctly'. — [7, 8] *í Ǫngulseyjarsundi*: 'in the sound of Angelsey', the Menai Strait, between the island of Anglesey and the mainland of Wales. It would be nearly impossible to use a word this long (six syllables, the length of an entire l.) in *dróttkvætt* without tmesis.

32. Víst hafði lið lestir	Þó réð hann at hvǫru
    linns þrimr hlutum minna	(hǫnum tjóði vel móður)
    heiptar mildr at hjaldri	(hór feksk af því) (hlýri)
    — harðr fundr vas sá — grundar.	(hagnaðr) ór styr gagni.

Víst hafði heiptar mildr lestir linns grundar þrimr hlutum minna lið at hjaldri; sá fundr vas harðr. Þó at hvǫru réð hann gagni ór styr; af því feksk hór hagnaðr; hlýri móður tjóði hǫnum vel.

Clearly the strife-generous damager of the snake's land [GOLD > GENEROUS MAN = Gutthormr] had three times fewer men at the battle; that meeting was hard. Yet notwithstanding he won victory in the battle; great advantage was gained from that; the brother of [his] mother [= Óláfr] helped him well.

Ms.: **Bb**(117vb). — Readings: [6] móður: móðir Bb [7] feksk: fekst Bb.

Editions: Skj Einarr Skúlason, 6. Geisli 32: AI, 465, BI, 435, Skald I, 214, NN §1794; Cederschiöld 1873, 5, Chase 2005, 82, 148.

Notes: [2] þó réð hann at hvǫru: The rhyme of the l. depends on hearing þór- as a rhyme with hvǫr. — [6] móður 'mother': Ms. móðir is nom. in C12th Icel., but this form is frequently used as dat. sg. in late medieval/early modern Icel. Cf. Anon Pét 5/6, 37/2 and 49/2. See, e.g., Bandle 1956, 263-7 and references.

33. Ǫld hefr opt inn mildi	Greitt má gumnum létta
    *u*nnar bliks frá miklu*m*	guðs ríðari stríðum;
    — Krist*s* mærik li*m* — leysta	rǫskr þiggr allt, sem œskir,
    litrauðs konungr nauðum.	Óláfr af gram sólar.

Konungr inn mildi litrauðs bliks *u*nnar hefr opt leysta ǫld frá miklu*m* nauðum; mærik li*m* Krist*s*. Guðs ríðari má greitt létta stríðum gumnum; rǫskr Óláfr þiggr allt, sem œskir, af gram sólar.

The king, generous with the red-coloured light of the wave [GOLD], has often rescued men from great need; I praise the limb of Christ [SAINT = Óláfr]. God's knight [SAINT = Óláfr] can easily alleviate afflictions for men; brave Óláfr gets all he desires from the king of the sun [= God].

Ms.: **Bb**(117vb). — Readings: [2] *u*nnar: 'aunnar' Bb; miklu*m*: miklu Bb [3] Krist*s*: krist Bb; li*m*: 'lin' Bb [5-8]: abbrev. as 'Greitt m. g. l.' Bb.

Editions: Skj Einarr Skúlason, 6. Geisli 33: AI, 465, BI, 435, Skald I, 215; Cederschiöld 1873, 5, Chase 2005, 83, 148-9.

Notes: [1, 2, 4] konungr inn mildi litrauðs bliks *u*nnar 'the king, generous with the red-coloured light of the wave [GOLD]': The kenning may be understood on several levels. It clearly refers to Óláfr, but the light imagery also recalls Christ, 'the king of the sun', whose radiance is associated with the saint. The 'king' in this multivalent metaphor can be the mortal Óláfr, generous with gold; the heavenly Óláfr, generous with miracles; or Christ, generous with the grace of his saints. Cederschiöld proposed emending Bb's 'aunnar' (l. 2) to u*nn*ar, and this has been followed by all eds. — [2] *miklu*m 'great': The ms. reads 'miklu', the n. dat. sg. form, which is grammatically impossible (there is no corresponding noun in the *helmingr*). — [3] *mærik li*m *Krist*s 'I praise the limb of Christ': Previous eds (Cederschiöld, *Skj* B and *Skald*) have emended ms 'lin' to *lim* and 'Krist' to *Krists*, creating a kenning, 'limb of Christ', for Óláfr (cf. *lim konungs himna sals* 'limb of the king of the hall of heaven', 66/6). A recent suggestion in Chase 2005, 83 and 149 has been to emend to *linan* and construe *Krist mærik linan* 'I praise merciful Christ'. However, the l. then becomes unmetrical, as the word in question must be monosyllabic (there is no resolution on a word in position 4 in an XE l. until C14th; for the terminology see Gade 1995). — [3] *leysta* 'rescued': The form is acc. sg. f., in agreement with *ǫld* 'men' (l. 1) rather than the usual sg. n. inflection. This was an accepted means of forming the perf. (*ANG* §541), and Einarr used it here to provide the requisite trochee at the end of the l.

34. Satts, at silfri skreytta   Þat hafa menn at minnum
    seggjum hollr ok golli   meir; jartegna þeira
    hér lét Gutthormr gerva   mark stendr Krists í kirkju
    — grams hróðr *v*as þat — róðu.   — konungs niðr gaf þat — miðri.

Satts, at Gutthormr, hollr seggjum, hér lét gerva róðu, skreytta silfri ok golli; þat *v*as hróðr grams. Þat hafa menn meir at minnum: mark þeira jartegna stendr í miðri Krists kirkju; konungs niðr gaf þat.

It is true that Gutthormr, devoted to men, here had an image made, ornamented with silver and gold; that was praise of the king. Men have that still as a reminder: the mark of those miracles stands in the middle of Kristkirken; the king's relative [= Gutthormr] gave that.

Mss: **Flat**(2rb), Bb(117vb). — *Readings*: [1] Satts ('Satt er'): *so* Bb, Satt var Flat [2] hollr: hollz Bb; ok: af Bb [3] Gutthormr: *so* Bb, 'guthorm' Flat; gerva: *so* Bb, 'g[...]fa' Flat [4] grams hróðr *v*as þat róðu: '[...]ar þat [...]du' Flat, grams hróðr er þat róðu Bb [5] Þat: slíkt Bb [8] niðr: *so* Bb, '[...]' Flat; gaf þat miðri: *so* Bb, 'g[...]f [...]id[...]' Flat.

Editions: *Skj* Einarr Skúlason, 6. *Geisli* 34: AI, 465, BI, 435, *Skald* I, 215, *NN* §§938, 2247D; *Flat* 1860-8, I, 4, Cederschiöld 1873, 5, Chase 2005, 84, 149-50.

Notes: [All]: *HómNo* and *ÓHLeg* use language strikingly similar to this st. in their accounts of Gutthormr's donation of the memorial cross: *ok let gera þegar roðo sva myccla ór silfri at allz coftar er hon lengri ok mæri en manzvaxtar. ok prýddi þegar þef hælga manz húf með þærri dýrð sér til falo-bota. ok til minni ok fra-fagnar iarteina þærra en hinn helgi Oláfr konungr gerði þa við hann* 'and he immediately had such a large silver image made, that it is at least taller and bigger than a man. And he immediately ornamented the house of this holy man with that treasure for the salvation of his soul and as a reminder and a record of the miracles which the holy King Óláfr performed then for him' (*HómNo*, 113; cf. *ÓHLeg* 1982, 212). — [2] *hollr* 'devoted': Finnur Jónsson and Kock choose *hollz*, the Bb reading. Finnur construes, *Gutthormr lét her gerva róðu grams, seggjum holls, skreytta silfri ok golli; þat es hróðr* 'Gutthormr had men make the image of the king, true to men, adorned with silver and gold; that is praise' (*Skj* B). Kock's version is smoother: he construes *seggjum holls grams* with *hróðr*: 'that is praise of the king, friendly to men' (*NN* §§938 and 2247D). The Flat text can also be read as it stands, as given above. — [3, 4, 8]: Flat's text is all but illegible in ll. 3, 4 and 8. In these cases, Bb is the only witness now, although earlier eds were able to read more of Flat. *Skj* A reports Flat's *viðr* for Bb's *niðr* in l. 8. — [6] *þeira jartegna* 'of those miracles': This phrase may be taken either with *mark* (l. 7), as here, or in the first cl. of *helmingr* b, with *at minnum* 'as a reminder of those miracles'. — [7, 8] *í miðri Krists kirkju* 'in the middle of Kristkirken': This can be understood as a simple reference to the position of Gutthormr's crucifix in the church, or as a more grandiose claim that the sign of Óláfr's honour holds a central place in Christendom. The Norwegians were proud of the popularity of Trondheim as a pilgrimage goal. — [8] *niðr* 'relative': According to earlier eds, Flat read *viðr* 'wood', which has obvious associations with the image of the Cross, but makes no sense as the only possible subject of *gaf* 'gave'.

35. Menn hafa sagt, at svanni
 sunnr, Skǫnungum kunnir,
 oss, um Óláfs messu
 almilds baka vildi.

 Enn þás brúðr at brauði
 brennheitu tók leita,
 þá varð grjón at grǫnu
 grjóti danskrar snótar.

Menn, kunnir Skǫnungum, hafa sagt oss, at svanni sunnr vildi baka um almilds Óláfs messu. Enn þás brúðr tók leita at brennheitu brauði, þá varð grjón danskrar snótar at grǫnu grjóti.

Men, known to the Skǫnungar, have told us that a woman in the south wanted to bake on all-generous Óláfr's feast day. Yet, when the woman went to seek the burning-hot bread, then the dough of the Danish woman had become a grey stone.

Mss: Flat(2rb), Bb(117vb). — *Readings*: [2] sunnr: suðr Bb; Skǫnungum: Skǫneyjum Bb [3] um: at Bb [4] almilds: ómildr Bb [7] grǫnu: 'grænu' Bb [8] danskrar: danskar Bb; snótar: *so* Bb, '[...]n[...]' Flat.

Editions: *Skj* Einarr Skúlason, 6. *Geisli* 35: AI, 465, BI, 435-6, *Skald* I, 215; Flat 1860-8, I, 4, Cederschiöld 1873, 5-6, Chase 2005, 85, 150.

Notes: [All]: Sts 35-6 narrate the miracle of a woman (from Trøndelag according to *ÓHLeg* 1982, 214-15), forced by her master, an evil Danish count, to bake bread on S. Óláfr's feast day. (Punishment for working on a saint's feast day is a common hagiographical motif.) She prayed to S. Óláfr for vengeance, and the loaves were turned to stone in the oven, while the count was blinded. This narrative, which comes from the legendary tradition, follows the Gutthormr miracle in a number of sources (e.g. *ÓHLeg* 1982, 214; *Passio Olaui* in

Metcalfe 1881, 78-9; *HómNo*, 115; *Hkr*, *ÍF* 28, 137-8; *ÓH* 1941, 636-7), both accounting for relics that were to be seen in Trondheim cathedral, the silver cross and three rocks kept at Óláfr's shrine until the Reformation. Many Icel. churches also displayed stones as a reminder of the story: 'Óláfssteinar' were kept in the churchyard at Þingvellir as late as 1873 (*DI* I, 1264-5; see further Chase 2005, 39 and nn. 110 and 111). The miracle of the loaves is also said to account for the fact that the feast of S. Óláfr was observed throughout Denmark (cf. st. 36). — [2] *sunnr* 'south': An early form of *suðr* (*ANG* §261), used here for the sake of the *aðalhending* with *kunnir* (and *liðhenda* with *Skǫnungum*). — [4] *almilds* (m. gen. sg.) 'all-generous': Cf. 'sa mildi konungr' (*HómNo*, 115); 'sa milldr konongr' (*ÓHLeg* 1982, 214). — [7-8] *þá varð grjón at grǫnu grjóti* 'then the dough had become a grey stone': Cf. *brauð þat allt varð at griote* 'all that bread turned to stone' *HómNo*, 115, *ÓHLeg* 1982, 214.

36. Hildings hefir haldin
    hǫtíð verit síðan
    — sannspurt es þat sunnan —
    snjalls of Danmǫrk alla.

    Greitt má gumnum létta
    guðs ríðari stríðum;
    rǫskr þiggr allt sem œskir,
    Óláfr af gram sólar.

Síðan hefir hǫtíð snjalls hildings verit haldin of alla Danmǫrk; þat es sannspurt sunnan. Guðs ríðari má greitt létta stríðum gumnum; rǫskr Óláfr þiggr allt, sem œskir, af gram sólar.

Since then the feast of the clever warrior has been observed throughout all Denmark; that is truly learned from the south. God's knight [SAINT = Óláfr] can easily alleviate afflictions for men; brave Óláfr gets all he desires from the king of the sun [= God].

Mss: **Flat**(2rb), Bb(117vb). — *Readings*: [1] Hildings: Mildings Bb [4] of: so Bb, um Flat [5-8]: *abbrev. as* 'Greitt' Flat, 'Greitt m.' Bb.

Editions: *Skj* Einarr Skúlason, 6. *Geisli* 36: AI, 465, BI, 436, *Skald* I, 215, *NN* §2971; *Flat* 1860-8, I, 4, Cederschiöld 1873, 6, Chase 2005, 86, 150.

Notes: [3] *sunnan* 'from the south': This adv. is construed as part of the intercalary cl. in l. 3 *sannspurt es þat sunnan* 'that is truly known from the south' (so *Skj* B), but Kock argues that it belongs with the main cl., and this interpretation is also followed in Chase 2005, 86 and 150. Kock cites a number of examples of similar one-l. parentheses in the poem where the final word of the l. is clearly not to be construed with the preceding phrase and construes 'Since then the feast of the clever warrior has been observed in the south, throughout all Denmark; that is truly learned' (*NN* §2791B). The problem with this reading, however, is that *sunnan* does not normally mean 'in the south'; there is also a measure of redundancy in 'in the south, throughout all Denmark'.

37. Gǫfug réð Hǫrn ór hǫfði   Þann sǫ́m vér, es vǫ́rum,
hvítings um sǫk lítla   válaust numinn máli
auðar aumum beiði   hodda njót, þars heitir
ungs manns skera tungu.   Hlíð, fǫ́m vikum síðan.

Gǫfug Hǫrn hvítings réð skera tungu ór hǫfði aumum beiði auðar um sǫk lítla ungs manns. Vér sǫ́m þann njót hodda, válaust numinn máli, es vǫ́rum fǫ́m vikum síðan, þars heitir Hlíð.

A noble Hǫrn <= Freyja> of the drinking horn [WOMAN] decided to cut the tongue out of the head of a poor seeker of riches [MAN] for little fault of the young man. We [I] saw that user of treasure [MAN], without doubt deprived of speech, when we were [I was] a few weeks later at the place called Lia.

Mss: **Flat**(2rb), Bb(117vb); K^x(624r-v), 39(40vb), E(46r) (*Hkr*); Holm2(77v), 73a^x(221r-v), Holm4(70vb), Tóm(164r), Bb(208vb), Flat(128va) (*ÓH*).

Readings: [1] réð: skar Bb(117vb), Holm2, lét K^x, 39, E, 73a^x, Holm4, Tóm, Flat(128va), 'lot' Bb(208vb); Hǫrn: heyrn Holm2; hǫfði: *so* Bb(117vb), K^x, 39, E, Holm2, 73a^x, Holm4, Tóm, Bb(208vb), Flat(128va), hofi Flat(2rb) [2] hvítings: 'hiorrungs' Tóm; um: fyr Tóm [3] aumum: aumir Tóm; beiði: beiða Tóm [4] ungs manns skera: ungr maðr var sá Bb(117vb), Holm2, Tóm; skera: 'kera' 39, skerða Tóm [5] sǫ́m: sá K^x, 39, E, sann Tóm [7] hodda njót: hodda brjót Bb(117vb), 39, E, Holm2, 73a^x, Holm4, hoddbrjót K^x, odda njót Tóm, hoddu brjóst Bb(208vb), hodda brjótr Flat(128va); þars ('þar er'): þar ór Bb(208vb) [8] síðan: síðar Bb(117vb), K^x, 39, E, Holm2, 73a^x, Holm4, Tóm, Bb(208vb), Flat(128va).

Editions: *Skj* Einarr Skúlason, 6. *Geisli* 37: AI, 465-6, BI, 436, *Skald* I, 215, *NN* §939; *Flat* 1860-8, I, 4, II, 285-6, Cederschiöld 1873, 6, Chase 2005, 87, 150-1; *Hkr*, *ÍF* 28, 271-2 (*Msona* ch. 33); *ÓH* 1941, 648-9.

Context: This st. is quoted in *Hkr*, *Msona*, ch. 33 (mss 39, E, and K^x) and in *ÓH* (Flat, Bb, Holm2, Holm4, 73a^x, Tóm). It is introduced by the following prose passage (as normalized in *Hkr*, *ÍF* 28, 271-2): *Kolbeinn hét maðr, ungr ok fátœkr, en Þóra, móðir Sigurðar konungs Jórsalafara, lét skera tungu ór hǫfði honum, ok var til þess eigi meiri sǫk en sá inn ungi maðr, Kolbeinn, hafði etit stykki hálft af diski konungsmóður ok sagði, at steikari hafði gefit honum, en hann þorði eigi við at ganga fyrir henni. Síðan fór sá maðr mállauss langa hríð. Þess getr Einarr Skúlason í Óláfsdrápu* 'There was a man named Kolbeinn, young and poor, and Þóra, the mother of King Sigurðr the Jerusalem-traveller (*sic*), had his tongue cut out, and there was no more reason for this than that the young man, Kolbeinn, had eaten half a morsel from the plate of the king's mother, and said that the cook (who was afraid to confess this to her) had given it to him. After that the man went around unable to speak for a long time. Einarr Skúlason reports this in *Óláfsdrápa*.' Following the st., the sagas continue: *Hann sótti síðan til Þrándheims ok til Niðaróss ok vakði at Kristskirkju. En um óttusǫng Óláfsvǫkudag inn síðara þá sofnaði hann ok þóttisk sjá Óláf konung inn helga koma til sín ok taka hendi sinni í stúfinn tungunnar ok heimta. En hann vaknaði heill ok þakkaði várum dróttni feginsamliga ok inum helga Óláfi konungi, er hann hafði heilsu ok miskunn af þegit, hafði farit þannug mállauss ok sótti hans heilagt skrín, en þaðan fór hann heill ok skorinorðr* 'He later went to Trondheim and Niðaróss and kept a watch at Kristkirken. And about the time of matins on the eve of the second feast of S. Óláfr he fell asleep and thought he saw the holy King Óláfr come to him and take with his hand the stump of his tongue and pull on it. And he awoke healed and joyfully thanked our Lord and the holy King Óláfr, from whom he had obtained health and mercy. He had come to that place without speech and sought out his holy shrine, and he went home well and articulate'. — *Notes*: [All]: Sts 37-9 recount a miracle of a servant whose tongue had been cut out for a minor offence on the order of the mother of King Sigurðr munnr, Þóra Gutthormsdóttir. The man, named Kolbeinn, made a pilgrimage to S. Óláfr's shrine, where he fell asleep. Óláfr appeared to him then and pulled the stump of his tongue. The pain awakened him and found himself cured. This must have been a rather risky narrative for Einarr to tell in the presence of Sigurðr and with the king's own mother labelled a wrongdoer. It is perhaps for this reason that *Geisl* adds the corroborative, supposedly eyewitness detail of ll. 5-8. — [All]: This st. is also in AM 61 fol, but is illegible. — [1-4]: Cf. the verbal parallels in the early prose versions: *þoːa gothoːms. dottir modir sigvrdar k(onungs) let [s]cera tungo oː hofði maɴi er kolbeiɴ het of eigi meiri sakar en hann hafdi tekit af krasadiski heɴar* 'Þóra Gutthormsdaughter, the mother of King Sigurðr, had the tongue cut out of the head of a man named Kolbeinn for no more reason than that he had taken from her plate of dainties' (Louis-Jensen 1970, 36); *Þora het kona, Guðþorms dotter, moðer Sigurðar, er skera let tungu or hofði manne, þæim er Kolbæinn het, firir æingi mæiri soc, en hann hafðe tækit af krasadisci hænnar nokcot* 'Þóra was the name of a woman, the daughter of Gutthormr, the mother of Sigurðr, who had the tongue cut out of the head of the man named Kolbeinn, for no more reason, than that he had taken something from her plate of dainties' (*ÓHLeg* 1982, 228). — [1] *Hǫrn*: *Hǫrn* is an alternative name for the goddess Freyja, here used as the base-word of a woman-kenning; the basic sense of *hvítingr* is 'white one' and can be applied to a range of light-coloured or shining referents, including drinking horns. — [3] *aumum beiði auðar* 'poor seeker of riches': Just as Einarr often compares Óláfr the miracle dispenser to a chieftain generous with his gold, he likens the beneficiary of the miracle to a 'poor seeker of riches'. — [7] *njót hodda* 'user of treasure': This kenning echoes *aumum beiði auðar* 'poor seeker of riches' in l. 2. — [8] *Hlíð* 'Lia': *Hlíð* (*lit.* 'Mountainside') was a popular farm name in medieval Norway (Rygh 1897-1936 lists over sixty examples). Storm 1900, 698 n. 1 identifies this Hlíð as the modern Lien (current Lia), a farmstead in Bratsberg county, Strinda, Sørtrøndelag.

38. Frétt hefk, at sá sótti   Hér fekk hann — en byrja
síðan malma stríðir   hótt kvæði skalk — bæði
heim, þanns hjǫlp gefr aumum   snáka vangs of slǫngvi
harmskerðanda, ferðum.   slungins mál ok tungu.

Frétt hefk, at sá stríðir malma síðan sótti heim harmskerðanda, þanns gefr hjǫlp aumum ferðum. Hér fekk hann bæði mál ok tungu; en skalk byrja hótt kvæði of slǫngvi vangs slungins snáka.

I have heard, that that enemy of weapons [WARRIOR = Kolbeinn] then sought the home of the harm-diminisher [SAINT = Óláfr], the one who gives help to wretched men. Here he received both speech and tongue; and I shall deliver an elevated poem about the distributor of the field of the coiled snake [GOLD > GENEROUS MAN].

Mss: **Flat**(2rb), Bb(117vb). — *Readings*: [4] harmskerðanda: *so* Bb, 'hardskerdand[...]' Flat [7] of: ok Bb; slǫngvi: 'slavnge' Bb [8] slungins: *so* Bb, slungin Flat.

Editions: *Skj* Einarr Skúlason, 6. *Geisli* 38: AI, 466, BI, 436, *Skald* I, 215, *NN* §940; *Flat* 1860-8, I, 4, Cederschiöld 1873, 6, Chase 2005, 88, 151.

Notes: [4] *harmskerðanda* (gen. sg.) 'of the harm-diminisher': The Bb version of this *hap. leg.* must be the correct reading. Flat reads 'harskerdand[...]' (the final letter in doubt, probably either 'a' or 'i'), which is nonsense in context. 'Harm-diminisher' emphasises the image of Óláfr expressed by the *stef*, and is analogous to *fárskerðandi* 'misfortune-diminisher' in 63/7.

39. Dýrð es ágæt orðin   Greitt má gumnum létta
ǫðlings ríks af slíku;   guðs ríðari stríðum;
mærð ríðr mildings Hǫrða   rǫskr þiggr allt, sem œskir,
mest um heims byggð flesta.   Óláfr af gram sólar.

Dýrð ríks ǫðlings es orðin ágæt af slíku; mest mærð mildings Hǫrða ríðr um flesta byggð heims. Guðs ríðari má greitt létta stríðum gumnum; rǫskr Óláfr þiggr allt, sem œskir, af gram sólar.

The fame of the powerful nobleman has become renowned from such things; the greatest praise of the king of the Hǫrðar [= Óláfr] travels over the whole [*lit.* the most] dwelling of the world. God's knight [SAINT = Óláfr] can easily alleviate afflictions for men; brave Óláfr gets all he desires from the king of the sun [= God].

Mss: **Flat**(2rb), Bb(117vb). — *Readings*: [3] ríðr: nemi Bb [4] um: of Bb; flesta: *so* Bb, 'flest[...]' Flat [5-8]: *abbrev. as* 'G' Flat, 'Greitt· m.' Bb.

Editions: *Skj* Einarr Skúlason, 6. *Geisli* 39: AI, 466, BI, 436-7, *Skald* I, 215; *Flat* 1860-8, I, 4, Cederschiöld 1873, 6, Chase 2005, 89, 151.

Notes: [1] *dýrð ... es orðin ágæt* 'the fame ... has become renowned': A formula: cf. st. 11/5. — [2] *slíku* 'such': To be understood substantively, 'from such things'.

40. Veitk, at Vinðr fyr skauti
 (verðr bragr af því) skerði
 gjalfrs Niðbranda grundar
 (greiddr) sárliga meiddu,
 ok endr frá trú týndir
 tírar sterks ór kverkum
 auðskýfanda óðar
 ǫ́r grimmliga skǫ́ru.

Veitk, at Vinðr meiddu skerði Niðbranda sárliga fyr skauti grundar gjalfrs; bragr verðr greiddr af því; ok týndir endr frá trú skǫ́ru grimmliga ǫ́r óðar ór kverkum auðskýfanda, tírar sterks.

I know that the Wends mutilated the diminisher of Nið <river>-flames [GOLD > GENEROUS MAN] painfully by the edge of the land of ocean-din [SEA]; poetry is made from that; and [men] lost long ago from the faith cut horribly the oar of poetry [TONGUE] from the throat of the distributor of riches [GENEROUS MAN], strong in honour.

Mss: **Bb**(117vb), Flat(2rb). — *Readings*: [2] *af því skerði*: *en þeir skerðu* Flat [3] *Niðbranda*: 'nidranda' Flat [4] *greiddr*: 'greiddra' Flat [5] *frá*: *fyr* Flat; *týndir* ('tindir'): 'tindri' Flat.

Editions: *Skj* Einarr Skúlason, 6. *Geisli* 40: AI, 466, BI, 437, *Skald* I, 215, *NN* §1794; *Flat* 1860-8, I, 4, Cederschiöld 1873, 6, Chase 2005, 90, 151-2.

Notes: [All]: The text above is based mainly on Bb (as in *Skj* B and *Skald*) on the grounds that it produces better and less syntactically strained sense, especially in l. 1 (*fyr skauti*) and l. 4, where Flat's text requires *sárliga* to be set off by two different sentence boundaries. — [All]: Sts 40-1 recount a miracle of S. Óláfr which is also told in the prose versions (see Chase 2005, 40-1 and n. 120). A group of Wends took a man named Halldórr and cut out his tongue. Halldórr then visited Óláfr's shrine on his feast day and was cured. The account in AM 325 4° IV (Louis-Jensen 1970) says that this took place while Cardinal Nicholas Breakspear was in Norway, in the year before *Geisl*'s recital, and that this and the cure involving Kolbeinn (see sts 37-9) were witnessed by a monk named Hallr. *Geisl* is the only account of the miracle that specifies a location for the maiming (according to the interpretation below). — [All]: Chase 2005, 90 presents the following text, based on Flat:

> Veitk, at Vinðr fyr skauti
> verðr bragr (en þeir skerðu)
> gjalfrs niðranda grundar
> greiddr (sárliga) meiddu,
> ok endr fyr trú týndir
> tírar sterks ór kverkum
> auðskýfanda óðar
> ǫ́r grimmliga skǫ́ru.

Veitk, at Vinðr meiddu skauti grundar gjalfrs fyr niðranda, en þeir skerðu sárliga – bragr verðr greiddr; ok endr fyr trú týndir skǫ́ru grimmliga óðar ǫ́r ór kverkum tírar sterks auðskýfanda 'I know that the Wends mutilated the twig of the land of noise [MOUTH > TONGUE] on the riverbank, and they cut [it] painfully. Poetry is made; and men lost from the faith long ago horribly cut the oar of poetry [TONGUE] from the throat of the most honourable distributor of riches [MAN]'. In this interpretation *skauti* (dat. sg.) (l.1) is understood as 'twig' (lit. 'corner, flap, edge' of something) and taken with *grundar gjalfrs* to produce a tongue-kenning, while Flat's *niðranda* (l.3) is taken with *fyr* (l. 1) to produce the sense 'on the riverbank'. *Nið* is here understood as referring to any body of water, and *randi* is taken as a poetic form of *rǫnd* 'rim, edge'. *Fyr niðranda* means 'beside the seacoast' or 'on the riverbank', perhaps a pun on the name *Niðaróss* 'estuary of the Nið'. — [2] *skerði* (dat. sg.) 'the diminisher': *Skerðir* 'diminisher, destroyer' is frequently a base-word of man-kennings that have 'gold' as the determinant, as here. Flat's text requires *skerðu* 'they cut', 3rd pers. pl. pret. indic. of *skerða* 'to cut a notch, diminish, harm'. — [3] *Niðbranda* 'of Nið <river>-flames': A kenning for gold, in which the name of the river Nið (Norw. Nidelven) that flows through Niðaróss, the older name for Trondheim, functions as a river-*heiti*, though one that may well also have had specific reference in this context, see *LP*: 2 *Nið*.

41. Sótti skrín it skreytta ok þeim, es vel vakði
    skíðrennandi síðan (veitk sǫnn) Hugins teiti,
    — orð finnask mér — unnar máls fekk hilmir heilsu
    Óláfs dreka bóli, heilagr (á því deili).

Unnar skíðrennandi sótti síðan Óláfs skrín it skreytta bóli dreka; orð finnask mér; ok heilagr hilmir fekk heilsu máls þeim, es vel vakði teiti Hugins; veitk sǫnn deili á því.

The runner of the ski of the wave [(*lit.* 'ski-runner of the wave') SHIP > SEAFARER] then sought Óláfr's shrine, the one ornamented with the dwelling of the dragon [GOLD]; words come to me; and the holy prince got the health of speech for that man who had well aroused the gladness of Huginn <raven>; I know true proof of that.

Mss: **Flat**(2rb), Bb(117vb). — *Readings*: [5] vel: val Bb [8] deili: deilir Bb.

Editions: Skj Einarr Skúlason, 6. Geisli 41: AI, 466, BI, 437, Skald I, 215; Flat 1860-8, I, 4, Cederschiöld 1873, 6, Chase 2005, 91, 152.

Notes: [All]: Cf. verbal echoes in the prose accounts: *Biðr miok gratande hinn hælga Olaf konong lia ser mals oc hæilsu. Þui næst feck hann mal oc miskunn af þæim goða kononge* 'Weeping greatly, he beseeches the holy king Óláfr to grant him speech and health. Immediately he obtained speech and mercy from the good king' (*ÓHLeg* 1982, 226: the sentence also appears in *HómNo*, 116). — [4] *bóli dreka* 'with the dwelling of the dragon [GOLD]': The gold-kenning (to be construed with *skreytta* 'ornamented') is a conventional allusion to the dragon Fáfnir and his hoard. — [5, 6] *es vel vakði teiti Hugins* 'who well aroused the gladness of Huginn': The rel. cl. is equivalent to kennings referring to warriors or men as promoters of the joy of carrion beasts and birds, by slaying enemies and so providing them with food; cf. 43/3-4. It applies to the beneficiary of the miracle.

42. Hǫ*s lætr helgan ræsi
    heims dómari sóma
    — fyllir framlyndr stillir
    ferð himneska — verðan.

Greitt má gumnum létta
guðs ríðari stríðum;
rǫskr þiggr allt, sem œskir,
Óláfr af gram sólar.

Dómari heims lætr helgan ræsi verðan hǫ*s sóma; framlyndr stillir fyllir himneska ferð. Guðs ríðari má greitt létta stríðum gumnum; rǫskr Óláfr þiggr allt, sem œskir, af gram sólar.

The judge of the world [= God] causes the holy king to be worthy of high honour; the bold-minded king completes the heavenly band. God's knight [SAINT = Óláfr] can easily alleviate afflictions for men; brave Óláfr gets all he desires from the king of the sun [= God].

Mss: **Flat**(2rb), Bb(117vb). — *Readings*: [1] Hǫ*s: 'Hærs' Flat, 'Hars' Bb [2] dómari: *so* Bb, 'domara domara' Flat [4] verðan: *so* Bb, verða Flat [5-8]: *abbrev. as* 'Gre' Flat, 'Greitt m. g. l. g.' Bb.

Editions: *Skj* Einarr Skúlason, 6. *Geisli* 42: AI, 466, BI, 437, *Skald* I, 215; *Flat* 1860-8, I, 4, Cederschiöld 1873, 6, Chase 2005, 92, 153.

43. Hneitir, frák, at héti,
    hjaldrs at vápna galdri,
    Óláfs hjǫrr, þess's orra
    ilbleikum gaf steikar.

Þeim klauf þengill Rauma
þunnvaxin ský gunnar
— rekin bitu stól — á Stikla-
stǫðum valbastar rǫðli.

Frák, at hjǫrr Óláfs, þess's gaf steikar ilbleikum orra hjaldrs at galdri vápna, héti Hneitir. Þeim rǫðli valbastar klauf þengill Rauma þunnvaxin ský gunnar á Stiklastǫðum; rekin stól bitu.

I heard that the sword of Óláfr, who gave meat to the pale-footed blackcock of battle [RAVEN] at the chant of weapons [BATTLE], was called Hneitir. With that sun of the sword-hilt [SWORD] the king of the Raumar [= Óláfr] clove the thin-grown clouds of battle [SHIELDS] at Stiklestad; inlaid steel weapons bit.

Mss: **Flat**(2rb), Bb(117vb-118ra). — *Readings*: [2] at: af Bb [3] Óláfs: ǫðlings Bb [4] steikar: *so* Bb, 'stikar' Flat [6] -vaxin: vaxins Bb [7] Stikla-: 'stika' Flat, 'stiklar' Bb.

Editions: *Skj* Einarr Skúlason, 6. *Geisli* 43: AI, 467, BI, 437-8, *Skald* I, 216, *NN* §§941, 942; *Flat* 1860-8, I, 5, Cederschiöld 1873, 6-7, Chase 2005, 93, 153-4.

Notes: [All]: Sts 43-50 are occupied with the story of the fate of King Óláfr's sword Hneitir 'cutter'. According to *Óláfs þáttr Geirstaðaálfs* (*Flat* 1860-8, II, 6-9; *Fms* 4, 37-8), this sword had belonged to Óláfr Geirstaðaálfr. When he died, it was buried with him, but he later appeared in a dream to Hrani Hróason and instructed him to break into the burial mound, take the sword, and give it to Ásta, then in labour with the birth of her son, S. Óláfr, who received it from his mother at the age of eight. Some versions of *Óláfs saga* report that after killing a huge boar with the sword, Óláfr changed its name from Bæsingr 'son of an exiled mother' to Hneitir 'cutter', *því at honum þótti þat hneita ǫnnur sverð fur hvassleika sakir* 'because it seemed to him to outdo other swords where sharpness is concerned' (*Fms* 4, 57-8). The story of what happened to Hneitir after S. Óláfr's death is the longest miracle account in *Geisl* and is not found in any of the prose legends. Einarr may well have known of it from oral tradition (see Chase 2005, 41-2 and nn. 121-6) and Snorri Sturluson evidently knew it from Einarr's *drápa*, which he mentions specifically in *Hkr* (*ÍF* 28, 369-71). Hneitir is there said to have been picked up after the battle at Stiklestad by a Swedish soldier and to have passed down in his family until it came into the possession of a member of the Varangian guard in Byzantium. The sword was bought by the Byzantine emperor after it appeared to have miraculous powers and was hung over the altar of a church the Varangians had dedicated to S. Óláfr. — [6] *þunnvaxin* (n. acc. pl.) 'thin-grown': This adj. presumably implies that the shields became thinner as they were hacked by swords. — [8] *rǫðli valbastar* 'with the sun of the sword-hilt [SWORD]': *Valbǫst* f. is the name of a decorative metal plate on the handle of a sword (cf. *LT*, 275); cf. Egill Lv 42/8ⱽ *eld valbasta* 'fire of sword-hilts [SWORD]'. Schrodt 1975 argues that *valbǫst* is a sword-*heiti* meaning 'corpse-striker'.

44. Tók, þás fell inn frœkni
  fylkis kundr til grundar,
  sverð, es sókn vas orðin,
  sœnskr maðr af gram þrœnzkum.
  Sá vas hjǫrr ins hóva
  hrings stríðanda síðan
  gulli merktr í Girkja
  gunndjarfs liði fundinn.

Sœnskr maðr tók sverð af þrœnzkum gram, þás inn frœkni kundr fylkis fell til grundar, es sókn vas orðin. Sá hjǫrr, gulli merktr, ins hóva gunndjarfs stríðanda hrings vas síðan fundinn í liði Girkja.

A Swedish man took the sword from the king from Trøndelag when the brave descendant of a king [= Óláfr] fell to the ground, when the battle was over. That sword, decorated with gold, of the tall, battle-eager enemy of the ring [GENEROUS MAN = Óláfr] was later found in the army of the Greeks.

Mss: **Flat**(2rb), Bb(118ra). — *Readings*: [1] inn: *so* Bb, '[...]nn' Flat [3] es: hinn Bb; sókn vas: sœkja Bb; orðin: þorði Bb [5] vas: *so* Bb, 'hefir' Flat [6] hrings: harm Bb; stríðanda: *so* Bb, stríðandi Flat [8] fundinn: *so* Bb, fundizk Flat

Editions: Skj Einarr Skúlason, 6. *Geisli* 44: AI, 467, BI, 438, *Skald* I, 216, *Flat* 1860-8, I, 5, Cederschiöld 1873, 7, Chase 2005, 94, 154.

Notes: [2] *kundr fylkis* 'descendant of a king': It is unclear whether any specific one of Óláfr's royal predecessors is implied in this kenning. The reference may be to either Haraldr hárfagri or Óláfr Tryggvason, both of whom he claimed as ancestors. — [5]: After *hjǫrr*, the scribe of Flat has erased a word, which is no longer legible. — [5, 8] *vas ... fundinn* 'was ... found': Although Flat's *hefr ... fundisk* is grammatically possible, '(that sword) ... has (later) been found', l. 5 then lacks internal rhyme, which Bb's reading (*sá vas* ...

hǫva) provides. — [6] *stríðanda* 'enemy': Bb's reading must be the correct one, since the nom. form *stríðandi* is not grammatically feasible in the *helmingr*. — [7, 8] *í liði Girkja* 'in the army of the Greeks': The Greek army referred to here is that of the Byzantine emperor called Kirjalax in Nordic sources, variously identified as Alexios I Komnenos (r. 1081-1118) or his son John II Komnenos (r. 1118-43). See further Note to 47/7.

45. Nú fremr, þanns gaf gumnum, Greitt má gumnum létta
    gǫfug dyrð jǫfur fyrða,   guðs ríðari stríðum;
    (slǫng Eindriði ungi)   rǫskr þiggr allt, sem œskir,
    armglœðr (í brag rœðu).   Óláfr af gram sólar.

Nú fremr gǫfug dyrð jǫfur fyrða, þanns gaf gumnum armglœðr; Eindriði ungi slǫng rœðu í brag. Guðs ríðari má greitt létta stríðum gumnum; rǫskr Óláfr þiggr allt, sem œskir, af gram sólar.

Now excellent fame promotes the prince of men [= Óláfr], the one who gave men arm-embers [GOLD]; Eindriði ungi ('the Young') cast the story into the poem. God's knight [SAINT = Óláfr] can easily alleviate afflictions for men; brave Óláfr gets all he desires from the king of the sun [= God].

Mss: **Flat**(2rb), Bb(118ra). — *Readings*: [1] þanns ('þann er'): *so* Bb, sá er Flat [2] jǫfur: konungr Bb [3] Eindriði: 'ein riðe' Bb [5-8]: *abbrev. as* 'G' Flat, 'Greitt· m· g· l·' Bb.

Editions: Skj Einarr Skúlason, 6. *Geisli* 45: AI, 467, BI, 438, *Skald* I, 216; *Flat* 1860-8, I, 5, Cederschiöld 1873, 7, Chase 2005, 95, 154.

Notes: [3] *Eindriði ungi*: Eindriði the Young was a well-known Norwegian contemporary of Einarr Skúlason. He travelled extensively and spent many years as a mercenary in Constantinople (see *Orkn*, *ÍF* 34, 193-224, 236-7; *Hkr*, *ÍF* 28, 370-1). The mention of his name is meant to enhance the story's authenticity and to indicate that he was one of Einarr's oral sources.

46. Mérs — því mærð skal skýra   þvít tǫkn, þess's lið læknar,
    mildings, þess's gaf hringa,   lofðungs himintungla
    styrjar snjalls — of stilli   — ljós kemr raun of ræsi —
    styrkjan vant at yrkja,   ranns ferr hvert á annat.

Mérs vant, at yrkja of styrkjan stilli — því skal skýra mærð styrjar snjalls mildings, þess's gaf hringa — þvít tǫkn lofðungs ranns himintungla, þess's lið læknar, ferr hvert á annat; ljós raun kemr of ræsi.

It is difficult for me to compose [poetry] about the strong ruler — therefore I shall make clear the praise of the clever-in-battle prince who gave rings — because miracles of the prince of the house of heavenly bodies [SKY/HEAVEN > = God (= Christ)], who heals men, go one after another; clear proof appears about the king.

Mss: Flat(2rb), Bb(118ra). — *Readings*: [1] því: en Bb; skýra: stæra Bb [3] snjalls: *so* Bb, 'snallz' Flat [4] styrkjan: *so* Bb, 'styrkann' Flat [5] læknar: læknir Bb [6] himin-: vinar Bb [7] kemr: verðr Bb; of: *so* Bb, um Flat.

Editions: *Skj* Einarr Skúlason, 6. *Geisli* 46: AI, 467, BI, 438, *Skald* I, 216; *Flat* 1860-8, I, 5, Cederschiöld 1873, 7, Chase 2005, 96, 154-5.

Notes: [4] *styrkjan* (m. acc. sg.) 'strong': *Styrkr* is an alternative form of the adj. *sterkr* showing the effect of ablaut (*ANG* §167). It is presumably used here for the sake of the rhyme with *yrkja*. — [5-8]: The *helmingr* works at two levels. The primary meaning is that Óláfr's miracles are signs given by God as proof of the saint's holiness. *Þess's lið læknar* 'the one who heals men' (l. 5) and *lofðungs ranns himintungla* 'of the prince of the house of heavenly bodies' (ll. 6, 8) clearly refer to Christ. But they can also refer to Óláfr: although the miracles are ultimately God's, a point which Einarr emphasizes, they are also Óláfr's in the sense that he is their efficient cause. The variant reading *vinar* 'of the friend' (*vinar lofðungs ranns tungla* 'of the friend of the prince of the house of heavenly bodies [= God > = Óláfr]'), adopted in *Skj* B and *Skald*, makes the reference to Óláfr the Saint explicit in the Bb text. The two *helmingar* of st. 46 juxtapose not only Óláfr and Christ, but also the Óláfr who gave rings and the Óláfr who heals. These eight ll. thus concisely express the theme of the *drápa*, as is fitting for the st. that begins its *slæmr*, or concluding section.

47. Gyrðisk hála herðum
    heldr síðarla á kveldi
    glaumkennandi gunnar
    glaðr véttrima* naðri.
    Drengr réð dýrr á vangi
    — dagr rofnaðisk — sofna
    ítrs landreka undir
    ógnfimr berum himni.

Glaðr glaumkennandi gunnar gyrðisk hála herðum naðri véttrima* heldr síðarla á kveldi. Dýrr ógnfimr drengr ítrs landreka réð sofna á vangi undir berum himni; dagr rofnaðisk.

The happy noise-tester of battle [WARRIOR] girded himself with the well-hardened snake of sword-rings [SWORD] rather late in the evening. The valuable, battle-deft soldier of the splendid land-ruler [= Byzantine emperor] decided to sleep in a field in the open air [*lit.* under the bare sky]; the day was waning.

Mss: Flat(2rb), Bb(118ra). — *Readings*: [1] Gyrðisk: *so* Bb, Gerðisk Flat [2] síðarla ('sidallá'): 'naliga' Bb; á· at Bb [3] -kennandi: vekjandr Bb; gunnar: 'grimo' Bb [4] véttrima*: 'vetþryma' Flat, vettrimar Bb [5] réð: nam Bb [8] ógn-: *so* Bb, orm- Flat.

Editions: *Skj* Einarr Skúlason, 6. *Geisli* 47: AI, 467, BI, 438-9, *Skald* I, 216; *Flat* 1860-8, I, 5, Cederschiöld 1873, 7, Chase 2005, 97, 155.

Notes: [All]: Sts 47-50 conclude the narrative of Óláfr's sword, Hneitir. A soldier in the army of the Greeks (44/7, 8) had the sword under his head one night, as he slept in the open air. When he woke, he found that the sword had moved and was lying on the ground some distance from him (st. 48). This miraculous happening took place on three successive nights (st. 49) and came to the attention of the Byzantine emperor, who bought it from the soldier and had it mounted over the altar of a church (st. 50). — [4] *naðri véttrima** 'snake of sword-rings': The meaning of *véttrim* is obscure, but it is usually understood to refer to a metal ring either between the sword guard and the sword handle or between the pommel and the sword handle; see *LP*: *véttrim*; *LT*, 290. For possible etymologies see Sijmons and Gering 1903-31, III.2, 210. *Naðr véttrima* is clearly a kenning for 'sword', and Einarr's choice of *naðr* 'snake' as the base-word may evoke the image of the sword creeping away from the man like a serpent. The emendation adopted here requires *véttrima* to be gen. pl., while Bb's reading, adopted by both *Skj* and *Skald*, makes it sg. — [7] *landreka* '[of the] land-ruler': According to Snorri Sturluson (*Hkr*, *ÍF* 28, 370), this man was the Byzantine emperor Kirjalax, who was identified by Metcalfe (1881, 76 n. 6) as Alexios I Komnenos, who reigned 1081-1118. More recently, however, Benedikz (1978, 122) has proposed an identity with Alexios's son John II Komnenos. — [8] *ógnfimr* 'battle-deft': The reading of Bb. Flat's *ormfimr* can only make sense in context if *orm-* 'snake-' is construed as meaning 'sword', in connection with sword-kennings with *ormr* as the base-word. See Chase 2005, 155 n.

48. Missti maðr, es lýsti,
    — morginn vas þá — borgar
    styrks mundriða steindrar
    styrsnjallr roðins galla.

    Nýtr gat séð á sléttri
    seimþiggjandi liggja
    grundu gylðis kindar
    gómsparra sér fjarri.

Styrsnjallr maðr missti styrks, roðins galla steindrar borgar mundriða, es lýsti; morginn vas þá. Nýtr seimþiggjandi gat séð gómsparra gylðis kindar liggja fjarri sér á sléttri grundu.

The battle-bold man missed the strong, reddened destruction of the stained stronghold of the sword-hilt [SHIELD > SWORD] when it grew light; it was morning then. The useful gold-receiver [MAN] was able to see the gum-spar of the wolf's offspring [SWORD] lying far from him on the flat ground.

Mss: **Flat**(2rb), Bb(118ra). — *Readings*: [3] steindrar: *so* Bb, steindra Flat [4] styrsnjallr: *so* Bb, styrs bráðr Flat; roðins: *so* Bb, regins Flat; galla: *so* Bb, 'væda' Flat [5] Nýtr gat séð: Þátti sinn Bb [6] -þiggjandi: -þiggjandr Bb.

Editions: *Skj* Einarr Skúlason, 6. Geisli 48: AI, 468, BI, 439, *Skald* I, 216; *Flat* 1860-8, I, 5, Cederschiöld 1873, 7, Chase 2005, 98, 155-6.

Notes: [1-4]: There is a considerable disparity between Flat's and Bb's texts of the first *helmingr*, but Bb's must be preferred as Flat's ll. 3-4 are ungrammatical as they stand and the sword-kenning possible in these ll. is unsatisfactory. One would have to read *styrks steindrar mundriða borgar Regins váða* '(the man missed) the strong sword hilt of the fortress of Reginn's peril [SWORD > SHIELD > SWORD]', with Bb's *steindrar* for Flat's *steindra* (gen. pl.), understanding *mundriði* (lit. 'that which causes the hand to move quickly') as a metonym for a sword. *Borgar Regins váða* would provide both a sword- and a shield-kenning. According to the Vǫlsung legends, the dwarf Reginn made his foster son

Sigurðr a powerful sword named Gramr, with which Sigurðr killed the dragon Fáfnir and later Reginn himself. 'Reginn's peril' would thus be a kenning for sword; its fortress is the shield. The *mundriði* of the shield is in turn another sword-kenning. But this is not very plausible, and Bb's reading of ll. 3-4 is better on several counts, even though *galla* (l. 4; nom. *galli*), which normally means 'defect, fault' has to be taken in the more abstract sense of 'destruction'. — [4] *styrsnjallr* 'battle-bold': Bb's reading *styrsnjallr* 'battle-bold' is preferred here to Flat's *styrs bráðr* 'battle-quick' and is also adopted by *Skj* B and *Skald*. Both mss' readings (-*snjallr* : *gall-* and *bráðr* : *váð-*) provide *aðalhending*. — [7-8] *gómsparra gylðis kindar* 'the gum-spar of the wolf's offspring [SWORD]': An allusion to a story told in the *Gylf* section of *SnE* (1982, 29): the Æsir fended off the wolf Fenrir by wedging a sword between his gaping jaws. This is the only such sword-kenning in skaldic poetry.

49. Þríar grímur vann þeima áðr þrekhvǫssum þessar
    þjóðnýtr Haralds bróðir (þingdjarfs) firar inga
    rauknstefnanda Reifnis   (bjǫrt eru bauga snyrtis
    ríkr bendingar slíkar,   brǫgð) jartegnir sǫgðu.

Ríkr, þjóðnýtr bróðir Haralds vann slíkar bendingar þeima Reifnis rauknstefnanda þríar grímur, áðr firar sǫgðu þessar jartegnir þrekhvǫssum inga; brǫgð þingdjarfs snyrtis bauga eru bjǫrt.

The powerful, very bountiful brother of Haraldr [= Óláfr] gave such signs to that driver of the ox of Reifnir <sea-king> [(*lit.* 'to that ox-driver of Reifnir') SHIP > SEAFARER] for three nights, before men told these miracles to the strength-keen *ingi* <king>; the deeds of the battle-brave polisher of rings [MAN = Óláfr] are bright.

Mss: **Flat**(2rb), Bb(118ra). — *Readings*: [1] grímur: *so* Bb, 'grimar' Flat [2] bróðir: *so* Bb, bróður Flat [3] raukn-: *so* Bb, 'rauck' Flat [5] þrekhvǫssum: *so* Bb, þrifhvassir Flat; þessar: *so* Bb, þessir Flat [6] inga: 'yngva' Bb [7] snyrtis: 'snytris' Bb.

Editions: *Skj* Einarr Skúlason, 6. *Geisli* 49: AI, 468, BI, 439, *Skald* I, 216, *NN* §§943, 3396T; *Flat* 1860-8, I, 5, Cederschiöld 1873, 7, Chase 2005, 99, 156-7.

Notes: [2] *bróðir Haralds* 'brother of Haraldr': The sense of the *helmingr* makes it clear that *bróðir* is the subject of the sentence, and the nom. form of the word in Bb must be the correct reading. The epithet for Óláfr refers to his half-brother Haraldr Sigurðarson (Haraldr harðráði 'the Hard-ruler'), the son of Óláfr's mother and step-father, Sigurðr sýr 'Sow'. Haraldr fought alongside Óláfr at Stiklestad, and was sole king in Norway after Magnús the Good (1047-66). He died in the battle of Stamford Bridge. — [6] *inga* (dat. sg.): Ingi is a variant of the name Yngvi, given to the god Freyr, and to kings considered to have been his descendants, including the Swed. and Norw. royal houses, the Ynglingar. The name functions in skaldic poetry as a king-*heiti*, and here refers to the Byzantine emperor who bought the sword as a relic. However, Einarr may have chosen it with his royal audience in mind, one of whom bore the name Ingi.

50. Mós frák jarðar eisu
    alls vald fyr hjǫr gjalda,
    (sléttik óð) þanns átti
    Óláfr (bragar tólum).

    Yfirskjǫldungr lét jǫfra
    oddhríðar þar síðan
    garðs *of* golli vǫrðu
    grand altári standa.

Frák vald alls gjalda eisu mós jarðar fyr hjǫr, þanns Óláfr átti; sléttik óð tólum bragar. Yfirskjǫldungr jǫfra lét síðan grand garðs oddhríðar standa þar *of* altári vǫrðu golli.

I heard [that] the ruler of all [= Byzantine emperor] paid with the fire of the gull's land [SEA > GOLD] for the sword which Óláfr had owned; I smooth [my] poem with the tools of poetry [ORGANS OF SPEECH]. The supreme king of princes [= Byzantine emperor] then caused the harm of the yard of the point-storm [BATTLE > SHIELD > SWORD] to stand there over the altar adorned with gold.

Mss: **Flat**(2rb), Bb(118ra). — *Readings*: [1] Mós: Meiðs Bb; frák ('frá ek'): *so* Bb, lét Flat [2] alls vald: *so* Bb, allvalds Flat [7] *of*: af Flat, á Bb.

Editions: Skj Einarr Skúlason, 6. Geisli 50: AI, 468, BI, 439, Skald I, 216; Flat 1860-8, I, 5, Cederschiöld 1873, 7, Chase 2005, 100, 157.

Notes: [1-4]: Bb's readings have been followed here for the most part; Flat's *allvalds* (l. 2) would have to be taken with *hjǫr* '(for the) sword of the all-ruler', and that would then make the rel. cl. *þanns Óláfr átti* 'which Óláfr owned' (ll. 3, 4) redundant. — [4] *tólum bragar* 'with the tools of poetry [ORGANS OF SPEECH]': A kenning for the tongue and possibly the other speech organs (lips, teeth) and the voice. Cf. st. 19/8 *máltól* 'speech-tools'. — [5-8]: These ll. refer to the Byzantine emperor's purchase of Óláfr's sword for a high price and his causing it to be hung over the altar of a church the Varangians had dedicated to Óláfr (see Chase 2005, 42 and references for the possible identity of this church).

51. Tókn gerir bjǫrt, þaus birta
    brandél á Girklandi,
    — mál finnsk of þat mǫnnum —
    margþarfr Haralds arfi.

    Fregnk, at allt (né ógnar
    innendr, meguð finna)
    dýrð Óláfs ríðr dála
    dagræfrs (konung hæfra).

Haralds margþarfr arfi gerir bjǫrt tókn, þaus brandél birta á Girklandi; mál finnsk mǫnnum of þat. Fregnk, at Óláfs dýrð ríðr allt dála dagræfrs, né meguð, innendr ógnar, finna hæfra konung.

Haraldr's very useful heir [= Óláfr] makes clear signs, which sword-showers [BATTLES] manifest in Greece; talk arises among men about that. I hear that Óláfr's fame rides all across the day-roof [SKY/HEAVEN]; you, doers of battle, will not be able to find a more worthy king.

Mss: **Flat**(2rb), Bb(118ra). — *Readings*: [1] gerir: *so* Bb, eru Flat;   birta: *so* Bb, birtask Flat   [3] mál: mærð Bb;   of: *so* Bb, um Flat   [4] margþarfr: 'marg þarfr' *corrected from* 'marg þaþr' Flat, 'man þarfr' Bb   [5] at: *om*. Bb;   allt: alls Bb;   ógnar: *so* Bb, 'aungir' Flat   [7] ríðr: viðr Bb.

Editions: *Skj* Einarr Skúlason, 6. *Geisli* 51: AI, 468, BI, 439-40, *Skald* I, 216-17, *NN* §2053; *Flat* 1860-8, I, 5, Cederschiöld 1873, 8, Chase 2005, 101, 157-8.

Notes: [1-4]: Bb's text is preferred here (as in *Skj* B and *Skald*), as Flat's raises difficulties of w.o. (especially in l. 3) and sense. Chase 2005, 101 offers a reading based on Flat. — [4] *Haralds arfi* 'Haraldr's heir': A reference to Óláfr's father Haraldr grenski ('the one from Grenland') and perhaps also an allusion to his ancestor Haraldr hárfagri ('Fine-hair'), with whom Óláfr liked to associate himself, claiming that the kingdom of Norway established by Haraldr hárfagri was his rightful paternal inheritance (*Hkr*, *ÍF* 27, 44). — [6] *né meguð* 'you will not be able': The form is 2nd pers. pl., a direct address to the audience. Both *Skj* B and *Skald* emend to *megu*, making the verb 3rd pers. pl., but this is not necessary. The topic of outdoing is already familiar from sts 11, 13, 14, and 21. — [8] *dagræfrs* (gen. sg.) 'day-roof [SKY/HEAVEN]': On the poetic use of the gen. to designate place, see *NS* §141.

52.   Háðisk hjaldr á víðum
— hungr sløkði vel þungan
gunnar mór í geira
gǫll — Pézínavǫllum.

Þar, svát þjóð fyr hjǫrvi
þúsundum laut, undan
— hríð óx Hamðis klæða
hjalmskœð — Grikir flœðu.

Hjaldr háðisk á víðum Pézínavǫllum; mór gunnar sløkði vel þungan hungr í gǫll geira. Þar flœðu Grikir undan, svát þjóð laut þúsundum fyr hjǫrvi; hjalmskœð hríð Hamðis klæða óx.

A battle was held on the wide Pezina plains; the gull of battle [RAVEN] slaked well [its] heavy hunger in the noise of spears [BATTLE]. There the Greeks fled away, so that people sank by the thousands before the sword; the helmet-harming storm of Hamðir's <warrior> clothing [ARMOUR > BATTLE] increased.

Mss: **Flat**(2rb), Bb(118ra). — *Readings*: [1] hjaldr: hildr Bb   [4] Pézína-: 'pecina' *or* 'perina' Flat, 'peizima' Bb   [5] Þar: *so* Bb, þars Flat   [6] laut: *so* Bb, fell Flat   [7] óx: *so* Bb, 'ǫr' Flat; Hamðis: 'handis' Bb.

Editions: *Skj* Finarr Skúlason, 6. *Geisli* 52: AI, 468-9, BI, 440, *Skald* I, 217, *NN* §1161B; *Flat* 1860-8, I, 5, Cederschiöld 1873, 8, Chase 2005, 102, 158.

Notes: [All]: Sts 52 and 53 are written in a different hand from the main hand of Flat. — [All]: Sts 52-6 cover another miracle attributed to Óláfr affecting the Varangians in the service of the Byzantine emperor. It is mentioned in numerous ON versions of the Óláfr legend (see Chase 2005, 42 and nn. 127-30 for references). The Varangians were losing a fight against a group of Petchenegs (a Turkic people who occupied a large area of the lower Danube, Ukraine, Moldavia and Wallachia) at a place called *Pézínavellir* in ON sources. (This is the only use of the name in skaldic verse; it was probably coined by the Varangians who fought in the battle. *Vellir* [m. pl.] means 'plains', and *Pézína* is an adaptation of

Πετζινάκοι, the Greek name for the Petchenegs.) The army prayed to Óláfr for victory and vowed to build a church in his honour if they were victorious, which they were. The battle may be the same as the one described by the Byzantine chronicler John Kinnamos (c. 1180) as taking place between the Byzantine emperor John II Komnenos and the Petchenegs in the winter of 1121-2 near Beroe (Stara Zagora) in Bulgaria. — [5-8]: Bb's readings *þar* (l. 5) and *laut* (l. 6) have been adopted here in order to avoid the difficulty caused by Flat's *þars svát* ... (l. 5), which requires understanding *svát ... Grikir flœðu ... undan* 'so that the Greeks fled away' (ll. 5, 6, 8), a very strained w.o., with *þars* introducing a further cl. *þars þjóð fell þúsundum fyr hjǫrvi* 'where people fell by thousands before the sword'. — [8] *Grikir* 'the Greeks': On this form of the name, see *ANG* §§279.1, 315 and 389.

53. Myndi mest und fjǫndum
    Miklagarðr ok jarðir
    (hryggs dugði lið) liggja
    (lagar eldbrota) veldi,
    nema rǫnd í byr branda
    (barðrau*k*ns) fáir harða
    (rǫðuls bliku vǫpn í veðri)
    Væringjar framm bæri.

Mest veldi, Miklagarðr ok jarðir, myndi liggja und fjǫndum — lið hryggs lagar eldbrota dugði —, nema harða fáir Væringjar bæri rǫnd framm í byr branda; vǫpn bliku í veðri rǫðuls barðrau*k*ns.

Most of the kingdom, Constantinople and the territories, would have lain under enemies — the army of the sorrowful breaker of the flame of the sea [(*lit.* 'sorrowful flame-breaker of the sea') GOLD > GENEROUS RULER = Byzantine king] did well —, except that a very few Varangians pushed [their] shields forward in the fair breeze of swords [BATTLE]; weapons gleamed in the storm of the sun of the prow-ox [SHIP > SHIELD > BATTLE].

Mss: **Flat**(2rb), Bb(118ra). — *Readings*: [2] -garðr: garðs Bb; jarðir: jarðar Bb [3] dugði: dugðit Bb [6] barðrau*k*ns: 'barraugn' Flat, 'bard ravgns' Bb; fáir: *so* Bb, 'faıt' Flat.

Editions: *Skj* Einarr Skúlason, 6. Geisli 53: AI, 469, BI, 440, *Skald* I, 217, *NN* §944; *Flat* 1860-8, I, 5-6, Cederschiöld 1873, 8, Chase 2005, 103, 158.

Notes: [3-4] *lið hryggs lagar eldbrota dugði* 'the army of the sorrowful flame-breaker of the sea did well': The reference is probably to the Byzantine army and its leader. The structure of this intercalary cl. follows *Skald* and *NN* §944 rather than *Skj* B, which fragments l. 3 syntactically. However, both *Skj* B and *Skald* adopt Bb's *dugðit* 'did not do well', with suffixed negative, rather than the positive 3rd pers. sg. pret. of Flat. Both readings are possible, and it could be argued that Bb's is better on grounds of sense, viz. the Byzantine army did *not* do well but was saved by the brave Varangians.

54. Hétu hart á ítran / hraustir menn af trausti / — stríð svall ógnar eyðis — / Óláf í gný stála, / þars of einn í ǫrva / (undbǫru) flug vǫru / (roðin klofnuðu Reifnis / rǫnn) sex tigir manna.

Hraustir menn hétu hart af trausti á ítran Óláf í gný stála — stríð eyðis ógnar svall —, þars sex tigir manna vǫru of einn í flug ǫrva; Reifnis rǫnn, roðin undbǫru, klofnuðu.

Strong men called hard with confidence on glorious Óláfr in the noise of steel weapons [BATTLE] — the distress of the destroyer of terror [RULER = Byzantine emperor] increased —, where sixty men [*lit.* six tens of men] were against one in the flight of arrows [BATTLE]; Reifnir's <sea-king> houses [SHIELDS], reddened with the wound-wave [BLOOD], were cloven.

Mss: **Flat**(2rb), Bb(118ra-b). — *Readings*: [3] svall: *so* Bb, stall Flat; ógnar: ógn þá er Bb; eyðis: óðusk Bb [4] Óláf: *so* Bb, Óláfr Flat [5] einn: *so* Bb, einum Flat [6] undbǫru: *so* Bb, 'undb̯ar a' Flat [7] roðin: *so* Bb, rofin Flat; klofnuðu: *so* Bb, klofnaði Flat.

Editions: *Skj* Einarr Skúlason, 6. Geisli 54: AI, 469, BI, 440-1, *Skald* I, 217, *NN* §945; *Flat* 1860-8, I, 6, Cederschiöld 1873, 8, Chase 2005, 104, 158-9.

Notes: [2] *af trausti* 'with confidence': cf. *HómNo*, 112: *á hann hafa callat með trauſti* 'they have called on him with confidence'. — [3] *stríð eyðis ógnar svall* 'the distress of the destroyer of terror increased': Flat's reading is followed here, except for the verb; *Skj* B and *Skald* follow Bb, understanding an intercalary *stríð ógn svall* 'tough battle raged', while construing *þás óðusk* with *í stála gný* 'when they were afraid in the noise of steel weapons [BATTLE]'. — [5-8]: Bb's text is better than Flat's and has been followed here. — [8] *sex tigir* 'six tens': The ON prose versions also mention the sixty-to-one advantage of the Petchenegs over the Varangians (Louis-Jensen 1970, 35; *ÓHLeg* 1982, 214; *Hkr*, *ÍF* 28, 372; *ÓH* 1941, 636).

55. Vas, sem reyk (af ríki / regn dreif stáls) í gegnum / hjalm-Njǫrðungum, harðan, / heiðingja lið, gingi. / Halft fimta vann heimtan / hundrað, brimi*s sunda, / nýztan tír, þars nœra, / Norðmanna, val þorðu.

Lið heiðingja vas hjalm-Njǫrðungum, sem gingi harðan í gegnum reyk; regn stáls dreif af ríki. Halft fimta hundrað Norðmanna vann heimtan nýztan tír, þars þorðu nœra val sunda brimi*s.

The host of heathens was to the helmet-Nirðir <gods> [WARRIORS] as if they were going hard through smoke; the rain of steel [BATTLE] drove mightily. Four and a half hundreds of Norwegians laid claim to very useful honour, where they dared to feed the falcon of the bays of the sword [BLOOD > RAVEN].

Mss: **Flat**(2rb), Bb(118rb). — *Readings*: [1] Vas sem: *so* Bb, Þá es Flat;   reyk: *so* Bb, rauk Flat [2] stáls: *so* Bb, stál Flat;   í: *so* Bb, á Flat;   gegnum: *so* Bb, þegna Flat   [3] -Njǫrðungum: 'niord vnar' Bb;   harðan: *so* Bb, harða Flat   [6] brimi*s: brimils Flat, brimirs Bb   [7] þars ('þar er'): 'þat er' Bb;   nœra: *so* Bb, nærri Flat   [8] þorðu: þorði Bb.

Editions: *Skj* Einarr Skúlason, 6. *Geisli* 55: AI, 469, BI, 441, *Skald* I, 217, *NN* §946; *Flat* 1860-8, I, 6, Cederschiöld 1873, 8, Chase 2005, 105, 159-60.

Notes: [1-4]: The syntax is awkward, whichever ms. is adopted as base. Here Flat's l. 1 has been deemed syntactically impossible, and Bb has been followed for ll. 1-4. — [3] *hjalm-Njǫrðungum* (dat. pl.) 'helmet-Nirðir': Pl. *Njǫrðungar*, derived from the name of the god Njǫrðr, is used in skaldic poetry (only as the second element of cpd nouns) as a base-word in kennings for men. According to Snorri Sturluson, Njǫrðr controls wind and fire (*SnE* 1982, 23), and Einarr may have used his name in this *hap. leg.* kenning to emphasize the imagery of smoke and storm. — [5, 6] *halft fimta hundrað* 'four and a half hundreds': Lit. 'half of the fifth hundred'; i.e. four 'hundreds' and half of another. In the Norse system of reckoning, a *hundrað* was 120, so the reference is to 540 men. — [7] *þars* 'where': *Skj* B and *Skald* follow Bb here, with *þats* (n. sg.) referring back to *halft* (l. 5), hence 'the one that dared to feed...'.

56. Ruddu gumnar gladdir   Nennir ǫll at inna
     — gǫfugr þengill barg drengjum —   øngr brimloga slǫngvir
     vagna borg, þars vargar   dǫglings verk, þess's dýrkar,
     vápnsundrat hræ fundu.   dáðsnjalls, verǫld alla.

Gladdir gumnar ruddu borg vagna, þars vargar fundu vápnsundrat hræ; gǫfugr þengill barg drengjum. Øngr slǫngvir brimloga nennir at inna ǫll verk dáðsnjalls dǫglings, þess's dýrkar alla verǫld.

The happy warriors cleared the fortress of wagons, where wolves found the weapon-torn carrion; the noble king saved men. No slinger of sea-fire [GOLD > GENEROUS MAN] is minded to tell all the deeds of the quick-acting ruler, the one who glorifies the whole world.

Mss: **Flat**(2rb), Bb(118rb). — *Readings*: [1] Ruddu: Eyddu Bb   [2] gǫfugr: 'gavfur gr' Bb   [4] -sundrat: sundruð Bb   [5] ǫll: *so* Bb, ǫld Flat   [6] øngr ('eingr'): *so* Bb, ungr Flat;   slǫngvir: slungins Flat, 'slaungir' Bb   [7] þess's: *so* Bb, 'þau er' Flat;   dýrkar: *so* Bb, dýrka Flat   [8] verǫld: veroll Bb.

Editions: *Skj* Einarr Skúlason, 6. *Geisli* 56: AI, 469, BI, 441; *Skald* I, 217; *Flat* 1860-8, I, 6, Cederschiöld 1873, 8, Chase 2005, 106, 160.

Notes: [1-4]: Flat is followed here, though Bb, which is followed by *Skj* B and *Skald*, also makes good sense. Differences are that Bb reads *eyddu* 'they emptied, laid waste, destroyed' in l. 1 and has pl. *vápnsundruð hræ* 'the weapon-torn corpses' in l. 4. — [3] *borg vagna* 'the fortress of wagons': Both Snorri (*Hkr*, *ÍF* 28, 371) and John Kinnamos (in Brand 1976, 16) describe the Petchenegs' tactic of drawing their wagons into a fortified circle. — [5-8]: Both ms. versions of this *helmingr* pose problems and both may be corrupt. Here Bb has been followed (so also *Skj* B and *Skald*), and Flat's version is discussed below. Bb's version requires one emendation (*sløngvir*, l. 6; *Skj* A reads 'slaungvir', but no 'v' is visible in the ms.) and the sense required for *dýrkar* (l. 7) is somewhat unusual (*Skj* B *som forherliger hele verden* 'who glorifies the whole world'). The problems produced by Flat's version are as follows: — [5] *inna* 'tell, relate': A verb used frequently in religious poetry. However, the syntax of its usage in Flat, *ungr nennir at inna ǫld verk* 'a young [man] is minded to tell men the works', requires *inna* to be used with the dat, which is unprecedented. — [6] *ungr* 'young': The adj. in Flat must be understood as a noun, possibly referring to the skald, though, if so, the reference to youth is merely conventional, since Einarr was hardly young at the time he recited *Geisl*. — [7, 8, 6] *verk dáðsnjalls dǫglings slungins brimloga* 'the works of the quick-acting ruler of scattered sea-fire': There are two reasons to be suspicious of this kenning; the first is that *dǫglingr* is never used as the base-word of a kenning for a secular ruler, only for God or Christ, and this is borne out by one other example in st. 5/7, and the second is that *dǫglingr* is not the right sort of base-word in a kenning for a generous ruler, which should belong to a category such as 'distributor', 'spender', 'waster' or similar.

57. Nús oss, þaus vann vísir,   Krapt skulum guðs, en giptu,
    verk fyr þjóð at merkja   gunnstyrks lofi dýrka,
    nauðr í nýjum óði,   lér hjaldrfrǫmum hórar
    næst; ríðrat þat smæstu.   heims læknir gram þeima.

Nús oss nauðr at merkja fyr þjóð í nýjum óði verk, þaus vísir vann næst; ríðrat þat smæstu. Skulum dýrka lofi krapt gunnstyrks guðs, en læknir heims lér hórar giptu þeima hjaldrfrǫmum gram.

Now it is a necessity for us [me] to make known to people, in new poetry, the deeds which the king accomplished next; that is not least important. We should honour with praise the power of the battle-strong God, for the healer of the world [= God] grants great fortune to the battle-prominent king.

Mss: **Flat**(2rb), Bb(118rb). — *Readings*: [1] oss: *so* Bb, *om*. Flat; vísir: vísi Bb   [4] ríðrat: 'ridr a' Bb; smæstu: smæstum Bb   [5] en: *so* Bb, 'þess er' Flat   [6] gunn-: geð- Bb   [7] hjaldr-: *so* Bb, 'halld' Flat   [8] læknir: *so* Bb, læknis Flat.

Editions: *Skj* Einarr Skúlason, 6. *Geisli* 57: AI, 470, BI, 441; *Skald* I, 217; *Flat* 1860-8, I, 6, Cederschiöld 1873, 8, Chase 2005, 107, 160.

Notes: [1, 3] *nús oss nauðr* 'now it is a necessity for us [me]': Bb's addition of *oss* must be adopted here, in order to provide the correct number of syllables and internal rhyme. — [5-8]: Flat's version of l. 5, *Krapt skulum guðs, þess's giptu* is both unmetrical and presents a syntactic problem for the interpretation of the second *helmingr*, for *þess's* 'the one who' can only refer to God, but this connection leaves *heims læknis* dangling. The only way to resolve the difficulty is to adopt Bb's readings *en* (l. 5) and *læknir* (l. 8), as do *Skj* B and *Skald*. — [6] *gunnstyrks* (gen. sg.) 'battle-strong': This epithet, applied to God, is varied in Bb as *geðstyrks* 'mind-strong, resolute'. — [6] *dýrka* 'honour': The rhyme with *-styrks* is irregular, unless shortening of <ý> is assumed to have occurred (*ANG* §127.5); cf. 7/4. — [7] *hjaldrfrǫmum* 'battle-prominent': Flat's reading, *haldfrǫmum* 'tenaciously prominent', if it is not an error, is *hap. leg.* and difficult to make sense of. Bb's *hjaldrfrǫmum* 'battle-prominent' is both easier to understand and more conventional (compounds in *hjaldr-* are fairly common in skaldic verse). — [8] *læknir heims* 'the healer of the world': Cf. 21/4 *græðari alls* 'healer of all'. The kenning anticipates the miracle of healing in the following sts.

58. Angrfyldrar varð aldar
 (illr gerisk hugr af villu)
 mildings þjónn fyr manna
 (margfaldr) ǫfund kaldri.

 Lygi hefr bragna brugðit
 (brýtr stundum frið) nýtra
 (hermðar kraptr) til heiptar
 hjaldrstríð skapi blíðu.

Þjónn mildings angrfyldrar aldar varð fyr kaldri ǫfund manna; margfaldr hugr gerisk illr af villu. Hjaldrstríð lygi hefr brugðit blíðu skapi nýtra bragna til heiptar; kraptr hermðar brýtr stundum frið.

The servant of the king of sinful humankind [= God > PRIEST = Ríkarðr] was up against the cold hatred of men; the many-sided mind becomes evil from delusion. Battle-hard lying has turned the happy mind of able men to hatred; the power of anger sometimes breaks the peace.

Mss: **Flat**(2rb), Bb(118rb). — *Readings*: [1] Angrfyldrar: *so* Bb, 'Angrs fylldir' Flat [5] bragna: *so* Bb, 'b[...]gna' Flat [7] heiptar: heipta Bb [8] hjaldrstríð: 'hialld stridr' Bb.

Editions: *Skj* Einarr Skúlason, 6. Geisli 58: AI, 470, BI, 441-2, *Skald* I, 217, *NN* §§948, 2271; *Flat* 1860-8, I, 6, Cederschiöld 1873, 8-9, Chase 2005, 108, 160.

Notes: [All]: Sts 58-61, like sts 37-9, mention a miracle of S. Óláfr that must have been a little delicate for Einarr to treat, as it again involved the mother of King Sigurðr munnr, Þóra Gutthormsdóttir, and her brothers Einarr and Andréas. It concerned an English priest named Ríkarðr who, Einarr and Andréas believed, was having an affair with Þóra. In order to punish him for this supposed insult to the family honour, they persuaded him to undertake a short journey and, on the way, they, with a servant, attacked him with an axe, breaking a leg, knocking out his eyes from their sockets, and cutting out his tongue. He did not die, but took refuge with a peasant household where he prayed to S. Óláfr. The saint appeared to him in a dream and cured his injuries. This narrative is found in all prose versions of the legend of S. Óláfr (Chase 2005, 43 and n. 132). The rather oblique and general statements of st. 58 are presumably Einarr Skúlason's way of deflecting absolute blame for the attack on a priest from Sigurðr's mother's brothers onto generalised rumour-mongering, while at the same time implying the priest Ríkarðr's innocence. — [5-8]: There are at least three ways of reading this *helmingr*. The one adopted here depends on reading Flat's adj. *hjaldrstríð* 'battle-hard' (l. 8, f. nom. sg.) as agreeing with *lygi* 'lying' (l. 5). Both *Skj* B and *Skald* prefer Bb's slightly emended reading *hjaldrstríðr* (m. nom. sg.) agreeing with *kraptr hermðar* 'the power of anger' (l. 7). Finnur Jónsson (*Skj* B) construes *lygi hefr brugðit blíðu skapi nýtra bragna til heiptar; hjaldrstríðr kraptr hermðar brýtr stundum frið* 'lying has transformed the happy mind of able men to indignation; the battle-strong power of anger sometimes breaks the peace'. Kock (*Skald* and *NN* §948) prefers *lygi hefr brugðit blíðu skapi bragna – stundum brýtr hjaldrstríðr kraptr hermðar frið nýtra til heipta* 'lying has transformed the happy mind of men – sometimes the battle-strong power of anger forces the peace of good [men] to feuds'. — [5] *bragna* 'of men': The 'ra' abbreviation of this word in Flat was legible to Finnur Jónsson (*Skj* A), but cannot now be read.

59. Lustu sundr á sandi
     seggs marglitendr eggja
     (hǫrð grœr fjón af fyrða)
     fót (aldrtrega rótum);
     ok prest, þeirs lǫg lestu
     líknar krǫfð, ór hǫfði
     — hætt mál vas þat — heila
     himintungl firar stungu.

Marglitendr eggja lustu sundr seggs fót á sandi; hǫrð fjón grœr af rótum aldrtrega fyrða; ok firar, þeirs lestu lǫg, líknar krǫfð, stungu himintungl heila ór hǫfði prest; þat vas hætt mál.

Frequent-stainers of blades [WARRIORS = Einarr and Andréas] broke the man's leg on the beach; hard hatred grows from the roots of the lifelong sorrows of men; and men, those who broke the law, from which mercy was demanded, struck the heavenly bodies of the brain [EYES] from the head of the priest; that was a dangerous undertaking.

Mss: **Flat**(2rb), Bb(118rb); W(169) (*SnE*, ll. 5-8). — *Readings*: [1] sundr: *so* Bb, í sundr Flat; á: *so* Bb, í Flat [2] seggs: 'se⸍g⸍x' *corrected from* 'sex' *in a different hand* Flat, sex Bb; marglitendr: *so* Bb, marglituðr Flat; eggja: eggi Bb [3] grœr ('grerr'): *so* Bb, greri Flat; af: *so* Bb, með Flat [5] prest: fyrst W; lǫg: *so* Bb, W, lim Flat; lestu: *so* Bb, W, leystu Flat [6] líknar: *so* Bb, 'feyfdar' Flat, leygðar W; krǫfð: krǫf W [8] firar: þegar W.

Editions: *Skj* Einarr Skúlason, 6. *Geisli* 59: AI, 470, BI, 442, *Skald* I, 217-18, *NN* §949; *Flat* 1860-8, I, 6, Cederschiöld 1873, 9, Chase 2005, 109, 160-1; *SnE* 1924, 112.

Context: In addition to st. 59's presence in Flat and Bb, ll. 5-8 are quoted in the W text of *SnE* (1924, 112) in a section listing *heiti* and kennings for the eyes. — *Notes*: [1] *lustu sundr á sandi* 'broke ... on the beach': Bb's readings must be preferred here, both for metrical reasons, and for sense (*á sandi*). — [3-4]: Bb's reading of l. 3 is again followed, although Flat's *greri* 'grew' would also be possible. Kock's understanding of the intercalary (*Skald* and *NN* §949) is followed here, rather than *Skj* B's *hǫrð fjón aldrtrega fyrða grœr af rótum* 'mændenes hårde dødelige had havde rodfæstet sig' ('mankind's hard deadly hatred had taken root'). — [5] *prest* (gen. sg.) 'of the priest': An occasionally-occurring alternative gen. form of *prestr*, which probably arose because of the difficulty of pronouncing the final consonant cluster in *prests* (see *ANG* §358.2, Anm. 3). *Skj* B and *Skald* emend to *prests*, but this is unnecessary.

60. Tungan vas með tangar
    tírkunns numin munni
    (vasa sem vænst) ok þrysvar
    (viðrlíf) skorin knífi.
    Auðskiptir lá eptir
    (ǫnd lætr maðr) á strǫndu
    (margr of minni sorgir)
    meinsamliga hamlaðr.

Tungan tírkunns vas numin með tangar munni ok þrysvar skorin knífi; vasa viðrlíf sem vænst. Auðskiptir lá eptir á strǫndu meinsamliga hamlaðr; margr maðr lætr ǫnd of minni sorgir.

The tongue of the one accustomed to praise was taken by the tong's mouth and cut three times with a knife; that was not a very hopeful treatment. The wealth-distributor [MAN] remained lying on the beach painfully mutilated; many a man gives up the ghost from fewer afflictions.

Mss: **Flat**(2rb), Bb(118rb). — *Readings*: [1] Tungan: Tunga Bb [2] -kunns: -kunn Bb; numin: *so* Bb, lokin Flat [3] þrysvar: 'tysvar' Bb [5] Auð-: aur- Bb.

Editions: *Skj* Einarr Skúlason, 6. *Geisli* 60: AI, 470, BI, 442, *Skald* I, 218, *NN* §§2054, 2792; *Flat* 1860-8, I, 6, Cederschiöld 1873, 9, Chase 2005, 110, 161-2.

Notes: [1, 2] *tungan tírkunns* 'the tongue of the one accustomed to praise': In Flat's version, also followed in *Skald*, understood as a reference to the priest Ríkarðr; Bb's adj. *tírkunn* (f. nom. sg.) can be construed with *tunga* 'the tongue accustomed to praise [God]'; so *Skj* B. — [2] *numin* 'taken': Bb's reading makes sense, while Flat's *lokin*, from *luka* 'to close, bring to an end', does not. — [6] *þrysvar* 'three times': This detail is explained in the prose accounts: *sidan drogo þeir ut tvngo hans oc skoro af mikit oc spurdo ef hann metti mela en hann leitaði vid at mela þa toko þeir i tungo stufiN oc skoro af tysvar þadan af oc i tungo rotom it sidarsta siN* 'then they drew out his tongue and cut off a big piece and asked if he could speak, and he tried to speak; then they took the stump of the tongue and cut off two more pieces, the last time cutting out the root of the tongue' (Louis-Jensen 1970, 37; cf. *Hkr*, *ÍF* 28, 336; *ÓH* 1941, 652-3). — [6] *á strǫndu* 'on the beach': The prose versions tell us that the incident took place on the shore of a lake. Einarr specifies a similar location in his account of the man mutilated by the Wends (st. 40); he may have confused the circumstances of the two miracles.

61. Leyfðrs, sás lét of stýfðrar   Hǫnd Óláfs vann heilan
lamins fótar, gramr, njóta   hreins gǫrvallra meina
ítran þegn sem augna   (gǫr munu gjǫld, þeims byrja)
út stunginna ok tungu.   guðs þræl (ǫfugmæli).

Leyfðrs gramr, sás lét ítran þegn njóta lamins fótar sem út stunginna augna ok of stýfðrar tungu. Hǫnd hreins Óláfs vann guðs þræl heilan gǫrvallra meina; gǫr munu gjǫld, þeims byrja ǫfugmæli.

Praised is the king who let the excellent man enjoy his lame leg, as well as his stabbed-out eyes and cut-off tongue. The hand of pure Óláfr healed God's servant [PRIEST] of all his injuries; ample will be the payments for those who spread slander.

Mss: **Flat**(2rb), Bb(118rb). — *Readings*: [1] of: ok Bb; stýfðrar: 'styfdar' Flat, Bb [2] lamins: lamiðs Bb; gramr: *so* Bb, gram Flat [3] ítran: ungan Bb; sem: *so* Bb, til Flat [4] ok: *om.* Bb [6] gǫrvallra: grimligra Bb [7] byrja: *so* Flat, byrjar Flat.

Editions: Skj Einarr Skúlason, 6. Geisli 61: AI, 470-1, BI, 442-3, Skald I, 218; *Flat* 1860-8, I, 6, Cederschiöld 1873, 9, Chase 2005, 111, 162-3.

Notes: [1-4]: The language parallels the Norw. homily on S. Óláfr's miracles: *ftyfðu af tungunni. ok ftungu bæði ǫugun or hǫfði honum* 'they cut off the tongue and stabbed both eyes out of his head' (*HómNo*, 117). — [1] *stýfðrar* (p.p.) 'cut': Although both mss read 'styfdar', the grammar of the cl. demands the p.p. be f. gen. sg. to agree with *tungu* (l. 4). — [3] *sem* 'as well as': Bb's reading must be preferred over Flat's *til* 'to' here, as the syntax of the cl. (with *njóta* 'to enjoy, make use of' + gen. object) is otherwise impossible. — [7-8]: Einarr expresses similar admonitory sentiments in sts 17 and 37, but his tone here is uncharacteristically sharp. The comment may have been *ad hominem*: Einarr does not use names, but his audience must have known that the assault on the priest Ríkarðr was linked to Sigurðr munnr's family, and the two brothers Einarr and Andréas may themselves have been present.

62. Bíðr allskonar œðri   þvít lausnara lýsir
— ǫruggt mælik þat — sælu   (liðs valdr) numinn aldri
dýrðar váttr með dróttni   vinr (firði sik synðum)
dyggr, an þjóð of hyggi,   slík verk á jarðríki.

Dyggr váttr dýrðar bíðr með dróttni allskonar sælu, œðri an þjóð of hyggi — ǫruggt mælik þat —, þvít vinr lausnara, numinn aldri, lýsir slík verk á jarðríki; valdr liðs firði sik synðum.

The valiant witness of glory [MARTYR] experiences with the Lord all kinds of blessedness, higher than people can imagine — I say that fearlessly —, because the friend of the Saviour [SAINT], taken from life, proclaims such works in the earthly kingdom; the ruler of men kept himself from sin.

Mss: **Flat**(2rb), Bb(118rb). — *Readings*: [2] mælik ('mæli ek'): *so* Bb, 'mæl ek' Flat [4] dyggr: *so* Bb, dyggri Flat [5] þvít: ef Bb; lýsir: *so* Bb, leysi Flat [7] vinr: *so* Bb, langvinr Flat.

Editions: *Skj* Einarr Skúlason, 6. Geisli 62: AI, 471, BI, 443, *Skald* I, 218, *NN* §2537; *Flat* 1860-8, I, 6, Cederschiöld 1873, 9, Chase 2005, 112, 163.

Notes: [2] *øruggt* 'fearlessly': The word ordinarily means 'certainly' or 'confidently', but its literal meaning is 'without fear', and here it may refer to Einarr's unrestrained comments on the crimes of Sigurðr's mother and brothers. — [3] *váttr dýrðar* 'witness of glory': The kenning for Óláfr translates the concept 'witness', which is conveyed by the Church Lat. (ultimately Gk) *martyr*; cf. st. 6/1 and *Pl* 26/3. — [4] *dyggr* (m. nom. sg.) 'valiant': Bb's adj. must be preferred here over Flat's *dyggri* (comparative adj.), unless the latter is to be understood in a superlative sense 'most valiant'. — [5] *lýsir* (3rd pers. sg. pres. indic.) 'proclaims': Bb's reading, preferable to Flat's *leysi* 'may loosen, determine' (3rd pers. sg. pres. subj.), which does not give good sense in context. — [5, 6] *vinr lausnara* 'the friend of the Saviour': 'Friend of God' is one of Einarr's favourite periphrases for Óláfr. Cf. *langvinr lausnara* st. 68/1-2; also sts 9/6-8, 63/1-4 and 64/8. Flat reads *langvinr* (l.7), but this would produce an unmetrical l. — [6] *numinn aldri* 'taken from life': Cf. *numin lifi* 'taken from life', st. 17/8 and *numinn ungr heðan frá miklu angri* 'taken young from here, from great affliction' 63/1, 4.

63. Heðan vas ungr frá angri
    — alls mest vini flesta
    guð reynir svá sína —
    siklingr numinn miklu.

Nú lifir hraustr í hæstri
himna valds, þars aldri,
fárskerðandi fyrða
friðarsýn, gleði týnisk.

Siklingr vas numinn ungr heðan frá miklu angri; guð reynir svá flesta vini sína alls mest. Nú lifir hraustr fárskerðandi fyrða í hæstri friðarsýn valds himna, þars gleði aldri týnisk.

The king was taken young from here, from great affliction; God tests thus most of his friends very frequently. Now the valiant misfortune-diminisher of men [SAINT] lives in the highest vision of peace of the ruler of the heavens [= God], where joy never ceases.

Mss: **Flat**(2va), Bb(118rb). — *Readings*: [2] vini: *so* Bb, vinir Bb; flesta: *so* Bb, flestir Flat [5] í: *so* Bb, af Flat.

Editions: *Skj* Einarr Skúlason, 6. Geisli 63: AI, 471, BI, 443, *Skald* I, 218, *NN* §2055; *Flat* 1860-8, I, 6-7, Cederschiöld 1873, 9, Chase 2005, 113, 163.

Notes: [7] *fárskerðandi* 'misfortune-diminisher': Cf. *harmskerðanda* 'harm-diminisher', st. 38/4. — [8] *friðarsýn* 'vision of peace': I.e. 'the Heavenly Jerusalem'. The cpd is a direct translation of Lat. *visio pacis*, which was believed to be the meaning of the name Jerusalem (Augustinus Hipponensis, *Enarrationes in Psalmos*, col. 598). This etymology was well known in the Middle Ages and appears frequently in theological writings and in hymns, the most famous being *Urbs beata Hierusalem, dicta pacis visio* (*AH* 51, 119; *Ordo Nidr.*, 292-3, 335-6). The image of the martyrs and confessors living in endless heavenly bliss, ultimately derived from Scripture (Rev. VII.13-17, XXI. 3-4, etc.), is a commonplace in hymns for the feasts of saints. Cf. Ník *Jóndr* 2/3 *himna sýnar* 'a vision of the heavens' and the Icel. Christmas homily: *Méttem ver þa fǫþor oc sun oc anda helgan i eino velde. oc fagrt eþle yver engla. þar monom ver siá helga friþar sýn þa er vár bíþr meþ sinom trúlegom borgmǫnom* 'We will then meet the Father and the Son and the Holy Spirit in one kingdom. And [it will be] a beautiful homeland above the angels. There we will see the holy vision of peace which awaits us with its faithful citizens' (*HómÍsl* 1993, fol. 23v).

64. Hverrs svá horskr, at byrjar
hans vegs megi of segja
ljóss í lífi þessu
lofðungs gjafar tunga,
þars hreggsalar hyggjum
heitfastr jǫfurr veitir
— skreytt megu skatnar líta
skrín — dýrðar vin sínum?

Hverrs svá horskr, at hans tunga megi of segja gjafar lofðungs ljóss vegs byrjar í lífi þessu, þars hyggjum heitfastr jǫfurr hreggsalar veitir dýrðar vin sínum? Skatnar megu líta skreytt skrín.

Who is so wise that his tongue can tell of the gifts of the prince of the bright path of fair wind [SKY/HEAVEN > = God] in this life, where we think [that] the oath-firm king of the storm-hall [SKY/HEAVEN > = God] gives honours to his friend? Men can see the ornamented shrine.

Mss: Flat(2va), Bb(118rb-va). — *Readings*: [1] byrjar: *so* Bb, hyrjar Flat [2] hans: háss Bb; vegs: *so* Bb, veg Flat; of: *om*. Bb [4] tunga: tungna Bb [5] þars ('þar er'): 'þær er' Bb; hreggsalar hyggjum: hims ok himna Bb [7] megu: er of Bb; skatnar: skatna Bb; líta: dróttinn Bb [8] sínum: þínum Bb.

Editions: *Skj* Einarr Skúlason, 6. Geisli 64: AI, 471, BI, 443, *Skald* I, 218, *NN* §950; *Flat* 1860-8, I, 7, Cederschiöld 1873, 9, Chase 2005, 114, 164.

Notes: [1] *byrjar* 'of fair wind': Bb's reading is superior to Flat's *hyrjar* 'of fire' because the latter produces three alliterative staves rather than the expected two. Additionally, the heaven-kenning produced with this reading, *ljóss vegs hyrjar* 'of the bright path of fire' (ll. 1, 2, 3), is abnormal (cf. *Meissner*, 106). — [5-8]: The second *helmingr* differs substantially between Flat and Bb, and neither is fully satisfactory. Here Flat's version is followed, beginning with a subordinate cl., ('in this life, where') and assuming a suppressed *at* (which is quite irregular), while Bb's (followed by *Skj* B and *Skald*), begins with the rel. pron. *þær es* (f. pl.), referring directly back to *gjafar* (l. 4). Following the Bb text (with minor emendation of 'hims' to *heims* in l. 5 and *skrín* to *skríns* in l. 8) gives the following sense: *þærs heitfastr jǫfurr heims ok himna veitir sínum dýrðarvin – skreytt skríns of dróttinn skatna* '(the gifts) which the oath-firm king of the world and the heavens grants to his honoured friend – an ornamented shrine stands [*lit.* is] above the lord of men'.

65. Heims hykk hingat kvǫmu
    hǫfuðsmenn í stað þenna
    — snarr tyggi bergr seggjum
    sólar — erkistóli.

Hérs af himna gervis
heilagr viðr — sem biðjum,
yfirskjǫldungr, bjarg, aldar,
oss — píningar krossi.

Hykk hǫfuðsmenn heims kvǫmu erkistóli hingat í stað þenna; snarr tyggi sólar bergr seggjum. Hérs heilagr viðr af krossi píningar gervis himna; yfirskjǫldungr aldar, bjarg oss, sem biðjum.

I know that the rulers of the world brought an archbishopric here to this place; the quick prince of the sun [= God (= Christ)] saves men. Here there is holy wood from the Cross of torture of the maker of the heavens [= God (= Christ)]; supreme king of men [= God], protect us as we pray.

Mss: **Flat**(2va), Bb(118va). — *Readings*: [2] hǫfuðsmenn: *so* Bb, hǫfuð manns Flat [3] snarr: snart Bb [4] erkistóli: *so* Bb, 'erchistolar' *corrected from* 'erchisolar' Flat [7] bjarg: *so* Bb, bjarg þú Flat.

Editions: *Skj* Einarr Skúlason, 6. *Geisli* 65: AI, 471, BI, 443-4, *Skald* I, 218; *Flat* 1860-8, I, 7, Cederschiöld 1873, 9, Chase 2005, 115, 164-5.

Notes: [1-4]: A reference to the establishment of the archdiocese of Trondheim in 1152, the visit of Cardinal Nicholas Breakspear to Norway, and his consecration of Jón Birgisson (who was in Einarr's audience) as its first archbishop. — [5] *gervis himna* 'of the maker of the heavens': A kenning for Christ, the creative word through whom God made the universe (Heb. I.1-2). The image of Christ as creator occurs frequently in hymns; Einarr would have known, e.g., *Conditor alme siderum* (*AH* 51, 46; *Ordo Nidr.*, 131, 133, 135, 137-41, 144-5, 149-50); *Regni cælestis conditor* (*AH* 51, 3); *Christe, cælorum conditor* (*AH* 51, 41). Cf. also Mark Frag 1[III]. — [6, 8] *heilagr viðr af krossi píningar* 'holy wood from the Cross of torture': King Sigurðr Jórsalafari ('Jerusalem-traveller') brought the relic of Christ's Cross to Trondheim after receiving it as a gift from Baldwin I of Jerusalem during a trip to Palestine in 1110 (*Ágr*, 50-1; Storm 1888, 66; *Hkr*, III, 250). — [7] *yfirskjǫldungr aldar* 'supreme king of men [= God]': The God-kenning reflects the kenning for the hierarchy in the first *helmingr*: the pope may be the head-man of the world, but God is 'over-king of mankind', the supreme ruler of everything. Cf. *hæstr skjǫldungr* 'highest prince', st. 6/7 and *ins hæsta hilmis* 'of the highest king', st. 67/7.

66. Ǫld nýtr Óláfs mildi
    — jǫfurs dýrð hǫfum skýrða —
    þróttar hvass a*t* þessum
    þreksnjǫll frama ǫllum.

Lúti landsfolk ítrum
lim salkonung*s* himna;
sæll es hverr, es hollan
hann gervir sér, manna.

Þreksnjǫll ǫld nýtr mildi Óláfs hvass þróttar a*t* ǫllum þessum frama; hǫfum skýrða dýrð jǫfurs. Landsfolk lúti himna salkonung*s* ítrum lim; sæll es hverr manna, es gervir hann hollan sér.

Strong and bold mankind enjoys the mercy of Óláfr, keen of strength with regard to all these [instances of] honour; we [I] have made clear the fame of the king. Let the people of the land bow before the bright limb of the king of the hall of the heavens [(*lit.* 'the bright limb of the hall-king of the heavens') SKY/HEAVEN > = God (= Christ) > SAINT = Óláfr]; blessed is every man who makes him friendly to himself.

Mss: **Flat**(2va), Bb(118va). — *Readings*: [3] þróttar: *so* Bb, þrotnar Flat; hvass: *so* Bb, hárs Flat; *at*: frá Flat, af Bb [4] þreksnjǫll: *so* Bb, þingsnjalls Flat; frama: *so* Bb, verǫld Flat; ǫllum: *so* Bb, alla Flat [5] Lúti: 'loti' Bb; lands-: land Bb [6] sal-: *so* Bb, '-salmls' Flat; -konungs: konungi Flat, konunguns Bb [7] hollan: hyllan Bb.

Editions: *Skj* Einarr Skúlason, 6. *Geisli* 66: AI, 471-2, BI, 444, *Skald* I, 218; *Flat* 1860-8, I, 7, Cederschiöld 1873, 10, Chase 2005, 116, 165-6.

Notes: [All]: Some emendation is necessary to make sense of this st., whichever ms. is taken as base; however, Flat's version poses more serious problems, especially in the first *helmingr*, in terms of syntax, metre and sense, so Bb's has been followed for the most part. Line 3 in the Flat version has no *hending*, and the epithet *hárs* 'old' (m. gen. sg.) can only qualify *Óláfs* (l. 1), and is not plausible in context; *þrotnar* 'dwindles away' (3rd pers. sg. pres. indic.) is similarly implausible, and has no obvious subject, *verǫld alla* 'all the world' being acc. — [6] *salkonung*s 'of the hall-king': Emendation is necessary here, as neither ms. is satisfactory.

67. Talðak fátt ór fjǫlða Bóls fái seggr, hverrs sólar
    friðgegns af jartegnum siklings, þess's guð miklar,
    (ber koma orð frá órum) hilmis ǫ́st ins hæsta,
    Óláfs (bragar stóli). heiðbjartrar lof reiðir,

Talðak fátt ór fjǫlða af jartegnum friðgegns Óláfs; ber orð koma frá órum stóli bragar. Hverr seggr, [e]s reiðir lof siklings bóls heiðbjartrar sólar, þess's guð miklar, fái ǫ́st ins hæsta hilmis,

I have told little from the multitude of miracles of peace-loving Óláfr; clear words come from our [my] seat of poetry [MOUTH]. May each man who spreads the praise of the lord of the dwelling-place of the cloud-free sun [SKY/HEAVEN > = Óláfr], whom God makes great, receive the love of the highest Lord,

Mss: **Flat**(2va), Bb(118va). — *Readings*: [1] ór: *so* Bb, í Flat [3] frá: *so* Bb, af Flat [5] fái: taki Bb; hverrs ('huerr er'): hverr Bb [6] þess's guð ('þess er guð'). *so* Bb, hefir Flat; miklar: *so* Bb, mikla Flat [7] hilmis: hilmir Bb [8] heiðbjartrar: *so* Bb, heiðbjartr er Flat; reiðir: greiðir Bb.

Editions: *Skj* Einarr Skúlason, 6. *Geisli* 67: AI, 472, BI, 444, *Skald* I, 219, *NN* §§951, 3281; *Flat* 1860-8, I, 7, Cederschiöld 1873, 10, Chase 2005, 117, 166.

Notes: [1] *fátt ór fjǫlða* 'little from the multitude': This is presumably intended as a modesty topos, given the number of miracles Einarr has just included in his poem. Bb's reading is preferred by both *Skj* B and *Skald*. — [2] *friðgegns* (m. gen. sg.) 'peace-loving': The epithet has decidedly Christian connotations: Óláfr now dwells in peace in the heavenly Jerusalem.

— [3] *koma frá* 'come from': Here Bb's reading is adopted, as Flat's *koma af* means 'descend from' (in a genealogical sense) and is inappropriate here. — [4] *stóli bragar* 'seat of poetry [MOUTH]': The kenning is multivalent. *LP* identifies it as a reference to the poet's breast or soul, but it could also refer to his voice or mouth, or even (secondarily) to the seat from which he proclaimed his poem to the audience. — [5-8]: There are considerable differences between Flat and Bb in the second *helmingr*. Neither version is unproblematic, so readings have been taken from both. The sense of ll. 5-8 is continued by the *svát*-cl. introducing st. 68. The interpretation offered here differs slightly from both *Skj* B and Kock (*Skald* and *NN* §951). Kock reads ll. 6-7 as an intercalary, adopting Flat's l. 6, though with emendation of *siklings* to *siklingr*, and another emendation in l. 8 (*heiðbjarts*). *Skj* B takes *lof hilmis* 'praise of the prince' (Óláfr) together and constructs the kenning *(ǫ́st ens hæsta) siklings heiðbjartrar sólar bóls* '(the highest love) of the king of the dwelling-place of the cloud-free sun [SKY/HEAVEN > = God]'. The cl. *þess's guð miklar* 'whom God makes great' then depends on gen. sg. *hilmis* (l. 7), referring to Óláfr, which avoids the difficulty in the interpretation adopted here that the gen. phrase is the kenning *siklings bóls heiðbjartrar sólar* 'lord of the dwelling-place of the cloud-free sun', which must be assumed to refer, unusually, to the saint rather than to God.

68. svát lausnara leysi   víga skýs, þeirs vísa,
     langvinr frá kvǫl strangri   veljendr, framan telja
     nýta þjóð ór nauðum   ǫflugs Krists af ǫ́stum
     nafnkuðr við trú jafnan,   alnennins brag þenna.

svát nafnkuðr langvinr lausnara leysi jafnan nýta þjóð frá strangri kvǫl, ór nauðum við trú, veljendr skýs víga, þeirs telja þenna framan brag alnennins vísa af ǫ́stum ǫflugs Krists.

so that the well-known old friend of the Saviour [= Óláfr] might constantly release able people from the great torment, from distress on account of the faith, those choosers of the cloud of battle [SHIELD > WARRIORS] who tell this splendid poem of the energetic prince about the love of mighty Christ.

Mss: **Flat**(2va), Bb(118va). — *Readings*: [2] langvinr: *so* Bb, 'lang vinn' Flat [3] ór: ok Bb [4] nafnkuðr: 'nagl kvaddr' Bb; jafnan: stadda Bb [5] þeirs ('þeir er'): 'þar er' Bb [6] veljendr: 'velendr' Flat, 'velivndr' Bb; framan: glaðir Bb [7] Krists: Krist Bb [8] alnennins: *so* Bb, 'almenins' Flat.

Editions: *Skj* Einarr Skúlason, 6. *Geisli* 68: AI, 472, BI, 444, *Skald* I, 219, *NN* §§952, 3396T; *Flat* 1860-8, I, 7, Cederschiöld 1873, 10, Chase 2005, 118, 167.

Notes: [1] *svát* 'so that': St. 68, joined to the preceding ll. by this subordinating conj., continues the prayer begun in the second *helmingr* of st. 67. — [3, 4] *ór nauðum við trú* 'from distress on account of the faith': Taking Flat's *ór* rather than Bb's *ok* (favoured by both *Skj* B and *Skald*), the phrase must be read as in apposition to *frá strangri kvǫl* 'from great torment' (l. 2). Bb's text allows the reading *frá strangri kvǫl ok nauðum við trú* 'from great torment and distress on account of the faith'. — [5] *þeirs* 'those ... who': The eds of *Skj* B and *Skald* prefer Bb's reading *þars* 'where'. — [6] *framan* 'splendid': The reading of Flat, here understood as an adj. qualifying *þenna brag* 'this poem' (l. 8). Other eds choose Bb's reading *glaðir* 'happy' (l. 6), which can be construed with the base-word of the kenning for warriors, *veljendr*.

69. Óláfs hǫfum jǫfra Laun fǫ́m holl, ef hónum
     orðhags kyni sagðar (hræsíks þrimu) líkar,
     (fylgir hugr) ins helga gǫfugs óðar (hjalp gœðum
     happsdáðir (því ráði). guðs blessan) lofs þessa.

Hǫfum sagðar kyni jǫfra happsdáðir orðhags Óláfs ins helga; fylgir hugr því ráði. Fǫ́m holl laun gǫfugs óðar, þessa lofs, ef hónum líkar; guðs blessan, hjalp gœðum þrimu hræsíks.

We [I] have told the family of the kings the blessed deeds of eloquent Óláfr the holy; the mind supports that undertaking. We [I] shall receive a kind reward for the splendid poem, this praise, if it pleases him [Óláfr]; God's blessing, help the increasers of the storm of the corpse-fish [SWORD > BATTLE > WARRIORS].

Mss: **Flat**(2va), Bb(118va). — *Readings*: [1] jǫfra: *so* Bb, jǫfri Flat   [3] fylgir: fylgði Bb   [4] happsdáðir: happsdáða Bb   [5] fǫ́m: 'fæ ek' Bb; ef: *so* Bb, af Flat; hónum: hreinum Bb   [7] hjalp: lét Bb; gœðum: 'gæðir' Bb   [8] blessan: 'blezon' Flat, 'blezun' Bb; lofs: liðs Bb.

Editions: *Skj* Einarr Skúlason, 6. *Geisli* 69: AI, 472, BI, 444-5, *Skald* I, 219, *NN* §953; Flat 1860-8, I, 7, Cederschiöld 1873, 10, Chase 2005, 119, 168.

Notes: [All]: The order of this st. and the following one is reversed in Bb. — [2] *orðhags* (m. gen. sg.) 'eloquent': The epithet is puzzling in this context, but it may refer to Óláfr's power as an intercessor. — [2, 1] *kyni jǫfra* 'the family of the kings': Bb's *jǫfra* must be the preferred reading here, as Flat's *jǫfri* (dat. sg.) leaves *kyni* (l. 2) syntactically isolated. Presumably Einarr uses the gen. pl. *jǫfra* to refer to the three kings Eysteinn, Sigurðr and Ingi, who were in his audience; the phrase could also flatter them by suggesting that they, as sons of Haraldr gilli, were descendants of S. Óláfr. — [3] *fylgir* 'supports': Bb's pret. *fylgði* 'supported' is preferred by *Skj* B and *Skald*, and could be taken to refer to Einarr's nearly completed performance of his encomium. — [4] *happsdáðir* 'blessed deeds': Cf. *happmætu* 'rich in blessing', st 19/7. — [5-8]: The second *helmingr* is difficult to understand. Both *Skj* B and *Skald* adopt Bb's *hreinum* (l. 5), *ef* (l. 5) and 'let' (l. 7), which Finnur Jónsson interprets as *létt* 'easily' and Kock emends to *lát* 'sound'. Chase 2005, 119 adopts *hjǫlp* 'help', based on Flat's 'hialp'. Line 7 is problematic for metrical reasons, as eds have long recognised, but the cause has not previously been adequately addressed, viz. that the word in position 4 cannot be either a noun or an adv., but must be a verb. Both Flat's and Bb's readings point in that direction. The present interpretation takes Flat's text in all instances except for *ef* (l. 5) instead of *af*. — [6, 7] *gœðum þrimu hræsíks* 'the increasers of the storm of the corpse-fish [SWORD > BATTLE > WARRIOR]': This warrior-kenning may refer to the three kings in Einarr's audience. Alternatively, if emendation of the base-word to *gœði* (dat. sg.) is preferred (so *Skj* B, following Cederschiöld), the kenning may refer to Einarr himself or to his patron King Eysteinn. — [7] *hræsíks* 'of the corpse-fish [SWORD]': The *síkr* is a kind of whitefish (*Coregonus lavaretus*).

70. Myndi bragr nú brǫnd*um*
  baugness vesa þessi
  — kannk rausnarskap ræsis —
  raundýrliga launaðr,
  ef lofða gramr lifði
  leikmildr Sigurðr Hildar
  — þess lýsik veg vísa —
  vellum grimmr inn ellri.

Þessi bragr myndi nú vesa raundýrliga launaðr brǫnd*um* baugness — kannk rausnarskap ræsis —, ef Sigurðr inn ellri, gramr lofða, grimmr vellum, Hildar leikmildr, lifði; lýsik veg þess vísa.

This poem would now be magnificently rewarded with the fires of the bracelet-headland [ARM > GOLD] — I know the munificence of the king —, if Sigurðr the elder, king of men, fierce to gold, generous with the play of Hildr [BATTLE] [*lit.* play-generous of Hildr] were alive; I praise the honour of this king.

Mss: Flat(2va), Bb(118va). — *Readings*: [1] Myndi bragr: Bragr myndi Bb; nú: *so* Bb, ins Flat; brǫnd*um*: 'brenda' Flat, 'grondv' Bb [2] -ness: *so* Bb, hvers Flat [3] kann-: man Bb [4] launaðr: launat Bb [7] lýsik ('lysek'): 'hrosa ek' Bb [8] grimmr: 'grims' Bb.

Editions: *Skj* Einarr Skúlason, 6. *Geisli* 70: AI, 472, BI, 445, *Skald* I, 219; *Flat* 1860-8, I, 7, Cederschiöld 1873, 10, Chase 2005, 120, 169.

Notes: [All]: The poet puts pressure on the kings for a reward. The *helmingar* are linked by a subordinating conj. (*ef*), and the bond between the two is reinforced by the alliteration of the last word in l. 4 with the *stuðlar* in l. 5. The entire st. is a single sentence with two intercalaries interposed. — [1] *nú* 'now': The reading of Bb, preferred here, as Flat's *ins* (def. art. n. gen. sg.) can only refer to *baugness* (l. 2) from which it is separated. — [1] *brǫndum* 'with the fires': Neither ms. has an acceptable reading; the emendation was first proposed by Cederschiöld. — [6, 8] *Sigurðr inn ellri* 'Sigurðr the elder': King Sigurðr Jórsalafari 'Jerusalem-traveller' Magnússon (r. 1103-30), who was renowned for his generosity.

71. Bœn hefk, þengill, þína,
  þrekrammr, stoðat framla;
  iflaust hǫfum jǫfri
  unnit mærð, sem kunnum.
  Ágætr, segið, ítran,
  Eysteinn, hvé brag leystak
  — hós elskið veg vísa
  vagnræfrs — en ek þagna.

Þrekrammr þengill, hefk framla stoðat bœn þína; iflaust hǫfum unnit jǫfri mærð, sem kunnum. Ágætr Eysteinn, segið, hvé leystak ítran brag; elskið veg vísa hós vagnræfrs; en ek þagna.

Courage-strong prince, I have excellently fulfilled your request; without a doubt we [I] have made praise to the king as we are [I am] able. Excellent Eysteinn, say how I have delivered the outstanding poem; love the honour of the king of the high wagon-roof [SKY/HEAVEN > = God]; and I fall silent.

Mss: **Flat**(2va), Bb(118va). — *Readings*: [1] þengill: 'þeimgill' *corrected from* 'femgit' *or* 'feingit' Bb   [5] segið: *so* Bb, segir Flat; ítran: *so* Bb, œztan Flat   [6] Eysteinn: *so* Bb, *om.* Flat; hvé: *so* Bb, 'hue ek' Flat; leystak: *so* Bb, leysta Flat   [7] elskið: *so* Bb, 'elskig' Flat.

Editions: *Skj* Einarr Skúlason, 6. Geisli 71: AI, 472-3, BI, 445, *Skald* I, 219, *NN* §2056; *Flat* 1860-8, I, 7, Cederschiöld 1873, 10, Chase 2005, 121, 169-70.

Notes: [1] *bœn* 'prayer, request': The word (pl. *bœnir* 1/1) appears in key position in the first l. of the poem, and it is with a sense of symmetry that Einarr uses it here. — [5, 7]: *segið* 'say' and *elskið* 'love' (both 2nd pers. pl. imp.), which are Bb's readings, are preferred here, and constitute a direct exhortation to Eysteinn. Flat's 'elskik' (l. 7), if taken as *elskak* 'I love' or 'may I love', is also possible, if understood as a pious, self-reflexive exclamation by the poet. See Chase 2005, 121 and 169-70 for such a reading. — [7, 8] *veg vísa hós vagnræfrs* 'the honour of the king of the high wagon-roof': The cpd *vagnræfr* 'wagon-roof' is a kenning for heaven: *Karlsvagn* was the ON name for the constellation Ursa Major; see Ník *Jóndr* 3/6 *tyggi vagnbryggju* 'ruler of the wagon-bridge' and Note *ad loc.* The adj. *hás* 'high' (m. gen. sg.) can be construed with either *vísa* 'king' or *vagnræfrs*. *Vegr* has two meanings: 'way, path' and 'honour', and Einarr may have intended both senses to be in play. — [8] *en ek þagna* 'and I fall silent': The abrupt conclusion is typical of medieval European poetry (see Curtius 1953, 89-91), and, although the small number of complete *drápur* makes it impossible to generalize, it is probably typical of skaldic poetry as well. The phrase appears again at the conclusion of HSt *Rst*[l].

Níkulás Bergsson

Biography

Modern scholars consider the Icelandic Benedictine monk Níkulás Bergsson (d. 1159 or 1160) to be the 'Abbot Nikulás' who wrote *Leiðarvísir* ('Guide pointing out the way'), a guidebook for pilgrims about the routes from Northern Europe to Rome and Jerusalem (Hill 1993a, 390). Níkulás became the abbot of the Benedictine monastery at Þverá (Munkaþverá, founded 1155) in Northern Iceland (Eyjafjörður).

Jónsdrápa postula

Edited by Beatrice La Farge

Introduction

Three sts of a *dróttkvætt* poem *Jónsdrápa postula* '*Drápa* about the Apostle John' (Ník *Jóndr*) composed by Níkulás Bergsson in honour of John the Apostle, to whom the fourth Gospel and the Book of Revelation were traditionally attributed, are preserved in a sole manuscript, AM 649 a 4° (649a), c. 1350-1400, where they are quoted at the end of a version of *Jóns saga postula* (*Jón⁴*; see Widding, Bekker-Nielsen and Shook 1963, 316; on S. John and the authorship of various books of the Bible see Kasper *et al.* 1993-2001, V, 866-71). In this ms. the saga is called *Litla Jóns saga postola ok guðsspiallamannz* 'Little saga of the Apostle and Evangelist Jón' (*Jón⁴* 1874, 466).

649a is of interest because it contains the only OIcel. prose saint's life to include skaldic verse in praise of the saint, though the verse comes at the end of the text and is not integrated into the prose narrative. It contains a note on fol. 48v, in a hand of c. 1400, stating that the ms. belonged to the church of John the Evangelist at Hof in Vatnsdalur. It has a faded miniature of the saint on fol. 1v, followed by his saga, and concludes by mentioning four individuals who paid special honour to him. These are Bishop Jörundr of Hólar (1267-1313) and (in this order) the three poets Níkulás Bergsson, Gamli kanóki and Kolbeinn Tumason, all of whom composed poetry in praise of John. Sts from compositions of all three poets are cited and there is a later Lat. poem in honour of John on fol. 48v (published by Lehmann 1936-7, II, 118-19). See further Gamlkan *Jóndr*, Kolb *Jónv* and Cormack 1994, 41-2 and 113-14.

In *Jón⁴* Níkulás is identified as the first abbot of the monastery at Munkaþverá in Eyjafjörður. His three sts are introduced with the remark: *Hann orti drapu sęlum Johanni, ok þar af lystir til minnis inn leiða sem eina þria puncta með þeim skilning er signadum Johanni bera mesta tign, þat er su frumtignut elska, er hann oðlaðiz af sialfum syni guðs nęst virðuligri Marie drotning; þar af segir hann sva* 'He [i.e. Níkulás] composed a *drápa* to blessed John, and from it one wishes to include, that it not be forgotten as three instances, the wording which brings blessed John the greatest honour, that is the pre-eminent love which he won from God's son himself, second only to the meritorious queen Mary; of this he [i.e. Níkulás] says as follows'.

In *Jón*[4] the three sts by Níkulás are quoted in the same order as they appear below, with short explanations before each st. The sts are evidently extracts from a longer *drápa*, but, given the paucity of information, it is virtually impossible to make assertions about the content of the rest of this poem or about the position of the three sts within it (cf. Lange 1958a, 80-1).

In *Jón*[4] Níkulás' poem is referred to as a *drápa* (see the passage quoted above), hence the title used by previous eds and here as well. The three sts quoted in *Jón*[4] stress John's privileged position in comparison with that of the other Apostles, thus the inclusion of the word *postula* (gen. sg.) in the title seems justified. Since the name of the Apostle appears in st. 3 as *Jón* this form has been adopted in the title, whereas Finnur Jónsson used the more latinate form *Jóan* in *Skj* A (but not in *Skj* B).

Ník *Jóndr* has been previously edited by Unger 1874 and, as an appendix to Unger's edn of *Jón*[4], by Sophus Bugge (1874, 932-3), as well as by Lange 1958a, Finnur Jónsson (*Skj*) and Kock (*Skald*).

1. Unni all*r*a manna
alskýrr ok mey dýrri
heilagr Kristr ins hæsta
hreinlífis þér einum.

   Valði heims ok hǫlða
haukshnjallr konungr allrar
sér til sýslu stjóra
sárvæginn þik frægjan.

Alskýrr heilagr Kristr unni þér einum all*r*a manna ok dýrri mey ins hæsta hreinlífis. Hauksnjallr konungr heims ok hǫlða, sárvæginn, valði þik frægjan sér til stjóra allrar sýslu.

Completely pure [and] holy Christ granted to you alone of all men and to the precious maiden the highest degree of chastity. Courageous as a hawk the king of the world and men, merciful to sin[ners] [= God], chose you, famous one, for himself as steward of all business.

Ms.: **649a**(46r) (*Jón*[4]). — *Reading*: [1] all*r*a: 'all[...]a' 649a.

Editions: *Skj* Níkulás Bergsson, 1. *Jóansdrápa postola* 1: AI, 560, BI, 546, *Skald* I, 265; *Jón*[4] 1874, 509, Bugge 1874, 932, Lange 1958a, 78.

Context: See Introduction. — *Notes*: [All]: The statement that S. John is second to Mary alone in purity is the highest form of praise, since Mary is the Virgin Mother of God. S. John was considered to be a virgin (Kirschbaum *et al.* 1968-76, VII, 112, 114), in contrast to the other Apostles, who were held to be married men. — [1] *allra* 'of all': Earlier eds read <r> without comment, but the letter is now no longer visible. — [8] *sárvæginn* 'merciful to sin[ners]': Finnur Jónsson (*Skj* B) interprets this cpd as 'merciful to wounds' or 'merciful to the wounded' and regards *sár* (noun 'wound' or adj. 'wounded') as a metaphorical expression for 'sin' or 'sinners' (*LP*: *sárvæginn*).

2. Þeim unni guð geymi
   guðdóms, es vel sómir,
   hreinum himna sýnar,
   hirðar vist með Kristi.

   Jón, heyrðir þú orða
   eilífs fǫður deili,
   hollr við oss, ok allan
   almǫtt séa knáttir.

Guð unni sýnar himna þeim hreinum geymi guðdóms, es vist hirðar með Kristi vel sómir. Jón, hollr við oss, þú heyrðir deili orða eilífs fǫður ok knáttir séa allan almǫtt.

God granted a vision of the heavens to that pure guardian of divinity [APOSTLE], whom an abode in the court with Christ well beseems. John, gracious towards us, you heard the distinctive features of the words of the eternal Father and were able to see all [his] omnipotence.

Ms.: **649a**(46r) (*Jón⁴*).

Editions: *Skj* Níkulás Bergsson, 1. *Jóansdrápa postola* 2: AI, 560, BI, 546, *Skald* I, 265; *Jón⁴* 1874, 509-10, Bugge 1874, 933, Lange 1958a, 78.

Context: In *Jón⁴* this st. is introduced with the remark: *Af somu elsku talar hann i oðrum stað, hvert innsigli sonr guðs lagði til hennar i Pathmós, þa er hann segir sva* 'Of this love [i.e. which Christ bore S. John] and of what confirmation the son of God placed upon it in Patmos he [i.e. Níkulás] speaks in another place [i.e. in the poem], where he says as follows'. — *Notes*: [All]: This st. appears to refer to the vision granted to John, upon which the biblical Book of Revelation is based (cf. the remark in *Jón⁴* 1874, 509; Rev. I.9-20; Lange 1958a, 81, 83). — [5-8]: A reference to the Revelation of John on Patmos, for which the phrase *himna sýn* is attested for the first time in ON. It is also in *Veraldar saga* (Jakob Benediktsson 1944, 54): *Þar* [on Patmos] *sa Joan postvli himna syn ok het sv bok Apokalipsis er hann gerþi þar* 'There John the Apostle saw a vision of the heavens and was called the book he wrote there "Apocalypse"'. The same idea is in Gamlkan *Jóndr* 2. Bugge (1874, 933) takes the gen. phrase *eilífs fǫður* 'of the eternal father' to modify *allmátt* 'omnipotence' rather than *deili orða* 'distinctive features of words'.

3. Sjalfr unni þér sinna
   snjallr postola allra
   sal deilandi sólar
   siklingr framast miklu.

   Hátt gengr vegr, sás veitir
   vagnbryggju þér tyggi;
   Jón, est hreinstr und háva
   hjarlborg skapaðr karla.

Sjalfr snjallr siklingr, deilandi sal sólar, unni þér miklu framast allra sinna postola; vegr, sás tyggi vagnbryggju veitir þér, gengr hátt; Jón, est skapaðr hreinstr karla und háva hjarlborg.

The wise Lord himself, sharing out the hall of the sun [SKY/HEAVEN], loved you by far the most of all his Apostles. The honour which the ruler of the wagon-bridge [SKY/HEAVEN > =

God] grants to you rises high; John, you are created the most pure of men under the high earth-castle [SKY/HEAVEN].

Ms.: **649a**(46r) (*Jón⁴*).

Editions: *Skj* Níkulás Bergsson, 1. *Jóansdrápa postola* 3: AI, 560, BI, 546, *Skald* I, 265; *Jón⁴* 1874, 510, Bugge 1874, 933, Lange 1958a, 79.

Context: In *Jón⁴* this st. is introduced with the remark: *Í þriði stað segir hann sva blezaðr af sama sętleik elskunnar* 'In third place [in the poem] it says that he [John] was thus blessed with the same sweetness of love'. — *Notes*: [All]: This st. refers to S. John's status as 'the Apostle whom Jesus loved' (cf. John XIII.23, XIX.26, XXI.7 and 20). — [2-3] *deilandi sal sólar* 'sharing out the hall of the sun': Following Bugge (1874, 933), this phrase is understood as 'who gives/is giving (men) a share in the hall of the sun [HEAVEN]' and thus as a reference to the entrance to heaven granted by Christ to men by means of his death on the Cross. — [6] *vagnbryggju* 'of the wagon-bridge': That is, bridge of the Great Bear. The constellation Ursa Major 'Great Bear' or 'Big Dipper' is called *vagn* 'Wagon' in ON (*AÍ* II, cxlv, 250), cf. the OE name for this constellation, *carles wæn* 'wagon of the churl', later 'Charles's Wain'. The word 'wagon' is appropriate to the metaphor 'bridge of the Wagon' as a kenning for sky or heaven.

Gamli kanóki

Biography

Gamli kanóki 'canon Gamli' (where the name Gamli, 'the old one' may itself be a nickname) is best known as the author of the poem *Harmsól* 'Sun of Sorrow', which is explicitly ascribed to him in a marginal note at the beginning of the poem on fol. 12r, l. 42 of the sole surviving ms., AM 757 a 4° (B): *Harmsol er gamle orti kanoke* '*Harmsól*, which canon Gamli composed'. Gamli is also mentioned by name in *Jóns saga postula* (*Jón[4]*), where the author of the prose text prefaces the quotation of four sts from Gamli's *Jónsdrápa* with the information: *Annan mann til óðgirðar signaðum Johanni nefnum vér Gamla kanunk austr í Þykkvabæ, hann orti drápu dyrligum Johanni* 'As the second man to have composed a poem to blessed John we [I] name canon Gamli in the east at Þykkvabær, he composed a *drápa* to S. John' (*Jón[4]* 1874, 510). In a remark before the fourth st. Gamli is referred to as *bróðir Gamli* 'Brother Gamli' (*Jón[4]* 1874, 511). Þykkvabær was an Augustinian monastery in south-eastern Iceland founded in 1168; Gamli was thus an Augustinian canon (or canon regular) of this community. His *floruit* can be inferred from the date of the foundation of Þykkvabær as being in the mid- to late C12th.

Harmsól

Edited by Katrina Attwood

Introduction

Harmsól 'Sun of Sorrow' (Gamlkan *Has*) is preserved complete in AM 757 a 4° (B) of c. 1400 on fols 12r-13v. The poem, a *drápa* in *dróttkvætt* metre, appears to have a dual function. It is a praise-poem addressed to Christ, whose purity, magnificence, creative power and holiness are stressed throughout the work in a series of magnificently crafted kennings. *Has* is also a versified sermon, in which the narrator urges his *systkin* 'brothers and sisters' (a liturgical phrase used in 45/6, 62/1-4, 64/1-8) to repentance. Having secured God's help in his composition and the audience's attention and silence (sts 1-5), Gamli launches into an evocation of human frailty and inadequacy, using a detailed confession of his own failings as illustration (sts 7-16). The confession focuses on Gamli's spiritual blemishes, and there is a subtle use of the *Confiteor* to structure this section of the poem. The *stefjabálkr* (sts 17-45) develops this penitential theme, explaining how Christ, in his Incarnation, sought to resolve the disparity between man and God. A description of the Nativity (frequently echoed in later Christian poems, most notably Anon *Lil*) is followed by a haunting evocation of the Crucifixion (sts 21-7), which focuses on Christ's generous response to the penitent thief. This partially dramatised account is the emotional centre of the poem, and Gamli's mastery and manipulation of the skaldic genre is clear as he simplifies his diction and w.o. to exploit the full pathos and starkness of the scene. The narrative is suspended in st. 27, as Gamli delays his account of the Resurrection to force his audience to pause at the foot of the Cross and meditate on the magnitude of the events described. The emotional impact of this, following closely on a sequence in which the poem's stylistic displays have been pared down to an austere, resonant minimum, is profound. The Passion scene gives way to accounts of the Resurrection and Ascension (sts 28-9). There follows, as part of the poem's admonitory scheme, a promise of the imminence of the Second Coming and Last Judgement (st. 31), which draws on accounts of Ragnarǫk such as we find in the eddic *Vsp*. The *stefjabálkr* is completed by a picturesque description of the fate of the impenitent (sts 38-9), followed by an account of the rewards of the just (st. 40), the entire section punctuated with urgent exhortations to repent before it is too late. The *slœmr* (sts 46-65) further illustrates the benefits of penitence by recounting the *exempla* of three sinners to whom God responded with mercy: King David (sts 48-9), S. Peter (sts 50-1) and Mary Magdalene (st. 52). After a further series of appeals to Christ and the Virgin for mercy and mediation on behalf of mankind in general and Gamli in particular, the poem closes with a request that the poem's hearers should pray for the soul of its author.

Harmsól is a complex and haunting poem, one of the masterpieces of Christian skaldic verse. To judge from the extensive echoes of it in later poetry, it was admired by successive generations of Christian skalds. It is clear from the poem's numerous literary allusions that Gamli was fully immersed in both the Norse literary tradition — *Has* echoes several eddic works and is intimately related to contemporary skaldic poems, notably ESk *Geisl* and Anon *Leið* — and in latinate liturgical, homiletic, hagiographic and hymnodic works, though no direct sources have been traced. Gamli's mastery of the skaldic form is particularly evinced by a series of kennings for God which characterise heaven as the home or kingdom of stormy weather, over which God rules. Although the ultimate inspiration for these figures is likely to be biblical, the kennings reveal an intimate appreciation of the power and beauty of the weather that is purely Icel.

Harmsól has long been recognised (Skard 1953; Attwood 1996b) as part of a group of four interrelated Christian *drápur* dating from the C12th. Other members of the group are *Geisl* and the anonymous *Pl* and *Leið*. These poems share a remarkable number of dictional and structural parallels, the most important of which are detailed in the Notes to this edn and in Attwood 1996b. Although all four poems can be reliably dated to the C12th, there is little trustworthy evidence either for the precise dating of individual texts or for the establishment of a relative chronology. A *terminus ante quem* is provided by the unique *Pl* ms., AM 673 b 4°, which is one of the earliest surviving Icel. mss, dated c. 1200 (Louis-Jensen 1998, 89). The other fixed point is supplied by *Geisl* (see Introduction to *Geisl* for circumstantial details) which is likely to have been recited sometime between winter 1152-3 and summer 1154. As Finnur Jónsson asserts (*LH* II, 115), linguistic evidence in *Has* — notably the coexistence of *ór-* and *ár-*forms in words like *vára* (18/8, 21/4, 57/8 etc.) and the *tjalds : alla* rhyme in 65/6 — also suggests a date from c. 1200 or the last quarter of the C12th.

Although all 65 sts of *Has* are preserved in B, that ms. is in a very poor state of preservation, dark and badly worn. It has therefore been necessary to rely selectively on previous transcriptions and eds of the poem to reconstruct the text where B is defective. Lbs 444 4°ˣ (444ˣ) is a bundle of loose papers which appear to be the working papers for Sveinbjörn Egilsson's printed edn of four Christian poems (1844). 444ˣ's transcription of *Has* is likely to be the work of Brynjólfur Snorrason, an Icel. student at the Arnamagnæan Institute in Copenhagen from 1842-50 (Attwood 1996a, 32-3). Brynjólfur's transcription was copied by Jón Sigurðsson in JS 399a-b 4°ˣ (399a-bˣ), and both this transcription and 444ˣ are heavily annotated by Sveinbjörn Egilsson. The 399a-bˣ transcript is identical in all respects to that preserved in 444ˣ, and the reference '399a-bˣ' in the textual apparatus should be taken as shorthand for both transcripts. The 444ˣ bundle also contains a series of notes in Sveinbjörn Egilsson's hand, in which a tentative prose arrangement of *Has* is worked out. Extensive use has also been made of Hugo Rydberg's transcription of B in Rydberg 1907, which is generally reliable, though less conservative than the 444ˣ transcription, in that Rydberg incorporates speculative reconstructions (always annotated) into his transcription. When Rydberg's transcription is referred to in the Readings it appears as B*Rydberg*, while Finnur Jónsson's transcription in *Skj* A, which relies heavily on Rydberg, is designated B*FJ*. The text of *Has* in Lbs 1152 8°ˣ (1152ˣ) fols 1-26 has also been consulted. This is Sveinbjörn Egilsson's clean, print copy for his 1844 edn. There are four minor discrepancies between this copy and the printed text — accents are included in *áðr* (29/5), *Ítr* (30/1) and *Úngr* (42/1), and Sveinbjörn's footnote to st. 7 has *konúngs*, rather than *konúngr*. References in the edited text below are to the 1844 printed text, rather than to 1152ˣ.

The first modern edn of *Has* was published by Sveinbjörn Egilsson, in his *Fjøgur gømul kvæði* (1844, 1-34). This partially-normalised text, which was prepared as a teaching text for use at the Lat. School at Bessastaðir, relies heavily on Brynjólfur Snorrason's transcription in 444ˣ and Jón Sigurðsson's annotated copy of that transcription in 399a-bˣ. Sveinbjörn's printed edn forms the basis of Hjalmar Kempff's 1867 edn, the Swedish translations and notes of which also draw heavily on Sveinbjörn's interpretations in *LP* (1860). Hugo Rydberg's 1907 doctoral dissertation contains a diplomatic transcription of *Has*, but does not supply a normalised prose arrangement, on the ground that Kempff's edn was available. *Has* is also ed. by Finnur Jónsson (*Skj* A and B) and by E. A. Kock (*Skald*). Diplomatic and normalised texts of the poem are presented in Elizabeth Black's Oxford BLitt dissertation (Black 1971). An annotated diplomatic transcription of the text in B is presented on pp. 83-102 of the doctoral thesis Attwood 1996a, and a normalised edn on pp. 222-302. Although the present edn draws heavily on that presented in the thesis, there are significant differences.

1. *H*ár stillir, lúk heilli mjúk svát mættik auka
    hreggtjalda, mér, aldar, mǫl gný/undum stála
    upp, þús allar skaptir, miska bót af mætu
    óðborgar hlið góðu, mín fulltingi þínu.

*H*ár stillir hreggtjalda, þús skaptir allar aldar, lúk mér upp hlið óðborgar góðu heilli, svát mættik auka mjúk mǫl mín, bót miska, stála gný/undum af mætu fulltingi þínu.

High ruler of the storm-tents [SKY/HEAVEN > = God], you who created all humans, open up for me the gate of the fortress of poetry [BREAST > MOUTH] with good grace, so that I might augment my soft words, the remedy for misdeeds, for trees of the din of swords [(*lit.* 'din-trees of swords') BATTLE > WARRIORS] with your excellent help.

Mss: **B**(12r), 399a-b[x]. — *Readings*: [1] *H*ár: '[...]rr' B, '[...]arr' 399a-b[x] [4] óð-: *so all others*, '[...]' B [5] svát ('suo at'): *so* 399a-b[x], B*FJ*, 'suo [...]t' B, 'suo (a)t'(?) B*Rydberg*; auka: *so* 399a-b[x], B*FJ*, 'au[...]a' B, 'au(k)a'(?) B*Rydberg* [6] gný/undum: 'gný[...]unndum' B, 'gnýunndum' 399a-b[x], 'gnýiunndum' B*Rydberg*, B*FJ* [8] mín fulltingi: *so* 399a-b[x], 'mi[...]lltinge' B.

Editions: *Skj* Gamli kanóki, 2. *Harmsól* 1: AI, 562, BI, 548, *Skald* I, 266, *NN* §2926; Sveinbjörn Egilsson 1844, 13, Kempff 1867, 1, Rydberg 1907, 20, Jón Helgason 1935-6, 252, Black 1971, 134, Attwood 1996a, 222.

Notes: [All]: The title and authorship of the poem are given in a marginal note, in the scribal hand, beside ll. 42 and 43 of fol. 12r: 'harmsol er gam|le orte ka|noke'. On Gamli, see Skald Biography. — [1] *hár* 'high': The beginning of this word is lost in a hole in B. The scribe's usual practice was to leave a space for a larger initial to mark the beginning of the poem, and the indentation of ll. 42 and 43 by some 11mm suggests that this was also the case here. 399a-b[x] is certain of the second letter. — [1-2] *hár stillir hreggtjalda* 'high ruler of the storm-tents [SKY/HEAVEN > = GOD]': The first in a series of kennings for God whose determinants contain circumlocutions for heaven involving *hregg* 'storm, rain', often with the adj. *hár* 'high, exalted'. Cf., e.g., 5/5-6, 45/1-4 and 57/6-7. These kennings may be influenced by similar constructions in other Christian *drápur*, most notably *Geisl*, the text of which in *Flat* has *jǫfurr hreggsalar* 'king of the storm-hall' at 64/5-6, and *Leið*, which has three God-kennings with *hreggrann* 'storm-house' as the determinant (2/1-3, 17/1-2 and 25/5 6), the first two of which also contain *hár*. The relative complexity of the variations on the patterns in *Has* might indicate that the poem is somewhat later than, and influenced by, *Leið* (see Skard 1953, 101, 108 and the discussion of Skard's analysis in Attwood 1996b, 236-7). That *hregg*- compounds were a particular favourite of Gamli's is perhaps suggested by the appearance of *jǫfurr hreggskríns* 'lord of the storm-shrine' (so also in Anon *Mgr* 49/6) in his *Jóndr* 2/4. — [1-4] *lúk mér upp hlið óðborgar* 'open up for me the gate of the fortress of poetry [BREAST > MOUTH]': Paasche (1914a, 143) suggests that this striking image might be an echo of Col. IV.3 *orantes simul et pro nobis ostium sermonis ad loquendum mysterium Christi* 'praying withal for us also, that God may open unto us a door of speech to speak the mystery of Christ'. The resemblance between the texts, however, is somewhat oblique, and Finnur Jónsson's intimation (*LH* II, 114) that the phrase is original is doubtless correct. — [6] *gnýlundum* (dat. pl.): Lit. 'din-trees'. B is badly worn at this point, and one cannot be certain of the fourth letter. Finnur Jónsson and Rydberg read 'gnýiunndum' with confidence, while the 399a-b[x] copyist is certain of 'gnýunndum'. There have been several attempts to make sense of this reading. Neither Sveinbjörn Egilsson nor Kempff saw any need to emend, both taking *gnýundum stála* to be a man-kenning, Sveinbjörn (1860, 257a) relating *gnýundum* to *gnúa* 'to rub' and Kempff (1867, 22) assuming it to derive from *gnýja* 'to sound'. Finnur Jónsson (*Skj* B) emends to *gnýviðum* (dat. pl.) 'din-trees'. Jón Helgason (1935-6, 252) rejects the interpretations of both Sveinbjörn and Kempff, and notes that, since the hole in B is over what previous eds read as an 'i', 'there is nothing against our assuming that this letter was an "l", the upper part of which is now missing'. Jón's reconstruction, which is adopted here, is therefore in accord with the spirit of Finnur's emendation but, as he says, 'is closer to what survives than *gnýviðum*'. Although the cpd *gnýlundum* 'din-trees' is not otherwise attested, *gnýlundum stála* would be partially paralleled by the warrior-kenning *lundr stála* 'tree of spears', which occurs in a poorly-preserved *lv.* attributed to Bjhít Lv 15/6[V] (*ÍF* 3, 155). — [7] *miska bót* 'the remedy for misdeeds': Sveinbjörn Egilsson and Finnur Jónsson both take *bót* as acc. sg. of *bót* 'cure, remedy' and connect it with *miska*, gen. sg. or pl. of *miski* 'misdeed, offence', as the object of *auka*, the subject of which is *mjúk mál mín*. In this, they are followed by Kock and Black (1971, 134). The present edn follows Kempff (1867, 1) in taking *miska bót* with *mjúk mál mín* as parallel objects of *auka*. It is clear from the general tone of *Has*, as well as from the lengthy confession in sts 7-17, that the entire poem is an act of penance, principally for Gamli but also for his hearers.

2. Eng*r* má elda sløngvir
 — allvíst es þat — Mistar
 maklig orð til mærðar
 minn *dróttinn* þér finna,
þars, élhallar, ǫllu
est, skýrr konungr, dýrri,
rómu linns þvís runnar
rammglyggs megi of hyggja.

Eng*r* sløngvir elda Mistar má finna maklig orð þér til mærðar, *dróttinn* minn — þat es allvíst —, þars est, skýrr konungr élhallar, dýrri ǫllu, þvís runnar rammglyggs linns rómu megi of hyggja.

No slinger of the fires of Mist <valkyrie> [SWORDS > WARRIOR] can find fitting words in praise of you, my Lord — that is altogether true — because you are, pure king of the storm-hall [SKY/HEAVEN > = God], more precious than all that which bushes of the strong storm of the snake of battle [SWORD > BATTLE > WARRIORS] may imagine.

Mss: **B**(12r), 399a-b[x]. — *Readings*: [1] Eng*r*: 'Eíngí' B [4] *dróttinn*: '[...]' B, 'dr̩ǫ̩tt̩iṇṇ' 399a-b[x], 'd[...]' B*Rydberg*.

Editions: *Skj* Gamli kanóki, 2. Harmsól 2: AI, 562, BI, 549, *Skald* I, 266, *NN* §§2070D, 2338D; Sveinbjörn Egilsson 1844, 13-14, Kempff 1867, 1, Rydberg 1907, 20, Black 1971, 138, Attwood 1996a, 222.

Notes: [1-2] *sløngvir elda Mistar* 'slinger of the fires of Mist [SWORDS > WARRIOR]': Mist is named as a valkyrie in *Grí* 36/1, and her name is often used as a battle-*heiti* in man-kennings such as *runnr Mistar* 'bush of Mist' (Anon *Nkt* 69/4[II]). *Viðir linns Mistar* 'trees of the snake of Mist' in 5/2-3 recalls both this kenning and the *rekit* man-kenning in the second *helmingr*. — [4] *dróttinn* 'Lord': No traces of this word are visible in B. 399a-b[x] reads *dróttinn*, but indicates uncertainty. All other eds adopt this reading.

3. Send þú yðvarn anda,   Alls megu ekki þollar
   einskepjandi, hreinan   án fremja þess hónum
   mér, þanns mitt of fœri   súða viggs, es seggjum
   munar grand heðan, landa.   siðabót af því hljótisk.

Send þú mér hreinan anda yðvarn, einskepjandi landa, þanns of fœri heðan munar grand mitt. Alls ekki megu þollar viggs súða fremja þess án hónum, es siðabót hljótisk seggjum af því.

Send your pure spirit to me, sole creator of lands [= God], the one which may carry hence my sorrow of mind. Trees of the steed of planking [SHIP > SEAFARERS] can by no means achieve this without it [*lit.* him, viz. the Holy Spirit], because moral amendment may proceed for men from it.

Mss: **B**(12r), 399a-b[x]. — *Readings*: [3] fœri: 'fę[...]e' B, 'ferį' 399a-b[x], 'fæ(ræ)'(?) B*Rydberg*, 'fère' B*FJ* [5] megu: *so all others*, 'meg[...]' B.

Editions: *Skj* Gamli kanóki, 2. *Harmsól* 3: AI, 562, BI, 549, *Skald* I, 266, *NN* §2926; Sveinbjörn Egilsson 1844, 14, Kempff 1867, 1, Rydberg 1907, 20, Jón Helgason 1935-6, 253, Black 1971, 140, Attwood 1996a, 222.

Notes: [5] *án hónum* 'without it [*lit.* him]': The reference is to the Holy Spirit (*heilagr andi*). In MIcel, the prep. *án* is invariably followed by the gen. Constructions with both acc. and dat. were permissible in ON (see *ONP*: *án, ón*). It is possible, as Kempff (1867, 24) suggests, that the *aðalhending* was not without influence in the choice of case here. — [7] *þollar viggs súða* 'trees of the steed of planking [SHIP > SEAFARERS]': *Súð* f. (here in gen. pl. *súða*) is a term for the overlapping planks that form the hull of a clinker-built ship (Jesch 2001, 139-40). Although the word occurs several times as a *heiti* for 'ship' (see *LP*: *súð*), this is its only occurrence as part of a ship-kenning. Jón Helgason (1935-6, 253), presumably influenced by the uniqueness of the kenning and its apparent tautology, objected to Finnur Jónsson's transcription of B in *Skj* A: 'The first word is written *suda* in the manuscript, and there is a hole over the *u*. The possibility that what was there was *sūda* = *sunda* must thus be considered'. Kock (*NN* §2926) and Black (1971, 340 and 141) adopt this suggestion and emend to *sunda* gen. sg. of *sund* 'a body of water', taking the kenning to be *þollar viggs sunda* 'trees of the steed of the water'. Although there is indeed a hole in B, it is considerably above and to the left of *súða*, and does not interfere with the text at this point. It is not conceivable that a nasal stroke, which would be expected to sit very close to the letter and extend over its full width, has been lost here. B's *súða* is therefore retained in this edn.

4. Mér vil ek ok eirar þótt óverðum orðum,
    — oss byrjar þat — hnossa ítr fylkir, mik lít*ir*
    himins stillandi hollrar víst fyr v*á*s ok lǫstu,
    hæst*r* miskunnar æsta, veðrhallar, þik kveðja.

Ek vil æsta mér hollrar miskunnar ok eirar, hæst*r* stillandi hnossa himins — þat byrjar oss —, þótt lít*ir* mik, ítr fylkir veðrhallar, kveðja þik óverðum orðum, víst fyr v*á*s ok lǫstu.

I wish to ask on my own behalf for wholesome grace and clemency, highest regulator of the ornaments of heaven [HEAVENLY BODIES > = God] — that is fitting for us [me] —, though you see me, glorious king of the storm-hall [SKY/HEAVEN > = God], call on you with unworthy words, surely because of sinfulness and flaws.

Mss: **B**(12r), 399a-b[x]. — *Readings*: [4] hæst*r*: 'h*ê*st' *all* [6] fylkir: *so* 399a-b[x], B*FJ*, '[...]lker' B, (fý)lkir(?) B*Rydberg*; lít*ir*: líta B [7] fyr: *so* 399a-b[x], B*Rydberg*, B*FJ*, '[...]r' B; v*á*s: '[...]os' B, 'vos' 399a-b[x], '(v)os'(?) B*Rydberg*, B*FJ* [8] kveðja: *so* 399a-b[x], 'kue[...]ia' B, 'kue(d)ia'(?) B*Rydberg*, B*FJ*.

Editions: *Skj* Gamli kanóki, 2. Harmsól 4: AI, 562, BI, 549, *Skald* I, 266, *NN* §§2926, 2927; Sveinbjörn Egilsson 1844, 14, Kempff 1867, 2, Rydberg 1907, 20-1, Black 1971, 134, Attwood 1996a, 222.

Notes: [2-4]: Finnur Jónsson (*Skj* B) understands *hnossa hollrar miskunnar* 'ornaments of wholesome mercy' as the object of the verb *æsta*, which takes the gen. of the thing requested (l. 4), and he translates *din kendte miskundheds goder* 'the benefits of your well-known mercy'. Jón Helgason (1935-6, 252), anticipated by Kempff (1867, 24) takes *hnossa* 'ornaments' to be part of the God-kenning *stillandi hnossa himins* 'regulator of the ornaments of heaven'. This recalls the God-kenning *harri fagrgims hás hreggranns* 'king of the fair jewel of the high storm-house [SKY/HEAVEN > SUN > = God]' in *Leið* 2/1-4. This arrangement is adopted by Kock (*NN* §2927) and Black (1971, 144). In *NN* §2803, Kock suggests the arrangement *hollrar miskunnar ok hnossa eirar* 'of wholesome mercy and treasures of clemency', which he rejects in §2927. — [4] *hæst*r 'highest': Sveinbjörn Egilsson (note in 444[x]) suggests that B drops the final 'r' for the sake of euphony. He corrects to *hæst*r, m. sg. nom. of the sup. of *hár* (adj.) 'high'. This emendation has been adopted by all subsequent eds. — [7] *víst fyr v*á*s ok lǫstu*: Cf. Anon *Líkn* 12/7: *víst fyr vára lǫstu* 'surely on account of our flaws'.

5. Þú býðr ǫll* með iðran, ok, hábrautar, heitið
   einn Kristr, viðum Mis*tar* hreggvǫrðr, þegar seggjum
   linns fyr lærðum mǫnnum sannri líkn ok syknu,
   lýti sín at tína, snjallr, fyr vás ok galla.

Þú, einn Kristr, býðr viðum linns Mis*tar* at tína ǫll* lýti sín með iðran fyr lærðum mǫnnum, ok heitið þegar seggjum, snjallr hábrautar hreggvǫrðr, sannri líkn ok syknu fyr vás ok galla.

You, the one Christ, command trees of the snake of Mist <valkyrie> [SWORD > WARRIORS] to enumerate all their faults with repentence before learned men; and you promise straight away to men, excellent warden of the high path of the storm [SKY/HEAVEN > = God], true mercy and acquittal for sinfulness and flaws.

Mss: **B**(12r-v), 399a-b[x]. — *Readings*: [1] *ǫll**: 'ǫlld' B [2] Mis*tar*: 'm[...]s[...]' B, 'mist(ar)'(?) 399a-b[x], 'mi(st)[...]'(?) B*Rydberg*, 'mis(tar)'(?) B*FJ* [5] hábrautar heitið: 'habra[...]ítið' B, hábrautar heit(ir)(?) 399a-b[x], 'habra[...](hæ)itið'(?) B*Rydberg*, 'habra(utar h)eitið'(?) B*FJ* [7] sannri: *so* 399a-b[x], B*FJ*, 's[...]nnre' B, 's(annræ)' B*Rydberg*.

Editions: *Skj* Gamli kanóki, 2. *Harmsól* 5: AI, 562, BI, 549, *Skald* I, 266; Sveinbjörn Egilsson 1844, 14, Kempff 1867, 2, Rydberg 1907, 21, Black 1971, 148, Attwood 1996a, 223.

Notes: [1] *ǫll**: B reads 'ǫlld'. With all previous eds of the text, the present edn adopts Sveinbjörn Egilsson's correction, which is suggested in a marginal note to the 444[x] transcript. — [5-8]: Compare 1 John I.9 *si confiteamur peccata nostra fidelis est et iustus ut remittat nobis peccata et emundet nos ab omni iniquitate* 'If we confess our sins he is faithful and just, to forgive us our sins and cleanse us from all iniquity'. — [7] *syknu* 'acquittal': This is the only occurrence of *sykna* f. 'freedom from guilt, blamelessness, declared innocence' in skaldic verse. The adj. *sykn* 'acquitted' occurs only in *Líkn* 31/4, in the context of a description of the Redemption of mankind through the Crucifixion. In prose, it occurs frequently in legal texts (*Fritzner*: *sykn*, *sykna*; *CVC*: *sykn*).

6. Oss verðr *ey*, nema þessum hver þvít hætt rǫ́ð *b*ǫrva
   aldr várn boðum haldim hl*j*óms á øfsta dómi
   (menn búisk mǫrgu sinni) upp fyr allri skepnu
   meiri ógn (við þeiri), ósǫgð koma lǫgðis.

Oss verðr *ey* meiri ógn, nema haldim þessum boðum aldr várn; menn búisk við þeiri mǫrgu sinni, þvít hver ósǫgð hætt rǫ́ð *b*ǫrva hljóms lǫgðis koma upp fyr allri skepnu á øfsta dómi.

Our terror will always increase unless we keep these commands during our lives; let men prepare themselves for it many a time, since all unconfessed, dangerous counsels of the trees of the sound of the sword [BATTLE > WARRIORS] will become known before all creation at the Last Judgement.

Mss: **B**(12v), 399a-b^x. — *Readings*: [1] *ey*: '[...]' B, B*Rydberg*, (ei)(?) 399a-b^x, B*FJ* [2] haldim: *so* 399a-b^x, 'halldi[...]' B, 'halldi(m)'(?) B*Rydberg*, B*FJ* [5] *bǫrva*: horfa B [6] hl*j*óms: 'hl[...]' B, 'hl(ioms)'(?) 399a-b^x, B*Rydberg*, 'hlioms' B*FJ* [7] skepnu: *so* 399a-b^x, 'sk[...]pnu' B.

Editions: *Skj* Gamli kanóki, 2. *Harmsól* 6: AI, 563, BI, 550, *Skald* I, 266; Sveinbjörn Egilsson 1844, 15, Kempff 1867, 2, Rydberg 1907, 21, Black 1971, 151, Attwood 1996a, 223.

Notes: [1] *ey* 'always': B is badly worn, and no traces of the word are now visible. All previous eds have accepted 399a-b^x's reading *ei*, even though the transcript indicates some uncertainty here. — [5-8]: There have been several attempts to interpret the second *helmingr*, which is a continuation of the exhortation to repentance begun in st. 5. B's *horfa* overloads the *h*-alliteration in the l. Even so, Sveinbjörn Egilsson (1844, 15 n. 6) retains this reading. He takes *horfa* as gen. pl. of *horfir* which is not otherwise attested in poetry, but is presumably a *nomen agentis* from *horfa* 'to look' and would mean 'one who looks'. Sveinbjörn understands a man-kenning *horfir hljóms lǫgðis* 'spectator of the din of the sword, spectator of battle', and glosses *horfir* as *præliator* 'spectator, eyewitness' (*LP* (1860): *horfir*). Apart from this, Sveinbjörn's prose arrangement, detailed in his working notes in 444^x, is identical to the one presented above. Kempff (1867, 25-6) takes *hætt rǫð* 'dangerous counsels' (l. 5) to be the subject of *horfa upp* 'to face upwards, come to light' (cf. *Fritzner*: *horfa*). He construes *þvíat hætt rǫð horfa á efsta dómi upp fyr allri skepnu* 'because dangerous counsels will come to light at the Last Judgement in the presence of all creation'. Kempff arranges the second cl. *hver koma hljóms lǫgðis* [*er*] *ósǫgð*, which he glosses *hvarje strid kommer obodad* 'every battle arrives unbidden'. It seems likely that Kempff's interpretation is influenced by S. Paul's assertion that *dies Domini sicut fur in nocte ita veniet* 'the day of the Lord shall so come, as a thief in the night' (1 Thess. V.2), but it is unlikely that Gamli would suggest that the antagonism of God towards sinners will come unannounced. This edn follows Kock and Black in adopting Finnur Jónsson's emendation of *horfa* (l. 5) to *bǫrva*, gen. pl. of *bǫrr* 'tree'. This is a paleographically straightforward emendation, and *bǫrva* then forms the base-word of a man-kenning *bǫrvar hljóms lǫgðis* 'trees of the sound of the sword'. — [8] *ósǫgð* 'unconfessed, unsaid': The adj. is taken in apposition to *hætt* 'dangerous' (l. 5), qualifying *rǫð* 'counsels'. *Ósǫgð hætt rǫð* are men's unconfessed designs, which will become known (*koma upp*) at Judgement.

7. Ungr vǫndumk ek, yngvi, Enn snørak jafnan inni,
    opt *dj*arf*liga at hv*a*rfa, illt ráð þás mik villti,
    (lítt gáðak þá) þjóðar, dýrðhittandi dróttinn
    (þín) ept vilja mínum. dáðrakkr, við þér hnakka.

Yngvi þjóðar, ungr vǫndumk ek opt *dj*arf*liga at hv*a*rfa ept mínum vilja; gáðak þá þín lítt. Enn snørak jafnan inni hnakka við þér, dáðrakkr dýrðhittandi dróttinn, þás illt ráð villti mik.

Prince of the people [= God], as a young man I often presumptuously developed the habit of wandering according to my desire; I paid you little heed then. Further I always turned my back on you inwardly, deed-bold, glory-finding Lord, when evil counsel led my heart astray.

Mss: **B**(12v), 399a-b^x. — *Readings*: [2] *dj*arf*liga: 'erfilega' B; hvarfa: hverfa B   [3] gáðak ('gáði ek'): *so* 399a-b^x, 'ga[...]ek' B, 'ga(...)æk'(?) B*Rydberg*, 'ga(da) ek'(?) B*FJ*   [5] inni: *so* 399a-b^x, '[...]ne' B.

Editions: *Skj* Gamli kanóki, 2. *Harmsól* 7: AI, 563, BI, 550, *Skald* I, 267, *NN* §2928; Sveinbjörn Egilsson 1844, 15, Kempff 1867, 2, Rydberg 1907, 21, Jón Helgason 1935-6, 253-4, Black 1971, 153, Attwood 1996a, 223.

Notes: [All]: Repentance for sins committed in youth is a common feature of biblical confessions. Job, for example, mentions the possibility that his sufferings are intended as a punishment for youthful sins: *scribis enim contra me amaritudines et consumere me vis peccatis adulescentiae meae* 'for thou writest bitter things against me, and wilt consume me for the sins of my youth' (Job XIII.26). Perhaps a more likely source for Gamli's inspiration is the Penitential Psalm XXIV, which contains the verse *delicta iuventutis meae et ignorantias meas ne memineris secundum misericordiam tuam memento mei tu; propter bonitatem tuam Domine* 'the sins of my youth and my ignorances do not remember. According to thy mercy remember thou me: for thy goodness' sake, O Lord' (Ps. XXIV.7). — [1] *yngvi*: B's text reads 'yng' with a superscript 'i' above the 'g', which may be understood as either *yngvi* or *yngri*. Finnur Jónsson (*Skj* A) understood it as *yngvi*, which makes sense in context, while Sveinbjörn Egilsson read *yngri*, which he emended to *yngvi* (note in 444^x and 1844 edn). — [2] dj*arf*liga* 'boldly, presumptuously': It is not possible to make sense of B's reading *opt erfiliga* 'often with difficulty' in this context, and various suggestions for emendation have been made. Finnur Jónsson modifies Sveinbjörn Egilsson's *ofderfilega* (1844, adopted by Kempff 1867, 2) to *ofderfil*a, hap. leg.*, which he glosses *dristigt* 'boldly, audaciously' (*LP*). Kock (*NN* §2928) suggests *ofherfliga* 'very wickedly', comparing Gamli's confession of sinful behaviour in 53/3-4 *pótt atferðin ór yrði stórum herfilig* 'even though my behaviour were to become very shameful'. Jón Helgason (1935-6, 253-4) observes that the poet often uses phrases with *opt*, and suggests a further emendation of Finnur's text to *opt derfila* 'often presumptuously'. Since *derfila* is not otherwise attested, he makes two alternative suggestions: *óperfila* 'useless, inconvenient' and *opt djarfliga* 'often presumptuously'. Although emendation to *opt djarfliga* necessitates a further emendation, to *hvarfa*, to satisfy the *aðalhending* in l. 2, this edn, with Black (1971, 154), follows Jón's suggestion, on the ground that it preserves B's *opt*. — [7] *dýrðhittandi dróttinn* 'glory-finding Lord': Cf. Anon *Pl* 18/1, where the epithet *dýrðhittir* 'glory-finder', used of Plácitus, alliterates with *dróttinn*. Although neither *dýrðhittir* nor *dýrðhittandi* is attested elsewhere, *LP*: *dýrðhittir* compares *dáðhittir* 'finder of [good] deeds', which is used of Bishop Páll Jónsson by ÁmÁrn *Lv* 3/1^{IV} (see also Attwood 1996b, 227). Once again, the alliteration is with *dróttinn*. With Finnur Jónsson (*Skj* B), Kock (*NN* §2929), Kempff (1867, 26), Rydberg (1907, xxvi) and Sveinbjörn Egilsson (444^x) this edn takes *dýrðhittandi* as adjectival, paralleling *dáðrakkr* and qualifying *dróttinn*. Jón Helgason (1935-6, 254) objects to this interpretation on the grounds that *dýrðhittir* is not 'a suitable expression' for God and that, in *Pl*, the epithet denotes Plácitus, not God. Jón therefore emends *dróttinn* to *drótta*, gen. pl. of *drótt* 'people, company', asserting that *dróttinn* is a straightforward scribal error. *Dýrðhittandi drótta* is understood to mean 'people who attain blessedness', and is construed with an emended *sinnir* in l. 5, to give the God-kenning *dáðrakkr sinnir dýrðhittandi drótta* 'valiant helper of men who are striving for glory'. Jón has, however, overlooked the epithet *dýrðargjarn* 'glory-eager' (st. 34/4), which is an exact parallel for *dýrðhittandi*.

8. Ofloskvan ho*fum* œsku   ítr, þás opt á móti
    aldr várn spanit sjaldan   ófríð risu blíðum,
    — barkat bl*ó*m á verkum   mærðvinnandi manna,
    bráðgort — frá ódǿðum,   mín ve*rk* boðum *þ*ínum.

Hofum sjaldan spanit várn ofloskvan aldr œsku frá ódǿðum — barkat bráðgort bl*ó*m á verkum —, þás ófríð ve*rk* mín risu opt á móti *þ*ínum blíðum boðum, ítr mærðvinnandi manna.

We [I] have rarely enticed our [my] lazy age of youth away from misdeeds — I did not bear easily ripened fruit on account of my deeds —, when my ugly deeds often rose against your friendly commands, glorious praise-winner of men [= God].

Mss: **B**(12v), 399a-b[x]. — *Readings*: [1] hofum: 'hǫf' B   [2] sjaldan: *so* 399a-b[x], B*Rydberg*, B*FJ*, 'sialld[...]' B   [3] blóm: 'bl[...]' B, 'bloma'(?) 399a-b[x], (blom)(?) B*Rydberg*, blom B*FJ*   [8] ve*rk* boðum *þ*ínum: 'v[...]odum[...]' B, 've*rk* boðum *þ*inum' 399a-b[x], 'væ(rk) (b)odum (þi)[...]'(?) B*Rydberg*, 've(rk) bodum þ(inum)'(?) B*FJ*.

Editions: *Skj* Gamli kanóki, 2. Harmsól 8: AI, 563, BI, 550, *Skald* I, 267; Sveinbjörn Egilsson 1844, 15, Kempff 1867, 3, Rydberg 1907, 21-2, Black 1971, 157, Attwood 1996a, 223.

Notes: [1] *hǫfum* 'we [I] have': B reads 'hǫf', Rydberg (1907, 21 n. 11) noting the possible presence of a nasal stroke over 'f', and *Skj* A presuming its existence. 399a-b[x], followed by Sveinbjörn Egilsson and Kempff, interprets the sign as an accent. *Skj* A suggests reconstruction to *hǫfum*, which is adopted by *Skald*, Black and here. — [3-4] *barkat bráðgort blóm á verkum* 'I did not bear easily ripened fruit on account of [my] deeds': Finnur Jónsson emends B's *á* (l. 3) to *af* and translates *jeg høstede ikke tidlig modnet frugt af mine gærninger* 'I did not harvest early ripened fruit from my deeds' (*Skj* B), though he indicates his uncertainty with a question mark. Jón Helgason's interpretation, *jeg bar ikke tidlig blomst paa mine gerninger [det vil sige] mine ungdomsgerninger var ikke skønne* 'I did not bear early flower on account of my deeds [that is to say] the deeds of my youth were not pretty' (1935-6, 254) may be the more correct. There appears to be no direct source for the expression, though it is possible that the parable of the trees and fruit in Matt. VII.16-20 may have influenced Gamli's thought here.

9. Gerðak opt í orðum,
eljunsterkr, sem verkum,
hreggs bjartloga, ok hyggju,
hróts, í gǫgn þér, dróttinn.

Þræll hefr þinn í allan
þann, lífgjaf*i* manna,
ó*fs* grǫndugrar andar
ástsn*au*ðr hratat da*u*ða.

Gerðak opt í gǫgn þ*ér* í orðum, sem verkum ok hyggju, eljunsterkr dróttinn bjartloga hróts hreggs. Lífgjaf*i* manna, ástsn*au*ðr þræll þinn hefr hratat í allan þann da*u*ða ó*fs* grǫndugrar andar.

I often acted against you in words, as in deeds and thought, energy-strong lord of the bright flame of the roof of the storm [SKY/HEAVEN > SUN > = God]; lifegiver of men [= God], your love-bereft servant has stumbled into the total death of an excessively sinful soul.

Mss: **B**(12v), 399a-b[x]. — *Readings*: [4] *þér*: '[...]' B, þ(ér)(?) 399a-b[x] [6] lífgjaf*i*: lífgjafa B [7] ó*fs*: oss B [8] ástsn*au*ðr: 'asts[...]udr' B, 'astsnạudr' 399a-b[x], 'ast s[...](a)udr'(?) B*Rydberg*, 'ast s(n)audr' B*FJ*; da*u*ða: 'da[...]' B, 'dau(da)'(?) 399a-b[x], 'da(uda)' B*Rydberg*, 'da(u)da' B*FJ*.

Editions: Skj Gamli kanóki, 2. *Harmsól* 9: AI, 563, BI, 550-1, *Skald* I, 267; Sveinbjörn Egilsson 1844, 16, Kempff 1867, 3, Rydberg 1907, 22, Black 1971, 160, Attwood 1996a, 224.

Notes: [1-4] *gerðak opt í gǫgn þér í orðum, sem verkum ok hyggju* 'I often acted against you in words, as in deeds and thought': Confession of sins in thought, word and deed is an article of the *Confiteor*. *Confiteor Deo omnipotenti ... quia peccavi nimis cogitatione, verbo et opera, mea culpa, mea culpa, mea maxima culpa* 'I confess to almighty God ... that I have sinned exceedingly in thought, word and deed, through my fault, through my fault, through my most grievous fault' (Lefebure 1924, 7). Gamli's re-ordering of the articles of confession, which is required by the alliterative demands of his st., informs the subject-matter of the three following sts: in st. 10, he confesses to swearing oaths, a sin 'in word', st. 11 concerns his sins 'in deed', and st. 12 his sinful thoughts, which rendered him technically unfit to take part in the Eucharist. — [5] *þræll þinn* 'your servant': The figure of the Christian as God's servant or slave has its origin in Rom. VI.22 *nunc vero liberati a peccato servi autem facti Deo habetis fructum vestrum in sanctificationem finem vero vitam aeternam* 'but now being made free from sin, and become servants to God, you have your fruit unto sanctification, and the end life everlasting'. It occurs several times in ON-Icel. Christian poetry. By far the most famous use is in the so-called 'death-song' of Kolbeinn Tumason (d. 1208), the first st. of which ends with the couplet *ek em þrællinn þinn,* | *þú'st dróttinn minn* 'I am your servant, you are my master' (Kolb Lv 8/7-8[IV]). In *Geisl* 61/8, S. Óláfr is referred to as *goðs þræll* 'God's servant', while men are called *þrælar konungs fróns* 'servants of the king of the land' in *Líkn* 33/1-2. Gamli repeats this concept in 10/3 and 58/8. — [6] *lífgjafi* 'lifegiver': It has not been possible to make sense of B's reading *lífgjafa*. Sveinbjörn Egilsson (note in 444[x] transcript and 1844 edn) suggested emendation to *lífgjafi*, nom., which has been adopted by all subsequent eds. — [7] *ófs* 'excessively': Sveinbjörn Egilsson (note in 444[x] transcript and 1844 edn) suggested emendation to *ófs*, adverbial gen., which has been adopted by all subsequent eds. — [8]: B is very badly worn, and the 399a-b[x] transcriber was unable to make complete sense of either the first or last word. That his reconstruction is correct is confirmed by the *auð-aðalhending*, of which sufficient traces remain.

10. Þinn hefir þunglig unnit
    (þat fœrir mjǫk) sœri
    synðugr þjónn (frá svinnu)
    sóltjalds konungr (aldir).

    Mæltak mart, þats spillti,
    (mætr, vissir þat, gætir
    ranns) í rausan minni,
    (rǫðuls) fyr mér ok ǫðrum.

Konungr sóltjalds, synðugr þjónn þinn hefir unnit þunglig sœri; þat fœrir aldir mjǫk frá svinnu. Mæltak mart í rausan minni, þats spillti fyr mér ok ǫðrum; vissir þat, mætr gætir ranns rǫðuls.

King of the sun-tent [SKY/HEAVEN > = God], your sinful servant has sworn heavy oaths; that removes men a lot from good sense. I said many things in my bragging which had a corrupting effect on myself and others; you knew that, excellent keeper of the house of the sun [SKY/HEAVEN > = God].

Mss: **B**(12v), 399a-b[x]. — *Readings*: [1] Þinn: *so* 399a-b[x], 'Þí[...]' B [2] mjǫk: mik B.

Editions: *Skj* Gamli kanóki, 2. *Harmsól* 10: AI, 551, BI, 563, *Skald* I, 267; Sveinbjörn Egilsson 1844, 16, Kempff 1867, 3-4, Rydberg 1907, 22, Black 1971, 163, Attwood 1996a, 224.

Notes: [2] *mjǫk* 'very': Sveinbjörn Egilsson (note to 444[x] transcript and 1844 edn) suggests emendation of B's *mik* to *mjǫk*, which has been adopted by all subsequent eds. — [4] *konungr sóltjalds* 'king of the sun-tent [SKY/HEAVEN > = God]': Cf. 14/6-8 and the God-kenning *stillir sóltjalda* 'regulator of the sun-tents' in Arn *Rǫgndr* 3/1-2[III]. The heaven-kenning may derive its inspiration from Ps. XVIII.6: *in sole posuit tabernaculum suum* 'he hath set his tabernacle in the sun'.

11. Ókynnin gatk annan
    optsinnis þar vinna
    víga* ljóss, es vissak,
    veðr-Þrótt, á mik dróttinn.

    Lítt bark ǫnn ok ótta,
    undgjalfrs, fyr mér sjǫlfum,
    grálinns geymirunn*a*
    gla*ðr* *pás* dœmðak aðra.

Gatk optsinnis annan ljóss víga* veðr-Þrótt vinna ókynnin þar, es vissak á mik, dróttinn. Bark lítt ǫnn ok ótta fyr mér sjǫlfum, *pás* dœmðak glaðr aðra geymirunn*a* grálinns undgjalfrs.

I declared oftentimes [that] another Þróttr <= Óðinn> of the storm of the flame of battles [(*lit*. 'storm-Þróttr of the flame of battles') SWORD > BATTLE > WARRIOR] was committing the sins there which I knew myself to be guilty of [*lit*. (were) in myself], Lord. I had little worry and fear for myself, when I gladly [*lit*. glad] judged other protecting bushes of the grey serpent of the wound-surge [BLOOD > SWORD > WARRIORS].

Mss: B(12v), 399a-b^x. — *Readings*: [3] víga*: vígar B   [6] undgjalfrs: *so all others*, 'vnn[...]gialfrs' B   [7] geymirunn*a*: geymirunnum B   [8] glað*r þás*: 'gla[...]' B, 'gla(dr þa)'(?) 399a-b^x, B*FJ*, 'gla(d)[...]'(?) B*Rydberg*.

Editions: *Skj* Gamli kanóki, 2. *Harmsól* 11: AI, 563, BI, 551, *Skald* I, 267, *NN* §2110; Sveinbjörn Egilsson 1844, 16-17, Kempff 1867, 4, Konráð Gíslason and Eiríkur Jónsson 1875-89, II, 271, Rydberg 1907, 22, Jón Helgason 1935-6, 195, Black 1971, 166, Attwood 1996a, 86-7, 224.

Notes: [1-4]: Finnur Jónsson (*Skj* B) construes this *helmingr* as follows: *Gatk optsinnis vinna ókynni á mik þar, es vissak annan vigrar veðr-Þrótt, dróttinn ljóss*, and translates *ofte gjorde jeg mig skyldig i unoder, hvor jeg vidste, at andre mænd gjorde det, lysets herre* 'I was often guilty of bad habits where I knew that other men were doing it, lord of light'. Kock (*NN* §2110) objects to Finnur's interpretation as 'modern', substituting his own prose arrangement: *Gatk optsinnis vinna þar ókynni, er ek vissa annan víga ljóss veðr-Þrótt á mik, dróttinn* which Black (1971, 167) paraphrases 'I have often behaved ignobly when I knew that another man was treating me in that manner, Lord'. Whether consciously or not, this largely accords with Sveinbjörn Egilsson's understanding in 444^x, which reads: *Ek gat optsinnis vinna ókynnin, þar er ek vissa annan Þrótt á mik, dróttinn ljóss veðrvegar* 'I have often behaved badly when I knew another man (*lit*. Þrótt = Óðinn) to be doing so towards me, Lord of the bright weather-way [SKY/HEAVEN > = God]'. This interpretation (and the emendation to *vegar* in l. 3) is adopted by Kempff (1867, 28). In the context of Gamli's confession of former sins, Kock's suggestion that Gamli is confessing to behaving badly seems more plausible than Finnur's, in which he tries to shift the blame for his misdeeds. As Jón Helgason (1935-6, 195) explains, there are some difficulties with Kock's interpretation. The main problem is that the construction *vinna á e-n* is otherwise unattested: *Fritzner*: *vinna* gives examples of the phrase only with dat. or gen. objects. Furthermore, as Jón says, it is difficult to justify the separation of the acc. *annan* in l. 1 from the immediately adjacent verb *geta*. Jón's suggestion, which is adopted by Black (1971, 166) and here, depends on the assumption that the phrasal verb *vita á sik* 'to know oneself, to be guilty of' with objects meaning 'fault', 'blame' or, as here, 'sin' existed in C12th usage. This use is common in MIcel, and *Fritzner*: *vita* has several examples of the similar phrase *at vita e-t eptir e-m* with this meaning in medieval religious prose, though *Fritzner* lists no examples of *vita* in conjunction with either *á* or *sik*. Even so, Jón's interpretation makes for a much simpler and smoother prose arrangement than does either Kock's or Finnur's, and fits better with the tone of both the second *helmingr* and Gamli's self-accusatory confession in sts 7-16. — [6-7] *geymirunna grálinns undgjalfrs* 'protecting bushes of the grey serpent of the wound-surge [BLOOD > SWORD > WARRIORS]': Konráð Gíslason and Eiríkur Jónsson (1875-89, II, 271) suggested emendation of B's *geymirunnum* (dat. pl.) to *geymirunna* (acc. pl), which has been adopted by all subsequent eds. *Geymirunnr* 'protecting bush' occurs elsewhere only in poetry dated to C12th: it is used twice in HSt *Rst* 25/3 and 32/5^I in the identical man-kennings *geymirunnr gunnelds* 'protecting bush of the fire of battle' and also in a poorly-preserved st. from RvHbreiðm *Hl* 5^{III}, where it seems to provide the base-word of a man-kenning. It is interesting to note that the HSt *Rst* examples share the basic conceit of Gamli's more elaborate kenning here. *Undgjalfr* 'wound-surge' is not attested elsewhere, but is conceptually related to *undbára* 'wound-wave' in *Geisl* 54/6.

12. Bergðak brjósti saurgu, Þó sék, þengill skýja
    byrjar hlunns, sem munni, þrifskjótr, — meginljótir
    hreins, ok holdi þínu, hagir sýnask mér mínir
    huggóðr jǫfurr, blóði. margir — þar til bjargar.

Bergðak blóði ok holdi þínu saurgu brjósti sem munni, huggóðr jǫfurr hlunns hreins byrjar. Þó sék þar til bjargar, þrifskjótr þengill skýja; margir hagir mínir sýnask mér meginljótir.

I tasted your blood and body with an unclean heart and mouth, merciful prince of the launching-roller of the fair [*lit.* pure] breeze [SKY/HEAVEN > = God (= Christ)]. Nevertheless I look there [i.e. to the body and blood of Christ] for help, prosperity-swift king of the clouds [= God (= Christ)]; many of my actions seem to me extremely ugly.

Mss: **B**(12v), 399a-b[x]. — *Readings*:   [3] hreins: 'hre[...]ns' B, 'hreins' 399a-b[x], hreins B*FJ*; holdi: 'h[...]' B, 'hǫlldę' 399a-b[x]   [6] þrifskjótr: *so* 399a-b[x], B*Rydberg*, B*FJ*, 'þrif skí[...]tr' B.

Editions: *Skj* Gamli kanóki, 2. Harmsól 12: AI, 564, BI, 551, *Skald* I, 267, *NN* §2804; Sveinbjörn Egilsson 1844, 17, Kempff 1867, 4, Rydberg 1907, 22, Black 1971, 169, Attwood 1996a, 224.

Notes: [1-4]: Gamli's confession is presumably a response to S. Paul's warning in 1 Cor. XI. 26-9: *quotienscumque enim manducabitis panem hunc et calicem bibetis mortem Domini adnuntiatis donec veniat itaque quicumque manducaverit panem vel biberit calicem Domini indigne reus erit corporis et sanguinis Domini probet autem se ipsum homo et sic de pane illo edat et de calice bibat qui enim manducat et bibit indigne iudicium sibi manducat et bibit non diudicans corpus* 'for as often as you shall eat this bread, and drink the chalice, you shall shew the death of the Lord, until he come. Therefore whosoever shall eat this bread, or drink the chalice of the Lord unworthily, shall be guilty of the body and of the blood of the Lord. But let a man prove himself: and so let him eat of that bread, and drink of the chalice. For he that eateth and drinketh unworthily eateth and drinketh judgement to himself not discerning the body [of the Lord]'. The same sentiment is found elsewhere in ON-Icel. religious literature. A Christmas day sermon in *HómÍsl* (*HómÍsl* 1872, 215), for example, warns its hearers that *sa es criz licama etr. Oc hans blóþ drekcr ómaclega. Hann etr sér afallz dóm oc dreckr* 'whoever eats Christ's body and drinks his blood unworthily eats and drinks a severe judgement for himself'. The Magister of *Eluc* (*Eluc* 1989, 83) is even more explicit in his condemnation of unworthy communicants: *en þa er þeir hondla holld drottens vars syndvgvm hondom ok vhreinvm hvat gera þeir þa nema crossfesta kristr* 'and when they touch our Lord's flesh with sinful and unclean hands, what are they doing then except crucifying Christ?' — [5-6] *þrifskjótr þengill skýja* 'prosperity-swift king of the clouds [= God (= Christ)]': The identical Christ-kenning occurs in *Líkn* 43/1, where the alliterative pattern and qualifying adj. may suggest that *Has* is the inspiration. Although the adj.

þrifskjótr appears to be *hap. leg.*, it recalls the nouns *þrifvaldr* 'promoter of well-being' used of God in 22/2 (providing the *hǫfuðstafr*, as *þrifskjótr* does here), and *þrifnuðr* 'well-being', a quality imparted to men by God in *Pl* 5/3 and *Geisl* 3/5, and to his followers by Magnús inn góði in Arn *Hryn* 3/8[II]. — [8] *margir – þar til bjargar* 'many there for help': Cf. *Leið* 20/8 *margri þjóð til bjargar*.

13. Létk í ljós fyr gautum seggja kind at sýndisk,
    láðs nǫkkurar dáðir   (setrs) þokka mun betri,
    laxa fróns, en leyndak   (vísi hár) an vær*ak*
    lǫskum þótt, sem máttak, (vel kunnum því, sunnu).

Létk nǫkkurar dáðir í ljós fyr gautum fróns laxa láðs, en leyndak lǫskum þótt sem máttak, at sýndisk seggja kind þokka mun betri an vær*ak*; vel kunnum því, hár vísi setrs sunnu.

I allowed certain deeds to come to light before the men of the land of the land of the salmon [SEA > GOLD > MEN], but I concealed my weaknesses as best I could, so that I should appear to the race of men [MANKIND] a great deal better than I was; we were [I was] well pleased with that, high king of the seat of the sun [SKY/HEAVEN > = God].

Mss: **B**(12v), 399a-b[x]. — *Readings*: [3] leyndak ('ek leynda'): *so* 399a-b[x], '[...]k ley[...]da' B [7] vísi: *so* 399a-b[x], 'v[...]' B; vær*ak*: væri B.

Editions: *Skj* Gamli kanóki, 2. *Harmsól* 13: AI, 564, BI, 551, *Skald* I, 267, *NN* §§2926, 2930; Sveinbjörn Egilsson 1844, 17, Kempff 1867, 4, Rydberg 1907, 22, Jón Helgason 1935-6, 255, Black 1971, 172, Attwood 1996a, 225.

Notes: [3] *laxa fróns en leyndak*: B's reading produces an irregular *skothending fróns* : *leynda*. That *fróns* may be an interpolation is suggested by the context, since the gold-kenning *frón laxa láðs* 'land of the salmon of the land', is somewhat clumsy and repetitious. Jón Helgason (1935-6, 255) suggested emendation of *fróns* to *brands* gen. sg. of *brandr* 'fire, flame'. This emendation gives a *-nd* : *-nd* rhyme and makes for a more conventional gold-kenning, *gautar brands láðs laxa* 'men of the fire of the land of the salmon'. — [5-8]: There have been several attempts to interpret the second *helmingr*. This edn follows Finnur Jónsson in *Skj* B. Finnur emended *væri* (l. 7) to *værak*, and construed *at sýndisk seggja kind þokka mun betri an værak*, which he translated *(jeg skulte min efterladenhed, sem jeg kunde,) for at jeg skulde syndes betydelig bedre end jeg var* '[I covered my negligence as well as I could,] so that I might appear considerably better than I was'. Jón Helgason (1935-6, 255) retained *væri* (l. 7), taking *seggja kind* as the subject, translating *jeg var fornøyet med at menneskene vilde synes betydelig bedre end de var, himlens høje kong* 'I was pleased that men wanted to appear considerably better than they were, high king of heaven'. Kock (*NN* §2930), perhaps following Kempff and Sveinbjörn Egilsson, objects to *seggja kind* as the subject, and interprets the *helmingr* in much the same way as Finnur does. — [6-8] *hár vísi setrs sunnu* 'high king of the seat of the sun [SKY/HEAVEN > = God]': Cf. the God-kennings *harri setrs* *sunnu* 'ruler of the seat of the sun' in 49/5-8 and *siklingr setrs sunnu* 'prince of the seat of the sun' in *Leið* 13/7-8.

14. Hendak hverjar stundir, Miðr óttuðumk yðra*
    Hlakkar borðs, es þorðak, ósjaldan, gramr tjalda,
    miskaráð fyr meiðum, — því vasa hags*k*ipt — hyrjar
    minn lífgjafi, at vinna. heiðs, an gumna reiði.

Hendak hverjar stundir, es þorðak at vinna miskaráð fyr meiðum Hlakkar borðs, lífgjafi minn. Ósjaldan óttuðumk miðr yðra* reiði an gumna, gramr tjalda hyrjar heiðs; því vasa hags*k*ipt.

I seized on all the times when I dared to commit misdeeds before trees of Hlǫkk's <valkyrie> board [SHIELD > WARRIORS], my life-giver [= God]. Not seldom I feared your wrath less than men's, king of the tents of the fire of the clear sky [SUN > SKY/HEAVEN > = God]; in that regard it was not a fair exchange.

Mss: **B**(12v), 399a-b^x. — *Readings*: [5] *yðra**: 'ydrar' B   [7] hags*k*ipt: 'h[...]g[...]ppt' B, 'hags̩leppt' 399a-b^x, 'hag s(l)[...]pt'(?) B*Rydberg*, 'hagsleppt' B*FJ*.

Editions: *Skj* Gamli kanóki, 2. *Harmsól* 14: AI, 564, BI, 552, *Skald* I, 267, *NN* §§2089, 2926; Sveinbjörn Egilsson 1844, 17, Kempff 1867, 5, Rydberg 1907, 22-3, Jón Helgason 1935-6, 255, Black 1971, 175, Attwood 1996a, 225.

Notes: [5] *yðra** 'your': Sveinbjörn Egilsson (note to 444^x transcript) suggests emendation of B's 'ydrar' to *yðra*, which has been accepted by all subsequent eds. — [7] *hags*kipt 'a fair exchange': B is very badly worn, and only 'h[...]g[...]ppt' can now be read with certainty. Although Finnur Jónsson (*Skj* A) does not indicate any uncertainty about his reading, previous transcribers of B are uncertain as to precisely what remains (see Readings). *Skj* B follows Sveinbjörn Egilsson and Kempff in reconstructing *hagslept*, from *hagsleppr*, adj. There are, however, some difficulties in assigning a meaning to *hagsleppr* here. Sveinbjörn (*LP* (1860)) suggests two possibilities: the first interprets *hagsleppr* as a cpd of *hagr* 'state, condition' and an adj. derived from the verb *sleppa* 'to slip, miss, escape'. The n. form *hagslept* is glossed as *amissio commodi* 'loss of advantage, profit'. The cl. *því vasa hagslept* would then mean 'for that reason there was no loss of advantage'. For this to make sense in context, it would surely have to be understood ironically. Sveinbjörn's second suggestion is that the adj. means 'easily thrown away, abandoned', with the sense that Gamli is declaring that he could not easily abandon his godless ways. In *Skj* B, Finnur Jónsson translates *det kunde jeg ikke let holde op med* 'I could not easily stop that', while *LP*: *hagsleppr*, gesturing towards *hagr* 'advantage', suggests *det kunde jeg ikke med fordel slippe* 'I could not escape that with advantage'. Although this is a possible interpretation, it does seem, as Jón Helgason (1935-6, 255) contends, to be the opposite of Gamli's intention here, since the sinner's neglect of God's anger in favour of men's approval can only be to his advantage, at least in the short term. Jón therefore reconstructs *hagskipt*, which he derives from *hagskipti* 'a fair or advantageous exchange'. Jón's interpretation, which is followed by Kock (*NN* §2926),

Black (1971, 176) and here, implies that the poet's exchanging his concern for God's wrath for a greater concern for men's approval is not profitable for his soul.

15. Hétk opt fyr lið láta   Enn snørumk ey til minna
 lasta verk til fasta   aptr, landreki krapta,
 þér, en þekkjask dýrar,   (esa vanði sá) syn*ð*a
 þeyláðs konungr, dáðir.   (sjaldreyndr kyni aldar).

Hétk þér opt til fasta láta lasta verk fyr lið, en þekkjask dýrar dáðir, konungr þeyláðs. Enn snørumk ey aptr til minna syn*ð*a, landreki krapta; sá vanði esa sjaldreyndr kyni aldar.

I often promised you firmly to lay sinful acts [*lit.* acts of vices] aside and be content with good deeds, king of the thawing wind's land [SKY/HEAVEN > = God]. I always again turned back to my sins, land-governor of powers [= God]; that custom is not infrequently tested by the kinsfolk of men [MANKIND].

Mss: **B**(12v), 399a-b˟. — *Readings*: [2] lasta: so 399a-b˟, 'l[...]sta' B [3] þekkjask: so 399a-b˟, 'þ[...]' B [7] syn*ð*a: 'sy[...]' B, 'synnḍa' 399a-b˟, 'sy(nn)[...]'(?) B*Rydberg*, 'syn(da)'(?) B*FJ*.

Editions: *Skj* Gamli kanóki, 2. *Harmsól* 15: AI, 564, BI, 552, *Skald* I, 268, *NN* §§2070, 2338B, 3125, 3242; Sveinbjörn Egilsson 1844, 18, Kempff 1867, 5, Rydberg 1907, 23, Black 1971, 178, Attwood 1996a, 225.

Notes: [1] *láta fyr lið* 'to lay aside': Kock (*NN* §3242) cites several examples of this phrase in *Fritzner*: *hlið* 2, and compares the German and English equivalents 'beseitigen' and 'to put aside'. He concludes that *lið* here is likely to be a variant of *hlið* 'side' (on the loss of initial <h>, see *ANG* §289). Finnur Jónsson's interpretative translation *at opgive lastefulde gærninger* 'to give up sinful deeds' seems to anticipate Kock here. — [6] *landreki krapta* 'land-governor of powers [= God]': Kempff (1867, 31) and Finnur Jónsson (*Skj* B) take *kraptr* to mean 'a work of power, a miracle' (so *Fritzner*: *kraptr* 3), and take the kenning to mean 'king of miracles'. Kock (*NN* §§3073, 3125) suggests that *krapta* is gen. pl. of *kraptr* 'supernatural power', here, by extension, 'the heavenly host'. In *NN* §2134, he compares the God-kenning *stýrir engla* in *Pl* 25/1, and the biblical *Dominus Sabaoth* (Rom. IX.29 and *passim*).

16. Hefr, at hvern of rifja*k*,   elsku kuðr, alls yðvarr,
 harri minn, til fjarri,   ǫðlingr, hefik, rǫðla,
 grandi firðr, þann*s* gerðak   aumligr þræll í ǫllum
 geig, es sék þik eigi,   afgerðum mik vafðan.

Hefr til fjarri, at of rifja*k* hvern geig, þann*s* gerðak, es sék þik eigi, harri minn, grandi firðr, alls, yðvarr aumligr þræll, hefik mik vafðan í ǫllum afgerðum, ǫðlingr rǫðla, elsku kuðr.

It is far [from the case] that I can enumerate every injury that I have committed when I do not see you, my Lord, removed from sin, since I, your wretched servant, have wrapped myself in all [kinds of] misdeeds, prince of heavenly bodies [= God], renowned for love.

Mss: **B**(12v), 399a-b^x. — *Readings*: [1] rifjak: 'rifiat' B [3] þann*s*: þann B; gerðak ('gordag'): *so* 399a-b^x, B*FJ*, 'gðr[...]' B [7] aumligr: *so* 399a-b^x, 'aumle[...]' B.

Editions: *Skj* Gamli kanóki, 2. Harmsól 16: AI, 564, BI, 552, *Skald* I, 268; Sveinbjörn Egilsson 1844, 18, Kempff 1867, 5, Rydberg 1907, 23, Black 1971, 181, Attwood 1996a, 88, 225.

Notes: [1] *rifja*k 'I ennumerate': It is not possible to make sense of B's reading 'rifiat'. Sveinbjörn Egilsson (1844, 18 n. 22) suggested emendation to *rifjak*, 1st pers. sg. pres. of *rifja* 'to rake hay into rows' with the figurative meaning 'to go over with oneself, reckon up, enumerate' (see *CVC*: *rifja*). This emendation has been adopted by all subsequent eds. — [3] *þann*s 'the one that': It is necessary to add the suffixed rel. particle for syntactic reasons. — [6] *ǫðlingr rǫðla* 'prince of heavenly bodies [= God]': The identical kenning appears in *Leið* 32/2. What one would expect to be a popular rhyming pair, in Christian poetry at least, occurs elsewhere only in a fragment of a poem about Sveinn tjúguskegg attributed to Þorleifr jarlsskáld Rauðfeldarson (Þjsk *Sveindr* 1/2¹) and *Mgr* 3/2.

17. Hverr es greppr, sás ge*r*ra,   Þú biðr ǫlð, en aðrir,
     grunnúðigr, þér unna,   almáttigr guð, sátta,
     — slíkr hǫfum synða auki   ýta ferð at yrði
     sótt — heimstǫðu dróttinn.   aldýr, sǫkum valda.

Hverr greppr, sás ge*r*ra unna þér, es grunnúðigr, dróttinn heimstǫðu; slíkr auki synða hǫfum sótt. Almáttigr guð, þú biðr ǫlð sátta, at ýta ferð yrði aldýr, en aðrir valda sǫkum.

Every man who does not love you is simple-minded, Lord of the world [= God]; such an increase of sins has visited us [me]. Almighty God, you ask mankind for settlement, so that the race of men [MANKIND] might become blessed, but others cause offences.

Mss: **B**(12v), 399a-b^x. — *Readings*: [1] ge*r*ra: 'geira' B [3] synða: *so* 399a-b^x, 'synd[...]' B [8] aldýr: *so* 399a-b^x, 'alldy[...]' B.

Editions: *Skj* Gamli kanóki, 2. Harmsól 17: AI, 564, BI, 552, *Skald* I, 268; *NN* §2931; Sveinbjörn Egilsson 1844, 18, Kempff 1867, 5-6, Konráð Gíslason and Eiríkur Jónsson 1875-89, II, 253, Rydberg 1907, 23, Jón Helgason 1935-6, 256-7, Black 1971, 183, Attwood 1996a, 226.

Notes: [1] *ge*rra 'does not': B's 'geira' does not make sense in context. The emendation to *gerra*, 3rd pers. sg. pres. indic. of *gera* 'to make, do, perform' with suffixed negative *-a* was first proposed in *Skj* B. — [3] *synða* 'of sins': 399a-b^x's reading has been followed here. Both *Skj* B and *Skald* supply the gen. sg. *synðar*. — [7-8] *ýta ferð at yrði aldýr* 'so that the race of men might become blessed': There have been several attempts to interpret this cl. Finnur Jónsson construes *þú biðr ǫlð sátta, almáttigr goð, en aðrir valda sǫkum, at ýta ferð yrði aldýr*, translating *du beder menneskeheden om forlig, almægtige gud, men andre volder, at* *menneskeheden blev meget dyr* 'you ask mankind for a settlement, almighty God, but others bring it about that mankind became very costly'. His implication is presumably that, as a result of sin, mankind became very costly for God to redeem (by the Crucifixion). The main problem with this, as Jón Helgason explains (1935-6, 256; see also Black 1971, 184) is in the interpretation of *aldýr*. Konráð Gíslason (and Eiríkur Jónsson 1875-89, II, 253) objects to the use of *aldýr* here to refer to men, as it is used elsewhere in *Has* (as at 29/6, for example) only to refer to God. As Black (1971, 184) points out, the distinction seems to be between *alldýrr*, in which the prefix *all-* is an intensifier, meaning 'very', and *aldýrr*, where *al-* (cognate with OE *eall*) means 'wholly'. The B scribe retains this distinction, writing *almáttigr* and *aldýrr*, and *al-* is required here for *aðalhending* with *valda*. Jón Helgason (1935-6, 256-7) follows Sveinbjörn Egilsson in construing the *at-*clause with *sátta*, but objects to his translation of *aldýr* as *præstantissimus, egregrius* 'most excellent' (*LP* (1860): *aldýr*). Instead, Jón quotes the expressions *eilíf dýrð* 'eternal glory' and *at fara til dýrðarlífs* 'to go to the life of glory' (Unger 1877, I, 289; see *Fritzner: dýrð*), and the angel-kenning *drótt dýrðar* 'company of glory' in *Has* 36/1-2 in support of his interpretation of *aldýr* as meaning 'members of the company of the blessed'.

18. Ítr, lýstir þú ástar,
    élserkjar gramr, merki
    láðs við lyptimeiða
    linns í hérvist þinni.

    Guð, rétt guðdóm yðvarn
    (glatask mein af því) hreina*n*
    (hǫlða lids) at hylja,
    hár, manndómi vǫrum.

Ítr gramr élserkjar, þú lýstir merki ástar við lyptimeiða láðs linns í hérvist þinni. Hár guð, rétt at hylja yðvarn hreina*n* guðdóm manndómi vǫrum; mein lids hǫlða glatask af því.

Glorious prince of the storm-shirt [SKY/HEAVEN > = God (= Christ)], you showed a sign of your love towards the lifting-poles of the land of the serpent [GOLD > MEN] in your sojourn here. Exalted God, you decided to cover your pure divinity with our humanity; the harm of the race of men [SIN] is destroyed by that.

Mss: **B**(12v), 399a-b^x. — *Readings*: [3] við: til 399a-b^x [6] hreina*n*: hreina B.

Editions: Skj Gamli kanóki, 2. *Harmsól* 18: AI, 564, BI, 553, *Skald* I, 268; Sveinbjörn Egilsson 1844, 18-19, Kempff 1867, 6, Konráð Gíslason and Eiríkur Jónsson 1875-89 II, 256, Rydberg 1907, 23, Black 1971, 186, Attwood 1996a, 226.

Notes: [2] *élserkjar* 'of the storm-shirt': Gamli's choice of *serkr* (m.) 'shirt' as the base-word of this *hap. leg.* heaven-kenning is particularly appropriate in a st. which concentrates on Christ's clothing (*hylja*, l. 7) his godhead in humanity. — [3] *við* 'towards': B's reading, understanding *lyptimeiða* as acc. pl. Both *Skj* B and *Skald* choose 399a-b^x's *til*, understanding *lyptimeiða* as gen. pl. — [3] *láðs við lyptimeiða*: Cf. *Leið* 4/3: *láðs fyr lyptimeiðum*. The identical man-kenning, *lyptimeiðar láðs linns*, also occurs in *Leið* 4/2-3. — [6] *hreina*n 'pure': Konráð Gíslason (and Eiríkur Jónsson 1875-89, II, 256) suggested emendation to *hreinan* (acc.), which has been adopted by all eds.

19. Þú vast, mæztr, frá meyju,   Sæll bart óstyrkð alla,
    — mikil dýrð es þat fyrðum —   ágætr, ok meinlæti,
    hauðrs, í heim með lýðum,   skrýðir skýja slóðar
    hildingr, borinn mild*r*i.   *skr*íns, á líkam þínum.

Mæztr hildingr hauðrs, þú vast borinn í heim með lýðum frá mild*r*i meyju; þat es mikil dýrð fyrðum. Ágætr skrýðir *skr*íns slóðar skýja, bart sæll alla óstyrkð ok meinlæti á líkam þínum.

Most precious prince of the earth [= God (= Christ)], you were born into the world amongst men of a gentle maiden; that is a great honour to mankind. Glorious adorner of the shrine of the path of the clouds [HEAVEN > = God (= Christ)], you gladly bore all weaknesses and sufferings on your body.

Mss: **B**(12v), 399a-b˟. — *Readings*: [4] mild*r*i: mildi B   [7] skýja: *so all others*, 'sk[...]ia' B   [7, 8] slóðar *skr*íns: 's[...]' B, 'slóðar ṣḳrins'(?) 399a-b˟, 'sl(odar skrins)'(?) B*Rydberg*, 'sl(oð)ar s(k)rins'(?) B*FJ*.

Editions: *Skj* Gamli kanóki, 2. *Harmsól* 19: AI, 565, BI, 553, *Skald* I, 268, *NN* §2926; Sveinbjörn Egilsson 1844, 19, Kempff 1867, 6, Rydberg 1907, 23, Black 1971, 188, Attwood 1996a, 226.

Notes: [1-4]: Cf. the account of the Nativity in *Leið* 23/3-4: *mæztr frá meyju betri* | *mildingr* [*lét*] *berask hingað* 'the most praiseworthy prince [allowed] himself to be born here of the best maiden'. — [4] *mild*r*i* (f. dat. sg) 'gentle': If the adj. qualifies *meyju* (l. 1), the ms. reading must be emended (so *Skj* B, *Skald* and *NN* §2926). Sveinbjörn Egilsson (note to 444˟ transcript), followed by Kempff, construes *Mæztr hildingr mildi, þú vast borinn frá meyju í heim með lýðum* 'Most honoured king of gentleness, you were born of a maiden into the world with men'. — [7-8] *skrýðir skríns slóðar skýja* 'adorner of the shrine of the path of the clouds [HEAVEN > = God (= Christ)]': A similar sun-kenning occurs in *Leið* 32/5-6 [*skjǫldungr*] *skríns skýja* '[king] of the shrine of the clouds'. Although *skrín skýja* 'shrine of the clouds' is popular in later poetry, it does not seem to occur earlier than here (see *LP*: *skrín*).

20. Skjǫldungi róm skyldir   Ern skóp hauðr ok hlýrni
    skýja tjalds ok aldar   heims valdr sem kyn beima;
    greitt, sem gǫfgast *m*ætti,   ǫrrs ok ǫllu dýrri
    *gr*andlausum stef vanda.   élsetrs konungr betri.

Róm skyldir vanda greitt stef, sem gǫfgast *m*ætti, *gr*andlausum skjǫldungi tjalds skýja ok aldar. Ern valdr heims skóp hauðr ok hlýrni sem kyn beima; ǫrr konungr élsetrs [e]s ǫllu betri ok dýrri.

We are [I am] obliged to fashion a free-flowing refrain, as excellent as may [be], for the sinless prince of the tent of the clouds [SKY/HEAVEN > = God (= Christ)] and of mankind. The powerful ruler of the world [= God] created earth and heaven as well as the kinsfolk of men [MANKIND]; the generous king of the storm-seat [SKY/HEAVEN > = God] is better and more precious than all.

Mss: **B**(12v), 399a-b^x. — *Readings*: [3] mætti: '[...]tti' B, '(m)ętt(e)'(?) 399a-b^x, '[...]æ')tt[...]'(?) B*Rydberg*, '(m)ȩ̂tt(e)'(?) B*FJ* [4] *gra*nd-: '[...]nd' B, '(gra)nd-'(?) 399a-b^x, '(g)[...]nd-'(?) B*Rydberg*, (gra)nd- B*FJ* [6] valdr: *so all others*, 'ual[...]r' B [8] betri: *so* 399a-b^x, '[...]ri' B.

Editions: *Skj* Gamli kanóki, 2. *Harmsól* 20: AI, 565, BI, 553, *Skald* I, 268, *NN* §2932; Sveinbjörn Egilsson 1844, 19, Kempff 1867, 6, Rydberg 1907, 23-4, Jón Helgason 1935-6, 257, Black 1971, 190, Attwood 1996a, 226.

Notes: [1] *róm* 'we are [I am]': The short form, rather than B's *erum*, must be adopted here, otherwise the l. is unmetrical. Cf. *ANG* §532.3 Anm. 1. — [1-2] *skjǫldungi tjalds skýja* 'for the prince of the tent of the clouds [SKY/HEAVEN = God (= Christ)]': Black (1971, 191) compares Isa. XL.22, where God is described as *qui extendit velut nihilum caelos et expandit eos sicut tabernaculum ad inhabitandum* 'he that stretcheth out the heavens as nothing, and spreadeth them out as a tent to dwell in'. The identical heaven-kenning occurs in 65/5-6, where God is described as *vǫrðr skýtjalds* 'warden of the cloud-tent'. — [3] *greitt* 'free-flowing': May be taken either adjectivally (as in the translation here) or adverbially. — [5-8]: That this is the refrain (*stef*) is indicated by an obelos in the left-hand margin (fol. 12v, l. 31). The first couplet of the refrain is similar in both sense and sound-structure to the opening of the second *Leið* refrain (25/5-6), which reads: *Gramr skóp hauðr ok himna | hreggranns sem kyn seggja* 'the king of the gale-house made land and skies, as well as the race of men'. Lines 7-8 recall the final couplet of the first refrain in *Leið* (13/7-8): *Einn er siklingr sunnu | setrs hvívetna betri* 'the king of the seat of the sun is alone better than everything else'. The sense of the couplets is identical, and both feature a cpd Christ-kenning including a heaven-kenning with the base-word *setr*. Both also exploit the *setrs* : *betri* rhyme. — [8] *betri* 'better': Jón Helgason (1935-6, 257) supposed that the two comparatives *dýrri* and *betri* cause difficulties of a stylistic kind. He therefore emended *betri* to *letri*, from *letr* 'letter', interpreting the final couplet as meaning that God is more holy (*dýrri*) than any description, but this seems not a good ground for emendation.

21. Endr vast barðr ok bundinn,
    buðlungr, meginþungar,
    hlýrnis elds, af hǫldum,
    hár, fyr sekðir várar.

    Enn lézt, ǫldu run*n*a
    angrstríðir, þik síðan,
    viggs, meðal vándra seggja,
    vegligr, á tré negla.

Endr vast barðr ok bundinn af hǫldum fyr várar meginþungar sekðir, hár buðlungr elds hlýrnis. Enn lézt síðan negla þik á tré meðal vándra seggja, vegligr angrstríðir run*n*a viggs ǫldu.

Once you were beaten and bound by men because of our very heavy sins, high king of the fire of the sky [SUN > = God (= Christ)]. Further you allowed yourself afterwards to be nailed to a tree between wicked men, magnificent sin-fighter of the trees of the steed of the wave [SHIP > SEAFARERS > = God (= Christ)].

Mss: **B**(12v), 399a-b^x. — *Readings*: [2] buðlungr: *so* 399a-b^x, '[...]udlu[...]' B [5] run*n*a: 'ru[...]a' B, 'runa' 399a-b^x, runna B*Rydberg*, B*FJ* [6] angr-: *so* 399a-b^x, 'an[...]' B.

Editions: *Skj* Gamli kanóki, 2. *Harmsól* 21: AI, 565, BI, 553, *Skald* I, 268; Sveinbjörn Egilsson 1844, 19-20, Kempff 1867, 6-7, Rydberg 1907, 24, Black 1971, 193, Attwood 1996a, 227.

Notes: [All]: This st. represents the thematic centre of the poem, and introduces a haunting evocation of, and meditation on, the Crucifixion (sts 21-7), which focusses on Christ's merciful response to the penitent thief. Gamli's mastery and manipulation of the skaldic genre is clear as he simplifies both his diction and his w.o. from this point to exploit the full pathos of the scene in a stark narrative reproduced almost verbatim from the account of the Passion in the Gospel of Luke. As Fidjestøl (1993, 223) points out, *Has* is very carefully structured, and st. 21 is the beginning of the 25-st. *stefjabálkr*, which carries the central meditation, in contrast to the surrounding sermon material. — [1] *barðr ok bundinn* 'beaten and bound': This theme is also present in *Líkn*'s account of the Crucifixion (15/7-8): *píndr var hann berr ok bundinn barðr* 'bare he was tortured and beaten bound'. — [7] *meðal vándra seggja* 'between wicked men': The homiletic nature of the language is confirmed by comparison with the phraseology of *HómÍsl*'s *Passio Domini* sermon: *Cristr lét sér sóma at deyia meþal vandra manna* 'Christ made it fitting for himself to die between wicked men' (*HómÍsl* 1872, 68).

22. Þjófr annarr tók þannig,
    þrifvaldr gǫfugr, aldar
    — sól vas hans ófs ok ælig
    ósæl — við gram mæla:
    'Nú sýn afl, ins eina
    alls þú guðs son*r* kallask,
    ok með ǫflgu ríki,
    oss, stíg niðr af krossi!'

Annarr þjófr — sól hans vas ófs ósæl ok ælig — tók mæla þannig við gram aldar, gǫfugr þrifvaldr: 'Nú sýn oss afl, alls þú kallask son*r* ins eina guðs, ok stíg niðr af krossi með ǫflgu ríki!'

One thief — his soul was excessively wretched and vile — began to speak thus to the prince of men [= God (= Christ)], noble promoter of well-being [= God (= Christ)]: 'Now show us your might, since you call yourself the son of the one God, and step down from the Cross with your mighty power!'

Mss: **B**(12v), 399a-b[x]. — *Readings*: [1] tók þannig: *so* 399a-b[x], 't[...]k þ[...]neg' B [5] eina: *so* 399a-b[x], 'e[...]a' B [6] son*r*: son B.

Editions: *Skj* Gamli kanóki, 2. *Harmsól* 22: AI, 565, BI, 555, *Skald* I, 268, *NN* §1192; Sveinbjörn Egilsson 1844, 20, Kempff 1867, 7, Rydberg 1907, 24, Black 1971, 196, Attwood 1996a, 227.

Notes: [All]: The story of the two thieves, one repentant, the other not, is found only in S. Luke's Gospel (XXIII.39-43). The other synoptic gospels state baldly that both thieves joined the bystanders in mocking Christ (cf. Matt. XXVII.44, Mark XV.32). Gamli appears to be conflating the thief's words *si tu es Christus salvum fac temet ipsum et nos* 'if thou be Christ, save thyself and us' (Luke XXIII.39) with the more specific jibes of the bystanders: *si Filius Dei es descende de cruce* 'if thou be the Son of God, come down from the Cross' (Matt. XXVII.40; cf. Matt. XXVII.42, Mark XV.30). The effect is to heighten the dramatic irony of the taunt. — [3] *ófs* 'excessively': Kock (*NN* §1192) suggests that the manuscript reading *ófs*, which he takes to be an intensifying adverbial expression meaning 'excessively', is preferable to *ofs*, which was suggested by Sveinbjörn Egilsson in a note to 444ˣ, and was adopted by *Skj* B. *LP* lists no other occurrence of *ofs*, which is glossed *overmodig* 'arrogant', as it is in *Skj* B, though the form is common in MIcel. The intensifier *ófs* is found also in *Has* 9/7, and is the preferred reading here.

23. Yðr nam annarr kveðja 'minnsk þú, mildingr sunnu,
    illvirki svá, stillir mín,' kvað bauga tínir,
    hás, þás hræddisk píslir, 'þ*itt — ák hag til hættan
    hríðar nausts, með trausti: heldr — es kemr í veldi.'

Annarr illvirki nam kveðja yðr svá með trausti, þás hræddisk píslir, stillir hás nausts hríðar: 'mildingr sunnu, minnsk þú mín,' kvað tínir bauga, 'es kemr í veldi þ*itt: ák heldr til hættan hag.'

The other malefactor began to call on you thus with faith, when he dreaded torments, ruler of the high boatshed of the tempest [SKY/HEAVEN > = God (= Christ)]: 'prince of the sun [= God (= Christ)], remember me,' said the gatherer of rings [MAN], 'when you come into your kingdom: I am in a rather too perilous situation'.

Mss: **B**(12v), 399a-bˣ. — *Readings*: [1] kveðja: *so* 399a-bˣ, '[...]edia' B [5] mildingr: *so* 399a-bˣ, 'milld[...]r' B [7] þ*itt: 'þrott' B.

Editions: *Skj* Gamli kanóki, 2. *Harmsól* 23: AI, 565, BI, 554, *Skald* I, 269; Sveinbjörn Egilsson 1844, 20, Kempff 1867, 7, Rydberg 1907, 24, Black 1971, 198, Attwood 1996a, 227.

Notes: [2-4] *stillir hás nausts hríðar* 'ruler of the high boatshed of the tempest [SKY/HEAVEN > = God (= Christ)]': A similar concept – *stillir* + 'abode of the storm' – also lies behind the God-kennings *stillir býrskríns* 'regulator of the shrine of the breeze' in *Pl* 3/2-3 and *hár stillir hreggtjalda* 'high ruler of the storm-tents' *Has* 1/1-2. — [6] *tínir bauga* 'gatherer of rings': Possibly an ironic use of a variation on a conventional kenning-type (*Meissner*, 256), when applied to a thief. Cf. *auðbrjótr* 'destroyer of riches' in 24/2. — [7] *þ*itt* 'your': Sveinbjörn Egilsson (note to 444ˣ transcript and 1844, 20 n. 29) suggests this emendation, which has been adopted by all subsequent eds. B's reading *þrótt* m. acc. sg. is undoubtedly caused by the scribe's eye-skip forward to *hring-Þrótt* (where Þróttr is a name for Óðinn) in 25/2 (fol. 12v l. 41), influenced by *bauga* in l. 6.

24. Hlaut af yðr sem aðrir Sókndeili* hézt sælu,
    auðbrjótr meginskjóta, sannvíss, paradísar,
    láðs, þeirs lǫstum eyða, — gæf reyndusk þau þjófi
    líkn, skepjandi ríkis. þín heit — friðar veitir.

Auðbrjótr hlaut meginskjóta líkn af yðr, skepjandi ríkis láðs, sem aðrir, þeirs eyða lǫstum. Sannvíss veitir friðar hézt sókndeili* sælu paradísar; þau heit þín reyndusk þjófi gæf.

The destroyer of riches [GENEROUS MAN] received very swift mercy from you, creator of the kingdom of the land [EARTH > = God (= Christ)], like those others who leave off sins. Truly certain giver of peace [= God (= Christ)] you promised the battle-dealer [WARRIOR] the bliss of Paradise; those promises of yours proved beneficial to the thief.

Mss: **B**(12v), 399a-b[x]. — *Readings*: [1] aðrir: *so* 399a-b[x], 'adr[...]' B [3] láðs: 'ladr' B [4] ríkis: ríki B [5] -deili*: '-deilerr' B; hézt: 'he[...]' B, 'het' 399a-b[x], B*FJ*, 'h(æt)'(?) B*Rydberg*.

Editions: *Skj* Gamli kanóki, 2. *Harmsól* 24: AI, 565, BI, 555, *Skald* I, 269; Sveinbjörn Egilsson 1844, 20-1, Kempff 1867, 7, Rydberg 1907, 24, Jón Helgason 1935-6, 257, Black 1971, 200, Attwood 1996a, 90-1, 227.

Notes: [3] *láð*s 'of the land': Sveinbjörn Egilsson (note to 444[x] and 1844, 20 n. 30) suggested emendation to gen. *láðs*, which has been adopted by all subsequent eds. — [4] *ríki*s 'of the kingdom': In his prose arrangement in 444[x] Sveinbjörn Egilsson retains B's reading, *ríki*, which he takes to be the weak m. nom. sg. form of *ríkr* 'powerful', qualifying *skepjandi*. Kempff (1867, 37) also adopts this interpretation. There is no other example of the weak form of the adj. in such a vocative expression elsewhere in *Has*. In MIcel., too, the strong form is invariably used, as, for example, in such expressions as *almáttigur guð* 'Almighty God' or *guð minn góður* 'my good God'. This edn therefore follows Finnur Jónsson in taking the ms.'s 'ríki' to represent *ríki* n. 'kingdom, empire' and emends to *ríkis*, governed by *skepjandi* (l. 4). Although there is not an exact parallel to the resultant earth-kenning *láðs ríki* (*LP*: *ríki*), a similar concept is found in common expressions like *himinríki* 'kingdom of heaven' and in the God-kenning *konungr fróns* 'king of earth' in *Líkn* 33/1-2, and there is no difficulty in characterising God as the creator (*skepjandi*) of either heaven or earth. — [5] *sókndeili** (dat. sg.) 'the battle-dealer': Sveinbjörn Egilsson (note to 444[x] and 1844, 21 n. 31) first proposed this emendation of B's *sókndeilir*, which has been followed by all subsequent eds. — [5] *hézt* 'you promised': This edn follows Jón Helgason (1935-6, 257) in taking *veitir friðar* 'giver of peace' as vocative, rather than as the subject of the verb *heita*, and reconstructs to *hézt* 2nd pers. sg. pret. of *heita* 'to promise', rather than the 3rd sg. *hét*. This arrangement makes for a better parallel with the first *helmingr*, where the appellation – as commonly in *Has* – is again vocative. — [6] *paradísar* 'of paradise': The first occurrence of this loan word in skaldic poetry (see *LP*: *paradís*). — [8] *þín heit friðar veitir*: A strikingly similar l. – *sín heit friðar veitir* – occurs at *Pl* 31/8.

25. Hollostu gefr *hæ*sta
    hring-Þrótt með sér dróttinn
    saðr, þeims sinna iðrask
    synða, lausn ok ynði.

    Ern skóp hauðr ok hlýrni
    heims valdr sem kyn beima;
    ǫrrs ok ǫllu dýrri
    élsetrs konungr betri.

Saðr dróttinn gefr hring-Þrótt, þeims iðrask synða sinna, *hæ*sta hollostu, lausn ok ynði með sér. Ern valdr heims skóp hauðr ok hlýrni sem kyn beima; ǫrr konungr élsetrs [e]s ǫllu betri ok dýrri.

The true Lord gives the ring-Þróttr <Óðinn> [MAN] who repents of his sins the highest faith, absolution and delight with him. The powerful ruler of the world [= God] created earth and heaven as well as the kinsfolk of men [MANKIND]; the generous king of the storm-seat [SKY/HEAVEN > = God] is better and more precious than everything.

Mss: **B**(12v), 399a-b[x]. — *Readings*:   [1] *hæ*sta: '[...]' B, 'hẹsta' 399a-b[x], 'h(æs)ta'(?) B*Rydberg*, 'h(êsta)'(?) B*FJ*   [3] *sað*r: *so* 399a-b[x], 'sad[...]' B; *þeims* ('þeim er'): *so* 399a-b[x], '[...]m er' B   [5-8]: *abbrev. as* 'Ern skop haudr [...] hlyrni' B.

Editions: *Skj* Gamli kanóki, 2. *Harmsól* 25: AI, 565, BI, 555, *Skald* I, 269, *NN* §1193; Sveinbjörn Egilsson 1844, 21, Kempff 1867, 8, Rydberg 1907, 24, Black 1971, 203, Attwood 1996a, 228.

Notes: [1-4]: Finnur Jónsson (*Skj* B) construes *saðr dróttinn gefr hring-Þrótt, þeims íðrask, hæsta hollostu með sér, lausn synða sinna ok yndi* 'the true Lord gives the man, the one who repents, the highest favour with him, freedom from his sins and delight'. The prose arrangement adopted here, which accords with those of Kock (*NN* §1193) and Black (1971, 203), makes for a smoother w.o. — [1] *hæsta* 'highest': There is a hole in the ms. at this point, and nothing is legible, except for a possible ascender to the left of the hole. 399a-b[x] reads 'hesta', but indicates uncertainty about the first three letters. Rydberg was certain of the <h> and the final <ta>, and reconstructed to 'hæsta'. Finnur Jónsson (*Skj* A) was sure only of the <h>, but accepted Rydberg's reconstruction, which has been adopted by all subsequent eds. — [2] *hring-Þrótt* 'ring-Þróttr': See Note to 11/4. The allusion to a repentant sinner as a 'ring-god' may be intended to remind one of the description of the penitent thief as *tínir bauga* 'gatherer of rings' (23/6) and *auðbrjótr* 'destroyer of riches' (24/2), and may tie Gamli's more general moralisation into the meditation on the Crucifixion scene. — [5-8]: The first l. of the *stef* is written out. Although the scribe of B usually indicates repetition of a *stef* (in this case, from st. 20) by means of a marginal obelos, the mark is omitted here.

26. Hverr myndi *svá h*endir   at, þreknenninn, þinni
    harðgeðr loga fjarðar,   ..., sættandi, mætti
    éla ranns (ef ynni)   ógrátandi, ýta,
    ítr ... (þér) rítar,   ormlands hjá kvǫl standa?

Ítr ... rítar ranns éla, hverr *h*endir loga fjarðar myndi *svá* harðgeðr, ef ynni þér, at ... ormlands mætti standa ógrátandi hjá þinni kvǫl, þreknenninn sættandi ýta?

Glorious ... of the shield of the house of storms [SKY/HEAVEN > SUN > = ?God (= Christ)], which distributor of the fire of the fjord [GOLD > GENEROUS MAN] could [be] so hard-minded, if he loved you, that [he], a ... of the land of the snake [GOLD > ?MAN] might stand unweeping by your Passion, powerful reconciler of men [= God (= Christ)]?

Mss: **B**(12v), 399a-b[x]. — *Readings*:   [1] *svá h*endir: 's[...]nnder' B, '[...]h[...]nnder' 399a-b[x], '(s)[...] [...](æ)nnder'(?) B*Rydberg*, 's(va) [...]nndir'(?) B*FJ*   [4] ...: '[...]' B, 399a-b[x]   [6] ...: '[...]' B, 399a-b[x].

Editions: *Skj* Gamli kanóki, 2. *Harmsól* 26: AI, 565-6, BI, 555, *Skald* I, 269; Sveinbjörn Egilsson 1844, 21, Kempff 1867, 5-6, Rydberg 1907, 24-5, Black 1971, 205, Attwood 1996a, 228.

Notes: [1] *svá* he*ndir*: B is very dark and badly worn; <h> is confirmed by the alliteration. Reconstruction to *svá hendir* is suggested by Sveinbjörn Egilsson in a marginal note to 444ˣ, and has been adopted by all eds. — [4] ...: The ms. is badly torn. Traces of a tall letter, possibly an <f> and an abbreviation remain, but these are uncertain. Sveinbjörn Egilsson's reconstruction to *festir* 'fastener', an agent noun from the verb *festa* 'to fasten' is perhaps inspired by the similar ll. at 50/2-3 *ítr postoli rítar* | *fróns musteris festir*. Rydberg (1907, lxxi) claims to see traces of a <g> here, and reconstructs *gervir* 'creator', which is adopted by Finnur Jónsson, Kock and Black. This seems unlikely, however, since the previous transcribers of the ms., those responsible for 399a-bˣ, record no trace of it. Rydberg compares *Geisl* 65/5, where God is referred to as *gervir himna* 'maker of the heavens', in support of his reconstruction. Clearly, there is a God-kenning here, but the base-word cannot be supplied with any certainty. — [5] *þreknenninn* 'powerful': Sveinbjörn Egilsson (note to 444ˣ), followed by Kempff, construes with his reconstruction *Þrór* 'Óðinn' in l. 6 (see following Note). — [6] ...: Once again, B is badly worn and no one has been able to discern any trace of the missing letters. The alliterative scheme requires a word with initial <þ>, which must serve as the base-word of a man-kenning with the determinant *ormlands* ('of the land of the snake [GOLD]'). Man-kennings of this type elsewhere in the poem and generally suggest that a noun meaning 'destroyer' or 'distributer', a god-name or a tree-name would be appropriate choices. Sveinbjörn Egilsson (1844, 21 n. 35), followed by Kempff, suggests reconstruction to *Þrór*, an Óðinn-*heiti*. *Skj* B suggests reconstruction to *þollr* 'tree', which has been adopted by all subsequent eds. — [6-7] *sættandi ýta* 'reconciler of men [= God (= Christ)]': This is a particularly appropriate Christ-kenning, given that Gamli is here challenging his hearers to consider their responses to Christ's attempt to make peace between themselves and God. Compare the similar assertion in st. 17, which seeks to manipulate the hearer's response to Christ as peacemaker (see especially ll. 5-6).

27. Sæll, tókt einn fyr allar
    óverðr guma ferðir,
    sannstýrandi, sáran,
    sólhauðrs, á þik dauða,

    ok liðfasta (leystir)
    lífs unnir þú runnum
    (hǫlða ferð ór harðri
    harms gnótt) fira dróttinn.

Sæll sannstýrandi sólhauðrs, einn óverðr, tókt sáran dauða á þik fyr allar ferðir guma, ok þú unnir runnum liðfasta lífs, dróttinn fira; leystir ferð hǫlða ór harðri gnótt harms.

Blessed true-steerer of the sun-land [SKY/HEAVEN > = God (= Christ)], alone, undeserving, you took a painful death upon yourself for all the hosts of men [MANKIND], and you granted life to bushes of arm-fires [GOLD RINGS > MEN], lord of men [= God (= Christ)]; you freed the host of men [MANKIND] from a cruel abundance of grief.

Mss: **B**(12v), 399a-bˣ. — *Readings*: [5] leystir: *so* 399a-bˣ, 'le[...]st[...]' B [7] hǫlða: 'h[...]' B, 'hǫ̣lda'(?) 399a-bˣ, 'h(ǫlda)'(?) B*Rydberg*, 'h(old)a'(?) B*FJ*.

Editions: *Skj* Gamli kanóki, 2. *Harmsól* 27: AI, 567, BI, 555, *Skald* I, 269, *NN* §1194; Sveinbjörn Egilsson 1844, 21-2, Kempff 1867, 8, Rydberg 1907, 25, Black 1971, 208, Attwood 1996a, 228.

Notes: [3-4] *sannstýrandi sólhauðrs* 'true-steerer of the sun-land [SKY/HEAVEN > = God (= Christ)]': An identical heaven-kenning is at the heart of the Christ-kenning *sonr hauðrs sólar* 'son of the land of the sun' in *Leið* 31/3-4. According to *LP*: *sólhauðr*, the cpd is a *hap. leg.*, and no other occurrence of *sólar hauðrs* is attested, though the concept is common.

28. Hilmir, reist, ins hæsta
    hríðtjalds, ór grǫf síðan,
    flýtileygs, á frægjum,
    friðsamr, degi þriðja,
    ok rá*ðvísa, ræsir
    regnhallar, vannt fegna,
    áðr þás yðvarr dauði,
    aldyggr, fira hryggði.

Friðsamr hilmir flýtileygs ins hæsta hríðtjalds, reist síðan ór grǫf á frægjum þriðja degi, ok, aldyggr ræsir regnhallar, vannt fegna rá*ðvísa fira, þás yðvarr dauði hryggði áðr.

Peaceful prince of the swift fire of the highest storm-tent [SKY/HEAVEN > SUN > = God (= Christ)], you rose then from the grave on the famous third day, and, altogether honourable king of the rain-hall [SKY/HEAVEN > = God (= Christ)], you made glad the counsel-wise people whom your death had saddened previously.

Mss: **B**(12v), 399a-b^x. — *Readings*: [1] reist ('reis þu'): *so* 399a-b^x, 'r[...]s þ[...]' B, 'ræis þ(u)'(?) B*Rydberg*, 'reis þ[...]' B*FJ* [5] rá*ðvísa: 'raud uisa' B.

Editions: *Skj* Gamli kanóki, 2. *Harmsól* 28: AI, 566, BI, 555, *Skald* I, 269; Sveinbjörn Egilsson 1844, 22, Kempff 1867, 8-9, Rydberg 1907, 25, Jón Helgason 1935-6, 257, Black 1971, 210; Attwood 1996a, 228.

Notes: [1] *reist* 'you rose': This edn follows Kock and Black in adopting Jón Helgason's suggestion (1935-6, 257), anticipated by Sveinbjörn Egilsson in a marginal note to the 444^x transcript (which is less certain about B's text than was 399a-b^x) that the verb should be in the 2nd pers. sg. here, as in the second *helmingr* (*vant* l. 6). The ms. reading suggests that the 2nd pers. is intended and Gamli's habit elsewhere is to maintain a continuity of address throughout a st., as, e.g. in the preceding st., where all three verbs are in the 2nd pers. sg. — [1-4] *hilmir flýtileygs ens hæsta hríðtjalds* 'prince of the swift fire of the highest storm-tent [SKY/HEAVEN > SUN > = God (= Christ)]': Cf. *valdr blásinna tjalda hreggs* 'king of the windswept tents of the storm' in 57/6-7.

29. Leitt í lopt upp, dróttin*n*
    — litu gǫrla þat vitr*ir* —
    himins fylgjandi, helgu
    holdi skrýddr, af foldu.
    Áðr trúir ǫld ok síðan
    aldýran þik stýra,
    skríngeyp*nan*di, skepnu,
    skýstalls, sælu allri.

Fylgjandi dróttin*n* himins, leitt í lopt upp af foldu, skrýddr helgu holdi; vitr*ir* litu þat gǫrla. Skýstalls skrín geyp*nan*di, ǫld trúir áðr ok síðan þik aldýran stýra allri sælu skepnu.

Helping lord of heaven [= Christ], you rose up into the sky from earth, clothed with holy flesh; wise men saw that clearly. Holder of the shrine of the cloud-platform [(*lit.* 'cloud-platform's shrine-holder') SKY/HEAVEN > SUN > = God (= Christ)], mankind believes, before and since, that you, altogether glorious, govern all the bliss of creation.

Mss: **B**(12v), 399a-b˟. — *Readings*: [1] dróttinn: 'drotte[...]' B, 'drotte(nn)'(?) 399a-b˟, B*Rydberg*, 'drotten' B*FJ* [2] vitr*i*r: vitrar B [3] fylgjandi: *so* 399a-b˟, 'f[...]de' B [4] skrýddr: *so* 399a-b˟, '[...]yddr' B [7] -geyp*na*ndi: '-geyp[...]e' B, 399a-b˟, '-gæyp[...](n)dæ'(?) B*Rydberg*, '-geyp(na)nde'(?) B*FJ*.

Editions: *Skj* Gamli kanóki, 2. *Harmsól* 29: AI, 566, BI, 555-6, *Skald* I, 269, *NN* §2111; Sveinbjörn Egilsson 1844, 22, Kempff 1867, 9, Rydberg 1907, 25, Jón Helgason 1935-6, 254, Black 1971, 213, Attwood 1996a, 229.

Notes: [1-4]: There have been various attempts to interpret this *helmingr*. Kempff (1867, 41) follows Sveinbjörn Egilsson (prose arrangement in 444˟) in taking *vitrar* from *vitr* 'wise'. They construe this with *fylgjandi* (l. 3) to give the phrase *fylgjandi vitrar* 'wise followers', which Kempff interprets as a reference to the Apostles, who witnessed the Ascension. Finnur Jónsson appears to take *fylgjandi* as pres. part. of *fylgja* 'to accompany', adjectival in force, amplifying *skrýddr* in the expression *skrýddr, fylgjandi helgu holdi*, which he translates *forklaret følgende dit hellige legeme* 'transfigured (or glorified) following your holy body' (*Skj* B). As Kock (*NN* §2111) objects, Finnur's meaning is elusive. Kock quotes parallels from *Líkn* and *Lil* (see following Note) in support of his reading of *skrýddr helgu holdi* 'clothed with your holy flesh' as a logical unit, and construes *fylgjandi* (which he translated as 'helping') as part of the God-kenning *fylgjandi dróttinn himins* 'helping lord of heaven'. Black (1971, 213) adopts this arrangement, translating *fylgjandi* as 'gracious', an attempt to characterise the nature of Christ's 'help'. For uses of *fylgja* to mean 'help, assist, show kindness', which are by no means unusual, see *Fritzner*: *fylgja*. Kock's interpretation has been followed here, although it and that in *Skj* B also require emendation to *vitrir* nom. pl. in l. 2. Jón Helgason (1935-6, 254) suggests that B's 'drotte...' (l. 1) should be reconstructed *dróttir* nom. pl. of *drótt* 'people', which may be construed with B's reading *vitrar* 'wise' (l. 2). This has the advantage of avoiding the need to emend in l. 2, but leaves a Christ-kenning, *fylgjandi himins*, where *fylgjandi* (pres. part.) has to function as a noun. — [3-4] *skrýddr helgu holdi* 'clothed with holy flesh': Cf. *Líkn* 12/3-4: *skrýddi sik hjalmprýddan holdi* 'clothed himself, helmet-adorned, with flesh'. See also *Lil* 24/7-8. — [7-8] *skýstalls skríngeypnandi* 'cloud-platform's shrine-holder, holder of the shrine of the cloud platform [SKY/HEAVEN > SUN > = God (= Christ)]': A similar concept lies behind the God-kennings *umgeypnandi alls heims* 'holder in hand of the whole world' in *Geisl* 16/7-8 and *umgeypnandi allrar skepnu* 'holder in hand of all creation' in *Kálf Kátr* 36/3. The concept of God's holding creation in his hand also informs *frónspennir fagrtjalda* 'clasper of the fair tents of the land' in *Has* 44/5-6. The verb *geypna* derives from *gaupn* 'hollow of the hand' (see *AEW*: *gaupn* and Note to *Mgr* 2/5).

30. Ítr lofar engla sveitar   Ern skóp hauðr ok hlýrni
    allr herr salar fjalla   heims valdr sem kyn beima;
    víst með vegsemð hæstri   ǫrrs ok ǫllu dýrri
    vǫrð* ok menn á jǫrðu.   élsetrs konungr betri.

Allr ítr herr sveitar engla ok menn á jǫrðu lofar víst vǫrð* salar fjalla með hæstri vegsemð. Ern valdr heims skóp hauðr ok hlýrni sem kyn beima; ǫrr konungr élsetrs [e]s ǫllu betri ok dýrri.

All the glorious host of the company of angels and men on earth certainly praise the guardian of the hall of the mountains [SKY/HEAVEN > = God] with the highest honour. The powerful ruler of the world [= God] created earth and heaven as well as the kinsfolk of men [MANKIND]; the generous king of the storm-seat [SKY/HEAVEN > = God] is better and more precious than everything.

Mss: **B**(12v), 399a-b[x]. — *Readings*: [4] vǫrð*: 'vðrðr' B [5-8]: abbrev. as 'Ern skop haudr ok hlýr[...]' B.

Editions: *Skj* Gamli kanóki, 2. *Harmsól* 30: AI, 566, BI, 556, *Skald* I, 269, *NN* §2926; Sveinbjörn Egilsson 1844, 22-3, Kempff 1867, 9, Rydberg 1907, 25, Black 1971, 216, Attwood 1996a, 229.

Notes: [1-4]: Kock (*NN* §2926) follows Jón Helgason (1935-6, 252) in construing *allr herr salar fjalla lofar vǫrð sveitar engla* 'all the host of the hall of the mountains [SKY/HEAVEN > ANGELS] praises the guardian of the company of angels [= God]'. This edn follows Finnur Jónsson (*Skj* B) in taking *vǫrðr salar fjalla*, which is reminiscent of *harri salar fjalla* 'lord of the hall of the mountains' in *Leið* 1/2, to be the God-kenning here. The sentiment of this *helmingr* recalls that of the first *stef* in *Leið*, and it seems reasonable to assume some influence here, though it is impossible to say which of the two poems is the senior. — [1] *lofar* 'praise': Lit. 'praises'. The 444[x] copyist suggests this normalisation from B's 'lofuar', which has been adopted by all eds. Note that the verb is sg. but the subject pl. (cf. *NS* §70). — [2] *salar fjalla* '(of the) hall of the mountains [SKY/HEAVEN]': In addition to *Leið* 1/2 (see previous Note), the identical heaven-kenning occurs in a *lv.* in *Gunnl* (GunnlI Lv 8/2[V] [*Gunnl* 13]) and in a couplet from Hallv *Knútdr* 8/2[III]. — [4] *vǫrð* 'warden, guardian': Sveinbjörn Egilsson (n. to 444[x] transcription and 1844, 23) corrects to vǫrð, which has been accepted by all eds. — [5-8] *ern skóp ... konungr betri*: The first l. of the *stef* is written out. Repetition of the *stef* (from st. 20) is indicated by a marginal obelos.

31. Enn mun ǫðru sinni   Geisar eldr ok œsisk
    ǫðlingr koma hingat   ǫlna fold; ór moldu
    mána tjalds inn mildi   ferð vaknar þá fyrða
    meðr til dóms *at kveð*ja.   flest við ugg inn mesta.

Enn mun inn mildi ǫðlingr tjalds mána koma hingat ǫðru sinni *at kveð*ja meðr til dóms. Eldr geisar ok fold ǫlna œsisk; flest ferð fyrða vaknar þá ór moldu við inn mesta ugg.

Again the gentle ruler of the tent of the moon [SKY/HEAVEN > = God (= Christ)] will come here a second time to call men to judgement. Fire will rage and the land of the mackerel [SEA] will surge; most of the troop of men will awaken then from the grave [*lit.* from the soil] with the greatest terror.

Mss: **B**(13r), 399a-b^x. — *Readings*: [1] mun: *so* 399a-b^x, 'm[...]' B; ǫðru sinni: 'óðr[...]nne' B, 'ǫ́dru sinne'(?) 399a-b^x, 'óðr[...] (s)[...](nn)æ'(?) B*Rydberg*, 'ǫ́d(ru si)nne'(?) B*FJ*   [2] hingat: 'h[...]ngat' B, 'h(in)gat'(?) 399a-b^x   [3] mána: *so* 399a-b^x, '[...]ana' B; tjalds: *so* 399a-b^x, 't[...]lldz' B   [4] til dóms *at kveð*ja: '[...]m[...]ia' B, 'til dóms [...]ia' 399a-b^x, 'til doms a[...]dia' B*Rydberg*, 'til dóms [...]ia' B*FJ*   [7] fyrða: *so* 399a-b^x, '[...]da' B.

Editions: *Skj* Gamli kanóki, 2. *Harmsól* 31: AI, 566, BI, 556, *Skald* I, 270; Sveinbjörn Egilsson 1844, 23, Kempff 1867, 9-10, Rydberg 1907, 25, Black 1971, 218, Attwood 1996a, 229.

Notes: [All]: The turmoil associated with the Second Coming and Last Judgement is a recurrent theme in medieval eschatological literature and art. It is difficult to find precise parallels with Gamli's account. The *locus classicus* is Rev. XX, where the account includes mention of punishing fire and of the resurrection of the dead (Rev. XX.12, 15). The account of the 'Day of the Lord' in the Second Epistle of Peter (2 Pet III.10-11) stresses that destruction will be by fire, not by water, as in the days of Noah. The raising of the dead is also a tenet of Pauline eschatology (1 Cor. XV.52). Turville-Petre (1953, 163) and Lange (1958a, 146) note that there are some parallels between this st. and the account of Ragnarǫk in *Vsp* 54. — [1-4]: B fol. 13r, l.1 is dark and badly worn (partly as a result of earlier restoration attempts). It has therefore been necessary to rely heavily on previous transcriptions of the ms., most notably that of 399a-b^x, to reconstruct the text. Where earlier eds are uncertain of the reading (notably with *kveðja* in l. 4), rhyme and alliteration have been used as guides for confirmation of their reconstructions. — [4] *meðr* 'men': An early form of the nom. pl. of *maðr* 'man', which was later assimilated to *mennr* and eventually to *menn*. *CVC*: *maðr* lists several occurrences in poetry, all in texts dating from the C11th and C12th. On *meðr* and the assimilation of *þrðr* to *nnr*, which Noreen dates to the late Viking period, see *ANG* §§261, 277b. — [6] *fold ǫlna* 'land of the mackerel [SEA]': The identical kenning occurs in HSt *Rst* 27/7[1].

32. Engr mun alls á þingi
    ísheims vesa þvísa
    jóskreytandi ítrum
    óttalauss fyr dróttni,

    éla vangs þvít englar
    jǫfurs skjalfa þá sjalfir
    — ógn tekr mǫttug magnask —
    mæts við ugg ok hræzlu.

Alls engr ísheims jóskreytandi mun vesa óttalauss fyr ítrum dróttni á þvísa þingi, þvít sjalfir englar mæts jǫfurs vangs éla skjalfa þá við ugg ok hræzlu; mǫttug ógn tekr magnask.

Not a single adorner of the horse of the ice-world [(*lit.* 'horse-adorner of the ice-world') SEA > SHIP > SEAFARER] will be fearless before the glorious Lord at this assembly, for the very angels of the worthy king of the field of storms [SKY/HEAVEN > = God] will tremble then with fear and dread; mighty terror will begin to increase.

Mss: **B**(13r), 399a-b[x]. — *Readings*:   [1] Engr: engi B;   þingi: *so* 399a-b[x], 'þing[...]' B   [4] fyr: '[...]iri' B, til 399a-b[x];   dróttni: *so* 399a-b[x], '[...]rottne' B   [8] hræzlu: *so* 399a-b[x], 'hrę[...]' B.

Editions: Skj Gamli kanóki, 2. *Harmsól* 32: AI, 566, BI, 556, Skald I, 270; Sveinbjörn Egilsson 1844, 23, Kempff 1867, 10, Rydberg 1907, 26, Black 1971, 221, Attwood 1996a, 229.

Notes: [1] *eng*r: B's *engi* makes the l. hypermetrical, so has been emended to *engr*. — [1] *á þingi* 'at the assembly': For a similar use of the indigenous term *þing* 'assembly, meeting' to refer to the gathering of men at the Last Judgement, see *Líkn* 27/1 *á þingi þessu* and 26/6 *til alþingis*. — [1-3] *alls engr ísheims jóskreytandi* 'not a single adorner of the horse of the ice-world [SEA > SHIP > SEAFARER]': Cf. the man-kenning *jóskreytandi reggstrindar* 'adorner of the horse of the land of the ship' in Anon *Óldr* 4/1, 3[l]. *Ísheimr* is a *hap. leg.* (*LP*: *ísheimr*). — [2] *þvísa* 'this': Archaic n. dat. sg. form = *þessu* (*ANG* §470, Anm. 2), adopted to provide *aðalhending* with *ís-*. — [4] *óttalauss fyr dróttni* 'fearless before the Lord': Lines on this pattern occur frequently in Christian poetry. Cf. *Has* 36/6 *óttlaust af því móti* 'fearless from the meeting', and *Líkn* 52/6 *óttlaust með þér dróttinn* 'fearless with you, Lord'. Almost identical ll. occur three times in *Leið*, always in sts describing the peace of heaven, where the saved will live *óttalauss með dróttni* 'fearless with the Lord', either as a result of their own prayers (40/6), or of Christ's intervention at the Last Judgement (41/8). The first refrain in *Leið*, which describes the praise of angels and men, contains the l. *óttlaust ok lið dróttni* (13/6). — [5-6] *sjalfir englar ... skjalfa* 'the very angels [of the Lord] will tremble': Black (1971, 222) notes that *HómÍsl* sermon for All Saints' Day has an interesting parallel: *þar es ótte sva mikill oc andvare at þeim dóme at þa skiálfa englar guþs oc aller helger men* 'there will be such great terror and trepidation at the Judgement that the angels of God and all holy men will tremble' (*HómÍsl* 1872, 45). That the saints will tremble at the Second Coming is also mentioned in the sermon on the Holy Spirit: *enda muno skiálfa aller helger. mikil mon þa ógn í heime vera. es conungr kømr reiþr* 'and so all the saints will tremble, there will be great terror in the world, when the king comes in anger' (*HómÍsl* 1872, 214). That the earth, and its inhabitants, will tremble at the day of the Lord is a biblical commonplace (see, for example, Ps. CXIII.7; Joel II.1, 10).

33. Hǫrð munat hógligt verða   systkin mín, þvít sýnask
     hjalmstýranda ins dýra   sǫ́r ok kross fyr ossu
     sunnu syndgum mǫnnum   dróttins várs með dreyra
     sekðarorð at forðask,   dyggs augliti hryggu.

Munat verða hógligt syndgum mǫnnum at forðask hǫrð sekðarorð ins dýra sunnu hjalmstýranda, þvít, systkin mín, sǫ́r ok kross dyggs dróttins várs með dreyra sýnask fyr hryggu augliti ossu.

It will not be easy for sinful men to escape the harsh words of damnation of the precious ruler of the helmet of the sun [(*lit.* 'helmet-ruler of the sun') SKY/HEAVEN > = God (=

Christ)], because, my brothers and sisters, the wounds and Cross of our faithful Lord, as well as his blood, will appear before our rueful faces [*lit.* face].

Mss: **B**(13r), 399a-b˟. — *Reading*: [1] Hǫrð: *so* 399a-b˟, 'H[...]' B.

Editions: *Skj* Gamli kanóki, 2. *Harmsól* 33: AI, 566-7, BI, 556-7, *Skald* I, 270; Sveinbjörn Egilsson 1844, 23-4, Kempff 1867, 10, Rydberg 1907, 26, Black 1971, 223, Attwood 1996a, 230.

Notes: [All]: Paasche (1914a, 146) notes that the concept of the appearance of Christ's wounds at Judgement can be traced to biblical passages concerned with the Last Days. Zech. XII.10 describes the sorrow of the Jews at this time: *et aspicient ad me quem confixerunt et plangent eum planctu quasi super unigenitum* 'and they shall look upon me, whom they have pierced: and they shall mourn for him as one mourneth for an only son'. This v. is recalled at the opening of Rev. I.7: *ecce venit cum nubibus et videbit eum omnis oculus et qui eum pupugerunt et plangent se super eum omnes tribus terrae etiam* 'behold, he cometh with the clouds, and every eye shall see him, and they also that pierced him. And all the tribes of the earth shall bewail themselves because of him'. — [2-3] *hjalmstýranda sunnu* 'steerer of the helmet of the sun [SKY/HEAVEN > = God (= Christ)]': Although the sky- or heaven-kenning *sunnu hjalmr* is a *hap. leg.*, it recalls *hjalmr sólar* 'helmet of the sun' in Arnórr jarlaskáld's supposed fragment from a memorial poem for Gellir Þorkelsson (Arn Frag 1^III; cf. Whaley 1998, 134), the earliest surviving poetic account of the Last Judgement in ON. The helmet reference also occurs in *Leið* 30/5-8, where God is referred to as *ǫðlingr lopthjalms* 'king of the sky-helmet'.

34. Vér getk, fátt at fœrim
    framm í orða glammi
    at dáðgeymis *dómi*
    dýrð*ar*gjarns of varnir,
    *áð*r ef eigi réðum
    aldar kyns fyr synðir
    — heldr reynisk þat hǫlðum
    hætt — við gram til sættar.

Getk, at vér fœrim fátt framm of varnir í glammi orða at *dómi* dýrð*ar*gjarns dáðgeymis, ef réðum eigi *áð*r til sættar fyr synðir við gram aldarkyns; þat reynisk hǫlðum heldr hætt.

I believe that we will advance our defences poorly in a babble of words at the Judgement of the glory-eager deed-guardian [= God (= Christ)], if previously we have not made peace for our sins with the prince of the race of men [MANKIND > = God]; that will prove rather dangerous for men.

Mss: **B**(13r), 399a-b˟. — *Readings*: [1] at: *so* 399a-b˟, '[...]t' B [3] *dómi*: '[...]e' B, '(do)me'(?) 399a-b˟ [4] dýrð*ar*-: dýrð B; varnir: *so* 399a-b˟, B*FJ*, '[...]' B, (varnir)(?) B*Rydberg* [5] *áð*r ef: '[...]r ef B, '[...]dr ef' 399a-b˟, B*Rydberg*, '(e)ndr ef'(?) B*FJ*; réðum ('rèdum'): 'rẹndum'(?) 399a-b˟, 'rædum' B*Rydberg*, rendum B*FJ*.

Editions: *Skj* Gamli kanóki, 2. *Harmsól* 34: AI, 567, BI, 557, *Skald* I, 270, *NN* §2926; Sveinbjörn Egilsson 1844, 24, Kempff 1867, 10, Rydberg 1907, 26, Jón Helgason 1935-6, 258, Black 1971, 226, Attwood 1996a, 230.

Notes: [4] *dýrð*ar: It has not been possible to make sense of B's reading *dýrð* nom. sg. or acc. sing. of *dýrð* 'glory'. Emendation to the gen. sg. *dýrðar* was suggested by Sveinbjörn Egilsson (1844, 24), and has been adopted by all subsequent eds. — [5] *áðr ef eigi réðum*: The ms. is very badly worn at this point (fol. 13r, l. 7), and it has been very difficult to read this l. Although in *Skj* A he reads *rendum* with certainty, Finnur Jónsson in *Skj* B follows Kempff in adopting Sveinbjörn Egilsson's suggestion (1844, 24 n. 25), that the l. should read *endr ef eigi vendum*. The *endr* : *vendum* reconstruction, however, gives an *aðalhending*, rather than the expected *skothending*. The final word, 'rēdum', is legible on ultra-violet photographs, and is confirmed by Rydberg's transcription. Although the first word is now illegible, apart from the final *r*, Rydberg read '...dr' with certainty, and believed he saw traces of an initial *a* (1907, 26 n. 4). Jón Helgason (1935-6, 258) accepts Rydberg's reading, though he points out that *ræðum* (dat. pl.) 'speeches', which would be the usual interpretation of what appears to be hooked 'e', is hardly appropriate in the context. As Jón points out, however, there are several instances where the scribe writes a curved accent which is easily mistaken for a hook. If we take this to be the case here, the l. becomes *áðr ef eigi réðum*. Although the expression *ráða til sætta við e-n* 'to make peace with someone' is not found elsewhere, Jón Helgason cites *ráða til saka við e-n* (Fritzner: *ráða til* 4.) 'to blame someone' as a close parallel. The first word of l. 5 has been taken as either *endr* (so Kempff and *Skj* B), following a suggestion of Sveinbjörn Egilsson (1844, 24 n. 45), or *áðr* (so Rydberg, Jón Helgason, Kock, Black, Attwood 1996a and here).

35. Orð meg*u* v*ǫ*nduð verða
 víst aldrigi Kristi
 — guðs an gǫrvallt œðri
 gœzkufyldr — sem skyldi.

St*e*rk lofar drótt ok dýrkar
dagstalls konung snjallan;
himins es fylkir fremri
fróðr hvívetna góðu.

Orð meg*u* víst aldrigi verða v*ǫ*nduð Kristi, sem skyldi; gœzkufyldr guðs œðri an gǫrvallt. St*e*rk drótt lofar ok dýrkar snjallan konung dagstalls; fróðr fylkir himins es fremri hvívetna góðu.

Words can surely never be as carefully chosen for Christ as they should be; grace-filled God is higher than everything. The mighty host praises and worships the excellent king of the day-support [SKY/HEAVEN > = God]; the wise king of heaven [= God] is superior to everything that is good.

Mss: **B**(13r), 399a-b[x]. — *Readings*: [1] Orð: so 399a-b[x], '[...]rd' B; meg*u*: 'meg[...]' B, mega 399a-b[x] [5] St*e*rk: 'St[...]k' B, 'St(er)k'(?) 399a-b[x].

Editions: *Skj* Gamli kanóki, 2. *Harmsól* 35: AI, 567, BI, 557, *Skald* I, 270; Sveinbjörn Egilsson 1844, 24, Kempff 1867, 11, Rydberg 1907, 26, Black 1971, 229, Attwood 1996a, 230.

Notes: [1] meg*u* 'can': B's *mega*, as represented through 399a-b[x], must be emended to give the correct form of the 3rd pers. pl. pres. indic. of this pret.-pres. verb. — [3-4] *gœzkufyldr guðs* 'grace-filled God is': Cf. *Leið* 17/3-4, where God is described as *gœzkufimr* 'grace-skilled'. For the semantic field of *gœzka*, see Walter 1976, 69. — [5] *sterk* 'strong, mighty':

B is badly worn, and only 'St...k' is legible. The reading here is supplied from the next occurrence of the second *stef* at fol. 13r, l. 19 (st. 40), where the word is written out in full. An obelos in the right margin at fol. 13r, l. 9 indicates the beginning of the poem's second *stef*. — [6] *konung dagstalls* 'king of the day-support [SKY/HEAVEN > = God]': Cf. *Mdr* 24/3-4, where Mary is referred to as *drotning dagstalls* 'queen of the day-support', and the similar heaven-kenning *hǫll dags* 'hall of day', which occurs twice in characterisations of God in *Leið*: 15/5-8 (*snjallr dróttinn dags hallar* 'wise lord of the day's hall') and 45/6 (*gramr dags hallar* 'prince of the day's hall').

36. Dómsorði lýkr dýrðar Spǫnð lætr ǫll til yndis
     dróttar valdr á aldir, óttlaust af því móti
     þars greinisk lið ljóna sunnu hvéls ok sælu
     loks í tvenna flokka.   sín bǫrn konungr fjǫrnis.

Valdr dróttar dýrðar lýkr dómsorði á aldir, þars lið ljóna greinisk loks í tvenna flokka. Konungr fjǫrnis hvéls sunnu lætr spǫnð ǫll bǫrn sín óttlaust af því móti til yndis ok sælu.

The ruler of the company of glory [ANGELS > = God] will pass judgement on men, where the host of men [MANKIND] will finally divide into two groups. The king of the helmet of the wheel of the sun [SUN > SKY/HEAVEN > = God] causes all his children to be drawn without fear from that gathering to joy and bliss.

Mss: **B**(13r), 399a-bˣ.

Editions: *Skj* Gamli kanóki, 2. *Harmsól* 36: AI, 567, BI, 557, *Skald* I, 270, *NN* §§2112A, 2113; Sveinbjörn Egilsson 1844, 24-5, Kempff 1867, 11, Rydberg 1907, 26, Black 1971, 231, Attwood 1996a, 230.

Notes: [All]: The division of men into two groups at the Last Judgement is a commonplace of Christian eschatology. The *locus classicus* is the parable of the sheep and the goats in Matt. XXV.32: *et congregabuntur ante eum omnes gentes et separabit eos ab invicem sicut pastor segregat oves ab hedis* 'and all nations shall be gathered together before him, and he shall separate them one from another, as the shepherd separateth the sheep from the goats'. The same idea is expressed in Arnórr jarlaskáld's *helmingr* on the Last Judgement mentioned in the Note to st. 33/2-3. — [1] *dómsorði* 'judgement': The cpd refers specifically to Christ's Judgement of humanity. Cf. *Fritzner*: *dómsorð*; Lange 1958a, 148. — [1-2] *valdr dróttar dýrðar* 'the ruler of the company of glory [ANGELS > = God]': Finnur Jónsson (*Skj* B) understands this phrase as *han som giver mennesken hæder* 'he who gives men glory'. This seems dubious, since the cl. as a whole relates to God's passing judgement on men. Kock (*NN* §2112A) prefers to take both *dýrðar* and *dróttar* as gen., forming an angel-kenning meaning 'company of glory' or (if *dýrð* 'glory' can be used metaphorically, as in Modern English, to mean 'heaven') 'company of heaven'. The *valdr* 'ruler' of this company is God. — [5] *spǫnð lætr ǫll til yndis*: Cf. *Pl* 54/5, *spandi ítr til yndis*. — [6] *óttlaust af því móti*: See Note on 32/4. Kock (*NN* §2113) suggests that *óttlaust* 'without fear' in this context acts as a meaningless filler-word, with the sense 'certainly, assuredly'. — [8] *sín bǫrn* 'his children': The tone and phraseology recall Malachi's prophecy of the Day of the Lord: *et erunt mihi ait Dominus exercituum in die qua ego facio in peculium et parcam eis sicus parcit vir filio suo servienti sibi* 'and they shall be my special possession, saith the Lord of hosts, in the day that I do judgement: and I will spare them, as a man spareth his son that serveth him' (Mal. III.17).

37. Gumar líta þá gæti   Oss skyldi sú aldri
 — gengr allt við kjǫr drengjum   unaðsgnótt fira dróttins
 heilags Krists — í hæstum   — þars ǫrsløngvi engum
 himinljóma guðdómi.   angrsamt — ór hug *ganga*.

Gumar líta þá gæti himinljóma í hæstum guðdómi; allt gengr drengjum við kjǫr heilags Krists. Sú unaðsgnótt fira dróttins skyldi aldri *ganga* oss ór hug; þars engum ǫrsløngvi angrsamt.

Men will look then upon the guardian of the light of heaven [SUN > = God (= Christ)] in his highest Godhead; everything will go for men according to the decision of holy Christ. That abundant bliss [*lit.* bliss of abundance] of the men of the Lord [CHRISTIAN PEOPLE] should never pass out of our minds; no arrow-slinger [MAN] is sorrowful there.

Mss: **B**(13r), 399a-b[x]. — *Readings*: [1] Gumar: *so* 399a-b[x], '[...]umar' B   [5] Oss: *so* 399a-b[x], 'o[...]' B   [8] *ganga*: '[...]' B, 'ganga'(?) 399a-b[x], '[...](a)'(?) B*Rydberg*, (gang)a(?) B*FJ*.

Editions: *Skj* Gamli kanóki, 2. Harmsól 37: AI, 567, BI, 557-8, *Skald* I, 270, *NN* §2926; Sveinbjörn Egilsson 1844, 25, Kempff 1867, 11, Rydberg 1907, 26, Jón Helgason 1935-6, 252, Black 1971, 234, Attwood 1996a, 230.

Notes: [1-4]: Finnur Jónsson (*Skj* B) construes *gumar líta þá gæti himinljóma í hæstum guðdómi heilags Krists; alt gengr drengjum við kør*, which he translates *mændene vil da se himmelglansens vogter i den hellige Kristus' höjeste guddom; alt vil gå mændene efter ønske* 'men will then see the guardian of the light of heaven in the highest Godhead of the holy Christ; everything will go for men according to their wishes'. Despite the objections of Kock (*NN* §2926) and Black (1971, 235) that this is theologically untenable, Finnur may have meant only that good Christians will have their wish, to live in bliss. Jón Helgason (1935-6, 252) follows Sveinbjörn Egilsson and Kempff in arranging *alt gengr drengjum heilags Krists við kjǫr* 'everything goes for the men of holy Christ according to choice', suggesting that both *drengjum heilags Krists* 'the men of holy Christ' and *dróttins fira* 'men of the lord' refer to the chosen, that is, the saved. This arrangement is adopted by both Kock and Black. However, a more powerful argument is for *kjǫr* 'choice, decision' to be understood with *heilags Krists* to refer to Christ's role in deciding whether the souls of the dead are saved and allowed to enter heaven or damned, as described in st. 38. This interpretation has the support of John V.22 and the Apostles' Creed, which state that Christ is appointed to judge mankind: *neque enim Pater iudicat quemquam sed iudicium omne dedit Filio* 'for neither doth the Father judge any man, but hath given all judgement to the Son' (John V.22); *Credo in Jesum Christum ... inde venturus (est) judicare vivos et mortuos* 'I believe in Jesus Christ ... thence he shall come to judge the living and the dead' (Apostles' Creed). — [5-8]: This *helmingr* is very similar to *Leið* 35/5-8, which also concerns the Second Coming. — [6] *unaðsgnótt fira dróttins*: An almost identical l. occurs at 27/8, which reads *harms gnótt fira dróttinn*; also similar is the last l. of the poem *unaðsgnótt ok frið dróttinn* (65/8).

38. Þjóð á hart, sús hlýða
    hildings boðum vildat
    lofða kyns meðan lifði,
    lýtum kend fyr hendi.

    Sú rasar aum í aumar
    óvísligar píslir;
    ey grœtir þar ýta
    uggr, en vætki huggar.

Þjóð, kend lýtum, sús vildat hlýða boðum hildings kyns lofða meðan lifði, á hart fyr hendi. Sú rasar aum í aumar, óvísligar píslir; uggr grœtir þar ýta ey, en vætki huggar.

That group of people, known for sins, who would not heed the commandments of the prince of the race of men [MANKIND > RULER = Christ] while it lived, faces hardship. It rushes wretched into wretched, uncertain tortures; fear grieves people there perpetually, and nothing affords comfort.

Mss: **B**(13r), 399a-b[x]. — *Readings*: [4] kend: '[...]' B, 'k[...]nd' 399a-b[x] [8] huggar: *so* 399a-b[x], 'huga[...]' B.

Editions: *Skj* Gamli kanóki, 2. Harmsól 38: AI, 567, BI, 558, *Skald* I, 270, *NN* §§2805, 2926; Sveinbjörn Egilsson 1844, 25, Kempff 1867, 11-12, Rydberg 1907, 27, Black 1971, 236, Attwood 1996a, 231.

Notes: [4] *kend* 'known': B is badly worn, and it is not possible to identify the traces of possibly two letters which remain. 399a-b[x] read 'k...nd' with certainty, and a second hand (identified by Sveinbjörn Egilsson 1844, 25 n. 48, as that of Jón Sigurðsson) supplied 'kend'. This reconstruction is confirmed by the *aðalhending* with *hendi*, and has been adopted by all subsequent eds. — [6] *óvísligar* (f. acc. pl.) 'uncertain': So B, 399a-b[x], Kempff and Rydberg; *Skj* A reads *æ vísligar*, which is followed by *Skj* B, Kock, Jón Helgason (1935-6, 252) and Black, the first word being understood as the adv. *æ* 'always'. Finnur Jónsson (*Skj* B) construes *sú rasar æ aum í aumar vísligar píslir*, which he translates *de styrter altid elendige i elendige visse pinsler* 'they rush always miserable into miserable certain torments'. Kock (*NN* §2805) takes the *æ* 'always' as modifying *vísligar píslir*, understood in apposition to *aumar* 'wretched'.

39. Fnyk þola flærðar auknir
    fleygjendr þrimu leygjar
    — þar liggr elds á ǫldum
    íma — frost með bríma.

    Mǫrgs ǫnnur þar manna
    meiri ógn ok fleira
    angr, an ór megi tunga,
    óvegs, frá því segja.

Fleygjendr leygjar þrimu, auknir flærðar, þola fnyk, frost með bríma; þar liggr íma elds á ǫldum. Mǫrgs ǫnnur meiri ógn óvegs manna þar ok fleira angr, an tunga ór megi segja frá því.

Flingers of the flame of battle [SWORD > WARRIORS], swollen with falsehood, endure stench, frost with flame; there lie embers of fire upon men. Many another greater terror for dishonourable men is there and more sorrow than our [my] tongue is able to describe.

Mss: **B**(13r), 399a-b˟. — *Readings*: [4] bríma: *so* 399a-b˟, '[...]ma' B [5] Mǫrgs: mǫrg eru B.

Editions: *Skj* Gamli kanóki, 2. *Harmsól* 39: AI, 567-8, BI, 558, *Skald* I, 271, *NN* §§21, 2806; Sveinbjörn Egilsson 1844, 25-6, Kempff 1867, 12, Rydberg 1907, 27, Black 1971, 238, Attwood 1996a, 231.

Notes: [1] *auknir flærðar* 'swollen with falsehood': Kock (*NN* §21) suggests that *flærð* means 'folly', and that, in a religious text, it should be interpreted as 'godlessness' or 'recklessness'. — [2] *fleygjendr* 'flingers': *Skj* B normalises B's 'fleygendr' to *fleygjendr*, *nomen agentis* from *fleygja* (weak class 1) 'to make fly'. All subsequent eds have adopted this form. — [3-4] *þar liggr íma elds á ǫldum* 'there lie embers of fire upon men': The problem here concerns both the case and meaning of ms. 'ima'. There is a complex of semantically related nouns in ON: *ím* n. 'dust, ashes', *íma* f. 'battle, she-wolf ('dusky one'), and *ímr* m. 'wolf ('dusky') (see *LP*: *íma*, *ímr*). Sveinbjörn Egilsson (cf. *LP* (1860): *íma*) and Kempff retain the ms. reading *íma*, taking this as the nom. form of *íma* f. in the sense 'embers', for which there is no other attested example in either poetry or prose. Finnur Jónsson (*Skj* B) emends to *ímu*, and arranges *þar liggr frost með bríma á ímu elds ǫldum* 'there lies frost with flame on the men of the fire of battle [SWORD > WARRIORS]'. He takes *íma* f. to mean 'battle', a sense attested in several poems, whose *eldr* is a sword (see also *LP*: *íma*, *ǫld*). Kock accepts this emendation without comment. — [5] *mǫrgs*: B's reading *eru* must be emended both from a grammatical point of view (*ógn* is f. nom. sg.) and from a metrical point of view (in a type E l.).

40. Mjǫk gengr móttr ok ríki   Sterk lofar drótt ok dýrkar
     mæts varðanda jarðar   dagstalls konung snjallan;
     — lýð dugir helzt at hræðask   himins es fylkir fremri
     hann — of allt vit manna.   fróðr hvívetna góðu.

Móttr ok ríki mæts varðanda jarðar gengr mjǫk of allt vit manna; lýð dugir helzt at hræðask hann. Sterk drótt lofar ok dýrkar snjallan konung dagstalls; fróðr fylkir himins es fremri hvívetna góðu.

The might and power of the glorious guardian of the earth [= God] surpasses greatly all the understanding of men; it befits people most of all to fear him. The mighty host praises and glorifies the excellent king of the day-support [SKY/HEAVEN > = God]; the wise king of heaven [= God] is superior to everything that is good.

Mss: **B**(13r), 399a-b˟. — *Readings*: [4] vit: *so* 399a-b˟, '[...]it' B [5-8]: *abbrev. as* 'Sterk lofar drott ok d.' B.

Editions: *Skj* Gamli kanóki, 2. *Harmsól* 40: AI, 568, BI, 558, *Skald* I, 271; Sveinbjörn Egilsson 1844, 26, Kempff 1867, 12, Rydberg 1907, 27, Black 1971, 240, Attwood 1996a, 231.

Notes: [5-8]: Repetition of the *stef* is indicated by an obelos in the left margin at fol. 13r, l. 19.

41. Kosti hverr við harra
— hætts ella mjǫk — sættask
byrjar láðs — hvat bíðum?
bl*i*kvaldr þrimu tjald*a*.

Opt verðr Ægis leiptra
ein stund viðum grundar
— *n*auðr erumk ǫll at eyða
andar mein — at seinum.

Hverr bl*i*kvaldr tjald*a* þrimu kosti sættask við harra láðs byrjar; ella [e]s mjǫk hætt; hvat bíðum? Opt verðr ein stund at seinum viðum leiptra grundar Ægis; *n*auðr erumk at eyða ǫll mein andar.

Let every wielder of the gleam of the tents of battle [(*lit.* 'gleam-wielder of the tents of battle') SHIELDS > SWORD > WARRIOR] try to reconcile himself with the lord of the land of the fair wind [SKY/HEAVEN > = God]; otherwise, there is great danger; what are we waiting for? Often one hour will be too late for the trees of the lightnings of the plain of Ægir <sea-king> [SEA > GOLD > MEN]; it is a necessity for me to blot out all injuries of the spirit.

Mss: **B**(13r), 399a-b^x. — *Readings*: [3] láðs: *so* 399a-b^x, 'la[...]' B [4] bl*i*kvaldr: blakkvaldr B; tjald*a*: 'tiallde' B [7] *n*auðr: '[...]a[...]dr' B, '[...]auðr' 399a-b^x, B*Rydberg*, B*FJ*; eyða: *so* 399a-b^x, 'y[...]' B.

Editions: *Skj* Gamli kanóki, 2. Harmsól 41: AI, 568, BI, 558-9, *Skald* I, 271, *NN* §§2926, 2933; Sveinbjörn Egilsson 1844, 26, Kempff 1867, 12, Rydberg 1907, 27, Jón Helgason 1935-6, 258-9, Black 1971, 241, Attwood 1996a, 232.

Notes: [1-4]: The ms. reads *blakkvaldr þrimu tjaldi* (l. 4) and it is clear from the context that this is a man-kenning. Finnur Jónsson (*Skj* B) assumes the man-kenning here to be *blakkvaldr láðs byrjar* 'horse-steerer of the land of the wind [SEA > SHIP > SEAFARER]'. He then emends B's *þrimu* to *þrumu* gen. sg. of *þruma* 'thunder', to form the God-kenning *harri þrumu tjalda* 'king of the thunder-tents'. This makes for a rather cumbersome cl.-arrangement in the *helmingr*. Jón Helgason (1935-6, 258) dismisses Finnur's interpretation of *láðs byrjar* '[of the] land of the wind' as a sea-kenning as rather unlikely. Instead, he indicates that one would expect it to mean 'heaven', like, for example, *byrjar vegr* 'path of the wind', *éla vangr* 'field of the storm'. If this interpretation is correct, *láðs byrjar* must be construed with *harra* acc. sg. of *harri* 'lord' (l. 1) to give a straightforward God-kenning in the acc. case. The w.o. is thus simplified considerably. Finnur's emendation to *þruma* is unnecessary, since *þrimu* can be taken as gen. sing. of *þrima* 'thunder', which by a transfer of meaning is often used for 'battle' (see *LP*: *þrima*). Emendation to *tjalda*, gen. pl. would give *blakkvaldr þrimu tjalda* 'horse-steerer of the tents of battle [SHIELDS > SHIP > SEAFARER]'. Jón Helgason (1935-6, 258) suggests that this kenning's lack of regularity might be alleviated by a minor emendation to *blikvaldr* 'gleam-wielder'. *Blikvaldr þrimu tjalds* (or *tjalda*) would provide a straightforward warrior-kenning, 'wielder of the gleam of the tent(s) of battle [SHIELD(S) > SWORD > WARRIOR]'. Kock (*NN* §2933) concurs with Jón's arrangement, and with his interpretation of *láðs byrjar*. However, he argues that emendation may be unnecessary, since the connection between ships and shields in poetry is so close that a kenning 'shield's steed' for 'ship' is not impossible (cf. Black 1971, 243). Although, as Kock suggests, there are a small number of kennings for 'shield' which have 'ship' as their determinant (see *Meissner*, 166-9; *LP*: *skip*), this is scarcely grounds for arguing that the two entities were interchangeable, or that the poem's original hearers would have understood *blakkr tjalda prímu* 'horse of the tents of battle' to mean 'ship'. There is no comparable kenning in which a shield-*heiti* is used as the determinant of a ship-kenning. Sword-kennings like *blik prímu tjalda* on the 'light, flame of the shield' model are extremely common (see *Meissner*, 150-1; *LP*: *blik*), and *blik* here anticipates the man-kenning *viðir leiptra grundar Ægis* 'the trees of the lightnings of the plain of Ægir' in the second *helmingr*. Jón Helgason's emendation has been adopted here. — [2-3]: Kempff, Finnur Jónsson and Kock follow Sveinbjörn Egilsson in taking *hvat bíðum* (l. 3) as part of the same sentence as *hætts ella mjök* (l. 2). Finnur translates *ellers er det meget uvist hvad vi opnår* 'otherwise what we will receive is most uncertain' (*Skj* B). Jón Helgason (1935-6, 259) claims that there is no reason to believe that the two clauses are connected, and suggests that *hætts ella mjök* should be taken to mean 'otherwise, there is [*or* will be] great danger' while *hvat bíðum* is construed as a straightforward question 'what are we waiting for?' This makes for a more straightforward w.o. than does Sveinbjörn's arrangement, and makes a strong connection between the *helmingar*. Besides, as st. 39 makes clear, the poet is unlikely to imply that the fate of those who fail to reconcile themselves with God is in any way uncertain! — [5-6] *viðum leiptra grundar Ægis* 'for trees of the lightnings of the plain of Ægir [SEA > GOLD > MEN]': Cf. 53/5-8, where God is characterised as *láðvaldr glóða hróts leiptra* 'land-king of the fires of the roof of lightnings'. — [7] *nauðr*: B is badly damaged at this point and only '...a...dr' can be read. None of the previous readers of the ms. were able to supply the beginning of the word, though the scribe of the 399a-b[x] transcript read the remainder of the word with confidence as '...auðr'. Sveinbjörn Egilsson suggested in a note to Jón Sigurðsson's copy (444[x]) that the word might be *trauðir* m. nom. pl. of *trauðr* 'reluctant', and used the form *trauðr* in his 1844 edn and in his prose arrangement (preserved in 444[x]). Kempff and Finnur Jónsson adopted this reconstruction. It is unlikely, however, that the space for the initial letter at the beginning of fol. 13r, l. 21 is sufficient to account for the loss of *tr* here, and Rydberg (1907, lxxii) and Jón Helgason (1935-6, 259) are agreed that there is space for only one letter before *a*. Furthermore, as Rydberg (1907, 27 n. 7) notes, in the following l. (fol. 13r, l. 22), the 'a' in *trauð* is abbreviated with the ω-like sign. Rydberg is in no doubt that the traces of the original letter seen by him suggest that *nauðr* f. 'need, necessity' is the correct reading here. He compares the parallel construction in *Leið* 15/3-4, which reads *nauðr er þegnum þýðask þann veg* 'there is a need for men to receive that glory'. Kock adopts this reading (*Skald*) and it is also adopted here.

42. Ungr skyldi þat ǫldu
 eyktemjandi fremja,
 gífrs es gǫmlum hœfir
 gunntjalds boða at halda.

 Trauð verðr hǫnd, en hlýða
 hrynvengis má engum
 Gaut, nema gǫr verk bœti,
 grundar mens, af venju.

Ungr eyktemjandi ǫldu skyldi fremja þat es hœfir gǫmlum boða gífrs gunntjalds at halda. Hǫnd verðr trauð, en engum Gaut hrynvengis mens grundar má hlýða, nema bœti verk gǫr af venju.

A young tamer of the horse of the wave [(*lit.* 'horse-tamer of the wave') SHIP > SEAFARER] should do what it befits an old messenger of the troll-wife of the battle-tent [SHIELD > AXE > WARRIOR] to keep doing. The hand becomes unwilling, but no Gautr <= Óðinn> of the ringing-land of the necklace of the earth [= Miðgarðsormr > GOLD > MAN] may be saved, unless he makes reparation for deeds done out of habit.

Mss: **B**(13r), 399a-b[x]. — *Readings*:   [6] hrynvengis: 'hrǫn[...]engiss' B, 'hrǫnvengiss' 399a-b[x] [8] *af*: á B.

Editions: *Skj* Gamli kanóki, 2. *Harmsól* 42: AI, 568, BI, 559, *Skald* I, 271; Sveinbjörn Egilsson 1844, 26, Kempff 1867, 13, Rydberg 1907, 27, Black 1971, 244, Attwood 1996a, 232.

Notes: [All]: Gamli's injunction to his younger hearers recalls his confession of his own early sins in st. 7. The tone is reminiscent of Solomon's advice to his son in Eccl. XII.1 *memento creatoris tui in diebus iuventutis tuae antequam veniat tempus adflictionis et adpropinquent anni de quibus dicas non mihi placent* 'remember thy Creator in the days of thy youth, before the time of affliction come, and the years draw nigh of which thou shalt say: They please me not'. — [3] *gífr* 'hag, troll-woman': Commonly used as a *heiti* for a troll or, more often, a trollwife (see *Vsp* 52/6). By extension, *gífr* is often used, as here, to convey the notion of 'enemy', 'danger' or 'bane' and is frequently the base-word of kennings for the battle-axe (see *LP*: *gífr*). — [4] *gunntjalds* 'of the battle-tent [SHIELD]': Cf. 41/4. The cpd also occurs in Sturl *Hrafn* 20/4[II]. — [6] *hrynvengis* 'of the ringing-land [GOLD]': 399a-b[x] is certain that B's reading (now worn) was 'hrǫnvengis' 'of the wave-land [SEA]'. It is difficult to make sense of this cpd here, and this edn follows all others in adopting Kempff's emendation (1867, 49) to *hrynvengis*, giving the cpd *hrynvengi* 'resounding, ringing land', which, with a determinant denoting a serpent (here the Miðgarðsormr or World-Serpent) means 'gold'. Such kennings refer to legendary dragons lying on gold to guard it; cf. RvHbreiðm *Hl* 36/4[III] *hrynvengi sefþvengjar* 'ringing-land of the sedge-thong [SERPENT > GOLD]'. — [7-8] *gǫr af venju* 'done out of habit': Here this phrase is taken with the cl. *nema bœti verk* 'unless he makes reparation'. Other eds (*Skj* B, *Skald*) take it with *hǫnd verðr trauð* 'the hand becomes unwilling out of habit' (l. 5), and this interpretation is also possible. It suggests that, because it is difficult to break a habit, one should begin to perform good deeds while young. — [8] *mens grundar* 'of the necklace of the earth [= Miðgarðsormr]': Finnur Jónsson offers two possible interpretations in *LP*. In the entry on *grund*, this phrase is listed among the kennings for 'sea', presumably based on the assumption of ON myth that the round earth was encircled by the sea. In this case it is difficult to understand what might be meant by the sea's *hrynvengi* 'ringing land'. In the entry on *hrynvengi*, the translation *slangens klingende land* 'the serpent's ringing-land' is suggested. This is close to the kenning from RvHbreiðm *Hl*[III] cited above. In this case, *men grundar* may either be a kenning for a snake or, more likely in terms of the ON myth that placed the World Serpent in the ocean surrounding the earth, a specific allusion to Miðgarðsormr. It has been interpreted in the latter sense here. — [8] *af*: B is undamaged here, and 'a' is clear. Sveinbjörn Egilsson (1844, 27 n. 52) suggests *af*, which has been adopted by all subsequent eds.

43. Ræfrs esat lǫngu lífi   Þvís hringstyrja*r* hverjum
      lun*g*beit*ǫ*ndum heitit   hag sinn með trú fagri
      — r*au*n finna *þess* runnar yngra þoll ok ellra
      randéls — af gram landa.   einsætt at vel hreinsi.

Lun*g*beit*ǫ*ndum esat heitit lǫngu lífi af gram ræfrs landa; runnar randéls finna r*au*n *þess*. Þvís einsætt hverjum þoll hringstyrja*r*, yngra ok ellra, at hreinsi vel hag sinn með fagri trú.

Ship-steerers [MEN] are not promised long life by the prince of the roof of lands [SKY/HEAVEN > = God]; bushes of the shield-storm [BATTLE > WARRIORS] gain experience of that. Therefore it is evident to each fir-tree of the sword-din [BATTLE > WARRIOR], to young and old, that he should thoroughly purify his state with beautiful faith.

Mss: **B**(13r), 399a-b[x]. — *Readings*: [2] lun*g*beit*ǫ*ndum: 'lunndbeitundum' B   [3] r*au*n: 'rum' B; *þess*: þat B, 399a-b[x]   [5] hringstyrja*r*: 'hringstyr[...] a' B, 'hringstyri a' 399a-b[x].

Editions: *Skj* Gamli kanóki, 2. *Harmsól* 43: AI, 568, BI, 559, *Skald* I, 271; Sveinbjörn Egilsson 1844, 27, Kempff 1867, 13, Konráð Gíslason and Eiríkur Jónsson 1875-89, II, 356, Rydberg 1907, 27, Jón Helgason 1935-36, 259, Black 1971, 247, Attwood 1996a, 232.

Notes: [1-4] *gram ræfrs landa* 'prince of the roof of lands [SKY/HEAVEN = God]': Cf. *Leið* 10/1-2, where God is characterised as *vǫrðr vallræfrs* 'guardian of the plain-roof'. — [2] *lungbeitǫndum* 'to ship-steerers [MEN]': It is not possible to make sense of B's reading 'lunndbeitundum'. Sveinbjörn Egilsson (note to 444[x] transcript and 1844, 27 n. 5) corrects to *lungbeitǫndum*, which has been adopted by all subsequent eds. — [4] *randéls af gram landa*: B's reading of the first word is quite clear here, though *Skj* B and Kempff emend to *randelds* 'of the shield-fire'. B's reading is perhaps confirmed by the similar l. *brandél á Girklandi* in *Geisl* 51/2. — [5] *þvís hringstyrjar hverjum*: The ms. reading 'því er hringstýr...a huerium' is rather problematical. Konráð Gíslason suggested that the l. originally read 'því er hrings fira hverjum', but had been garbled in transmission. He postulated the arrangement *því er fira hverjum, hrings yngra þoll ok ellra* 'therefore is to each man, the younger tree of the ring and the older'. Sveinbjörn Egilsson, followed by Kempff, adopted the 399a-b[x] reading 'hringstyre' (from *hring stýri*), overlooking the final 'a' in B. Finnur Jónsson, who read 'hringstyre a' (*Skj* A), emended to *hringskúrar* ('of the ring [i.e. sword]-shower'), giving a battle- and (with *þollr* 'fir-tree') a warrior-kenning. Rydberg (1907, lxxiii) suggested a palaeographical solution to this difficulty. The scribe, he notes, uses <e> and <i> in word-final position without distinction. Rydberg suggests that the copyist interpreted the final <i> in 'hringstýri' as a final vowel, and altered it to an 'e' which is now lost in B. The <i> was in fact consonantal and was followed either by <a> (as the remains in B suggest) or by an *ar* abbreviation. The reading is then *hringstýrjar* (gen. sg.) 'of sword-din', which gives a man-kenning *þollr hringstýrjar* 'tree of the sword-din'. Rydberg's suggestion is perhaps confirmed by 399a-b[x]'s reading 'hringstýri a', which suggests that confusion over consonantal <i> (not, we note, normalised to <e>) originated with the B copyist. Rydberg's elegant solution is adopted by Jón Helgason (1935-

6, 259), Kock and Black, as well as here. — [5] *hag* 'state': This word, which is difficult to translate adequately, occurs several times in *Has*, always with reference to the effects of sin on a man's spiritual condition. Its resonances appear to be at once specific (as in 49/2) and general (12/6-8), and it seems to refer to situations palpable (49/2) and psychological (23/7, 43/6). In his confession of sin in thought, word and deed (st. 12), Gamli admits that *margir hagir mínir sýnask mér meginljótir* 'many of my actions seem to me extremely ugly' (12/6-8). The penitent thief fears that, unless Christ listens to his pleas for mercy, *ek á til hættan hag* 'I am in a rather too perilous situation' (23/7). Similarly, in st. 49, King David is said to have decided to ask God for mercy *eftir þungan hag* 'after his grievous (*lit.* 'heavy') sinfulness' (49/2), *hagr* presumably being used to allude to David's adultery with Bathsheba and the death of her husband, Uriah the Hittite (see Note to st. 48).

44. Leygs hefr dánardœgri
dáðreyndr jǫfurr leynða
svana flugreinar sínu
sviptendr jǫru skriptar,

því frónspennir finna
fagrtjalda vill aldri
dœlar seiðs við dauða
dúnmeiða vanbúna.

Dáðreyndr jǫfurr leygs flugreinar svana hefr leynða sviptendr skriptar jǫru dánardœgri sínu, því fagrtjalda frónspennir vill aldri finna dœlar seiðs dúnmeiða vanbúna við dauða.

The deed-proven prince of the flame of the flying-land of swans [SKY/HEAVEN > SUN > = God] has concealed from the brisk movers of the icon of battle [SHIELD > WARRIORS] their death-day, because the clasper of the fair tents of the earth [(*lit.* 'earth-clasper of the fair tents') SKY/HEAVEN > = God] wishes never to find the trees of the feather-bed of the fish of the dell [(*lit.* 'feather-bed-trees of the fish of the dell') SNAKE > GOLD > MEN] unprepared for death.

Mss: **B**(13r), 399a-b[x]. — *Reading*: [3] svana: 'suo na' B, 399a-b[x].

Editions: *Skj* Gamli kanóki, 2. Harmsól 44: AI, 568, BI, 559, *Skald* I, 271; Sveinbjörn Egilsson 1844, 27, Kempff 1867, 13, Konráð Gíslason and Eiríkur Jónsson 1875-89, II, 356, Rydberg 1907, 27-8, Black 1971, 250, Attwood 1996a, 233.

Notes: [1-3] *dáðreyndr jǫfurr leygs flugreinar svana* 'deed-proven prince of the flame of the flying-land of swans [SKY/HEAVEN > SUN > = God]': B's reading 'suo na' in l. 3 presents some difficulties. This edn follows Finnur Jónsson, Kock and Black in adopting Konráð Gíslason's (and Eiríkur Jónsson 1875-89, II, 356) emendation to *svana* (gen. pl.), which makes for an acceptable Christ-kenning. A conceptually similar, though less complex, God-kenning occurs in *Pl* 28/2-3 *ítr stillir leiðar gagls* 'glorious ruler of the path of the goose'. — [5-6] *frónspennir fagrtjalda* 'clasper of the fair tents of the earth [SKY/HEAVEN > = God]': See Note to *skríngeypnandi skýstalls* 29/7-8. — [7] *seiðs* (gen. sg.) 'fish': Specifically, the saithe or coalfish (*gadus virens*). Both Rydberg and Finnur Jónsson (*Skj* A) read the initial consonant as <l>, not <s>, and it is easy to see why: the letter in B has an ascender with right-leaning final stroke that is more similar to this scribe's <l>s than to his <s>s. However, Finnur may have changed his mind, for *Skj* B has *seiðr* here.

45. Háborgar, fæsk hvergi   Sterk lofar drótt ok dýrkar
hald, þats bresti aldri,   dagstalls konung snjallan;
hreggs nema horskum seggjum   himins es fylkir fremri
heitfastr jǫfurr veiti.   fróðr hvívetna góðu.

Hvergi fæsk hald, þats aldri bresti, nema heitfastr jǫfurr háborgar hreggs veiti horskum seggjum. Sterk drótt lofar ok dýrkar snjallan konung dagstalls; fróðr fylkir himins es fremri hvívetna góðu.

Nowhere is found that help which never fails, unless the promise-faithful prince of the high fortress of the storm [SKY/HEAVEN > = God] may grant [it] to prudent men. The mighty host praises and glorifies the glorious king of the day-support [SKY/HEAVEN > = God]; the excellent king of heaven [= God] is superior to everything that is good.

Mss: **B**(13r), 399a-bˣ. — *Readings*: [4] veiti: *so* 399a-bˣ, '[...](e)ite'(?) B   [5] Sterk lofar drótt: *abbrev. as* 'Sterk lofar drott ok d.' B.

Editions: *Skj* Gamli kanóki, 2. *Harmsól* 45: AI, 568, BI, 560, *Skald* I, 271, *NN* §1206; Sveinbjörn Egilsson 1844, 27-8, Kempff 1867, 13-14, Rydberg 1907, 28, Black 1971, 252, Attwood 1996a, 233.

Notes: [1-4] *jǫfurr háborgar hreggs* 'prince of the high fortress of the storm [SKY/HEAVEN > = God]': God-kennings involving the adj. *hár* 'high' in conjunction with a heaven-kenning meaning 'abode of the weather', where the 'weather' element is supplied by *hregg* 'storm' occur in both *Has* and *Leið*. Cf. the opening of *Has*, where God is hailed as *hár stillir hreggtjalda* 'high ruler of the storm-tents' (1/1-2) and *jǫfurr hás hreggranns* 'prince of the high storm-house' (*Leið* 17/1-2), a more complicated version of which occurs in 2/1-3: *harri hás hreggranns fagrgims* 'king of the high stormhouse of the fair jewel'. — [3] *horskum seggjum* 'to prudent men': Kock (*NN* §§224, 1206) notes that this phrase may be construed as belonging to either cl. in the first *helmingr*, giving either the arrangement adopted here, or that adopted by Finnur Jónsson (*Skj* B): *hvergi fæsk hald horskum seggjum, þats aldri bresti* 'nowhere is found help for prudent men which never fails'. — [5-8]: The third and final instance of *stef* 2.

46. Enn lætk sagðan svinnum   Þjóð mun sýna síðan
sárklungrs viðum þungan   slœmr miskunnar dœmi,
hótt, þats hvern dag ættim   — ek *sky*lda *þó* aldri
hræðask, framm í kvæði.   ugglauss — þaus mik hugga.

Enn lætk sagðan framm í kvæði svinnum viðum sárklungrs þungan hótt, þats ættim hræðask hvern dag. Slœmr mun síðan sýna þjóð dœmi miskunnar, þaus hugga mik — ek *sky*lda *þó* aldri ugglauss.

Further I will relate in the poem to the wise trees of the wound-thorn [SWORD > WARRIORS], the oppressive way of life concerning that which we should fear every day. The *slœmr* will then show people examples of mercy, which comfort me — yet I ought never [be] without fear.

Mss: **B**(13r), 399a-b˟. — *Readings*: [2] sárklungrs: sárklungr B   [3] þats hvern ('þat er hvern'): so 399a-b˟, 'þat [...]r' B   [7] sky*l*da þó: '[...]o' B, '[...]llda þó' 399a-b˟, '[...](a) þó'(?) B*Rydberg*, '[...](llda) þó'(?) B*FJ*.

Editions: *Skj* Gamli kanóki, 2. *Harmsól* 46: AI, 568-9, BI, 560, *Skald* I, 271, *NN* §1207; Sveinbjörn Egilsson 1844, 28, Kempff 1867, 14, Rydberg 1907, 28, Black 1971, 254, Attwood 1996a, 233.

Notes: [3] *þats* 'concerning that which': Because the antecedent *hǫtt* 'way of life' is m. acc. sg. and *þats* is n. nom. or acc. sg., the cl. cannot be a rel. one. Kock (*NN* §1207) suggests a nominal expression, expanded as a cl. *Skj* B's '*þats* (*þanns*)' in the prose order indicates uncertainty. — [6] *slœmr*: The concluding section of a *drápa*, which begins after the final *stef* of the middle section (*stefjabálkr*). — [7] sky*l*da þó 'ought yet': Sveinbjörn Egilsson (1844, 28 n. 58) suggests this reading, which has been adopted by all subsequent eds.

47. Lítk optliga ýta
    ólíkan mik fíkjum
    — aukumsk sǫ́r í slíku
    sótt — ástvinum dróttins.

    Þeir bundusk vel vándra
    verka ógnar sterkir,
    brigða skjótt ok bœttu
    bógsvells metendr, ella.

Lítk mik optliga fíkjum ólíkan ástvinum dróttins ýta; sǫ́r sótt aukumsk í slíku. Þeir metendr bógsvells, sterkir ógnar, bundusk vel vándra verka ok bœttu ella brigða skjótt.

I see myself often [as] terribly unlike the dear friends of the lord of men [= God > SAINTS]; bitter distress increases for me because of this. Those valuers of arm's ice [SILVER > MEN], strong in battle, kept themselves well away from evil deeds, or else made amends extremely quickly.

Mss: **B**(13r), 399a-b˟. — *Readings*: [3] í: so 399a-b˟, '[...]' B   [7] bœttu: 'b[...]' B, 'bȩ̄ṭṭu' 399a-b˟, 'b(ȇtt)[...]'(?) B*Rydberg*, 'bȇ(ttu)'(?) B*FJ*.

Editions: *Skj* Gamli kanóki, 2. *Harmsól* 47: AI, 569, BI, 560, *Skald* I, 272; Sveinbjörn Egilsson 1844, 28, Kempff 1867, 14, Rydberg 1907, 28, Black 1971, 256, Attwood 1996a, 233.

Notes: [1, 4] *ástvinum dróttins ýta* 'dear friends of the lord of men [= God > SAINTS]': *Ástvinr* 'dear friend' (lit. 'love-friend') is a popular designation of saints and Apostles in Christian poetry after Gamli and, apart from one appearance in Egill *St* 7/4^V, is found only in poetry dating from the C12th or later (*LP*: *ástvinr*). Arngrímr Brandsson's *drápa* on Guðmundr Árason twice characterises the bishop as *ástvinr ýta* 'dear friend of men' (Arngr *Gd* 18/1, 50/7^IV).

48. Frétt haf*a** dyggvar dróttir, Blíðr nam þengill þýðask
Dávíð konungr síðan — þats bann — konu annars,
snilli vanðr ept synðir en réð, svát bar brǫ́ðum,
siðabót at tók skjóta. búandmann* af því svanna.

Dyggvar dróttir haf*a** frétt, at Dávíð konungr, snilli vanðr, tók síðan skjóta siðabót ept synðir. Blíðr þengill nam þýðask konu annars — þats bann —, en réð af því búandmann* svanna, svát bar brǫ́ðum.

Worthy men have heard that King David, accustomed to eloquence, later made quick moral amends after his sins. The gentle king took pleasure in the wife of another man — that is forbidden — and for that reason brought about the death of the woman's husband, in such a way that it happened by surprise.

Mss: **B**(13r), 399a-b^x. — *Readings*: [1] haf*a**: 'hafum' B, 399a-b^x, 'hǫfum' B*Rydberg*, 'hofum' B*FJ* [4] siðabót: *so* 399a-b^x, 's[...]bot' B [8] búandmann*: '[...]uand mannz' B, 'buand mannz' 399a-b^x.

Editions: *Skj* Gamli kanóki, 2. *Harmsól* 48: AI, 569, BI, 272, *Skald* I, 272, *NN* §3243; Sveinbjörn Egilsson 1844, 28, Kempff 1867, 14, Rydberg 1907, 28, Black 1971, 258, Attwood 1996a, 234.

Notes: [1] *hafa** 'have': Finnur Jónsson, followed by Kock, Black, and this edn, emends B's 'hafum' (l. 1) to *hafa** in order to supply a verb in the 3rd pers. pl., and construes *dyggvar dróttir hafa frétt* 'worthy men have heard'. — [3] *snilli vanðr* 'accustomed to eloquence': Cf. *Leið* 6/6, where God is described as *snillifimr* 'prowess-nimble'. Both expressions appear to be *hap. leg*. Use of this cpd here to describe the Psalmist, David, is particularly appropriate. — [4] *siðabót* 'moral amends': Cf. 3/8. — [5-8]: The story of David's adultery with Bathsheba and the subsequent death of Bathsheba's husband, Uriah the Hittite, is recounted in 2 Sam. XI. — [8] *búandmann** 'husband': B's reading '[...]uand mannz' is gen. Sveinbjörn Egilsson (note to 444^x transcript and 1844, 28 n. 59) emends to *búandmann* acc., which has been adopted by all subsequent eds. — [8] *af því* 'for that reason': Kock (*NN* §3243) notes that the force of this phrase is consequential, rather than temporal. Gamli is implying that David arranged the death of Uriah as a consequence of his love for Bathsheba, not, as *Skj* B's translation *derefter* 'thereafter' suggests, merely after he had fallen in love with her.

49. Drengr réð brátt at beiða / buðlung ept hag þungan / hǫppum reifðr, sem hœfði, / himinríkis sér líkna. // Fekk an fyrr af sǫkkva / fríðr landreka síðan / — hann réttisk svá — sunnu / sætrs vingjafar mætri.

Drengr, hǫppum reifðr, réð brátt ept þungan hag at beiða buðlung himinríkis sér líkna, sem hœfði. Fríðr fekk síðan mætri vingjafar an fyrr af landreka sǫkkva sætrs sunnu; hann réttisk svá.

The man, endowed with successes, quickly resolved after his grievous sinfulness to beg the lord of the kingdom of heaven [= God] for mercies for himself, as was fitting. The noble one received then more glorious gifts of friendship than before from the land-ruler of the treasures of the seat of the sun [SKY/HEAVEN > HEAVENLY BODIES > = God]; he put himself right in this way.

Mss: **B**(13r), 399a-b^x. — *Readings*:   [3] hǫppum: *so* 399a-b^x, 'hǫpp[...]' B   [6] landrek*a*: landreki B   [7] réttisk: *so* 399a-b^x, 'retti[...]' B.

Editions: *Skj* Gamli kanóki, 2. *Harmsól* 49: AI, 569, BI, 560-1, *Skald* I, 272, *NN* §1208; Sveinbjörn Egilsson 1844, 29, Kempff 1867, 15, Rydberg 1907, 28, Jón Helgason 1935-6, 259-60, Black 1971, 261, Attwood 1996a, 234.

Notes: [All]: According to 2 Sam. XII, David's penance for his adultery and for the death of Uriah occurred only after considerable prompting from the prophet Nathan, and the death of his child by Bathsheba. Nonetheless, David is regularly presented as an example of repentance in medieval homiletic literature. Black (1971, 260) gives parallels in Gregory the Great's *Homilia* XXXIV (*Gregorius* I, cols 1256-7), which is cited in the ON-Icel. *Eluc* and in *HomÍsl* 1872, 63. — [2] *hag* 'sinfulness': See Note to 43/6. — [5-8]: Although the essential meaning and content of the second *helmingr* are clear, previous eds have encountered difficulties in resolving the w.o. and, more particularly, in identifying the God-kenning. At the heart of the problem is the ms. reading *sǫkkva* in l. 5, which is not in any doubt. Sveinbjörn Egilsson, followed by Kempff, construes the kenning *sǫkkvi sætrs sunnu*, which Kempff (1867, 52) translates 'creator of the seat of the sun'. No explanation is offered (but see *LP* (1860): *sǫkkvi*), and *sǫkkvi* meaning 'creator' is not attested elsewhere (see *LP*: *sǫkkvi*), the normal sense being 'adversary, enemy, slayer'. Finnur Jónsson (*Skj* B and *LP*: *sǫkkvi*) is unable to make sense of the ms. reading, and emends to *harra* gen. sg. of *harri* m. 'king, lord'. This creates the God-kenning *harri sætrs sunnu* 'king of the seat of the sun', which recalls the similar kennings *vísi setrs sunnu* (*Has* 13/6-8) and *siklingr setrs sunnu* (*Leið* 13/7-8). Kock (*NN* §§1057, 1208) takes *sǫkkva* as the gen. pl. of *sǫkk*, n., which he assumes to be cognate with OE *sinc*, meaning 'jewel, treasure'. Neither *AEW* nor Alexander Jóhannesson 1951-6 gives any etymology for *sǫkk* n., and the word is attested in neither *Fritzner* nor *CVC*. However, *sǫkk* seems to make one (other) appearance in skaldic poetry, in Egill *Arkv* 8/3^V, where it refers to the skald's eyes. If *sǫkk* is understood to mean 'jewel', the God-kenning, according to Kock, is then formed by taking *vinr* from *vingjafir* in l. 8, and construing either *vinr søkkva sunnu sætrs*, or *søkkvavinr sunnu sætrs* 'the generous lord of the seat of the sun [SKY/HEAVEN > = God]'. Jón Helgason (1935-6, 259-60) takes this one stage further. He accepts Kock's interpretation of *søkk* as meaning 'jewel' or 'treasure', but does not feel that *vinr søkkva sætrs sunnu* is compatible with other God-kennings in *Has*. Instead, Jón takes *søkk sætrs sunnu* to mean 'the treasure of heaven', in the sense of the heavenly bodies, which are described in similar terms in 4/2-3 (*hnossa himins* – see Note). Jón also notes that *landreki* 'ruler' (l. 6) is used elsewhere in *Has* only in kennings for God, viz. *landreki krapta* (15/6) and *landreki veðrs strandar* (61/6): 'I presume that *landreki* was originally part of the kenning for "God", which is found in this half-st. ..., but that a copyist, who believed that the word was used of King David here, altered a dat. *landreka* to the nom. *landreki*' (1935-6, 259). The God-kenning thus becomes *landreki søkkva sætrs sunnu* 'ruler of the jewels of the seat of the sun', which requires only minimal emendation, and fits well with the image-structure of the poem. Further evidence for *landreki*, rather than *vinr*, being the base-word here is afforded by the fact that the cpd *vingjǫf* (l. 8) is also used to describe the grace of God in *Pl* 28/7 and *Heildr* 17/8. This suggests that Jón's resistance to Kock's interpretation is well-founded.

50. Nítti einn við ótta
    ítr postoli rítar
    fróns musteris festi*
    forðum þýjar orða.

    Enn, þegars iðran sanna
    aldrprýðir fekk lýða,
    Pétr vann glœp með gráti
    grandlauss þvegit vandla.

Einn ítr postoli nítti forðum festi* rítar musteris fróns við ótta orða þýjar. Enn þegars aldrprýðir lýða fekk sanna iðran, vann grandlauss Pétr þvegit vandla glœp með gráti.

One glorious Apostle long ago denied the securer of the shield of the temple of the land [HEAVEN > SUN > = God (= Christ)] for fear of a bondswoman's words. But, as soon as the adorner of the lives of men [*lit*. life-adorner of men] [SAINT = Peter] experienced true repentance, the sinless Peter washed his wickedness away completely with weeping.

Mss: **B**(13r), 399a-b[x]. — *Readings*: [3] musteris: *so all others*, 'muster(i)[...]'(?) B; festi*: festir B   [4] forðum: *so* 399a-b[x], 'fo[...]um' B   [5] þegars: þegar B; iðran: *so* 399a-b[x], 'idra[...]' B   [8] grandlauss: *so* 399a-b[x], 'grand[...]uss' B.

Editions: *Skj* Gamli kanóki, 2. Harmsol 50: AI, 569, BI, 561, *Skáld* I, 272; Sveinbjörn Egilsson 1844, 29, Kempff 1867, 15, Rydberg 1907, 28-9, Black 1971, 263, Attwood 1996a, 234.

Notes: [All]: The Apostle Peter's denial of Christ after the latter's arrest is recounted in all four Gospels: Matt. XXVI.69-75, Mark XIV.66-72, Luke XXII.55-62 and John XVIII.16-18, 25-7. — [1] *nítti* 'denied': Sveinbjörn Egilsson (1844, 29 n. 60) claims that this is his correction, from B's 'Hítte'. In fact, 'Hítte' is Jón Sigurðsson's misreading (in the 444[x] transcript) of 399a-b's correct reading 'Nitte'. — [2] *ítr postoli rítar*: The *ítr* : *rítar* rhyme is also exploited in 26/4 and in *Leið* 42/2: *ítr túns himins rítar*. — [2-3] *festi* fróns musteris rítar* 'securer (dat.) of the shield of the temple of the land [HEAVEN > SUN > = God (=

Christ)]': This striking expression appears to be a conflation of two kenning-types found elsewhere in *Has*. In locutions like *rítar ranns éla* '(of the) shield of the house of storms' (26/3-4), the sun is characterised as the shield of heaven. The lexical parallels noted above may indicate that Gamli intends his readers/hearers to recall that image here. He superimposes it on the concept of heaven as a shrine or temple, which occurs in *skrín skýja* 'shrine of the clouds' (19/7-8) and *skrín skýstalls* 'shrine of the sky-platform' (29/7-8). Gamli uses the OFr loanword *musteri*, which derives from Lat. *monasterium* (*AEW*: *mustari*) and is used to designate a Christian or Jewish temple or church, rather than a *hof*, a heathen temple (*CVC*: *musteri*). The word is used of a Christian church in Anon *Vitn* 15/3 and Anon *Mv I* 15/2. — [5] *þegar*s 'as soon as': The emendation is necessary, as *þegar* functions here as a conj. (*þegar er*), rather than an adv. — [6] *aldrprýðir* 'life-adorner [of men]': This is *hap. leg.* Quite what the significance of this epithet is, in application to S. Peter, is uncertain, though there may be an oblique allusion to his traditional roles as founder of the church and holder of the keys to the gate of heaven.

51. Því lét seggja sveitar at bæri mun meiri
    sinn postola finna malmrunnum várkunnir,
    — raun lýsir þat — ræsir menn þótt misgǫrt vinni,
    ríkr óstyrkðir slíkar, margfríðr skǫrungr síðan.

Því lét ríkr ræsir sveitar seggja postola sinn finna slíkar óstyrkðir — raun lýsir þat —, at margfríðr skǫrungr bæri síðan mun meiri várkunnir malmrunnum, þótt menn vinni misgǫrt.

For this reason the powerful king of the company of men [MANKIND > = God (= Christ)] caused his Apostle to feel such weaknesses — experience shows that —, so that the very beautiful leader should later have considerably greater compassion for sword-trees [WARRIORS], even though men commit sins.

Mss: **B**(13r), 399a-b^x. — *Readings*: [4] óstyrkðir: *so* 399a-b^x, 'os[...]kter' B [5] meiri: *so* 399a-b^x, '[...]eire' B [8] skǫrungr: *so* 399a-b^x, '[...]rungr' B.

Editions: *Skj* Gamli kanóki, 2. Harmsól 51: AI, 569, BI, 561, Skald I, 272; Sveinbjörn Egilsson 1844, 29, Kempff 1867, 15, Rydberg 1907, 29, Jón Helgason 1935-6, 252, Black 1971, 265, Attwood 1996a, 234.

Notes: [3] *raun lýsir þat* 'experience shows that': Cf. 43/3, where the intercalated phrase is *raun finna þess* '[men] gain experience of that'. — [7] *vinni* (3rd pers. pl. pres. subj.) 'commit': *Skj* B emends to *ynni*, 3rd pers. pl. pret subj., but the pres. tense makes good sense here. — [8] *margfríðr skǫrungr* 'the very beautiful leader': The Apostle Peter. Cf. *Geisl* 26/2, where S. Óláfr is described as *margfríðr jǫfurr* 'very beautiful prince'. Given that the two ll. are remarkably similar – *Geisli* has *margfríðr jǫfurr síðan* –, and that *margfríðr* is not otherwise attested in ON poetry or prose, it is possible that Gamli is borrowing from Einarr Skúlason here.

52. Hlaut María mætum
miskunn af gram sunnu,
*ví*ns þás virða reynis
Vǫr þó fœtr með tárum.

Snjallr vann snót frá ǫllum
senn misgerðum hennar
*gumn*a vǫrðr, þeims gerði,
— guði treystisk Bil — leysta.

María hlaut miskunn af mætum gram sunnu, þás Vǫr *ví*ns þó fœtr reynis virða með tárum. Snjallr vǫrðr *gumn*a vann senn leysta snót frá ǫllum misgerðum hennar, þeims gerði; Bil treystisk guði.

Mary received mercy from the illustrious prince of the sun [= God (= Christ)], when the Vǫr <goddess> of wine [WOMAN = Mary Magdalene] washed the feet of the tester of men [= God (= Christ)] with her tears. The wise guardian of men [= God (= Christ)] immediately released the woman from all her sins, which she had committed; Bil <goddess> trusted in God.

Mss: **B**(13r), 399a-b^x. — *Readings*:   [3] *ví*ns: 'v[...]s' B, 'ṿịṇs' 399a-b^x, 'vi(ns)'(?) B*Rydberg*, 'vi(n)s'(?) B*FJ*   [4] fœtr með: so 399a-b^x, '[...]ed' B   [7] *gumn*a: '[...]a' B, 'g̣ụṃṇa' 399a-b^x, '[...](n)a'(?) B*Rydberg*, '(gumn)a'(?) B*FJ*.

Editions: *Skj* Gamli kanóki, 2. *Harmsól* 52: AI, 569, BI, 561, *Skald* I, 271, *NN* §1209; Sveinbjörn Egilsson 1844, 29-30, Kempff 1867, 15-16, Konrað Gíslason and Eiríkur Jónsson 1875-89, II, 356, Rydberg 1907, 29, Black 1971, 267, Attwood 1996a, 235.

Notes: [1] *María* 'Mary [Magdalene]': Bugge (1889, 22) wrongly interprets this as a reference to the Virgin Mary. The identification of the repentant sinner who anoints Christ's feet in Luke VII.36-9 with the woman who does the same thing, but is not described as a sinner, in Mark XIV.3-9 and Matt. XXVI.6-13 is a logical one. The identification of this conflated character with Mary Magdalene, which seems to date at least from C6th (Warner 2000, 226-8), is presumably due to a literal interpretation of Christ's words *mittens enim haec unguentum hoc in corpus meum ad sepeliendum me fecit* 'for she in pouring this ointment upon my body, hath done it for my burial' (Matt. XXVI.12). Mary Magdalene's repentance is also the subject of Anon *Mey* 11-13. Her cult is generally held to have begun after 1200 in Iceland; there was reportedly an image of her at Þykkvabær monastery, though its age cannot be determined, and may well have dated from after Gamli's time (Cormack 1994, 130). — [2] *miskunn af gram sunnu* 'mercy from the prince of the sun': The *miskunn:sunnu* rhyme is also exploited at 65/4 *miskunn jǫfurr sunnu*. This l. also occurs in *Leið* 42/6. — [8] *Bil* 'Bil <goddess>': Kock (*NN* §1209) notes that previous eds have been reluctant to accept that *Bil* can stand alone as a half-kenning. There is, as he says, an undue concern for the plight of *oklädda guddinor* 'naked goddesses', that is, goddess names that are not qualified by a term for gold or treasure or some female attribute (cf. *LP*: *Bil*). Finnur Jónsson (*Skj* B) attempts to provide such an attribute by emending *gerði* (l. 7) to *gerðu*, gen. sg. of *gerða* 'feminine attire', producing the woman-kenning *Bil gerðu* 'goddess of clothing'. This necessitates the omission of *þeim* (l. 7). Rydberg (1907, lxxiv) approves Finnur's emendation, and suggests that *þá er* could be substituted for the ms. reading here, taking the intercalated phrase to be *þá er Bil gerðu treystisk guði* 'when the goddess of clothing trusted God'. As Kock (*NN* §§1209, 1072) suggests, this 'prudery' is a feature of Finnur's edn: it is interesting to note that, of the four occurrences of *gerða* listed in *LP*, three appear in conjunction with a goddess-name, and two of those depend on emendation. There is no obvious reason why the ms. reading cannot be retained here, and *Bil* treated, as Kock (*NN* §1209) suggests, as a half-kenning for 'woman'.

53. Slík styrkja mik merki,   leiptra hróts at láta
    minn guð, ... þinna,   láðvaldr muni aldr*i*
    þótt atferðin yrði   gla*ð*r, ef glœpa iðrumk,
    ór herfilig stórum,   glóða mik fyr róða.

Slík merki *þ*inna ... styrkja mik, minn guð, þótt ór atferðin yrði stórum herfilig, at *glað*r láðvaldr glóða hróts leiptra muni aldr*i* láta mik fyr róða, ef iðrumk glœpa.

Such tokens of your ... strengthen me, my God, even though our [my] behaviour were to become very shameful, that the glad ruler of the land of the fires of the roof of lightnings [(*lit*. 'land-ruler of the fires of the roof of lightnings') SKY/HEAVEN > HEAVENLY BODIES > SKY/HEAVEN > = God] will never cast me to the winds, if I repent of my sins.

Mss: **B**(13r), 399a-b[x]. — *Readings*: [1] Slík: *so* 399a-b[x], 'Sli[...]' B [2] ... *þ*inna: '[...]nna' B, 'un[...](þi)nna'(?) 399a-b[x], 'v(n)[...]inna'(?) B*Rydberg*, 'vn[...](þi)nna'(?) B*FJ* [4] ór: '[...]ðr' B, 'vǫr' 399a-b[x], '(v)ðr'(?) B*Rydberg*, B*FJ* [6] aldr*i*: 'a[...]' B, 'alldr[...]' 399a-b[x], 'a(lld)[...]'(?) B*Rydberg*, 'all[...]' B*FJ* [7] *glað*r: '[...]dr' B, 'gla̧ðr' 399a-b[x], '[...]dr' B*Rydberg*, '(gla)dr'(?) B*FJ*.

Editions: *Skj* Gamli kanóki, 2. *Harmsól* 53: AI, 569-70, BI, 561-2, *Skald* I, 271, *NN* §§1210, 2926, 2934; Sveinbjörn Egilsson 1844, 30, Kempff 1867, 16, Rydberg 1907, 29, Jón Helgason 1935-6, 260, Black 1971, 270, Attwood 1996a, 235.

Notes: [2] ...: B is very badly worn here. The end of the word is completely obliterated by a hole, and only the vaguest traces remain of two (?) initial letters. Of these, only the very first downstroke is at all certain, and this might just as well represent the vestige of an <n> as a <u>. Sveinbjörn Egilsson adopts the suggestion made in a marginal note by the 399a-b[x] copyist (mediated to Sveinbjörn via Jón Sigurðsson's 444[x] transcript of 399a-b[x]) that the ms. reading should be *undra*, gen. pl. of *undr* 'wonder, miracle'. In this, he is followed by Kempff and Finnur Jónsson (*Skj* B). Jón Helgason (1935-6, 260) comments that 'the word *undr* fits very badly here, where the discussion does not concern God's miracles but his mercy'. Jón reconstructs *náða* 'mercies', and is followed by Kock (*NN* §2926) and Black. — [4] *ór* 'our': The mss' form, with initial 'v', must be normalised here to the earlier *ór* (*ANG* §467.2) to supply *aðalhending* with *stór*-. — [5, 8] *at láta fyr róða* 'to leave, cast to the winds, abandon': Cf. the prayer to the Virgin preserved in *HómÍsl* 1872, 195: *eige mic fyr rópa láta í náupsyn* mi*N*e 'do not abandon me in my need'. The phrase is common in both verse and prose (cf. *Fritzner*: *róði*), and it is clear that the essential meaning is 'to abandon'. Several different interpretations of *róði* have been offered, perhaps the most satisfactory being Finnur Jónsson's suggestion (*LP*: *róði*) that *róði* should be understood as a *heiti* for the wind. This certainly renders the phrase at once vivid and accessible, and fits extremely well with the image-structure of *Has*. — [7] *glaðr* 'glad': The beginning of this word is lost, though the two final letters are quite clear. The alliteration requires initial <g>. Previous eds have tended to agree that *glaðr* is the most acceptable reconstruction. Finnur Jónsson (*Skj* B) construes this as part of the conditional cl. *ef iðrumk glaðr glœpa* 'if I repent of my sins gladly'. Jón Helgason (1935-6, 260) objects that 'it hardly accords with the sincerity of the penitent soul that the sinner should be glad'. He suggests that *greiðr* 'willing' would be a more appropriate adj. here. Kock (*NN* §2934) is not altogether convinced by this suggestion, but accepts that, if *glaðr* is understood to refer to the speaker-sinner, it strikes a wrong note. As Black (1971, 272) points out, there is some appropriateness in the suggestion that sinners should repent cheerfully, in the expectation of mercy. Kock suggests that *glaðr* be retained, but that it be construed as part of the main cl., rather than the conditional one. In this, he is anticipated by Sveinbjörn Egilsson's prose arrangement in 444[x], which is adopted here.

54. Sólu veittak, sættir,
 — sárrs minn ... —
 *b*ana hættligar *b*enjar,
 bragna kyns, fyr syn*ð*ir.

 Nú beiðum *þ*ik, þjóðar
 þrekfœðandi, grœð*a*
 *and*ar sór, þaus óru
 ósvífr glata lífi.

Sættir kyns bragna, veittak ... sólu hættligar benjar bana fyr synðir; sárrs minn .... Nú beiðum *þ*ik, þrekfœðandi þjóðar, grœða andar sór, þaus ósvífr glata lífi óru.

Reconciler of the kindred of heroes [MEN > = God], I dealt ... soul dangerous wounds of death because of my sins; bitter is my .... Now we [I] beg you, strength-nourisher of the people [= God], to heal the soul's wounds which, relentless, destroy our [my] life.

Mss: **B**(13r), 399a-b[x]. — *Readings*: [1] Sól*u*: 'Sals' B   [2] ...: , '[...]re[...]' B, 399a-b[x], 'træ(g)i'(?) B*Rydberg*, '(t)re[...]' B*FJ*   [3] *b*ana: '[...]na' B, '[...]ana' 399a-b[x], '[...]na' B*Rydberg*, B*FJ*   [5] *þ*ik: *om.* B   [6] grœða: 'gręd[...]' B, 399a-b[x]   [7] *and*ar: '[...]ar' B, 'a̠ndar' 399a-b[x], '[...](dar)'(?) B*Rydberg*, (an)dar(?) B*FJ*   [8] lífi: *so* 399a-b[x], '[...]' B.

Editions: *Skj* Gamli kanóki, 2. *Harmsól* 54: AI, 570, BI, 562, *Skald* I, 272; Sveinbjörn Egilsson 1844, 30, Kempff 1867, 16, Rydberg 1907, 29, Black 1971, 274, Attwood 1996a, 235.

Notes: [1] *sól*u (dat. sg.) 'soul': B reads *Sáls* gen. sg. Sveinbjörn Egilsson suggests emendation to *Sálu* dat. (unsigned note in 444[x] and 1844, 30 n. 64). That reading has been adopted by all subsequent eds. — [2-3] ... *bana*: B is very badly damaged, and traces of only one letter and a superscript *re* abbreviation are visible (fol. 13r, ll. 45-6). The 399a-b[x] copyist was able to read only one further letter in the second word '...ana'. Reconstruction of this word thus relies on this reading and on the fact that initial <b> is required for alliteration. Other eds have made valiant attempts to reconstruct the missing text here, which is likely to comprise two words. Sveinbjörn Egilsson (444[x] and 1844) postulates *sárr es minn hugr* þinni | *bana*. He is followed by Kempff and Finnur Jónsson (*Skj* B), who construes *Sǫ́lu þinni veittak benjar fyr bana hættiligar synðir, sættir bragna kyns; sárr es hugr minn* 'I dealt wounds to your soul by means of my deathly dangerous sins, reconciler of the kindred of heroes; my soul is wounded'. Rydberg (1907, xxiii) rejects this interpretation on the grounds that the remaining traces of the text will not sustain it. He asserts (1907, 29 n. 9) that he once was able to read a number of letter forms no longer visible in 1907, and reconstructs the text *sarr er minn tregi varri bana*, construing *veittak várri sǫ́lu hættiligar benjar bana fyr synðir; minn tregi es sárr* 'I dealt our [my] soul dangerous death-wounds because of [my] sins; my grief is bitter'. Sveinbjörn's reconstruction requires *þinni* to be construed with *sǫ́lu*, as in Finnur's prose arrangement. The continuation of the theme through the st., however, suggests that, as in the second *helmingr*, the injured soul here is not likely to be Christ's, but rather that of the sinner-narrator, who refers to himself in the 1st pers. throughout. — [5] *þik* 'you': B is short of an alliterating syllable here. Sveinbjörn Egilsson (1844, 30 n. 67) supplies the acc. sg. pron. *þik*, which has been adopted by all eds.

55. Brigðr es heimr, sás hugðak,   Eykr, sás eigi rœkir
— hann døkkvir sið manna —   orð þín, friðar tínir,
... verðr lýðr á láði   hjǫrva þollr, en hylli
lastauðigr, vinfastan.   hans leitar, sér vansa.

Heimr, sás hugðak vinfastan, es brigðr; hann døkkvir sið manna; lýðr á láði ... verðr lastauðigr. Þollr hjǫrva, sás eigi rœkir orð þín en leitar hylli hans, eykr sér vansa, tínir friðar.

The world, which I thought steadfast as a friend, is fickle; it darkens men's behaviour; people on earth ... become rich in sin. The fir-tree of swords [WARRIOR], who does not heed your words but seeks its [the world's] favour, increases his own shame, gatherer of peace [= God].

Mss: **B**(13r), 399a-b[x]. — *Readings*: [2] manna: *so* 399a-b[x], '[...]' B [3] ...: '[...]' *all*; verðr: '[...]dr' B, '[...]erdr' 399a-b[x], B*Rydberg*, '[...]erdr' B*FJ* [4] vinfastan: *so* 399a-b[x], 'vinfast[...]' B.

Editions: *Skj* Gamli kanóki, 2. Harmsól 55: AI, 570, BI, 562, *Skald* I, 273; Sveinbjörn Egilsson 1844, 30-1, Kempff 1867, 16-17, Rydberg 1907, 29-30, Black 1971, 277, Attwood 1996a, 235.

Notes: [3] ... *verðr lýðr á láði*: Sveinbjörn Egilsson (1844, 30 n. 68) reconstructs the first word of the l. as *opt* 'often', giving the second cl. *lýðr á láði opt verðr lastauðigr* 'people on earth often become rich in sin'. This suggestion is adopted by *Skj* B, *Skald* and Black. — [6] *orð þín, friðar tínir* 'your words, gatherer of peace [= God]': This l. recalls the account of the Passion of Christ in sts 23 and 24. The God-kenning, *tínir friðar* 'gatherer of peace', may be a deliberate echo of *tínir bauga* 'gatherer of rings', which characterises the penitent thief in 23/6. The diction and content also parallel the description of God's promises, which offer the thief hope in 24/8 *þín heit, veitir friðar* 'your promises, giver of peace'.

56. Tregr emk ljót at láta
lastaverk til fasta
— mér *br*agar opt fyr augum —
æligs móðs fyr róða.

Þess ák mér at meir*a*
margríkr jǫfurr, líknar,
*fl*eygs ok foldar œgis,
friðar sjalfan þik biðja.

Emk tregr at láta til fasta ljót lastaverk æligs móðs fyr róða; mér *br*agar opt fyr augum. Þess ák at meir*a* biðja þik friðar sjalfan mér, margríkr jǫfurr líknar ok *fl*eygs œgis foldar.

I am reluctant to abandon the ugly sins of a vile soul too completely; it [i.e. sin] often glimmers before my eyes. Therefore I must beg you the more for peace for myself, very powerful king of mercy and of the swirling helmet of the land [SKY/HEAVEN > = God].

Mss: **B**(13r), 399a-b[x]. — *Readings*: [3] *br*agar: '[...]agar' B, 'ḅagḷ[...]' 399a-b[x], '(b)agaz'(?) B*Rydberg*, 'hagar' B*FJ* [7] *fl*eygs: '[...]leýgs' B.

Editions: *Skj* Gamli kanóki, 2. *Harmsól* 56: AI, 570, BI, 562-3, *Skald* I, 273, *NN* §§174, 1212, 2935, 3014; Sveinbjörn Egilsson 1844, 31, Kempff 1867, 17, Rydberg 1907, 30, Jón Helgason 1935-6, 260-1, Black 1971, 279, Attwood 1996a, 236.

Notes: [1, 4] *at láta fyr róða* 'to cast to the winds, abandon': See Note to 53/5-8. — [3] br*agar* 'it glimmers': The beginning of this word is extremely badly worn and affected by misalignment. Traces of an initial tall letter are visible, but cannot be identified with any certainty, and this was so when 399a-b[x] was written, either 'b' or 'h' being suggested then. Rydberg (1907, 30) suggests *bagar* (see below). Finnur Jónsson (*Skj* A and B) reads *hagar*, which he takes to be the 3rd pers. sg. pres. tense of *haga*. Various meanings of *haga* exist, none of which seems entirely appropriate here (see *Fritzner*: *haga*), including 'to manage, organise, arrange, suit'. Finnur construes *mér hagar opt fyr augum*, which he translates *de (lastens gærninger) er ofte fordelagtige for mine öjne* 'they (sinful deeds) are often advantageous in my eyes' though he indicates that he is uncertain of this interpretation. In *LP*: *haga* he suggests that it should be understood as an impersonal construction, and glosses *det [onde] viser sig ofte som godt i mine öjne* '[evil] often reveals itself as good in my eyes'. Kock (*NN* §174) rejects the notion that the verb is impersonal, preferring to translate *den [onde] är ofte behaglig i mina ögon* 'the [evil one] is often pleasant in my eyes'. Sveinbjörn Egilsson (1844, 31 n. 69) anticipates Rydberg's reading, reconstructing *bagar*, which he takes to be a formation from *bagi* 'difficulty, impediment'. He translates *det hindrer mig* 'that hinders me'. Jón Helgason (1935-6, 260-1) picks up on a suggestion made by Sveinbjörn Egilsson in a marginal note in Jón Sigurðsson's copy of 399a-b[x] (i.e. 444[x]). He emends to *bragar*, 1st pers. sg. pres. indic. of *braga* 'to glimmer, flicker, flash', and construes *æligs móðs* (l. 4) as part of the intercalated cl., which he translates *ofte flimrer det for min elendige sjæls øjne* 'it often flickers before the eyes of my wretched soul'. This poetic and elegant interpretation avoids the problems associated with *haga*, and the necessity of postulating a back-formation *bagar*, and this emendation is adopted here. — [4] *æligs móðs* 'of a vile soul': Finnur Jónsson (*Skj* B) construes this with *lastaverk*, giving *tregr emk at láta til* *fasta ljót lasta verk æligs móðs fyr róða* 'I am reluctant to abandon too completely the ugly sins of a vile soul'. This edn follows his interpretation. However, Sveinbjörn Egilsson and Jón Helgason (see previous Note) take the phrase as part of the intercalated cl. — [5-8]: Several interpretations of the second *helmingr* have been offered, none entirely satisfactory. Jón Helgason (1935-6, 261) suggests that *at meiri* should be emended to *at meira*, which he takes to be adverbial, amplifying *ák biðja þik*. He reads the God-kenning as having two determinants, *jǫfurr líknar ok fleygs foldar ægis*, and translates *naadens og den rullende himmels konge* 'king of mercy and of the turbulent heaven'. *Friðar* (l. 8) is taken to be part of the main cl., and the *helmingr* is construed *þess ák at meira biðja þik friðar sjalfan mér, margríkr jǫfurr líknar ok fleygs foldar ægis* 'therefore I must beg you the more for peace for myself, very powerful king of mercy and of the turbulent heaven'. This edn follows Jón's interpretation. Kock (*NN* §2935) objects to this interpretation, claiming that God's attributes of mercy (*líkn*) and heaven (*fleygr foldar ægir*) are too disparate to be governed by the same noun (*jǫfurr*). He (*NN* §1212) agrees with Finnur Jónsson that *friðr* 'peace', and *líkn* should be taken together as the object of *biðja* 'to beg, pray', but assumes that they are asyndetic. The conj. *ok* (l. 7) is thus freed, and Kock reads it *in situ*, linking *fleygs* and *foldar*. He then interprets *ægir* as a reference to the sea, and takes the complete God-kenning to be *jǫfurr foldar ok fleygs ægis* 'king of the earth and the tumultuous sea'. A third interpretation is that of Sveinbjörn Egilsson, which is also followed by Finnur Jónsson and Kempff. Sveinbjörn (1844, 31 n. 70) concurs with Kock in taking both *friðr* and *líkn* as the object of *biðja*, but chooses to link them with the conj. *ok*. This separates *ok* from its syntactic environment and cannot be paralleled in the corpus of skaldic poetry.

57. Heldr dœmðu mik, hǫlða
happvinnandi, þinni
meir af miskunn dýrri,
mætastr, an réttlæti.

Lít ok virð, sem vættik,
*v*aldr blásinna tjalda
hreggs, at hjǫlp of þiggi,
hár, óstyrkðir várar.

Mætastr happvinnandi hǫlða, dœmðu mik heldr meir af þinni dýrri miskunn *an* réttlæti. Lít ok virð óstyrkðir várar, sem vættik, at of þiggi hjǫlp, hár *v*aldr blásinna tjalda hreggs.

Most illustrious luck-worker of men [= God], judge me rather more out of your precious mercy than justice. Consider and evaluate our [my] frailties, which, I expect, may receive help, high ruler of the windswept tents of the storm [SKY/HEAVEN > = God].

Mss: **B**(13r-v), 399a-b[x]. — *Readings*: [2] happvinnandi þinni: *so* 399a-b[x], 'h[...]pvin[...]e[...]' B [3] meir af miskunn: *so* 399a-b[x], 'meirr[...]iskunn' B [4] mætastr a*n* réttlæti: '[...]ẹtaz[...]ettlẹti' B, 'mẹtaz e(n) réttlẹti'(?) 399a-b[x] [8] hár: *so* 399a-b[x], 'h[...]r' B.

Editions: *Skj* Gamli kanóki, 2. Harmsól 57: AI, 570, BII, 563, *Skald* I, 273, *NN* §1213; Sveinbjörn Egilsson 1844, 31, Kempff 1867, 17, Rydberg 1907, 30, Black 1971, 282, Attwood 1996a, 236.

Notes: [6-7] v*aldr blásinna tjalda hreggs* 'ruler of the windswept tents of the storm [SKY/HEAVEN > = God]': Cf. *Geisl* 7/5-6, where heaven is described as *hríðblásinn salr heiða* 'storm-blown hall of the heaths'. On the frequency of heaven-kennings involving *hár* and *hreggr* in C12th *drápur*, see Notes to 1/1-2 and 45/1-4. — [8] *óstyrkðir várar* 'our frailties': The edn follows Finnur Jónsson (*Skj* B) and Kempff (1907, 56) in adopting Sveinbjörn Egilsson's suggestion (note to 444ˣ transcript) that this phrase is the object of *Lít ok virð* 'consider and evaluate' (l. 5). Kock (*NN* §1213) objects that this sense is rather unlikely, since God's nature is not to look upon sin, and thereby to destroy it, but rather to avert his eyes from it (cf. Exod. XXXIII.20, Ps. LI.9). Kock therefore takes *óstyrkðir várar* as part of the *at*-cl., construing the entire cl. *at óstyrkðir várar hjǫlp of þiggi* 'that our frailties may receive help' as the object of *Lít ok virð*.

58.   Hvar meg*im* oss, inn ǫrvi   nema lastauknum líkna,
      ýta *k*yns, fyr syndir   logskríns, vilir þínum
      sǫ́r eða sekðir órar,   sjalfr, þeims syndir skelfa,
      sættir, skjóls of vætta,   sæll gervandi, þræli?

Hvar meg*im* of vætta oss skjóls fyr syndir, sǫ́r eða sekðir órar, inn ǫrvi sættir *k*yns ýta, nema vilir sjalfr líkna þínum lastauknum þræli, þeims syndir skelfa, sæll gervandi logskríns?.

Where may we expect shelter because of our sins, griefs or guilts, generous reconciler of the kinsfolk of men [HUMANS > = God], unless you yourself desire to have mercy on your sin-laden servant, whom sins cause to tremble, blessed creator of the flame-shrine [SKY/HEAVEN > = God]?

Mss: **B**(13v), 399a-bˣ. — *Readings*:   [1] meg*im*: mega B   [2] ýta *k*yns: 'y[...]yns' B, 'ýṭạ kyns' 399a-bˣ   [6] vilir: *so* 399a-bˣ, 'ui[...]er' B; þínum: *so* 399a-bˣ, '[...]num' B.

Editions: *Skj* Gamli kanóki, 2. *Harmsól* 58: AI, 570, BI, 563, *Skald* I, 273, *NN* §2926; Sveinbjörn Egilsson 1844, 31-2, Kempff 1867, 17-18, Rydberg 1907, 30, Black 1971, 285, Attwood 1996a, 236.

Notes: [1-4]: The first *helmingr* has been variously interpreted and corrected. At the heart of the problem are the difficulties eds have encountered in deciphering the beginning of l. 3. This edn agrees with Rydberg (1907, 30) in reading 'sár ẽ', interpreted as *sǫ́r eða*. The hooked <e> is often used to abbreviate *eða* in the prose section of B (as, for example, at fol. 5r, l. 27 and 8v, l. 35), and is quite unlike the *er*-abbreviation. Lines 2 and 3 may therefore be read as a straightforward paralleling of acc. pls, *syndir* 'sins' *sǫ́r* 'griefs' and *sekðir* 'guilts', without the need for emendation, though it is syntactically odd, as *eða* in a group of three nouns is unusual. Other eds have suspected scribal error. Jón Helgason (1935-6, 261) reads *sár er* here, normalising to *sárir*. This he takes to be the f. acc. pl. of *sárr* adj. 'sore, aching', qualifying *sekðir*. *Sárir sekðir órar* 'our aching guilts' is then taken as parallel to *syndir* 'sins' and the verb is emended to *megim* (subj.). The *helmingr* is thus construed *hvar megim of vætta oss skjóls fyrir syndir, sárir sekðir órar* 'where might we expect to find a refuge in the face of our sins, our aching guilts'. Kock (*NN* §2926) approves this change. Finnur Jónsson (followed by Kock in *Skald*) normalises to *sárar*, which he assumes to be adjectival, qualifying *synðar sekðir órar*, which he translates *vore synders svære skyld* 'our sins' heavy guilt'. — [8] *præli* 'servant': On the Christian as God's servant, see Note to 9/5.

59. Hlut meguð hv*er*n til gotna,
 happkunnig, miskunnar
 ramligs bús af ræsi
 rǫðuls, María, ǫðlask.

 Vest ávalt at trausti,
 vegstýris, *m*ér dýru,
 mild, at missak aldri,
 móðir *, yðvars góða.

Happkunnig María, meguð ǫðlask hv*er*n hlut af ræsi ramligs bús rǫðuls til miskunnar gotna. Vest ávalt *m*ér at dýru trausti, mild móðir * vegstýris, at missak aldri góða yðvars.

Mary, renowned for good fortune, you can obtain everything from the king of the strong homestead of the sun [SKY/HEAVEN > = God] for mercy for men. Always be a precious support to me, gentle mother of the honour-controller [= God (= Christ) > = Mary], so that I may never lose your goodwill.

Mss: **B**(13v), 399a-b^x. — *Readings*: [1] hv*er*n: 'hu[...]n' B, 'hu(er)n'(?) 399a-b^x [6] *m*ér: '[...]' B, '[...]er' 399a-b^x [8] móðir *: 'moder guds' B; yðvars: *so* 399a-b^x, 'ydu[...]' B.

Editions: *Skj* Gamli kanóki, 2. Harmsól 59: AI, 571, BI, 563, *Skald* I, 273; Sveinbjörn Egilsson 1844, 32, Kempff 1867, 18, Rydberg 1907, 30, Jón Helgason 1935-36, 262, Black 1971, 287, Attwood 1996a, 236.

Notes: [1] *happkunnig* 'renowned for good fortune': Cf. 57/1-2, where Christ is characterised as *happvinnandi hǫlða* 'luck-worker of men'. — [3] *ramligs bús af ræsi*: A strikingly similar l. occurs in *Leið* 43/7 *ramligt hús, þars reistum*. Jón Helgason (1935-6, 262) objects to the Christ-kenning *ræsir bús rǫðuls* 'king of the dwelling of the sun', as *rǫðuls bú* 'sun's dwelling' is apparently without parallel in the skaldic corpus. Jón suggests that *bús* be emended to *býs*, which gives the Christ-kenning *ræsir býs rǫðuls* 'king of the farm of the sun', which occurs again at *Líkn* 19/3. The ms. reading is certain, and the *Líkn* kenning could well be an 'embroidery' on *Has*. There seems little justification for adopting Jón's emendation here. — [8] *móðir * yðvars góða*: B's *guðs* is metrically otiose, and also, as indicated by the prose order above, semantically so. Its inclusion in B is probably best explained as a lapse by the copyist, distracted by the coexistence of the words *María* and *móðir* into writing the liturgical commonplace *móðir guðs* 'mother of God'.

60. Vættik oss með ótta,
 alskírt himins birti
 hǫfuðmusteri *in*s hæsta
 h*i*ldings, af þér mildi,

 hauðrs, þvít hugga fríðir
 hug minn siðir þínir,
 grams kastali inn glæsti
 glyggs, en várt líf hryggvir.

Vættik oss með ótta mildi af þér, alskírt hǫfuðmusteri *ins* hæsta *h*ildings himins birti, því þínir fríðir siðir hugga hug minn, en líf várt hryggvir, inn glæsti kastali grams hauðrs glyggs.

I hope for us [for myself] with fear for mercy from you, altogether brilliant chief temple of the highest prince of heaven's brightness [SUN > = God (= Christ)], because your fine virtues comfort my mind, but our [my] way of life distresses [it], splendid fortress of the prince of the land of the wind [SKY/HEAVEN > = God (= Christ)].

Mss: **B**(13v), 399a-b˟. — *Readings*:   [3] i*ns* hæsta: 'e[...]hęs[...]' B, 'e(ns) hęsta'(?) 399a-b˟   [4] *h*ildings: 'h[...]' B, 'h(illdings)'(?) 399a-b˟   [8] glyggs: *so* 399a-b˟, '[...]yggs' B.

Editions: *Skj* Gamli kanóki, 2. *Harmsól* 60: AI, 571, BI, 563-4, *Skald* I, 273; Sveinbjörn Egilsson 1844, 32, Kempff 1867, 18, Rydberg 1907, 30-31, Black 1971, 290, Attwood 1996a, 237.

Notes: [3] *hǫfuðmusteri* 'chief temple': The only other use of this cpd in skaldic poetry, also with reference to the Virgin Mary, is *Mdr* 14/3. — [4] *h*ildings 'prince's': Although the 399a-b˟ copyist is not certain of the reading, the reconstruction here is confirmed by *aðalhending* with *mildi*. — [5-8] *kastali grams hauðrs glyggs* 'fortress of the prince of the land of the wind': Cf. *Mdr* 1/7, where Mary is praised as God's *hæstr hǫfuðkastali* 'highest chief fortress'. It is possible that the *Mdr* poet consciously imitated the two appellations for Mary used in this st. Gamli's use of kenning-types that compare the Virgin Mary to a building, especially a sacred or royal one, the receptacle for Christ's incarnation, is among the earliest in skaldic verse and is based on Old Testament typology (*templum Domini* 'the temple of the Lord', *solium Salomonis* 'the throne of Solomon'), whereby Solomon's temple is a type or allegorical figure of the Virgin and she in turn is a type of the Church (Schottmann 1973, 47-51, 76).

61. Verðrat, blíðr, fyr borði
    brjótr, hǫfðingi snóta,
    — mjǫk treystumk því — Mistar
    myrkleygs, sás þik dýrkar,
    því vegskjótum* veita,
    veðrs landreka strandar,
    vilt, svinn, ok mátt mǫnnum,
    móðir, allt it góða.

Brjótr Mistar myrkleygs, sás dýrkar þik, blíðr hǫfðingi snóta, verðrat fyr borði — mjǫk treystumk því —, því vilt ok mátt veita vegskjótum* mǫnnum allt it góða, svinn móðir landreka strandar veðrs.

The destroyer of Mist's <valkyrie> dark flame [SWORD > WARRIOR], who worships you, gentle chief of women, will not be lost — we [I] greatly rely on that — because you are willing and able to grant men, swift in glory, all that is good, wise mother of the land-ruler of the shore of the wind [SKY/HEAVEN > = God (= Christ) > = Mary].

Mss: **B**(13v), 399a-b˟. — *Reading*:   [5] vegskjótum*: 'vegskiotumz' B.

Editions: *Skj* Gamli kanóki, 2. *Harmsól* 61: AI, 571, BI, 564, *Skald* I, 273; Sveinbjörn Egilsson 1844, 32-3, Kempff 1867, 18, Rydberg 1907, 31, Black 1971, 292, Attwood 1996a, 237.

Notes: [1] *blíðr* 'blessed': The m. nom. sg. of the adj. *blíðr* 'blessed, happy', which could be construed as qualifying either *brjótr* (l. 2) or *hǫfðingi snóta* 'chief of women' (l. 2). It is most plausibly regarded as part of the kenning-like periphrasis for the Virgin Mary, probably modelled on Lat. *regina virginum* 'queen of virgins' (cf. Paasche 1914a, 115; Lange 1958a, 224). Cf. *konungr vífa* lit. 'king of women', *Mdr* 5/2. — [2-4] *brjótr Mistar myrkleygs* 'the destroyer of Mist's <valkyrie> dark flame [SWORD > WARRIOR]': Cf. the man-kenning *slǫngvir Mistar elda* 'slinger of Mist's fires' in 2/1. There are thematic and dictional echoes here of st. 5, where men, characterised as *viðir Mistar linns* 'trees of Mist's snake', are promised *sannri líkn ok sýknu fyr vás ok galla* 'true mercy and acquittal for sinfulness and flaws', by Christ. — [5] *vegskjótum** 'swift in glory': B reads 'vegskiotumz'. Finnur Jónsson (*Skj* B) emends to *vegskjótust*, f. nom. sg. of the superlative adj. *vegskjótastr*. He construes this as qualifying the periphrasis for the Virgin, and glosses *rask til at give hæder* 'swift to give honour'. Finnur's interpretation is accepted without comment by Kock and Black. Sveinbjörn Egilsson (1844) takes B's 'vegskiotumz' as an error for *vegskjótum*, which he understands as the m. dat. pl. of *vegskjótr*, qualifying *mǫnnum* (l. 7). In either case, the first element of the cpd is understood as *vegr* 'glory, renown, honour', Sveinbjörn's gloss for *vegskjótr* in *LP* (1860) being *ad gloriam promptus, honoris cupidus* 'ready for glory, desirous of honour'. Sveinbjörn's interpretation requires least emendation, and Gamli's use of coinages on this model is confirmed by the similar adjectival form *þrifskjótr* 'swift to prosperity', in a God-kenning in 12/6.

62. Hvern biðk hald ok árnan
    helgan m*ann* ins sanna,
    (trús) við tírar ræsi
    (trausts leitak) mér veita,
    svát óbœttan ættim
    en*gi* kost, þá*s* drengja
    jǫfurr vill andar krefja
    ástnenninn hal þenna.

Biðk hvern helgan m*ann* veita mér hald ok árnan við ræsi ins sanna tírar — leitak trús trausts —, svát ættim en*gi* kost óbœttan, þá*s* ástnenninn jǫfurr drengja vill krefja þenna hal andar.

I ask every holy man to grant me support and intercession with the king of the true glory — I am seeking certain protection —, so that we [I] might have no circumstance unatoned for when the love-disposed prince of men [= God (= Christ)] will ask this man for his soul.

Mss: **B**(13v), 399a-b[x]. — *Readings*: [2] helgan: *so* 399a-b[x], 'h[...]lgan' B; m*ann*: '[...]' B, m(ann)(?) 399a-b[x] [6] en*gi*: 'ein[...]' B, 'eingi' 399a-b[x], 'æin[...](i)'(?) B*Rydberg*, 'ein(gi)'(?) B*FJ*; þá*s*: 'þa[...]' B, 399a-b[x], þá (er)(?) B*Rydberg*, þá (e)r(?) B*FJ*.

Editions: *Skj* Gamli kanóki, 2. *Harmsól* 62: AI, 571, BI, 564, *Skald* I, 273, ; *NN* §3126; Sveinbjörn Egilsson 1844, 33, Kempff 1867, 19, Rydberg 1907, 31, Jón Helgason 1935-36, 262, Black 1971, 294, Attwood 1996a, 237.

Notes: [1-2] *hvern helgan m*ann 'every holy man': That is, every saint. — [2-3] *við ræsi ens sanna tírar* 'with the king of true glory': A kenning-like periphrasis for Christ, probably based on Lat. *rex gloriae* 'king of glory'. — [4] *mér* 'to me': As Kock (*NN* §3126) observes, the dat. sg. pers. pron. may be construed with either *veita* 'to grant' (l. 1) or *leita* 'to seek' (l. 4), giving either the prose order above or the intercalated phrase *ek leita mér trús trausts* 'I am seeking certain protection for myself'. — [6] *kost* 'circumstance': Jón Helgason (1935-6, 262) objects to the ms. reading here, on the ground that *kostr* 'condition, circumstance' is usually only used of positive circumstances. He suggests an emendation to *lǫst*, acc. sing. of *lǫstr* m. 'fault, flaw'. However, as Black (1971, 295) notes, *Fritzner*: *kostr* gives examples of the morally neutral meaning 'situation, circumstance', which is followed in the translation here. — [8] *ástnenninn* 'love-disposed, -inclined': B is quite clear at this point, and the reading is confirmed by all transcribers of the ms. Sveinbjörn Egilsson adopts this form, the m. nom. sg. of the *hap. leg.* adj. *ástnenninn* 'love-disposed' in his 1844 edn, but suggests emendation to a m. sg. acc. form *ástnennin* in a note in 444[x], which produces a prose rearrangement *þás jǫfurr drengja vill krefja þenna ástnennin hal andar* 'when the prince of men will ask this love-disposed man for his soul'. This reading is adopted by Kempff. Ms. evidence apart, *ástnenninn* 'love-disposed', would seem more suitable as an appellation for the merciful Christ than for the sinful poet and his hearers in the context of this st.

63. Ér látið þau, ýta, svát frá yðr í ítru
     atferðar lok *verða*, — oss kjósum þat — ljósi,
     miskunnandi, minnar, veglyndr veðra grundar
     margríkr, at þér líki, valdr, skiljumk ek aldri.

Margríkr miskunnandi ýta, ér látið þau lok atferðar minnar *verða*, at líki þér, svát ek skiljumk aldri frá yðr í ítru ljósi, veglyndr valdr grundar veðra; kjósum oss þat.

Very powerful pardoner of men [= Christ], you allow the endings of my life's course to turn out in such a way that it pleases you, so that I will never be parted from you in glorious light, honour-minded ruler of the plain of the winds [SKY/HEAVEN > = God]; we [I] choose that for ourselves [myself].

Mss: **B**(13v), 399a-b[x]. — *Readings*: [2] atferðar lok *verða*: 'atferd[...]k[...]' B, 'atferdar lok verð(a)'(?) 399a-b[x] [7] veg-: 'v[...]' B, 'vegh' 399a-b[x].

Editions: *Skj* Gamli kanóki, 2. *Harmsól* 63: AI, 571, BI, 564; *Skald* I, 274; Sveinbjörn Egilsson 1844, 33, Kempff 1867, 19, Rydberg 1907, 31, Black 1971, 296, Attwood 1996a, 237.

Notes: [1] *ér* 'you': An accent is written over the *r*. Sveinbjörn Egilsson (1844), who is followed by Kempff, follows the 399a-b[x] copyist in interpreting the accent as the common nasal abbreviation, producing 'Ern'. Rydberg concurs, though he notes (1907, 31 n. 10) that *Ér* in *Líkn* 44/1 (fol 12r, l. 24) is remarkably similar to the form here. There is no doubt that *Ér* is the correct reading in that case. Sveinbjörn takes *ern* to be the nom. sg. of *ern* adj. 'vigorous', qualifying the God-kenning *miskunnandi ýta* in apposition with *margríkr*. He construes *Ern miskunnandi ýta margríkr, látið þau lok verða atferðar minnar...* 'Vigorous, very powerful pardoner of men [= God (= Christ)]], you allow the endings of my life's course to turn out...'. This edn follows Finnur Jónsson (*Skj* B), Black (1971, 296) and Kock (*Skald*) in reading *Ér*, the archaic form of the honorific pl. pron. (see *ANG* §§464, Anm. 5 and 465, Anm. 5), construed with the adjacent *látið* 'you allow' (l. 1). — [6] *margríkr* 'very powerful': *LP* lists no occurrence of this cpd. outside *Has*. Cf. 56/6 *margríkr* : *líknar*.

64. Létum hróðr, þanns heitir
    Harmsól, fe*t*ilkjó*l*a
    fyr hugprúða hríðar
    herðendr borinn verða.

Mér biði hverr, es heyrir,
heimspenni, brag þenna,
œski-Þrór ok eirar
unnrǫðla miskunnar.

Létum hróðr, þanns heitir Harmsól, verða borinn fyr hugprúða herðendr hríðar fe*t*ilkjó*l*a. Hverr œski-Þrór unnrǫðla, es heyrir þenna brag, biði mér heimspenni miskunnar ok eirar.

We [I] caused the praise-poem, which is called 'Harmsól', to be borne before strong-minded hardeners of the storm of strap-ships [SHIELDS > BATTLE > WARRIORS]. May each craving-Þrór <ÓÐINN> of wave-suns [GOLD > MAN] who hears this poem, ask the world-clasper [= God] for mercy and compassion for me.

Mss: **B**(13v), 399a-b[x]. — *Readings*: [1] þanns: þann B [2] fe*t*ilkjó*l*a: 'fe[...]l kiosa' B, 'fe(ti)lkiosa'(?) 399a-b[x], 'fæ[...](i)l kiosa'(?) B*Rydberg*, 'fe (ti)l kiosa'(?) B*FJ* [6] þenna: *so* 399a-b[x], 'þenn[...]' B.

Editions: *Skj* Gamli kanóki, 2. Harmsól 64: AI, 571, BI, 564-5, *Skald* I, 274, *NN* §2114; Sveinbjörn Egilsson 1844, 33-4; Kempff 1867, 19, Rydberg 1907, 31-2, Black 1971, 298, Attwood 1996a, 238.

Notes: [2] *Harmsól*: Lit. 'sorrow-sun'. The title of the poem draws together many of its central themes. *Harmsól* may be taken as a kenning for Christ, whose *harmr* 'pain, injury' is the subject of the poem's central meditation, and who is apostrophised throughout the poem in kennings referring to his mastery of the weather and his lordship over the heavenly halls of the sun. At another level, the poem itself, as a public act of penance and a meditation on the grace of God, has acted as a 'sun', dissipating the clouds of the poet's own *harmr* 'sorrow', his grief and shame at his own sinfulness. See further Paasche 1914a, 116-18. — [2] *fetilkjóla* 'of strap-ships': Although the ms. is very badly worn, all previous eds concur that the second element is *kjósa*, and they follow the 399a-b[x] copyist in reconstructing the first element as *fetil*. Sveinbjörn Egilsson's emendation to *fetilkjóla* (1844, 33 n. 81), which provides an expected *aðalhending*, is adopted here, though not without reservation. The interpretation of this cpd presents considerable difficulties. It is clear from the remainder of the man-kenning *herðendr* 'hardeners' and *hríðar* 'of the storm' (ll. 3-4), that an expression for a weapon of some kind is required. *Fetill* designates a strap or belt, and is often used specifically of a sword-belt or a shield-strap (*Fritzner: fetill*). Sveinbjörn Egilsson (1844, 33 n. 81) resolves this, by a transfer of meaning (*pars pro toto*), as a *heiti* for 'sword'. Finnur Jónsson (*LP*: *fetilhjól*) regards the ms. reading as meaningless, and emends the second element of the cpd to *fetilhjól* 'strap-wheel', a shield-*heiti*. Kock

(*NN* §2114) dismisses this emendation as providing an excess of alliteration on the <h>, interpreting *fetilkjóll* 'strap-ship [SHIELD]' (ON *kjóll* a kind of large ship, cognate with OE *ceol*). This he derives from a lost myth of the ship of the Norse god Ullr, possibly involving Ullr's use of a shield as a boat. There is no doubt that several instances of the use of the phrase 'Ullr's ship' as shield-kennings are listed in *SnE* (1998, I, 43 (verse 143/3 *Ullar kjóll* attributed to Eyvindr skáldaspillir, Eyv Lv 9[I]), 67 (*Skjǫldr er ok kallaðr skip Ullar* 'a shield is also called Ullr's ship') and 69 (verse 236/2 *Ullar skip*, probably from ÞjóðA Frag 3/2[II]). Whether a word for 'ship', without explicit reference to the god Ullr, was an acceptable element in shield-kennings remains an open question, though the cpd *fetilkjóll* has been understood here to fit into this pattern. Louis-Jensen (2003, 317-18) doubts whether a ship-word without reference to Ullr can give a shield-kenning. She argues that the cpd is more likely to be a sword-kenning, and proposes emendation to *fetilnjóla*, a cpd in which the second element *-njóli* (found only in compounds in ON) has the basic sense of 'stem, stalk'. — [7] *œski-Þrór* 'craving-Þrór': That is, each man who craves wave-suns, i.e. gold. *Þrór* is listed as a *heiti* for Óðinn in *Gylf* (*SnE* 1982, 22). Although it occurs rather infrequently in man-kennings, (*LP*: *Þrór*), it is interesting to compare the warrior-kenning *Þrós þingveljandi* 'decider of Þrór's assembly' in *Pl* 49/3-4.

65. Án lát engan þína, Vǫrðr, laða skatna skírða,
    angrlestandi, mesta skýtjalds, saman alla,
    mann — deilir þat máli — ítr, þars aldri þrjóti
    miskunn, jǫfurr sunnu. unaðsgnótt ok frið, dróttinn.

Lát engan mann án mesta miskunn þína, angrlestandi jǫfurr sunnu; þat deilir máli. Ítr dróttinn, vǫrðr skýtjalds, laða saman alla skírða skatna, þars aldri þrjóti unaðsgnótt ok frið.

Let no man [be] without your very great mercy, sorrow-injuring prince of the sun [= God (= Christ)]; that is of prime importance. Glorious Lord, warden of the cloud-tent [SKY/HEAVEN > = God], invite together all baptised men, to where an abundance of happiness and peace will never end.

Mss: **B**(13v), 399a-b[x]. — *Readings*: [1] engan: *so* 399a-b[x], 'ǫnngua[...]' B [2] angrlestandi: *so* 399a-b[x], 'anngrlestan[...]e' B [8] frið dróttinn: *so* 399a-b[x], 'fri[...]rotinn' B.

Editions: *Skj* Gamli kanóki, 2. *Harmsól* 65: AI, 572, BI, 565, *Skald* I, 274, Sveinbjörn Egilsson 1844, 34, Kempff 1867, 20, Konráð Gíslason 1897, 253-4, Rydberg 1907, 32, Jón Helgason 1935-6, 262, Black 1971, 301, Attwood 1996a, 238.

Notes: [2-3]: Jón Helgason (1935-6, 262) expands B's 'm[n]' (l. 3) to *menn* (acc. pl.) and assumes the intercalated phrase to be *þat deilir menn mestu máli*, taking *þat deilir máli* to mean 'that settles the case, is of importance'. This requires emendation of the ms.'s *mesta* to *mestu* 'great', to agree with *máli* dat. sg. Although the intercalated phrase often encompasses the third l. of a *helmingr* in its entirety (as at 8/3, 17/3, 22/3 and 35/3), it does not always do so (cf., e.g., 61/3). The ms. reading *mesta* may be preserved here by taking it as qualifying *miskunn* 'mercy' (l. 4) and, in agreement with Sveinbjörn Egilsson, Finnur Jónsson and Black, expanding 'mⁿ' to *mann*, and construing this as part of the main cl. — [4] *miskunn, jǫfurr sunnu*: The identical l. occurs at *Leið* 42/6. These are the only occurrences of the Christ-kenning *jǫfurr sunnu* 'prince of the sun', but the symbolic equation of God with the sun and Christ as the sun's rays is central to *Geisl* (see Chase 2005, 21-5). — [6] *skýtjalds saman alla*: The *tjalds* : *alla* rhyme is dubious in a poem purporting to date from before C13th and is, indeed, one of the late linguistic features which led Finnur Jónsson (*LH* II, 115) to suggest that the poem can hardly be older than from c. 1200, if the reading does not involve error. Konráð Gíslason (and Eiríkur Jónsson 1875-89, II, 253-4) suggests that the original reading was *skýstalls*, gen. sg. of *skýstallr* m. 'pedestal, altar of the sky', but that a later copyist substituted *tjalds*. Rydberg (1907, lxvi) agrees that *stallr*, which is used by Gamli at 29/8 and 35/5, would fit well with *vǫrðr* 'warden, guardian' (l. 5). Jón Helgason (1935-6, 262) suggests that *alla* should be emended to *alda*, gen. pl. of *ǫld* f. 'people', the kenning *skýtjalds aldir* 'people of the tent of cloud' being a reference to the blessed, whose *vǫrðr* 'guardian' is God. The B scribe, however, has correctly rendered *skýstalls* in 29/8, where there is a full rhyme with *allri*. The *tjald* : *alla* rhyme again occurs in a strikingly similar l. in *Líkn* 25/4, *heiðtjalds saman alla*. As Kock (*NN* §2328) points out, the pronunciation of *lds* as *lls* can be exemplified from slightly later verse (Játg Lv 1/2^{II}, Sturl Hákkv 18/5^{II}) and a similar process accounts for the *aðalhendingar vindsamt* : *finna* in Halli XI *Fl* 3/8^{II} (*Skj* B emends to *vinnsamt* here), considerably earlier than Gamli. This edn therefore follows Kock in assuming that *tjalds* : *alla* is an acceptable full rhyme, and retains the ms. reading.

Gamli kanóki, *Jónsdrápa*

Edited by Beatrice La Farge

Introduction

Four sts of *Jónsdrápa* 'Drápa about the Apostle John' (Gamlkan *Jóndr*) composed by Gamli kanóki in honour of John the Apostle, to whom the fourth Gospel and the Book of Revelation were traditionally attributed, are preserved in a sole ms., AM 649 a 4° (649a, c. 1350-1400), where they are quoted at the end of a version of *Jóns saga postula* (*Jón*[4]; on this ms., see Introduction to Ník *Jóndr* and Widding, Bekker-Nielsen and Shook 1963, 316). Three of the sts emphasise the special privileges granted to John; the fourth st. is a prayer for the forgiveness of sin.

In *Jón*[4] the four sts are quoted in the same order as they appear below, with short explanations before each st. The sts are evidently extracts from a longer poem, as the remark made before the fourth st. quoted indicates: *Nærr enda drápunnar setr bróðir Gamli bænarform* ... 'Near the end of the *drápa* Brother Gamli places a st. in the form of a prayer ...' (*Jón*[4] 1874, 511). Given the paucity of information, it is virtually impossible to make assertions about the content of the rest of this poem or about the position of the other three sts within it (see Lange 1958a, 83-4). The sts are composed in the metre *hrynhent*.

In *Jón*[4] Gamli's poem is twice called a *drápa*, hence the title used by previous eds and here as well. Since the name of the Apostle appears in st. 3 as *Jón*, this form has been adopted in the title, whereas Finnur Jónsson used the earlier form *Jóan* in *Skj* A and B.

Gamlkan *Jóndr* has been previously edited by Unger 1874 and, as an appendix to Unger's edn of *Jón*[4], by Sophus Bugge (1874, 933-4), as well as by Lange 1958a, Finnur Jónsson (*Skj*) and Kock (*Skald*).

1. Tígnar frák þik upphaf eignask   sólar ranns at siklingr unni
   — eigi mistir blezan Kristi —   seima brjót* í þessum heimi
   ráðeflandi, risnu prúðan,   mærðar kœnn, ok móður sinni
   rekka liðs, af flærðar hnekki,   mætra lífs, an aðrir gæti.

Ráðeflandi liðs rekka, frák þik, prúðan risnu, eignask upphaf tígnar af hnekki flærðar — eigi mistir blezan Kristi — at mærðar kœnn siklingr ranns sólar unni brjót* seima ok sinni móður mætra lífs í þessum heimi, an aðrir gæti.

Counsel-provider of the troop of men [MANKIND > APOSTLE], I have heard that you, splendid in munificence, acquired for yourself elevation in honour from the suppressor of falsehood [= God (= Christ)] — you did not go without the blessing of Christ — that the famous lord of the hall of the sun [SKY/HEAVEN > = God (= Christ)] granted to the breaker of gold wires [GENEROUS MAN] and to his own mother a more worthy life in this world than others were able to obtain.

Ms.: **649a**(46v) (*Jón⁴*). — *Reading*: [6] brjót*: brjótr 649a.

Editions: *Skj* Gamli kanóki, 1. *Jóansdrápa* 1: AI, 561, BI, 547, *Skald* I, 265, *NN* §3124; *Jón⁴* 1874, 510, Bugge 1874, 933, Lange 1958a, 81.

Context: Prefaced to this st. is the remark: *ok kveðr svá til ástarlófs Jesu Cristi, er hann veitti sínum frænda* 'and he [Gamli] says this in praise of the love that Jesus Christ granted to his relative [John]' (*Jón⁴* 1874, 510). On the idea of John as Christ's relative, see Note to st. 2/4. — *Notes*: [3-4] *ráðeflandi liðs rekka* 'counsel-provider of the troop of men [MANKIND > APOSTLE]': Since the base-word of this kenning ([*ráð*]*eflandi*) is in the nom. and the st. is addressed to S. John, Lange (1958a, 82) plausibly regards the nom. form *eflandi* as a vocative; the kenning is thus an apostrophe addressed to S. John. Finnur Jónsson (*Skj* B) takes *ráð ... liðs* to be a phrase standing in apposition to the pron. *þik* 'you'. As Lange points out, one would then expect an acc. form *eflanda*, rather than the nom. Bugge takes the kenning to be part of the intercalary cl. *eigi mistir blezan Kristi*, but it is more likely that he takes it as a vocative addressed to S. John than as a phrase standing in apposition to the gen. *Kristi*, as Lange asserts. The kenning reflects the Christian view that it was the function of the Apostles to teach mankind (cf. Matt. XXVIII.20). — [6] *brjót**: The ms. reading is 'brjotr' (nom. sg.). The subject of the sentence is the kenning *siklingr ranns sólar* 'lord of the hall of the sun' [SKY/HEAVEN > = God (= Christ)]; since the st. is addressed to S. John, it is to be expected that he be mentioned in the second part of the st. as well as in the first. All eds since Bugge therefore emend the nom. form *brjótr* to the dat. sg. *brjót** (1874, 933 n. 3) assuming a m. dat. sg. a-stem noun without dat. ending *-i* (*ANG* §358.3). The man-kenning *brjót seima* 'breaker of gold wires' [GENEROUS MAN] then designates the Apostle John and forms part of the indirect object in the construction *unni mætra lífs seima brjót ok móður sinni* 'granted a more worthy life to the breaker of gold wires [GENEROUS MAN = John] and to his mother'. — [6] *í þessum heimi* 'in this world': Bugge, Finnur Jónsson (*Skj* B) and Lange (1958b, 17) regard this prepositional phrase as part of the subordinate cl. *an aðrir gæti* 'than others were able to obtain'; Kock (*NN* §3124) argues that the w.o. suggests rather that *í þessum heimi* forms part of the cl. *at siklingr ranns sólar unni seima brjót ok móður sinni mætra líf*. — [7] *mærðar kœnn* 'famous': This phrase can be translated as 'wise in fame' and is interpreted by Finnur Jónsson (*Skj* B; *LP*: *mærð*), Kahle (1901, 138) and Lange (1958b, 17) as 'famous, much praised' or (less plausibly) as 'praised for his wisdom' (*LP*: *kœnn*).

2. Brigð kómu þess brátt, es hugði
bǫlfyldr konungr verða skyldu,
harðla fljótt, þvít huggan veitti
hreggskríns jǫfurr frænda sínum.

Alla náði eirar stillis
ítr postoli dýrð at líta,
humra nausts þás hǫfðu flestir
hrein*a* þollar fréttir einar.

Brigð kómu brátt þess, es bǫlfyldr konungr hugði skyldu verða, þvít jǫfurr hreggskríns veitti huggan frænda sínum harðla fljótt. Ítr postoli náði at líta alla dýrð stillis eirar, þás flestir þollar hrein*a* nausts humra hǫfðu einar fréttir.

Changes came about abruptly in that which the baleful king thought should happen, for the lord of the storm-shrine [HEAVEN > = God] granted comfort to his relative very quickly. The noble Apostle was able to see all the glory of the disposer of mercy [= God], of which most fir-trees of the reindeer of the boat-house of lobsters [SEA > SHIP > SEAFARERS] have only reports.

Ms.: **649a**(46v) (*Jón⁴*). — *Reading*: [8] hrein*a*: hreinir 649a.

Editions: *Skj* Gamli kanóki, 1. *Jóansdrápa* 2: AI, 561, BI, 547, *Skald* I, 265; *Jón⁴* 1874, 510, Bugge 1874, 934, Lange 1958a, 82.

Context: Prefaced to this st. is the explanation: *Af eitrliga grímd Domiciani keisara ok veizlum várs dróttins til Johannem i Pathmos segir hann svá* 'About the poisonous enmity of the emperor Domitian and the aid of Our Lord to John on Patmos he says the following' (*Jón⁴* 1874, 510). This is a reference to the torture to which Domitian is said to have subjected John in Rome (he was placed in a vat of boiling oil, from which he emerged unscathed) and to John's banishment to the stone-quarries on the island of Patmos, where he was granted the visions described in the Book of Revelation (cf. *Jón⁴* 1874, 474-8). — *Notes*: [4] *frænda sínum* 'to his relative': John is called Christ's *frændi* 'relative' because his mother was thought to be a sister of Christ's mother Mary (*Jón⁴* 1874, 466, *AÍ* I, 56, *HómÍsl* 1993, 94; cf. the designation of John as *systrungr ... ýta hilmis* 'son of the sister [*systrungr*] of the protector of men' in st. 3/1-2). — [8] *hreina* '(gen. pl.) of reindeer': The ms. reading is *hreinir*, which would be nom. pl. of the adj. *hreinn* 'pure'. The subject of the sentence is evidently an extended (*rekit*) man-kenning whose base-word is a term for 'tree' (*þollar* 'fir-trees'). The last part of the determinant is clearly itself a kenning for 'sea' (*humra naust* 'boat-house of lobsters'). Since a man-kenning 'tree of the sea' would be without parallel, all eds follow Bugge and emend *hreinir* to *hreina* (gen. pl. of *hreinn* 'reindeer'; Bugge 1874, 934 nn. 1 and 4). This yields a man-kenning of the type 'tree of the ship' (cf. *Meissner*, 278).

3. Systrungr hefr nú alt, þat*s* æstir   Dróttinn valði drengja sætti
   ýta hilmis giptu flýti,   dyggra líf, an menn of hyggi,
   sólar vangs með sjǫlfum deili   — alla hlaut af engla stilli
   synðalauss í fullu ynði.   Jón postoli dýrð — ok kosti.

Systrungr hilmis ýta hefr nú alt, þats æstir flýti giptu, synðalauss í fullu ynði með deili vangs sólar sjǫlfum; dróttinn valði sætti drengja dyggra líf ok kosti, an menn of hyggi; Jón postoli hlaut alla dýrð af engla stilli.

The cousin of the protector of men [RULER = God (= Christ) > = John] has now all that he asks of the conveyor of grace [= God (= Christ)], sinless in perfect joy with the ruler of the meadow of the sun [SKY/HEAVEN > = God] himself; the Lord chose for the reconciler of valiant men [HOLY MAN = John] a more virtuous life and circumstances than men can imagine; John the Apostle was allotted all glory by the ruler of the angels [= God].

Ms.: **649a**(46v) (*Jón⁴*). — *Reading*: [1] þats: þat 649a.

Editions: *Skj* Gamli kanóki, 1. *Jóansdrápa* 3: AI, 561, BI, 548, *Skald* I, 266; *Jón⁴* 1874, 511, Bugge 1874, 934, Lange 1958a, 82.

Context: This st. is prefaced with the remark: *Af náveru hifneskrar Jerusalem í sælu Johannis segir hann svá* 'About the presence of John in the bliss of the heavenly Jerusalem [*lit*. the presence of the heavenly Jerusalem in the bliss of John] he says as follows' (*Jón⁴* 1874, 510). — *Notes*: [1] *þat*s 'that': Since the rel. particle *es*/*er* is required at the beginning of the subordinate cl. *æstir ýta hilmis giptu flýti*, all eds follow Bugge in emending *þat* to *þat*s (= *þat es*; 1874, 934 n. 2). — [5] *sætti drengja* 'reconciler of valiant men': Paasche (1914a, 109) interprets the designation of John as *sættir drengia* 'reconciler of valiant men' as an allusion to an admonition ascribed to the aged John by S. Jerome: *filioli, diligite alterutrum* 'little children, love one another'. Lange (1958a, 83) regards it an example of the application to John of a term ordinarily used of God or Christ.

4. Hǫrðu lát mik hverju firðan, Flotna, vildak frá þér aldri,
hreinlífr faðir dróttar, meini, ferðgeymandi, skiliðr verða;
— síðan mætti ór of eyðask uggr es mér, hvárt þá mák þiggja
andar sǫr — þvís ljónum grandar. þessa gipt, es heimar skiptask.

Hreinlífr faðir dróttar, lát mik firðan hverju hǫrðu meini, þvís grandar ljónum; mætti ór sǫr andar síðan of eyðask. Flotna ferðgeymandi, vildak aldri verða skiliðr frá þér; uggr es mér, hvárt þá mák þiggja þessa gipt, es heimar skiptask.

Pure-living Father of the host [= God], let me be removed from every hard evil which injures men; may our wounds of the soul [SINS] then be wiped out. Guardian of the troop of mariners [MANKIND > = God], I would wish never to be parted from you; I am anxious whether I shall be able to receive this grace at the time when worlds are exchanged.

Ms.: **649a**(47r) (*Jón⁴*). — *Readings*: [6] ferðgeymandi: friðgeymandi 649a [7] þá: þat 649a.

Editions: *Skj* Gamli kanóki, 1. *Jóansdrápa* 4: AI, 561, BI, 548, *Skald* I, 266; *Jón⁴* 1874, 511, Bugge 1874, 934, Lange 1958a, 82.

Notes: [6] *ferðgeymandi, skiliðr verða*: All eds follow Unger in emending the ms. reading *frið* 'peace' to *ferð* 'journey, troop' since the metre requires *aðalhending* with *verð-* (Bugge 1874, 934 n. 1). — [7] *þá* 'then': The ms. reading is *þat* 'that'. All eds follow Bugge in emending the demonstrative pron. *þat* 'that' to the adv. *þá* 'then' (cf. Bugge 1874, 934 n. 2). — [8]: The cl. *es heimar skiptask* refers to the departure from 'this world' to 'the other' or 'the next' at death (cf. Bugge 1874, 934 n. 3).

Anonymous, *Leiðarvísan*

Edited by Katrina Attwood

Introduction

Leiðarvísan 'Way-Guidance' (Anon *Leið*) is a *drápa* of forty-five sts in *dróttkvætt* metre. Its name is given in st. 44/8. The poem is a version of the so-called Sunday Letter or 'Epistle from Heaven', in which Christ enjoins his followers, on pain of various cruel torments, to respect the sanctity of Sunday, to observe the festivals of the church and (in some versions) to fulfil various obligations of the Christian life.

After a conventional opening with requests to God for inspiration and to his audience for a hearing, the poet describes the Letter's arrival in sts 6-7: written by Christ himself with golden letters, it was found in Jerusalem on a Sunday and scrutinised by 'wise men'. They found in it a message to the effect that people who work on a Sunday (st. 8), who fail to observe holy days (st. 9) or who fail to pay the correct tithe (st. 10) will be punished severely. By contrast, baptised people who respect the sanctity of Sunday (sts 11-12) are promised prosperity and peace. The *stefjabálkr* (sts 13-33) illustrates the significance of Sunday observance in an enumeration of important events from biblical history and religious tradition, all of which are said to have happened on a Sunday. Two refrains occurring at intervals of four sts divide this list into sections concerning 'Genesis events' (the creation and Noah, sts 14-16), 'Exodus events' (Moses and the Israelites, sts 18-20), 'Christ events' (the Annunciation, Birth and Baptism, sts 22-4), Miracles (Cana and the feeding of the Five Thousand, sts 26-8) and events expressing Christ's triumph and glory (Triumphal entry into Jerusalem, Resurrection and Pentecost, sts 30-2). Thematic parallels between the chosen events, and verbal echoes within the poem, help to establish the theme. The *slæmr* (sts 34-45) balances the *upphaf* in both length and subject-matter. St. 34 echoes the opening requests for inspiration, the poet reiterating that he is powerless without help from God. He then goes on to warn that the Second Coming and Day of Judgement (which will, apparently, also take place on a Sunday) are imminent, and urges people to respect Sundays accordingly (sts 35-7). He promises deliverance, peace, eternal life and general happiness to those who love God and pray regularly (sts 37-9), and exhorts all Christians to implore God to grant them a place beside the Holy Cross (st. 40). The poem ends with four sts (42-5) in which the poet prays for himself, thanks one *prestr* ... *Rúnolfr* ('Rúnolfr the priest'; see below) for his help with the composition of the poem, then names the poem *Leiðarvísan* 'Way-Guidance', before commending it, with a last bidding-prayer, to its audience.

The legend of a letter from Christ concerning Sunday observance enjoyed a widespread and recurrent celebrity during the Middle Ages. Versions are extant in Lat. and in several vernaculars, dating from the C6th until well into the C14th. Exactly where the letter originated is unclear, although Priebsch (1936, 26-34) suggests, from a detailed comparison of its contents with more mainstream theological writings — notably those of Caesarius of Arles — that its history may have begun in Spain or the Moorish Empire. The widespread distribution and relative simplicity of the theme, however, suggest that versions of the Letter may well have appeared more or less independently in widely differing countries and cultures as and when the perceived need for it arose. Delehaye (1899), Priebsch (1936) and Lees (1990) give detailed accounts of the history and reception of the Letter in Western Europe, while the eastern recensions (many of which seem to derive from Gk texts produced in the C12th and thus considerably later than the earliest Lat. versions) are treated at length in Bittner (1906). Attwood (2003, 59-67) provides a summary of the history of the Letter, drawing particular attention to its apparent connections with the Crusades and the rush of pilgrim journeys — and travelogues — which they inspired.

It may be in this connection that the Letter reached Scandinavia. Apart from *Leið* — whose title perhaps tantalises us with suggestions of pilgrimage, as well as with more conventional connotations of the way of (Christian) life, — there are two known references to the text in ON-Icel. literature, both occurring in works directly concerned with pilgrim journeys to Jerusalem, one real, one imaginary. The *Leiðarvísir* 'Itinerary' is a prose account of a pilgrimage made in the mid-C12th by one 'Níkulás', usually identified with Níkulás Bergsson (d. 1159/1160), who became abbot of the Benedictine house at Munkaþverá shortly after its foundation in 1155 and is named elsewhere as the author of a *Jónsdrápa postula* (see skald biography in Ník *Jóndr*) and a *Kristsdrápa* (Hill 1983, 1993a, 1993b; for an alternative attribution of *Leiðarvísir* to abbot Níkulás Sæmundsson of Þingeyrar, see Riant 1865, 80).

The longer version of *Leiðarvísir* includes the following description of a side-chapel in the Church of the Holy Sepulchre: *Þar suðr frá því við veggin er alltari sancti Simeonis, þar kom ofan brefit gull-ritna* 'South of there [the main sepulchre] by the wall is the altar of S. Simeon, where the letter written in gold came down' (*AÍ* I, 26-7). There can be little doubt that it is to the Sunday Letter, reproductions of which may have been among the souvenirs on sale to medieval pilgrims to Jerusalem, that Níkulás refers. The similarity between the title of his itinerary and that of *Leið* has led to suggestions that Níkulás Bergsson might be the author of the *drápa* (Kedar and Westergaard-Nielsen 1978-9, 195; Astås 1993, 390). Although this attribution cannot be made for certain, it is likely that the poet had his background in the same monastic circles as Níkulás did. The Sunday Letter is also mentioned in the description of the Church of the Holy Sepulchre in the C14th *Kirialax saga*, which draws heavily on the longer version of *Leiðarvísir*: *Þar stendr Simions kirkia, ok er þar vardveittr hanndleggr hans yfir alltari; þar kom ofan bref þat er sialfr drottin ritaði sinum haundum gullstaufum um hin helga sunnudag* 'S. Simeon's chapel is there, and his armbone is preserved above the altar; the letter about holy Sunday which the Lord himself wrote in golden letters with his own hand came down there' (Kålund 1917, 65, quoted in Kedar and Westergård-Nielsen 1978-9, 210).

Some of the extant versions of the Sunday Letter also contain a Sunday List, an enumeration of scriptural and pseudo-scriptural events which are said to have occurred on

Sunday. The purpose is presumably to reinforce the Letter's message concerning Sunday observance. Lees (1990) gives a detailed account of the textual relationships between surviving Lat., OE and OIr. versions of the Sunday Letter and the Sunday List. There is general agreement that the surviving Western European versions of the Sunday Letter can be divided, on the basis of their accounts of the circumstances of the Letter's arrival on earth and its content, into three recensions. Attwood (2003, 68-77) undertakes a detailed comparison of *Leið* with representative texts of these three recensions and concludes that, although the direct source for *Leið* is not known, the account of the Sunday Letter in the poem most closely resembles that found in texts from the first recension. There are some thematic parallels between *Leið* and the late OE homily *Sermo angelorum nomina* (Pseudo-Wulfstan Homily XLV, in Napier 1883, 226-32) and its likely source, now represented by a late C14th Lat. text *Epistola Salvatoris Domini nostri Jesu Christi* (Priebsch 1899, 130-4), though it is unlikely that the poet had direct access to either text (Attwood 2003, 76-7). Attwood (2003, 70-5) also indicates several similarities between the Sunday List preserved in the *stefjabálkr* of *Leið* (sts 13-33) and those found in two MHG versions of the Sunday List which make no mention of the Sunday Letter: the homily *De die dominico*, which is preserved in a C15th ms. from the Benedictine monastery of S. Emmeram in Regensburg (Strauch 1895, 148-150), and a Sunday List transmitted in a C12th copy of the homily collection known as the *Speculum Ecclesiae*, preserved in the monastery at Benediktbeuern (Melbourn 1944, 147-8). Both these texts were known in Scandinavia, and they have been shown to have exerted considerable influence on the *HómÍsl* sermon *In natiuitate Domini* (Tveitane 1966). There is considerable similarity between *Leið*'s list and that found in the S. Emmeram homily (Attwood 2003, 74-5), although there are some minor omissions and alterations in *Leið*'s narrative. It is probably safest, however, to assume that none of the surviving Sunday Letters or Sunday Lists is the immediate source of *Leið*, but that the existence of the German and OE analogues suggest probable transmission routes for the material to Iceland.

Leið can be confidently dated to the second half of the C12th, on the basis of its relationship with other Christian *drápur* of this period (Skard 1953; Attwood 1996b). Other members of the group are Gamlkan *Has*, ESk *Geisl* and Anon *Pl*. These poems share a remarkable number of dictional and structural parallels, the most important of which are detailed in the Notes to this edn and in Attwood 1996b. The chronology of the poems is discussed in the Introductions to Gamlkan *Has* and Anon *Pl*. We have no reliable information about the authorship of *Leið*, although there is a possible hint in st. 43, where the poet thanks a certain *gǫfugr prestr* 'noble priest' called Rúnolfr for his help in composing the poem. Rúnolfr cannot be identified with certainty, although, as discussed in the Notes to st. 43, speculation has generally centred on two priests of that name mentioned in a *Prestatal* of 1143 (*DI* I, 180-94). These are Rúnolfr Dálksson, the nephew of Bishop Ketill Þorsteinsson of Hólar (bishop 1122-45) and Rúnolfr Ketilsson (d. 1186), the son of the same bishop. Both men are known to have had an active interest in skaldic poetry, and it is clear that, whoever the author of *Leið* was, he is likely to have moved in the priestly community, rich in scholarship, which would have been afforded by either Rúnolfr's connection with Bishop Ketill.

Leið is preserved complete in AM 757a 4° (B) of c. 1400 on fols 10r l. 39 - 11r l. 38. The first thirty-five sts are also found in AM 624 4° (624), which dates from the late C15th (Kålund 1888-94, II, 179). In neither case, however, is the preservation entirely satisfactory: B is extremely dark and difficult to read, and, like all of the other poems preserved in that ms. (Gamlkan *Has*, Anon *Líkn*, Anon *Heildr*, Anon *Gyð*, and Anon *Mdr*), the text is badly affected by wearing and lacunae. The 624 version seems to have been copied from B, and hence is useful as a witness to B's readings at a time when that ms. was in a far better state of preservation. Although 624 is clearly legible, words and phrases are often wrongly ordered, and the text has many misunderstandings and miscopyings (see Attwood 1996a, 41). It has been used selectively in this edn, along with the transcripts described below, when B is defective.

Lbs 444 4°ˣ (444ˣ) is a bundle of loose papers, among which are what appear to have been the working papers for Sveinbjörn Egilsson's printed edn of four Christian poems (1844). 444ˣ's transcription of *Leið* from B is likely to be the work of Brynjólfur Snorrason, an Icel. student at the Arnamagnæan Institute in Copenhagen from 1842-50 (Attwood 1996a, 32-3). The reference '444ˣ' in the textual apparatus refers to this transcription of B. Brynjólfur's transcription was copied by Jón Sigurðsson in JS 399a-b 4°ˣ (399a-bˣ), and both this transcription and 444ˣ are heavily annotated by Sveinbjörn Egilsson. The 399a-bˣ transcript is identical in all respects to that preserved in 444ˣ, and the reference '399a-bˣ' in the Readings should be taken as shorthand for both transcripts. The 444ˣ bundle also contains other material related to *Leið*. For ease of reference, this additional material is designated by bracketed numerals, in the form '444(1)ˣ' etc. 444(1)ˣ is a single paper bifolium comprising a diplomatic transcription of sts 1-2 and 35 from 624. The hand is that of Konráð Gíslason. 444(2)ˣ is an untitled diplomatic transcription of 624 in Jón Sigurðsson's hand. The text is lightly annotated by both Jón and Sveinbjörn Egilsson. 444(3)ˣ is a partially normalised transcription of 624 in Sveinbjörn's hand. The text is heavily annotated and prose recastings of sts 1-4, 8, 14-18, explanations of complex kennings and a schematic résumé of the poem, all in Sveinbjörn's hand, are scribbled in the margins. Extensive use has also been made of Hugo Rydberg's transcription of B in Rydberg 1907, which is generally reliable, though less conservative than the 444ˣ transcription, in that Rydberg incorporates speculative reconstructions (always annotated) into his transcription. Where readings from Rydberg 1907 are given among the Readings, they are designated B*Rydberg*. The text of *Leið* in Lbs 1152 8°ˣ fols 53-69 has also been consulted. This is Sveinbjörn Egilsson's clean, print copy for his 1844 edn. There are four minor discrepancies between this copy and the printed text (to which reference is made below): accents are included in *áðr* (49/5), *hánum* (37/8), and *orðvápn* (44/4), while the printed text adds an accent in *sképnu* (15/8) which does not appear in Lbs 1152 8°ˣ. Reidar Astås's annotated Norw. translation of *Leið* in Astås 1970 has also been consulted, as has Attwood 1996a, which is the present ed.'s doctoral thesis.

1. Þinn óð sem ek inni
allskjótt, salar fjalla,
harðla brátt til hróðrar,
harri, munn ok varrar.

Mér gefi dǫglingr dýra
dœmistóls ok sólar,
enn svát ek mega, sanna
orðgnótt, lofa dróttin.

Ek sem inni þinn óð, munn ok varrar, allskjótt, harðla brátt til hróðrar, harri salar fjalla. Dǫglingr dœmistóls ok sólar gefi mér dýra, sanna orðgnótt, svát ek mega enn lofa dróttin.

I arrange your poem inwardly, [and] my mouth and lips very quickly, very briskly for praise, lord of the hall of the mountains [SKY/HEAVEN > = God]. May the king of the judgement-seat and of the sun [= God] give me precious, true word-abundance, so that I may again praise the Lord.

Mss: **B**(10r), 624(85). — *Reading*: [1] Þinn: *so* 624, '[...]inn' B.

Editions: *Skj* Anonyme digte og vers [XII], G [2]. *Leiðarvísan* 1: AI, 618, BI, 622, *Skald* I, 302, *NN* §§1257, 1258, 2991D; Sveinbjörn Egilsson 1844, 57, Rydberg 1907, 4, Attwood 1996a 60, 171.

Notes: [All]: Sts 1-5 constitute an appeal to God and the other members of the Trinity to help the poet compose his poem, represented as a praise-poem (*hróðr*, *mærðr*). Each st. marks a stage in the poet's progression towards the realisation of his goal. In st. 1 he has barely begun to prepare his mind and the organs of speech for a quick composition; in st. 2 he asks God to give him plenty of words and predicts that his speech-organs will be stirred into action; in st. 3 he begs the Father and Son to straighten out the poem's form, while asking the Holy Spirit to strengthen the work. St. 4 sees the poet more confident in his abundance of words, and ready to recite his poem before a human audience, while in st. 5 he asks his audience for a formal hearing and announces his subject: advice about Sunday. — [1] *Þinn*: In B, the beginnings of 10r, 39 and 10r, 40 are indented by some 9mm, to allow space for a larger initial to mark the beginning of the poem, which has not been supplied. All previous eds and transcribers have reconstructed this letter as <Þ>. — [1] *sem ek inni* 'I arrange inwardly': *Skj* B, followed by *Skald*, treats both *sem* and *inni* as 1st pers. sg. pres. indic. verbs, adding the enclitic pronouns. This requires emendation of *ek* to *ok* and *inni* to *innik*. They thus read *semk ok innik*. Finnur Jónsson takes *munn ok varrar* (l. 4) as the object of *semja* 'to arrange, compose', and *þinn óð* (l. 1) as the object of *inna* 'to perform, relate, tell, achieve'. He construes *innik þinn óð ... ok semk munn ok varrar* 'I produce your poem ... and arrange [my] mouth and lips'. Kock (*NN* §1257) argues that this is an example of *zeugma*, with *óð* 'poem' the object of both verbs and *munn ok varrar harðla brátt til hróðrar* 'mouth and lips very eager to praise' the object of *semk*. Attwood 1996a retains the ms. reading by treating *sem* as a conj. meaning 'just as, as well as' and *ek inni þinn óð* 'I compose your poem' and *sem munn ok varrar* 'just as [I compose my] mouth and lips' as parallel clauses, with *óð* and *munn ok varrar* as the objects of *inna* in the sense 'to compose'. The problem with this reading is that *inna* does not mean 'to compose' (as *semja* does) but 'to perform, relate' and thus does not suit both postulated objects. The only other way to keep the ms. reading (and the one adopted here) is to consider *sem ek* the verb with two objects and regard *inni* as the adv. 'inside, indoors', usually used in a concrete sense, but here meaning 'inwardly, in my breast', where poetry resided according to skaldic convention (cf. *Meissner*, 134-6). Another example of *inni* used in a metaphorical sense is in Gamlkan *Has* 7/5. — [2] *salar fjalla* 'hall of the mountains [SKY/HEAVEN]': A common kenning for the sky or heavens; cf. GunnlI Lv 8/2^V, Hallv *Knútdr* 8/2^{III} and *Has* 30/2. — [6] *dǫglingr dǿmistóls* 'king of the judgement-seat [= God]': This kenning also occurs in Kálf *Kátr* 47/5-6. Cf. also *drottinn dǿmistóls* 'lord of the judgement-seat' in Kálf *Kátr* 1/1-2 and 21/1-2. — [7] *enn* 'again': This adv. suggests that the poet has composed poetry in praise of God before; cf. Anon *Mgr* 2/8 and Anon *Vitn* 2/7. — [7] *sanna* 'true': *Skj* B, followed by *Skald*, emends to *sannan*, m. acc. sg. to agree with *dróttin* 'lord' (l. 8). The ms. reading is retained here by taking *sanna* as f. acc. sg., qualifying *orðgnótt* 'word-abundance', amplifying *dýra* 'precious'.

2. Fyrr kveðk frægjan harra
    fagrgims, þanns ræðr himni,
    hás at hróðri þessum
    hreggranns an kyn seggja.
    Æstik aflamestan
    orðgnóttar mér dróttin;
    hrœrð skulu mín til mærðar
    málgǫgn, en lið þagni.

Kveðk frægjan harra fagrgims hás hreggranns, þanns ræðr himni, at hróðri þessum fyrr an kyn seggja. Æstik aflamestan dróttin orðgnóttar mér; málgǫgn mín skulu hrœrð til mærðar, en lið þagni.

I call upon the famous king of the fair jewel of the high storm-house [SKY/HEAVEN > SUN > = God], the one who rules heaven, [to hear] this praise-poem before the kinsfolk of men. I request the most powerful lord for word-abundance for myself; my speech-organs shall be stirred into praise, and let the people keep silent.

Mss: **B**(10r), 624(85), 399a-b^x. — *Reading*: [6] orðgnóttar: *so* 624, 399a-b^x, 'ord gno[...]r' B.

Editions: *Skj* Anonyme digte og vers [XII], G [2]. *Leiðarvísan* 2: AI, 618, BI, 622, *Skald* I, 302-3; Sveinbjörn Egilsson 1844, 57, Rydberg 1907, 4, Attwood 1996a, 60, 171.

Notes: [1-4] *harra fagrgims hás hreggranns* 'king of the fair jewel of the high storm-house [SKY/HEAVEN > SUN > = God]': Heaven-kennings of the 'abode of the storm' type are very common in the C12th *drápur* and seem to be a favourite of the *Leið* poet. Cf. *jǫfurr hás hreggranns* 'prince of the high storm-house' (17/1-2) and *gramr hreggranns* 'prince of the storm-house' (25/5-6). For comparable kennings, see *Has* 1/1-2, *Geisl* 64/5-6 and *Mdr* 24/2. Also comparable in terms of reference to God as lord of the sun, is *Geisl* 18/8. — [6] *orðgnóttar mér dróttin*: Cf. *Geisl* 10/2: *orðgnóttar biðk dróttin*.

3. Fǫður biðk ok son síðan
   slétt óðarlag rétta;
   minn styrki vel verka
   vandan heilagr andi.

   Ór munu aldar stýri
   óþægilig frægjum
   orð, nema mér til mærðar
   málsgnótt fái dróttinn.

Síðan biðk fǫður ok son rétta slétt óðarlag; heilagr andi styrki vel vandan verka minn. Orð ór munu óþægilig frægjum stýri aldar, nema dróttinn fái mér málsgnótt til mærðar.

Then I ask the Father and Son to straighten out a smooth poem form; may the Holy Spirit strengthen my awkward work well. Our [my] words will be displeasing to the famous steerer of men [= God], unless the Lord gives me an abundance of language for the praise-poem.

Mss: **B**(10r), 624(85).

Editions: *Skj* Anonyme digte og vers [XII], G [2]. *Leiðarvísan* 3: AI, 619, BI, 623, *Skald* I, 303, *NN* §3137; Sveinbjörn Egilsson 1844, 57-8, Rydberg 1907, 4, Attwood 1996a, 60, 171.

Notes: [4] *vandan* 'awkward': Finnur Jónsson translates *vanskelige* 'difficult, awkward', but Kock (*NN* §3137) objects to the interpretation of this term as pejorative, on the grounds that the poet speaks positively of his creation elsewhere (see, for example, 4/2, 43/7, 44). He suggests the meaning 'wearisome, exhausting' for *vandan*. That the poet does find his work wearisome is clear from 44/1-4, but Finnur's interpretation is preferable here, as it seems to capture the parallelism between the *slétt óðarlag* 'smooth poem-form' that the Father and Son are asked to create in l. 2 and the *vandan verk* 'awkward work' for which the Holy Spirit is asked for help in the second cl. — [8] *málsgnótt* 'abundance of language': This cpd is *hap. leg.*, but is obviously on the same model as *orðgnótt* 'word-abundance' (1/8, 2/6, 4/8; *Geisl* 10/2). This kind of variation supports the parallelism of theme and diction between the second *helmingar* of the first four sts.

4. Víst emk fúss at freista
   — fæk ljósum brag hrósat —
   láðs fyr lyptimeiðum
   linns orðspeki minn*ar*.

   Því hefr hreggþjalma hilmir
   hreinlyndr gefit eina
   oss, til óðar þessa
   orðgnótt, at skalk njóta.

Víst emk fúss at freista orðspeki minn*ar* fyr lyptimeiðum linns láðs; fæk hrósat ljósum brag. Því eina hefr hreinlyndr hilmir hreggþjalma gefit oss orðgnótt, at skalk njóta til óðar þessa.

Truly I am eager to try my word-wisdom before the lifting-poles of the serpent's land [GOLD > MEN]; I can praise the bright poem. For that purpose only has the pure-minded prince of the storm-enclosure [SKY/HEAVEN > = God] given us [me] word-abundance, so that I can use [it] for this poem.

Mss: **B**(10r), 624(86). — *Reading*: [4] minn*ar*: minni B, 624.

Editions: *Skj* Anonyme digte og vers [XII], G [2]. *Leiðarvísan* 4: AI, 619, BI, 623, *Skald* I, 303; Sveinbjörn Egilsson 1844, 58, Rydberg 1907, 4, Attwood 1996a, 60-1, 171.

Notes: [3] *láðs fyr lyptimeiðum*: Cf. *Has* 18/3 *láðs við lyptimeiða*, and the phonetically-similar l. *Pl* 31/3 *láðhofs lypti-Móða*. In the *Leið* and *Has* examples, the man-kennings completed by the alliterating word in the following ll. are identical. — [4] *minn* 'my': *Skj* B and *Skald* emend to *minnar* to agree with *orðspeki* 'word-wisdom' f. gen. sg., since *freista* (l.1) takes a gen. object.

5. Hljóð gefi hirðimeiðar Vilk, meðan varrar telja,
    hrælinns at brag svinnir — vegskrýðendr mér hlýði —
    — gegn vilk þjóð at þagni frá dáðmǫttugs dróttins
    þá stund, es kveðk — sunda. degi nǫkkur rǫk segja.

Svinnir hirðimeiðar linns hræsunda gefi hljóð at brag; vilk, at gegn þjóð þagni þá stund, es kveðk. Vilk, meðan varrar telja, segja nǫkkur rǫk frá degi dáðmǫttugs dróttins; vegskrýðendr hlýði mér.

May the wise guarding-poles of the serpent of carrion-channels [BLOOD > SWORD > MEN] give a hearing to the poem; I desire that the honest people keep silence while I am reciting. I want, while my lips declaim, to utter some lore concerning the day of the deed-mighty Lord; way-adorners [MEN] should hear me.

Mss: **B**(10r), 624(86), 399a-b[x]. — *Reading*: [1] gefi: *so* 624, 399a-b[x], 'ge[...]' B.

Editions: *Skj* Anonyme digte og vers [XII], G [2]. *Leiðarvísan* 5: AI, 619, BI, 623, *Skald* I, 303, *NN* §1259; Sveinbjörn Egilsson 1844, 58, Rydberg 1907, 4-5, Attwood 1996a, 61, 172.

Notes: [5-6]: To accommodate the emendation of *vegskrýðendr* described below under Note to l. 6, Finnur Jónsson construes *varrar viggskrýðendr hlýði mér, meðan teljak* 'the adorners of the horse of the wash should hear me, while I recite'. Kock (*NN* §1259) objects to this, on the grounds that it is impossible to split the temporal cl. (*meðan telja*) with part of the subject of the main cl. (*varrar*). Instead, he prefers to preserve the ms. reading *telja*, which Finnur had emended, and to take *varrar* as nom. pl. of *vǫrr* f. 'lip', referring back to the lips first mentioned in 1/4. His reading is followed here. Sveinbjörn Egilsson, who first suggested the emendation to *viggskrýðendr*, also assumed *varrar* to be the subject of the temporal cl., giving the arrangement *hlýði viggskrýðendr mér meðan* [*minnar*] *varrar telja* 'may horse-adorners [MEN] listen to me while [my] lips declaim' (note to Sveinbjörn's transcription of the 624 text in 444(3)[x]). — [6] *vegskrýðendr* 'way-adorners': Finnur Jónsson (*Skj* B) follows Sveinbjörn Egilsson's suggestion (1844, 58 n. 2) that *veg*- m. 'way, path' should be emended to *vigg*- n. 'horse, steed', to give the man-kenning *viggskrýðendr* 'horse-adorners'. Finnur extends this kenning by taking *varrar* (l. 5) as nom. pl. of m. *vǫrr* 'pull of the oar, wash or wake left by a ship', which is often used poetically for the sea. He thus forms the inverted man-kenning *viggskrýðendr varrar* 'adorners of the horse of the wash' [SHIP > MEN]. Although *viggskrýðendr varrar* would anticipate *blakkskreytendr brautar borðs* 'decorators of the horse of the path of the plank' in 8/3-4, B's reading *vegskrýðendr* 'way-adorners' makes acceptable grammatical sense and is likely to be a man-kenning, given that the poem's title gestures towards the familiar Christian figure of life as a journey, possibly a pilgrimage. Alternatively, *veg-* could have the sense of 'honour' in this cpd. — [7] *dáðmǫttugs* 'deed-mighty': This is the first of a series of adjectival compounds beginning *dáð-* used to describe God and his miracles. Compounds of this type are quite common in the Christian *drápur*, though relatively uncommon elsewhere in the skaldic corpus (see *LP*: *dáðmǫttugr*). They appear to be a particular favourite of the *Leið*-poet: God is described as *dáðfimr* 'deed-agile' 26/6; *dáðhress* 'deed-hearty' 45/4; *dáðsnjallr* 'deed-eager' 23/6; *dáðsterkr* 'deed-strong' 20/2, 36/6. Christ establishes peace that is *dáðskreytr* 'deed-adorned' 15/5, the angel host is characterised as *dáðstett dags lands* 'the deed-host of day's land' 24/5 and the crowd of five thousand fed by Christ is *dáðgladdr* 'deed-gladdened' 28/2. Most of these compounds appear to be neologisms, though similar forms are found in both *Geisl* (where God is *dáðmildr* 'deed-kind' 25/8, and *dáðvandr* 'zealous for [good] deeds' 6/2, and S. Óláfr is *dáðsnjallr* 'deed-eager' 56/8) and *Has* (where God is described as *dáðgeymir* 'hoarder of [good] deeds' 34/3; *dáðrakkr* 'deed-bold' 7/8; *dáðreyndr* 'deed-proven' 44/2).

6. Tekk til orðs, þars urðu
alfregnar jartegnir
— tǫkn eru sýnd í slíku
sǫnn — Jórsalamǫnnum.

Sendi salvǫrðr grundar
snillifimr af himni
borgar lýð til bjargar
bréf gollstǫfum sollit.

Tekk til orðs, þars alfregnar jartegnir urðu Jórsalamǫnnum; sǫnn tǫkn eru sýnd í slíku. Snillifimr grundar salvǫrðr sendi bréf af himni, sollit gollstǫfum, til bjargar lýð borgar.

I begin to speak at the point when renowned miracles befell the people of Jerusalem; true tokens are shown in such [a thing]. The prowess-nimble warden of the hall of the earth [(*lit.* 'earth's hall-warden') SKY/HEAVEN > = God] sent a letter from heaven, embellished [*lit.* swollen] with golden letters, as a help for the townspeople.

Mss: **B**(10v), 624(86), 399a-b[x]. — *Readings*: [1] Tekk ('tek ek'): *so all others*, 'Tek [...]k' B [8] gollstǫfum sollit ('gullstöfum sullet'): 'gullstǫfum sullath' 624.

Editions: *SkJ* Anonyme digte og vers [XII], G [2]. *Leiðarvísan* 6: AI, 619, BI, 623, *Skald* I, 303; Sveinbjörn Egilsson 1844, 58, Rydberg 1907, 5, Attwood 1996a, 61, 172.

Notes: [2] *jartegnir* 'miracles': On the spelling here, see Note to 26/4. — [5] *sendi salvǫrðr grundar*: Cf. *Geisl* 19/3: *sýndi salvǫrðr grundar*. — [6] *snillifimr* 'prowess-nimble': This cpd adj. is *hap. leg.*, but a similar construction is found at *Has* 48/3, where King David is described as *snilli vanðr* 'accustomed to eloquence'. — [8] *gollstǫfum* 'with golden letters': Sunday Letter texts of the first and second recensions conventionally describe the letter as having golden calligraphy (Attwood 2003, 72). Both Abbot Níkulás of Munkaþverá and the author of *Kirialax saga* mention this in their descriptions of the chapel of S. Simeon, part of the Basilica of the Holy Sepulchre in Jerusalem, where the letter was reputed to have landed. For details, see the Introduction. — [8] *sollit gollstǫfum* 'embellished [*lit.* swollen] with golden letters': Normalisation of B's 'sullet' is necessary to preserve the correct sequence of vowels in a Class III strong verb (cf. *ANG* §489). This in turn necessitates normalisation to *goll-* in order to preserve the rhyme. Although *goll* and *gull* coexisted for a while (*ANG* §61.1), *goll* was the more usual form in the early period. For the sake of consistency, *gullstǫfum* in 7/8 has also been normalised to *gollstǫfum*, though the rhyme is not affected there.

7. Varð bréf, þats guð gerði
    geðsnjallr ok lét falla
    — vóns á gipt — á grœna
    grund, sunnudag fundit.

    Bók* réðu þá blíðir
    byrskíðs viðir síðan
    — verðr, sás vensk á dýrðir,
    vítr — gollstǫfum ritna.

Bréf, þats geðsnjallr guð gerði ok lét falla á grœna grund, varð fundit sunnudag; vóns á gipt. Blíðir viðir byrskíðs réðu síðan þá bók*, ritna gollstǫfum; verðr vítr, sás vensk á dýrðir.

The letter, which valiant-minded God made and let fall onto the green ground, was discovered on a Sunday; there is an expectation of grace. Gentle trees of the wind-ski [SHIP > SEAFARERS] later interpreted that book, written with gold letters; he will become wise who accustoms himself to glories.

Mss: **B**(10v), 624(86),. — *Reading*: [5] *Bók**: 'becks' B, 624.

Editions: *Skj* Anonyme digte og vers [XII], G [2]. *Leiðarvísan* 7: AI, 619, BI, 624, *Skald* I, 303, *NN* §3248; Sveinbjörn Egilsson 1844, 59, Rydberg 1907, 5, Attwood 1996a, 61, 172.

Notes: [5] *bók** 'book': It is not possible to use B's and 624's reading 'becks'. Although *bekkr* 'bench' may be compounded with expressions for the sea in ship-kennings (as, for example, in SnSt *Ht* 75/2[III]: *hafbekkr* 'sea-bench'), the man-kenning *viðir bekks byrskíðs* 'trees of the bench of the wind-ski', which seems to be the only possible arrangement, would be tautologous: *byrskíð* 'wind-ski' is already an acceptable ship-kenning. Kock (*NN* §3248) suggests that *þá* (l. 5), interpreted as an adv., should be construed with *síðan* (l. 6), but even this arrangement does not solve the problem of 'becks', since it would leave *réðu* (l. 5) without an object. With Rydberg and Finnur Jónsson this edn adopts Sveinbjörn Egilsson's emendation to *bók**, understood as a reference to the Sunday Letter, and qualified by the adj. *ritna* 'written' (l. 8).

8. Sagði bréf, hvat brygði
bitr fár guma ári,
blakks skreytendum brautar
borðs frá dróttins orðum.

'Hljóta víst', kvað veitir
vegfróðr hluta góðra,
'menn þeirs minn dag vinna,
mest angr af því flestir.'

Bréf sagði skreytendum blakks brautar borðs frá orðum dróttins, hvat bitr fár brygði ári guma. Vegfróðr veitir góðra hluta kvað: 'Flestir menn, þeirs vinna dag minn, hljóta víst mest angr af því'.

The letter told the furnishers of the horse of the path of the plank [SEA > SHIP > SEAFARERS] about the Lord's words, what bitter harm could alter the good fortune of men. The way-wise giver of good things [= God] said: 'Most men who work on my day will certainly gain the greatest sorrow from it'.

Mss: **B**(10v), 624(86), 399a-b[x]. — *Readings*: [2] guma: gumna 624 [4] borðs: borð B, 624 [8] angr: so 624, 399a-b[x], '[...]gr' B.

Editions: *Skj* Anonyme digte og vers [XII], G [2]. *Leiðarvísan* 8: AI, 619-20, BI, 624, *Skald* I, 303, *NN* §2140; Sveinbjörn Egilsson 1844, 59, Rydberg 1907, 5, Attwood 1996a, 61, 172.

Notes: [1] *hvat* 'what': Finnur Jónsson (*Skj* B) emends B's 'huad' to *hver*, considering the phrase *hver bitr fár* to be pl. and the verb *brygði* (l. 1) also pl., translating *hvilke bitre mén skadede mændenes lykke* 'what bitter injuries damaged peoples' good fortune'. *Brygði* can also be 3rd pers. sg. pret. subj. and could thus have a sg. subject. Kock (*NN* §2140) reads *hvat bitr fár* (sg.) with a sg. verb, and this reading is followed here. — [2] *guma* 'of men': A rarer variant than *gumna* (so 624): see *ANG* §401.3. — [3-4] *skreytendum blakks brautar borðs* 'furnishers of the horse of the path of the plank [SEA > SHIPS > SEAFARERS]': That the apparent retention of B's reading *borð* nom. or acc. 'plank' in Sveinbjörn Egilsson's 1844 edn is a misprint is confirmed by Lbs. 1152 8[ox] (Sveinbjörn's print copy) which has *borðs* gen. Sveinbjörn himself first suggested the emendation to *borðs* in a note to 444[x]. — [6] *vegfróðr* 'way-wise': *Skj* B understands as *hæderkyndig* 'honour-wise', which is further glossed in *LP* as *i besiddelse af hæder* 'in possession of honour' (cf. *LP* (1860)'s gloss *gloriosus* 'famous, renowned'). Though this interpretation is perfectly possible, the first element of the cpd may also be understood as acc. of m. *vegr* 'way', path'. *Vegfróðr* 'way-wise' is a suitable adj. to describe God; see Note to *vegskrýðendr* (5/6) above.

9. Hætt kveðr heilagr dróttinn
hyrskerðǫndum verða
arms, þeims eigi þyrma
alfríðs sonar tíðum.

Því ro fluggreddar fœddir
fleins með ýmsum meinum;
bæði bǫrn ok móðir
báglundask fyr stundum.

Heilagr dróttinn kveðr verða hætt arms hyrskerðǫndum, þeims eigi þyrma tíðum alfríðs sonar; því ro fleins fluggreddar fœddir með ýmsum meinum; bæði bǫrn ok móðir báglundask fyr stundum.

The Holy Lord says it will become dangerous for the diminishers of the fire of the arm [(*lit.* 'arm's fire-diminishers') GOLD > GENEROUS MEN], for those who do not respect the festivals of the altogether beautiful Son. Therefore nourishers of spear-flight [(*lit.* 'flight-nourishers of the spear') BATTLE > WARRIORS] are born with various defects; both children and their mother quarrel from time to time.

Mss: **B**(10v), 624(86-7), 399a-b[x]. — *Readings*: [3] þyrma: *so* 624, 'þýr[...]' B, þyr(m)a(?) 399a-b[x]   [5] -greddar: -raddar B, 624   [7] bǫrn: *so* 624, 399a-b[x], '[...]ǫrn' B;   ok: *so* 624, '[...]' B; móðir: *so* 399a-b[x], '[...]oder' B, 'mædur' 624.

Editions: *Skj* Anonyme digte og vers [XII], G [2]. *Leiðarvísan* 9: AI, 620, BI, 624, *Skald* I, 303, *NN* §§1260, 2557; Sveinbjörn Egilsson 1844, 59, Rydberg 1907, 5, Attwood 1996a, 61-2, 173.

Notes: [5-8]: Attwood 1996a, 191-2 understood this *helmingr* to refer to the nature of the torments which will befall those who do not respect the festivals of the Church, drawing parallels with much more graphic and detailed descriptions in other versions of the Sunday Letter. However, it would be equally possible to understand st. 9 as stating that life will become dangerous for those who do not keep Christian observances because mankind is imperfect and sinful and there are even disagreements between those one would expect to be most harmonious, viz. mothers and their children. — [5-8]: These ll. are difficult to construe, largely because of the uncertain status of the kenning in ll. 5-6. Readings that attempt to construct a man-kenning here involve considerable emendation. On the other hand, failure to emend results in what appears to be a battle-kenning *flugraddar fleins* 'flight-voices of the arrow', which does not make sense in context and does not agree with *fæddir* (m. nom. pl.) 'born'. It is possible that *–raddar* (l. 5) is a corruption of some agent noun designating men or warriors. Here it is assumed to form the base-word of a kenning for warriors by emending *-raddar* to *-greddar* 'feeders, nourishers', following a suggestion of Kari Ellen Gade. In ll. 5-6 B reads 'þui eru flugraddar fędder fleins med ymsum meinum'. Sveinbjörn Egilsson (notes preserved in 444[x] and 1844, 59) suggested normalisation of 'fędder' to *fæddir*, m. nom. pl. of the participial adj. formed from *fæða* 'to give birth to, be born, be brought up', taken with B's pl. verb *eru* (l. 5). He is followed by *Skj* B and this edn. Sveinbjörn and *Skj* B also emend l. 8 to *bág lundar ferr stundum*, constructing a man-kenning *lundar fleins flugraddar* 'groves of the arrow's flight-voice' [BATTLE > WARRIORS]. The *helmingr* is then construed *því eru fleins flugraddar lundar fæddir með ymsum meinum; bæði bǫrn ok móðir ferr stundum bág* 'therefore the groves of the arrow's flight-voice are born with various defects; both children and the mother sometimes suffer difficulty'. Kock (*NN* §1260 and *Skald*), followed by Attwood 1996a, emend B's 'fędder' to *fæðir* 'feeder', which requires only minor additional emendation to the sg. *es* 'is' in l. 5. This produces a warrior-kenning, *fæðir fluggraddar fleins* 'feeder of the flight-voice of the arrow' and a statement that he, presumably representing mankind, has various pains. The sg. usage here is rather curious, however, if the poet is alluding to human imperfections in general. In *NN* §2557 (and *Skald*), Kock introduces a further emendation to *flughríðar fæðir* 'feeder of the flight-storm', claiming that *raddar* is a garbled form of *ríðar*, i.e. *hríðar*.

Although *flugrǫdd* 'flight-voice' is not attested elsewhere, battle-kennings on the model 'weapon + *rǫdd*' are very common in the skaldic corpus (see *LP*: *rǫdd*), though it is worth noting that *LP* does not list another cpd using an abstract concept such as *flug* instead of the word for 'weapon'. — [8] *báglundask fyrir stundum*: Although the verb *báglunda* 'to become obstreperous, quarrel' is not otherwise attested in either poetry or prose, there is both a noun and adj. *bágr* 'difficul(ty), trouble(some)' (see *ONP*) and the adj. *báglundr* 'spiteful, warlike' occurs in Gestr Lv 1/6[III], where Snorri goði is characterised as *báglundr goði* 'a spiteful priest'. See also *Fritzner*: *lundaðr* 'minded, of a particular disposition' = *lyndr*.

10.   'Munk', kvað vǫrðr, 'í virða',   ef vegrunnar vinna
    vallræfrs, 'liðu alla   varrelgs daga helga
    — stríð þjá drótt til dauða   elds eða eigi gjalda
    drjúghvasst — e*ld*um kasta,   allþétt tíund rétta.'

Vǫrðr vallræfrs kvað: 'Munk kasta e*ld*um í alla liðu virða — stríð þjá drjúghvasst drótt til dauða —, ef varrelgs veg- elds -runnar vinna allþétt helga daga eða gjalda eigi rétta tíund'.

The warden of the plain-roof [SKY/HEAVEN > = God] said: 'I will cast fires into all the limbs of men — afflictions will plague mankind severely unto death — if the trees of the fire of the way of the wake-elk [(*lit.* 'way-trees of the fire of the wake-elk') SHIP > SEA > GOLD > MEN] work very energetically on holy days or do not pay the correct tithe'.

Mss: **B**(10v), 624(87), 399a-b[x]. — *Readings*: [1] vǫrðr: *so all others*, 'vǫrd[...]' B [2] -ræfrs ('-ręfrss'): 'ræfuls' 624 [4] e*ld*um: 'ęttum' B, ættum 624, 'ęllum' 399a-b[x] [6] varrelgs: 'vareelgs' B, 'vardegls' B*Rydberg*, 624, 399a-b[x]; helga: *so* 624, 'helg[...]' B [7] elds: *so* 624, '[...]ll[...]z' B.

Editions: *Skj* Anonyme digte og vers [XII], G [2]. *Leiðarvísan* 10: AI, 620, BI, 624, *NN* §§2141, 3249; Sveinbjörn Egilsson 1844, 59-60, Rydberg 1907, 5, Attwood 1996a, 62, 173.

Notes: [4] *eldum* (dat. pl.) 'fires': The dat. is needed with *kasta*. It has not been possible to make sense of B's reading 'ęttum', possibly dat. pl. of f. *ætt*, either an astronomical term referring to a portion, or 'quarter' of the heavens or, more commonly, a reference to kinship relations or family pedigree (cf. *Fritzner*: *ætt*). The word is clearly intended as the instrument of God's threat to punish mankind for its failure to observe Sundays by throwing (*kasta*, l. 4) something painful into men's limbs. Finnur Jónsson's emendation (*Skj* B) to *trega*, dat. sg. of *tregi* 'woe, sorrow', bears no relation to the ms. reading. Kock's suggestion (*NN* §2141) of *eitrum* or *eitri*, dat. pl. or dat. sg. of *eitr* 'poison' makes sense in the context and is in keeping with the threatening tone of the st. Most other versions of the Sunday Letter include fire as one of the punishments for failing to observe the sanctity of Sunday (Attwood 2003, 72). Thus emendation has been made to *eldum*, dat. pl. of *eldr* 'fire'. — [5, 6, 7] *vinna allþétt helga daga eða eigi gjalda rétta tíund* '[they] work very energetically on holy days or do not pay the correct tithe': Kock (*NN* §3249) offers an alternative prose rendition, requiring a slight emendation, though he did not adopt it in

Skald: vinna all[a] helga daga, eða gjalda eigi þétt rétta tíund 'work on all holy days, or do not eagerly pay the correct tithe'. — [5, 6, 7] *vegrunnar elds varrelgs* 'way-trees of the fire of the wake-elk [SHIP > SEA > GOLD > SEAFARERS]': Sveinbjörn Egilsson (1844, 60) follows 624's and 399a-b^x's readings to give *varðelg* 'guardian-elk', but B reads 'vareelgs', though it is possible that the first <e> is meant to be a <d> (cf. Rydberg 1907, 5 n. 14). *Skj* B and Kock emend to *varrelg*, compounding *elgr* 'elk' with the poetic word *vǫrr* 'wake of a ship'. Although *varrelgr* is not otherwise attested, *elgr* is often used in kennings for ships (*LP*: *elgr*). *Vegr varrelgs* 'way of the wake-elk' i.e. 'way of the ship' makes for an acceptable sea-kenning.

11. Fárskerðir býðr fyrðum
    friðkunnan dag sunnu
    ýtum hollr of allan
    aldr dýrliga at halda.

    Gefa kvezk mætr í móti
    meinhrjóðandi þjóðum
    ár með ǫllum tíri
    einart ok frið hreinan.

Fárskerðir, hollr ýtum, býðr fyrðum at halda dýrliga friðkunnan sunnu dag of allan aldr. Mætr meinhrjóðandi kvezk gefa þjóðum í móti einart ár ok hreinan frið með ǫllum tíri.

The misfortune-diminisher [= God], gracious to men, commands men to observe ceremoniously the peace-known day of the sun thoughout all ages. The worthy harm-destroyer [= God] says he will give the peoples in return reliable abundance and pure peace with all glory.

Mss: **B**(10v), 624(87), 399a-b^x. — *Readings*: [1] Fárskerðir: *so* 624, 399a-b^x, 'Fár[...]kerðir' B [2] frið-: friðan 624, friðar 399a-b^x; -kunnan: *so* 624, 'kunna[...]' B, kunna(n)(?) 399a-b^x [4] at: *so* 624, 'a[...]' B, a(ð)(?) 399a-b^x [5] í: *so* 624, á B [6] meinhrjóðandi: *so* 624, 399a-b^x, 'mei[...]hrjoðannde' B [7] ǫllum: *so* 624, 399a-b^x, 'ǫll[...]m' B; tíri: *so* 624, 'tír[...]' B, tír(i)(?) 399a-b^x [8] einart: *so* 624, 399a-b^x, '[...]inart' B.

Editions: *Skj* Anonyme digte og vers [XII], G [2]. *Leiðarvísan* 11: AI, 620, BI, 625, *Skald* I, 304; Sveinbjörn Egilsson 1844, 60, Rydberg 1907, 5-6, Attwood 1996a, 62-3, 173.

Notes: [1] *fárskerðir* 'misfortune-diminisher': This epithet recalls *fárskerðandi* m. 'misfortune-diminisher', used of S. Óláfr in *Geisl* 63/7. Neither cpd is attested elsewhere. The two ll. are strikingly similar, the rhyme being with a form of *fyrðar* 'men, warriors' in each case. — [2] *friðkunnan* 'peace-known': Sveinbjörn Egilsson (1844, 60), Finnur Jónsson (*Skj* B) and Kock follow the 399a-b^x transcriber in reading *friðar kunnan*, while B reads *frið*. Interestingly, st. 63/8 in *Geisl* begins with the cpd *friðarsyn* 'vision of peace'.

12. Án meg*u* engir dýnu   Orð munu eigi verða
    otrs, þeirs skírn hafa hlotna,   órbrennd, þaus goð kenndi;
    — gótts meiðum þrif þýðask —   mjǫks sá*rvita sœkir
    þat kaup hafa skatnar.   sanns dulðr, ef hyggr annat.

Engir skatnar dýnu otrs, þeirs hafa hlotna skírn, meg*u* hafa þat án kaup; gótts meiðum þýðask þrif. Orð, þaus goð kenndi, munu eigi verða órbrennd; sœkir sá*rvita [e]s mjǫk dulðr sanns, ef hyggr annat.

No chieftains of the feather-bed of the otter [GOLD > MEN], who have received baptism, may have that [baptism] without a bargain; it is good for men to acquire well-being. The words that God taught will never be destroyed; the attacker of the wound-flame [SWORD > WARRIOR] has the truth very much concealed from him, if he thinks otherwise.

Mss: **B**(10v), 624(87), 399a-b[x]. — *Readings*: [1] meg*u*: mega B, 624 [3] meiðum: *so* 624, 399a-b[x], '[...]eidum' B [4] hafa: *so* 624, 'hafe' B [6] ór-: 'a' 624 [7] sá*rvita: 'sa er vita' B, 'sa a̠rvita' 624.

Editions: *Skj* Anonyme digte og vers [XII], G [2]. *Leiðarvísan* 12: AI, 620, BI, 625, *Skald* I, 304, *NN* §1261; Sveinbjörn Egilsson 1844, 60, Rydberg 1907, 6, Attwood 1996a, 63, 173.

Notes: [1-2] *dýnu otrs* 'of the feather-bed of the otter [GOLD]': *Skj* B emends to *launa otrs* 'of the reward of the otter', presumably on the grounds that it is more in keeping with the myth of the slaying of Otr, son of Hreiðmarr and brother of Fáfnir and Reginn, which is recounted in *Reg* (*NK* 173-9), and in *Skm* (*SnE* 1998, I, 45-6). Gold-kennings alluding to this myth usually rely on the idea of ransom or payment, in that the mound of gold served as the blood-price of the slain Otr (see *LP*: *otr*). There are, however, several gold-kennings with the base-word *dýna* 'pillow, feather-bed' (*LP*: *dýna*), usually taken as a reference to the myth of Otr's brother, Fáfnir, who took the ransom gold after slaying Hreiðmarr and, as Snorri explains: *fór upp á Gnitaheiði ok gerði sér þar ból ok brásk í orms líki ok lagðisk á gullit* 'went up on to Gnita-heath and made himself a lair there and turned into a serpent and lay down on the gold' (*SnE* 1998, I, 46; Faulkes 1987, 101) until his death at the hands of Sigurðr. The poet of *Leið* appears to have generalised this kenning-type from Fáfnir to Otr, though somewhat inappropriately in terms of the legend, for the carcass of Otr is not said to have been lying on the gold. Instead, according to both *Reg* (*NK*, 174, prose interpolation) and *Skm* (*SnE* 1998, I, 45), the pelt is first stuffed with gold, then covered by it. Although, as Kock (*NN* §1261) implies, it is possible that the stuffed carcass may have rested on a layer of gold before being covered, this hardly justifies the use of *dýna*. *Otrs* alliterates correctly with both *án* and *engir* (l. 1) and rhymes with *hlotna* (l. 2), and there is no reason to emend it on metrical grounds. In *LP*: *Dýna*, Finnur Jónsson suggested that *dýnu* shold be taken as gen. of *Dýna*, the ON name for the river Dvina, and that *Dýnu otrs* 'of the otter of the Dvina' is a ship-kenning. This is not paralleled elsewhere in the corpus, and is unconvincing. — [4] *hafa* 'have': Sveinbjörn Egilsson's emendation of B's 'hafe' to accord with 624's *hafa* is adopted by *Skj* B and by Rydberg, as well as here. Kock (*NN* §1261) suggests emendation to *megu fara* 'are able to go, i.e. can survive', construing *engir skatnar dýnu otrs megu fara án þat kaup* 'no distributers of the feather-bed of the otter can survive without that reward', the *kaup* 'reward' in question being *skírn* (l. 2) 'baptism'. — [7] *sá*rvita* 'wound-flame [SWORD]': Although B's reading 'sa er vita' is clear, it does not make sense. The 624 copyist attempts to reproduce B's letter-forms, indicating his uncertainty about the phrase using points beneath the text. Sveinbjörn Egilsson suggests, in a marginal note to the 444ˣ transcript of B, that the text should be emended to *sárvita* gen. sg. of *sárviti* 'wound-flame'. Sveinbjörn's emendation is adopted by Rydberg, *Skj* B, Kock and here.

13. Stef skal hátt — né hætta Lúta englar ítrum
     hykk enn tǫlu dyggva —   óttlaust ok lið dróttni;
     fljótt, ef finna mættak   einn es siklingr sunnu
     fríð orð, goði smíðat.   setrs hvívetna betri.

Hátt stef skal smíðat goði fljótt, ef mættak finna fríð orð; né hykk enn hætta dyggva tǫlu. Englar ok lið lúta óttlaust ítrum dróttni; siklingr setrs sunnu es einn betri hvívetna.

A loud refrain shall be made quickly for God, if I am able to find beautiful words; nor do I yet intend to desist from good speech. Angels and people bow down fearlessly before the glorious Lord; the king of the seat of the sun [SKY/HEAVEN > = God] is alone better than everything else.

Mss: **B**(10v), 624(87). — *Readings*: [3] mættak ('ec mætta'): *so* 624, 'ek mętte' B [4] smíðat: 'smidut' B, 'smidud' 624 [8] hvívetna: 'huetuetnu' 624.

Editions: *Skj* Anonyme digte og vers [XII], G [2]. *Leiðarvísan* 13: AI, 620-1, BI, 625, *Skald* I, 304, *NN* §2558; Sveinbjörn Egilsson 1844, 60-1, Rydberg 1907, 6, Attwood 1996a, 63, 174.

Notes: [All]: There is an obelos in the left margin indicating the beginning of *Leið*'s first *stef* (refrain). — [1-4]: Several interpretations of these ll. are possible. With Sveinbjörn Egilsson and *Skj* B *fljótt* (l. 3) is understood here as an adv. 'quickly', describing the composition of the refrain. However, Kock (*NN* §2558) takes *fljótt* 'swift-running' and *hátt* 'loud' (l. 1) as grammatically parallel adjectives. He thus construes *hátt, fljótt stef skal smíðat goði* 'a loud, swift-running refrain shall be composed for God'. It is also possible (Peter Foote, pers. comm.) that *fljótt* (adv.) might be construed with *hætta* 'to stop, desist' (l. 1), rendering the second clause *né hykk enn hætta fljótt* 'nor do I intend to desist (i.e. bring the poem to an end) soon'. — [5-8]: Considerable similarities of diction, structure and sentiment exist between this refrain and other *helmingar* in the Christian skaldic corpus, especially that of C12th. On these similarities, especially between *Leið* 13/5-8, *Pl* 32/1-4, *Geisl* 66/5-6 and *Has* 20/7-8, and their possible implications for the relative chronology of the C12th *drápur*, see Attwood 1996b, 232-4. — [7-8] *siklingr setrs sunnu* 'prince of the seat of the sun [SKY/HEAVEN > = God]': Cf. the God-kennings *Has* 13/6-8:

vísi setrs sunnu 'king of the seat of the sun', and 49/5-8: *harri setrs sunnu* 'ruler of the seat of the sun'. Cf. the heaven-kenning *Geisl* 3/2-4: *setrs rǫðuls* 'of the seat of the sun'. In each case, *setrs* provides the *hǫfuðstafr*. *Konungr élsetrs* 'king of the storm-seat' (*Has* 20/8) is also on the same model, and the same concept informs *dǫglingr stóls sólar* 'king of the seat of the sun' (*Leið* 1/5-6).

14. Yfirþengill skóp engla   Ok heimstýri*r*, harr*a*,
    einn sunnudag hreina;   heppinn, þás skóp skepnu
    sǫnn hefr siklingr unnit   þann setti dag, dróttinn
    slík verk himinríkis.   dýrðar mildr, til hvíldar.

Einn yfirþengill skóp hreina engla sunnudag; siklingr himinríkis hefr unnit slík sǫnn verk; ok heppinn heimstýri*r* setti þann dag til hvíldar, þás dróttinn harr*a*, dýrðar mildr, skóp skepnu.

The one overlord created the pure angels on a Sunday; the king of the heaven-kingdom [= God] has performed true deeds such as these; and the fortunate world-ruler [= God] established that day for rest, when the lord of lords [= God], generous in glory, brought creation into being.

Mss: **B**(10v), 624(87). — *Readings*: [5] heimstýrir: heimstýris B, 624;   harra: 'harre' B, 624.

Editions: *Skj* Anonyme digte og vers [XII], G [2]. *Leiðarvísan* 14: AI, 621, BI, 625-6, *Skald* I, 304, *NN* §1262; Sveinbjörn Egilsson 1844, 61, Rydberg 1907, 6, Attwood 1996a, 63, 174.

Notes: [All]: St. 14 begins the *stefjabalkr*, in which the poet enumerates a number of significant events in Christian history that took place on a Sunday. Sts 14-16 deal with events from the Book of Genesis. — [1-2] *einn yfirþengill skóp hreina engla sunnudag* 'the one overlord created the pure angels on a Sunday': *Einn* 'one' could also be construed with *sunnudag* 'Sunday' (l. 2). Although the creation of the angels is not biblical, references to it are widespread in early apocryphal tradition, as, for example in the *Book of Jubilees* II.2; see Charles 1913, II, 13 and Lees 1985, 140. It is often mentioned in the Sunday Lists included in versions of the Sunday Letter, across all recensions. In the two MHG homilies containing freestanding Sunday Lists (see Introduction), the creation of the angels is the first event listed. On the relationships between *Leið*, the MHG sermons and other texts in the Sunday Letter/List traditions, see Attwood 2003. — [5-6]: These ll. are echoed in 21/3-4: *heims stýrandinn hár*i | hallar skepnu allri*. — [5-8]: God's establishment of Sunday as a day of rest is recorded in Gen. II.2: *conplevitque Deus die septimo opus suum quod fecerat et requievit die septimo ab universo opere quod patrarat* 'and on the seventh day God ended his work which he had made: and he rested on the seventh day from all his work which he had done'. — [5-8]: Sveinbjörn Egilson offers an alternative interpretation in a marginal note to Jón Sigurðsson's transcription of the 624 text in 444(2)ˣ. He retains B's readings *heimstýris harri* in l. 5, taking *heimstýrir* 'steerer of the world' as a kenning for the sun, whose *harri* m. 'lord, king' is God. He construes *ok þá's heppinn harri heimstýris skóp skepnu, setti dýrðarmildr dróttinn þann dag til hvíldar* 'and when the fortunate lord of the steerer of the world [SUN > = God] created the race of men, the glory-generous lord established that day as a time of rest'. This makes for a neat, balanced arrangement, in which the two couplets make independent sense. However, the sun is not generally, in *Leið* or the other C12th *drápur*, designated by a cpd, figurative expression, but is invariably the prosaic element in kennings for both heaven and God, rendered by *sunna*, *sól* or *rǫðull*. *Stýrir* appears elsewhere in *Leið* only in expressions for God (see 3/5, 27/2, 21/3). It therefore seems unlikely that *Leið* would adopt such a different technique only here as Sveinbjörn's interpretation would require. Here ms. 'harre' has been emended to *harra* 'of lords' to produce a God-kenning; cf. *Geisl* 25/7-8 *dyrr lét dróttinn harra* | *dáðmilds*.

15. Kristr setti frið fastan　　　　　ok dáðskreyttan dróttinn
    fimr meðal láðs ok himna　　　　dags hallar frið lagði
    — nauðr es þegnum þýðask　　　— þat vas sunnudag — sinnar
    þann veg — goðs ok manna,　　　snjallr meðal skepnu allrar.

Fimr Kristr setti fastan frið meðal láðs ok himna, goðs ok manna — nauðr es þegnum þýðask þann veg —, ok snjallr dróttinn dags hallar lagði dáðskreyttan frið meðal allrar skepnu sinnar; þat vas sunnudag.

Nimble Christ established firm peace between earth and heavens, God and men — it is necessary for men to receive that glory —, and the valiant lord of the day's hall [SKY/HEAVEN > = God] laid down deed-adorned peace throughout his entire creation; that was on a Sunday.

Mss: **B**(10v), 624(88). — *Readings*: [5] dáðskreyttan: skreyttan dáð 624　[8] skepnu: *so* 624, 'skepn[...]' B.

Editions: *Skj* Anonyme digte og vers [XII], G [2]. *Leiðarvísan* 15: AI, 621, BI, 626, *Skald* I, 304, *NN* §2983; Sveinbjörn Egilsson 1844, 61, Rydberg 1907, 6, Attwood 1996a, 63-4, 174.

Notes: [1-2] *fimr Kristr setti fastan frið meðal láðs ok himna* 'nimble Christ established firm peace between earth and heavens': This event is not directly paralleled in any other version of the Sunday List. It may be an oblique reference to the Fall of Lucifer described in Isa. XIV.12-20. — [5-6] *dáðskreyttan frið* 'deed-adorned peace': See Note to *dáðmáttugr* 'deed-mighty' (5/7). *Leið* often characterises God in terms of his good works. Here, as in the cpd *dáðstétt* 'deed-host' used for the angel-host in 24/5, this renown is transferred to God's creation. — [5-6] *dróttinn dags hallar* 'lord of the day's hall [SKY/HEAVEN > = God]': Cf. *gramr dags hallar* 'prince of the day's hall' in 45/6.

16. Reiddi rǫngum studdan   en, þás ǫrk á landi
ra*m*n þjóðtraðar Glamma   ólesta vel festi,
flóð, áðr foldu næði   þjóð af þram-Val prúðum
fjǫlkœnn Nói grœnni,   — þat vas dróttins dag — sótti*.

Flóð reiddi rǫngum studdan ra*m*n þjóðtraðar Glamma, áðr fjǫlkœnn Nói næði grœnni foldu, en, þás ǫrk festi vel ólesta á landi, sótti* þjóð af prúðum þram-Val; þat vas dróttins dag.

A flood tossed the rib-supported raven of the highway of Glammi <sea king> [SEA > SHIP], before very wise Noah could reach green land, and once the Ark was moored quite unbroken to the land, the people proceeded from the magnificent rim-Valr <horse> [SHIP]; that was on the Lord's day.

Mss: **B**(10v), 624(88). — *Readings*: [2] ra*m*n: 'rañ' B, 'ran' 624   [5] þás ('þa er'): þá 624   [7] -Val: vel 624   [8] sótti*: 'sottizt' B, 624.

Editions: *Skj* Anonyme digte og vers [XII], G [2]. *Leiðarvísan* 16: AI, 621, BI, 626, *Skald* I, 304, *NN* §2983; Sveinbjörn Egilsson 1844, 61, Rydberg 1907, 6, Attwood 1996a, 64, 174.

Notes: [All]: The story of Noah's flood is recounted in Gen. VI.9-IX.17. The exodus from the Ark is described in Gen. VIII.13-IX.17. Although the Noah story appears in the Sunday Lists preserved in Pseudo-Wulfstan Sermon XLV and the OIr. *Cáin Domnaig*, the Flood and the exodus from the Ark occur together, apart from here, only in the MHG homilies (see Introduction; Attwood 2003, 73). — [2] ra*m*n 'raven': B has 'rañ', which one would expect to be expanded 'rann', nom. or acc. sg. of *rann* 'house'. The 624 scribe, whose exemplar is B, writes 'ran'. It is not possible to make sense of *rann* here, and *m* is required for *aðalhending* with *Glamma*. Sveinbjörn Egilsson first made the emendation to *ramn* in a marginal note to Jón Sigurðsson's transcript of the 624 text, suggesting that the nasal stroke might have been misplaced, and that the exemplar read 'rān'. A similar spelling variant (*hramn*) of *hrafn* m. 'raven' occurs in GSvert *Hrafndr* 7/3[IV]. *Hramn* is probably to be construed as a horse-*heiti*, after King Áli's horse of that name; cf. *LP*: 2. *Hrafn*. — [5] *ǫrk* '[Noah's] ark': The only reference to Noah's Ark in skaldic poetry. — [7] *þram-Val* 'rim Valr <horse>': The cpd is *hap. leg.*, but Valr is named in Anon *Kálfv* 2/1[III] as the horse of one Vésteinn, and appears very frequently in ship-kennings (see *LP*: *Valr* 2). The word is clearly related to *valr*, cognate with the first element in OE *wealhhafoc* 'hawk, falcon' (*AEW*: *valr* 2). The ornithological resonances shared by the two ship-kennings in this st. make for an interesting parallelism between the *helmingar*. — [8]: B's 'sottizt', indicating m.v. *sóttisk* 'to be advanced (of a work in hand), be passed (of a road or distance)', does not fit the context here. *Skj* B (following a suggestion of Konráð Gíslason mentioned in a n. to *Skj* A) and *Skald* emend to *sótti** and this is followed here.

17. Hás ræðr heimi þessum
   hreggranns jǫfur*r* — seggjum
   goð lætr gótt líf ǫðlask
   gœzkufimr — sem himnum.

   Lúta englar ítrum
   óttlaust ok lið dróttni;
   einn es siklingr sunnu
   setrs hvívetna betri.

Jǫfur*r* hás hreggranns ræðr þessum heimi sem himnum; goð, gœzkufimr, lætr seggjum ǫðlask gótt líf. Englar ok lið lúta óttlaust ítrum dróttni; siklingr setrs sunnu es einn betri hvívetna.

The prince of the high storm-house [SKY/HEAVEN > = God] rules this world as well as the heavens; God, agile of grace, makes it possible for men to achieve a good life. Angels and people bow down fearlessly before the glorious Lord; the king of the seat of the sun [SKY/HEAVEN > = God] is alone better than everything else.

Mss: **B**(10v), 624(88). — *Readings*: [2] jǫfur*r*: 'iðfu[...]' B, 'iofur' 624   [5-8]: *abbrev. as* 'Luta einglar itrum' B, 624.

Editions: *Skj* Anonyme digte og vers [XII], G [2]. *Leiðarvísan* 17: AI, 621, BI, 626, *Skald* I, 304; Sveinbjörn Egilsson 1844, 62, Rydberg 1907, 6, Attwood 1996a, 64, 175.

Notes: [1-2] *jǫfurr hás hreggranns* 'prince of the high storm-house [SKY/HEAVEN > = God]': See Note to 2/1-4 above. — [4] *gœzkufimr* 'agile of grace': Presumably a reference to God's generosity in bestowing grace on humans in a variety of circumstances. This adj. describes God in *Mgr* 45/2; cf. *gœzkufyldr guð* 'God, filled with grace' in *Has* 35/4. — [5-8]: First repetition of the first *stef*, indicated by an obelos in the left-hand margin of fol. 10v.

18. Fylgði lýðr af láði
   lagavísum Móísi;
   sundr sprakk vágr fyr vendi;
   vas þat sunnudag unnit.

   Þusti hafs með hreysti
   heiðit folk á leiðir;
   brátt vann lǫgr inn ljóti
   líftjón Pharaóni.

Lýðr fylgði lagavísum Móísi af láði; vágr sprakk sundr fyr vendi; þat vas unnit sunnudag. Heiðit folk þusti með hreysti á leiðir hafs; brátt vann inn ljóti lǫgr Pharaóni líftjón.

The people followed law-wise Moses from the land; the sea burst apart before the staff; that was accomplished on a Sunday. The heathen people rushed with valour onto the ocean's paths; quickly the ugly sea brought about a loss of life for Pharaoh.

Mss: **B**(10v), 624(88).

Editions: *Skj* Anonyme digte og vers [XII], G [2]. *Leiðarvísan* 18: AI, 621, BI, 626-7, *Skald* I, 304-5; Sveinbjörn Egilsson 1844, 62, Rydberg 1907, 6-7, Attwood 1996a, 64, 175.

Notes: [All]: Sts 18-20 tell of events in the Old Testament book of Exodus. The account of the exodus from Egypt is in Exod. XII.31-42. The Egyptians' pursuit of the Israelites, and the subsequent drowning of the Pharaonic army in the Red Sea is described in Exod.

XIV.23-8. — [2] *lagavísum Móísi* (dat.) 'law-wise Moses': Moses is *lagavíss* 'law-wise', since it was he who received the law from God on Mt Sinai (Exod. XIX-XXXI). Although, according to biblical chronology, this event took place some three months after the exodus (Exod. XIX.1), the *Leið*-poet's use of this adj. to describe Moses here anticipates the subject-matter of st. 19. On the form of the name Moses, see Note to 19/4.

19. Tunglbryggju gaf tyggi ok þrekprúðum þjóðar
     tíu orð laga forðum þann veg yfirmanni
     — fríðr af fǫstu mœðisk — várr dróttinn lét veittan
     fjǫlhress goðs vin Móises, víðkunnan dag sunnu.

Fjǫlhress tyggi tunglbryggju gaf forðum Móises, goðs vin, tíu orð laga — fríðr mœðisk af fǫstu —, ok dróttinn várr lét veittan þrekprúðum yfirmanni þjóðar þann víðkunnan veg sunnu dag.

The very hearty king of the moon-pier [SKY/HEAVEN > = God] once gave Moses, God's friend, ten words of law — the handsome one grows weary from fasting —, and our Lord let the strength-magnificent overseer of the people [RULER = Moses] be granted that widely-known honour on a Sunday.

Mss: **B**(10v), 624(88). — *Reading*: [5] þjóðar: so 624, 'þ[...]ar' B.

Editions: *Skj* Anonyme digte og vers [XII], G [2]. *Leiðarvísan* 19: AI, 622, BI, 626-7, *Skald* I, 305, *NN* §§1263, 2559, 3250; Sveinbjörn Egilsson 1844, 62, Rydberg 1907, 7, Attwood 1996a, 64-5, 175.

Notes: [All]: Moses's receipt of the Ten Commandments (*tíu orð laga*, l. 2) is documented in Exod. XX.3-17. Although no fast (l. 3) is mentioned at this point in the biblical narrative, Moses is later (Exod. XXXIV.28) said to have spent forty days and nights in conversation with God on Mt Sinai and to have fasted there: *fecit ergo ibi cum Domino quadraginta dies et quadraginta noctes panem non comedit et aquam non bibit et scripsit in tabulis verba foederis decem* 'and he was there with the Lord forty days and forty nights: he neither ate bread nor drank water, and he wrote upon the tables the ten words of the covenant'. — [3-4]: *Skj* B emends *vin* (dat. sg.) 'friend' (l. 4), to the nom. form *vinr*, and takes the resulting kenning *goðs vinr* 'God's friend' as part of the intercalary cl., modified by *fríðr* (l. 3). In this, he is followed by Kock (*NN* §§1263, 2559), who also takes *fjǫlvíss* 'very wise' (l. 4) (on the emendation, see following Note) as in apposition to *fríðr* 'handsome'. This gives *fríðr fjǫlhress vinr goðs mœðisk af fǫstu* 'the fair, very wise friend of God grows weary from fasting'. However, it is not necessary to emend *vin*, if it is taken, as the w.o. suggests, with *Móises* (l. 4). — [4] *fjǫlhress* 'very hearty': *Skj* B and *Skald* emend to *fjǫlvíss* (adj.) 'very wise', which produces a better rhyme, but only if Moses' name assumed the form *Móises* (see Note below) Although *fjǫlhress* produces a less good rhyme, it makes good sense here (cf. *dáðhress* 'deed-healthy' 45/4, also used of God). Although *hress* 'healthy, hearty' does not occur very frequently in compounds in skaldic verse, it is interesting to compare several other examples in the C12th *drápur*. *Pl* describes its hero as *móðhress* 'hearty in courage' 29/6 and the Emperor Trajan as *víghress* 'hearty in battle' 58/1, while S. Óláfr is characterised as *eljunhress* 'energy-filled' in *Geisl* 11/6. — [4] *Móises* 'Moses': The name must here be disyllabic, as a third syllable, such as we have in 18/2, would render the l. hypermetrical. Kock (*NN* §3250 and *Skald*) emends to *Móísi*, which makes the l. too long. Like OE, ON adopted the Hebrew diphthong (cf. Lat. Mōȳsēs; Goth. and Gk Mōsēs). It is very difficult to ascertain stress and length, which seem to vary according to metrical environment. In Hebrew, the first element of the diphthong is long, but the tokens seem to indicate that internal rhyme could be on both elements of the diphthong, which could be rendered *ói* or *óí* (cf. Lat. ōȳ). It could well be that, in its disyllabic form, the name was pronounced 'Mojses'. — [6] *þrekprúðum* 'strength-magnificent': Compounds with *þrekr* 'strength, prowess' are fairly common in the Christian *drápur*, although this is the only occurrence in *Leið*. Cf. *Pl* 20/3: *þrekmaðr* 'doughty man'; *Has* 26/5: *þreknenninn* 'active in power'; *Geisl* 71/2: *þrekrammr* 'mighty in strength'; *Geisl* 66/4, *Líkn* 43/2: *þreksnjallr* 'swift in strength'.

20. Sinn skreytti dag dróttinn   * Ráðmegninn lét rigna
    dáðsterkr framaverkum,   risnufimr af himni
    rekkum*s rann til drykkjar   mat, þeims manna heitir,
    reint vatn fram ór steini.   margri þjóð til bjargar.

Dáðsterkr dróttinn skreytti sinn dag framaverkum, *[e]s reint vatn rann fram ór steini til drykkjar rekkum. * Ráðmegninn, risnufimr, lét rigna af himni mat, þeims heitir manna, til bjargar margri þjóð.

The deed-strong Lord adorned his day with deeds of distinction, when pure water flowed forth from a rock as a drink for men. The one strong in counsel, quick with hospitality, caused that food which is called manna to rain from heaven as a help to many people.

Mss: **B**(10v), 624(88). — *Readings*:   [3] rekkum*s: rekkum þá er B, 624   [5] *: ok B, 624; Ráðmegninn: ráðmeginn B, 624.

Editions: *Skj* Anonyme digte og vers [XII], G [2]. *Leiðarvísan* 20: AI, 622, BI, 627, *Skald* I, 305; Sveinbjörn Egilsson 1844, 62-3, Rydberg 1907, 7, Attwood 1996a, 65, 175.

Notes: [All]: Two separate accounts of God's feeding the hungry Israelites during their desert wanderings are alluded to in this st. Lines 1-4 refer to Moses' striking the rock at Horeb with his staff, providing drinking water. This event is recorded in Exod. XVII.1-7, and is widely referred to in later Hebrew hymns and Scriptures (see, for example, Ps. LXXVIII.15-16, XLVIII. 48.21). Lines 5-8 relate the more famous incident of the provision of manna, *panes de caelo* 'bread from heaven' (Exod. XVI.4), which is recorded in Exod. XVI.1-36. It is interesting to note that the *Leið*-poet has reversed the biblical chronology in sts 19-20. In Exod., the provision of manna is recorded as taking place before the striking of the rock at Horeb (the relative chronology is confirmed by the geographical progression indicated in Exod. XVI.1 and Exod. XVII.1), both of which take place before the Israelites reach Sinai, where Moses receives the Law. None of the surviving recensions of the Sunday Letter actually contains accounts of all three of these incidents, and only the S. Emmeram Homily version of the Sunday List has accounts of both the miracle at Horeb and the receipt of the Ten Commandments, these being presented there in strict biblical order (see Attwood 2003, 73). Either the *Leið*-poet was working from some hitherto undiscovered exemplar, or there is some artistic purpose behind the chronology here. Imagery established in these events, in which God provides nourishment for his people, is traditionally considered in Christian thought to refer to Christ, who is described in the New Testament as a provider of life-giving water and as the bread of life: *sed aqua quam dabo ei fiet in eo fons aquae salientis in vitam aeternam* 'the water that I will give him shall become in him a fountain of water, springing up into life everlasting' (John IV.14); *ego sum panis vitae* 'I am the bread of life' (John VI.35). Read in this light, st. 20 prefigures the Incarnation, which is the subject of the next narrative st. (as opposed to refrain st.), st. 22. It is perhaps churlish to point out that the Exod. account implies that manna did not fall on the Sabbath – the Israelites were told to collect a double ration on the sixth day and keep the seventh as a day of rest (Exod. XVI.23-6). — [2] *dáðsterkr* 'deed-strong': See Note on 5/7: *dáðmáttugr* 'deed-mighty'. — [3] *rekkum*s*: The omission of B's *þá* was first suggested by Konráð Gíslason (and Eiríkur Jónsson 1875-89, II, 907, 926) to produce a 6-syllable l., and has been followed by *Skj* B and *Skald*. — [5]: Similarly, Konráð Gíslason (and Eiríkur Jónsson 1875-89, II, 907) proposed the omission of B's *ok* at the beginning of this l., to produce a regular 6-syllable l. — [5] *ráðmegn*inn 'the one strong in counsel': Both B and 624 read *ráðmeginn*, but emendation to the substantivised adj. + def. art. is adopted here to provide a long syllable in metrical position 2. — [7] *manna* 'manna': The only reference in skaldic poetry to this miraculous biblical food. — [8] *margri þjóð til bjargar*: 'Filler' ll. on this model occur elsewhere in the Christian skaldic corpus. Cf. 6/7: *borgar lýð til bjargar*, Has 12/8: *margir þar til bjargar*.

21. Einn es sælstr of sinni   Lúta englar ítrum
    — samir lýðum trú þýðask —   óttlaust ok lið dróttni;
    heims stýrandinn hár*i   einn es siklingr sunnu
    hallar skepnu allri.   setrs hvívetna betri.

Stýrandinn hallar heims es einn sælstr of allri sinni hár*i skepnu; lýðum samir þýðask trú. Englar ok lið lúta óttlaust ítrum dróttni; siklingr setrs sunnu es einn betri hvívetna.

The steerer of the hall of the world [SKY/HEAVEN > = God] is alone most blessed throughout all his exalted creation; it befits people to submit to the faith. Angels and people bow down fearlessly before the glorious Lord; the king of the seat of the sun [SKY/HEAVEN > = God] is alone better than everything else.

Mss: **B**(10v), 624(88). — *Readings*: [3] hár*i: 'harri' B, 'harre' 624   [5-8]: *abbrev. as* 'Luta einglar itru.' B, 'Luta en' 624.

Editions: *Skj* Anonyme digte og vers [XII], G [2]. *Leiðarvísan* 21: AI, 622, BI, 627, *Skald* I, 305, *NN* §2560; Sveinbjörn Egilsson 1844, 63, Rydberg 1907, 7, Attwood 1996a, 65, 176.

Notes: [1] *einn* 'alone': Finnur Jónsson construes *einn stýrandi heims hallar* which he glosses *himlens eneste styrer* 'heaven's sole steerer' (*Skj* B). Kock's arrangement, adopted here (see *NN* §2560) takes *einn* as a predicative adj. 'alone'. This interpretation is anticipated by Sveinbjörn Egilsson in a marginal note to Jón Sigurðsson's transcription of the 624 text in 444(2)[x]. *Fritzner*: *einn* cites several examples in which *einn* or *einna* is followed by a sup. adj. The same construction, with the comp. form of the adj., is found in the first refrain (13/5-8; 17/5-8; 21/5-8*)*, thus providing parallelism between the two *helmingar* of this st. — [3-4]: On the similarities between these ll. and 14/5-6, see Notes to st. 14. — [3] *stýrandinn* 'the steerer': Both *Skj* B and *Skald* emend to *stýrandi*, but this is unnecessary. — [5-8]: The second repeat of *stef* 1, noted by an obleos in the left-hand margin of B's fol. 10v.

22. Engill kom við unga   Brims tók bjǫrk in fremsta
     allheppinn mey spjalla,   brands við helgum anda;
     burð ok buðlungs dýrð*a*r   sú hefk frétt at dag dróttins
     bauð hann frǫmum svanna.   dýrð framm komin yrði.

Allheppinn engill kom spjalla við unga mey, ok hann bauð frǫmum svanna burð buðlungs dýrð*a*r. In fremsta bjǫrk brands brims tók við helgum anda; hefk frétt, at sú dýrð yrði framm komin dróttins dag.

An altogether fortunate angel came to speak with a young maiden, and he announced to the foremost lady the birth of the king of glory [= God (= Christ)]. The foremost birch of the fire of the sea [GOLD > WOMAN] received the Holy Spirit; I have heard that this glory was brought about on the Lord's day.

Mss: **B**(10v), 624(88). — *Readings*: [1] við: *om.* 624   [3] dýrðar: dýrðir B, 624   [5] Brims: *corrected from* 'grims' *in margin in a different hand* 624   [6] brands: 'banndz' B, 624   [7] hefk ('hefe ec'): *so* 624, 'hefer ek' B.

Editions: *Skj* Anonyme digte og vers [XII], G [2]. *Leiðarvísan* 22: AI, 622, BI, 627-8, *Skald* I, 305; Sveinbjörn Egilsson 1844, 63, Rydberg 1907, 7, Attwood 1996a, 65, 176.

Notes: [All]: Sts 22-4 recount events leading up to the birth and baptism of Christ. Gabriel's Annunciation of the birth of Christ to the Virgin Mary is recounted in Luke I.26-38. The account in *Leið* has some conceptual similarities to that found in the sermon for the Feast of the Assumption in *HómÍsl* 1872, 138: *seɴdi guþ drottiɴ engil siɴ ɢabriel til fundar viþ mario meþ þui eyrende at segia henni þat at guþ siálfr kaus hana til móþor sér. oc hon scyllde verþa hafandi at guþs syni. en þat eyreɴdi bar engilleɴ heɴi a þessom degi er nu hǫlldom vér* 'The Lord God sent his angel Gabriel to meet with Mary with the purpose of telling her that God himself chose her to be his own mother, and she would bear God's son. And the angel brought her that message on this day which we now celebrate'. — [1-2] *allheppinn engill* 'altogether fortunate angel': Cf. *heppinn heimstýrir* 'fortunate lord of the world' 14/5-6. — [3] *dýrðar* 'of glory': B's *dýrðir* must be emended to provide the correct gen. sg. form, an emendation first suggested by Sveinbjörn Egilsson in a marginal note to the 444ˣ transcript. — [5-6] *bjǫrk brims brands* 'birch of the fire of the sea [GOLD > WOMAN]': A kenning for 'woman' is clearly required here. In that context, it has not been possible to make sense of B's reading 'banndz', which could be gen. sg. of *band* 'a bond, fetter, team, confederacy etc.', sometimes used in pl. of the Norse gods. In a n. to Jón Sigurðsson's transcript of 624 in 444(2)ˣ, Sveinbjörn Egilsson suggested emendation to *beins*, gen. sg. of *beinn* 'ebony', which is listed among *heiti* for 'tree' in a *þula* but is not attested elesewhere (*LP*: 1. *beinn*). Aside from its rarity, the noun does not work in a kenning which already has a tree-element, *bjǫrk* f. 'birch' in l. 5. Sveinbjörn rethought this emendation in preparing his printed edn (1844, 62 n. 10), in which he emended to *brands* gen. sg. of m. *brandr* 'fire, flame'. This creates the gold-kenning, *brandr brims* 'flame of the sea', whose *bjǫrk* is a woman, in this case the Virgin Mary. Sveinbjörn's second emendation has been adopted by all subsequent eds.

23. Dagmærir lét dýrðar
    dróttins tíð fyr óttu
    mæztr frá meyju beztri
    mildingr berask hingat.

    Þvís rétt, at dag dróttins
    dáðsnjalls hǫfuð kallim
    — gerðisk fǫgnuðr fyrðum
    fríðr — annarra tíða.

Dagmærir, mæztr mildingr dýrðar, lét berask hingat dróttins tíð fyr óttu frá beztri meyju. Þvís rétt, at kallim dag dáðsnjalls dróttins hǫfuð annarra tíða; fríðr fǫgnuðr gerðisk fyrðum.

The day-glorifier, the most praiseworthy prince of glory [= God (= Christ)], allowed himself to be born here at the Lord's time before dawn from the best maiden. Therefore it is right that we should call the day of the deed-eager Lord chief of other times; fair welcome was prepared for men.

Mss: **B**(10v), 624(89), 399a-bˣ. — *Readings*: [1] -mærir: *so* 624, 'męriʀʀ' B; dýrðar: *so* 624, 'dyrrar' B [3] beztri: *so* 624, 399a-bˣ, 'bezt[...]' B [6] kallim: 'kalle' 624.

Editions: *Skj* Anonyme digte og vers [XII], G [2]. *Leiðarvísan* 23: AI, 622, BI, 627-8, *Skald* I, 305, *NN* §1264; Sveinbjörn Egilsson 1844, 63, Rydberg 1907, 7, Attwood 1996a, 65-6, 176.

Notes: [All]: The birth of Christ is described in detail only in Luke II.1-20, though there is also a reference to it in Matt. I.25. — [1] *dagmærir* 'the day-glorifier': *Skj* B emends *-mærir*, the reading of 624 (B has '-męriʀʀ'), to *mærri** and takes this as the fem. dat. sg. comp. form of *mærr* 'glorious, great'. He regards this as parallel with *beztri* 'best' (l. 3) qualifying *meyju* 'maiden' (l. 3) and construes *mæztr mildingr dýrðar lét berask hingat fyr óttu tíð dróttins dag frá mærri, beztri meyju* 'the most praiseworthy prince of glory allowed himself to be born here before dawn on the Lord's day from the most glorious, best maiden'. Kock (*NN* §1264) objects to Finnur's w.o. and reinstates B's reading, commenting that the kenning-like expression 'day-glorifier' is appropriate in the context of a poem seeking to show how God allowed all great and remarkable things to happen on Sundays in order to endow that day with holiness and lustre. Sveinbjörn Egilsson (1844, 63 n. 11) emended to *dagmærar*, f. gen. sg. of *dagmærr*, *hap. leg.*, which he regarded as a *heiti* for 'heaven' (*LP* (1860): *dagmærr*), construing it with *mildingr dýrrar* (retaining B's reading for the second word) to give the God-kenning *mildingr dýrrar dagmærar* glossed as *rex almi cæli* 'king of the bountiful heaven'. — [3] *mæztr frá meyju*: Cf. *Has* 19/1: *Þú vast mæztr frá meyju*. This st. is also concerned with the birth of Christ. — [5-6] *dáðsnjalls dróttins* 'of the deed-eager Lord': Cf. *Geisl* 56/7-8, where S. Óláfr is described as *dáðsnjallr døglingr* 'quick-acting ruler'.

24. Lét Jóhannem ítran
     einn dýrðarmann hreinan
     ár í Jórðán stýrir
     alls tírar sik skíra.

     Dáðstéttar kom dróttni
     dags ok krismu lagði
     líknarfúss í lesni
     lands inn helgi andi.

Stýrir alls tírar lét ítran Jóhannem, einn hreinan dýrðarmann, skíra sik ár í Jórðán. Inn helgi andi kom líknarfúss ok lagði krismu í lesni dróttni dáðstéttar dags lands.

The steerer of all glory [= God (= Christ)] allowed the remarkable John, a certain pure man of glory, to baptise him long ago in the [River] Jordan. The Holy Spirit came, eager with grace, and laid chrism in the headband of the Lord of the deed-host of day's land [SKY/HEAVEN > ANGELS > = God (= Christ)].

Mss: **B**(10v), 624(89), 399a-b[x].

Editions: *Skj* Anonyme digte og vers [XII], G [2]. *Leiðarvísan* 24: AI, 622-3, BI, 628, *Skald* I, 305, *NN* §1265; Sveinbjörn Egilsson 1844, 64, Rydberg 1907, 7-8, Attwood 1996a, 66, 176.

Notes: [2] *einn* 'a certain': Once again (cf. Note to 21/1) Finnur Jónsson (*Skj* B) understands *einn* to qualify *stýrir alls tírar* in the sense *den eneste styrer af al hæder* 'the sole steerer of all glory', referring to Christ. Here *einn* is construed with *hreinan dýrðarmann* as 'a certain pure man of glory' (l. 2). — [5-8]: It is interesting to compare this *helmingr* with a *lv.* on Christ's baptism preserved in the text of *Skm* in AM 242 fol and attributed there to Skáld-Þórir (Skáldþ Lv[III]). This poet is otherwise unknown (he is tentatively assigned by *Skj* B to the C12th). The noun *krisma* 'chrism' appears only in these two places in the skaldic corpus. — [6-7] *lagði krismu í lesni* 'laid chrism in the headband': Anointing with chrism (a mixture of consecrated oil and balsam) was a standard part of medieval baptismal practice. That Iceland was no exception to the norm is confirmed by Bishop Árni Þorláksson's 'Boðskapur' (*DI* II, 23-37), a series of instructions to clergy in his Skálholt diocese, which are dated September 1269, shortly after Árni's accession to the see. They claim to confirm and update a similar document of Bishop Magnús Gizurarson (bishop of Skálholt 1216-29, 1231-7; *DI* I, 423-63) which is dated 1224, but does not include detail of baptismal practice. The version of Árni's 'Boðskapur' preserved in AM 456 12° fols 130-6 discusses infant baptism at some length: ... *þa skal [prestrinn] signa þat*

[barn] *ok gefa sallt vigt ok lesa gudspiall yfir ok giora krossa yfir med hraka sinum fyri eyrum ok nosum ok leida i kirkiu. smyria sidan ä brioste ok millum herde med oleo sancto ok sidan med krisma j hǫfdi. færa j skirnar klædi ok fa kerti loganda j hond* ... 'Then the priest must sign the child and give it consecrated salt and read the gospel over it and make the sign of the cross over its ears and nose with his saliva and lead it into the church; then [the priest must] annoint [the child's] breast and between its shoulders with holy oil and then annoint its head with chrism, put it into baptismal clothes and set a burning candle in its hand...' (*DI* II, 26). An alternative version of Árni's instructions, preserved in AM 456 12° fols 93-4, gives further details of the headband used to seal the chrism (*DI* II, 51): *dregla suo langa at uel megi knyta um hǫfudit. ok suo breida at hyli krisma krossinu. ... Þriar nætur skulu dreglar um hǫfudit barnanna ok skulu mædurnar at geyma ok lata eigi at falla ... sidan skulu puozt hǫfud barnanna j lut ok j uormu uatni ok kasta j elld dreglinum* 'the band [should be] so long that it can be wound around the head, and so broad as to hide the chrism cross ... the children must wear the bands round their heads for three nights and their mothers must look after them and not allow them to fall ... then they must wash the heads of the children in lye and warm water and throw the bands into the fire'. Tveitane (1966, 131 n. 3) argued that the use of the word *krisma* 'chrism' indicates a direct borrowing from the Pseudo-Wulfstan homily *Sermo angelorum nomina* (Pseudo-Wulfstan Homily XLV, in Napier 1883, 226-32). However, there are considerable differences between the two accounts of the baptism. In the OE text, and its Lat. source *Epistola Salvatoris Domini nostri Jesu Christi* (Priebsch 1899, 130-4), Christ is anointed with both oil and chrism, while *Leið* mentions only chrism. Although the Lat. text includes no account of Christ's salutation as the Son of God, the OE indicates that, after John had baptised and anointed him, an angel came from heaven and announced: *Þis is min leofa sunu, on þæm ic me wel gelicode, geherað him wel* 'This is my dear son, in whom I am well pleased. Listen carefully to him' (Napier 1883, 229). *Leið* credits John only with the baptism itself and asserts that the Holy Spirit performed the anointing (24/5-8).

25. Enn vilda ek annat
    alfríðustum smíða
    hátt í hróðri sléttum
    himins gotna stef dróttni.

    Gramr skóp hauðr ok himna
    hreggranns sem kyn seggja;
    einns salkonungr sólar
    snjallr hjalpari allra.

Enn vilda ek smíða annat hátt stef í sléttum hróðri alfríðustum dróttni gotna himins. Gramr hreggranns skóp hauðr ok himna sem kyn seggja; snjallr sólar salkonungr [e]s einn hjalpari allra.

Further I would like to fashion another exalted refrain in the smooth praise-poem for the altogether fairest lord of the men of heaven [ANGELS > = God]. The king of the storm-house [SKY/HEAVEN > = God] created land and heavens, as well as the race of men; the excellent king of the hall of the sun [(*lit.* 'the excellent hall-king of the sun') SKY/HEAVEN > = God] is alone the helper of all.

Mss: **B**(10v), 624(89), 399a-b˟. — *Readings*: [3] hátt: 'ha[...]' 624; sléttum: *so* 624, 399a-b˟, 'sle[...]' B.

Editions: *Skj* Anonyme digte og vers [XII], G [2]. *Leiðarvísan* 25: AI, 623, BI, 628, *Skald* I, 305; Sveinbjörn Egilsson 1844, 64, Rydberg 1907, 8, Attwood 1996a, 66, 177.

Notes: [2] *alfríðustum* 'for the altogether fairest': See also 9/4 and 36/4. *Alfríðr* provides the *hǫfuðstafr* in each case. — [3] *í sléttum hróðri* 'in the smooth praise-poem': Cf. the poet's prayer for a *slétt óðarlag* 'smooth poem-form' in 3/2. These comments on the 'smoothness' of the poem are presumably intended to call attention to its apparently effortless artistry, though in fact much about the poem is rather self-conscious. Cf. the introductions to the refrains in 13/1-4 and 25/1-4, the prayers for inspiration and a hearing which occupy almost half of the *upphaf* and the expression of gratitude to *prestr... Rúnolfr* in st. 43 — [3-4] *hátt stef* 'exalted refrain': The identical phrase is used to describe the first refrain in 13/1. — [5-8]: The first instance of the second refrain. The opening couplet of this refrain is very similar to that of the first refrain in *Has* 20/5-6: *Ern skóp hauðr ok hlýrni | heims valdr sem kyn beima* 'The powerful ruler of the world [= God] created earth and heaven as well as the kinsfolk of men'. The *helmingr* as a whole is similar to one preserved in *Skm* and attributed there to Markús Skeggjason (d. 1107) (Mark Frag[III]), probably from a poem about Christ (*SnE* 1998, I, 77 and 201). — [5-6] *gramr hreggranns* 'king of the storm-house [SKY/HEAVEN > = God]': See also 2/4 and 17/2 and cf. the God-kenning *konungr hreggranns* 'king of the storm-house' in *Mdr* 24/2. — [7] *salkonungr sólar* 'hall-king of the sun': I.e. 'king of the hall of the sun', 'king of heaven [= God]'. Cf. *Geisl* 66/6, where God is described as *salkonungr himna* 'hall-king of the heavens'. *Salkonungr sólar* is used twice in God-kennings in *Heildr* (13/1, 17/5).

26. Sýndi sólar landa
    siklingr með trú mikla
    horskum lýð á hauðri
    hreinn skjótar jarteinir.
    Frítt gerði dag dróttins
    dáðfimr jǫfurr himna
    vín ór vatni einu;
    varð þjóð fegin harðla.

Hreinn siklingr landa sólar sýndi horskum lýð á hauðri skjótar jarteinir með mikla trú. Dáðfimr jǫfurr himna gerði frítt vín ór vatni einu dróttins dag; þjóð varð harðla fegin.

The pure prince of the lands of the sun [SKY/HEAVEN > = God (= Christ)] showed wise people on earth swift miracles with great faith. The deed-agile prince of the heavens [= God (= Christ)] made beautiful wine out of water alone on the Lord's day; people became very happy.

Mss: **B**(10v), 624(89), 399a-b˟. — *Readings*: [5] dróttins: dróttinn 399a-b˟ [8] þjóð: *om.* 624.

Editions: *Skj* Anonyme digte og vers [XII], G [2]. *Leiðarvísan* 26: AI, 623, BI, 628-9, *Skald* I, 305, *NN* §3133C; Sveinbjörn Egilsson 1844, 64, Rydberg 1907, 8, Attwood 1996a, 66, 177.

Notes: [All]: Sts 26-8 treat two of Christ's miracles; the wedding at Cana, where he turned water into wine (st. 26), and the feeding of the Five Thousand (sts 27-8). — [4] *jarteinir* 'miracles': B's <ei> spelling is required here to preserve the rhyme with *hreinn*, but cf. 6/2, where the <gn> spelling is used, to rhyme with *alfegnar*. The <gn> form also occurs in *Geisl* 67/2, where the rhyme is with *friðgegn*. It appears likely that the <ei> form is the younger (see *ANG* §§292.3, 318.5; *LP*: *jartegn, jartein*). — [5-8]: The reference here is to Christ's turning water into wine at the wedding at Cana, recounted in John II.1-10. The miracle is also the subject of a sermon preserved in *HómÍsl* 1872, 187-91, and occurs in texts from all three recensions of the Sunday Letter and the MHG sermons. — [5] *dróttins* 'the Lord's': Brynjólfur Snorrason, the writer of the 444ˣ transcript, miscopied this word as *dróttinn*. This error was carried over into Jón Sigurðsson's copy of 444ˣ, 399a-bˣ, which was used by Sveinbjörn Egilsson as the basis of his 1844 edn. Sveinbjörn corrected to *dróttins* in a marginal n. to 444ˣ, though he notes *drottinn* as the 'MS reading' in 1844, 64 n. 13.

27. Sinn veitti dag dróttinn Rǫskr vann fljótt af fiskum
    dýr tǫkn himins stýrir, friðkennandi tvennum
    lýð þás lítlu brauði fjǫlða lýðs ok fríðum
    lofkvaddan goð saddi. fimm hleifum vel reifa*n*.

Dróttinn, stýrir himins, veitti dýr tǫkn dag sinn, þás goð saddi lofkvaddan lýð lítlu brauði. Rǫskr friðkennandi vann fljótt fjǫlða lýðs vel reifan af tvennum fiskum ok fimm fríðum hleifum.

The Lord, steerer of heaven [= God], granted precious tokens on his day, when God fed the famous multitude with little bread. The valiant peace-bringer [= God (= Christ)] quickly made a multitude of people very happy with two fishes and five beautiful loaves.

Mss: **B**(10v-11r), 624(89), 399a-bˣ. — *Readings*: [4] -kvaddan: *so* 624, 399a-bˣ, '-[...]ddan' B [7] fríðum: 'fyrdum' 624 [8] hleifum: 'leife' 624; reifa*n*: reifa B, 'refi' *added in margin* 624.

Editions: *Skj* Anonyme digte og vers [XII], G [2]. *Leiðarvísan* 27: AI, 623, BI, 629, *Skald* I, 306, *NN* §§1845, 2142; Sveinbjörn Egilsson 1844, 64-5, Rydberg 1907, 8, Attwood 1996a, 66-7, 177.

Notes: [All]: The order of sts 27 and 28 is reversed in B, though marginal notes in the scribal hand indicate the correct order, which is confirmed by the content of the sts. — [1]: Finnur Jónsson (*Skj* B), followed by Kock (*Skald*), emends to *Sín veitti dag dróttins*, construing *sín* with *dýr tǫkn* (l. 2) 'his precious tokens'. *Dróttins* is construed with *dag*, to give *himins stýrir veitti dag dróttins sín dýr tǫkn* 'the steerer of heaven granted his precious tokens on the day of the Lord'. — [2] *stýrir himins* 'steerer of heaven [= God]': God-kennings involving *stýrir* m. 'steerer' are a common feature of the image-structure of *Leið*. Cf. *stýrir aldar* 'steerer of men' 3/5; *stýrir alls tírar* 'steerer of all glory' 24/3-4; *stýrir heims* 'steerer of the world' 14/5. — [8] *reifan*: Finnur Jónsson emended B's *reifa* 'to enrich, present with' to *reifan*, m. acc. sg. of *reifr* 'glad, cheerful', agreeing with *fjǫlða* (l. 7) and this emendation is accepted here. Kock (*NN* §2142) construed B's *reifa* with *vann* (l. 5), to give the sense 'succeeded in enriching', but *vinna* is nowhere attested with the inf., other than in Kock's own readings proposed in this note.

28. Hátt gengr dýrð, sús dróttinn   Tolf, segi*r* e*l*da elfar
    dáðgladdan her saddi   Ullr, vandlaupar fullir
    — opt es kuðr at krapti   — matr vannsk mǫnnum snotrum —
    Kristr — á lítlum vistum.   mikill fengr at af gengi.

Hátt gengr dýrð sús dróttinn saddi dáðgladdan her á lítlum vistum; Kristr es opt kuðr at krapti. Ullr e*l*da elfa*r* segir, at mikill fengr, tolf vandlaupar fullir, gengi af; matr vannsk snotrum mǫnnum.

Far and wide spreads the glory [from the fact] that the Lord fed the deed-gladdened host with few provisions; Christ is often known for his strength. An Ullr <god> of the fires of the river [GOLD > MAN] says that a huge catch, twelve baskets full, was left over; the food sufficed for the wise men.

Mss: **B**(10v), 624(89). — *Readings*: [5] segi*r*: segja B, 624; e*l*da: edda B, enda 624   [6] Ullr: 'ullt' 624.

Editions: *Skj* Anonyme digte og vers [XII], G [2]. *Leiðarvísan* 28: AI, 623, BI, 629, *Skald* I, 306, *NN* §1266; Sveinbjörn Egilsson 1844, 65, Rydberg 1907, 8, Attwood 1996a, 66, 177.

Notes: [5] *segir*: B reads 'segia', regarded by Finnur Jónsson (*Skj* B) as the 3rd pers. pl. pres. tense of the verb *segja* 'to say', used in the sense 'people say'. He emends *Ullr* (l. 6) to *Ull* (so also *Skald*) and translates *man fortæller mig, at ...* 'people tell me that ...'. However, *segja* renders the l. hypermetrical, and here Ullr has been retained as nom. sg., with emendation of *segja* to the necessary sg. verb, *segir* 'says'. — [5-6] *Ullr elda elfar* 'Ullr <god> of the fires of the river [GOLD > MAN]': The man-kenning (possibly a reference to the witness of one of the evangelists) relies on an emendation of B's 'edda' to *elda* 'of fires'. Finnur Jónsson (*Skj* A, n.) claimed that B's <dd> was an alteration, and read 'ellda', but this is difficult to ratify from the present state of the ms. Rydberg read <dd> without comment. All previous eds have adopted Sveinbjörn Egilsson's emendation (1844, 65) to *elda elfar*, which makes for a conventional gold-kenning. — [8] *mikill fengr* 'a huge catch': Kock (*Skald* and *NN* §1266) takes this phrase with the intercalary cl. and emends *matr* (l. 7) to *matar* (gen. sg.), which he takes with the main cl.

29. Ótraulla má ǫllu   Gramr skóp hauðr ok himna
    aldýrr faðir stýra;   hreggranns sem kyn seggja;
    sterkr es engr, svát orki   einns salkonungr sólar
    aptrat dróttins krapti.   snjallr hjalpari allra.

Aldýrr faðir má stýra ǫllu ótraulla; engr es sterkr, svát orki aptrat krapti dróttins. Gramr hreggranns skóp hauðr ok himna sem kyn seggja; snjallr sólar salkonungr [e]s einn hjalpari allra.

The altogether precious father is able to govern everything indefatigably; no one is so strong that he is able to impede the Lord's power. The king of the storm-house [SKY/HEAVEN > = God] made land and heavens as well as the race of men; the excellent king of the hall of the sun [(*lit.* 'hall-king of the sun') SKY/HEAVEN > = God] is alone the helper of all.

Mss: **B**(11r), 624(89), 399a-b^x. — *Readings*: [1] ǫllu: *so* 624, 'ǫll[...]' B [3] engr: engi 624; orki: *so* 624, 399a-b^x, 'or[...]i' B [4] krapti: *so* 399a-b^x, 'k[...]apti' B, kraptr 624 [5-8]: *abbrev. as* 'Gramr skop h.' B, 'gramr skop haudr' 624.

Editions: *Skj* Anonyme digte og vers [XII], G [2]. *Leiðarvísan* 29: AI, 623-4, BI, 629, *Skald* I, 306; Sveinbjörn Egilsson 1844, 65, Rydberg 1907, 8, Attwood 1996a, 67, 178.

Notes: [1] *ótraulla* 'indefatigably, with perseverance': A variant of *ótrauðla*, used to provide *skothending* with *ǫllu*. — [5-8]: The first repeat of the second refrain, indicated in B by an obelos in the right-hand margin.

30. Dag reið sinn með sigri
    siklingr blíðr til víðrar
    sólbryggju — hratt seggja
    sorg — Jórsalaborgar.

    En fyr ǫðling ríkjan
    óhræðinn litklæði
    þar vann lýðr á láði
    lopthjalms borit palma.

Blíðr siklingr sólbryggju reið dag sinn með sigri til víðrar Jórsalaborgar — sorg seggja hratt —, en lýðr þar á láði vann borit litklæði, palma fyr óhræðinn, ríkjan ǫðling lopthjalms.

The joyful prince of the sun-pier [SKY/HEAVEN > = God (= Christ)] rode on his day with victory to the extensive city of Jerusalem — men's sorrow was ended —, and the people in that country put coloured cloths [and] palms before the fearless, powerful prince of the sky-helmet [SKY/HEAVEN > = God (= Christ)].

Mss: **B**(11r), 624(90), 399a-b^x. — *Readings*: [1] reið: réð B, 624 [2] víðrar: *so* 624, 399a-b^x, 'vid[...]ar' B [3] hratt: *so* 399a-b^x, 'hr[...]tt' B, 'hrat' 624.

Editions: *Skj* Anonyme digte og vers [XII], G [2]. *Leiðarvísan* 30: AI, 624, BI, 629-30, *Skald* I, 306, *NN* §2561; Sveinbjörn Egilsson 1844, 65-6, Rydberg 1907, 8-9, Attwood 1996a, 67-8, 178.

Notes: [All]: Sts 30, 31 and 32 describe, respectively, Christ's entry into Jerusalem on Palm Sunday, his Resurrection from the dead on Easter Sunday, and the granting of the Holy Spirit to the Apostles at Pentecost. Christ's triumphal entry into Jerusalem on Palm Sunday is described in Matt. XXI.1-11, Mark XI.1-10, Luke XIX.28-44 and John XII.12-15. The accounts in Matt. and Mark mention that the crowd spread cloaks and branches on the road before him. — [2-3] *siklingr sólbryggju* 'prince of the sun-pier [SKY/HEAVEN > = God (= Christ)]': Cf. 19/1: *tyggi tunglbryggju* 'king of the moon-pier'. This model for heaven-kennings is also used in *hirðir mánabryggju* 'guardian of the moon-pier' in *Mgr* 46/5-6. — [5-8]: Kock (*NN* §2561) proposed that *óhræðinn* 'unafraid, fearless' (l. 6) should be taken in apposition to *ríkjan* 'powerful' (l. 5), qualifying *ǫðlingr* 'king' (l. 5). Although there is no reason why the adj., which may be interpreted as nom. or acc. here, should not be taken, as *Skj* B does, as describing the *lýðr* 'people' (l. 7), it may, as Kock suggests, suit Christ better at this juncture than the people strewing cloths and palms before him. However, it could be argued equally well that the adj. applies to people whose sorrow is said to have been removed from them (ll. 3-4).

31. Dag reis sinn með sigri Áðr batt flærðarfróðan
     snjallastr faðir allra   fjanda heilagr andi
     — sonr huggaði seggi   fast ok fyrða leysti
     sólar hauðrs — af dauða. fremðarstyrkr ór myrkrum.

Snjallastr faðir allra reis af dauða með sigri dag sinn; sonr hauðrs sólar huggaði seggi. Áðr batt fremðarstyrkr heilagr andi fast flærðarfróðan fjanda ok leysti fyrða ór myrkrum.

The most valiant father of all [= God (= Christ)] rose from death with victory on his day; the son of the land of the sun [SKY/HEAVEN > = God (= Christ)] comforted men. Previously the honour-strong Holy Spirit bound fast the deceit-learned fiend and released men from darkness.

Mss: **B**(11r), 624(90), 399a-b[x]. — *Readings*: [1] reis: réð B, 624 [3] seggi: *so* 624, 399a-b[x], 's[...]ggi' B [4] hauðrs: *so* 624, 'hau[...]' B, hauð(r)s(?) 399a-b[x] [8] fremðar-: *so* 624, 399a-b[x], '[...]emdar' B.

Editions: *Skj* Anonyme digte og vers [XII], G [2]. *Leiðarvísan* 31: AI, 624, BI, 630, *Skald* I, 306, *NN* §§1268, 2143; Sveinbjörn Egilsson 1844, 66, Rydberg 1907, 9, Attwood 1996a, 68, 178.

Notes: [1-4]: Christ's Resurrection from the dead on Easter Sunday is described in Matt. XXVIII.1-8, Mark XVI.1-8, and Luke XXIV.1-10. — [1] *reis* '[he] rose': Line 1 echoes 30/1. The similarity of the ll. accounts for B's scribal error, repeating 'réð' here. Sveinbjörn Egilsson makes the obvious correction to *reis* 'rose' in a marginal note to Jón Sigurðsson's 444[x] transcription. — [3] *sonr* 'son': The Christ-kenning *sonr hauðrs sólar* 'son of the land of the sun', based on a hypothetical kenning-type 'son of heaven' is without parallel in the skaldic corpus. Presumably for this reason Finnur Jónsson (*Skj* B) emends *sonr* to *sjóli* 'prince'. This destroys the subtle theological structure of the st., however. Christ is referred to successively as all three persons of the Trinity: it is as *faðir allra* 'father of all' that he rises from the dead (l. 2), as *sonr hauðrs sólar* 'son of the land of the sun' that he comforts mankind (ll. 3-4) and as *heilagr andi* 'holy spirit' that he harrows hell (ll. 5-8). — [4] *hauðrs sólar* 'of the land of the sun': This phrase appears as the second element in Christ kennings in *Líkn* 23/4 (also an account of the Resurrection), and in the Crucifixion account in *Mgr* 23/2-3. On the same model are *hildingr hauðrs hvels mána* 'prince of the land of the wheel of the moon' in *Líkn* 7/1-3 and *skjǫldungr hauðrs skýja* 'prince of the land of the clouds' in *Mgr* 25/3-4.

32. Vǫru ǫðlings ærir
    alkunnan dag sunnu
    heiðar bœs í húsi
    hreins luktaðir einu.

Þá gaf skjǫldungr skýja
skríns postolum sínum
— ítr firri goð gotna
grandi — helgan anda.

Ærir ǫðlings hreins bœs heiðar vǫru luktaðir í einu húsi alkunnan sunnudag. Þá gaf skjǫldungr skríns skýja postolum sínum helgan anda; ítr goð firri gotna grandi.

The envoys of the prince of the pure dwelling of the heath [SKY/HEAVEN > = God (= Christ) > APOSTLES] were shut up in a certain house on a well-known Sunday. Then the king of the shrine of the clouds [HEAVEN > = God] gave his Apostles the Holy Spirit; may glorious God save men from harm.

Mss: **B**(11r), 624(90), 399a-b[x]. — *Readings*: [1] *ǫðlings*: egg þings B*Rydberg*, B, af þingi 624, 'af þings' 399a-b[x] [2] -kunnan: 'kvna' 624 [3] húsi: *so* 624, 399a-b[x], '[...]' B [4] hreins: hrein B, hreinn 624; einu: *so* 399a-b[x], 'ein[...]' B, einni 624 [7] firri: fyrir 624.

Editions: *Skj* Anonyme digte og vers [XII], G [2]. *Leiðarvísan* 32: AI, 624, BI, 630, *Skald* I, 306, *NN* §2144; Sveinbjörn Egilsson 1844, 66, Rydberg 1907, 9, Attwood 1996a, 68, 178.

Notes: [All]: The granting of the Holy Spirit to the Apostles at Pentecost is recounted in Acts II.1-4, and occurs in Sunday Letters from all three recensions. — [1, 3, 4] *Ærir ǫðlings hreins bœs heiðar* 'servants of the prince of the pure dwelling of the heath [SKY/HEAVEN > = God (= Christ) > APOSTLES]': The ms. readings of the first part of the second word of l. 1 are confusing, though they seem to agree on the second part, presenting it as some form of the noun *þing* 'meeting, assembly'. This is, however, difficult to fit into what appears to be a kenning for the Apostles as the subject of the first *helmingr*. If B's reading *eggþings* 'blade-meeting [BATTLE]' is kept (so *Skald* and *NN* §2144), a standard kenning results: *eggþings ærir* 'envoys of the blade-meeting [BATTLE > WARRIORS]', but *heiðar bœs* 'of the dwelling of the heath [SKY/HEAVEN]' is unaccounted for, unless the idea of 'heaven's warriors', invoked by Kock in *NN* is correct. Finnur Jónsson's suggested emendation of B's *eggþings* to *ǫðlings* 'prince, ruler' has been followed here, except that *hreins* 'pure' is taken with *bœs* rather than *ǫðlings*. The resulting kenning is parallel to *ǫðlingr salar rǫðla* 'prince of the hall of heavenly bodies [SKY/HEAVEN > = God]' in 33/2. — [3] *hreins bœs heiðar* 'of the pure dwelling of the heath [SKY/HEAVEN]': Cf. the heaven-kennings *salr heiðar* 'hall of the heath' in *Geisl* 7/5-6 and *tjald heiða* 'tent of the heaths' in *Líkn* 12/3. — [5-6] *skríns skýja* 'of the shrine of the clouds [HEAVEN]': The conceit of heaven as a shrine, whose jewel is the sun, is a popular one. This heaven-kenning occurs twice in *Has* (19/7-8, 29/7-8), *skrín* providing the *hǫfuðstafr* (as it does here) both times.

33.   Gefr, sás ǫllum efri,
         ǫðlingr salar rǫðla
         — goð magnar þrif þegna —
         þjóðum allt it góða.

Gramr skóp hauðr ok himna
hreggranns sem kyn seggja;
einns salkonungr sólar
snjallr hjalpari allra.

Ǫðlingr salar rǫðla, sás efri ǫllum, gefr þjóðum allt it góða; goð magnar þrif þegna. Gramr hreggranns skóp hauðr ok himna sem kyn seggja; snjallr sólar salkonungr [e]s einn hjalpari allra.

The prince of the hall of heavenly bodies [SKY/HEAVEN > = God], who is higher than all, gives to people all that is good — God strengthens the prosperity of his servants. The king of the storm-house [SKY/HEAVEN > = God] made land and skies as well as the race of men; the excellent king of the hall of the sun [(*lit.* 'the excellent hall-king of the sun') SKY/HEAVEN > = God] is alone the helper of all.

Mss: **B**(11r), 624(90), 399a-b^x. — *Readings:* [4] þjóðum: *so* 624, 399a-b^x, 'þi[...]um' B [5-8]: *abbrev. as* 'Gramr skop h.' B, 'Gramur' 624.

Editions: *Skj* Anonyme digte og vers [XII], G [2]. *Leiðarvísan* 33: AI, 624, BI, 630, *Skald* I, 306; Sveinbjörn Egilsson 1844, 66, Rydberg 1907, 9, Attwood 1996a, 68-9, 179.

Notes: [2] *ǫðlingr salar rǫðla* 'prince of the hall of heavenly bodies [SKY/HEAVEN > = God]': Cf. *Has* 16/6: *ǫðlingr, hefik, rǫðla.* The same rhyming pair also appears elsewhere in Þjsk Sveindr^1 and in *Mgr* 3/2. — [5-8]: The third and final iteration of the second refrain, with which the *stefjabálkr* of *Leið* concludes. B marks the *stef* with an obelos in the right-hand margin.

34.   Slœm skalk upp af aumu
         — eru stef liðin — hefja,
         mætr ef mér vil láta
         málfinni goð vinnask.

Styrk ávalt til verka,
vegs gnóttar, mik, dróttinn;
verðk at engu orði
einhlítr, nema goð beini.

Skalk hefja upp slœm af aumu, ef mætr goð vil láta málfinni vinnask mér; stef eru liðin. Dróttinn gnóttar vegs, styrk mik ávalt til verka; verðk einhlítr at engu orði, nema goð beini.

I will begin a conclusion from a state of wretchedness, if glorious God will grant that eloquence be achieved for me; the refrains are complete. Lord of the abundance of glory [= God], assist me always in [the composition of] poems; I will be fully sufficient for not one word, unless God helps [me].

Mss: **B**(11r), 624(90), 399a-b^x. — *Readings:* [2] hefja: *so* 399a-b^x, '[...]fia' B, 'hefur' 624 [6] vegs gnóttar ('vex gnottar'): *so* 624, '[...]e[...]s[...]ottar' B, 'vegs[...]ttar' B*Rydberg*, vegsnóttar 399a-b^x.

Editions: *Skj* Anonyme digte og vers [XII], G [2]. *Leiðarvísan* 34: AI, 624, BI, 630-1, *Skald* I, 306; Sveinbjörn Egilsson 1844, 67, Rydberg 1907, 9, Attwood 1996a, 69, 179.

Notes: [All]: St. 34 begins the *slœmr* or concluding section of the poem, as the poet says. As befits a Christian skald whose inspiration comes from God alone, the *Leið* poet introduces a modesty topos disclaiming poetic proficiency, unless God helps him. Cf. *Mgr* 3/5-6 with ll. 7-8. — [1] *af aumu* 'from a state of wretchedness': The adj. *aumr* means 'poor, wretched, miserable' (*ONP*: *aumr*, adj., *auma*, f. the latter only in the expression *sjá aumu* 'to feel pity for'), but in this context expresses the poet's feeling of inadequacy to his task. Sveinbjörn Egilsson (1844, 67 n. 21) suggested that the phrase may refer to the poet's miserable subject-matter, given that he is to discuss the fates of men at the Last Judgement in st. 35, but this seems unlikely in context. — [4] *málfinni* 'eloquence': An assimilated variant of *málfimni*, introduced to form an *aðalhending* with *vinn-*.

35. Þats rétt, at dag dróttins
 døglingr myni hingat
 lopts ok lýðum skipta
 ljósgims koma af himnum.
 Oss skyldi sú aldri
 ógnartíð in stríða
 — drótt biði sikling sátta
 sólvangs — ór hug ganga.

Þats rétt, at døglingr lopts ljósgims myni koma hingat af himnum dróttins dag ok skipta lýðum. Sú in stríða ógnartíð skyldi oss aldri ganga ór hug; drótt biði sikling sólvangs sátta.

It is true that the king of the loft of the light-jewel [SUN > SKY/HEAVEN > = God (= Christ)] will come here from the heavens on the Lord's day and divide people. That severe time of terror should never go out of our minds; let the people beg the prince of the sun-plain [SKY/HEAVEN > = God (= Christ)] for reconciliation.

Mss: **B**(11r), 624(90). — *Readings:* [2] myni: 'mune' B, 624 [4] ljósgims: ljóðgims B, 'hliod fims' 624.

Editions: Skj Anonyme digte og vers [XII], G [2]. *Leiðarvísan* 35: AI, 624-5, BI, 631, *Skald* I, 306; Sveinbjörn Egilsson 1844, 67, Rydberg 1907, 9, Attwood 1996a, 69, 179.

Notes: [All]: St. 35 is the last in 624. — [4] *ljósgims* 'of the light-jewel [SUN]': B reads *ljóðgims*, a *hap. leg.* which can be glossed 'poem-gem', but is difficult to make sense of here. Sveinbjörn Egilsson emended (n. to 444(2)ˣ) to *ljósgim* 'light-jewel' (cf. the sun-*heiti fagrgim* 'fair jewel' in 2/2). — [5-8]: This *helmingr* is very similar to the account of the Second Coming and Last Judgement in *Has* 37/5-8 — [7-8] *sikling sólvangs* 'the prince of the sun-plain [SKY/HEAVEN > = God (= Christ)]': Although *sólvangr* 'sun-plain' is *hap. leg.*, the kenning is reminiscent of *siklingr landa sólar* 'prince of the lands of the sun', used of Christ in 26/1-2. Similar are the God-kennings *siklingr bóls sólar* 'prince of the abode of the sun' in *Geisl* 67/5-6 and *siklingr ranns sólar* 'prince of the house of the sun' in Gamlkan *Jóndr* 1/5.

36. Dag metr sinn at sǫnnu
snjallastr konungr allra
eljunkuðr of aðrar
alfríðar hátíðir.

Dýrka dýrligs verka
dáðsterks hǫfuðmerki
— rétt segjum — dag dróttins
drjúgmǫrg himintǫrgu.

Snjallastr konungr allra, eljunkuðr, metr dag sinn at sǫnnu of aðrar alfríðar hátíðir. Drjúgmǫrg hǫfuðmerki verka dýrka dag dýrligs dáðsterks dróttins himintǫrgu; segjum rétt.

The most valiant king of all [= God], known for his energy, rates his day in truth higher than other most glorious festivals. Very numerous chief testimonies of deeds [HOLY WRITINGS] celebrate the day of the glorious, deed-strong lord of the heaven-shield [SKY/HEAVEN > = God]; we [I] tell it correctly.

Mss: **B**(11r), 399a-b[x]. — *Reading*: [4] alfríðar: *so* 399a-b[x], 'alf[...]dar' B.

Editions: *Skj* Anonyme digte og vers [XII], G [2]. *Leiðarvísan* 36: AI, 625, BI, 631, *Skald* I, 307; Sveinbjörn Egilsson 1844, 67, Rydberg 1907, 9-10, Attwood 1996a, 69, 179.

Notes: [1] *dag metr sinn*: Note the deliberate similarity to the opening ll. of sts. 30 – *Dag reið sinn* – and 31 – *Dag reis sinn*. — [8] *himintǫrgu* 'of the heaven-shield [SUN]': This particular kenning occurs in only one other place in skaldic verse, Eil *Þdr* 5/2[III], where it is part of a *rekit* kenning for a giantess (cf. *LP*: himintarga). Cf. also 42/2 *rítar himins* 'of the shield of heaven [SUN]'.

37. Menn skulu œztum unna
angrs hrjóðanda þjóðar
— mér berr máls á stýri
mart — af ǫllu hjarta.

Siðminningr fær sannan
seima Þróttr af dróttni
(Kristr gefr fyrðum) fasta
(friðar vón, þeims ann hónum).

Menn skulu unna œztum hrjóðanda angrs þjóðar af ǫllu hjarta; mart berr mér á stýri máls. Siðminningr Þróttr seima fær sannan fasta af dróttni; Kristr gefr fyrðum, þeims ann hónum, friðar vón.

Men must love the most excellent destroyer of the harm of people [SIN > = God] with all their hearts; many a thing comes to my rudder of speech [TONGUE]. The faithful Þróttr <= Óðinn> of riches [MAN] receives true strength from the Lord; Christ gives to men who love him the hope of peace.

Mss: **B**(11r), 399a-b[x].

Editions: *Skj* Anonyme digte og vers [XII], G [2]. *Leiðarvísan* 37: AI, 625, BI, 631, *Skald* I, 307; Sveinbjörn Egilsson 1844, 67-8, Rydberg 1907, 10, Attwood 1996a, 69, 180.

Notes: [7-8]: Cf. 42/7-8: *Kristr gefr fyrðum fastan | frið en ek kunna biðja.*

38. Verðim vér ok fyrðar   ok heim dýrstr frá dómi
    — vili svá faðir skilja —   dagskeiðs jǫfurr leiði
    hilmis frægs til hœgri   oss frá ótta hvǫssum
    handar allra landa,   ǫll til himna hallar.

Verðim vér ok fyrðar til hœgri handar frægs hilmis allra landa — vili faðir skilja svá —, ok dýrstr jǫfurr dagskeiðs leiði oss ǫll frá hvǫssum ótta, frá dómi, heim til hallar himna.

May we [I] and [other] men be at the right hand of the famous ruler of all lands [= God] — may the Father be willing to decide thus — and may the most dear prince of the day-course [SKY/HEAVEN > = God (= Christ)] lead us all from acute fear, from judgement, home to the hall of the heavens [SKY/HEAVEN].

Mss: **B**(11r), 399a-b[x].

Editions: *Skj* Anonyme digte og vers [XII], G [2]. *Leiðarvísan* 38: AI, 625, BI, 631-2, *Skald* I, 307, *NN* §3251; Sveinbjörn Egilsson 1844, 68, Rydberg 1907, 10, Attwood 1996a, 69, 180.

Notes: [1] *fyrðar* (m. nom. pl.) 'men': Finnur Jónsson (*Skj* B) emends to *fyrða* (gen. pl.) 'of men', which he construes with *faðir* (l. 2) to form the God-kenning *faðir fyrða* 'father of men'. This kenning then forms part of the intercalary cl. *ok vili faðir fyrða skilja svá* 'and may the father of men be willing to decide so'. Kock (*NN* §3251) retains Finnur Jónsson's emendation, which he takes as acc. pl. He construes the intercalary cl. *ok faðir vili skilja svá fyrða* 'and may the father be willing to divide men thus', understanding *skilja* in the sense 'divide' rather than 'decide'. It is possible, however, to retain the ms. reading *fyrðar* and assume a double subject 'other men and I', whom the poet wishes to be among the saved at the Last Judgement (on the right hand of God). The intercalary cl. then underlines this wish.

39. Vér skulum opt með tǫrum   at, þás ǫflugr eflir
    — verðr mein, ef því seinum —   alls sóma lýkr dómi,
    — kostum flærð at forðask —   fara næðim vér fríða
    friðar helgan goð biðja,   fljótt í dýrð með dróttni.

Vér skulum opt biðja helgan goð friðar með tǫrum — mein verðr, ef seinum því; kostum at forðask flærð —, at, þás ǫflugr eflir alls sóma lýkr dómi, næðim vér fara fljótt í fríða dýrð með dróttni.

We must often pray holy God for peace with tears — harm will result, if we delay that; we must try to shun deceit —, so that when the powerful strengthener of all honour [= God] finishes judgement, we may succeed in going swiftly into splendid glory with the Lord.

Mss: **B**(11r), 399a-b[x].

Editions: *Skj* Anonyme digte og vers [XII], G [2]. *Leiðarvísan* 39: AI, 625, BI, 632, *Skald* I, 307, *NN* §21B; Sveinbjörn Egilsson 1844, 68, Rydberg 1907, 10, Attwood 1996a, 69-70, 180.

Notes: [1] *opt* 'often': As it stands in B, l. 1 lacks a second alliterating syllable. Konráð Gíslason (and Eiríkur Jónsson 1875-89, II, 31-4) suggested emending to *víst* 'certainly', and this has been adopted by Finnur Jónsson (*Skj* B) and Kock (*Skald*).

40. Kostum allir æsta
    oss at helgum krossi
    kœnir menn, sem kunnum,
    Krist eilífrar vistar.

    Staðr es ǫllum œðri
    — óttalaus með dróttni
    þjóð lifir glǫð, sús gœði*
    getr — munligri ok betri.

Allir kœnir menn, sem kunnum, kostum æsta Krist oss eilífrar vistar at helgum krossi. Staðr es ǫllum œðri, munligri ok betri; glǫð þjóð, sús getr gœði*, lifir óttalaus með dróttni.

Let all wise men, as we are able, strive to ask Christ for an eternal abode for ourselves beside the holy Cross. That place is higher, more desirable and better than all; the happy [group of] people that obtains good things will live fearlessly with the Lord.

Mss: **B**(11r), 399a-b[x]. — *Reading*: [7] gœði*: 'gęðir' B, 399a-b[x].

Editions: *Skj* Anonyme digte og vers [XII], G [2]. *Leiðarvísan* 40: AI, 625, BI, 632, *Skald* I, 307, *NN* §1269; Sveinbjörn Egilsson 1844, 68-9, Rydberg 1907, 10, Attwood 1996a, 70, 180.

Notes: [5-8]: Several interpretations of this *helmingr* are possible. The one favoured here assumes l. 5 *staðr es ǫllum œðri* 'the place is higher than all' to refer back to the first *helmingr*, in which the poet advocates that humans seek a place in heaven beside the holy Cross; *munligri ok betri* 'more desirable and better' (l. 8) qualify *staðr* (l. 5). The remainder of the *helmingr* may then be understood as an intercalary sentence. Finnur Jónsson (*Skj* B) takes *með dróttni* 'with the Lord' (l. 6) as qualifying *staðr* 'place' (l. 5) and *óttalauss* 'fearless' (l. 6) as part of the intercalary cl., qualifying *þjóð lifir* 'the people live' (l. 7). He construes *staðr með dróttni es ǫllum æðri, munnligri ok betri; glǫð þjóð ... lifir óttalaus* 'A place with the Lord is higher, more pleasant and better than all others; the happy people ... lives without fear'. Kock (*NN* §1269) agrees with Finnur's understanding of *með dróttni* and promotes *óttalaus*, emended to *óttalauss* to agree with *staðr*, to the main cl., construing *staðr óttalauss með dróttni* 'a fearless place with the Lord'. — [6] *óttalaus með dróttni*: The identical l. occurs at 41/8, while 13/6 reads *óttalaust ok lið dróttni*. Cf. the strikingly similar *óttalaus fyr dróttni* in *Has* 32/4. — [7] *gœði* * 'good things': Sveinbjörn's emendation (1844, 69 n. 23) has been adopted by all subsequent eds.

41. Haldi oss frá eldi / svát ǫll í frið fullan
eilífr skapa deilir / farim heim, es skilr beima
Kristr styrkr ok myrkrum / alls stýrandi, órum
menn, es heim líðr þenna, / óttalaus með dróttni.

Eilífr deilir skapa, styrkr Kristr, haldi oss menn frá eldi ok myrkrum, es líðr þenna heim, svát farim ǫll heim í fullan frið, óttalaus með órum dróttni, es stýrandi alls skilr beima.

May the eternal ruler of fates [= God (= Christ)], powerful Christ, keep us men from fire and darkness, when this world passes away, so that we may all go home into complete peace, fearlessly with our Lord, when the steerer of all [= God] divides men.

Mss: **B**(11r), 399a-b[x]. — *Reading*: [7] stýrand*i*: stýranda B, 399a-b[x].

Editions: *Skj* Anonyme digte og vers [XII], G [2]. *Leiðarvísan* 41: AI, 625-6, BI, 632, *Skald* I, 307, *NN* §1270; Sveinbjörn Egilsson 1844, 69, Rydberg 1907, 10, Attwood 1996a, 70, 181.

Notes: [3] *styrkr* 'strong, powerful': The ms. reading has been retained here, although it disturbs the alliteration, which requires a word beginning with <m>. Sveinbjörn Egilsson, acknowledging Jón Sigurðsson's suggestion (in a n. to 444(2)[x]), and Kock (*NN* §1270) independently suggested that the word should be *merkir*, 3rd pers. sg. pres. indic. of *merkja* in the sense 'to set a value on'. They take *Kristr* 'Christ' (l. 3) to be the subject and *menn* the object in an intercalary cl. *Kristr merkir menn* 'Christ values men'. Finnur Jónsson (*Skj* B) omits the word altogether, marking the space with dots. — [4, 6] *heim* '[this world, place of abode]', *heim* (adv.) 'home, homewards': The poet plays on the similarity between these two words and the disparity between the first, which refers to the temporal world, and the second, which holds out the prospect of heavenly bliss. — [5] *ǫll* 'all': The poet's use of the n. pl. form of the adj. allows for the possibility that women as well as men may go to heaven. — [7] *stýrandi alls* 'steerer of all [= God]': Sveinbjörn Egilsson's correction (note to 444(2)[x]) is adopted by all subsequent eds. Cf. the kenning *stýrandi hallar heims* 'steerer of the hall of the world [SKY/HEAVEN > = God]' in 21/3-4. *Alls stýrandi* is used in Mark *Eirdr* 29/2[II].

42. Yfirstillir firr ǫllu / Mér fái miklu hæri
ítr túns himins rítar / miskunn jǫfurr sunnu,
— harmsfullum ræðk halli / — Kristr gefr fyrðum fastan
hugstrandar — mik grandi. / frið — en ek kunna biðja.

Ítr yfirstillir túns rítar himins, firr mik ǫllu grandi; ræðk harmsfullum halli hugstrandar. Jǫfurr sunnu fái mér miklu hæri miskunn, en ek kunna biðja; Kristr gefr fyrðum fastan frið.

Glorious overseer of the home-field of the shield of heaven [SUN > SKY/HEAVEN > = God], distance me from all harm; I govern a sorrowful stone of the shore of thought [BREAST >

HEART]. May the prince of the sun [= God (= Christ)] grant me much higher mercy than I could ask for; Christ gives people secure peace.

Mss: **B**(11r), 399a-b[x]. — *Readings*: [1] Yfirstillir: 'Y[...]ir[...]i[...]' B, 'Yfirṣṭiller' 399a-b[x]   [4] hugstrandar: *so* 399a-b[x], 'hugstrannda[...]' B;   grandi: *so* 399a-b[x], 'g[...]nnde' B.

Editions: *Skj* Anonyme digte og vers [XII], G [2]. *Leiðarvísan* 42: AI, 626, BI, 632-3, *Skald* I, 307; Sveinbjörn Egilsson 1844, 69, Rydberg 1907, 10-11, Attwood 1996a, 70, 181.

Notes: [1-2] *ítr yfirstillir túns himins rítar* 'glorious overseer of the home-field of the shield of heaven [SUN > SKY/HEAVEN > = God]': Cf. the God-kenning in *Has* 26/3-4. *Ítr* provides the *hǫfuðstafr* in each case. — [7-8]: The intercalary cl. in 37/7-8 is almost identical to the one here.

43. Réð með oss, at óði
     — es fróðr, sás vensk góðu —
     greitt, hvé grundvǫll settak,
     gǫfugr prestr at hlut mestum.

     Orð* mun allra verða
     auðsætt, bragar þætti,
     ramligt hús þars reistum,
     Rúnolfr, hvé fekk snúnat.

Gǫfugr prestr réð greitt með oss at mestum hlut, hvé settak grundvǫll at óði; es fróðr, sás vensk góðu. Orð* allra mun verða auðsætt, þars reistum ramligt hús, Rúnolfr, hvé fekk snúnat þætti bragar.

A noble priest readily gave us [me] advice, for the most part, about how I should establish the foundation of the poem; he is wise who accustoms himself to what is good. The words of all will become readily apparent, where we [I] raised a strong building, Rúnolfr, how I was able to compose the poem [*lit.* weave together the strand of the poem].

Mss: **B**(11r), 399a-b[x]. — *Readings*: [4] mestum: *so* 399a-b[x], '[...]estum' B   [5] Orð*: Yðr B   [7] ramligt: ramligs B   [8] fekk: ferr B.

Editions: *Skj* Anonyme digte og vers [XII], G [2]. *Leiðarvísan* 43: AI, 626, BI, 633, *Skald* I, 307; Sveinbjörn Egilsson 1844, 69-70, Rydberg 1907, 11, Attwood 1996a, 70, 181.

Notes: [5] Orð* 'words': All eds follow Sveinbjörn Egilsson (1844, 69 n. 25) in emending to *orð* 'word'. This is construed with *allra* (gen. pl.) 'of all' (l. 5) to give *orð allra mun verða auðsætt* 'everyone's words (i.e. public opinion) will be obvious'. B's reading *yðr* does not provide *skothending* and is difficult syntactically. — [7] *ramligt hús þars reistum* 'where we [I] raised a strong building': Cf. *Has* 59/3 *ramligs bús af ræsi*. B's *ramligs* must be emended to *ramligt*, to agree with *hús* (n. acc. sg.). Both Finnur Jónsson (*Skj* B) and Kock (*Skald*) emend thus. The poet appears to be thanking Rúnolfr (see Note below) for helping him establish the foundation (*grundvǫllr*, l. 3) of *Leið*, presumably its basic structure, and he continues this metaphorical comparison here between composing a poem and building a house. Cf. Egill *Arkv* 25[V] and Kálf *Kátr* 1/4 for similar comparisons. — [8] *Rúnolfr*: Rúnolfr is usually taken to be the name of the *gǫfugr prestr* 'noble priest' of l. 4, possibly the poet's teacher or mentor. There are two priests of that name mentioned in a *Prestatal* of

1143, attributed to Ári Þorgilsson (*DI* I, 180-94). The first is Rúnolfr Dálksson, nephew of Bishop Ketill Þorsteinsson of Hólar (bishop 1122-45). He is probably identical with the Rúnolfr Dagsson named in ch. 19 of *BjH* (*ÍF* 3, 163 n. 2) as the source of information concerning Bjǫrn Hítdœlakappi's composition of religious poetry and said in *Sturlu saga* ch. 29 (*Stu* 1988, 88-9) to have been a monk at Helgafell c. 1170 (see Astås 1970, 266-7 n. 15; Attwood 1996b, 226). The other possibility is Bishop Ketill's son, Rúnolfr Ketilsson (d. 1186), who was the author of a poem celebrating the new church built at Skálholt by Klœngr Þorsteinsson (bishop 1152-76), one st. of which (RKet Lv[IV]) survives in *Hungrvaka*. As a known poet, Rúnolfr Ketilsson is often considered to have the better claim, but *BjH*'s evidence for Rúnolfr Dálksson/Dagsson's interest in skaldic poetry bolsters his claim also.

44. Mœðask mér á óði
      — mest þarf hóf at flestu —
      (brands hefr ǫrr til enda)
      orðvǫpn* (kveðit drópu).

      Skulu eldviðir ǫldu
      alljósan brag kalla
      — þjóð hafi þekt á kvæði
      þvísa — Leiðarvísan.

Orðvǫpn* mœðask mér á óði; mest hóf þarf at flestu; ǫrr brands hefr kveðit drópu til enda. Ǫldu eldviðir skulu kalla alljósan brag Leiðarvísan; þjóð hafi þekt á kvæði þvísa.

My word-weapons [ORGANS OF SPEECH] become exhausted from the poem; the greatest moderation is needed in most things; the sword-blade's messenger [MAN] has recited the poem to the end. Trees of the fire of the wave [(*lit.* 'fire-trees of the wave') GOLD > MEN] shall call the very bright poem 'Leiðarvísan'; may people derive pleasure from this poem.

Mss: **B**(11r), 399a-b[x]. — *Readings*: [2] þarf: '[...]arf' B, '(þ)arf(?) 399a-b[x] [4] -vǫpn*: 'vǫpns' B [5] eldviðir: *so* 399a-b[x], 'e[...]d u[...]ir' B.

Editions: Skj Anonyme digte og vers [XII], G [2]. *Leiðarvísan* 44: AI, 626, BI, 633, Skald I, 308; Sveinbjörn Egilsson 1844, 70, Rydberg 1907, 11, Attwood 1996a, 70-1, 181.

Notes: [3] *brands* 'of the sword-blade': Sveinbjörn Egilsson (1844, 70) considered this to be the pers. n. *Brandr*, and construed (with emendation) *Brandr hefr ǫrr kveðit drápa til enda* 'Brandr has spoken the poem to the end'. He argued that the poet is giving his own name here, as he has named his mentor in 43/8. In the introduction to his 1844 edn (vi) and in 444(3)[x], Sveinbjörn identified this Brandr as Brandr Jónsson, Abbot of Þykkvabœr 1247-62 and Bishop of Skálholt 1263-4. Brandr is credited with authorship of several religious texts, most notably *Gyðinga saga* (Wolf 1995). If, however, *Leið* can be dated to the mid to late C12th, as is argued in the Introduction, this attribution becomes chronologically implausible. Finnur Jónsson (*LH* II, 118) pointed out that Sveinbjörn's emendation is unnecessary, since *ǫrr brands* 'the messenger of the sword-blade' makes a perfectly acceptable man-kenning (*LP*: 2. *brandr*). — [5] *ǫldu eldviðir* 'the trees of the fire of the wave [(*lit.* 'the fire-trees of the wave') GOLD > MEN]': The identical kenning occurs in a verse spoken by Skarphéðinn Njálsson in *Nj* (Skarp Lv 9/7[V]) and in a *lv.* preserved in *Víga-*

Glúms saga and attributed to Víga-Glúmr (VGl Lv 4/3ᵛ). — [6] *alljósan brag* 'very bright poem': Cf. 4/2 *ljósum brag* 'bright poem'. — [8] *Leiðarvísan*: Lit. 'Way-guidance'. The poem's title draws attention to the conceit of the Christian life as a journey, possibly a pilgrimage, for which the poet has provided guidance concerning penitence, sinless living and Sunday observance. On the title, see the Introduction. *Has* 64/2 also gives the name of the poem in the penultimate st., as do the anonymous poets of *Sól* and *Lil*.

45. Nú skal drótt á lok líta   Heim laði dýrr frá dómi
    — lopthjalms dǫgum optar   dags hallar gramr allan
    dýrkim dǫglings verka   — þjóð hjali kersk of kvæði —
    dáðhress — bragar þessa.   kristinn lýð til vistar.

Nú skal drótt líta á lok bragar þessa; dýrkim dǫgum optar verka dáðhress dǫglings lopthjalms. Dýrr gramr dags hallar laði allan kristinn lýð heim frá dómi til vistar; þjóð hjali kersk of kvæði.

The company shall now look on the end of this poem; let us praise more often than [there are] days the works of the deed-hearty king of the sky-helmet [SKY/HEAVEN > = God]. May the glorious prince of day's hall [SKY/HEAVEN > = God (= Christ)] invite all Christian folk home from judgement to his dwelling place; may people chatter cheerfully about the poem.

Mss: **B**(11r), 399a-bˣ.

Editions: *Skj* Anonyme digte og vers [XII], G [2]. *Leiðarvísan* 45: AI, 626, BI, 633, *Skald* I, 308, *NN* §2562; Sveinbjörn Egilsson 1844, 70, Rydberg 1907, 11, Attwood 1996a, 71, 182.

Notes: [1] *nú skal* 'now shall': Kock (*NN* §2562), observing that the l. is septasyllabic, omits *skal* and emends to *Nú's* 'now is'. — [1] *drótt* 'company': In skaldic court poetry, *drótt* refers to a king's or earl's retinue, but here the nature of the poet's audience is not courtly. It is probably most likely to be monastic or ecclesiastical, but it may be a lay or mixed audience. — [2] *dǫgum optar* 'more often than [there are] days': The same expression is in Anon *Nkt* 73/6ᴵᴵ, but nowhere else in the skaldic corpus. — [3-4] *dǫglings lopthjalms* 'of the king of the sky-helmet [SKY/HEAVEN > = God]': Cf. 30/5, 8: *dǫgling lopthjalms* 'prince of the sky-helmet' (of Christ). — [4] *dáðhress* 'deed-hearty': See Notes to *dáðmáttugr* (5/7) and *fjǫlhress* (19/4). Having described his own exhaustion in 44/1-4, the poet here draws attention to the hearty freshness of God's creative energy. — [6] *gramr dags hallar* 'prince of day's hall': Cf. *dróttinn dags hallar* 'lord of day's hall [SKY/HEAVEN > = God (= Christ)]' in 15/5-6.

Anonymous, *Plácitusdrápa*

Edited by Jonna Louis-Jensen and Tarrin Wills

Introduction

Plácitusdrápa 'Drápa about Plácitus' (Anon *Pl*) is the only C12th Icel. poem to be preserved in a near-contemporary ms.: AM 673 b 4° (673b), dated to c. 1200. Ms. 673b contains a number of mistakes which indicate that it is a transcript of an older ms., not an original. Since no other copy of the poem has survived, some of these errors are difficult or impossible to correct, but the transmission of *Pl* would nevertheless have compared favourably with that of other early poetry if the *codex unicus* had not been badly damaged by wear and tear. The preserved leaves are disfigured by numerous small holes in the vellum and by stains, possibly caused by damp, that have more or less obliterated large areas of writing. It is to be hoped that better methods than the ones presently used to decipher worn and indistinct writing will be developed in the future, but for the time being the only way to recover the passages that are torn or mouldered away remains conjecture, which of course carries varying degrees of conviction.

There are some discrepancies between certain eds and transcribers regarding the actual ms. readings. The available versions include: Þorsteinn Helgason's transcript, used by Sveinbjörn Egilsson (cf. Louis-Jensen 1998, 89n.) and printed in his edn after Sveinbjörn's normalised text, referred to in the apparatus as 673b*ÞH*; Halldór Einarson's transcripts (673b*HE*) which are included as variants to 673b*ÞH* in Sveinbjörn's edn; Sveinbjörn's own notes to the transcripts (673b*SE*); Finnur Jónsson's readings in 1887 (673b*FJ*) and *Skj* A (673b*Skj*); and Jón Helgason's readings in 1932-3 (673b*JH*). Many of these works have readings that are now no longer visible: such readings are included in the textual apparatus. Where these eds have indicated a reading as uncertain, the reading is followed by '(?)'.

Conjectures to *Pl* are found chiefly in Sveinbjörn Egilsson (1833), Finnur Jónsson (1887), *Skj*, and also in an article by Jón Helgason (1932-3) and a number of paragraphs in *NN*. Reference should also be made to Konráð Gíslason's edn of *Nj* (with Eiríkur Jónsson 1875-89, II); the comments on *Pl* made there were used by Finnur Jónsson in his 1887 edn and *Skj*. It should be emphasised that it is difficult to distinguish between reading of the ms., conjecture and emendation in some of these sources. Unless otherwise noted, conjectures are those proposed by Sveinbjörn Egilsson 1833.

Conjectures are incorporated into the main text in the following cases: where a previous ed. has been able to read the text in the ms. with some degree of certainty, even if the ms. is now no longer legible; where some text of a line survives and a missing word can be conjectured on the basis of the metre, the prose version or some other evidence indicating the precise wording; or where the emendation is of a minor or grammatical nature. Other plausible conjectures made by eds are included in the Notes.

The edn of Louis-Jensen 1998 is a version of the *Pl* text and translation in *Skj* B, updated with readings and emendations from Jón Helgason 1932-3. The present edn is based on Louis-Jensen 1998, but has been compared with the unique ms. by Jonna Louis-Jensen and Tarrin Wills. As a result, a few of the readings presented here differ from those in Louis-Jensen 1998. The English translation in Louis-Jensen 1998 is based on John Tucker's unpublished translation of the Danish prose version in *Skj* B. The present translation and prose word order have been independently revised by Tarrin Wills and Margaret Clunies Ross, while the deconstruction of kennings was prepared by Jonna Louis-Jensen. The Introduction, Variant readings and Notes are based on Louis-Jensen 1998, with revisions and additions by Tarrin Wills and Margaret Clunies Ross.

The ms. fragment 673b is likely to have originally been part of a larger compilation, which probably included the also fragmentary AM 673 a II 4° (Louis-Jensen 1998, xcii-iii). The latter includes the remains of an Icel. translation of the Lat. *Physiologus*, probably from an English source, and parts of two sermons, on the religious-symbolic meanings associated with parts of a ship, and on the symbolism of the rainbow (Larsson 1891; Hamre 1949). While 673b is itself dated c. 1200, scholars agree that its text of *Pl* is a copy at one or more removes from the original written text. This allows for the possibility that the poem was composed as early as c. 1150 or as late as c. 1200; for the various arguments, see Louis-Jensen 1998, xcic-cii. The scribe was an Icelander, and there is no reason to doubt that the composer of *Pl* was also an Icelander, despite arguments by Seip (1949) that both were Norw. It appears, however, from marginal additions to both ms. fragments, that the compilation was in Norway in the late C14th.

Louis-Jensen (1998, ciii-cxxv) has demonstrated that *Pl* may be compared to versions A and C of the four extant prose redactions of *Plácitus saga* (see Tucker 1993 and 1998 for a discussion of the prose texts), though all extant mss of these versions of the prose saga are considerably later than 673b. She shows by means of detailed comparisons that *Pl* descends from the same translation as A and C, and that it shows a particular affinity to C, whose scribe is likely to have been influenced by *Pl*. She also queries Finnur Jónsson's proposal (1887, 257-8) that the poet of *Pl* may have worked directly from an abbreviated Lat. source. These deductions are of considerable interest for the literary and stylistic study of Christian skaldic poetry.

The legend of Placidus is one of the most exciting in Christian hagiography. It tells of a Roman general and favourite of the Emperor Trajan (r. 98-117), who converted to Christianity after an encounter with Christ in the form of a stag, changed his name to Eustace, was subjected to various trials, being deprived of his wife by a lecherous ship's captain and of his two sons by wild beasts, and was then reunited with his family before they were all martyred together in an ox-shaped oven of brass for refusing to sacrifice to pagan gods for the success of the new Emperor, Hadrian (r. 117-38).

The legend of Placidus/Eustace exists in several Greek and Lat. versions, and probably took shape under the dual influence of Greek romance and the Christian Bible. From the C9th the legend became popular in Carolingian circles and spread from there to England, where vernacular versions in both prose and verse developed and attained considerable popularity during the C11th (Lapidge 1988). Knowledge of the legend may have spread to Scandinavia from France, Germany or England, the latter being perhaps the most likely source. The various Norse redactions of the prose saga of Plácitus, the earliest of which is a fragment written c. 1150 in Trondheim, together with the unique early ms. of *Pl*, bear witness to the popularity of the legend in medieval Iceland from C12th onwards. This may be in part because of the genuine interest of the narrative, in part because, as an example of a virtuous pagan, the figure of Placidus struck a chord in a society concerned with the fate of its own 'noble heathens', as a number of sagas of Icelanders reveal. Oddly enough, in spite of the popularity of his legend, Plácitus was not himself the subject of any recorded cult in Iceland (Cormack 1994), even though surviving Icel. calendars from before 1400 attest to the liturgical importance of his feast (Tucker 1998, xxxi).

Pl is a fragmentary *drápa* in *dróttkvætt* metre, preserved on 5 leaves of 673b. Louis-Jensen has calculated that at least a first and a last leaf have been lost (1998, xcii; cf. Finnur Jónsson 1887, 254; Lange 1958a, 100-1). It is clear from the structure of the *drápa* and the extant 59 sts that 11 sts have been lost at the opening and 8 at the end, making up an original number of 78 sts. 10 sts remain of an original 21-st. introduction (*upphaf*). The central section of the poem (*stefjabálkr*), comprising 36 sts, begins at st. 11 with the first refrain (*stef*), which is repeated at sts 18 and 25. *Stef* 2 occurs at sts 32, 39 and 46. The concluding *slæmr* begins at st. 47 and runs to st. 59, but it is presumed to have comprised 8 more sts to a total of 21, in parallel with the *upphaf*.

The anonymous poet of *Pl* adapted his narrative very skilfully to skaldic conventions. As Louis-Jensen has demonstrated (1998, cvii-cxxv), he was often able to echo words and phrases in the prose version of the legend he was presumably working from, while adapting them to the considerable metrical constraints of *dróttkvætt*. In addition, as his was a narrative poem, he had to tell a story while at the same time observing the micro-structural divisions of the *stefjabálkr*. This may be why he sometimes rearranges the sequence of events in the narrative, in comparison with the normal prose sequence of the legend. Of outstanding interest, particularly in comparison with other C12th *drápur*, is the poet's copious use of kennings to ornament his narrative. These fall particularly into the traditional categories of kennings for man, warrior, seafarer, generous man and woman, alongside kennings of a newer, Christian type for God, Christ, holy man and priest. Noteworthy also is the poet's skilful use of direct speech (where the prose texts sometimes have reported speech) to enliven the narrative.

1. ...
... gengit,
fjǫrnis valdr kv*að* foldar
frægr: 'nú mun *þ*ér lægjask.

Mjúks, skalt mannra*un* sl*í*ka,
morðlinns boði, finna
— vestu í frægri *f*reis*t*ni
framr — sem Jób inn gamli'.

...gengit, frægr valdr fjǫrnis foldar kv*að*: 'nú mun *þ*ér lægjask. Finna skalt, boði mjúks morðlinns, sl*í*ka mannra*un* sem Jób inn gamli; vestu framr í frægri *f*reis*t*ni'.

...gone, the renowned ruler of the helmet of the earth [SKY/HEAVEN > = God] spoke: 'now you will be humbled. Messenger of the smooth battle-serpent [SWORD > WARRIOR], you will undergo such an ordeal as Job the old [did]; be bold in a trial [which will be] famous.

Ms.: 673b(1r). — *Readings*: [3] kv*að*: 'q[...]' 673b, 'quaþft' 673b*ÞH*, 'quaþ' 673b*HE*, 673b*FJ*; foldar: '[...]' 673b [4] *þ*ér: 'er' 673b [5] mannra*un*: 'mannra[...]' 673b, mannraun 673b*HE*; sl*í*ka: '[...]ca' 673b, 'flica' 673b*ÞH* [7] *f*reis*t*ni: 'f[...]ne' 673b, 'frestne' 673b*ÞH*.

Editions: Skj Anonyme digte og vers [XII], G [1]. *Plácítúsdrápa* 1: AI, 607, BI, 606-7, *Skald* I, 295; Sveinbjörn Egilsson 1833, 11, 39, Finnur Jónsson 1887, 230, Louis-Jensen 1998, 93.

Notes: [All]: The beginning of the poem must have introduced Plácitus as a righteous pagan in the service of the Emperor Trajan, and told of the stag hunt that Plácitus and other men undertook, during which he became isolated from the others and confronted a hart larger than the rest of the herd with a crucifix between its horns, which revealed itself as a manifestation of Christ. In the prose texts, Christ's indication that Plácitus must be tried like Job comes after his baptism and his return to meet the Christ-hart for a second time (see sts 7-10). — [4] *þ*ér 'you': *er* is interpreted as the dat. sing. *þ*ér by Sveinbjörn Egilsson 1833, but cf. Finnur Jónsson 1887, 245 and Konráð Gíslason and Eiríkur Jónsson 1875-89, II, 46-7. — [5] *mannra*un 'ordeal, trial of strength': Also st. 12/4, when Plácitus is tried by having all his animals and household perish; in this instance *mannraun* also appears in the C text of the prose saga (Tucker 1998, 31, l. 101). The word is also used in Anon *Mhkv* 7/8^{III} of the ordeal of the biblical hero Eleazar (Eljárnir), who was crushed beneath an elephant (1 Macc. VI.43-7). — [8] *sem Jób inn gamli; vestu framr í frægri f*reis*t*ni 'as Job the old [did]; be bold in a trial [which will be] famous': Cf. the C text of the prose saga *og þola freistingar með Yób hinum gamla* 'and endure temptations with [?like] Job the old' (Tucker 1998, 27, l. 82; Louis-Jensen 1998, cxxi). The designation of Job as *inn gamli* only occurs in *Pl* and C, and Louis-Jensen (1998, cxi-ii) has argued that the *Pl* poet introduced it to satisfy the demands of *aðalhending*, proffering this as an example to support the thesis that the author of the C redaction of the saga knew and was influenced by *Pl*. Both the Lat. and other ON prose texts make the comparison with the suffering of the Old Testament figure Job, and it comes up again in st. 26/8. On references to the Book of Job in OIcel. texts, see Kirby 1976-80, I, 24-30.

2. Lundr reis gjalfrs frá grundu
goðs orðum ... skorðaðr
elds; vas áðr til foldar
ormstalls boði fallinn.

Logstýfir b*að* leyfa
ljó*ss* engla sér þengil
Vánar vífi sínu
*v*egs þessi r*o*k segja.

Lundr elds gjalfrs reis frá grundu ... skorðaðr orðum goðs; boði ormstalls vas áðr fallinn til foldar. Vánar logstýfir b*að* þengil ljó*ss v*egs engla leyfa sér segja vífi sínu þessi r*o*k.

The tree of the fire of the sea [GOLD > MAN] rose from the ground ... supported by the words of God; the messenger of the serpent-lair [GOLD > MAN] had previously fallen to earth. The snipper of the fire of Vǫn <river> [(*lit.* 'the fire-snipper of Vǫn') GOLD > GENEROUS MAN] asked the ruler of the bright path of angels [HEAVEN > = God] to permit him to tell his wife about these omens.

Ms.: **673b**(1r). — *Readings*: [2] ...: *om.* 673b [5] b*að*: 'b*e*þ' 673b [6] ljó*ss*: ljós 673b [8] *v*egs: '[...]egs' 673b, 'uegs' 673b*ÞH*, 673b*FJ*.

Editions: *Skj* Anonyme digte og vers [XII], G [1]. *Plácitúsdrápa* 2: AI, 607-8, BI, 607, *Skald* I, 295; Sveinbjörn Egilsson 1833, 11-12, 39, Finnur Jónsson 1887, 230, Louis-Jensen 1998, 93-4.

Notes: [2] ...: Konráð Gíslason proposed adding *vel* 'well' to fill the metrical lacuna here (Konráð Gíslason and Eiríkur Jónsson 1875-89, II, 252). — [6] *ljóss* 'bright': Emendation proposed in *Skj* B. — [8] *vegs* 'of the path': Both Þorsteinn Helgason and Finnur Jónsson thought they could read the <v> or <u> in the ms. While the letter is no longer visible, it is determined by the alliteration.

3. 'Bei*ð*ir, segðu ok brúði',
byrskríns, 'sonum þínum,
*o*ll vilk yðr', kvað stillir,
'ormstalls, í trú kalla.

Hyrsl*ø*ngvir, kom hingat
hvalranns, *um* dag annan;
þá munk yðr, þats *...
— *y*fir þegjum nú — segja'.

'Bei*ð*ir ormstalls, segðu sonum þínum ok brúði', kvað stillir byrskríns, 'vilk kalla yðr *o*ll í trú. Hvalranns hyrsl*ø*ngvir, kom hingat *um* annan dag; munk þá segja yðr, þats *...; *y*fir þegjum nú'.

'Demander of the serpent-lair [GOLD > MAN], tell your sons and wife', said the ruler of the wind-shrine [SKY/HEAVEN > = God], 'I will call you all to the faith. Flinger of the fire of the whale-house [(*lit.* 'fire-flinger of the whale-house') SEA > GOLD > GENEROUS MAN], come here tomorrow; I will then tell you about that which ...; we are [I am] silent now about [it]'.

Ms.: **673b**(1r). — *Readings*: [1] Bei*ð*ir: 'Bei[...]' 673b, 'Beiþ' 673b*ÞH* [2] byrskríns: 'byrscrns' 673b [5] -sl*ø*ngvir: 'sclavgvir' 673b [6] *um*: '[...]' 673b [7, 8] *... *y*fir: 'høf[...] hvfer' 673b, 'þof n vfer' 673b*FJ*.

Editions: *Skj* Anonyme digte og vers [XII], G [1]. *Plácítúsdrápa* 3: AI, 608, BI, 607, *Skald* I, 295-6, *NN* §2490; Sveinbjörn Egilsson 1833, 12, 40, Finnur Jónsson 1887, 230, Jón Helgason 1932-3, 151, Louis-Jensen 1998, 94.

Notes: [All]: On verbal correspondences between this st. and the A and C versions of the prose text, see Louis-Jensen 1998, cxvii. — [6] um: Supplied by Finnur Jónsson (1887). *Skj* B has 'of'. — [7-8] ... *yfir* '... about [it]': Sveinbjörn Egilsson (1833) emended ms. 'høf.. hvfer' to *ófir*, supposedly a variant of *váfir* (*yfir*) 'is imminent, threatens'. Finnur Jónsson read 'þof..n vfer' (1887) and later 'þof..r yfer' (*Skj* A), but in *Skj* B he followed Sveinbjörn in emending the word to *ófir* and connecting it with *yfir*. Jón Helgason (1932-3) accepted the older reading 'høf..' and explained the <h> in 'hvfer' (=*yfir*) at the beginning of the following l. as an attempt to restore alliteration which had been disturbed by the evidently intrusive 'h' in 'høf..'. While doubting the existence of the form *ófir* = *váfir*, Jón offered no alternative explanation. It seems at least as likely that *yfir* should belong with *þegja* to form the expression *þegja yfir e-u* 'keep silent about something'. Kock suggested *hǫfum* = *œfum* (from Low German *oven* 'exercise, do' [*NN* §2490]), but one does not expect a Low German loan-word in a text of this date.

4. Heim kom hodda *geymir*; (*Seims*) kvað sér í draumi,
    hagat ... vel þvís sagði (svǫr veitti þau bǫr*v*i)
    viggþollr ... dyggva *men*reið mána slóðar
    Vinnils konu sinni. mjúklynd kon*ung* sýndan.

Geymir hodda kom heim; Vinnils viggþollr ... vel hagat, þvís sagði konu sinni dyggva ... Mjúklynd *men*reið *kvað* kon*ung* slóðar mána sýndan sér í draumi; veitti þau svǫr bǫr*v*i *seims*.

The keeper of hoards [MAN] came home; the tree of the horse of Vinnill <sea-king> [(*lit*. 'the horse-tree of Vinnill') SHIP > SEAFARER] ... behaved well in telling his wife the excellent ... The gentle necklace-bearer [WOMAN] said that the king of the path of the moon [SKY/HEAVEN > = God] had appeared to her in a dream; she gave these answers to the tree of gold [MAN].

Ms.: **673b**(1r). — *Readings*: [1] *geymir*: '[...]' 673b, geymir 673b*FJ* [5] Sei*ms*: 'seis' 673b, 673b*ÞH*, seims 673b*FJ*; *kvað sér*: '[...]' 673b, 'qvaþ ser' 673b*FJ* [6] svǫr: 'suar' 673b; bǫr*v*i: 'bavr[...](e)'(?) 673b, 'bavrve' 673b*ÞH*, 673b*FJ* [7] *men*reið: '[...]reiþ' 673b, 'men reiþ' 673b*FJ* [8] kon*ung*: 'kon[...]' 673b, 673b*HE*, kona 673b*ÞH*, konung 673b*FJ*.

Editions: *Skj* Anonyme digte og vers [XII], G [1]. *Plácítúsdrápa* 4: AI, 608, BI, 607, *Skald* I, 296, *NN* §2491; Sveinbjörn Egilsson 1833, 12, 40, Finnur Jónsson 1887, 230, Jón Helgason 1932-3, 151-2, Louis-Jensen 1998, 94-5.

Notes: [2] ... *vel*: Jón Helgason proposed *lét*, which would fit well with the p.p. *hagat*. Kock proposed *vann* (*NN* §2491). *Skj* B omits as here. — [3] ...: The metre requires a two-syllable word starting with *v*. Jón Helgason suggested *vitrun* 'vision', which was adopted in *Skald* and in Louis-Jensen 1998. However, *vitrun* is otherwise only found in C14th poetry. *Skj* B has *of vann*. — [5-8]: Cf. the wording of these ll. with C, 54-5: *Mier sýndist í nótt í svefni ... sem hann siálfur kiæmi til mýn* 'It appeared to me last night in a dream ... as if he himself came to me' (Louis-Jensen 1998, cxxii). — [8] *mjúklynd ... sýndan*: The same *aðalhending* (*-lyndum ... sýndisk*) occurs in st. 7/4. Such rhymes become increasingly common after C12th, usually when the vowels are followed by more than one consonant (cf. Kuhn 1977, 528).

5. Ok bæði hjú blíðan
    byskups fund — at mundum
    þeim hykk þrifnuð kómu —
    þá nótt með veg sóttu,

    ok tveir með þeim þeira
    — þýðr gaf lærdóms prýðir
    holdum hilmis foldar
    hirðnofn — synir skírðusk.

Ok bæði hjú sóttu þá nótt blíðan fund byskups með veg — hykk þrifnuð kómu þeim at mundum — ok tveir synir þeira skírðusk með þeim; þýðr prýðir lærdóms gaf holdum foldar hilmis hirðnofn.

And both husband and wife had that night a gracious reception from the bishop with honour — I think good fortune came within their grasp — and their two sons were baptised with them; the kindly adorner of learning [BISHOP] gave the men names of the court of the ruler of the earth [(*lit.* 'court-names of the ruler of the earth') = God > HEAVEN].

Ms.: **673b**(1r-v). — *Readings*: [2] byskups: 'by(sco)[...]'(?) 673b, byskups 673b*ÞH*, 673b*FJ* [3] þrifnuð: 'þrifn[...]' 673b, 'þri[...]' 673b*ÞH*, 'þrif(na)'(?) 673b*HE*, 'þrifnoþ' 673b*FJ* [5] ok tveir: 'O[...]' 673b, 'oc [...]' 673b*ÞH*, 'oc tueir' 673b*FJ* [6] gaf lærdóms: 'gøfler doms' 673b [7] holdum: 'halldo' 673b [8] hirðnofn: 'hiþnøfn' 673b.

Editions: *Skj* Anonyme digte og vers [XII], G [1]. *Plácítúsdrápa* 5: AI, 608, BI, 607-8, *Skald* I, 296, *NN* §1243; Sveinbjörn Egilsson 1833, 13, 41, Finnur Jónsson 1887, 231, Louis-Jensen 1998, 95.

Notes: [6, 7] *gaf lærdóms ... holdu*m: Emendations proposed by Finnur Jónsson 1887. — [8] *hirðnofn* 'court-names': That is, names that show these persons belong to the *hirð* 'court' of God. The names Eustace, Theopista, Agapitus and Theopistus are given in the next st., where they all contribute to *aðalhendingar*. The latinate forms in *Pl* are closer to the Lat. prose text and version A of the saga than they are to version C (Louis-Jensen 1998, cxviii). Cf. also the use of another *hirð-* cpd in connection with God in st. 7/8.

6. Snjallr gat orr frá illu
    Evstákíus vaknat;
    kvón réð þegns at þjóna
    Þeopista vel Kristi.

    Ungr nam atferð drengja
    Ágapítus fága,
    þýðr né þengils lýða
    Þeopistus trú missti.

Snjallr Evstákíus gat orr vaknat frá illu; þegns kvón, Þeopista, réð at þjóna vel Kristi. Ungr Ágapítus nam fága atferð drengja, né missti þýðr Þeopistus trú þengils lýða.

Brave Eustace was able to wake, prompt, from evil; the man's wife, Theopista, undertook to serve Christ well. Young Agapitus began to cultivate the behaviour of good men, nor did the mild Theopistus lack faith in the ruler of mankind [= God].

Ms.: 673b(1v). — *Readings*: [3] *þjóna*: 'þjono' 673b [6] *fága*: 'fregia' 673b.

Editions: *Skj* Anonyme digte og vers [XII], G [1]. *Plácítúsdrápa* 6: AI, 608, BI, 608, *Skald* I, 296, *NN* §§2970E, 3133B; Sveinbjörn Egilsson 1833, 13, 41, Finnur Jónsson 1887, 231, Louis-Jensen 1998, 96.

Notes: [2] *Evstákíus* 'Eustace': Cf. *NN* §§2970E, 3133B. — [6] *fága* 'to cultivate': Emendation proposed by Finnur Jónsson 1887. Cf. st. 8/3.

7. Ok annan dag unnar
    elg-Þróttr í stað sótti,
    fyrr þanns flærðar þverri
    framlynd*um* *goð* sýndisk.

    Sannhugguðr leit seggja
    snildar framr á hamri
    hauks í hjartar líki
    hirðvand*an* gram standa.

Ok annan dag sótti unnar elg-Þróttr í stað, þanns *goð* sýndisk fyrr framlynd*um* þverri flærðar. Sannhugguðr hauks, framr snildar, leit hirðvand*an* gram seggja standa á hamri í líki hjartar.

And the next day the Þróttr <= Óðinn> of the elk of the wave [(*lit.* 'the elk-Þróttr of the wave') SHIP > SEAFARER] sought the place where God had shown himself previously to the brave diminisher of falsehood [HOLY MAN]. The true comforter of the hawk [WARRIOR], outstanding in courage, beheld the ruler of men, careful chooser of his retainers, [= God] standing on a cliff in the shape of a hart.

Ms.: 673b(1v). — *Readings*: [4] framlynd*um*: 'framlund[...]' 673b, framlyndum 673b*Þ*H; *goð*: *om.* 673b [8] -vand*an*: -vandin 673b, bandin 673b*Þ*H.

Editions: *Skj* Anonyme digte og vers [XII], G [1]. *Plácítúsdrápa* 7: AI, 608-9, BI, 608, *Skald* I, 296; Sveinbjörn Egilsson 1833, 13-14, 42, Finnur Jónsson 1887, 231, Louis-Jensen 1998, 96.

Notes: [All]: According to the Eustace legend, the morning after Plácitus and his family had been baptised, Plácitus went back to the place where he had first encountered the Christ-hart, and was granted a second vision. It is at this point that Christ tells him that he must be tried for his faith. — [4] *goð* 'God': This emendation was proposed by Sveinbjörn Egilsson. It reflects the wording of the C version of the saga: *enn um moruninn fór Evst(asius) til þess sama stadar sem gud hafdi ádur vitr[ast honum ...]* (Tucker 1998, 23) 'and the next day Eustace went to the same place where God had previously appeared to him'. — [5, 7] *sannhugguðr hauks* 'the true comforter of the hawk [WARRIOR]': Slightly unusual, in that the determinant in kennings of this type is normally an expression for raven or eagle, sometimes in the form of a kenning with *haukr* as its base-word; see *Meissner*, 310 (including examples with *haukr*), 346. — [7-8]: Cf. the wording of the C text *síndist honum hann þar kominn í hiartarmind þeirri* 'he [God] appeared to him to have come there in the form of the hart' (Louis-Jensen 1998, cxxii). The alliterating *á hamri* 'on a cliff' (l. 6) reflects the demands of the poetic form and is based on the location of Plácitus's vision on a mountain (*mons*) in the Lat. text (cf. the A version's *fjall*). The symbolic significance of the hart was particularly appropriate to the legend of the Christian convert Plácitus and would have been well understood by the poet and audience of *Pl*. On the one hand, the hart panting for cooling streams mentioned in Ps. XLII.1 was understood to represent the soul saved through baptism, and, on the other, the hart who tramples a serpent was understood as a type of Christ overcoming Satan according to the *Physiologus*. If 673b was originally part of a compilation together with 673a, there would have been a thematic connection between *Pl* and the *Physiologus* text in 673a, which includes the hart among the animals whose allegorical meaning is expounded (Halldórr Hermansson 1938, 20).

8. Unnit engla kennir
   aldyggr við bǫl styggum
   lýteigs lengi at fága
   logbeiði sið heiðinn,

   þás sinnar trú sv*i*nnan
   sjaldspurðum at*b*urði
   fleinrjóð fylkir lýða
   flærðvarr gǫtu lærði.

Aldyggr kennir engla unnit lýteigs log beiði, styggum við bǫl, at fága lengi heiðinn sið, þás flærðvarr fylkir lýða lærði sv*i*nnan fleinrjóð gǫtu sinnar trú sjaldspurðum at*b*urði.

The all-good knower of angels [= God] did not allow the demander of the fire of the fish-field [(*lit.* 'the fish-field's fire-demander') SEA > GOLD > MAN], shy of evil, to cultivate heathen practice[s] for long, when the deceit-wary ruler of mankind [= God] taught the wise spear-reddener [WARRIOR] the way of his faith by an unusual event.

Ms.: **673b**(1v). — *Readings*: [3] lýteigs: 'lyteigir' 673b [5] sv*i*nnan: 'suennan' 673b [6] at*b*urði: 'at þvrþi' 673b [8] gǫtu: 'g[...]to' 673b, 'goto' 673b*PH*.

Editions: *Skj* Anonyme digte og vers [XII], G [1]. *Plácítúsdrápa* 8: AI, 609, BI, 608-9, *Skald* I, 296; Sveinbjörn Egilsson 1833, 14, 42, Finnur Jónsson 1887, 231, Louis-Jensen 1998, 97.

Notes: [8] gǫtu 'the way': Emendation supplied by Finnur Jónsson 1887; Sveinbjörn Egilsson has 'gøto'.

9. 'Hræzkat vǫrðr, þótt verðir,
   — v*e*st traust*r* ok ger h*r*aust*l*a —
   fremðar lystr, *í* freistni,
   fránsk*í*ðs, af mér, Vánar.

   Þin*n* mun huggun hreinni,
   hers skins, trega minka,
   enn skalt, ǫrr, til þinnar
   ástskýrðr koma dýrðar.'

'Hræzkat, fremðar lystr vǫrðr fránsk*í*ðs Vánar, þótt verðir *í* freistni af mér; v*e*st traust*r* ok ger h*r*aust*l*a. Hreinni huggun mun minka trega þin*n*; ǫrr skins hers, enn skalt koma, ástskýrðr, til dýrðar þinnar.'

'Do not fear, glory-desiring keeper of the shining ski of Vǫn <river> [SHIP > SEAFARER], even though you come into trial through me; be confident and act bravely. With pure consolation I will lessen your sorrow; messenger of the shine of war [SWORD > WARRIOR], yet you shall come, purified by love, to your glory.'

Ms.: **673b**(1v). — *Readings*: [1] verðir: 'verþr' 673b, 'verþir' 673b*ÞH* [2] v*e*st: 'vist[...]' 673b, 'vactu' *or* 'vastu' 673b*ÞH*, 'vist þu' 673b*FJ*; traustr: 'travstc' 673b; hr*a*us*t*la: 'hrvsla' 673b, 673b*FJ*, 'hrvsra' 673b*ÞH* [3] *í*: '[...]' 673b, 'i' 673b*ÞH*, 673b*FJ* [4] -sk*í*ðs: -skeiðs 673b; V*á*n*a*r: 'vaner' 673b [5] Þin*n*: 'þin' 673b [7] ǫ́rr: ór 673b.

Editions: *Skj* Anonyme digte og vers [XII], G [1]. *Plácítúsdrápa* 9: AI, 609, BI, 609, *Skald* I, 296, *NN* §2131; Sveinbjörn Egilsson 1833, 14, 43, Finnur Jónsson 1887, 232, Jón Helgason 1932-3, 152-3, Louis-Jensen 1998, 97.

Notes: [2] *ve*st 'be': Finnur Jónsson (1887) read *vist*, but noted the *i* as indistinct; cf. Jón Helgason 1932-3. An extrametrical pronoun, *þú*, following this verb is noted as indistinct by Finnur Jónsson (1887 and *Skj* A) and as illegible by Jón Helgason 1932-3. — [4] -sk*í*ðs ... V*á*nar '-ski ... of Vǫ́n': Emendations proposed by Finnur Jónsson (1887). — [5-6] *hreinni huggun mun mink*a *trega þin*n 'with pure consolation [I] will lessen your sorrow': *Skj* B translates *en renere trøst vil forminske din sorg* 'a purer consolation will lessen your sorrow', but *hreinni* is dat. The above reading follows *NN* §2131, which has *hreinni* as instrumental dat. and reads *mun* as representing *munk*. *Huggan* 'consolation, comfort' is an important concept in *Pl*, and recurs in sts 31/5, 36/6 and 54/7. The only other occurrence of the word in skaldic verse is Gamlkan *Jóndr* 2/3.

10. B*r*aut var*ð* hjǫrtr frá hreyti
     — heim fór at þat — seima;
     Krist bað frægr við freistni
     fultings boði hringa.

     Sagði drengr, þaus dugðu,
     (dolglinns*) konu sinni
     (rǫskr gat hug við háska)
     heit goðssonar (beitir).

Hjǫrtr var*ð* b*r*aut frá hreyti seima; fór heim at þat; frægr boði hringa bað Krist fultings við freistni. Drengr sagði konu sinni heit goðssonar, þaus dugðu; rǫskr beitir dolglinns* gat hug við háska.

The hart went away from the flinger of gold [GENEROUS MAN]; he went home after that; the famous offerer of rings [GENEROUS MAN] asked Christ for help in the face of his trial. The man told his wife the promises of God's son [= Christ], which were powerful; the brave handler of the battle-serpent [SWORD > WARRIOR] received courage against danger.

Ms.: **673b**(1v-2r). — *Readings*: [1] B*r*aut: baut 673b; var*ð*: varf 673b [3] freistni: 'frei' *touched up by a later hand* 673b [6] -linns*: '-linnsc' 673b.

Editions: *Skj* Anonyme digte og vers [XII], G [1]. *Plácítúsdrápa* 10: AI, 609, BI, 609, *Skald* I, 296, *NN* §1244; Sveinbjörn Egilsson 1833, 15, 43, Finnur Jónsson 1887, 232, Louis-Jensen 1998, 98.

Notes: [All]: For the several verbal echoes between this st. and the C text of the saga, see Louis-Jensen 1998, cxii. — [1] *varð* 'went': So emended by Louis-Jensen 1998. Finnur Jónsson (1887 and *Skj* B) emended to *hvarf*.

11. Fúss emk fremðar lýsi Hlaut, sás œztr es ýta,
     fritt, ef þat mák hitta, íðn Plácitus fríða;
     — Kristr fr*em*r hodda hr*i*sti — Evstákíus ævi
     hugblíðum stef smíða. albazta sér valði.

Emk fúss smíða hugblíðum lýsi fremðar fritt stef, ef mák hitta þat; Kristr fr*em*r hr*i*sti hodda. Plácitus, sás œztr es ýta, hlaut fríða íðn; Evstákíus valði sér albazta ævi.

I am eager to compose an attractive refrain for the gentle illuminator of honour [HONOURABLE MAN = Plácitus], if I may come upon it; Christ promotes the shaker of hoards [GENEROUS MAN]. Plácitus, who is the highest of men, was allotted a glorious task; Eustace chose for himself the very best life.

Ms.: **673b**(2r). — *Readings:* [3] fr*em*r: 'frør' 673b; hr*i*sti: 'hr[...]ste' 673b, 'hroste' 673b*Þ*H, 'hrosre' *or* 'hruste' 673b*H*E, 'hriste' 673b*F*J.

Editions: Skj Anonyme digte og vers [XII], G [1]. *Plácítúsdrápa* 11: AI, 609, BI, 609, *Skald* I, 296-7, *NN* §§3133B, 3134, 3247; Sveinbjörn Egilsson 1833, 15, 44, Finnur Jónsson 1887, 232, Louis-Jensen 1998, 98.

Notes: [3] *fremr* 'promotes': Emendation proposed by Finnur Jónsson 1887. — [5-8]: The ll. comprise the first *stef*.

12. Brátt kom fram, þats flýti Hjǫrð tók hodda skerðis
     friðbragða goð sagði; hyggjusnjalls at falla
     næst varð meiðr í mestri — fúrlestir stóðsk freistni
     mannraun dra*s*ils hranna. fleygarðs — en hjú deyja.

Kom brátt fram, þats goð sagði flýti friðbragða; meiðr dra*s*ils hranna varð næst í mestri mannraun. Hjǫrð hyggjusnjalls skerðis hodda tók at falla, en hjú deyja; fleygarðs fúrlestir stóðsk freistni.

What God had told the advancer of acts of kindness [HOLY MAN] soon came to pass; the tree of the steed of the waves [SHIP > SEAFARER] came immediately into the greatest ordeal. The herd of the brave-souled diminisher of hoards [GENEROUS MAN] began to perish and [his] household to die; the wrecker of the fire of the ship-fence [(*lit.* 'the fire-wrecker of the ship-fence') SHIELD > SWORD > WARRIOR] endured the trial.

Ms.: **673b**(2r). — *Readings:* [4] dra*s*ils: 'dra[...]els' 673b, '[...]els' 673b*Þ*H, 'dr(as)els'(?) 673b*K*G, 'drasels' 673b*F*J.

Editions: *Skj* Anonyme digte og vers [XII], G [1]. *Plácítúsdrápa* 12: AI, 609-10, BI, 609-10, *Skald* I, 297; Sveinbjörn Egilsson 1833, 15-16, 44, Finnur Jónsson 1887, 232, Louis-Jensen 1998, 99.

Notes: [4] *drasils* 'of the steed': Reading first proposed by Konráð Gíslason and Eiríkur Jónsson 1875-89, II, 300-1.

13. Hús brutu heip*tar fúsir   Ǫll réð flærð*ar* fellir
     — hófsk freistni svá — þjófar;   fétjón, þaus beið ljóna
     út bǫr*u* þeir aura   — snauðr varð* ǫrr at auði
     ǫldurmanns ór ranni.   un*n*blakks — goði þakka.

Þjófar fúsir heip*tar brutu hús; svá hófsk freistni; *þeir bǫru aura* út ór ǫldurmanns ranni. Fellir ljóna flærð*ar* réð þakka goði ǫll fétjón, þaus beið; ǫrr un*n*blakks varð* snauðr at auði.

Thieves eager for harm broke into the house; thus the trial began; they carried valuables out of the nobleman's house. The destroyer of men's falsehood [HOLY MAN] gave thanks to God for all the losses which he suffered; the messenger of the wave-horse [SHIP > SEAFARER] became bereft of wealth.

Ms.: **673b**(2r). — *Readings*: [3, 4] bǫr*u* þeir aura ǫldur-: 'bor[...]alldor' 673b, 'bore[...]alldor' 673b*ÞH*, 'boro þeir avra ølldor' 673b*FJ*   [5] flærð*ar*: 'flęrþ(a)[...]'(?) 673b, 'flęrþar' 673b*ÞH* [7] varð*: varðr 673b   [8] un*n*-: und 673b.

Editions: *Skj* Anonyme digte og vers [XII], G [1]. *Plácítúsdrápa* 13: AI, 610, BI, 610, *Skald* I, 297, *NN* §1245; Sveinbjörn Egilsson 1833, 16, 45, Finnur Jónsson 1887, 233, Louis-Jensen 1998, 99.

Notes: [All]: For verbal correspondences between sts 12 and 13 and the C text of the prose saga, see Louis-Jensen 1998, cxxii-iii. — [4] *ǫldurmanns* 'the nobleman's': A loan word from English (cf. OE *aldormann, ealdormann*, *OED*: *alderman* 1a), found in skaldic verse only here and in two poems where Anglophone influence is also likely, Bjbp *Jóms* 11/2[I] and GunnLeif *Merl I* 63/4[VIII]. This word is not used in any of the prose versions of the legend.

14. 'Hvat hafim, Sjǫfn, at sitja,   'Eigum oss at lægja,
     seims' (mælti þat) 'heima?'   einn réttr þvíat goð bei*nir*,
     (*e*lda njótr við ítra   — reyndrs, sás stríð má standask
     ulfvíns konu sína).   stór — *far*naði órum.'

'Hvat hafim, Sjǫfn seims, at sitja heima?'; njótr *e*lda ulfvíns mælti þat við ítra konu sína. 'Eigum at lægja oss, þvíat einn réttr goð bei*nir far*naði órum; reyndrs, sás má standask stór stríð.'

'What do we gain, Sjǫfn <goddess> of gold [WOMAN], by staying at home?'; the user of the fires of wolf-wine [BLOOD > SWORDS > WARRIOR] said that to his splendid wife. 'We must humble ourselves because the one true God furthers our fortune; that one is well-proven who can endure great distresses.'

Ms.: **673b**(2r). — *Readings*:   [6] þvíat: 'þūat' 673b;   bei*n*ir: 'be(i)e(ck)'(?) 673b, 'beteck' 673b*ÞH*, 'beiegk' 673b*FJ*   [8] stór*far*naði: 'sto[...]naþe' 673b.

Editions: *Skj* Anonyme digte og vers [XII], G [1]. *Plácitúsdrápa* 14: AI, 610, BI, 610, *Skald* I, 297, *NN* §§2132, 2492; Sveinbjörn Egilsson 1833, 16, 45, Finnur Jónsson 1887, 233, Jón Helgason 1932-3, 153-4, Louis-Jensen 1998, 100.

Notes: [6] *einn réttr* 'the one true': The letters are partially damaged but legible nevertheless. This reading is found in Sveinbjörn Egilsson 1833, but Finnur Jónsson (1887 and *Skj* A) and Kock (cf. *NN* §2132) apparently could not read the 're'. Sveinbjörn's reading was restored by Jón Helgason 1932. Kock suggested *einréttr* (*NN* §§2132, 2492). — [6] *þvíat* 'because': Emendation proposed by Jón Helgason 1932-3. — [6] *beinir* 'furthers': Emendation proposed by Kock (*NN* §2132). There may possibly have been a nasal stroke over the first 'i' which is no longer visible. — [8] *farnaði* 'fortune': Emendation proposed (along with the alternative *lifnaði* 'conduct of life') by Jón Helgason 1932-3. Finnur Jónsson (1887 and *Skj* B) has *búnaði* 'household'.

15. Réð ór Rúmsborg víðri
    rausnar valdr at halda,
    hǫppum reifðr þás hafði
    hringþollr skaða fingit.

    Fóru *braut með beiti
    byrstóðs synir fróðum
    tilstýranda tírar
    tveir ok móðir þeira.

Valdr rausnar réð at halda ór víðri Rúmsborg, þás hringþollr hǫppum reifðr hafði fingit skaða. Tveir synir tilstýranda tírar ok móðir þeira fóru *braut með fróðum beiti byrstóðs.

The possessor of splendour [NOBLEMAN] left the great city of Rome, when the ring-fir, blessed with victories [MAN], had received injury. The two sons of the pursuer of renown [NOBLEMAN] and their mother went abroad with the wise steerer of the wind-horse [SHIP > SEAFARER].

Ms.: **673b**(2r). — *Readings*:   [5] Fóru: 'for' 673b;   *braut: 'abrot' *touched up by a later hand* 673b   [7] tilstýranda: 'til st[...]randa' 673b.

Editions: *Skj* Anonyme digte og vers [XII], G [1]. *Plácitúsdrápa* 15: AI, 610, BI, 610, *Skald* I, 297, *NN* §2133; Sveinbjörn Egilsson 1833, 17, 45-5, Finnur Jónsson 1887, 233, Jón Helgason 1932-3, 154, Louis-Jensen 1998, 100.

Notes: [1] *Rúmsborg* 'city of Rome': The C text echoes this p. n.; both the Lat. and other ON texts state only that Plácitus and his family set out for Egypt (see Louis-Jensen 1998, cxxiii). — [5] *fóru* 'went': Emendation proposed by Finnur Jónsson 1887. — [5] *braut 'abroad': Emendation proposed by Jón Helgason 1932-3. — [7] *tilstýranda* 'of the pursuer': Emendation proposed by Kock (*NN* §2133).

16. Sik *bað* stríða stǫðvir
 stirðs, es at kom firði,
 hy*r*lund heiðni kenndan
 herleiks of sæ *ferja*.

Veittit fremðar flýti
flugstyggum aldyggva
fetrjóðr Fenris jóða
farning inn bǫlgjarni,

Stǫðvir stríða, es kom at firði, *bað* stirðs herleiks hy*r*lund, kenndan heiðni, *ferja* sik of sæ. Inn bǫlgjarni fetrjóðr jóða Fenris veittit aldyggva farning flugstyggum flýti fremðar,

The calmer of distress [HOLY MAN], when [he] came to the bay, asked the tree of the fire of harsh army-play [(*lit*. 'fire-tree of harsh army-play') SWORD > WARRIOR], known for paganism, to ferry them over the sea. The evil-eager paw-reddener of the offspring of Fenrir <wolf> [WOLVES > WARRIOR] did not provide reliable transportation for the flight-shy begetter of honour [HOLY MAN],

Ms.: 673b(2r-v). — *Readings*: [1] *bað*: '[...]' 673b, 'baþ' 673b*FJ*   [3] hy*r*-: 'h(y)[...]'(?) 673b, 'hot' 673b*PH*, 'hyr' 673b*FJ*   [4] *ferja*: '[...]' 673b.

Editions: *Skj* Anonyme digte og vers [XII], G [1]. *Plácítúsdrápa* 16: AI, 610, BI, 610-11, *Skald* I, 297; Sveinbjörn Egilsson 1833, 17, 46, Finnur Jónsson 1887, 233, Louis-Jensen 1998, 101.

Notes: [All]: In the legend, Plácitus and his family seek passage to Egypt with a ship's captain who is variously described as *dominus ... barbarus* 'the barbarous master' and *scips drottin ...heiþiɴ oc grímr* 'the ship's captain ... heathen and cruel' (A¹) (Tucker 1998, 32). The warrior-kennings in sts 16 and 17 refer to this man, who quickly sees that the family is destitute and decides to seize Theopista, whom he finds very attractive, in payment for the crossing. — [3] *hy*r*lund* 'fire-tree': Proposed by Finnur Jónsson 1887, who could apparently read the now-illegible letters in the ms. — [4] *herleiks* 'of army-play [BATTLE]': This cpd is treated as a kenning in *Meissner* (199); however, terms for 'warriors' are rare as determinants of battle-kennings (cf. *Meissner*, 177, 194).

17. þás auðskiptis eptir
 almilds konu dvaldi
 — væn leizk hodd-Gefn hónum —
 hjǫrlundr á skæ sunda.

Hreins varð heggr við sína
hraustr, þás gekk af flausti,
auðar eiginbrúði
óviljandi at ski*lj*ask.

Þás hjǫrlundr dvaldi konu almilds auðskiptis eptir á skæ sunda; hodd-Gefn leizk hónum væn. Hraustr heggr hreins auðar varð óviljandi at ski*lj*ask við eiginbrúði sína, þás gekk af flausti.

when the sword-tree [WARRIOR] kept the wife of the most generous wealth-distributor [GENEROUS MAN] back on the horse of channels [SHIP]; the hoard-Gefn <= Freyja> [WOMAN] looked beautiful to him. The brave tree of shining wealth [MAN] had to part with his wife against his will, when he left the ship.

Ms.: 673b(2v). — *Reading*: [8] ski*lj*ask: 'scialsc' 673b.

Editions: *Skj* Anonyme digte og vers [XII], G [1]. *Plácítúsdrápa* 17: AI, 610-11, BI, 611, *Skald* I, 297; Sveinbjörn Egilsson 1833, 18, 46, Finnur Jónsson 1887, 234, Louis-Jensen 1998, 101.

Notes: [5] *heggr* 'tree': The bird-cherry tree, *prunus padus*.

18. Dýrðhittir bað dróttin
    dagbœjar sér tœja;
    hæst gat hrjóðr við freistni
    hugborð móins storðar.
    Hlaut, sás œztr es ýta,
    íðn Plácitus fríða;
    Evstákíus ævi
    albazta sér valði.

Dýrðhittir bað dróttin dagbœjar tœja sér; hrjóðr storðar móins gat hæst hugborð við freistni. Plácitus, sás œztr es ýta, hlaut fríða íðn; Evstákíus valði sér albazta ævi.

The acquirer of glory [HOLY MAN] bade the lord of the daylight-home [SKY/HEAVEN > = God] help him; the destroyer of the ground of the serpent [GOLD > GENEROUS MAN] received the highest mind-board [COURAGE] in the face of trial. Plácitus, who is the best of men, was allotted a glorious task; Eustace chose for himself the very best life.

Ms.: 673b(2v). — *Reading*: [5-8]: abbrev. *as* 'hlaut sa es e. e.i.' 673b.

Editions: *Skj* Anonyme digte og vers [XII], G [1]. *Plácítúsdrápa* 18: AI, 611, BI, 611, *Skald* I, 297; Sveinbjörn Egilsson 1833, 18, 47, Finnur Jónsson 1887, 234, Louis-Jensen 1998, 102.

Notes: [4] *hugborð* 'mind-board': I.e. breast and consequently courage (cf. *Meissner*, 135). The only other instance in skaldic poetry is Þorm Lv 3/4^V, but the word is also found in prose in *Saga Sigurðar Jórsalafara* (*Fms* 7, 143/13; cf. *Fritzner*: *hugborð*). — [5-8]: *Stef* 1, cf. st. 11.

19. Fljóð varð heim með heiðnum
    hlunndýrs fara runni;
    kona bað sér við synðum
    saurlífis goð hlífa.
    Blíðr dugði svá brúði
    brátt, at saurgask máttit,
    himna valdr, af Hildar
    hauknistis samvistu.

Fljóð varð fara heim með heiðnum runni hlunndýrs; kona bað goð hlífa sér við synðum saurlífis. Blíðr valdr himna dugði brátt brúði svá, at máttit saurgask af samvistu Hildar hauknistis.

The woman had to go home with the heathen tree of the animal of the launching-roller [SHIP > SEAFARER]; the woman asked God to protect her against the sins of impure living. The gentle ruler of the heavens [= God] quickly helped the woman so that she could not be polluted by cohabitation with the feeder of the hawk of Hildr <valkyrie> [(*lit.* 'hawk-feeder of Hildr') RAVEN > WARRIOR].

Ms.: 673b(2v).

Editions: *Skj* Anonyme digte og vers [XII], G [1]. *Plácítúsdrápa* 19: AI, 611, BI, 611, *Skald* I, 297; Sveinbjörn Egilsson 1833, 18-19, 47, Finnur Jónsson 1887, 234, Louis-Jensen 1998, 102.

Notes: [All]: The description of the fate of Plácitus' wife comes earlier in the narrative sequence in both *Pl* and the C text of the saga than in the Lat. and A text (Louis-Jensen 1998, cxxiii). This restructuring has the effect of increasing the dramatic tension concerning Theopista's suffering at the hands of her captor.

20. Sýnir gekk með sína
    seggja trausts af flausti
    — þá vas þrekmanns ævi
    þung — tvá sonu unga.
    Seimtýnir *kom* sveinum,
    søkkmeiðr, at ǫ́ breiðri,
    borðs* né báða þorði
    bera senn yfir nenninn.

Sýnir trausts seggja gekk með tvá unga sonu sína af flausti; þrekmanns ævi vas þá þung. Seimtýnir *kom* sveinum at breiðri ǫ́; nenninn borðs* søkkmeiðr né þorði bera báða senn yfir.

The demonstrator of support to men [RULER] went with his two young sons from the ship; the powerful man's life was heavy then. The gold-destroyer [GENEROUS MAN] brought the boys to a broad river; the brave tree of the jewel of the gunwale [(*lit.* 'jewel-tree of the gunwale') SHIELD > SEAFARER] did not dare to carry both over at once.

Ms.: **673b**(2v). — *Readings*: [2] trausts: 'trauste' *or* 'traustc' *or* 'trausts' 673b*Þ*H, 'traustc' 673b*FJ* [5] *kom*: *om.* 673b [6] søkk-: 'sc[...]k' 673b, 'scok' 673b*Þ*H, 's.ok' 673b*FJ* [7] borðs*: 'borþsc' 673b.

Editions: *Skj* Anonyme digte og vers [XII], G [1]. *Plácítúsdrápa* 20: AI, 611, BI, 611-12, *Skald* I, 298, *NN* §1246; Sveinbjörn Egilsson 1833, 19, 47, Finnur Jónsson 1887, 234, Jón Helgason 1932-3, 154-5, Louis-Jensen 1998, 102-3.

Notes: [5] *sveinum* 'the boys': Cf. *NN* §1246. Finnur Jónsson (1887 and *Skj* B) emends to *sveina* and reads with *báða* 'both', but transitive *koma* 'bring' with dat. object is unproblematic. — [6] *søkk-* 'jewel-': Emendation proposed by Jón Helgason 1932-3. *Skj* B has *sól-* 'sun' but this involves further emendation of the 'k' visible in the ms.

21. Sinn bar of ǫ́, þás annan,
    ástvitjuðr, lét sitja,
    hraustr erfingja, hristir
    Hlakkar skins á bakka.
    Ok þás annan sœkja
    auðgildir son vildi,
    stóð umb *ok* sásk síðan
    sviðr þegn a*t* ǫ́ miðri.

Ástvitjuðr bar erfingja sinn of ǫ́, þás hraustr hristir skins Hlakkar lét annan sitja á bakka. Ok þás auðgildir vildi sœkja annan son, stóð sviðr þegn a*t* miðri ǫ́ *ok* sásk síðan umb.

The seeker of love [HOLY MAN] carried his heir over the river, while the strong shaker of the gleam of Hlǫkk <valkyrie> [SWORD > WARRIOR] left the other sitting on the bank.

And when the wealth-payer [GENEROUS MAN] wanted to fetch his other son, the wise man stopped in the middle of the river and then looked about him.

Ms.: **673b**(2v). — *Readings*: [7] *ok*: *om*. 673b [8] *at*: 'a[...]' 673b, 'at' 673bÞH, 673bFJ.

Editions: *Skj* Anonyme digte og vers [XII], G [1]. *Plácítúsdrápa* 21: AI, 611, BI, 612, *Skald* I, 298, *NN* §2553; Sveinbjörn Egilsson 1833, 19-20, 48, Finnur Jónsson 1887, 235, Louis-Jensen 1998, 103.

Notes: [7] u*m*b ok 'about him ... and': Previous eds have read 'umb', but all but the second minim of the 'u' is obscured by a hole and the 'b' by a fold (cf. Konráð Gíslason and Eiríkur Jónsson 1875-89, II, 302). The addition of *ok* was originally proposed by Konráð Gíslason (and Eiríkur Jónsson 1875-89, II, 302 and 958) and adopted by Finnur Jónsson in *Skj* B.

22. Dýr leit *fr*óns it frána
     fleinrjóðr koma at sveini,
     — hryggr varð við þat harða
     hann — en vargr tók annan;

     ok baugfergir bjarga
     brátt hvǫrungi má*tt*i,
     dýr þás dyggva hlýra
     drógu braut til skógar.

Fleinrjóðr leit it frána dýr *fr*óns koma at sveini, en vargr tók annan; hann varð harða hryggr við þat; ok baugfergir má*tt*i hvǫrungi bjarga brátt, þás dýr drógu dyggva hlýra braut til skógar.

The spear-reddener [WARRIOR] saw the fierce animal of the land approach the boy, and a wolf took the other one; he became very distraught at that; and the ring-destroyer [GENEROUS MAN] could save neither of them quickly [enough], as the beasts dragged the excellent brothers away to the wood.

Ms.: **673b**(2v-3r). — *Readings*: [1] *fr*óns: '(f)[...]ons'(?) 673b, 'frons' 673bÞH, 673bFJ [6] má*tt*i: '(ma)[...]'(?) 673b, 'matte' 673bÞH, 673bFJ.

Editions: *Skj* Anonyme digte og vers [XII], G [1]. *Plácítúsdrápa* 22: AI, 611, BI, 612, *Skald* I, 298; Sveinbjörn Egilsson 1833, 20, 48, Finnur Jónsson 1887, 235, Louis-Jensen 1998, 103-4.

Notes: [1] *it frána dýr fr*óns 'the fierce animal of the land': I.e. a lion (*óarga dýr* 'wild animal' in the prose versions [Tucker 1988, 34-5]); cf. Beck 1972. The action is conventionally supposed to have taken place in Egypt. — [3-4] *hann varð harða hryggr við þat* 'he became very distraught at that': Cf. the verbal echo in the C text of the saga *Við þad vard hann mióg [hrig]gur* 'At that he became very distraught' (Tucker 1998, 35).

23. Hlaut sve*i*nn hj*a*rðar gætis
    — hugstœðr léo flœði —
    (akrmenn gripu annan)
    œzta bjǫrg (frá vǫrgum).

    Fjǫrnæms fœddu bǫrvar
    fleins í þorpi einu
    brœðr (glygg*s* h*v*atendr) báða
    (blóðíss né til vissusk).

Sve*i*nn hlaut *œzta* bjǫrg gætis hj*a*rðar; hugstœðr léo flœði; akrmenn gripu annan frá vǫrgum. Bǫrvar fjǫrnæms fleins fœddu báða brœðr í einu þorpi; né h*v*atendr glygg*s* blóðíss vissusk til.

[One] boy received the most excellent help from a herdsman [*lit.* guardian of the herd]; the hateful lion fled; farmhands seized the other from the wolves. Trees of the life-taking spear [WARRIORS] raised both brothers in the same village; the hasteners of the storm of the blood-ice [SWORD > BATTLE > WARRIORS] did not know of one another.

Ms.: 673b(3r). — *Readings*: [1] sve*i*nn: 'svenn' 673b; hj*a*rðar: hirðar 673b [2] -stœðr ('-støþr'): '-scøþr' 673b*FJ* [4] *œzta*: 'øts(ta)'(?) 673b, 'øtser' 673b*ÞH*, 'øt[...]' 673b*FJ*, 'øt(sta)'(?) 673b*Skj* [5] bǫrvar ('bǫrvar'): 'borvar' 673b*ÞH*, 'b[...]ruar' 673b*FJ* [7] glygg*s* h*v*atendr: 'glygg ih*a*atendr' 673b.

Editions: *Skj* Anonyme digte og vers [XII], G [1]. *Plácítúsdrápa* 23: AI, 611-12, BI, 612, *Skald* I, 298, *NN* §§1247, 2247B; Sveinbjörn Egilsson 1833, 20, 48-9, Finnur Jónsson 1887, 235, Jón Helgason 1932-3, 156, Louis-Jensen 1998, 104.

Notes: [2] *hugstœðr* 'the hateful': Finnur Jónsson (1887 and *Skj* A) read *hugskœðr* 'evil-/injury-minded' (the <t>/<c> is partially missing). Jón Helgason, however, was sure of the 't' reading.

24. Lifði halr, sás hafði
    hranne*lds tekit svanna,
    *b*lótum gnœgðr, frá brigði
    blíðum, fá vetr síðan.

    Hús átti sér hættin
    hǫrstrengs * *at* þat lengi
    Jǫrð í aldingarði
    ógntvist ok helt kristni.

*B*lótum gnœgðr halr, sás hafði tekit svanna frá blíðum brigði hranne*lds, lifði fá vetr síðan. Hættin Jǫrð hǫrstrengs átti sér lengi * *at* þat hús í aldingarði ok helt, ógntvist, kristni.

The man, steeped in heathen practices, who had taken the woman from the gentle breaker of the wave-fire [GOLD > GENEROUS MAN], lived few winters longer. The virtuous Jǫrð <goddess> of the linen-ribbon [WOMAN] owned for a long time after that a house in an orchard and kept [her] Christian faith, although muted by [impending] danger.

Ms.: 673b(3r). — *Readings*: [2] hranne*lds: 'hraɴenllds' 673b [3] *b*lótum: '[...]lotum' *ascender visible on first letter* 673b, 'blotum' 673b*ÞH*, 673b*FJ* [6] *: ok 673b; *at*: '[...]' 673b, at 673b*ÞH*, '[...]t' 673b*FJ*.

Editions: *Skj* Anonyme digte og vers [XII], G [1]. *Plácítúsdrápa* 24: AI, 612, BI, 612-13, *Skald* I, 298; Sveinbjörn Egilsson 1833, 21, 49, Finnur Jónsson 1887, 235, Louis-Jensen 1998, 104-5.

Notes: [All]: There are several distinctive verbal correspondences between st. 24 and the C version of the saga (Louis-Jensen 1998, cxxiii-iv), including *blótum gnægðr* 'steeped in heathen practices' (l. 3) and *mikill blótmaðr* 'great [pagan] sacrificer' (C); *halr lifði … fá vetr síðan* 'the man lived few winters longer' (ll. 1, 4) and *og lifdi litla stund* 'and lived for a short time' (C); [*hun*] *átti sér lengi at þat hús í aldingarði ok helt … kristni* (ll. 5, 6, 7, 8) '[she] owned for a long time after that a house in an orchard and kept … [her] Christian faith' and *átti hun sjer þjá hús í einum alldinngardi lifdi þar vel hiellt sinn c[hristinndom stadfastlega* 'then she owned a house in an orchard [and] lived there [and] kept her Christian faith steadfastly' (C).

25. Ǫrr hefr engla stýris   Hlaut, sás œztr es ýta,
    ástlaun af gram raunar   íðn Plácitus fríða;
    hraustr, sás hér stóðsk freistni   Evstákíus ævi
    heimsiklings vel mikla.   albazta sér valði.

Hraustr ǫrr stýris, sás stóðsk vel mikla freistni heimsiklings hér, hefr ástlaun raunar af gram engla. Plácitus, sás œztr es ýta, hlaut fríða íðn; Evstákíus valði sér albazta ævi.

The strong messenger of the rudder [SEAFARER], who stood up well to the world-ruler's [= God] great trial here, receives a loving reward for his ordeal from the prince of angels [= God]. Plácitus, who is the best of men, was allotted a glorious task; Eustace chose for himself the very best life.

Mss.: 673b(3r). — *Readings*: [2] *ástlaun*: '[…]st lovn' 673b, 673b*FJ*, '. ost lovn' 673b*ÞH* [5-8]: *abbrev. as* 'hlaut sa· e·' 673b.

Editions: *Skj* Anonyme digte og vers [XII], G [1]. *Plácítúsdrápa* 25: AI, 612, BI, 613, *Skald* I, 298, *NN* §2134; Sveinbjörn Egilsson 1833, 21, 49, Finnur Jónsson 1887, 236, Louis-Jensen 1998, 105.

Notes: [5-8]: Stef 1.

26. Ok þás heiptar hnekkir   'Éls, halt við mik máli
    harmtvistr sona missti,   (*mí*ns freistat nú) þínu,
    dýrðar vǫttr — við dróttin   frægr valderir foldar
    dælt gerði sér — mæ*lti: (framar en Jóbs ins gamla).

Ok þás harmtvistr hnekkir heiptar missti sona, mæ*lti vǫttr dýrðar — gerði sér dælt við dróttin —: 'Halt við mik máli þínu, frægr valderir foldar éls; nús mín freistat framar en ins gamla Jóbs.

And when the sorrow-muted subduer of wrath [HOLY MAN] lost his sons, the witness of glory [MARTYR] spoke — addressed the Lord familiarly —: 'Keep your promise to me, renowned ruler of the ground of the storm [SKY/HEAVEN > = God]; now I have been tried harder than Job the old [was].

Ms.: **673b**(3r). — *Readings*: [4] mæ*lti: 'metlte' 673b   [6] m*í*ns: 'mier' 673b   [7] f*o*ldar: 'f[...]dar' 673b, foldar 673b*ÞH*, 673b*FJ*.

Editions: *Skj* Anonyme digte og vers [XII], G [1]. *Plácítúsdrápa* 26: AI, 612, BI, 613, *Skald* I, 298, *NN* §1248; Sveinbjörn Egilsson 1833, 21-2, 50, Finnur Jónsson 1887, 236, Louis-Jensen 1998, 105-6.

Notes: [1] *heiptar* 'of wrath': Ms. 'heifstar'. The 's' may be etymological (cf. *ANG* §291, Anm. 2 and §237, Anm. 2). Cf. 31/3. — [3] *v*ǫ*ttr dýrðar* 'witness of glory': With this expression for a martyr, cf. the same phrase in ESk *Geisl* 62/3 and Note *ad loc.* — [3] *við dróttin* 'the Lord': Kock (*NN* §1248) points out that this prepositional phrase could just as well belong to the cl. with *mælti*, i.e. '... spoke to the Lord – addressed [him] familiarly...'.

27. 'Hyrgey*mi* frák heima   Ek em í útlegð stokkinn
    (hans vitjuðu) sitja   afkárr vinum fjarri;
    — kvǫn vas holds með hónum — kvǫns braut frá mér; m*í*na
    haukborðs (vi*nir* forðum).   me*i*ndýr *gripu* sveina.

'Frák haukborðs hyrgey*mi* sitja heima; vi*nir* vitjuðu hans forðum; kvǫn holds vas með hónum. Ek em stokkinn í útlegð, afkárr fjarri vinum; kvǫns braut frá mér; me*i*ndýr *gripu* sveina m*í*na.

'I have heard that the keeper of the fire of the hawk-table [(*lit.* 'fire-keeper of the hawk-table') ARM > GOLD > MAN] sat at home; friends visited him in days gone by; the man's wife was with him. [But] I am driven into outlawry, distraught, far from my friends; my wife has been taken from me; fierce beasts have seized my sons.

Ms.: **673b**(3r). — *Readings*: [1] Hyrgey*mi*: 'Hurg(e)y[...]'(?) 673b, 673b*HE*, 'Hurgdys' 673b*ÞH*, 'Hurgeyme' 673b*FJ*   [4] vi*nir*: 'vi þ[...]' 673b, 'viþa' *or* 'viþir', 'vinir' 673b*ÞH*, 'viþa' 673b*FJ*   [7] m*í*na: 'm[...](a)'(?) 673b   [8] me*i*ndýr: mendýr 673b; *gripu*: *om.* 673b.

Editions: *Skj* Anonyme digte og vers [XII], G [1]. *Plácítúsdrápa* 27: AI, 612, BI, 613-14, *Skald* I, 298, *NN* §§1249, 1797, 2135A, 2991C; Sveinbjörn Egilsson 1833, 22, 50, Finnur Jónsson 1887, 236, Jón Helgason 1932-3, 156, Louis-Jensen 1998, 106.

Notes: [All]: As all versions of the prose text make clear (Tucker 1998, 38-9), Plácitus is here making an unfavourable comparison between his own sad condition and that of Job, arguing to God that his own trials have been far worse than that of the biblical figure. — [3] v*i*nir *forðum* 'friends ... in days gone by': *Skj* B takes *forðum* with the cl. ... *sitja heim*, which creates a tripartite l. The present reading was suggested by Kock (*NN* §1248). — [6] *afkárr* 'distraught': This word is defined variously as '?difficult, contrary' (*ONP*); *vanskelig at komme tilrette med* 'difficult to come to agreement with' (*Fritzner*); *meget kraftig, ... voldsom* 'very strong, ... violent' (*LP*); 'strange, prodigious' (*CVC*). — [8] gripu 'have seized': Emendation proposed by Finnur Jónsson 1887. Kock suggested *rifu* 'have torn (up)' (*NN* §2135B), citing the more common collocation of the verb *rífa* with animals. Jón Helgason, however, pointed out that *grípa* matches the prose text (cf. Tucker 1998, 39); in any case, the prose and poetic texts are all clear that the boys survive.

28. 'Gjalta*t*, goð, *þótt* mæltak,   Sett fyr munn, alls minnumk,
(ga*gl*s leiðar) mér reiði,   minn, vingjafa þinna,
(ítrs stillis þarfk all*r*ar   (veit oss várkunn) dróttinn,
eirar) þurftum fleir*a*.   varðhald (konungr aldar).'

'Gjalta*t* mér reiði, goð, *þótt* mæltak þurftum fleir*a*; þarfk all*r*ar eirar ítrs stillis leiðar ga*gl*s. Sett varðhald fyr munn minn, dróttinn, alls minnumk þinna vingjafa; veit oss várkunn, konungr aldar.'

'Do not repay me with anger, God, although I spoke more than is necessary; I need all the mercy of the glorious ruler of the path of the goose [SKY/HEAVEN > = God]. Set a watch before my mouth, Lord, since I remember your gifts of friendship; give us [me] pardon, king of mankind [= God].'

Ms.: **673b**(3r-v). — *Readings*: [1] Gjalta*t*: gjaltaðu 673b; *þótt*: 'þo […]' 673b, 673b*ÞH*, 'þo at' 673b*FJ* [2] ga*gl*s: galgs 673b [3] all*r*ar: allar 673b [4] fleir*a*: 'fleir[…]' 673b, 'fleire' *or* 'fleira' 673b*ÞH*, fleira 673b*FJ* [6] -gjafa: '-gia(f)a'(?) 673b, '-giara' *or* '-giava' 673b*ÞH*, '-giafa' 673b*FJ*.

Editions: *Skj* Anonyme digte og vers [XII], G [1]. *Plácítúsdrápa* 28: AI, 612-13, BI, 614, *Skald* I, 299, *NN* §2554; Sveinbjörn Egilsson 1833, 22, 50-1, Finnur Jónsson 1887, 236, Louis-Jensen 1998, 106-7.

Notes: [5, 8, 6, 7] *sett varðhald fyr munn minn, dróttinn* 'set a watch before my mouth, Lord': Also found in the A and C versions of the prose saga, from Ps. CXLIII.3 *Pone domine custodiam ori meo* 'Place, Lord, a watch on my mouth'.

29. Morðsólar veik máli   Menfergir vas margan
meiðir; sinnar leiðar   móthress í bœ þessum
gekk ramms hǫtuðr rekka   vetr, ok vann til mætrar
rógs í þorp ór skógi.   vargnistir sér bjargar.

Meiðir morðsólar veik máli; hǫtuðr ramms rógs rekka gekk leiðar sinnar ór skógi í þorp. Móthress menfergir vas margan vetr í þessum bœ, ok vargnistir vann sér til mætrar bjargar.

The destroyer of the war-sun [SHIELD > WARRIOR] broke off his speech; the hater of the fierce strife of men [SIN > HOLY MAN] went his way from the forest into a village. The battle-fierce neckring-destroyer [GENEROUS MAN] was many a winter in that town and the wolf-feeder [WARRIOR] earned a good living.

Ms.: **673b**(3v).

Editions: *Skj* Anonyme digte og vers [XII], G [1]. *Plácítúsdrápa* 29: AI, 613, BI, 614, *Skald* I, 299, *NN* §2136; Sveinbjörn Egilsson 1833, 23, 51, Finnur Jónsson 1887, 237, Louis-Jensen 1998, 107.

Notes: [6] *móthress* 'brave': Lit. 'battle-fierce'. Ms. has *mót-*; cf. *NN* §2136; Sveinbjörn Egilsson (1833), Finnur Jónsson (1887 and *Skj* B) have *móð-* 'mind-' (cf. *sit* = *sið-* 31/7).

30. Ok til aumra rekka
    atvinnu gaf Þvinnils
    vigg-Baldr víðrar foldar
    verkkaup, þats sér merkði.

    Fast helt lundr ok leyndi
    linnvengis trú sinni
    hlunndýrs heiðna runna
    hǫttnæfr við goð sóttum,

Ok Þvinnils víðrar foldar vigg-Baldr gaf verkkaup, þats merkði sér, til atvinnu aumra rekka. Hǫttnæfr lundr linnvengis helt fast sóttum við goð ok leyndi trú sinni heiðna runna hlunndýrs,

And the Baldr <god> of the horse of the wide land of Þvinnill <sea-king> [(*lit.* 'horse-Baldr of the wide land of Þvinnill') SEA > SHIP > SEAFARER] gave the wages, which he had set aside for himself, for the support of poor men. The virtuous tree of the serpent-ground [GOLD > MAN] held fast to his agreements with God and concealed his faith from the heathen trees of the animal of the launching-roller [SHIP > SEAFARERS],

Ms.: **673b**(3v). — *Readings*: [2] Þvinnils: 'þuɴils' 673b [3] foldar: 'f[...]dar' 673b, 673b*FJ*, foldar 673b*ÞH* [7] hlunndýrs: 'hlvɴ dv[...]s' 673b, 'hlyra dyrs' 673b*ÞH*, 'hlvɴ dvrs' 673b*FJ* [8] hǫttnæfr: 'hactnæfr' 673b, 673b*ÞH*, 'hattnæfr' 673b*FJ*.

Editions: *Skj* Anonyme digte og vers [XII], G [1]. *Plácitúsdrápa* 30: AI, 613, BI, 614, *Skald* I, 299; Sveinbjörn Egilsson 1833, 23, 51, Finnur Jónsson 1887, 237, Louis-Jensen 1998, 107-8.

Notes: [All]: The wording of this st. corresponds very closely to the C text of the prose saga (Louis-Jensen 1998, cxxiv), except for the kennings, while the Lat. and A texts state only that Plácitus took his wages, and do not refer to his giving of alms or his concealing his Christian faith from heathens. — [2] *Þvinnils* 'of Þvinnill': Emendation proposed by Konráð Gíslason (and Eiríkur Jónsson 1875-89, II). Sveinbjörn Egilsson emended to *þynnils, although it is unclear what this word should mean. — [4] *verkkaup* 'wages': This is the only example of this word in poetry, and it is repeated in the C text. Cf. A^2 version, where *tók kaup* translates the Lat. *mercedem accipiens* 'receiving a wage'.

31. unz hvardyggvan hugga
    happmildr konungr vildi
    láðhofs lyp*ti-Móða
    leggjar farms í harmi,

    þás við huggun hóva
    herstefni* réð efna
    siðbjóðr snotra lýða
    sín heit friðar veitir.

unz happmildr konungr láðhofs vildi hugga lyp*ti-Móða farms leggjar, hvardyggvan, í harmi, þás siðbjóðr snotra lýða, veitir friðar, réð efna heit sín herstefni* við hóva huggun.

until the mercy-granting king of the earth-temple [SKY/HEAVEN > = God] wished to comfort the bearing-Móði <god> of the cargo of the arm [GOLD > MAN], honourable in everything, in his sorrow, when the faith-bringer to wise men [= Christ], the giver of peace [= Christ], fulfilled his promise to the army-ruler [WARRIOR] with supreme consolation.

Ms.: **673b**(3v). — *Readings*: [1] -dyggva*n*: -dyggva *corrected from* '-dyggvan' 673b [2] -mil*d*r: 'mill[...]' 673b [3] lyp*ti-: 'lyfste' 673b [6] -stefni*: -stefnir 673b.

Editions: *Skj* Anonyme digte og vers [XII], G [1]. *Plácitúsdrápa* 31: AI, 613, BI, 614-15, *Skald* I, 299, *NN* §1250; Sveinbjörn Egilsson 1833, 23-4, 52, Finnur Jónsson 1887, 237, Louis-Jensen 1998, 108.

Notes: [1, 6] *-dyggva*n, *-stef*ni 'honourable, -ruler': Emendations proposed in Konráð Gíslason and Eiríkur Jónsson 1875-89, II, 52. — [2] *happmil*dr 'mercy-granting': Lit. 'fortune-generous' or 'fortune-pious', the only example of this cpd in poetry. — [3] *lypti-* 'bearing-': Ms. 'lyfste': cf. st. 26/1. — [5] *pás* 'when': Finnur Jónsson (*Skj* B) emended to *þá* 'then' to make a main cl. here, but a main cl. would require a verb in syntactic position 2 and is in any case unnecessary. — [7] *siðbjóðr* 'faith-bringer': Ms. 'sit'; there seems to be some interchangeability of <t>/<ð> after vowels in the ms.: cf. *mót*/ *móð* in st. 29/6.

32. Lýtr engla lið ítrum
    angrhrjóðanda ok þjóðir;
    einn es ǫllu hreinni,
    allt gótt sás skóp, *drótt*inn.

Lið engla ok þjóðir lýtr ítrum angrhrjóðanda; einn *drótt*inn, sás skóp allt gótt, es ǫllu hreinni.

The band of angels and humankind bows to the glorious destroyer of sin [= God]; the one Lord, who created everything good, is purer than all.

Ms.: **673b**(3v). — *Readings*: [2] þjóðir: 'þio[...]' 673b, 'þiodar' 673b*ÞH*, 'þioþer' 673b*FJ* [4] *drótt*inn: '[...]en' 673b, 'drotteɴ h. s. e.' 673b*ÞH*, 'droteɴ' 673b*FJ*.

Editions: *Skj* Anonyme digte og vers [XII], G [1]. *Plácitúsdrápa* 32: AI, 613, BI, 615, *Skald* I, 299, *NN* §§3134, 3143A; Sveinbjörn Egilsson 1833, 24, 52, Finnur Jónsson 1887, 237, Louis-Jensen 1998, 108.

Notes: [All]: *Stef* 2. A cross in the margin on the previous l. marks the new *stef*. There is a gap in the ms. of about half a l. at the end of the *helmingr* and Þorsteinn Helgason claimed to read an abbreviation of the first *stef* in this space. Sveinbjörn Egilsson includes the first *stef* directly after the new *stef* (following 673b*ÞH*), which would be consistent with the first *stef* occurring every 7 sts (previously in sts 11, 18, 25). However, there are no remaining traces of the abbreviation in the ms. and the repetition of the first *stef* directly after the second would be very unusual. — [3, 4] *einn drótt*inn ... *es ǫllu hreinni* 'the one Lord is purer than all': Kock (*NN* §3143A) takes this as equivalent to the idiomatic *einn* + sup., in which case it would be translated 'the Lord is the purest of all'. Cf. GunnLeif *MerlI* 56/1[VIII].

33. Gǫr vas guðr, en verjask,
gramr þurfti her samna
trautt, áðr tíg*inn* mætti
Trájánus vel ráni.

Bauð landre*ki* lýða
liði ríðara fríðu
snildar framr at sam*na*
s*verð*hríðar til víða.

Guðr vas gǫr, en áðr tíg*inn* Trájánus mætti vel verjask ráni, þurfti gramr samna her trautt. Snildar framr landre*ki* lýða bauð at sam*na* víða fríðu *liði* ríðara til s*verð*hríðar.

Battle was begun, but before the noble Trajan could protect himself properly against plundering, the king had to gather an army with difficulty. The king of men, outstanding in prowess, bade [his men] gather from far and wide a fine band of knights for the swordstorm [BATTLE].

Ms.: **673b**(3v). — *Readings*: [3] tíg*inn*: 'tig[...]' 673b, 'tiginn' 673b*Þ*H, 'tigeɴ' 673b*FJ* [5] landre*ki*: 'landre[...]' 673b, 'landreki [...]' 673b*Þ*H, 'landreke' 673b*FJ* [6] *liði*: om. 673b [7] sam*na*: 'sam[...]' 673b, 673b*FJ*, 'samre' 673b*Þ*H [8] s*verð*-: '(s)[...]þ'(?) 673b, 'suerd' 673b*Þ*H, 'suerþ' 673b*FJ*.

Editions: *Skj* Anonyme digte og vers [XII], G [1]. *Plácítúsdrápa* 33: AI, 613, BI, 615, *Skald* I, 299, *NN* §§1251, 2315n., 2369, 2811, 2812; Sveinbjörn Egilsson 1833, 24, 52, Finnur Jónsson 1887, 238, Jón Helgason 1932-3, 156, Louis-Jensen 1998, 109.

Notes: [All]: According to the legend, an unnamed army began ravaging the Roman empire and Trajan needed to rally his forces against it. He remembered his former cavalry commander Plácitus, and asked his men where Plácitus was, but no one knew. He offered a reward to anyone who found him (st. 34), and this impelled two former soldiers who had served with Plácitus to go looking for him (st. 35). — [4] *Trájánus* 'Trajan': Ms. 'træyanus'. On the vowel lengths in the name cf. *NN* §3247.

34. Minntisk gra*mr*, þá*s* gumna
gunndjarfra vas þarfi,
Yggjar *leik* hvé auka
endr Plácitus kenndi.

Vel/meiðis bað víða
vígteitr konungr leita;
gnótt hét góðs, þeims mætti,
gramr, svinnan hal finna.

Gra*mr* minntisk, hvé Plácitus kenndi endr auka *leik* Yggjar, þá*s* vas þarfi gunndjarfra gumna. Vígteitr konungr bað leita vel*l*meið*is* víða; gramr hét gnótt góð*s*, þeims mætti finna svinnan hal.

The king recalled how Plácitus once knew how to intensify the game of Yggr <= Óðinn> [BATTLE], when he was in need of battle-bold men. The strife-glad king bade [his men] search for the gold-destroyer [GENEROUS MAN] far and wide; the king promised an abundance of riches to the one who might find the wise man.

Ms.: **673b**(3v-4r). — *Readings*: [1] gra*mr*: 'graar' 673b; þá*s*: 'þa [...]' 673b, 'þa er' 673b*Þ*H, 673b*FJ* [3] Yggjar: 'ygg[...]ar' 673b, 673b*FJ*, 'yggiar' 673b*Þ*H; *leik*: '[...]' 673b, 'læik' noted as *unclear* 673b*Þ*H, 'leik' 673b*FJ*   [5] Vel*l*meið*i*s: 'vel[...]mei[...]' 673b, 'vellmeidrs' *or* 'vellmeidis' 673b*Þ*H, 'vel[...] meiþer' 673b*FJ*.

Editions: *Skj* Anonyme digte og vers [XII], G [1]. *Plácítúsdrápa* 34: AI, 613-14, BI, 615, *Skald* I, 299; Sveinbjörn Egilsson 1833, 25, 53, Finnur Jónsson 1887, 238, Louis-Jensen 1998, 109.

35. Brœðr riðu Byrfils skíða   Fundu Gylfa *g*rundar
     beitis tveir at leita   glaðríðanda umb síðir;
     ár, þeirs ítrum vǫru   unnar fúrs né *æ*rir
     endr Plácito á hendi.   afrendan bǫr kenndu.

Tveir brœðr, þeirs vǫru endr á hendi ítrum Plácito, riðu ár at leita beitis skíða Byrfils. Fundu umb síðir *g*rundar Gylfa glaðríðanda; *æ*rir né kenndu afrendan bǫr fúrs unnar.

Two brothers, who were formerly in the service of the glorious Plácitus, rode out early to look for the steerer of the skis of Byrfill <sea-king> [SHIPS > SEAFARER]. At length they found the rider of the horse of the ground of Gylfi <sea-king> [(*lit.* 'the horse-rider of the ground of Gylfi') SEA > SHIP > SEAFARER]; the messengers did not recognise the powerful tree of the fire of the wave [GOLD > MAN].

Ms.: **673b**(4r). — *Readings*:   [5] *g*rundar: '[...]undar' 673b, 673b*FJ*, 'grundar' 673b*Þ*H   [7] *æ*rir: '[...]rer' 673b, 673b*FJ*, 'ærer' 673b*Þ*H.

Editions: *Skj* Anonyme digte og vers [XII], G [1]. *Plácítúsdrápa* 35: AI, 614, BI, 615-16, *Skald* I, 299, *NN* §1252; Sveinbjörn Egilsson 1833, 25, 53, Finnur Jónsson 1887, 238, Louis-Jensen 1998, 110.

36. Værr tók vegs ins fyrra   Sér *l*eitaði særir
     viggfinnandi at minnask   seims huggunar beima
     sunds, þás sína kenndi   brátt *í* bœn *af* dróttni
     snarlundaðr húskarla.   bilstyggr, þás tók hryggvask.

Værr sunds viggfinnandi tók at minnask ins fyrra vegs, þás snarlundaðr kenndi húskarla sína. Bilstyggr særir seims *l*eitaði sér brátt huggunar *af* dróttni beima *í* bœn, þás tók hryggvask.

The peace-loving provider of the horse of the sound [(*lit.* 'the sound's horse-provider') SHIP > SEAFARER] began to remember his former glory, when the eager-minded one recognised his retainers. The delay-shunning harmer of gold [GENEROUS MAN] quickly sought for himself consolation from the lord of mankind [= God] in prayer, as he began to grow sad.

Ms.: **673b**(4r). — *Readings*.   [5] *l*eitaði: '[...]eitaþe' 673b, 673b*FJ*, '. er aþe' 673b*Þ*H, 'leitaþe' 673b*HE*   [7] *í*: '[...]' 673b;   *af*: '[...]' 673b, 'af' 673b*Þ*H, 673b*FJ*.

Editions: *Skj* Anonyme digte og vers [XII], G [1]. *Plácítúsdrápa* 36: AI, 614, BI, 616, *Skald* I, 299-300; Sveinbjörn Egilsson 1833, 25-6, 54, Finnur Jónsson 1887, 238, Louis-Jensen 1998, 110.

37. Kvaddi krapti prýddan
    Krists rǫdd ara nisti:
    'Dýrð hittir þik dróttins
    dygg; skal*a þú nú hryggvask.

Tíð kømr, sóknar seiða
sendir, þér at hendi
enn, sús yðr mun finna
auð ok veg fyr nauðir'.

Rǫdd Krists kvaddi nisti ara, prýddan krapti: 'Skal*a þú nú hryggvask; dygg dýrð dróttins hittir þik. Tíð kømr enn at hendi þér, sendir seiða sóknar, sús mun finna yðr auð ok veg fyr nauðir'.

The voice of Christ spoke to the feeder of the eagle [WARRIOR], adorned with power: 'You shall not now be sorrowful; the noble glory of the Lord will come upon you. The time is yet to come for you, mover of the fish of attack [SWORD > WARRIOR], which will bring you riches and honour instead of affliction'.

Ms.: **673b**(4r). — *Readings*: [2] Krists: 'crist' 673b; ara: '[...]ra' 673b, 673bFJ, 'ata' 673bÞH; nisti: 'nist[...]' 673b, 'niste' 673bÞH, 'nister' 673bFJ [4] skal*a: 'skalla' 673b.

Editions: Skj Anonyme digte og vers [XII], G [1]. *Plácítúsdrápa* 37: AI, 614, BI, 616, Skald I, 300; Sveinbjörn Egilsson 1833, 26, 54, Finnur Jónsson 1887, 239, Louis-Jensen 1998, 111.

Notes: [1] *krapti* 'with power': Or possibly 'with virtue' — [4] *skal*a* 'shall not': Emendation proposed by Finnur Jónsson 1887. Cf. Konráð Gíslason and Eiríkur Jónsson 1875-89, II, 51-2. — [5] *seiða* (gen. pl.) 'of the fish': *Seiðr* is a saithe or coalfish.

38. Bliktýnir vann beina
    (bauglestanda) gestum
    sunds (tóksk harmr af hǫndum
    hór), þeims komnir vǫru.

Útbeiti frák Áta
undrask brœðr, þás fundu,
skíðs, á skrautvals beiði
skokks áhyggju þokka.

Sunds bliktýnir vann beina gestum, þeims vǫru komnir; hór harmr tóksk af hǫndum bauglestanda. Frák brœðr undrask útbeiti skíðs Áta, þás fundu þokka áhyggju á beiði skrautvals skokks.

The destroyer of the shine of the channel [(*lit.* 'shine-destroyer of the channel') GOLD > GENEROUS MAN] gave hospitality to the guests who had arrived; deep sorrow lifted from the ring-destroyer [GENEROUS MAN]. I have heard that the brothers wondered at the steerer of the ski of Áti <sea-king> [SHIP > SEAFARER], when they sensed a disposition of anxiety in the demander of the adornment-horse of the deck-plank [SHIP > SEAFARER].

Ms.: **673b**(4r). — *Readings*: [3] tóksk: 'tocs[...]' 673b, 'tocst' 673bÞH, 'tocsk' 673bFJ, 'iocsk' 673bJH [4] vǫru: 'u[...]r[...]' 673b, 'uaro' 673bÞH, 'uoro' 673bFJ [6] þás: 'þ[...] er' 673b, 'þa er' 673bÞH, 673bFJ [8] skokks: 's[...]' 673b, 'scokk' 673bÞH, 673bFJ.

Editions: Skj Anonyme digte og vers [XII], G [1]. *Plácítúsdrápa* 38: AI, 614, BI, 616, Skald I, 300, *NN* §1793; Sveinbjörn Egilsson 1833, 26, 54-5, Finnur Jónsson 1887, 239, Jón Helgason 1932-3, 157, Louis-Jensen 1998, 111.

Notes: [3] *tóksk af* 'passed from, lifted': *Tóksk* is very faint in the ms. and Jón Helgason (1932-3) read 'iocsk' (*jóksk* 'increased'). The <f> is unfinished in *af* and Jón emends to *at*, producing a reading 'deep sorrow increased for [Plácitus]'. In support of this reading, he cites the saga, which at this point states that Plácitus's sorrow increases: ... *og minntist hinnz fyrra lyfsinnz og matti ey uatnne hallda, af miklum hrigdleyk* '[he] remembered his former life and could not stop himself from weeping from his great affliction' (Tucker 1998, 81); also other uses of *at hǫndum, at hendi* in the poem in sts 37/6 and 44/7. However, although faint, the ms. is more likely to read 'tocsk' and 'af' than Jón's suggestions. — [8] *skokks* 'of the deck-plank': The word *skokkr* appears to refer to part of a ship (*LP*). Jesch (2001, 151-3) and Lindquist 1928, on the basis of its usage in Arn *Þorfdr* 21[II] and Bǫlv *Hardr* 4[II], argue that it is synonymous with *þilja* 'deck-plank (of a ship)'.

39. Friðbeiðir gefr fríðan   Lýtr engla lið ítrum
    fǫgnuð með sér brǫgnum   angrhrjóðanda ok þjóðir;
    hǫppum glæstr, þeims hraustla   einn es ǫllu hreinni,
    hǫrð mein bera á jǫrðu.   allt gótt sás skóp, dróttinn.

Friðbeiðir glæstr hǫppum gefr brǫgnum, þeims bera hǫrð mein hraustla á jǫrðu, fríðan fǫgnuð með sér. Lið engla ok þjóðir lýtr ítrum angrhrjóðanda; einn dróttinn, sás skóp allt gótt, es ǫllu hreinni.

The peace-promoter, shining with victories [= God], gives men who bear hard suffering bravely on earth glorious joy with him. The band of angels and humankind bows to the glorious destroyer of sin [= God]; the one Lord, who created everything good, is purer than all.

Ms.: 673b(4r). — *Readings*: [1] fríðan: 'frıþ[...]n' 673b, 'friþan' 673b*ÞH*, 673b*FJ* [3] glæstr: 'gl[...]s[...]' 673b, 'glæstr' 673b*ÞH*, 673b*FJ*, 'gløstr' 673b*HE* [4] mein: 'm[...]n' 673b, 'mein' 673b*ÞH*, 'me[...]n' 673b*FJ*; jǫrðu: '[...]þu' 673b, 'iorþu' 673b*ÞH*, 673b*FJ* [5-8]: abbrev. as 'lytr:' 673b.

Editions: *Skj* Anonyme digte og vers [XII], G [1]. *Plácítúsdrápa* 39: AI, 614, BI, 616-17, *Skald* I, 300; Sveinbjörn Egilsson 1833, 27, 55, Finnur Jónsson 1887, 239, Louis-Jensen 1998, 112.

Notes: [5-8]: *Stef* 2, cf. st. 32.

40. Hugðu brœðr at beiði   unz hyr-Þróttar hittu
    brandéls meginvandla,   hjaldrserks ...
    þóttusk mildi mætan   ... hǫfðu
    menn Plácitus kenna,   hoddsendi rétt kenndan.

Brœðr hugðu meginvandla at beiði brandéls — menn þóttusk kenna mildi mætan Plácitus —, unz hjaldrserks hyr-Þróttar hittu ... hǫfðu rétt kenndan hoddsendi.

The brothers considered carefully the demander of the sword-storm [BATTLE > WARRIOR] — the men thought they recognised Plácitus, renowned for generosity [*or* piety] —, until the Þróttar <= Óðinns> of the fire of the war-shirt [(*lit.* 'the fire-Þróttar of the war shirt') MAIL-SHIRT > SWORD > WARRIORS] met ... they had correctly recognised the gold-distributor [GENEROUS MAN].

Ms.: **673b**(4r-v). — *Readings*:   [2] br*andéls*: 'br[...]e[...]s' 673b, 'br[...]egs' 673b*ÞH*, 'bran[...]e[...]s' 673b*FJ*   [3] mæ*tan*: 'mæ[...]' 673b, 'mæra' 673b*ÞH*, 'metan' 673b*FJ*   [5] -Þróttar: 'þrotta[...]' 673b, 'þrottar' 673b*ÞH*, 673b*FJ*   [6] ...: '[...]ar[...]' 673b, 'kloker[...]' 673b*FJ*   [7] *hǫf*ðu: '[...]þv' 673b   [8] *k*enndan: '[...]endan' 673b, '*k*endan' 673b*FJ*.

Editions: *Skj* Anonyme digte og vers [XII], G [1]. *Plácitúsdrápa* 40: AI, 614-15, BI, 617, *Skald* I, 300, *NN* §2137; Sveinbjörn Egilsson 1833, 27, 55, Finnur Jónsson 1887, 239, Jón Helgason 1932-3, 157-8, Louis-Jensen 1998, 112.

Notes: [6-7] *hjaldrserks* ...: In the prose versions at this point, Plácitus is recognised by a scar on his neck (Tucker 1998, 46-7). The first two ll. of fol. 4v in 673b are very damaged from rubbing. Finnur Jónsson (1887 and *Skj* A) thought he could make out 'kloker' (i.e. *klókir* 'clever'; cf. *NN* §§2137, 2491), but his reading was disputed by Jón Helgason (1932-3). The word *klókir* is of German origin and therefore unlikely to occur in a text of this date, besides being too heavy to fill the metrical position. Jón Helgason suggested *ørugg merki* | *at hringdrífar hǫfðu* (i.e. 'until the [men] found the safe sign, so that the ring-scatterers [GENEROUS MEN] had correctly recognised the [man]'), but only as one possibility among others. As an alternative to *ørugg merki*, he suggested *ǫrr á kverkum* 'scar on the throat', cf. *ǫrr á hálsi* in the prose text.

41. Bǫ́ru orð*, ok urð*u*,
    odd*r*egns hvat*endr, fegnir,
    heiðins grams af hljóði,
    hjǫrva lund es *fu*ndu.

    Hodda Baldr til hildar
    hug*f*ylldr koma skyldi
    alla tígn ok eignask,
    en*dr* þás lét af hendi.

Hvat*endr oddregns bǫ́ru orð* heiðins grams af hljóði ok urð*u* fegnir, es *fu*ndu lund hjǫrva. Hug*f*ylldr Baldr hodda skyldi koma til hildar ok eignask alla tígn, þás lét en*dr* af hendi.

The inciters of the spear-rain [BATTLE > WARRIORS] carried the word of the heathen king in secret and became glad when they found the tree of swords [WARRIOR]. The courage-filled Baldr <god> of hoards [MAN] was to come to the battle and regain all the honour which he had previously abandoned.

Ms.: **673b**(4v). — *Readings*:   [1] orð*: 'orðr' 673b;   urð*u*: 'vrþ[...]' 673b, 'vrþo' 673b*FJ*   [2] oddregns: 'odd[...](e)gns'(?) 673b, 'oddregns' 673b*ÞH*, 673b*FJ*;   hvat*endr: 'huatiendr' 673b   [4] *fu*ndu: '[...]ndo' 673b, 'fvndo' 673b*ÞH*, 'f[...]ndo' 673b*FJ*   [6] hug*f*ylldr: 'hug[...]ylldr' 673b, '[...]ylldr' 673b*ÞH*, 'hug fylldr' 673b*FJ*   [8] en*dr* þá-: 'en[...]þa' 673b, 'en[...]a' 673b*ÞH*, 'endr þa' 673b*FJ*.

Editions: Skj Anonyme digte og vers [XII], G [1]. *Plácítúsdrápa* 41: AI, 615, BI, 617, *Skald* I, 300; Sveinbjörn Egilsson 1833, 27-8, 56, Finnur Jónsson 1887, 240, Louis-Jensen 1998, 113.

Notes: [All]: There is a close similarity in wording between this st. and the C text of the prose saga, in contrast to the Lat. and A texts (Louis-Jensen 1998, cxxiv).

42. Brátt rézk í fǫr flýtir
    flœðar elds með brœðrum;
    maðr kunni þá manni
    megintíðendi at segja.

    Sóttu fund, es frétt*i*,
    f*á*kr*í*ðanda víð*is*,
    lofða sveit, at lifði
    leng*r* Pl*á*c*it*us, drengir.

Flýtir elds flœðar rézk brátt í fǫr með brœðrum; maðr kunni þá at segja manni megintíðendi. Drengir sóttu fund víð*is* f*á*kr*í*ðanda, es sveit lofða frétt*i* at Pl*á*c*it*us lifði leng*r*.

The hastener of the fire of the flood [GOLD > GENEROUS MAN] set out at once on the journey with the brothers; [each] man could then tell [the other] man the important news. Men sought a meeting with the rider of the horse of the ocean [(*lit.* 'horse-rider of the ocean') SHIP > SEAFARER] when the band of men heard that Plácitus still lived.

Ms.: **673b**(4v). — *Readings*: [5] frétt*i*: fréttu 673b [6] f*á*k-: 'f[...]' 673b, 'far*N*er' 673bÞH, 'fark' 673bFJ; víð*is*: víða 673b [8] leng*r*: 'lengr' *or* 'lengi' 673b, 'lengi' 673bÞH, '[...]ngi' 673bFJ; Pl*á*c*it*us: 'pl[...]us' 673b, 'placidus' 673bÞH, 'placitus' 673bFJ.

Editions: Skj Anonyme digte og vers [XII], G [1]. *Plácítúsdrápa* 42: AI, 615, BI, 617-18, *Skald* I, 300; Sveinbjörn Egilsson 1833, 28, 56, Finnur Jónsson 1887, 240, Louis-Jensen 1998, 113.

Notes: [All]: All emendations in this st. were originally proposed by Finnur Jónsson (1887).

43. Fúss gerði veg vísi
    — varð gr*am*r *feg*inn harða,
    heim es happs kom geymir —
    hringlest*and*a mestan.

    Setti þengill Þróttar
    þingb*e*iði h*ǫ*fðingja
    ǫflugs lýðs, ok auði
    ulfs fœði tók *gœ*ða.

Vísi gerði fúss mestan veg hringlest*and*a; gr*am*r varð harða *feg*inn, es geymir happs kom heim. Þengill setti Þróttar þingb*e*iði h*ǫ*fðingja ǫflugs lýðs, ok tók *gœ*ða fœði ulfs auði.

The ruler eagerly bestowed the greatest honour on the ring-destroyer [GENEROUS MAN]; the king became very glad when the minder of good luck [MAN] came home. The prince appointed the demander of the assembly of Þróttr <= Óðinn> [(*lit.* 'the assembly-demander of Þróttr') BATTLE > WARRIOR] leader of the powerful troop and began to endow the feeder of the wolf [WARRIOR] with riches.

Ms.: **673b**(4v). — *Readings*: [2] gr*am*r: 'gr[...]r' 673b, 673bFJ, 'gramr' 673bÞH; *feg*inn: '[...]en' 673b, '[...]ar' 673bÞH, 'fegen' 673bFJ [4] -lest*and*a: 'lest[...]a' 673b, '[...]est[...]' 673bÞH, '[...]standa' 673bFJ [6] -*e*iði: 'b[...]iþi' 673b, 673bFJ, 'bliþi' 673bÞH; h*ǫ*fðingja:

'[...]fþingia' 673b, '[...]' 673b*ÞH*, 'høfþingia' 673b*HE*, 673b*FJ* [8] *gæða*: '[...]' 673b, 'gøþa'(?) 673b*ÞH*, 673b*FJ*.

Editions: *Skj* Anonyme digte og vers [XII], G [1]. *Plácítúsdrápa* 43: AI, 615, BI, 618, *Skald* I, 300, *NN* §2138; Sveinbjörn Egilsson 1833, 28, 57, Finnur Jónsson 1887, 240, Louis-Jensen 1998, 114.

Notes: [5-8]: The wording of this *helmingr* shows similarities with the C text of the prose saga in contrast to the Lat. and A texts (Louis-Jensen 1998, cxxv). — [6] *þingbeiði* 'assembly-demander': Emendation proposed by Kock *NN* §2138. Previous eds have *þingblíðan* 'assembly-mild'.

44. En*n* bað ungra manna   *Svinn*s kómu þá seima
    ítr gramr fira sam*na*   sendis heim (né kenndi
    fljótt, ef fámeðr þœttisk   *hyr*jar lunda) at hǫndum
    ferð, Plácitus verða.   (haukláðs) synir báð*ir*.

Ítr gramr bað en*n* fira sam*na fljótt* ferð ungra manna, ef Plácitus þœttisk verða fámeðr. Báð*ir* synir *svinn*s sendis seima kómu þá heim at hǫndum; né kenndi lund*a hyr*jar haukláðs.

The glorious king then asked the men to gather quickly a troop of young men, if Plácitus found himself short of men. Both sons of the wise distributor of gold [GENEROUS MAN > = Agapitus and Theopistus] then came home to him [*lit.* to his hands]; he did not recognise the trees of the fire of the hawk-ground [ARM > GOLD > MEN].

Ms.: **673b**(4v). — *Readings*: [1] En*n*: '(E)n[...]'(?) 673b, Enn 673b*ÞH*, 673b*FJ* [2] sam*na*: 'sam[...]' 673b, 673b*FJ*, 'samna' 673b*ÞH* [3] *fljótt*: '[...]' 673b, 673b*ÞH*, 'fliott' 673b*FJ* [5] *Svinn*s: '[...]s' 673b, 673b*ÞH*, 'saman' 673b*FJ* [7] *hyr*jar: '[...]r' 673b, '[...](i)ar'(?) 673b*ÞH*, 'hyriar' 673b*FJ*; lund*a*: lund 673b [8] báð*ir*: 'baþ[...]' 673b, 673b*FJ*, 'baþo' 673b*ÞH*.

Editions: *Skj* Anonyme digte og vers [XII], G [1]. *Plácítúsdrápa* 44: AI, 615, BI, 618, *Skald* I, 300, *NN* §2812; Sveinbjörn Egilsson 1833, 29, 57, Finnur Jónsson 1887, 240, Louis-Jensen 1998, 114.

Notes: [All]: According to the legend, once Plácitus had been reinstated as commander of the Emperor's cavalry, he recognised that he needed new recruits, so he sent word to all parts of the empire to summon young men to the army, and his own sons answered the call. — [5] svinn*s* 'of the wise': Finnur Jónsson (1887 and *Skj* B) supplied *saman*, noting the word as indistinct. The *-s* is, however, visible on an infra-red photograph.

45. Þá *réð* brims á brœðrum
　　blakkrennandi kenna,
　　*skíðs at skr*eytendr réðu
　　skokks stórmennis *þ*okka.

　　Þi*ngs* lét þessa drengi
　　þráhvetjandi *setja*
　　sóknar fráns í s*í*na
　　sveit, þás œzt vas *teit*i.

Brims blakkrennandi *réð þá* kenna á brœðrum *at skr*eytendr *skíðs* skokks réðu *þ*okka stórmennis. Þráhvetjandi *þi*ngs fráns sóknar lét *setja* þessa drengi í s*í*na sveit, þás vas œzt *teit*i.

The driver of the horse of the surf [(*lit.* 'horse-driver of the surf') SHIP > SEAFARER] then recognised in the brothers that the adorners of the ski of the deck-plank [SHIP > SEAFARERS] had the disposition of great men. The eager inciter of the assembly of the serpent of attack [SWORD > BATTLE > WARRIOR] had these men placed in his own company, which was foremost in high spirits.

Ms.: **673b**(4v). — *Readings*:　[1] *Þá réð*: '[...]' 673b, 673b*ÞH*, 'þa reþ' 673b*FJ*　[3] *skíðs at skr*eytendr: '[...]aeytendr' 673b, 673b*ÞH*, 'sk[...]skr aeytendr' 673b*FJ*　[4] *þ*okka: '[...]ca' 673b, '[...]' 673b*ÞH*, 'þocka' 673b*FJ*　[5] Þi*ngs*: 'þi[...]' 673b, '[...]' 673b*ÞH*, 'þings' 673b*FJ*　[6] -hvetjandi: '-hevetiande' 673b;　*setja*: '[...]' 673b, 673b*ÞH*, 'setia' 673b*FJ*　[7] s*í*na: 'syna' 673b　[8] þás: þá 673b;　*teit*i: '[...]i' 673b, '[...]' 673b*ÞH*, 'teiti' 673b*FJ*.

Editions: *Skj* Anonyme digte og vers [XII], G [1]. *Plácítúsdrápa* 45: AI, 615-16, BI, 618, *Skald* I, 301, *NN* §§1255, 2493A, 2555; Sveinbjörn Egilsson 1833, 29, 58, Finnur Jónsson 1887, 241, Jón Helgason 1932-3, 158-9, Louis-Jensen 1998, 115.

Notes: [1] *þá réð kenna* 'then recognised': Finnur Jónsson (1887) claimed to be able to read 'þa reþ', but in *Skj* A marked all but the last letter as unclear. — [3] *skíðs* 'of the ski': Emendation proposed by Lindquist 1928. — [3, 4] *réðu þokka stórmennis* 'had the disposition of great men': Reading suggested by Jón Helgason (1932-3, 159). — [5] *þings* 'of the assembly': While the transcripts of *ÞH* and *HE* could not make out any letters at this point, Sveinbjörn reconstructed the word on the basis of the alliteration and *skothending*. Finnur's 1887 transcription, however, claims to read the whole word. — [8] *þás* 'which': Emendation proposed by Finnur Jónsson 1887. — [8] *þás vas œzt* teiti 'which was foremost in high spirits': Reading suggested by Jón Helgason (1932-3, 159).

46. Dýrr *es* himna harri;
　　hann eignask ve*g sannan*;
　　aldrgǫfgu r*æð*r aldar
　　*a*flsteldr ... *veldi*.

　　Lýtr engla lið ítrum
　　angrhrjóðanda ok þjóðir;
　　einn es ǫllu hreinni,
　　allt gótt sás skóp, dróttinn.

Harri himna *es* dýrr; hann eignask *sannan* ve*g*; r*æð*r *a*flsteldr *a*ldrgǫfgu ... *veldi* aldar. Lið engla ok þjóðir lýtr ítrum angrhrjóðanda; einn dróttinn, sás skóp allt gótt, es ǫllu hreinni.

The king of the heavens [= God] is glorious; he gains true honour; he rules, mighty, over the age-noble ...-power of the age. The band of angels and humankind bows to the glorious destroyer of sin [= God]; the one Lord, who created everything good, is purer than all.

Ms.: 673b(4v). — *Readings*: [1] *es*: '[...]r' 673b [2] veg *sannan*: 've[...]' 673b [3] ræðr: 'r[...]þr' 673b, '[...]þr' 673bÞH [4] *a*flsteldr: '[...]fll steldr' 673b, 673bÞH, 'afll stelldr' 673bFJ; ... *veldi*: '[...]' 673b, 673bÞH, '[...]uelde' 673bFJ [5-8]: *abbrev. as* 'lytr.' 673b.

Editions: Skj Anonyme digte og vers [XII], G [1]. *Plácítúsdrápa* 46: AI, 616, BI, 618, Skald I, 301; Sveinbjörn Egilsson 1833, 29-30, 58, Finnur Jónsson 1887, 241, Louis-Jensen 1998, 115-16.

Notes: [1, 3] *es ... ræðr* 'is ... rules': Emendations proposed by Sveinbjörn Egilsson (1833). All other conjectures in this st. proposed by Finnur Jónsson (1887). — [4] *a*flsteldr 'mighty': This is the only occurrence of this cpd in ON. In *LP*, Finnur Jónsson suggests that the second element is from a verb **stella*, related to the late OIcel. *stelling* 'mast-step' (MIcel. 'posture, stance'). — [4] ... *veldi* '...-power': Sveinbjörn Egilsson proposed *meginveldi* 'mighty kingdom' here, but there is no evidence for the first element of his conjecture.

47. Hermanna fór h*ra*nna
    hyr*br*jótr *l*iði at móti,
    samr vas *í* só*kn* at f*r*emja
    sik Plácit*us*, m*iklu*.

Ógn stóð angrs af hegni;
ulfgœðendr þá flœðu;
þegn hlaut goðs fyr g*a*gni —
gu*ð*r háðisk vel — *r*áða.

H*ra*nna hyr*br*jótr fór at móti m*iklu l*iði hermanna; Plácit*us* vas samr at fremja sik *í* sókn. Ógn stóð af hegni angrs; ulfgœðendr flœðu þá; þegn goðs hlaut *r*áða fyr g*a*gni; gu*ð*r háðisk vel.

The destroyer of the fire of the waves [(*lit.* 'fire-destroyer of the waves') GOLD > GENEROUS MAN] went to meet a great host of warriors; Plácitus was disposed to distinguish himself in battle. Menace issued from the suppressor of sin [HOLY MAN]; the wolf-feeders [WARRIORS] fled then; God's retainer [HOLY MAN] was able to gain the victory; the battle was fought well.

Ms.: 673b(4v-5r). — *Readings*: [1] h*ra*nna: 'h[...]ɴa' 673b, 'hraɴa' 673bÞH [2] hyr*br*jótr *l*iði: 'hyr[...]iþe' 673b, 'hyr[...]e' 673bÞH, 'hyr(briotr) liþe'(?) 673bFJ [3] *í*: ok 673b; só*kn*: 'so[...]' 673b; f*r*emja: 'f[...]emia' 673b, '[...]mia' 673bÞH, 'fremia' 673bFJ [4] Plácit*us*: 'placit' *abbreviation not visible* 673b, 'placitus' 673bÞH, 673bFJ; m*iklu*: 'm[...]' 673b, 'mikli' *or* 'mikla' 673bSE, '[...]' 673bÞH, 'mikló' 673bFJ [7] g*a*gni: 'g[...]gne' 673b, 'gegne' 673bÞH, 673bFJ [8] gu*ð*r: 'gavtr' 673b; *r*áða: '[...]aþa' 673b, 'raþa' 673bÞH.

Editions: Skj Anonyme digte og vers [XII], G [1]. *Plácítúsdrápa* 47: AI, 616, BI, 619, Skald I, 301, *NN* §§1255, 2493A, 2555; Sveinbjörn Egilsson 1833, 30, 59, Finnur Jónsson 1887, 241, Jón Helgason 1932-3, 159-60, Louis-Jensen 1998, 116.

Notes: [1-3] h*ra*nna hyr*br*jótr *f*ór *a*t móti *m*iklu *l*iði *h*ermanna 'the destroyer of the fire of the waves [GOLD > GENEROUS MAN] went to meet a great host of warriors': Finnur Jónsson

(1887) claimed to read 'hyrbriotr liþe' but emended to -*brióts*, while reading *Herr manna* for the opening 'Her maɴa', making: *Herr manna fór at móti miklu liði hranna hyrbrjóts* 'An army of men came towards the [man's] great army'. Jón Helgason questioned the validity of normalising to *herr* as well as Finnur's reading of the final <r> in the very unclear 'hyrbriotr'. Jón's interpretation is reproduced here. — [3] *í* 'in': Emendation proposed by Louis-Jensen 1998. Finnur retained the ms. *ok*, but *sókn* needs a prep. Kock (*NN* §§1255, 2493A) suggested *at*. — [5-8]: The wording of this *helmingr* is much closer to the C text of the prose saga than to the Lat. and A texts (Louis-Jensen 1998, cxxv).

48. Herferðar rak harðan   áðr fyr rán, þats réðu
    hyr-Þróttr í styr flótta   randlinns stafar vinna,
    odda þings ok eyddi   gjald, sem goðs þegn vildi,
    eirlaust heruð þeira,   gjalfrhests metendr festu.

Odda þings hyr-Þróttr rak harðan flótta herferðar í styr ok eyddi eirlaust heruð þeira, áðr metendr gjalfrhests festu gjald, sem þegn goðs vildi, fyr rán, þats stafar randlinns réðu vinna.

The Þróttr <= Óðinn> of the fire of the assembly of spears [(*lit.* 'fire-Þróttr of the assembly of spears') BATTLE > SWORD > WARRIOR] vigorously pursued the retreat of the troops in battle and mercilessly harried their districts, until the appraisers of the sea-stallion [SHIP > SEAFARERS] fixed such compensation as God's retainer [HOLY MAN] wished for the pillaging, which the staves of the shield-serpent [SWORD > WARRIORS] had committed.

Ms.: **673b**(5r). — *Readings*: [1] harðan: 'h[...]þan' 673b, 'harþan' 673bÞH, 673bFJ [3] eyddi: '[...]de' 673b, 'eydde' 673bSE, 673bFJ, 'rydde' 673bÞH [4] heruð: 'horoþ' 673b [5] þats réðu: 'þat[...]' 673b, 673bÞH, 'þat er reþo'(?) 673bSE, 'þat es reþo' 673bFJ [7] vildi: '[...]lde' 673b, 'vildi'(?) 673bSE, 'vallde' 673bÞH, 'valde' 673bFJ [8] gjalfrhests: 'giafr hestc' 673b, 673bFJ, 'giafr betsc' 673bÞH; festu: '(f)esto'(?) 673b, 673bFJ, 'lesto' 673bÞH.

Editions: Skj Anonyme digte og vers [XII], G [1]. *Plácítúsdrápa* 48: AI, 616, BI, 619, *Skald* I, 301; Sveinbjörn Egilsson 1833, 30, 59, Finnur Jónsson 1887, 241, Louis-Jensen 1998, 116-17.

Notes: [8] *gjalfrhests* 'of the sea-stallion': Emendation proposed in Konráð Gíslason and Eiríkur Jónsson 1875-89, II, 45-6

49. Hyrgildir ... hvíldar   Létu of eins hvers ýtis
    hrafnvíns liði sínu;   apaldrgarð brimis kapla
    garpr bauð þ... í þorpi   lundar búðum lýðar
    þingveljondum dveljask.   lungs umbhverfis slungit.

Hrafnvíns hyr-gildir ... liði sínu hvíldar; garpr bauð þ... þingveljondum dveljask í þorpi. Lýðar lundar lungs létu búðum slungit umbhverfis of apaldrgarð eins hvers ýtis kapla brimis.

The appraiser of the fire of raven-wine [BLOOD > SWORD > WARRIOR] ... his men rest; the champion bade the choosers of the assembly of þ... [(*lit.* 'assembly-choosers of þ...') ?BATTLE > WARRIORS] stay in a village. The troops of the tree of the ship [SEAFARER] pitched camp around the orchard of a certain launcher of the horses of the sea [SHIPS > SEAFARER].

Ms.: **673b**(5r). — *Readings*: [1] Hyrgi*ldir*: 'hyrgi[...]' 673b, 'hyrgilldir' 673b*ÞH*, 'hyrgilldr' 673b*HE*, 'hyrgilder' 673b*FJ*;   ...: '[...]' 673b [3] garp*r*: 'garp[...]' 673b, 'garpr' 673b*ÞH*, 673b*FJ*;   þ...: 'þ[...]' 673b, 673b*ÞH*, 'þuþr'(?) 673b*HE*, 'þro(t)'(?) 673b*FJ* [5] *Létu of* eins: '[...]et[...](ei)[...]'(?) 673b, 'sett or eins' 673b*ÞH*, 'sette of eins' 673b*FJ*; *of*: 'of *or* 'or' 673b*HE*; *hvers*: '[...]ve[...]s' 673b, 'hvers' 673b*ÞH*, 'hve[...]' 673b*FJ* [6] apald*r*-: 'apald[...]' 673b, 'apaldrs' 673b*ÞH*, 'apaldrer' 673b*FJ* [7] *lundar bú*ðum l*ý*ðar: 'l[...] b[...]þum l[...]þar' 673b, 'lattas [...] þ[...]v lyþer' 673b*ÞH*, '[...]u lyþar' 673b*FJ*; *lundar*: 'lattat' 673b*HE* [8] slungit: 'stungit' 673b*ÞH*, 673b*FJ*.

Editions: Skj Anonyme digte og vers [XII], G [1]. *Plácítúsdrápa* 49: AI, 616, BI, 619, *Skald* I, 301; Sveinbjörn Egilsson 1833, 31, 60, Finnur Jónsson 1887, 242, Jón Helgason 1932-3, 160-1, Louis-Jensen 1998, 117.

Notes: [1] ...: Sveinbjörn proposed *fekk* 'got, granted' for this lacuna, but there is no evidence from the *hendingar* or alliteration. — [3] *þ*...: Finnur Jónsson (*Skj* B) supplied *Þrós* 'Þrór's <= Óðinn>' to provide a determinant for the battle-kenning. He earlier (1887) used *Þrótts* (another name for Óðinn); Sveinbjörn Egilsson (1833) emended to *þýðr* 'gentle'. — [5-8]: Words in this *helmingr* correspond to vocabulary in either the A or C texts of the prose saga, including *apaldrgarð* (l. 6, a word not used elsewhere in skaldic poetry, providing *aðalhending* with *kapla*; the C text has *aldingarðr* as in *Pl* st. 24/7) and *umbhverfis* (l. 8) (Louis-Jensen 1998, cxxi). — [5-8]: All the conjectural emendations in this *helmingr* derive from Jón Helgason 1932-3, except *lýðar*, originally proposed by Finnur Jónsson (1887). — [8] *slungit* 'pitched': Sveinbjörn Egilsson (1833) and Finnur Jónsson (1887) both read *stungit* 'stuck' here, but Jón Helgason pointed out that what appears to be a line coming off the second letter is in fact part of the following letter 'u'. Jón also points to a comparable phrase in *Knýtl* (*ÍF* 35, 292).

50. Hús *át*ti sér hættin
    hress í garði þessum
    (*f*ekk *stre*ngjar *þ*ar Þungra)
    Þeopista (sér vistar),
    síz jarðar *fj*ǫr *f*irr*ð*isk,
    fránbaugs, sás tók hána,
    undins lát*r*s, *f*rá ítrum
    endr Plácito, sendir.

Hættin, hress Þeopista *át*ti sér hús í garði þessum; Þungra *stre*ngjar *f*ekk sér *þ*ar vistar, síz sendir lát*r*s undins fránbaugs jarðar, sás tók hána endr *f*rá ítrum Plácito, *f*irr*ð*isk fjǫr.

The virtuous, energetic Theopista had a house in this orchard; the Þungra <= Freyja> of the ribbon [WOMAN] settled there after the distributor of the ground of the twisted shining ring of the earth [= Miðgarðsormr > GOLD > GENEROUS MAN], the one who had once taken her from the glorious Placitus, left this life.

Ms.: **673b**(5r). — *Readings*: [1] H*ús á*tti: 'H[...]ti' 673b, 673b*ÞH*, 'hus atte'(?) 673b*HE*, 'Hus [...]te' 673b*FJ* [2] þessum: 'þessu' 673b*FJ* [3] *f*ekk *streng*jar *þa*r: 'sek [...]giar [...]r' 673b, 'seks [...]engiar þar' 673b*ÞH*, 'seks þuengiar er' 673b*FJ* [5] fjǫr: 'f[...]' 673b, 'fra' 673b*ÞH*, 673b*FJ*; *firrðisk*: '[...]' 673b, 673b*FJ*, 'firþisc' 673b*ÞH* [6] fránbaugs: 'fran bavgs' 673b, 673b*FJ*, 'stan havgs' 673b*ÞH*; frán-: 'fran' *or* 'stan' 673b*HE* [7] lát*r*s: 'lat[...]s' 673b, 'sætes' 673b*ÞH*, 'ætes' 673b*HE*, 'latrs' 673b*FJ*; *fr*á: '[...]a' 673b.

Editions: *Skj* Anonyme digte og vers [XII], G [1]. *Plácítúsdrápa* 50: AI, 616, BI, 619, *Skald* I, 301, *NN* §1256; Sveinbjörn Egilsson 1833, 31, 60, Finnur Jónsson 1887, 242, Louis-Jensen 1998, 117-18.

Notes: [3] str*eng*jar 'of the ribbon': Emendation proposed by Louis-Jensen (1998). Sveinbjörn Egilsson had '-s engiar' and Finnur Jónsson *þveng*jar (1887, remarking that <þu> is very unclear). The reading *þveng*jar would produce excessive alliteration (if the following word is *þar*) and *þveng*r is not found elsewhere as an element of a kenning for woman. *Streng*jar seems preferable, although the gen. of this word ends in *-s* in st. 24. — [3, 4] fekk sér vistar 'settled': Emendation proposed in *NN* §1256, but already suggested by Sveinbjörn Egilsson (1833) in a note. — [6] -*baugs* '-ring': Originally proposed by Finnur Jónsson (1887). Sveinbjörn Egilsson has 'haugs'. Part of the <b> is, however, visible.

51. Ok inn í sal sinnar
    siðfróðastir móður
    — brœðr hlutu œzta *blíðu* —
    *brynþ*ings viðir gingu;

en ítrfoldar el*da*
Endils so*n*u kenndit
hirðigótt, þótt hit*ti*
h...ðir móður,

Ok viðir *bryn*þ*ings*, siðfróðastir, gingu inn í sal móður sinnar; brœðr hlutu œzta *blíðu*; en hirðigótt el*da* ítrfoldar *Endils* kenndit so*n*u, þótt h...ðir hit*ti* móður,

And the trees of the mailcoat-assembly [BATTLE > WARRIORS], very well instructed in religion, went into their mother's hall; the brothers received the best hospitality; but the nursing-tree of the fires of the glorious ground of Endill <sea-king> [SEA > GOLD > WOMAN] did not recognise her sons, although ... met their mother,

Ms.: **673b**(5r). — *Readings*: [3, 4] œzta *blíðu bryn*þ*ings*: 'øtsta [...] þ[...]gs' 673b, 'østrar iþ(io) en(gg)is [...]egs' 673b*ÞH*, 'øtstan [...]gs' 673b*FJ* [5, 6] el*da Endils* so*n*u: 'e(l)[...] s[...]o'(?) 673b, 'elld[...]o' 673b*ÞH*, 'elld[...]livo' 673b*HE* [7, 8] hit*ti* h...ðir: 'hit[...]þer' 673b, 'hitte h[...]þer' 673b*ÞH*, 'hitte [...]þer' 673b*FJ*.

Editions: *Skj* Anonyme digte og vers [XII], G [1]. *Plácítúsdrápa* 51: AI, 617, BI, 620, *Skald* I, 301, *NN* §2556; Sveinbjörn Egilsson 1833, 31-2, 61, Finnur Jónsson 1887, 242, Jón Helgason 1932-3, 161-2, Louis-Jensen 1998, 118.

Notes: [3-4] blíðu brynþ*ings*: Emendation proposed in *Skj* B. — [6] Endils so*n*u: Emendation proposed by Finnur Jónsson 1887. — [8] h...ðir: The 'h' is predicted by the alliteration. Jón Helgason (1932-3) suggested several possibilities for filling this l., including *hǫldar fróðir* 'the wise men' and *harða fróðir* 'the very wise ones' but recommended *hljóðlundaðir* 'the quiet-minded ones'; Kock (*NN* §2556) suggested *hróðrglýjaðir* 'the fame-glad ones'.

52. unz tírrœkir tœki   Þollr gat ... inn el*lri*
     tv*eir* brœðr of þat rœða   ... fyr bróður
     orð, hvat œski-Nir*ðir*   lýst ok langa freistni
     ... framast myndi.   ... hlífar,

unz tv*eir* tírrœkir br*œ*ðr tœki rœða orð of þat, hvat œski-Nir*ð*ir ... myndi framast; inn el*lri* þollr ... hlífar gat lýst ... ok langa freistni ... fyr bróður,

until the two renown-cultivating brothers began to speak of that which the wishing-Nirðir <gods> ... [?MEN] first remembered; the older tree ... of the shield [?BATTLE > WARRIOR] was able to describe ... and long ordeal ... to his brother,

Ms.: **673b**(5r). — *Readings*: [1, 2] tœki tv*eir* br*œ*ðr: 't[...](c)[...] tu[...]þr'(?) 673b, 'tœce tu[...]þr' 673b*PH*, 'tœce tueir brøþr' 673b*FJ*   [3, 4] -Nir*ð*ir ...: 'nir[...]' 673b, 'nirþer [...]' 673b*PH*, 673b*FJ*, 'nirþ[...]' 673b*JH*   [5, 6] el*lri* ...: 'el[...]' 673b, 'all[...]' 673b*PH*, '[...]' 673b*FJ*, '[...]ll[...]þ[...]' 673b*JH*   [8] ...: '[...]' 673b, 673b*FJ*, 'l[...]' 673b*PH*, '[...]sc[...]' 673b*JH*.

Editions: *Skj* Anonyme digte og vers [XII], G [1]. *Plácítúsdrápa* 52: AI, 617, BI, 620, *Skald* I, 301; Sveinbjörn Egilsson 1833, 32, 61, Finnur Jónsson 1887, 242, Jón Helgason 1932-3, 162-3, Louis-Jensen 1998, 119.

Notes: [3] -*Nir*ðir: This is the nom. pl. of the name Njǫrðr, a member of the Vanir group of gods, and often regarded as the god of the sea in Norse mythology. — [4] ...: A determinant of a man-kenning appears to be required here, but the metre predicts only that the two syllables should begin with a vowel and contain -*yn*. Sveinbjörn Egilsson's conjecture, *undlinns* 'of the wound-snake [SWORD]', was rejected by Jón Helgason because it produces a poor rhyme. Finnur had *yndis* 'of happiness' and added *of* before *myndi* to fill out the metre. Jón proposed instead *odddyns* 'of the spear-din [BATTLE]'. — [5] ...: The l. requires a long syllable alliterating with *ellri* or *þollr* (unless a conjecture in l. 6 is made), forming the base-word of a kenning. Jón Helgason proposed *éls* 'of the storm', forming a battle-kenning, but *éls* would produce three internal rhymes. — [6] ...: The alliteration requires that the missing three syllables start with a vowel and contain the *aðalhending* -*óð*-. Jón Helgason suggested *óðaljǫrð* 'ancestral home' here, based in part on his own reading of the ms. ('[...]ll[...]þ'), but this is largely conjectural. — [8] ...: Jón read two letters ('sc') in this lacuna, and suggested *lindskífanda* 'the shield-slicer's'; a four-syllable sequence containing *líf*... *sk*... is also possible on the basis of the metre and Jón's reading of the ms.

53. frá því's fri*ð*gin, nýja,   Ok bjartglóða beið*r*
fjǫg*ur endr*, síz trú kenndu,   *brag*ðvíss gripinn sagðisk
ráð ór Rúmsborg *víðri*   frár af frœknu dýri
... mœðila flœðu.   fló*ðs*, en vargr tók bróður.

frá þvís fjǫgur friðgin *endr* mœðila flœðu ... ráð ór *víðri* Rúmsborg, síz kenndu nýja trú. Ok *brag*ðvíss frár beiðir bjartglóða fló*ðs* sagðisk gripinn af frœknu dýri, en vargr tók bróður.

about how the four, parents [and children], once fled with difficulty from their ... circumstances from the great city of Rome, after they embraced the new faith. And the plucky, agile demander of the bright embers of the flood [GOLD > MAN] described himself being taken by a fierce beast, and [how] a wolf took his brother.

Ms.: **673b**(5r-v). — *Readings*: [1] friðgin: 'fr[...]þgin' 673b, 'friþgin' 673b*ÞH*, 673b*FJ* [2] fjǫg*ur endr*: 'fiog[...]' 673b, 'fi[...]' 673b*ÞH*, 'fiogur [...]' 673b*FJ* [3, 4] víðri ...: '[...]' 673b [5, 6] beiðir *brag*ðvíss: 'beiþ(e)[...]þuiss'(?) 673b, 'beiþer [...]þuiss' 673b*ÞH*, 673b*FJ* [8] fló*ðs*: 'floþ[...]' 673b, 673b*ÞH*, 'floþs' 673b*FJ*

Editions: Skj Anonyme digte og vers [XII], G [1]. *Plácitúsdrápa* 53: AI, 617, BI, 620, Skald I, 301-2; Sveinbjörn Egilsson 1833, 32, 62, Finnur Jónsson 1887, 243, Jón Helgason 1932-3, 164, Louis-Jensen 1998, 119-20.

Notes: [1] *friðgin* 'parents [and children]': Lit. '(married) couple'. *Hap. leg.* in poetry. — [2] *endr* 'once': Emendation proposed by Finnur Jónsson 1887. — [3] *ór víðri Rúmsborg* 'from the great city of Rome': The C text of the prose saga also mentions Rome, both here and in the passage corresponding to st. 57/5, while the Lat. and A texts do not (Louis-Jensen 1998, cxxv). Cf. Note to 15/1. — [4] ...: Finnur Jónsson (1887 and *Skj* B) has *raunmœðila* 'with very great difficulty' to fill this gap in the ms., but his reading requires further emendation of ms. *ráð* to *ráði* (to agree with *því*). Jón Helgason suggested *rýrt* 'poor, reduced', but only the first letter is determined by the metre.

54. Kenndusk, órr þás end*i*   Spandi ítr til yndis
unnfress sǫgu þessa,   †eir goð...† þe*i*ra,
mildir brœðr en móðir   þvíat hrygg saga huggun
mei*n*stygg sonu dyggva.   hoddskerð*ǫndum* ge*r*ði.

Mildir brœðr kenndusk, þás órr unnfress end*i* sǫgu þessa, en mei*n*stygg móðir dyggva sonu. Ítr †eir goð...† spandi ... þe*i*ra til yndis, þvíat hrygg saga gerði huggun hoddskerð*ǫndum*.

The pious brothers recognised each other, when the messenger of the wave-bear [SHIP > SEAFARER] finished this story, and the sin-shy mother her excellent sons. The glorious ... won their ... over to happiness, because the sad story brought comfort to the hoard-diminishers [GENEROUS MEN].

Ms.: **673b**(5v). — *Readings*: [1, 2] end*i* unn*f*ress: 'end[...](u)Nfress'(?) 673b, 'end[...]ir[...]fress' 673b*ÞH*, 'end[...]fress' 673b*HE*, 'end[...] vn fress' 673b*FJ*   [4] mei*n*stygg: 'mei[...]st(y)gg'(?) 673b, 'me[...]' 673b*ÞH*, 'meinstygg' 673b*FJ*   [6] †eir goð...†: 'eir guþ[...]' 673b, 673b*FJ*, 'eyr guþ[...]a' 673b*ÞH*;   þ*e*ira: 'þerra' 673b   [8] -skerð*ǫ*n*dum ge*rði: 'scerþo[...]rþi' 673b, 'scerþe[...]þe' 673b*ÞH*, 'scerþeþa gørþe' 673b*FJ*.

Editions: *Skj* Anonyme digte og vers [XII], G [1]. *Plácítúsdrápa* 54: AI, 617, BI, 620, Skald I, 302, *NN* §2139; Sveinbjörn Egilsson 1833, 33, 62, Finnur Jónsson 1887, 243, Louis-Jensen 1998, 120.

Notes: [2] unn*fress* 'wave-bear': Sveinbjörn Egilsson suggested *undfress* 'wound-bear', a wolf-kenning, but it does not fit well with *ǫrr* to form a man-kenning. Finnur Jónsson (1887), however, claimed to read 'uN' in the ms. and provides the reading given here. — [6] †eir goð...†: Kock (*NN* §2139) dismissed Finnur Jónsson's conjecture, *Eir goð mjaðar* (*Skj* B), on the grounds that it creates 'fyrtaktighet' (a term not explained in *NN*, but which seems to mean 'four beats to a line'). His own suggestion, *Eir guðvefjar* 'the Eir <goddess> of velvet [WOMAN]', however, has the defect of leaving *spanði* without an object. Unless the couplet is irreparably corrupt, the illegible passage must have contained the sentence object, in which case 'fyrtaktighet' can hardly be avoided. Louis-Jensen suggests the following, but with strong reservations on account of the metrics: either *Eir goðvefs hug* 'the Eir <goddess> of velvet [won their] minds', or, since the mother is not designated as chief comforter in the prose texts: *eir goðlig hug* 'the divine grace of God [won their] minds' (cf. 28.4, where *eir* = 'the grace of God'), and the close parallel in Gamlkan *Has* 36: *spǫnð lætr ǫll til yndis ... sín bǫrn* 'guides all his children to bliss', where the sentence subject is God. Kari Ellen Gade, in reviewing the present edn, suggested *eir guðs hugi* 'the grace of God [won their] minds [over to happiness]', which, while metrically correct, still involves a great deal of conjecture.

55. Ok fjǫlkostig fýstisk
    fóstr*l*anda til *stranda*
    hauka klifs, þás hafði,
    hyrgrund, so*nu* fundna.

    Fljótt bað fylgju veita
    fenglóðar *sér tróð*a
    liðs hǫfðingja leyfðan
    Langbarða *til jarðar*.

Ok fjǫlkostig klifs hauka hyrgrund fýstisk til strand*a* fóstr*l*anda, þás hafði fundna so*nu*. Tróð*a* fenglóðar bað fljótt leyfðan hǫfðingja liðs veita *sér* fylgju *til jarðar* Langbarða.

And the many-virtued ground of the fire of the cliff of the hawks [(*lit.* 'fire-ground of the hawks' cliff) ARM > GOLD > WOMAN] longed for the shores of her homeland after she had found her sons. The stick of the fen-fire [GOLD > WOMAN] quickly asked the esteemed commander of the army to give her escort to the land of the Langobards [= Italy].

Ms.: **673b**(5v). — *Readings*:   [2] fóstr*l*anda: 'fost[...] landa' 673b;   *stranda*: '[...]' 673b, 673b*ÞH*, 673b*FJ*, 'branda'(?) 673b*SE*, 'stranda'(?) 673b*SkjA*   [4] so*nu*: 'so[...]' 673b, 'sono' 673b*ÞH*, 673b*FJ*   [6] *sér tróð*a: '[...]a' 673b, 'ser troþa' 673b*SE*, 673b*FJ*   [8] *til jarðar*: '[...]' 673b, 673b*ÞH*, 'til iarþar' 673b*SE*, 673b*FJ*.

Editions: *Skj* Anonyme digte og vers [XII], G [1]. *Plácítúsdrápa* 55: AI, 617, BI, 621, *Skald* I, 302; Sveinbjörn Egilsson 1833, 33, 63, Finnur Jónsson 1887, 243, Louis-Jensen 1998, 121.

Notes: [All]: Cf. the A² version of the prose text *Bid eg þig ... ad þú flytir mig aptur til minar fosturjardar* 'I ask you ... that you take me back to my homeland' (Tucker 1998, 59, ll. 297-8). — [2] stranda (gen. pl.) 'coast': Finnur Jónsson in *Skj* A claimed this reading in the ms. was *temlig sikkert* 'fairly certain', although the transcription in his 1887 edn indicates the ms. was then illegible at this point, as it is now. Sveinbjörn Egilsson read (or conjectured?) *branda*, but had to emend *til* to *á vit* to make sense of the text.

56. *K*enndusk hjú, þás handa   Beiði-Þrór við báða
    h... þǫp...   b*u*ri *k*anna*ð*isk sanna,
    atburð elda Nirði   armlinns, œsku sinnar
    ormv*ang*s, *hv*é kom þangat.   ...ld... þ...ðu.

Hjú *k*enndusk, þás *h*... þǫp... ormv*ang*s ... Nirði elda handa atburð, *hv*é kom þangat. Beiði-Þrór armlinns *k*anna*ð*isk við báða b*u*ri sanna ... œsku sinnar.

The husband and wife recognised each other when the ... of the serpent-ground [GOLD > ?WOMAN] [told] the Njǫrðr <god> of the fires of arms [ARM-RINGS > MAN] the events, how she had got there. The demanding-Þrór <= Óðinn> of the arm-snake [ARM-RING > MAN] acknowledged both as his true sons ... of their youth.

Ms.: **673b**(5v). — *Readings*: [1] *K*enndusk: '[...]enndosc' 673b, '[...]nndosc' 673b*ÞH*, '*K*enndosc' 673b*FJ*   [2] *h*... þǫp...: '[...]þæp[...]' 673b, 673b*FJ*, '[...]þauf[...]ne' 673b*ÞH*, '[...]þaup[...]ne' *or* '[...]þauʀ[...]ne' 673b*HE*   [4] ormv*ang*s *hv*é: 'orm u[...]s [...]' 673b, 673b*FJ*, 'ormu [...]' 673b*ÞH*   [6] b*u*ri *k*anna*ð*isk: 'b[...]ri[...]' 673b   [8] ...ld... þ...ðu: '[...]ld[...]þ[...]þo' 673b, '[...]ld[...]rþ[...]þo' 673b*ÞH*, 673b*FJ*.

Editions: *Skj* Anonyme digte og vers [XII], G [1]. *Plácítúsdrápa* 56: AI, 617, BI, 621, *Skald* I, 302, *NN* §§3135, 3136, 3396X; Sveinbjörn Egilsson 1833, 33-4, 63, Finnur Jónsson 1887, 243, Jón Helgason 1932-3, 164-6, Louis-Jensen 1998, 121-2.

Notes: [2] *h*... þǫp...: The 'h' is predicted by the alliteration in the first l. Kock's conjecture *Hlín Þeópista tíndi* (*NN* §3135), puts the name in a metrical position which it does not otherwise fill; also, the second of the visible letters is certainly <æ> not <eo>. Jón Helgason 1932-3 saw no possibility other than reconstructing the l. as *hýr þopta nam skýra* 'the friendly thwart ... [WOMAN] began to explain' or *hrein þopta nam greina* 'the pure thwart ... [WOMAN] began to expound', suggestions that depend on the likelihood that 'æ' can represent 'o', either intentionally or by mistake. — [6] b*u*ri, *k*anna*ð*isk: Emendations proposed by Finnur Jónsson 1887. — [8]: Instead of the first <þ> and the preceding word space, Sveinbjörn Egilsson (1833) read <rþ>, which was repeated in *Skj* A and B. Jón Helgason 1932-3 suggested *aldýrð þegar es skýrðu* 'when [they] explained ... glorious' but was not satisfied with *aldýrð* (according to the prose text, the brothers told each other *alla sǫgu sem gengit hafði yfir þá* 'all the events which had happened to them', not merely their happy memories). Another possibility which would be compatible with the legible remains of the words as described in Jón Helgason 1932-3 is *aldrs bǫl þegars tǫlðu* 'when [they] told of the misfortunes of [their] life' (Louis-Jensen 1998, 122). The conjecture in *NN* §3136 (*ǫld es furðu tǫlðu*) contains an unsatisfactory rhyme.

57. Gerðu, grœnnar jarðar,   áðr til Rúms frá rómu
    gǫfug es ...izk hǫfðu,   rekka sveit með teitri
    eklaust ítrum þakkir   sigrgladdr snilli prýddri
    ǫll ... gram snjǫllum,   sóknstærandi fœri.

Ǫll gerðu eklaust þakkir ítrum, snjǫllum gram ... grœnnar jarðar, *es* gǫfug hǫfðu ...izk, áðr sigrgladdr *sóknstæra*ndi fœri frá rómu til Rúms með teitri, snilli *prýd*dri sveit rekka.

They all gave thanks profusely to the glorious, brave ruler ... of the green earth [?SKY/HEAVEN > = God], when the noble ones had ..., before the victory-glad attack-increaser [WARRIOR] returned from the battle to Rome with the cheerful, courage-adorned band of men.

Ms.: **673b**(5v). — *Readings*: [2] *gǫfug es* ...*izk*: 'go[...]o[...]esck' 673b, 'gott[...]resck' 673b*ÞH*, 'goþu[...]resck' 673b*HE*, 'go[...]esck' 673b*FJ*   [4] *ǫll* ...: '[...]' 673b, 673b*ÞH*, '[...]gu' 673b*FJ*   [6] *rekka sveit*: '[...]' 673b, 673b*ÞH*, rekka sveit(?) 673b*SE*, '[...]it' 673b*FJ*   [7] *prýddri*: '[...]rvd[...]' 673b, '[...]ruþ[...]' 673b*ÞH*, '[...]rvd[...]' 673b*FJ*   [8] *sóknstærandi*: '[...]nde' 673b, '[...]ande' 673b*ÞH*, 673b*FJ*, sóknstærandi(?) 673b*SE*.

Editions: *Skj* Anonyme digte og vers [XII], G [1]. *Plácítúsdrápa* 57: AI, 618, BI, 621, *Skald* I, 302, *NN* §2813; Sveinbjörn Egilsson 1833, 34, 64, Finnur Jónsson 1887, 244, Jón Helgason 1932-3, 166-7, Louis-Jensen 1998, 122.

Notes: [2] *es gǫfu*g 'when the noble ones': Emendation proposed by Jón Helgason 1932-3. — [2] ...*izk*: Finnur (*Skj* A) conjectured *fundizk* 'been reunited' for this lacuna, but there is no evidence from the *hendingar* or alliteration. — [3] *ǫll* 'all': Emendation proposed by Finnur Jónsson 1887. Although the ms. is illegible here, *ǫll* is very likely to be the correct reading on the basis of the rhyme and alliteration. — [4] ...: Jón Helgason 1932-3, who thought he could make out two <a>s, proposed *tjalda* 'of the tents' here. Finnur Jónsson 1887 (but not *Skj* A) read the last two letters of the word as <gu>. — [7] rekka sveit 'band of men': This reading is found in Sveinbjörn Egilsson's notes to the transcription of the poem, but is not incorporated into his text of *Pl*. — [7] *prýd*dri 'adorned': Emendation proposed by Finnur Jónsson 1887.

58. Né víghressa vissi   Óþǫrfu bað erfi
      †vel... ...is†   ítrstyrkr ...
      tírmildr tiggja þeira   andrán Adriánus
       — Trájánus ...   ǫrva móts ...

Trájánus ...; né vissi tírmildr †vel... ...is† þeira víghressa tiggja. Ítrstyrkr Adriánus bað andrán ... móts ǫrva óþǫrfu erfi ...

Trajan ...; the gloriously merciful ... did not know ... of their battle-zealous prince. The magnificently powerful Hadrian gave orders that the death ... of the meeting of arrows [BATTLE > ?WARRIOR] ... with a harmful funeral feast ...

Ms.: **673b**(5v). — *Readings*: [2] †vel... ...is†: 'uel[...]is' 673b, 'uel[...]s' 673b*ÞH*, 'uel[...]eldes' 673b*FJ*, '(u)el[...]tis' 673b*JH*   [4] Trájánus ...: 'trai[...]r' 673b, 673b*FJ*, 673b*JH*, 'trau[...]' 673b*ÞH*   [6] ítrstyrkr ...: 'itr str[...]r[...]ur[...]a' 673b, 'itr str [...] urþa' 673b*ÞH*, 'itr str[...]r[...]sika' 673b*FJ*, 'it(r) str(k)r [...]yr(k)a'(?) 673b*JH*   [8] móts ...: 'mots [...]' 673b, 'mets [...]' 673b*ÞH*, 'm[...]ts [...]' 673b*FJ*.

Editions: Skj Anonyme digte og vers [XII], G [1]. *Plácitúsdrápa* 58: AI, 618, BI, 621, Skald I, 302, NN §3; Sveinbjörn Egilsson 1833, 34, 64, Finnur Jónsson 1887, 244, Jón Helgason 1932-3, 167-8, Louis-Jensen 1998, 122-3.

Notes: [All]: At this point in the prose versions, the Emperor Trajan dies and the new Emperor, Hadrian, orders the preparation of a pagan funeral feast involving sacrifices. — [All]: Jón Helgason 1932-3 proposed the following conjectures for this st. In l. 2, *vel*lsviptandi skipt*is* 'the gold-discarder' (the subject of the cl.) and 'the replacement' (the object of his conjecture for l. 4 *vánir*). In l. 4, *Tráj*ánus dó; ... vánir 'Trajan died; ... expected'. In l. 6, *ítr*styrk*r* viðar dýrka 'magnificently powerful ... of the tree ... be commemorated'. For l. 8 he suggested *at blóti* 'with sacrifices' but also gave alternatives, including *ok blóti* (taken with *erfi*), *ok blóta* (inf. of verb) and *með blóti*. The resulting st. would then read *Trájánus dó; né vissi tírmildr vellsviptandi vánir skiptis þeira víghressa tiggja. Ítrstyrkr Adriánus bað dýrka andrán viðar móts ǫrva óþǫrfu erfi at blóti* 'Trajan died; the gloriously merciful gold-discarder [GENEROUS MAN] had not expected the replacement of their battle-zealous prince. The magnificently powerful Hadrian gave orders that the death of the tree of the meeting of arrows [BATTLE > WARRIOR] be commemorated with a harmful funeral feast with sacrifices'.

59. Inn bað með sér svinna*n*
snar*fengr í h*of þengill
— ítr hnekkir stóð úti
*angr*s — Plá*c*itum ganga.

'Blót', kvað gramr *inn grimmi*,
'*gagni* í sókn ok fagna
kvǫn hittir þú ...'

Snar*fengr* þengill bað svinna*n* Plá*c*itum ganga með sér inn *í h*of; ítr hnekkir *angrs* stóð úti. 'Blót', kvað *inn grimmi* gramr, 'ok fagna *gagni* í sókn; þú hittir kvǫn ...'

The vigorous prince told the wise Plácitus to go with him into the temple; the glorious subduer of sin [HOLY MAN] stood outside. 'Sacrifice', said the fierce king, 'and rejoice for your victory in battle; you found your wife ...'

Ms.: **673b**(5v). — *Readings*: [1] svinna*n*: svinnat 673b [2] snar*fengr í h*of: 'snar[...]of' 673b, snarfengr í hof(?) 673b*SE* [4] *angrs* Plá*c*itum: '[...]itum' 673b, '[...] placitum' 673b*FJ* [5, 6] *inn grimmi gagni* í sókn: '[...]isocn' 673b, 673b*FJ*, '[...]socn' 673b*ÞH*, '[...]son' 673b*HE*.

Editions: *Skj* Anonyme digte og vers [XII], G [1]. *Plácítúsdrápa* 59: AI, 618, BI, 622, *Skald* I, 302; Sveinbjörn Egilsson 1833, 34, 65, Finnur Jónsson 1887, 244, Louis-Jensen 1998, 123.

Notes: [5-6] inn grimmi ... gagni 'the fierce ... for your victory': Emendation proposed by Finnur Jónsson 1887.

The Thirteenth Century

Kolbeinn Tumason

Biography in Volume IV

Jónsvísur

Edited by Beatrice La Farge

Introduction

Five sts from a *dróttkvætt* poem *Jónsvísur* 'Vísur about John the Apostle' (Kolb *Jónv*) composed by Kolbeinn Tumason (1173-1208) in honour of John the Apostle, to whom the fourth Gospel and the Book of Revelation were traditionally attributed, are preserved in a sole ms., AM 649 a 4° (649a), c. 1350-1400, where they are quoted at the end of a version of *Jóns saga postula* (*Jón⁴*; for further details of the ms., see Introduction to Ník *Jóndr*; see also Widding, Bekker-Nielsen and Shook 1963, 316).

In *Jón⁴* the five sts are quoted in the same order as they appear below. In the saga they are preceded by a short introduction which states that Kolbeinn's poem had forty-seven sts. The prose introduction (fol. 47r) mentions that Kolbeinn entitled his poem *Jóns vísur*, *þviat verki sa er eigi stefsettr* 'because the work is not provided with a refrain'. The introduction also indicates that the first four sts quoted are from the first part of the poem, while the fifth is from *nærr enda sins verks* 'near the end of his poem'. The sts emphasise John's virginity and his special position in relation to Christ, as the prose introduction to the poem in *Jón⁴* states with reference to the first four sts quoted: *I ondverðu briosti þess kvæðis setr hann þa dyrðarástuð, er guðs son veitti Johanni, ok hversu gudsriddarinn stóð i striði várs græðara undir krossinum, ok hveria tign hann oðlaðiz i umboði teknu at geyma drotning himinrikis* 'In the beginning of the first part of this poem he sets forth the special love which God's son bore to John, and how God's knight stood at the foot of the Cross during the agony of our Saviour and what honour he gained in accepting the charge of protecting the queen of the kingdom of heaven [Mary]' (*Jón⁴* 1874, 511). For further information on Kolbein's devotion to the Virgin Mary and S. John see his biography in vol. IV.

Kolb *Jóndr* has been previously edited by Unger 1874 and, as an appendix to Unger's edn of *Jón⁴*, by Sophus Bugge (1874, 935-6), as well as by Lange 1958a, Finnur Jónsson (*Skj*) and Kock (*Skald*).

1. Angrfellir, vast ǫllum
   einn postolum hreinni
   heilags Krists í hæstu,
   happskeytr, fǫruneyti.
   Unni engum manni
   jafnheitt friðar veitir
   þýðr sem þér ok móður
   — þats minniligt — sinni.

Happskeytr angrfellir, vast einn hreinni ǫllum postolum í hæstu fǫruneyti heilags Krists. Þýðr veitir friðar unni engum manni jafnheitt sem þér ok móður sinni — þats minniligt.

Lucky-shooting sorrow-feller [APOSTLE], you were alone purer than all the Apostles in the highest company of holy Christ. The friendly granter of peace [= God (= Christ)] loved no-one as ardently as you and his mother — that is worthy of remembrance.

Ms.: **649a**(47r) (*Jón⁴*).

Editions: *Skj* Kolbeinn Tumason, 1. *Jónsvísur* 1: AII, 37, BII, 45-46, *Skald* II, 28, *NN* §2560; *Jón⁴* 1874, 511, Bugge 1874, 935, *GBpB*, 570n.

Context: See Introduction. — *Notes*: [1, 4] *happskeytr angrfellir* 'lucky-shooting sorrow-feller': Both cpds in this kenning for a saint or, here, specifically the Apostle John, are *hap. leg.* — [5-8]: Kolbeinn here makes the traditional identification of John with the unnamed 'disciple whom Jesus loved' (cf. John XIII.23, XXI.7, 20; Anon *Alpost* 4).

2. Miðr gekt einn an aðrir
   ǫðlings frá píningu,
   svikbannandi, sunnu,
   snjallr, postolar allir,
   því drengr í styr strǫngum
   stótt þú hjá kvǫl dróttins
   blíð ok bragnings móðir
   byrstrandar grátandi.

Snjallr svikbannandi, einn gekt frá píningu ǫðlings sunnu miðr an allir aðrir postolar, þvít þú, drengr í strǫngum styr, ok grátandi blíð móðir bragnings byrstrandar stótt hjá kvǫl dróttins.

Courageous one who bans falsity [APOSTLE], you alone fled from the torment of the king of the sun [= God (= Christ)] less than all the other Apostles, for you, a valiant man in the hard battle, and the weeping gentle mother of the ruler of the wind-beach [SKY/HEAVEN > = God (= Christ) > = Mary] stood close by at the torture of the Lord.

Ms.: **649a**(47v) (*Jón⁴*).

Editions: *Skj* Kolbeinn Tumason, 1. *Jónsvísur* 2: AII, 37, BII, 46, *Skald* II, 29, *NN* §2560; *Jón⁴* 1874, 512, Bugge 1874, 935, *GBpB* 570n.

Context: See Introduction. — *Notes*: [All]: This st. and sts 3-4 refer to the scene described in S. John's gospel (John XIX.25-7): *Stabant autem iuxta crucem Iesu mater eius et soror matris eius Maria Cleopae et Maria Magdalene cum vidisset ergo Iesus matrem et discipulum stantem quem diligebat dicit matri suae mulier ecce filius tuus deinde dicit discipulo ecce mater tua et ex illa hora accepit eam discipulus in sua* 'Now there stood by the Cross of Jesus his mother, and his mother's sister, Mary of Cleophas, and Mary Magdalen. When Jesus therefore had seen his mother and the disciple whom he loved, he saith to his mother: "Woman, behold thy son". And after that, he saith to the disciple: "Behold thy mother". And from that hour, the disciple took her to his own'. — [5-8]: Although this *helmingr* contains two subjects (*þú* 'you' and *móðir* 'mother') the verb form *stótt* (2nd pers. sg. pret. indic. of *standa* 'to stand') is congruent with *þú*. This phenomenon may occur when the verb precedes subjects in differing persons: in such cases the verb agrees with the subject nearest to it (in this case *þú*, cf. *NS* §69).

3. Sjalfr kallaði sællar
    sólknarr*ar* þik harri
    son Máríe sær*ir*
    sundhyrs, í kvǫl bundinn.

    Ráð fal ræsir lýða
    risnu kendr á hendi,
    díks, áðr dauðann tœki,
    dagrennir, þér hennar.

Sjálfr harri sólknarr*ar* bundinn í kvǫl, kallaði þik son sællar Máríe, sær*ir* sundhyrs. Ræsir lýða, risnu kendr, fal hennar ráð ráð hendi þér, áðr dauðann tœki, díks dagrennir.

The lord of the sunship himself [SKY/HEAVEN > = God (= Christ)], bound in torment, called you the son of the blessed Mary, wounder of strait-fire [GOLD > GENEROUS MAN]. The impeller of peoples [= God (= Christ)], known for his munificence, placed her wellbeing in your hands before he took death, mover of the day of the ditch [(*lit.* 'day-mover of the ditch') GOLD > GENEROUS MAN].

Ms.: **649a**(47v) (*Jón⁴*). — *Readings*: [2] sólknarr*ar*: sólknarri 649a [3] sær*ir*: 'sęrar' 649a.

Editions: *Skj* Kolbeinn Tumason, 1. *Jónsvísur* 3: AII, 37, BII, 46, *Skald* II, 29; *Jón⁴* 1874, 512, Bugge 1874, 935, *GBpB*, 570n., Konráð Gíslason 1877, 20-1, 32-3.

Context: See Introduction. — *Notes*: [2] *harri sólknarrar* 'lord of the sun-ship [SKY/HEAVEN > = God (= Christ)]': The ms. reading is *sólknarri*, which could be interpreted as a nom. form meaning 'little ship of the sun' (the form *knarri* 'little ship' is attested as a diminutive of *knǫrr* 'ship', cf. *LP*: knarri; *Skj* AI, 333; Arn *Hryn* 1/2¹¹). However the subject of the sentence *Sjalfr ... bundinn* 'himself ... bound' is *harri* 'lord', referring to Christ. All eds agree that the form *sólknarri* is an error and emend it to a gen. form *sólknarra* (gen. sg. or pl. of -*knarri*, *Jón⁴* 1874, 935n., *GBpB*, 570n.; cf. Konráð Gíslason 1877, 20-1) or *sólknarrar* (gen. sg. of *knǫrr*, *Skj* B; *Skald*). The emended gen. form is regarded as the determinant in a kenning for Christ. Konráð Gíslason argues that a diminutive form *sólknarri* 'little ship of the sun' is not appropriate as a kenning for heaven (1877, 32) and suggests the emendation to *sólknarrar* (gen. sg. of *sólknǫrr*) adopted here. — [3-4] *særir sundhyrs* 'wounder of strait-fire [GOLD > GENEROUS MAN]': The ms. reading is 'sęrar', which Bugge normalises to *særar*. This would be a nom. pl. of *særir* 'sower' and the base-word of a conventional man-kenning. Such a pl. *særar sundhyrs* 'sowers of the strait-fire [GOLD > GENEROUS MEN]', would be a vocative addressing the audience of the poem. Konráð Gíslason argues that it is implausible that a statement addressed directly to John (cf. *þik* 'you' 3/2) should contain an expression addressed directly to the audience of the poem as well. Since all the other sts quoted are addressed to John, Konráð Gíslason regards 'sęrar' = (*særar*) as a scribal error and suggests emendation to the sg. *sæ*r*ir* 'sower': the kenning *særir sundhyrs* 'sower of the strait-fire [GOLD > GENEROUS MAN]' would then be a term addressed to John, as in the case of the synonymous kenning *díks dagrennir* 'mover of the day of the ditch [GOLD > GENEROUS MAN]' in 3/7-8. — [7] *áðr dauðann tæki* 'before he took death, died': *Skj* B and *Skald* omit the enclitic art. and normalise *dauðann* to *dauða* (acc. sg. of *dauði* 'death'). The use of the subj. after the conj. *áðr* is very common (*NS* §§301-2B, Anm., 304).

4. Kœnn, lé*zt þú hag hreinnar
    hǫfðingi, drótningar,
    hafs meðan hyrþǫll lifði,
    hugat blíðliga síðan.

Þér var hón, sem hárar
hildingr skipa vildi
(ykr lofar) éla þekju,
(ǫll þjóð) í stað móður.

Kœnn hǫfðingi, þú lé*zt hag hreinnar drótningar hugat blíðliga síðan, meðan hafs hyrþǫll lifði. Hón var í stað móður þér, sem hildingr hárar þekju éla vildi skipa; ǫll þjóð lofar ykr.

Wise chieftain, you let the circumstances of the pure queen be attended to kindly thereafter, as long as the fir sapling of the fire of the sea [(*lit*. 'sea's fire-fir sapling') GOLD > WOMAN = Mary] lived. She was in the position of a mother to you, as the warlord of the high thatch of snowstorms [SKY/HEAVEN > = God (= Christ)] wanted it arranged; all people praise you.

Ms.: **649a**(47v) (*Jón*⁴). — *Reading*: [1] lé*zt: 'leitz' 649a.

Editions: *Skj* Kolbeinn Tumason, 1. *Jónsvísur* 4: AII, 37, BII, 46; *Skald* II, 29; *Jón*⁴ 1874, 512; Bugge 1874, 935-6, *GBpB*, 570n.

Context: See Introduction. — *Notes*: [1, 2, 4] *þú lézt hag hreinnar drótningar hugat blíðliga síðan* 'you let the circumstances of the pure queen be attended to kindly thereafter': The ms. reading 'leitz' could be interpreted as the 2nd pers. sg. pret. indic. form of the verb *líta* 'to look', *leizt* 'looked' or as the corresponding m.v. form 'looked at yourself/for yourself'. Neither verb form makes sense in the passage at hand and all eds follow Bugge's emendation to *lézt* (= 2nd pers. sg. pret. indic. form of the verb *láta* 'let'; *Jón*⁴ 1874, 935). Bugge's emendation of *hugat* 'attended to' to *huggat* 'comforted' (*Jón*⁴ 1874, 935 n. 2) makes the l. too long by introducing a long plus a short syllable (= 2 syllables).

5. Frami gengr hátt, sás himna
    herteitir þér veitir,
    snardeilandi sólar
    sunds, á margar lundir.

Hárs á hvern veg meiri
hyrbjóðr, an kyn þjóðar,
Alda garðs, með orðum
yðra dýrð geti skýrða.

Frami, sás himna her teitir veitir þér, gengr hátt á margar lundir, snardeilandi sólar sunds. Hár Alda garðs hyrbjóðr [e]s meiri á hvern veg, an kyn þjóðar geti skýrða yðra dýrð með orðum.

That distinction which the gladdener of the host of the heavens [(*lit.* 'host-gladdener of the heavens') ANGELS > = God (= Christ)] grants you rises high in many ways, speedy distributer of the sun of the sound [GOLD > GENEROUS MAN]. The high offerer of the fire of the fence of Alden <island> [(*lit.* 'high fire-offerer of the Alden-fence') SEA > GOLD > GENEROUS MAN] is greater in every way than the family of people [MANKIND] are able to expound your glory with words.

Ms.: **649a**(47v) (*Jón⁴*). — *Reading*: [5] Hárs: 'hárr er' 649a.

Editions: *Skj* Kolbeinn Tumason, 1. *Jónsvísur* 5: AII, 37, BII, 46, *Skald* II, 29, *NN* §2165; *Jón⁴* 1874, 512, Bugge 1874, 936, *GBpB*, 570n.

Context: In *Jón⁴* 1874, 512 this st. is prefaced with the remark: *Nærr enda sins verks setr Ko*[*l*]*beinn þessa visu af guðligum veitzlum ok verðleikum sęls Johannis; hann segir sva* 'Near the end of his poem Kolbeinn places this st. about the divine gifts and merits of blessed John; he says as follows'. — *Notes*: [6-7] *hárs*: The ms. reading is 'háʀ er'. The reading 'háʀ' could be normalised to *hárr* 'hoary, grey-haired' (m. nom. sg.) or to *hár* 'high' (m. nom. sg.; <ʀ> appears in mss as a grapheme for [rr] or for [r], cf. Lindblad 1954, 73, 206-7). Since the adj. is part of an honorific term for S. John, all previous interpreters take 'háʀ' to be *hár* 'high'. The reading *er* is evidently the predicate in the main cl., the 3rd pers. sg. indic. of *vera* 'to be'. Since *hár er* produces a seven-syllable l., *Skj* B normalises to *hárs*. Kock (*NN* §2165) argues that it is implausible that John should be spoken of in the 3rd pers. in a sentence containing a subordinate cl. which addresses him in the 2nd pers. pl. (*yðra dýrð* 'your glory' 5/8) and in a st. whose first *helmingr* also addresses him in the 2nd pers. (*þér* 'to you' 5/2). He therefore emends the verb form to *est/ert* 'you are' (cf. the translation in Lange 1958b, 19). He indicates that the problem of the seven-syllable l. could be solved by the omission of the prep. *á*, which is not required by the syntax of the construction *á hvern veg* 'in every way'. — [7] *Alda*: Interpreted as an island-*heiti*, the gen. sg. of a Norw. island named Aldi, Alden in Søndfjord (cf. *LP*: *Aldi*); the 'fence of Aldi' (*garðr Alda*) designates the surrounding sea.

Anonymous, *Líknarbraut*

Edited by George S. Tate

Introduction

Líknarbraut 'The Way of Grace' (Anon *Líkn*) is an anonymous late C13th Icel. devotional *drápa* in *dróttkvætt* metre celebrating Christ's Passion and the virtues of the Cross. In the prologue (*upphaf*, sts 1-12), the poet prays for poetic inspiration ('sprinkle my mind's land with precious heavenly seed' 5/1-4), acknowledges sins of the tongue (he is *ungr* 'young' 2/7 and impetuous of speech), appeals to 'brothers and sisters' for supportive prayers (8/1-4), and explores the commingling of joy and sorrow that his subject evokes in him (9-10). St. 12 concerns the Nativity, and in the next st. the poet, as if present, offers Christ a *hátt stef* 'sublime refrain' as a gift as he begins the central 'narrative' refrain section (*stefjabálkr*, sts 13-29). The four-l. *stef* extolling the power of the Cross recurs in every fourth st. (13, 17, 21, 25, 29) as the poet depicts the Passion, Harrowing of Hell, Resurrection, and the appearance of the Cross at the Last Judgement. Sts 30-45 constitute an *adoratio crucis* 'adoration of the Cross' and draw heavily on that portion of Good Friday liturgy. The poet alludes to 'creeping to the Cross' (30/1), quotes the recurrent phrase *Popule meus* 'O my people' (*mín þjóð* 45/1) from the Reproaches, and borrows details from the Cross hymns of Venantius Fortunatus, *Pange lingua* and *Vexilla regis*, both used in the rite. Several sts (31-7) of this section are devoted to exegetical figures of the Cross (key, flower, ship, ladder, bridge, scales, and altar). Sts 46-52 contain the elements usually associated with the *slœmr* 'conclusion': the poet confesses his unworthiness, requests a blessing as a reward, and names the poem in the penultimate st. (51/4), as is done in his C12th models *Harmsól* and *Leiðarvísan* (Gamlkan *Has* and Anon *Leið*). The title is also given at the beginning in the right margin of the sole medieval ms., B (see below).

An oddity of *Líkn* is its apparently lopsided structure (*upphaf* 12 sts, *stefjabálkr* 17, *slœmr* 23), lacking the second *stef* 'refrain' one finds in other Christian *drápur*, including its models *Has* and *Leið*. A possible explanation for this is that the poet, by evoking in the *adoratio crucis* section (sts 30-45) the richly polyphonic texture of the liturgical rite — with its elaborately interwoven phrases (including the use of st. 8 of *Pange lingua* as a two-part refrain) — calls attention to its intricate patterns of recurrence through contrast, by omitting the *stef* in the corresponding section of the poem. Sts 30-45 would then function — as they seem to do — as the equivalent of a second *stefjamél* 'refrain section'. If so, the poem's structure is both more symmetrical — 12-33(17+16)-7 (like most Christian *drápur*, for instance, *Has* 20-25-20, *Leið* 12-21-12) — and based on symbolic numbers (see Tate 1978). The high frequency of *ár* '(year's) abundance' may support de Vries's suggestion (1964-7, II, 76) that the total number of sts (52) may represent the weeks of the year.

The poem gives evidence of the range of the anonymous poet's learning: earlier skaldic poetry, Icel. homilies (one of which, on the Cross, he follows closely in sts 38-41), and Lat. liturgy, hymns, and exegetical literature, such as a passage by Honorius Augustodunensis from which he draws the image of the Cross as a ladder whose side-poles represent 'twofold love' (34/1-4). The poet was probably a cleric (possibly a monk), and the poem's close connection to Good Friday liturgy suggests that it may originally have functioned, like ESk *Geisl* (1152/3), as a verse sermon. (On the literary milieu generally see Guðrún Nordal 2001.)

The dating of the poem is based on its borrowings from *Has* and *Leið* (later C12th), its influence on C14th *drápur* (most especially Árni Jónsson's *Guðmundardrápa*, Árni Gd^{IV} mid-C14th), on formal elements suggesting transition (reduction in kenning frequency, averaging 1.9 per st., 3 with none, 14 with only one), on linguistic features such as full rhyme of historical *œ* : *æ* in *brœðr*: *kvæði* (8/2), and on its iconographic and emotional concord with contemplative Franciscan Passion poetry of the late C13th and C14th (see Tate 1974, 28-33; Holtsmark 1965, 554).

The normalised text is based upon the sole medieval ms., AM 757 a 4° (B), c. 1400 (probably from northern Iceland), which has many lacunae and other defects. Most of the approximately 70 restorations are based upon an early C19th transcription, arranged in verses, by Jón Sigurðsson (and others), JS 399 a-b 4^{ox}, made when B was in a better condition than now; many of these restorations are supported by alliteration or internal rhyme. Lbs 444 4^{ox}, a transcription (including the notes) of 399a-b^x, with additional marginal annotations in preparation for Sveinbjörn Egilsson's 1844 edn, has also been consulted and is occasionally cited in the Notes. (Sveinbjörn Egilsson's printer's copy also exists as Lbs 1152 8^{ox}.)

Among Christian *drápur*, *Líkn* is unusual in having been twice set to music: in excerpts by Nystedt 1975 (*Nådvegen*) and in its entirety by Plagge 2000, both employing Norw. translations. (The poem was translated into English verse by Pilcher in 1954, first published in Barwell and Kennedy 1994, 47-59.)

Introduction adapted by permission from Tate 1986. At an earlier stage of this edn the ed. has benefitted from helpful comments by Roberta Frank, James W. Marchand, and Maureen Thomas.

1. Einn, lúk upp, sem ek bæni,   Þinn vil ek kross, sem kunnum,
   óðrann ok gef sanna   (Kristr styrki mik) dýrka
   mér, þú er* alls átt ærit,   (örr, sá er ýta firrir
   orðgnótt, himins dróttinn.   allri nauð ok dauða).

Himins dróttinn, þú er* einn átt ærit alls, lúk upp óðrann, sem ek bæni, ok gef mér sanna orðgnótt. Ek vil dýrka þinn kross, sem kunnum; Kristr styrki mik, örr, sá er firrir ýta allri nauð ok dauða.

Heaven's Lord [= God], you who alone possess a fullness of all, open up my poetry-house [BREAST], as I pray, and give me true word-abundance. I desire to glorify your Cross as [well as] we [I] can; may Christ strengthen me, the bountiful one, who removes men from all distress and death.

Mss: B(11r), 399a-b^x. — *Readings*: [1] Einn: '[...]inn' B, Ẹinn 399a-b^x [2] óðrann: óð*ar* rann *perceived abbrev. expanded* 399a-b^x [3] er*: ert B, 399a-b^x [6] Kristr: '[...]ristr' B, 399a-b^x.

Editions: Skj Anonyme digte og vers [XIII], C. 1. *Líknarbraut* 1: AII, 150, BII, 160, *Skald* II, 85; Sveinbjörn Egilsson 1844, 35, Rydberg 1907, 11, 47, Kock and Meissner 1931, I, 91, Tate 1974, 46.

Notes: [All]: The opening st. in which the poet appeals for divine inspiration in composing his poem, juxtaposes God's fullness *ærit alls* 'a fullness of all' (l. 3), and the poet's need as he pleads for the abundance *-gnótt* (l. 4) he lacks. — [1] *einn* 'one, alone': Restoration based upon 399a-b^x, supported by the need for vowel alliteration. Despite its presence in 399a-b^x, the 'E' may not actually have been legible to Jón Sigurðsson; as with the beginnings of other poems (except Anon *Heildr*) in B, space was left in the ms. for a possible rubricated capital which was never supplied. — [2] *óðrann* 'poetry-house [BREAST]': The kenning has typically been construed as [BREAST], the place of emotion or thought (thus *LP*: *rann*, also Meissner, 136-7; cf. *hugar rann* 'house of thought' 7/4), but in her analysis of C13th body-part kennings, Guðrún Nordal 2001, 250 considers it more likely to depict the mouth. — [3] *er**'who': All eds emend from ms. *ert*, an error (verb for rel. particle) following *þú*. — [6] *Kristr* 'Christ': The <k> is lost in a lacuna; required by alliteration and context. — [6] *styrk-: dýrk-*: This same full rhyme of short and long <y> occurs also in *Geisl* 7/4, 57/6, and *Heildr* 16/8; see also 13/8, 28/2 (*dýrð-: fyrð-*).

2. Víst má ek hræddr, *in*s hæsta   ár því at ek má stórum
   heið*s* algöfug*r*, beiða,   ungr hógsettrar tungu
   mér at munnshöfn dýra   frá afgerðum orða
   mærðteitr jöfurr veiti,   ofsjaldan vel halda.

Víst má ek hræddr beiða, at algöfug*r* mærðteitr jöfurr *in*s hæsta heið*s* veiti mér dýra munnshöfn, því at ungr má ek ofsjaldan halda ár orða vel frá stórum afgerðum hógsettrar tungu.

Surely I must, fearful, entreat that the completely noble, fame-glad prince of the highest clear-heaven [= God] grant me precious mouth-content [SPEECH], for, [being] young, I can all too seldom keep my oar of words [TONGUE] well from great offences of an easily-employed tongue.

Mss: **B**(11r), 399a-b[x]. — *Readings*: [1] ek: *so* 399a-b[x], '[...]k' B; ins: '[...]ss' B, 399a-b[x] [2] heiðs algöfugr: heiðr algöfugs B, 399a-b[x] [4] mærðteitr: *so* 399a-b[x], 'mêrd [...]eítr' B [7] orða: *so* 399a-b[x], '[...]a' B.

Editions: *Skj* Anonyme digte og vers [XIII], C. 1. *Líknarbraut* 2: AII, 150-1, BII, 160, *Skald* II, 85, *NN* §§1385, 1853B, 2584; Sveinbjörn Egilsson 1844, 35, Rydberg 1907, 11, 47, Tate 1974, 47.

Notes: [All]: The st.'s concern with sins of the tongue may be inspired by Jas. I.26 and III.5-10 as well as, in a monastic context, by ch. 6 of the Benedictine Rule and the Ambrosian hymn for prime, *Iam lucis orto sidere* 2/1: *linguam refrenans* 'bridling the tongue' (*AH* 51, 40 and *Ordo Nidr.*, 183-4, 242, 260, 264). With reference to the nautical imagery (below, and sts 33-4), see also the OIcel. ship allegory, where the tongue is likened to a rudder (rather than an oar): *Styret iarteiner tungu mannz, fyr þvi at stiórnen styrer skipeno sem tunga mannz styrer ǫllum mannenom til gopra hluta eþa illra ... Sva fyrerferr oc sá maþr ser, er illa styrer tungu sinne ... En ef han gæter væl tungu sinnar, þa styrer hann sér til himinrikis* 'The rudder signifies the tongue of man, because the rudder steers the ship just as the tongue of man steers all men (*sic* 'the whole man') to good or evil things ... Thus the man who poorly governs his tongue also perishes ... But if he governs his tongue well he then steers himself to heaven' (Larsson 1891, 246, glossed by Marchand 1976a, 244-7). — [2] *heiðs algöfugr* 'of clear-heaven ... completely noble': Despite Kock's effort (*NN* §1385) to maintain the ms. reading (*heiðr algöfugs*), there seems to be no way around the need to emend l. 2. Kock's construction depends upon 1) an otherwise unattested sense of *heiðr* 'glory' as *bistånd* 'assistance', 2) inverting the acc. and gen. objects in the idiom *at beiða e-n e-s* 'to ask someone for something', and 3) mixing weak and strong adjectives following the def. art. (*ins hæsta, göfugs*). Sveinbjörn Egilsson 1844, 35 n. (supported by Konráð Gíslason 1877, 23 n.) proposed *heiðtjalls* (i.e. *-tjalds* '-tent') for B's 'heiðr al'; so Rydberg 1907, 47 and *Skj* B. While this, with the end of l. 1, would be analogous to *ins hæsta hríðtjalds* in *Has* 28/1-2, a C12th *drápa* from which *Líkn* draws various details, it is unlikely that the poet would use exactly the same sky kenning twice (cf. *heiðtjalds* 25/4). A 'king of heaven'-kenning can be achieved less radically by emending *heiðr* to *heiðs* 'of the (highest) clear-heaven'. (An alternative would be *heiðrs* 'of (the highest) glory'; i.e. *rex summae gloriae*.) Emendation of *algöfugs* 'completely noble' to nom. *algöfugr* (*Skj* B *göfugr*), while less essential, seems justified to avoid apposition of weak and strong adjs following *ins* 'the', but also by the marginal appropriateness of *algöfugs* as a modifier of 'sky'. — [3] *munnshöfn* 'mouth-content/resource [SPEECH]': This is the only occurrence in poetry, but the cpd is also found in ON hagiographic prose (*Matheus saga, Þorláks saga in yngri*); cf. ODan. cognates *munnhæfþe, munnhæfth* (*Fritzner*: *munnshöfn* fig. 'mode of expression'; also *Meissner*, 436 'mouth-content' = 'speech'). Guðrún Nordal 2001, 251-2 proposes that the poet here 'construes a *nýgjǫrvingr* ..., calling the tongue *orða ár* ("oar of words") and the mouth *munnshǫfn* ("the harbour of the mouth"). Poetry is pushed out of the harbour through the strength of the poet who commands the oar'. This is an attractive reading in the abstract, and no doubt the *nýgjǫrving* is present, but 'harbour of the mouth' does not seem suitable in context as the direct object of *veiti* 'grant' (l. 4). (See the similar dual possibility with *orða ár* below.) — [4] *mærðteitr* 'fame-glad': Restoration of <t> based upon 399a-b^x, supported by *teit-* : *veit-* rhymes in *Geisl* 41/6 and Anon *Mdr* 27/4, which occasionally borrows from *Líkn*; cf. synonymous *mærðarblíðr* Mark *Eirdr* 4/5^{II}. — [5] *stórum* 'great': *Skj* B construes adverbially ('very'); Rydberg 1907, 47 and *NN* §2584, as here, with *afgerðum* 'offences'. — [5, 7] *ár orða* 'oar of words [TONGUE]': Restoration of 'orð' based upon 399a-b^x; <rð> confirmed by *skothending*. The tongue-kenning mixes oddly with the plain noun *tungu* 'tongue' (l. 7) in the same *helmingr*. Since *ár* can mean 'abundance' (from 'year's yield', Lat. *annona*) as well as 'oar', *orða ár* might also play off *orðgnótt* 'word-abundance' (1/4) in the previous st., in which case the poet would be contrasting his own surfeit of words – a sin of the tongue – with the true abundance of inspired words for which he has just prayed.

3. Hneig, er veitir vægðir allr týnumz ek ella,
vígrunni, miskunnar ítr, sem þú mátt líta,
hreina hugðubænum guð, nema gæzku saðrar
heyrn þína, guð, mínum; gipt þín of mér skíni.

Guð, er veitir vægðir vígrunni, hneig þína hreina heyrn miskunnar mínum hugðubænum; ella týnumz ek allr, sem þú, ítr guð, mátt líta, nema þín gipt saðrar gæzku skíni of mér.

God, [you] who grant mercies to the battle-bush [WARRIOR], incline your pure ear [*lit.* hearing] of mercy to my loving prayers; otherwise I am completely lost, as you, glorious God, can see, unless your gift of true grace shine upon me.

Mss: **B**(11r), 399a-b^x. — *Reading*: [8] of: yfir B, 399a-b^x.

Editions: *Skj* Anonyme digte og vers [XIII], C. 1. *Líknarbraut* 3: AII, 151, BII, 161, *Skald* II, 85, *NN* §3277B; Sveinbjörn Egilsson 1844, 35-6, Rydberg 1907, 11-12, 47, Tate 1974, 48.

Notes: [All]: The movement of the st., in which *guð* 'God' and the idea of mercy or grace appear in each *helmingr*, is from the aural image *heyrn* 'hearing' (l. 4) of the first half-st. to the visual *líta* 'see' (l. 6), *skíni* 'shine' (l. 8) of the second. Following upon the 'tongue's offences' in the previous st., it is as if sound now resolves in quietude. The final word *skíni* 'shine' anticipates the light imagery of the next st., in which the verb *skína* is repeated (4/2). — [2] *vígrunni* 'to the battle-bush [WARRIOR]': The source of the st.'s lone kenning may be HSt *Rst* 8/7^1 (C12th), the only other occurrence of *vígrunnr*, also rhymed with *kunn-*. — [2] *miskunnar* 'of mercy': *Apo koinu*; the gen. can go either with *vægðir* 'mercies' (so *Skj* B) or *heyrn* 'hearing', or even *guð* 'God'. Analogues to the first, a tautology, are found in the OIcel. Nativity homily *lícn miscuNar* 'grace of mercy' (*HómÍsl* 1993, 23v; *HómÍsl*

1872, 48) and in liturgical Lat. (*clementia misericordiae* 'mercy of compassion', Manz 1941, 112, no. 165). The second (*heyrn*), favoured by Rydberg 1907, 47, is also echoed in the liturgy (*aures clementiae, aures misericordiae* 'ears of mercy, compassion', Manz 1941, 80-1, nos 91-2) and in the late medieval Icel. *Rósa* 1/3-4 (probably influenced by *Líkn*): *hneig þu þitt enn helgi drottenn | heyrenda myskunnar eyra* 'Holy Lord, incline your listening ear of mercy' (*ÍM* I.2, 6). — [3] *hugðubænum* 'loving prayers': Lit. 'prayers of love, sincerity'. *Skj* B (followed by *Skald*) emends *hugðu* unnecessarily to *hugðum* (from adj. *hugaðr* 'minded, disposed, righteous'), assuming perhaps a missing nasal stroke. Sveinbjörn Egilsson 1844, 36 and Rydberg 1907, 47 follow B. *LP* (1860) translates *hugðu bænir* as *preces sincerae* 'sincere prayers'; cf. *CVC*: *hugð, hugða* 'love, interest, affection'; *hugðumaðr* 'intimate friend'. *Hugða* also occurs with a slightly different sense in 41/7.

4. Þrifgæðir, lát, þjóðar,   þat er misverka myrkrum,
   þíns anda mér skína   munar, hrindi, svá blindi
   ástarljós, sem ek æsti,   míns, ór mælsku túni,
   albjart í sal hjarta,   móðs vandliga hrjóði.

Þrifgæðir þjóðar lát albjart ástarljós þíns anda skína mér í hjarta sal, sem ek æsti, þat er hrjóði vandliga myrkrum misverka ór mælsku túni, hrindi svá blindi míns móðs munar.

Prosperity-endower of the people [= God (= Christ)], let the wholly radiant light of love of your spirit shine in my heart's hall [BREAST], as I entreat that which may clear away completely the darkness of misdeeds from my field of eloquence [BREAST], [and] so drive out the blindness of my despondent mind.

Mss: **B**(11r), 399a-b[x]. — *Readings*: [7] mælsku: 'mæ[...]ku' B, 'me[...]u' *corrected from* 'me[...]a' 399a-b[x].

Editions: *Skj* Anonyme digte og vers [XIII], C. 1. *Líknarbraut* 4: AII, 151, BII, 161, *Skald* II, 85, *NN* §1386; Sveinbjörn Egilsson 1844, 36. Rydberg 1907, 12, 48, Tate 1974, 49.

Notes: [All]: The plea for divine light to dispel the soul's darkness is a Psalmic motif (e.g. XVII.29 *Deus meus, illumina tenebras meas* 'O my God, enlighten my darkness') occurring also in liturgical hymns: e.g. Ambrose's *Aufer tenebras mentium* 'remove the darkness of our minds' and *Tu lux, refulge sensibus* 'You light, shine upon our senses' (*AH* 51, 28 and 50, 10 respectively; cf. *Brev. Nidr., fer iii ad mat.*, c.vi and *off. dieb. ad laud.*, a.viii). — [1] *Þrifgæðir* 'prosperity-endower [= God (= Christ)]': This *kenning* can refer to God or Christ. See the etymology, among early fragments of Icel. Christian learning, *Jesus þýdiz þrifgjafi eða græðari* 'Jesus means bounteous giver or healer' (Þorvaldur Bjarnason 1878, 152). *Þrifgjafi* also occurs in the OIcel. Annunciation homily (*HómÍsl* 1993, 63v; *HómÍsl* 1872, 140); cf. *þrifvaldr* 'prosperity-ruler' *Has* 22/2. — [5-8]: The words of the *helmingr* can be (and have been) arranged in a variety of ways, depending upon which of several meanings are assigned to *munar* (l. 6) and *móðs* (l. 8) and whether *ór mælsku túni* is taken with the first or second cl. — [5] *misverka* 'misdeeds': Either gen. pl. of *misverk* n. or gen. sg. of *misverki* m. (so *LP*); the only occurrence of either in poetry. — [6] *munar* (gen. sg.) 'mind': The range of possible meanings of *munr* ('mind, soul, desire, longing, will, love, object of love, difference' etc.) makes w.o. and translation somewhat uncertain; cf. *Has* 3/4 *munar grand* 'soul's injury'. — [6] *svá* 'thus': *Skj* B emends to rel. pron. *sem*; *NN* §1386 objects but translates *svá* as *liksom också* 'as well as', a meaning no ON dictionary gives. Since B is a C14th ms., it is possible that there is an underlying deleted *at* (*svá at* = *svá*: see *Introduction* 9. *Normalisation of Fourteenth-Century Poetry* II. B. 3.) — [7] *mælsku túni* '(hedged) enclosure, field of eloquence [BREAST]': In a note on the lacuna in B, 399a-b^x (Jón Sigurðsson) conjectures 'mĕlzku' (revised from 'mĕrðar'), which all eds have adopted. Guðrún Nordal 2001, 258 observes that *mælska* does not fit the typical pattern of determinants in chest-kennings and that it is 'probably closer to the point to interpret [*mælsku tún*] as mouth'. (Cf. *Meissner*, 136 who, while construing it as 'breast', acknowledges that it could by itself be a kenning for 'mouth'.) This suggestion seems however less probable with reference to the context. While *myrkrum misverka* 'darkness of misdeeds' (l. 5) could refer back to sins of the tongue in st. 2, it seems less likely that the poet is here praying to have his mouth cleansed than to have his heart purified. This is especially true because of the counterbalancing of two kennings – one in each *helmingr* – for the same locus. Surely it is the darkness now residing in his *mælsku tún* 'enclosure of eloquence [BREAST]' which he prays to have cleared away as light infuses his *sal hjarta* 'hall of the heart [BREAST]' (l. 4). The second element of the prayer, that the light clear away the *blindi móðs munar* 'blindness of despondent mind' (ll. 6, 8, 6), simply restates the entreaty of the first – that the darkness be driven from the poet's breast (the seat of the mind). (See Note on *lyndis láð* 'mind's land [BREAST]' at 5/3-4.) — [8] *móðs* (gen. sg. m.) 'despondent': Although construed here as adj. (following *Skj* B), *móðr* may also be taken as a noun: 'mind, soul, passion, anger, worry' (so *LP* (1860), Rydberg and *NN* §1386).

5. Dreifðu, láðs ok lofða ár svá at ávöxt færak,
    lífstýrir, mér dýru, alls kannandi, sannan,
    leyfðar *k*endr, í lyndis elsku kuðr, af yðru
    láð himnesku sáði, óþornuðu korni.

Lífstýrir láðs ok lofða, *k*endr leyfðar, dreifðu mér í lyndis láð dýru himnesku sáði, svá at færak ár, sannan ávöxt af yðru óþornuðu korni, kannandi alls, elsku kuðr.

Ruler of land and the life of men [(*lit.* 'life-ruler of land and men') = God], acknowledged in praise, sprinkle my mind's land [BREAST] with precious heavenly seed, so that I may bring forth an abundance, true fruit from your unwithered seed, tester of all [= God], renowned for love.

Mss: **B**(11r-v), 399a-b^x. — *Readings*: [3] *k*endr: '[...]dr' B, '[...]ndr' 399a-b^x [7] elsku: *so* 399a-b^x, 'elsk[...]' B [8] korni: 'ko[...]i' B, 'korn̨e' 399a-b^x.

Editions: *Skj* Anonyme digte og vers [XIII], C. 1. *Líknarbraut* 5: AII, 151, BII, 161, *Skald* II, 86; Sveinbjörn Egilsson 1844, 36, Rydberg 1907, 12, 48, Kock and Meissner 1931, I, 91, Tate 1974, 50.

Notes: [All]: The st.'s dominant image, that of God as sower whose seed is his word, depends upon such passages as I Cor. III.7-9 (God as husbandman who gives increase, cf. *ár* below) and the parable of the sower in Mark IV.3-20. See the OIcel. homily on ember-days (*HómÍsl* 1993, 16v-17r; *HómÍsl* 1872, 36): *sva scolom vér nu haɬda þa. at vér náem andlego áre í hiortom órom ... Þa keomr orþa sáp hans i hugscoz iorþ óra* 'thus we should now hold them [i.e. ember-days] that we might receive a spiritual abundance in our hearts ... Then the seed of his word will come into our mind's ground' (cf. *lyndis láð* below). With reference to this st., Paasche 1914a, 127, who noted this homiletic analogue, has also assembled relevant appellatives of Christ from church Lat.: e.g. *verus et summus agricola* 'true and supreme husbandman', *sator universi* 'sower of the universe', *auctor sprituialium fructum* 'creator of spiritual fruits'; cf. liturgical *agricola caelestis* 'celestial husbandman' (Manz 1941, 60, no. 34). — [1] *dreifðu* 'sprinkle you': One of only two instances in the poem (cf. *látattu* 6/5) of B's several suffixed 2nd pers. pronouns necessary for a six-syllable l. — [3] ken*dr* 'acknowledged, known': Restoration of 'ken' based upon Jón Sigurðsson's note in 399a-b[x], supported by an ascender of possible 'k' and an 'n' that was visible to Jón and to Rydberg 1907, 12; Jón's suggestion has been accepted by all eds. — [3-4] *lyndis láð* 'mind's land [BREAST]': According to Guðrún Nordal 2001, 258, 'the poetic imagery that supposes that the mind resides in the chest is dominant in chest-kennings in the thirteenth century', but already we find *vilja byrgi* 'enclosure of desire' in Þjóð *Yt* 4/2[1] (C10th); cf. *rann hugar* 'house of the mind' 7/4 and *tún hyggju* 'field of the mind' 40/3. — [5] *ár* '(year's) abundance': Cf. Lat. *annona* 'year's yield'. *Skj* B (cf. *LP*) and Kock and Meissner 1931, II, 10 construe *ár* as adv. 'soon, quickly', giving the sense *svát ár færak sanna ávöxt* 'so that I may bring forth early (i.e. promptly) true fruit'. Though this is possible, the frequency of *ár* as 'year' or 'year's abundance' in the poem, especially in kennings for God or Christ (10/2, 17/1, 20/5, 46/3, 47/3), together with the sowing imagery of the st., argues against it. A similar joint occurrence of *ár* and *ávöxtr* as synonyms is found in the ONorw. homily on the parable of the sower: *þa fec hann þar mikit ár ok margfaldan á-vöxt* 'then he received a great abundance and manifold yield' (*HómNo*, 70). — [6] *kannandi alls* 'tester of all [= God]': On the idea of God as tester, cf. *reynir munka* 'tester of monks' Anon *Hafg* 1[IV], possibly the earliest of all ON Christian kennings; see Lange 1958a, 59 on the surprise the kenning must have evoked, even though *reynir* had a long history in pagan kennings. — [7] *elsku kuðr* 'renowned for love': Restoration of 'u' based upon 399a-b[x] and occurrence of *elsku kuðr* in *Has* 16/5, one of the chief models for *Líkn*; cf. *elsku kunnr*, Arngr *Gd* 32/2[IV]. — [8] *korni* 'seed': Restoration based upon 399a-b[x] and *aðalhending*.

6. Þann, er af mínum munni S... látattu sveitir,
margr til andar bjargar siðskjótr, af því hljóta
sér megi randa rýrir gumna kind at grandi,
röðuls framkvæmd*an* öðlaz. guð minn, laga þinna.

Þann er margr rýrir randa röðuls megi öðlaz sér til andar bjargar framkvæmd*an* af mínum munni. Minn guð, siðskjótr, látattu sveitir hljóta af því s... þinna laga, at grandi kind gumna.

Such [fruit] that many a destroyer of shields' sun [SWORDS > WARRIOR] might gain benefit from for his soul's salvation [produced] from my mouth. My God, quick to promote virtue, let not men suffer from it [a perversion?] of your laws, to the injury of the race of men.

Mss: **B**(11v), 399a-b[x]. — *Readings*: [4] framkvæmd*an*: framkvæmd B, 399a-b[x]; öðlaz: *so* 399a-b[x], 'ðdl[...]z' B [5] S...: , 's[...]' B, 399a-b[x] [7] at grandi: 'at gra[...]e' B, 'at grande̦' *corrected from* 'af grande̦' 399a-b[x] [8] þinna: 'þ[...]a' B, 'þi̯nna̯' 399a-b[x].

Editions: *Skj* Anonyme digte og vers [XIII], C. 1. *Líknarbraut* 6: AII, 151, BII, 161, *Skald* II, 86, *NN* §§1387-8; Sveinbjörn Egilsson 1844, 36-7, Rydberg 1907, 12, 48, Tate 1974, 51.

Notes: [1] *þann* 'such [fruit]': The demonstrative pron. refers back to *ávöxt* 'fruit' (5/5). Snorri Sturluson calls such a concatenation of sts *langlokum* 'with late conclusions' or 'with long enclosings' (*SnE* 1999, 10-11, 124 and cf. SnSt *Ht* 14-15[III]). — [4] *framkvæmd*an: As it stands, the l. is unmetrical and must have had an unstressed syllable after -*kvæmd*. For this reason, *Skj* B emends to *framkvæmdan* 'obtained, produced' (cf. *LP*: *framkvæmðr*, adj. only occurrence). *Skald* follows Sveinbjörn Egilsson, giving *framkvæmð* 'furtherance (*bátnað*)', and adds an enclitic *of* before *ǫðlaz* (cf. *NN* §1387); this is unmetrical. — [4] *öðlaz*: Restoration of 'a' based upon 399a-b[x]. — [5] *s...*: Lacuna in B; a minim follows 's', with perhaps the tip of a second (suggesting possible 'u'). Judging from the space, the missing word is probably monosyllabic but could be disyllabic, in which case the suffixed pron. of *látattu* 'let not' would be dropped. (A suffixed 2nd pers. pron. is otherwise only metrically necessary in 5/1.) Sveinbjörn Egilsson conjectures *svík*, a nominal form of *svíkja* 'to betray'; cf. Rydberg *sveik* (or *sút* 'sorrow, affliction'). *Skj* B does not try to supply the missing letters, but speculates that the damaged word might mean 'punishment'. *Skald* (cf. *NN* §1388) posits *svarf* (from *svarfa* [*sverfa*?] 'to bring something out of its proper position', i.e., here, a wrenching or twisting of the law). This proposal seems reasonable; hence 'perversion'. As Kock (*Skald*) observes, the st. juxtaposes the good effects of inspired poetry (in the first *helmingr*) with the possible evil effects (in the second) if the poet's prayer for divine help goes unanswered. — [6] *af því* 'from it, on its account': Lacks a noun antecedent; *kvæði* 'poem' is understood.

7. Hauðrs, veit helgar ræður,   Öll eru orð þín gulli,
    hildingr, ok kenningar,   alhreinn, ok gimsteinum
    mána hvéls, ór mínu,   vísi sæll, ór völlum,
    mannvandr, hugar ranni.   vegs, bjartari ok fegri.

Hildingr hauðrs mána hvéls, mannvandr, veit helgar ræður ok kenningar ór mínu ranni hugar. Alhreinn, sæll vísi vegs, öll þín orð eru bjartari ok fegri gulli ok gimsteinum ór völlum.

King of the land of the moon's wheel [MOON > SKY/HEAVEN > = God], exacting of man, direct holy discourses and doctrines out of my house of thought [BREAST]. Completely pure, blessed prince of glory, all your words are brighter and fairer than gold and gems from the fields.

Mss: **B**(11v), 399a-b[x]. — *Reading*: [3] hvéls: 'huols' 399a-b[x].

Editions: *Skj* Anonyme digte og vers [XIII], C. 1. *Líknarbraut* 7: AII, 151, BII, 160-17, *Skald* II, 86, *NN* §3278; Sveinbjörn Egilsson 1844, 37, Rydberg 1907, 12, 48, Tate 1974, 52.

Notes: [3] *mána hvéls* 'of the moon's wheel': A tautological kenning in which the determinant contains the same concept as its referent: 'moon's wheel [MOON]'. The idea of a heavenly body as wheel may depend in part upon the celestial wheels in Ezek. I and X; cf. the common Lat. phrase *solis rota* 'wheel of the sun' and *Has* 36/7 *sunnu hvéls* 'of the sun's wheel'. — [4] *mannvandr* 'exacting of man': *Vandr* has a range of meanings, including 'difficult, painstaking, zealous, chosen'. In this context, the cpd suggests both 'zealous or painstaking on man's behalf' and 'exacting of man', i.e. dissatisfied until human beings become what they should become; cf. *hirðvandr* (of Christ) 'careful in selecting his following' Anon *Pl* 7/8. — [7] *ór völlum* 'from the fields': Sveinbjörn Egilsson, followed by Rydberg, emends to *gjørvöllum* 'all', adj. modifying *gimsteinum* 'gems'; *Skj* B and *Skald* emend to *ok vellum* 'and (than) golden things' (i.e. pl. redundancy with *gulli*). But the ms. reading makes sense if the poet is implicitly contrasting *earthly* riches (extracted from the ground) with the heavenly riches alluded to in such biblical passages as Jer. XLI.8 *quia habemus thesauros in agro* 'for we have treasures in the field' and Matt. XIII.44 in which the kingdom of heaven is likened to a *thesauro abscondito in agro* 'treasure hidden in a field'. — [7, 8] *sæll vísi vegs* 'blessed prince of glory': Cf. Ps. XXIII.10 *rex gloriae* 'king of glory', with further liturgical instances in Manz 1941, 424, no. 854; as a kenning type, see Meissner, 371. *NN* §3278 rejects *LP*'s suggestion of possible tmesis (*LP*: *vegssæll* 'blessed with glory'). — [8, 5, 6] *bjartari ok fegri ... gulli ok gimsteinum* 'brighter and fairer than gold or gems': Cf. *gimsteinum fegra* 'fairer than gems' 36/2, of Christ as the 'price of the world' and Ps. XVIII.11 *desiderabilia super aurum et lapidum pretiosum multum* 'more to be desired than gold or many precious gems'.

8. Beiðandi kveð ek bæði   vizku stærðr at virðiz
    bræðr ok systr at kvæði;   veðrskríns jöfurr mínum
    öll veiti þér ítran   — nýtr er, n*á*ð sem heitir —
    yðarn tænað mér bæna,   nálægr vera málum.

Beiðandi kveð ek bæði bræðr ok systr at kvæði; veiti þér öll mér yðarn ítran tænað bæna, at jöfurr veðrskríns, vizku stærðr, virðiz vera nálægr mínum málum; nýtr er, sem heitir n*á*ð.

Entreating, I summon both brothers and sisters to my poem; may you all grant me your excellent help of prayers, that the prince of the storm-shrine [HEAVEN > = God], very great in wisdom, might deign to be close to my utterances; potent is [he] who promises grace.

Mss: **B**(11v), 399a-b^x. — *Readings*: [5] stærðr: 's[...]dr' B, 'stir̨dr' 399a-b^x [6] veðrskríns: *so* 399a-b^x, 'v[...]d[...]skrins' B [7] n*á*ð sem: nauð sem B, 399a-b^x.

Editions: *Skj* Anonyme digte og vers [XIII], C. 1. *Líknarbraut* 8: AII, 152, BII, 162, *Skald* II, 86, *NN* §1389; Sveinbjörn Egilsson 1844, 37, Rydberg 1907, 12-13, 48, Tate 1974, 53.

Notes: [1-2] *bæði brœðr ok systr at kvæði* 'both brothers and sisters to my poem': Metrically the first couplet is unusual on two grounds: the *runhenda*-like end-rhyme of *bæði* and *kvæði*, and *aðalhending* of historical <œ> (*brœðr* < *bróðir*) and <æ> (*kvæði*) in l. 2. Troubled by these features, and noting that in all other instances the poem is consistent in matching historical <œ>-rhymes (3 times, including *tænað*: *bæna* (l. 4)) and <æ>-rhymes (8 times), Konráð Gíslason 1869, 146 suggested emending *kvæði* to *frœði* 'learning, history', which Rydberg adopts and *Skj* B cites as an alternative in the prose arrangement. Even though the *aðalhending* here is anomalous, emendation is unnecessary. By C13th, the distinction in ligatures was lost in Iceland; <œ> was absorbed into <æ> (Halldór Halldórsson 1950, 47; cf. *CVC*: *æ*). B does not differentiate, using <ê> for both. Addressing a congregation as 'brothers and sisters' is common in homilies (e.g. *HómÍsl* 1993, 4v, 22r, 40r; *HómÍsl* 1872, 10, 45, 87); cf. *systkyn* 'brothers and sisters' 46/7. — [5] *stærðr* 'increased, very great': B 's[...]dr'; 399a-b^x *stirðr* 'stiff', but in a n. possibly *stirðum* even though the final 'r' is clear. The 't' was visible at the time of the 399a-b^x transcription; a remnant of a hook, suggesting 'ê' or 'ð', can still be seen; and *skothending* with *virð*- requires <r> before <ð>. In a marginal note to 444^x, Sveinbjörn Egilsson first suggested *skýrðr* 'made clear' (so *Skj* B), but crossed it out and replaced it with *stærðr*, which he employs in his edn (1844, 37); so also Rydberg 1907, 48 and *Skald* (cf. *NN* §1389). In poetry *stærðr* often functions as an intensive of *stórr* 'great', i.e. 'very great' (cf. *afli stærðr* 'very strong' Ólhv *Hryn* 12/1^{II} and *prekstærðr* 'very powerful' Bjbp *Jóms* 34/5^I, Sturl *Hrafn* 12/5^{II}), and this sense seems appropriate here. — [6] *veðrskríns* 'of the storm-shrine [HEAVEN]': Restoration based on 399a-b^x. Here and at 25/2, 31/6, and 48/4, -*skrín* has been translated with its cognate 'shrine', resonant with holy connotation (so also *LP*: *skrín*; *CVC*; *Meissner*, 378: 'Schrein', and Attwood 1996b, 229-30), recognising that its more limited sense is 'casket' (Guðrún Nordal 2001, 294, 381). On God as keeper of the winds, see Jer. XLIX.36. — [7] *n*á*ð* 'grace': B, 399a-b^x *nauð*.

Sveinbjörn Egilsson emends to *náð* 'grace', adopted by Rydberg and here. Salvaging ms. *nauð* 'need' would require a stretched meaning of *heita* – 'useful is he (i.e. the poet) who names (i.e. points out)/promises need' – but this is not very satisfactory. *Skj* B (followed by *Skald*), having emended ms. *nauð sem* to *nauðsyn* 'necessity' construes *er nauðsyn heitir* to mean 'as necessity demands', but no ON dictionary gives 'demand' as a meaning for *heita*. (Despite this emendation in *Skj* B, *LP* under *nýtr* has *nýtr es nǫð sem heitir*, i.e., as here, 'useful, potent is he who promises grace'.) In its theological sense, *náð* 'grace' (otherwise 'rest, peace', both of which could also work here) appears rather late in Icel. *CVC* dates it to C14th, but *Fritzner* gives some C13th instances. If the emendation is correct, this would be the earliest such use in poetry; cf. Anon *Lil* 12/4, Kálf *Kátr* 48/6, EGils *Guðkv* 28/7[IV], Árni *Gd* 41/4[IV], and Anon *Vitn* 14/4 (*nýtar náðir*).

9. Hróðr stofna ek h*ei*ðar   *ok* mun árum þykkja
    hjálmspennanda þenna   eggmóts, of hvárttveggja
    bæði hryggr ok blíðan   vísi ljóss ef vissi,
    bjartr ok glaðr í hjarta,   vera sök til þ*ess* nökkur.

Bæði hryggr ok bjartr ok glaðr í hjarta stofna ek þenna blíðan hróðr heiðar hjálmspennanda, *ok* mun þykkja árum eggmóts vera nökkur sök til *þess*, ef ljóss vísi vissi of hvárttveggja.

Both sorrowful and bright and glad at heart, I begin this joyful encomium for him who spans the heath's helmet [(*lit.* 'helmet-spanner of the heath') SKY/HEAVEN > = God], and it will seem to messengers of the edge-meeting [BATTLE > WARRIORS] that there is some cause for this, if a bright prince might know of both [i.e. sorrow and joy].

Mss: **B**(11v), 399a-b[x]. — *Readings*: [1] *heið*ar: '[...]dar' B, 'h[...]ðar' 399a-b[x] [3] *blíðan*: *bliðr* 399a-b[x] [5] *ok*: '[...]' B, 399a-b[x] [8] *þess*: '[...]' B, 'þ[...]' 399a-b[x].

Editions: *Skj* Anonyme digte og vers [XIII], C. 1. *Líknarbraut* 9: AII, 152, BII, 162, *Skald* II, 86, *NN* §§1390-1; Sveinbjörn Egilsson 1844, 37-8, Rydberg 1907, 13, 48, Tate 1974, 54.

Notes: [1] *stofna* 'to institute, begin': Used with respect to beginning a poem also in RvHbreiðm *Hl* 43/2[III] (C12th). — [1] *heiðar* 'of the heath': Restoration based in part upon <h> in 399a-b[x] (required also by alliteration); *heiðar* suggested by Sveinbjörn Egilsson accepted by all subsequent eds. — [3-4]: The second couplet has been subject to various readings and emendations. — [3] *blíðan* 'joyful': 399a-b[x] and all previous eds, except Rydberg (1907, 13 and 48), read the superscript <n> (for *-an*, i.e. acc. m. adj.; cf. *æztan* 13/7, *sáran* 16/2) as an 'r/er'-abbreviation, i.e. *blíðr* or (so *Skald*) *blíðir*. To avoid having the l. then end with a stressed syllable (*blíðr*), Sveinbjörn Egilsson, followed by Konráð Gíslason (in Konráð Gíslason and Eiríkur Jónsson 1875-89, II.1, 30) and *Skj* B, transposes to *blíðr ok hryggr bæði*, thus allowing the l. to end with a trochee. Konráð Gíslason and *Skj* B also add a second *ok* (between *hryggr* and *bæði*) to give the l. six syllables. *NN* §1390 (cf. *Skald*), choosing *blíðir* (construed as an otherwise unattested m. noun 'joyful one') over *blíðr*, maintains the ms. word order, which allows six syllables and a final trochee. Sensing the need for contrasting pairs, Konráð Gíslason also emends *glaðr* 'glad' (l. 4) to *myrkr* 'dark' (i.e. *blíðr ok hryggr | bjartr ok myrkr* 'joyful and sorrowful, bright and dark'); *Skj* B follows this thinking but prefers *dapr* 'downcast'. Although the symmetry is appealing, the point seems to be that the joy (*bjartr ok glaðr* 'bright/happy and glad' and *blíðan hróðr* 'joyful encomium') outweighs the sorrow, though the subject of the Crucifixion causes the poet to experience both (cf. Árni Gd 1/2^{IV} *dyggur ok bjartur í mínu hjarta*, amplified in 24/5-8). — [4] *bæði* 'both': Although technically only relating two elements, *bæði* can also introduce an extended series (here *hryggr ... ok bjartr ok glaðr* (ll. 3-4); see *Fritzner: bæði* n. pl. — [5] *ok*: Restoration proposed by Sveinbjörn Egilsson adopted by all subsequent eds; the <k> is supported by *skothending* and the <o> by the need for an alliterating vowel. — [6] *of hvárttveggja* 'of both': *Of*, prep. (= *um*, i.e. *vita um e-t* 'to know about something'); *hvárttveggja* 'both, each of two' taken to refer back to the joy and sorrow of the first *helmingr*. — [7] *ljóss* 'bright': Adj. *Skj* B construes as gen. sg. of *ljós* 'light', taking it as base-word in a sword-kenning *eggmóts ljós* 'light of edge-meeting [BATTLE > SWORD]' (ll. 7, 6) (so also Guðrún Nordal 2001, 293). *Skj* B further emends *vísi* 'prince' (l. 7) to *vísum* 'wise', agreeing with dat. pl. *árum* 'messengers, men'. Sveinbjörn Egilsson followed by Rydberg forms a cpd *vísiljós(s)*, defined in *LP* (1860) as *ignis praenuntiativus* 'announcing fire' (from *vísa* 'to show, demonstrate'), again as a base-word in a sword-kenning. Both of these readings have the advantage of dispensing with the somewhat awkward shift from pl. *árum* to sg. *vísi*, both referring to the same unspecified person, but necessity of emendation in the one and the somewhat unlikely compound *vísiljós* in the other make both undesirable. The present reading favours that of Kock (*NN* §1391) who follows the ms.; the only difference is that he translates *vísi ljóss* as *förståndig hövding* 'intelligent, wise chieftain' whereas the adj. usually refers to physical appearance. *Vísi* 'prince' is construed here to have generalised reference, 'a person'. — [8] *til þess* 'for this': Restoration proposed by Sveinbjörn Egilsson and adopted by all subsequent eds; the <þ> was legible to Jón Sigurðsson in 399a-b^x, and there is no space in B for further characters, hence the standard abbreviation for *þess*, made more sure by the preceding *til*.

10. Því ber ek angr, at engu   Þó gleðr enn sem aðra
     árs launa ek sárar   oss, sú er hlauz af krossi
     skírs, sem skyldugt væri,   lýð ok lofðungs dauða,
     skilfingi píningar.   líkn dýr, himinríkis.

Því ber ek angr, at ek launa engu, sem væri skyldugt, skilfingi skírs árs sárar píningar. Þó gleðr enn oss sem aðra dýr líkn, sú er hlauz lýð af krossi ok dauða lofðungs himinríkis.

On this account I bear sorrow, that I requite not at all, as would be due, the king of bright abundance [= God (= Christ)] for his sore torments. Yet there still gladdens us [me] as [well as] others precious grace, which was allotted to people from the Cross and from the death of the king of heaven's kingdom [= God (= Christ)].

Mss: **B**(11v), 399a-bˣ. — *Readings*: [5] gleðr: *so* 399a-bˣ, 'gl[...]dr' B   [7] lofðungs: *so* 399a-bˣ, 'löfdunngs' B.

Editions: *Skj* Anonyme digte og vers [XIII], C. 1. *Líknarbraut* 10: AII, 152, BII, 162-3, *Skald* II, 86, *NN* §2327; Sveinbjörn Egilsson 1844, 38, Rydberg 1907, 13, 48, Tate 1974, 55.

Notes: [All]: The st. explains the poet's ambivalent feelings of sorrow and joy introduced in st. 9. — [2] *ek launa* 'I requite': *Skj* B emends to *launum vér*, apparently to avoid the possibility of elision and for agreement with *oss* 'us'; *NN* §2327 objects, and indeed 1st pers. sg. and pl. regularly alternate in skaldic poetry, especially with reference to the poet. — [3, 2, 4] *skilfingi skírs árs* (dat.) 'king of bright abundance [= God (= Christ)]': This is the poem's first of several uses of *ár* in a kenning for God or Christ; cf. 17/1 *árstillir* 'instituter of abundance', 20/5 *árveitir* 'abundance giver', 46/2-3 *árs öðlingr* 'prince of year's abundance', 47/3 *árs eflir* 'strengthener of year's abundance'. In each of these, either the temporal sense 'year' or the beneficent concept of '(year's) abundance' (cf. Lat. *annona*) accords with the divine referent, as creator of time or as giver of bounty and good fortune. Such kennings only occur in *Líkn*, and the concentration of them, together with other instances of the word (see Notes to 5/5 and possibly 2/5), may support de Vries's speculation (1964-7, II, 76) that the overall number of sts is symbolic of the fifty-two weeks of the year. Snorri Sturluson (*SnE* 1931, 184; *SnE* 1998, I, 103) defines *skilfingr* 'king, prince' (l. 4) as a descendent of the legendary warrior king *Skelfir*, cf. OE *scylfingas*. Used of Christ or God only here, the *heiti* also occurs in *Geisl* 13/3 of S. Óláfr. — [6] *af krossi* 'from the Cross': The prep. can also mean 'by means of'; as in st. 39 and possibly 1/5-8 the Cross may be construed here as instrumental. — [6, 8, 6] *dýr líkn, sú er hlauz lýð* 'precious grace which was allotted to mankind': Cf. *hlaut* and *líkn* in *Has* 24/1-4. Rydberg 1907, 48 (cf. lxii) emends *lýð* '(common) people, mankind' (l. 7) to acc. pl. *lýða*, taken in conjunction with *sem aðra* (l. 5) as object of *gleðr*, i.e. 'which gladdens us as well as other people'.

11. Kosti alls af ástum
— einsætt er þat — hrein*um*
(magn stýri því) meira
maðr hverr (svika þverri*s*);

þvít margfalda mildi,
minn lausnari, þína
hverja stund at höndum
hlífrunnum lætr svífa.

Hverr maðr kosti alls meira af hrein*um* ástum; þat er einsætt; magn þverri*s* svika stýri því; þvít, minn lausnari, lætr þína margfalda mildi svífa hverja stund at höndum hlífrunnum.

Let each man strive all the more out of pure loves; that is the only choice; may the power of the diminisher of falsehoods [VIRTUOUS RULER = Christ] govern it; because, my Saviour, you allow your manifold mercy to glide every hour into the hands of shield-bushes [WARRIORS].

Mss: **B**(11v), 399a-b˟. — *Readings*: [1] ástum: ástar 399a-b˟ [2] einsætt: 'eíns(e)t'(?) B, einsæt 399a-b˟; hrein*um*: hreinan B, 399a-b˟ [4] þverris: 'þu[...]e' B, 'þuerre' 399a-b˟ [5] mildi: '[...]llde' B, 'ṃịḷḍe' 399a-b˟.

Editions: *Skj* Anonyme digte og vers [XIII], C. 1. *Líknarbraut* 11: AII, 152, BII, 163, *Skald* II, 86; Sveinbjörn Egilsson 1844, 38, Rydberg 1907, 13, 48, Tate 1974, 56.

Notes: [All]: At 11v l. 13 of ms. B *full vel* 'very well' appears as a marginal comment in a later hand. — [1-4]: The first *helmingr* presents difficulties, and none of the several possibilities is fully satisfactory. Sveinbjörn Egilsson and Rydberg maintain the ms. readings of *hreinan* (l. 2) and *þverri* (l. 4); Sveinbjörn also emends *af* (l. 1) to *of* and reads *ástar* for ms. *ástum* (l. 1). His arrangement, given in *LP* (1860): *kosta*, is *hverr maðr kosti alls meira* (= *öllu fremr*) *ástar of hreinan svíka þverri*, which, using a sense of *kosta* otherwise unattested, he translates loosely as 'let each man show love (*amorem erga quem exhibere, aliquem amare*) all the more for the pure diminisher of falsehoods'. Without emendation, Rydberg construes as follows: *hverr maðr kosti hreinan svíka þverri alls meira af ástum — þat er einsætt — magn stýri því* 'let each man prove/cost (?) the pure diminisher of falsehoods all the more out of love(s) — that is the only choice — may might govern it (?)'. The crux is the verb *kosta* (related to *kjósa* 'to choose'). In the meaning 'to try, put to the test' it takes a gen. object (or inf. 'to try to'); if 'to cost' or 'defray expenses' it takes acc. 'Let each man cost Christ all the more out of love' make no sense. If, however, an acc. object could work for 'try, prove', there would be a good biblical analogue in Mal. III.10 in which the Lord invites his people to try him (*probate me*) to see if he will not bless them abundantly. Another issue is whether *stýri* (l. 3) could be, rather than subj. of *stýra* 'to rule, govern', the acc. of *stýrir* in a Christ-kenning *magnstýrir* 'might-ruler' (or even *magnstýrir alls* 'might-ruler of all/the universe' (ll. 3,1)); cf. *lífstýrir* 'life-ruler' 5/2, *himinstýrir* 'ruler of heaven' 38/4, and *vegstýrir* 'glory-ruler' *Has* 59/6. Assuming, again, an acc. object of *kosta* and taking *magnstýri* in apposition to *svíka þverri* (l. 4), this would give *hverr maðr kosti því meira hreinan magnstýri alls, svíka þverri, af ástum — þat er einsætt* 'let each man the more prove the pure might-ruler of all, the diminisher of falsehoods, out of loves — that is the only choice'. Not having found another attestation of *kosta* 'try, prove' with acc. object, however, this ed. reluctantly follows *Skj* B and *Skald* in emending ms. *hreinan* to *hreinum* and *þverri* to gen. *þverris* and in construing the *helmingr* with the w.o. above. — [1] *ástum* 'loves': The pl. may result from the skaldic practice of occasionally substituting pl. for sg. (or vice versa) or might allude to the two loves (of God and of neighbour) in Matt. XX.37-9; cf. *tvennrar ástar* 'of twofold love' in 34/3. — [2] *hreinum* 'pure': *Skj* B and *Skald* emend from ms. *hreinan* for agreement with *ástum*. — [4] *þverris svika* 'diminisher of falsehoods [VIRTUOUS RULER = Christ]': Restoration of 'err' based upon 399a-b˟, supported by traces of the missing letters around the lacuna and by *aðalhending*. *Skj* B, followed by *Skald*, emends ms. acc. (or dat.) to gen. *þverris*. Cf. *angrþverrir* 'grief-diminisher' (of the Holy Ghost) *Heildr* 15/2 and *þverrir flærðar* 'diminisher of falsehood' *Pl* 7/3 (both C12th). — [5] *mildi* 'mercy, tenderness': Restoration based upon 399a-b˟, supported by alliteration. The noun occurs again in 44/5;

an important theme of the poem is that of Christ's tender mercy. — [6] *minn* : *pína*: The short/long rhyme *i* : *í* also occurs at 47/2 (*píns* : *inna*) and 52/2 (*minn* : *skína*).

12. Sá * baztr frá mey mæztri
mildingr beraz vildi
heiða tjalds ok holdi
hjálmprýddan sik skrýddi;
en nauð á sik *síðan*
sjálfráði tók dáða
víst fyr vára löstu
vísi sjálfr með píslum.

Sá * baztr mildingr heiða tjalds vildi beraz frá mæztri mey ok skrýddi sik hjálmprýddan holdi; en *síðan* tók vísi sjálfr, sjálfráði dáða, nauð á sik með píslum, víst fyr vára löstu.

The best prince of heaths' tent [SKY/HEAVEN > = God] willed to be born from a most precious maiden and clothed himself, helmet-adorned, with flesh; and later the prince himself, independently with regard to his deeds, took distress upon himself with torments, certainly for our errors.

Mss: **B**(11v), 399a-b^x. — *Readings*: [1] Sá * baztr: Sá er baztr B, 399a-b^x; mæztri: 'mez[...]' B, 'ṃě̈ztri' 399a-b^x [2] mildingr: '[...]lldin[...]' B, 'ṃilldingr' 399a-b^x [5] sik *síðan*: 'si[...]' B, 'ṣịḳ s[...]' 399a-b^x.

Editions: *Skj* Anonyme digte og vers [XIII], C. 1. *Líknarbraut* 12: AII, 152, BII, 163, *Skald* II, 86; Sveinbjörn Egilsson 1844, 38-9, Rydberg 1907, 13, 49, Tate 1974, 57.

Notes: [1-2]: The first couplet echoes descriptions of the Nativity in the poet's two chief C12th models: *Leið* 23/3-4 and *Has* 19/1-4. — [1] *sá*: Ms. 'Sá er'; the relative particle *er* as pron. is problematic, and this ed. follows *Skj* B and *Skald* in omitting it. A scribal error seems possible both because of the infrequency of *sá* + strong adj. + noun constructions and because of recent occurrences of *sá er* (1/7) and *sú er* (10/6). Sveinbjörn Egilsson and Rydberg retain *er*, but this is problematic since it requires deferring the relative particle syntactically ('The best prince ... *who* willed to be born') rather than keeping it contiguous with *sá* (i.e. 'That one who'). Such postponement would not allow *Sá er* to be cliticised and would thus produce a seventh syllable. Then, too, it would seem odd, construing *ok* as 'also' (or 'in addition'), to say 'The best prince ... who willed to be born ... *also* took on flesh'. — [2] *mildingr* 'prince, generous ruler': Restoration based upon 399a-b^x, confirmed in part by alliteration and *aðalhending*. — [3] *heiða tjalds* 'of heaths' tent [SKY/HEAVEN]': This is the poem's first use of *tjald* 'tent' in a heaven-kenning extended as a *tvíkennt* kenning for God or Christ; cf. 24/5-7 *fróns tjald* 'earth's tent', 25/4 *heiðtjald* 'heath-tent', 50/8 *veðra tjald* 'winds' canopy'. The greatest concentration of this kenning type occurs in Christian poetry and especially in *Líkn*'s model *Has* 1/2, 10/4, 14/6-8, 20/2, 28/2, 31/3, 41/4, 44/5-6, and 65/6. Such kennings may be informed by the biblical idea of the heavens as a tabernacle; see Isa. XL.22 *qui extendit velut nihilum caelos et expandit eos sicut tabernaculum ad inhabitandum* 'he that stretcheth out the heavens as nothing and spreadeth them out as a tent to dwell in'. (With respect to God's 'stretching out the heavens' see *-spennandi* 'who spans [the heavens]' 9/2.) See Eisler 1910, II for comparative discussion of the *Himmelszelt* 'tent of heaven' in ancient cultures. — [4] *hjálmprýddan* 'helmet-adorned': *Skj* B (cf. *LP*), followed by *Skald*, apparently concerned about the seeming incongruity between God's being 'helmet-adorned' yet clothing himself with flesh, emends to *hjálpprýddan* 'equipped with help, salvation'. But *hjalmprýddr* suggests metaphorically that the second person of the Trinity enters the world as a warrior prepared for battle, a metaphor that also occurs in OE Christian poetry and in the OS *Heliand*. The helmet was a royal as much as a warrior adornment in the Middle Ages. — [5] *sik síðan* 'himself ... later': Restoration based upon 399a-b[x] (including conjecture '*síðan*?' in Jón Sigurðsson's note), supported in part by the needs of alliteration and *skothending*; a trace of possible 'k' followed by descender of possible 's' remain. A six-syllable l. requires that the final word be disyllabic, but the lacuna has space for only three letters, with possible abbreviation ('-an', '-ar'). — [6] *sjálfráði* 'by his own will/choice, independently [*lit.* self-counsel]': Cf. Kálf *Kátr* 9/5-6 *Sjalfráður á sik tók dauða* | *sára písl fyr glæpi vára* 'at his own choice he took upon himself death, a painful torment for our misdeeds'.

13. Vilda ek vitra hölda
    vegs gæti*, meinlætum,
    hátt, þeim er hörðum mætti,
    hvargóðum stef bjóða.

    Krists vinnr krapt ins hæsta
    krossmark viðum hnossa
    alls bezt; lofar æztan
    öll dýrð konung fyrða.

Ek vilda bjóða hátt stef hvargóðum gæti* vegs vitra hölda, þeim er mætti hörðum meinlætum. Krossmark ins hæsta Krists vinnr krapt alls bezt viðum hnossa; öll dýrð lofar æztan konung fyrða.

I would like to offer a sublime refrain to the ever-good guardian of the way of wise men [= God (= Christ)], who met with hard tribulations. The cross-sign of the most high Christ gains power best of all for trees of treasures [MEN]; all glory exalts the highest king of men [RULER (= Christ)].

Mss: **B**(11v), 399a-b[x]. — *Readings*: [2] vegs gæti*: 'vegsgētiss' B, 399a-b[x] [5] Krists: Kristr B, 399a-b[x].

Editions: *Skj* Anonyme digte og vers [XIII], C. 1. *Líknarbraut* 13: AII, 153, BII, 163-4, *Skald* II, 87; Sveinbjörn Egilsson 1844, 39, Rydberg 1907, 13-14, 49, Kock and Meissner 1931, I, 91, Tate 1974, 58.

Notes: [All]: Having alluded to the Nativity in st. 12, the poet, as if present, now offers Christ a *hátt stef* 'sublime refrain' as a gift as he begins the refrain section (*stefjabálkr*). — [1-2] *gæti* vitra hölda vegs* (dat.) 'guardian of the way of wise men': The ms. has gen. *-gætis* for *gæti* 'guardian' (dat. sg.). All eds emend: Sveinbjörn Egilsson 1844, 39 to nom. *gætir* (speculating in a note that the <s> may derive from misreading an abbreviation stroke in an earlier ms.); all others to dat. *gæti*. Two strained readings are possible if the ms. gen. were retained. 1) the kenning could modify *meinlætum* 'tribulations' (l. 2) (as the scribe may have assumed), giving 'I would like to offer a high refrain to that ever-good one who met with the hard torments of the guardian of the way of wise men' (i.e. redundantly 'to Christ who suffered Christ's torments'. 2) The kenning could modify *stef* 'refrain' (l. 4), i.e. 'I would like to offer the sublime *stef* of the guardian of the way of wise men who suffered hard torments'. In this case, 'the guardian of the way of wise men' might refer to the Cross. Both readings seem unsatisfactory. — [4] *stef* 'refrain': The word is also used formally to introduce the first *stef* of the *stefjabálkr* in *Leið* 13/1 (as here *hátt stef*), *Has* 20/4, *Pl* 11/4 and *Geisl* 18/4. — [5]: A marginal ms. obelos (†) indicates occurrence of the *stef* here and at later occurrences. — [5] *Krists*: Kristr in ms. B; all eds assume a scribal error (because of *vinnr*: i.e. Kristr vinnr krapt), repeated in subsequent incipits of the *stef* (17/5, 21/5, 25/5, 29/5). — [5] *krapt* 'power': The word may have a richer theological connotation, for in the ON *Elucidarius* Lat. *gratia* 'grace' is sometimes translated as *kraptr* (Salvesen 1968, 42; cf. Walter 1976, 43). — [6] *krossmark* 'cross-sign': In *Niðrst¹* I.8 Christ makes the *crossmarc* 'sign of the cross' over the captives as he leads them up out of hell at the Harrowing. On the early history of the term 'sign' (σημεῖον, or *signum*) for the Cross, see Reijners 1965, 118-23, 160-87. — [7] *alls bezt* 'best of all': *Skj* B, *Skald*, and Kock and Meissner include with the rest of ll. 7-8 as a single syntactic unit. — [8] *dýrð* : *fyrða*: Ms. *fyrða*; *Skj* B shortens *dýrð* to *dyrð*. This same rhyme (*dýrð*- : *fyrð*-) of long and short 'y' occurs also 28/2 as well as in *Geisl* 24/2, 45/2, *Mdr* 33/8 and *Lil* 68/8, 74/2; cf. 1/6 *styrki* : *dýrka*.

14. Veittu menn, sem máttu,
    marga lund á grundu,
    grimmúðgastir gumnar,
    guði sælum harmkvæli.

    Lét fyr ljóna sveitum
    limu sína guð pína,
    framar en flestir gumnar,
    fjöldyggr, megi hyggja.

Grimmúðgastir gumnar — menn sem máttu — veittu sælum guði harmkvæli marga lund á grundu. Fjöldyggr guð lét sína limu pína fyr sveitum ljóna, framar en flestir gumnar megi hyggja.

The most grim-minded men — men who were able — gave blessed God sorrowful torments in many ways on earth. Very faithful God let his limbs be tortured for the hosts of men more than most men might imagine.

Mss: **B**(11v), 399a-b[x]. — *Readings*: [2] marga lund: 'mar[...]a [...]unnd' B, 'marga lund' 399a-b[x].

Editions. *Skj* Anonyme digte og vers [XIII], C. 1. *Líknarbraut* 14: AII, 153, BII, 164, *Skald* II, 87, *NN* §§1353H, 1956; Sveinbjörn Egilsson 1844, 39, Rydberg 1907, 14, 49, Tate 1974, 59.

Notes: [8] *fjöldyggr* 'very faithful': Sveinbjörn Egilsson, following 399a-b[x], expands the abbreviation above <g> as pl. -*ir*, construing the adj. to modify *gumnar* 'men'. But the *er/ir* abbreviation can also be expanded simply as <r> (Hreinn Benediktsson 1965, 92).

15. Þoldi halshögg hölda
    hildingr með spýtingum;
    vörðr hlaut fróns af fyrðum
    flest skaup ok kinnhesta.

    Hann bar hneyxl af mönnum
    hverja lund ok stundir
    — píndr var hann berr ok bundinn
    barðr — viðfarar harðar.

Hildingr hölda þoldi halshögg með spýtingum; fróns vörðr hlaut af fyrðum flest skaup ok kinnhesta. Hann bar hneyxl hverja lund af mönnum ok harðar stundir viðfarar; berr var hann píndr ok barðr, bundinn.

The king of men [RULER = Christ] endured neck-blows along with spittings; earth's guardian [RULER = Christ] received from men extreme mockery and slaps. He bore disgrace in every way from men and hard hours of mistreatment; bare, he was tortured and bound, beaten.

Mss: **B**(11v), 399a-b^x.

Editions: *Skj* Anonyme digte og vers [XIII], C. 1. *Líknarbraut* 15: AII, 153, BII, 164, *Skald* II, 87, *NN* §1853C; Sveinbjörn Egilsson 1844, 39-40, Rydberg 1907, 14, 49, Tate 1974, 60.

Notes: [All]: The st. is remarkably similar to a passage from the OIcel. Lenten sermon (*HómÍsl* 1993, 49v; *HómÍsl* 1872, 109): *oc hann þolþe bond. oc hálshogg. kinhesta. oc hrækingar. oc bardaga* 'and he endured binding, and neck-blows, slaps, and spittings, and beating'. — [3] *fróns vörðr* 'earth's guardian [RULER = Christ]': Elsewhere kennings employing *vörðr* 'guardian' as base-word and some form of 'land' or 'earth' as determinant (e.g. *vörðr foldar* 'guardian of the earth', *vörðr grundar* 'guardian of the plain', *landvörðr* 'land-guardian', *láðvörðr* 'land-guardian') refer only to earthly kings. On the need for context to determine whether such a kenning refers to Christ or an earthly king, see Snorri Sturluson's discussion in *Skm* (*SnE* 1998 1, 78). Typically when *vörðr* is used in a God-kenning it is combined with 'heaven' or a heaven-kenning, as in *Geisl* 19/3, *Leið* 10/1, *Hás* 30/4. The poet uses the latter in 29/3-4 (*vörðr sólar slóðar* 'guardian of the sun's track [SKY/HEAVEN > = God]'). The poet's choice of two kennings for ruler in this st. is probably intended to point up a contrast between the true status of Christ and his humiliation during the Flagellation. His humanity is underscored by the omission of kenning ornament in the second *helmingr* and by the repetition of the plain pron. *hann*, which is, however, unmetrical in l. 7. Stylistically the *helmingr*, like Christ at the Flagellation, is 'bare'.

16. Nisti ferð í frosti
    fárlunduð við tré sáran
    — vasa hann verðugr písla —
    várn græðara járnum.

    Glymr varð hár af hömrum
    heyrðr, þá er nagla keyrðu
    hjálms gnýviðir hilmi
    hófs í ristr ok lófa.

Fárlunduð ferð nisti várn sáran græðara járnum við tré í frosti; hann vasa verðugr písla. Hár glymr varð heyrðr af hömrum, þá er hjálms gnýviðir keyrðu nagla í ristr ok lófa hilmi hófs.

A harm-minded host nailed our wounded Saviour with irons to the tree in the frost; he was not deserving of torment. High clanging was heard from hammers, when the trees of the din of the helmet [(*lit.* 'din-trees of the helmet') BATTLE > WARRIORS] drove nails into the insteps and palms of the prince of moderation [VIRTUOUS RULER = Christ].

Mss: **B**(11v), 399a-b[x]. — *Readings*: [6] keyrðu: 'keyr[...]' B, 'keyrðu' 399a-b[x].

Editions: *Skj* Anonyme digte og vers [XIII], C. 1. *Líknarbraut* 16: AII, 153, BII, 164, *Skald* II, 87; Sveinbjörn Egilsson 1844, 40, Rydberg 1907, 14, 49, Tate 1974, 61.

Notes: [1] *nisti* 'nailed, pinned': The verb is often used in the sense of 'to pin, transfix' with a spear or arrow, which is consonant with the warrior imagery of the st. Except in 32/4 *nista* does not appear to be used of the Crucifixion elsewhere in ON until late medieval poetry: see *Píslargrátur* 37/4, *Krossvísur I*, 9/3 and 40/4 and *Krossvísur II*, 8/3-4 (*ÍM* I.2, 204, 254, 260, 263). — [1] *í frosti* 'in the frost': *LP* translates as *ved vintertid* 'in wintertime', but winter does not square well with the season of Holy Week. Coldness is often glossed in a moral sense as infidelity or as malice or absence of charity (see Hill 1968, 522-32); cf. the prayer in the OIcel. ember-days homily that God might drive *grimléics frost* 'the frost of cruelty' from our hearts (*HómÍsl* 1993, 17r; *HómÍsl* 1872, 36). Later poetry extends the moral sense, e.g. *frost glæpa* 'frost of sins' *Lil* 81/8; related is C15th *jǫkul synda* 'glacier of sins' *Máríublóm* 3/8 (*ÍM* I.2, 173). Closest to *Líkn*, in the context of Passion narrative, is the late medieval *Niðrstv* 19/5, which refers to Christ's being beaten *bædi j grimd ok frosti* 'both in fierceness and frost' (*ibid.* 228). — [2] *fárlunduð* 'harm-minded': Line 2 is unmetrical. Rydberg 1907, 49 (following Konráð Gíslason and Eiríkur Jónsson 1875-89, II.1, 257 and II.3, 925) emends to *fárlynd* to achieve a six-syllable l.; *Skj* B and *Skald* to *fárlund*. — [3] *vasa* 'was not': Both B and 399a b[x] read 'vara'; the older form *vasa* is required by *skothending* with *písla*, but contrast the *ertu : hjarta* rhyme at 40/5. — [4] *hömrum* 'hammers': Lindow 1994, 493 notes as rare this use of *hamarr* in a context that does not involve Þórr, where it is typically a weapon rather than hammer *per se*. — [7] *hjálms gnýviðir* 'trees of the din of the helmet [*lit.* din-trees of the helmet] [BATTLE > WARRIORS]': The kenning draws together each dominant image of the st.: the *glymr* 'clanging' of the hammers, the tree (*tré*) of the Cross, and the *hilmir* 'prince [*lit.* helmet-granter]' who is Christ. The relationship of *hjálms* 'helmet's' and *hilmi* 'prince, helmeter' at either end of the l. is underscored not only by alliteration but also through polyptoton, the close repetition of a word or stem but in different form. Cf. Glúmr *Gráf* 4/1[1]. — [7, 8]

hilmi hófs 'of the prince of moderation [VIRTUOUS RULER = Christ]': Etymologically *hilmir* 'prince' means 'helmeter'; with reference to Christ this may also have a religious sense, for Eph. VI.17 exhorts men to put on the *galea salutis* 'helmet of salvation'. Christ's 'moderation' (*hóf*) contrasts with the extremes of frost and loud ringing.

17. Árstillir vann alla
    oss, þá er hekk á krossi
    (eitt er um þat) dróttinn,
    (almæli) fullsæla.

    Krist*s* vinnr krapt ins hæsta
    krossmark viðum hnossa
    alls bezt; lofar æztan
    öll dýrð konung fyrða.

Árstillir vann oss alla fullsæla, þá er dróttinn hekk á krossi; eitt almæli er um þat. Krossmark ins hæsta Krist*s* vinnr krapt alls bezt viðum hnossa; öll dýrð lofar æztan konung fyrða.

The instituter of abundance [= God] made us all fully fortunate, when the Lord hung on the Cross; all agree about that. The Cross-sign of the most-high Christ gains power best of all for trees of treasures [MEN]; all glory exalts the highest king of men [RULER = Christ].

Mss: **B**(11v), 399a-b[x]. — *Reading*: [5-8]: *abbrev. as* 'Kristr var krapt ins h-' B, 399a-b[x].

Editions: *Skj* Anonyme digte og vers [XIII], C. 1. *Líknarbraut* 17: AII, 153, BII, 165, *Skald* II, 87; Sveinbjörn Egilsson 1844, 40, Rydberg 1907, 14, 49, Tate 1974, 62.

Notes: [1] *Árstillir* 'instituter of abundance': The kenning is able to bear both meanings of both its elements: *ár* 'year' and 'abundance or fruitfulness'; *stillir* from *stilla* 'to calm' or 'to institute or rule', of which *LP* (1860) favours the former (*moderator*) and *LP* the latter (*styrer* 'ruler'). 'Ruler of year's fruitfulness' accords well with the biblical *dominus messis* 'Lord of the harvest' (Matt. IX.38, Luke X.2). — [3, 4] *eitt almæli er um þat* 'all agree about that': Lit. 'there is one common saying about that'. — [4] *fullsæla* 'fully fortunate, blessed': In poetry only here and 35/4. The word can have the technical sense of 'saved', possessing *fullsæla* 'salvation' (*Fritzner*).

18. Guðs var mær ok móðir
    má*n*a hauðrs við dauða
    hýr með hjarta sáru
    hildings ok píningar.

    Víst bar víf it hæsta
    vátar kiðr af gráti,
    son*r*, þá er sárr af benjum
    siðnenninn dó hennar.

Hýr mær ok móðir guðs var með sáru hjarta við dauða ok píningar hildings má*n*a hauðrs. Víst bar it hæsta víf kiðr vátar af gráti, þá er hennar siðnenninn son*r* dó, sárr af benjum.

The mild maiden and mother of God [= Mary] was with a sore heart at the death and torments of the king of the moon's land [SKY/HEAVEN > = God (= Christ)]. Certainly the highest woman bore cheeks wet from weeping when her virtue-striving son died, sore from wounds.

Mss: B(11v), 399a-b[x]. — *Readings*: [2] má**n**a hauðrs: 'má[...]hau[...]s' B, 'm[...]a hau̱ḍ̱rs' 399a-b[x] [6] gráti: '[...]e' B, 'gráte' 399a-b[x] [7] son**r**: son B, 399a-b[x].

Editions: *Skj* Anonyme digte og vers [XIII], C. 1. *Líknarbraut* 18: AII, 153-4, BII, 165, *Skald* II, 87; Sveinbjörn Egilsson 1844, 40-1, Rydberg 1907, 14, 49, Tate 1974, 63.

Notes: [All]: Mary standing at the foot of the Cross weeping (*stabat mater dolorosa*) is a recurrent motif in poetry of the Passion. — [1] *mær ok móðir* 'maiden and mother': This is the first pairing of these alliterative appellatives in ON poetry. The pair appears in the C14th in *Lil* 3/1, 34/3 (*mey*), Anon *Pét* 6, 3/4, and Anon *Mv II* 22/1-2, later also in *Náð* 5/1-2, *María móðirin skæra* 1/1-2, *Máríublóm* 40/1, etc. (*ÍM* II, 5; II, 48; I.2. 180). — [2] *má*n*a hauðrs* 'moon's land [SKY/HEAVEN]': Restoration based upon 399a-b[x] (including Jón Sigurðsson's note 'likely *mánahauðrs*') as well as <ð> for *aðalhending*. The same kenning recurs (and, as here, *hauð-* is rhymed with *dauð-*) in *Mgr* 30/2 and 34/8, again with reference to Mary's weeping at Jesus's death. The alliterative linkage of *máni* 'moon' with Mary (*mær ok móðir* 'maiden and mother' (l. 1)) may evoke the widespread association of Mary with the moon in the patristic period (as the Christmas moon from whose radiance Christ as 'sun of justice' proceeds, Rahner 1963, 161-7) and with the growth of Marian devotion in the C12th-13th (see Salzer 1886-93, 377-84). In his Sermon on the Nativity of our Lady, S. Anthony of Padua (early C13th) writes, e.g., that Mary is called the full moon (*luna plena*) of Eccles. L.6 *quia ex omni parte perfecta* 'because she is in every way perfect' (Costa, Frasson and Luisetto 1979, II, 107-8). Cf. the *Speculum Beatae Mariae Virginis* of Conrad of Saxony (C13th), long attributed to Bonaventure; commenting on *pulchra ut luna* 'fair as the moon' in Cant. VI.9, he writes: *Luna ergo est Maria.... Lunae plenae bene Maria comparata est, quae lumine sapientiae et veritatis a sole aeterno plene illuminata est* 'The moon is therefore Mary.... Well is Mary likened to the full moon, which is fully illuminated by the eternal sun with the light of wisdom and truth' (VII.1; Martinez 1975, 269-70, cf. 378). Mary is also often identified with the radiant woman standing on the moon (*et luna sub pedibus eius*) in Rev. XII.1 (see Kirschbaum *et al.* 1968-76, I, 146-8). — [3] *hýr* 'mild': Construing the adj. as predicate and translating it as 'glad', *Skj* B and *Skald* add the neg. particle '-a' to *var* 'was' (l. 1), i.e., '[Mary] was not happy at the death ...'. This is unnecessary if the adj. is considered attributive to *mær* 'maid'; and, indeed, adding the particle runs the danger of making l. 1 seem initially to suggest that 'God's mother was not a maiden'. The sense 'mild' or 'kindly disposed' is not uncommon; *hýrr* can be synonymous with *mildr* and *hlýrr*, both of which qualify Mary elsewhere (e.g. *Mdr* 1/1 and *Geisl* 32/6-7). This meaning is also found in the OIcel. homily on the Circumcision: *bergia oc siá hve hy*r *drótteN es* 'taste and see how mild/kind the Lord is' (*HómÍsl* 1993, 27v; *HómÍsl* 1872, 56). — [6] *gráti* 'weeping': Restoration based upon 399a-b[x] and *aðalhending* ('át'); there is also in B only space for an abbreviation ('ra'). — [7] *son*r 'son': Final <r> is frequently omitted in C14th mss, but has been restored here, as *Líkn* is a C13th poem. Rydberg, *Skj* B, and *Skald* all emend to *sonr*. — [8] *siðnenninn* 'virtue-striving': Occurs as a cpd only here; cf. *ástnenninn* 'love-striving' *Has* 62/8 and *dáðnenninn* 'deed-striving' *Mdr* 12/4.

19. Hvat megi heldr of græta   er dýrr á sik sáran
    hvern mann, er þat kannar,   siklingr ept kvöl mikla
    röðla býs en ræsis   hreinn til hjálpar mönnum
    ríks píningar slíkar,   hauðrfjörnis tók dauða?

Hvat megi heldr of græta hvern mann, er kannar þat, en slíkar píningar ríks ræsis röðla býs, er dýrr, hreinn siklingr hauðrfjörnis tók sáran dauða á sik ept kvöl mikla til hjálpar mönnum?

What could be more able to make weep each man who ponders it than such torments of the mighty ruler of suns' dwelling [SKY/HEAVEN > = God (= Christ)], when the precious, pure king of earth's helmet [SKY/HEAVEN > = God (= Christ)] took bitter death upon himself after great torture for the salvation [*lit.* help] of men?

Mss: **B**(11v), 399a-b^x. — *Readings*: [2] þat: 'þ[...]' B, 'þạṭ' 399a-b^x.

Editions: *Skj* Anonyme digte og vers [XIII], C. 1. *Líknarbraut* 19: AII, 154, BII, 165, *Skald* II, 87; Sveinbjörn Egilsson 1844, 41, Rydberg 1907, 14, 49, Tate 1974, 64.

Notes: [All]: The two kennings of this st. emphasise the theological point that humans crucified God himself when Jesus died on the Cross. — [2] *kannar* 'ponders': The usual meaning of the verb is to search through/out something in order to gain knowledge of it (*Fritzner*). Here the sense seems to be 'to ponder, contemplate', perhaps even imaginatively to share in the sufferings of Christ through compassion. The verb is used again in 22/4 in the sense 'to explore, search out' with reference to the Harrowing of Hell. — [3] *ræsis röðla býs* 'of the ruler of suns' dwelling [SKY/HEAVEN > = God (= Christ)]': Cf. *Has* 59/3-4 and Kálf *Kátr* 39/3-4. The gen. pl. *röðla* 'of suns' (contrasting with the sg. in *Has* 59/4) is attested elsewhere; the extended sense is probably 'heavenly bodies', i.e. sun and stars. (Guðrún Nordal 2001, 292 translates it as sg. 'lord of the dwelling of the sun', and indeed pl. forms can substitute for sg. in skaldic poetry.) — [7] *hjálpar* (gen. sg.) 'salvation [*lit.* help]': The extended sense of *hjálp* 'help' as 'salvation' occurs also in 24/4, 32/2 and 41/3. — [8] *hauðrfjörnis* 'of earth's, land's helmet [SKY/HEAVEN]': *Fjörnir* 'helmet', lit. 'protector of life' (from *fjör* 'life'). The kenning occurs also in Anon (*FoGT*) 12/4^{III}; cf. *Pl* 1/2 *foldar fjörnir* 'earth's helmet'.

20. Enn und hægri hendi   Árveitis rann ýta
    hyggjublíðr á síðu   eirsanns ór ben þeiri
    hlaut af hvössu spjóti   — hugum skyldu þat höldar
    höfugt sár konungr jöfra.   heyra — vatn ok dreyri.

Enn á síðu und hægri hendi hlaut hyggjublíðr konungr jöfra höfugt sár af hvössu spjóti. Vatn ok dreyri rann ór þeiri ben eirsanns árveitis ýta; höldar skyldu heyra þat hugum.

Yet on his side under the right arm the thought-tender king of princes [RULER = Christ] received a heavy wound from a sharp spear. Water and blood flowed out of that wound of the mercy-true abundance-giver of men [= God (= Christ)]; men should hear that in their thoughts.

Mss: **B**(11v), 399a-b[x].

Editions: *Skj* Anonyme digte og vers [XIII], C. 1. *Líknarbraut* 20: AII, 154, BII, 165, *Skald* II, 87, *NN* §3279; Sveinbjörn Egilsson 1844, 41, Rydberg 1907, 14-15, 50, Tate 1974, 65.

Notes: [1] *enn* 'yet': Sveinbjörn Egilsson, Rydberg and *Skj* B all normalise ms. *enn* as *en* 'but'. As *NN* §3279 suggests, however, the adv., as opposed to the conj., is appropriate given the cumulation of tortures over the previous sts; cf. similar use of *enn* in 26/1. — [1, 2] *á síðu und hægri hendi* 'on his side under the right arm': This specific iconographic detail locating the wound from the lance on the right side accords with the more common medieval tradition. Mâle 1958, 190-5 indicates that the wound on the right side represents the founding of the church (Ecclesia), but the tradition is not fixed. See Gurewich 1957, 358-62, who suggests that when on the left, the wound points to Christ's 'bleeding heart'. Late medieval Icel. Passion poems vary the position of the wound, either leaving it unspecified but penetrating the heart (*Rósa* 106), locating it on the right side (*Blómarós* 55), or on the right but still reaching to the heart (*Gimsteinn* 55) (*ÍM* I.2, 29; I.2, 93; I.2, 316). — [2] *hyggjublíðr* 'thought-tender': Cf. *hugblíðr* (also of Christ) in RKet Lv 1[IV]. — [5, 6, 8] *vatn ok dreyri rann ór þeiri ben ... árveitis ýta* 'water and blood flowed out of the wound ... of the abundance-giver of men [= God (= Christ)]': The conflation of the kenning with the image may suggest that the blood and water which flow from Christ's wound are themselves symbols of his nurturing 'abundance'. On this effluence as a representation of Christ's grace, related to the 'rivers of living water' in John VII.38, see Rahner 1964, 177-238. — [6] *eirsanns* (gen.) 'mercy-true': An otherwise unattested cpd; all previous eds unnecessarily emend ms. *-sanns* to *-sams*, in part because *eirsamr* 'peaceful, mild' occurs in st. 49/6. As an adj. for Christ, however, the cpd *eirsannr* is well conceived. In addition to the meaning 'true', *-sannr* can, by association with the noun *sannr* m. 'justice', suggest Christ's justice while *eir-* points to his tender mercy, an idea which dominates the st.

21. Lýsti miskunn mesta Krist*s* vinnr krapt ins hæsta
    mildr, þá er saklauss vildi krossmark viðum hnossa
    einn fyr öllum mönnum, alls bezt; lofar æztan
    eyhjálms konungr, deyja. öll dýrð konung fyrða.

Mildr konungr eyhjálms lýsti mesta miskunn, þá er einn vildi deyja saklauss fyr öllum mönnum. Krossmark ins hæsta Krist*s* vinnr krapt alls bezt viðum hnossa; öll dýrð lofar æztan konung fyrða.

The tender king of the island-helmet [SKY/HEAVEN > = God (= Christ)] showed the greatest mercy when he alone willed to die guiltless for all men. The cross-sign of the most-high Christ gains power best of all for trees of treasures [MEN]; all glory exalts the highest king of men [RULER = Christ].

Mss: **B**(11v), 399a-b^x. — *Readings*: [2] saklauss: *so* 399a-b^x, 'saklau[...]s' B [5-8]: *abbrev. as* 'Kristr vinnr kr-' B, 399a-b^x.

Editions: *Skj* Anonyme digte og vers [XIII], C. 1. *Líknarbraut* 21: AII, 154, BII, 166, *Skald* II, 87; Sveinbjörn Egilsson 1844, 41, Rydberg 1907, 15, 50, Tate 1974, 66.

Notes: [2] *saklauss* 'guiltless': Restoration of 's' based upon 399a-b and grammatical need (m. nom. sg.). — [4] *eyhjálms* 'of the island-helmet': This is the only instance in skaldic poetry of *ey* 'island' in a sky-kenning.

22. Kvaliðr sté öll*um* æðri
    ítr gramr til helvítis
    dægra láðs ept dauða
    djöfla rann at kanna.

    Leysti sinn at *sö*nnu
    *só*lhallar gramr allan
    lýð fyr lífstré þjóðar
    líknarstyrkr frá myrkrum.

Kvaliðr ítr gramr dægra láðs, öll*um* æðri, sté ept dauða til helvítis at kanna rann djöfla. Líknarstyrkr gramr *só*lhallar leysti at *sö*nnu allan sinn lýð frá myrkrum fyr lífstré þjóðar.

The tormented glorious king of days' land [SKY/HEAVEN > = God (= Christ)], higher than all, descended after death to Hell to explore the house of devils [HELL]. The mercy-strong king of sun's hall [SKY/HEAVEN > = God (= Christ)] freed truly all his people from darkness by means of the life-tree of mankind [CROSS].

Mss: **B**(11v), 399a-b^x. — *Readings*: [1] öll*um* æðri: 'öll[...] ed[...]' B, 'öll[...]' 399a-b^x [5] at sönnu: '[...]t s[...]nnu' B, 'at sęðnnu' 399a-b^x [6] *só*lhallar: '[...]hallar' B, 's[...]hallar' 399a-b^x.

Editions: *Skj* Anonyme digte og vers [XIII], C. 1. *Líknarbraut* 22: AII, 154, BII, 166, *Skald* II, 88, *NN* §30; Sveinbjörn Egilsson 1844, 42, Rydberg 1907, 15, 50, Tate 1974, 67.

Notes: [All]: A frequent motif in representations of the Harrowing of Hell is that of light – associated here with Christ through *sól* 'sun' (l. 6) and perhaps *dægra láð* 'days' land' (l. 3) in the kennings – penetrating the darkness (*myrkrum*, dat. pl., l. 8) as it moves from the highest realm to the lowest. See, e.g., *Niðrst*[1] l.7: *Cristr ferr her nu oc rekr a braut með liose guðdoms sins dauþa myrcr...* 'Now Christ goes here and dispels the darkness of death with the light of his godhead...' (*Hms* II, 6). — [1] *öll*um *æðri* 'higher than all': A plausible conjecture by Sveinbjörn Egilsson 1844, 42, adopted by all subsequent eds. In B only 'e' for <æ> is visible, but the hook 'ȩ' was likely lost in the split above the letter. — [2, 6] *gramr* 'king': The same noun appears, unusually, as base-word of a Christ-kenning in each *helmingr*, each time in the second l. Of Christ in the context of the Harrowing, the choice is also somewhat odd; deriving from the adj. *gramr* 'angry, hostile', the pl. is often used substantively of 'fiends' (cf. *djöfla rann*, l. 4), the very beings his radiance overcomes. — [5] *sönnu* 'in truth, truly': Restoration based upon 399a-b^x, including superscript notation; either <o> (<ð>) or <e> is possible from the remnants. — [5, 6, 7] *leysti ... allan sinn lýð* 'freed all his people': Cf. the late medieval *Niðurstigningsvísur* 35/6 *leyste alla lydi sin* and *þu leyster alla lydi* 37/3 (*ÍM* I.2, 234). — [6] *sólhallar* 'of the sun's hall': In B lower tips of possible long <s> and <l> remain; Sveinbjörn Egilsson (1844, 42) suggests *sólhallar*, which all have accepted. 'Sun' + 'building' is a common kenning type for 'heaven'. — [7] *fyr lífstré* 'by means of the tree of life': Tree of life (*arbor vitae*) is ubiquitous in reference to the Cross. The instrumentality of the Cross at the Harrowing is also a common iconographic detail. In *Niðrst*[1] I. 7-8, e.g., after Christ has broken down the portals of hell, the liberated captives tell Satan that it is *fyrer crosstre* 'by means of the cross-tree' that he has been vanquished, and Adam praises Christ for rescuing them with his might and with the *marki cross* 'sign of the cross' (*Hms* II, 6-7). The late medieval *Krosskvæði* 26/3-4 echoes this idea: *ok i hendi bar | sigrmerki sitt* 'and he bore in his hand his victory-sign' at the Harrowing (*ÍM* I.2, 281). The prep. *fyr* also introduces the instrumentality of the Cross in 31/6 where it is by means of the Cross that Christ opened heaven for mankind. — [8] *líknarstyrkr ... frá myrkrum* 'mercy-strong ... from darkness': Cf. *Leið* 31/8, also of the Harrowing.

23. Lík fór kennir keykja
krapts með önd til graptar
sitt, ok sæll reis dróttinn
sólar hauðrs af dauða.

Urðu allir fyrðar
angrhegnanda fegnir,
áðr þá er elsku fæðis
aldyggs ban*i* hryggði.

Kennir krapts fór til graptar keykja lík sitt með önd, ok sæll dróttinn sólar hauðrs reis af dauða. Allir fyrðar urðu fegnir angrhegnanda, þá er ban*i* aldyggs fæðis elsku áðr hryggði.

The knower of strength [POWERFUL MAN = Christ] went to the grave to quicken his body with spirit, and the blessed Lord of sun's land [SKY/HEAVEN > = God (= Christ)] arose from death. All men became glad at the harm-suppressor [= God (= Christ)], those whom the death of the fully loyal nourisher of love [= God (= Christ)] earlier grieved.

Mss: **B**(11v), 399a-b[x]. — *Readings*: [3] reis: 're[...]' B, reiş 399a-b[x] [8] ban*i*: bana B, 399a-b[x].

Editions: *Skj* Anonyme digte og vers [XIII], C. 1. *Líknarbraut* 23: AII, 154, BII, 166, *Skald* II, 88; Sveinbjörn Egilsson 1844, 42, Rydberg 1907, 15, 50, Tate 1974, 68.

Notes: [1] *keykja* 'to quicken': *Skj* B and *Skald* emend to the usual *keykva*. The *-ja* form does not appear in *LP*, *CVC*, or *Fritzner* but occurs as a headword in *AEW*. This is the only occurrence of either in ON poetry. The verb is rich in christological significance; cf., with respect to Resurrection, Lat. *vivifico* (Gk ζωοποιέω) 'to quicken, give life' in such passages as John V.21, Rom. IV.17, and VIII.11. — [1, 2] *kennir krapts* 'knower of strength [POWERFUL MAN = Christ]': The agent noun *kennir* occurs only in poetry; of God elsewhere only in *Pl* 8/1 *kennir engla* 'knower of the angels'. Besides 'knower' *kennir* (from *kenna*) might also mean 'perceiver', 'tester', 'announcer', or 'teacher'. The kenning is a variation on a common type, in which a man is described as a *kennir* of gold, battle, weapons, etc. — [3-4] *dróttinn sólar hauðrs reis af dauða* 'the Lord of sun's land [SKY/HEAVEN > = God (= Christ)] arose from death': In combination with the kenning, the verb equates Christ's Resurrection with the rising of the sun, a common theme in hymns for prime. Line 4 is identical to *Leið* 31/4, which also concerns the Resurrection. — [5-8]: Generally analogous to the second *helmingr* is a passage from the OIcel. Resurrection homily: *Sa vas oc margfaldr fǫgnoþr i þessom heime af upriso criz es tóko ástmeN hans. þeir áþr vǫro hryGver oc daprer af dauþa hans* 'Thus there was also manifold happiness in this world at the Resurrection of Christ when he met his beloved [followers]; they were before despondent and downcast at his death' (*HómÍsl* 1993, 34r; *HómÍsl* 1872, 72). — [7] *fæðis elsku* 'of the nourisher of love [= God (= Christ)]': *Fæðir* might have the extended sense here of 'creator'; cf. *líknfæðir* 'author of grace' 47/8 and *fæðir fremðarráðs* 'nourisher of propitious counsel' 26/7. Both senses play off the theme of abundance in the poem. — [8] *ban*i (nom.) 'the death, slayer of': Ms. *bana*. All subsequent eds accept the emendation of Sveinbjörn Egilsson, which is supported, as he notes, by the similar nom. *dauði* 'the death of' in *Has* 28/7, a st. also on the Resurrection and which employs in its final l., as here, the rhyme *aldygg-* : *hryggði* (l. 8), as well as *fegn-* : *áðr þá* in the same positions in ll. 6-7.

24. Lands sté gramr af grundu
    guðblíðr dögum síðarr
    — eykz af öllu *slí*ku
    ór hjálp — tugum fjórum.

Fróns skal sikling* sínu
sveit, hin er Krists vill leita,
tjalds í tígnarveldi
trúa mann ok guð sannan.

Guðblíðr gramr lands sté af grundu fjórum tugum dögum síðarr; ór hjálp eykz af öllu *slí*ku. Sveit, hin er vill leita Krists, skal trúa sikling* fróns tjalds sannan mann ok guð í sínu tígnarveldi.

The godly-tender king of the earth [= God (= Christ)] ascended from the ground forty days later; our salvation is increased by all such [acts]. The company that wishes to seek Christ must believe the king of the earth's tent [SKY/HEAVEN > = God (= Christ)] [to be] true man and [true] God in his glorious power.

Mss: B(11v), 399a-b[x]. — *Readings*: [3] eykz: 'eyksz' B, 'eyks ok' 399a-b[x]; *slí*ku: '[...]ku' B, 399a-b[x] [4] ór: 'vðr' B, 399a-b[x] [5] sikling*: siklings B, 399a-b[x] [7] tjalds: 'tialld[...]' B, tjalds̩ 399a-b[x].

Editions: *Skj* Anonyme digte og vers [XIII], C. 1. *Líknarbraut* 24: AII, 154-5, BII, 166, *Skald* II, 88; Sveinbjörn Egilsson 1844, 42, Rydberg 1907, 15, 50, Tate 1974, 69.

Notes: [2, 1] *guðblíðr gramr lands* 'the godly-tender king of the earth [= God (= Christ)]': Apparently in an effort to achieve a heaven-kenning *Skj* B (cf. *LP*: *guðblíðr*), followed by *Skald*, separates *guð* and emends it to *glyggs* (i.e. *glyggs gramr lands* 'king of gale's land'). However, the kenning type earth + king for God is not uncommon; *Meissner*, 328 lists nine instances including (from *Líkn*) *fróns vörðr* 'the earth's guardian' 15/3 and *fróns konungr* 'the earth's king' 33/1-2, as well as *Pl* 57/1, 4 *jarðar gramr* 'the earth's king'. The st. concerns itself with Christ's human and divine natures (*mann ok guð* 'man and God', l. 8). The kenning of the first *helmingr* ('king of the earth') may emphasise his humanity, while that of the second underscores his divinity ('king of the earth's tent [SKY/HEAVEN]'). The adj. *guðblíðr* also occurs (of the sun) in Skúli Lv 1/2[III]. An alternative arrangement would be to separate its elements and place them in apposition to *gramr lands*, i.e. 'the king of the earth, tender God, ascended'. — [3] *eykz* 'is increased': Following 399a-b[x], Sveinbjörn Egilsson construes the final <z> of ms. 'eyksz' as Tironian nota, i.e. *eyks ok* 'is also increased'. — [3] *slíku* 'such': Proposed by Sveinbjörn Egilsson, the restoration has been accepted by all subsequent eds; the referent is unspecified. — [4] *ór* 'our': Ms. 'vðr' (*vár*); normalisation as variant *ór* allows rhyme with *fjórum* and vowel alliteration with *eykz* and *öllu* (l. 3). — [5] *sikling** 'king': Ms. *siklings*; Sveinbjörn Egilsson's emendation has been accepted by all subsequent eds. Salvaging the ms. reading leaves one with a strained construction: *sveit siklings fróns tjalds, hin er vill leita Krists í tignarveldi sínu, skal trúa mann ok guð sannan* 'the company of the king of the earth's tent, which desires to seek Christ in his glorious power, must believe man and God true'. — [7] *tígnarveldi* (dat. sg.) 'glorious power': The basic meaning of *veldi* is 'power', but its extended sense is 'empire' or 'kingdom'; hence *Skj* B translates the cpd as *höjheds rige* 'kingdom of sovereignty'. — [8] *trúa sannan mann ok guð* 'believe [him to be] true man and [true] God': The adj. *sannan* 'true' can qualify both *mann* 'man' and *guð* 'God', or only one of the two nouns. Although in the Nicene Creed 'true' qualifies only God: *Deum verum de deo vero ... et homo factus est* 'true God of true God ... and was made man', the later Council of Chalcedon (451) assigns 'true' to Christ's human nature as well. This position is reflected in a number of Lat. and ON texts. See e.g. the hymn ll. *Ut deus verus / homo verus fieret* 'that he might become true God and true man' (Mone 1853-5, I, 113/5), *Mar* (Unger 1871, 416) *hann er ... sannr guð ok sannr maðr* 'he is ... true God and true man', and *Mdr* 16/8 *guð og mann borinn sannan* 'true God and man born [of your womb]'.

25. Geypnir skjöldungr skepnu   Krists vinnr krapt ins hæsta
     skríns styrkliga sína   krossmark viðum hnossa
     (ern er hilmir) hlýrna   alls bezt; lofar æztan
     (heiðtjalds) saman alla.   öll dýrð konung fyrða.

Skjöldungr skríns hlýrna geypnir styrkliga sína skepnu alla saman; hilmir heiðtjalds er ern. Krossmark ins hæsta Krists vinnr krapt alls bezt viðum hnossa; öll dýrð lofar æztan konung fyrða.

The ruler of the shrine of heavenly bodies [HEAVEN > = God] holds in his hand mightily his creation all at once; the prince of the heath's tent [SKY/HEAVEN > = God] is valiant. The cross-sign of the most high Christ gains power best of all for trees of treasures [MEN]; all glory exalts the highest king of men [RULER = Christ].

Mss: **B**(11v), 399a-b[x]. — *Reading*: [5-8]: abbrev. as 'Kristr vinnr kr-' B, 399a-b[x].

Editions: *Skj* Anonyme digte og vers [XIII], C. 1. *Líknarbraut* 25: AII, 155, BII, 166-7, *Skald* II, 88, *NN* §2328; Sveinbjörn Egilsson 1844, 43, Rydberg 1907, 15, 50, Tate 1974, 70.

Notes: [1] *geypnir* 'holds, gathers in his hand': The verb (from *gaupn*, f. 'hollow of the hand') occurs only in Christian skaldic poetry, primarily in kennings depicting God or Christ as pantocrator 'ruler of the universe'. See, e.g., *Has* 29/7-8, *Geisl* 16/7-8, Kálf *Kátr* 36/3 and *Mgr* 2/5. On the iconography of Christ as pantocrator, see Kirschbaum *et al.* 1968-76, I, 392-4. A good example from the period is from the early C13th painted ceiling of S. Michael's, Hildesheim; in the final roundel of the tree of Jesse, Christ appears enthroned against a blue field, surrounded by sun, moon, and stars. — [2] *skríns* 'shrine's': Rydberg 1907, 50 (so also Guðrún Nordal 2001, 300) takes *skríns* and *heiðtjalds* 'heath-tent's' (l. 4) (emended to *heiðstalls* 'heath-ledge's'; see below) together as a *tvíkent* heaven-kenning, making l. 3 parenthetical: *ern er hilmir hlýrna* 'valiant is the prince of heavenly bodies'. The *tvíkennt* kenning of this reading is analogous to *Has* 29/7-8 (above), and the use of *hlýrna* as determinant in the kenning of the interjection is similar to *gramr hlýrna* 'king of heavenly bodies' Anon (*FoGT*) 35/3^{III}. Following *Skj* B and *Skald*, however, this ed. prefers the balanced pairing of *skjöldungr skríns hlýrna* 'prince of the shrine of heavenly bodies' (ll. 1, 3, 2) and *hilmir heiðtjalds* (*Skj* B -*stalls*) 'prince of the heath's tent' (ll. 3, 4), the first of which recalls *Leið* 32/5-6. — [4] *heiðtjalds* 'of the heath's tent': Sveinbjörn Egilsson 1844, 43 normalises ms. '-tialldz' to -*tjallz* to improve rhyme with *alla* 'all'. Konráð Gíslason 1877, 23-4, pointing out instances of *tjald*: *ald*- rhymes in *Has* (*tjalds*: *aldir* 10/4, *tjalds*: *halda* 20/7) and *Líkn* (*tjalds* [ms. 'tíalldz']: *aldir* 50/8), concludes that the scribe mistakenly substituted -*tjalds* for -*stalls* 'ledge's', not only here but in *Has* 65/6 (ms. 'tialldz': *alla*). (Cf. *Has* 29/8 *skýstalls*: *allri*.) Rydberg 1907, 50 and *Skj* B accordingly emend to *heiðstalls*. But it is puzzling that the scribe of B (the same for both *Has* and *Líkn*) who got -*stalls* (ms. 'stallz') right in *Has* 29/8 would then substitute 'tialldz' (-*tjalds*) for -*stalls* in 65/6 and then again here. As Kock (*NN* §2328) argues, the pronunciation of '-lds-' as '-lls-' is not unusual in the period (analogous to *kall* for *karl*). This ed., with *Skald*, maintains the ms. reading and assumes that -*tjalds* (at least -*al*-) is intended to rhyme with *alla*. Cf. Játg Lv 2^{II} *hjald*-: *fjalli* and, similarly, Halli XI *Fl* 3/8^{II} *vind*-: *finna* (*Skj* B and *Skald* both emend to *vinn*-).

26. Enn mun kross dýrð kynnaz
 — kemr ótti þá — dróttins
 fyr hnigstöfum hjörva
 hljóms at efsta dómi.

 Meiðr skal hverr ór hauðri
 hringmóts til alþingis
 fremðarráðs á fæðis
 fund hvatliga skunda.

Dýrð dróttins kross mun enn kynnaz fyr hnigstöfum hljóms hjörva at efsta dómi; ótti kemr þá. Hverr meiðr hringmóts skal skunda hvatliga ór hauðri til alþingis á fund fæðis fremðarráðs.

The glory of the Lord's Cross will yet be made known to bowing staves of swords' din [BATTLE > WARRIORS] at the Last Judgement; fear will come then. Each tree of the sword-meeting [BATTLE > WARRIOR] shall hasten quickly from out of the ground to the Althing to meet the nourisher of propitious counsel [= God (= Christ)].

Mss: **B**(11v), 399a-b^x.

Editions: *Skj* Anonyme digte og vers [XIII], C. 1. *Líknarbraut* 26: AII, 155, BII, 167, *Skald* II, 88; Sveinbjörn Egilsson 1844, 43, Rydberg 1907, 15, 50, Tate 1974, 71.

Notes: [3-4] *hnigstǫfum hljóms hjǫrva* 'bowing-staves of swords' din [BATTLE > WARRIORS]': The identical battle-kenning (*hjǫrva hljómr*) occurs previously in Tindr Hákdr 10/5-6[1] (C10th). *LP* finds the *hnig-* element of *hnigstafr* 'bowing-stave' problematic, having no particular transitive meaning as *LP* (1860) had posited (*praelium inclinare faciens* 'causing the battle to bend'); *LP* suggests something like 'those who themselves move or cause movement' in battle. But *hnig-* is from intrans. *hníga* 'to bow down, sink, fall (gently)', the p.p. of which (*hniginn*) often means 'bent with age' or 'fallen in battle' (cf. Lat. *occubitus*). Here, however, the allusion is likely to be to men bowing before God or the Cross. — [4] *hljóms at efsta dómi*: Probably based upon Has 6/6 *hljóms á efsta dómi*. — [6] *til alþingis* 'to the Althing': This conception of the Last Judgement in terms of the Althing is apparently unique in ON. In an Icel. poem the term cannot but evoke the country's general assembly, the highest court of the land, though in Norway the cpd has a less specific sense, simply 'a general meeting' (*Fritzner*). The Last Judgement is also characterised as a *þing* 'assembly' (not *alþingi*) in 27/1, Has 32/1, Likn 27/1, Lil 72/1, and in the late medieval *Píslardrápa* 32/1, 34/1 (*ÍM* I.2, 62); cf. *mót* 'meeting' in the ONorw. Doomsday homily (*HómNo*, 101). In poetry, *alþingi* otherwise occurs only in HǫrðG Lv 7/2 (*Harð* 14)[V], where it refers to the Icel. general assembly. — [7] *fœðis fremðarráðs* 'the nourisher of propitious counsel [= God (= Christ)]': Cf. *fœðir fremðarráða* 'king of famous deeds' (of King Eiríkr Sveinsson of Denmark; Mark Eirdr 4/1[II]). *LP* defines *fremðarráð* (*fremðar róð*, under *fremð*) as 'a deed which wins fame'. Adapted to Christ, the kenning is enriched, more capable of simultaneously suggesting the semantic range of each of its elements: *ráð* 'counsel, plan, authority, deed', perhaps even 'judgement'; *fremð* (here translated adjectively) 'furtherance, aid, fame, nobility'; *fœðir* 'nourisher, author'. Christ's counsels and deeds are both worthy of fame and furthering of salvation.

27. Kross mun á þingi þessu Líta seggja sveitir,
    þjóðum sýndr með blóði   svipur ok spjót á móti
    — uggs fyllaz þá allir   sér ok sjá með dreyra
    aumir menn — ok saumi.   sjálfs Krists viðir Mistar.

Á þessu þingi mun kross sýndr þjóðum með blóði ok saumi; allir aumir menn fyllaz þá uggs. Sveitir seggja líta ok viðir Mistar sjá á móti sér svipur ok spjót með dreyra Krists sjálfs.

At this assembly the Cross will be shown to the people [*lit.* pl.] with blood and nails; all wretched men will be filled then with terror. Hosts of men look, and the trees of Mist <valkyrie> [WARRIORS] see before them the whips and spear with the blood of Christ himself.

Mss: **B**(11v), 399a-b[x]. — *Readings*: [2] með: *so* 399a-b[x], '[...]' B [5] sveitir: *so* 399a-b[x], 'sue[...]' B [7] ok: *so* 399a-b[x], '[...]' B.

Editions: Skj Anonyme digte og vers [XIII], C. 1. *Líknarbraut* 27: AII, 155, BII, 167, Skald II, 88, *NN* §§1392, 2710A, cf. 3040; Sveinbjörn Egilsson 1844, 43, Rydberg 1907, 15-16, 50, Tate 1974, 72.

Notes: [All]: The appearance of the Cross in the heavens (often with other instruments of the Passion) at the Last Judgement is an iconographic and liturgical commonplace. The response *Hoc signum crucis erit in coelo cum Dominus ad judicandum venerit; tunc manifesta abscondita cordis nostri* 'This sign of the cross will be in the heaven when the Lord comes to render judgement; then will be manifest the hidden things of our heart' recurs in the Feast of the Invention of the Cross (3 May) and in the Feast of the Exaltation of the Cross (14 September) (See *Ordo Nidr.*, 339, 394, 414). The appearance of the blood-covered Cross is part of the chilling imagery of the Judgement in *Has* 32-3, in which the terror is so great that even the angels quake with fear and dread (*ugg ok hrælu* 32/8) – a detail occurring also in the Icel. homily on All Saints (*HómÍsl* 1993, 21v; *HómÍsl* 1872, 45) and in the late medieval *Rósa* 124/2 (*ÍM* I.2, 33). The appearance of the Cross at Judgement is likewise mentioned in *Píslardrápa* 31/4 (*ÍM* I.2, 62) and *Milska* 67 (*ÍM* I.2, 53), the latter with other instruments of the Passion. These instruments, the *arma Christi*, are also depicted in the *Íslensk tegnebog* (Fett 1910, pl. 4). — [4] *saumi* 'nails': See Note to 32/1, 4. — [5] *sveitir* 'hosts': Restoration of <itir> based upon 399a-b[x]; <t> confirmed by *skothending*. — [5-7] *líta ... ok sjá* 'look ... and see': Cf. Icel. homily (above), with reference to the Last Judgement, where God's enemies will be required *at siá oc at líta* 'to see and look' toward the Lord. — [6-7] *á móti sér* 'before them': *Skj* B takes *á móti* to mean 'at the assembly' and *sjá sér* as 'become fearful' (cf. *LP* on this passage, the usage otherwise unattested). *NN* §1392 rightly objects to this, but construes *með* 'with' as *ocksá* 'as well' (i.e. 'blood as well as whips and spear'). Surely, however, *með dreyra* 'with blood' describes the condition of *svipur ok spjót* 'whips and spear'. — [8] *viðir Mistar* 'the trees of Mist <valkyrie> [WARRIORS]': Mist is a valkyrie named in *Grm* (*NK* 64; *SnE* 1982, 30) and *Þul Ásynja* 4[III] and *Valkyrja* 1[III]. This is the only occurrence of a mythological name in *Líkn*. Rhymed with *Krists*, and in the context of judgement, it may suggest the juxtaposition of pagan and Christian realms.

28. Heim laðar hvern frá dómi
 himins fyrða til dýrðar
 — gipt þrýtrat þá — gætir
 glyggranns með sér dyggra;
 en veglausum vísar
 vándum lýð til fjánda
 birtiranns at brenna
 byrjar valdr of aldir.

Gætir glyggranns laðar hvern dyggra fyrða heim með sér frá dómi til himins dýrðar; gipt þrýtrat þá; en valdr birtiranns byrjar vísar veglausum vándum lýð til fjánda at brenna of aldir.

The guardian of the storm-house [SKY/HEAVEN > = God (= Christ)] invites each of the faithful men home with him from the Judgement to heaven's glory; grace will not fail then; but the ruler of the radiant house of the wind [SKY/HEAVEN > = God (= Christ)] consigns the inglorious, wicked host to devils to burn forever.

Mss: **B**(11v), 399a-b[x]. — *Readings*: [1] *frá: so* 399a-b[x], '[...]a' B [2] til: '[...]' B, til 399a-b[x] [4] glyggranns: *so* 399a-b[x], 'g[...]ýggrannz' B [6] vándum lýð: 'vǫnnd[...]ýd' B, 'vǫnndum lýð' 399a-b[x].

Editions: *Skj* Anonyme digte og vers [XIII], C. 1. *Líknarbraut* 28: AII, 155, BII, 167, *Skald* II, 88; Sveinbjörn Egilsson 1844, 43-4, Rydberg 1907, 16, 50, Tate 1974, 73.

Notes: [All]: On the division of the multitudes at the Last Judgement, see *Has* 36-9 and the Icel. homily on All Saints (*HómÍsl* 1993, 21v; *HómÍsl* 1872, 45); the fullest ON account, based largely on Matt. XXV.32-46, is the ONorw. homily on Doomsday (*HómNo*, 168-71). — [1] *laðar hvern ... heim frá dómi* 'invites each ... home from the Judgement': Cf. *Leið* 45/5 and *Lil* 68/8. — [3-4] *gætir glyggranns* 'guardian of the storm-house [SKY/HEAVEN > = God (= Christ)]': The source of *glyggrann* may be Mark Frag 1/2[III] where the *glygg-* : *dygg-* rhyme also occurs. The full kenning (with *gætir*) is repeated in *Mdr* 21/1. — [5] *veglausum* (m. dat. sg.) 'inglorious': Possibly also 'pathless, lacking the way', appropriate given the poem's emphasis on 'way': *vegr* (sometimes, as here, ambiguously 'glory' or 'path') and *braut* 'way', as in the title; i.e. those found to be without glory or honour are those who have abandoned 'the way of grace' (see Note to 51/4). — [6] *vándum lýð* 'wicked host': Restoration based upon 399a-b[x]; initial vowel (<ð> in B) adjusted for rhyme and sense by all eds.

29. Hljóta ey með ítrum Krists vinnr krapt ins hæsta
    alfegnastir þegnar   krossmark viðum hnossa
    sólar vörð í sælu   alls bezt; lofar æztan
    slóðar alt it góða.   öll dýrð konung fyrða.

Þegnar alfegnastir hljóta ey alt it góða í sælu með ítrum vörð sólar slóðar. Krossmark ins hæsta Krists vinnr krapt alls bezt viðum hnossa; öll dýrð lofar æztan konung fyrða.

Thanes joyous beyond measure obtain forever every good thing in blessedness with the glorious guardian of the sun's track [SKY/HEAVEN > = God]. The cross-sign of the most-high Christ gains power best of all for trees of treasures [MEN]; all glory exalts the highest king of men [RULER = Christ].

Mss: **B**(11v), 399a-b[x]. — *Reading*: [5-8]: abbrev. as 'Kristr vinnr k-' B, 399a-b[x].

Editions: *Skj* Anonyme digte og vers [XIII], C. 1. *Líknarbraut* 29: AII, 155, BII, 168, *Skald* II, 88, *NN* §1392, 2710A, cf. 3040; Sveinbjörn Egilsson 1844, 44, Rydberg 1907, 16, 50, Tate 1974, 74.

Notes: [3-4] *sólar slóðar* 'of the sun's track [SKY/HEAVEN]': *Slóð* 'track, path' is a base-word in heaven-kennings also in *Has* 19/7-8 (*skýja slóð* 'clouds' track') and *Pl* 4/7 (*mána slóð* 'moon's path'). 'Narrow path' and 'light' are also combined in the liturgical phrase *semita lucis* (Manz 1941, 457, no. 909).

30. Krýp ek til kross, en glæpa Dýrt kveð ek hræddu hjarta
     knosuð bönd af því losna, huggóðs drifit blóði
     óttafullr með öllu grams píslartré geisla
     innan brjósts frá þjósti. grundar sköpum bundinn.

Með öllu óttafullr innan brjósts krýp ek til kross frá þjósti, en bönd glæpa, knosuð af því, losna. Hræddu hjarta, bundinn sköpum, kveð ek dýrt píslartré, drifit blóði, huggóðs grams grundar geisla.

Wholly fearful within my breast, I creep to the Cross away from anger, and the bonds of sin, torn thereby, are loosened. With a fearful heart, bound by fate, I address the precious Passion-tree [CROSS], besprinkled with blood, of the benevolent king of the land of rays [SKY/HEAVEN > = God (= Christ)].

Mss: **B**(11v), 399a-b^x. — *Readings*: [3] óttafullr: 'ótta f[...]llr' B, 'ótta fullr' 399a-b^x; öllu: '[...]llu' B, ǫllu 399a-b^x [6] blóði: 'bl[...]de' B, blóði 399a-b^x.

Editions: *Skj* Anonyme digte og vers [XIII], C. 1. *Líknarbraut* 30: AII, 155-6, BII, 168, *Skald* II, 89, *NN* §1393; Sveinbjörn Egilsson 1844, 44, Rydberg 1907, 16, 50-1, Tate 1974, 75.

Notes: [All]: This st. marks the beginning of the poem's several direct references to the liturgy for Good Friday, including the Adoration of the Cross (*adoratio crucis*) and the Reproaches (*improperia*) of Christ from the Cross (see sts 43-5), signalled by the phrase *Mín þjóð* 'O my people' 45/1, echoing the recurrent *Popule meus* of the rite. Between these two markers (sts 30 and 45), the poet draws occasional images from the two famous Cross hymns by Venantius Fortunatus (C6th), *Pange lingua* (sung during the Adoration) and *Vexilla regis* (the processional hymn at its conclusion); these allusions are pointed out in the Notes. On the history of the rite, see Römer 1955 and Schmidt 1956-7, II, 789-803; for Scandinavia, Gjerløw 1961 and Björkman 1957, 266-7, 282-5; on *Líkn*, Tate 1978. — [1] *krýp ek til kross* 'I creep to the Cross': The phrase alludes to the Adoration of the Cross on Good Friday. See, e.g., the fragment (AM 266 4°, c. 1400) of the Gufudalr Ordinary, adapted from that of Nidaros: *Þui næst skal prestr fara vr messu hökli ok af skoou[m] ok hosum ok kriupi til kross berrfættr ok syngia þad er til er skipat* 'Then shall the priest remove the chasuble and his shoes and hose and creep barefoot to the crucifix and sing that which is specified' (Magnus Már Lárusson 1958, 209). The phrase 'creep to the Cross' only occurs in Germanic vernaculars (see *OED*: *creep* 3; cf. Swed. *krypa till krysse* (C16th), Ahnlund 1924, 180); Lat. employs less descriptive verbs (*procedo, venio ad crucem salutandam*), but more is meant by *krjúpa* here than *LP*'s 'to prostrate oneself or fall upon one's knees'. The verb denotes moving forward in veneration or penitence rather than static kneeling or prostration and is attested in skaldic verse as early as Þloft *Glækv* 8/4[1] (C11th). — [1-2] *bönd glæpa* 'bonds of sin': Cf. Prov. V.22 *funibus peccatorum suorum constringitur* 'fettered by the bonds of his sins'. *Skj* B takes *bönd* with *knosuð* (l. 2) (i.e. 'broken bonds') and *glæpa* with *þjósti* (l. 4); *NN* §1393, unable to see how broken bands can then be loosened, rejects this reading. — [4] *frá þjósti* 'away from anger': Approaching the Cross (on the altar) 'away from anger' may allude to Christ's exhortation in the Sermon on the Mount to put away anger and be reconciled with one's brother before making an offering at the altar (Matt. V.22, 24-5), an injunction especially appropriate in a monastic context. The *þjóst-* : *brjóst-* rhyme also occurs in EGils *Guðkv* 30/2^{IV} and *Lil* 48/8.

31. Heill ver kross, er kallaz,
    Krists mark, himins vistar
    lýðs af læknis dauða
    lykill mannkyni syknu;
    örr því at upp lauk* harri
    élskríns fyr þik sínum,
    áðr þá er læst var lýðum,
    lífs höll vinum öllum.

Heill ver kross, Krists mark, er kallaz lykill himins vistar mannkyni syknu af dauða lýðs læknis; því at örr harri élskríns lauk* upp fyr þik lífs höll öllum sínum vinum þá er áðr var læst lýðum.

Hail Cross, Christ's sign [CROSS], which is called the key of heaven's dwelling for mankind, acquitted through the death of mankind's healer [= Christ]; for the generous lord of the storm-shrine [HEAVEN > = God (= Christ)] opened by means of you life's hall [SKY/HEAVEN] for all his friends, which was earlier locked to men.

Mss: **B**(11v), 399a-b^x. — *Readings*: [5] upp lauk*: '[...]pp laukt' B, upplaukt 399a-b^x [7] er: *so* 399a-b^x, 'e[...]' B; var: *so* 399a-b^x, '[...]' B.

Editions: Skj Anonyme digte og vers [XIII], C. 1. *Líknarbraut* 31: AII, 156, BII, 168, Skald II, 89; Sveinbjörn Egilsson 1844, 44-5, Rydberg 1907, 16, 51, Kock and Meissner 1931, I, 91, Tate 1974, 76.

Notes: [All]: This st. is the first in a catalogue (sts 31-7) devoted to figures of the Cross: as key, blossom, ship, ladder, bridge, scales and altar. Several of these figures, with attendant details, appear in *Pange lingua* and *Vexilla regis*, the famous Cross hymns of Venantius Fortunatus (C6th) used in Good Friday liturgy as well as in feasts of the Cross (Connelly 1957, 79). Almost all of them occur in the Lat. hymns collected by Dreves and Blume in *AH*, which range from mid C11th to early C13th, as well as in exegetical texts and iconography. (Such analogues are pointed out in the Notes to the individual sts.) The late medieval *Gimsteinn* (102-15) contains a similar catalogue of *figurur* (102/1): ladder, road, altar, Noah's ark, ointment, key, rod of Aaron, David's staff (*ÍM* I.2, 327-30). — [1] *heill ver kross* 'hail, Cross': A characteristic beginning of hymns on the Cross. e.g. *Salve crux sancta* 'Hail, holy Cross' (Mone 1853-5, I, 111; cf. 103, 109), *Salve crux, arbor / vitae praeclara* 'Hail, Cross, celebrated tree of life' (*AH* 54, 192; cf. 194); cf. the late medieval *Krossþulur* 2/1 *Heill serttu krucius | kross enn helge* 'Hail, excruciating holy Cross' (*ÍM* I.2, 240). — [2] *Krists mark* 'Christ's sign [CROSS]': Cf. *Geisl* 34/7 *Mark stendr Krists í kirkju* 'the sign of Christ stands in the church'. *Meissner*, 432 lists *Krists mark* among Cross-kennings; on the term 'sign' for the Cross, see Reijners 1965, 118-23, 160-87 (cf. *krossmark* 'cross-sign' 13/6 and *friðarmerki* 'peace-sign' 32/2). — [3] *af dauða lýðs læknis* 'from the death of mankind's [*lit.* people's] healer [= Christ]': The letter form of <a> in *af* is unusual, like an alpha;

Rydberg 1907, 16 reads *of* but emends to *af* (51). Christ is also called *læknir* 'healer, physician' in *Geisl* 57/8 and *Mdr* 14/1. This common appellation is based upon Christ's reference to himself as *medicus* 'physician' in Matt. IX.12 (Mark II.17, Luke V.31). For liturgical occurrences see Manz 1941, 292, no. 588-91 (*medicus bonus, m. caelistis, m. salutaris, m. verus*); Augustine's use of the metaphor is discussed by Arbesmann 1954, 1-28. It is, of course, a sacred paradox that the physician heals by means of his own death. (On the Cross as healer, see Note to 40/1.) — [4] *lykill* 'key': Only occurrence in skaldic poetry. The Cross as key is a fairly common image, based primarily upon the 'key of David' in Isa. XXII.22 and Rev. III.7. See, e.g., Augustine, *Enarrationes in Psalmos* XLV (Augustinus Hipponensis, col. 514) *crux Domini nostri clavis fuit, qua clausa aperirentur* 'the Cross of our Lord was a key by which closed things were opened' and Bonaventure *ipsa crux ... comparatur et assimilitatur in Sacra Scriptura clavi domus David* 'the Cross itself is compared and in holy scripture likened to the key of the house of David' (Bonaventure 1882-1902, IX, 222). The image is also found in Cross hymns, often, as here, with specific reference to opening heaven: e.g. *Ave, clavis reserans / Portas paradisi / Adam quas exasperans / Clausit* 'Hail, key, unlocking the gates of Paradise, which Adam, making them harsh, closed' (*AH* 38, 88, cf. 128; 40, 33; 8, 30); see also *Gimsteinn* 111/1 *Hægur lykill himna ʀikis* 'convenient key of heaven' (*ÍM* I.2, 329). — [5] *lauk upp* 'opened': All eds emend from ms. 'laukt', which the scribe apparently understood to refer to *kross* 'Cross' (l. 1), perhaps construing *harri* 'lord' (l. 5) as vocative, hence 2nd pers. But the subject of the verb has to be *harri*, with *þik* 'you' (l. 6) referring to the Cross. Restoration of <u> based upon 399a-b^x. — [7] *élskríns* 'of the storm-shrine [HEAVEN]': Cf. *veðrskrín* 'storm-shrine' 8/6. The proper object of *lauk upp* 'opened up' (l. 5) is, of course, *lífs höll* 'life's hall [SKY/HEAVEN]' (l. 8), but an associative transfer to the kenning's base-word (*skrín*) may suggest that the Cross opens heaven just as a key opens a casket or shrine. — [8] *er var læst* 'which was locked': Restoration of <r> (*er*) and *var* based upon 399a-b^x and trace of possible <v> in B. Cf. *Gimsteinn* 110/5-6 *Lukuzt vpp dyr þær eʀ læstar voru | með lykli* 'The doors which were locked were opened with a key' (*ÍM* I.2, 329).

32. Heims, bart hvössum saumi, Mátt af dreyra dróttins
     hjálpsterkr, friðarmerki, dags reitar því heita
     lýðr at lausn of næði, blíðs ok bitrum dauða
     limu Krists við þik nista. blómi helgra dóma.

Hjálpsterkr, friðarmerki heims, bart limu Krists nista við þik hvössum saumi at lýðr of næði lausn. Því mátt heita blómi helgra dóma af dreyra ok bitrum dauða blíðs dróttins dags reitar.

Help-strong one, peace-sign of the world [CROSS], you bore the limbs of Christ pinned to you with sharp nail-stitching, so that mankind might obtain liberation. Therefore you can be called the blossom of relics on account of the blood and bitter death of the tender lord of day's furrow [SKY/HEAVEN > = God (= Christ)].

Mss: **B**(11v-12r), 399a-b˟. — *Readings*: [1] hvössum: 'huð[...]um' B, 'huð⸒ȅ⸌[...]um' 399a-b˟ [8] helgra: *so* 399a-b˟, 'he[...]' B.

Editions: *Skj* Anonyme digte og vers [XIII], C. 1. *Líknarbraut* 32: AII, 156, BII, 168, *Skald* II, 89, *NN* §1394; Sveinbjörn Egilsson 1844, 45, Rydberg 1907, 16-17, 51, Tate 1974, 77.

Notes: [1, 4] *nista ... hvössum saumi* 'pinned ... with sharp nail-stitching': Restoration of <ss> suggested by Sveinbjörn Egilsson 1844, 45, accepted by all subsequent eds. *Hvössum* is also used in 36/3 with reference to the Cross as scales. Besides 'seam, stitching' (from *sauma* 'to sew, make a seam'), *saumr* by extension also means 'nail' in ship-making, with reference to seam-like rows of nails along the ship's ribs and gunwales. The sg. is used of ship's nails in Bragi *Rdr* 5/4[III]; cf. *Þul Skipa* 6/4[III]. With reference to the Crucifixion *saumr* occurs elsewhere only at 27/4; its use here adumbrates the next st. in which the Cross is described as a ship. On *nista* see Note to 16/1. — [2] *hjálpsterkr* 'help, salvation-strong': *Skj* B and *Skald* emend to *hjálpsterkt* for agreement with *merki* 'sign', but the adj. can function alone as substantive, in apposition to *friðarmerki* 'peace-sign', the m. referring back to *kross* 'Cross' (or even *lykill* 'key') in the previous st. — [2, 1] *friðarmerki heims* 'peace-sign of the world [CROSS]': *NN* §1394, objecting to *Skj* B's construction *hjálpsterkt merki heims friðar* 'help-strong sign of the world's peace' suggests the cpd *friðarmerki*, analogous to *friðarmark* and *friðartákn* (Fritzner); cf. *signum pacis* 'sign of peace' in a Cross hymn (*AH* 8, 30). — [6] *dags reitar* 'of day's furrow [SKY/HEAVEN]': A somewhat unusual heaven-kenning; cf. *dags land* 'day's land' *Leið* 24/8. *Reitr* (from *ríta* 'to scratch, engrave, write') 'furrow', by extension 'cultivated land', 'a marked out space'. Alternatively the kenning can be read as 'the space inscribed/marked out by the day', or simply as 'day's land'. This is the first use of *reitr* as a base-word in a heaven-kenning (cf. *Lil* 11/4, 26/2). As 'furrow' or 'cultivated land' the noun accords well, however, with the agrarian imagery of the *blómi* 'blossom' (l. 8) watered (rained upon) by the *dreyri* 'blood' of Christ (cf. the use of such imagery as metaphor for inspiration in sts 4-5 and the recurrence of *ár* in the sense of 'year's abundance'; see Note to 5/5). — [8] *blómi helgra dóma* 'the blossom of relics': In the phrase *helgir dómar*, *dómar* has the sense 'relics'; see Mark *Eirdr* 10/2[II] in which Eiríkr *sótti Haralds ... helga dóma út frá Rómi* 'sought Haraldr's relics from Rome'. As in this example, *blóm* or *blómi* 'blossom, flower; flowering' can be abstract, meaning simply 'premier exemplar'. The Cross itself as blossom or flower is unusual, though Jón Arason uses the image later in a poem about the Cross at Réttarholt (1548): *Má það einginn maðr skýra | mektar blóm hvert krossinn er* 'No man can describe what a flower of might the Cross is' (Jón Sigurðsson and Guðbrandr Vigfússon 1858-78, II, 574). Floral imagery is, however, common in poems on the Cross or the Passion, in which the redness of Christ's blood (or Christ himself) is likened to a flower, often a rose: e.g. Fortunatus' *Pange lingua*, st. 8 *Crux fidelis, inter omnes arbor una nobilis – | nulla talem silva profert flore fronde germine* 'Faithful Cross, tree alone notable among others – no forest produces such a one in flower, foliage, or seed' (Bulst 1956, 128; Szövérffy 1976, 15 takes *germine* to mean 'roots' or 'effects'); from another hymn *O Crux, ave, frutex gratus | coeli flore fecundatus | Rubens agni sanguine* 'Hail, Cross, pleasing stalk, made fruitful with the flower of heaven, reddening with the blood of the Lamb' (*AH* 9, 28). It is, however, typically Christ, rather than the Cross itself, that is the flower, based upon S. of S. II.1 *flos campi* 'flower of the field' and Isa. XI.1 where Mary (*virgo*) is interpreted as the 'rod [*virga*] of Jesse' and Christ as the flower that springs from the rod. Cf. (of Christ) the late medieval poems *Blómarós* 165/3, 187/2, 207/3 and *Máríublóm* 16/3, 18/1, 23/1 (*ÍM* I.2, 90 ff.; I.2, 176-7). Bonaventure (C13th) entitles ch. 17 of his tract *Vitis mystica* the 'Rosa passionis', in which he likens the Passion to a rose made red by the blood of Christ (Bonaventure 1882-1902, VIII, 182-3). The phrase *blómi af dreyra ok bitrum dauða dróttins* 'blossom from the Lord's blood and bitter death' (ll. 8, 5, 7) is in this tradition. In the end, however, *blómi helgra dóma* (l. 8) may simply mean 'the flower [i.e. the greatest] of holy relics'.

33. Skeið ert fróns und fríðum Þú snýr böls hjá bárum
farsæl konungs þrælum — boðar kasta þér lasta —
fljót ok farmi ítrum lýðs und líknar auði
fóstrlands á vit strandar. lífs hafnar til stafni.

Ert farsæl, fljót skeið und fríðum þrælum konungs fróns ok ítrum farmi á vit strandar fóstrlands. Þú snýr stafni hjá bárum böls til lífs hafnar und auði líknar lýðs; boðar lasta kasta þér.

You are a voyage-prosperous, swift warship bearing [*lit*. under] beloved servants of the king of earth [RULER = Christ] and a glorious cargo towards the shore of our native land. You turn your prow past the waves of evil to life's haven bearing the wealth of grace for mankind; billows of vices toss you.

Mss: **B**(12r), 399a-b^x. — *Reading*: [3] fljót: *so* 399a-b^x, 'fli[...]' B.

Editions: Skj Anonyme digte og vers [XIII], C. 1. *Líknarbraut* 33: AII, 156, BII, 168-9, Skald II, 89; Sveinbjörn Egilsson 1844, 45, Rydberg 1907, 17, 51, Tate 1974, 78.

Notes: [All]: If *Líkn* had a second *stefjamél* 'refrain section' (see Note to st. 30), its first *stef* would occur here. Instead of a *stef* we encounter a ship, whose *stafn* 'prow' (etymologically connected to *stef*) guides surely to the heavenly port. — [1] *skeið* 'ship': Technically a warship of the long-ship (*langskip*) class (Falk 1912, 104-5; Jesch 2001, 123-4). The noun can also mean 'course, track' (e.g. *sunnu skeið* 'sun's track' in C14th Árni *Gd* 66/1^IV), and the poet's choice of word for 'ship' may be calculated to play on the Cross as *braut* 'way' (*Líknarbraut*) and on the poem's frequent 'way, path' images (see Note to 51/4). The Cross as ship is a patristic and medieval commonplace, based mostly on commentary on Noah's ark, which is usually glossed as the Ship of the Church, with the Cross as mast. But this is often simplified to the Cross itself as ship, as in a l. from the hymn *Salve lignum sanctae crucis* which addresses the Cross as: *veri nautae vera nauta* 'true ship of the true seaman' (*AH* 54, 194). Through reverse typology, Noah's ark is sometimes represented as having been made from the wood of the Cross: *ligno crucis fabricatur / Arca Noe* (*AH* 8, 29). In the late medieval *Gimsteinn* 105/1 the Cross also *makliga merkiʀ* 'fittingly symbolises' Noah's ark (*ÍM* I.2, 327). On the history of these ideas see Rahner 1964, 239-564 'Antenna crucis'. —

[1-2] *und fríðum þrælum* 'bearing [*lit.* under] beloved servants': For *fríðum* 399a-b^x reads *firðum* 'fjords'; so Sveinbjörn Egilsson 1844, 45 (although in a marginal note to 444 Sveinbjörn wrote *fríðum*). *Und* 'under' also governs the dat. *farmi* 'cargo' (l. 3) (on Christ as the cargo, and possibly as captain, see Notes to ll. 3 and 7). The 'beloved servants' are perhaps the saints or more generally the righteous, possibly even the clergy who guide the faithful. — [3] *fljót* 'swift': Restoration of 'ót' based upon 399a-b^x, with 't' confirmed by *skothending*. The lit. sense 'floating' (from *fljóta* 'to float') suits the nautical context. — [3] *ítrum farmi* (dat. sg.) 'glorious cargo': 399a-b^x, expanding the abbreviation differently, reads *frami* 'forward, in front'; so also Sveinbjörn Egilsson. The cargo is either the crucified Christ or the salvation (cf. *auðr líknar* 'wealth of grace', l. 7) won by his suffering. The Cross is often called 'salvation-bearing' (*crux salutifera*), in liturgy (Manz 1941, 132, no. 213), poetry (Bonaventure 1882-1902, VIII, 667, st. 7), and elsewhere: e.g. Dungal (Dungalus Reclusus C9th), who, in defending the veneration of images, writes how hopeless it is for mankind to try to navigate the stormy sea of this world *sine nave salutiferae crucis* 'without the ship of the salvation-bearing Cross' (Dungalus Reclusus, col. 489). — [3] *á vit strandar fóstrlands* 'toward the shore of our native land': Cf. *Pl* 55/2. This is the only skaldic occurrence of *fóstrland* 'foster-land, native land' as heavenly homeland; cf. *ad caelestem patriam* 'to the heavenly fatherland' (*AH* 54, 194). *Á vit*, with gen., lit. 'on a visit with'. — [5] *hjá bárum böls* 'past the waves of evil': 399a-b^x (so also Sveinbjörn Egilsson 1844, 45) reads *barmi* 'brim'; in a marginal note 444 has *bárum* (so all other eds). Together with *boðar lasta* 'billows of vices' the phrase, possibly a kenning-like circumlocution for sin, evokes the widespread idea that this world is like a perilous sea, its surging waves and raging storms representing various aspects of evil, by which mankind is easily shipwrecked. For discussion see Rahner 1964, 272-303 and 432-72; cf. the common liturgical phrase *mare saeculi* 'sea of the world' (Manz 1941, 291, no. 586). Fortunatus' *Pange lingua* evokes this tradition in the ll.: *Sola digna tu fuisti ferre pretium saecli / atque portum praeparare nauta mundo naufrago* 'You alone were worthy to bear the price of the world (Christ) and, like the seaman, to make ready a haven for a shipwrecked world' (Bulst 1956, 128, st. 10); in later liturgical use *nauta* was replaced by *arca* 'ark' to strengthen the idea of the Cross as ship (see Connelly 1957, 85). — [6] *boðar lasta kasta þér* 'billows of vices toss you': Rydberg includes *hjá böls bárum* 'past the waves of sin' (l. 5) in this intercalary cl. *Skj* B and *Skald* add a negative particle (*kastat* 'do not toss'), but this misses the point that the voyage *is* rough and that mankind's only safety in such peril is the Cross and what it represents. Peter Chrysologus (C5th), e.g., writes that the ship *tunditur ... non mergitur* 'is pounded but not sunk' (Petrus Chrysologus, *Sermo* 21, col. 258); Augustine, too, describes the sea as so turbulent that even those who are borne upon the cross-tree can scarcely (*vix*) traverse it (Augustinus Hipponensis, *Confessionum*, I, XVI.25, col. 672; O'Donnell 1992, I, 12). The etymology of *boði* in a marine context is disputed. Most ON dictionaries see it as deriving from *boða* 'to announce' (*boði* 'messenger, proclaimer'), i.e. a wave which, breaking over a submerged reef or skerry, 'announces' or 'bodes' the hidden rocks (so *CVC*, *LP*, and *Fritzner*). Ulvestad and Beeler 1957 believe this to be a folk etymology and conclude that it is 'more appropriate to regard "submerged reef" (semantically unrelated to *boða*) as the

primary meaning, and "wave" or "breaker" as the secondary' (214). For yet another view, see *AEW*: *boði* 2. With the verb *kasta* 'to throw, toss', however, 'billow' seems the preferable sense; a ship that strikes a reef in a storm does not survive to continue its journey. It is possible that the poet is also playing on the lit. sense in which *boðar lasta* means simply 'proclaimers, preachers of vices'; these, too, are sometimes associated with threatening waves, as in the Epistle of Jude, who likens false teachers to *fluctus feri maris despumantes suas confusiones* 'waves of the raging sea, foaming out their own confusion' (13). — [7] *und auði líknar lýðs* 'bearing [*lit.* under] the wealth of grace for mankind': A reference to Christ's Passion and mankind's consequent salvation, parallel to *ítrum farmi* 'glorious cargo' (l. 3). On 'wealth of grace', cf. the liturgical phrases *copia miserationum* 'abundance of compassions' and *immensa clementia* 'immense mercy' (Manz 1941, 124 §194; 225 §431).

34. Stigi nefniz þú stafna
    stálfríðundum smíði
    traustr af tvennrar ástar
    — tek ek minni þess — kinnum.

Framm kemr hverr á himna
hræskóðs ok fær góða
stétt, þá er stig þín hittir,
styrjar lundr af grundu.

Þú nefniz stigi, traustr af kinnum tvennrar ástar, smíði stafna stálfríðundum; ek tek minni þess. Hverr lundr styrjar hræskóðs kemr framm ok fær góða stétt af grundu á himna, þá er hittir þín stig.

You are called a ladder, trusty on account of side-poles of twofold love, a smith-work of stems for prow-adorners [SEAFARERS]; I take remembrance of this. Each tree of the tumult of the corpse-scathe [WEAPON > BATTLE > WARRIOR] advances and receives a good pathway from the earth to the heavens, when he gains your steps.

Mss: **B**(12r), 399a-b[x]. — *Readings*: [3] traustr: 'trau[...]r' B, trauṣṭṛ 399a-b[x] [6] góða: *so* 399a-b[x], 'g[...]da' B.

Editions: Skj Anonyme digte og vers [XIII], C. 1. *Líknarbraut* 34: AII, 156, BII, 169, *Skald* II, 89, *NN* §1395; Sveinbjörn Egilsson 1844, 45-6, Rydberg 1907, 17, 51, Tate 1974, 79.

Notes: [All]: The dominant image of the st., the Cross as ladder, is an exegetical commonplace deriving from commentary on Jacob's vision of a ladder extending to heaven (Gen. XXVIII.12-13). E.g., in a sermon that circulated under Augustine's authority in the Middle Ages, Caesarius of Arles (C6th) writes: *Scala ipsa usque ad caelos attingens, crucis figuram habuit* 'The ladder itself extending to the heavens held the figure of the Cross' (*Sermo* 87 in Morin 1953, 360; cf. *Classis prima*, auctor incertus [Augustinus Hipponensis?], col. 1761). The connection of Jacob's ladder with the Cross also occurs in the late medieval Icel. *Gimsteinn* 102/5-03/4 (*ÍM* I.2, 327). Medieval commentators often gloss the parts of the ladder – e.g., the side-poles or stiles (*latera*) as Christ's two natures, the two Testaments, etc. The probable source for *kinnum tvennrar ástar* 'side-poles of twofold love' (ll. 3-4), i.e. love of God and neighbour (Matt. XXII.37-9), is Honorius

Augustodunensis (C12th), who was known in Iceland mainly through his *Eluc* and *Gemma animae*, both of which were translated into ON. In his sermon on Quinquagesima Sunday in *Speculum ecclesiae*, and again in *Scala coeli minor*, Honorius allegorises the parts of a ladder of love which is clearly the Cross. Of the side-poles he writes: *Hujus scalae vero latera sunt geminae dilectionis, Dei scilicet et proximi dilectio* 'The side-poles of this ladder are indeed twofold love, i.e. love of God and neighbour' (cols 869 and 1239). An analogue (noted by Paasche 1914a, 130) is in the Icel. homily on the Cross, which allegorises the arms of the Cross as *óst við goþ oc meN* 'love for God and men' (*HómÍsl* 1993, 17v; *HómÍsl* 1872, 38; cf. *HómNo*, 104). Árni Jónsson later borrows several details from *Líkn* for his *Gd*[V], including the 'ladder of twofold love' *elsku tvennrar stigi* (72/6-7); see Tate 1978-9. — [2-3] *smíði stafna stálfriðundum* 'a smith-work of prows for stem-adorners [SEAFARERS]': The nautical image looks back to the Cross as ship in the preceding st. Probably because the phrase seems to refer twice to the same thing – according to *LP*: *stafn* and *stál* can both mean prow – *Skj* B emends to *stafna stóðríðǫndum* 'for riders of prow-horses [SHIPS > SEAFARERS]' (cf. *LP*: *stálfriðandi*), a change *NN* §1395 rejects, arguing that *stál* is part of, not synonymous with, *stafn*. This distinction is confirmed by Falk 1912, 36 and 84; *stál* is the rising keel beam or beak of the prow, *stafn* the stem, or prow deck. Cf. Jesch 2001, 145 and 150, who observes that *stafn* is the generic term for either end of a viking ship and cites skaldic examples supporting Falk's interpretation of *stál* as the stem-post of the prow or fore-stem. Sveinbjörn Egilsson 1844, 45, followed by Rydberg 1907, 51, combines *stál* with *smíði* by means of tmesis: i.e., 'a steel/sturdy [*firmissima*] structure for adorners of prows' (*LP* (1860): *stál-smíði*). The interpretation here accords with a suggestion of Edith Marold, that images of the Cross might have decorated the prows of Scandinavian ships; thus the Cross could be described as *smíði stafna* 'a smith-work of prows' for sailors who used it to decorate their ships, so 'stem-adorners' (*stálfriðundum*). — [3] *traustr* 'trusty': Restoration based upon 399a-b[x], supported by *skothending*. The m. sg. adj. modifies *stigi* 'ladder'. Though *Skj* A acknowledges the trace of <r> in a note, it is not included in the diplomatic text; hence *Skj* B and *Skald* emend unnecessarily to n. *traust* for agreement with *smíði* 'smith-work', construed here as appositive. — [4] *tek ek*: *Skj* B and *Skald* emend to cliticised pret. *tókk*. — [4] *kinnum* (dat. pl.) 'side-poles': Lit. 'cheeks'. This is the only ON occurrence of *kinn* 'cheek' in this sense, though it (and more commonly its derivative *kinnungr*) is used of a ship's bow (*Fritzner*: *kinnungr* 2). The underlying idea seems to be 'cheeks' as parallel (or converging) members, whether side-poles (stiles) of a ladder or forward gunwales of a ship. (Cf. the synonym *hlýr* 'cheek', used metaphorically of sides of axe, blade, or ship's bow, and, with respect to the last, Jesch 2001, 147 construes *hlýr* as 'imagining the ship as a face seen head-on'. — [6] *góða* 'good': Restoration of <ó> based upon 399a-b[x], confirmed by rhyme. — [6, 8] *lundr styrjar hræskóðs* 'tree of corpse-scathe's tumult [BATTLE > WEAPON > WARRIOR]': The weapon kenning *hræskóð* (not so much something that harms corpses but a scathe that makes corpses of men) occurs also in the primary ms. of Hfr *Óldr* 4/2[I], with a variant reading *hjálmskóð* 'helmet-scathe', which *Skj* B accepts for Hfr while allowing *hræskóð* to stand in *Líkn*. Perhaps extrapolating from the variant in Hfr, *Skald* emends *Líkn* also to *hjálmskóð*, overturning the evidence of primary mss of two different poems. (Cf. analogous *valskóð* 'slaughter scathe' in GOdds Lv 4/2^IV.) The conflation of 'tumult' (*styrr*) and 'tree' (*lundr*) recalls the imagery of 'din-trees' (*gnýviðir*) in 16/7. — [7] *þín stig* 'your steps': The only occurrence of *stig* in poetry; *Skald*, construing acc. sg. of *stigr* m. 'pathway', emends *þín* to *þinn*.

35. Bezt ert brú til ástar, Færir ganga þik fyrðar
     brýn þó at torgeng sýniz fimir í lið til himna;
     gumna kind, af grundu hallaz af þér, er illrar
     guðs þrælum fullsælum. óvenju til spenjaz.

Ert bezt brú til ástar af grundu fullsælum þrælum guðs, brýn þó at sýniz torgeng kind gumna. Færir fyrðar, fimir í lið, ganga þik til himna; hallaz af þér, er spenjaz til illrar óvenju.

You are the best bridge to love from earth for the fully blessed servants of God, though you seem conspicuous, difficult to traverse for the children of men. Capable men, agile in limb, traverse you to the heavens; they fall off you who are allured to evil misconduct.

Mss: **B**(12r), 399a-b^x. — *Readings*: [3] grundu: *so* 399a-b^x, 'g[...]du' B [5] Færir: 'fè[...]er' B, 'fè[...]ir' 399a-b^x [8] spenjaz: 'spe[...]azth' B, 'spennazth' 399a-b^x.

Editions: *Skj* Anonyme digte og vers [XIII], C. 1. *Líknarbraut* 35: AII, 156-7, BII, 169, *Skald* II, 89, *NN* §2329; Sveinbjörn Egilsson 1844, 46, Rydberg 1907, 17, 51, Kock and Meissner 1931, I, 91, Tate 1974, 80.

Notes: [All]: The Cross as way is inherent in the poem's title *Líknarbraut* 'way of grace' (see Note to 51/4). Here that way is a bridge (*brú*, l. 1), apparently difficult to traverse, leading to heaven. This image is in the tradition of various obstacle bridges crossing a water barrier to the Otherworld (see Patch 1950, *passim*; for ON, see Boberg 1966, nos F152 and A657.1). The motif received its classical formulation in Gregory's *Dialogues* (Gregorius I, *Dialogorum* IV, chs 37-38, cols 384-8; ON translation in *Hms* I, 249-51, differently numbered and, because of a gap in fragments, missing Gregory's explication). A soldier who dies of the plague but shortly comes back to life tells how he saw a bridge over a black river, on the other side of which were lovely meadows and gleaming mansions. The bridge is such that if a wicked man attempts to cross it he falls into the river, but the righteous are able to cross safely. Questioned by his interlocutor, Gregory explains that the bridge teaches us that *angusta valde est semita quae ducit ad vitam* 'very narrow is the way that leads to life' (cf. Matt. VII.14), and that the black river represents the vice and corruption of the world. This text is important background for this st., not only because it was known in Iceland, but because Gregory uses Matt. VII.14 to explicate the bridge. It is this passage in turn that underlies the frequent medieval representations of the Cross as way, e.g. Hildebert of Lavardin's *Liber de sacra eucharista crux... via vitae* 'the Cross is the way of life' (Hildebertus Cenomanensis [C12th], col. 1205) and, from hymns, *AH* 9, 27 *Crux est coelorum via* 'The Cross is the way of/to heaven'. In subsequent formulations the narrowness or difficulty of the bridge is emphasised; it is often sharp-edged or spiked. In *Duggals leiðsla* (C13th trans.

of C12th *Visio Tnugdali*), e.g., such a bridge is described as only a hand's breadth and studded with sharp steel spikes (*Hms* I, 339; Cahill 1983, 40); for further medieval examples, including sword bridges, see Patch 1950, 73, 98, 123, 284 and 303-5. While the bridge of this st. is clearly in this tradition, specific references to the Cross itself as bridge are rare; unlike most of the poem's other figures of the Cross, this image is not a recurrent motif in hymns and exegetical literature. The wood of the Cross *does* appear as a footbridge in legends of the cross-tree before the Crucifixion; beginning in the C12th, these occur in various versions with varying details (see Meyer 1882). The popular *Legenda aurea* version (C13th) recounts that when workmen were unable to fit the cross-tree's wood into any part of Solomon's temple, they cast it across a pond for use as a footbridge (*pons*). When later the Queen of Sheba, visiting Solomon, was about to cross the bridge, she saw in spirit (*uidit in spiritu*) that the Saviour of the world was destined to hang from the beam, and she immediately knelt in veneration (Meyer 1882, 124). In the later Icel. version, she has goose feet, which are transformed into those of a human as she removes her shoes in reverence before crossing the bridge (Overgaard 1968, 41). In some versions, a small bridge of the same wood (*a tre þat the cros was made offe*) is laid across the brook Cedron (e.g., in C14th *Mandeville's Travels*, see Hamelius 1919-23, I, 62; cf. Meyer 1882, 163); in others the beam is made into a footbridge for people going to the temple, symbolising, as Meyer 1882, 161 notes, that the Cross of Christ is the bridge to heaven (*die Brücke zum Himmel*). The idea of a bridge to suggest mediation is also used of Mary in the late medieval poem *María heyr mig háleitt víf* 4/5, where she is called *hjálpar brú* 'bridge of salvation' (*ÍM* II, 258). — [2] *brýn* 'conspicuous': For this sense see *ONP*: *brýnn* adj. 1. *Skj* B translates loosely as 'leading (to love)', and all eds other than Kock and Meissner 1931, I, 91 (see glossary 'steep, narrow', II, 21) appear to construe the adj. as a positive contrast to *torgeng* 'difficult to traverse' – a contrast supported by the position of the adj. just before *þó at torgeng syniz* 'though you seem difficult to traverse' in l. 2. *LP* gives 'sharp-edged' as the first meaning but gives 'easy to traverse' for this occurrence. — [2] *torgeng* 'difficult to traverse': Cf. synonymous *torfærr* (Fritzner). *Gengr* commonly refers to the capacity to walk but can also refer to passability; e.g. *illgengr* is used both of a horse with rough gait and of something '"bad to pass" of ice, crags, or the like' (*CVC*). — [3] *grundu* (dat.) 'earth': Restoration based upon 399a-b^x, with <n> supported by *skothending* and by a nasal stroke over the damaged third letter, of which the lower tip of a minim remains. — [5] *færir* 'capable': Sveinbjörn Egilsson 1844, 46 conjectures *færðir* 'are brought'; for *færðir í lið LP* (1860) gives *ordinatim instructi* 'arranged in succession'. That the '-er' abbreviation is, however, directly over the third letter (remnant of possible 'r') in B argues against -*rðir*, even if space of the lacuna might allow a further letter. The single <r> of *færir* is also sufficient for *skothending* with *fyrðar* 'men'. — [6] *fimir* 'agile, clever': A favourite adj. in *Leið* (6/6, 15/2, 17/4, 26/6), where all instances rhyme, as here, with *himn*-. — [7] *þér er*: *NN* §2329 (cf. *Skald*), objecting to *er* 'who' as overly elliptical for '[those] who', suggests that the '-er' abbreviation of *þér* 'you' be expanded to form *þeir* 'they'. But there is no other instance of the abbreviation as '-eir', and the ms. reading makes perfectly good sense. — [8] *spenjaz* 'are allured': Restoration based upon 399a-b^x's reading of <n> and *aðalhending* with *óvenju*.

With the exception of *eigniz* 'might obtain' 52/7 (ms. 'eígnezt'), this is the poem's only instance of '-zt(h)' as m.v. ending, elsewhere consistently '-z'. Sveinbjörn Egilsson, based upon 399a-b[x], has *spennazth*.

36. Heims lézt verð ok virða
    vegit gimsteinum fegra,
    himna ljóss, í hvössum,
    háleitr, friðar skálum.

    Vág erat víst né frægri
    (vétt sýnir þú rétta)
    ófs til ýta gæfu
    (alsetrs vera) betri.

Háleitr, ljóss himna, lézt vegit verð heims ok virða, fegra gimsteinum, í hvössum skálum friðar. Erat víst betri né frægri *vág* til ýta ófs gæfu; þú sýnir rétta vétt alsetrs vera.

High, radiant one of the heavens [CROSS], you weighed the price of the world and men, fairer than gems, in sharp scales of peace. Surely there is not a better or more famous balance for men's bounteous good fortune; you show the just weight of the common seat of men [WORLD].

Mss: **B**(12r), 399a-b[x]. — *Reading*: [5] *Vág*: '[...]' B, 399a-b[x].

Editions: *Skj* Anonyme digte og vers [XIII], C. 1. *Líknarbraut* 36: AII, 157, BII, 169, *Skald* II, 89, *NN* §§1394, 1396; Sveinbjörn Egilsson 1844, 46, Rydberg 1907, 17, 51, Tate 1974, 81.

Notes: [All]: Like other images in this catalogue of Cross figures (sts 31-7), the idea of the Cross as scales (*skálum*, l. 4; *vág*, l. 5) in which Christ, the 'price of the world' (*verð heims*, l. 1) is weighed, is also found in one of Fortunatus' hymns, sung in Good Friday liturgy. St. 6 of *Vexilla regis*, addressed to the Cross, reads: *Beata, cuius brachiis / pretium pependit saeculi, / statera facta corporis / praedam tulitque tartari* 'Blessed (tree), on whose branches the price of the world was weighed; [it was] made the scales of [Christ's] body, and it lifted up the plunder of hell' (Bulst 1956, 129). *Pretium saeculi* occurs in *Pange lingua* 10 as well (Bulst 1956, 128); cf. 1 Cor. VI.20 *Empti enim estis pretio magno* 'For you are bought with a great price'. In a passage noted by Paasche 1914a, 130, Alan of Lille (C12th) also articulates this idea in his *Distinctiones*: *Statera ... dicitur crux Christi, in qua ponderatum est pretium nostrae redemptionis, id est corpus Christi* 'The Cross is said to be the scales of Christ, in which has been weighed the price of our redemption, i.e. the body of Christ' (Alanus de Insulis, col. 955). The phrase *statera crucis* 'scales of the Cross' occurs in liturgy (Manz 1941, 472, no. 942) and in hymns (e.g. *AH* 53, 193); on the iconography of the image see Wormald 1937-8, 276-80. — [1-2] *lézt vegit* 'you weighed': *Láta vegit* can mean either 'to cause, allow to be weighed' or simply 'to weigh'. — [2] *fegra gimsteinum* 'fairer than gems': The phrase also occurs, of God's words, in 7/6, 8. — [3-4] *hvössum skálum friðar* 'in sharp scales of peace': The adj. *hvass* typically means 'sharp, acute', here referring to Christ's suffering. *Friðar* 'of peace' seems more suitable with *skálum* 'scales' than with *himna ljóss* (see below), both because of proximity and because it is through the balance of the Cross that the atonement (at-one-ment) is effected, whereby peace is won for mankind. — [4, 3] *háleitr ljóss himna* 'high, radiant one of the heavens [CROSS]': *Ljóss* 'radiant' is here construed as a substantival adj., which with *háleitr* 'high' qualifies the 2nd pers. subject, deriving m. gender from implied *kross* 'Cross'. *LP* (1860), construing a sun-kenning, renders the phrase *alte in solem suspiciens* 'gazing [from *-leitr*] high toward the sun'. *Skj* B and *Skald* emend to n. *háleitt ljós* and combine the phrase with *friðar* 'of peace' (l. 4). *Skj* B (cf. *LP*: *háleitr*) then takes this to refer to God, but *NN* §1394 to the Cross as 'peace-light of heaven'. (Using *Skj* B's emended text, Guðrún Nordal 2001, 293 cites *himna ljós* 'light of the heavens' as the only time *ljós* occurs as a base-word in a kenning for Christ in C12th-C13th.) — [5] *vág* 'balance-scales': Lacuna in B; upper right of possible <g> remains. Alliteration and l. length require a monosyllabic word beginning with <v>. Sveinbjörn Egilsson 1844, 46 suggests *vag*, which (as *vág*) has been accepted by all subsequent eds. — [6] *vétt* 'weight': Possibly *vett* (ms. *vétt*, but accents are inconsistent). Only *LP* gives *vétt* as a headword (here for *aðalhending* with *rétta*); *CVC*, *AEW*, and *Fritzner* see *vett* as an alternative spelling of *vætt* 'weight'. In either case, this is the only occurrence in skaldic poetry. It is unclear, however, whether the word refers to Christ (like *pretium saeculi* / *heims verð*, l. 1) or, perhaps more likely, to the weight of the sin-laden world which Christ's sacrifice outweighs. — [7] *ófs* (gen. sg.) 'bounteous': Lit. 'of great quantity'. *Skj* B (*LP*) construes as *overmod* 'pride'; Finnur Jónsson 1901, 24 suggests that *ófs* is a contraction of *óhóf* 'immoderation'. The gen. sg., however, often functions as an intensive, 'greatly, very'; *LP* (1860), Rydberg 1907, 51, and *NN* §1396 read it this way but apply it to *rétta*, i.e. 'very just'. Here, however, it is taken with *gæfu*, i.e. 'bounteous good-fortune', with reference to the immeasurable grace extended to mankind through the Passion. — [8] *alsetrs vera* 'of the common seat of men [EARTH]': *Skj* B separates and emends the prefix to *alls*, assigning the adj. to the intercalary clause to modify *ófs* (i.e., 'the just weight of all pride'), but the *al-* prefix means simply 'general, common' as in *alþingi* 'general assembly'. *Alsetrs vera*, a kenning for 'of the whole world' (*NN* §1396); cf. *Meissner*, 87, based on *Skj* B: *vera setr* as earth-kenning, i.e. 'the earth as dwelling place of mankind'. The sense here is probably more 'world' (*saeculum* with its moral implications), than 'earth' *per se*; it is not physical creation that is weighed in the balance of the Cross. — [8] *betri* 'better': The abbreviation, here expanded as '-ri' can also be expanded '-ir'; in 399a-b[x] Jón Sigurðsson adopts the former in his transcription but notes 'bet*ir* ms.' in margin.

37. Sæfðu lamb guðs lofðar
 ljóst (hafa þess í brjóstum)
 ok ert enn í slíku
 altári (lög sára),
 því at lautviðir létu
 lastbundnir helgasta
 linns, þá er lausn gaf mönnum,
 lífs fórn á þik borna.

Lofðar sæfðu ljóst lamb guðs — hafa þess lög sára í brjóstum — ok ert enn altári í slíku, því at lastbundnirlinns lautviðir létu helgasta fórn lífs, þá er gaf mönnum lausn, borna á þik.

Men slaughtered the radiant Lamb of God — they have its sea of wounds [BLOOD] in their breasts — and you are still an altar in such [offering], for sin-bound trees of the serpent's dell [(*lit.* 'dell-trees of the serpent') GOLD > MEN] caused the holiest sacrifice of life, that which gave men liberation, to be placed upon you.

Mss: **B**(12r), 399a-b˟. — *Reading*: [1] lamb: *so* 399a-b˟, '[...]amb' B.

Editions: *Skj* Anonyme digte og vers [XIII], C. 1. *Líknarbraut* 37: AII, 157, BII, 170, *Skald* II, 89-90, *NN* §§1397, 2331; Sveinbjörn Egilsson 1844, 46-7, Rydberg 1907, 17-18, 51, Tate 1974, 82.

Notes: [All]: The Cross as altar (*altári*, l. 4), on which the Lamb of God is sacrificed, is a frequent Christian image. See, e.g., the final st. of Fortunatus' *Vexilla regis* which begins *Salve, ara, salve victima* 'Hail, altar, hail, victim' (Bulst 1956, 129), and st. 5 of the sequence *Laudes crucis attollamus*, attr. Adam of S. Victor (C12th) *O quam felix, quam praeclara / Fuit haec salutis ara / Rubens agni sanguine* 'O how blessed, O how famous, was this altar of salvation, growing red with the blood of the Lamb' (*AH* 54, 188; cf. *AH* 8, 26 and 30). The idea occurs also in Icel. liturgical mss: *ara crucis* 'altar of the Cross' in *De sancta cruce missa*, AM 98 I 8° (C13th, Gjerløw 1980, I, 35) and *tu amara crucis ara* 'you bitter altar of the Cross' in the hymn for Vespers, attr. Bonaventure (C13th), in AM 241 a fol (early C14th, Gjerløw 1980, I, 223); cf. *Gimsteinn* 104/1 *Alltare erttu gudz* 'you are the altar of God' (*ÍM* I.2, 327). — [1] *lamb guðs* 'Lamb of God': Restoration of <l> based upon 399a-b˟ and alliteration; a kenning-like formulation from Lat. *agnus Dei*, based on John I.29. — [2] *ljóst* 'radiant': Sveinbjörn Egilsson 1844, 46 and Rydberg 1907, 51 construe as adv. 'brightly' with *hafa* 'have' (l. 2). — [2] *hafa* 'they have': Ms. 'h' with superscript 'a'; *NN* §1397 suggests reading ms. abbreviation as *hefr* '(you) have', agreeing with an implied 2nd pers. subj.; cf. *ert* (ms. *ertu*) (l. 3). While addressing the intercalary clause to the Cross would accord with frequent descriptions of the altar covered with blood, the pl. *í brjóstum* 'in (their) breasts' supports the pl. verb. In *NN* §1397 Kock renders *þess* 'its' (l. 2) as 'for its sake' but in §1397 construes it as a rel. pron. referring to *lamb* (l. 1). — [3-4] *ert enn altári í slíku* 'you are still an altar in such [offering]': The inexactness of *í slíku* 'in such (a thing)' makes the phrase somewhat vague; the reference may be to the role of the Cross in the eucharistic offering of the mass, which symbolically renews the sacrifice of the Lamb. — [4] *altári* 'altar': The second <a> is long, as in Lat. *altāri*. The noun occurs four times in skaldic poetry, but only here in a rhyme position. — [5-8]: The same alliterative pattern ('l') occurs throughout the *helmingr*, echoing that of the st.'s first couplet. The recurrence of 'l', not only in regular alliteration but elsewhere (*slíku*, l. 3; *altári, lög*, l. 4; *helgasta*, l. 6), continually ties the st. back to the *lamb* 'Lamb' (l. 1). — [6, 5, 7] *lastbundnir lautviðir linns* 'sin-bound dell-trees of the serpent [GOLD > MEN]': *Laut* 'dell', is a small, wooded hollow or valley, by extension simply 'land'. Analogous to *lastbundnir* 'sin-bound' is *bönd glæpa* 'bonds of sin' 30/1-2 (cf. Prov. V.22). The combination here of tree, serpent, and sin may be consciously intended to evoke the fall of Adam. If so, the st. has an implicit typological structure, counterbalancing Adam (*figura Christi*, Rom. V.14) with Christ (the New Adam, 1 Cor. XV.45-9), the Tree of Knowledge with the Tree of Life (the Cross), and original sin with its remedy through the atonement of Christ, the *helgasta fórn lífs* 'holiest sacrifice of life' (ll. 6, 8). From Origen forward, the exegetical and iconographic tradition has placed Adam's grave (as represented by a skull, see Kirschbaum *et al.* 1968-76, IV, 343) on Calvary at the foot of the Cross, so that the blood of the Second Adam pours over the first, prefiguring for Adam and his posterity liberation from death and the effects of sin. — [7] *lausn* 'liberation, release': Within the *helmingr*'s pattern of contrasts, the noun *lausn* (from *leysa* 'to loosen, unbind') plays against, and provides the solution for, *lastbundnir* 'sin-bound' (cf. *lausnari* 'releaser, redeemer').

38. Snjallr, ert orðinn öllum   Leggr andskota undan
     ofrníðingum síðan   ætt fyr göfgum mætti
     djöflum leiðr ept dauða,   opt ok yðrum krapti
     dýrr kross, himinstýris.   óttagjörn á flótta.

Dýrr kross, ert snjallr orðinn öllum ofrníðingum síðan, djöflum leiðr ept dauða himinstýris. Andskota ætt, óttagjörn, leggr undan opt á flótta fyr yðrum göfgum mætti ok krapti.

Precious Cross, you have afterwards attained power over all arch-villains, [you are] hateful to devils since the death of heaven's ruler [= God (= Christ)]. The devil's clan, eager with fear, flees often before your noble might and power.

Mss: **B**(12r), 399a-b[x].

Editions: *Skj* Anonyme digte og vers [XIII], C. 1. *Líknarbraut* 38: AII, 157, BII, 170, *Skald* II, 90; Sveinbjörn Egilsson 1844, 47, Rydberg 1907, 18, 51, Tate 1974, 83.

Notes: [All]: Sts 38-41 (especially 39-40) appear to be based largely on a list of virtues and powers of the Cross in the Icel. homily *De sancta cruce* (*HómÍsl* 1993, 18r; *HómÍsl* 1872, 39; cf. *HómNo*, 105), beginning with *fyr crosse drotteɴs fløia dioflar. hræpesc helvite* 'devils flee before the Cross of the Lord; hell is afraid'. The devils' fear of, or flight from, the Cross (or its sign) is a common motif. See, e.g., Pseudo-Augustine, *Sermo* 247 (Auctor incertus [Augustinus Hipponensis?], col. 2203) *Hoc signo daemones fugantur* 'At this sign demons are put to flight', and, from hymns, *O crux praeclara, / quam impia / tremunt tartara* 'O famous Cross, which the ungodly, infernal regions fear' (*AH* 9, 25); the idea occurs also in the late medieval Icel. *Gimsteinn* 113/8 *enn giædi hans* [i.e. *krossins*] *munu dioflaʀ hrædazt* 'but devils will fear its [the Cross's] virtue' (*ÍM* I.2, 329; cf. *Máríublóm* 18/5-6, *ÍM* I.2, 176). — [1] *snjallr* 'powerful, valiant'. Perhaps striving for equality in adj. distribution, *Skj* B, followed by *Skald*, emends to gen. *snjalls* to modify *himinstýris* 'heaven's ruler' (l. 4), but this is unnecessary. — [4] *himinstýris* 'of heaven's ruler [= God (= Christ)]': The kenning occurs elsewhere only in *Mdr* 40/4, where *dýr-* and *stýr-* are again rhymed. — [5] *leggr undan … á flótta* 'flees': *Skj* B construes *undan* as prep. with *krapti*, i.e. 'under [your] power', but *LP* (1860): *leggja*, translates *leggja undan* (adv.) *á flótta* simply as 'to flee'. The verbal phrase combines *leggja undan* (e.g. GunnLeif *Merl I* 18/8[VIII]) and *leggja á flótta* (e.g. *Geisl* 29/5-6), both of which mean 'to flee'. — [5] *andskota* 'the devil's': Lit. 'counter-shooter'; although the noun occurs frequently in the general sense 'enemy', it occurs in skaldic poetry only here and in Jón *Lv* 1/3[IV] in its theological sense (common in prose) 'the devil'.

39. Crúx, lemið angr en æxlið   Opt ert éls í höptum
    alt gótt liði dróttins;   ítr lausn viðum rítar;
    sýndr ert seggja kindum,   guma forðar þú gerla
    sigrtrúr í gný vigra.   grandi holds ok andar.

Crúx, lemið angr en æxlið alt gótt dróttins liði; ert sýndr seggja kindum, sigrtrúr í gný vigra. Opt ert ítr lausn viðum rítar éls í höptum; þú forðar gerla guma grandi holds ok andar.

Cross, you cripple grief but cause all good things to increase for the Lord's retinue; you are visible to men's offspring, victory-faithful in the din of spears [BATTLE]. Often you are a glorious liberation to trees of the shield's storm [BATTLE > WARRIORS] in fetters; you rescue men completely from injury of flesh and spirit.

Mss: **B**(12r), 399a-b[x]. — *Readings*:   [1] Crúx: *so* 399a-b[x], '[...]' B   [4] vigra: *so* 399a-b[x], '[...]gr[...]' B.

Editions: *Skj* Anonyme digte og vers [XIII], C. 1. *Líknarbraut* 39: AII, 157, BII, 170, *Skald* II, 90; Sveinbjörn Egilsson 1844, 47, Rydberg 1907, 18, 52, Tate 1974, 84.

Notes: [All]: The enumerative quality of the st., in which each couplet is a separate syntactic unit, focusing on a particular virtue of the Cross, derives from its rather close following of the powers of the Cross listed in the Icel. homily *De sancta cruce* (*HómÍsl* 1993, 18r; *HómÍsl* 1872, 39; cf. *HómNo*, 105). — [1] *Crúx* 'Cross': Lacuna; restoration based upon 399a-b[x], supported by *skothending*. Here and in 52/1 (*mæztr/crúcis*) *Skj* B and *Skald* employ an Icelandicised paradigm for Lat. *crux/crucis* (i.e. *krúx/krúzis*); cf. *LP* and Lange 1958a, 90. The evidence for such a paradigm does not seem strong. In addition to the two instances in *Líkn*, the only other occurrences *LP* lists (the Icel. forms do not appear in *CVC* or *Fritzner*) are EKúl *Kristdr*1/1[III] (*Skj* A *hroz/kruzi*, B *hróts/krúzi*) and Anon *Bjúgvís*[III] (*Skj* A *hves/krusi*, B *hvé's/krúsi*), both C12th. In each case rhyme is a possible indicator, but each of the rhymes is different, which may suggest nothing more than confusion about (or variety in) the pronunciation of Lat. *crucis/cruci*. — [1] *lemið angr* 'you cripple grief': In 399a-b[x] Jón Sigurðsson reads 'lein' with superscript tittle, but in a note he writes '(m)' over 'in' and is uncertain whether the abbreviation is <ið> or <er>. *Lemið* and *æxlið* (l. 1) are 2nd pers. pl. forms used here (perhaps honorifically) with a sg. subject; cf. sg. *ert* 'are' (l. 3) of the same subject. Cf. also *yðrum* 'your' (pl.) 38/7. The power of the Cross to console in grief is addressed in the homily above, where it is described as *huɢon við harme* 'a comfort in sorrow'. — [3-4]: This couplet refers to the medieval use of the Cross as a sign of victory in battle. In the homily the *Heilagr cros es sigrmarc goþs* 'The holy Cross is the victory-sign of God' and *sigr i orrostom* 'triumph in battles' (cf. *sigrstoð* 'victory pillar' 42/2). The idea depends ultimately on Constantine's famous dream before the Battle of the Milvian Bridge (Eusebius, *De vita Constantini* I, 28 in Winkelmann 1991, 29-30). — [5-6] *ítr lausn ... í höptum* 'a glorious liberation ... [to men] in fetters': In the homily (above) the Cross is described as *laúsn i hoftom* 'liberation in [from] bonds' and *laúsnarmarc maɴa* 'sign of men's liberation'. — [7-8]: Cf. the homily, in which the Cross is *leipretteng fra synþum* 'redress from sins'.

40. Veit mér líkn, er læknar   Ert fyr hvers manns hjarta
ljóna kind frá blindi   hreins við öllum meinum
hyggju túns ok hreinsar,   hæstr ok harðri freistni
heims prýði, kyn lýða.   hlífiskjöldr í lífi.

Heims prýði, veit mér líkn, er læknar ljóna kind frá blindi hyggju túns ok hreinsar kyn lýða. Ert hæstr hlífiskjöldr fyr hjarta hvers hreins manns við öllum meinum ok harðri freistni í lífi.

World's adornment [CROSS], grant me mercy, you who heal men's offspring from blindness of thought's enclosure [BREAST] and purify the race of men. You are the highest protective-shield before the heart of each pure man against all injuries and hard temptation in life.

Mss: **B**(12r), 399a-b[x].

Editions: *Skj* Anonyme digte og vers [XIII], C. 1. *Líknarbraut* 40: AII, 157, BII, 170-1, *Skald* II, 90; Sveinbjörn Egilsson 1844, 47, Rydberg 1907, 18, 52, Tate 1974, 85.

Notes: [1]: The consonance of *líkn* 'grace' and *lækn-* 'heal' calls attention to their conceptual relationship, for it is through grace that healing is effected. (On Christ as *læknir* 'healer' see 31/3.) The subject of *læknar* is ambiguous, either *líkn* 'mercy' or the implied 2nd pers. *þú* 'you' (ms. *veittu*), but the tradition of the Cross as healer or medicine makes the latter perhaps more likely. In this st., the poet continues to draw upon the Icel. homily *De sancta cruce* (*HómÍsl* 1993, 18r; *HómÍsl* 1872, 39; cf. *HómNo*, 105), in which the Cross is called *læcning við sóttom* 'a cure/medicine for illnesses'; cf. *AH* 8, 24 where the Cross is *medicina corporalis / christianis et mentalis* 'physical and spiritual medicine for Christians'. These ideas probably depend upon Num. XXI.9, in which the brazen serpent with its healing power is a type of the Crucifixion; cf. *Veraldar saga*'s allegorical reading: *Eitrormr sa er i tre hieck er hver vard heill er til leit. merkir Jesvm Christvm hanganda a krossinvm, er græder oll sär anda vora* 'The brazen serpent which hung on the wood, as each one was healed who looked upon it, signifies Jesus Christ hanging on the Cross, who heals all the wounds of our souls' (Jakob Benediktsson 1944, 84). — [3-8]: The 'h'-alliteration extends for 6 ll., cf. 33/1-4, 37/5-8 (and 1-2). — [3] *hyggju túns* 'of thought's enclosure [BREAST]': *Tún* lit. 'hedge' is a 'hedged plot, field' or simply 'enclosure'; Guðrún Nordal 2001, 256 translates the kenning 'field of the mind'. — [4] *heims prýði* 'world's adornment': Cf. Alcuin's famous acrostic hymn *Crux decus est mundi* 'The Cross is the adornment of the world' (Szövérffy 1976, 25; Dümmler 1881, 224-5), and from a later hymn *salve mundi gloria / ... dulce decus saeculi* 'hail, glory of the world, ... sweet adornment of the world' (Mone 1853-5, I, 111). Mary is called *heims prýði* in *Mdr* 11/2. — [8, 6, 7] *hlífiskjöldr við öllum meinum ok harðri freistni* 'a protective-shield against all injuries and hard temptation': This follows the homily (above) closely: *heilagr cros er hlífskioldr við méinom ... en efling við allre freístne* 'a protective shield against injuries ... and strength against all temptation'; cf. the late medieval *Gimsteinn* 117/8, in which the Cross is *hlíf ok skiolldur mot fiandans golldrum* 'a protection and shield against the devil's spells'. The Cross as protection (*praesidium*) is also a motif in hymns, e.g. *Christi crux et passio / Nobis est praesidio, / Si credamus* 'Christ's Cross and Passion are [*lit.* is] to us for a protection if we believe' (*AH* 54, 223); it is described as a shield in a ME lyric: *Crux est ... / a targe to weren fro detly woundes* 'The Cross is a shield to protect from deadly wounds' (Brown and Robbins 1943, no. 23).

41. Eng*r* fær töld með tungu Æxt*r* ferr valt til vaxtar
    tákn þín, er nú skína, vegr þinn, er berr fegri,
    hjálpar hneigistólpi hreinn, en hugðu vinnim,
    heims alls, *of* kyn beima. hverja dýrð, *of* skýrða.

Hneigistólpi alls heims hjálpar, eng*r* fær töld með tungu tákn þín, er nú skína *of* kyn beima. Hreinn vegr þinn, er berr hverja dýrð fegri en vinnim *of* skýrða hugðu, ferr valt æxt*r* til vaxtar.

Inclining pillar of all the world's salvation [CROSS], none can enumerate with tongue your signs, which now shine upon the race of men. Your pure honour, which bears every glory fairer than we might express in thought, grows continually greater.

Mss: **B**(12r), 399a-b[x]. — *Readings*: [1] Eng*r*: engi B, 399a-b[x]; fær töld: 'ferr töl[...]' B, 'ferr töld' 399a-b[x] [4] *of*: ok B, 399a-b[x] [5] Æxt*r*: æxt B, 399a-b[x] [8] *of*: ór B, 399a-b[x].

Editions: *Skj* Anonyme digte og vers [XIII], C. 1. *Líknarbraut* 41: AII, 157-8, BII, 171, *Skald* II, 90, *NN* §1398; Sveinbjörn Egilsson 1844, 47-8, Rydberg 1907, 18, 52, Tate 1974, 86.

Notes: [1] *engr fær töld með tungu tákn þín* 'none can enumerate with tongue your signs': Cf. Arngr *Gd* 51/1, 3[IV], a C14th poem which borrows from *Líkn* several details, *táknin öll ... eingi fær þau talt með tungu* 'all the signs ... none can ennumerate them with tongue'. Ineffability is a topos of mystical poetry in particular, as in the Bernardine *Jubilus* (*AH* 19, 190) *nec lingua potest dicere* 'nor can tongue express'. In order to achieve a six-syllable l. Rydberg, *Skj* B, and *Skald* normalise, as here, ms. 'Eingí' to the early variant *engr*. — [1] *fær töld* 'can enumerate': Since the 'er'-abbreviation can also represent <ẽr> (<ær>), as in *væri* 10/3, this is not strictly an emendation (as first proposed by Sveinbjörn Egilsson), and cf. *ferr* (l. 5). — [3] *hneigistólpi ... hjálpar* 'inclining pillar ... of salvation [CROSS]': *Stólpi* 'pillar, column', is used in *Veraldar saga* to translate the pillar of light that guided the Israelites in Exod. XIII (Jakob Benediktsson 1944, 26 and 83). The Cross as column or pillar is a rare image (cf. *sigrstóð* 'victory-post' 42/2). Rabanus Maurus (C9th) calls the Cross *columna et firmamentum veritatis* 'the column and mainstay of truth' (*De laudibus sanctae crucis*, col. 169; Perrin 1997, 59). Possibly influenced by *Líkn*, the image occurs in *Mgr* 13/2-3 where Mary tells how she watched as Christ bore on his shoulders the *hjálpar stólpa til píslar* 'pillar of salvation [CROSS] to the torment'. (Mary herself is called *hjálpar stólpi* in *Mdr* 41/5 and *Pét* 5/7). 'Inclining' (*hneigi-*, from *hneigja* 'incline, bow down', as in 3/1-4 *hneig heyrn þína* 'incline your hearing') may, as *LP* (1860) and *LP* propose, suggest the idea of leaning forward as if proffering a gift; cf. the kenning in Kálf *Kátr* 45/6-7 *hneigiþollr öglis túna* 'giving tree of hawk's home fields [ARM > GENEROUS MAN]'. But here the image is more likely based upon st. 9 of Fortunatus' *Pange lingua*, in which the poet tenderly entreats the Cross to bend in order to ease Christ's suffering: *Flecte ramos, arbor alta, tensa laxa viscera / et rigor lentescat ille, quem dedit nativitas* 'Bend your branches, noble tree; relax your tense fibres, and let the firmness nature gave you become pliant' (Bulst 1957, 128). — [4] *alls* 'all the world's': *LP* (1860) and Rydberg 1907, 52 assign this phrase to *kyn beima* 'race of men' (l. 4), but it seems more suitable to *hjálpar*, i.e. (inclining pillar) 'of all the world's salvation'. (*Heims* and *kyn beima* are also rhymed in *Has* 20/6.) — [4] *of* 'upon': Ms. *ok* (abbreviation); Sveinbjörn Egilsson's 1844, 48 emendation, adopted by all subsequent eds, seems unavoidable; a preposition is clearly necessary. — [5-8]: The *helmingr* is problematic and cannot be resolved without emendation. This edn follows Rydberg's emendation *of* (l. 8), and *Skj* B's *Æxt*r (l. 5). The various approaches can be characterised as follows: Sveinbjörn Egilsson 1844, 48 attempts to salvage the ms. readings, normalising only adv. *valt* to n. *vald* 'power'. His construction, found in *LP* (1860): *æxti* and *berr*, is *æxt vald ferr til fegri vaxtar, en vinnim hugðu ór skýrða hverja dýrð – þinn hreinn vegr er berr*, or to translate his Lat. 'The distinguished power (of the Cross) rises into growths too beautiful for us to be able in thought to explicate its every excellent virtue – your clear glory is manifest'. But this is awkward, loosely translated, and depends on inexact meanings, e.g. *berr* (*manifesta* 'manifest'). Rydberg 1907, 52 follows this construction but emends *ór* (l. 8) to *of*. He understands *hugðu* (dat.) (l. 7) simply as 'in [our] thought', as does this edn. *Skj* B emends (as here) *æxt* to *æxtr* and (like Rydberg) *ór* to *of*, construing *hugðu* (l. 7) as p.p. of *hyggja* (*LP*: *hugðu fegri* 'fairer than is thought'); Finnur Jónsson then arranges the subordinate clause as *er berr hverja dýrð hugðu fegri en of vinnim skýrða* 'which bears each glory, more beautiful than can be thought (and more beautiful) than we can express'. *NN* §1398 (cf. *Skald*), accepting *æxtr* for *æxt*, emends *hugðu* to *hugða*, paralleling *skýrða* (l. 8), and *ór* (*Skj* B *of*) to *ok* (l. 8); Kock then translates 'Your honour, the pure, which possesses every beauty, (is) fairer than we can think or express'. But this is again rather free and requires three emendations. — [5] *æxtr* 'augmented, (made) greater': P.p. of *æxla* 'to cause to grow, increase' (only *CVC* gives *æxa*, causal from *vaxa*, as a headword separate from *æxla*). — [5] *ferr valt til vaxtar* 'grows continually': The verbal phrase *fara* (or *ganga*) *til vaxtar* means simply 'to grow'. Adv. *valt*, short for *ávalt* 'continually', from adj. *valr* 'round, in a circle'. The short adv. form *valt* also occurs in Bjbp *Jóms* 38/1[1] and Anon *Mhkv* 28/1[III]. A minor reason for taking *valt* as adv. rather than as n. *vald* 'power' (like Sveinbjörn Egilsson and Rydberg) is that the longer form *ávalt* and *veg*- appear in the same positions in *Has* 59/5-6 and Anon 34/5-6, the two poems from which *Líkn* draws the most details. — [7-8] *vinnim skýrða* 'we might express, explain [*lit.* might make expressed, explained]': *Vinna* with predicative adj. or (as here) part. 'to make _-ed'; i.e. with *skýrða* 'to make told, explained' or simply 'to express, explain'. The form is pres. subj.; the antecedent of *skýrða* (acc. f. p.p.) is *dýrð* 'glory' (l. 8). On *dýrð : skýrða* cf. *Geisl* 66/2 and EGils *Guðv* 4/3-4[IV].

42. Sett hefr sína dróttar   Sjá má hverr í heimi
     sigrstoð konungr roðna   hnossa brjótr, á krossi
     blikmeiðundum blóði   dyggr hvé sinn faðm seggjum
     bauga láðs fyr augu.   sólstéttar gramr réttir.

Konungr dróttar hefr sett sína sigrstoð roðna blóði fyr augu láðs bauga blik meiðundum. Hverr brjótr hnossa í heimi má *sjá*, hvé dyggr gramr sólstéttar á krossi réttir seggjum faðm sinn.

The king of the host [RULER = Christ] has set his victory-post [CROSS], reddened with blood, before the eyes of harmers of the radiance of the land of rings [(*lit.* 'radiance-harmers of the land of rings') ARM > GOLD > GENEROUS MEN]. Each breaker of treasures [GENEROUS MAN] in the world may see how the faithful king of the sun's path [SKY/HEAVEN > = God (= Christ)] on the Cross extends his embrace to men.

Mss: **B**(12r), 399a-b^x. — *Readings*: [5] *Sjá*: '[...]' B, '[...]a' 399a-b^x.

Editions: *Skj* Anonyme digte og vers [XIII], C. 1. *Líknarbraut* 42: AII, 158, BII, 171, *Skald* II, 90, *NN* §1399; Sveinbjörn Egilsson 1844, 48, Rydberg 1907, 18, 52, Tate 1974, 87.

Notes: [2] *sigrstoð* 'victory-post [CROSS]': Cf. *-stólpi* 'pillar' 41/3. The kenning (cited by Meissner, 432) may well be a translation of Lat. *trop(h)aeum* 'victory memorial' (originally a tree trunk bedecked with captured arms), a common appellative of the Cross. (Cf. the Gk cognate σταυροῦ τρόπαιον 'trophy of the Cross' in Eusebius' account of Constantine's dream, by which sign the emperor was instructed to conquer [*De vita Constantini* I, 28 in Winkelmann 1991, 30]. See, e.g., Fortunatus' *Pange lingua*, st. 2: *et super crucis trophaeo dic triumphum nobilem* 'and over the trophy of the Cross, sound the noble triumph' (Bulst 1956, 128), in which *trophaeo* alliterates (with *triumphum*) just as does *sigrstoð* (with *sétt* and *sína*). (In his Genesis commentary, Alcuin also refers to *crucis trophaeum*. Alcuinus, *Epistolae* XCVII, col. 307.) On the early history of the Cross as *trophaeum*, see Reijners 1965, 192-3. — [5] *sjá má hverr í heimi*: The restoration of *sjá*, proposed marginally by Jón Sigurðsson in 399a-b^x and adopted by all eds, is supported by an accent indicating possible <í> followed by trace of possible <a>. *Skothending* is achieved by eliding the <á> of *sjá* and the <m> of *má* to rhyme with *heimi*. — [7] *faðm* 'embrace': Cf. *faðm miskunnar* 'embrace of mercy' 45/5-8. — [8] *gramr sólstéttar* 'king of the sun's path' [SKY/HEAVEN > = God (= Christ)]': 'Sun's path' in a kenning for Christ on the Cross may evoke the patristic idea that his proffered embrace was cosmic in scope, encompassing the whole world (see Rahner 1963, 51; Reijners 1965, 195-6). Moving from active (placing the victory-pillar) to passive (stretched upon on the Cross), the st. thus juxtaposes Christ's justice and mercy.

43. Þá er, sem þengill skýja
þreksnjallr kveði alla
oss með orðum þessum
ágætr fyr meinlæti:

'Mín hefi ek sár at sýna
seggjum góð með blóði;
maðr sjái hverr á hauðri
hingat til píninga.

Þá er, sem þreksnjallr þengill skýja, ágætr fyr meinlæti, kveði oss alla með þessum orðum: 'Ek hefi mín góð sár með blóði at sýna seggjum; hverr maðr á hauðri sjái hingat til píninga.

Then it is as if the strength-bold king of clouds [= God (= Christ)], famed on account of agonies, addresses us all with these words: 'I have my good wounds with blood to show to men; let each man on earth look hither at [these] torments.

Mss: **B**(12r), 399a-b^x.

Editions: *Skj* Anonyme digte og vers [XIII], C. 1. *Líknarbraut* 43: AII, 158, BII, 171, *Skald* II, 90; Sveinbjörn Egilsson 1844, 48, Rydberg 1907, 18, 52, Tate 1974, 88.

Notes: [All]: The address of Christ from the Cross is a topos of medieval poetry on the Passion, though this is the only instance in skaldic poetry. The address usually takes the form of a complaint; Christ calls attention to his suffering and reproaches his people (or an individual) for being ungrateful, often exhorting to repentance (see Woolf 1968, 36-44). An example is a C13th lyric by Philip the Chancellor, *Homo vide, quae pro te patior* 'O man, see what things I suffer for you' (*AH* 21, 10) in which Christ calls upon the listener, for whom he is dying, to behold his sufferings, the nails with which he is pierced, and to consider that however great his physical torment may be, his inward anguish is yet greater because of ingratitude. An influential early instance in which Christ evokes the torments of the Cross while accusing man of ingratitude is Caesarius of Arles' (C6th) *Sermo* 57 (Morin 1953, 253-4). Ultimately the topos derives from Old Testament sentences which were interpreted as the speech of Christ: *Popule meus, quid feci tibi?* 'O my people, what have I done to you' (Mic. VI.3), *O vos omnes qui transitis per viam, attendite et videte si est dolor sicut dolor meus* 'O all ye that pass by the way, attend, and see whether there be any sorrow like to my sorrow' (Lam. I.12), and *Quid est quod debui ultra facere?* 'What is there that I ought to do more?' (Isa. V.4). The first of these, *Popule meus* (cf. *þjóð mín* 'my people' 45/1), recurs throughout the Reproaches (*improperia*) which accompany the Adoration of the Cross in Good Friday liturgy, and the third occurs in the same context. The second is found in the Hours of the Passion, attr. Bonaventure (C13th), attested in Iceland in the early C14th AM 241 a fol (Gjerløw 1980, I, 217). On the liturgy for Good Friday more generally see Notes to st. 30. — [1] *þengill skýja* 'the king of clouds [= God (= Christ)]': The kenning occurs earlier in *Has* 12/4. — [2] *þreksnjallr* 'strength-bold': The adj. occurs previously in *Geisl* 66/4 and subsequently, in a pattern suggesting *Líkn*'s influence, in Anon *Ól* 2/3[1] (C14th). — [4] *ágætr fyr meinlæti* 'famed on account of agonies': *Meinlæti* may be sg. or pl. Cf. *Has* 19/6.

44. 'Ér meguð undir stórar   mín því at mildi raunar
     yðars grædis sjá blæða;   mest ok yðrir lestir
     þær eru sýnt, þó at sárar, veldr því, at verða skyldi
     saklausum mér vaktar,   vísi lýðs fyr píslum.

'Ér meguð sjá yðars grædis stórar undir blæða; þær eru, þó at sárar, sýnt vaktar mér saklausum, því at raunar veldr mest mín mildi ok yðrir lestir því, at vísi lýðs skyldi verða fyr píslum.

'You may see your healer's great wounds bleed; they are, though grievous, clearly dealt me guiltless, for in reality my mercy and your sins most cause it, that the prince of the people should be subjected to torments.

Mss: **B**(12r), 399a-b[x]. — *Readings*: [5] því at: *so* 399a-b[x], '[...]t' B [8] vísi: 'visí' *corrected from* 'vist' B, vist 399a-b[x].

Editions: *Skj* Anonyme digte og vers [XIII], C. 1. *Líknarbraut* 44: AII, 158, BII, 172, *Skald* II, 90, *NN* §§1400, 2332; Sveinbjörn Egilsson 1844, 48-9, Rydberg 1907, 18-19, 52, Tate 1974, 89.

Notes: [2] *grædis* 'healer's': Just as in 31/3, when *lýðs læknir* 'mankind's healer [= Christ]' dies, the use of *grædir* is paradoxical here; the one who heals is himself afflicted with wounds. The *nomen agentis*, formed from *græða* 'to grow, nourish, heal' also resonates with the poem's recurrent use of *ár* '(year's) abundance' in kennings for God or Christ. — [4] *vaktar* (p.p.) 'dealt': *Vekja e-m undir* lit. 'to awaken wounds (in) someone' is otherwise unattested; *LP* does not cite the occurrence, *LP* (1860) gives *vulnera infligere cui* 'to inflict wounds on someone'. Somewhat similar, however, are *vekja blóð* 'call forth blood' and *vekja víg* 'awaken battle'. *Vekja* can also mean 'to rouse, begin, cause'; possibly 'to cause someone wounds'. — [5] *raunar* 'in reality': Gen. sg. of *raun* 'reality, test' used adverbially. — [7] *veldr* 'cause(s)': The 3rd pers. sg. verb is governed by its first subject *mildi* 'mercy' even though the subject is compounded by *yðrir lestir* 'your sins' (see *NS* §70). — [7-8] *vísi lýðs skyldi* 'the prince of the people should': 399a-b[x], Sveinbjörn Egilsson, *Skj*, and *Skald* all read *víst* 'certainly' for *vísi* 'prince'; the scribe of B appears first to have begun to write 'vist' then to have corrected it to 'visí' with a heavy accent. *Skyldi* 'should' is 3rd pers. subj., whose subject *Skj* takes to be an understood *hann*; this, however, agrees awkwardly with *mín* (l. 5), hence *Skj* B translates *at han (jeg) skulde* 'that he (I) should'. *NN* §2332 attempts to improve agreement by arguing that ms. 'skullde' simply reflects the later 1st pers. sg. (Icel. *skyldi*) and should be 'normalised' to *skylda*. Both the awkwardness and emendation are avoided with the reading *vísi* 'prince'.

45. 'Mín snúz þjóð ok þjóna
— þat er ráðuligt — dáðum
glæpum vön frá greypu
grandi mér til handa.

Því býð ek faðm, at feðmik
fúss ok glaðr með saðri
ást, hvern er iðraz lasta,
unninna, miskunnar.'

'Þjóð mín, vön glæpum, snúz frá greypu grandi mér til handa ok þjóna dáðum; þat er ráðuligt. Því býð ek faðm miskunnar, at fúss ok glaðr feðmik með saðri ást, hvern er iðraz unninna lasta.'

'My people, accustomed to sins, turn away from fierce injury to me and serve with deeds; that is advisable. Therefore I offer the embrace of mercy, because, willing and glad, I embrace with true love each one who repents of sins committed.'

Mss: **B**(12r), 399a-b^x.

Editions: *Skj* Anonyme digte og vers [XIII], C. 1. *Líknarbraut* 45: AII, 158, BII, 172, *Skald* II, 90-1; Sveinbjörn Egilsson 1844, 49, Rydberg 1907, 19, 52, Tate 1974, 90.

Notes: [1] *Þjóð mín* 'my people': On the relation to the recurrent *Popule meus* 'O my people' in the Reproaches of the Good Friday liturgy, see Notes to st. 43. — [3-4] *vön glæpum ... frá greypu grandi* 'accustomed to sin ... from fierce injury': Possibly influenced Árni *Gd* 18/5^{IV} and *Mdr* 8/7-8, both C14th. — [5] *feðmik* 'I embrace': *Feðma* 'to embrace' (from *faðmr* 'embrace') is a rare variant of *faðma*. The proximity of *faðm* and *feðmik* is an instance of polyptoton. — [5, 8] *Því býð ek faðm ... miskunnar* 'Therefore I offer the embrace of mercy': See the Icel. homily on the Cross: *þuiat haN býþr faþm miscvNar siNar. ǫl þeim er haN elsca* 'for he offers the embrace of mercy to all those who love him' (*HómÍsl* 1993, 17v; *HómÍsl* 1872, 38; cf. *HómNo*, 104). — [7-8] *iðraz lasta unninna* 'repents of sins committed': Cf. *Has* 53/7 *glæpa iðrumk*, the only other occurrence of *iðrask* + sins in skaldic poetry.

46. Minnumz á hvat unni
öðlingr í píningu
árs, þá er orð slík heyrum,
oss deyjandi á krossi.

Leiðum hörð á hauðri
hjarta várs með tárum,
systkin mín, fyr sjónir
siðgætis meinlæti.

Minnumz á, þá er heyrum slík orð, hvat öðlingr árs, deyjandi á krossi, unni oss í píningu. Systkin mín, leiðum hörð meinlæti siðgætis á hauðri fyr várs hjarta sjónir með tárum.

Let us remember, when we hear such words, how the prince of the year's abundance [= Christ], dying on the Cross, loved us in his Passion. My brothers and sisters, let us bring the hard torments of the faith-guardian [= God (= Christ)] on earth before our heart's eyes with tears.

Mss: **B**(12r), 399a-b^x. — *Reading*: [5] hörð: *so* 399a-b^x, 'hðr[...]' B.

Editions: Skj Anonyme digte og vers [XIII], C. 1. *Líknarbraut* 46: AII, 158, BII, 172, *Skald* II, 91, *NN* §2448A; Sveinbjörn Egilsson 1844, 49, Rydberg 1907, 19, 52, Tate 1974, 91.

Notes: [5-8] *leiðum ... fyr várs hjarta sjónir ... meinlæti* 'let us bring ... before our heart's eyes ... the torments': The idiom is *leiða e-t augum* 'to lead something to the eyes, to make something the object of sight' (see e.g. *Hym* 13/7-8 [*NK* 90] and *Fritzner: leiða* 7). This seems to be the only occurrence with *fyr(ir)* (but cf. *setja fyr augu* 'set before the eyes' 42/4); it may suggest not only bringing but holding the object before one in sustained contemplation. — [6-7] *hjarta sjónir* 'heart's eyes': *Sjón* 'sight, appearance' > 'faculty of sight' > 'eye'. Rydberg makes *hjarta* part of a kenning for God: *várs hjarta siðgætis* 'virtue-guardian of our heart'. But *hjarta sjónir* translates the *oculi cordis* 'eyes of the heart' of Eph. I.18, which occurs also in the liturgy (Manz 1941, 330, no. 653). — [8] *siðgætis* (gen. sg.) 'faith-guardian, i.e., guardian of the faith [= God (= Christ)]': *Siðr* 'custom, conduct, virtue, faith, religion'. Cf. *siðskjótr* 'quick to promote virtue/faith' 6/6 and *siðnenninn* 'virtue-striving' 18/8 – both as divine attributes.

47. Réðum krapt í kvæði
kross þíns fyr þjóð inna,
árs, þó at, eflir, værak
allítt til þess fallinn.

Sízt em ek samr of baztan
sýnt — öngrumz því löngum —
fyr lundfasta löstu,
líknfæðir, þik ræða.

Eflir árs, réðum inna fyr þjóð krapt kross þíns í kvæði, þó at værak allítt fallinn til þess. Sýnt em ek sízt samr, líknfæðir, ræða of þik baztan fyr lundfasta löstu; því öngrumz löngum.

Strengthener of year's abundance [= God (= Christ)], we [I] undertook to relate to the people the power of your Cross in a poem, even though I was poorly equipped to do so. Clearly I am least suited, begetter of grace [= God (= Christ)], to speak of you, the best, on account of mind-fixed sins; for that reason we are [I am] continuously troubled.

Mss: B(12r), 399a-b[x]. — *Readings*: [1] Réðum: 'rèdum' *with very light tittle, poss. erased* B, *ink blotted obscuring accent or hook on 'e'* 399a-b[x]; í kvæði: '[...]' B, 'í kva̧ȩði' 399a-b[x] [5] *em*: *so* 399a-b[x], 'e[...])' B; samr: 's[...]' B, 's[...]nʼmʼr' 399a-b[x].

Editions: Skj Anonyme digte og vers [XIII], C. 1. *Líknarbraut* 47: AII, 158-9, BII, 172-3, *Skald* II, 91; Sveinbjörn Egilsson 1844, 49, Rydberg 1907, 19, 52, Tate 1974, 92.

Notes: [1] *réðum* 'we [I] undertook': Ms. 'rèdum' (*ræðum* 'we speak'); all eds emend to (or read as, so Sveinbjörn Egilsson) *réðum*. The frequency of *ráða* + inf. 'to undertake to' (see *LP: ráða* 12), the lightness of the tittle (indicating possible attempted erasure), and the fact that (if restoration of *kvæði* is correct) the l. would be *aðalhent* rather than *skothent*, all argue against *ræðum*. — [2] *þíns: inna*: The long/short rhyme *í : i* also occurs at 11/6 (*minn : þína*) and 52/2 (*minn : skína*). — [3] *eflir árs* 'strengthener of year's abundance [= God (= Christ)]': *Eflir* (< *efla* < *afl* 'strength') is used of God or Christ elsewhere only in *Leið* 39/5 (also as base-word). — [5] *em ek samr* 'I am suited': Restoration is based upon 399a-b[x], including note; all subsequent eds follow Sveinbjörn Egilsson here. The sense 'suited to, fitting' for *samr* occurs only in poetry (*LP*: *samr* 2). — [7] *lundfasta* 'mind-fixed, firmly fixed temperament': The cpd does not occur elsewhere.

48. Bæn heyr, bragningr, mína,
 bila muntat þú vilja
 veita vægð at móti,
 veðrskríns, lofi þínu.

 Sjálfr eggjar þú seggja
 sveit á þik at heita
 (þat viðr), gumna gætir,
 (gerbænan mik) hverja.

Bragningr veðrskríns, heyr mína bæn; þú muntat vilja bila veita vægð at móti lofi þínu. Sjálfr eggjar þú hverja seggja sveit at heita á þik, gumna gætir; þat viðr mik gerbænan.

King of the storm-shrine [HEAVEN > = God], hear my prayer; you will not desire to fail to grant mercy in return for praise of you [*lit.* your praise]. You yourself urge each host of men to call upon you, guardian of men [= God]; that makes me prayer-eager.

Mss: **B**(12r), 399a-b[x]. — *Readings*: [2] muntat: munat B, 399a-b[x] [4] veðrskríns: vegskríns B, 399a-b[x] [6] sveit: *so* 399a-b[x], 'su[...]' B.

Editions: *Skj* Anonyme digte og vers [XIII], C. 1. *Líknarbraut* 48: AII, 159, BII, 173, *Skald* II, 91, *NN* §§ 1401, 2333; Sveinbjörn Egilsson 1844, 49-50, Rydberg 1907, 19, 53, Tate 1974, 93.

Notes: [2] *muntat* 'will not': The ms. form 'munat' is unmetrical, because it would resolve under full stress. Therefore the older form *munt-at* with long syllable in the second metrical position must be adopted. — [3] *veita vægð* 'to grant mercy': See 3/1 in which the poet appeals to God, *er veitir vægðir* '(you) who grant mercies' — [4] *veðrskríns* 'of the storm-shrine [HEAVEN]': B reads *vegskríns* 'of the way-shrine' or 'of the glory-shrine', neither of which provides a conventional kenning type for sky/heaven. On analogy with other wind/storm + *skrín* kennings for sky/heaven, *Skj* B (cf. *LP*) and *Skald* emend to *veðrskríns* 'of the storm-shrine', a kenning the poet employs at 8/6. *LP* 1860 takes *vegr* here to mean *terra* 'earth'; so also Konráð Gíslason 1877, 28. *Skj* B's emendation has been adopted here. — [4] *lofi* (nom. *lof*) 'praise': On its extended sense 'encomium, eulogy' *LP* cites *SnE* 1848-87, I, 468 (*SnE* 1998, I, 84) where Snorri, commenting on the use of *lof* in ÚlfrU *Húsdr* 12/4[III], identifies it as a poetic genre. — [8] *gerbænan* 'prayer-eager': Ms. 'gjör bænan'; the orthographic variant *ger-* is necessary for rhyme with *hverja* 'every' (so Konráð Gíslason 1877, 41 n).

49. Vilda ek af þér, aldar
 angrstríðandi, síðarr
 enn fyr óðgerð mína
 eiga gjöld með leigum.

 Áðr hefi ek önnur gæði,
 eirsamr, hlotit meiri
 þín, en ek þér fá launat
 — þat óttumz ek — dróttinn.

Angrstríðandi aldar, ek vilda enn síðarr eiga gjöld með leigum af þér fyr óðgerð mína. Áðr hefi ek hlotit önnur meiri gæði þín, en ek þér fá launat, eirsamr dróttinn; þat óttumz ek.

Grief-fighter of mankind, I would like still later to gain recompense with interest from you for my poetry-making. Previously I have received other and greater blessings from you, than I can repay you, merciful Lord; that frightens me.

Mss: **B**(12r), 399a-b^x. — *Readings*: [7] en: '[...]' B, eņ 399a-b^x.

Editions: *Skj* Anonyme digte og vers [XIII], C. 1. *Líknarbraut* 49: AII, 159, BII, 173, *Skald* II, 91, *NN* §2584 Anm.; Sveinbjörn Egilsson 1844, 50, Rydberg 1907, 19-20, 53, Tate 1974, 94.

Notes: [2] *angstríðandi* 'grief-fighter': A circumlocution for Christ as the saviour of mankind from despair on account of sin. Cf. *Has* 21/6. *LP* extends the basic sense of *angr* 'grief, worry' to 'sorrow for sins'. Cf. *angrhegnandi* 'grief/harm suppressor' 23/6 and *angrskerðandi* 'grief-diminisher' 51/6. — [2] *síðarr* 'later': *Skj* B, followed by *Skald*, emends *síðarr* to *síðan*, translating *enn* (l. 3) *síðan* as *fremdeles engang* 'further someday'. But *síðar(r)* 'later' (so also Sveinbjörn Egilsson and Rydberg) makes sense if understood to refer to future reward; the poet requests that the poem be counted to his soul's good after death. — [3] *óðgerð* 'verse, poetry-making': The cpd occurs earlier in *Geisl* 10/3. — [5] *gæði* 'good things, blessings': Related to adj. *góðr* 'good'; in the sense of religious blessing, even salvation, also in *Leið* 40/7. *NN* §2584, Anm. changes *Skj* B's translation *goder* 'goods' to *väljärningar* 'kind deeds'.

50. Æsti ek öllu trausti,
    ítr, þik er görst kant líta
    með réttvísi, ræsir
    regnsals, hvat er mér gegnir.
    Lát mik laun fyr þetta
    lof þitt, konungr, hitta
    víst, þau er varðar mestu,
    veðra tjalds, of aldir.

Ítr ræsir regnsals, öllu trausti æsti ek þik, er görst kant líta með réttvísi, hvat er mér gegnir. Konungr veðra tjalds, lát mik víst hitta fyr þetta þitt lof laun, þau er mestu varðar of aldir.

Glorious lord of the rain-hall [SKY/HEAVEN > = God], in all trust I ask of you, who can most perfectly see with justice, whatever is fitting for me. King of the storms' pavilion [SKY/HEAVEN > = God], let me certainly attain for this your encomium those rewards which are of greatest worth forever.

Mss: **B**(12r), 399a-b^x. — *Readings*: [3] réttvísi: 're[...]vise' B, 'réṭtvíse' 399a-b^x.

Editions: *Skj* Anonyme digte og vers [XIII], C. 1. *Líknarbraut* 50: AII, 159, BII, 173, *Skald* II, 91, *NN* §2584 Anm.; Sveinbjörn Egilsson 1844, 50, Rydberg 1907, 19-20, 53, Tate 1974, 94.

Notes: [3] *réttvísi*: Restoration is based upon 399a-b^x and occurrence of similar wording in *Heildr* 7/1-2. — [3-4] *ræsir regnsals* 'lord of the rain-hall [SKY/HEAVEN > = God]': The same kenning occurs later in *Mgr* 48/5; cf. *ræsir regnhallar* 'lord of the rain-hall' *Has* 28/5-6. — [8] *veðra tjalds* 'of the storms' pavilion [SKY/HEAVEN]': This sky-kenning, combined with 'ruler' [= God], is of a type particularly common to *Has*, e.g. *hreggtjald* 'gale-tent' 1/2, *skýja tjald* 'clouds' canopy' 20/2, *hríðtjald* 'storm-tent' 28/2 — the first two of which rhyme, as here, with *ald-*. (Cf. *Líkn* 8/6 *veðrskrín* 'storm-shrine' and *Has* 4/8 *veðrhöll* 'wind-hall'). The two cosmic kennings for God in this st. are the last elaborate ones of the poem. By the final st. the style becomes plain; God is simply *dróttinn jöfra* 'lord of princes' 52/5-6.

51. Framm bar ek foldar humra   Sæll lát oss ok allri
    (fæ ek heitis svá leitat)   angrskerðandi verða
    leiðar (ljósu kvæði)   þjóð, sem þurft vár beiðir
    Líknarbraut fyr gauta.   þenna hróðr at góðu.

Ek bar framm Líknarbraut — svá fæ ek leitat heitis ljósu kvæði — fyr gauta leiðar foldar humra. Sæll angrskerðandi, lát þenna hróðr verða oss ok allri þjóð at góðu, sem þurft vár beiðir.

I have presented 'Líknarbraut' — thus I find a name for the bright poem — before men of the path of the realm of lobsters [SEA > SEA PATH > SEAFARERS]. Blessed grief-diminisher [= Christ], let this encomium be for the good of us and all people, as our need entreats.

Mss: **B**(12r), 399a-b[x]. — *Reading*: [7] vár: vör 399a-b[x].

Editions: *Skj* Anonyme digte og vers [XIII], C. 1. *Líknarbraut* 51: AII, 159, BII, 174, *Skald* II, 91, *NN* §1197; Sveinbjörn Egilsson 1844, 50-1, Rydberg 1907, 20, 53, Kock and Meissner 1931, I, 91, Tate 1974, 96.

Notes: [All]: By naming the poem in the penultimate st., the poet is following the pattern of his two main models, *Has* (64/2) and *Leið* (44/8); cf. Anon *Sól* 81/4 and *Lil* 98/8. — [1, 3-4] *gauta leiðar foldar humra* 'men of the path of the realm of lobsters [SEA > SEA PATH > SEAFARERS]': *LP* (1860), *LP*, and *Meissner*, 238 all construe *foldar humra* as 'land-lobsters' (i.e. 'snakes'), whose *leið* 'path' is 'gold'. (Cf. *orma leið*, *linns leið*, etc., *Meissner*, 238.) This ed., however, follows *NN* §1197 in construing *humra fold* 'land/realm of lobsters' as 'sea', whose *leið* 'path' is the 'sea-path' seafarers cross. All other instances of *humarr* 'lobster' in kennings are in sea-kennings (e.g. *humra heiðr* 'lobsters' heath', *humra fjöll* 'lobsters' mountain'; see *Meissner*, 96). The semi-redundancy of *fold* 'land' and *leið* 'path' is similar to the sea-kenning *holmfjöturs leið* 'island fetter's path' (Hallv *Knútdr* 5/2[III]), where 'island fetter' itself is a kenning for 'sea'. (See also *Líkn* 7/1, 3 *mána hvéls hauðr* 'land of the moon's wheel' where 'wheel' simply refines the concept of 'moon'). 'Men of the sea' or 'seafarers' accords well with the 'sea of the world' allegory and the Cross as ship in st. 33; see also the seafarer-kenning at 34/1-2. — [3] *ljósu kvæði* 'for the bright poem': Cf. *ljóss bragr* and *alljóss bragr* 'completely radiant poem' *Leið* 4/2, 44/6, the latter, as here, in the st. naming the poem. — [4] *Líknarbraut*: 'The Way of Grace/Mercy'. The poem's title may itself be construed as a kenning for its subject, the Cross. On the idea of 'way', note the recurrence of *vegr* 'way' or 'glory' in the poem, at times in kennings for God or Christ (7/8, 13/2, 28/5, 41/6, 48/4); cf. *brú* 'bridge' 35/1 and *leið* 'path' 51/3. *Líkn* 'grace, mercy' also occurs at 10/8, 22/8, 33/7 and 40/1.

52. Mæztr, lát merki crúcis, svá at eilífrar, jöfra,
    minn lausnari, skína,   óttlaust með þér, dróttinn,
    örr, í atferð várri   eigniz æztan fögnuð
    alla stund á grundu,   unaðs vistar lið kristit.

Mæztr, örr lausnari minn, lát merki crúcis skína í várri atferð alla stund á grundu, svá at kristit lið eigniz óttlaust með þér, dróttinn jöfra, æztan fögnuð eilífrar vistar unaðs.

My most glorious, bountiful Saviour, let the sign of the Cross shine in our conduct every hour on earth, so that the Christian host might obtain without fear along with you, lord of princes [= God], the highest joy of the eternal abode of happiness.

Mss: B(12r), 399a-b[x]. — *Readings*: [5] eilífrar: eilifra B, 399a-b[x] [6] óttlaust: *so* 399a-b[x], '[...]ttlaust' B [7] eigniz: 'eígnezt' B, 399a-b[x] [8] vistar: *so* 399a-b[x], '[...]istar' B.

Editions: *Skj* Anonyme digte og vers [XIII], C. 1. *Líknarbraut* 52: AII, 159, BII, 174, *Skald* II, 91, *NN* §2113; Sveinbjörn Egilsson 1844, 51, Rydberg 1907, 20, 53, Tate 1974, 97.

Notes: [All]: This prayer for the sign of the cross to shine in all our *atferð* 'conduct' is reminiscent of the first 45 ll. of Bonaventure's famous poem (also C13th) *Laudismus de sancta cruce* (1882-1902, VIII, 667) in which the audience is exhorted to let the Cross be present in – and govern – body, tongue, heart, mouth, limbs, mind, meditation – in short, to be active in one's whole conduct: *In praeclara cruce stude / Et in ipsa te reclude / Magna cum laetitia* 'Desire to repose in the radiant Cross, and enclose yourself in it, with great gladness' (43-5). — [1] *crúcis* 'of the Cross': See Note to 39/1. — [2] *minn : skína*: The short/long rhyme *i : í* also occurs at 11/6 (*minn : þína*) and 47/2 (*þíns : inna*). — [5] *eilífrar* 'eternal': Ms. *eilífra*; the scribe apparently construed the adj. as gen. pl. modifying contiguous *jöfra* 'princes'. Sveinbjörn Egilsson's (1844, 51) emendation to gen. sg. modifying *vistar* 'abode' (l. 8), adopted by all subsequent eds, seems preferable to 'lord of eternal princes'. The emendation (as well as 399a-b[x]'s clear reading of initial 'v' in *vistar* (l. 8)) finds further support from *Leið* 40/4 (*eilífrar vistar*), since the poet often borrowed directly from *Leið*. — [5-6] *dróttinn jöfra* 'lord of princes [= God (= Christ)]': The exact kenning occurs elsewhere only of an earthly king, in Sturl *Hryn* 13/3[II], but cf. (of God) *konungr jöfra* 'king of princes' *Líkn* 20/4 and *vísa dróttinn* 'lord of princes' EGils *Guðv* 10/6[IV]. — [6] *óttlaust með þér dróttinn* 'without fear with you, lord': Restoration based upon 399a-b[x]; the 'ó' (all but the accent of which is now lost in a lacuna) was legible in 1973 when the present ed. first worked with the poem and can still be seen in photographs from that time. Cf. *Óttlaust með sér dróttinn*, *Mdr* 43/6. Kock (*NN* §2113) translates *óttlaust* as *förvisso* 'assuredly'. — [7] *eigniz* 'might obtain': Ms. 'eígnezt'; on <z> for <zt/st>, see Note to 35/8. — [8] *kristit lið ... vistar unaðs* 'The Christian host ... of the abode of happiness': Perhaps as a final acknowledgment of his debt to his two principal models, the poet combines in his last l. elements of the final ll. of *Has* and *Leið*: *unaðs* 'of happiness' (in same position) *Has* 65/8 and *kristinn lýð til vistar* 'Christian people to [a heavenly] abode' *Leið* 45/8.

Anonymous, *Sólarljóð*

Edited by Carolyne Larrington and Peter Robinson

Introduction

Sólarljóð 'Song of the Sun' (Anon *Sól*) is preserved only in paper mss, the oldest of which dates from the C17th; thus its age is uncertain, although it is generally presumed to be of C13th date (see below). It is composed, like other OIcel. wisdom verse, in *ljóðaháttr* 'song metre', and in its present form comprises eighty-three sts, the last of which is probably a later addition. Like a number of other Christian poems (Gamlkan *Has*, Anon *Leið*, Anon *Lil*), *Sól*'s name is given in what was probably the originally penultimate st., 81/4.

Sól is essentially a fusion of two genres, the first being the indigenous pre-Christian wisdom poetry genre, exemplified by *Hávamál* (*Hávm* 'Words of the High One') in the *Poetic Edda*, while the second is the popular Christian type of the Other World vision. Wholly Christian in outlook, *Sól* nevertheless employs pagan or pseudo-pagan figures for rhetorical effect. It also has affiliations with other genres or subgenres (*undergenrer* as Fidjestøl 1979, 30-1 calls them): the *exemplum*, the list, lyric, allegory and perhaps the riddle (Fidjestøl 1979, 57-8).

The poem has many verbal parallels with other eddic wisdom poetry, which doubtless provided models for the first section (Clunies Ross 1982-3, 113), and with *Hugsvinnsmál* 'Sayings of the Wise-minded One' (Anon *Hsv*), the OIcel. translation of the Lat. wisdom poem *Disticha Catonis* 'The Distichs of Cato'. *Sól* has many parallels of phrasing and of sentiment with eddic poetry, particularly the gnomic verses of *Hávm* (most strikingly in *Sól* 8-9 and *Hávm* 78 on the unreliability of earthly good fortune) and the poems of the hero Sigurðr's youth (*Gríp*, *Reg*, *Sigrdr*); these are noted below. The majority of eddic parallels occur in the first two sections of the poem, comprising the *exempla* and gnomic advice. These sts also have the largest number of parallels with *Hsv*, a consequence of their similarity of subject matter. Whether *Sól* is dependent on *Hsv*, or whether the later redaction of *Hsv* has in turn been influenced by *Sól*, is impossible to say, given the uncertainties of dating both poems. Larrington 2002, 180 summarises critical views about the poem's date.

Falk 1914, 58 argued that *Sól* was dependent on *Hsv*, and thus should be dated to the second half of the C13th. Björn M. Ólsen 1915, 67 suggested that the two poems might even be the work of the same author, though there is insufficient evidence to support this hypothesis. Other eds have suggested a range of dates for the poem, from Guðbrandur Vigfússon's confident identification of the poem's provenance in the British Isles in the latter part of the C11th (Gudbrand Vigfusson 1878, clxxxviii) to Finnur Jónsson's argument on metrical and linguistic grounds that there is no evidence for a date later than 1200 (*LH* II, 131). Some scholars have felt that *Sól* might well be later than Finnur's estimate: Falk (1914, 40) thought that the depiction of punishments in Hell has similarities to accounts of the persecution of heretics and witches, and thus dates the poem c. 1250. He was also struck by the absence of any reference to the poem in *SnE* (1914, 56). Björn M. Ólsen suggested the end of the C13th, since he thought that *Hsv* dates from this time, adducing three morphological forms: *svikit* 'betrayed' in st. 6/6 for the older form *svikvit*; *utan* 'from outside' for *útan* in st. 44/6, and *gá* for *ganga* 'go' in st. 25/6 (1915, 72-3). These forms may, however, be later scribal alterations. Given the late date of the mss, the enormous variety of orthographical variants, and the complexity of the relationship with *Hsv*, it is not possible to date the poem with any greater accuracy than to suggest a date of composition some time in the C13th, and probably after 1250. Normalisation of the text in this edn has been carried out on this assumption.

As far as metrical evidence is concerned, *Sól* usually avoids trochees in the last foot of a full l., while permitting them in long ll.; such metrical scrupulousness could be consistent with a date before 1250 and suggests that the poet was well aware of metrical rules. Across the mss, however, *Sól* has a considerable number of metrical and alliterative irregularities; most of these are doubtless the result of its complex transmission history and the late date of the mss. Alliteration is defective in at least nineteen ll.: sts 1/ 4-5, 2/6, 7/5-6, 17/1, 26/1-2, 30/2, 41/5, 46/2, 46/5, 57/6, 62/3, 62/6, 73/2, 70/4-6, 75/4-6, 76/1-2, 76/4-5, 77/6, 80/1, 80/6. Metrical irregularities occur in sts 1/4-5, 2/3, 2/6, 3/6, 4/2, 8/3, 19/2, 19/4, 20/3, 21/3, 25/6, 33/6. 36/5, 38/6, 39/4, 40/5, 41/3, 48/4, 51/6, 52/5, 63/6, 68/3, 68/6, 69/5, 70/4-6. *Skj* B and *Skald* normalise the text to reflect pre-1250 usage; this edn normalises both spelling and syntax to conform to a date between 1250 and 1300. Particles (particularly *er* and *at*) that are missing in the mss are silently restored, and verbal endings are normalised.

The poem begins *in medias res* with its protagonist and narrator rehearsing a series of *exempla* with moral import. The first anecdote is the most developed, narrating how a robber, in a moment of human sympathy, decides against murdering his guest, only to be killed in his turn by the very man he had spared. The robber's late impulse of repentance saves his soul, while his murderer not only suffers the consequences of his own action, but takes on the sins of his victim too (sts 1-7). This *exemplum* is followed by a series of vignettes in which characters with semi-allegorical names demonstrate the folly of trusting in riches and health (sts 8-9); the enmity which love of the same woman can bring about between good friends (sts 10-14); the consequences of arrogance (sts 15-18), and the dangers of trusting one's enemies (sts 19-24). These anecdotal *exempla* are followed by a list of seven more formal counsels (sts 25-32), enumerated in the final st. of the section. These sts parallel most markedly the verbal expressions and sentiments of *Hsv*. In the next section the protagonist reveals something of his identity — he is a dead Christian man, perhaps a revenant — as he narrates his own death (sts 33-52). Taking painful leave of a world which he loves, the speaker recounts his fatal illness and death-bed agonies. In an anaphoric series of lyrical sts, he describes the central, mystical and salvific vision of the sun which accompanies his transition from this world to the next and which give the poem its name (sts 39-45); the death is followed by an interval in which his soul apparently hovers between Heaven and Hell (sts 46-52). Finally (sts 53-74), the dead man sets out into the

Other World, where he sees a number of enigmatic sights: a dragon (st. 54), the *sólar hjörtr* 'hart of the sun' who appears to represent Christ (st. 55), and the seven sons of 'the dark phases of the moon' (the *niðja synir* of st. 56) before he witnesses the torments of the damned and the bliss of Heaven. The sins and merits of those whose Other-World fates the speaker recounts frequently recall the *exempla* and admonitions of the poem's opening wisdom sections. In the last sts of the poem (sts 75-82), the speaker invokes the Trinity, conjures up a nightmarish vision of malevolent pagan figures who are still active in this world, and reveals (st. 78) that he has been addressing his son. More obscure references to quasi-mythological figures follow (sts. 78-80), before, with a final admonition to heed and disseminate the wisdom imparted in *Sól*, the speaker concludes by giving the poem its name (st. 81/4). A final st. promises that father and son, but also reciter and audience, will meet again on Judgement Day and offers a prayer for the dead (st. 82). Thirty-two mss record an additional and probably later st. (st. 83) which reiterates the wisdom-value of the poem and names it once again.

The vision section of the poem shares some motifs with medieval European vision accounts: parallels can be found for both the alternation of damned souls between frost and fire (st. 18), one of the earliest and most widespread characteristics of descriptions of Hell, and also for more individualised details such as the comparison of singed souls (st. 53) to birds. This also occurs in the C8th Anglo-Saxon 'Vision of the Monk of Wenlock' (recorded by Boniface in Epistle 10 to Abbess Eadburg of Thanet) and, though the souls are not in bird-form, in the mid-C13th OIcel. translation of the c. 1150 Irish *Visio Tnugdali, Duggals Leiðsla* (*Dugg*), and in the *Visio Alberici* of Settefrati, c. 1117, recorded in a ms. from Monte Cassino. The *brunnr Baugreyris* 'well of Baugreyrir' (st. 56/6) may recall the 'well of living water' in *Dugg*; the unusual flaming clothes and the ridicule of the proud man (st. 66) are also found in the 1206 *Visio Thurkilli* from Essex, recorded in a ms. from the mid-C13th. There are also a number of biblical echoes; both Paasche (1914b, 61; 1948, 189-90, 196, 202) and Njörður P. Njarðvík (1991, 193-5) argue that the Revelation of S. John may be the key to understanding the obscure symbolism towards the end of the poem, while echoes of the Gospels and the Psalms underscore the Christian teaching and phraseology in earlier sections. *Sól* is likely to have originated in a milieu where there was a broad knowledge of European Christian literature as well as an antiquarian interest in eddic themes and styles.

Recent critical discussion such as Tate 1985, Amory 1985, 1990 and 1993 and Larrington 2002, all following to some extent Fidjestøl 1979, has particularly engaged with the poem's syncretic features. Fidjestøl 1979, 42-3 argues that the poet intends his diction to be multivalent; that the metaphors of the later part of the poem refer to concepts which are Christian, but in terms that have pagan resonances, such as the *mála-dísir... dróttins* 'the confidential-*dísir* of the Lord' (st. 25/1-2), probably the *sanctae virgines* or holy virgins who intercede with God, but are referred to in terms of female pagan spirits. Likewise, Fidjestøl (1979, 42) notes that, while the *heljar meyjar* 'Hell's (or Hel's) maidens' (st. 38/4) seem to be pagan figures, the word *mær* has strong Christian associations. Amory (1985, 8-9; 1990, 258) argues that the reference to the *dísir... dróttins mála* in st. 25 represents a kind of syncretism 'which upgraded the tutelary deities of an established Norse cult', but, as Larrington 2002 argues, such syncretism is always only at a referential and linguistic level, and is not presented as a matter of belief. Thus the linguistic and rhetorical syncretism of the poem is 'a secondary *interpretatio christiana* ... fashioned ... imaginatively from diverse literary, legendary and biblical materials' (Amory 1985, 10; 1990, 259), which 'did not qualify doctrinally the faith of the *Sólarljóð* poet or of his audience' (Amory 1985, 3; 1990, 253). For Tate the relationship of paganism to Christianity in *Sól* is one of 'serious confrontation'; the poet intends to 'consign the apparatus of the old mythology to Hell' (1985, 1028). However, Larrington argues that the poem's apparent syncretic elements are largely rhetorical and ornamental, a 'late pastiche of paganism' (2002, 192) of the sort found in *Svipdagsmál*. Although the poet of *Sól* makes use of pagan images to emphasise the identification of the former pagan gods with diabolical forces, he also employs symbols which have a positive value in Norse pagan thinking: the mead, the well and runes are associated with wisdom.

Sól was first published in 1787 in *Edda rhytmica seu antiqvior, vulgo Sæmundina dicta, Pars I* by Guðmundur Magnússon (1787-1828). It was accompanied by a Lat. translation and textual notes. The next major edn was that of Sophus Bugge in *Norrœn Fornkvæði* (1867), followed by Guðbrandur Vigfússon and F. York Powell's version in *Corpus poeticum boreale* (*CPB* I, 202-17). These two scholars divided the text into two distinct poems: 'Sun-song' and 'The Christian's Wisdom'. As Fidjestøl (1979, 10) notes, in Norway interest in *Sól* and the poem *Draumkvædet* went hand-in-hand. Jørgen Moe, the first ed. of *Draumkvædet*, suggested that this poem was a version of *Sól*, reworked as a romance (Moe 1877, 10). Hjalmar Falk's edn of *Sól* (1914) was the product of a joint project with Moltke Moe on *Draumkvædet* and *Sól*. The year after Falk's edn appeared, Björn M. Ólsen produced the first Icel. edn of the poem. These were boom years for *Sól* (Fidejestøl 1979, 12): as well as the two eds and the *Skj* texts of *Sól*, Fredrik Paasche's discussion of *Sól* in his doctoral thesis (1914a) and in Paasche 1914b engaged closely with the poem. An extended discussion of *Sól* is in Paasche 1948, 170-203. A lively debate between Finnur Jónsson, Paasche, Falk and Björn M. Ólsen ensued in the Icel. journal *Edda* after Finnur wrote an article criticising the other three scholars. He argued against the structural unity that the other scholars saw in *Sól*, and they in turn replied to his arguments in the same number (Finnur Jónsson *et al.* 1916). In *Et lille gensvar* 'A little reply' Finnur has the last word.

Little new work, either critical or editorial — apart from Kock's *Skald* and his accompanying textual notes on certain verses in *NN* — was done on *Sól* until 1979 when Bjarne Fidjestøl published an important interpretation of the poem. His reading of *Sól* is based on hermeneutic principles, and avoids relying on the large number of parallels found by other eds in Norse and Christian literature as a basis for explaining the poem. Fidjestøl provides a version of Falk's 1914 text, with most of Falk's emendations removed, as the basis for his interpretation, but makes no claim to have edited or re-edited the poem. The Icel. scholar Njörður P. Njarðvík undertook a thorough reassessment of the *Sól* ms. tradition in his Gothenburg doctoral thesis of 1993, producing a conservative edn of the poem based on forty-four mss. A modernised edn of the poem, based on the doctoral work and accompanied by extensive textual notes, was published by Njörður in 1991. *Sól* was first translated into English by Guðbrandur Vigfússon and F. York Powell in *CPB* (1883). W. H. Auden and P. B. Taylor collaborated on a trans. of *Sól* in *The Elder Edda: A Selection translated from the Icelandic* (1969). Though this trans. has Auden's typical muscularity of expression, it is a very free version of the Icel. text.

Selection of mss represented in the apparatus

Sól is preserved only in paper copies dating from the C17th onwards. Seventy-three copies are known to the eds, in a total of 71 mss (with 2 mss each containing 2 distinct copies). All these copies were transcribed in full, collated, and the record of agreements and disagreements analysed to give a view of the relations among the mss. Thirty-two of these mss also contain copies of the narrative sequence *Svipdagsmál*. It appears that this poem has a similar textual history to *Sól* and conclusions about the relations of the mss for *Svipdagsmál* were used to check the conclusions reached for *Sól*. From this analysis, 9 of the 73 extant copies were selected as the basis for the present edn.

Like *Svipdagsmál*, all extant copies of *Sól* derive from a single copy surviving into the C17th. Thus, all copies contain six common errors likely to have been present in this single archetype: *sofandi* (5/5; emended to *sofanda*); *virta* (or *virtra* / *virtar* 13/6, emended to *virkta*); *gala* (or *hala* 26/4, emended to *gæla*); *á væl, á vil* etc. (28/4, emended to *á mis*); the omission of a word in 80/1 (*bölvi* supplied), *undir* (80/6). In addition to these six errors, it is likely that some of the sixteen places where readings are supplied from post-1700 copies (see below) also represent errors present in the archetype.

Five copies, dating from between 1650 and 1700, appear to descend independently from the lost archetype. These five, used in this edn, are:

1. **AM 166b 8°ˣ** fols 45v-48v (166bˣ): mid-C17th, used as the base ms. for this edn. Some eight later copies, including 427ˣ, 428ˣ, 1871ˣ and 21 6 7ˣ, appear to descend from this copy. 166bˣ is the oldest copy and preserves several important and distinctive readings found in no other early copy (*ynðisheimi* 33/3, *seig* 37/5, *harðla* 43/5, *munaðarlausir* 48/4, *sýnduz* 59/5, *ok himna skript* 70/6, *illum* 80/6; the whole of st. 83).

2. AM 167 b 8°ˣ fols 1r-4v (167b 6ˣ): second half of the C17th (contains sts 1-26 and 56-82). Textually close to 738ˣ (no. 5) with which it may share an exemplar below the archetype.

3. AM 155 a V 8°ˣ (155aˣ): second half of the C17th (contains only sts. 1-5).

4. Holm papp 15 8°ˣ 1r-8r (papp15ˣ): c. 1675. This has the best text of *Svipdagsmál*, and contains a text of *Sól* independent of any other early copy (so differing at some 150 places from 166bˣ and 738ˣ). It supplies ten readings to this edn. found in no other of the pre-1700 copies here used (*válígr* 4/6, *kallaðr* 29/2, *mér* 50/5, *véltu* 63/3, *eign* 63/3, *höfðu* 67/2, *myrðir* 74/5, *Bjúgvör* 76/1, *móðug á munað* 77/3, *ór* 78/5). In terms of its influence on later copies, this is the most important single copy of *Sól*: some 25 later copies (including all

other pre-1700 copies) descend from papp15^x. No previous ed. has used this ms., though several have relied on copies descended from it (notably 1866^x, used by Sophus Bugge 1867, and 1867^x, used by Finnur Jónsson in *Skj*).

5. AM 738 4^{ox} pp. 70-84 (738^x): dated 1680. 167b 6^x, 1872^x and another five later copies may descend from 738^x. In *Svipdagsmál* the 'b' group of mss associated with 214^x also appears descended from 738^x, and this may also be true of the same mss in *Sól*.

The range of readings present in these five mss suggest that the first scribes had difficulty reading the lost archetype. The frequent disagreement on readings likely to have arisen from expansion of abbreviations (e.g., the *Sváfar/Sváfur* forms in st. 80) suggest that this archetype made heavy use of abbreviation, as indeed does 166b^x especially. Of these five early copies, 166b^x is the clear choice as the base text for an edn, since the distinctive and important readings listed above are present only in 166b^x among these early copies. However, at some 73 places 166b^x has a reading which appears to be inferior, and a reading found in other mss is preferred. The importance of the other pre-1700 mss can be demonstrated easily: 57 of the 73 readings accepted from other mss beside 166b^x come from one of the other four pre-1700 mss, with papp15^x being the most productive. In these cases, we can presume that 166b^x has miscopied its exemplar, while at least one (and often all) of the other pre-1700 mss has preserved the archetypal readings. These presumed errors in 166b^x, which are here corrected from the other four pre-1700 mss, most frequently involve omission or addition of function words (e.g. *er* 4/2, 29/6, 38/3, 69/2, *en* 21/6) or mishandling of abbreviations (e.g. *himni* 7/2, *þæ* 13/1; perhaps *gá* 25/6). Other errors are more serious: e.g. the omission of *naktir þeir urðu* in 9/4. Overall, however, 166b^x remains considerably closer to this edited text than is any other early copy: both papp15^x and 738^x differ from the text printed here in some 150 places, compared to the 86 where 166bx differs (the 73 places here mentioned, where readings are supplied from other mss, plus the thirteen points where we emend, to give a reading found in no ms).

As with *Svipdagsmál*, all extant copies descend from a single copy surviving into the C17th, a copy itself containing many errors. Thus, at ten points all copies contain the same error, or readings manifestly derived from the same error, suggesting this single copy itself contained erroneous readings at those ten points. Accordingly, emendation is required at all those points. Thus: 'harða' 2/2 (or 'harla'); 'sofandi' 5/5; 'æ lifa' 7/5; 'virta' 13/6 (or 'virtra/virtar'); 'gala' 26/4 (or 'hala'); 'inzta' 41/5, 'glæddum' 59/3; the omission of 'it' 71/6 and of 'inn' 75/2; the omission of a word (possibly *bölvi*) in 80/1. At three other points, the mss show a range of impossible readings suggesting (most likely) varying attempts by the scribes to make sense of an impossible reading in the archetype, though the extent of variation makes it impossible to be sure what that original reading was: thus, the readings at 27/6, 28/4 and 49/5. In fact, there were certainly many more errors in this lost archetype than just these thirteen. It is likely that some of the places where readings are supplied from post-1700 copies also represent errors present in the archetype: thus the fifteen readings (six found in 2797^x alone) listed in the discussion of the four post-1700 mss used in this edn. Finally, there is 16/6, where all but two mss have 'eldi'. There reading 'elda', present in only two very late mss, is considered to have been an independent scribal emendation.

On the basis of an analysis of the history of the *Sól* tradition (alongside that of *Svipdagsmál*), four post-1700 mss are also used in this edn, in addition to the five pre-1700 copies described above. These four are:

1. Lbs 214 4°ˣ fols 149r-152v (214ˣ): written by Vigfúss Jónsson after 1723, probably c. 1736. In both *Sól* and *Svipdagsmál* this is the ancestor of a group of some eight mss (including 215ˣ, 329ˣ, 64934ˣ, 818ˣ, 21 5 2ˣ) labelled as the 'b' text of *Svipdagsmál*. For both poems there is evidence suggesting that this 'b' text derives ultimately from the copy in 738ˣ.

2. Lbs 1441 4°ˣ fols 581r-588v (1441ˣ): (1760) this contains a text of *Svipdagsmál* independent of any earlier copy, and the same appears true for its text of *Sól*; several later copies appear descended from this ms.

3. British Library Add. 10575 Bˣ (10575ˣ): C18th (only text in ms.); contains a text of *Sól* apparently independent of any earlier copy; several later copies appear descended from this ms.

4. Lbs 2797 4°ˣ 230-58 (2797ˣ): written by Gísli Konráðsson in 1820. Gísli (father of Professor Konráð Gíslason) was widely learned, and may have had access to mss no longer extant. His text contains six readings found only in 2797ˣ among the mss here chosen, and which are accepted into this text (thus *vályndr* 3/6, *þat kveða sálu sama* 26/6, *náum* 33/6, *skýdrúpnis* 51/6, *hungri* 71/3, *þruma* 77/6). It is not possible to determine whether these are Gísli's intelligent emendations or readings derived from now-lost mss. They are treated as readings in this edn.

These four mss give a sense of the later variation found in the tradition. Further, at least two of these four (1441ˣ and 10575ˣ), and possibly also 214ˣ, appear to represent lines of descent independent of the pre-1700 copies, and so might preserve archetypal readings not present in those copies. This may be the case with the nine readings *þegjanda* 28/6 (1441ˣ, 10575ˣ, 2797ˣ), *leiz á marga vegu* 40/4-5 (1441ˣ, 2797ˣ), *höfðu* 72/2 (214ˣ, 10575ˣ, 2797ˣ); *eigu* 74/3 (1441ˣ, 2797ˣ), *mæzti* 75/2 (10575ˣ, 2797ˣ); *skilja* 75/4 (214ˣ, 2797ˣ); *eymðum* 75/6 (214ˣ, 2797ˣ); *firum* 76/6 (10575ˣ, 2797ˣ); *Böðveig* 79/4 (10575ˣ). Of these nine readings, all except that in 79/4 are present in 2797ˣ, which may also represent independent descent.

Altogether, fifteen readings are adopted from these later four copies: six found only in 2797ˣ among these copies, and apparently arising by emendation from Gísli Konráðsson; and nine found in at least one of the other three (of which eight are also in 2797ˣ), possibly by independent descent from the lost archetype. One other reading, *elda* in 16/6, is found in two post-1700 mss, and is considered a scribal emendation. Thus, the edited text differs from the base ms. 166bˣ in 86 places as follows:

1. 13 emendations found in no copy
2. 57 readings preferred from the other four pre-1700 copies
3. 15 readings preferred from four post-1700 copies
4. 1 reading preferred from the other 64 copies

Mss not recorded in the apparatus to this edn

All variants present in the nine mss described in the last section are recorded in the Readings. Beside these nine, the sixty-two other mss known to contain texts of *Sól* (64 texts, with 2 mss each containing 2 distinct texts) are listed here. As stated above, the texts of all these were transcribed and collated, and the selection of the nine mss used based on analysis of this collation. None of these sixty-two can be shown to derive independently from the archetype as can many of the nine here used. Indeed, it can be demonstrated that many of these sixty-two derive from mss among these nine: thus the 25 (approximately) descending from papp15^x, the 8 descending from 166b^x, another 8 descending from 214^x. Evidence of these ms. relations for the text of *Svipdagsmál* in these mss may be found in Robinson 1991; the eds propose to give a full discussion of the ms. relations for both *Svipdagsmál* and *Sól* in a separate publication. While the readings in these mss may be of interest to (for example) cultural historians investigating the reception of older Christian poetry in C18th Iceland, they are of diminishing value where the aim is the establishment of a best text for modern readers.

The 62 mss are:

Copenhagen: AM 427 fol^x (427^x) fols 29r-36r: 1756; AM 428 fol^x (428^x) pp. 70-87: 2nd half of C18th; AM 750 4^{ox} (AM750 4^{ox}) fol. 36v: 2nd half of C17th (contains only sts. 1-10 and part of st. 11); NKS 1108 fol^x (1108^x) pp. 255-66: c. 1750; NKS 1109 fol^x (1109^x) pp. 482-501: c. 1770; NKS 1110 fol^x (1110^x) fols 3r-6v: C18th; NKS 1111 fol^x (1111^x) pp. 449-67: c. 1750; NKS 1866 4^{ox} (1866^x) pp. 349-55: 1750; NKS 1867 4^{ox} (1867^x) pp. 67-72 : 1760, written by Ólafur Brynjólfsson; NKS 1869 4^{ox} (1869^x) pp. 647-71: c. 1770; NKS 1870 4^{ox} (1870^x) fols 2r-8v, 161r-2v: after 1689, c. 1700; NKS 1871 4^{ox} (1871^x) pp. 127-52: 2nd half of C18th; NKS 1872 4^{ox} (1872^x) pp. 229-58: 2nd half of C18th; NKS 1891 4^{ox} (1891^x) pp. 179-91: c. 1770 (contains sts. 1-26, 57-82); Thott 773 a fol^x (773a^x) pp. 446-60: c. 1770; Thott 1492 4^{ox} (1492^x) fols 156r-62v: c. 1770.

Reykjavík: Lbs 215 4^{ox} (215^x) fols 262r-8v: date as for 214^x, c. 1736, also written by Vigfúss Jónsson; Lbs 437^x (Lbs437^x) fols 30v-3v: 1770-80?; Lbs 709 8^{ox} (709^x) pp. 79-94: C18th; Lbs 1199 4^{ox} (1199^x) fols 93r-5v: 1650-1860?; Lbs 1249 8^{ox} (1249^x) 62r-7r: 1791-1805; Lbs 1393 8^{ox} (1393^x) pp. 1-11: C19th (contains sts. 1-49); Lbs 1458 8^{ox} (1458^x) fols 36r-42v: 2nd half C19th; Lbs 1562^x 4° (1562^x) fols 7r-12v: c. 1770 (contains sts. 11.2-82); Lbs 1588^x (1588^x) fols 140r-3v: 1750-99?; Lbs 1692 8^{ox} (1692^x) fols 2r-12v: 1st half C19th; Lbs 1765 4^{ox} (1765^x) fols 17r-26v: 1854-75?; Lbs 2298 8^{ox} (2298^x) pp. 1-11: 1835-6; Lbs 631 4^{ox} (631^x) fols 90r-2v: C18th-19th; Lbs 636 4^{ox} (636^x) pp. 96-105: c. 1750; Lbs 719 8^{ox} (719^x) fols 1r-6v: c. 1750; Lbs 756 4^{ox} (Lbs756^x) fols 115v-19r: 1777; Lbs 818 4^{ox} (818^x) fols 20r-2v: 2nd half of C18th; Lbs 932 4^{ox} (932^x) fols 75r-8v: C18th;

Lbs 966 4°ˣ (966ˣ) fols 17v-21v: c. 1792, written by Ólafur Jónsson of Purkey; Lbs 903 8°ˣ (903ˣ) fols 69v-72v: 2nd half C18th, c. 1760; JS 36 4°ˣ (JS36ˣ) fols 2r-3v: c. 1800; JS 84 8° (84) fols 170v-5r: C18th-19th; JS 542 4°ˣ (with Lat. translation) (542ˣ and 542aˣ) fols 26r-38r (marked 1-13) and 40r-3r (marked 16-19): C17th and 19th hands (contains 2 copies of poem); JS 648 4°ˣ (648ˣ) pp. 112-17 : C19th; ÍB 13 8°ˣ (13ˣ) fols 67r-72v: C18th; ÍB 539 8°ˣ (539ˣ) fols 5r-10vb (small leaf with st. 83 attached to 10v): 1836; ÍBR 36 4°ˣ (ÍBR36ˣ) pp. 309-18: first half of C19th; ÍBR 24 8°ˣ (24ˣ) pp. 97-106: c. 1840.

Edinburgh: Adv 21 4 7ˣ (21 4 7ˣ) pp. 270-82: c. 1750, possibly written by Eggert Ólafsson; Adv 21 5 2ˣ (21 5 2ˣ) pp. 462-81: written by Oddur Jónsson c. 1755; Adv 21 6 7 aˣ (21 6 7 aˣ) pp. 95-101: before 1750; Adv 21 6 7 bˣ (21 6 7 bˣ) fols 133r-8v: before 1750.

Dublin: Trinity College, Dublin 1027ˣ (1027ˣ) fols 128r-38v: C19th.

Uppsala: UppsUB R 691 4°ˣ (R691ˣ) fols 42r-49r: 2nd half C18th; UppsUB R 692 4°ˣ (R692ˣ) pp. 12-16: C18th (unreadable after v. 70); UppsUB R 682 folˣ (R682ˣ) fols 2r-9v: end C18th; UppsUB R 682 Aˣ fol (R682 Aˣ) pp. 9-45: c. 1685; a copy by Helgi Ólaffson of papp46ˣ.

London: BLAdd 4877ˣ (4877ˣ) pp. 439-55: C18th; BLAdd 11165ˣ (11165ˣ) pp. 139-44: c. 1770; BLAdd 6121ˣ (6121ˣ) fols 71v-7r: C18th; BLAdd 11173ˣ (11173ˣ) fols 11r-19r: C18th.

Stockholm: Holm papp 11 folˣ (papp11ˣ) pp. 1-27: after 1687, a copy of papp34ˣ; Holm papp 34 folˣ (papp34ˣ) pp. 285-99: c. 1684, a copy of papp15ˣ by Helgi Ólaffson; Holm papp 46 4°ˣ (papp46ˣ) pp. 3-12: c. 1682, a copy of papp15ˣ by Guðmundr Ólaffson; Nordiska Museet St. 64.934ˣ (64934ˣ) unpaginated: c. 1725.

Berlin: Berlin Staatsbibliotek Ms. germ. qu. 329ˣ (329ˣ) fols 210v-15r: written by Oddur Jónsson c. 1755.

Harvard: Houghton Library Ms Icel. 47ˣ (47ˣ) pp. 342-52: c. 1756, a copy of 1866ˣ by Jón Eíriksson. This manuscript appears to have been the base of the 1787 Arnamagnaean edn (see Robinson 1991).

1. Fé ok fjörvi   rænti fyrða kind
    sá inn grimmi greppr;
    yfir þá götu,   er hann varðaði,
    mátti enginn kvikr komaz.

Sá inn grimmi greppr rænti kind fyrða fé ok fjörvi; enginn mátti komaz kvikr yfir þá götu, er hann varðaði.

The fierce man stole property and life from the offspring of men; no one might pass alive over that road which he guarded.

Mss: **166b**[x](45v), papp15[x](1r), 738[x](80r), 155a[x](8v), 167b 6[x](1r), 214[x](149r), 1441[x](581), 10575[x](1r), 2797[x](230).

Readings: [2] rænti: ræntu papp15[x]   [5] varðaði: varði 10575[x]   [6] mátti: náði papp15[x], 738[x], 155a[x], 167b 6[x], 1441[x], 10575[x], 2797[x]; kvikr: *so all others*, kviðr 166b[x].

Editions: *Skj* Anonyme digte og vers [XII], G [6]. *Sólarljóð* 1: AI, 628, BI, 635, *Skald* I, 308; Bugge 1867, 357, Falk 1914, 1, Björn M. Ólsen 1915, 6, Fidjestøl 1979, 60, Njörður Njarðvík 1991, 43, Njörður Njarðvík 1993, 7, 90.

Notes: [All]: The poem appears to start *in medias res*. — [3] *greppr* 'man': Although some mss capitalise *greppr*, they also erratically capitalise other nouns throughout the poem. Björn M. Ólsen (1915, 26-7) contends that both *greppr* and *gestr* (2/6) are pers. names, but this cannot be substantiated. — [4-5]: The alliteration is defective here and *götu* is unmetrical; the reading may have been imported from 2/6. *Skj* B and *Skald*, following Bugge, emend to *of þann veg* 'over that road' to eliminate the metrical problem. — [6]: *mátti* 'might' and *náði* 'managed to' appear in free variation across the whole ms. tradition, but *náði* is preferred by the majority of mss listed among the Readings. — [6] *kvikr* 'alive': This reading occurs in 62 mss; 166b[x]'s *kviðr* 'belly, womb', makes little sense in context.

2. Einn hann át,   opt, harð*li*ga;
    aldri bauð hann manni til matar,
    áðr en móðr   ok meginlítill
    gestr gangandi af götu kom.

Hann át einn, opt, harð*li*ga; hann bauð aldri manni til matar, áðr en móðr ok meginlítill gestr kom gangandi af götu.

He ate alone, often, sternly; he never invited anyone for a meal, before a weary, exhausted stranger came walking from the road.

Mss: **166b**[x](45v), papp15[x](1r), 738[x](80r), 155a[x](8v), 167b 6[x](1r), 214[x](149r), 1441[x](581), 10575[x](1r-v), 2797[x](230).

Readings: [1] hann át: hann hann át 155a[x], át hann 1441[x]   [2] harðliga: harðla 166b[x], papp15[x], 10575[x], 2797[x], 'harla' 738[x], 155a[x], 167b 6[x], 214[x], 1441[x]   [3] hann: *om.* 1441[x]   [6] af götu: at garði 155a[x], um götu 2797[x].

Editions: Skj Anonyme digte og vers [XII], G [6]. *Sólarljóð* 2: AI, 628, BI, 635, *Skald* I, 308, *NN* §57; Bugge 1867, 357, Falk 1914, 1, Björn M. Ólsen 1915, 6, Fidjestøl 1979, 60, Njörður Njarðvík 1991, 43-4, Njörður Njarðvík 1993, 8, 91.

Notes: [2] *harðliga* 'sternly': The emendation produces a metrically regular l. 166b[x] and a number of other mss have *harðla* 'very'. Aside from the metrical irregularity this produces, it does not make a great deal of sense after *opt*. Skj B encloses *opt harðla* in inverted commas and in the translation describes the l. as *forvansket* 'corrupted'. Only one, early C19th, ms., 1765[x], not listed among the variants here, reads *harðliga*, and this is probably a scribal emendation. — [6] *gangandi* 'walking': Appears in all mss but one, despite the excessive alliteration for a *ljóðaháttr* long l. Njörður Njarðvík (1991, 44) suggests that l. 6 corresponds to 2 ll. of *fornyrðislag*.

3.   Drykks of þurfi   lézk inn dæsti maðr
        ok vanmettr vera;
     hræddu hjarta   hann lézk trúa,
        þeim er áðr hafði vályndr verit.

Inn dæsti maðr lézk of þurfi drykks ok vera vanmettr; hræddu hjarta lézk hann trúa, þeim er áðr hafði vályndr verit.

The weary man said he was in need of a drink and was very hungry; with a fearful heart he said he trusted the man who before had been hostile.

Mss: **166b**[x](45v), papp15[x](1r), 738[x](80r), 155a[x](8v), 167b 6[x](1r-v), 214[x](149r), 1441[x](581), 10575[x](1v), 2797[x](231).

Readings: [1] þurfi: þurfti papp15[x], 1441[x]   [2, 3] lézk inn dæsti maðr ok: inn dæsti maðr ok lézk papp15[x], 1441[x], 2797[x]   [3] -mettr: -máttigr 738[x], 1441[x], 10575[x], 2797[x]   [4-5]: '[...]' 167b 6[x]   [5] trúa: *so* papp15[x], 738[x], 155a[x], 214[x], 1441[x], 10575[x], 2797[x], 'tau' 166b[x]   [6] þeim: '[...]' 167b 6[x]; hafði: *om.* papp15[x], 'he' 1441[x]; vályndr: *so* 2797[x], 'vællindr' 166b[x], 214[x], 'volendr' papp15[x], 'volindr' 738[x], 155a[x], 167b 6[x], 1441[x], 10575[x].

Editions: Skj Anonyme digte og vers [XII], G [6]. *Sólarljóð* 3: AI, 628, BI, 635, *Skald* I, 309; Bugge 1867, 357, Falk 1914, 1, Björn M. Ólsen 1915, 6, Fidjestøl 1979, 60, Njörður Njarðvík 1991, 44, Njörður Njarðvík 1993, 9, 91.

4. Mat ok drykk   veitti hann, þeim er móðr var,
      alt af heilum hug;
   guðs hann gáði,   góðu honum beindi,
      þvít hann hugðiz váligr vera.

Hann veitti mat ok drykk, þeim er móðr var, alt af heilum hug; hann gáði guðs, beindi honum góðu, þvít hann hugðiz vera váligr.

He offered food and drink to the one who was tired, all with a good intention; he paid heed to God, offered him good things, although he [the robber] realised he was wicked.

Mss: **166b**[x](45v), papp15[x](1r-v), 738[x](80r), 155a[x](8v), 167b 6[x](1v), 214[x](149r), 1441[x](581), 10575[x](1v), 2797[x](231).

Readings: [1] drykk: drykkju papp15[x], 1441[x], 2797[x], drykkinn 167b 6[x] [2] veitti: inn veitti 167b 6[x]; er: *so* papp15[x], 738[x], 155a[x], 167b 6[x], 1441[x], 10575[x], 2797[x], *om.* 166b[x], 214[x] [5] honum: hann 1441[x] [6] váligr: *so* papp15[x], 1441[x], 'vælligr' 166b[x], 738[x], 155a[x], 214[x], 'vælligr' *corrected from* 'væ' 167b 6[x], 'voligr' 10575[x], 2797[x].

Editions: *Skj* Anonyme digte og vers [XII], G [6]. *Sólarljóð* 4: AI, 628, BI, 636, *Skald* I, 309, *NN* §§2814, 2145; Bugge 1867, 358, Falk 1914, 1, Björn M. Ólsen 1915, 7, Fidjestøl 1979, 60, Njörður Njarðvík 1991, 44-5, Njörður Njarðvík 1993, 10, 92.

Notes: [6] *váligr* 'wicked': The reading of papp15[x] and 1441[x], explained by *LP*: *forfærdelig, som man kan vænte noget slemt af* 'frightening, from whom one can expect something bad'. 166b[x], 738[x], 155a[x] and 214[x] have the otherwise unknown word 'vælligr'. Björn M. Ólsen (1915, 27) argues that this is a form of *værligr* derived from *værr* 'cheerful', implying that the robber is intending to do good. Interpretation of l. 6 has been problematic: *Skj* B emends the verb to a negative (*hugðit*) and translates *ti han trode ikke at han var svigfuld* 'for he did not think that he [the guest] was treacherous'. The present translation, following Falk (1914a, 3) and Fidjestøl (1979, 23), indicates that the robber has repented of his previous wickedness and now recognises the obligations of hospitality, though this will cost him his life in the next st. Njörður Njarðvík (1991, 185-6) notes a verbal similarity with *Hsv* 110/6 *ok þykkiz válaðr vera* 'and thinks himself to be wretched'. Falk (1914a, 3) traces the thought that it is possible to atone for the sin of murder with one's life to the *Visio Gottschalchi*, ch. 43 (Assmann 1979, 126-7). There however, murderers are warned that if their victim is Christian, they will not be freed from punishment before the Last Judgement, even though they repent of their sin.

5. Upp hinn stóð;   ilt hann hugði;
    eigi var þarfsamliga þegit;
    synð hans svall;   sofand*a* myrði
    fróðan fjölvaran.

Hinn stóð upp; hann hugði ilt; eigi var þegit þarfsamliga; synð hans svall; myrði fróðan fjölvaran sofand*a*.

That one [the guest] got up; he had evil in mind; it [the host's generosity] was not received gratefully; his sin swelled up; he murdered the wise, very cautious sleeping man.

Mss: **166b**[x](45v), papp15[x](1v), 738[x](80r), 155a[x](8v), 167b 6[x](1v), 214[x](149r), 1441[x](581), 10575[x](1v), 2797[x](231).

Readings: [1] hinn: hann papp15[x], 738[x], 155a[x], 167b 6[x], 214[x], 1441[x], 10575[x]   [5] sofand*a*: sofandi *all*;   myrði: (brjósti) myrði 738[x]   [6] fróðan: 'frömann' 155a[x], fróðan *corrected from* 'frömann' 167b 6[x].

Editions: *Skj* Anonyme digte og vers [XII], G [6]. *Sólarljóð* 5: AI, 628-9, BI, 635, *Skald* I, 309, *NN* §89; Bugge 1867, 358, Falk 1914, 1, Björn M. Ólsen 1915, 7, Fidjestøl 1979, 60, Njörður Njarðvík 1991, 45, Njorður Njarðvík 1993, 11, 92.

Notes: [5] *sofand*a 'sleeping (man)': The mss without exception infer the sleeping man to be the subject of the verb and read *sofandi*. All eds emend to *sofanda*. — [5] *myrði* 'murdered': 155a[x] ends with this st.

6. Himna guð   bað hann hjálpa sér,
    þá er hann veginn vaknaði,
    en sá gat   við syndum taka,
    er hann hafði saklausan svikit.

Hann bað himna guð hjálpa sér, þá er hann vaknaði veginn, en sá, er hafði svikit hann saklausan, gat taka við syndum.

He asked God of the heavens to help him when he awoke slain, and the one [the guest] who had betrayed him without cause took on his sins.

Mss: **166b**[x](45v), papp15[x](1v), 738[x](80r), 167b 6[x](1v), 214[x](149r), 1441[x](581), 10575[x](2r), 2797[x](231).

Readings: [5] við: '[...] við' 10575[x];   taka: 'taka[...]' 167b 6[x]   [6] hafði: hefði 738[x].

Editions: *Skj* Anonyme digte og vers [XII], G [6]. *Sólarljóð* 6: AI, 629, BI, 636, *Skald* I, 309; Bugge 1867, 358, Falk 1914, 1, Björn M. Ólsen 1915, 7, Fidjestøl 1979, 60, Njörður Njarðvík 1991, 45, Njörður Njarðvík 1993, 12, 92.

Notes: [4-5] *en sá gat við syndum taka* 'but the one took on his sins': Falk (1914a, 3) draws the parallel between Christ and the good thief who was crucified with him in Luke XXIII.40-3. Njörður Njarðvík (1991, 197) compares the appearance of the thief in heaven in *Niðrst*[2] (13-14). The idea that a malefactor takes on the sins of his victim is a theological oddity, which most commentators have ignored.

7. Helgir englar   kómu ór himnum ofan
      ok tóku sál hans til sín;
   í hreinu lífi   hon skal *lifa*
      æ með almátkum guði.

Helgir englar kómu ofan ór himnum ok tóku sál hans til sín; hon skal *lifa* í hreinu lífi æ með almátkum guði.

Holy angels came down from the heavens above, and gathered his soul to themselves; it will live in a pure existence forever with almighty God.

Mss: **166b**^{x}(45v), papp15^x(1v), 738^x(80r), 167b 6^x(1v), 214^x(149r), 1441^x(581), 10575^x(2r), 2797^x(231).

Readings: [2] kómu: 'kuami' 10575^x; ór: af 214^x, 1441^x; himnum: *so* papp15^x, 738^x, 167b 6^x, 1441^x, 2797^x, himni 166b^x, 214^x, 10575^x [4] í: *om.* 1441^x;   hreinu lífi: hreinlífi papp15^x, 1441^x, 10575^x [5, 6] hon skal *lifa æ*: hon skal æ lifa *all.*

Editions: Skj Anonyme digte og vers [XII], G [6]. *Sólarljóð* 7: AI, 629, BI, 636, *Skald* I, 309; Bugge 1867, 358, Falk 1914, 1, Björn M. Ólsen 1915, 7, Fidjestøl 1979, 60, Njörður Njarðvík 1991, 45-6, Njörður Njarðvík 1993, 13, 93.

Notes: [2] *ór himnum* 'from the heavens': Occurs as sg. *himni* in 166b^x, but the pl. is in papp15^x, 738^x and 42 other mss. — [5-6] *hon skal* lifa æ *með almátkum guði* 'it [*lit.* she, *viz.* the soul] will live ... forever with almighty God': In keeping with earlier eds (*Skj* B; *Skald*; Bugge) *æ* 'forever' (l. 5) has been moved to l. 6 to provide the necessary alliteration.

8. Auði né heilsu   ræðr enginn maðr,
      þótt honum gangi greitt;
   margan þat sækir,   er minst of varir;
      enginn ræðr sættum sjálfr.

Enginn maðr ræðr auði né heilsu, þótt honum gangi greitt; þat sækir margan, er minst of varir; enginn ræðr sjálfr sættum.

No man has control over riches or health, though it may go smoothly for him; what he least expects comes upon many a man; no one can set his own terms.

Mss: **166b**^{x}(45v), papp15^x(1v), 738^x(80r), 167b 6^x(1v), 214^x(149r), 1441^x(581), 10575^x(2r), 2797^x(231).

Readings: [1] Auði: auð papp15ˣ, 10575ˣ, 2797ˣ;   heilsu: '[...]lsu' 738ˣ   [3] honum: *so* papp15ˣ, 738ˣ, 167b 6ˣ, 1441ˣ, 10575ˣ, 2797ˣ, hann 166bˣ   [4] sækir: hendir 10575ˣ   [5] er: *om.* papp15ˣ;   varir: varar papp15ˣ, 1441ˣ   [6] ræðr: 'r[...]' 10575ˣ;   sættum: sættum *corrected from* 'sáttum' 738ˣ.

Editions: *Skj* Anonyme digte og vers [XII], G [6]. *Sólarljóð* 8: AI, 629, BI, 636, *Skald* I, 309, *NN* §2146; Bugge 1867, 358, Falk 1914, 4, Björn M. Ólsen 1915, 8, Fidjestøl 1979, 61, Njörður Njarðvík 1991, 47, Njörður Njarðvík 1993, 14, 94.

Notes: [All]: The thought of sts 8-9 is paralleled in *Hávm* 78, which tells of the misfortune of Fitjungr's sons. — [1-2] *auði né heilsu ræðr enginn maðr* 'no man has control over riches or health': cf. *Hsv* 35/4-5 *aldrlagi sínu ræðr engi maðr* 'No man has power over his life-span', and *Hsv* 112 which also couples concepts of riches and health. — [3] *honum* 'for him': *hann* 'he' is the reading of 166bˣ and 20 other mss. Papp15ˣ, 738ˣ, and the great majority (49) of mss have *honum* 'for him' here, giving an impersonal cl. 'though it may go smoothly for him'.

9.   Ekki þeir hugðu   Unnarr ok Sævaldi,
       at þeim mundi heill hrapa;
     nøktir þeir urðu   ok næmðir hvervetna
       ok runnu sem vargar til viðar.

Þeir Unnarr ok Sævaldi hugðu ekki at heill mundi hrapa þeim; þeir urðu nøktir ok næmðir hvervetna, ok runnu sem vargar til viðar.

Unnarr and Sævaldi did not think that their good fortune would tumble down; they became naked and deprived everywhere, and ran like wolves to the woods.

Mss: **166bˣ**(45v), papp15ˣ(1v), 738ˣ(80r), 167b 6ˣ(1v), 214ˣ(149r-v), 1441ˣ(581), 10575ˣ(2r-v), 2797ˣ(231).

Readings: [1] þeir: þau 214ˣ   [2] Unnarr: *so* papp15ˣ, 738ˣ, 167b 6ˣ, 10575ˣ, 2797ˣ, 'unr' 166bˣ, Unn 214ˣ   [4] nøktir þeir urðu: *so* papp15ˣ, 738ˣ, 167b 6ˣ, 214ˣ, 1441ˣ, 10575ˣ, 2797ˣ; nøktir: *blank space* 166bˣ   [5] ok: '[...]ok' 214ˣ;   næmðir: næmir papp15ˣ, 167b 6ˣ, 214ˣ, 1441ˣ, 10575ˣ, 2797ˣ;   hvervetna: hvivetna 2797ˣ   [6] vargar: vargr 1441ˣ, 10575ˣ.

Editions: *Skj* Anonyme digte og vers [XII], G [6]. *Sólarljóð* 9: AI, 629, BI, 636, *Skald* I, 309; Bugge 1867, 358, Falk 1914, 4, Björn M. Ólsen 1915, 8, Fidjestøl 1979, 61, Njörður Njarðvík 1991, 47-9, Njörður Njarðvík 1993, 15ˣ, 94.

Notes: [All]: Unnarr and Sævaldi are the first of a number of characters in the poem whose quasi-allegorical names are apparently invented, though they may consist of pre-existing name elements such as *-ulfr* '-wolf' or *-ný* (cf. *AEW*: *-ný*). (*Sörli* and *Vígólfr* in st. 20 as attested pers. names are the exception.) That four of the five *exempla* in the first section of *Sól* concern paired allegorically-named characters motivates Falk, following Bugge and Vigfússon, to move st. 80, with its isolated reference to *Sváfr* and *Sváfrlogi* to initial position in the poem (Falk 1914, 2). There is a comparable use of invented names in *Fj*.

— [2] *Unnarr* (male pers. n.) 'Unnarr': There is some doubt about *Unnarr*, a name form which occurs in papp15[x], 738[x], and 43 other mss. Eight mss, including 166b[x], have the indeterminate 'unr'; 11 mss have Unnr or a similar form which could be f., and accordingly give a n. pron. *þau*. — [3] *þeim mundi heill hrapa* 'their good fortune would tumble down': Although the sense is somewhat different, cf. *Reg* 25/6 *illt er fyr heill at hrapa* 'it is bad to stumble when good fortune is needed'. According to *LP*: 3. *heill*, these two instances are the only collocations of *heill* and *hrapa* in the corpus. Njörður Njarðvík (1991, 180) suggests somewhat improbably that this may be evidence of a direct link between the two poems. — [4]: This l. is missing in 166b[x]. — [5] *næmðir* 'deprived': P.p. of *næma* 'to deprive', found in 8 mss including 166b[x], as against papp15[x], 738[x], and the majority of mss which show *næmir* 'able to be caught, taken' (*LP*: *næmr*, in the passive sense). Both senses are possible. — [6] *vargar* 'wolves': Cf. *HHund II* 33: *ef þú værir vargr á viðom úti* 'if you were a wolf out in the woods'.

10. Munaðar ríki hefr margan tregat;
  opt verðr kvalræði af konum;
 meingar þær urðu, þótt inn mátki guð
  skapaði skírliga.

Ríki munaðar hefr margan tregat; kvalræði verðr opt af konum; þær urðu meingar, þótt inn mátki guð skapaði skírliga.

The power of desire has brought many a man to grief; torment often stems from women; they become harmful, though the mighty God created them purely.

Mss: **166b**[x](45v), papp15[x](1v-2r), 738[x](80v), 167b 6[x](1v), 214[x](149v), 1441[x](581), 10575[x](2v), 2797[x](231).

Readings: [1] Munaðar: Mundar 738[x], 167b 6[x] [2] tregat: tregat *corrected from* 'svikit' 1441[x] [3] verðr: verða 10575[x] [5] inn: honum 214[x] [6] skapaði: 'sk padi' 167b 6[x], skapti 214[x], 10575[x], 2797[x]; skírliga: '[...]' 167b 6[x].

Editions: *Skj* Anonyme digte og vers [XII], G [6]. *Sólarljóð* 10: AI, 629, BI, 637, *Skald* I, 309; Bugge 1867, 358, Falk 1914, 5, Björn M. Ólsen 1915, 8, Fidjestøl 1979, 61, Njörður Njarðvík 1991, 50, Njörður Njarðvík 1993, 16, 96.

Notes: [All]: The unreliability and harmfulness of women is a staple of gnomic poetry; cf. *Hávm* 84, *Hsv* 12, 105. — [2] *tregat* 'brought to grief': This is the reading of 60 mss. 166b[x] reads 'togd' here; probably superscript <r> has been accidentally omitted. — [6]: 167b[x] has a damaged leaf; 'sk padi' is supplied from the catchword of the preceding page.

11. Sáttir þeir urðu   Sváfaðr ok Skartheðinn;
      hvárgi mátti annars án vera,
   fyrr en þeir ædduz   fyr einni konu;
      hon var þeim til lýta lagin.

Þeir Sváfaðr ok Skartheðinn urðu sáttir; hvárgi mátti vera án annars, fyrr en þeir ædduz fyr einni konu; hon var lagin þeim til lýta.

Sváfaðr and Skartheðinn were on good terms; neither could be without the other, until they went mad over a single woman; she was destined to bring disgrace to them.

Mss: **166b**[x](45v-46r), papp15[x](2r), 738[x](80v), 167b 6[x](2r), 214[x](149), 1441[x](581-2), 10575[x](2v), 2797[x](231).

Readings: [1] Sáttir þeir urðu: '[...]' 167b 6[x]; Sáttir: sættir 738[x]; urðu: váru 2797[x] [2] Sváfaðr: 'suafødur' 738[x], '[...]ur' 167b 6[x]; Skartheðinn: Skarpheðinn 10575[x] [3] án: '[...] án' 167b 6[x] [5] einni: eina 214[x] [6] lagin: login 214[x].

Editions: *Skj* Anonyme digte og vers [XII], G [6]. *Sólarljóð* 11: AI, 629, BI, 637, *Skald* I, 309; Bugge 1867, 359, Falk 1914, 5, Björn M. Ólsen 1915, 8, Fidjestøl 1979, 61, Njörður Njarðvík 1991, 51, Njörður Njarðvík 1993, 17, 97.

Notes: [All]: Falk (1914a, 6) and Björn M. Ólsen (1915, 31) suggest that this *exemplum* (sts 11-14) is based on *Gunnl*, but Njörður Njarðvík (1991, 202-3) argues that there is only a general similarity of two friends loving the same woman, and suggests that *Hávm* 84, 97 and 114 are better parallels to this narrative. — [1]: 167b[x]'s damaged leaf makes the first l. impossible to read. — [5] *fyr einni konu* (dat.) 'over a single woman': Found in 166b[x], papp15[x], 738[x], and the great majority of mss; the dative implies 'in the presence of'. 214[x], and 11 other mss mostly derived from it, have *eina konu* (acc.), the implication of *fyr* + acc. being 'on account of, for the sake of'.

12. Hvárskis þeir gáðu   fyr þá hvítu mey
      leiks né ljóssa daga;
   engan hlut   máttu þeir annan muna
      en þat ljósa lík.

Þeir gáðu hvárskis, leiks né ljóssa daga, fyr þá hvítu mey; þeir máttu engan annan hlut muna en þat ljósa lík.

They paid no heed to anything, neither sport nor the radiant days, because of the shining girl; they could think about no other thing than that radiant body.

Mss: **166b**[x](46r), papp15[x](2r), 738[x](80v), 167b 6[x](2r), 214[x](149v), 1441[x](582), 10575[x](2v), 2797[x](231).

Readings: [2] hvítu: hvita 214ˣ [3] leiks: leigis 1441ˣ [4, 5] hlut máttu: *so* papp15ˣ, 738ˣ, 167b 6ˣ, 1441ˣ, 10575ˣ, 2797ˣ, máttu hlut 166bˣ, hlut mátt 214ˣ.

Editions: *Skj* Anonyme digte og vers [XII], G [6]. *Sólarljóð* 12: AI, 629-39, BI, 637, *Skald* I, 309; Bugge 1867, 359, Falk 1914, 6, Björn M. Ólsen 1915, 8, Fidjestøl 1979, 61, Njörður Njarðvík 1991, 52, Njörður Njarðvík 1993, 18, 98.

Notes: [All]: The distraction and sleeplessness caused by love is paralleled in *Hávm* 97, 114.

13. Daprar þeim urðu   inar dimmu nætr;
    engan máttu þeir sætan sofa;
   en af þeim harmi   rann heipt saman
    millum vir*k*tavina.

Inar dimmu nætr urðu þeim daprar; þeir máttu engan sætan sofa; en heipt rann saman af þeim harmi millum vir*k*tavina.

The dark nights became gloomy for them; they could sleep no sweet [sleep]; but enmity sprang up from that grief between those affectionate friends.

Mss: **166bˣ**(46r), papp15ˣ(2r), 738ˣ(80v), 167b 6ˣ(2r), 214ˣ(149v), 1441ˣ(582), 10575ˣ(2v-3r), 2797ˣ(231).

Readings: [1] þeim: *so* papp15ˣ, 738ˣ, 167b 6ˣ, 1441ˣ, 10575ˣ, 2797ˣ, þær 166bˣ [2] dimmu: dökkvu 214ˣ [4] af: gaf 167b 6ˣ [6] millum: milli 214ˣ, 10575ˣ; vir*k*tavina: 'virta' 166bˣ, virtra papp15ˣ, 738ˣ, 167b 6ˣ, 214ˣ, 1441ˣ, 10575ˣ, 'virtar' 2797ˣ.

Editions: *Skj* Anonyme digte og vers [XII], G [6]. *Sólarljóð* 13: AI, 630, BI, 637, *Skald* I, 309-10, *NN* §1272; Bugge 1867, 359, Falk 1914, 6, Björn M. Ólsen 1915, 9, Fidjestøl 1979, 61, Njörður Njarðvík 1991, Njörður Njarðvík 1993, 19, 99.

Notes: [3] *sætan* 'sweet': This adj. has no noun referent. *Svefn* m. 'sleep' or a similar word is implied. — [6] *virkta-* 'dear, kind, affectionate': Some kind of emendation is necessary here, as 166bˣ's 'virta' does not give sense. 'Virtra' 'honoured', possibly a correction of 'virta', is found in 32 mss including papp15ˣ and 738ˣ, but does not give very good sense in context. *Virkta-* is assumed here to be the first element of a cpd *virktavinr* (cf. *Fritzner: virktavinr*), the adv. *virkta*, formed from the gen. pl. of *virkt* f. 'tender care, affection', This emendation was first proposed by Munch (1847, 179), and adopted by Falk, Björn M. Ólsen, Fidjestøl, Njörður Njarðvík (1991) and *Skj* B (*virkða vina*). Kock (*Skald* and *NN* §1272) emends to *millum virkra vina* 'between valued friends'.

14. Fádæmi verða   í flestum stöðum
       goldin grimliga;
    á hólm þeir gengu   fyr it horska víf,
       ok fengu báðir bana.

Fádæmi verða goldin grimliga í flestum stöðum; þeir gengu á hólm fyr it horska víf, ok báðir fengu bana.

Abnormal events are repaid fiercely in most places; they went to duel for the wise lady, and both were killed.

Mss: **166b**[x](46r), papp15[x](2r), 738[x](80v), 167b 6[x](2r), 214[x](149v), 1441[x](582), 10575[x](3r), 2797[x](232).

Reading: [5] it: þat 1441[x].

Editions: *Skj* Anonyme digte og vers [XII], G [6]. *Sólarljóð* 14: AI, 630, BI, 637, *Skald* I, 310; Bugge 1867, 359, Falk 1914, 6, Björn M. Ólsen 1915, 9, Fidjestøl 1979, 61, Njörður Njarðvík 1991, 53, Njörður Njarðvík 1993, 20, 9.

Notes: [All]: Four mss not chosen for the variant apparatus to this edn, transpose ll.1-3 and ll. 4-6, thus providing the st. with a gnomic conclusion.

15. Ofmetnað drýgja   skyldi engi maðr,
       — þat hefk sannliga sét —
    þvít þeir hverfa,   er honum fylgja,
       flestir guði frá.

Engi maðr skyldi drýgja ofmetnað — þat hefk sannliga sét — þvít flestir þeir er honum fylgja, hverfa frá guði.

No man should cultivate pride — I have truly seen that — because most of those who pursue it turn away from God.

Mss. **166b**[x](46r), papp15[x](2r-v), 738[x](80v), 167b 6[x](2r), 214[x](149v), 1441[x](582), 10575[x](3r), 2797[x](232).

Readings: [1] drýgja: 'deya' papp15[x] [2] skyldi: skyli 2797[x] [4] þeir: *om.* papp15[x], 1441[x]; hverfa: *so* papp15[x], 738[x], 167b 6[x], 214[x], 1441[x], 10575[x], 2797[x], 'huofu' 166b[x] [5] honum: *so* papp15[x], 738[x], 167b 6[x], 214[x], 1441[x], 10575[x], 2797[x], þeim 166b[x] [6] guði frá: frá guði papp15[x], 738[x], 167b 6[x], 1441[x], 10575[x].

Editions: *Skj* Anonyme digte og vers [XII], G [6]. *Sólarljóð* 15: AI, 630, BI, 637, *Skald* I, 310; Bugge 1867, 359, Falk 1914, 6, Björn M. Ólsen 1915, 9, Fidjestøl 1979, 61, Njörður Njarðvík 1991, 53, Njörður Njarðvík 1993, 21, 101.

Notes: [5] *honum* (dat.) 'it': That is, *ofmetnaðr* m. 'pride'. 166b^x has *þeim*, m. dat. sg. of *sá*, giving a similar meaning.

16. Rík þau urðu   Ráðný ok Véboði
      ok hugðuz gótt eitt gera;
   nú þau sitja   ok sárum snúa
      ýmsum eld*a* til.

Þau Ráðný ok Véboði urðu rík ok hugðuz gótt eitt gera; nú sitja þau ok snúa ýmsum sárum til eld*a*.

Ráðný and Véboði became powerful and thought to do only good; now they sit and turn now one, now another wound towards the fires.

Mss: **166b^x**(46r), papp15^x(2v), 738^x(80v), 167b 6^x(2r), 214^x(149v), 1441^x(582), 10575^x(3r), 2797^x(232).

Readings: [1] þau urðu: þau váru papp15^x, 167b 6^x, 214^x, 1441^x, 10575^x, 2797^x, váru þau 738^x   [2] -ný: -ey papp15^x, 1441^x, -ri 214^x;   -boði: -bogi papp15^x, 10575^x, 2797^x, -logi 1441^x   [3] eitt: *om*. 214^x   [4] nú: enn nú 10575^x   [6] eld*a*: eldi *all*; til: at 1441^x, 2797^x.

Editions: *Skj* Anonyme digte og vers [XII], G [6]. *Sólarljóð* 16: AI, 630, BI, 638, *Skald* I, 310, *NN* §§2147A, 2148; Bugge 1867, 359, Falk 1914, 7, Björn M. Ólsen 1915, 9, Fidjestøl 1979, 62, Njörður Njarðvík 1991, 54-5, Njörður Njarðvík 1993, 22, 101.

Notes: [All]: The st. is rather cryptic, but the sense seems to be that those who trust in their own power (rather than in God's, cf. st. 17) come to grief, even though they intend to do good. The implication of *hugðuz gótt eitt gera* (l. 3) could be, as given here, 'thought to do, i.e. intended to do only good', or 'thought they were doing only good'. — [5-6] *ok snúa ýmsum sárum* 'and turn now one, now another wound': The sense of *ýmiss* (adj.), usually used in the pl., is 'various, now this, now that, by turns'. — [6] *elda* (gen. pl.) 'fires': The noun must be gen. pl., governed by *til*; the ungrammatical *eldi* dat. sg. is found in all but 2 mss (539^x and 24^x) not used in this edn. Eds uniformly make the emendation, following Bugge's initial suggestion (1867, 359).

17. Á sik þau trúðu   ok þóttuz ein vera
      allri þjóð yfir,
   en þó leiz   þeira hagr
      annan veg almátkum guði.

Þau trúðu á sik ok þóttuz vera ein yfir allri þjóð, en þó leiz hagr þeira annan veg almátkum guði.

They trusted in themselves and thought that they alone were above all people, but yet their condition seemed quite different to almighty God.

Mss: **166b^x**(46r), papp15^x(2v), 738^x(80v), 167b 6^x(2r), 214^x(149v), 1441^x(582), 10575^x(3r-v), 2797^x(232).

Readings: [2] þóttuz ein: ein þóttuz 738^x;   vera: *om.* papp15^x, 738^x, 167b 6^x, 1441^x.

Editions: *Skj* Anonyme digte og vers [XII], G [6]. *Sólarljóð* 17: AI, 630, BI, 638, *Skald* I, 310, *NN* §2147B; Bugge 1867, 360, Falk 1914, 7, Björn M. Ólsen 1915, 9, Fidjestøl 1979, 62, Njörður Njarðvík 1991, 55, Njörður Njarðvík 1993, 23, 102.

18. Munað þau drýgðu   á marga vegu
     ok höfðu gull fyrir gaman;
  nú er þeim goldit,   er þau ganga skulu
     meðal frosts ok funa.

Þau drýgðu munað á marga vegu ok höfðu gull fyrir gaman; nú er þeim goldit, er þau skulu ganga meðal frosts ok funa.

They experienced sensuality in many ways and had gold for pleasure; now they are repaid, since they have to walk between frost and fire.

Mss: **166b^x**(46r), papp15^x(2v), 738^x(80v), 167b 6^x(2r), 214^x(149v), 1441^x(582), 10575^x(3v), 2797^x(232).

Readings: [1] Munað: munaðlífi papp15^x, 738^x, 167b 6^x, 1441^x, 10575^x, 2797^x [2] vegu: vega 167b 6^x [3] fyrir: at 10575^x;   gaman: gamni papp15^x, 10575^x, 2797^x [4] er: at papp15^x, 738^x, 167b 6^x, 1441^x, 10575^x [6] meðal: milli papp15^x, 738^x, 167b 6^x, 1441^x, 10575^x, 2797^x, millum 214^x.

Editions: *Skj* Anonyme digte og vers [XII], G [6]. *Sólarljóð* 18: AI, 630, BI, 638, *Skald* I, 310; Bugge 1867, 360, Falk 1914, 7, Björn M. Ólsen 1915, 9, Fidjestøl 1979, 62, Njörður Njarðvík 1991, 55-6, Njörður Njarðvík 1993, 24, 102.

Notes: [1] *munað* 'sensuality': *Munaðlífi* 'a life of sensuality' is the majority reading in the other mss, but this makes the l. too long as Björn M. Ólsen (1915, 32-3) points out. — [3] *gaman* 'pleasure': So 166b^x and 33 other mss. *Gamni* (dat.) appears in 32 mss in total. — [5-6] *ganga meðal* 'to walk between': The reading of 166b^x. However, it could be argued that the majority reading, *ganga milli*, meaning 'to mediate', gives better sense, or at least as good sense, here. — [6] *frosts ok funa* (gen.) 'frost and fire': This alternation of fire and frost is frequent in visions of Hell; cf. 'The Vision of Dryhthelm' in Bede's *Historia Ecclesiastica* (Colgrave and Mynors 1969, 488-91), *Dugg* (Cahill 1981, 28-9), the Vision of Othloh of S. Emmeram (Othlonus S. Emmerammi, *Visio*, col. 380), *Visio Thurkilli* (Schmidt 1978, 28) and the Revelation of the Monk of Eynsham (Easting 2002, 48-9). *Has* 39 also couples frost and fire.

19. Óvinum þínum   trú þú aldrigi,
    þótt fagrt mæli fyr þér;
    góðu þú heit;   gótt er annars
    víti hafa at varnaði.

Trú þú aldrigi óvinum þínum, þótt mæli fagrt fyr þér; heit þú góðu; gótt er hafa annars víti at varnaði.

Never trust your enemies, though they speak fair words to you; promise good things; it is good to have another's punishment as a warning.

Mss: **166b**ˣ(46r), papp15ˣ(2v), 738ˣ(80v), 167b 6ˣ(2v), 214ˣ(149v), 1441ˣ(582), 10575ˣ(3v), 2797ˣ(232).

Readings: [2] trú þú: 'tr[...]' 167b 6ˣ [3] þótt: *om.* 167b 6ˣ; fagrt mæli fyr þér: þeir fagrt mæli fyr þér papp15ˣ, 167b 6ˣ, 1441ˣ, 10575ˣ, þeir fagrt fyr þér mæli 738ˣ, fagrt mæli fyr 214ˣ, þeir fagrt mæli fyr 2797ˣ [6] víti hafa at varnaði: vit at hafa fyrir varnaði papp15ˣ, víti sér varnaðar vita *corrected from* 'víti sér varnaðar vefia' 738ˣ, víti at hafa fyr varnaði 167b 6ˣ, 1441ˣ, 10575ˣ, 2797ˣ.

Editions: *Skj* Anonyme digte og vers [XII], G [6]. *Sólarljóð* 19: AI, 630, BI, 638, *Skald* I, 310, *NN* §1921F; Bugge 1867, 360, Falk 1914, 10, Björn M. Ólsen 1915, 10, Fidjestøl 1979, 62, Njörður Njarðvík 1991, 57, Njörður Njarðvík 1993, 25, 104.

Notes: [All]: The *exemplum* of sts 19-24 recalls the admonitions in *Sigrdr* 23 and 35 against swearing oaths unless reconciliation has truly been achieved and against trusting those whose kin you have killed. Amory (1985, 16; 1990, 264-5) suggests a reference to Matt. X.16, warning against trusting one's enemies. — [2] *trú þú aldrigi* 'never trust': *Skj* B, followed by *Skald*, normalises all mss' *aldri* to *aldrigi* to give a metrical l. — [3] *þótt fagrt mæli fyr þér* 'though they speak fair words to you': The l. requires alliteration on <f>, not <þ>. Most eds regularise (so *Skj* B, *Skald*) by using the more archaic form of the prep. *fyrir* (which receives full stress) and deleting *þér*. For the sentiment, cf. *Hsv* 42/2-3: *þótt fagrt mæli | þarftu eigi þeim at trúa* 'though they speak well, you need not trust in them'. — [4] *góðu þú heit* 'promise good things': *Þú* is omitted by both *Skj* B and *Skald*. Falk (1914a, 11) suggests, but does not incorporate into his text, the emendation *góðu þó heiti* 'though they promise good things', a suggestion followed by Björn M. Ólsen (1915, 34). This continues the admonition of the preceding ll. — [6] *hafa annars víti at varnaði* 'have another's punishment as a warning': Cf. *Hsv* 98/4-5: *annars manns víti | láti sér at varnaði* 'he should let the punishment of another [be] a warning to him'. Cf. also *Hávm* 45, 91, 124 and *Hsv* 42.

20. Svá honum gafz   Sörla inum góðráða,
    þá er hann lagði á vald hans Vígolfs;
    tryggliga hann trúði,   en hinn at tálum varð,
    sínum bróðurbana.

Svá gafz honum Sörla inum góðráða, þá er hann lagði á vald hans Vígolfs; hann trúði sínum bróðurbana tryggliga, en hinn varð at tálum.

So it turned out for Sörli the well-meaning, when he put the matter in Vígolfr's power; he trusted securely in his brother's killer, but that man engaged in deceit.

Mss: **166b**[x](46r), papp15[x](2v), 738[x](80v), 167b 6[x](2v), 214[x](149v), 1441[x](582), 10575[x](3v), 2797[x](232).

Readings: [1] honum: hinn 738[x] [2] góðráða: *om.* 738[x] [3] er: *om.* 214[x]; lagði: lagða 738[x]; hans: *om.* 1441[x]; -olfs ('-ulfs'): -olf 738[x], 167b 6[x] [4] trygg-: *so* 167b 6[x], treg- 166b[x], triggi- 738[x], trú- 214[x] [5] tálum: 'talmi' 1441[x].

Editions: *Skj* Anonyme digte og vers [XII], G [6]. *Sólarljóð* 20: AI, 631, BI, 638, *Skald* I, 310, *NN* §3252; Bugge 1867, 360, Falk 1914, 10, Björn M. Ólsen 1915, 10, Fidjestøl 1979, 62, Njörður Njarðvík 1991, 58, Njörður Njarðvík 1993, 26, 105.

Notes: [6] *bróðurbana* (dat.) 'brother's killer': Cf. *Hávm* 89 which counsels against trusting one's brother's slayer.

21. Grið hann þeim seldi   af góðum hug,
    en þeir hétu honum gulli í gegn;
    sáttir létuz,   meðan saman drukku,
    en þó kómu flærðir fram.

Hann seldi þeim grið af góðum hug, en þeir hétu honum gulli í gegn; sáttir létuz, meðan saman drukku, en þó kómu flærðir fram.

He offered them a truce with a good intention, and they promised him gold in exchange; they pretended to be reconciled while they drank together, but yet falsehoods emerged.

Mss: **166b**[x](46r), papp15[x](3r), 738[x](81r), 167b 6[x](2v), 214[x](150r), 1441[x](582), 10575[x](3v-4r), 2797[x](232).

Readings: [2] hug: huga 1441[x], 2797[x] [3] en þeir hétu honum gulli í gegn: þó kómu flærðir fram 214[x]; hétu: 'heti' 10575[x]; honum: *om.* 738[x]; gulli: gull papp15[x], 167b 6[x] [4] létuz: þeir létuz 738[x] [6] en: *so* papp15[x], 738[x], 214[x], 1441[x], 10575[x], 2797[x], *om.* 166b[x]; þó kómu flærðir fram: þeir hétu honum gulli í gegn 214[x].

Editions: *Skj* Anonyme digte og vers [XII], G [6]. *Sólarljóð* 21: AI, 631, BI, 638, *Skald* I, 310; Bugge 1867, 360, Falk 1914, 10, Björn M. Ólsen 1915, 10, Fidjestøl 1979, 62, Njörður Njarðvík 1991, 58, Njörður Njarðvík 1993, 27, 106.

Notes: [6] *en* 'but': Although 166b[x] omits this, it is well-supported by all the other major mss. 214[x] transposes ll. 3 and 6. Line 6 is close in phrasing to *Hsv* 64/6.

22. En þá eptir   á öðrum degi,
        er þeir höfðu í Rýgjardal riðit,
    sverðum þeir meiddu,   þann er saklauss var,
        ok létu hans fjörvi farit.

En þá eptir á öðrum degi, er þeir höfðu riðit í Rýgjardal, meiddu þeir sverðum, þann er saklauss var, ok létu farit fjörvi hans.

And then afterwards on the second day, when they had ridden into Rýgjardalr, they maimed with swords the man who was innocent and deprived him of life.

Mss: **166b**[x](46r), papp15[x](3r), 738[x](81r), 167b 6[x](2v), 214[x](150r), 1441[x](582), 10575[x](4r), 2797[x](232).

Readings: [3] höfðu: höfði 10575[x]; í: á 738[x]; Rýgjar- ('ryar-'): eyrar- papp15[x], 1441[x], eyar- 738[x], 167b 6[x], 10575[x], rygja- 2797[x]   [4] meiddu: myrðu 10575[x]   [5] er: *om.* papp15[x], 214[x], 1441[x].

Editions: *Skj* Anonyme digte og vers [XII], G [6]. *Sólarljóð* 22: AI, 631, BI, 638, *Skald* I, 310; Bugge 1867, 360, Falk 1914, 10, Björn M. Ólsen 1915, 10, Fidjestøl 1979, 63, Njörður Njarðvík 1991, 58-9, Njörður Njarðvík 1993, 28, 107.

Notes: [3] *Rýgjardal* 'valley of the ogress': On the scribal form, see *ANG* §203.2. This highly appropriate and alliteratively correct, though elsewhere unattested, p. n. is frequently substituted with actual place names, e.g. *Eyrardal* in papp15[x], or *Eyjardal* in other mss. There is an Eyrardalur in Suður-Múlasýsla and another in Vestur Ísafjarða-sýsla; Eyjadalur is in the Eyjafjörður district (see Icelandic Gazetteer: Geographical Information System <http://gis.bofh.is/ornefnaskra/>). — [6] *létu farit fjörvi hans* 'deprived him of life': cf. *Lok* 57/6 *verðr þá píno fjǫrvi um farit* 'then your life will have gone' and *Fáfn* 5/3.

23. Lík hans þeir drógu   á leynigötu
        ok brytjuðu í brunn niðr;
    dylja þeir vildu,   en dróttinn sá
        heilagr himni af.

Þeir drógu lík hans á leynigötu ok brytjuðu niðr í brunn; þeir vildu dylja, en heilagr dróttinn sá af himni.

They dragged his body along a secret path and dismembered it [putting it] down into a well; they wanted to conceal it, but the holy Lord saw it from heaven.

Mss: **166b**[x](46v), papp15[x](3r), 738[x](81r), 167b 6[x](2v), 214[x](150r), 1441[x](582-3), 10575[x](4r), 2797[x](232).

Readings: [1] þeir: *om.* 2797ˣ [3] brytjuðu: brytjuði 10575ˣ [4] þeir: þér 167b 6ˣ [6] heilagr: *so* papp15ˣ, 738ˣ, 167b 6ˣ, 1441ˣ, 2797ˣ, helgr 166bˣ, 214ˣ, 10575ˣ; himni: himnum papp15ˣ, 738ˣ, 167b 6ˣ, 1441ˣ, 10575ˣ, 2797ˣ.

Editions: *Skj* Anonyme digte og vers [XII], G [6]. *Sólarljóð* 23: AI, 631, BI, 639, *Skald* I, 310; Bugge 1867, 360, Falk 1914, 10, Björn M. Ólsen 1915, 11, Fidjestøl 1979, 63, Njörður Njarðvík 1991, 59, Njörður Njarðvík 1993, 29, 107.

Notes: [6] *himni* (dat. sg.) 'heaven': Either 166bˣ's reading or the dat. pl. reading of the other mss is possible.

24. Sál hans bað   inn sanni guð
       í sinn fögnuð fara;
    en sökudólgar   hygg ek síðla myni
       kallaðir frá kvölum.

Inn sanni guð bað sál hans fara í fögnuð sinn; en ek hygg sökudólgar myni síðla kallaðir frá kvölum.

The true God commanded his soul to journey into his joy; but I think that his enemies will be summoned late from torments.

Mss: 166bˣ(46v), papp15ˣ(3r), 738ˣ(81r), 167b 6ˣ(2v), 214ˣ(150r), 1441ˣ(583), 10575ˣ(4r), 2797ˣ(232).

Readings: [1] bað: bauð 738ˣ, 10575ˣ, 2797ˣ [2] inn: heim papp15ˣ, heim inn 10575ˣ, 2797ˣ [4] en: *om.* papp15ˣ, 738ˣ, 167b 6ˣ, 214ˣ [5] síðla: *corrected from* 'síðar' 738ˣ; myni ('mune'): *so* papp15ˣ, 167b 6ˣ, 214ˣ, 1441ˣ, 2797ˣ, munu 166bˣ, muni *corrected from* 'mun' 738ˣ, 'mano' 10575ˣ.

Editions: *Skj* Anonyme digte og vers [XII], G [6]. *Sólarljóð* 24: AI, 631, BI, 639, *Skald* I, 310-11; Bugge 1867, 360-1, Falk 1914, 10, Björn M. Ólsen 1915, 11, Fidjestøl 1979, 63, Njörður Njarðvík 1991, 59-60, Njörður Njarðvík 1993, 30, 107.

Notes: [3] *fögnuð* 'joy': Also describes heaven in Anon *Líkn* 52. — [5-6]: An example of litotes; the speaker thinks that the man's assailants will never be released from torments. — [6] *kallaðir frá kvölum* 'summoned from torments': Cf. st. 45/6.

25. Dísir bið þú þér   dróttins mála
       vera hollar í hugum;
    viku eptir   mun þér vilja þíns
       alt at óskum gá.

Bið þú mála-dísir dróttins vera þér hollar í hugum; viku eptir mun alt gá þér at óskum vilja þíns.

Ask the confidential-*dísir* of the Lord to be gracious to you in their thoughts; one week later everything will go according to the desires of your will.

Mss: **166b**[x](46v), papp15[x](3r), 738[x](81r), 167b 6[x](2v), 214[x](150r), 1441[x](583), 10575[x](4r), 2797[x](232-3).

Readings: [1] Dísir: *so* papp15[x], 738[x], 1441[x], 10575[x], 2797[x], 'dysi' 166b[x], 167b 6[x], 214[x]; bið þú: þú bið 1441[x]   [5] mun: man 10575[x], 2797[x]   [6] alt: *so* papp15[x], 738[x], 167b 6[x], 214[x], 1441[x], 10575[x], 2797[x], at 166b[x];   óskum: 'audnu' papp15[x], 167b 6[x], 10575[x], 2797[x], 'audnu' *corrected from* 'óskum' 738[x], öðru 1441[x]; gá: ganga 738[x], 167b 6[x].

Editions: *Skj* Anonyme digte og vers [XII], G [6]. *Sólarljóð* 25: AI, 631, BI, 639, *Skald* I, 311; Bugge 1867, 361, Falk 1914, 13, Björn M. Ólsen 1915, 11, Fidjestøl 1979, 63, Njörður Njarðvík 1991, 61, Njörður Njarðvík 1993, 31, 108-9.

Notes: [1] *dísir* '*dísir*, female spirits': Not in 166b[x], but in many other mss. The distribution of 'dysi' however is wide enough to suggest an archetype error. In pre-Christian belief, *dísir* were female tutelary spirits of the family or of an individual (Turville-Petre 1964, 221-6). Here they seem to have been transferred syncretically to a Christian context. — [1-2] *mála-dísir dróttins* 'the confidential-*dísir* of the Lord': It is not clear whether *mála* should be regarded as part of a cpd noun, or as a simplex. If the latter (see below), emendation is required. Falk (1914a, 15), Björn M. Ólsen (1915, 36), and Fidejstøl (1979, 42-3) understand *mála-dísir* as *de diser sem taler med Gud* 'the *dísir* who talk with God', that is, God's confidantes; Falk compares *málvinr* 'a friend one habitually talks to, a close friend, confidant' (*LP*: *málvina, málvinr*). *Skj* B, followed by *Skald,* emends *mála* to *málur* acc. pl. (*LP*: *mála* 'confidential female friend'), and construes *bið þér dísir, dróttins málur* 'pray to the *dísir*, the Lord's confidantes'. The *mála-dísir* or *dróttins málur* may be, Falk and Björn M. Ólsen suggest, virgin saints who have an intercessory role. Falk notes that they appear in *Visio Tnugdali* (Cahill 1983, 104-5), *Visio Alberici* (Mirra 1932, 99) and *Visio Thurkilli* (Schmidt 1978, 36), near the throne of God. For Fidjestøl's and Amory's views of the syncretic tendencies of *Sól*, particularly in this st., see Introduction. — [6] *alt at óskum gá* 'go according to your desires': *gá* 'go' is the form found in 166b[x] and a number of other mss. This form is normally thought to be post-1400 (*ANG* §504 n. 4); *ganga* may well have stood in the original text, but not in final position, as it would be unmetrical there. Gering (1902, 454-5) proposed adopting *ganga* and reversing its position with that of *alt* to give a regular l., thus: *at óskum ganga alt*. This suggestion was adopted by *Skj* B and *Skald*. The l. is paralleled in *Hsv* 78/3: *þótt gangi at óskum alt* 'although everything goes as wished'.

26. Reiðiverk,   þau er þú unnit hefr,
    bæt þú eigi illu yfir;
  grættan gæla   skaltu með góðum hlutum;
    þat kveða sálu sama.

Reiðiverk, þau er þú hefr unnit, bæt þú eigi illu yfir; skaltu gæla grættan með góðum hlutum; þat kveða sama sálu.

The angry deeds that you have committed, do not compensate for them with wickedness; you must comfort the weeping one with good things; they say that befits the soul.

Mss: **166b**ˣ(46v), papp15ˣ(3r-v), 738ˣ(81r), 167b 6ˣ(2v) (l. 1), 214ˣ(150r), 1441ˣ(583), 10575ˣ(4v), 2797ˣ(233).

Readings: [2-6]: *om.* 167b 6ˣ [2] þú: er 1441ˣ [3] þú: *om.* 10575ˣ, 2797ˣ [4] gæla: gala 166bˣ, 738ˣ, 214ˣ, 1441ˣ, 10575ˣ, 2797ˣ, hala papp15ˣ [5] skaltu: skalt 10575ˣ [6] þat kveða sálu sama: á vinna aptr 1441ˣ; kveða: *so* 2797ˣ, *om.* 166bˣ, papp15ˣ, 214ˣ, 10575ˣ, er 738ˣ.

Editions: *Skj* Anonyme digte og vers [XII], G [6]. *Sólarljóð* 26: AI, 632, BI, 639, *Skald* I, 311, *NN* §2147C; Bugge 1867, 361, Falk 1914, 13, Björn M. Ólsen 1915, 11, Fidjestøl 1979, 63, Njörður Njarðvík 1991, 62, Njörður Njarðvík 1993, 32, 109.

Notes: [1-2]: Most eds, following Bugge, regularise ll. 1-2 by adding 'er' to l. 2, and combining it with *þau* (l. 1) in order to regularise the syntax. However, ll. 1-2 lack alliteration. — [2-6]: These ll. are omitted in 167b 6ˣ, as are all succeeding sts up to and including 55. — [3] *bæt þú eigi illu yfir* 'do not compensate for them with wickedness': Cf. *Hsv* 87. — [4] *gæla* 'to comfort, soothe': Bugge's emendation. *Gala* 'to chant' is preferred by most of the main mss to papp15ˣ's *hala*, possibly related to *halda* 'to hold, maintain'. Neither of these variants makes sense in context. — [6] *kveða* 'they [people] say': The reading (or possibly the emendation) of 2797ˣ, adopted by 4 related later mss (1692ˣ, 2298ˣ, IBR36ˣ and 1458ˣ). It is likely that the majority of mss have omitted a verb here. This reading has been adopted by all subsequent eds.

27. Á guð skaltu heita   til góðra hluta,
    þann er hefr skatna skapat;
  mjök fyrir verðr   manna hverr,
    er sér finn*r*at föður.

Skaltu heita á guð til góðra hluta, þann er hefr skapat skatna; hverr manna verðr mjök fyrir, er sér finn*r*at föður.

You must pray to God for good things, the one who has created men; each man perishes who does not find the Father for himself.

Mss: **166b**ˣ(46v), papp15ˣ(3v), 738ˣ(81r), 214ˣ(150r), 1441ˣ(583), 10575ˣ(4v), 2797ˣ(233).

Readings: [1] skaltu: skal papp15ˣ, 10575ˣ, 2797ˣ, skalt 1441ˣ [6] sér: seint papp15ˣ, sinn 1441ˣ, 10575ˣ, 2797ˣ; finn*r*at: 'fjóna' 166bˣ, 1441ˣ, 10575ˣ, 2797ˣ, þjóna papp15ˣ, finna 738ˣ, 214ˣ.

Editions: *Skj* Anonyme digte og vers [XII], G [6]. *Sólarljóð* 27: AI, 632, BI, 639-40, *Skald* I, 311, *NN* §1934D; Bugge 1867, 361, Falk 1914, 13, Björn M. Ólsen 1915, 11-12, Fidjestøl 1979, 63, Njörður Njarðvík 1991, 62-3, Njörður Njarðvík 1993, 33, 110.

Notes: [6] *er sér finn*rat *föður* 'who does not find the Father for himself': This l. is problematic in all mss, and is likely to have been corrupted. The verb and subject of the main cl. is sg. (*hverr manna* 'each man, lit. 'each of men'), but the verb of the rel. cl. in all ms. readings appears to be pl. Thus either the verb of the rel. cl. is corrupted (the view taken here), or some other distortion of the text has occurred. *Finna* is the most acceptable of the ms. readings and also provides good alliteration. If the final <a> is what remains of an original neg. enclitic particle *–at*, the sg. verb *finnrat* can be reconstructed by slight emendation. *Skj* B and *Skald* also emend thus. The mss also vary considerably in the second word of l. 6. 166b[x]'s *sér* 'for himself' has been accepted here. Other eds either choose one of the other variants or emend; *Skj* B and *Skald* adopt *sinn*, giving the sense 'who does not find his Father'. Bugge (1867, 361) emended papp15[x]'s reading *seint* (adv.) 'late' to *seinar* (comp. adv.) 'later' (*seint* appears in 23 mss, though never in combination with *finna*). This solves the problem of the pl. verb and sg. subject for the rel. cl., but there is still a switch between sg. and pl. as between main cl. and rel. cl. The danger inherent in coming to God late is paralleled in *Has* 41 and *Leið* 39.

28. Æsta þykkir   einkum vandliga,
    þess er þykkir vant vera;
    alls á mis verðr,   sá er einskis biðr;
    fár hyggr þegjanda þörf.

Þykkir æsta einkum vandliga, þess er þykkir vant vera; sá er einskis biðr, verðr alls á mis; fár hyggr þörf þegjanda.

It seems [right] to ask especially carefully for what seems to be lacking; he who asks for nothing, will go amiss in everything; few consider the need of the one who is silent.

Mss: **166b[x]**(46v), papp15[x](3v), 738[x](81r), 214[x](150r), 1441[x](583), 10575[x](4v), 2797[x](233).

Readings: [1] Æsta: 'æsca' papp15[x], 'æskia' 10575[x], æstandi 2797[x]; þykkir: þarftu 1441[x] [2] vand-: var- papp15[x] [3] þykkir vant: vant þykkir 2797[x]; vera: *om.* 2797[x] [4] á mis: 'a væl' 166b[x], 214[x], 'ami' papp15[x], á vil 738[x], 'a ne' 1441[x], 'a nei' 10575[x], 'ani' 2797[x] [5] sá er: þeir 214[x] [6] þegjanda: *so* 1441[x], 10575[x], 2797[x], þegjandi 166b[x], papp15[x], 738[x], 214[x].

Editions: *Skj* Anonyme digte og vers [XII], G [6]. *Sólarljóð* 28: AI, 632, BI, 639-40, *Skald* I, 311, *NN* §2149; Bugge 1867, 361-2, Falk 1914, 13, Björn M. Ólsen 1915, 12, Fidjestøl 1979, 63, Njörður Njarðvík 1991, 62-3, Njörður Njarðvík 1993, 34, 110.

Notes: [1, 3] *þykkir* 'it seems': The repetition of *þykkir* has tempted eds, following Bugge, to emend the first *þykkir* to *dugir* 'it helps, is of advantage' (so Falk, Björn M. Ólsen, *Skj* B, *Skald*, Fidjestøl) but *þykkir* is found in 166b[x] and 58 other mss; *þarftu* 'you need' in 1441[x] looks like an intelligent scribal emendation. — [4] *a mis*: The mss have a variety of readings, providing variants on 'væl', 'mi' and 'ne'. *Skj* B's conjecture *mis* (followed by Björn M. Ólsen and Njörður Njarðvík) is supported by papp15[x] and possibly by the various 'ne' readings. *Verða á mis(s)* + gen. means 'to go wrong, go amiss' and suits the context well. *Á víl* (which is suggested by the readings of 738[x] and 166b[x]) does not take the gen. of what goes astray or amiss, as is required here. Kock (*NN* §2149 and *Skald*) conjectures *áveill* 'wretched, miserable'. Bugge emended to *án æ* 'always without'; some support for this may be offered by 7 mss reading 'an', 'ani' or 'a nei', as 10575[x] does. Falk, followed by Fidjestøl, emended to *án* 'alone', *als án verðr* 'he will get nothing'. This emendation provides an effective contrast with asking for nothing (l. 5); cf. Matt. VII.7-8: *petite et dabitur vobis quaerite et invenietis pulsate et aperietur vobis | omnis enim qui petit accipit et qui quaerit invenit et pulsanti aperietur* 'ask, and it shall be given you: seek, and you shall find: knock, and it shall be opened to you. For every one that asketh, receiveth: and he that seeketh, findeth: and to him that knocketh, it shall be opened' (cf. Luke XI.9-10). — [6] *þegjanda* 'of the one who is silent': 166b[x] has *þegjandi*, but a nom. case can scarcely be correct. About 10 mss have *þegjanda* however, probably by independent emendation; no doubt nom. *fár* 'few' has encouraged the use of *þegjandi* in agreement. Cf. *Hávm* 104: *fátt gat ek þegjandi þar* 'little did I get there by being silent', and *Hsv* 46 for a similar sentiment.

29. Síðla ek kom   snemma kallaðr
    til dómsvalds dura;
þangat ek ætlumz;   því mér heitit var;
    sá hefr krás, er krefr.

Ek kom síðla, kallaðr snemma til dura dómsvalds; ek ætlumz þangat; því var mér heitit; sá hefr krás, er krefr.

I came late, [I was] called early to the doors of the ruler of judgement; I intend to go there; that was promised to me; he who asks gets the delicacy.

Mss: **166b[x]**(46v), papp15[x](3v), 738[x](81r), 214[x](150r), 1441[x](583), 10575[x](4v), 2797[x](233).

Readings: [2] kallaðr: *so* papp15[x], 10575[x], 2797[x], ek kallaði 166b[x], ek kolladusk 214[x]　[3] dura: *so* 2797[x], dyra 166b[x], 738[x], 214[x], 1441[x], 10575[x], dyrir papp15[x]　[5] því: því at papp15[x], 738[x], 2797[x], þat 1441[x]　[6] er: *so* papp15[x], 738[x], 214[x], 1441[x], 10575[x], 2797[x], *om.* 166b[x].

Editions: *Skj* Anonyme digte og vers [XII]. G [6]. *Sólarljóð* 29: AI, 632, BI, 640, *Skald* I, 311, *NN* §2150; Bugge 1867, 362, Falk 1914, 14, Björn M. Ólsen 1915, 12, Fidjestøl 1979, 64, Njörður Njarðvík 1991, 63-4, Njörður Njarðvík 1993, 35, 111.

Notes: [2] *kallaðr* 'called': 166b[x] has *ek kallaði* 'I called', but the verb has no object; the contrast between being called early and coming late seems to be what is intended. — [6] *er* 'who': Omitted by 166b[x] only, but is required by the syntax. Cf. John X.9: *ego sum ostium per me si quis introierit salvabitur et ingredietur et egredietur et pascua inveniet* 'I am the door. By me, if any man enter in, he shall be saved: and he shall go in and go out, and shall find pastures'.

30. Synðir því valda,   at vér hryggvir förum
      ægisheimi ór;
   engi óttaz,   nema ilt geri;
      gótt er vammalausum vera.

Synðir valda því, at vér förum hryggvir ór ægisheimi; engi óttaz, nema ilt geri; gótt er vera vammalausum.

Sins cause this, that sorrowful we journey out of the terrible world; no-one is afraid, unless he does wrong; it is good to be without stains.

Mss: **166b**[x](46v), papp15[x](3v), 738[x](81r), 214[x](150r), 1441[x](583), 10575[x](5r), 2797[x](233).

Readings: [2] hryggvir: syrgir 2797[x]   [6] vammalausum: vammalaus 214[x], vammlausum 10575[x]; vera: at vera 214[x].

Editions: *Skj* Anonyme digte og vers [XII], G [6]. *Sólarljóð* 30: AI, 632, BI, 640, *Skald* I, 311; Bugge 1867, 362, Falk 1914, 14, Björn M. Ólsen 1915, 12, Fidjestøl 1979, 64, Njörður Njarðvík 1991, 64, Njörður Njarðvík 1993, 36, 111.

Notes: [2] *hryggvir* 'sorrowful': 2797[x]'s reading *syrgir* (?for *saurgir* 'stained') is an attempt to improve the alliteration; otherwise ll. 1 and 2 are unmetrical. — [3] *ægisheimi* (dat. sg.) 'terrible world': A *hap. leg.*, perhaps calqued on *ægishjálmr* lit. 'helmet of terror', the helmet owned by Fáfnir in *Fáfn* 16, 17, and related to *ægir* (*LP*: *skrækindjager* 'one who induces terror'). — [6] *vammalausum vera* 'to be without stains', lit. '[it is good] for the stainless ones to exist': Cf. *Sigrdr* 22/3: *vammalauss verir* 'be without stains'; *Hsv* 3/3: *vammalauss lífa* 'to live without stains', and more distantly, *Hávm* 68; Rom. XIII.4.

31. Úlfum líkir   þykkja allir þeir,
      sem eiga hverfan hug;
   svá mun gefaz,   þeim er ganga skal
      þær inar glæddu götur.

Allir þeir, sem eiga hverfan hug, þykkja líkir úlfum; svá mun gefaz, þeim er skal ganga þær inar glæddu götur.

All those who have a changeable heart seem like wolves; it shall turn out thus for the one who has to tread the glowing-hot paths.

Mss: **166b**[x](46v), papp15[x](3v), 738[x](81r), 214[x](150r), 1441[x](583), 10575[x](5r), 2797[x](233).

Readings: [2] allir: vera allir 738[x]   [3] sem: sin papp15[x]; eiga: hafa 1441[x], eigu 10575[x]   [4] mun: mun ok 738[x], man 10575[x], 2797[x]   [5] er: sem papp15[x], er *corrected from* sem 10575[x]; skal: *om.* papp15[x], 738[x], 1441[x], 10575[x].

Editions: *Skj* Anonyme digte og vers [XII], G [6]. *Sólarljóð* 31: AI, 632, BI, 640, *Skald* I, 311; Bugge 1867, 362, Falk 1914, 14, Björn M. Ólsen 1915, 12-13, Fidjestøl 1979, 64, Njörður Njarðvík 1991, 64-5, Njörður Njarðvík 1993, 37, 112.

Notes: [1] *líkir úlfum* 'like wolves': cf. Matt. VII.15: *adtendite a falsis prophetis qui veniunt ad vos in vestimentis ovium intrinsecus autem sunt lupi rapaces* 'beware of false prophets, who come to you in the clothing of sheep, but inwardly they are ravening wolves'. — [6] *inar glæddu götur* 'the glowing-hot paths': Cf. st. 59 and *Dugg* (Cahill 1983, 25-6).

32. Vinsamlig ráð   ok viti bundin
    kenni ek þér sjau saman;
görla þau mun   ok glata aldri;
    öll eru þau nýt at nema.

Ek kenni þér sjau ráð saman, vinsamlig ok bundin viti; mun þau görla ok glata aldri; þau eru öll nýt at nema.

I teach you seven counsels in all, friendly and bound with wit; remember them fully and never forget them; they are all useful to learn.

Mss: 166b^x(46v), papp15^x(3v-4r), 738^x(81v), 214^x(150v), 1441^x(583), 10575^x(5r), 2797^x(233).

Readings: [3] kenni: *so* papp15^x, 738^x, 214^x, 1441^x, 10575^x, 2797^x, kunni 166b^x [4] þau: þú papp15^x, 738^x, 1441^x, 2797^x; mun: nem papp15^x, 10575^x, 2797^x, man 1441^x.

Editions: *Skj* Anonyme digte og vers [XII], G [6]. *Sólarljóð* 32: AI, 633, BI, 640, *Skald* I, 311, *NN* §2564A; Bugge 1867, 362, Falk 1914, 14, Björn M. Ólsen 1915, 13, Fidjestøl 1979, 64, Njörður Njarðvík 1991, 65, Njörður Njarðvík 1993, 38, 113.

Notes: [3] *kenni* '[I] teach': 166b^x has *kunni* 'I know', but this cannot take an indirect object. — [3] *sjau* 'seven': A number with Christian associations, contrasting with the nine *fimbulljóð* 'mighty spells' of Óðinn in *Hávm* 140. For pagan and Christian number symbolism in *Sól* see Tate 1985, 1031 and more generally Laugesen 1959. The seven counsels are given in sts 25-32. — [6] *öll eru þau nýt at nema* 'they are all useful to learn': Cf. *Hávm* sts 112-37: *nióta mundo, ef þú nemr* 'they will be useful if you learn them'; *Hávm* 162/8 *nýt, ef þú nemr* 'useful if you learn'; *Hsv* 86/3 *nýtt at nema* 'useful to learn'. Cf. also *Gróg* 16; *Hsv* 2, 148; Prov. VII.1-2 for the adjuration to memorise imparted wisdom.

33. Frá því er at segja,   hvé sæll ek var
    yndisheimi í;
ok inu öðru,   hvé ýta synir
    verða nauðgir at náum.

Frá því er at segja, hvé sæll ek var í yndisheimi; ok inu öðru, hvé ýta synir verða nauðgir at náum.

It is to be told how happy I was in the delightful world; and the other thing, how the sons of men are forced to become corpses.

Mss: **166b**ˣ(46v), papp15ˣ(4r), 738ˣ(81v), 214ˣ(150v), 1441ˣ(583), 10575ˣ(5r-v), 2797ˣ(233).

Readings: [2] hvé: hvat papp15ˣ, 738ˣ, 214ˣ, 1441ˣ, 10575ˣ [3] yndis-: ægis- papp15ˣ, 738ˣ, 214ˣ, 1441ˣ, 10575ˣ, 2797ˣ [6] náum ('nám'): *so* 2797ˣ, námi 166bˣ, papp15ˣ, 738ˣ, 214ˣ, 1441ˣ, 10575ˣ.

Editions: *Skj* Anonyme digte og vers [XII], G [6]. *Sólarljóð* 33: AI, 633, BI, 640-1, *Skald* I, 311; Bugge 1867, 362, Falk 1914, 18, Björn M. Ólsen 1915, 13, Fidjestøl 1979, 64, Njörður Njarðvík 1991, 67, Njörður Njarðvík 1993, 39, 114.

Notes: [All]: 214ˣ and related mss transpose sts 33 and 34. — [3] *yndisheimi* 'the delightful world': So 166bˣ, and two other mss. All other mss including papp15ˣ and 738ˣ, have *ægisheimi* 'the terrible world', or variants of it, probably imported from st. 30. — [6] *náum*: Gísli Konráðsson, scribe of 2797ˣ, copied or emended his text as *nám*, probably recognising that the majority mss' *námi* is unmetrical in final position. Even though his reading has support only from 7 mostly unimportant mss, it is likely to be correct, both on metrical grounds, and on grounds of sense. *Nám* or *náum* (dat. pl.) 'corpses' was adopted as an emendation by Bugge and accepted by *Skj* B, *Skald*, Falk, Björn Ólsen and Fidjestøl. The expression *verða at nám* 'to become corpses' occurs in *HHund II* 28/4: *at nám orðnir*. If the majority mss' reading *verða at námi* is retained, as Njörður Njarðvík does (1991, 67), the sense must be that the second thing the speaker mentions is that sons of men are forced to set about learning (*nám* n.), a sentiment certainly relevant to the injunction to learn in st. 32.

34. Vil ok dul   tælir virða sonu,
        þá er fíkjaz á fé;
    ljósir aurar   verða at löngum trega;
        margan hefr auðr apat.

Vil ok dul tælir sonu virða, þá er fíkjaz á fé; ljósir aurar verða trega at löngum; auðr hefr apat margan.

Desire and delusion trap the sons of men, those who are greedy for wealth; shining pieces of silver turn to grief in the long run; riches have made a monkey of many a man.

Mss: **166b**ˣ(46v), papp15ˣ(4r), 738ˣ(81v), 214ˣ(150v), 1441ˣ(583), 10575ˣ(5v), 2797ˣ(233).

Readings: [3] fíkjaz: 'fykast' 214ˣ [5] verða: verði 10575ˣ.

Editions: *Skj* Anonyme digte og vers [XII], G [6]. *Sólarljóð* 34: AI, 633, BI, 641, *Skald* I, 311; *NN* §1779D; Bugge 1867, 362, Falk 1914, 18, Björn M. Ólsen 1915, 13, Fidjestøl 1979, 64, Njörður Njarðvík 1991, 67-8, Njörður Njarðvík 1993, 40, 114.

Notes: [1] *vil ok dul* 'desire and delusion': Cf. Hfr *ErfÓl* 25/8[1] and *dularheim* 'world of delusion' in st. 35/4. — [2] *tælir* 'entrap': 3rd pers. sg. verb for pl. subject comprising two distinct entities. For warnings against trusting in riches, cf. *Hsv* 34/6: *ilt er auði at trúa* 'it is bad to trust in wealth', and more distantly *Hsv* 22, 66, 80; *Hávm* 75, and Matt. VI.19-21; against trusting in worldly things in general, cf. *Hsv* 106.

35. Glaðr at mörgu   þótta ek gumnum vera,
         því ek vissa fátt fyrir;
    dularheim   hefr dróttinn skapat
         munafullan mjök.

Ek þótta gumnum vera glaðr at mörgu, því ek vissa fátt fyrir; dróttinn hefr skapat mjök munafullan dularheim.

I seemed to men to be happy at many a thing, because I knew little of what lay ahead; the Lord has created a world of delusion very full of pleasures.

Mss: **166b**[x](46v), papp15[x](4r), 738[x](81v), 214[x](150v), 1441[x](584), 10575[x](5v), 2797[x](233).

Readings: [4] dular-: dvalar- papp15[x], 738[x], 214[x], 10575[x], 2797[x]   [6] munafullan: munaþfullan 214[x].

Editions: *Skj* Anonyme digte og vers [XII], G [6]. *Sólarljóð* 35: AI, 633, BI, 641, *Skald* I, 312; Bugge 1867, 363, Falk 1914, 18, Björn M. Ólsen 1915, 13, Fidjestøl 1979, 64, Njörður Njarðvík 1991, 68, Njörður Njarðvík 1993, 41, 114-5.

Notes: [4] *dularheim* 'world of delusion': Is in 166b[x], and a limited range of other mss, cf. *dul* 'delusion' in 34/1. *Dvalarheim* 'world where we stay', as in papp15[x] and 738[x], is elsewhere the dominant reading and has been adopted by all other eds. For the sentiment that happiness is the result of not knowing one's fate, cf. *Hávm* 55, 56.

36. Lútr ek sat;   lengi ek hölluðumz;
         mjök var ek þá lystr at lifa;
    en sá réð,   sem ríkr var;
         frammi eru feigs götur.

Ek sat lútr; ek hölluðumz lengi; ek var þá mjök lystr at lifa; en sá réð, sem ríkr var; götur feigs eru frammi.

I sat bowed; I was leaning over for a long time; I was then very eager to live; but he prevailed, who was powerful; the doomed man's roads are at an end.

Mss: **166b**[x](46v), papp15[x](4r), 738[x](81v), 214[x](150v), 1441[x](584), 10575[x](5v), 2797[x](233-4).

Readings: [1] Lútr: latr papp15ˣ;   ek: ok papp15ˣ, 738ˣ, 1441ˣ, 10575ˣ, 2797ˣ   [2] hölluðumz: hallaður 1441ˣ   [4] réð: réði 10575ˣ, 2797ˣ   [5] ríkr: ríki 1441ˣ   [6] frammi: fram 10575ˣ, 2797ˣ.

Editions: Skj Anonyme digte og vers [XII], G [6]. *Sólarljóð* 36: AI, 633, BI, 641, *Skald* I, 312; Bugge 1867, 363, Falk 1914, 18, Björn M. Ólsen 1915, 14, Fidjestøl 1979, 65, Njörður Njarðvík 1991, 68, Njörður Njarðvík 1993, 42, 115.

Notes: [5] *ríkr* 'powerful': So Bugge, Fidjestøl and Njörður Njarðvík. Falk, Björn M. Ólsen, *Skj* B and *Skald* emend to *ríkri* 'more powerful', following *CPB* I, 204, which would be metrically correct. — [6] *götur feigs eru frammi* 'the doomed man's roads are at an end': This may be proverbial; *feigr* frequently collocates with *fara* 'to go' in proverbs, see Finnur Jónsson (1913-14, 82-3) and Harris (In progress), for similar proverbs in *Grettis saga*.

37. Heljar reip   kómu harðliga
       sveigð at síðum mér;
    slíta ek vilda,   en þau seig váru;
       létt er lauss at fara.

Reip heljar kómu at síðum mér, harðliga sveigð; ek vilda slíta, en þau váru seig; létt er at fara lauss.

The ropes of Hell came around my sides, powerfully twisted; I wanted to tear them but they were tough; it is easy to move unbound.

Mss: **166b**ˣ(46v-47r), papp15ˣ(4r), 738ˣ(81v), 214ˣ(150v), 1441ˣ(584), 10575ˣ(5v-6r), 2797ˣ(234).

Readings: [3] sveigð: sveig 1441ˣ;   síðum: síðo 214ˣ   [5] seig: sterk papp15ˣ, 738ˣ, 214ˣ, 1441ˣ, 10575ˣ, 2797ˣ.

Editions: Skj Anonyme digte og vers [XII], G [6]. *Sólarljóð* 37: AI, 633, BI, 641, *Skald* I, 312; Bugge 1867, 363, Falk 1914, 18, Björn M. Ólsen 1915, 14, Fidjestøl 1991, 65, Njörður Njarðvík 1991, 69, Njörður Njarðvík 1993, 43, 115.

Notes: [1] *heljar* 'of Hell': Primarily the Christian Hell, but allusion to Hel, the pagan goddess of the dead may also be intended; cf. Psalm XVII.5-6: *circumdederunt me funes mortis et torrentes diabuli terruerunt me / funes inferi circumdederunt me praevenerunt me laquei mortis* 'the sorrows of death surrounded me: and the torrents of iniquity troubled me. The sorrows of Hell encompassed me: and the snares of death prevented me', and similarly 2 Sam. XXII.6. — [5] *seig* 'tough': The *lectio difficilior*. The reading is in 166bˣ and 10 other mss to which it is closely related. *Seig* provides correct alliteration, unlike *sterk* 'strong', which is the majority reading.

38. Einn ek vissa,   hvé alla vegu
        sullu sútir mér;
    heljar meyjar   mér hrolla buðu
        heim á hverju kveldi.

Ek einn vissa hvé sútir sullu mér alla vegu; heljar meyjar buðu mér heim hrolla á hverju kveldi.

I alone knew how agonies surged over me in all directions; Hell's maidens dealt shivers home to me every evening.

Mss: **166b**[x](47r), papp15[x](4r-v), 738[x](81v), 214[x](150v), 1441[x](584), 10575[x](6r), 2797[x](234).

Readings: [1] vissa: vissi 166b[x], papp15[x], 738[x], 1441[x], 10575[x], 2797[x], 'viss[...]' 214[x] [2] hvé: hversu papp15[x], 738[x], 214[x], 1441[x]; alla: á 1441[x]; vegu: vega papp15[x], 1441[x], 2797[x] [3] mér: so papp15[x], 738[x], 214[x], 1441[x], 10575[x], 2797[x], er mér 166b[x] [5] hrolla: 'hroll[...]' 214[x].

Editions: *Skj* Anonyme digte og vers [XII], G [6]. *Sólarljóð* 38: AI, 633, BI, 641, *Skald* I, 312, *NN* §§2151, 2564B; Bugge 1867, 363, Falk 1914, 18, Björn M. Ólsen 1915, 14, Fidjestøl 1979, 65, Njörður Njarðvík 1991, 69-70, Njörður Njarðvík 1993, 44, 116.

Notes: [1] *mér* 'to me': 166b[x] has *er* 'which' before *mér*, but it is not present in most mss. Njörður Njarðvík (1993, 116) notes similarly redundant *er* in sts 49 and 50 (though in fact 166b[x] has *ec* rather than *er* in st. 49). — [4-6] *heljar meyjar buðu mér heim hrolla á hverju kveldi* 'Hell's maidens dealt shivers home to me every evening': Several interpretations of these ll. have been offered. Njörður Njarðvík (1993, 116) suggests *hrolla-heim* as a cpd object of *buðu* 'offered me a world of shivers', but observes that the poem does not normally split compounds like this. *Skj* B and *LP*: *hrolla* make *heim* the acc. in an acc.-inf. construction with *hrolla*, a verb meaning 'to shiver' or 'to collapse', *hver aften skulde verden gyse (være kold) for mig* 'every evening the world would shiver (be cold) for me' (*Skj*), or *verden skulde for mig være som ved at falde sammen* 'the world should be for me as if it were collapsing' (*LP*). It is preferable to take *heim* as adverbial, meaning lit. 'home', metaphorically (and untranslatably) 'right to me' (as in English 'to hit home') and *hrolla* as acc. pl. of *hrollr* 'shiver'; here we follow Marold's suggestion in Whaley *et al.* 2002, 72. The fever that racks the speaker every evening is sent by maidens from Hell. Who these women might be is unclear; Björn M. Ólsen (1915, 41) suggests they are personifications of sickness, but the figures seem rather to be evidence of the poem's syncretic tendencies, paralleled by the *dísir* of 25/1. As Fidjestøl (1979, 42) points out, the context does not exclude the possibility that norns or valkyries may be part of the phrase's frame of reference, and thus that Hel, the goddess, is also intended. — [6] *heim á hverju kveldi*: As it stands, the l. is unmetrical. *Skj* B and *Skald*, following Gering (1902, 465-6), have produced a metrically regular l. by reversing the position of *heim* and *kveldi*, *á hverju kveldi heim*.

39. Sól ek sá   sanna dagstjörnu
    drjúpa dynheimum í;
    en heljar grind   heyrða ek annan veg
    þjóta þungliga.

Ek sá sól, sanna dagstjörnu, drjúpa í dynheimum; en annan veg heyrða ek grind heljar þjóta þungliga.

I saw the sun, the true day-star, bow down in the noisy world; and in the other direction I heard the gate of Hell roaring weightily.

Mss: **166b**[x](47r), papp15[x](4v), 738[x](81v), 214[x](150v), 1441[x](584), 10575[x](6r), 2797[x](234).

Readings: [2] sanna dagstjörnu: samað at stjörnu 738[x]   [3] drjúpa: drúpa 2797[x]; dynheimum í: *so* 738[x], 1441[x], 10575[x], 2797[x], 'dimheimum i' *or* 'dinheimum i' 166b[x], 'dyrheimum i' papp15[x], 'i dynheimum' 214[x]   [4] heljar grind: *so* 10575[x], 2797[x], helgrind 166b[x], heljar grund papp15[x]   [5] heyrða: *so* papp15[x], 738[x], 1441[x], 10575[x], 2797[x], 'hedi' 166b[x], heyrði 214[x]; ek: *om.* 214[x]; annan: á annan papp15[x], 2797[x].

Editions: *Skj* Anonyme digte og vers [XII], G [6]. *Sólarljóð* 39: AI, 634, BI, 641-2, *Skald* I, 312; Bugge 1867, 363, Falk 1914, 19, Björn M. Ólsen 1915, 14, Fidjestøl 1979, 65, Njörður Njarðvík 1991, 70-1, Njörður Njarðvík 1993, 45, 117.

Notes: [All]: This st. is the first of a series of anaphoric sts (39-45), beginning *Sól ek sá* 'I saw the sun'. The significance of the sun in these sts is disputed: Falk 1914, 22 interprets it as symbolising Christ; Björn M. Ólsen 1915, 42 sees it as the actual sun, seen with the narrator's dying eyes. Paasche 1948, 181 argues that the sun is to be interpreted on both naturalistic and symbolic levels, an argument broadly endorsed by Fidjestøl 1979, 46. — [2] *sanna dagstjörnu* 'true day-star': cf. Rev. XXII.16: *stella splendida et matitutina* 'the bright and morning star'. Lange 1958a, 188, 243-5 discusses the possibility of sun-worship among early Icel. settlers; see also Amory 1985, 5-8; 1990, 255-6 for extensive discussion of the *sol salutis* 'the sun of salvation' and the *sol iustitiae* 'the sun of justice' in Carolingian and later theology. — [3] *dynheimum* (dat. pl.) 'noisy world': As in 738[x], and a large number of other mss, pl. is taken for sg. here. 166b[x]'s common mark of abbreviation could be read as giving *din-* (*dyn-* 'noise') or *dim-* (*dimm-* 'dark') *heimum* 'dark world', and both are plausible readings in context. Falk, *Skj* B and *Skald* have *dynheimum*. *Dýrheimum* 'precious world', found in papp15[x] and 7 other mss is also an attractive reading. — [4] *heljar grind* 'gate of Hell': Two late mss, 10575[x] and 2797[x], have this reading, which produces a metrically regular *fornyrðislag* l., whereas the cpd *helgrind*, the reading of 166b[x], 738[x], and a significant number of other mss gives a *kviðuháttr* l. Papp15[x] reads *heljar grund* 'the abyss of Hell', as do 13 other mss; this is also metrically acceptable, and roaring might be more likely from an abyss than a gate. However the gates of death (*portae mortis*) are referred to in Job XXXVIII.17, Psalm IX.15 and the gates of Hell (*portae inferi*) in Matt.

XVI.18. The image is also present in a pagan context, cf. *nágrindr* 'corpse-gate' *Ski* 35/3, *Lok* 63/6 and *helgrindr* 'Hell-gate' *SnE* 1982, 9, 47.

40. Sól ek sá   setta dreyrstöfum;
       mjök var ek þá ór heimi hallr;
       máttug hon leiz   á marga vegu
       frá því, sem fyrri var.

Ek sá sól, setta dreyrstöfum; ek var þá mjök hallr ór heimi; hon leiz máttug á marga vegu frá því, sem var fyrri.

I saw the sun, set with bloody staves; I was then forcefully tilting out of this world; it appeared mighty in many ways compared with how it was before.

Mss: **166b**[x](47r),   papp15[x](4v),   738[x](81v),   214[x](150v),   1441[x](584),   10575[x](6r),   2797[x](234).

Readings: [4] hon: *om.* papp15[x];   leiz ('lietst'): *so* 1441[x], 2797[x], 'liest' 166b[x], leysti papp15[x], 738[x], 'lei[...]' 214[x]   [5] á: *om.* papp15[x], 738[x], 10575[x];   marga: margan 10575[x];   vegu: *om.* papp15[x], 738[x], 10575[x].

Editions: Skj Anonyme digte og vers [XII], G [6]. *Sólarljóð* 40: AI, 634, BI, 642, *Skald* I, 312; Bugge 1867, 363, Falk 1914, 19, Björn M. Ólsen 1915, 14, Fidjestøl 1979, 65, Njörður Njarðvík 1991, 70-1, Njörður Njarðvík 1993, 46, 118.

Notes: [2] *dreyrstöfum* 'with bloody staves': For Falk (1914a, 23) these are bloody tokens of the end of the world; for Björn M. Ólsen (1915, 42) they are the red rays of the setting sun, while Paasche (1948, 181) interprets them as the bloody wounds of Christ. *Skj* B and *LP*: *dreyrstafir* suggest the translation 'bloody runes' and this may have been the poet's intended meaning, as later (70/6) he uses the word *skript* 'writing' to refer to angels reading written texts from holy books, presumably in the roman alphabet, while the cpd *feiknstafir* 'terrible staves' (60/6), similar to *dreyrstafir*, applies to inscriptions on 'heathen stars' which appear over the heads of sinners. — [4-6]: There are three possible readings of these ll., depending on which of three verbs (*leiz, lézk, leysti*) is chosen in l. 4. These are: a) *máttug hon leiz á marga vegu frá því sem var fyrri* 'mighty it [the sun] appeared in many ways compared with how it was before'; b) *máttug hon lezk á marga vegu vegu frá því sem var fyrri* 'mighty it called itself in many ways compared with how it was before'; c) *máttug leysti margan/marga frá því sem var fyrri* 'the mighty one released many a person (or 'many men') from that which was before'. Although reading b) is found in 166b[x], in the unnormalised form 'liest', this is its only occurrence, and the sun does not speak elsewhere in the *sól ek sá*-sts. The preferred reading a) appears in 1441[x] and 2797[x], and a number of other mss. Reading c) requires the sun to be personified (which it is not in other *sól ek sá*-sts), meaning '[she] released many a man (or 'many men')', presumably from earthly life. This creates metrical problems: l. 5 then lacks a second lift. The sentiment is comparable with *Hsv* 80.

41. Sól ek sá;   svá þótti mér,
         sem ek sæja á göfgan guð;
     henni ek laut   *h*inzta sinni
         aldaheimi í.

Ek sá sól; svá þótti mér, sem ek sæja á göfgan guð; ek laut henni *h*inzta sinni í aldaheimi.

I saw the sun; it seemed to me as if I were looking at worshipful God; I bowed to it for the last time in the world of men.

Mss: **166b**[x](47r),   papp15[x](4v),   738[x](81v),   214[x](150v),   1441[x](584),   10575[x](6r-v), 2797[x](234).

Readings: [3] á: *om.* 214[x], 2797[x]   [4] henni ek: ek henni 214[x]   [5] *h*inzta: inzta *all.*

Editions: *Skj* Anonyme digte og vers [XII], G [6]. *Sólarljóð* 41: AI, 634, BI, 662, *Skald* I, 312, Bugge 1867, 363, Falk 1914, 19, Björn M. Ólsen 1915, 14, Fidjestøl 1979, 65, Njörður Njarðvík 1991, 72, Njörður Njarðvík 1993, 47, 119.

Notes: [5] h*inzta* 'the last': *Skj* B, *Skald*, Bugge, Falk and Björn M. Ólsen restore the <h> to mss' *inzta* to provide alliteration (Fidjestøl has (*h*)*inzta*), though the reading is found in no ms.

42. Sól ek sá;   svá hon geislaði,
         at ek þóttumz vætki vita;
     en gylfar straumar   grenjuðu annan veg
         blandnir mjök við blóð.

Ek sá sól; hon geislaði svá at ek þóttumz vita vætki; en straumar gylfar grenjuðu annan veg, blandnir mjök við blóð.

I saw the sun; it dazzled so much that I seemed to know nothing; but the currents of the sea roared in the other direction, greatly mingled with blood.

Mss: **166b**[x](47r),   papp15[x](4v),   738[x](81v),   214[x](150v),   1441[x](584),   10575[x](6v), 2797[x](234).

Readings: [4] gylfar: gilnar papp15[x], gylfu 1441[x]   [5] grenjuðu: grenjuði 10575[x];   annan: á annan 738[x], 1441[x], 2797[x]   [6] blandnir: blandaðir papp15[x], blandnar 738[x];   mjök: *om.* 214[x].

Editions: *Skj* Anonyme digte og vers [XII], G [6]. *Sólarljóð* 42: AI, 634, BI, 642, *Skald* I, 312; Bugge 1867, 363, Falk 1914, 19, Björn M. Ólsen 1915, 15, Fidjestøl 1979, 65, Njörður Njarðvík 1991, 72-3, Njörður Njarðvík 1993, 48, 119.

Notes: [3] *þóttumz* 'I seemed': Lit. 'I seemed (to myself)'; the phrase probably implies that the speaker loses consciousness, cf. Njörður Njarðvík (1991, 73). — [4] *gylfar* 'of the sea':

This word occurs only here in OIcel. and does not exist in MIcel. Bugge (1867, 364), though he adduces ON *gjálfr* 'the sound of the sea' and by extension 'sea' (*LP*: *gjálfr*), reads *Gylfar* as a gen. pers. n., derived from **Gylfr*, meaning 'gulf, body of water'. However, there is no such word recorded in ON. Falk (1914, 26) relates it to a Norw. dialect word he gives as *gyl* 'mountain-cleft', cf. *OED*: *gill* n.2, noting that the entrance to the ON underworld is sometimes envisaged as a headland (Egill *St* 25^V; *Fáfn* 11/2) and linking a water-filled cleft to the *vötn fjalla* 'mountain waters' of 45/4. *LP*: *Gylfr* (?), f. (?) notes the obscurity of the word's form and meaning. *Skj* B, as also *Skald*, gives *Gilfar*, a pers. n., apparently derived from **Gylfr*. Björn M. Ólsen (1915, 43) emends to *Gylfa*, from *Gylfi*, a sea-king name, and thus interprets *Gylfa straumar* 'the currents of Gylfi' as a kenning for the sea. It seems likely that the word does have some association with the sea (cf. *AEW*: *Gylfi*, which cites *gylfr*, f. a river name, also 'wave, sea' as cognate); whether it is a common noun or a pers. n. is uncertain.

43. Sól ek sá   á sjónum skjálfandi
          hrælufullr ok hnipinn,
     þvít hjarta mitt   var harðla mjök
          runnit sundr í sega.

Hrælufullr ok hnipinn, sá ek sól, skjálfandi á sjónum, þvít hjarta mitt var harðla mjök runnit sundr í sega.

Terrified and cowed, I saw the sun, trembling in my eyes, for my heart had completely turned to shreds.

Mss: **166b**^x(47r), papp15^x(4v), 738^x(82r), 214^x(150v), 1441^x(584), 10575^x(6v), 2797^x(234).

Readings: [2] á: *om*. 2797^x [4] hjarta: 'hiar[...]' 214^x [5] harðla: *om*. papp15^x, 10575^x, heldr 738^x, 214^x, 1441^x, 2797^x [6] sega: siga papp15^x, 1441^x, 10575^x, 2797^x, sefa 214^x.

Editions: *Skj* Anonyme digte og vers [XII], G [6]. *Sólarljóð* 43: AI, 634, BI, 642, *Skald* I, 312; Bugge 1867, 363-4, Falk 1914, 19, Björn M. Ólsen 1915, 15, Fidjestøl 1979, 65, Njörður Njarðvík 1991, 73-4, Njörður Njarðvík 1993, 49, 120-1.

Notes: [All]: 738^x transposes sts 43 and 44. — [2] *skjálfandi á sjónum* 'trembling in [my] eyes': *Sjónir* (f. pl.) means 'eyes' or 'sight', though it is possible to take it, as Björn M. Ólsen does (1915, 44) as dat. sg. of *sjór* 'sea'. *Skjálfandi* is universal in the mss; it could refer to *sól* 'sun' (f. acc. sg.) or *ek* 'I' (masc. nom. sg.); *á* is in almost all mss; *Skj* B omits it, and emends l. 2 to *sjónum skjalföndum*, translated *med bævende öjne* 'with trembling eyes'; *Skald* includes *á* at the end of l. 1, while Falk, Björn M. Ólsen and Njörður Njarðvík retain *á* (as here) in l. 2. While the majority of eds conclude with *Skj* B that the narrator's sight is trembling, Falk (1914a, 23) suggests that the sun appears to tremble to the frightened narrator, while Björn M. Ólsen (1915, 43) contends that the image is naturalistic; the sun appears to shiver as it sinks into the sea. — [6] *runnit sundr í sega* 'completely turned to shreds': Björn M. Ólsen

(1915, 44) and Njörður Njarðvík (1991, 74-5) relate this to *contritio cordis* 'contrition of the heart' or sorrow for sin, the first stage of the sacrament of penance, cf. Psalm L.19, discussed in *HómÍsl* 1872, 168.

44. Sól ek sá   sjaldan hryggvari;
    mjök var ek þá ór heimi hallr;
  tunga mín   var til trés metin
    ok kólnat at fyrir utan.

Ek sá sól, sjaldan hryggvari; ek var þá mjök hallr ór heimi; tunga mín var metin til trés ok kólnat at fyrir utan.

I saw the sun, [I was] seldom more grief-stricken; I was then forcefully tilting out of this world; my tongue was as if turned to wood and it was chilled on the outside.

Mss: **166b^x**(47r), papp15^x(4v-5r), 738^x(82r), 214^x(150v-151r), 1441^x(584), 10575^x(6v), 2797^x(234).

Readings: [3] mjök: ok 738^x;   ór: mjök ór 738^x, '[...]' 214^x [5] til: *om.* 1441^x [6] kólnat: *so* 738^x, 'kolnud' 166b^x, klofnat papp15^x; at: *om.* papp15^x, 738^x, 10575^x.

Editions: *Skj* Anonyme digte og vers [XII], G [6]. *Sólarljóð* 44: AI, 634, BI, 642, *Skald* I, 312, *NN* §2152; Bugge 1867, 364, Falk 1914, 19, Björn M. Ólsen 1915, 15, Fidjestøl 1979, 66, Njörður Njarðvík 1991, 75, Njörður Njarðvík 1993, 50, 122.

Notes: [3]: The same l. occurs at 40/3. — [4-5] *tunga mín var metin til trés* 'my tongue was as if turned to wood': *Metin* from *meta* 'to estimate, value, assess as, regard, perceive as'. — [6] *kólnat* 'it was chilled': The verb must be impers. here, as the n. p.p. cannot modify *tunga* f. (l. 4). *Skald* follows 166b^x and emends to allow this: *ok kólnuð allt fyr utan*.

45. Sól ek sá   síðan aldri
    eptir þann dapra dag,
  þvít fjalla vötn   lukðuz fyrir mér saman,
    en ek hvarf kaldr frá kvölum.

Ek sá sól aldri síðan eptir þann dapra dag, þvít vötn fjalla lukðuz saman fyrir mér, en ek hvarf kaldr frá kvölum.

I saw the sun never again after that gloomy day, for the waters of the mountains closed together in front of me, and I turned away cold from the torments.

Mss: **166b^x**(47r), papp15^x(5r), 738^x(82r), 214^x(151r), 1441^x(584), 10575^x(6v-7r), 2797^x(234).

Readings: [3] dapra: in dapra   [5] fyrir: yfir 10575^x [6] kaldr: kallaðr papp15^x, 2797^x.

Editions: *Skj* Anonyme digte og vers [XII], G [6]. *Sólarljóð* 45: AI, 634-5, BI, 642, *Skald* I, 312; Bugge 1867, 364, Falk 1914, 19, Björn M. Ólsen 1915, 15, Fidjestøl 1979, 66, Njörður Njarðvík 1991, 75-6, Njörður Njarðvík 1993, 51, 122.

Notes: [4] *vötn fjalla* 'the waters of the mountains': Falk (1914a, 26-7) relates these to the *straumar gylfar* of 42/4; water and mountain are part of the landscape of the entrance to the Other World. Paasche (1914a, 146) and Björn M. Ólsen (1915, 44) construe *vötn fjalla* as 'lakes of the mountains'; for Paasche these close together, *lukðusk saman*, as the soul flies above the earth. Björn M. Ólsen objects to the presence of mountain-lakes in the seascape he imagines, and emends *fjalla* to *fjarla* 'distant'. Njörður Njarðvík (1991, 76) compares the eschatological prophecy of Isa. XXX.25: *et erunt super omnem montem excelsum et super omnem collem elevatum rivi currentium aquarum in die interfectionis multorum cum ceciderint turres* 'and there shall be upon every high mountain, and upon every elevated hill rivers of running waters on the day of the slaughter of many, when the towers shall fall'. — [6] *kaldr* 'cold': This adj. appears in 166b[x] and in many other mss, making reasonable sense, and is accepted by *Skj* B and *Skald*. *Kallaðr* 'called' in papp15[x], 2797[x] and another 28 mss was adopted by Bugge, Falk, Björn M. Ólsen, Fidjestøl and Njörður Njarðvík. Since it often collocates with *kvölum*, cf. st. 24/6, it may have been attracted into the st. for that reason.

46. Vánarstjarna fló   — þá var ek fæddr —
    burt frá brjósti mér;
hátt at hon fló;   hvergi hon settiz,
    svát hon mætti hvíld hafa.

Vánarstjarna fló burt frá brjósti mér; þá var ek fæddr; hon fló hátt at; hon settiz hvergi, svát hon mætti hafa hvíld.

A star of hope flew away from my breast; then I was born; it flew on high; nowhere did it come down so that it might have rest.

Mss: **166b[x]**(47r), papp15[x](5r), 738[x](82r), 214[x](151r), 1441[x](584-5), 10575[x](7r), 2797[x](234).

Readings: [2] þá var ek: var ek þá 10575[x]   [3] brjósti: brjóstum 214[x]   [5] hon: *om.* papp15[x], 738[x], 214[x], 10575[x], 2797[x]   [6] hon: at hon 10575[x], 2797[x].

Editions: *Skj* Anonyme digte og vers [XII], G [6]. *Sólarljóð* 46: AI, 635, BI, 642-3, *Skald* I, 313, *NN* §2815; Bugge 1867, 364, Falk 1914, 19, Björn M. Ólsen 1915, 16, Fidjestøl 1979, 66, Njörður Njarðvík 1991, 77, Njörður Njarðvík 1993, 52, 128.

Notes: [1] *vánarstjarna* 'a star of hope': Falk (1914a, 27-8) compares *Mar* 1871, 936: *dagstjarna sannrar vánar* 'the day-star of true hope'. For Paasche (1914a, 146) and Björn M. Ólsen 1915, the star represents the soul leaving the body. — [2] *þá var ek fæddr* 'then I was born': The sense seems to be that the narrator is now being born in spirit into the next life; he hopes, but cannot yet be certain, that he will find rest among the blessed. *Skj* B normalises to *þás fæddr of vask* to regularise the metre, while *Skald* emends *fæddr* to *hræddr* 'afraid'. — [4] *at*: Present in all mss, but its significance is uncertain. Some eds (e.g. *Skj* B, Falk) delete, but, if retained (so Bugge, Björn M. Ólsen, *Skald*, Fidjestøl and Njörður Njarðvík), it must be part of a verb-adv. collocation, *hon fló hátt at* 'it flew on high'. — [5] *hon* 'it': That is, the star-soul. The pron. is f.

47. Öllum lengri   var sú in eina nótt,
        er ek lá stirðr á stráum;
     þat merkir þat,   er guð mælti,
        at maðr er moldu samr.

Sú in eina nótt, er ek lá stirðr á stráum, var lengri öllum; þat merkir þat, er guð mælti, at maðr er moldu samr.

That one night, when I lay stiff on the straw, was longer than all; that demonstrates what God has spoken, that man is the same as earth.

Mss: **166b**[x](47r), papp15[x](5r), 738[x](82r), 214[x](151r), 1441[x](585), 10575[x](7r), 2797[x](234).

Readings: [2] var: *so* papp15[x], 738[x], 214[x], 1441[x], 10575[x], 2797[x], er 166b[x]; in: *om.* papp15[x], 738[x], 214[x], 1441[x], 10575[x], 2797[x]   [3, 4] stráum þat: strám þá *corrected from* 'strámi þá' papp15[x], fram strám þá 2797[x]   [4] merkir: merktak 1441[x]   [5] er: *om.* papp15[x], 214[x], 10575[x], 2797[x]; mælti: mæli 2797[x]   [6] at: áðr at 214[x], *om.* 2797[x]; moldu: moldar papp15[x], 1441[x]; samr: *so* 738[x], 214[x], 10575[x], 2797[x], sami 166b[x], sannr *corrected from* 'samr' papp15[x], sonr 1441[x].

Editions: *Skj* Anonyme digte og vers [XII], G [6]. *Sólarljóð* 47: AI, 635, BI, 643, *Skald* I, 313, *NN* §2564C; Bugge 1867, 364, Falk 1914, 19, Björn M. Ólsen 1915, 16, Fidjestøl 1979, 66, Njörður Njarðvík 1991, 77-8, Njörður Njarðvík 1993, 53, 124.

Notes: [2] *var* 'was': Found in all mss except for 166b[x] and one other. The past tense is required here to match *lá* 'lay'. — [5] *er guð mælti* 'what God has spoken': *Skj* B, *Skald* and Falk emend to *es mælti goð* to give a regular alliterating l. — [6] *maðr er moldu samr* 'man is the same as earth': Cf. Gen. III.19: *quia pulvis es et in pulverem reverteris* 'for dust thou art and into dust thou shalt return' and *HómÍsl* 1872, ch. 26. Similar sentiments are found in the ON and OIcel. *Rune Poems* for the letter M: *maðr er moldar auki* 'man is the augmentation of earth'. It is likely that the sentiment is semi-proverbial. — [6] *samr* 'same': 166b[x] has the weak form *sami*, as well as 6 other mss which follow it closely. *Samr* as in 738[x], 10575[x] and 2797[x] is grammatically correct.

48. Virði þat ok viti   inn virki guð,
    sá er skóp hauðr ok himin,
hversu munaðarlausir   margir fara,
    þótt við skylda skili.

Inn virki guð, sá er skóp hauðr ok himin, virði þat ok viti: hversu margir fara munaðarlausir, þótt við skylda skili.

May the precious God, who created earth and heaven, value and know that, how many journey loveless, though they part from their kin.

Mss: **166b**[x](47r), papp15[x](5r), 738[x](82r), 214[x](151r), 1441[x](585), 10575[x](7r), 2797[x](235).

Readings: [1] þat ok viti: ok viti þat papp15[x], 1441[x], 10575[x]   [2] inn: sá inn papp15[x]   [4] hversu: hversi 10575[x]; munaðarlausir: einmana papp15[x], 1441[x], 2797[x], einmunalausir 738[x], einmanalausir 10575[x]   [5] fara: lifa fara 214[x].

Editions: *Skj* Anonyme digte og vers [XII], G [6]. *Sólarljóð* 48: AI, 635, BI, 643, *Skald* I, 313; Bugge 1867, 365, Falk 1914, 19, Björn M. Ólsen 1915, 16, Fidjestøl 1979, 66, Njörður Njarðvík 1991, 78, Njörður Njarðvík 1993, 54, 124-5.

Notes: [4] *munaðarlausir* (m. nom. pl.) 'loveless': Found in 166b[x] and a number of other mss; other usages of *munaðr* and *munuðr* 'desire, voluptuousness' elsewhere in the poem (10/1, 18/1, 77/3) usually refer to sexual desire, which does not seem to be the case here. It is possible that the first element of the cpd was originally *munar* from *munr* m. 'mind, delight, love'; an emendation to *munarlausir* 'without love, loveless' is adopted by *Skj* B and *Skald*. Papp15[x] and 1441[x] have *einmana* indeclinable adj. 'solitary, lonely', and Falk accepts this reading; the forms of 738[x], and 10575[x] seem to be a blend of the two readings, with uncertain meaning. The l. is hypermetrical; accordingly *Skj* B and *Skald* substitute *hvé* for *hversu*, and produce a lesser number of syllables through emending to *munarlausir*. — [5] *margir fara*: *Skj* B and *Skald* add *of*, enclitic particle, to give *margir of fara* in order to regularise the metre. The meaning is unchanged.

49. Sinna verka   nýtr seggja hverr;
    sæll er sá, sem gótt gerir;
auði frá   * mér ætluð var
    sandi orpin sæng.

Seggja hverr nýtr verka sinna; sæll er sá, sem gótt gerir; frá auði var * mér ætluð sæng orpin sandi.

Every man benefits from his deeds; fortunate is he who does good; away from riches there was intended for me a bed heaped up with sand.

Mss: **166b**[x](47r), papp15[x](5r), 738[x](82r), 214[x](151r), 1441[x](585), 10575[x](7r-v), 2797[x](235).

Readings: [3] sem: er 214ˣ, 2797ˣ   [5] * mér: ek mér 166bˣ, er mér papp15ˣ, 738ˣ, 214ˣ, 1441ˣ, 10575ˣ, 2797ˣ; var: *om.* 1441ˣ   [6] sandi: í sandi 738ˣ, 214ˣ.

Editions: Skj Anonyme digte og vers [XII], G [6]. *Sólarljóð* 49: AI, 635, BI, 643, *Skald* I, 313, *NN* §2564B; Bugge 1867, 365, Falk 1914, 20, Björn M. Ólsen 1915, 16, Fidjestøl 1979, 66, Njörður Njarðvík 1991, 78-9, Njörður Njarðvík 1993, 55, 125.

Notes: [5] *mér* 'for me': All mss but two add an unnecessary rel. *er* before *mér*; 166bˣ and one other have *ek* 'I', probably an error in abbreviation. — [6] *sæng orpin sandi* 'a bed heaped up with sand': The grave, a typical contrast with the comforts which life had offered.

50. Hörundar hungr   tælir hölða opt;
    hann hefr margr til mikinn;
    laugavatn   mér leiðast var
    eitt allra hluta.

Hörundar hungr tælir hölða opt; margr hefr hann til mikinn; laugavatn var mér eitt leiðast allra hluta.

The hunger of the flesh often entraps men; many a one possesses it in the extreme; washing water was alone to me most hateful of all things.

Mss: **166bˣ**(47r-v), papp15ˣ(5r), 738ˣ(82r), 214ˣ(151r), 1441ˣ(585), 10575ˣ(7v), 2797ˣ(235).

Readings: [3] hann: þann 1441ˣ; mikinn: mikit 2797ˣ   [4] lauga-: langa 738ˣ, 1441ˣ   [5] mér: *so* papp15ˣ, eitt er mér 166bˣ, er mér 738ˣ, 214ˣ, 1441ˣ, 10575ˣ, 2797ˣ; leiðast: leiðist 214ˣ; var: varð papp15ˣ, 738ˣ, 214ˣ, 1441ˣ.

Editions: Skj Anonyme digte og vers [XII], G [6]. *Sólarljóð* 50: AI, 635, BI, 643, *Skald* I, 313, *NN* §2564B; Bugge 1867, 365, Falk 1914, 20, Björn M. Ólsen 1915, 16, Fidjestøl 1979, 67, Njörður Njarðvík 1991, 79, Njörður Njarðvík 1993, 56, 125.

Notes: [4] *laugavatn* 'A bath, washing water': The significance of this reference is unclear. Some eds assume that the water symbolises repentance and absolution, cf. the heavenly maidens of st. 74 who wash souls clean. Falk (1914a, 29), following *CVC: laug*, makes the connection with the Saturday (*laugardagr*) bath, as physical and spiritual preparation for Sunday. Björn M. Ólsen (1915, 46; also Paasche 1948, 183) suggests the bath represents the hot tears of remorse and penitence; cf. Njörður Njarðvík (1991, 79). Njörður Njarðvík (1991, 197-8) contributes a parallel from the *Dialogues of Gregory*, referring to washing as a way of removing sin produced by intercourse with women (Unger 1877, I, 246). If water symbolises spiritual cleansing here, then the narrator presumably alludes to his former life of debauchery when he was not yet ready to undergo penance. Earlier commentators, as Fidjestøl (1979, 47-8) notes, regarded the bath as the kind of luxury which the body now no longer requires. — [5] *mér* 'to me': *Er* 'which' appears in the majority of mss before *mér* but makes the last half of the st. ungrammatical, unless *laugavatn* is construed as in apposition to *hörundar hungr* (l. 1). *Skj* B omits it, though Falk, *Skald*, Björn M. Ólsen and Njörður Njarðvík 1991 do not.

51. Á norna stóli   sat ek níu daga;
         þaðan var ek á hest hafinn;
   gýgjar sólir   skinu grimmliga
         ór skýdrúpnis skýjum.

Ek sat níu daga á stóli norna; þaðan var ek hafinn á hest; sólir gýgjar skinu grimmliga ór skýjum skýdrúpnis.

I sat for nine days on the norns' seat; from there I was lifted onto a horse; the ogress's suns shone fiercely out of the cloud-lowerer's clouds.

Mss: **166b**[x](47v), papp15[x](5r-v), 738[x](82r), 214[x](151r), 1441[x](585), 10575[x](7v), 2797[x](235).

Readings: [1] stóli: *so* papp15[x], 738[x], 214[x], 1441[x], 10575[x], 2797[x], stól 166b[x]   [4, 5] sólir skinu: sól er skein papp15[x], 10575[x], 2797[x]   [6] skýdrúpnis: *so* 2797[x], skýdripnis 166b[x], papp15[x], 214[x], 10575[x], 'skyd dripnis' 738[x], 'skýdeipnis' 1441[x]; skýjum: 'skirmi' papp15[x].

Editions: *Skj* Anonyme digte og vers [XII], G [6]. *Sólarljóð* 51: AI, 635, BI, 643, *Skald* I, 313, *NN* §2564B; Bugge 1867, 365, Falk 1914, 20, Björn M. Ólsen 1915, 17, Fidjestøl 1979, 67, Njörður Njarðvík 1991, 80-1, Njörður Njarðvík 1993, 57, 126.

Notes: [1] *á stóli norna* 'on the norns' seat': 166b[x] has *stól* in error for *stóli*. The norns are pagan figures who determine fate, cf. *Vsp* 20, *SnE* 1982, 18-19, though they are not normally associated with a seat. The throne of judgement is a Christian image; thus, as with other syncretic ideas in the poem, such as the *dísir* in 25/1, the poet has translated a Christian concept into its imagined pagan equivalent. However Óðinn's high-seat *Hliðskjálf* (*Skí* prose; *Grí* prose; *SnE* 1982, 13) permits a view into other worlds. *Hávm* 138 tells of Óðinn's sacrifice hanging on the World-Tree, Yggdrasill 'Steed of the Terrifying One' which brings him occult knowledge. For Falk (1914a, 29) and Paasche (1914a, 183) the nine days on the norns' seat refers back to the narrator's sickness, an explanation with which Njörður Njarðvík (1991, 80) concurs. However as Björn M. Ólsen (1915, 46-9) objects, the fatal illness is concluded in st. 45. He argues that *Nornastóll* is a mountain-name, and refers to the soul's sojourn in purgatorial fires, situated on a peak in the Other World. Since in st. 46 the narrator has apparently been born into the next world, it seems likely that the period on the seat is a transitional time of waiting in the next world, though not necessarily spent in Purgatory. — [2] *níu daga* 'for nine days': The number nine is significant in Norse myth (there are nine worlds according to *Vsp* 2; nine nights in *Hávm* 138 and in *Skí* 39, 41). Seven is, in contrast, a Christian number: 52/3 makes reference to seven victory-worlds *sigrheima sjau*; see Note to 32/3. — [3] *hafinn á hest* 'lifted onto a horse': For Paasche (1948, 184) the ride on the horse is part of the corpse's journey to the grave; Falk (1914a, 30) envisages a horse in the Other World which conducts the soul further on its journey, even though no horse is mentioned subsequently. Björn M. Ólsen (1915, 49) emends to *hæst* 'highest'; the narrator is lifted onto the highest peak of the mountain *Nornastóll*. — [4] *sólir gýgjar* 'the ogress's suns': Falk (1914a, 30), assumes this periphrasis refers to the moon, taking sg. for pl. as Njörður Njarðvík (1991, 81) notes. Björn M. Ólsen (1915, 49) argues for an underworld sun, similar to the *urðarmáni* 'fate-moon' of *Eyrbyggja saga* ch. 52 (*ÍF* 4, 146). — [6] *skýdrúpnis* 'of the cloud-lowerer': *Hap. leg.*, presumably a periphrasis for the heavily overcast sky (cf. *LP*: *skýdrúpnir*). Though the form of 166b^x occurs in 38 mss in total, *dripnir* is unknown outside the poem. Four mss give *drúpnis* from *drúpa* 'to bow one's head, to lower', usually as a sign of sorrow, see st. 39/3. The repetition of *ský-* and *skýjum* is clumsy; while *skýjum* is unmetrical (with a trochaic final foot to the full l., a practice this poet avoids elsewhere), it is found almost universally across the tradition. Papp15^x and related mss try to avoid this repetition with 'skirmi', not otherwise attested.

52. Utan ok innan   þóttumz ek alla fara
       sigrheima sjau;
     upp ok niðr   leitaða ek æðra vegar,
       hvar mér væri greiðastar götur.

Ek þóttumz fara utan ok innan alla sjau sigrheima; upp ok niðr leitaða ek æðra vegar, hvar væri mér greiðastar götur.

It seemed to me that I travelled outside and inside all the seven victory-worlds; up and down I looked for better ways where the roads would be easiest for me.

Mss: **166b^x**(47v), papp15^x(5v), 738^x(82r), 214^x(151r), 1441^x(585), 10575^x(7v), 2797^x(235).

Readings: [2] þóttumz: þóttist papp15^x, 1441^x; alla: *om.* 2797^x [3] -heima: -himna 738^x [4] upp: uppi 214^x, 2797^x; niðr: niðri 214^x, 2797^x [5] æðra: *so* 738^x, 2797^x, æðri 166b^x, papp15^x, 214^x, 1441^x, 10575^x; vegar: vegr 1441^x.

Editions: *Skj* Anonyme digte og vers [XII], G [6]. *Sólarljóð* 52: AI, 635-6, BI, 643-4, *Skald* I, 313; Bugge 1867, 365, Falk 1914, 20, Björn M. Ólsen 1915, 17, Fidjestøl 1979, 67, Njörður Njarðvík 1991, 81, Njörður Njarðvík 1993, 58, 128.

Notes: [3] *sjau sigrheima* 'seven victory-worlds': The Christian number seven contrasts with the pagan number nine, as in st. 51; see Note to 32/3. — [5] *æðra*: Although many of the earlier mss have the form *æðri*, this form, occurring in 18 mss, is grammatically correct. Njörður Njarðvík (1991, 81), compares the dream-verse Anon (*Hrafn*) 8/1-4^{IV}: *Se þú, hvé hvarfa | heima í milli | syndauðigra | sálir manna* 'see how between worlds, the souls of sinrich men hover'.

53. Frá því er at segja,   hvat ek fyrst um sá,
        þá er ek var í kvölheima kominn;
    sviðnir fuglar,   er sálir váru,
        flugu svá margir sem mý.

Frá því er at segja, hvat ek fyrst um sá, þá er ek var kominn í kvölheima; sviðnir fuglar, er sálir váru, flugu svá margir sem mý.

It must be related what I saw first when I came into the worlds of torment; singed birds, which were souls, flew as many as midges.

Mss: **166b**[x](47v), papp15[x](5v), 738[x](82r), 214[x](151r), 1441[x](585), 10575[x](7v-8r), 2797[x](235).

Readings: [2] ek: *om.* 10575[x]   [3] ek var: var ek 738[x]   [5] er: en 10575[x]   [6] svá: *so* papp15[x], 738[x], 214[x], 1441[x], 10575[x], 2797[x], *om.* 166b[x].

Editions: *Skj* Anonyme digte og vers [XII], G [6]. *Sólarljóð* 53: AI, 636, BI, 644, *Skald* I, 313; Bugge 1867, 365, Falk 1914, 31, Björn M. Ólsen 1915, 17, Fidjestøl 1979, 67, Njörður Njarðvík 1991, 82, Njörður Njarðvík 1993, 59, 128.

Notes: [4] *sviðnir fuglar* 'singed birds': Njörður Njarðvík (1991, 82) compares an account of an eruption of the Icel. volcano Hekla where onlookers, seeing birds flying into the flames of the eruption, interpreted the sight as souls flying in Hell in *Flat* (*Flat* 1860-8, III, 559). For souls as black birds in the flames of Hell cf. the 'Vision of the Monk of Wenlock' (Tangl 1916, 11) where the visionary sees *miserorum hominum spiritus in similitudine nigrarum avium* 'spirits of wretched men in the likeness of black birds'; the *Visio Alberici* (Mirra 1932, 91) depicts souls swarming like flies in diabolic fire; *Dugg* (Cahill 1983, 47) records souls singed in fire.

54. Vestan sá ek fljúga   vánardreka
        ok fell á Glævalds götu;
    vængi þeir skóku,   svát víða þótti mér
        springa hauðr ok himinn.

Vestan sá ek vánardreka fljúga ok fell á götu Glævalds; þeir skóku vængi, svát hauðr ok himinn þótti mér springa víða.

From the west I saw a dragon of expectation flying and it landed on Glævaldr's road; they shook their wings, so that earth and heaven seemed to me to spring widely apart.

Mss: **166b**[x](47v), papp15[x](5v), 738[x](82r-v), 214[x](151r), 1441[x](585), 10575[x](8r), 2797[x](235).

Readings: [1] Vestan: vitar 738[x], 214[x]   [3] fell: felli 10575[x]   [4] þeir skóku: skóku þeir 10575[x]   [5] þótti mér: þótti meir 738[x], mér þótti 2797[x].

Editions: *Skj* Anonyme digte og vers [XII], G [6]. *Sólarljóð* 54: AI, 636, BI, 644, *Skald* I, 313; Bugge 1867, 365-6, Falk 1914, 31, Björn M. Ólsen 1915, 17, Fidjestøl 1979, 67, Njörður Njarðvík 1991, 83-4, Njörður Njarðvík 1993, 60, 129.

Notes: [1-2]: *Skj* B and *Skald* divide these ll. thus: *Vestan sák | fljúga vánardreka*. — [1] *vestan* 'from the west': See Note to 55/2 for the significance of cardinal directions in the poem. — [2] *vánardreka* 'dragon of expectation': The meaning of *vánar-* is not entirely clear; presumably the dragon expects to prey on souls. Björn M. Ólsen (1915, 50-1) takes *Ván* as a river-*heiti*, as in *Grí* 28/8, and interprets the creature as Leviathan (Job XLI). The number of dragons is also unclear; more than one dragon is suggested by *þeir skóku* 'they shook' in l. 4, but *fell* 'fell' in l. 3 is universally sg. in the mss. — [3] *fell á götu Glævalds* 'fell on Glævaldr's road': Njörður Njarðvík (1991, 83-4) suggests that it is the narrator's soul which lands there, hence the sg. verb. *Glævaldr* has been taken by most eds as an otherwise unknown pers. n., though *Skj* B and *LP*: *glævaldr* take it as a common noun cpd of uncertain meaning, suggesting the first element is either associated with *glær* 'sea' or with *glær* adj. 'transparent, clear, shining'. Bugge (1867, 366) tentatively suggests *glæv-ellds* 'of glowing flame'. Following Bugge, Falk (1914, 31-2) reads *fella glævalds götu*, translating *efterladende en lysende ildstripe* 'leaving a glowing trail', eliminating the sg. verb. — [4] *þeir skóku* 'they shook': *Skj* B and *Skald* emend the pl. verb to sg. *skók*. Njörður Njarðvík (1991, 84) explains the pl. by assuming that the dragon of l. 2 is accompanied by others. Björn M. Ólsen (1915, 51) suggests that the pl. verb refers both to the *vánardreki* and to Glævaldr, also envisaged as a winged being. Njörður Njarðvik (1991, 194) notes earlier eds' comparison of the dragon with the dragon of Revelations XII. Many visions have similar dragon-like beasts who devour souls, e.g. *Dugg* (Cahill 1983, 58-61).

55. Sólar hjört   leit ek sunnan fara;
        hann teymðu tveir saman;
    fætr hans   stóðu foldu á,
        en tóku horn til himins.

Ek leit hjört sólar fara sunnan; tveir saman teymðu hann; fætr hans stóðu á foldu, en horn tóku til himins.

I saw the hart of the sun journey from the south; two together had bridled him; his feet stood on the earth, and his horns reached to heaven.

Mss: 166b^x(47v), papp15^x(5v), 738^x(82v), 214^x(151r-v), 1441^x(585), 10575^x(8r), 2797^x(235).

Reading: [6] tóku: toki 10575^x.

Editions: *Skj* Anonyme digte og vers [XII], G [6]. *Sólarljóð* 55: AI, 636, BI, 644, *Skald* I, 313; Bugge 1867, 366, Falk 1914, 32, Björn M. Ólsen 1915, 17-18, Fidjestøl 1979, 67, Njörður Njarðvík 1991, 84-5, Njörður Njarðvík 1993, 61, 130.

Notes: [1] *hjört sólar* 'the hart of the sun': In Christian iconography the hart is a symbol of Christ. This significance was well known in Iceland from an early date, witness the Icel. *Physiologus* (Halldór Hermannsson 1938, 20) and the legend of S. Eustace/Plácitus, available in Icel. translation and poetry from at least the late C12th. See further Introduction to Anon *Pl* and Note to *Pl* 7/7-8. A *hjartarhorn* 'hart's horn', most likely signifying Christ's Cross, is mentioned in 78/4. The hart is also a symbol of nobility in eddic poetry, cf. *HHund II* 38 where Helgi is compared to an animal whose *horn glóa við himinn siálfan* 'horns glow up to the very sky', as also *Guðr II* 2/5. The image, like many others in the poem, clearly partakes both of Christian and indigenous mythological associations; see Amory (1985, especially 9-12 and 1990, 258-60). — [2] *sunnan* 'from the south': cf. *vestan* 'from the west' in 54/1 and *norðan* 'from the north' in 56/1. Different cardinal directions are normally associated with good and evil in both pagan and Christian thinking; see Tate (1985, 1030-1) who notes that the south and north are respectively associated with the positive and the negative in both Christian and pagan lore. The east is the home of giants in Norse myth, however, while the east is sacred for Christians. Evil can come from the west for Christians, hence the western origin of the *vánardreki* in 54/1. — [3] *tveir saman teymðu hann* 'two together had bridled him': The two are usually thought to be the other persons of the Trinity (so Falk). Björn M. Ólsen (1915, 52) argues that Christ (*hann*) is the subject of the cl., that the m. nom. *tveir* 'two' may be a misunderstanding of the roman numeral ii (= *tvá*, m. acc.) in the original ms., and that the hart is driving Glævaldr and the *vánardreki* before him. He therefore emends *teymðu* 3rd pers. pl. pret. to *teymði* 3rd pers. sg. pret. Amory (1990, 260) identifies the two with the prophets Isaiah and Daniel, released from Hell at the Harrowing, or with the two alleged authors of the *Gospel of Nicodemus* (*Niðrst*[1]). — [4-6] *fœtr hans stóðu á foldu, en horn tóku til himins* 'his feet stood on the earth, and his horns reached to heaven': Cf. Isa. LXVI.1 *caelum sedis mea et terra scabillum pedum meorum* 'heaven is my throne and the earth my footstool'.

56. Norðan sá ek ríða   niðja sonu
     ok váru sjau saman;
   hornum fullum   drukku þeir inn hreina mjöð
     ór brunni Baugreyr*is*.

Ek sá sonu niðja ríða norðan ok váru sjau saman; þeir drukku inn hreina mjöð ór brunni Baugreyr*is* fullum hornum.

I saw the sons of the dark phases of the moon riding from the north, and they were seven together; they drank the pure mead from the well of Baugreyrir out of full horns.

Mss: **166b**[x](47v), papp15[x], 738[x](82v), 167b 6[x](3r), 214[x](151v), 1441[x](585), 10575[x](8r), 2797[x](235).

Readings: [5] þeir: *om.* 214[x]; hreina: hreinu 10575[x]   [6] brunni: brunn 214[x]; -reyr*is*: '-reirs' 166b[x], 214[x], '-reins' papp15[x], 1441[x], 10575[x], 2797[x], '-reyens' 738[x], '-reyrs' 167b 6[x].

Editions: *Skj* Anonyme digte og vers [XII], G [6]. *Sólarljóð* 56: AI, 636, BI, 644, *Skald* I, 314; Bugge 1867, 366, Falk 1914, 32, Björn M. Ólsen 1915, 18, Fidjestøl 1979, 67, Njörður Njarðvík 1991, 86-8, Njörður Njarðvík 1993, 62, 132.

Notes: [All]: 167b 6ˣ resumes with the final <a> of *hreina* in l. 5, having previously left off at st. 26/1. — [1] *norðan* 'from the north': See Note to 55/2. — [2] *sonu niðja* 'the sons of the dark phases of the moon': In ON there are two words, *nið* n. and *niðar* f. pl. (*LP*: 1. *nið* n. and *niðar* f. pl.) that mean both the waning moon and the time before the new moon (cf. *Vsp* 6/5, *Vafþr* 24/6). There is no equivalent English word, so the translation here 'the dark phases of the moon' attempts to approximate the ON with a phrase. The f. pl. form *niðar* has facultative <j> in gen. pl. Who 'the sons of the dark phases of the moon' are is uncertain; Falk (1914a, 35-6), as also Paasche (1948, 188-9), see them as angels or archangels coming to Christ's aid. Björn M. Ólsen (1915, 53-4) argues that they are the inhabitants of a Norse *limbus patrum*, the wise pagans who cannot enter Heaven or Hell. Njörður Njarðvík (1991, 88) also sees these men as the denizens of Purgatory, neither good enough to join the hart of st. 55 nor wicked enough to be the prey of the dragon of st. 54. — [5] *inn hreina mjöð* 'the pure mead': Larrington (2002, 189) notes that mead, well and horn are symbolic of wisdom in mythological poetry, in particular where they appear together in *Sigrdr* 13-18; here they also have positive associations. — [6] *brunni Baugreyris* 'from the well of Baugreyrir': Falk (1914a, 36) and Björn M. Ólsen (1915, 53-4) connect the well with the well of Mímir in *Vsp* 28, but for Falk, as also for Paasche (1914b, 61 and 1948, 189-90), the well is the *vitae fontes aquarum* 'the fountains of the waters of life' of Rev. VII.17 and XXII.1, the *fons misericordiae* 'the fountain of mercy' of *HómÍsl* (1872, 76). Here the ring (*baugr*) symbolises God's mercy. Njörður Njarðvík (1991, 87) compares the heavenly *brunnr lifanda vatns* 'the well of living water' in *Dugg* (Cahill 1983, 85-7). 166bˣ's *baugreirs* is understood here as the name Baugreyrir; 167b 6ˣ shows a similar form as do c. 18 other mss. *Baugreyrir* 'ring-stirrer', perhaps 'generous lord', parallels *Óðre(y)rir* 'mind-stirrer' in *Hávm* 140 and *SnE* (1998, I, 3-4), the name of the vat where the mead of poetry is stored. Alternatively, the original form may have been Baugrerir (cf. *LP*: *Óðrørir*). Thus the poet makes allusion to poetry, like the mead of Baugreyrir's well, as a potent drink, which, though pagan in origin, is capable of being used for Christian purposes. Papp15ˣ's equally plausible *Baugrein*, and 738ˣ's *Baugreyin*, probably to be normalised to *Baugreginn* 'ring-god, divine power' (*LP*: *baugreginn*), is shared by 23 other mss and is adopted by *Skj* B, *Skald*, and most other eds. It may or may not be a pers. n.

57. Vindr þagði;   vötn stöðvaði;
    þá heyrða ek grimligan gný;
  sínum mönnum   svipvísar konur
    moluðu mold til matar.

Vindr þagði; vötn stöðvaði; þá heyrða ek grimligan gný; svipvísar konur moluðu mold til matar mönnum sínum.

The wind fell silent; the waters stood still; then I heard a terrible din; treacherous women were crushing earth into food for their men.

Mss: **166b^x**(47v), papp15^x(5v-6r), 738^x(82v), 167b 6^x(3r), 214^x(151v), 1441^x(586), 10575^x(8r-v), 2797^x(235).

Readings: [1] þagði: þagnaði 10575^x [2] vötn: víti papp15^x; stöðvaði: stöðvaðiz 10575^x [3] heyrða: so papp15^x, 738^x, 167b 6^x, 214^x, 1441^x, 10575^x, heyrði 166b^x, 2797^x [6] moluðu: 'moto' 10575^x, mólu 2797^x.

Editions: Skj Anonyme digte og vers [XII], G [6]. *Sólarljóð* 57: AI, 636, BI, 644, Skald I, 314; Bugge 1867, 366, Falk 1914, 38, Björn M. Ólsen 1915, 18, Fidjestøl 1979, 68, Njörður Njarðvík 1991, 88-9, Njörður Njarðvík 1993, 63, 135.

Notes: [5] *svipvísar konur* 'treacherous women': Falk (1914, 39-40) argues that these women have been practising magic and that the *rýgjar blóði* 'ogress's blood' of 59/6 connects these women to the men who must walk on red-hot paths in that st., but there is no clear evidence of what the women's sin is. — [6] *moluðu* 'they were crushing': The reading of the majority of mss, 3rd pers. pret. pl. of *mola* (weak verb) 'to crush, break into small pieces'. 2797^x has *mólu*, 3rd pers. pret. pl. of *mala* (strong verb, class 6) 'to grind', and this probable emendation (reportedly first suggested by Jón Ólafsson of Grunnavík – so Bugge and *Skj* A) has been adopted by almost all eds. It reduces the syllable count of the l., even though it still has too many alliterating staves. — [6] *moluðu mold til matar* 'they were crushing earth into food': Cf. *Grott* where the giantesses Fenja and Menja are condemned to grind out gold from a magic mill. Njörður Njarðvík (1991, 88-9) notes that earth does not need grinding (though it may need crushing!), and that this is therefore an unending task. A similar punishment appears in the 'Vision of the Monk of Wenlock' (Tangl 1916, 13).

58. Dreyrga steina   þær inar dökku konur
      drógu daprliga;
   blóðug hjörtu   hengu þeim fyr brjóst utan
      mædd við miklum trega.

Þær inar dökku konur drógu daprliga dreyrga steina; blóðug hjörtu hengu þeim fyr brjóst utan, mædd við miklum trega.

Those dark women were sorrowfully dragging gory stones; bloody hearts hung outside their breasts, exhausted by great grief.

Mss: **166b^x**(47v), papp15^x(6r), 738^x(82v), 167b 6^x(3r), 214^x(151v), 1441^x(586), 10575^x(8v), 2797^x(235-6).

Readings: [2] inar: hinu 738^x, 'hinan' 167b 6^x [5] brjóst: brjósti papp15^x, 1441^x, 2797^x [6] við: með papp15^x, 1441^x; miklum: mikinn 214^x.

Editions: *Skj* Anonyme digte og vers [XII], G [6]. *Sólarljóð* 58: AI, 636, BI, 644-5, *Skald* I, 314; Bugge 1867, 366, Falk 1914, 38, Björn M. Ólsen 1915, 18, Fidjestøl 1979, 68, Njörður Njarðvík 1991, 89-90, Njörður Njarðvík 1993, 64, 136.

Notes: [1] *dreyrga steina* 'gory stones': If the women of this st. are the same as those of the previous one, then (if *mólu* was the original reading of 57/6, see Note) the stones here may well be their grinding stones. — [5]: The l. is hypermetrical. Torn breasts are mentioned as a punishment in the *Visio Alberici* (Mirra 1932, 88) where sinful women are forced to suckle snakes because they would not feed orphan children.

59. Margan mann sá ek meiddan fara
 á þeim glæddu*m* götum;
andlit þeira sýnduz mér öll vera
 rýgjar blóði roðin.

Ek sá margan meiddan mann fara á þeim glæddu*m* götum; öll andlit þeira sýnduz mér vera roðin blóði rýgjar.

I saw many a maimed man journey on the glowing paths; all their faces seemed to me to be reddened with an ogress's blood.

Mss: **166b**ˣ(47v), papp15ˣ(6r), 738ˣ(82v), 167b 6ˣ(3r), 214ˣ(151v), 1441ˣ(586), 10575ˣ(8v), 2797ˣ(236).

Readings: [3] glæddu*m*: glæddu *all* [5] sýnduz: þótti papp15ˣ, 167b 6ˣ, 1441ˣ, 10575ˣ, þóttu 738ˣ, 214ˣ, 2797ˣ [6] blóði: blóð 10575ˣ.

Editions: *Skj* Anonyme digte og vers [XII], G [6]. *Sólarljóð* 59: AI, 637, BI, 645, *Skald* I, 314; Bugge 1867, 366, Falk 1914, 38, Björn M. Ólsen 1915, 18, Fidjestøl 1979, 68, Njörður Njarðvík 1991, 90-1, Njörður Njarðvík 1993, 65, 137.

Notes: [3] *á þeim glæddu*m *götum*: Cf. st. 31/6: *þær inar glæddu götur*. The adj. (f. dat. pl. weak) must be emended to *glæddum* to agree with *götum*, although both *Skj* B and *Skald* retain the ms. form.

60. Marga menn sá ek moldar gengna,
 þá er eigi máttu þjónustu ná;
heiðnar stjörnur stóðu yfir höfði þeim
 fáðar feiknstöfum.

Ek sá marga menn gengna moldar, þá er eigi máttu ná þjónustu; heiðnar stjörnur stóðu yfir höfði þeim, fáðar feiknstöfum.

I saw many men gone into earth, those who had not managed to obtain the sacrament; heathen stars stood over their heads, coloured with terrible staves.

Mss: **166b**[x](47v), papp15[x](6r), 738[x](82v), 167b 6[x](3r), 214[x](151v), 1441[x](586), 10575[x](8v), 2797[x](236).

Readings: [1, 2] Marga menn sá ek: Marga menn papp15[x], Menn sá ek marga 738[x], Margan mann sá ek 167b 6[x]   [4] heiðnar: heiðvar 738[x], 167b 6[x], 214[x]; stjörnur: stjörnu 214[x]   [5] stóðu: stóði 10575[x].

Editions: *Skj* Anonyme digte og vers [XII], G [6]. *Sólarljóð* 60: AI, 637, BI, 645, *Skald* I, 314; Bugge 1867, 366, Falk 1914, 38, Björn M. Ólsen 1915, 19, Fidjestøl 1979, 68, Njörður Njarðvík 1991, 91, Njörður Njarðvík 1993, 66, 138.

Notes: [3] *þjónustu* (dat.) 'the sacrament': Björn M. Ólsen (1915, 55) thinks that these men are being punished for failing to receive the last rites, but as Njörður Njarðvík (1991, 91) notes, the first *exemplum* has shown that salvation without the last rites is possible. Njörður Njarðvík follows Paasche (1948, 191-2) and Falk (1914a, 40-1), who suggest that these sinners were excommunicated and were thus refused the sacraments – including the last rites. — [4, 6] *heiðnar stjörnur ... fáðar feiknstöfum* 'heathen stars ... coloured with terrible staves': Most likely a reference to runic staves, as is clearly the case in st. 61/4. Cf. *dreyrstöfum* 'with bloody staves' 40/2 and contrast the *hreinar kyndlar* 'pure candles', *helgar bækr* 'holy books', and *himna skript* 'heavenly writing' of 69/4 and 70/5-6; cf. Tate 1985, 1031-2.

61. Menn sá ek þá,   er mjök ala
       öfund um annars hagi;
   blóðgar rúnir   váru á brjósti þeim
       merkðar meinliga.

Ek sá menn þá, er mjök ala öfund um hagi annars; blóðgar rúnir váru merkðar meinliga á brjósti þeim.

I saw men then who greatly nourish envy of another's affairs; bloody runes were painfully marked on their breasts [*lit.* breast].

Mss: **166b**[x](47v), papp15[x](6r), 738[x](82v), 167b 6[x](3r), 214[x](151v), 1441[x](586), 10575[x](8v), 2797[x](236).

Readings: [1] sá ek: *so* papp15[x], 738[x], 167b 6[x], 214[x], 1441[x], 10575[x], 2797[x], ek sá 166b[x]   [2] ala: *so* papp15[x], 738[x], 167b 6[x], 214[x], 1441[x], 10575[x], 2797[x], ala *corrected from* 'hafa ala' 166b[x]   [6] meinliga: meinlegu papp15[x].

Editions: *Skj* Anonyme digte og vers [XII], G [6]. *Sólarljóð* 61: AI, 637, BI, 645, *Skald* I, 314; Bugge 1867, 366-7, Falk 1914, 38, Björn M. Ólsen 1915, 19, Fidjestøl 1979, 68, Njörður Njarðvík 1991, 91-2, Njörður Njarðvík 1993, 66, 138.

Notes: [All]: Each st. of sts 61-7 begins with the same formula *Menn sá ek þá* 'I saw men then', describing various torments of the damned; cf. the same stylistic technique used in the *sól ek sá* sts 39-45. — [1] *sá ek* 'I saw': 166b[x] here and in the following st. transposes *sá* and *ek*. Assuming that the poet intended the same formula throughout this sequence, the majority ms. reading has been adopted. — [3] *um hagi annars* 'of, concerning another's affairs': If *hagi* is regarded as dat. sg., the phrase is grammatically aberrant, for *um* in the sense 'of, concerning' takes the acc., not the dat. Some eds (e.g. *Skj* B, *Skald*) emend to *af*, presumably assuming an earlier scribal confusion between original *af* and the prep. *of*, which is replaced by *um* in later mss. Here, however, *hagi* is judged to be acc. pl., so *um* has been retained. — [4-6]: Falk compares Rev. XIII.16 for the mark of the beast and VII.2-3 for the sealing of the blessed.

62. Menn sá ek þá   marga ófegna;
    þeir váru villir vega;
    þat kaupir sá,   er þessa heims
    apaz at óheillum.

Ek sá marga ófegna menn þá; þeir váru villir vega; sá kaupir þat, er apaz at óheillum þessa heims.

I saw many unhappy men then; they had gone astray [*lit.* were erring with regard to ways]; he purchases that [unhappiness], who fools himself into the misfortunes of this world.

Mss: **166b^x**(47v-48r), papp15^x(6r), 738^x(82v), 167b 6^x(3r), 214^x(151v), 1441^x(586), 10575^x(8v-9r), 2797^x(236).

Readings: [1] sá ek: *so* papp15^x, 738^x, 167b 6^x, 214^x, 1441^x, 10575^x, 2797^x, ek sá 166b^x; þá: *so* 214^x, 1441^x, þar 166b^x, papp15^x, 738^x, 167b 6^x, 10575^x, 2797^x [2] marga: er marga 214^x, 1441^x, margu 10575^x; ófegna: ófegri 738^x, ófegri *corrected from* 'ofegrgra' 167b 6^x, ófegra 214^x, fegna 10575^x [3] villir: allir villir papp15^x, 2797^x; vega: vegar 214^x, 10575^x [6] apaz: apar papp15^x.

Editions: *Skj* Anonyme digte og vers [XII], G [6]. *Sólarljóð* 62: AI, 637, BI, 645, *Skald* I, 314, *NN* §2147D; Bugge 1867, 367, Falk 1914, 38, Björn M. Ólsen 1915, 19, Fidjestøl 1979, 68, Njörður Njarðvík 1991, 92, Njörður Njarðvík 1993, 68, 139.

Notes: [1] sá ek þá 'I saw then': See Note to 61/1. Here also the reading *þá* has been chosen to preserve stylistic uniformity in preference to 166b^x's and other mss' *þar*. — [6] *óheillum* 'misfortunes': Being unfortunate is not one of the usual sins, unlike *öfund* 'envy' (st. 61), covetousness (st. 63), theft (st. 64), failure to attend divine service (st. 65), pride (st. 66) and slander (st. 67) which can be paralleled in other visions of Hell, and in sermon *exempla*. The word produces an unmetrical l., so it is possible that originally a different noun stood in its place. *NN* §2147D and *Skald* change the w.o. of the l. to *at óheillum apask*. Njörður Njarðvík (1991, 92) suggests that worldliness has led these men from the path of righteousness.

63. Menn sá ek þá, er mörgum hlutum
 véltu um annars eign;
 flokkum þeir fóru til Fégjarns borgar
 ok höfðu byrðar af blýi.

Ek sá menn þá, er véltu um eign annars mörgum hlutum; þeir fóru flokkum til borgar Fégjarns ok höfðu byrðar af blýi.

I saw men then, who have defrauded another of property in many things; they travelled in crowds to Fégjarn's fortress, and carried burdens of lead.

Mss: 166b^x(48r), papp15^x(6r-v), 738^x(82v), 167b 6^x(3r-v), 214^x(151v), 1441^x(86), 10575^x(9r), 2797^x(236).

Readings: [2] hlutum: hlut 1441^x [3] véltu: *so* papp15^x, 1441^x, 10575^x, 2797^x, viltu 166b^x, 738^x, 167b 6^x, 214^x; eign: *so* papp15^x, 10575^x, eigu 166b^x, 738^x, 167b 6^x, 214^x, 1441^x, 2797^x [5] Fégjarns: 'feyg yarns' 738^x, Fégjarns Fégjarns 167b 6^x, 'fegarins' 214^x [6] byrðar: *so* 738^x, byrðir 167b 6^x, 214^x, 'by[...]' 167b 6^x; blýi: 'býi' papp15^x, '[...]' 167b 6^x.

Editions: *Skj* Anonyme digte og vers [XII], G [6]. *Sólarljóð* 63: AI, 637, BI, 645, *Skald* I, 314, *NN* §2153; Bugge 1867, 367, Falk 1914, 38, Björn M. Ólsen 1915, 19, Fidjestøl 1979, 68, Njörður Njarðvík 1991, 92, Njörður Njarðvík 1993, 69, 139.

Notes: [All]: Ms. 2797^x transposes sts 63 and 64. — [3] *véltu* 'they defrauded': The mss are divided on whether the verb is *véltu* from *véla* 'to defraud, betray' or *viltu* from *villa* 'to lead astray, falsify, wilfully destroy'. In the last sense *viltu* would fit the present context, and is chosen by some eds (e.g. *Skj* B); *véltu* is the choice of Björn M. Ólsen, *Skald*, Fidjestøl and Njörður Njarðvík. — [3] *eign* 'property': The mss again divide between *eign* f. and *eigu* from *eiga* f., both with the same sense. Although *eiga* is attested in poetry, e.g. *Lok* 65 and *Sigsk* 47, *eign* is to be preferred here because it produces a metrical l., whereas *eigu* does not. — [5] *fégjarns* (gen. sg.): Lit. 'eager for money'. Interpreted by all eds as a pers. n. of transparent etymology. Falk (1914a, 41-2) suggests it is a term for Mammon. Cf. *Hávm* 78's use of the invented name *Fitjungr* (Evans 1986, 113). That Fégjarn should possess a fortress where ill-gotten gains are stored is reminiscent of a typical trope of sermon literature. Heito's *Visio Wettini* has a sinful monk enclosed within a box of lead inside a castle in Purgatory (Dümmler 1883-4, 270). On avarice cf. in particular *Hsv* 44; cf also *Hsv* 22, 73, 96 and 97. — [6] *blýi* 'lead': The final *–i* is unlikely to have been pronounced (*ANG* §135). The lead is the hellish equivalent of the gold which the avaricious coveted in life.

64. Menn sá ek þá,   er margan höfðu
       fé ok fjörvi rænt;
    brjóst í gegnum   rendu brögnum þeim
       öflgir eitrdrekar.

Ek sá menn þá, er höfðu rænt margan fé ok fjörvi; öflgir eitrdrekar rendu í gegnum brjóst þeim brögnum.

I saw men then who had robbed many a one of property and life; mighty poisonous dragons ran through the breasts of those men.

Mss: **166b**^{x}(48r), papp15^x(6v), 738^x(82v), 167b 6^x(3v), 214^x(151v), 1441^x(586), 10575^x(9r), 2797^x(236).

Readings: [4] brjóst: brjósti 167b 6^x, bifrost 214^x [6] öflgir: oflugir papp15^x, 1441^x, ofleigir 214^x, 'aufligir' 2797^x.

Editions: *Skj* Anonyme digte og vers [XII], G [6]. *Sólarljóð* 64: AI, 637, BI, 645-6, *Skald* I, 314; Bugge 1867, 367, Falk 1914, 38, Björn M. Ólsen 1915, 19, Fidjestøl 1979, 69, Njörður Njarðvík 1991, 93, Njörður Njarðvík 1993, 70, 139.

Notes: [6] *öflgir eitrdrekar* 'mighty poisonous dragons': Cf. *Vsp* 39 for the dragon Níðhǫggr who devours the corpses of evil-doers and the *vánardreki* of st. 54/2.

65. Menn sá ek þá,   er minst vildu
       halda helga daga;
    hendr þeira   váru á heitum steinum
       negldar nauðliga.

Ek sá menn þá, er minst vildu halda helga daga; hendr þeira váru negldar nauðliga á heitum steinum.

I saw men then who least wished to observe holy days; their hands were nailed painfully onto hot stones.

Mss: **166b**^{x}(48r), papp15^x(6v), 738^x(83r), 167b 6^x(3v), 214^x(151v), 1441^x(586), 10575^x(9r), 2797^x(236).

Readings: [1] sá ek: *so* papp15^x, 738^x, 167b 6^x, 214^x, 1441^x, 10575^x, 2797^x, ek sá 166b^x;   þá: þar papp15^x [5] heitum: beitum 214^x.

Editions: *Skj* Anonyme digte og vers [XII], G [6]. *Sólarljóð* 65: AI, 637, BI, 646, *Skald* I, 314; Bugge 1867, 367, Falk 1914, 38, Björn M. Ólsen 1915, 19-20, Fidjestøl 1979, 69, Njörður Njarðvík 1991, 93, Njörður Njarðvík 1993, 71, 140.

Notes: [All]: Limbs pierced by red-hot nails are frequent in medieval European vision literature. See, e.g., *St Patrick's Purgatory* (Easting 1991, 52-3, 131), the *Revelation of the Monk of Evesham* (Easting 2002, 44-5) and *Visio Thurkilli* (Schmidt 1978, 21).

66. Menn sá ek þá,   er af mikillæti
    virðuz vánum framar;
  klæði þeira   váru kýmiliga
    eldi um slegin.

Ek sá menn þá, er af mikillæti virðuz framar vánum; klæði þeira váru kýmiliga um slegin eldi.

I saw men then who from pride esteemed themselves beyond expectation; their clothes were amusingly set on fire.

Mss: **166b**[x](48r), papp15[x](6v), 738[x](83r), 167b 6[x](3v), 214[x](151v), 1441[x](586), 10575[x](9r-v), 2797[x](236).

Readings: [3] virðuz: réðuz papp15[x], virðaz 738[x], 167b 6[x] [5] kýmiliga: kynliga 1441[x], 10575[x] [6] slegin: *so* papp15[x], 738[x], 167b 6[x], 214[x], 10575[x], 2797[x], 'skiginn' 166b[x], ausin 1441[x].

Editions: *Skj* Anonyme digte og vers [XII], G [6]. *Sólarljóð* 66: AI, 638, BI, 646, *Skald* I, 314; Bugge 1867, 367, Falk 1914, 38, Björn M. Ólsen 1915, 20, Fidjestøl 1979, 69, Njörður Njarðvík 1991, 93-4, Njörður Njarðvík 1993, 72, 140.

Notes: [5] *kýmiliga* 'amusingly': Bugge, *Skj* B, Falk, Björn M. Ólsen, *Skald* and Fidjestøl all emend to *kynliga* 'strangely', occurring in 1441[x], 10575[x] and one other ms., but 166b[x]'s reading is overwhelmingly attested across the tradition. Njörður Njarðvík (1991, 94), adopting *kýmiliga*, cites a striking parallel in the *Visio Thurkilli* where a proud man is made to parade in a theatre for the amusement of devils; while he is strutting his clothes suddenly catch fire (Schmidt 1978, 20-1). — [6] *slegin eldi* 'set on fire': 166b[x]'s 'skigin' occurs only in one other ms.; *ausin* 'drenched, soaked', unique to 1441[x], is a suggestive evocation of the flames permeating the garments of the proud.

67. Menn sá ek þá,   er margt höfðu
    orð á annan logit;
  heljar hrafnar   ór höfði þeim
    harðliga sjónir slitu.

Ek sá menn þá, er höfðu logit margt orð á annan; hrafnar heljar slitu harðliga sjónir ór höfði þeim.

I saw men then who had greatly slandered another; Hell's ravens violently tore the eyes out of their heads.

Mss: **166b**[x](48r), papp15[x](6v), 738[x](83r), 167b 6[x](3v), 214[x](151v), 1441[x](586), 10575[x](9v), 2797[x](236).

Readings: [1] þá: þar 2797ˣ [2] höfðu: *so* papp15ˣ, 214ˣ, 1441ˣ, 2797ˣ, hafa 166bˣ, 738ˣ, 167b 6ˣ, 10575ˣ [3] orð: 'o[...]' 214ˣ [6] harðliga sjónir slitu: slitu harðliga sjónir 738ˣ, 'hardleg[...] sjónir slitu' 214ˣ, sárliga sjónir slitu 2797ˣ.

Editions: *Skj* Anonyme digte og vers [XII], G [6]. *Sólarljóð* 67: AI, 638, BI, 646, *Skald* I, 314-15; Bugge 1867, 367, Falk 1914, 39, Björn M. Ólsen 1915, 20, Fidjestøl 1979, 69, Njörður Njarðvík 1991, 94-5, Njörður Njarðvík 1993, 73, 141.

Notes: [2] *höfðu* 'had': The past tense is generally used in this section to refer to sinners' lives on earth, though see 61/2. — [4] *hrafnar heljar* 'Hell's ravens': These ravens may be associated with the pagan goddess of death, Hel (although Óðinn was traditionally the owner of ravens; cf. Tate 1985, 1032), as well as with the Christian realm of punishment; see Note to 38/4. — [6] *slitu sjónir* 'tore the eyes (out)': In *Fj* 45/1-3 Svipdagr is threatened with having his eyes pecked out by ravens as a punishment for lying: *horskir hrafnar | skulu þér á hám gálga | slíta sjónir úr | ef þú þat lýgr* 'wise ravens shall, on high gallows, tear out your eyes if you are lying about that'.

68. Allar ógnir   fær þú eigi vitat,
    þær sem helgengnir hafa;
  sætar syndir   verða at sárum bótum;
    æ koma mein eptir munuð.

Þú fær eigi vitat allar ógnir, þær sem helgengnir hafa; sætar syndir verða at sárum bótum; mein koma æ eptir munuð.

You will never get to know all the terrors which those who have gone to Hell have; sweet sins turn into bitter compensations; injuries always come after pleasure.

Mss: **166bˣ**(48r), papp15ˣ(6v), 738ˣ(83r), 167b 6ˣ(3v), 214ˣ(151v-152r), 1441ˣ(586), 10575ˣ(9v), 2797ˣ(236).

Readings: [3] þær: *om.* papp15ˣ, 1441ˣ, 10575ˣ, þá 214ˣ [5] verða: verði 10575ˣ; at: á papp15ˣ, 738ˣ, 167b 6ˣ, 1441ˣ; bótum: ljótum 738ˣ [6] æ: er 738ˣ; mein: menn 738ˣ, 167b 6ˣ.

Editions: *Skj* Anonyme digte og vers [XII], G [6]. *Sólarljóð* 68: AI, 638, BI, 646, *Skald* I, 315; Bugge 1867, 367, Falk 1914, 39, Björn M. Ólsen 1915, 20, Fidjestøl 1979, 69, Njörður Njarðvík 1991, 95, Njörður Njarðvík 1993, 74, 142.

Notes: [2] *fær þú eigi vitat* 'you will never get to know': Njörður Njarðvík (1991, 95) notes a parallel use of the inexpressibility topos for the torments of Hell in *Has* 39. — [6] *æ koma mein eptir munuð*: The l. sounds proverbial; Paasche (1914b, 52) notes a close parallel in Peter Damian's C10th poem *Rhythmus de die mortis*, st. 7 where *dulcedo carnis* 'the sweetness of the flesh' is turned into bitterness.

69. Menn sá ek þá,   er margt höfðu
       gefit at guðs lögum;
    hreinir kyndlar   váru yfir höfði þeim
       brendir bjartliga.

Ek sá menn þá, er margt höfðu gefit at guðs lögum; hreinir kyndlar váru brendir bjartliga yfir höfði þeim.

I saw men then who had given much according to God's laws; pure candles were being burned brightly over their heads.

Mss: **166b**[x](48r), papp15[x](6v-7r), 738[x](83r), 167b 6[x](3v), 214[x](152r), 1441[x](587), 10575[x](9v), 2797[x](236-7).

Readings: [1] sá ek: *so* papp15[x], 738[x], 214[x], 1441[x], 10575[x], 2797[x], ek sá 166b[x], 167b 6[x];   þá: þar 738[x]   [2] er: *so* papp15[x], 738[x], 167b 6[x], 214[x], 1441[x], 2797[x], *om.* 166b[x], sem 10575[x]; margt: mark 167b 6[x], 214[x]   [3] lögum: vilja 1441[x]   [5] yfir: of 10575[x]   [6] brendir: *so* papp15[x], 738[x], 167b 6[x], 214[x], 1441[x], 10575[x], 2797[x], breiddir 166b[x].

Editions: Skj Anonyme digte og vers [XII], G [6]. *Sólarljóð* 69: AI, 638, BI, 646, *Skald* I, 315; Bugge 1867, 368, Falk 1914, 45, Björn M. Ólsen 1915, 20, Fidjestøl 1979, 69, Njörður Njarðvík 1991, 96, Njörður Njarðvík 1993, 75, 142.

Notes: [All]: Sts 69-72 employ the *Menn sá ek þá* formula, by contrast with sts 61-7, to give examples of people who had performed good deeds. — [1] *sá ek* 'I saw': See Note to 61/1 above. — [2] *er* 'who': See Note to 4/2 above. — [2] *margt* 'much': The virtue of charity is rewarded, but if *mark* 'heed' is adopted from 167b 6[x] and 214[x] in place of *margt*, as Fidjestøl (1979, 55-6) advocates, it becomes a more generalised sentiment about paying heed to God's laws. — [6] *brendir* '(being) burned': 166b[x]'s *breiddir* 'spread' is a possible if less convincing reading, but it occurs in only one other ms.

70. Menn sá ek þá,   er af miklum hug
       veittu fátækum frama;
    lásu englar   helgar bækr
       ok himna skript yfir höfði þeim.

Ek sá menn þá, er af miklum hug veittu fátækum frama; englar lásu helgar bækr ok himna skript yfir höfði þeim.

I saw men then who from a generous spirit offered support to the poor; angels read holy books and heavenly writing [*lit.* writing of the heavens] over their heads.

Mss: **166b**[x](48r), papp15[x](7r), 738[x](83r), 167b 6[x](3v), 214[x](152r), 1441[x](587), 10575[x](10r), 2797[x](237).

Readings: [1] sá ek: ek sá 167b 6ˣ [2] af: *om.* 738ˣ, 167b 6ˣ, 2797ˣ [3] fátækum: 'fakękom' 10575ˣ [6] ok himna skript: *om.* papp15ˣ, 738ˣ, 167b 6ˣ, 214ˣ, 1441ˣ, 10575ˣ, 2797ˣ.

Editions: Skj Anonyme digte og vers [XII], G [6]. *Sólarljóð* 70: AI, 638, BI, 646-7, *Skald* I, 315; Bugge 1867, 368, Falk 1914, 45, Björn M. Ólsen 1915, 20-1, Fidjestøl 1979, 69, Njörður Njarðvík 1991, 96-7, Njörður Njarðvík 1993, 76, 143.

Notes: [All]: In a vision recounted in the *Annals of S. Bertin*, attributed to a 'religious English man', boys, who represent the blessed, read books with red and black script in alternating lines; the red ink recounts the deeds of the wicked, the black tells of good deeds (Grat *et al.* 1964, 29-30). Larrington (2002, 184) notes the preponderance of loan-words and references to church accoutrements in the description of the pleasures of heaven. — [4-6] *lásu englar helgar bækr ok himna skript yfir höfði þeim* 'angels read holy books and heavenly writing over their heads': Both alliteration and metre have gone awry in the last half of this st. There is no alliteration in ll. 4-5 and, although it supplies alliteration, the phrase *ok himna skript* makes l. 6 much too long. It is found only in 166bˣ and 8 other mss closely related to 166bˣ. Other eds have improved ll. 4-6 by altering the w.o.: *Skj* B, followed by *Skald*, have *helgar bækr | ok himna skript | lǫ́su þeim englar yfir*; Falk gives *helgar bækr | ok himna skript*; Fidjestøl puts *ok himna skript* in brackets, but leaves it at the beginning of l. 6.

71. Menn sá ek þá,   er mjök höfðu
     hungri farit hörund;
 englar guðs   lutu öllum þeim;
     þat er *it* æzta unað.

Ek sá menn þá, er mjök höfðu farit hörund hungri; englar guðs lutu þeim öllum; þat er *it* æzta unað.

I saw men then who had greatly afflicted their flesh with hunger; God's angels bowed to them all; that is the highest delight.

Mss: **166bˣ**(48r), papp15ˣ(7r), 738ˣ(83r), 167b 6ˣ(3v-4r), 214ˣ(152r), 1441ˣ(587), 10575ˣ(10r), 2797ˣ(237).

Readings: [1] sá ek: ek sá 738ˣ, 167b 6ˣ [2] höfðu: hafa 738ˣ, hafði 1441ˣ [3] hungri: *so* 2797ˣ, hungrí 166bˣ, papp15ˣ, 738ˣ, 167b 6ˣ, 214ˣ, 1441ˣ, 10575ˣ; farit hörund: hörund farit 1441ˣ [5] lutu öllum þeim: '[...]' 167b 6ˣ [6] þat er *it* æzta unað: þat ek æzta unað 166bˣ, þat er æzta unað papp15ˣ, 738ˣ, 214ˣ, 1441ˣ, 10575ˣ, 2797ˣ, '[...]' 167b 6ˣ.

Editions: Skj Anonyme digte og vers [XII], G [6]. *Sólarljóð* 71: AI, 638, BI, 647, *Skald* I, 315; *NN* §2564D; Bugge 1867, 368, Falk 1914, 45, Björn M. Ólsen 1915, 21, Fidjestøl 1979, 69, Njörður Njarðvík 1991, 69, Njörður Njarðvík 1993, 77, 143.

Notes: [3] *hungri* 'with hunger': This is the reading of about half the mss, while the others share the reading of 166bˣ, probably originating in a mistake in word division. — [5-6]: These ll. are missing or semi-legible in 167b 6ˣ due to a damaged leaf. For praise of the ascetic life, cf. *Hsv* 116. — [6]: Emendation is required here. It is necessary to insert the n. def. art. *it* to accompany *æzta* n. nom. sg. weak adj.

72. Menn sá ek þá,   er móður höfðu
         látit mat í munn;
     hvílur þeira   váru á himingeislum
         hafðar hagliga.

Ek sá menn þá, er höfðu látit mat í munn móður; hvílur þeira váru hafðar hagliga á himingeislum.

I saw men then who had placed food in the mouth of their mothers [*lit.* mother]; their resting-places were comfortably appointed on heavenly rays.

Mss: **166b**^{x}(48r), papp15^x(7r), 738^x(83r), 167b 6^x(4r), 214^x(152r), 1441^x(587), 10575^x(10r), 2797^x(237).

Readings: [1] sá ek: ek sá 738^x, 167b 6^x [2] höfðu: *so* 214^x, 10575^x, 2797^x, hafa 166b^x, papp15^x, 738^x, 167b 6^x, 1441^x [3] munn: mann 738^x [5] á: *so* papp15^x, 738^x, 167b 6^x, 214^x, 1441^x, 10575^x, 2797^x, af 166b^x;   himin-: himins- 167b 6^x.

Editions: *Skj* Anonyme digte og vers [XII], G [6]. *Sólarljóð* 72: AI, 638-9, BI, 647, *Skald* I, 315; Bugge 1867, 368, Falk 1914, 45, Björn M. Ólsen 1915, 21, Fidjestøl 1979, 70, Njörður Njarðvík 1991, 97-8, Njörður Njarðvík 1993, 78, 144.

Notes: [2] *höfðu* 'had': See Note to 67/2 and 73/6 below. Falk (1914a, 47) and Paasche (1948, 191) compare the Fourth Commandment, the adjuration to honour one's parents. Cf. *Hsv* 3, 108.

73. Helgar meyjar   höfðu hreinliga
         sál af syndum þvegit
     manna þeira,   er á mörgum degi
         pína sjálfa sik.

Helgar meyjar höfðu hreinliga þvegit af syndum sál manna þeira, er á mörgum degi pína sjálfa sik.

Holy maidens had washed clean [*lit.* cleanly] of sin the souls of those men who on many a day mortify themselves.

Mss: **166b**^{x}(48r), papp15^x(7r), 738^x(83r), 167b 6^x(4r), 214^x(152r), 1441^x(587), 10575^x(10r-v), 2797^x(237).

Readings: [2] hreinliga: hreinligan 214^x [4] manna þeira: menn þeir 738^x [5] mörgum: helgum papp15^x, morgun- 1441^x.

Editions: *Skj* Anonyme digte og vers [XII], G [6]. *Sólarljóð* 73: AI, 639, BI, 647, *Skald* I, 315; Bugge 1867, 368, Falk 1914, 45, Björn M. Ólsen 1915, 21, Fidjestøl 1979, 70, Njörður Njarðvík 1991, 98, Njörður Njarðvík 1993, 79, 144.

Notes: [1] *helgar meyjar* 'holy maidens': Cf. *mála-dísir dróttins* 'confidential *dísir* of the Lord' in 25/1 and contrast *meyjar heljar* 'Hell's maidens' in 38/4. — [4-6]: Paasche (1948, 193) compares the adjuration to mortification of the flesh in *HómÍsl* 1872, 60. — [6] *pína* '[they] mortify, torture': So also Bugge, Fidjestøl and Njörður Njarðvík. *Skj* B, Falk, Björn M. Ólsen and *Skald* emend the 3rd pers. pl. pres. indic. *pína* to 3rd pers. pl. pret. indic. *píndu*, presumably on grounds of sense, that men's self-mortification must have preceded their absolution by the holy maidens. A similar use of the pres. tense is at 61/2 *ala* 'they nourish'.

74. Hávar reiðir   sá ek með himnum fara;
       þær eigu götur til guðs;
     menn þeim stýra,   er myrðir eru
       alls fyrir öngvar sakir.

Ek sá hávar reiðir fara með himnum; þær eigu götur til guðs; menn stýra þeim, er eru myrðir fyrir alls öngvar sakir.

I saw tall wagons journeying along the heavens; they have paths to God; men drive them who are murdered for no cause [*lit.* causes] at all.

Mss: **166b**[x](48r), papp15[x](7r), 738[x](83r), 167b 6[x](4r), 214[x](152r), 1441[x](587), 10575[x](10v), 2797[x](237).

Readings: [1] Hávar: hair papp15[x], 1441[x];   reiðir: *so* papp15[x], 738[x], 167b 6[x], 1441[x], reiðar 166b[x], 214[x], 10575[x], 2797[x]   [2] ek: *om.* papp15[x], 738[x], 167b 6[x]   [3] eigu: *so* 1441[x], 2797[x], eiga 166b[x], papp15[x], 738[x], 167b 6[x], 214[x], 10575[x]; götur: götu 738[x], 214[x]   [4] menn: enn 214[x]; þeim: þeir 214[x]   [5] er: sem papp15[x], 1441[x], 10575[x]; myrðir: *so* papp15[x], 214[x], 10575[x], 2797[x], 'mindir' 166b[x], 'marder' 738[x], 'mirder' *corrected from* 'm[...]rder' 167b 6[x], myrðtir 1441[x]   [6] öngvar: öngvan 167b 6[x], 'aungr' 1441[x].

Editions: *Skj* Anonyme digte og vers [XII], G [6]. *Sólarljóð* 74: AI, 639, BI, 647, *Skald* I, 315; Bugge 1867, 368, Falk 1914, 45, Björn M. Ólsen 1915, 21, Fidjestøl 1979, 70, Njörður Njarðvík 1991, 98, Njörður Njarðvík 1993, 80, 145.

Notes: [1] *hávar reiðir* 'tall wagons': Paasche (1948, 194) and Njörður Njarðvík (1991, 98) compare the flaming chariot which bears Elias to heaven in 2 Kings II.11. — [5-6] *myrðir ... fyrir alls öngvar sakir* 'murdered ... for no cause at all': A theme sounded earlier in the poem, e.g sts 1-7 and 20-4.

75. Inn mátki faðir,   *inn* mæzti sonr,
    heilagr andi himins!
Þik bið ek skilja,   sem skapat hefr,
    oss alla eymðum frá.

Inn mátki faðir, *inn* mæzti sonr, heilagr andi himins! Ek bið þik, sem hefr skapat, skilja oss alla frá eymðum.

Mighty Father, most glorious Son, Holy Spirit of heaven! I ask you who have created [us] to release us all from miseries.

Mss: **166b**[x](48r), papp15[x](7r-v), 738[x](83r), 167b 6[x](4r), 214[x](152r), 1441[x](587), 10575[x](10v), 2797[x](237).

Readings: [2] *inn*: *om. all*; mæzti: *so* 10575[x], 2797[x], mestr 166b[x], papp15[x], 738[x], 167b 6[x], 214[x], 1441[x] [3] heilagr: H. 166b[x] [4] bið: biðr papp15[x], 2797[x]; ek: *om.* papp15[x]; skilja: *so* 214[x], 2797[x], leysa *all others* [5] sem: er 214[x], 10575[x], 2797[x]; skapat: skapat *corrected from* 'spapad' 214[x] [6] eymðum: *so* 214[x], 2797[x], synðum *all others*.

Editions: Skj Anonyme digte og vers [XII], G [6]. *Sólarljóð* 75: AI, 639, BI, 647, *Skald* I, 315; Bugge 1867, 368-9, Falk 1914, 5, Björn M. Ólsen 1915, 22, Fidjestøl 1979, 70, Njörður Njarðvík 1991, 99, Njörður Njarðvík 1993, 81, 145.

Notes: [All]: There are a number of metrical and alliterative irregularities affecting this st., as it is presented in 166b[x] and other early modern mss. Probably as a result of scribal awareness of these irregularities, several later mss present texts that correct them, and these readings have been adopted here, in ll. 2, 4 and 6. — [2]: 166b[x]'s 'mestr sonr' is unmetrical; adopting the weak form of the adj., preceded by the def. art. *inn*, restores metrical regularity to the l. — [6] *eymðum* 'miseries, wretchedness': 43 mss read *synðum* 'sins', but a substantial minority (21) read *eymðum*, which is the *lectio difficilior* and improves the alliteration, as this cannot rest on *oss alla*; the reading is accepted by *Skj* B, *Skald*, Björn M. Ólsen, Falk and Fidjestøl and adopted here.

76. Bjúgvör ok Listvör   sitja í Herðis dyrum
    organs stóli á;
járnadreyri   fellr ór nösum þeim;
    sá vekr fjón með firum.

Bjúgvör ok Listvör sitja á organs stóli í Herðis dyrum; járnadreyri fellr ór nösum þeim; sá vekr fjón með firum.

Bjúgvör and Listvör sit on an organ stool in Herðir's doorway; iron blood falls from their nostrils; that awakens hatred among men.

Mss: 166b[x](48v), papp15[x](7v), 738[x](83r-v), 167b 6[x](4r), 214[x](152r), 1441[x](587), 10575[x](10v), 2797[x](237).

Readings: [1] Bjúgvör: *so* papp15[x], 10575[x], 2797[x], Bingvör 166b[x], Vingvör 738[x];   Listvör: Litvör 1441[x]   [4] járna-: *so* papp15[x], 167b 6[x], 1441[x], 10575[x], 2797[x], járn- 166b[x], í arna- 738[x]   [6] fjón: fjör 738[x]; firum: *so* 10575[x], 2797[x], fyrðum *all others*.

Editions: *Skj* Anonyme digte og vers [XII], G [6]. *Sólarljóð* 76: AI, 639, BI, 647-8, *Skald* I, 315, *NN* §§1273, 2564E; Bugge 1867, 369, Falk 1914, 48, Björn M. Ólsen 1915, 22, Fidjestøl 1979, 70, Njörður Njarðvík 1991, 99-100, Njörður Njarðvík 1993, 82, 146.

Notes: [All]: Both this st. and st. 77 sketch the power of what are presented as malevolent female figures, who awaken feelings of hatred (st. 76) and lust (st. 77) among men. — [1] *Bjúgvör ok Listvör* 'Bjúgvör and Listvör': The names of these probably invented mythical female figures are transmitted in a number of variant forms. 166b[x]'s *Bing-* does not appear to be a likely or meaningful name element; papp15[x]'s *Bjúg-* 'bent' gives a more plausible designation for a troll-like female. Other invented names in the sts which follow are equally prone to variation. It is not known whether these figures are pure inventions or were known from other contexts. — [2] *Herðis* 'of Herðir': The identity of this figure is also obscure. Bugge and Falk emend to *Lævíss*, a name for Loki, because of the defective alliteration. However, if Listvör (l. 1) were emended to *Hlistvör*, alliteration would be restored. For Björn M. Ólsen 1915, 60, Herðir is 'the hardener' (of hearts), i.e. the devil, an epithet which, he argues, may have been suggested to the poet by its similarity to *Herebi* 'Erebus' in Walter de Chatillon's *Alexandreis* X, l.31 (Colker 1978, 254), translated into Icel. as *Alexanders saga* (*Alex*) by abbot Brandr Jónsson (Unger 1848). — [3] *á organs stóli* 'on an organ stool': Why this quintessentially Christian instrument should be associated with the troll-like females is not at all clear; Björn M. Ólsen (1915, 61) suggests the function of the music is to attract men to sin, like the Sirens of the *Odyssey*. Paasche (1914a, 158) notes a parallel with Eggþér in *Vsp* 42, whose harp-playing signals the onset of *ragna rök* 'the doom of the gods'. Fidjestøl (1979, 57) compares an OSwed. proverb, *wärldslik qwinna är diäfwulsins orgha* 'worldly women are the devil's organ', but here the devil plays upon the women, rather than the women playing the instrument. — [4-5] *járnadreyri fellr ór nösum þeim* 'iron blood falls from their nostrils': The ll. lack alliteration in their present form, as vocalic alliteration cannot be carried by *ór*. (*Skald* deals with this problem by placing *ór* first in l. 5.) 166b[x]'s reading *járn-* is also unmetrical. The element *járna-* in *járnadreyri* may be understood as adjectival, 'iron blood' (lit. gen. pl. 'of weapons'), as here and in *Skj* B (*jærn-væske* 'iron-snot'), or as nominal, as Fidjestøl interprets it (*våpen-væska* 'weapon-snot'), i.e. 'snot produced by weapons', and *dreyri* may be understood in its normal sense of 'blood' or more narrowly to refer to nasal discharge. Björn M. Ólsen 1915, following Rask, suggests *norna* 'of Norns' rather than *járna-*, as in 51/1 *norna stóli* 'the seat of the Norns'. The idea of blood rousing hostility can be paralleled in Anon *Darr*[V], as Falk (1914a, 49) points out. — [6] *firum* (dat. pl.) 'men': This reading is preferable to the majority mss' *fyrðum*, which is unmetrical.

77. Óðins kván   rær á jarðar skipi
    móðug á munað;
    seglum hennar   verðr síð hlaðit,
    þeim er á þráreipum þruma.

Óðins kván, móðug á munað, rær á skipi jarðar; seglum hennar verðr síð hlaðit, þeim er þruma á þráreipum.

Óðinn's wife, mighty in desire, rows on the ship of the earth; her sails will be late furled, those which hang on the ropes of longing.

Mss: **166b**[x](48v), papp15[x](7v), 738[x](83v), 167b 6[x](4r), 214[x](152r), 1441[x](587), 10575[x](10v-11r), 2797[x](237).

Readings: [1] kván: kon 1441[x] [2] jarðar: jarður 214[x] [3] móðug á munað: *so* papp15[x], 214[x], 10575[x], í móðugum munað 166b[x], 214[x], í móðug á munað 738[x], 167b 6[x], 1441[x] [6] þruma: *so* 2797[x], 'þumu' 166b[x], 'þumar' papp15[x], 214[x], 1441[x], 'þrymur' 738[x], 'þrimur' 167b 6[x], þrumir 10575[x].

Editions: Skj Anonyme digte og vers [XII], G [6]. *Sólarljóð* 77: AI, 639, BI, 648, Skald I, 315; Bugge 1867, 369, Falk 1914, 48, Björn M. Ólsen 1915, 22, Fidjestøl 1979, 70, Njörður Njarðvík 1991, 101-2, Njörður Njarðvík 1993, 83, 147.

Notes: [1] *Óðins kván* 'Óðinn's wife': Frigg, or conceivably Freyja, as Björn M. Ólsen (1915, 59) and Paasche (1914a, 158) suggest. Both goddesses are associated with Venus in homiletic writing, both in ON and OE, symbolising sexual desire. Ælfric of Eynsham names Frigg as *þære sceamleasan gydenan* 'the shameless goddess' (Pope 1967-8, 686); Freyja is noted as *Freyja portkona* 'Freyja the whore' in *Heilagra manna søgur* (Unger 1877, I, 417; II, 233). — [2] *skipi jarðar* 'on the ship of the earth': That the world can be symbolised by a ship is a homiletic commonplace; cf. Lange (1958a, 257-8) who adduces a homily about the ship of the earth in AM 673 a 4°. Here, however, the Christian symbol is given a traditional ON context, and associated with the persistent force of sexual desire, linked with the dominance of female powers. The metaphor of the world as a ship is elaborated in the second half of the st.; see Fidjestøl 1979, 56-7. — [3] *móðug á munað* 'mighty in desire'. 166b[x]'s reading, as well as those of many of the other mss, seems to be the result of confusion about word division. — [6] *þruma* 'hang': 2797[x]'s reading looks like an intelligent guess for a word which most mss had difficulty with; the form is found in 5 other mss and as a correction in a further 3. The readings of 738[x], 10575[x] and a further 15 mss may also derive from *þruma*, which gives good sense, even if the word is not widely attested with this meaning, as Njörður Njarðvík (1991, 101) points out. Its normal sense is 'to stand, sit, fast, loiter, mope'.

78. Arfi, faðir   einn ek ráðit hefi,
    ok þeir Sólkötlu synir
    hjartarhorn,   þat er ór haugi bar
    inn vitri Vígdvalinn.

Arfi, ek einn, faðir, ok þeir synir Sólkötlu, hefi ráðit hjartarhorn, þat er inn vitri Vígdvalinn bar ór haugi.

Heir, I alone, the father, and the sons of Sólkatla, have interpreted the hart's horn which the wise Vígdvalinn carried out of the burial mound.

Mss: **166b**[x](48v), papp15[x](7v), 738[x](83v), 167b 6[x](4r), 214[x](152r), 1441[x](587), 10575[x](11r), 2797[x](237).

Readings: [2] ek: þér papp15[x], 1441[x], 10575[x], 2797[x];   ráðit: *so all others*, 'rad' *with smudged superscript letter* 166b[x]   [3] þeir: *om.* papp15[x], 10575[x]   [5] þat er: er 738[x], 214[x], sem 10575[x]; ór: *so* papp15[x], 214[x], 1441[x], 10575[x], 2797[x], *om.* 166b[x], vor 738[x], 167b 6[x];   haugi: *so* papp15[x], 738[x], 167b 6[x], 214[x], 1441[x], 10575[x], 2797[x], hugi 166b[x]   [6] vitri: *om.* 214[x]; Vígdvalinn: 'vijgdarannlinn' 738[x].

Editions: *Skj* Anonyme digte og vers [XII], G [6]. *Sólarljóð* 78: AI, 639-40, BI, 648, *Skald* I, 316, *NN* §2816; Bugge 1867, 369, Falk 1914, 50, Björn M. Ólsen 1915, 22-3, Fidjestøl 1979, 71, Njörður Njarðvík 1991, 102-5, Njörður Njarðvík 1993, 84, 148-9.

Notes: [All]: This st. for the first time clarifies the discursive framework of the poem – a father addresses his son – and yet ll. 1-4 are capable of two different interpretations. *Arfi* (l. 1) may be either the m. noun 'son, heir' nom., the subject of direct address, or the m. dat. sg. of *arfr* 'inheritance', object of *ráða* 'to possess, have at one's disposal' (which takes the dat. case). *Skj* B and *Skald* follow the latter line of interpretation, which also requires them to emend *faðir* to *fǫður* (gen. sg). *Skj* B construes *Faders arv har jeg ene rådet over og de Solkatlas sönner* 'I alone, and Solkatla's sons, have had the father's inheritance at my disposal'. *Hjartarhorn* (l. 4), presumably in apposition to *fǫður arfi* (l. 1) should then also be in the dat. case, and *Skald* emends to *hjartarhorni*, though *Skj* B does not. The other possibility, and that adopted here, is that the father addresses his son directly and that *ek einn, faðir* is to be understood as 'I alone, the father ...'. *Ráða* (l. 2) is then to be understood as meaning 'to interpret' (in this sense it takes the acc. case) with *hjartarhorn* (l. 4) as object of *ek hefi ráðit* (l. 2). This sense fits better with the remainder of st. 78 and looks forward to st. 79. — [1] *arfi* 'heir, son': The convention of a father addressing his son is frequent in wisdom poetry, as in *Hsv* 1. The dead father's heir(s) are also the audience of the poem; 'father' may also denote a priest and his son(s) the congregation as Njörður Njarðvík (1991, 102) notes. Under what circumstances, whether in a dream or in a vision, the father narrates the poem to his son is never made explicit, but the notion of occult wisdom being revealed to a young man by his senior male kinsmen is found in ON myth, as well as in stock motifs of *fornaldarsögur*. — [2] *ráðit* 'interpreted': 166b[x]'s 'rad' is followed by a smudged superscript which is likely to be a <t>, giving the same reading as the other mss. — [3] *synir Sólkötlu* 'the sons of Sólkatla': The woman's name is otherwise unknown. It is etymologically transparent, from *sól* 'sun' + f. form of *ketill* 'cauldron, container'. For Falk (1914a, 53), as also for Amory (1985, 12); 1990, 261-2, Sólkatla is the *mulier amictae sole* 'woman clothed with the sun' of Rev. XII.1, the Virgin Mary, the Church and the New Jerusalem at once. Her sons are the citizens of the New Jerusalem, the righteous. Björn M. Ólsen (1915, 62) contends that the sons of Sólkatla are the father's companions in heaven, and that their mother is a virtuous dead woman; there may be some connections with *Sólblinda synir* 'the sons of Sun-Blind' in *Fj* 10. Brennecke 1985 comments extensively on this st.; he notes Paasche's reference to the epithet *vas gratiae* 'the vessel of grace' for the Virgin Mary in Finnur Jónsson *et al.* (1916, 174) and compares a number of similar epithets in later German religious verse. The sons of Sólkatla would thus be the Apostles, since Christ designated the Apostle John as Mary's son in John XIX.26. Njörður Njarðvík (1991, 103) more simply suggests that *sólkatla* may be a *heiti* for heaven; the sons of heaven are then the righteous. — [4] *hjartarhorn* 'hart's horn': For Björn M. Ólsen (1915, 51-2) the horn is a surface on which the runes of the next st. are carved; for Bugge and Paasche (1914a, 159 and 1914b, 71) the hart's horn is the weapon used in Christ's (the *sólar hjört* 'hart of the sun' of st. 55) fight with the devil in serpent or dragon form, i.e. the Cross. After this he casts off his old horns and grows new ones, a token of redemption which he brings out of the grave-mound in l. 4. Falk (1914a, 51-2) cites Anon *Mhkv* 8/4[III]: *Niðjungr skóf af haugi horn* 'Niðjungr shaved (*sc.* brought into being a new) horn from the mound', suggesting that the horn is the horn of our salvation (*cornu salutis nobis*) of Luke I.69, though Amory (1985, 24 n. 42 and 1990, 262 n. 43) argues that in this st. the word *horn* means the corner of the *haugr*. Cf. also *Hávm* 139 where Óðinn brings up occult wisdom from below. Amory (1985, 12; 1990, 261) suggests that the runes carry the message of sin and its consequences from beyond the grave (*haugr*) and are to be equated with the Gospel. Brennecke's suggestion that the reference is to Christ the unicorn has little merit. — [5] *ór haugi* 'out of the burial mound': The scribe of 166b[x] may have had an exemplar which omitted *ór*, thus causing confusion about the following word. — [6] *Vígdvalinn* 'Vígdvalinn': This name, though composed of elements familiar from eddic poetry, made no sense to the scribe of 738[x]. There has been much debate as to the meaning of the name, summarised by Njörður Njarðvík (1991, 104). Brennecke (1985, 106) notes that Dvalinn can be a deer name, as well as that of a dwarf, or meaning 'one who delays'. Whatever the precise implications of the name, as Njörður Njarðvík (1991, 105) notes, some scholars think that the second half of the st. refers to Christ bringing salvation for mankind at his Resurrection, though Amory (1985, 12-13; 1990, 262) interprets Vígdvalinn as Peter, the first pope, communicating the teachings of Christ to the faithful as a father does to his son.

79. Hér eru þær rúnir,   sem ristit hafa
    Njarðar dætr níu,
    Böðveig in elzta   ok Kreppvör in yngsta
    ok þeira systr sjau.

Hér eru þær rúnir sem níu dætr Njarðar hafa ristit, Böðveig in elzta ok Kreppvör in yngsta ok sjau systr þeira.

Here are the runes which the nine daughters of Njǫrðr have carved, Böðveig the eldest and Kreppvör the youngest and their seven sisters.

Mss: **166b**[x](48v), papp15[x](7v), 738[x](83v), 167b 6[x](4v), 214[x](152r), 1441[x](587), 10575[x](11r), 2797[x](237-8).

Readings: [1] Hér: Þetti 10575[x]; þær: *om.* papp15[x], 738[x], 1441[x], 10575[x], 2797[x] [2] sem: er 214[x], 2797[x]; hafa: hafar 214[x] [3] Njarðar: 'nirdar' 167b 6[x] [4] Böðveig: *so* 10575[x], 'Baðveing' 166b[x], Baugveig papp15[x], 1441[x], 'Baudveing' 738[x], 167b 6[x], Skaðveig 214[x], Baugvör 2797[x]; elzta: '[...]sta' 214[x] [5] Kreppvör: Krippvör papp15[x], 167b 6[x], 214[x], 1441[x], 10575[x], 'kryppvar keypp' 738[x].

Editions: *Skj* Anonyme digte og vers [XII], G [6]. *Sólarljóð* 79: AI, 640, BI, 648, *Skald* I, 316, *NN* §2564F; Bugge 1867, 369, Falk 1914, 50, Björn M. Ólsen 1915, 23, Fidjestøl 1979, 71, Njörður Njarðvík 1991, 105-6, Njörður Njarðvík 1993, 84, 152.

Notes: [All]: It is unusual for women to be associated with the carving of runes. — [1-2]: These ll. are missing in 167b 6[x] because of a damaged leaf. — [3] *níu dætr Njarðar* 'Njǫrðr's nine daughters': The only daughter of the sea-god Njǫrðr known by name from ON myth is Freyja. Ægir, a sea-deity like Njǫrðr, is however said to have nine daughters in *SnE* (1998, I, 36); these are normally regarded as personifications of the waves. It is likely that Ægir and Njǫrðr have been assimilated to one another here. Björn M. Ólsen (1915, 62-3) and Njörður Njarðvík (1991, 105) suggest the daughters are the Deadly Sins, usually thought of as seven in number, but given as nine both in the *Alexandreis* X, ll. 32-57 (Colker 1978, 254-5) and in *Alex* (Unger 1848, 152-3). This fits the pagan associations of the number nine elsewhere in the poem. Falk (1914a, 52-3) and Björn M. Ólsen (1915, 61-2) assume that the daughters of Njǫrðr have carved runes on the horn of salvation; Njörður Njarðvík (1991, 105) objects to such pagan lettering on a Christian symbol, while Tate (1985, 1032-3) thinks that the runes of this st. are not carved on the hart's horn (which would surely carry a Christian message in *himna skript* 'heavenly script'), but must be some other runes. — [4] *Böðveig*: There is little to choose between the variants of this name; Böðveig and Baugveig are both possible, though 166b[x]'s 'Baðveing' can hardly be right. Attempts to link the names of the st. with individual Deadly Sins have not proved convincing, cf. Björn M. Ólsen 1915, 62.

80. Hverju *bölvi*   þeir belt hafa
       Sváfr ok Sváfrlogi;
   blóð þeir vöktu   ok benjar sugu
       ey undir illum vana.

Hverju *bölvi* hafa þeir belt, Sváfr ok Sváfrlogi; þeir vöktu blóð ok sugu benjar, ey undir illum vana.

Every evil they have ventured, Sváfr and Sváfrlogi; they awakened blood and sucked wounds, always with a bad habit.

Mss: **166b**^{x}(48v), papp15^x(7v), 738^x(83v), 167b 6^x(4v), 214^x(152r-v), 1441^x(587), 10575^x(11r-v), 2797^x(238).

Readings: [1] *bölvi*: *om. all*   [2] belt hafa: hafa belt 2797^x;   belt: 'billt' 738^x, 167b 6^x, '[...]illt' 214^x [3] Sváfr: sváfni 738^x, sváfar 10575^x;   Sváfr-: Sváfar papp15^x, 738^x, 167b 6^x, 1441^x, 10575^x [4] vöktu: 'vok[...]' 167b 6^x [5] benjar: beinar 167b 6^x [6] ey undir illum vana: undir illum ey vana 166b^x;   illum: öllum papp15^x, 738^x, 167b 6^x, 214^x, 1441^x, 10575^x, 2797^x.

Editions: *Skj* Anonyme digte og vers [XII], G [6]. *Sólarljóð* 80: AI, 640, BI, 648, *Skald* I, 316, *NN* §§2154, 2218B; Bugge 1867, 370, Falk 1914, 1, Björn M. Ólsen 1915, 23, Fidjestøl 1979, 71, Njörður Njarðvík 1991, 106-8, Njörður Njarðvík 1993, 86, 154.

Notes: [All]: Falk, Guðbrandur Vigfússon (*CPB* I, 211) and Bugge all move this st. to the beginning of the poem in order to provide names for the characters in the first *exemplum*. There is no justification for this move. — [1] *bölvi* (n. dat. sg.) 'evil': The required noun is missing in all mss. It must have alliterated on <b>; Bugge, followed by most other eds, supplies *bölvi*, which makes good sense. — [3] *Sváfr ok Sváfrlogi* 'Sváfr and Sváfrlogi': It is not clear who these figures are; for the names, cf. one of Óðinn's names, Sváfnir 'one who puts to sleep' (*LP*: *Sváfnir*). For Björn M. Ólsen 1915, they are men who have fallen completely under the influence of the Deadly Sins. — [6] *ey undir illum vana* 'always with a bad habit': The l., as it stands in the mss, is problematical. Here the w.o. of 166b^x has been reversed and prep. *undir* has been construed with *vana* from *vani* weak m. noun 'custom', 'habit'. Bugge suggests the scribes may have understood *undir* as 'wounds', parallel to *benjar* in l. 5, rather than as a prep. 'under'. Bugge, *Skj* B, *Skald* and Björn M. Ólsen omit *undir* and read the l. as *illum ey vana*, which *Skj* B translates as *med en altid slet skik* 'with an always bad practice'. Njörður Njarðvík (1991, 106-7) accepts *undir* but does not explain what he thinks the l. means. Lbs 437^x, a ms. not used in the present edn, has *vandir* 'wicked', a reading adopted by Falk and Fidjestøl.

81. Kvæði þetta,   er þér kent hefi,
          skaltu fyr kvikum kveða,
     Sólarljóð,   er sýnaz munu
          minst at mörgu login.

Þetta kvæði, er hefi kent þér, skaltu kveða fyr kvikum, Sólarljóð, er munu sýnaz at mörgu minst login.

This poem which I have taught you, you must recite before living people, 'Sólarljóð' which will appear in many ways to be least untruthful [*lit.* lying].

Mss: **166b**[x](48v), papp15[x](7v-8r), 738[x](83v), 167b 6[x](4v), 214[x](152v), 1441[x](587), 10575[x](11v), 2797[x](238).

Readings: [2] er: ek 214[x], 2797[x] [3] kvikum: *om.* 10575[x] [5] er: *om.* papp15[x], 738[x], 167b 6[x], 1441[x], 10575[x]; munu: manu 10575[x] [6] mörgu: mörgum 738[x], 214[x], 1441[x].

Editions: *Skj* Anonyme digte og vers [XII], G [6]. *Sólarljóð* 81: AI, 640, BI, 648, *Skald* I, 316; Bugge 1867, 370, Falk 1914, 50, Björn M. Ólsen 1915, 23, Fidjestøl 1979, 71, Njörður Njarðvík 1991, 108, Njörður Njarðvík 1993, 87, 155.

Notes: [4] *Sólarljóð* 'Songs of the Sun': The n. *ljóð* is indicated as pl. here by the verb *munu* (l. 5), though st. 83 understands it as sg. Naming the poem in the closing or penultimate st., and the injunction to take its lessons to heart are paralleled in *Hsv* 148 and 149 and *Hávm* 164. *Has* 64 and *Leið* 44, as Paasche (1914a, 162) points out, also name the poem in the second to last st., as does *Lil*, leaving the final st. for a valedictory prayer.

82. Hér vit skiljumz   ok hittaz munum
          á feginsdegi fira;
     dróttinn minn   gefi þeim dauðum ró
          ok hinum líkn, er lifa.

Hér skiljumz vit ok munum hittaz á feginsdegi fira; dróttinn minn gefi þeim dauðum ró ok líkn hinum, er lifa.

Here we two part and we will meet on men's day of joy; may my Lord give to the dead peace, and grace to those who live.

Mss: **166b**[x](48v), papp15[x](8r), 738[x](83v), 167b 6[x](4v), 214[x](152v), 1441[x](588), 10575[x](11v), 2797[x](238).

Readings: [2] munum: manum 10575[x] [3] feginsdegi: 'ferginsdegi' papp15[x], 214[x], 'frigñiz deigi' *corrected from* 'fiørgiṅz deigi' 738[x], feginsdegi *corrected from* 'ferginsdegi' 167b 6[x]; fira: fira *corrected from* 'finum' 738[x], 'fina' 167b 6[x], 214[x] [4] minn: *om.* 214[x] [5] þeim: *om.* papp15[x], 1441[x], 10575[x], 2797[x]; dauðum: *so* papp15[x], 167b 6[x], 1441[x], 10575[x], 2797[x], 'daudu' 166b[x], 738[x], 214[x]   [6] ok: *om.* papp15[x], 1441[x], 10575[x], 2797[x], en 738[x], 167b 6[x], 214[x].

Editions: Skj Anonyme digte og vers [XII], G [6]. *Sólarljóð* 82: AI, 640, BI, 648, *Skald* I, 316; Bugge 1867, 370, Falk 1914, 50, Björn M. Ólsen 1915, 23-4, Fidjestøl 1979, 71, Njörður Njarðvík 1991, 108-9, Njörður Njarðvík 1993, 88, 156.

Notes: [All]: Many eds have regarded this as the final st. of the original *Sólarljóð* and do not include st. 83. — [3] *feginsdegi* 'day of joy': In poetry only here and in the form *feginsdœgr* in QrvOdd *Ævdr* 36[VIII]. The cpd is not difficult to construe: it is clearly a term for Judgement Day. Njörður Njarðvík (1991, 109) notes the phrase occurring in this sense in prose in *Sv* (*Sv* 1920, 42). It seems, however, to have caused later scribes a great deal of difficulty. — [5] *gefi þeim dauðum ró* 'give the dead peace': Paasche (1914a, 162) suggests this is a quotation from the Requiem Mass, *requiem aeternam dona eis, Domine!* 'Lord, give them eternal rest!'. The Day of Judgement is evoked, and a final prayer pronounced for the living and the dead.

83.   Dásamligt fræði   var þér draumi kvadd,
        en þú sázt it sanna;
    fyrða engi   var svá fróðr skapaðr,
        er áðr hefði heyrt Sólarljóðs sögu.

Dásamligt fræði var kvadd þér draumi, en þú sázt it sanna; engi fyrða var skapaðr svá fróðr, er áðr hefði heyrt Sólarljóðs sögu.

Admirable advice was addressed to you in a dream, but you feared the truth; no man was created so wise that he would have heard 'Sólarljóð's' tale before.

Mss: **166b[x]**(48v), 214[x](152v), 10575[x](11v), 2797[x](238). — *Readings*: [2] draumi: í draumi 10575[x], 2797[x]; kvadd: í kvatt 214[x]   [3] sázt: sátt 10575[x], 2797[x]   [5] skapaðr: of skapaðr 10575[x], 2797[x]   [6] hefði heyrt: heyrði 214[x], 10575[x], 2797[x].

Editions: Skj Anonyme digte og vers [XII], G [6]. *Sólarljóð* 83: AI, 640; Bugge 1867, 370, Njörður Njarðvík 1993, 89.

Notes: [All]: This st. occurs in 32 mss though eds have usually rejected it as a later addition. Certainly it adds nothing to st. 82, but as Bugge observes, this is not an adequate reason for deleting it. It imposes on the poem the dream-framework common in literary and in later medieval visions (Dinzelbacher 1981, 229-65).

Anonymous, *Hugsvinnsmál*

Edited by Tarrin Wills and Stefanie Würth

Introduction

Hugsvinnsmál ('Sayings of the Wise-minded One', Anon *Hsv*) is an anonymous translation of the *Dicta* or *Disticha Catonis*, a Lat. didactic poem from the C2nd or C3rd AD. The title of the poem is mentioned in the last st. In Lbs 1199 4^{ox} (1199^x) the poem has the title *Hugsvinnsmál: harðla nýtsöm* 'Hugsvinnsmál: very useful'. The Icel. title indicates that the Lat. *Catonis* ('of Cato') must have been thought to derive from the adj. *catus* 'clear-sighted, intelligent'. *Hsv* belongs to so-called gnomic or wisdom literature, and it shares the eddic *ljóðaháttr* metre with other didactic poems including, among others, large parts of *Hávm*.

Hsv is one of very few ON-Icel. translations in verse. It is presented as a conversation between father and son and is a rather free adaptation of the *disticha* as well as of the prose passages in the Lat. original. *Hsv* has been dated to the C13th on the basis of its metre, style and vocabulary (Tuvestrand 1977, 12-13). It is difficult to determine the exact dating, but for the purposes of normalisation, the text is presumed here to be from the second half of the C13th. The *First Grammatical Treatise*, written in the mid-C12th, quotes one of the Lat. *Disticha* with a translation (*FGT* 1972, 228-9), but its wording does not correspond to that of mss of the complete *Hsv*. Thus it cannot be concluded that there already existed a complete ON-Icel. translation of the *Disticha Catonis* at this time.

During the Middle Ages the *Disticha* were very popular. The text was widely used as a school book and translated into many European languages. The poem begins with an *epistula* in which the father gives reasons for the work's composition. The *epistula* also includes 55 *breves sententiae* 'brief opinions', hortatory commands such as 'love your parents' or 'do not drink too much wine'. These *sententiae* may have been added to the text in Carolingian times. The introduction is followed by four books with approximately 140 gnomic rules for a good life, each book beginning with a prose introduction. These books are written in two-line hexameters, i.e. the so-called *disticha*. All parts of the *Disticha*, including the prose and the *breves sententiae*, are rendered in the *ljóðaháttr* metre in *Hsv*. There are some lacunae and adjustments to the order, including the use of the prefaces to books III and IV at the end of the poem.

Much of the advice given in the *disticha* often represents basic rules of human behaviour. Therefore in many cases it remains uncertain whether similar rules in vernacular languages can be traced back to their influence. Many problems connected to the Lat. text are still unsolved. The identity of the Cato of the title is uncertain as well as the dating of the different text layers. We do not know how many distichs belong to the original collection nor how many were added during transmission. As a school book the *Disticha* were very often copied, glossed and translated. Many classical and medieval texts allude to the *Disticha* or quote from them. Since the largest part of the work was composed in pre-Christian times, it was often commented upon and interpreted from a Christian point of view in medieval mss (see Schiesaro 1996).

The transmission of *Hsv* is complex. It is preserved in at least forty-four mss, three of them containing more then one version. At least twenty-three mss preserve the complete text. Most mss are paper and written in the C18th and C19th. The oldest nearly-complete extant version was written in the C15th (AM 624 4°). Lbs 1199 4°ˣ (1199ˣ, late C17th) represents a text of the whole poem. Related to it are AM 720 a IV 4° (720a IV, C16th), preserving sts 13-25, 111-19, 123, 130, 138, 143 and 147) and AM 723 a 4°ˣ (723aˣ, C17th), preserving sixty-eight sts. Another, possibly older group is represented by JS 401 4°ˣ (401ˣ, C18th), preserving most of sts 20-58; and AM 696 XV 4° (696XV, c. 1500), which preserves thirty-four sts in the first part of the poem. This last ms., while important in the stemma and relatively old, is a poorly-preserved fragment of a leaf and is missing the ends of most ms. lines. Since the dating of the individual mss is quite often very difficult, a stemma can be most reliably established according to internal criteria. There are two main versions of the poem, neither of them identical with the presumed archetype. Tuvestrand 1977 provides the most comprehensive treatment of the mss and their transmission. In agreement with previous eds she established a stemma with two branches. The following is a modified version:

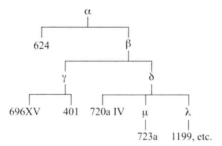

In several passages the two versions differ considerably, and comparison with the Lat. text does not help to answer the question of which version is closer to the original, or even if there was a single original. Concerning the order of the distichs, however, the first version is usually closer to the Lat. text. In cases where the two versions have a completely different text, comparison with the Lat. text reveals that both versions represent equally good translations. Tuvestrand suggests that the translator may have made several translations, and therefore she thinks it is impossible to assume an archetype. According to her the oral transmission of *Hsv* also has to be taken into account. For this reason she decided to give both versions in her edn.

Skj A's text is based on the oldest ms. of the first version, AM 624 4° (624). However, *Skj* B departs so significantly and routinely from 624's readings that it has to be considered as an edn of the second version. Because the second version is generally more metrically sound and apparently less corrupt, it is also used as the basis of the present edn. The present edn takes a selection of mss representative of the two main versions. 1199ˣ represents the best ms. of the second version which preserves the text in full, and is used as the basis of this edn. Also included in the apparatus are 720a IV, 723a^x, 401^x, 696XV. Finally, readings from 624 are also included in the apparatus as the only independent witness to the first version. In addition, readings are occasionally taken from Hallgrímur Scheving's edn of the poem (1831), although these are marked as emendations when there is no other evidence. Hallgrímur Scheving appears to have had access to a now-lost ms., but it is difficult to establish the textual status of his edn because he may have emended the text himself (cf. Tuvestrand 1977, 58). The readings in his edn, however, are very close to those in 1199^x. In addition to these eds, the main contributions to the editing of *Hsv* are by Konráð Gíslason (1860) and Hugo Gering (1907). There are also brief notes to the poem by 'J. S. H.' in Halldór Hermannsson 1958, 81-3.

All mss coincide in the order of the sts (where recorded) up to st. 51. The order of sts in the present edn largely follows that of 1199^x, but a number of modifications have been made on the basis of other mss to bring the order closer to that of the Lat.

The language of the Lat. poem is simple and clear, but the syntax sometimes seems to be rather monotonous, which may be related to limited possibilities for variation within the Lat. hexameters. For this reason the *Disticha* are easily comprehensible and were therefore very popular in the classroom. For a long time there was only one known tradition of the *Disticha Catonis*, called the vulgate version. Since *Hsv* only contains *Disticha* that are also found in this vulgate version of the Lat. text, its exemplar must have belonged to this version. *Hsv* is also composed in a very simple style with an easily comprehensible and not very large vocabulary. But since it renders the Lat. text very freely or rather paraphrases it, it might not have been intended as a translation aid for school children. The Icel. poem uses the eddic metre *ljóðaháttr* throughout as an equivalent of the hexameter of the Lat. poem. *Ljóðaháttr* was the metre typically used for vernacular gnomic poetry during the Middle Ages. As in other vernacular versions of the *Disticha* there is a strong Christian influence in *Hsv*. Because of parallels in content and phrasing, a close connection between *Sól* and *Hsv* has been suggested. It is striking that most of these parallels can be found in mss of the second version of *Hsv*. Therefore they might be related to the revision of the poem by a later redactor. In addition a relationship between *Hsv* and the *ljóðaháttr* parts of *Hávm* has been pointed out, although there is still ongoing discussion concerning the direction of the influence (cf. von See 1972 and Hermann Pálsson 1985). It may, however, be wrong to suggest only one direction of influence. The many and rather late mss of *Hsv* indicate the enduring popularity of the poem. It is interesting that the metre is more regular in the second version of *Hsv*. There may have been a long process of revision with influence from poems originally younger than *Hsv* and which in former times had themselves been influenced by *Hsv* or even directly by the Lat. *Disticha*.

In the C17th the Lat. poem was again translated into Icel. by Jón Bjarnason (d. 1635) and by Bjarni Gizurarson (c. 1621-1712), but the latter translation only contains the first two books of the *Disticha Catonis*. Halldór Hermannsson 1958 contains an edn of Jón Bjarnason's translation.

The editorial practice here follows the general principles, and those specifically for *ljóðaháttr*, outlined in the Introduction to this volume. In particular, the present edn uses ms. readings which produce alliteration according to the rules of *ljóðaháttr*, and readings are prefered which conform to the specific metrical rules for *ljóðaháttr*. However, the present edn does not emend on metrical grounds where no ms. evidence exists. Lines that do not conform to the metrical rules are discussed in the Notes. All mss of the poem use post-1300 orthography, (such as *ie* for *é* and often interchangeable *i* and *y*) but are silently changed here to c. 1250-1300 norms. There is considerable variation between mss in their use of pre- and post-1300 syntax (such as the omission of *at* and the relative particle *er* (e.g. st. 25/2), which are taken here to be post-1300), but these are silently normalised on the basis of the C13th dating.

Kari Ellen Gade has provided extensive advice on the text, including a number of notes. The text of the Lat. *Disticha* included here is from Marcus Boas 1952 and the present English translation is of the Boas text. Other accessible English translations of the Lat., text such as the Loeb (Goold 1982) and the electronic text on the Labyrinth website <www.georgetown.edu/labyrinth> are based on different versions of the Lat.

1. Heyri seggir,   þeir er vilja at sið lifa
    ok góð verk gera,
    horsklig ráð,   þau er heiðinn maðr
    kendi sínum syni.

Seggir, þeir er vilja lifa at sið ok gera góð verk, heyri horsklig ráð, þau er heiðinn maðr kendi syni sínum.

Men who want to live with good conduct and do good works should listen to the wise advice that a heathen man taught his son.

Mss: **1199**[x](72r), 624(140). — *Readings*: [1] Heyri: Hlýði 624 [2] er: *so* 624, eð 1199[x]; sið: lið 624; lifa: lifi 624 [3] gera: geri 624 [6] sínum syni: *so* 624, syni sínum 1199[x].

Editions: *Skj* Anonyme digte og vers [XIII], [C. E/5]. *Hugsvinnsmál* 1: AII, 167-8, BII, 185, *Skald* II, 96; Hallgrímur Scheving 1831, 7, Konráð Gíslason 1860, 549, Gering 1907, 1, Tuvestrand 1977, 71, Hermann Pálsson 1985, 24.

Notes: [All]: Lat. parallel: (*Epistula*) *Cum animadverterem quam plurimos graviter in via morum errare, succurrendum opinioni eorum et consulendum famae existimavi, maxime ut gloriose viverent et honorem contingerent* 'Since I am aware of how very many people go seriously astray in the path of morals, I thought I should come to the aid of their understanding and take their reputations into account, so that they might live with greatest glory and obtain honour'. The st. translates the first part of the introductory letter (*Epistula*) preceding the Lat. poem. — [4] *ráð* 'advice': Lit. pl.: 'pieces of advice'. *Ráð* is usually used in the pl. but translated here and elsewhere in the sg. — [6] *syni sínum* 'his son': The 624 reading of l. 6 is more correct in *ljóðaháttr*, since long-stemmed disyllabic words are generally avoided in the final two positions.

2. Ástsamlig ráð   kenni ek þér, minn einkason;
   mun þú þau eptir öll;
   gálauss þú verðr,   ef þú gleyma vilt,
   því er þarf horskr at hafa.

Ek kenni þér, einkason minn, ástsamlig ráð; mun þú þau öll eptir; þú verðr gálauss, ef þú vilt gleyma, því er horskr þarf at hafa.

I will teach you, my only son, loving advice; remember all of it; you will be careless if you forget what a wise [man] needs to have.

Mss: **1199**[x](72r), 624(140). — *Reading*: [3] eptir öll: öll eptir 624.

Editions: *Skj* Anonyme digte og vers [XIII], [C. E/5]. *Hugsvinnsmál* 2: AII, 168, BII, 186, *Skald* II, 96-7; Hallgrímur Scheving 1831, 7, Konráð Gíslason 1860, 549, Gering 1907, 1, Tuvestrand 1977, 71, Hermann Pálsson 1985, 25.

Notes: [All]: Lat. parallel: (*Epistula*, cont.) *Nunc te, fili carissime, docebo quo pacto morem animi tui componas. Igitur praecepta mea ita legito ut intellegas. Legere enim et non intellegere neglegere est* 'I will teach you by what agreement you may devise a moral system for your own mind. Therefore read my precepts in such a way that you may understand; to read and not to understand is to disregard them'. This st. translates the second part of the *Epistula*.

3. Þarflátr ok þakklátr   skaltu fyrir þínum guði
   ok vammalauss vera;
   föður ok móður   unn þú fróðhugaðr;
   ræktu þína alla ætt.

Skaltu vera þarflátr ok þakklátr ok vammalauss fyrir guði þínum; unn þú fróðhugaðr föður ok móður; ræktu alla ætt þína.

You must be humble and thankful and unblemished before your God; love your father and mother as a man with intelligence; take care of all your family.

Mss: **1199**[x](72r), 696XV(1r) (l. 6), 624(140). — *Readings*: [2] guði: guði vera 624 [3] vera: lifa 624 [5] unn þú: una 624 [6] ræktu: '[...]' 696XV; ætt: '[...]' 696XV.

Editions: *Skj* Anonyme digte og vers [XIII], [C. E/5]. *Hugsvinnsmál* 3: AII, 168, BII, 186, *Skald* II, 97; Hallgrímur Scheving 1831, 7, Konráð Gíslason 1860, 549, Gering 1907, 1, Tuvestrand 1977, 72, Hermann Pálsson 1985, 25.

Notes: [All]: Lat. parallels: (*sententia* 1) *Deo supplica* 'pray to God'; (*sent*. 2) *parentes ama* 'love your parents'; (*sent*. 3) *cognatos cole* 'respect your kindred'. The sts 3-16 translate the short gnomic sentences (*breves sententiae*), following the *Epistula* in the Lat. text. — [1-3]: These ll. correspond in both content and phrasing to Anon *Sól* 30. Cf. also the phrasing in *Hsv* 21 (*vamma varr* 'free of blemish') and the content of *Hsv* 73. — [3] *vammalauss vera* 'be unblemished': This might have been influenced by *Lok* 53/4-6 (*NK*, 107): *heldr þú hana eina* | *látir með ása sonom* | *vammalausa vera* 'you should admit, among the children of the Æsir, that I alone am blameless' (Larrington 1996, 93).

4. Ef þér góðan grip   gefa hollir vinir,
    eiga þú skalt ok unna allvel;
góðu þú fylg,   en gakk illu frá;
    hvergi þú fyrir ráð rasir.

Ef hollir vinir gefa þér góðan grip, skalt þú eiga ok unna allvel; fylg þú góðu, en gakk frá illu; þú rasir hvergi fyrir ráð.

If loyal friends give you a precious thing, you must own it and enjoy it well; follow good and keep away from evil; by no means rush in headlong.

Mss: **1199**[x](72r), 696XV(1r) (ll. 4-6). — *Reading*: [6] rasir: 'rasa[...]' 696XV.

Editions: *Skj* Anonyme digte og vers [XIII], [C. E/5]. *Hugsvinnsmál* 4: AII, 168, BII, 186, *Skald* II, 97, *NN* §110; Hallgrímur Scheving 1831, 7, Gering 1907, 2, Tuvestrand 1977, 72, Hermann Pálsson 1985, 26.

Notes: [All]: Lat. parallels: (*sent*. 4) *datum serva* 'look after what is given to you'; (*sent*. 6) *cum bonis ambula* 'keep company with good people'; (*sent*. 7) *antequam* † *ne accesseris*. 'do not [go] until called'. — [6]: The last l. of this st. corresponds to an Icel. saying: *Illt er að rasa fyrir ráð fram* 'It is bad to rush in headlong'.

5. Hreinlífr þú vert,   ok hræztu þinn læriföður;
    halt þú heiðsæi.

Vert þú hreinlífr, ok hræztu læriföður þinn; halt þú heiðsæi.

Be pure of life and fear your teacher; preserve your reverence.

Mss: **1199**[x](73v), 624(140). — *Readings*: [2] ok: *om*. 624; hræztu: *so* 624, hræðaz 1199[x] [3] heiðsæi: *so* 624, eiðsæri 1199[x].

Editions: *Skj* Anonyme digte og vers [XIII], [C. E/5]. *Hugsvinnsmál* 5: AII, 168, BII, 186, *Skald* II, 97, *NN* §3266B Anm.; Gering 1907, 2, Tuvestrand 1977, 73, Hermann Pálsson 1985, 27.

Notes: [All]: Lat. parallels: (*sent*. 8) *mundus esto* 'keep neat'; (*sent*. 11) *magistratum metue* 'fear a magistrate'; (*sent*. 12) *verecundiam serva* 'preserve modesty'. This st. occurs after st. 65 in

1199ˣ, very much out of the order of the *disticha*. — [3] *heiðsæi* 'reverence': 1199ˣ's *eiðsæri* 'oath-swearing' does not provide alliteration and is further from the Lat. *verecundiam* 'modesty'.

6.   Bragna hvern,   er þú á brautu finnr,
       kveð þú hann kunnliga;
    ófróðr er sá,   er einskis spyrr,
      ef finnr at máli mann.

Hvern bragna, er þú finnr á brautu, kveð þú hann kunnliga; sá, er einskis spyrr, er ófróðr, ef finnr mann at máli.

Each man whom you meet on the road, greet him intimately; he who does not ask is unwise, if he finds a man to talk to.

Mss: **1199ˣ**(72r), 696XV(1r) (ll. 2-6), 624(140) (ll. 1-5). — *Readings*: [2] er þú á: '[...]' 696XV; brautu: braut 624   [3] kunnliga: kunnliga ok góðum orðum 624   [4] ófróðr: þvíat ófróðr 624; er: þykkir 696XV   [5] er: sem 624; einskis spyrr: 'ein[...]' 696XV   [6] ef finnr: '[...]' 696XV.

Editions: *Skj* Anonyme digte og vers [XIII], [C. E/5]. *Hugsvinnsmál* 6: AII, 168, BII, 186, *Skald* II, 97; Hallgrímur Scheving 1831, 7, Gering 1907, 2, Tuvestrand 1977, 73, Hermann Pálsson 1985, 27.

Notes: [All]: Lat. parallel: (*sent*. 9) *saluta libenter* 'greet willingly'. The idea that one should talk to other people and ask them for news is also expressed in some sts of *Hávm*. Cf. *Hávm* 63 (*NK*, 27): *Fregna oc segia | scal fróðra hverr, | sás vill heitinn horskr* 'Asking questions and answering, this every wise man should do, he who wants to be reputed intelligent' (Larrington 1996, 22). Cf. also *Hávm* 28 (*NK*, 21): *Fróðr sá þycciz, | es fregna kann, | oc segia hit sama* 'Wise that man seems who knows how to question and how to answer as well' (Larrington 1996, 18). — [All]: The version in 624 reads: *Bragna hvern, | er þú á braut finnr, | kveð þú hann kunnliga | ok góðum orðum, | þvíat ófróðr er sá, | sem einskis spyrr* 'Greet intimately and with friendly words every man you meet on the road, because he who does not ask is unwise'. The additional l., however, lacks alliteration.

7.   Afli deila   þú skalt aldrigi
       þér við máttugra mann;
    athuga öflgann   skaltu við alt hafa,
      ok ræk þín hús ok hjú.

Þú skalt aldrigi deila þér afli við máttugra mann; skaltu hafa öflgann athuga við alt, ok ræk þín hús ok hjú.

You must never test your strength with a mightier man; you must have strengthened attention for everything, and take care of your house and household.

Mss: **1199**^x(72r), 696XV(1r), 624(140). — *Readings*: [1, 2] deila þú: *so* 624, þú deila 1199^x, deila 696XV   [2] aldrigi: '[...]' 696XV   [3] þér við: *so* 696XV, 624, '[...]' 1199^x;   máttugra mann: meiri menn 624   [4] athuga: athafa 624;   öflgann: 'aulfgan' 696XV, 'afgan' 624   [6] ok ræk þín hús: '[...]' 624.

Editions: *Skj* Anonyme digte og vers [XIII], [C. E/5]. *Hugsvinnsmál* 7: AII, 169, BII, 186, *Skald* II, 97; Hallgrímur Scheving 1831, 8, Gering 1907, 2, Tuvestrand 1977, 74, Hermann Pálsson 1985, 28.

Notes: [All]: Lat. parallels: (*sent.* 10) *maiori concede* 'give way to your superior'; (*sent.* 14) *diligentiam adhibe* 'practise diligence'; (*sent.* 15) *familiam cura* 'take care of your household'.

8. Blíðmæltr vera skalt   við bragna lið,
      ok hirð þitt fengit fé;
    minni ok mannvit   nem þú á margan veg,
      ok kenn þat síðan sonum.

Blíðmæltr skalt vera við lið bragna, ok hirð fengit fé þitt; nem þú á margan veg minni ok mannvit, ok kenn þat síðan sonum.

You must be affably spoken with a company of men, and take care of the money you have gained; learn in many a way memory and understanding, and teach it later to your sons.

Mss: **1199**^x(72r), 696XV(1r), 624(140). — *Readings*: [1] vera: þú 624; skalt: *so* 624, skaltu 1199^x, 696XV   [3] ok hirð: 'h[...]' 696XV, hirtu 624; þitt fengit: '[...]' 696XV   [4] ok: þat síða finnz 624   [5] nem: nema 624;   margan veg: marga vega 696XV, 624   [6] ok kenn þat síðan sonum: 'og kenn þad si[...]' 696XV, kennir 624.

Editions: *Skj* Anonyme digte og vers [XIII], [C. E/5]. *Hugsvinnsmál* 8: AII, 169, BII, 187, *Skald* II, 97; Hallgrímur Scheving 1831, 8, Gering 1907, 2-3, Tuvestrand 1977, 74, Hermann Pálsson 1985, 29.

Notes: [All]: Lat. parallels: (*sent.* 29) *blandus esto* 'be pleasant'; (*sent.* 13) *rem tuam custodi* 'look after your property'; (*sent.* 27) *quae legeris memento* 'remember what you read'; (*sent.* 28) *liberos erudi* 'teach your children'.

9. Hatri þú hafna,   ok hlæ þú at öngum;
      gjalt gjöf við gjöf;
    vakr þú vera skalt,   ok ver nær staddr
      lýða lögskilum.

Hafna þú hatri, ok hlæ þú at öngum; gjalt gjöf við gjöf; þú skalt vera vakr, ok ver nær staddr lögskilum lýða.

Abandon hatred and laugh at no-one; repay a gift with a gift; you must be alert and be situated near people's legal proceedings.

Mss: **1199ˣ**(72r), 696XV(1r), 624(140). — *Readings*: [2] ok: *om*. 696XV, 624; hlæ: hlægi 624; þú: *so* 696XV, eigi 1199ˣ, þú eigi 624; at öngum: í manngi 624 [3] gjalt: gjaltu 696XV, 624; við gjöf: '[...]' 696XV [4] vakr þú: '[...]' 696XV; vera skalt: '[...] skaltv' 696XV, þú vert 624 [5] ok ver: ok vera 696XV, vertu 624; staddr: 'sta[...]ur' 696XV, *om*. 624.

Editions: *Skj* Anonyme digte og vers [XIII], [C. E/5]. *Hugsvinnsmál* 9: AII, 169, BII, 187, *Skald* II, 97, *NN* §3266B Anm.; Hallgrímur Scheving 1831, 8, Gering 1907, 3, Tuvestrand 1977, 75, Hermann Pálsson 1985, 29-30.

Notes: [All]: Lat. parallels: (*sent.* 30) *irascere ob rem* [*noli*] '[do not] get angry for no reason'; (*sent.* 31) *neminem riseris* 'do not laugh at anybody'; (*sent.* 16) *mutuum da* 'make a loan'; (*sent.* 19) *quod satis est dormi* 'sleep a sufficiency'; (*sent.* 32) *in iudicium adesto* 'stand by [a friend] in court'; (*sent.* 33) *ad praetorium stato* 'keep in good standing at the praetor's residence'.

10. Sjaldan þú sitja   skalt sumblum at,
     ok drekk varliga vín;
  eiginkonu þinni   þú skalt unna vel;
     hyggðu fyrir hverri gjöf.

Þú skalt sjaldan sitja at sumblum, ok drekk varliga vín; þú skalt vel unna eiginkonu þinni; hyggðu fyrir hverri gjöf.

You must seldom attend banquets, and drink wine cautiously; you must love your wife dearly; take heed of every gift.

Mss: **1199ˣ**(72r), 696XV(1r), 624(140). — *Readings*: [1] Sjaldan þú: 'Si[...]' 696XV [1, 2] sitja skalt: '[...]' 696XV, skalt sitja 624 [2] sumblum: 'sablvm' 696XV [3] ok drekk: drekk 696XV, drekktu 624; vín: '[...]' 696XV [5] þú skalt unna: 'skaltu [...]' 696XV, unna skaltu 624 [6] hyggðu: '[...] þu' 696XV.

Editions: *Skj* Anonyme digte og vers [XIII], [C. E/5]. *Hugsvinnsmál* 10: AII, 169, BII, 187, *Skald* II, 97; Hallgrímur Scheving 1831, 8, Gering 1907, 3, Tuvestrand 1977, 75, Hermann Pálsson 1985, 30.

Notes: [All]: Lat. parallels: (*sent.* 18) *Conviva raro* 'attend banquets rarely'; (*sent.* 22) *vino tempera* 'do not drink too much wine'; (*sent.* 20) *coniugem ama* 'love your wife'; (*sent.* 17) *cui des videto* 'think carefully about the person to whom you should give'.

11. Oddi ok eggju   ver þú þína óðaljörð,
    ok eigi auðtryggr ver;
fyrir orðum ok eiðum   hyggðu öllum vel,
    ok halt við fyrða heit.

Ver þú óðaljörð þína oddi ok eggju, ok ver eigi auðtryggr; hyggðu vel fyrir öllum orðum ok eiðum, ok halt heit við fyrða.

Defend your native land with point and edge and do not be credulous; think well about all your words and oaths and keep promises to people.

Mss: **1199ˣ**(72r), 696XV(1r), 624(140). — *Readings*: [1] ok eggju: '[...]iu' 696XV [2] óðaljörð: 'odo[...]' 696XV [3] ok eigi: '[...]' 696XV, eigi þú 624; auðtryggr ver: *so* 624, á tryggðar veg 1199ˣ, '[...] ud tryggur uert' 696XV [4] ok eiðum: '[...]d[...]' 696XV, ok orðum 624 [5] vel: 'u[...]' 696XV [6] ok halt við fyrða heit: '[...]it víd fyrda' 696XV, haltu þín heit við fira 624.

Editions: *Skj* Anonyme digte og vers [XIII], [C. E/5]. *Hugsvinnsmál* 11: AII, 170, BII, 187, *Skald* II, 97; Hallgrímur Scheving 1831, 8, Gering 1907, 3, Tuvestrand 1977, 76, Hermann Pálsson 1985, 31.

Notes: [All]: Lat. parallels: (*sent*. 21) *iusiurandum serva* 'keep your oath'; (*sent*. 23) *pugna pro patria* 'fight for your native land'; (*sent*. 24) *nihil temere credideris* 'believe nothing without consideration'. In 624, the order of the two halves is reversed. — [2] *óðaljörð* 'native land': In Norw. this would mean 'allodial estate', but the Icel. sense (where the Norw. *óðal* system was not applied) is closer to the Lat. — [6] *ok halt heit við fyrða* 'and keep promises to people': Most eds adopt 624's *haltu þín heit við fira*, which has the same sense.

12. Bækr ok rúnir   kenn þú blíðliga;
    ger þú við góða vel;
illra kvenna   firr þú þik öllu lagi,
    ok ráð hverjum heilt.

Kenn þú blíðliga bækr ok rúnir, ger þú vel við góða; firr þú þik öllu lagi illra kvenna, ok ráð hverjum heilt.

Teach with kindness books and runes; treat the good well; keep away from bad women by all means, and give everybody good advice.

Mss: **1199ˣ**(72r), 696XV(1r), 624(140). — *Readings*: [2] kenn: nem 696XV, 624; blíðliga: 'blid[...]' 696XV [3] ger þú við: '[...]' 696XV; góða: góðan 696XV [4] illra: *om*. 624 [5] lagi: samlagi 696XV [6] ok ráð hverjum: '[...]' 696XV.

Editions: *Skj* Anonyme digte og vers [XIII], [C. E/5]. *Hugsvinnsmál* 12: AII, 170, BII, 187, *Skald* II, 97; Hallgrímur Scheving 1831, 8, Gering 1907, 4, Tuvestrand 1977, 76, Hermann Pálsson 1985, 31.

Notes: [All]: Lat. parallels: (*sent*. 26) *libros lege* 'read books'; (*sent*. 38) *litteras disce* 'study literature'; (*sent*. 39) *bono benefacito* 'do good to a good man'; (*sent*. 25) *meretricem fuge* 'avoid a prostitute'; (sent 40) *tute consule* 'give safe advice'. Two mss have *nem* 'learn' (l. 2) (so *Skj* B and *Skald*), and the Lat. parallels have more to do with learning than teaching. The importance of education is also mentioned in *Sól* 49. *Hávm* 118/3 parallels the *illra kvenna* of 1199^x (*NK*, 36). — [1] *rúnir* 'runes': The word is used widely as a metonymic expression for reading and writing, but in this context probably has a more specific meaning.

13. Ráðhollr ok réttdæmr   ok í reiði stiltr,
    mæltu eigi við ýta ilt;
  kostum þú safna,   ok kynn þik við góða menn;
    vinn eigi löst né lygi.

Ráðhollr ok réttdæmr ok stiltr í reiði, mæltu eigi ilt við ýta; safna þú kostum, ok kynn þik við góða menn; vinn eigi löst né lygi.

Loyal in advice and just in judgement and moderate in anger, do not speak evil to men; gather virtues and make friends with good men; cultivate neither vices nor lies.

Mss: **1199^x**(72r), 720a IV(1r), 696XV(1r), 624(140-1). — *Readings*:   [1] réttdæmr: *so* 624, réttdæmr vertu 1199^x, 720a IV, þú ver 696XV   [2] ok í reiði stiltr: 'þu uer ok reí[...]' 696XV   [3] eigi við: við eigi 696XV   [5] ok: *om*. 720a IV, 696XV;   kynn þik við góða: 'k[...]' 696XV; menn: til 624   [6] vinn: vinn þú 720a IV, 696XV, 624; lygi: *om*. 624.

Editions: *Skj* Anonyme digte og vers [XIII], [C. E/5]. *Hugsvinnsmál* 13: AII, 170, BII, 187, *Skald* II, 98; Hallgrímur Scheving 1831, 8, Gering 1907, 4, Tuvestrand 1977, 77, Hermann Pálsson 1985, 32-3.

Notes: [All]: Lat. parallels: (*sent*. 43) *aequum iudica* 'judge fairly'; (*sent*. 45) *iracundiam rege* 'control your anger'; (*sent*. 41) *maledicus ne esto* 'do not be abusive'; (*sent*. 42) *existimationem retine* 'hold on to your reputation'; (*sent*. 35) *virtute utere* 'practise virtue'; (*sent*. 44) *nihil mentire* 'do not lie'.

14. Ókunna menn   né ölmosur
     skaltu eigi at hlátri hafa,
þótt fornmannligir   fyrðar sé;
þolinmóðr þú vert,   ok bregð eigi af þeim lögum,
     sem sjálfr settir þú.

Skaltu eigi hafa ókunna menn né ölmosur at hlátri, þótt sé fornmannligir fyrðar; vert þú þolinmóðr, ok bregð eigi af þeim lögum, sem þú settir sjálfr.

You must not make a laughing stock of unknown men or beggars, even though they are old-fashioned men; be patient and do not break the rules that you yourself made.

Mss: **1199ˣ**(72r), 720a IV(1r), 696XV(1r), 624(141). — *Readings*: [1] Ókunna menn: 'ogaufg[...]' 696XV, Ógöfgann mann 624   [2] né: *so* 624, ok 1199ˣ, '[...]' 696XV; ölmosur: '[...]osur' 696XV   [4] fornmannligir: fornmannligi 720a IV, fornmálugir 624   [4-5]: *om.* 696XV   [6] þú vert: 'þ[...]lid' 696XV   [7] ok bregð: bregð þú 720a IV, 624; þeim lögum: lögum þeim 720a IV, 624   [8] sem: er 720a IV; sjálfr settir þú: *so* 720a IV, 624, þú sjálfr settir 1199ˣ, 'þu setur si[...]' 696XV.

Editions: *Skj* Anonyme digte og vers [XIII], [C. E/5]. *Hugsvinnsmál* 14: AII, 170-1, BII, 188, *Skald* II, 98; Hallgrímur Scheving 1831, 9, Gering 1907, 4, Tuvestrand 1977, 78, Hermann Pálsson 1985, 33.

Notes: [All]: Lat. parallels: (*sent.* 47) *minorem ne contempseris* 'do not despise your inferior'; (*sent.* 52) *miserum noli inridere* 'do not ridicule the poor'; (*sent.* 46 variant) *patienter vince minorem necque contempseris* 'with patience overcome an inferior but do not despise [him]'; (*sent.* 49) *patere legem quam ipse tuleris* 'keep the law you made yourself. — [1] *ókunna menn* 'unknown men': 624's *ógöfgan mann* 'un-noble man, commoner', is closer to the Lat. text. — [4-8]: The st. has eight ll. rather than the normal six, and no ms. version of ll. 4-5 corresponds with the Lat. text. Finnur Jónsson (*Skj* B) removes these ll. and renders the remaining three: *þolinmóðr ver,* | *bregðat af þeim lǫgum,* | *er þú settir sjálfr* 'be patient, do not break the rules you yourself made'.

15. Af afli þínu   vertu óhræsinn,
     ok launa þú góðu gott;
annars eign   girnztu aldrigi;
     unn, þeim er elskar þik.

Vertu óhræsinn af afli þínu, ok launa þú góðu gott; girnztu aldrigi annars eign; unn, þeim er elskar þik.

Do not be boastful about your strength, and return good with good; never desire somebody else's property; love the one who loves you.

Mss: **1199ˣ**(72r), 720a IV(1r), 696XV(1r), 624(141). — *Readings*: [1] Af afli: '[...]li' 696XV [2] vertu: *so* 720a IV, 696XV, 624, vera skaltu 1199ˣ; óhræsinn: eigi hræsinn 720a IV [3-6]: 'þo at þu hafer megn[...]þ jafnt ueiter þad e[...] miog hæl[...]z og er [...]' 696XV; ok: *om.* 720a IV, 624 [4] annars: á annars 720a IV [6] unn: unn þú 720a IV, 624.

Editions: *Skj* Anonyme digte og vers [XIII], [C. E/5]. *Hugsvinnsmál* 15: AII, 171, BII, 188, *Skald* II, 98, *NN* §3266B Anm.; Hallgrímur Scheving 1831, 9, Gering 1907, 4-5, Tuvestrand 1977, 79, Hermann Pálsson 1985, 34.

Notes: [All]: Lat. parallels: (*sent.* 48) *nihil arbitrio virium feceris* 'do not do anything with the authority of force'; (*sent.* 50) *benefici accepti esto memor* 'remember a benefit [you have] received'; (*sent.* 54) *alienum noli concupiscere* 'do not covet what belongs to someone else'; (*sent.* 56) *libenter amorem ferto* 'show affection freely'.

16. Fámálugr þú vert,   er með fyrðum kemr
    ok at sumblum sitr;
  annan fýsa   skaltu eigi illra hluta;
  mæl þú gott ok ger.

Vert þú fámálugr, er kemr með fyrðum ok sitr at sumblum; skaltu eigi fýsa annan illra hluta; mæl þú ok ger gott.

Be reticent when you come among men and sit at banquets; you must not encourage another [to do] bad things; speak and do good.

Mss: **1199ˣ**(72r), 720a IV(1r), 723aˣ(77) (l. 6), 696XV(1r), 624(141). — *Readings*: [1] Fámálugr: '[...]' 696XV; vert: ver 696XV [2] er: er þú 624 [3] sumblum: sumlu 720a IV, samkundum 696XV, samkundu 624; sitr: 'sit[...]' 696XV [4] annan fýsa: '[...]ann [...]' 696XV [5] skaltu: þú skaltu 720a IV, '[...]' 696XV [6] mæl: '[...]' 723aˣ, annaz 624.

Editions: *Skj* Anonyme digte og vers [XIII], [C. E/5]. *Hugsvinnsmál* 16: AII, 171, BII, 188, *Skald* II, 98, *NN* §3266B Anm.; Hallgrímur Scheving 1831, 9, Gering 1907, 5, Tuvestrand 1977, 79, Hermann Pálsson 1985, 35.

Notes: [All]: Lat. parallels: (*sent.* 51) *pauca in convivio loquere* 'say few words at a banquet'; (*sent.* 55) *illud adgredere quod iustum est* 'undertake what is rightful'. A similar topic is dealt with in *Hsv* 104. In ON-Icel. literature it seems to have been common advice to be cautious among strangers and to listen carefully before speaking oneself. Cf. for instance *Hávm* 27 and *Sól* 19. — [6] *mæl* 'speak': The main ms. reading does not correspond to the Lat. text, whereas the reading of 624 (*annaz* 'concern yourself with, take care of') is closer to the Lat.

17. Allra ráða   tel ek þat einna bezt
       at göfga æztan guð;
    með hreinu hjarta   skaltu á hann trúa
       ok elska af öllum hug.

Ek tel þat einna bezt allra ráða at göfga æztan guð; skaltu trúa á hann með hreinu hjarta ok elska af öllum hug.

I consider this the best of all advice to worship the highest God; you must believe in him with a pure heart and love him with all your mind.

Mss: **1199**[x](72r), 720a IV(1r), 723a[x](77), 624(141). — *Readings*:   [2] einna bezt: *so* 723a[x], bezt vera 1199[x], 624, bezt 720a IV   [4] með hreinu hjarta: þú 624   [5] skaltu: skalt 624   [6] ok: *om.* 723a[x]; af: '[...]' 723a[x].

Editions: *Skj* Anonyme digte og vers [XIII], [C. E/5]. *Hugsvinnsmál* 17: AII, 171, BII, 188, *Skald* II, 98; Hallgrímur Scheving 1831, 9, Konráð Gíslason 1860, 549, Gering 1907, 5, Tuvestrand 1977, 80, Hermann Pálsson 1985, 35.

Notes: [All]: Lat. parallel: (*Dist.* I, 1) *Si deus est animus nobis ut carmina dicunt, / hic tibi praecipue sit pura mente colendus* 'If God is a spirit, as songs tell us, he is to be worshipped by you above all with a pure mind'. With this st. the translation of the *Disticha* proper starts. — [2]: This l. lacks alliteration in mss other than 723a[x], so *Skj* B and *Skald* adopt the reading *einna bezt*, as here. — [4] *með hreinu hjarta* 'with a pure heart': This reading, missing from 624, might have been influenced by *Sól* 3. *Unna af öllum hug* (or *allz hugar*) is found in eddic poetry esp. denoting the love of a woman for a man: cf. *Grp* 32/7-8; *HHund* II, 15/1-2, etc.

18. Ofsvefni tæla   láttu þik aldrigi;
       kosta vakr at vera;
    leti ok lasta   verðr, þeim er lengi sefr,
       auðit iðugliga.

Láttu þik aldrigi tæla ofsvefni; kosta at vera vakr; verðr leti ok lasta iðugliga auðit, þeim er lengi sefr.

Never let too much sleepiness entice you; try to stay awake; laziness and vices frequently fall to the lot of the one who sleeps for a long time.

Mss: **1199**[x](72r), 720a IV(1r), 723a[x](77), 696XV(1r), 624(141). — *Readings*:   [1] Ofsvefni: ofsefn 723a[x], ofsvefna 624;   tæla: 'tel[...]' 696XV, *om.* 624   [2] láttu þik: '[...]' 696XV; aldrigi: '[...]' 696XV, eigi tæla 624   [3] kosta: kosta þú 720a IV, 696XV, 624;   vera: ver 624   [4] lasta: losta 696XV, 624   [5, 6] er lengi sefr auðit: '[...]' 696XV.

Editions: Skj Anonyme digte og vers [XIII], [C. E/5]. *Hugsvinnsmál* 18: AII, 171, BII, 188, *Skald* II, 98; Hallgrímur Scheving 1831, 10, Konráð Gíslason 1860, 549, Gering 1907, 5, Tuvestrand 1977, 80, Hermann Pálsson 1985, 36.

Notes: [All]: Lat. parallel: (*Dist.* I, 2) *Plus vigila semper nec somno deditus esto; / nam diuturna quies vitiis alimenta ministrat* 'Always keep more alert, nor be given to sleep; for continuous idleness offers food for vice'. The text of 1199[x] is closer than that of 624 to the Lat.; in 624 the whole st. seems corrupt. The advice to be alert is also expressed in *Hsv* 9. Similar advice is also given in *Grp* 29 (*NK*, 168).

19. Ómálugr skal   ok stilla orðum vel,
    sá er vill guðs ást geta;
    æðra krapt   fær maðr aldrigi,
    en hann sé með tungu trúr.

Skal ómálugr ok stilla vel orðum, sá er vill geta ást guðs; maðr fær aldrigi æðra krapt, en hann sé trúr með tungu.

He must [be] close-mouthed and control words well, who wants to gain the love of God; a man never obtains more strength than by being true with his tongue.

Mss: **1199[x]**(72r-v), 720a IV(1r-v), 723a[x](77), 624(141). — *Readings*: [1] skal: skalt þú 720a IV, þú vert 624   [2] stilla orðum: orðum stilla 723a[x], stilt orðum 624   [3] ást: ástar 720a IV, *om*. 723a[x];   geta: *so* 720a IV, 723a[x], 624, gefa 1199[x]   [6] hann sé með: at vera í 720a IV, vera í 723a[x], 624.

Editions: Skj Anonyme digte og vers [XIII], [C. E/5]. *Hugsvinnsmál* 19: AII, 172, BII, 188, *Skald* II, 98; Hallgrímur Scheving 1831, 10, Konráð Gíslason 1860, 549, Gering 1907, 6, Tuvestrand 1977, 81, Hermann Pálsson 1985, 36.

Notes: [All]: Lat. parallel: (*Dist.* I, 3) *Virtutem primam esse puta conpescere linguam; / proximus ille deo est, qui scit ratione tacere* 'I think the first virtue to be curbing your tongue; he is closest to God who knows how to keep quiet properly'. The advice to listen rather than to speak in a circle of strangers is parallelled in *Hsv* 16, but this st. concentrates on discretion as a general virtue. A similar idea is expressed in *Hávm* 103 (cf. *NK*, 33).

20. Ýmisgjarn   vertu aldrigi,
    ok sáttr vertu við sjálfan þik;
    seggjum öngum   verðr samhuga,
    ef hann er sundrþykkr við sik.

Vertu aldrigi ýmisgjarn, ok vertu sáttr við þik sjálfan; verðr samhuga öngum seggjum, ef hann er sundrþykkr við sik.

Never be wayward, and be at peace with yourself; [one] comes to agreement with no-one, if he is not in agreement with himself.

Mss: **1199ˣ**(72v), 720a IV(1v), 723aˣ(77), 696XV(1r), 401ˣ(1r) (ll. 2-6), 624(141).

Readings: [1] Ýmisgjarn: 'Omis giar[...]' 696XV   [3] ok: *om.* 720a IV, 723aˣ, 696XV, 624; sáttr: sæzt 723aˣ;   vertu: *om.* 723aˣ, 401ˣ;   sjálfan þik: '[...]' 696XV   [4] seggjum: við seggja 720a IV, 723aˣ, 'vid [...]' 696XV   [5] verðr: verðr sá 720a IV, 624, verðr manni 696XV, verðr maðr sá 401ˣ;   samhuga: samhugi 401ˣ   [6] ef: er 720a IV, 723aˣ, 'ef hega' 696XV;   hann er: *om.* 723aˣ;   sundrþykkr: sundrþykkiz 723aˣ, 'sund[...]' 696XV;   við sik: '[...]' 696XV, 'við s[...]' 401ˣ, við sjálfan sik 624.

Editions: *Skj* Anonyme digte og vers [XIII], [C. E/5]. *Hugsvinnsmál* 20: AII, 173, BII, 189, *Skald* II, 98, *NN* §3266B Anm.; Hallgrímur Scheving 1831, 10, Konráð Gíslason 1860, 549, Gering 1907, 6, Tuvestrand 1977, 82, Hermann Pálsson 1985, 37.

Notes: [All]: Lat. parallel: (*Dist.* I, 4) *Sperne repugnando tibi tu contrarius esse: / conveniet nulli, qui secum dissidet ipse* 'Strongly avoid being contrary to yourself; he agrees with no one who disagrees with himself'.

21.   Ef at ýta lífi   hyggr þú öllu saman
          ok sér þeira siðu,
      þat þú þá finnr,   er fira reynir:
          fár er vamma varr.

Ef þú hyggr at ýta lífi öllu saman ok sér þeira siðu, þá finnr þú þat, er reynir fira: fár er varr vamma.

If you consider men's life altogether and look at their customs, then you notice that, when you try people: few are free of blemishes.

Mss: **1199ˣ**(72v), 720a IV(1v), 723aˣ(77), 696XV(1r), 401ˣ(1r), 624(141).

Readings: [1] Ef at: '[...]' 696XV; lífi: liði 696XV   [2] öllu saman: allra saman 696XV, vandliga 624   [3] sér: 'si[...]ä' 696XV, sér þú 401ˣ;   þeira siðu: þeira siðu grant 723aˣ, 'siðu þeir[...]' 696XV   [4] þat þú: '[...]' 696XV;   þá: *om.* 720a IV, 723aˣ, 401ˣ, 624, '[...]' 696XV;   finnr: finnr þá 723aˣ, '[...]' 696XV   [5] er: so 696XV, ef 1199ˣ, ef þú 720a IV, þá 723aˣ, þat þú 401ˣ, er þú 624;   fira: so 624, fyrða 1199ˣ, 720a IV, 723aˣ, 696XV, *om.* 401ˣ;   reynir: 'reyne[...]' 401ˣ   [6] fár er: at fáir er 723aˣ, 696XV, at fáir eru 401ˣ, er færri 624;   vamma: vámi 696XV.

Editions: *Skj* Anonyme digte og vers [XIII], [C. E/5]. *Hugsvinnsmál* 21: AII, 172, BII, 189, *Skald* II, 98; Hallgrímur Scheving 1831, 10, Konráð Gíslason 1860, 549, Gering 1907, 6, Tuvestrand 1977, 82, Hermann Pálsson 1985, 38.

Notes: [All]: Lat. parallel: (*Dist.* I, 5) *Si vitam inspicias hominum, si denique mores, / cum culpant alios: nemo sine crimine vivit* 'If you look at the life of those men (and their ways of life) who find fault with others, [you will find that] nobody lives without fault'. — [6] *fár er varr vamma* 'few are free of blemishes': This l. is a variant of a common OIcel. saying. Cf. *Hávm* 22/6 (*NK*, 20): *hann era vamma vanr* 'he is not free of blemishes'.

22. Ef þú eyri átt,   þann er þér ekki stóðar,
         eða þú hlýtr ógagn af,
    gef þú hann burt,   þótt þér góðr þykki;
         mart er fríðara en fé.

Ef þú átt eyri, þann er þér stóðar ekki, eða þú hlýtr ógagn af, gef þú hann burt, þótt þér góðr þykki; mart er fríðara en fé.

If you own money which is not of any use to you or which leads to harm for you, give it away, even though it may seem good to you; much is better than money.

Mss: **1199**[x](72v), 720a IV(1v), 723a[x](77), 696XV(1r), 401[x](1r), 624(141).

Readings: [1-3]: 'Ef [...] ogagn af ecki hann þier storum stodur' 696XV   [2] er: *so* 401[x], *om.* 1199[x], 720a IV, 723a[x], 696XV, 624   [3] þú hlýtr: hlýtr þú 720a IV, hlýtr 723a[x]   [4] gef þú hann burt: gef þú hann á burt 720a IV, gef þú þér góðr 696XV, gef hann í burt 401[x], burt skaltu hann gefa 624   [5] þótt: *so* 720a IV, þó 1199[x], 723a[x], 401[x], þú 696XV, *om.* 624.

Editions: *Skj* Anonyme digte og vers [XIII], [C. E/5]. *Hugsvinnsmál* 22: AII, 172, BII, 189, *Skald* II, 98; Hallgrímur Scheving 1831, 10, Gering 1907, 7, Tuvestrand 1977, 83, Hermann Pálsson 1985, 39.

Notes: [All]: Lat. parallel: (*Dist*. I, 6) *Quae nocitura tenes, quamvis sint cara, relinque: / utilitas opibus praeponi tempore debet* 'Things you have which are harmful, though they are dear, let go; in time, usefulness should be put before wealth'.

23. Blíðr þú vert   en stundum bráðskapaðr,
         ef geraz þarfir þess;
    vel má þat verða   at skipti vitr maðr geði,
         þótt hann lastvarr lifi.

Vert þú blíðr en stundum bráðskapaðr, ef geraz þarfir þess; þat má vel verða, at vitr maðr skipti geði, þótt hann lifi lastvarr.

Be friendly but sometimes of hasty disposition if it becomes necessary; it can well happen, that a wise man becomes angry, although he lives virtuously.

Mss: **1199**[x](72v), 720a IV(1v), 723a[x](77), 401[x](1r), 624(141). — *Readings*: [4] má þat verða: 'ma verd[...]' 401[x], þat þykkir 624   [5] at: þó 624;   skipti vitr maðr: vitr maðr skipti 723a[x], skipti vinr 401[x], skipti vitr 624;   geði: reiði 624   [6] þótt: þó 723a[x], 401[x]; hann: *om.* 723a[x].

Editions: *Skj* Anonyme digte og vers [XIII], [C. E/5]. *Hugsvinnsmál* 23: AII, 173, BII, 189, *Skald* II, 98-9; Hallgrímur Scheving 1831, 10, Gering 1907, 7, Tuvestrand 1977, 83, Hermann Pálsson 1985, 39-40.

Notes: [All]: Lat. parallel: (*Dist.* I, 7) *Clemens et constans, ut res expostulat, esto: | temporibus mores sapiens sine crimine mutat* 'Be constant and kind, as the case demands; the wise man changes his ways without fault as the times require'. — [1]: The advice to be *blíðr* 'affable' or *blíðmæltr* 'affable, bland' is also given in *Hsv* 8 and 90.

24. Konu þinnar   hlýð þú eigi kveinstöfum,
        þótt hon þræla saki;
    opt hon þann hatar,   er þér hollr geriz,
        reyndu, hvat it sanna sé.

Hlýð þú eigi kveinstöfum konu þinnar, þótt hon saki þræla; hon hatar opt þann, er geriz þér hollr; reyndu, hvat it sanna sé.

Do not listen to your wife's complaints, although she may blame the servants; often she hates him who is loyal to you; test out what is the truth.

Mss: **1199ˣ**(72v), 1199ˣ(74v) (ll. 1-2), 720a IV(1v), 723aˣ(77-8), 401ˣ(1r), 624(141). — *Readings*: [1] Konu: 'Kvonar' 401ˣ   [2] hlýð þú eigi kveinstöfum: hlyð eigi kveinstofum 1199ˣ(74v), 723aˣ, 'kveinstofum hlyd[...]' 401ˣ, kveinstöfum þarftu eigi at trúa 624   [3] þótt: *so* 401ˣ, 624, þó 1199ˣ(72v), 723aˣ, þótti 720a IV; þræla: þína þræla 401ˣ; saki: 'sa[...]' 723aˣ, þinna áviti opt 624   [4] opt hon þann: hon þann opt 624   [5] geriz: er 624   [6] it: *so* 720a IV, 723aˣ, 401ˣ, 624, at 1199ˣ(72v).

Editions: *Skj* Anonyme digte og vers [XIII], [C. E/5]. *Hugsvinnsmál* 24: AII, 173, BII, 189, *Skald* II, 99; Hallgrímur Scheving 1831, 11, Gering 1907, 7, Tuvestrand 1977, 84, Hermann Pálsson 1985, 40.

Notes: [All]: Lat. parallel: (*Dist.* I, 8) *Nil temere uxori de servis crede querenti: | semper enim mulier, quem coniux diligit, odit* 'Believe nothing rashly of a wife complaining about the servants; for often a woman hates the one her husband likes'. The last l. has no equivalent in the Lat. text. — [1-3]: The wording of 624 is quite different, although the sense is roughly the same: *Konu þinnar | kveinstöfum þarftu eigi at trúa, | þótt hún þræla þinna áviti opt* 'You need not believe your wife's complaints, although she may often accuse your servants'.

25. Ef þú vin átt,   þann er þér vildr sé,
        fýs þú hann gott at gera;
    orða þinna   þótt hann kunni öngva þökk,
        þó skaltu hann við vammi vara.

Ef þú átt vin, þann er sé þér vildr, fýs þú hann at gera gott; þótt hann kunni öngva þökk orða þinna, skaltu hann þó vara við vammi.

If you have a friend who is agreeable to you, encourage him to do good; although he might be ungrateful for your words, you must nonetheless warn him against wrongdoing.

Mss: **1199**[x](72v), 720a IV(1v) (ll. 1-5), 723a[x](78), 401[x](1r), 624(141). — *Readings*: [2] vildr sé: hollr geriz 624   [4] orða: þó orða 723a[x]   [5] kunni öngva þökk: 'kunne au[...]' 720a IV, öngva þökk kunni 401[x], óþökk kunni 624   [6] þó: *so* 624, þá 1199[x], 723a[x], *om.* 401[x]; skaltu: skalt 723a[x].

Editions: *Skj* Anonyme digte og vers [XIII], [C. E/5]. *Hugsvinnsmál* 25: AII, 173, BII, 189, *Skald* II, 99; Hallgrímur Scheving 1831, 11, Gering 1907, 7, Tuvestrand 1977, 84, Hermann Pálsson 1985, 41.

Notes: [All]: Lat. parallel (*Dist.* I, 9): *Cum moneas aliquem nec se velit ille moneri, / si tibi sit carus, noli desistere coeptis* 'When you warn somebody even though he does not want to be warned, if he is dear to you, do not desist in what you have begun'. — [1-3]: These ll. are parallelled in *Hávm* 44 (*NK*, 24): *Veiztu, ef þú vin átt, | þann er þú vel trúir, | oc vill þú af hánom gott geta...* 'You know, if you've a friend whom you really trust / and from whom you want nothing but good...' (Larrington 1996, 20). The reading *vildr* 'pleasant, agreeable' in 1199[x] may have been influenced by *Hávm* 124/4 (*NK*, 37): *era sá vinr ǫðrom, | er vilt eitt segir* 'he is no true friend who only says pleasant things' (Larrington 1996, 31).

26. Hirtu eigi at senna,   þótt þú satt vitir,
        við hvassorðan hal;
      málskálp mikit   er mörgum gefit;
        fár er at hyggju horskr.

Hirtu eigi at senna við hvassorðan hal, þótt þú vitir satt; mikit málskálp er gefit mörgum; fár er horskr at hyggju.

Take care not to quarrel with a sharp-worded man, even though you may know the truth; great loquacity is granted to many; few are wise in mind.

Mss: **1199**[x](72v), 723a[x](78), 401[x](1r), 624(141). — *Readings*: [1] at senna: *so* 723a[x], at seggja 1199[x], sina 401[x], at sverja 624   [2] þótt: *so* 401[x], þó 1199[x], 723a[x], *om.* 624; vitir: *om.* 624   [3] hal: há 624   [4] málskálp: *so* 401[x], málskap 1199[x], 723a[x], því málskálp 624   [5] er: verðr 723a[x], 401[x]; mörgum: 'm[...]' 401[x]   [6] at: í 401[x], 624.

Editions: *Skj* Anonyme digte og vers [XIII], [C. E/5]. *Hugsvinnsmál* 26: AII, 173, BII, 190, *Skald* II, 99, *NN* §1915; Hallgrímur Scheving 1831, 11, Konráð Gíslason 1860, 550, Gering 1907, 8, Tuvestrand 1977, 85, Hermann Pálsson 1985, 42.

Notes: [All]: Lat. parallel: (*Dist.* I, 10) *Contra verbosos noli contendere verbis: / sermo datur cunctis, animi sapientia paucis* 'Do not exchange words with wordy people; speech is given to all, wisdom of mind to few'. The corresponding st. of the distichs is also cited in *FGT*. There the Lat. text is followed by a translation: *Hirð eigi þú at þræta við málrófsmenn; málróf er gefit mǫrgum, en spekin fám* 'Do not quarrel with loquacious people; loquacity is given to many, but wisdom to few' (*FGT* 1972, 228-9). — [2] The second l. has no equivalent in the Lat. text. — [4] *málskálp* 'loquacity': 624 does not agree with the other mss of the first version but with 401ˣ, which is usually considered as a representative of the second version.

27. Þann dugnað veitt   vinum þínum,
         sem eigi fylgir mein til mikit;
    annars illsku   láttu aldrigi
         standa þér fyrir þrifum.

Veitt vinum þínum þann dugnað, sem eigi fylgir til mikit mein; láttu aldrigi annars illsku standa þér fyrir þrifum.

Give your friends that [kind of] assistance which is not accompanied by too much harm; never let another's ill will stand in the way of your wellbeing.

Mss: **1199ˣ**(72v), 723aˣ(78), 624(141). — *Readings*: [1] dugnað: dugnað þú skalt 624 [2] vinum þínum: þínum vin 723aˣ [3] sem eigi fylgir mein til mikit: so 624, at eigi fylgi mikit mein 1199ˣ, 723aˣ [4] illsku: eigin 624 [5] láttu: girnztu 624 [6] standa: eða lát standa 624.

Editions: *Skj* Anonyme digte og vers [XIII], [C. E/5]. *Hugsvinnsmál* 27: AII, 173-4, BII, 190, *Skald* II, 99; Hallgrímur Scheving 1831, 11, Gering 1907, 8, Tuvestrand 1977, 85, Hermann Pálsson 1985, 43.

Notes: [All]: Lat. parallel: (*Dist*. I, 11) *Dilige sic alios, ut sis tibi carus amicus; / sic bonus esto bonis, ne te mala damna sequantur* 'Love others in such a way that you are a dear friend to yourself; so be good to the good, so that bad losses will not happen to you'. The mutual respect among friends is also mentioned in *Hsv* 15. — [3] *sem eigi fylgir til mikit mein* 'which is not accompanied by too much harm': 624's reading is chosen here. The scribe of 1199ˣ may not have understood the intensifier *til*. — [4-6]: These ll. have no exact equivalent in the Lat. text, but the phrasing of 1199ˣ might be interpreted as trying to render the *sic bonus esto bonis* 'so be good to the good' in the redactor's own words.

28. Öll tíðindi,   þau er upp koma,
         ræð þú eigi fyrstr með firum;
    betra er at þegja   en þat at segja,
         sem lýðum reyniz at lygi.

Ræð þú eigi fyrstr með firum öll tíðindi, þau er upp koma; betra er at þegja en at segja þat, sem reyniz lýðum at lygi.

Do not be the first to discuss with men all the news that comes up; it is better to keep silent than to say what proves in public to be a lie.

Mss: **1199ˣ**(72v), 723aˣ(78), 696XV(1v), 401ˣ(1r), 624(141-2). — *Readings*: [1] Öll: '[...]' 696XV, ill 401ˣ; tíðindi: '[...]e[...]' 696XV [3] ræð þú: hreyfðu 723aˣ, reif þú 696XV; eigi: 'e[...]' 696XV, '[...]' 401ˣ; firum: so 624, fyrðum 1199ˣ, 401ˣ, 'fyrd[...]' 696XV [4] betra er: 'bet[...] e[...]' 696XV, því betra er 624 [6] sem lýðum reyniz: sem lýðum 723aˣ, '[...]zt kyind at lygi' 696XV, er reyniz lýðum 401ˣ, sem síðan reyniz 624;   at lygi: at lygi reyniz 723aˣ, 'at [...]' 401ˣ.

Editions: *Skj* Anonyme digte og vers [XIII], [C. E/5]. *Hugsvinnsmál* 28: AII, 174, BII, 190, *Skald* II, 99; Hallgrímur Scheving 1831, 11, Konráð Gíslason 1860, 550, Gering 1907, 8, Tuvestrand 1977, 86, Hermann Pálsson 1985, 43.

Notes: [All]: Lat. parallel: (*Dist.* I, 12) *Rumores fuge, ne incipias novus auctor haberi, / nam nulli tacuisse nocet, nocet esse locutum* 'Flee from rumours, and do not try to be taken as the recent author of them, for it does not harm anyone to be silent, [but] to have spoken may harm'. — [6]: This l. might have been influenced by *Sigrdr* 25 (*NK*, 195): *Alt er vant, | ef þú við þegir; | þá þiccir þú með bleyði borinn | eða sǫnno sagðr; | ... Annars dags | láttu hans ǫndo farit | oc launa svá lýðom lygi!* 'Everything is lost if you are silent in response; then you seem to be born a coward or else it is spoken truly; ... on another day let his spirit pass on and thus repay his lies in public' (Larrington 1996, 170).

29. Öðrum heita   skaltu eigi því,
        er undir öðrum átt;
     opt þik tælir,   sá er þú trúat hefir;
        brigð eru beggja heit.

Skaltu eigi heita öðrum því, er átt undir öðrum; tælir þik opt, sá er þú hefir trúat; heit beggja eru brigð.

You must not promise another what you have lent to somebody else; that one may often trick you, whom you have trusted; the promises of both are fickle.

Mss: **1199ˣ**(74v), 696XV(1v), 624(142). — *Readings*:   [2] skaltu eigi því: skaltu öngum því 696XV, þú skalt eigi gjöf þeiri 624   [3] er undir: 'sem [...]' 696XV, er þú at 624; öðrum átt: '[...]' 696XV   [4-6]: símálugs orð þykkir snotrum hól vindi líkt vera 624.

Editions: *Skj* Anonyme digte og vers [XIII], [C. E/5]. *Hugsvinnsmál* 29: AII, 174, BII, 190, *Skald* II, 99; Hallgrímur Scheving 1831, 12, Gering 1907, 8-9, Tuvestrand 1977, 86, Hermann Pálsson 1985, 44.

Notes: [All]: Lat. parallel: (*Dist.* I, 13) *Spem tibi promissi certam promittere noli: / rara fides ideo est, quia multi multa locuntur* 'Do not hold out certain hope of something promised to you; surety is rare, because many say many things'. The first 3 ll. are parallelled in *Hsv* 41. The text of 624 is closer to the Lat. — [4-6]: The reading in 624 differs considerably: *símálugs orð | þykkir snotrum hól | vindi líkt vera*, which requires emendation of *hól* 'praise, flattery' to *hal* 'man', thus: 'to a wise man the words of a long-winded man seem like the wind'. — [6] *heit beggja* 'the promises of both': It is possible *beggja* refers to the two parties in ll. 1-3, but it is by no means clear. Finnur (*Skj* B) emends to *bragna orð* 'men's word(s)'.

30. Metnað þinn,   þótt þik menn lofi,
   lát eigi magnaz til mjök;
hælins manns orði   þarftu eigi hverju at trúa;
   sjálfr kunn þú sjálfan þik.

Lát eigi metnað þinn magnaz til mjök, þótt menn lofi þik; þarftu eigi at trúa hverju orði hælins manns; kunn þú sjálfr þik sjálfan.

Do not let your pride become too great, even though people are praising you; you do not need to believe every word of a boastful man; you yourself [must] know yourself.

Mss: **1199**[x](72v), 723a[x](78), 696XV(1v), 401[x](1r), 624(142). — *Readings*: [1] Metnað þinn: '[...]inn' 696XV   [2] þótt: þó 723a[x], 696XV, 401[x], 624;   þik menn: *so* 723a[x], 624, menn þik 1199[x], 696XV, 401[x]   [3] lát: láttu 696XV, 401[x], 624;   magnaz: vaxa við 723a[x], miklaz 624;   til: *so* 624, *om.* 1199[x], 696XV, of 723a[x], því 401[x];   mjök: mikit 723a[x]   [4] manns orði: '[...]huergí' 696XV   [5] þarftu: '[...]to' 401[x];   at: *om.* 624   [6] sjálfr: *so* 723a[x], 696XV, 401[x], 624, sjálfan 1199[x];   kunn: kenn 624;   þú: *om.* 723a[x];   sjálfan þik: þik sjálfan 624.

Editions: *Skj* Anonyme digte og vers [XIII], [C. E/5]. *Hugsvinnsmál* 30: AII, 174, BII, 190, *Skald* II, 99; Hallgrímur Scheving 1831, 12, Konráð Gíslason 1860, 550, Gering 1907, 9, Tuvestrand 1977, 87, Hermann Pálsson 1985, 45.

Notes: [All]: Lat. parallel: (*Dist.* I, 14) *Cum te aliquis laudat, iudex tuus esse memento; / plus aliis de te quam tu tibi credere noli* 'When someone praises you, remember to be your own judge; do not believe more from others about yourself than you believe of yourself'. The first half is parallelled in *Hsv* 66. — [6]: This l. has no equivalent in the Lat. text.

31. Allan þann dugnað,   er þér annarr gerir,
   mun þú ok mörgum seg;
vinum þínum   þótt þú vel dugir,
   hirð þú eigi at hrósa því.

Allan þann dugnað, er annarr gerir þér, mun þú ok seg mörgum; þótt þú dugir vel vinum þínum, hirð þú eigi at hrósa því.

All that assistance which another provides you with, remember [it] and tell it to many; even if you help your friends well, do not care about praising it.

Mss: **1199**[x](72v), 723a[x](78), 696XV(1v), 401[x](1r), 624(142). — *Readings*: [1] Allan: *om.* 723a[x]   [1, 2] þann dugnað er: góða þann 696XV   [2] annarr: gumna 723a[x], '[...]' 696XV, annar veitir eða þú öðrum 624;   gerir: gera 723a[x], '[...]' 696XV   [3] mun þú: '[...]u' 696XV;   ok: hann ok 624   [5] þótt þú: *so* 723a[x], þó þú 1199[x], 696XV, 401[x], þá 624;   dugir: *so* 723a[x], 696XV, 401[x], 624, gerir 1199[x]   [6] þú: *om.* 723a[x];   hrósa: '[...]' 696XV, hrós 624;   því: '[...]' 696XV.

Editions: *Skj* Anonyme digte og vers [XIII], [C. E/5]. *Hugsvinnsmál* 31: AII, 174-5, BII, 190, *Skald* II, 99; Hallgrímur Scheving 1831, 12, Gering 1907, 9, Tuvestrand 1977, 88, Hermann Pálsson 1985, 46.

Notes: [All]: Lat. parallel: (*Dist.* I, 15) *Officium alterius multis narrare memento, / at quaecumque aliis benefeceris ipse, sileto* 'Remember to tell many about the kindness of another, but be silent about whatever good you yourself do to others'.

32. Ungr skal venjaz   því er þarf aldraðr at hafa;
    varaztu við löst, meðan lifir;
  ávítunarlaust   máttu eigi elligar
    dæma um seggja siðu.

Ungr skal venjaz því er aldraðr þarf at hafa; varaztu við löst, meðan lifir; máttu eigi elligar dæma ávítunarlaust um siðu seggja.

When young one must get used to what is needed when old; beware of faults while you are alive; otherwise you cannot judge men's morals without blame.

Mss: **1199**[x](72v), 723a[x](78), 696XV(1v), 401[x](1r), 624(142). — *Readings*: [1] Ungr skal: '[...]skyldi' 696XV   [2] þarf: *om.* 723a[x], skal 696XV; aldraðr: 'aldraur' 696XV, gamall 624; at: 'ætte [...]' 723a[x]   [3] varaztu: ok varaz 696XV, 'var[...]' 401[x]; við: *om.* 723a[x]; löst: *so* 401[x], 624, löstu 1199[x], löstu æ 723a[x], laus 696XV; lifir: '[...]' 696XV, 'li[...]' 624   [4] ávítunarlaust: '[...]ítalaust' 696XV, ávítalaust 401[x], þvíat ávítunarlaust 624   [5] eigi: aldri 723a[x]; elligar: *om.* 624   [6] seggja: annarra manna 624; siðu: 'si[...]' 401[x], siðu alla 624.

Editions: *Skj* Anonyme digte og vers [XIII], [C. E/5]. *Hugsvinnsmál* 32: AII, 175, BII, 191, *Skald* II, 99; Hallgrímur Scheving 1831, 12, Gering 1907, 9, Tuvestrand 1977, 89, Hermann Pálsson 1985, 46/47.

Notes: [All]: Lat. parallel: (*Dist.* I, 16) *Multorum cum facta senex et dicta reprendas, / fac tibi succurrant, iuvenis quae feceris ipse* 'When, having grown old, you censure the deeds and sayings of many, let those things come to your mind that you yourself did as a youth'. The content is quite similar to *Has* 42.

33. Einmæli manna   ræk þú aldrigi;
    þarftu eigi til þess at hlera;
  um sik ræða   ætla seggja hverr,
    hinn er veit á sik sakir.

Ræk þú aldrigi einmæli manna; þarftu eigi at hlera til þess; hverr seggja, hinn er veit sakir á sik, ætla ræða um sik.

Never pay attention to men's private conversation; you do not need to listen to it; every man who knows he is guilty thinks [people] are talking about him.

Mss: 1199ˣ(72v), 723aˣ(78), 696XV(1v), 401ˣ(1r), 624(142). — *Readings*: [1] Einmæli: 'ein[...]' 696XV, um einmæli 624; manna: mann 723aˣ, '[...]' 696XV [2] ræk þú aldrigi: *om.* 624 [3] þarftu eigi til þess: tak þú til 401ˣ, hirtu aldrigi 624; hlera: hlæja 401ˣ [4] um: *so* 723aˣ, 696XV, 401ˣ, 624, um sjálfan 1199ˣ [4, 5] ræða ætla seggja hverr: *so* 723aˣ, 401ˣ, ætla ræða seggja hverr 1199ˣ, 'ræ[...] huer' 696XV, seggja hvern ræða ætla 624 [6] hinn: '[...]' 723aˣ, sá 696XV, *om.* 624; er: sem 723aˣ; sik: baki sér 624.

Editions: Skj Anonyme digte og vers [XIII], [C. E/5]. *Hugsvinnsmál* 33: AII, 175, BII, 191, *Skald* II, 99, *NN* §3166; Hallgrímur Scheving 1831, 12, Gering 1907, 10, Tuvestrand 1977, 89, Hermann Pálsson 1985, 47.

Notes: [All]: Lat. parallel: (*Dist.* I, 17) *Ne cures, si quis tacito sermone loquatur: / conscius ipse sibi de se putat omnia dici* 'Do not pay any attention if someone talks behind your back [*lit.* with silent speech]; the guilty man thinks everything is said about him'. Both versions render the Lat. text equally well, but 401ˣ and 1199ˣ correspond better to the rules of *ljóðaháttr*. 624 is metrically deficient in the first two ll. — [6]: The last l. corresponds to *Hsv* 102/3.

34. Við meinum varna   skaltu á margan veg,
    þótt þú sért fullsterkr at fé;
    margr er sá aumr,   er aurum ræðr;
    ilt er auði at trúa.

Skaltu varna við meinum á margan veg, þótt þú sért fullsterkr at fé; margr er sá aumr, er ræðr aurum; ilt er at trúa auði.

You must beware of harm in many a way, although you are very well off with money; many a one is poor who possesses money; it is bad to trust in wealth.

Mss: 1199ˣ(72v), 723aˣ(79), 696XV(1v), 401ˣ(1r), 624(142). — *Readings*: [1] varna: varaz 696XV, *om.* 624 [2] skaltu: þú skalt 696XV; á margan veg: 'ǽ [...]' 696XV, '[...] margan hatt' 401ˣ, á marga vega varaz 624 [3] þótt þú: þó þú 723aˣ, '[...]' 696XV; sért: vitir þik 624; fullsterkr: fullríkr 696XV, 401ˣ, vel auðgan 624 [4] margr: opt 624; er: verðr 696XV; sá aumr: aumr sá 723aˣ, 696XV, aumr 401ˣ [5] aurum: fyrir aurum 696XV, 401ˣ; ræðr: '[...]' 696XV, 'r[...]' 401ˣ [6] ilt er auði at trúa: ilt er at trúa auð 723aˣ, '[...]d at trua' 696XV, ilt er auð at trúa 401ˣ, ok verðr varr sanns 624.

Editions: Skj Anonyme digte og vers [XIII], [C. E/5]. *Hugsvinnsmál* 34: AII, 175, BII, 191, *Skald* II, 99-100; Hallgrímur Scheving 1831, 12, Gering 1907, 10, Tuvestrand 1977, 90, Hermann Pálsson 1985, 48.

Notes: [All]: Lat. parallel: (*Dist.* I, 18) *Cum fueris felix, quae sunt adversa, caveto: / non eodem cursu respondent ultima primis* 'When you are happy, be on your guard against adverse things; the end does not always follow the same course as that begun'. The text of 1199ˣ might have been influenced by *Sól* 34. The dangers of being rich are also mentioned in, e.g., *Hávm* 10/4-5 (*NK*, 18): *auði betra | þiccir þat í ókunnom stað* 'better than riches [common sense] will seem in an unfamiliar place' (Larrington 1996, 15).

35. Af annars dauða   væntu aldrigi,
       at þér gagn geriz;
    aldrlagi sínu   ræðr engi maðr;
       nær stendr höldum hel.

Væntu aldrigi, at þér gagn geriz af annars dauða; engi maðr ræðr aldrlagi sínu; hel stendr nær höldum.

Never hope that you may profit from another's death; nobody controls his own life's end; death is close to men.

Mss: **1199ˣ**(72v), 723aˣ(79), 696XV(1v), 401ˣ(1r), 624(142). — *Readings*: [2] væntu: væntu þér 696XV, glez þú 624   [3] þér: '[...]' 696XV; gagn: '[...]' 696XV, 401ˣ; geriz: '[...]' 696XV, geri 624   [4] aldrlagi: '[...]gí' 696XV   [5] ræðr: kvíði 401ˣ   [6] nær: því nær 401ˣ, þvíat nær 624; höldum hel: 'haulld[...]m[...]' 401ˣ, 'holl hol' 624.

Editions: *Skj* Anonyme digte og vers [XIII], [C. E/5]. *Hugsvinnsmál* 35: AII, 175-6, BII, 191, *Skald* II, 100; Hallgrímur Scheving 1831, 13, Gering 1907, 10, Tuvestrand 1977, 90, Hermann Pálsson 1985, 49.

Notes: [All]: Lat. parallel: (*Dist*. I, 19) *Cum dubia et fragilis nobis sit vita tributa, / in mortem alterius spem tu tibi ponere noli* 'Since the life given to us is doubtful and fragile, do not place your hope in the death of another'. — [6] *höldum hel* 'to men ... death': The reading in 624 ('nær stendr holl hol') might indicate that the scribe of that ms. no longer understood the allusion to the role of Hel as the abode of the dead in Norse mythology or did not expect an allusion to pre-Christian mythology in a Christian poem.

36. Ef þér litla gjöf   gefr af léttum hug
       vinr, sá sem válaðr er,
    þiggja þú skalt   ok þakklátr geraz;
       ást fylgir aums gjöfum.

Ef vinr, sá sem válaðr er, gefr þér litla gjöf af léttum hug, skalt þú þiggja ok geraz þakklátr; ást fylgir gjöfum aums.

If a friend who is poor gives you a small gift from a happy disposition, you must accept it and be grateful; love accompanies the gifts of a poor person.

Mss: **1199ˣ**(72v), 723aˣ(79), 696XV(1v), 401ˣ(1r), 624(142). — *Readings*: [1] litla gjöf: 'l[...]' 696XV   [2] gefr af léttum: '[...]godum' 696XV   [3] sem: *om*. 723aˣ, 696XV, 401ˣ, er 624   [4] þú skalt: 'þ[...]' 401ˣ   [5] þakklátr: 'þack[...]' 696XV; geraz: '[...]' 696XV, 401ˣ, vera 624   [6] ást: '[...]' 696XV, því ást 624; fylgir: '[...]ger' 696XV.

Editions: Skj Anonyme digte og vers [XIII], [C. E/5]. *Hugsvinnsmál* 36: AII, 176, BII, 191, *Skald* II, 100; Hallgrímur Scheving 1831, 13, Konráð Gíslason 1860, 550, Gering 1907, 11, Tuvestrand 1977, 91, Hermann Pálsson 1985, 50.

Notes: [All]: Lat. parallel: (*Dist.* I, 20) *Exiguum munus cum det tibi pauper amicus, / accipito placide, plene laudare memento* 'When your poor friend gives you a small gift, accept it happily and remember to praise [it] fully'.

37. Öreign þína   lát þér eigi gera
         harðan hugtrega;
    minztu þess,   er þik móðir bar,
         svát þér fylgdi eigi fé.

Lát eigi öreign þína gera þér harðan hugtrega; minztu þess, er þik móðir bar, svát þér fylgdi eigi fé.

Do not let your destitution cause you severe heartbreak; remember this, that your mother bore you [i.e. gave birth to you] in such a way that no money came with you.

Mss: **1199**[x](72v), 723a[x](79), 696XV(1v), 401[x](1r), 624(142). — *Readings*: [1] Öreign: öreigu 624   [2] lát: láttu 723a[x], 696XV, 401[x], 624;   þér eigi gera: aldri gera 723a[x], eigi gera þér 401[x], þik eigi hryggvan 624   [3] harðan hugtrega: 'hriggvann [...]' 723a[x], 'he[...]' 696XV, hrygt í hug 401[x], hryggvan gera 624   [4] minztu þess: þat þú minnz 723a[x], þú þat minnz 696XV, 'þess þ[...]' 401[x], 'hins þu minn[...]' 624   [5] er: at 723a[x]   [6] svát ('so ad'): svá 723a[x], 401[x], 624; eigi fé: '[...]' 696XV.

Editions: Skj Anonyme digte og vers [XIII], [C. E/5]. *Hugsvinnsmál* 37: AII, 176, BII, 191, *Skald* II, 100; Hallgrímur Scheving 1831, 13, Konráð Gíslason 1860, 550, Gering 1907, 11, Tuvestrand 1977, 91, Hermann Pálsson 1985, 51.

Notes: [All]: Lat. parallel: (*Dist.* I, 21) *Infantem nudum cum te natura crearit, / paupertatis onus patienter ferre memento* 'Since nature created you as a naked infant, remember to bear the burden of poverty patiently'. The ll. of the Lat. distich are rendered in reverse order in *Hsv*.

38. Aldrlagi sínu   kvíði engi maðr
         né um þat önn ali;
    dugir eigi dægr,   þeim er dauða forðaz;
         enginn feigð um flýr.

Engi maðr kvíði aldrlagi sínu né ali önn um þat; dægr dugir eigi þeim er dauða forðaz; enginn um flýr feigð.

Nobody should dread his death or nourish fear about it; a day and night are not enough for him who wants to avoid death; no one escapes a fated death.

Mss: **1199ˣ**(72v), 723aˣ(79), 696XV(1v), 401ˣ(1r), 624(142) (ll. 4-6). — *Readings*: [1] Aldrlagi: '[...]' 696XV   [2] kvíði engi: 'kuid[...]' 401ˣ   [5] þeim er dauða: '[...]' 696XV; forðaz: *so* 624, kvíðir 1199ˣ, kvíða 723aˣ, '[...]' 696XV, óaz 401ˣ   [6] enginn: '[...]ygi' 696XV, 'ei[...]' 401ˣ, hvergi 624;   feigð: hann feigð 696XV, 624, '[...]' 401ˣ.

Editions: Skj Anonyme digte og vers [XIII], [C. E/5]. *Hugsvinnsmál* 38: AII, 176, BII, 192, *Skald* II, 100; Hallgrímur Scheving 1831, 13, Konráð Gíslason 1860, 550, Gering 1907, 11, Tuvestrand 1977, 92, Hermann Pálsson 1985, 52.

Notes: [All]: Lat. parallel: (*Dist*. I, 22) *Ne timeas illam, quae vitae est ultima finis: / qui mortem metuit, quod vivit, perdit id ipsum* 'Do not fear that which is the final end of life: whoever fears death while he is alive, loses life itself'. 624 has only ll. 4-6. As the two *helmingar* in 1199ˣ each render more or less the sense of the Lat. distich, ll. 1-3 in the second version mss may not be original. Unavoidable death has already been mentioned in *Hsv* 35. Lines 4-5 may also mean 'a day and a night has no value for the one who wants to avoid death', i.e. people waste their time fearing death. This seems to be the sense of the Lat.

39. Vinir þínir   þótt þér verr dugi,
        en þú þykkiz verðr vera,
     þess meins völd   kenn þú eigi þínum guði,
        saka þú heldr sjálfan þik.

Þótt vinir þínir dugi þér verr, en þú þykkiz verðr vera, kenn þú eigi þess meins völd guði þínum; saka þú heldr þik sjálfan.

Although your friends may help you less than you think you deserve, do not fault your God for the cause of that evil; you should instead blame yourself.

Mss: **1199ˣ**(72v-73r), 723aˣ(79), 696XV(1v) (ll. 1-5), 401ˣ(1r), 624(142). — *Readings*: [2] þótt: þó 723aˣ, 401ˣ, ef 624; þér: '[...]' 401ˣ; dugi: duga 696XV, 624   [3] en þú þykkiz verðr vera: en þú verðr þykkiz 723aˣ, '[...]r verra' 696XV   [4] þess meins völd: *so* 696XV, 401ˣ, 624, þess manns völd 1199ˣ, *om*. 723aˣ   [5] kenn þú eigi: kenn þú þat eigi 723aˣ, kenndu ekki 696XV, kenna áttu eigi 624; guði: *om*. 401ˣ   [6] heldr: *om*. 401ˣ, 624; þik: 'þi[...]' 401ˣ.

Editions: Skj Anonyme digte og vers [XIII], [C. E/5]. *Hugsvinnsmál* 39: AII, 176, BII, 192, *Skald* II, 100; Hallgrímur Scheving 1831, 13, Konráð Gíslason 1860, 550, Gering 1907, 11, Tuvestrand 1977, 92, Hermann Pálsson 1985, 53.

Notes: [All]: Lat. parallel: (*Dist*. I, 23) *Si tibi pro meritis nemo respondet amicus, / incusare deos noli, sed te ipse coerce* 'If no friend stands up for you according to your deserts, do not accuse the gods, but restrain yourself'. — [4] *meins* 'of evil': Comparison with the Lat. text does not allow any conclusion as to whether the main ms. reading, *manns* 'man's', is the original.

40. Aura afla skaltu á alla vegu,
   sem drengmanni dugir;
 aura þinna skaltu eigi til ónýts hafa,
   þótt þú þik vel auðgan vitir.

Skaltu afla aura á alla vegu, sem drengmanni dugir; skaltu eigi hafa aura þinna til ónýts, þótt þú vitir þik vel auðgan.

You must acquire money in all ways which befit an independent man; you must not use your money for something useless, although you know yourself [to be] very wealthy.

Mss: **1199**ˣ(73r), 723aˣ(79), 696XV(1v), 401ˣ(1v), 624(142). — *Readings*: [1] Aura: auðs 723aˣ, auðar 624 [2] skaltu: 'skalt[...]' 624; á alla vegu: á marga vega 696XV, þeim 401ˣ, alla veg 624 [3] sem: svá sem 696XV, er 401ˣ; drengmanni dugir: 'dreing[...]' 696XV, 'dreingmenne dug[...]' 401ˣ [4] aura þinna: '[...]' 696XV [5] skaltu: skalt 723aˣ, '[...]' 696XV [6] þótt þú: þó 723aˣ, þóttu 696XV, þótt 401ˣ; vel: '[...]' 624; auðgan: '[...]gdan' 401ˣ; vitir: '[...]' 696XV.

Editions: *Skj* Anonyme digte og vers [XIII], [C. E/5]. *Hugsvinnsmál* 40: AII, 177, BII, 192, *Skald* II, 100; Hallgrímur Scheving 1831, 13, Gering 1907, 12, Tuvestrand 1977, 93, Hermann Pálsson 1985, 54.

Notes: [All]: Lat. parallel: (*Dist*. I, 24) *Ne tibi quid desit, quaesitis utere parce, / utque quod est serves, semper deesse putato* 'So that you will not be lacking anything, keep from using up what you have gained, and, so that you may keep what you have, always pretend to be without it'. The phrasing is paralleled in *Hsv* 57.

41. Sinni optar heittu eigi seggjum gjöf,
   þeirri er þú veita vilt;
 símálugs orð þykkja snotrum hal
   vindi lík vera.

Heittu eigi sinni optar seggjum gjöf, þeirri er þú vilt veita; snotrum hal þykkja símálugs orð vera lík vindi.

Do not promise people more than once the gift that you intend to give; to a wise man the words of a long-winded man seem like the wind.

Mss: **1199**ˣ(73r), 723aˣ(79), 696XV(1v) (ll. 2-6), 401ˣ(1v), 624(142) (ll. 1-3). — *Readings*: [2] heittu eigi seggjum: heit eigi sömu 723aˣ, skaltu eigi hcita 624 [3] þeirri er: ef 723aˣ; veita vilt: at öðrum átt 624 [4] símálugs: '[...]r' 696XV [5] þykkja: þykkir 401ˣ.

Editions: *Skj* Anonyme digte og vers [XIII], [C. E/5]. *Hugsvinnsmál* 41: AII, 177, BII, 192, *Skald* II, 100; Hallgrímur Scheving 1831, 14, Gering 1907, 12, Tuvestrand 1977, 93, Hermann Pálsson 1985, 54.

Notes: [All]: Lat. parallel: (*Dist.* I, 25) *Quod praestare potes, ne bis promiseris ulli, | ne sis ventosus, dum vis bonus esse videris* 'That which you are able to lend do not promise twice to anyone, do not be a windbag if you want to seem to be a good man'. This st. is parallelled in *Hsv* 29. — [1-3]: The first version (i.e. 624) only consists of these ll., but has a similar text to ll. 4-6 in its version of st. 29/4-6. The ll. here also read somewhat differently from the other mss: *Sinni optar | skaltu eigi heita gjöf | þeirri er þú at öðrum átt* 'You must not promise more than once a gift which you have due from others'.

42. Fláráðs manns orði,   þótt fagrt mæli,
       þarftu eigi þeim at trúa;
    glyslig orð   lát þú í gegn koma,
       ok gjalt svá líku líkt.

Þarftu eigi at trúa þeim orði fláráðs manns, þótt fagrt mæli; lát þú í gegn koma glyslig orð, ok gjalt svá líku líkt.

You need not believe the word of a deceitful man, even though he may speak fair; let specious words counter them, and thus repay like with like.

Mss: **1199ˣ**(73r), 723aˣ(79), 696XV(1v), 401ˣ(1v), 624(142). — *Readings*: [1] Fláráðs manns orði: Fláráðs manns orðum 723aˣ, 624, 'Flara[...]' 696XV, Fláráðr maðr 401ˣ   [2] þótt fagrt: þótt hann fagrt 723aˣ, 401ˣ, 624, '[...]' 696XV   [3] þarftu: '[...]' 723aˣ, 'þarf[...]v' 401ˣ; þeim: so 723aˣ, 624, til honum 1199ˣ, honum 696XV, því 401ˣ   [5] í gegn koma: 'j [...]' 723aˣ   [6] ok gjalt svá: '[...]' 723aˣ, '[...]tu' 696XV, gjaltu 401ˣ, gjaltu svá 624.

Editions: Skj Anonyme digte og vers [XIII], [C. E/5]. *Hugsvinnsmál* 42: AII, 177, BII, 192, *Skald* II, 100; Hallgrímur Scheving 1831, 14, Konráð Gíslason 1860, 550, Gering 1907, 12, Tuvestrand 1977, 94, Hermann Pálsson 1985, 55.

Notes: [All]: Lat. parallel: (*Dist.* I, 26) *Qui simulat verbis nec corde est fidus amicus, | tu qui fac simile: sic ars deluditur acte* 'Whoever dissimulates in words and is not a faithful friend at heart, treat him the same way: thus artifice is deluded by action'. The advice to be sceptical if somebody praises you too much is quite common in ON-Icel. poetry. Usually the adj. *flár* is used to denote untruthful or false speech. Cf. for instance Anon *Mhkv* 28[III]. Parallels in phrasing occur in *Hávm* 45 (*NK*, 24): *Ef þú átt annan, | þannz þú illa trúir, | vildu af hánom þó gott geta: | fagrt scaltu við þann mæla, | en flátt hyggia | oc gialda lausung við lygi* 'if you've another, whom you don't trust, but from whom you want nothing but good, speak fairly to him but think falsely and repay treachery with lies' (Larrington 1996, 20). Cf. also the phrasing in *Sól* 19, although the st. deals with a different topic.

43. Ef þér erfingja   auðit verðr,
        ok ertu fáskrúðigr at fé,
    jóðum þínum   kenn þú íþróttir,
        þær er þeim fæzlu fái.

Ef þér verðr erfingja auðit, ok ertu fáskrúðigr at fé, kenn þú jóðum þínum íþróttir, þær er fái þeim fæzlu.

If you come to have an heir and you are poor in possessions, teach your children the skills which may provide them with food.

Mss: **1199**[x](73r), 723a[x](80), 696XV(1v), 401[x](1v), 624(142). — *Readings*: [1, 2] erfingja auðit verðr: *so* 723a[x], erfingja verðr auðit eiga 1199[x], erfingja verðr eiga skapat 696XV, 401[x], verðr erfingja 624   [3] ok ertu fáskrúðigr: '[...]gigur' 696XV, ok sértu fátækr 401[x]   [6] er þeim fæzlu fái: '[...]' 696XV.

Editions: *Skj* Anonyme digte og vers [XIII], [C. E/5]. *Hugsvinnsmál* 43: AII, 177, BII, 192, *Skald* II, 100; Hallgrímur Scheving 1831, 14, Gering 1907, 12, Tuvestrand 1977, 95, Hermann Pálsson 1985, 56.

Notes: [All]: Lat. parallel: (*Dist*. I, 28) *Cum tibi sint nati nec opes, tunc artibus illos / instrue, quo possint inopem defendere vitam* 'When you have sons rather than riches, then instruct them in the arts, by means of which they may be able to maintain a life without riches'. *Dist*. I, 27 (*Noli homines blando nimium sermone probare; / fistula dulce canit, volucrem dum decipit auceps* 'Do not approve too much of men with flattering speech; the pipe sings sweetly, when the fowler deceives the bird') is not translated in *Hsv*.

44. Fé þik eigi tæla lát,   þótt þér fagrt sýniz,
        né til síngirnu snúi;
    annars eign   girniz illr at hafa;
        sæll er, sá er sínu unir.

Lát eigi fé tæla þik, né snúi til síngirnu, þótt sýniz þér fagrt; illr girniz annars eign at hafa; sæll er, sá er unir sínu.

Do not let money entice you nor turn [you] to covetousness, although it may seem attractive to you; a bad person desires to own another's possession; he is fortunate, who is content with his own.

Mss: **1199**[x](73r), 723a[x](80), 696XV(1v), 401[x](1v), 624(142). — *Readings*: [1] þik eigi tæla lát: þik eigi tæla 723a[x], láttu þik eigi tæla 696XV, '[...] fagvrt se' 624   [2] þótt: *so* 696XV, 401[x], þótt at 1199[x], þat 723a[x], *om*. 624; þér fagrt sýniz: 'þier fagurt [...]' 696XV, lát þú þik eigi tæla 624   [3] né til síngirnu snúi: *so* 624, þat til þín girnd snúiz 1199[x], þó þér komi girnd í geð 723a[x], '[...] snuazt' 696XV, eða til sinkr snúiz 401[x]   [5] girniz: girnstu 401[x], fýsiz 624; illr: aldri 401[x]; at: 'a[...]' 624; hafa: 'h[...]' 696XV   [6] sæll: snotr 624.

Editions: *Skj* Anonyme digte og vers [XIII], [C. E/5]. *Hugsvinnsmál* 44: AII, 177-8, BII, 193, *Skald* II, 100; Hallgrímur Scheving 1831, 14, Gering 1907, 13, Tuvestrand 1977, 95, Hermann Pálsson 1985, 56.

Notes: [All]: Lat. parallel: (*Dist.* I, 29) *Quod vile est carum, quod carum vile putato:* | *sic tu nec cupidus nec avarus nosceris ulli* 'Take that which is cheap to be dear, that dear to be cheap; thus you will be known to no-one as greedy nor avaricious'. Although the phrasing in both versions of ll. 1-3 is quite different, they both render the Lat. distich equally correctly. Therefore it remains uncertain which version is closer to the original translation. Avarice is quite a common topic in medieval literature. In *Hsv* it is also mentioned in sts 22, 73, 96, and 97. There is a parallel in content in *Sól* 63. — [1-2]: 624 reads quite differently: *Fé [þótt] fagrt sé | lát þú þik eigi tæla* 'Do not let money entice you, although it seems attractive' (AM 148 8° has *þó*). — [3] *né snúi til síngirnu* 'nor turn [you] to covetousness': 624's reading is taken here following *Skj* B. Although it differs substantially from the other mss, they all have problems. 1199[x]'s reading *þat snúiz til þín girnd* 'it may turn desire to you' alliterates somewhat irregularly on *þat* and *þín* and could be corrupt; additionally, *snúaz* cannot take an acc. object. Hermann Pálsson bases his text on 401[x], which requires emendation: *eða til sínku snúisk* 'or turn [you] to covetousness'. 696XV has a lacuna. 723a[x] has yet another version: *þó þér komi girnd í geð* 'although desire comes to your mind', but does not fit very well semantically with the previous ll. *Skj* takes 624's version but emends *síngirnu* (from *síngirna*) to *síngirni*, although the former is attested.

45. Ljótlig vömm   ef þú lasta vilt,
    drýgðu eigi sjálfr in sömu;
  annan samir þér   eigi at lasta,
    ef þú ert syndauðigr sjálfr.

Ef þú vilt lasta ljótlig vömm, drýgðu eigi sjálfr in sömu; samir þér eigi at lasta annan, ef þú ert syndauðigr sjálfr.

If you want to censure ugly faults, do not commit the same yourself; it does not beseem you to blame another if you are sinful yourself.

Mss: **1199**[x](73r), 723a[x](80), 401[x](1v), 624(142). — *Readings*: [1] vömm: verk 624   [2] lasta vilt: '[...]asta vill' 401[x]   [3] in sömu: it sama 723a[x], 401[x], *om.* 624   [4] annan: því 624   [4, 5] samir þér eigi at lasta: lasta samir þér eigi vel 401[x], lýta samir þér eigi 624   [6] ert syndauðigr sjálfr: veiz þik syndugan sjálfan 624.

Editions: *Skj* Anonyme digte og vers [XIII], [C. E/5]. *Hugsvinnsmál* 45: AII, 178, BII, 193, *Skald* II, 100-1; Hallgrímur Scheving 1831, 14, Gering 1907, 13, Tuvestrand 1977, 96, Hermann Pálsson 1985, 57.

Notes: [All]: Lat. parallel: (*Dist.* I, 30) *Quae culpare soles, ea tu ne feceris ipse:* | *turpe est doctori, cum culpa redarguat ipsum* 'Those things you are accustomed to blame do not do yourself; it is bad for a teacher when his fault refutes himself. The same topic is dealt with in *Sól* 15.

— [4-5] *annan samir þér eigi at lasta* 'it does not beseem you to blame another': 401ˣ has a different w.o. but is more or less the same, apart from the addition of the adv. *vel*. *Skj* B uses 624, *því annan lýta | samir þér eigi* 'because it does not beseem you to disgrace another', but reverses the last two words to produce correct alliteration.

46. Einskis biðja   samir þér annan þess,
    er gengr af réttri rifi;
  ósvinnr maðr   biðr þess iðugliga,
    er hann þarf hvergi at hafa.

Samir þér biðja annan einskis þess, er gengr af réttri rifi; ósvinnr maðr biðr iðugliga þess, er hann þarf hvergi at hafa.

It befits you to ask another for nothing which departs from right reason; an unwise man frequently asks for that which he does not need to have.

Mss: **1199ˣ**(73r), 723aˣ(80), 401ˣ(1v), 624(142). — *Readings*: [1] Einskis: *so* 723aˣ, 401ˣ, 624, einski 1199ˣ [2] samir þér: þér samir vel 401ˣ, skaltu 624 [3] gengr af réttri rifi: er gengr af restu rifi 723aˣ, 'ei geingr af re[...]rife' 401ˣ, þú eigi þarft 624 [4] ósvinnr: ósnotr 624 [5] iðugliga: optliga 401ˣ.

Editions: *Skj* Anonyme digte og vers [XIII], [C. E/5]. *Hugsvinnsmál* 46: AII, 178, BII, 193, *Skald* II, 101, *NN* §2589; Hallgrímur Scheving 1831, 14, Konráð Gíslason 1860, 550, Gering 1907, 13, Tuvestrand 1977, 96, Hermann Pálsson 1985, 58.

Notes: [All]: Lat. parallel: (*Dist*. I, 31) *Quod iustum est petito vel quod videatur honestum, | nam stultum petere est quod possit iure negari* 'Ask for what is right or what seems proper, for it is foolish to ask for that which may rightly be denied'. The question of whom to ask for what and to be decent in one's pleas is also dealt with in *Hávm* and *Sól*. Cf. *Sól* 28. — [1-3]: The text in 624 departs from the Lat.: *Einskis biðja | skaltu annan þess | er þú eigi þarft* 'You must ask another for nothing which you do not need'.

47. Ókunnann mann   virð þú öngu framar
    en þinn vísan vin;
  margr er sá illr,   er læz alldyggr vera;
    brigð eru útlenzk orð.

Virð þú ókunnann mann öngu framar en vísan vin þinn; margr er sá illr, er læz alldyggr vera; orð útlenzk eru brigð.

Do not value an unknown man any more than your certain friend; many a one is bad who pretends to be very trustworthy; foreign words are fickle.

Mss: **1199ˣ**(73r), 723aˣ(80), 401ˣ(1v), 624(142-3). — *Readings*: [1] Ókunnann: '[...]kvnnann' 401ˣ [2] öngu: öngvan 401ˣ, eigi 624 [4] illr: slægr 624 [6] útlenzk: *so* 723aˣ, 401ˣ, 624, útlenzkra 1199ˣ.

Editions: *Skj* Anonyme digte og vers [XIII], [C. E/5]. *Hugsvinnsmál* 47: AII, 178, BII, 193, *Skald* II, 101; Hallgrímur Scheving 1831, 15, Gering 1907, 14, Tuvestrand 1977, 97, Hermann Pálsson 1985, 59.

Notes: [All]: Lat. parallels: (*Dist.* I, 32) *Ignotum tibi tu noli praeponere notis: / cognita iudicio constant, incognita casu* 'Do not prefer someone unknown to you over those who are known: known things are subject to judgement, unknown to chance'. — [6] *útlenzk orð* 'foreign words': *Skj* B has *útlendra orð* 'words of foreigners' here, from Hallgrímur Scheving's edn, which agrees better with the sense of the rest of the st.

48. Hvern dag, er þú heilsu náir,
    vertu þér at nokkru nýtr;
 sótt ok dauði kemr, þá er sízt varir;
    brigt er lýða líf.

Hvern dag, er þú náir heilsu, vertu nýtr þér at nokkru; sótt ok dauði kemr, þá er sízt varir; brigt er lýða líf.

Every day in which you enjoy good health, be useful to yourself in something; sickness and death come when one least expects them; humans' life is fickle.

Mss: **1199**^{x}(73r), 723a^x(80), 401^x(1v), 624(143). — *Readings*: [1] dag: dag frá öðrum 401^x, 624 [2] er þú: meðan þér 624; heilsu: heilsan 624; náir: hefr 723a^x, 401^x, gefz 624 [3] þér: *om.* 401^x [5] varir: vari 723a^x, at varir 624 [6] lýða: synda 624.

Editions: *Skj* Anonyme digte og vers [XIII], [C. E/5]. *Hugsvinnsmál* 48: AII, 178-9, BII, 193, *Skald* II, 101; Hallgrímur Scheving 1831, 15, Gering 1907, 14, Tuvestrand 1977, 97, Hermann Pálsson 1985, 60.

Notes: [All]: Lat. parallel: (*Dist.* I, 33) *Cum dubia incertis versetur vita periclis, / pro lucro tibi pone diem, quicumque sequetur* 'Since fickle life turns on uncertain perils, consider each day you struggle through a gain for yourself. Both versions are very free translations. — [1-2]: 624's reading, used by Hermann Pálsson and Finnur Jónsson, differs here: *Hvern dag frá öðrum, | meðan þér heilsan gefz* ... 'Every day to the next, while health is granted to you...'. — [6] *brigt er lýða líf* 'humans' life is fickle': The saying *brigt er...* is quite common in ON-Icel. literature. It is also used in *Has* 55/1. The unpredictability of health and wealth is also dealt with in *Sól* 8.

49. Þjarka eða þræta skaltu eigi við þína liða;
    heldr skaltu væginn vera;
 sanna elsku gerir samþykki,
    en þverúð af þrætum vex.

Skaltu eigi þjarka eða þræta við liða þína; skaltu heldr vera væginn; samþykki gerir sanna elsku, en þverúð vex af þrætum.

You must not dispute or argue with your followers; you should rather be balanced; concord makes true love, but discord grows from disputes.

Mss: **1199**[x](73r), 723a[x](80), 401[x](1v), 624(143). — *Readings*: [1] Þjarka eða þræta: þræta eða þjarka 723a[x], 624, þjarka né þræta 401[x] [2] eigi við: aldri við 723a[x], við 401[x], eigi við þér meira mann eða 624; liða: *corrected from* 'lika' 401[x], líka 624 [3] heldr skaltu væginn vera: væg þú opt fyrir vinum 401[x], væg þú fyrir vinum 624 [4] sanna elsku: inn sanna elska 723a[x], 401[x] [5] samþykki: 'sa[...]þycki' 401[x] [6] en: *om.* 401[x].

Editions: *Skj* Anonyme digte og vers [XIII], [C. E/5]. *Hugsvinnsmál* 49: AII, 179, BII, 193-4, *Skald* II, 101; Hallgrímur Scheving 1831, 50, Gering 1907, 15, Tuvestrand 1977, 98, Hermann Pálsson 1985, 62.

Notes: [All]: Lat. parallel: (*Dist.* I, 36) *Litem inferre cave cum quo tibi gratia iuncta est, / ira odium generat, concordia nutrit amorem* 'Beware of starting a fight with someone who is closely joined to you; anger brings about hatred; harmony nourishes love'. A similar topic is dealt with in *Hsv* 7. — [3] *skaltu heldr vera væginn* 'you should rather be balanced': 624 and 401[x] read: *væg þú* (*opt* 401[x]) *fyrir vinum* 'yield (often) to friends'.

50. Gjafir launa   skaltu við góðan hug,
          þær er þér veita vinir;
      rækt ok elska   helz með rekka liði
          þeim, er at þurftum dugir.

Skaltu við góðan hug launa gjafir, þær er vinir veita þér; rækt ok elska helz með þeim liði rekka, er dugir at þurftum.

You must with good intentions repay gifts which friends give you; affection and love stay with the company of men who support [each other] in need.

Mss: **1199**[x](73r), 723a[x](80), 401[x](1v), 624(143). — *Readings*: [1] Gjafir: '[...]iafer' 401[x] [3] þær: *om.* 401[x]; er: *om.* 723a[x]; veita vinir: vinir veita 401[x] [4] rækt: ræk 401[x] [5] með: '[...]d' 401[x] [6] þeim: þann 723a[x], þeira 624; at: *so* 723a[x], 401[x], 624, *om.* 1199[x]; þurftum: þörfum 624; dugir: dugaz 624.

Editions: *Skj* Anonyme digte og vers [XIII], [C. E/5]. *Hugsvinnsmál* 50: AII, 179, BII, 194, *Skald* II, 101; Hallgrímur Scheving 1831, 15, Konráð Gíslason 1860, 550, Gering 1907, 14-15, Tuvestrand 1977, 98, Hermann Pálsson 1985, 63.

Notes: [All]: Lat. parallel: (*Dist.* I, 35) *Ne dubita cum magna petas impendere parva: / his etenim rebus coniungit gratia caros* 'Do not hesitate, when you are seeking great things, to spend a little; for in such matters good behaviour requires expenditures'. On the topics of hospitality and generosity in ON-Icel. poetry, cf. for instance *Hávm* 48, 117 (*NK*, 24, 35), *Hárb* 21 (*NK*, 81).

51. Þrælum þínum   reiðz þú eigi þungliga,
    svát þú þeim grand gerir;
    því sjálfum sér   aflar síns skaða
    hverr, sem meiðir mann.

Reiðz þú eigi þungliga þrælum þínum, svát þú gerir þeim grand, því hverr, sem meiðir mann, aflar skaða síns sér sjálfum.

Do not become violently angry with your servants, so that you cause them an injury, because everybody who injures a man causes harm to himself.

Mss: **1199ˣ**(73r), 723aˣ(80), 401ˣ(1v). — *Readings*: [1] Þrælum: '[...]lumm' 723aˣ, '[...]rælum' 401ˣ   [2] þú: *om*. 723aˣ   [3] gerir: veitir 401ˣ   [4] því sjálfum sér: '[...]r' 723aˣ, 'þviat sia[...] sier' 401ˣ   [6] sem: er sinn 723aˣ, er sína 401ˣ; meiðir mann: menn meiðir 401ˣ.

Editions: *Skj* Anonyme digte og vers [XIII], [C. E/5]. *Hugsvinnsmál* 52: AII, 179-80, BII, 194, *Skald* II, 101, *NN* §2590; Hallgrímur Scheving 1831, 15, Gering 1907, 15, Tuvestrand 1977, 99, Hermann Pálsson 1985, 63.

Notes: [All]: Lat. parallels: (*Dist*. I, 37) *Servorum culpis cum te dolor urguet in iram, / ipse tibi moderare, tuis ut parcere possis* 'When the vexation of servants' faults pushes you to anger, control yourself, so that you may spare your own'. The topic is also dealt with in *Sól* 26, albeit without the hint of social differences. From this point onwards, the ordering and preservation of the sts in 1199ˣ, 624 and eds of *Hsv*, departs. The present edn follows 1199ˣ for the most part, but is modified slightly on the basis of the order in 624 where that ms. follows the order of the Lat. more closely.

52. Fyrir öðrum vægja   samir þér iðugliga,
    þótt þú meira megir;
    friðsamr við annan   skyldi fyrða hverr,
    sá er vill hæstan tír hafa.

Samir þér iðugliga vægja fyrir öðrum, þótt þú megir meira; hverr fyrða, sá er vill hafa hæstan tír, skyldi friðsamr við annan.

It often befits you to yield to others, although you may be capable of more; every man who wants to have the highest renown must [be] peaceful with another.

Mss: **1199ˣ**(73r), 723aˣ(80) (ll. 1-2), 401ˣ(1v) (ll. 1-3), 624(143) (ll. 1-3). — *Readings*: [1] Fyrir: '[...]' 401ˣ; vægja: vægum 624.

Editions: *Skj* Anonyme digte og vers [XIII], [C. E/5]. *Hugsvinnsmál* 51: AII, 179, BII, 194, *Skald* II, 101; Hallgrímur Scheving 1831, 15, Gering 1907, 14, Tuvestrand 1977, 100, Hermann Pálsson 1985, 64.

Notes: [All]: Lat. parallels: (*Dist.* I, 34) *Vincere cum possis, interdum cede sodali, / obsequio quoniam dulces retinentur amici* 'When you are able to win, now and again give in to a friend, since good friends are kept by giving in'; (*Dist.* I, 38) *Quem superare potes, interdum vince ferendo, / maxima enim morum semper patientia virtus* 'Conquer the one you can overcome now and again with tolerance, for the greatest virtue in behaviour is always patience'. The first two ll. echo *Hsv* 28.

53. Þolinmóðr þú skalt vera   við þegna lið;
     svá gerir sá, er vill hæverskan sið hafa.

Þú skalt vera þolinmóðr við þegna lið; svá gerir sá, er vill hafa hæverskan sið.

You must be patient with a host of men; he who wants to have courtly manners does this.

Mss: **624**(143), 148^x(71v).

Editions: *Skj* Anonyme digte og vers [XIII], [C. E/5]. *Hugsvinnsmál* 53: AII, 179-80, BII, 194, *Skald* II, 101; Hallgrímur Scheving 1831, 15, Gering 1907, 14, Tuvestrand 1977, 100, Hermann Pálsson 1985, 64.

Notes: [All]: Lat. parallel: *Dist.* I, 38 (cf. st. 52). In 624 the text seems somewhat corrupt, and is probably an alternative translation of st. 52/4-6.

54. Aura þína   skaltu eigi til ónýtis hafa;
     heldr neyt með hagspeki;
   válaðr verðr,   sá er eigi vinna má,
     ef hann hefr aurum amat.

Skaltu eigi hafa aura þína til ónýtis; *heldr* neyt með hagspeki; verðr válaðr, sá er eigi má vinna, ef hann hefr amat aurum.

You must not have your money for no use; rather use it with sense; he who cannot work becomes poor if he has squandered his money.

Mss: **1199^x**(73r), 401^x(1v), 624(143). — *Readings*: [1] Aura þína: '[...] þina' 401^x, eigur þínar 624 [2] ónýtis: ónýts 401^x, ofneyzlu 624 [3] *heldr*; ok 1199^x, hafna 401^x, *om.* 624, neyt með hagspeki: þú eigi hagspeki 401^x, *om.* 624 [4] válaðr verðr: opt verðr sá aumr 624 [5] sá er eigi vinna má: sá er vinna eigi má 401^x, er fyrir aurum ræðr 624 [6] ef hann hefr aurum amat: ok hefr öðrum á mót 624.

Editions: *Skj* Anonyme digte og vers [XIII], [C. E/5]. *Hugsvinnsmál* 54: AII, 180, BII, 194, *Skald* II, 101, *NN* §2590; Hallgrímur Scheving 1831, 16, Gering 1907, 15, Tuvestrand 1977, 101, Hermann Pálsson 1985, 64.

Notes: [All]: Lat. parallel: (*Dist.* I, 39) *Conserva potius, quae sunt iam parta labore; / cum labor in damno est, crescit mortalis egestas* 'Preserve with greater effort what you have already gained; when labour is set at naught, human poverty grows'. 624 has a very different reading:

> Eigur þínar   skaltu eigi til ofneyzlu hafa;
> opt verðr sá aumr,   er fyrir aurum ræðr,
>   ok hefir öðrum á mót.

Skaltu eigi hafa eigur þínar til ofneyzlu; sá verðr opt aumr, er ræðr fyrir aurum ok hefir öðrum á mót 'You shall not use your property for intemperance; he often becomes poor who rules over money and uses it against others'. 624 lacks a 3rd l. and there is no alliteration in the last l. The verbal correspondences in the first *helmingr*, however, suggest that both versions are ultimately derived from the same translation. — [3] heldr *neyt með hagspeki* 'rather use it with sense': This l. does not correspond to the Lat. text and is missing in 624. *Skj* B uses Hallgrímur Scheving's reading of a now-lost ms. (*heldr*) to produce the correct alliteration, which is also used here.

55. Örr af þurftum   skaltu við ýta lið,
        ok dugi vel vinum;
    sá mun þrífaz,   er þarfr geriz
        sér ok sínu liði.

Skaltu örr við lið ýta af þurftum, ok dugi vel vinum; sá mun þrífaz, er geriz þarfr sér ok liði sínu.

You must [be] open-handed with a host of men if needed, and help your friends well; he will prosper who is useful for himself and his men.

Mss: **1199**^{x}(73r), 401^x(1v), 624(143). — *Readings*: [1] Örr: '[...]' 401^x; af: at 401^x [2] skaltu: vertu vertu 624 [3] ok: *om.* 401^x, 624; dugi: *so* 624, dugir 1199^x, duga 401^x [5] þarfr: 'þarf[...]' 401^x; geriz: *so* 624, er 1199^x, '[...]z' 401^x.

Editions: *Skj* Anonyme digte og vers [XIII], [C. E/5]. *Hugsvinnsmál* 55: AII, 180, BII, 194-5, *Skald* II, 101, *NN* §111; Hallgrímur Scheving 1831, 16, Konráð Gíslason 1860, 550, Gering 1907, 16, Tuvestrand 1977, 101, Hermann Pálsson 1985, 65.

Notes: [All]: Lat. parallels: (*Dist*. I, 40) *Dapsilis interdum notis et carus amicis / dum fueris dando, semper tibi proximus esto* 'While you were a bountiful and dear friend sometimes to known friends, in giving always be nearest to yourself'.

56. Allsnotr maðr		ef íþróttir nema vill
	ok vel mart vita,
   bækr hann lesi,		þær er gerðu *bragnar* spakir,
	þeir er kendu fróðleik firum,
   því́t á fornum bókum		stendr til flestra hluta
	ráðafjölð ritin.

Ef allsnotr maðr vill nema íþróttir ok vita mart vel, lesi hann bækr, þær er spakir *bragnar* gerðu, þeir er kendu firum fróðleik, þvít ráðafjölð stendr ritin til flestra hluta á fornum bókum.

If a very wise man wants to learn accomplishments and know many things well, let him read the books which wise men who taught people knowledge wrote, because a great deal of advice stands written on most things in ancient books.

Mss: **1199**[x](73r), 624(143). — *Readings*: [2] ef: sá er vill 624; vill: *om*. 624 [4] lesi: nemi 624 [5] *bragnar*: gumnar 1199[x], þær er fyrðar 624 [6] þeir er: *so* 624, ok 1199[x]; firum: *so* 624, fyrðum 1199[x] [7] á fornum bókum: *so* 624, í flestum bókum fornum 1199[x] [8] flestra hluta: flest ráð 624.

Editions: *Skj* Anonyme digte og vers [XIII], [C. E/5]. *Hugsvinnsmál* 56-7: AII, 180, BII, 195, *Skald* II, 102, 107, *NN* §2591; Hallgrímur Scheving 1831, 16, Gering 1907, 16, Tuvestrand 1977, 102-3, Hermann Pálsson 1985, 66.

Notes: [All]: Sts 56-7 paraphrase the preface to Book II of the *Disticha*. The present st. corresponds roughly to the two opening ll.: (*Praefatio Libri* II/1-2) *Telluris si forte velis cognoscere cultus / Vergilium legito; quodsi mage nosse laboras...* 'If by chance you want to learn about tilling the soil, read Virgil; but if you seek to know rather...'; and l. 10: *Ergo ades, et quae sit sapientia disce legendo* 'So come closer and learn by reading what wisdom is'. The reference to Virgil is to his treatise on agriculture, the *Georgics*. Finnur Jónsson (*Skj* B) has two sts here, with the second (his st. 58) incomplete and based on 624: [*þvít*] *á fornum bókum | stendr til flests ráð*, which he translates *ti i gamle bøger står der råd for alt* 'for in old books there stands advice for everything'. — [5] bragnar 'men': Neither 1199[x]'s *gumnar* nor 624's *fyrðar* supply the necessary alliteration. *Skj* B has *bragnar* deriving from Hallgrímur Scheving's ms. (cf. also st. 64/6).

57. Gæzku safna		skal gumna hverr,
	sá er vill hyggindi hafa;
   æðri speki		fær maðr aldrigi,
	en hann við syndum sjái.

Hverr gumna, sá er vill hafa hyggindi, skal safna gæzku; maðr fær aldrigi æðri speki, en hann sjái við syndum.

Every man who wants to have wisdom must accumulate virtues; a man never gets more wisdom than [if] he guards himself against sins.

Mss: **1199ˣ**(73r), 624(143). — *Readings*: [1] safna: gerva 624 [2] skal: skyli 624 [3] vill hyggindi: hyggindi vill 624 [4] æðri: æðra 624; speki: spekt 624 [5] fær: getr 624 [6] hann við syndum sjái: lastvarr lifa 624.

Editions: *Skj* Anonyme digte og vers [XIII], [C. E/5]. *Hugsvinnsmál* 58: AII, 180-1, BII, 195, *Skald* II, 102; Gering 1907, 16, Tuvestrand 1977, 103, Hermann Pálsson 1985, 67.

Notes: [All]: Lat. parallel: (*Praefatio Libri* II, 6-9) *Si quid amare libet vel discere amare legendo, / Nasonem petito; sin autem cura tibi haec est, / Ut sapiens vivas, audi quae discere possis, / Per quae semotum vitiis deducitur aevum* 'If your fancy is to love something, or you want to learn of love by reading, seek out Ovid [Publius Ovidius Naso]; but if this is your concern, to live as a wise man, hear those things you may learn, from which a lifetime removed from vice is drawn'. The Icel. text of the preface to Book II avoids specific mention of the two Lat. authors Virgil and Ovid, in the latter case possibly because his *Ars Amatoria* 'Art of Love' appears to have been somewhat controversial in Icel. classrooms, to judge by the well-known incident reported in *Jóns saga helga* (*JBp* 2003, 19, 84, 125), in which Bishop Jón forbade the future bishop Klængr Þorsteinsson to study this and similar books.

58. Ókunnum samir þér opt at duga,
    ef þú vilt vinsæll vera;
   veldi betra þykkir vitrum hal
    at eiga víða vini.

Samir þér at duga ókunnum opt, ef þú vilt vera vinsæll; vitrum hal þykkir veldi betra at eiga víða vini.

It befits you to help an unknown man often, if you want to be popular; to a wise man it seems better than power to have friends far and wide.

Mss: **1199ˣ**(73r), 624(143). — *Readings*: [1] samir: manni samir 624 [2] opt: opt vel 624 [3] vinsæll vera: víðfrægr verða ok vinsæll 624 [4] veldi: *so* 624, verði 1199ˣ [6] eiga víða: öreigi eigi 624.

Editions: *Skj* Anonyme digte og vers [XIII], [C. E/5]. *Hugsvinnsmál* 59: AII, 181, BII, 195, *Skald* II, 102; Hallgrímur Scheving 1831, 17, Konráð Gíslason 1860, 550, Gering 1907, 17, Tuvestrand 1977, 104, Hermann Pálsson 1985, 68.

Notes: [All]: Lat. parallel: (*Dist.* II, 1) *Si potes, ignotis etiam prodesse memento: / utilius regno est, meritis adquirere amicos* 'If you can, even remember to help people you do not know; it is more beneficial than a kingdom to gain friends by kindness'.

59. Áhyggju bera   skaltu fyrir öngum hlut,
    þeim er leynir guð gum*a,
þvít himneska skepnu   megu eigi höldar vita,
    þeir er á jörðu búa.

Skaltu bera áhyggju fyrir öngum hlut, þeim er guð leynir gum*a, þvít höldar, þeir er á jörðu búa, megu eigi vita himneska skepnu.

You must not be concerned about anything which God conceals from men, because men who live on earth cannot know heavenly creation.

Mss: **1199ˣ**(73r-v), 624(143) (ll. 4-6). — *Readings*: [3] gum*a: gumna 1199ˣ   [4] þvít: *om.* 624; skepnu: hluti 624   [5] megu: mega 1199ˣ, 624.

Editions: *Skj* Anonyme digte og vers [XIII], [C. E/5]. *Hugsvinnsmál* 60: AII, 181, BII, 195, *Skald* II, 102; Hallgrímur Scheving 1831, 17, Gering 1907, 17, Tuvestrand 1977, 104, Hermann Pálsson 1985, 68.

Notes: [All]: Lat. parallel: (*Dist.* II, 2) *Mitte arcana dei caelumque inquirere quid sit,* / *[An di sint caelumque regant, ne quaere doceri]* / *cum sis mortalis quae sunt mortalia cura* 'Avoid asking what are the secret things of God and heaven; [do not seek to be told whether gods exist and rule the heaven] since you are human, worry about human things'. — [3] *gum*a* 'men': The word is unmetrical in 1199ˣ. This emendation is found in Hallgrímur Scheving's edn and is also adopted in *Skj* B. Cf. also *gumn-* emended to *gum*-* in this metrical position in sts 86/6, 87/3 (624 has *gunnum*), 121/3, 122/6 and 130/6. In general, the shorter, metrically correct form seems unknown to all scribes. — [5] *meg*u 'can': The mss have the subj. form *mega*, but an indic. verb is needed here (so *Skj* B, *Skald*). — [6] *er á jörðu búa* 'who live on earth': This l. lacks alliteration in both mss. Finnur (*Skj* B) has *þeir er í heimi hafaz* 'those who are on earth', which derives from Hallgrímur Scheving's edn.

60. Einskis þræta   skaltu óráðins hlutar
    reiðr við rekka lið,
þvít reiðr maðr   fylliz rangs hugar;
    eigi hann satt um sér.

Skaltu reiðr þræta einskis óráðins hlutar við rekka lið, þvít reiðr maðr fylliz rangs hugar; hann um sér eigi satt.

[When you are] angry, you must not debate undecided things with a host of men, because an angry man is filled with a wrong mind; he does not see the truth.

Mss: **1199ˣ**(73v), 624(143). — *Readings*: [1] þræta: hlutar 624   [2] skaltu óráðins hlutar: óráðins skaltu þinga 624   [3] reiðr: *om.* 624   [4] maðr: *so* 624, *om.* 1199ˣ   [6] eigi hann satt um sér: má hann eigi satt um sjá 624.

Editions: *Skj* Anonyme digte og vers [XIII], [C. E/5]. *Hugsvinnsmál* 61: AII, 181, BII, 195-6, *Skald* II, 102; Hallgrímur Scheving 1831, 17, Gering 1907, 17, Tuvestrand 1977, 105, Hermann Pálsson 1985, 69.

Notes: [All]: Lat. parallel: (*Dist.* II, 4) *Iratus de re incerta contendere noli, / impedit ira animum, ne possis cernere verum* 'Do not fight about something doubtful when you are angry; anger keeps the mind from being able to discern the truth'.

61. Fengins fjár   neyttu framarliga,
    ok vert þíns mildr matar;
aura njóta   láttu auma fira,
    ef geraz þarfir þess.

Neyttu framarliga fengins fjár, ok vert mildr matar þíns; láttu auma fira njóta aura, ef geraz þarfir þess.

Use valiantly the property you gained, and be generous with your food; let poor men have benefit of money if it becomes necessary.

Mss: **1199ˣ**(73v), 624(143). — *Readings*: [2] framarliga: framliga 624   [3] ok: *om.* 624   [4] njóta: *so* 624, þína 1199ˣ   [5] láttu auma fira: *so* 624, skaltu eigi til ónýtis hafa 1199ˣ.

Editions: *Skj* Anonyme digte og vers [XIII], [C. E/5]. *Hugsvinnsmál* 62: AII, 181, BII, 196, *Skald* II, 102; Hallgrímur Scheving 1831, 17, Gering 1907, 17, Tuvestrand 1977, 105, Hermann Pálsson 1985, 70.

Notes: [All]: Lat. parallel: (*Dist.* II, 5) *Fac sumptum propere, cum res desiderat ipsa: / dandum etenim est aliquid, cum tempus postulat aut res* 'Give goods quickly when the situation demands; a thing is to be given when the time or the situation demands'. — [4-6]: Lines 4-5 are the basically same as st. 54/1-2 in 1199ˣ and are probably the result of scribal error. These ll. in both mss have no parallel in the Lat. text.

62. Litlu láni   fagni lýða hverr,
    ok hafi eigi metnað mikinn;
í litlum polli   haldaz lengi skip,
    er síðan brýtr hregg í hafi.

Hverr lýða fagni litlu láni, ok hafi eigi metnað mikinn; skip haldaz lengi í litlum polli, er hregg brýtr í hafi síðan.

Let every man rejoice at small benefits, and let him not have great arrogance; ships stay safe for a long time in a small pool, which a storm at sea later wrecks.

Mss: **1199ˣ**(73v), 624(143). — *Readings*: [1] láni: hann 624   [2] fagni: fagna 624   [3] ok: *om.* 624; eigi: eigi maðr 624   [4] í: opt í 624   [6] er síðan: þau er 624; brýtr hregg: hregg brýtr 624; í: *so* 624, ór 1199ˣ.

Editions: *Skj* Anonyme digte og vers [XIII], [C. E/5]. *Hugsvinnsmál* 63: AII, 181, BII, 196, *Skald* II, 102; Hallgrímur Scheving 1831, 17, Konráð Gíslason 1860, 551, Gering 1907, 18, Tuvestrand 1977, 106, Hermann Pálsson 1985, 71.

Notes: [All]: Lat. parallel: (*Dist.* II, 6) *Quod nimium est fugito, parvo gaudere memento: / tuta mage est puppis, modico quae flumine fertur* 'Flee that which is excessive; remember to rejoice in small things; that craft is safer which is borne on a small stream'. Both versions render the Lat. distich equally well, but the text in 624 seems somewhat corrupt.

63. Ill tíðendi, þótt þú einn vitir,
    gerz þú þagmælskr af þeim;
allir þann lasta, ef einn geriz
    flærðar frumkveðill.

Þótt þú einn vitir ill tíðendi, gerz þú þagmælskr af þeim; allir lasta þann, ef einn geriz frumkveðill flærðar.

Even if you alone know of some bad news, be discreet about it; everyone blames him, if he alone becomes the originator of falsehood.

Mss: **1199**[x](73v), 624(143). — *Readings*: [2] þótt þú einn vitir: þau er upp koma 624 [3] gerz þú: vættu 624; þagmælskr af þeim: eigi fyrstr með firum 624 [4] allir þann lasta: vertu þögnmælskr 624 [5] einn geriz: allir lasta 624 [6] flærðar frumkveðill: er einn geriz frumkveðill at 624.

Editions: *Skj* Anonyme digte og vers [XIII], [C. E/5]. *Hugsvinnsmál* 64: AII, 181-2, BII, 196, *Skald* II, 102; Hallgrímur Scheving 1831, 17, Gering 1907, 18, Tuvestrand 1977, 106, Hermann Pálsson 1985, 72.

Notes: [All]: Lat. parallel: (*Dist.* II, 7) *Quod pudeat, socios prudens celare memento, / ne plures culpent id, quod tibi displicet uni* 'Remember, prudent [as you are], to keep that which makes you ashamed from your associates, so that many will not blame that which displeases you alone'. 1199[x] is closer to the Lat. text. 624 differs considerably:

    Ill tíðindi, þau er upp koma,
        vættu eigi fyrstr með firum;
    vertu þögnmælskr, ef allir þau lasta,
        er einn geriz frumkveðill at.

Vættu eigi fyrstr með firum ill tíðindi, þau er upp koma; vertu þögnmælskr, ef allir lasta þau, er einn geriz frumkveðill at 'Do not expect as the first among men bad news which comes up; be discreet, if all blame those [i.e. the news] of which one man is the instigator'. There is an implication of causality between the two *helmingar* which is lacking in the Lat. distich.

64. Ódyggra manna   skaltu eigi atferð nema,
    þótt þeim verði flærð at frama;
  löstum eigi   megu þeir lengi leyna;
    upp koma um síðir svik.

Skaltu eigi nema atferð ódyggra manna, þótt flærð verði þeim at frama; þeir megu eigi lengi leyna löstum; um síðir koma upp svik.

You must not learn the behaviour of unreliable people, although deceit may advance them; they cannot conceal vices for long; in time treachery comes out.

Mss: **1199**[x](73v), 624(144), 624(143). — *Readings*: [2] eigi: *om.* 624(143)   [3] frama: fé 624(144), 624(143)   [4] löstum: löstnum 624(143); eigi: *om.* 624(144), 624(143)   [5] megu þeir lengi leyna: mega þeir lengi leyna 624(143), leyna munu lengi 624(144)   [6] upp: en upp 624(143); um síðir svik: svik um síðir; síðir svik: *so* 624(144), 624(143).

Editions: Skj Anonyme digte og vers [XIII], [C. E/5]. *Hugsvinnsmál* 65: AII, 182, BII, 196, *Skald* II, 102; Hallgrímur Scheving 1831, 18, Gering 1907, 18, Tuvestrand 1977, 107, Hermann Pálsson 1985, 72.

Notes: [All]: Lat. parallel: (*Dist*. II, 8) *Nolo putes pravos homines peccata lucrari: / temporibus peccata latent et tempore parent* 'I do not want you to think that crimes enrich bad men; at times crimes are hidden, but with time they become obvious'. The topic is also dealt with in *Hávm* 28/4-6 (*NK*, 21): *eyvito leyna | mego ýta sønir, | því er gengr um guma* 'the sons of men cannot keep secret / what's already going around' (Larrington 1996, 18). The last l. is very close to the phrasing in *Sól* 21. 624 contains the same st. twice. Both sts in 624 are so similar in phrasing that the second st. seems to be a correction of the first one. This st. belongs to a small block of three sts quoted twice in 624. The repetition might be due to the fact that, according to the Lat., they should be placed later in the ordering of verses in that ms.

65. Engan þú fyrirlít,   þótt aflvani sé
    eða ljótr ok lágskapaðr;
  margr er hygginn,   þótt herviligr sé,
    ok mjök lítit megi.

Fyrirlít þú engan, þótt sé aflvani, eða ljótr ok lágskapaðr; margr er hygginn, þótt sé herviligr, ok megi mjök lítit.

You should not look down on anybody, although he may be deficient in strength or ugly and short; many a one is intelligent, although he may be wretched and is capable of very little.

Mss: **1199ˣ**(73v), 624(143), 624(144). — *Readings*:   [1] fyrirlít: fyrirlítir 624(144)   [2] þótt: þótt hann 624(143);   aflvani sé: sé álfvani 624(143), álfvani sé 624(144)   [3] eða: *om.* 624(143), 624(144);   lágskapaðr: lágr er margr skapaðr 624(143), lágr skapaðr margr er 624(144)   [4] margr er: þó er sá margr 624(143)   [5] þótt herviligr sé: er herviligr er sýnar 624(143), þótt sé herviligir 624(144)   [6] ok mjök lítit megi: so 624(144), eða ljótr ok lágskapaðr 1199ˣ, maðr þó lítit megi 624(143).

Editions: *Skj* Anonyme digte og vers [XIII], [C. E/5]. *Hugsvinnsmál* 66: AII, 182, BII, 196, *Skald* II, 102; Hallgrímur Scheving 1831, 18, Gering 1907, 18-19, Tuvestrand 1977, 108, Hermann Pálsson 1985, 73.

Notes: [All]: Lat. parallel: (*Dist.* II, 9) *Corporis exigui vires contemnere noli: / consilio pollet, cui vim natura negavit* 'Do not disdain the powers of a small body; [the man] to whom nature denied strength may be strong in counsel'. Cf. *Sól* 34. Further parallels occur in *Hávm* 10 and 75. — [3] *eða ljótr ok lágskapaðr* 'or ugly and short': The two versions in 624 are hypermetrical. Finnur Jónsson (*Skj* B) has *eða ljótr ok lágr skapaðr*. — [6]: The last l. in 1199ˣ is a repetition of l. 3 and appears to be the result of scribal error.

66. Friðsamr við annan   skyldi firða hverr,
    þótt hann meira megi;
opt sá hefniz,   er halloki verðr,
    ok vegr síðan sigr.

Hverr firða skyldi friðsamr við annan, þótt hann megi meira; opt hefniz sá, er halloki verðr, ok vegr sigr síðan.

Every man should be peaceable towards another, although he may be stronger; often he who is defeated avenges himself, and later wins victory.

Mss: **1199ˣ**(74v), 1199ˣ(73v), 401ˣ(1v) (ll. 1-3), 624(144), 624(143). — *Readings*:   [1] við annan: vera 1199ˣ(73v), 624(144), '[...] annan' 401ˣ, þú vert 624(143)   [2] skyldi firða hverr: við annan 624(143)   [3] hann meira: hann mikit 624(144), minna 624(143)   [4] sá hefniz: er sá hrendr 624(144)   [5] halloki: halloka 624(144), 624(143)   [6] vegr: vinnr 1199ˣ(73v); síðan: um síðir 624(144), 624(143).

Editions: *Skj* Anonyme digte og vers [XIII], [C. E/5]. *Hugsvinnsmál* 67: AII, 182, BII, 196-7, *Skald* II, 102-3; Hallgrímur Scheving 1831, 18, Gering 1907, 19, Tuvestrand 1977, 109, Hermann Pálsson 1985, 74.

Notes: [All]: Lat. parallel: (*Dist.* II, 10) *Cui scieris non esse parem te, tempore cede: / victorem a victo superari saepe videmus* 'Yield at times to one whom you know not to be your equal; we frequently see the victor conquered by the loser'. This st. occurs first between sts 67 and 68 in 1199ˣ but is placed here in accordance with the order of the *disticha*. — [1-2]: These ll. are the same as st. 52/4-5. — [4-6]: 401ˣ renders the rest of the st.: *sá er vill hæstan tír hafa* 'he who wants to have the highest glory'.

67. Forlǫgu sinnar   skal maðr eigi frétt reka
       né um þat ǫnn ala;
    guð veit bezt,   hverjum hann giptu ann,
       ok vita þat eigi fyrðar fyrir.

Maðr skal eigi reka frétt forlǫgu sinnar, né ala ǫnn um þat; guð veit bezt, hverjum hann ann giptu, ok fyrðar vita þat eigi fyrir.

A man must not enquire about his future fate nor worry about it; God knows best to whom he grants luck and men do not know that beforehand.

Mss: **1199ˣ**(73v), 624(144). — *Readings*: [1] Forlǫgu: til farsælu 624   [2] skal: þar 624; maðr eigi: engi maðr 624;   reka: at reka 624   [3] ǫnn ala: annála 624   [4] bezt: gerst 624   [6] ok vita: vitu 624.

Editions: *Skj* Anonyme digte og vers [XIII], [C. E/5]. *Hugsvinnsmál* 69: AII, 183, BII, 197, *Skald* II, 103; Hallgrímur Scheving 1831, 18, Konráð Gíslason 1860, 551, Gering 1907, 19, Tuvestrand 1977, 110, Hermann Pálsson 1985, 75.

Notes: [All]: Lat. parallel: (*Dist.* II, 12) *Quid deus intendat, noli perquirere sorte: / quid statuat de te, sine te deliberat ille* 'Do not seek out by divination what God intends; what he establishes for you, he determines without you'. In l. 3 there are parallels in phrasing to the third l. in the second version's text of *Hsv* 38. Lines 1-3 are paralleled by *Hsv* 126/1-3. Cf. also *Hávm* 56/4-5 (*NK*, 25): *ørlǫg sín | viti engi fyrir* 'no one may know his fate beforehand' (Larrington 1996, 21).

68. Ǫfund ok þrætur   skal ýta hverr
       forðaz, sem mest megi;
    þvít ǫfundsamt hjarta   mæða ofrtregar,
       ok eigi hann satt um sér.

Hverr ýta skal forðaz ǫfund ok þrætur, sem mest megi, þvít ofrtregar mæða ǫfundsamt hjarta, ok hann um sér eigi satt.

Every man must flee envy and disputes as much as he can, because too many sorrows exhaust the envious heart and he does not see the truth.

Ms.: **1199ˣ**(73v).

Editions: *Skj* Anonyme digte og vers [XIII], [C. E/5]. *Hugsvinnsmál* 68: AII, 182-3, BII, 197, *Skald* II, 103; Hallgrímur Scheving 1831, 18, Gering 1907, 19, Tuvestrand 1977, 110, Hermann Pálsson 1985, 75.

Notes: [All]: Lat. parallel: (*Dist.* II, 13) *Invidiam nimio cultu vitare memento; / quae si non laedit, tamen hanc sufferre molestum* 'Remember to avoid envy with extreme care, which, even if it is not harmful, nevertheless is troublesome to endure'. The phrasing of the last l. of the Icel. text is quite close to *Hsv* 64/6.

69. Ef þik ríkir menn   dæma rangliga,
    lát eigi þinn hryggja hug;
  litla stund   fagna því lýða synir,
    ef þeir sælaz á svikum.

Ef ríkir menn dæma þik rangliga, lát eigi hryggja hug þinn; lýða synir fagna því litla stund, ef þeir sælaz á svikum.

If powerful men judge you wrongly, do not let it distress your mind; the sons of men rejoice in it for a short time, if they become happy from treachery.

Mss: 1199ˣ(73v), 624(144). — *Readings*: [3] lát: ger 624; þinn: þér 624; hryggja: hryggt í 624   [4] litla stund: lengi njóta 624   [5] fagna því: mun þess 624   [6] ef: er 624.

Editions: Skj Anonyme digte og vers [XIII], [C. E/5]. *Hugsvinnsmál* 70: AII, 183, BII, 197, *Skald* II, 103; Hallgrímur Scheving 1831, 18, Gering 1907, 20, Tuvestrand 1977, 111, Hermann Pálsson 1985, 76.

Notes: [All]: Lat. parallel: (*Dist*. II, 14) *Forti animo esto libens, cum sis damnatus inique: / nemo diu gaudet, qui iudice vincit iniquo* 'Be of strong mind with good will when you are wrongly accused; no one is happy for long who wins with an unjust judgement'.

70. Liðnar heiptir   skaltu eigi lengi muna;
    vertu í trygðum trúr;
  sakir at sækja,   þær er sættar eru,
    þat kveða ódyggs manns eðli.

Skaltu eigi muna liðnar heiptir lengi; vertu trúr í trygðum; þat kveða eðli ódyggs manns at sækja sakir, þær er eru sættar.

You must not remember past wrath for long; be faithful to your plighted oath; it is said to be the nature of an unreliable man to pursue actions which have been settled.

Ms.: 1199ˣ(/3v). — *Reading*: [2] skaltu: skulu 1199ˣ.

Editions: Skj Anonyme digte og vers [XIII], [C. E/5]. *Hugsvinnsmál* 71: AII, 183, BII, 197, *Skald* II, 103, *NN* §8B; Hallgrímur Scheving 1831, 19, Gering 1907, 20, Tuvestrand 1977, 111, Hermann Pálsson 1985, 76-7.

Notes: [All]: Lat. parallel: (*Dist*. II, 15) *Litis praeteritae noli maledicta referre: / post inimicitias iram meminisse malorum est* 'Do not allude to the curses of a past quarrel; it is bad to remember anger after hostilities'. — [2] *skaltu* 'must': 1199ˣ's *skulu* might be the result of confusing *liðnar heiptir* as the subj. of the cl.

71. Sjálfan sik   skal eigi seggja hverr
        lasta mjök né lofa;
    þat gera þeir,   er göfgir þykkjaz
        ok vilja heims skraut hafa.

Hverr seggja skal eigi lasta né lofa mjök sjálfan sik; þeir, er göfgir þykkjaz ok vilja hafa heims skraut, gera þat.

Every man must neither blame nor praise himself a lot; those who seem noble and want to have the finery of the world do that.

Mss: **1199ˣ**(73v), 624(144). — *Readings*: [2] skal eigi: skyldi 624   [3] mjök: eigi 624   [4] þat gera þeir: þeir þat gera 624   [5] göfgir þykkjaz: ógegnir eru 624   [6] vilja: vilja þó 624.

Editions: *Skj* Anonyme digte og vers [XIII], [C. E/5]. *Hugsvinnsmál* 72: AII, 183, BII, 197, *Skald* II, 103; Hallgrímur Scheving 1831, 19, Konráð Gíslason 1860, 551, Gering 1907, 20, Tuvestrand 1977, 112, Hermann Pálsson 1985, 78.

Notes: [All]: Lat. parallels: (*Dist.* II, 16) *Nec te conlaudes nec te culpaveris ipse: / hoc faciunt stulti, quos gloria vexat inanis* 'Neither praise nor blame yourself; this foolish people do, whom empty fame troubles'. Modesty is also dealt with in *Hsv* 72 and 127.

72. Af hyggjandi sinni   skyldi maðr óhræsinn vera,
        nema geraz þarfir þess;
    opt at haldi   hefr ýtum komit,
        ef leyniz spakr at speki.

Maðr skyldi vera óhræsinn af hyggjandi sinni, nema geraz þarfir þess; opt hefr komit at haldi ýtum, ef spakr leyniz at speki.

A man should not be boastful [*lit.* should be unboastful] of his intelligence, unless need of it arises; often it has become a help to people, if a wise man conceals his wisdom.

Mss: **1199ˣ**(74v), 624(144). — *Readings*:   [1] sinni: þinni 624   [2] skyldi maðr: vertu 624; vera: *om.* 624   [3] nema: unz 624   [6] ef: at 624; leyniz: leynaz.

Editions: *Skj* Anonyme digte og vers [XIII], [C. E/5]. *Hugsvinnsmál* 73: AII, 183, BII, 197-8, *Skald* II, 103, *NN* §3282; Hallgrímur Scheving 1831, 19, Konráð Gíslason 1860, 551, Gering 1907, 20, Tuvestrand 1977, 112, Hermann Pálsson 1985, 78.

Notes: [All]: Lat. parallels: (*Dist.* II, 18) *Insipiens esto, cum tempus postulat ipsum, / stultitiam simulare loco, prudentia summa est* 'Be foolish when the occasion demands; to feign stupidity is at times the highest prudence'. For similar phrasing cf. *Hávm* 6/1-2 (*NK*, 18): *At hyggiandi sinni / scylit maðr hræsinn vera* 'about his intelligence no man should be boastful' (Larrington 1996, 15). This st. is included considerably further on in 1199ˣ, with other sts that seem very much out of order (29, 66). Its inclusion here follows 624 and the Lat. text.

73. Fégirni rangri   skaltu forða þér;
    ljót er líkams munúð;
    orðstír hærra   getr engi maðr,
    en hann við syndum sjái.

Skaltu forða þér rangri fégirni; líkams munúð er ljót; maðr getr engi hærra orðstír, en hann sjái við syndum.

You must save yourself from wrongful avarice; desire of the body is ugly; a man gets no better reputation than if he avoids sins.

Mss: **1199ˣ**(73v), 624(144). — *Readings*: [2] forða þér: firra þik 624 [4] hærra: góðan 624 [5] engi maðr: maðr aldri 624 [6] hann: *om*. 624; sjái: sjá 624.

Editions: *Skj* Anonyme digte og vers [XIII], [C. E/5]. *Hugsvinnsmál* 74: AII, 183, BII, 198, *Skald* II, 103, *NN* §112; Hallgrímur Scheving 1831, 19, Konráð Gíslason 1860, 551, Gering 1907, 21, Tuvestrand 1977, 113, Hermann Pálsson 1985, 79.

Notes: [All]: Lat. parallel: (*Dist*. II, 19) *Luxuriam fugito, simul et vitare memento / crimen avaritiae; nam sunt contraria famae* 'Shun luxury, and also remember to avoid the accusation of avarice; for they are inimical to good repute'. Avarice is also dealt with in *Hsv* 22, 44, 56, 96, 97. Cf. also *Sól* 10, 18.

74. Sögvísum manni   skaltu sjaldan trúa,
    þeim er með rógi rennr,
    þvít málugs manns   reynaz margar sögur
    lýða kind at lygi.

Skaltu sjaldan trúa sögvísum manni, þeim er rennr með rógi, þvít margar sögur málugs manns reynaz lýða kind at lygi.

You must seldom believe a tattling man who runs with slander, because many stories of a talkative man prove to be lies for the race of men.

Mss: **1199ˣ**(73v), 624(144). — *Reading*: [4] þvít málugs manns: málugra manna 624.

Editions: *Skj* Anonyme digte og vers [XIII], [C. E/5]. *Hugsvinnsmál* 75: AII, 183-4, BII, 198, *Skald* II, 103, *NN* §112; Hallgrímur Scheving 1831, 19, Konráð Gíslason 1860, 551, Gering 1907, 21, Tuvestrand 1977, 113, Hermann Pálsson 1985, 80.

Notes: [All]: Lat. parallel: (*Dist*. II, 20) *Noli tu quaedam referenti credere semper: / exigua est tribuenda fides, qui multa locuntur* 'Do not always believe someone who bears reports; little credence is to be paid to those who speak many things'.

75. Ofdrukkinn maðr,   ef hann ilt geri,
    er eigi várkunnar vert;
    sjálfr því veldr,   ef hann svá drekkr,
    at eigi at geð síns gáir.

Ofdrukkinn maðr, ef hann geri ilt, er eigi várkunnar vert; sjálfr veldr því, ef hann drekkr svá, at eigi gáir at geð síns.

If a man who has drunk too much does wrong, it does not deserve excusing; he causes it himself if he drinks so much that he is not aware of his senses.

Mss: **1199^x**(73v), 624(144). — *Readings*: [2] ef: *so* 624, þótt 1199^x; geri: gerir 624 [3] várkunnar: *so* 624, 'vorkinnar' 1199^x [5] ef: er 624 [6] eigi at geð síns: síns góðs eigi 624.

Editions: *Skj* Anonyme digte og vers [XIII], [C. E/5]. *Hugsvinnsmál* 76: AII, 184, BII, 198, *Skald* II, 103; Hallgrímur Scheving 1831, 20, Konráð Gíslason 1860, 551, Gering 1907, 21, Tuvestrand 1977, 114, Hermann Pálsson 1985, 80.

Notes: [All]: Lat. parallels: (*Dist.* II, 21) *Quae potus peccas, ignoscere tu tibi noli, / nam crimen nullum vini, sed culpa bibentis* 'The crimes you commit in drinking do not excuse in yourself; for there is no fault in wine, but the fault is that of the drinker'. The topic of drinking decently is dealt with in several sts of *Hávm*. Cf. for instance *Hávm* 11/4-6 (*NK*, 18): *vegnest verra | vegra hann velli at, | enn sé ofdryccia ǫls* 'a worse journey-provision he couldn't carry over the land / than to be too drunk on ale' (Larrington 1996, 15). Cf. also *Hávm* 12 and 19. In a less direct way it is also dealt with in *Sól* 21.

76. Mál hvert, eigi   er skyldu margir vita,
        ber þú fyrir ómálgan upp;
    hygginn maðr,   ef vill heilsu taka,
        lætr eptir góðum læknum gera.

Ber þú upp fyrir ómálgan mál hvert, er eigi margir skyldu vita; hygginn maðr lætr gera eptir góðum læknum, ef vill taka heilsu.

Tell to a taciturn person every matter that not many should know; the intelligent man sends for good doctors if he wants to gain health.

Mss: **1199^x**(73v), 624(144). — *Readings*: [1] Mál: mál þat 624 [2] er: *so* 624, *om.* 1199^x; skyldu: skulu 624 [3] ómálgan: ómálgum 624 [4] maðr: maðr skal 624 [5] ef: sá er 624; taka: *so* 624, geti 1199^x [6] lætr: *om.* 624; læknum: *so* 624, læknir 1199^x; gera: leita 624.

Editions: *Skj* Anonyme digte og vers [XIII], [C. E/5]. *Hugsvinnsmál* 77: AII, 184, BII, 198, *Skald* II, 103; Hallgrímur Scheving 1831, 20, Gering 1907, 21, Tuvestrand 1977, 115, Hermann Pálsson 1985, 81.

Notes: [All]: Lat. parallel: (*Dist.* II, 22) *Consilium arcanum tacito committe sodali / corporis auxilium medico committe fideli* 'Entrust a secret plan to a close-mouthed associate; entrust aid for the body to a trustworthy doctor'. The danger of telling important news in front of too many and too talkative people is also mentioned in *Hávm* 63.

77. Optlig mein skal maðr eigi illa bera,
  ef hann er vítis verðr.

Maðr skal eigi bera optlig mein illa, ef hann er verðr vítis.

A man must not bear frequent misfortunes badly, if he is deserving of punishment.

Mss: **1199**ˣ(74v), 624(144).

Editions: *Skj* Anonyme digte og vers [XIII], [C. E/5]. *Hugsvinnsmál* 78: AII, 184, BII, 198-9, *Skald* II, 104; Hallgrímur Scheving 1831, 25, 34, Gering 1907, 28, 27, Tuvestrand 1977, 115, Hermann Pálsson 1985, 81-2.

Notes: [All]: Lat. parallel: (*Dist.* II, 23) *Successus pravos noli tu ferre moleste: / indulget fortuna malis, ut laedere possit* 'Do not take badly unworthy successes; fortune indulges the evil that it may wound them'. These ll. are recorded in 1199ˣ together with some other sts which fall outside the usual order of the *disticha*. This st. is included here in accordance with the order in 624 and the Lat. text.

78. Búinn við meinum skal bragna hverr,
  þótt gangi at óskum alt;
 sterklig stríð, trú ek, standaz meg*i*
  hverr, er þeira bíðr búinn.

Hverr bragna skal búinn við meinum, þótt alt gangi at óskum; ek trú hverr meg*i* standaz sterklig stríð, er þeira bíðr búinn.

Every man must be prepared for misfortunes, although everything goes as wished; I believe everyone can endure serious calamities who waits prepared for them.

Mss: **1199**ˣ(73v), 624(144). — *Readings*: [2] skal: skyldi 624; hverr: *so* 624, *om.* 1199ˣ [4] sterklig: sterkligri 624 [5] trú: hyggz 624; ek: er 624; meg*i*: 'meg[...]' 1199ˣ, mega 624 [6] hverr: hverr maðr 624; er: *so* 624, *om.* 1199ˣ.

Editions: *Skj* Anonyme digte og vers [XIII], [C. E/5]. *Hugsvinnsmál* 79: AII, 184, BII, 199, *Skald* II, 104; Hallgrímur Scheving 1831, 20, Gering 1907, 22, Tuvestrand 1977, 116, Hermann Pálsson 1985, 83.

Notes: [All]: Lat. parallel: (*Dist.* II, 24) *Prospice qui veniant casus: hos esse ferendos; / nam levius laedit quidquid praevidimus ante* 'Foresee events that come to pass; they are to be endured; for whatever we have previously foreseen wounds us more lightly'. — [2]: The phrasing of this l. is reminiscent of *Sól* 25/6. — [6] *meg*i 'can': Emendation of the verb is required here for it to agree with *hverr*. It is possible that the illegible letter in 1199^x is 'i'. Emendation to *hvern* 'everyone' (so *Skj* B) is also possible, creating an acc. and inf. construction.

79. Margsnotr maðr,   sá er fyrir meinum verðr,
    láti sinn eigi hryggja hug;
  góðs at vænta   skal gumna hverr,
    þótt hann sé til dauða dæmdr.

Margsnotr maðr, sá er verðr fyrir meinum, láti eigi hryggja hug sinn; hverr gumna skal góðs at vænta, þótt hann sé dæmdr til dauða.

A very wise man who meets with misfortunes should not let them distress his mind; every man must expect good, although he may be sentenced to death.

Mss: **1199^x**(74v), 624(144). — *Readings*: [1] Margsnotr: margvitr 624 [2] sá: *om.* 624 [3] sinn eigi: eigi sinn 624 [5] skal: skyldi 624; gumna: seggja 1199^x, gunna 624.

Editions: *Skj* Anonyme digte og vers [XIII], [C. E/5]. *Hugsvinnsmál* 80: AII, 184, BII, 199, *Skald* II, 104; Hallgrímur Scheving 1831, 20, Konráð Gíslason 1860, 551, Gering 1907, 22, Tuvestrand 1977, 116, Hermann Pálsson 1985, 84.

Notes: [All]: Lat. parallel: (*Dist.* II, 25) *Rebus in adversis animum submittere noli; / spem retine: spes una hominem nec morte relinquit* 'Do not lower your courage when things go wrong; keep up hope: hope alone does not desert a man, not even in death'. The phrasing of the last two ll. is very close to *Hsv* 34. A similar topic is dealt with in *Sól* 34. — [5] *gumna* 'of men': 1199^x's *seggja* does not provide alliteration, whereas 624's *gunna* 'of wars' is clearly an error. AM 148 8^{ox}, a copy of 624, has *gumna*. Cf. sts 81/5 and 87/3, where the scribe of 624 also has written *gunn-* for *gumn-*.

80. Hársíðan mann   sá ek í hölða liði;
    þó var honum skalli skapaðr;
  svá er sá maðr,   sem mart á fjár
    ok verðr síðan snauðr.

Ek sá hársíðan mann í hölða liði; þó var honum skalli skapaðr; svá er sá maðr sem á mart fjár ok verðr snauðr síðan.

I saw a man with long hair in a host of men; he was, however, destined to be bald; like this is the man who has a lot of money but becomes poor later.

Mss: **1199^x**(74v), 624(144). — *Readings*: [2] liði: *so* 624, siði 1199^x [5] mart á: *so* 624, á auð 1199^x [6] síðan: um síðir 624.

Editions: *Skj* Anonyme digte og vers [XIII], [C. E/5]. *Hugsvinnsmál* 81: AII, 184-5, BII, 199, *Skald* II, 104; Hallgrímur Scheving 1831, 34, Gering 1907, 22, Tuvestrand 1977, 117, Hermann Pálsson 1985, 84.

Notes: [All]: Lat. parallel: (*Dist.* II, 26) *Rem tibi quam scieris aptam dimittere noli: / fronte capillata, post haec occasio calva* 'The thing which you know to be fitting for you, do not give up; chance has a forelock in front, behind [that] is bald'. The Lat. distich draws upon a literary and iconographical tradition, originating in ancient Greece but well known in the Middle Ages, that the figure of Kairos, god of the fleeting moment (Lat. *occasio*) had a forelock in front, which those who were able could grasp, while the back of his head was bald to prevent people taking hold of him from behind. This symbolises the notion that the favourable moment must be grasped immediately, otherwise it is gone and cannot be regained; see further Moreno 1999. Clearly, the Icel. translator of this distich was unaware of the classical tradition.

81. Um lítaz   þarf maðr á alla vegu
        ok við villu varaz;
    glöggþekkinn   skyldi gumna hverr
        ok fróðr ok forsjáll vera.

Maðr þarf lítaz um á alla vegu ok varaz við villu; hverr gumna skyldi vera glöggþekkinn ok fróðr ok forsjáll.

A man has to look around in all directions and beware of falsehood; every man should be clear-sighted and wise and foresighted.

Mss: **1199**^x(73v), 624(144). — *Readings*: [1] Um: um at 624   [2] á alla vegu: alla vega 624   [3] villu: víti 624;   varaz: at varaz 624   [5] gumna: gunna 624   [6] ok: *om*. 624.

Editions: *Skj* Anonyme digte og vers [XIII], [C. E/5]. *Hugsvinnsmál* 82: AII, 185, BII, 199, *Skald* II, 104; Hallgrímur Scheving 1831, 20, Gering 1907, 22, Tuvestrand 1977, 117, Hermann Pálsson 1985, 85.

Notes: [All]: Lat. parallel: (*Dist.* II, 27) *Quod sequitur specta quodque imminet ante, videto: / illum imitare deum, partem qui spectat utramque* 'Look at what has happened, and see that which is coming; imitate that god who looks in both directions [Janus]'. The Icel. text here does not reproduce the classical reference. Cf. also *Hsv* 98. In ON-Icel. poetry there are many parallels to the admonition in the first two ll. Cf. e.g. *Hávm* 1 (*NK*, 17): *Gáttir allar, | áðr gangi fram, | um scoðaz scyli, | um scygnaz scyli; | þvíat óvíst er at vita, | hvar óvinir | sitia á fleti fyrir* 'All the entrances, before you walk forward, you should look at, you should spy out; for you can't know for certain where enemies are sitting ahead in the hall' (Larrington 1996, 14). There is also a parallel in phrasing in *Sól* 19. Cf. also the topic of *Sól* 40. — [5] *gumna*: As this is the second instance in 624 where *gunna* is used instead of *gumna*, it has to be supposed that the scribe did not know the poetic word.

82. Áts né drykkju   neyt þú aldrigi,
         svát þitt minkiz megn;
    afl ok heilsu   þarft þú við alt at hafa;
         lif þú eigi mart at munúð.

Neyt þú aldrigi áts né drykkju, svát megn þitt minkiz; þú þarft at hafa afl ok heilsu við alt; lif þú eigi mart at munúð.

Never enjoy eating nor drinking to such an extent that your strength decreases; you need to have strength and health for everything; do not live [too] much for pleasure.

Mss: **1199**ˣ(73v-74r), 624(144). — *Readings*: [1] Áts né: 'Azt ok' 624 [4] afl ok heilsu: til álfs ok heils 624 [5] þarft þú: þartu 624; við: eigi 624 [6] lif þú: líf áttu 624.

Editions: *Skj* Anonyme digte og vers [XIII], [C. E/5]. *Hugsvinnsmál* 83: AII, 185, BII, 199, *Skald* II, 104; Hallgrímur Scheving 1831, 21, Konráð Gíslason 1860, 551, Gering 1907, 23, Tuvestrand 1977, 118, Hermann Pálsson 1985, 86.

Notes: [All]: Lat. parallel: (*Dist*. II, 28) *Fortius ut valeas, interdum parcior esto: / pauca voluptati debentur, plura saluti* 'Be more forceful so that you may be strong, occasionally be more sparing. A few things are owed to pleasure, more to health'. The topic of eating too much is dealt with in *Hávm* 20. — [4-5]: 624's reading of these ll. is possibly closer to the Lat.: *til álfs* [i.e. *afls*] *ok heils | þarftu eigi alt at hafa* 'you do not need to have everything for strength and good fortune'.

83. Alþýðuróm   lasta þú aldrigi,
         þann er lýðir lofa;
    öngum sá hugnar,   er öllum vill
         gagnmálugr geraz.

Lasta þú aldrigi alþýðuróm, þann er lýðir lofa; sá hugnar öngum, er vill geraz öllum gagnmálugr.

Never blame general acclamation which people praise; he who wants to become the opponent of everyone pleases nobody.

Mss: **1199**ˣ(74r), 624(144-5). — *Readings*: [2] aldrigi: eigi 624 [3] er: sem 624 [4] sá hugnar: hugnaz sá 624 [5] öllum vill: vill öllum 624.

Editions: *Skj* Anonyme digte og vers [XIII], [C. E/5]. *Hugsvinnsmál* 84: AII, 185, BII, 199-200, *Skald* II, 104; Hallgrímur Scheving 1831, 21, Konráð Gíslason 1860, 551, Gering 1907, 23, Tuvestrand 1977, 118, Hermann Pálsson 1985, 87.

Notes: [All]: Lat. parallel: (*Dist*. II, 29) *Iudicium populi numquam contempseris unus, / ne nulli placeas, dum vis contemnere multos* 'Never despise public opinion on your own, lest you please no one when you want to slight many'.

84. Dagráðs leita   þarf eigi til dugnaðar,
          sá er vill heilindi hafa;
    stundir eigi ráða,   þótt komi stríð um her;
          allar eru tíðir trúar.

Sá er vill hafa heilindi, þarf eigi leita dagráðs til dugnaðar; stundir ráða eigi, þótt stríð komi um her; allar tíðir eru trúar.

He who wants to have good health need not look for a convenient time for aid; hours do not determine whether strife spreads among the population; all times are appropriate.

Ms.: **1199**[x](74r).

Editions: *Skj* Anonyme digte og vers [XIII], [C. E/5]. *Hugsvinnsmál* 85: AII, 185, BII, 200, *Skald* II, 104; Hallgrímur Scheving 1831, 21, Gering 1907, 23, Tuvestrand 1977, 119, Hermann Pálsson 1985, 87.

Notes: [All]: Lat. parallel: (*Dist.* II, 30) *Sit tibi praecipue, quod primum est, cura salutis: / tempore ne culpes, cum sit tibi causa doloris* 'Let your health, which is foremost, be your main concern, nor blame the occasion, when you yourself are the cause of pain'. — [5] *um her* 'among the population': *Skj* B takes Hallgrímur Scheving's text, *þótt komi stríð eða hel* 'if strife or death may come'.

85. Draumum sínum   skulu eigi dróttir trúa;
          tæla þeir ýta opt;
    sofanda manni þykkir   þat, er sjálfr, þegar at vakir,
          æskir sér eða óaz.

Dróttir skulu eigi trúa draumum sínum; þeir tæla ýta opt; þat, er sjálfr æskir sér eða óaz, þegar at vakir, þykkir manni sofanda.

Men should not believe their dreams; they often deceive people; what he wishes for himself or fears when awake, appears to a man when asleep.

Mss: **1199**[x](74r), 624(145). — *Readings*: [1] Draumum: óvinum 624   [2] skulu eigi dróttir: skyldi dróttir eigi 624   [3] ýta: seggi 624   [4] sofand*a*: sofandi 1199[x], 624; manni: *om.* 624   [5] þegar at: meðan 624.

Editions: *Skj* Anonyme digte og vers [XIII], [C. E/5]. *Hugsvinnsmál* 86: AII, 185, BII, 200, *Skald* II, 104; Hallgrímur Scheving 1831, 21, Konráð Gíslason 1860, 551, Gering 1907, 23, Tuvestrand 1977, 119, Hermann Pálsson 1985, 88.

Notes: [All]: Lat. parallel: (*Dist.* II, 31) *Somnia ne cures, nam mens humana quod optat, / dum vigilat, sperat, per somnum cernit id ipsum* 'Do not pay attention to dreams; for the human mind hopes for what it wishes for while it is asleep, [and] through dreaming recognises that very thing [i.e. what it wishes for]'. — [1] *draumum* 'dreams': 624 and the copy of it in

AM 148 8ᵒˣ (fol. 73r, l. 18) have *óvinum* 'enemies', although *Skj* A reads 'Dvmum'. The reading in 624 might have been influenced by *Sól* 19.

86. Örr at kenna   skalt þú öðrum gott
    ok svá nýtr at nema;
  mörgum dugir,   sá er at mannviti kenniz;
    veitir gott ráð gum*um.

Þú skalt örr at kenna öðrum gott ok svá nýtr at nema; dugir mörgum, sá er kenniz at mannviti; veitir gum*um gott ráð.

You must be generous in teaching good to others and also capable in learning; he helps many, who acknowledges reason; he gives people good advice.

Mss: **1199ˣ**(74r), 624(145). — *Readings*: [1] Örr at: gott skal 624   [2] skalt þú öðrum gott: sá er vill grandvarr vera 624   [3] svá nýtr: kosta nýtt 624;   at: af 624   [5] kenniz: *om.* 624   [6] veitir gott ráð: kennir gott 624;   gum*um: gumnum 1199ˣ, 624.

Editions: *Skj* Anonyme digte og vers [XIII], [C. E/5]. *Hugsvinnsmál* 87: AII, 185-6, BII, 200, *Skald* II, 104; Hallgrímur Scheving 1831, 22, Gering 1907, 24, Tuvestrand 1977, 120, Hermann Pálsson 1985, 89.

Notes: [All]: Lat. parallel: (*Dist*. III, 1) *Instrue praeceptis animum, ne discere cessa; / nam sine doctrina vita est quasi mortis imago* 'Instruct your mind with precepts, nor cease to learn; for a life without learning is like the image of death'. This st. begins the main text of Book III, but there is no attempt to translate the preface to this book of the *Disticha*. — [All]: Hallgrímur Scheving includes ll. 1-3 with the same readings as here, but lacks ll. 4-6, which could be corrupt in 1199ˣ. 624 differs considerably, but is used by most eds (including *Skj*, *Skald* and Hermann Pálsson):

    Gott skal kenna,   sá er vill grandvarr vera,
      ok kosta nýtt at nema;
    mörgum dugir,   sá er af mannviti
      kennir gott gum*um.

*Skal kenna gott ok kosta nýtt at nema, sá er vill vera grandvarr; dugir mörgum, sá er af mannviti kennir gum*um gott* 'He who wants to be prudent must teach something good and strive to learn something useful; he helps many, who teaches people something good from understanding'. — [1-3]: For these ll. there is a parallel in content in *Sól* 32. — [2]: The reading of 1199ˣ *svá nýtr* in the second l. might have been influenced by *Hsv* 132. — [6] *gum*um* 'people': Cf. Note to st. 59/3.

87. Manndáð meiri   getr eigi fyrir mold ofan,
    en kenna góð ráð gum*um;
ódyggt líf   mundu ýtar hafa,
    ef bætti engi yfir.

Getr eigi meiri manndáð fyrir mold ofan en kenna gum*um góð ráð; ýtar mundu hafa ódyggt líf, ef engi bætti yfir.

There is no greater act of prowess on earth than to teach men good advice; people would have a worthless life if nobody were to improve it.

Mss: **1199ˣ**(74r), 624(145). — *Readings*: [1] Manndáð: manndýrð 624   [3] góð: gott 624; ráð: *om.* 624;   gum*um: gumnum 1199ˣ, gunnum 624   [4] ódyggt: fádyggt 624   [5] ýtar: flestir 624   [6] bætti engi: engi bætti 624.

Editions: Skj Anonyme digte og vers [XIII], [C. E/5]. *Hugsvinnsmál* 88: AII, 186, BII, 200, *Skald* II, 104; Hallgrímur Scheving 1831, 22, Konráð Gíslason 1860, 551-2, Gering 1907, 24, Tuvestrand 1977, 120, Hermann Pálsson 1985, 89.

Notes: [All]: Lat. parallel: (*Dist*. III, 1a) *Fortunae donis semper par esse memento: | non opibus bona fama datur, sed moribus ipsis* 'Always remember to be equal to the gifts of Fortune; a good reputation is given not on account of riches, but because of [one's] conduct'. The Lat. distich is a variant of III, 1 and the translation here is likewise a variant of st. 86. — [3] *gum*um* 'to men': Cf. Note to st. 59/3.

88. Löstum leyna   skaltu, sem lengst má,
    þeim er þú veiz með vinum;
halt trú til þess,   ok lát af hljóði fara,
    þat er sjálfan sakir.

Skaltu, sem lengst má, leyna löstum, þeim er þú veiz með vinum; halt trú til þess, ok lát fara af hljóði, þat er sakir sjálfan.

You must, as long as possible, hide the vices you know that friends have; be faithful to that, and let what is harmful to oneself dissipate in silence.

Mss: **1199ˣ**(74r), 624(145). — *Readings*: [2] má: ef mátt 624   [3] þeim: þat 624; með: eptir 624   [4] halt trú til þess: til þess alt 624   [5] fara: *so* 624, *om.* 1199ˣ   [6] þat: *om.* 624; sjálfan: þeir bæta sínar 624;   sakir: *so* 624, sækir 1199ˣ.

Editions: Skj Anonyme digte og vers [XIII], [C. E/5]. *Hugsvinnsmál* 90: AII, 186, BII, 200-1, *Skald* II, 105; Hallgrímur Scheving 1831, 22, Gering 1907, 25, Tuvestrand 1977, 121, Hermann Pálsson 1985, 90.

Notes: [All]: Lat. parallel: (*Dist*. III, 3) *Productus testis, salvo tamen ante pudore, | quantumcumque potes, celato crimen amici* 'When called as a witness, while still keeping your honour safe, as much as you can, hide the offence of a friend'. — [4-6]: The text here, from 1199ˣ, is the same as Hallgrímur Scheving's. 624's version, the basis of all other eds, is perhaps more intelligible (taking *Skj* B's emendation *alt* to *halt*): *til þess halt, | ok lát af hljóði fara, | er þeir bæta sínar sakir* 'make a point of it, that they make good their wrongs, but let it happen in secret'.

89. Illa áleitni   ræk þú aldrigi,
    ef þú lastvarr lifir;
  eigi er auðgætt,   þat er öllum líki;
    ger þú, svát góðr lofi.

Ræk þú aldrigi illa áleitni, ef þú lifir lastvarr; eigi er auðgætt, þat er öllum líki; ger þú, svát góðr lofi.

Never worry about evil rebuke if you live as a virtuous person; it is not easy [to do] what pleases everyone; behave in such a way that a good person praises [you].

Ms.: **1199ˣ**(74r).

Editions: *Skj* Anonyme digte og vers [XIII], [C. E/5]. *Hugsvinnsmál* 89: AII, 186, BII, 201, *Skald* II, 105; Hallgrímur Scheving 1831, 22, Gering 1907, 24, Tuvestrand 1977, 121, Hermann Pálsson 1985, 91.

Notes: [All]: Lat. parallel: (*Dist*. III, 2) *Cum recte vivas, ne cures verba malorum, | arbitri non est nostri, quid quisque loquatur* 'If you live rightly, do not worry about the words of bad people; it is not in our power to decide what each person says'.

90. Blíðum orðum   þótt þik bragnar kveði,
    þarftu eigi þeim at trúa;
  opt sá fagrt mælir,   er hefir flátt hugat;
    ráð er at sjá við svikum.

Þótt bragnar kveði þik blíðum orðum, þarftu eigi at trúa þeim; sá mælir opt fagrt, er hefir hugat flátt; ráð er at sjá við svikum.

Although men may greet you with pleasant words, you need not believe them; he often speaks fair, who has considered deceit; it is advisable to look out for treachery.

Mss: **1199ˣ**(74r), 624(145). — *Readings*: [2] kveði: lofi 624   [3] trúa: trúa við vel at varaz 624   [5] er: sem hann 624;   hugat: í huga 624   [6] ráð: gott 624.

Editions: *Skj* Anonyme digte og vers [XIII], [C. E/5]. *Hugsvinnsmál* 91: AII, 186, BII, 201, *Skald* II, 105, *NN* §2592; Hallgrímur Scheving 1831, 23, Gering 1907, 25, Tuvestrand 1977, 122, Hermann Pálsson 1985, 92.

Notes: [All]: Lat. parallel: (*Dist*. III, 4) *Sermones blandos blaesosque cavere memento: | simplicitas veri fama est, fraus ficta loquendi* 'Remember to watch out for smooth and lisping words; simplicity is the character of the true, deceit that of telling stories'. As in many other instances 1199[x] conforms better to the requirements of *ljóðaháttr*. 624 seems to combine several versions of this st., especially l. 3, which includes almost an extra l.: *við vel at varaz* 'be wary of tricks'. — [3]: The l. corresponds to st. 30/5. Similar advice is given in *Sól* 19.

91. Eigi skaltu lataz, ef þú vilt líf hafa,
    þat er drengmanni dugir;
    því fleira lýtir, sem færra nennir
    gott at vinna gumi.

Skaltu eigi lataz, ef þú vilt hafa líf, þat er dugir drengmanni; því fleira lýtir, sem gumi nennir færra gott at vinna.

You must not be lazy if you want to have a life which suits a good man; a man will blame the more, as he is inclined to do less [that is] good.

Mss: 1199[x](74r), 624(145). — *Readings*: [1] Eigi skaltu: skal eigi sá 624; lataz: latr 624   [2] ef þú vilt: er vill eigi 624   [4] lýtir: fýsir 624   [5] sem færra nennir: er fleira nemr 624   [6] vinna gumi: vilja 624.

Editions: *Skj* Anonyme digte og vers [XIII], [C. E/5]. *Hugsvinnsmál* 92: AII, 186, BII, 201, *Skald* II, 105; Hallgrímur Scheving 1831, 23, Gering 1907, 25, Tuvestrand 1977, 122, Hermann Pálsson 1985, 92.

Notes: [All]: Lat. parallel: (*Dist*. III, 5) *Segnitiem fugito, quae vitae ignavia fertur; / nam cum animus languet, consumit inertia corpus* 'Avoid sluggishness, which means laziness of life; for when the mind is weary, inertia consumes the body'. — [4-6]: 624 reads quite differently: *því fleira fýsir, / er fleira nemr, / gott at vilja* 'he who learns more is urged to want [to do] all the more good'. The last l. is hypometrical and lacks alliteration.

92. Höfugt erfiði ef þér at höndum kemr,
    vertu glaðmæltr gumi;
    fagnandi maðr neytir flest at vinna;
    öll eru lostverk létt.

Ef höfugt erfiði kemr at höndum þér, vertu glaðmæltr gumi; fagnandi maðr neytir at vinna flest; öll lostverk eru létt.

If a difficult problem comes your way, be a cheerfully-speaking man; a joyful man manages to achieve most things; all labours of love are easy.

Ms.: 1199[x](74r).

Editions: *Skj* Anonyme digte og vers [XIII], [C. E/5]. *Hugsvinnsmál* 93: AII, 187, BII, 201, *Skald* II, 105; Hallgrímur Scheving 1831, 23, Gering 1907, 25, Tuvestrand 1977, 123, Hermann Pálsson 1985, 93.

Notes: [All]: Lat. parallel: (*Dist.* III, 6) *Interpone tuis interdum gaudia curis, / ut possis animo quemvis sufferre laborem* 'Intersperse your cares now and again with joy, that you may be able to bear in your mind any kind of hardship'.

93. Eigi skaltu hlæja, ef þú vilt horskr vera,
    at annars ófǫrum;
  opt þeir hefnaz, er hlegnir eru,
    ok gjalda líku líkt.

Skaltu eigi hlæja at annars ófǫrum, ef þú vilt vera horskr; þeir hefnaz opt, er hlegnir eru, ok gjalda líku líkt.

You must not laugh at another's ill-luck, if you want to be wise; they who are laughed at often take revenge and repay like with like.

Mss: **1199**ˣ(74r), 624(145). — *Readings*: [1] Eigi skaltu: skaltu eigi 624 [2] vera: verat 624 [4] opt þeir: þeir opt 624 [6] gjalda: gjalda þeir 624.

Editions: *Skj* Anonyme digte og vers [XIII], [C. E/5]. *Hugsvinnsmál* 94: AII, 187, BII, 201, *Skald* II, 105; Hallgrímur Scheving 1831, 23, Gering 1907, 26, Tuvestrand 1977, 123, Hermann Pálsson 1985, 93.

Notes: [All]: Lat. parallel: (*Dist.* III, 7) *Alterius factum ac dictum ne carpseris umquam, / exemplo simili ne te derideat alter* 'Never criticise the saying or deed of another, lest the other man deride you in similar fashion'. — [4-5]: These ll. are similar to st. 56/4-5. A similar topic is dealt with in st. 121. Cf. also *Hávm* 132/5-7 (*NK*, 38): *at hæði né hlátri | hafðu aldregi | gest né ganganda* 'never hold up to scorn or mockery a guest or a wanderer' (Larrington 1996, 33).

94. Aldraðr maðr ef fyrir aurum ræðr
    ok dregr sekk saman,
  vinum sínum skal sá vel duga
    ok vera góðr gjafa.

Ef aldraðr maðr ræðr fyrir aurum ok dregr saman sekk, skal sá duga vinum sínum vel ok vera góðr gjafa.

If an elderly man has command of wealth and gathers together a hoard, he must help his friends well and be generous with gifts.

Mss: **1199**ˣ(74r), 624(145). — *Readings*: [2] fyrir aurum: eigi auði 624 [3] sekk: hann sǫkk 624.

Editions: *Skj* Anonyme digte og vers [XIII], [C. E/5]. *Hugsvinnsmál* 95: AII, 187, BII, 201, *Skald* II, 105; Hallgrímur Scheving 1831, 23, Gering 1907, 26, Tuvestrand 1977, 124, Hermann Pálsson 1985, 94.

Notes: [All]: Lat. parallel: (*Dist*. III, 9) *Cum tibi divitiae superent in fine senectae, / munificus facito vivas, non parcus, amicus* 'When riches abound for you at the end of old age, make sure to live as a generous friend, not a niggardly one'. *Hsv* 60 also deals with the topic of generosity towards friends.

95. Gott ráð nema skal gumna hverr,
    þótt kenni þý eða þræll;
  ánauðgan mann hygg ek opt vera
    frjálsum fróðara.

Hverr gumna skal nema gott ráð, þótt þý eða þræll kenni; ek hygg ánauðgan mann opt vera fróðara frjálsum.

Every person must take good advice, even if a female or male slave teaches it; I think an enslaved man is often wiser than a free one.

Mss: **1199**^{x}(74r), 624(145). — *Readings*: [2] skal: skuli 624   [3] kenni: ken 624   [4] ánauðgan: *so* 624, óauðgan 1199^x.

Editions: *Skj* Anonyme digte og vers [XIII], [C. E/5]. *Hugsvinnsmál* 96: AII, 187, BII, 201-2, *Skald* II, 105; Hallgrímur Scheving 1831, 24, Konráð Gíslason 1860, 552, Gering 1907, 26, Tuvestrand 1977, 124, Hermann Pálsson 1985, 94.

Notes: [All]: Lat. parallel: (*Dist*. III, 10) *Utile consilium dominus ne despice servi; / nullius sensum, si prodest, tempseris unquam* 'As a master do not despise the useful counsel of your servant [*or* slave]; never spurn anyone's advice, if it is useful'.

96. Aura tjón skal maðr eigi illa bera,
    þótt honum verði skapaðr skaði;
  hitt hann huggar, ef hann halda má:
    sæll er, sá er sínu unir.

Maðr skal eigi illa bera aura tjón, þótt verði skapaðr skaði honum; hitt huggar hann, ef hann má halda; sæll er, sá er unir sínu.

A man must not bear badly the loss of his wealth, although it may cause harm for him; what [remains] will comfort him, if he can keep it; he is fortunate who is content with what he has.

Ms.: **1199**^{x}(74r).

Editions: *Skj* Anonyme digte og vers [XIII], [C. E/5]. *Hugsvinnsmál* 136: AII, 195, BII, 208, *Skald* II, 109; Hallgrímur Scheving 1831, 31, Gering 1907, 37, Tuvestrand 1977, 125, Hermann Pálsson 1985, 95.

Notes: [All]: Lat. parallels: (*Dist.* III, 11) *Rebus et in censu si non est quod fuit ante, / fac vivas contentus eo, quod tempora praebent* 'If in goods and income things are not what they were, see that you live happy with that which the times offer'; (*Dist.* IV, 35) *Ereptis opibus noli maerere dolendo / sed gaude potius, tibi si contingat habere* 'Do not bewail grieving over stolen goods, rather be happy, if it happens that you have something [left]'. Finnur Jónsson (*Skj* B) takes the latter distich as the primary parallel and consequently includes this st. after his st. 135 (translating *Dist.* IV, 34). — [6]: This l. seems to be a variant of a common saying in Icel. Cf. *Hávm* 9/1-3 (*NK*, 18): *Sá er sæll, | er siálfr um á | lof oc vit, meðan lifir* 'That man is fortunate who, in himself, keeps his reputation and wits while he lives' (Larrington 1996, 15). There is similar phrasing in *Sól* 49.

97. Algegn maðr   með aurafjölð
    vill sér kjósa konu;
  þat þá reynir,   ef hann reyna skal
    mundargjöld til mikin.

Algegn maðr með aurafjölð vill kjósa sér konu; þat reynir þá, ef hann skal reyna til mikin mundargjöld.

A very upright man with a lot of money will want to choose a wife for himself; that [his wealth] is then put to the test, if he must test too great a bride-price settlement.

Ms.: **1199**[x](74r).

Editions: *Skj* Anonyme digte og vers [XIII], [C. E/5]. *Hugsvinnsmál* 97: AII, 187, BII, 202, *Skald* II, 105, *NN* FF §60; Hallgrímur Scheving 1831, 24, Gering 1907, 26, Tuvestrand 1977, 125, Hermann Pálsson 1985, 96.

Notes: [All]: Lat. parallel: (*Dist.* III, 12) *Uxorem fuge ne ducas sub nomine dotis, / nec retinere velis, si coeperit esse molesta* 'Flee from taking a wife for the sake of dowry, and do not wish to keep her if she begins to be burdensome'. — [4-6]: The sense seems to be: because it is known that the prospective groom is wealthy, the bride's family will attempt to ask for an excessive *mundr* or bride-price. The translation here reflects the difference between the ON system of bride-price and dowry and the dowry (*heimanfylgja*) system implied in the Lat. distich. — [6] *mundargjöld* 'bride-price settlement': This cpd is *hap. leg.*

98. Góðra dæma   leiti gumna hverr,
    sá er vill hyggindi hafa;
annars víti   láti sér at varnaði,
    ok geriz svá góðum líkr.

Hverr gumna, sá er vill hafa hyggindi, leiti góðra dæma; láti víti annars sér at varnaði, ok geriz svá líkr góðum.

Every man who wants to have wisdom, should look for good examples; he should let the punishment of another [be] a warning to him and thus become like good people.

Mss: **1199**[x](74r), 624(145). — *Readings*: [2] leiti: leiti sér 624   [3] sá: *om*. 624   [4] annars: vánds manns 624   [5] láti: lætr 624; varnaði: varnaði verða 624   [6] geriz svá: verðr 624.

Editions: *Skj* Anonyme digte og vers [XIII], [C. E/5]. *Hugsvinnsmál* 98: AII, 187, BII, 202, *Skald* II, 105; Hallgrímur Scheving 1831, 24, Gering 1907, 26, Tuvestrand 1977, 126, Hermann Pálsson 1985, 97.

Notes: [All]: Lat. parallel: (*Dist*. III, 13) *Multorum disce exemplo quae facta sequaris, / quae fugias, vita est nobis aliena magistra* 'Learn from the example of many what deeds you should emulate and which to avoid; the life of others is a teacher to us'.

99. Upp at hefja   sómir þér eigi vel
    meiri iðn, en þú megir;
algers verks,   þá er unnit er;
    æ spyrr lýðr at lokum.

Sómir þér eigi vel at hefja upp meiri iðn, en þú megir; lýðr spyrr æ at lokum algers verks, þá er unnit er.

It does not befit you to start a bigger business than you can manage; people always find out about the results of a completed work when it is finished.

Mss: **1199**[x](74r), 624(145). — *Readings*: [2] sómir: samir 624   [4] algers verks: algert verk dugir 624   [6] æ: at 624.

Editions: *Skj* Anonyme digte og vers [XIII], [C. E/5]. *Hugsvinnsmál* 99: AII, 187-8, BII, 202, *Skald* II, 105-6; Hallgrímur Scheving 1831, 24, Gering 1907, 27, Tuvestrand 1977, 126, Hermann Pálsson 1985, 98.

Notes: [All]: Lat. parallel: (*Dist*. III, 14) *Quod potes, id tempta: operis ne pondere pressus / succumbat labor, et frustra temptata relinquas* 'Whatever you can, try, lest under the weight of the burden of the task work collapses and you give up that tried in vain'. In 1199[x] there is additional text which serves as a paraphrase for the st.: *uppbyrja sæmir eigi iðju meiri en algert fáir* 'it is not fitting to undertake an activity greater than can be finished'.

100. Eigi skaltu þegja,   þóttu sért þess beðinn,
    um annars ósiðu;
illr þykkir sá,   er með öðrum hefir
    ljótu ráði leynt.

Skaltu eigi þegja um annars ósiðu, þóttu sért beðinn þess; sá þykkir illr, er hefir leynt ljótu ráði með öðrum.

You must not keep silent about another's immorality, although you may be asked to [keep silent]; he is considered bad, who has hidden a bad action [carried out] by another.

Mss: **1199^x**(74v), 723a^x(81) (l. 6), 624(145). — *Readings*: [1] Eigi skaltu: skaltu eigi 624   [3] um: yfir 624;   ósiðu: ósiðum 624   [4] illr: *so* 624, féligr 1199^x   [5] öðrum: *so* 624, öðru 1199^x;   hefir: *so* 624, *om*. 1199^x   [6] ljótu: '[...]' 723a^x, leynt 624;   ráði leynt: *so* 723a^x, leynir 1199^x, ljótu ráði 624.

Editions: *Skj* Anonyme digte og vers [XIII], [C. E/5]. *Hugsvinnsmál* 100: AII, 188, BII, 202, *Skald* II, 106, *NN* §113; Hallgrímur Scheving 1831, 24, Gering 1907, 27, Tuvestrand 1977, 127, Hermann Pálsson 1985, 98.

Notes: [All]: Lat. parallel: (*Dist*. III, 15) *Quod nosti factum prave, nolito silere, / ne videare malos imitari velle tacendo* 'That which you know to be wrongly done, do not be silent about, lest by keeping silence you seem to be willing to imitate wrongdoers'. — [4-6]: 1199^x is hypometrical in these ll. In l. 6, 723a^x resumes and supplies the metrically correct reading.

101. Liðs skal biðja,   þá er ráða lögskilum,
    ef maðr er lýtum loginn;
röngu verz,   ef réttu náir,
    maðr, sá er dómendr duga.

Ef maðr er loginn lýtum, skal biðja liðs, þá er ráða lögskilum; maðr, sá er dómendr duga, verz röngu, ef náir réttu.

If a man is unjustly accused of faults, he must ask for help from those who have command of legal procedure; a man whom the judges help, defends himself against something wrong, if he gets his rights.

Mss: **1199^x**(74r), 624(145). — *Readings*: [3] ef maðr er: sá er verðr 624   [4] röngu: röngu máli 624   [5] ef: sá er 624   [6] maðr sá er: hvar 624.

Editions: *Skj* Anonyme digte og vers [XIII], [C. E/5]. *Hugsvinnsmál* 101: AII, 188, BII, 202, *Skald* II, 106, *NN* §114; Hallgrímur Scheving 1831, 25, Gering 1907, 27, Tuvestrand 1977, 127, Hermann Pálsson 1985, 99.

Notes: [All]: Lat. parallel: (*Dist*. III, 16) *Iudicis auxilium sub † iniquitate rogato, / ipsae etiam leges cupiunt, ut iure rogentur* 'Beg for the aid of the judge in an unjust lawsuit, for the very laws themselves desire to be questioned properly'. — [4-6]: *Skj* B has the same text as here (except *sá er* (624) for *ef* (1199ˣ) or *en* (Hallgrímur Scheving) in l. 5). Kock (*NN* §114) questions the metre, particularly the stress on the non-pronominal *maðr*, which he omits in *Skald*.

102. Unnins vítis   dyli engi maðr,
       ef veit á sik sakir;
   sinna verka   mun seggja hverr
       laun með leigum taka.

Engi maðr dyli unnins vítis, ef veit sakir á sik; hverr seggja mun taka laun sinna verka með leigum.

No man may conceal a deserved punishment if he knows he is guilty; every man will take the reward for his deeds with interest.

Mss: 1199ˣ(74r-v), 624(144) (ll. 4-6). — *Reading*: [5] mun: skal 624.

Editions: *Skj* Anonyme digte og vers [XIII], [C. E/5]. *Hugsvinnsmál* 78 [var], 78: AII, 184, BII, 198-9, Hallgrímur Scheving 1831, 25, Gering 1907, 27, Tuvestrand 1977, 128, Hermann Pálsson 1985, 99.

Notes: [All]: Lat. parallel: (*Dist*. III, 17) *Quod merito pateris, patienter perfer id ipsum, / cumque reus tibi sis, ispum te iudice damna* 'That which you bear deservedly, endure it patiently, and when you stand as a defendant before yourself, judge yourself strictly'. Line 3 corresponds to st. 33/6. Lines 4-6 are the same as st. 77/4-6 in 624.

103. Gamansamlig ljóð   skaltu af greppum nema
       ok mörg fræði muna,
   þvít ágætlig ljóð   bera fyrir ýta sonu
       skáld til skemtanar.

Skaltu nema gamansamlig ljóð af greppum ok muna mörg fræði, þvít skáld bera ágætlig ljóð til skemtanar fyrir ýta sonu.

You must learn entertaining poems from poets and remember much knowledge, because poets deliver excellent poems as entertainment to the sons of men.

Mss: 1199ˣ(74v), 723aˣ(81), 624(145). — *Readings*: [1] ljóð: *so* 723aˣ, *om*. 1199ˣ, hljóð 624 [2] af: at 723aˣ, 624; greppum: görpum 624 [3] mörg fræði muna: *so* 723aˣ, 624, margfróðr vera 1199ˣ [4] þvít: *om*. 624; ágætlig: ágætt 723aˣ; ljóð: *so* 723aˣ, hljóð 1199ˣ, minni 624 [5] bera: bera þú 624; sonu: lið 624 [6] skáld: skála 624.

Editions: *Skj* Anonyme digte og vers [XIII], [C. E/5]. *Hugsvinnsmál* 102: AII, 188, BII, 202-3, *Skald* II, 106, *NN* §2593; Hallgrímur Scheving 1831, 25, Gering 1907, 28, Tuvestrand 1977, 128, Hermann Pálsson 1985, 99-100.

Notes: [All]: Lat. parallel: (*Dist*. III, 18) *Multa legas facito, perlectis perlege multa, / nam miranda canunt, sed non credenda poetae* 'See to it that you read many things, having read, forget many things; for poets write a lot of things to be wondered at, but not believed'. All ms. versions focus on the positive aspects of poetry, in contrast to the Lat. text. — [1, 4] *ljóð* 'poems, songs': 1199^x has *hljóð* 'sound(s), silence' for both instances of this word; cf. also st. 145/1. — [3]: 1199^x's reading *ok margfróðr vera* 'and be learned in many things' does not supply alliteration.

104. Fámálugr vera   skyldi fyrða hverr,
      er at samkundum sitr;
   manvits vant   verðr þeim, er mart talar;
      hljóðr er hygginn maðr.

Hverr fyrða, er sitr at samkundum, skyldi vera fámálugr; manvits vant verðr þeim, er mart talar; hygginn maðr er hljóðr.

Every man who is attending a feast should be taciturn; good sense is lacking in the one who speaks a lot; a wise man is silent.

Ms.: **624**(145).

Editions: *Skj* Anonyme digte og vers [XIII], [C. E/5]. *Hugsvinnsmál* 103: AII, 188, BII, 203, *Skald* II, 106; Hallgrímur Scheving 1831, 25, Konráð Gíslason 1860, 552, Gering 1907, 28, Tuvestrand 1977, 129, Hermann Pálsson 1985, 100.

Notes: [All]: Lat. parallel: (*Dist*. III, 19) *Inter convivas fac sis sermone modestus, / ne dicare loquax, cum vis urbanus haberi* 'At feasts make sure that you are moderate in speech, so that you will not be called loud-mouth when you want to be considered urbane'. A similar topic is dealt with in *Hsv* 16. The topic of taciturn guests also occurs in *Hávm*. Cf. *Hávm* 7/1-3 (*NK*, 18): *Inn vari gestr, | er til verðar kømr, | þunno hljóði þegir* 'The careful guest, who comes to a meal, keeps silent with hearing finely attuned' (Larrington 1996, 15).

105. Reiðrar konu   skaltu eigi rógi trúa
      né at því gaum gefa;
   kaldráð kona,   hygg ek, klökkvandi
      biði opt óþarfra hluta.

Skaltu eigi trúa rógi reiðrar konu né gefa gaum at því; ek hygg, kaldráð, klökkvandi kona biði opt óþarfra hluta.

You must not believe the slander of an angry woman nor pay attention to it; I think a calculating, crying woman may often ask for unnecessary things.

Mss: **1199^x**(74v) (ll. 4-6), **624**(145-6). — *Readings*: [3] gaum: geymd 624;   gefa: *so* 624, gæfir 1199^x [4, 5] kaldráð kona hygg ek klökkvandi: *om.* 624   [6] biði: vandi 624.

Editions: *Skj* Anonyme digte og vers [XIII], [C. E/5]. *Hugsvinnsmál* 104: AII, 188, BII, 203, *Skald* II, 106; Hallgrímur Scheving 1831, 25, 34, Gering 1907, 28, Tuvestrand 1977, 129, Hermann Pálsson 1985, 101.

Notes: [All]: Lat. parallel: (*Dist.* III, 20) *Coniugis iratae noli tu verba timere, / nam lacrimis struit insidias, cum femina plorat* 'Do not fear the words of an angry wife; for when a woman weeps, she heaps up the tears with treachery'. — [1-2]: In 1199^x these ll. are the same as st. 24/1-2 and consequently its readings are included with that st. in the apparatus. 624 is used here as the base ms. for these two ll. — [4-5]: In 624 these ll. are omitted, but the redactor has attempted to make sense of the remaining ll. — [4] *kaldráð* 'calculating': Lit. 'cold-advised'; cf. the Icel. proverb *köld eru kvenna ráð* 'the counsels of women are cold' (cf., e.g., *Gísla saga* ch. 19; *ÍF* 6, 61).

106. Á aura neyzlu   skaltu allri hafa
  hóf ok hagspeki;
annars þurfi   verðr sá iðugliga,
  er sínum hefr aurum amat.

Skaltu hafa hóf ok hagspeki á allri neyzlu aura; sá verðr iðugliga þurfi annars, er hefr amat aurum sínum.

You must have moderation and economy in all use of money; he who has squandered his money frequently becomes dependent on another.

Mss: **1199^x**(74v), **723a^x**(81), **624**(146). — *Readings*: [1] Á: at 723a^x [2] allri: aldri 723a^x [4] þurfi: þurfa 723a^x [5] sá iðugliga: hverr 624   [6] sínum hefr: hefir sínu 624;   aurum: auðum 723a^x, fé 624;   amat: farit 624.

Editions: *Skj* Anonyme digte og vers [XIII], [C. E/5]. *Hugsvinnsmál* 105: AII, 188-9, BII, 203, *Skald* II, 106, *NN* §2590; Hallgrímur Scheving 1831, 25, Gering 1907, 29, Tuvestrand 1977, 130, Hermann Pálsson 1985, 102.

Notes: [All]: Lat. parallel: (*Dist.* III, 21) *Utere quaesitis, sed ne videaris abuti: / qui sua consumunt, cum deest, aliena sequentur* 'Make use of your wealth, but do not appear to waste it; those who use up their own goods, when they are gone, follow those belonging to others'. — [6]: This l. is close to st. 54/6 in 1199^x. There is also a parallel in phrasing in *Sól* 34. 624 (also *Skj* B, *Skald*) reads: *er hefir sínu fé farit* 'who has lost his money'.

107. Bana sinn hræðaz   skal eigi bragna hverr,
    því́t hann er endir ills;
góðum mönnum,   þeim er grand varaz,
    dauði ok líf dugir.

Hverr bragna skal eigi hræðaz bana sinn, því́t hann er endir ills; dauði ok líf dugir góðum mönnum, þeim er varaz grand.

Every man must not fear his death, because it is the end of evil; death and life help good men who are wary of sin.

Mss: 1199^x(74v), 723a^x(81). — *Readings*: [2] skal: skalt 723a^x; hverr: lið 723a^x.

Editions: *Skj* Anonyme digte og vers [XIII], [C. E/5]. *Hugsvinnsmál* 106: AII, 189, BII, 203, *Skald* II, 106; Hallgrímur Scheving 1831, 27, Gering 1907, 29, Tuvestrand 1977, 130, Hermann Pálsson 1985, 103.

Notes: [All]: Lat. parallel: (*Dist*. III, 22) *Fac tibi proponas mortem non esse timendam, / quae bona si non est, finis tamen illa malorum est* 'Make sure to declare to yourself that death is not to be feared; for even if it is not good, it is the end of evils'.

108. Föður ok móður   unn þú fróðhugaðr
    jöfnum ástarhug;
hvárkis þeira   ræki maðr hylli svá,
    at týni annars ást.

Unn þú fróðhugaðr föður ok móður jöfnum ástarhug; maðr ræki hylli hvárkis þeira svá, at týni ást annars.

Love, wise-minded, your father and mother with equal affection; a man should not care for the favour of one of them such that he loses the other's love.

Mss: 1199^x(74v), 723a^x(81), 624(146). — *Readings*: [1] Föður: feðr 624   [2] unn þú fróðhugaðr: unni fyrða hverr 624   [3] jöfnum: *so* 723a^x, 624, ok jöfnum 1199^x [5] ræki: rækir 723a^x; maðr: *om*. 723a^x, hann 624   [6] týni: fyrir 723a^x, hann týni 624.

Editions: *Skj* Anonyme digte og vers [XIII], [C. E/5]. *Hugsvinnsmál* 107: AII, 189, BII, 203, *Skald* II, 106; Hallgrímur Scheving 1831, 26, Gering 1907, 29, Tuvestrand 1977, 131, Hermann Pálsson 1985, 103.

Notes: [All]: Lat. parallel: (*Dist*. III, 24) *Aequa diligito caros pietate parentes / nec matrem offendas, dum vis bonus esse parenti* 'Love your dear parents with equal filial affection, and do not offend your mother when you want to be good to your father'.

109. Á engum hlut   láttu þér elsku vera,
       þeim er aðrir eiga;
   sínu láni   skal seggja hverr
       una, því er eignaz hefir.

Láttu vera þér elsku á engum hlut, þeim er aðrir eiga; hverr seggja skal una láni sínu, því er hefir eignaz.

Do not let there be love for you in anything which others own; every man must be content with his property, which he has acquired.

Mss: **1199**[x](74v), 723a[x](81), 624(146). — *Readings*:   [2] láttu: skal 624;   elsku: elska 624;   vera: *om.* 723a[x]   [3] aðrir eiga: hugdyggvir hata 624   [5] skal: skyldi 624   [6] una: *so* 723a[x], 624, laun með launum taka unna 1199[x];   eignaz: *so* 723a[x], 624, elskat 1199[x].

Editions: *Skj* Anonyme digte og vers [XIII], [C. E/5]. *Hugsvinnsmál* 108: AII, 189, BII, 203-4, *Skald* II, 106; Hallgrímur Scheving 1831, 31, Gering 1907, 36, Tuvestrand 1977, 132, Hermann Pálsson 1985, 104.

Notes: [All]: Possible Lat. parallels: (*Dist.* IV, 1) *Despice divitias si vis animo esse beatus, / quas qui suspiciunt, mendicant semper avari* 'Spurn riches, if you wish to be happy in mind, for those who admire them always beg as misers'; (*Dist.* IV, 2) *Commoda naturae nullo tibi tempore deerunt, / si contentus eo fueris, quod postulat usus* 'Necessities from nature will never be lacking to you, if you are content with what need demands'. The topic of this st. recurs throughout the poem (cf., e.g. sts 22, 44, 96); it is therefore difficult to determine the exact equivalent among the Lat. *disticha*. Tuvestrand has suggested that in this and the next st. the translation of several distichs has been mingled. However, in all mss this st. and the next occur consistently in order between the translation of the end of the third book of the *Disticha* and distich 3 of the fourth book, which suggests *Dist.* IV, 1-2 are translated here, thus beginning the translation of Book IV. — [3] *þeim er aðrir eiga*: This l. is unmetrical in 1199[x] and 723a[x]. 624's reading is metrically correct: *þeim er hugdyggvir hata* 'which steadfast people hate'. — [6]: 1199[x] adds a further full l. here: *sínu láni | skal seggja hverr | laun með leigum taka | unna, því er elskat hefr* 'every man must take rewards with wages for his estate [and] love that which he has loved'. This neither corresponds to the Lat. nor makes much sense in itself.

110. Aumr maðr   telr sér einskis vant,
       ef sér atvinnu á,
   en inn fégjarni sýtir,   þótt fullsælu hafi,
       ok þykkiz válaðr vera.

Aumr maðr telr sér einskis vant, ef á sér atvinnu, en inn fégjarni sýtir, þótt hafi fullsælu, ok þykkiz vera válaðr.

A poor man thinks he lacks nothing if he has means of subsistence for himself, but the avaricious person complains even if he has great wealth, and thinks he is poverty-stricken.

Mss: **1199^x**(74v), 723a^x(81), 624(146). — *Readings*: [1] Aumr: angrlauss 624 [2-3]: *so* 723a^x, 624, ef sér atvinnu á telr sér einskis vant 1199^x [3] sér: hann 624; á: fær 723a^x [4] en: *om*. 723a^x; inn fégjarni: *so* 624, ágjarn 1199^x, 723a^x [5] þótt: þótt hann 624 [6] þykkiz: þykkiz æ 723a^x.

Editions: Skj Anonyme digte og vers [XIII], [C. E/5]. *Hugsvinnsmál* 109: AII, 189, BII, 204, *Skald* II, 106; Hallgrímur Scheving 1831, 27, Gering 1907, 30, Tuvestrand 1977, 132, Hermann Pálsson 1985, 105.

Notes: [All]: Lat. parallels: (*Dist*. IV, 4) *Dilige denarium, sed parce dilige formam. / quam nemo sanctus nec honestus captat habere* 'Love money, but love its appearance sparingly, which no one good and honest seeks to gain'; (*Dist*. IV, 16) *Utere quaesitis opibus, fuge nomen avari; / quid tibi divitias, si semper pauper abundas* 'Make use of riches you have gained, avoid the name of miser; what use are riches to you, if you always live like a poor man?'. — [2-3]: These ll. are reversed in 1199^x, which produces an unmetrical reading. — [4] *inn fégjarni* 'the avaricious person': 624's reading is preferred here to produce the correct alliteration.

111. Gálauss maðr,   sá er eigi vill gott nema,
    kann eigi við víti varaz;
  ógæfu sinni   veldr hann einn saman;
    engum er ilt skapat.

Gálauss maðr, sá er eigi vill nema gott, kann eigi varaz við víti; hann veldr einn saman ógæfu sinni; engum er ilt skapat.

The careless man who does not want to learn good cannot guard against punishment; he alone causes his bad luck; nobody is destined to something bad.

Mss: **1199^x**(74v), 720a IV(2r) (ll. 4-6), 723a^x(81), 624(146). — *Readings*: [2] er: *so* 624, *om*. 1199^x, 723a^x; nema: vinna 723a^x [3] við víti: víti at 723a^x, við vítum 624 [4] sinni: vinni 723a^x [5] einn: *so* 720a IV, 723a^x, 624, eirn 1199^x.

Editions: Skj Anonyme digte og vers [XIII], [C. E/5]. *Hugsvinnsmál* 110: AII, 190, BII, 204, *Skald* II, 106-7; Hallgrímur Scheving 1831, 27, Gering 1907, 30, Tuvestrand 1977, 133, Hermann Pálsson 1985, 106.

Notes: [All]: Lat. parallel: (*Dist*. IV, 3) *Cum sis incautus nec rem ratione gubernes, / noli fortunam, quae non est, dicere caecam* 'If you are careless and do not steer your affairs with reason, do not say that fortune is blind, which she is not'.

112. Líkama sinn   ræki lýða hverr;
       heilsa er höldum framar;
   aura njóta   þykkiz engi maðr,
       nema hann heilsu hafi.

Hverr lýða ræki líkama sinn; heilsa er framar höldum; engi maðr þykkiz njóta aura, nema hann hafi heilsu.

Every man should look after his body; health is very important to men; nobody thinks to enjoy his money, unless he is healthy.

Mss: **1199**^{x}(74v), 720a IV(2r), 723a^x(82). — *Readings*: [1] Líkama: líkam 720a IV, 723a^x [3] höldum: hverju 720a IV, 723a^x [5] engi: enginn 723a^x [6] hann: *om*. 723a^x.

Editions: Skj Anonyme digte og vers [XIII], [C. E/5]. *Hugsvinnsmál* 111: AII, 190, BII, 204, *Skald* II, 107; Hallgrímur Scheving 1831, 27, Gering 1907, 30, Tuvestrand 1977, 133, Hermann Pálsson 1985, 106-7.

Notes: [All]: Lat. parallel: (*Dist*. IV, 5) *Cum fueris locuples, corpus curare memento: / aeger dives habet nummos, se non habet ipsum* 'When you become rich, remember to take care of your body; a sick rich man has wealth, but he does not have himself. The contrast between wealth and health is also mentioned in *Sól* 8.

113. Þat skaltu gera,   sem þér gegnir vel,
       ok við villu varaz;
   mildr af þurftum   vertu í mörgum hlutum;
       gott er dyggum at duga.

Skaltu gera þat, sem gegnir þér vel, ok varaz við villu; vertu í mörgum hlutum mildr af þurftum; gott er at duga dyggum.

You must do what suits you well and beware of error; be in many things generous as necessary; it is good to help the trustworthy.

Mss: **1199**^{x}(74v), 720a IV(2r), 723a^x(82), 624(146). — *Readings*: [?] sem þér: er þér 720a IV, þér 723a^x, er 624 [3] ok: en 624; við villu varaz: varaz villu mest 723a^x [4] af: at 624 [5] vertu: skalt 723a^x [6] er: so 723a^x, 624, kveða 1199^x, kveð 720a IV.

Editions: Skj Anonyme digte og vers [XIII], [C. E/5]. *Hugsvinnsmál* 113: AII, 190, BII, 204, *Skald* II, 107, *NN* §111; Hallgrímur Scheving 1831, 27, Gering 1907, 31, Tuvestrand 1977, 134, Hermann Pálsson 1985, 107.

Notes: [All]: Lat. parallels: (*Dist*. IV, 7) *Res age quae prosunt, rursus vitare memento, / in quis error inest nec spes est certa laboris* 'Do things which are useful, but on the other hand remember to avoid those in which there is fault and no sure hope of work'; (*Dist*. IV, 8) *Quod donare potes gratis, ne vende roganti, / nam recte fecisse bonis, in parte lucrorum est* 'What you can give for nothing, do not sell to the asker; for to have done right with goods is to be considered as gain'.

114. Föður ok móður   gremz eigi fróðhugaðr
     orðum ok ávítum;
    reiðr er þér betri,   sá er rækja vill,
     en hinn, sem er hrekkvíss í hugum.

Gremz eigi fróðhugaðr orðum ok ávítum föður ok móður; sá er vill rækja, er betri þér reiðr, en hinn, sem er hrekkvíss í hugum.

Do not, wise-minded, become angry at the words and reprimands of your father and mother; he who is willing to look after you is better for you angry, than the one who is mischievous in his thoughts.

Mss: **1199**^{x}(74v), 720a IV(2r), 723a^x(82), 624(146). — *Readings*: [2] gremz eigi: *so* 723a^x, reynztu 1199^x, reiðz þú 720a IV, vertu 624   [3] orðum ok: *so* 723a^x, eigi með 1199^x, 720a IV, ok öngum 624   [5] er: þik 720a IV, 723a^x, er þik 624   [6] hinn sem er: *so* 720a IV, 723a^x, hinn sem hann er 1199^x, *om.* 624; hugum: hug 723a^x.

Editions: *Skj* Anonyme digte og vers [XIII], [C. E/5]. *Hugsvinnsmál* 112: AII, 190, BII, 204, *Skald* II, 107; Hallgrímur Scheving 1831, 27, Gering 1907, 31, Tuvestrand 1977, 134, Hermann Pálsson 1985, 108.

Notes: [All]: Lat. parallel: (*Dist*. IV, 6) *Verbera cum tuleris discens aliquando magistri, / fer patris imperium, cum verbis exit in iram* 'Just as you bear blows now and again from the teacher when learning, accept your father's authority when he breaks out in anger in words'. — [2-3]: All mss have made different attempts to make sense of this l. *Ávítum* is unmetrical in its position, probably an indication of an early corruption in transmission, and all mss share this reading. 1199^x's and 720a IV's *reynztu fróðhugaðr | eigi með ávítum* 'try to be wise-minded ... not with reprimands' makes little sense. 624 has *vertu fróðhugaðr | ok öngum ávítum reiðr* 'be wise-minded ... and not angry because of any reprimands', but the punctuation of the other mss and the alliteration make it clear that *reiðr* belongs to l. 4. 723a^x's reading is adopted here, but it leaves the unmetrical ending on l. 3. Hallgrímur Scheving has for l. 3 *er með ávítum aga* 'when they chastise you with reprimands', which is both metrically correct and makes sense.

115. Fljóta raun   skaltu við flest hafa,
     þat er grunsamligt geriz;
    leyndir lestir,   þeir er lengi felaz,
     gera mörgum mein.

Skaltu hafa fljóta raun við flest, þat er geriz grunsamligt; leyndir lestir, þeir er lengi felaz, gera mörgum mein.

You must have a quick test for everything that is suspicious; secret vices which have been hidden for a long time do many people harm.

Mss: 1199ˣ(74v), 720a IV(2r), 723aˣ(82), 624(146). — *Readings*: [1, 2] raun skaltu: skaltu raun 720a IV [3] er: sem 720a IV, 723aˣ [5] er: *om*. 720a IV, 723aˣ [6] gera: gera oft 720a IV, 723aˣ.

Editions: *Skj* Anonyme digte og vers [XIII], [C. E/5]. *Hugsvinnsmál* 114: AII, 190-1, BII, 204-5, *Skald* II, 107; Hallgrímur Scheving 1831, 28, Konráð Gíslason 1860, 552, Gering 1907, 31, Tuvestrand 1977, 135, Hermann Pálsson 1985, 109.

Notes: [All]: Lat. parallel: (*Dist.* IV, 9) *Quod tibi suspectum est, confestim discute, quid sit / namque solent, primo quae sunt neglecta, nocere* 'Whatever is suspect to you, immediately test what it is; for those things which are at first ignored are often accustomed to do harm'. Unusually, 1199ˣ and 624 present identical text for this st., with fairly minor variants occurring in the other mss.

116. Ofdrykkju forðaz;   * hon drýgir erfiði;
            svá skal við vífin varaz;
        líkams lestir   tæla lýða hvern,
            er í sællífi sitr.

Forðaz ofdrykkju; * hon drýgir erfiði; svá skal varaz við vífin; líkams lestir tæla hvern lýða, er sitr í sællífi.

Avoid too much drinking; * it causes hardship; thus one must guard against women; vices of the body entrap every man who keeps to a wealthy way of life.

Mss: 1199ˣ(74v-75r), 720a IV(2r), 723aˣ(82), 624(146). — *Readings*: [2] *: en 1199ˣ, því 720a IV, 723aˣ, ok 624; hon: *so* 720a IV, 723aˣ, *om*. 1199ˣ, 624; drýgir erfiði: *so* 720a IV, drýg erfiði 1199ˣ, 624, erfiði drýgir 723aˣ [3] skal: skal ok 720a IV, skaltu ok 723aˣ; við: *om*. 723aˣ; vífin: *so* 720a IV, 723aˣ, meinum 1199ˣ, vífni 624 [4] lestir: losti 624 [5] tæla: tælir 624.

Editions: *Skj* Anonyme digte og vers [XIII], [C. E/5]. *Hugsvinnsmál* 115: AII, 191, BII, 205, *Skald* II, 107, *NN* §2593; Hallgrímur Scheving 1831, 28, Gering 1907, 31, Tuvestrand 1977, 135, Hermann Pálsson 1985, 109.

Notes: [All]: Lat. parallels: (*Dist.* IV, 10) *Cum te detineat Veneris damnosa voluptas, / indulgere gulae noli, quae ventris amica est* 'When the cursed pleasure of Venus holds you in its grasp, do not indulge in gluttony, which is a friend of the stomach'. (*Dist.* IV, 24) *Hoc bibe, quo possis, si vis tu, vivere sanus: / morbi causa mali est homini quaecumque voluptas* 'Drink what you are able, if you wish to live healthy; the cause of bad disease to a man is most frequently some kind of pleasure'. Cf. also *Hsv* 133. The advice not to drink too much is also expressed in several sts of *Hávm* (e.g. 11, 12, 19). The advice to beware of physical desire is also mentioned in *Sól* 71. — [2] * *hon drýgir erfiði* '* it causes hardship': The reading in 1199ˣ, *en drýg erfiði* 'but suffer hardship' does not produce good sense. The reading here is that of 720a IV and 723a^x, and is adopted in *Skj* B. Both 720a IV and 723a^x begin with *því* here, but adopting their reading would require emendation to *því að* 'because...'.

117. Afl ok eljan   ef þú eignaz vilt,
       nem þú hyggindi hugar;
   beztr sá þykkir,   er bæði má
       vitr ok sterkr vera.

Ef þú vilt eignaz afl ok eljan, nem þú hyggindi hugar; sá þykkir beztr, er bæði má vera vitr ok sterkr.

If you want to acquire strength and energy, learn wisdom of mind; he appears best, who can be both intelligent and strong.

Mss: **1199^x**(75r), 720a IV(2r), 723a^x(82), 624(146). — *Readings*: [2] vilt: hefir 624   [4] beztr sá þykkir: æ sá beztr þykkir 720a IV, æ þykkir sá beztr 723a^x, sá betr virðiz 624;   beztr: *so* 720a IV, 723a^x, 'besti' 1199^x, betr 624.

Editions: *Skj* Anonyme digte og vers [XIII], [C. E/5]. *Hugsvinnsmál* 116: AII, 191, BII, 205, *Skald* II, 107; Hallgrímur Scheving 1831, 28, Gering 1907, 32, Tuvestrand 1977, 136, Hermann Pálsson 1985, 110.

Notes: [All]: Lat. parallel: (*Dist.* IV, 12) *Cum tibi praevalidae fuerint in corpore vires, / fac sapias: sic tu poteris vir fortis haberi* 'If your strength in body is great for you, see to it that you are wise; thus you will be considered a strong man'. — [1] *afl ok eljan*: The alliterating phrase is also used in *Rþ* 44/5 (*NK*, 286) and Angantýr Lv 11/5^{VIII} (*Heiðr* 48).

118. Upptekna sýslu   ef þú eigi
       orka mátt einsamall,
   tryggvan vin   bið þú ténaðar;
       vel kveða dyggva duga.

Ef þú eigi mátt orka einsamall upptekna sýslu, bið þú tryggvan vin ténaðar; kveða dyggva duga vel.

If you cannot manage alone a job [you have] started, ask a loyal friend for help; they say that reliable people help well.

Mss: **1199^x**(75r), 720a IV(2r-v), 723a^x(82). — *Readings*: [2] eigi: *om.* 723a^x [3] orka mátt einsamall: einn saman orka mátt 720a IV, eigi orkat getr 723a^x [6] kveða: munu 723a^x; dyggva: dyggvir 723a^x; duga: *so* 720a IV, 723a^x, dugaz 1199^x.

Editions: *Skj* Anonyme digte og vers [XIII], [C. E/5]. *Hugsvinnsmál* 117: AII, 191, BII, 205, *Skald* II, 107; Hallgrímur Scheving 1831, 28, Gering 1907, 32, Tuvestrand 1977, 136, Hermann Pálsson 1985, 111.

Notes: [All]: Lat. parallel: (*Dist.* IV, 13) *Auxilium a notis petito si forte labores; / nec quisquam melior medicus quam fidus amicus* 'Ask for aid from your associates when you are having difficulties; no one is a better doctor than a faithful friend'. — [1-3]: Line 2 is too short. *Skj* B and *Skald* have an alternative, metrically sound w.o. deriving from Hallgrímur Scheving's text: *Upp tekna sýslu | ef þú eigi mátt | orka einn saman*. — [6]: This l. is very similar to st. 113/6.

119. Blót né fórnir   þarf eigi til batnaðar at hafa
    fyrir afgerðir ýta;
heimskr er sá,   er ætlar sér til hjálpar,
    þótt hann sæfi smala,
þvít eins guðs elska   ok aldyggvir siðir
    bæta um gervan glæp.

Þarf eigi at hafa blót né fórnir til batnaðar fyrir afgerðir ýta; sá er heimskr, er ætlar sér til hjálpar, þótt hann sæfi smala, þvít eins guðs elska ok aldyggvir siðir bæta um gervan glæp.

It is not necessary to have sacrifices nor offerings as atonement for men's transgressions; he is foolish who thinks it is a help for him when he sacrifices [small] livestock, because the one God's love and very trustworthy morals compensate for a misdeed performed.

Mss: 1199^x(75r), 720a IV(2v), 723a^x(82). — *Readings*: [1] né: ok 723a^x [3] afgerðir ýta: ýta afgerðir 720a IV, 723a^x [4] heimskr er sá: sá er ofheimskr 723a^x [5] er: sem 723a^x; sér til: '[...]' 723a^x; hjálpar: sálubótar 720a IV, '[...]älu böt' 723a^x [7] eins: *so* 720a IV, 723a^x, *om.* 1199^x [8, 9] siðir bæta um: '[...]ta[...]' 723a^x [9] glæp: *so* 720a IV, 723a^x, grun 1199^x.

Editions: *Skj* Anonyme digte og vers [XIII], [C. E/5]. *Hugsvinnsmál* 118: AII, 191, BII, 205, *Skald* II, 107; Hallgrímur Scheving 1831, 28, 34, Gering 1907, 32, Tuvestrand 1977, 137, Hermann Pálsson 1985, 111.

Notes: [All]: Lat. parallel: (*Dist.* IV, 14) *Cum sis ipse nocens, moritur cur victima pro te? / stultitia est morte alterius sperare salutem* 'When you yourself are a killer, why should the victim die for you? It is foolishness to hope for salvation from the death of another'. — [3]: The l. is unmetrical in all mss. — [7-9]: The extra 3 ll. have perhaps been added from a lost st. or from a commentary in a schoolbook. It is also possible that the redactor's intention was to give the st. a more Christian touch, since the first six ll. deal with heathen sacrifices. The reading *eins* 'the one' in l. 7 is added from 720 a IV, 723a^x to make the l. metrical.

120. Trúnaðarmanns   leita þú trúliga,
         ef þú vilt góðan vin geta;
     at fésælu   kjós eigi fulltrúa
         heldr at sönnum siðum.

Leita þú trúliga trúnaðarmanns, ef þú vilt geta góðan vin; kjós eigi fulltrúa at fésælu, heldr at sönnum siðum.

Look faithfully for a confidant, if you want to get a good friend; do not choose a confidant on the basis of wealth, rather according to sound morals.

Mss: **1199ˣ**(74v), 723aˣ(81), 624(146). — *Readings*: [2] leita þú trúliga: leita at ef þér tryggs vilir 624   [3] ef þú vilt: ok 624   [4] fésælu: farsælu nógri kjósa 624   [5] kjós eigi: áttu eigi þér 624.

Editions: *Skj* Anonyme digte og vers [XIII], [C. E/5]. *Hugsvinnsmál* 119: AII, 191-2, BII, 205, *Skald* II, 107; Hallgrímur Scheving 1831, 28, Gering 1907, 32, Tuvestrand 1977, 137, Hermann Pálsson 1985, 112.

Notes: [All]: Lat. parallel: (*Dist*. IV, 15) *Cum tibi vel socium vel fidum quaeris amicum, / non tibi fortuna est hominis sed vita petenda* 'If you are looking for an associate or a faithful friend, it is for you to look not at the fortune but the life of the man'. This st. is included between sts 100 and 103 in 1199ˣ and 723aˣ (translating *Dist*. III, 15 and 18), but is included here in accordance with the order in 624 and the Lat. original. The text of 624 differs somewhat:

     Trúnaðarmanns at leita   ef þér tryggs vilir
         ok góðan vin geta,
     at farsælu nógri   kjósa áttu eigi þér fulltrúa
         heldr at sönnum siðum.

Ef vilir at leita þér tryggs trúnaðarmanns ok geta góðan vin, áttu eigi kjósa þér fulltrúa at farsælu nógri heldr at sönnum siðum 'If you want to look for a trustworthy confidant and to get a good friend, you must not choose for yourself a true friend according to great prosperity but rather according to sound morals'. *Skj* B omits *at* (l. 1) and compresses *kjósa áttu eigi* to *kjósat* (l. 5).

121. Almanna lof   ef þú eignaz vilt
         ok heita góðr með gum*um,
     annars ógæfu   fagna þú aldrigi;
         sé þín æ at góðu getit.

Ef þú vilt eignaz almanna lof ok heita góðr með gum*um, fagna þú aldrigi ógæfu annars; sé þín æ getit at góðu.

If you want to acquire general praise and be called good among men, never rejoice in another's misfortune; always be mentioned as good.

Mss: **1199**ˣ(75r), 723aˣ(83), 624(146). — *Readings*: [2] vilt: vilir 624 [3] gum*um: gumnum *all* [4] annars ógæfu: ógiptu annars 624 [6] sé þín æ: æ sé þin 723aˣ, ger þér 624; getit: gaman 624.

Editions: *Skj* Anonyme digte og vers [XIII], [C. E/5]. *Hugsvinnsmál* 120: AII, 192, BII, 205-6, *Skald* II, 107; Hallgrímur Scheving 1831, 29, Gering 1907, 33, Tuvestrand 1977, 138, Hermann Pálsson 1985, 113.

Notes: [All]: Lat. parallel: (*Dist*. IV, 17) *Si famam servare cupis, dum vivis, honestam, / fac fugias animo, quae sunt mala gaudia vitae* 'If you want to keep a good reputation while you are alive, make sure to avoid in mind those things which are evil joys of life'. — [3] *gum*um* 'men': Emended from ms. 'gumnum' for metrical purposes. Cf. Note to st. 59/3. — [6]: The l. in 624 (also *Skj* B, *Skald*) reads: *ger þér at góðu gaman* 'take pleasure in what is good'.

122. Eigi skaltu hlæja,   ef þú vilt horskr vera,
    at öldruðum afa;
opt þat ellibjúgr man,   sem ungr veit eigi,
    ok kennir gott gum*um.

Skaltu eigi hlæja at öldruðum afa, ef þú vilt vera horskr; ellibjúgr man opt þat, sem ungr veit eigi, ok kennir gum*um gott.

You must not laugh at an elderly grandfather, if you want to be wise; often one bowed down with age remembers what a young person does not know, and teaches men well.

Mss: **1199**ˣ(75r), 723aˣ(83), 624(146). — *Readings*: [1] Eigi skaltu hlæja: skal eigi sá hlægja 624 [2] ef þú vilt horskr: ef horskr vilt 723aˣ, er vill hoskr 624 [3] afa: *so* 723aˣ, veðrafa 1199ˣ, *om*. 624 [4] þat: veit þat 723aˣ, *om*. 624; man: maðr 723aˣ, veit 624 [5] sem: þat er 624; veit: mun 624; eigi: *so* 723aˣ, 624, eigi til 1199ˣ [6] ok: *so* 723aˣ, 624, *om*. 1199ˣ; gum*um: *all*.

Editions: *Skj* Anonyme digte og vers [XIII], [C. E/5]. *Hugsvinnsmál* 121: AII, 192, BII, 206, *Skald* II, 108, *NN* §2344; Hallgrímur Scheving 1831, 29, Gering 1907, 33, Tuvestrand 1977, 138, Hermann Pálsson 1985, 113.

Notes: [All]: Lat. parallel: (*Dist*. IV, 18) *Cum sapias animo, noli ridere senectam; / nam † quocumque † sene, puerilis sensus in illo est* 'Since you are wise in mind, do not mock old age; for whoever is growing old, there is a childish mind in him'. The OIcel. version has a much more positive view of old age than the Lat. distich. Concerning the advice not to laugh at elderly people cf. also *Hávm* 134/5-9 (*NK*, 39): *at három þul | hlæðu aldregi! | opt er gott, | þat er gamlir qveða; | opt ór scorpom belg | scilin orð koma* 'at a grey-haired sage you should never laugh! Often what the old say is good; often from a wrinkled bag come judicious words' (Larrington 1996, 33). — [3] *afa* 'grandfather': 723aˣ's reading is chosen here for alliteration. 1199^x's *veðrafa* (from *veðrafi* 'weather-grandfather') is a *hap. leg.* — [5]: The l. is unmetrical, having two alliterating staves in all mss. — [6] *gum*um* 'men': Cf. Note to st. 59/3.

123. Íþróttir margar þótt þú öðlaz hafir,
   kosta þú at vinna vel;
   erfiði drýgja þurfu alda synir,
   meðan þeir heilsu hafa.

Kosta þú at vinna vel, þótt þú hafir öðlaz margar íþróttir; alda synir þurfu drýgja erfiði, meðan þeir hafa heilsu.

Try to work well, even if you have attained many accomplishments; the sons of men need to endure hardship while they have their health.

Mss: **1199**^{x}(75r), 720a IV(2v), 723a^x(83), 624(146). — *Readings*: [2] þótt: ef 624; öðlaz: *so* 720a IV, 723a^x, 624, eignaz 1199^x; hafir: hefir 624 [3] þú: þó 720a IV, vel 723a^x [5] þurfu: *so* 624, þurfa 1199^x, 720a IV, 723a^x; alda: allir manns 723a^x [6] meðan: *om.* 723a^x; þeir: *so* 720a IV, 624, sína 1199^x, þeir eð 723a^x; hafa: halda 624.

Editions: *Skj* Anonyme digte og vers [XIII], [C. E/5]. *Hugsvinnsmál* 124: AII, 193, BII, 206, *Skald* II, 108; Hallgrímur Scheving 1831, 29, Gering 1907, 34, Tuvestrand 1977, 140, Hermann Pálsson 1985, 115.

Notes: [All]: Lat. parallel: (*Dist.* IV, 21) *Exerce studium, quamvis perceperis artem: / ut cura ingenium, sic et manus adiuvat usum* 'Practise zeal in whatever art you have taken up, that care and attention may aid talent, and practise likewise the hand'.

124. Málum hlýðir, ef með mörgum kemr
   höldum, hygginn maðr;
   af orðum kennaz ýta hagir;
   þokka hylr, sá er þegir.

Hygginn maðr hlýðir málum, ef kemr með mörgum höldum; hagir ýta kennaz af orðum; þokka hylr, sá er þegir.

A wise man listens to conversations, if he comes among many men; the affairs of men are known through words; the one who keeps silent conceals his thought.

Mss: **1199**^{x}(75r), 723a^x(84), 624(146). — *Readings*: [2] ef: þar 723a^x, er 624 [3] höldum: hölda 624 [4] af: þvíat af of 624; kennaz: kynnaz 723a^x, 624 [5] hagir: hugir 723a^x, 624 [6] er: *so* 723a^x, 624, *om.* 1199^x.

Editions: *Skj* Anonyme digte og vers [XIII], [C. E/5]. *Hugsvinnsmál* 123: AII, 192, BII, 206, *Skald* II, 108, *NN* §3277; Hallgrímur Scheving 1831, 29, Gering 1907, 33, Tuvestrand 1977, 139, Hermann Pálsson 1985, 115.

Notes: [All]: Lat. parallel: (*Dist.* IV, 20) *Perspicito cuncta tacitus, quid quisque loquatur: / sermo hominum mores et celat et indicat idem* 'Look silently upon all things that people say; the speech of men both hides and reveals their ways'. For the first half there is a parallel in content in *Hávm* 7 (cf. st. 104).

125. Íþróttum safna   skalt á alla vegu,
        sem drengmanni dugir;
     þær þér tjá,   þótt þú týnt hafir
        afli ok öllu fé.

Skalt safna íþróttum á alla vegu, sem dugir drengmanni; þær tjá þér, þótt þú hafir týnt afli ok öllu fé.

You must acquire accomplishments in all ways which are useful to a good man; they will serve you, even if you have lost strength and all your money.

Mss: **1199**ˣ(75r), 723aˣ(84). — *Readings*:   [2] vegu: vega 723aˣ   [3] sem: *so* 723aˣ, þat er 1199ˣ   [4] tjá: *so* 723aˣ, duga 1199ˣ.

Editions: *Skj* Anonyme digte og vers [XIII], [C. E/5]. Hugsvinnsmál 122: AII, 192, BII, 206, *Skald* II, 108; Hallgrímur Scheving 1831, 29, Gering 1907, 33, Tuvestrand 1977, 139, Hermann Pálsson 1985, 114.

Notes: [All]: Lat. parallels: (*Dist.* IV, 19): *Disce aliquid, nam, cum subito fortuna recessit, / ars remanet vitamque hominis non deserit umquam* 'Learn something; for when fortune suddenly leaves, skill remains and never leaves the life of a man'. — [4] *tjá* 'serve': 1199ˣ's reading, *duga* 'help', does not supply the required alliteration.

126. Örlög sín   viti engi fyrir
        né um þat önn ali;
     flestir þat vita,   at mun flærðvörum
        dauði ok líf duga.

Engi viti örlög sín fyrir né ali önn um þat; flestir vita þat, at dauði ok líf mun duga flærðvörum.

Let no-one know his destiny beforehand, nor show concern about it; most know that death and life will help the deceit-wary.

Mss: **1199**ˣ(75r), 723aˣ(84), 624(146). — *Readings*:   [2] viti: veit 723aˣ, skyldi 624;   fyrir: maðr fyrir 723aˣ, maðr 624   [3] önn ali: veit neitt tala 624   [4] flestir þat vita: hitt vita flestir 624   [5] mun: mun eigi 624;   -vörum: 'v[...]vdvm' 624.

Editions: *Skj* Anonyme digte og vers [XIII], [C. E/5]. Hugsvinnsmál 125: AII, 193, BII, 206, *Skald* II, 108, *NN* §21B; Hallgrímur Scheving 1831, 29, Gering 1907, 34, Tuvestrand 1977, 140, Hermann Pálsson 1985, 116.

Notes: [All]: Lat. parallel: (*Dist*. IV, 22) *Multum venturi ne cures tempora fati: / non metuit mortem, qui scit contemnere vitam* 'Do not worry much about the times of fate which will come; he does not fear death who knows how to spurn life'. — [1-3]: These ll. are close in content to *Hávm* 56/4-6.

127. Hyggindi þína láttu at haldi koma
  þér ok þínum vinum;
 æðri sýslu máttu eigi hafa,
  en kenna nýtt ok nema.

Láttu hyggindi þína koma at haldi þér ok vinum þínum; máttu eigi hafa æðri sýslu, en kenna ok nema nýtt.

Let your wisdom come to be a support for you and your friends; you cannot have a more important job than to teach and learn something useful.

Mss: **1199ˣ**(75r), 723aˣ(84), 624(146-7). — *Readings*: [1] Hyggindi: *so* 723aˣ, 624, hyggenda 1199ˣ; þína: þín 723aˣ, 624 [2] láttu: lát þér 624 [4] æðri: enga 624 [5] máttu eigi hafa: fær maðr aldri 723aˣ, máttu þér æðri geta 624 [6] nýtt: *so* 723aˣ, 624, gott 1199ˣ.

Editions: Skj Anonyme digte og vers [XIII], [C. E/5]. *Hugsvinnsmál* 126: AII, 193, BII, 206-7, Skald II, 108; Hallgrímur Scheving 1831, 34, Gering 1907, 34, Tuvestrand 1977, 141, Hermann Pálsson 1985, 116.

Notes: [All]: Lat. parallels: (*Dist*. IV, 23) *Disce sed a doctis, indoctos ipse doceto: / propaganda etenim est rerum doctrina bonarum* 'Learn, but from the learned; teach the unlearned yourself; for the knowledge of good things should be spread abroad'. (*Dist*. IV, 27) *Discere ne cessa, cura sapientia crescat: / rara datur longo prudentia temporis usu* 'Do not cease learning; taking pains increases wisdom; rarely is a long space of time given to prudence'. — [6] *nýtt* '(something) useful': 1199ˣ's reading *gott* '(something) good' does not provide alliteration, although it is closer to the Lat. text.

128. Illa láta skaltu yfir engum hlut,
  þeim er þú hælt hefir,
 né þat lasta, sem þú lofat hefir;
  ilt er vályndum at vera.

Skaltu láta illa yfir engum hlut, þeim er þú hefir hælt, né lasta þat, sem þú hefir lofat; vályndum er ilt at vera.

You must express disapproval about nothing that you have boasted about, nor deride what you have praised; it is bad to be fickle-minded.

Mss: **1199ˣ**(75r), 723aˣ(84), 624(147). — *Readings*: [3] er þú: áðr 723aˣ [4, 5] né þat lasta sem þú lofat: vel þat leyfug, er þú lastat 624 [6] vályndum: veillyndum 624.

Editions: *Skj* Anonyme digte og vers [XIII], [C. E/5]. *Hugsvinnsmál* 127: AII, 193, BII, 207, *Skald* II, 108; Hallgrímur Scheving 1831, 30, Gering 1907, 35, Tuvestrand 1977, 141, Hermann Pálsson 1985, 117.

Notes: [All]: Lat. parallel: (*Dist*. IV, 25) *Laudaris quodcumque palam, quodcumque probaris, / hoc vide ne rursus levitatis crimine damnes* 'Praise openly whatever you have tested out; live so that you are not then accused of the crime of flightiness'. — [6]: The last l. may have been influenced by *Sól* 3.

129. Vertu eigi svá aumr,   at þú eigi gáir
    at vænta ins vildara hlutar,
né svá auðugr,   at þér örvænt sé
    meins á marga vega.

Vertu eigi svá aumr, at þú gáir eigi at vænta ins vildara hlutar, né svá auðugr, at sé þér örvænt meins á marga vega.

Do not be so miserable that you do not remember to expect the more pleasant fate, nor so wealthy that you are not dismayed by injury in many ways.

Mss: **1199ˣ**(75r), 723aˣ(84), 624(147). — *Readings*: [2] at: *om*. 723aˣ [3] hlutar: *so* 723aˣ, 624, hluta 1199ˣ [4] auðugr: auðigr 624 [5] örvænt: aura annt 624 [6] marga vega: margan veg 624.

Editions: *Skj* Anonyme digte og vers [XIII], [C. E/5]. *Hugsvinnsmál* 128: AII, 193-4, BII, 207, *Skald* II, 108; Hallgrímur Scheving 1831, 30, Gering 1907, 35, Tuvestrand 1977, 142, Hermann Pálsson 1985, 117.

Notes: [All]: Lat. parallel: (*Dist*. IV, 26) *Tranquillis rebus semper adversa timeto: / rursus in adversis melius sperare memento* 'In peaceful circumstances always be on the lookout for adverse things, and again, in bad times, remember always to hope for better'. The same idea is expressed in several other sts of *Hsv*, as for instance in sts 24, 25, 80.

130. Mikit mæla   skaltu eigi um margan hlut;
    lasta þú fátt né lofa;
þvít á einni stundu   bregz, þat er ætlat hafa
    gott ok ilt gum*ar.

Skaltu eigi mæla mikit um margan hlut; lasta þú fátt né lofa, þvít á einni stundu bregz, þat er gum*ar hafa ætlat gott ok ilt.

You must not talk too much about many a thing; blame little and do not praise, because in a short while that which people have regarded as good and evil changes.

Mss: **1199ˣ**(75r), 723aˣ(84), 624(147). — *Readings*: [1, 2] mæla skaltu eigi: eigi mæla skaltu 723aˣ [5] bregz: 'brgdst' 723aˣ; er: *so* 624, *om.* 1199ˣ, 723aˣ; hafa: hefr 624 [6] ok ilt: eitt 624; gum*ar: gumnar 1199ˣ, gumnum 624.

Editions: *Skj* Anonyme digte og vers [XIII], [C. E/5]. *Hugsvinnsmál* 130: AII, 194, BII, 207, *Skald* II, 108; Hallgrímur Scheving 1831, 30, Gering 1907, 35, Tuvestrand 1977, 143, Hermann Pálsson 1985, 119.

Notes: [All]: Lat. parallel: (*Dist.* 28) *Parce laudato, nam quem tu saepe laudaris, / una dies, qualis fuerit, ostendit, amicus* 'Praise sparingly; for the one you have often put to the test, one day will show you what a friend he has been'. The advice to be careful about what you say is also given in sts 71 and 128. *Skj* B and *Skald* use mss from the second group, as in the present edn, as the basis for the text of this st. — [6] *gum*ar* 'people': Cf. Note to st. 59/3.

131. Fyrir augum vaxa   lát þér aldrigi
     at kenna nýtt ok nema,
  því holla speki   lofa hyggnir menn
     en lasta heimskan hal.

Lát þér aldrigi vaxa fyrir augum at kenna ok nema nýtt, þvít hyggnir menn lofa holla speki en lasta heimskan hal.

Never let yourself shrink from teaching and learning something useful, because wise men praise wholesome wisdom and censure a foolish man.

Mss: **1199ˣ**(75r), 723aˣ(84), 624(147). — *Readings*: [1] vaxa: *so* 723aˣ, 624, *om.* 1199ˣ [2] aldrigi: eigi 723aˣ [3] at kenna: *so* 723aˣ, vaxa nýtt kenna 1199ˣ, spyrja 624 [4] holla speki: hygginn maðr 624 [5] lofa hyggnir menn: lofar hölda í þokka 624 [6] lasta: lastar 624; heimskan: heimskar 624.

Editions: *Skj* Anonyme digte og vers [XIII], [C. E/5]. *Hugsvinnsmál* 131: AII, 194, BII, 207, *Skald* II, 108-9; Hallgrímur Scheving 1831, 30, Gering 1907, 35, Tuvestrand 1977, 143, Hermann Pálsson 1985, 119.

Notes: [All]: Lat. parallel: (*Dist.* IV, 29) *Ne pudeat quae nescieris te velle doceri: / scire aliquid laus est; culpa est nil discere velle* 'Do not be ashamed when you wish to be taught what you do not know; to know something is praiseworthy, blamable is to not want to learn anything'. — [3]: This l. is very close to *Hsv* 86/2. — [4-5]: 624 has: *þvít hygginn maðr | lofar hölda í þokka* (*Skj* B removes *í*) 'because a wise man praises men's opinion'.

132. Ill er ofdrykkja; ferr hon eigi einsömul;
  fylgir henni mart til meins
 angr ok þrætur ok óstilt lostasemi
  sótt ok synda fjölð.

Ofdrykkja er ill; hon ferr eigi einsömul; mart til meins fylgir henni: angr ok þrætur ok óstilt lostasemi, sótt ok fjölð synda.

Too much drinking is bad; it does not come alone; much harm accompanies it: grief and quarrels and unsatisfied carnal lust, sickness and a multitude of sins.

Mss: **1199**ˣ(75r), 624(147). — *Readings*: [2] einsömul: einsömun 624 [4] angr: öfund 624 [5] ok: *om.* 624 [6] fjölð: fjölði 624.

Editions: *Skj* Anonyme digte og vers [XIII], [C. E/5]. *Hugsvinnsmál* 132: AII, 194, BII, 207-8, *Skald* II, 109; Hallgrímur Scheving 1831, 31, Gering 1907, 36, Tuvestrand 1977, 144, Hermann Pálsson 1985, 120.

Notes: [All]: Lat. parallel: (*Dist.* IV, 30) *Cum Venere et Baccho vis est et iuncta voluptas: quod lautum est, animo complectere, sed fuge lites* 'Between Venus and Bacchus there is both struggle and pleasure; embrace that which is pleasant in your mind; but avoid the strife'. The warning not to drink too much is also expressed in st. 116. Cf. the commentary there. Once again, the Icel. poet avoids mentioning classical deities.

133. Mikit vatn gerir mörgum skaða,
  þótt eigi falli straumar strítt;
 svá er seggr slægr ok langþögull;
  þarf æ við þeim at sjá.

Mikit vatn gerir skaða mörgum, þótt straumar falli eigi strítt; svá er slægr ok langþögull seggr; þarf æ at sjá við þeim.

A large river does harm to many, although the currents do not run strong; so too is a sly and long-silent man; it is always necessary to beware of that one.

Mss: **1199**ˣ(75r-v), 624(147). — *Readings*: [1] vatn: vondt 624 [2] mörgum: *so* 624, mögum 1199ˣ [3] eigi falli: falli eigi 624; strítt: 'firitt' 624 [4] seggr: segir 624 [6] þarf æ: þörf er 624.

Editions: *Skj* Anonyme digte og vers [XIII], [C. E/5]. *Hugsvinnsmál* 133: AII, 194, BII, 208, *Skald* II, 109; Hallgrímur Scheving 1831, 31, Gering 1907, 36, Tuvestrand 1977, 144, Hermann Pálsson 1985, 121.

Notes: [All]: Lat. parallel: (*Dist.* IV, 31) *Demissos animo et tacitos vitare memento: / quod flumen placidum est, forsan latet altius unda* 'Remember to avoid those who are depressed and silent in their minds; when a river is peaceful, perhaps deeper water is hidden'. The same idea is expressed in st. 99, albeit in a less metaphorical way.

134. Fávíss maðr   ef verðr á firði staddr,
    ok getr eigi beinan byr,
 liðligra er honum   til lands at halda
    en sigla foldu frá.

Ef fávíss maðr verðr staddr á firði ok getr eigi beinan byr, er honum liðligra at halda til lands en sigla frá foldu.

If a not very wise man is stuck in a fjord and does not get a direct wind [for sailing], it is more useful for him to keep to the shore than to sail away from the land.

Mss: **1199ˣ**(75v), 624(147). — *Readings*: [3] ok: *om.* 624   [4] er honum: ráð 624   [5] til lans' 624; halda: snúa 624   [6] sigla: *om.* 624.

Editions: *Skj* Anonyme digte og vers [XIII], [C. E/5]. *Hugsvinnsmál* 134: AII, 195, BII, 208, *Skald* II, 109; Hallgrímur Scheving 1831, 31, Konráð Gíslason 1860, 552, Gering 1907, 36, Tuvestrand 1977, 145, Hermann Pálsson 1985, 121.

Notes: [All]: Lat. parallel: (*Dist.* IV, 33) *Quod potes id tempta: nam litus carpere remis / tutius est multo quam velum tendere in altum* 'Whatever you are able [to do], try it; for to seize the oar at the shore is far safer than to spread the sail on the high sea'.

135. Um engar sakir   skaltu aldri deila
    við hygginn hal;
 gjöld af guði   hygg ek garpa taka
    fyrir reiði rangs hugar.

Skaltu aldri deila við hygginn hal um engar sakir; ek hygg garpa taka gjöld af guði fyrir reiði rangs hugar.

You must never argue with an intelligent man for the sake of nothing; I think that bold men get repayment from God for the anger of a wrong mind.

Mss: **1199ˣ**(75v), 624(147). — *Readings*: [1] Um engar: *so* 624, fyrir unnar 1199ˣ   [2] deila: *so* 624, saka 1199ˣ   [3] við hygginn: *so* 624, aldyggvan 1199ˣ   [5] garpa taka: at gumnar taki 624   [6] fyrir: *om.* 624; rangs: konungs 624.

Editions: *Skj* Anonyme digte og vers [XIII], [C. E/5]. *Hugsvinnsmál* 135: AII, 195, BII, 208, *Skald* II, 109; Hallgrímur Scheving 1831, 31, Gering 1907, 37, Tuvestrand 1977, 145, Hermann Pálsson 1985, 122.

Notes: [All]: Lat. parallel: (*Dist.* IV, 34) *Contra hominem iustum prave contendere noli: / semper enim deus iniustas ulciscitur iras* 'Do not contend wrongly against a just man; for God is always angry at unjust anger'. A similar topic is dealt with in st. 70. — [1-3]: 624's reading is chosen here, because 1199ˣ seems corrupt: *Fyrir unnar sakir | skaltu aldri saka | aldyggvan hal* 'you must never accuse a very trustworthy man on account of committed crimes'; the repetition of *sakir/saka* is suspect, and l. 3 lacks alliteration. Emendation to *hugdyggvan hal* would restore the alliteration in l. 3 (Hallgrímur Scheving has *hugdyggva hali* for l. 3). *Skj* B takes 624's reading and emends l. 3 to *við hugdyggva hali*, based on Hallgrímur Scheving's text, but in doing so blends two quite separate ms. traditions.

136. Engi oftreysti,　　þótt eigi sé gamall,
　　　at muni lengi lifa;
　skugga sinn　　hygg ek eigi mega skatna flýja
　　　né heldr forðaz feigð.

Engi oftreysti, at muni lifa lengi, þótt sé eigi gamall; ek hygg skatna mega eigi flýja skugga sinn né heldr forðaz feigð.

Nobody may trust too much that he will live long, even if he is not old; I think that men cannot escape their shadow nor avoid the approach of death.

Mss: 1199ˣ(75v), 624(147). — *Readings*: [1] oftreysti: oftreystiz 624　[2] eigi sé: hann sé eigi 624　[3] muni: hann muni 624　[5] mega skatna flýja: skatna flýja mega 624.

Editions: *Skj* Anonyme digte og vers [XIII], [C. E/5]. *Hugsvinnsmál* 137: AII, 195, BII, 208, *Skald* II, 109; Hallgrímur Scheving 1831, 32, Gering 1907, 37, Tuvestrand 1977, 146, Hermann Pálsson 1985, 122.

Notes: [All]: Lat. parallel: (*Dist*. IV, 37) *Tempora longa tibi noli promittere vitae: | quocumque ingrederis, sequitur mors corporis umbra* 'Do not promise yourself a long stretch of life; wherever you go death, the shadow of the body, follows'. The advice to be wary of sudden death is also given in *Hsv* 38. Cf. also *Hávm* 16 (*NK*, 19): *Ósniallr maðr | hyggz muno ey lifa, | ef hann við víg varaz* 'The foolish man thinks he will live for ever, if he keeps away from fighting' (Larrington 1996, 16). The same idea is expressed in *Has* 43.

137. Hjarðir sæfa　　þarf eigi til hylli guðs;
　　　beit þú yxn fyrir arðr;
　reykelsis ilm,　　þann er kemr af réttum siðum,
　　　vill hann fyrir tafn taka.

Þarf eigi sæfa hjarðir til hylli guðs; beit þú yxn fyrir arðr; hann vill taka fyrir tafn reykelsis ilm, þann er kemr af réttum siðum.

It is not necessary to kill herds for the honour of God; harness oxen to a plough; He will accept in place of sacrifice the fragrance of incense which comes from correct religious observances.

Mss: 1199ˣ(75r), 720a IV(2v), 723aˣ(83), 624(147). — *Readings*: [2] þarf: skaltu 624;   hylli: *so* 720a IV, 723aˣ, 624, hylla 1199ˣ   [3] beit: bættu 624;   þú: þín 720a IV, 624, því 723aˣ   [4, 5] reykelsis ilm þann: þann reykelsis ilm 723aˣ   [5] er: sem 723aˣ   [6] vill: *so* 723aˣ, þat 1199ˣ, 720a IV, 624;   tafn: takn 624.

Editions: *Skj* Anonyme digte og vers [XIII], [C. E/5]. *Hugsvinnsmál* 138: AII, 195, BII, 208-9, *Skald* II, 109; Hallgrímur Scheving 1831, 32, Gering 1907, 37, Tuvestrand 1977, 146, Hermann Pálsson 1985, 123.

Notes: [All]: Lat. parallel: (*Dist.* IV, 38) *Ture deum placa, vitulum sine crescrat aratro: / ne credas gaudere deum, cum caede litatur* 'Please God with incense, that the calf may grow without the plough; do not think to please God when sacrifice is made to him by killing'. The same idea is expressed in *Hsv* 119, possibly deriving from Pss 49 and 50. — [3] *beit* 'harness, bite': There is a play here on the senses of *beita*: the expression *beita fyrir* 'to harness (an animal) to (a vehicle, plough, etc.)'; and the sense of the same verb, 'cause to bite, hunt', which can relate to the killing of animals for sacrifice mentioned in the first cl. — [6] *vill* 'will': The reading *þat* at the start of this l. in most mss does not seem to work grammatically, as *þat* n. cannot agree with *ilm* m. in l. 4.

138. Óreiðinn   skal ýta hverr
       ok sjá sem gerst við grunum;
    hugsjúkr maðr   kvíðir hvervetna;
       aldri honum dagr um dugir.

Hverr ýta skal óreiðinn ok sjá sem gerst við grunum; hugsjúkr maðr kvíðir hvervetna; dagr um dugir honum aldri.

Every man must [be] calm and be careful of suspicion as much as possible; an anxious man is afraid everywhere; the day never helps him.

Mss: 1199ˣ(75r), 720a IV(2v), 723aˣ(83). — *Readings*: [2] skal: skyldi 720a IV, 723aˣ   [4] hugsjúkr: hugsandi 720a IV, 723aˣ   [5] hvervetna: hvetvetna *all*.

Editions: *Skj* Anonyme digte og vers [XIII], [C. E/5]. *Hugsvinnsmál* 142: AII, 196, BII, 209, *Skald* II, 109-10; Hallgrímur Scheving 1831, 32, Gering 1907, 38, Tuvestrand 1977, 149, Hermann Pálsson 1985, 126.

Notes: [All]: Lat. parallel: (*Dist.* IV, 43) *Suspectus caveris, ne sis miser omnibus horis, / nam timidis et suspectis aptissima mors est* 'Avoid being suspected so that you will not be miserable forever, for death is most proper for the timid and suspected'. This st. is included between 137 and 146 in the mss (translating *Dist.* IV, 38 and 23/27/48 respectively) but all the sts at this point seem to correspond poorly to the Lat. It is included here in accordance with its position in the mss. Concerning content and phrasing cf. *Hávm* 23 (*NK*, 20): *Ósviðr maðr | vakir um allar nætr | oc hyggr at hvívetna; | þá er móðr, | er at morni kømr, | allt er víl, sem var* 'The foolish man lies awake all night and worries about things; he's tired out when the morning comes and everything's just as bad as it was'

(Larrington 1996, 17). Cf. also *Hávm* 48/4-5 (*NK*, 24): *en ósniallr maðr | uggir hotvetna* 'but the cowardly man is afraid of everything' (Larrington 1996, 20). — [5] *hvetvetna* 'everywhere': The mss' *hvetvetna* (acc.) cannot be the object of *kvíða*, which can only take a dat. object. It is possible that early in the ms. transmission <r> was mistaken for <t>.

139. Meinlæti drýgja   skal sá, er misgert hefir,
    ok bæta syndir svá;
    sárar atgerðir   þarf inn sjúki maðr
    sér til heilsu at hafa.

Sá, er hefir misgert skal drýgja meinlæti ok bæta svá syndir; inn sjúki maðr þarf at hafa sárar atgerðir til heilsu sér.

The one who has transgressed must practise self-chastisement and thus atone for sins; the sick man needs to have painful treatments for his health.

Mss: **1199**[x](75v), 624(147). — *Readings*: [2] skal sá er misgert hefir: skaltu ok margan veg 624 [3] bæta: hæða 624 [6] sér til: til sinnar 624.

Editions: *Skj* Anonyme digte og vers [XIII], [C. E/5]. *Hugsvinnsmál* 139: AII, 195-6, BII, 209, *Skald* II, 109; Hallgrímur Scheving 1831, 32, Gering 1907, 38, Tuvestrand 1977, 147, Hermann Pálsson 1985, 124.

Notes: [All]: Lat. parallel: (*Dist*. IV, 40) *Cum quid peccaris, castiga te ipse subinde: | vulnera dum sanas, dolor est medicina doloris* 'When you have sinned in some way, charge yourself right away; when you cure wounds pain is remedy for pain'.

140. Heiptarorða   gerz þú eigi hefnisamr;
    heldr skaltu væginn vera;
    af þeiri gæzku   máttu þér gera
    vísa fjándmenn at vinum.

Gerz þú eigi hefnisamr heiptarorða; heldr skaltu vera væginn; af þeiri gæzku máttu gera þér vísa fjándmenn at vinum.

Do not become vengeful because of words of hate; you must rather be yielding; from this kindness you can make certain enemies into friends for yourself.

Mss: **1199**[x](75v), 624(147). — *Reading*: [6] fjándmenn: fjándr 624.

Editions: *Skj* Anonyme digte og vers [XIII], [C. E/5]. *Hugsvinnsmál* 53: AII, 179-80, BII, 194, *Skald* II, 101; Hallgrímur Scheving 1831, 34, Konráð Gíslason 1860, 37, Tuvestrand 1977, 147, Hermann Pálsson 1985, 125.

Notes: [All]: Lat. parallel: (*Dist*. IV, 39) *Cede loco laesus, fortunae cede potenti: | laedere qui potuit, poterit prodesse aliquando* 'Give way to fortune when hurt, give way to the powerful;

whoever was able to harm might now and again be able to help'. Lines 4-6 are reminiscent of Egill *St* 24/5-8ᵛ: *... ok þat geð | es gerðak mér | vísa fjándr | af vélundum* '... and that temper with which I made certain enemies out of tricksters'.

141. Bölgjörnum manni,   ef þér brugðiz hefir,
    skaltu eigi grand gera,
   þvít af annars gæzku   batnar sá iðugliga,
    sá er hefir óvinauðigr verit.

Skaltu eigi gera grand bölgjörnum manni, ef hefir brugðiz þér, þvít sá batnar iðugliga af annars gæzku, sá er hefir verit óvinauðigr.

You must not do harm to a malicious man if he has deceived you, because the one who has not been rich in friends frequently improves from another's kindness.

Ms.: **624**(147).

Editions: *Skj* Anonyme digte og vers [XIII], [C. E/5]. *Hugsvinnsmál* 140: AII, 196, BII, 209, *Skald* II, 109; Gering 1907, 38, Tuvestrand 1977, 141, Hermann Pálsson 1985, 125-6.

Notes: [All]: Lat. parallel: (*Dist.* IV, 41) *Damnaris numquam post longum tempus amicum: / mutavit mores, sed pignera prima memento* 'Never condemn a friend of long standing, he has changed his ways, but remember his first merits'. — [6] *óvinauðigr* 'not rich in friends': i.e. without many friends. This word is a *hap. leg.*, possibly modelled on *vinsæll / óvinsæll* and *-auðigr* compounds (e.g. *féauðigr*). It could also be construed *óvin-auðigr* 'rich in enemies'. Gering and *Skj* B following him corrects to *óvinligr* 'unfriendly'.

142. Vel skaltu vinna,   ef þú átt í verkum hlut,
    ok geraz höldum hollr;
   sinni sýslu   týnir slægr maðr;
    ilt er verkþjófr at vera.

Ef þú átt hlut í verkum, skaltu vinna vel ok geraz hollr höldum; slægr maðr týnir sýslu sinni; ilt er at vera verkþjófr.

If you take part in work, you must work well and become loyal to men; a sly man forgets his work; it is bad to be a work-thief.

Mss: **1199**ˣ(75v), **624**(147). — *Readings*: [3] höldum: *om.* 624;   hollr: 'hollvr' *corrected from* 'holldvr' 624   [4] sinni sýslu: sýslu sinni 624   [5] týnir slægr: gleymir slækinn 624.

Editions: *Skj* Anonyme digte og vers [XIII], [C. E/5]. *Hugsvinnsmál* 141: AII, 196, BII, 209, *Skald* II, 109; Hallgrímur Scheving 1831, 34, Gering 1907, 38, Tuvestrand 1977, 148, Hermann Pálsson 1985, 126.

Notes: [All]: Lat. parallels: (*Dist.* IV, 42) *Gratior officiis, quo sis mage carior, esto, / ne nomen subeas, quod dicunt, officiperdi* 'Be more gracious in your business dealings to those to whom you may be dearer, so that you will not bear the name of "officiperdus" [*lit.* one who makes ill use of the favours of others]'. — [5] *slægr* 'sly': 624's *slækinn* 'slack' (i.e. 'lax, lazy') seems to suit the sense better. — [6] *verkþjófr* 'work-thief': This word, occurring in both mss, is a *hap. leg.* The Lat. word it translates, *officiperdus* 'one who makes ill use of the favours of others', is found only in this distich and an Isidore gloss.

143. Miskunnsamr   skaltu við menn vera,
    ef þú átt þræla þér,
  þvít jarðligt eðli   hygg ek jafnt hafa
    þý sem þjóðans mögr.

Skaltu vera miskunnsamr við menn, ef þú átt þér þræla, þvít ek hygg þý hafa jafnt jarðligt eðli sem þjóðans mögr.

You must be merciful with men if you own slaves, because I think a bondwoman has the same earthly nature as the kinsman of a prince.

Mss: **1199**[x](75v), 624(148). — *Readings*: [2] menn: mann 624 [4] þvít: *om.* 624; jarðligt: *so* 624, jarðligs 1199[x]; eðli: *om.* 624 [5] hygg ek: minztu 624; hafa: hefir 624 [6] þý sem: þræll ok 624; þjóðans: *so* 624, þjóðkóngs 1199[x].

Editions: *Skj* Anonyme digte og vers [XIII], [C. E/5]. *Hugsvinnsmál* 143: AII, 196, BII, 209, *Skald* II, 110; Hallgrímur Scheving 1831, 33, Konráð Gíslason 1860, 552, Gering 1907, 39, Tuvestrand 1977, 149, Hermann Pálsson 1985, 127.

Notes: [All]: Lat. parallel: (*Dist.* IV, 44) *Cum servos fueris proprios mercatus in usus / et famulos dicas, homines tamen esse memento* 'When you have bought your own slaves for your use, and you call them servants, remember they are still men'. — [4-6]: 624 reads quite differently here: *jarðligt minztu, | at jafnt hefir | þræll ok þjóðans mögr* (*minztu, at þræll ok þjóðans mögr hefir jafnt jarðligt* [*eðli*] 'remember that a slave and a ruler's kinsman have the same earthly [nature]'). — [6] *þjóðans* 'of a prince': The scribe of 1199[x] may have misunderstood the word (perhaps with *-an-* abbreviated) and replaced it with the more familiar form *þjóðkóngs*. *LP*: *þjóðann* cites a number of similar phrases.

144. Ódyggra manna   skaltu aldrigi
    fagna bráðum bana;
  hitt er sýnna,   at sælir munu
    dyggvir menn, þótt deyi.

Skaltu aldrigi fagna bráðum bana ódyggra manna; hitt er sýnna, at dyggvir menn munu sælir, þótt deyi.

You must never rejoice at the sudden death of wicked men; it is obvious that worthy men will [be] blessed when they die.

Mss: 1199[x](75v), 624(148). — *Readings*: [1] Ódyggra manna: *so* 624, ókunnra dyggra 1199[x] [2] aldrigi: *so* 624, eigi 1199[x] [3] fagna bráðum bana: *so* 624, bráðum dauða fagna 1199[x] [5] sælir munu: munu sælir vera 624.

Editions: *Skj* Anonyme digte og vers [XIII], [C. E/5]. *Hugsvinnsmál* 144: AII, 196-7, BII, 209-10, *Skald* II, 110; Hallgrímur Scheving 1831, 33, Konráð Gíslason 1860, 552, Gering 1907, 39, Tuvestrand 1977, 150, Hermann Pálsson 1985, 128.

Notes: [All]: Lat. parallel: (*Dist*. IV, 46) *Morte repentina noli gaudere malorum: / felices obeunt quorum sine crimine vita* 'Do not rejoice at the sudden death of evil-doers; happy die those whose life [is] without blemish'. The topic of gloating is also dealt with in *Hsv* 35. — [3]: 1199[x]'s *bráðum dauða fagna* lacks alliteration.

145. Þessi *ljóð,   ef þú þekkjaz vilt,
        efla þik til þrifa,
    en sá halr,   sem hafna vill,
        stríðir sjálfum sér.

Þessi *ljóð efla þik til þrifa, ef þú vilt þekkjaz, en sá halr, sem vill hafna, stríðir sér sjálfum.

This poem [*lit.* these poems] will help you to prosperity, if you want to receive it, but the man who wants to reject it, will harm himself.

Mss: 1199[x](75v), 624(148). — *Readings*: [1] *ljóð: hljóð 1199[x], ráð 624 [5] sem: er þeim 624 [6] stríðir: stríðir um 624.

Editions: *Skj* Anonyme digte og vers [XIII], [C. E/5]. *Hugsvinnsmál* 145: AII, 197, BII, 210, *Skald* II, 110; Hallgrímur Scheving 1831, 22, Gering 1907, 24, Tuvestrand 1977, 150, Hermann Pálsson 1985, 128.

Notes: [All]: Lat. parallel: (III, *Praefatio*) *Hoc quicumque voles carmen cognoscere lector / cum praecepta ferat, quae sunt gratissima vitae / commoda multa feres, sin autem spreveris illud, / non me scriptorem, sed te neglexeris ipse* 'Any reader who wishes to know this poem, since it brings precepts which are most applicable to life; you carry many useful things, but if you scorn it, you are not neglecting me, the author, but yourself'. The inclusion of an Icel. version of the prefaces to Books III-IV here is probably to supply an appropriate conclusion to the poem. The Lat. *disticha* end with IV, 49: *Miraris verbis nudis me scribere versus; / hoc brevitas fecit, sensu coniungere binos* 'You marvel that I write these verses in bare words; this brevity brings about, to join in one thought two (lines)'. — [1] *ljóð* 'poem': Lit. 'poems'. On 1199[x]'s use of *hljóð* for *ljóð*, cf. st. 103/1, 4 and Notes. 624's *ráð* 'advice' is further from the Lat. *carmen*.

146. At hyggnum mönnum   nem þú horsklig ráð
    ok lát þér í brjósti búa;
örþrífsráða   verðr sá aldrigi,
    sem girniz margt at muna.

Nem þú horsklig ráð at hyggnum mönnum ok lát búa í brjósti þér; sá verðr aldrigi örþrífsráða, sem girniz at muna margt.

Learn wise advice from intelligent men and let it live inside your breast; that one never becomes at a loss for what to do who is eager to remember much.

Mss: **1199**[x](75r), 720a IV(2v), 723a[x](83). — *Reading*: [3] brjósti: *so* 720a IV, 723a[x], *om.* 1199[x].

Editions: *Skj* Anonyme digte og vers [XIII], [C. E/5]. *Hugsvinnsmál* 129: AII, 193, BII, 207, *Skald* II, 108; Hallgrímur Scheving 1831, 30, Gering 1907, 34, Tuvestrand 1977, 142, Hermann Pálsson 1985, 118.

Notes: [All]: Lat. parallels: *Dist.* IV, 23, 27 – cf. st. 127; (*Dist.* IV, 48) *Cum tibi contingerit studio cognoscere multa, / fac discas multa, vita nescire doceri* 'If you come to know many things through study, see to it that you learn many things, from life you will not know to learn'. The topic of this st. occurs quite often in the *Disticha*, so it is difficult to determine which distich the translation is based on. In all 3 mss, the st. is included after st. 143, translating *Dist.* IV, 43, and before 147.

147. Í ljóðum þessum   megu lýðir nema,
    þat er drengmanni dugir:
gæzku ok mildi   glæpa viðrsjá
    ráð ok rétta siðu.

Í ljóðum þessum megu lýðir nema, þat er dugir drengmanni: gæzku ok mildi, viðrsjá glæpa, ráð ok rétta siðu.

In this poem [*lit.* these poems] men may learn what helps a good man: kindness and generosity, shunning of sins, advice and correct morals.

Mss: **1199**[x](75r), 720a IV(2v) (ll. 1-2), 723a[x](83), 624(148). — *Readings*: [2] megu: *so* 624, mega 1199[x], 720a IV, 723a[x]   [4] gæzku: *so* 723a[x], gæzka 1199[x], 624; ok: *om.* 723a[x]   [5] glæpa: glæpum 723a[x], 'gleppur' 624; viðrsjá: vit sér 624   [6] ráð ok rétta siðu: ráði ok réttum sið 723a[x].

Editions: *Skj* Anonyme digte og vers [XIII], [C. E/5]. *Hugsvinnsmál* 146: AII, 197, BII, 210, *Skald* II, 110; Hallgrímur Scheving 1831, 26, Gering 1907, 30, Tuvestrand 1977, 151, Hermann Pálsson 1985, 129.

Notes: [All]: Lat. parallel: (IV, *Praefatio*) *Securam quicumque cupis perducere vitam / nec vitiis haerere animo, quae moribus obsint* 'Whoever you are, if you wish to lead a safe life, do not fix your mind on faults which are contrary to character'.

148. Ástsamlig ráð   mun þú, einkason,
    þau er ek hefi í kvæði kent;
  fræði þessi   láttu fylgja þér
    alt til endadags.

Mun þú, einkason, ástsamlig ráð, þau er ek hefi kent í kvæði; láttu fræði þessi fylgja þér alt til endadags.

Remember, my only son, the affectionate advice which I have taught in the poem; let this knowledge accompany you to the very last day.

Mss: **1199**ˣ(75v), 624(148). — *Readings*: [2] mun þú: *so* 624, kenni ek þér minn 1199ˣ   [3] þau: *so* 624, þessi 1199ˣ; hefi í kvæði kent: *so* 624, kveðit hefi 1199ˣ   [4] þessi: þetta 624   [5] fylgja þér: *so* 624, þér fylgja 1199ˣ   [6] endadags: efsta dags 624.

Editions. *Skj* Anonyme digte og vers [XIII], [C. E/5]. *Hugsvinnsmál* 147: AII, 197, BII, 210, *Skald* II, 110; Hallgrímur Scheving 1831, 26, Gering 1907, 29, Tuvestrand 1977, 151, Hermann Pálsson 1985, 129.

Notes: [All]: Lat. parallel: (IV, *Praefatio* cont.) *haec praecepta tibi semper retinenda memento: / invenies aliquid* † *quod te vitare magistro* † 'Always remember that these precepts should be held fast by you; you will find something [text corrupt]'. In content and phrasing this st. is very close to *Sól* 81. — [1-3]: 1199ˣ's text has metrical problems: *Ástsamlig ráð | kenni ek þér, minn einkason, | þessi er ek kveðit hefi* 'I teach you affectionate advice, my only son, which I have composed'. It is also further from the Lat. than 624. Hallgrímur Scheving has the same ll. 1-2 as 1199ˣ (echoing st. 2/1-2), but *er hér kveðið hefi* 'which I have composed/recited here' for l. 3 to restore the alliteration. — [5]: The w.o. in 624 is needed to correct the metre.

149. Hugsvinnsmál   læt ek fyrir höldum kveðin,
    ok kenda ek rekkum ráð;
  hyggins manns   lýsta ek hugspeki;
    hér er nú ljóðum lokit.

Ek læt Hugsvinnsmál kveðin fyrir höldum, ok ek kenda rekkum ráð; ek lýsta hugspeki hyggins manns; hér er nú lokit ljóðum.

I let 'Hugsvinnsmál' be recited before people, and I taught men advice; I illuminated the foresight of a wise man; here the poem is now finished.

Mss: **1199ˣ**(75v), 624(148). — *Readings*: [1] -mál: *so* 624, *om.* 1199ˣ [2] læt ek fyrir höldum kveðin: *so* 624, hef ek nú hljóðin kveðit 1199ˣ [3] kenda: kendi 624; rekkum: *so* 624, ýtum 1199ˣ [5] lýsta: leysta 624; hugspeki: hölða speka 624 [6] lokit: lokinn 624.

Editions: *Skj* Anonyme digte og vers [XIII], [C. E/5]. *Hugsvinnsmál* 148: AII, 197, BII, 210, *Skald* II, 110; Hallgrímur Scheving 1831, 33, Konráð Gíslason 1860, 552, Gering 1907, 39, Tuvestrand 1977, 152, Hermann Pálsson 1985, 130.

Notes: [All]: The correspondence is not very close to the *disticha* here (cf. *Dist.* IV, 49, quoted in Notes to st. 145). The closing st. is probably the translator's own composition. — [1-3]: 1199ˣ's text again has problems: *Hugsvinns* | *hef ek nú hljóðin kveðit,* | *ok kenda ek ýtum ráð* 'I have now composed the ?sounds of a wise man and I taught advice to men'. Line 3 lacks alliteration. Likewise, if *hljóðin* is emended to **ljóðin* 'the verses, the poem', as in sts 103 and 145, to make sense of ll. 1-2, the alliteration is removed. 624's text is consequently used here.

Anonymous, *Heilags anda drápa*

Edited by Katrina Attwood

Introduction

Heilags anda drápa 'Drápa about the Holy Spirit' (Anon *Heildr*) is partially preserved on fol. 10r of AM 757 a 4° (B). Fourteen full sts and four *helmingar* remain, representing part of the *stefjabálkr* of a substantial skaldic *drápa*. The opening is lost in a lacuna before fol. 10r, and B's text breaks off at 10r, l. 38, at the beginning of Anon *Leið*. It is not possible to determine the extent of the missing text, though the abbreviated refrains (*stef*) in sts 2, 10 and 18 suggest that the poem originally had at least two refrains, each of which would have occurred at least three times with seven refrainless sts between them, giving a *stefjabálkr* of at least forty sts. If the poem was constructed on the model of the C12th Christian *drápur*, we can postulate an approximate ratio of *upphaf : stefjabálkr : slæmr* of 1:1.5:1, which would give a total length of some 94 sts, arranged 27:40:27.

The poor state of B means that it has been necessary to rely heavily on previous transcriptions and eds of the poems, in particular the transcription in JS 399 a-b 4°ˣ (399a-bˣ), a collection of transcripts of the Christian poems preserved in B made in the middle of C19th. The transcription of *Heildr*, unlike those of all of the other B poems, is in two hands, one of which is probably that of Brynjólfur Snorrason, an Icel. student at the Arnamagnæan Institute in Copenhagen from 1842-50 (see Attwood 1996a, 32-3 for a fuller discussion of this attribution). Finnur Jónsson identifies the other hand as that of Jón Þorkelsson (Attwood 1996a, 32). This transcript has been cited selectively in the Readings, where B is defective. Finnur Jónsson's own diplomatic edn of *Heildr* in *Skj* A has also been cited selectively in the Readings, designated B*FJ* and some use has also been made of Rydberg's transcription (1907, 1-4), designated B*Rydberg*. Both these eds were made when B was more legible than it is now.

Sveinbjörn Egilsson included *Heildr* in his edn of *Fjøgur gømul kvæði* (1844, 52-6), which was prepared as a teaching text for the Lat. School at Bessastaðir. His text made extensive use of the 399a-bˣ transcript. In addition to a conservative, diplomatic transcription of the six poetic texts preserved on fols 10r-14v of B and a detailed discussion of the ms.'s preservation and paleographical features, Hugo Rydberg's thesis (Rydberg 1907) includes normalised prose arrangements of four of the poems, with *Heildr* on pp. 45-7. *Heildr* is also edited by Finnur Jónsson in *Skj* AII, 160-3 and by E. A. Kock in *Skald* II, 92-4. An annotated diplomatic transcript of the text in B is presented on pp. 55-60 of the doctoral thesis, Attwood 1996a, and a normalised edn on pp. 151-70. Although the following edn draws on that presented in the thesis, there are significant differences.

The poem's title is editorial, and was bestowed in the form *Heilags anda vísur* 'The Holy Spirit's *vísur*' by Sveinbjörn Egilsson (1844, iii). It has been renamed *Heilags anda drápa* for this edn, as it is clear that what is left of the poem is part of a *drápa* with refrain.

Heildr itself provides scant dating evidence. A *terminus ante quem* is provided by B, which can be dated to the late C14th. Although there are few direct borrowings from earlier poems, some aspects of the diction seem to be inspired by the great C12th Christian *drápur* (see Notes to 2/1 and 10/4), and the poet's use of the two-refrain *drápa* structure is also likely to be inspired by these poems. This ed. follows Einar Ólafur Sveinsson in assigning the poem to the later C13th. This dating depends largely on the poem's subject-matter and on the presence of rhymes such as *bryst* : *þosta* (8/7), *er* : *sár-* (12/7) and *ver* : *forð-* (15/5). Finnur Jónsson (*LH* II, 112 and n. 1) considered it likely to be slightly later than Anon *Líkn*. Einar Ólafur has demonstrated (1942) that sts 11-16 are a direct translation of the Lat. Pentecost hymn *Veni Creator Spiritus*, which is usually ascribed to Hrabanus Maurus (d. 856). The translation is highly accurate and intricate, and is the only example of a metrical work being translated into *dróttkvætt* verse. Attribution to the later C13th, the period in which, as the dissemination of the *Second* and *Third Grammatical Treatises* demonstrates, both knowledge of Lat. poetry and an interest in reproducing it in the vernacular were emerging in scholarly (and therefore religious) contexts in Iceland, seems reasonable.

Heildr is a prayer of praise to the Holy Spirit. It is in *dróttkvætt* throughout. The tone is elevated, and there are several latinate echoes of biblical or liturgical phrases, such as the rather complex phrase in 3/5-8, where the Spirit is said to have *grænkat geðfjöll snjöllu liði blómi siðferðar* 'made green the mind-mountains for wise people with the bloom of moral conduct', which possibly recalls the Postcommunion Sentence of the Mass for Pentecost. Elsewhere, as in the parallel God-kennings *frömuðr hölda, rennir ranns hátunnu regns* 'promoter of men, setter in motion of the house of the high barrel of rain' (5/2-4) the phrasing recalls, and perhaps outdoes, that of earlier Christian *drápur*. There are numerous kenning-like periphrases for the Holy Spirit in the poem (see Introduction to this volume), unparalleled elsewhere in the skaldic corpus, which has very few periphrases that can be said to refer specifically to the Holy Spirit (*Meissner*, 371).

Recent work by Sverrir Tómasson on the influence of music on the composition of skaldic poetry in this period (2003, 87) raises the tantalising possibility that the hymn might have been sung in this translation, but, as Sverrir indicates, this is ultimately unprovable.

1. ... lífgaðra anda.   endrbornar hér, forna*.
 Blíðr, lífgar þrif þjóðar
 þinn blástr, frömuðr ástar,
 lemið synd ... eykr yndi,

... lífgaðra anda. Blíðr frömuðr ástar, þinn blástr lífgar þrif endrbornar þjóðar hér; lemið synd forna* ... eykr yndi.

... of revived souls. Blessed promoter of love [= God], your breath stimulates the prosperity of reborn people here; you suppress ancient sin ... it [Holy Spirit] augments joy.

Mss: **B**(10r), 399a-b^x. — *Readings*: [1] lífgaðra: *so* 399a-b^x, B*FJ*, 'lifg[...]dra' B, B*Rydberg* [4] lemið synd: 'lemid syn[...]' B, 'lennd syne' 399a-b^x, 'læmid syn(d)'(?) B*Rydberg*, 'lemid synd' B*FJ* [5] forna*: fornar *all*.

Editions: *Skj* Anonyme digte og vers [XIII], C. [3]. *Heilags anda vísur* 1: AII, 160, BII, 175, *Skald* II, 92, *NN* §1402; Sveinbjörn Egilsson 1844, 52, Rydberg 1907, 1, 45, Attwood 1996a, 55, 151.

Notes: [All]: Several pp. are missing from B before 10r. Despite the fact that, in B, the initial letters of sts are enlarged uncials, and that the first of these is *Fæsk* (fol. 10r, l. 2, 2/1), Sveinbjörn Egilsson (1844) assumes sts 1 and 2 to be matching *helmingar* and prints them as one st., omitting 2/5. His st. numbering thus remains one in arrears throughout the poem. — [4] *lemið* 'you suppress': This edn follows Rydberg and *Skj* B in retaining B's 'lemid', 2nd pers. pl. of *lemja* 'to beat, thrash, suppress', addressed to God, the *frömuðr ástar* 'promoter of love' of l. 3. Kock (*NN* §1402) proposes an emendation to *lemr*, 3rd pers. sg. pres. indic. of *lemja*, taking the three verbal forms *lífgar* (l. 2), *lemr* (l. 4) and *eykr* (l. 4) to be parallel references to the Holy Spirit. — [5] *endrbornar hér* 'of reborn (people) here': *Skj* B, followed by *Skald*, emends to *endrbornum*, taking *endrbornum her* 'the reborn army', i.e. Christians, as the dat. indirect object with *eykr yndi* 'he augments joy'. B's *endrbornar* can be retained if it is assumed to be a syncopated form of the f. gen. sg. form of the adj. *endrborinnar*, agreeing with *þjóðar* (l. 2), and if B's 'her' is construed as the adv. *hér* 'here'. Theologically, a soul is reborn at Baptism and thus exists on earth ('here') in a reborn spiritual state until earthly death brings it to its heavenly apotheosis. — [5] *forna**'ancient': This edn agrees with *Skj* B in emending B's *fornar* to *forna*, f. acc. sg. of adj. *forn* 'old', agreeing with *synd* (l. 4). Kock (*NN* §1402) takes *forna* as qualifying *yndi endrbornar*, translating *ökar forna fröjden för pånyttet folk* 'he [the Holy Spirit] augments ancient pleasure for reborn people'.

2. Fæsk, en frá líða lestir, Greindr skínn orð ok andi
   friðr, þeim er synda iðrask; ...
   hljóta menn af mætum
   miskunn lífsins brunni.

Friðr fæsk, þeim er iðrask synda, en lestir líða frá; menn hljóta miskunn af mætum brunni lífsins. Greindr andi skínn ok orð ...

Peace is obtained for those who who repent their sins, and flaws pass away; men receive mercy from the worthy spring of life. The discerning spirit shines and the word ...

Mss: **B**(10r), 399a-b^x. — *Readings*: [2] iðrask: *so* 399a-b^x, B*FJ*, 'i[...]' B, 'id[...](z)'(?) B*Rydberg* [5] Greindr: *so* 399a-b^x, B*Rydberg*, B*FJ*, 'Gr[...]índr' B.

Editions: *Skj* Anonyme digte og vers [XIII], C. [3]. *Heilags anda vísur* 2: AII, 160, BII, 175, *Skald* II, 92, *NN* §§2335, 2336, 3157; Sveinbjörn Egilsson 1844, 52, Rydberg 1907, 1, 45, Attwood 1996, 55, 151.

Notes: [1] *líða* 'pass away': Kock (*NN* §2335) objects to what he regards as excessive alliteration (on *f* and *l*) in this l., and emends to *hlíða*, 3rd pers. pl. pres. indic. of *hlíða* 'to give way, move aside', construed with *lestir* 'flaws' (l. 1). He is anticipated by Rydberg. — [2] *friðr... þeim er iðrask synda* 'peace ... for those who repent their sins': Recalls Gamlkan *Has* 25/3, which also occurs in a context concerning the promise of salvation to the penitent. — [4] *brunni lífsins* 'spring of life': This is one of a cluster of metaphors characterising the Holy Spirit as a spring or river. Compare *brunnr miskunnar* 'spring of mercy' in 8/4, *eilífr ok heilagr brunnr* 'eternal and holy spring' in 12/6, and *brunnr vits* 'spring of wisdom' in 16/2. Such epithets are widespread in medieval devotional literature and hymnody, and their ultimate source is undoubtedly biblical. *Brunnr lífsins* appears to be a calque on Jer. II.13, where God describes himself as *fons aquae vitae* 'the fountain of the water of life'. The image of God as the source of life-restoring water is one of the most common biblical metaphors, perhaps the most common occurrences of which are Ezekiel's vision of the river of life (Ezek. XLVII.1-12), S. John's parallel vision of the crystal-clear river in Rev. XXII.1-2, and Christ's claim to be the source of life-giving water in John IV.14. — [5] *greindr skínn ok orð andi* 'the discerning spirit shines and the word ...': Repetition of the first words of a *stef*, the remainder of which is lost in the lacuna preceding fol. 10r, is indicated by the obelos symbol in the right-hand margin.

3. Hugfyldra, blést, hölda   Sú hefr einkagjöf grænkat
   heilagra guð fögrum   geðfjöll liði snjöllu
   vitr, þeim er vísdóm betrir   (erat seggja trú) tryggva
   vandan, spektaranda.   (tóm) siðferðar blómi.

Vitr guð hugfyldra heilagra hölda, blést fögrum spektaranda, þeim er betrir vandan vísdóm. Sú tryggva einkagjöf hefr grænkat geðfjöll snjöllu liði blómi siðferðar; trú seggja erat tóm.

Wise God of courageous holy men, you inspired the beautiful spirit of understanding which improves hard-won wisdom. That true, unique gift has made green the mind-mountains [SOULS] for wise people with the bloom of moral conduct; the faith of men is not empty.

Mss: **B**(10r), 399a-b[x]. — *Reading*: [2] *fögrum*: fagra B, 399a-b[x].

Editions: *Skj* Anonyme digte og vers [XIII], C. [3]. *Heilags anda vísur* 3: AII, 160, BII, 175, *Skald* II, 92, *NN* §§1403, 2337, 2338B; Sveinbjörn Egilsson 1844, 52, Rydberg 1907, 1, 45, Attwood 1996a, 55, 151.

Notes: [2] *guð fögrum*: B's 'fagra' must be emended to *fögrum* after *blása* (which may take acc. or dat.) to provide a dat. antecedent for *þeim er* (l. 3). Finnur Jónsson (*Skj* B) emends to *guðs fögrum*, construing the first *helmingr*: *blést vitr fögrum spektaranda, þeims betrir vandan vísdóm hugfyldra heilagra hǫlda guðs* 'You, wise, exhaled the beautiful spirit of understanding, the one which improves the painstaking wisdom of courageous, holy men of God'. — [4] *vandan* 'hard-won': The adj. *vandr* is usually translated 'difficult, painstaking', and derives from the verb *vanda* 'to make elaborately, take care and pains in (a work or choice)' (*LP*: *vanda*). The reference may be to worldly understanding, which is utterly ineffectual unless bolstered by the Holy Spirit (see, for example, Eph. I.17-22, Col. I.9). *Vandr* is translated 'hard-won' here, in an attempt to exploit connotations of both the difficulty and the skill of the endeavour. — [4] *spektaranda* 'spirit of understanding': I.e. *andi spektar*. Cf. Eph. I.17, where the Holy Spirit is described as *spiritus sapientiae et revelationis* 'the spirit of wisdom and revelation'. This is a deliberate echo of the characterisation of the Spirit in Isa. XI.2: *spiritus sapientiae et intellectus spiritus consilii et fortitudinis spiritus scientiae et pietatis* 'the spirit of wisdom, and of understanding, the spirit of counsel, and of fortitude, the spirit of knowledge, and of godliness'. — [5-8] *hefr grænkat geðfjöll snjöllu liði blómi siðferðar* 'has made green the mind-mountains for wise people with the bloom of moral conduct': Morally upright behaviour is often described as the 'fruit' of the Holy Spirit in the New Testament (see, for example, Gal. V.22-3; Phil. I.11; Col. I.10; Jas III.17). It is interesting to compare the Postcommunion Sentence of the Mass for Pentecost: *Sancti Spiritus, Domine, corda nostra mundet infusio: et sui roris intima aspersione fœcundet* 'May the infusion of the Holy Spirit purify our hearts, O Lord, and make them fruitful by the inward sprinkling of His heavenly dew' (Lefebure 1924, 970). — [6] *geðfjöll* 'mind-mountains [SOULS]': Cf. the similar kenning *skóg hu*gar* 'forest of the mind [SOUL]' in 5/2. — [7] *tryggva* (f. sg. nom.) 'true': Here construed with *sú einkagjöf* (l. 5) as a weak adj. This requires no emendation. Both *Skj* B and *Skald* emend, Finnur Jónsson to *tryggu* (n. dat. sg.) agreeing with *blómi*, Kock to *tryggra*, m. gen. pl. agreeing with *seggja*, producing the intercalary cl. *trú tryggra seggja erat tóm* 'the faith of reliable men is not empty'.

4. Aflnægir seðr öflgu
    jóð — huggari þjóðar,
    átt, þann er aldri fættisk,
    auð — skilningar brauði,
    því er oss með hug hvössum
    hrein brjóst ok trú fóstrar;
    glöð lætr guðdóms e*ðli*
    guma kyn föður skynja.

Aflnægir seðr jóð öflgu brauði skilningar — huggari þjóðar, átt auð, þann er aldri fættisk — því er fóstrar oss hrein brjóst með hvössum hug ok trú; lætr glöð kyn guma skynja guðdóms e*ðli* föður.

The strength-granter satisfies his children with the powerful bread of understanding — you, comforter of people, have the wealth that never diminishes — which fosters in us pure hearts [*lit.* breasts] along with keen thought and faith; it allows the cheerful race of men [MANKIND] to comprehend the divine nature of the Father.

Mss: **B**(10r), 399a-b[x]. — *Readings*: [4] auð: *so* 399a-b[x], B*Rydberg*, B*FJ*, '[...]uð' B; brauði: *so* 399a-b[x], B*Rydberg*, B*FJ*, 'bra[...]ðe' B [6] brjóst: *so* 399a-b[x], B*Rydberg*, B*FJ*, '[...]riost' B [7] e*ðli*: 'e[...]' B, B*FJ*, '(æ[...]læ)'(?) B*Rydberg*.

Editions: *Skj* Anonyme digte og vers [XIII], C. [3]. *Heilags anda vísur* 4: AII, 160-1, BII, 175-6, *Skald* II, 92, *NN* §3162; Sveinbjörn Egilsson 1844, 52-3, Rydberg 1907, 1, 45, Attwood 1996a, 55, 151.

Notes: [1] *aflnægir* 'strength-granter': A kenning-like periphrasis for the Holy Spirit. There are very few specific periphrases for the Holy Spirit in skaldic verse, and most are in this poem; cf. *Meissner*, 371. — [2] *huggari þjóðar* 'comforter of people': Another kenning-like reference to the Holy Spirit. The figure of the Holy Spirit as 'comforter' is a commonplace of medieval hymnody and exegesis. Its origin seems to reside in the post-Vulgate, C7th Lat. translation of the Greek παράκλητως in John XIV.16 and XXVI.15 as *consolator* 'comforter' (Cross and Livingstone 1983: *Comforter, the*). Cf. st. 12/2 *huggari*. — [6] *guðdóms eðli* 'the divine nature': Lit. 'nature of divinity'. This edn follows Finnur Jónsson and Rydberg in adopting Sveinbjörn Egilsson's reconstruction of *eðli*, acc. sg. of n. *eðli* 'nature, character', here. Although Rydberg's tentative reading '(æ...læ) (?)' (i.e. *e...le*) cannot be taken on trust, since neither *Skj* A nor 399a-b^x is able to make out more than the initial letter, *ðl* is required for *skothending* with *glöð lætr* 'cheerful race' (l. 7).

5. Ok völdum her, hölda,   því er illlífis æfa
   h*ugar skóg, frömuðr, nógu,   andvígr hiti gran*dar*
   regns hátunnu rennir   — frem*d* er í gipt — *né* grimdar
   ranns, aldini faldið,   greypr élreki steypir.

Ok, frömuðr hölda, rennir ranns hátunnu regns, faldið skóg h*ugar völdum her nógu aldini, því er andvígr hiti illlífis æfa gran*dar* né greypr élreki grimdar steypir; frem*d* er í gipt.

And promoter of men [= God], impeller of the house of the high barrel of rain [CLOUD > SKY/HEAVEN > = God], you cover the forest of the mind [SOUL] for the chosen army with abundant fruit, which the pernicious heat of a wicked life's term will never damage nor the violent storm-driver [WIND] of wrath throw down; there is honour in grace.

Mss: **B**(10r), 399a-b^x. — *Readings*: [2] h*ugar: haugar *all*; nógu: so 399a-b^x, B*Rydberg*, B*FJ*, 'nóg[...]' B   [3] hátunnu: so 399a-b^x, B*Rydberg*, B*FJ*, 'hatunn[...]' B   [4] faldið: so 399a-b^x, B*Rydberg*, B*FJ*, 'f[...]lldit' B   [5] æfa: æfi *all*   [6, 7] gran*d*ar frem*d*: 'gra[...]fre[...]' B, 'gran[...]frem[...]' 399a-b^x, B*Rydberg*, B*FJ*   [7] *né*: en B*Rydberg*.

Editions: *Skj* Anonyme digte og vers [XIII], C. [3]. *Heilags anda vísur* 5: AII, 161, BII, 176, *Skald* II, 92, *NN* §§1405, 2338; Sveinbjörn Egilsson 1844, 53, Rydberg 1907, 1, 45, Attwood 1996a, 55, 152.

Notes: [1-4]: Previous eds have had difficulty in interpreting *rennir* (l. 3). Sveinbjörn Egilsson (*LP* (1860): *renna*) takes it to be 3rd pers. sg. pres. indic. of *renna* 'to run'. He construes *frǫmuðr regns hátunnu ranns rennir vǫldum hǫlda her hugar skóg, faldit nógu aldini*, and translates *ornator cæli conserit hominem pectora, velata copioso semine* 'the adorner of heaven binds the hearts [*lit.* breasts] of men, producing a lot of seed'. This is unsatisfactory, since *consero* 'to tie, join' is not a close translation of *renna*, and *skógr* 'forest' (l. 2) is m. and cannot agree with *faldit* (l. 4), which Sveinbjörn takes to be adjectival, without emendation. Rydberg (1907, 45 n. 3) proposes that it is 'natural' to take the 3rd pers. sg. pres. form *rennir* and the p.p. *faldit* together as a periphrastic phrase, presumably identical in meaning with *falda*. He offers the examples of *vinna* in *Has* 51/7 (*þótt menn vinni misgert* 'even though men had comitted sins') and Anon *Gyð* 2/4, 8 (*vann sier aflað frægðar* 'earned fame for himself'), and *orka* in *Leið* 29/3-4 (*sterkr er engr svát orki aptrat dróttins krapti* 'no one is so strong as to be able to impede the Lord's power'). As Kock (*NN* §2142) points out, the first two examples are not exact parallels, since *vinna* often functions as an auxiliary in certain constructions. Rydberg offers no evidence for the use of *renna* in parallel expressions elsewhere, and *Fritzner: renna* has no examples of such usage. Finnur Jónsson, who is followed by Kock, takes *rennir* to be a m. noun, base-word of a God-kenning *rennir ranns hátunu regns* 'impeller of the house of the high-barrel of rain'. He emends B's 'fraumudr' (l. 2) to *framiðr*, m. nom. sg. adj. 'outstanding', which qualifies the God-kenning. This edn agrees with Finnur in taking *rennir* as a m. sg. nom. noun, meaning 'one who makes something run, a spurrer-on, impeller', but adopts a normalized form of B's 'fraumudr', *frömuðr*, m. 'promoter, furtherer' being construed with *hölda* (l. 1) to form a kenning for God or the Holy Spirit, *frömuðr hölda* 'promoter of men', which is in apposition to *rennir ranns hátunu regns*; cf. *frömuðr ástar* 'promoter of love' 1/3.

6.   Enn móð í styr stríðum,   Prýðir önd í andar
     sterkr græðari, skæðu   orrostu mann*kost*um,
     eflið ýgra djöfla,   né drengjum þar þröngva
     aldar ... fyri valdi.   þrír óvinir skírum.

Sterkr græðari aldar, enn eflið móð ... í stríðum styr fyri skæðu valdi ýgra djöfla. Prýðir önd mann*kost*um í orrostu andar, né þröngva þrír óvinir þar skírum drengjum.

Mighty healer of mankind, you still strengthen courage ... in the harsh battle against the dangerous power of vicious devils. You equip the soul with virtues in the battle of the spirit, neither do the three enemies subdue pure men there.

Mss: **B**(10r), 399a-b[x]. — *Readings*:   [4] ...: '[...]' B, '[...]st' 399a-b[x], B*Rydberg*, B*FJ*   [6] mann*kost*um: 'mank[...]um' *all*   [7] né: *so* 399a-b[x], B*FJ*, '[...]' B   [8] skírum: *so* 399a-b[x], B*Rydberg*, B*FJ*, 'skír[...]' B.

Editions: *Skj* Anonyme digte og vers [XIII], C. [3]. *Heilags anda vísur* 6: AII, 161, BII, 176, *Skald* II, 92; Sveinbjörn Egilsson 1844, 53, Rydberg 1907, 1-2, 45, Attwood 1996a, 56, 152.

Notes: [1] *enn* 'still': So also *Skald*; *Skj* B understands *en* 'but'. — [2, 4] *sterkr græðari aldar* 'mighty healer of mankind': Another kenning-like construction referring to the Holy Spirit. — [4]: B is badly torn. Traces of the last letter (possibly a *t*) are visible, but no further traces remain. 399a-b[x], B*Rydberg* and B*FJ* read final *st* with certainty. Sveinbjörn Egilsson suggests reconstruction to adv. *mest* 'most', qualifying *eflið móð* 'you strengthen courage' (ll. 1, 3). This reconstruction is adopted by *Skj* B and *Skald*. Rydberg (1907, 1 n. 12) suggests emendation to *brjóst*, acc. sing. of *brjóstr* 'breast', construing *enn eflið (þér) í styr stríðum móð brjóst fyr skæðu valdi ygra diǫfla* 'still you strengthen your courage in the harsh battle against the dangerous power of vicious devils'. — [6] *mann*kost*um* 'virtues':

This edn follows all other eds in adopting Sveinbjörn Egilsson's reconstruction here. — [8] *þrír óvinir* 'three enemies': Presumably, as Sveinbjörn Egilsson (1844, 43 n. 1) and Rydberg suggest, these 'enemies' are the world, the flesh and the devil. — [8] *skírum* (m. dat. pl.) 'pure': Both *Skj* B and *Skald* take this adj. with *mannkostum* 'virtues' (l. 6).

7. Réttvísum kant, ræsir   glaðir hrinda því grandi
   regnbýs, hugum lýsa,   guðs menn, þeir er vel renna
   *svá*t skynja*r* veg vizku   — fremsk helgat lið — lymsku,
   vakr her*r* með trú spakri;   lífs braut, djöfuls skrauti.

Ræsir regnbýs, kant lýsa réttvísum hugum, *svá*t vakr her*r* skynja*r* veg vizku með spakri trú; því hrinda glaðir menn guðs, þeir er renna vel braut lífs, grandi, djöfuls lymsku skrauti; helgat lið fremsk.

King of the rain-dwelling [SKY/HEAVEN > = God], you are able to illuminate righteous minds, so that the watchful army understands the way of wisdom with serene faith; therefore, cheerful men of God, who run life's way well, cast away harm, the devil's treacherous finery; the holy troop gains honour.

Mss: **B**(10r), 399a-b[x]. — *Readings*: [3] *svá*t: '[...]t' *all*; skynja*r*: 'skynia' *all*   [4] her*r* með trú: 'her med [...]' B, 399a-b[x], 'her m[...] tru' B*Rydberg*, B*FJ*;   spakri: *so* 399a-b[x], B*Rydberg*, B*FJ*, 'spa[...]ri' B.

Editions: *Skj* Anonyme digte og vers [XIII], C. [3]. *Heilags anda vísur* 7: AII, 161, BII, 176-7, *Skald* II, 92, *NN* §§1406, 2338; Sveinbjörn Egilsson 1844, 53-4, Rydberg 1907, 2, 45-6, Attwood 1996a, 56, 152.

Notes: [1-4]: Rydberg takes *vakr* (l. 4) as an adj. meaning 'watchful, alert', qualifying *ræsir regnbýs* 'king of the rain-dwelling [SKY/HEAVEN > = God]'. He reconstructs *bezt* at the beginning of l. 3. His prose arrangement is *Vakr ræsir regnbýs, þú kannt bezt skynja réttvísum hugum hér með spakri trú [ok] lýsa vizku veg* 'Watchful king of the rain-dwelling, you are best able to understand righteous minds here with unassuming faith [and] illuminate the way of wisdom'. This edn adopts Finnur Jónsson's arrangement in *Skj* B (also *Skald*), *kant lýsa réttvísum hugum, svát vakr herr skynjar* 'you are able to illuminate righteous minds, so that the watchful army understands ...', which requires construal of B's *her* as m. *herr* 'army' and emendation of *skynja* to *skynjar*, 3rd pers. sg. pres. indic. of *skynja* 'to understand'. — [1] *réttvísum kant, ræsir*. Cf. *Kálf Kátr* 14/7. — [5-8]: Rydberg and Finnur Jónsson assume *skrauti* dat. sg. of n. *skraut* 'ornament' (l. 8) to be part of an intercalated phrase *helgat lið fremsk skrauti*, which Finnur (*Skj* B) paraphrases *de hellige mænd iføres skrud* 'the holy people dress in finery'. The significance of this phrase is not altogether clear and the interpretation seems inappropriate in context. Kock (*NN* §1406) suggests that *grandi* (l. 5) and *djǫfuls skrauti* (l. 8) be interpreted as parallel expressions, and that *lymsku* be taken as gen. sg. of f. *lymska* 'treachery', functioning adjectivally and qualifying *lífs braut* (l. 8) 'life's way of treachery, life's treacherous way'. However, *lymsku* is more easily construed as an adj., *lymskr* 'wily, cunning, treacherous', here understood as the strong dat. sg. n. form, qualifying *skrauti*.

8. Hvert mein þváið, hirtir
   hugar sjúks, liði mjúku,
   gegn, sá er góðu magnar,
   glöðum brunni miskunnar.
   Siðlátum eykr sætan
   sá bekkr, þeim er af drekka,
   (linar brysti þrá) þo*sta
   (þekkr elskugi) rekkum.

Gegn hirtir, sá er góðu magnar, þváið hvert mein sjúks hugar mjúku liði glöðum brunni miskunnar. Sá bekkr eykr sætan þo*sta siðlátum rekkum, þeim er af drekka; þekkr elskugi linar þrá brysti.

Fitting chastiser, who strengthens righteousness, you wash every stain of the sick mind with gentle help in the clear spring of mercy. That spring intensifies sweet thirst in those morally upright men who drink from it; delightful love alleviates longing in the breast.

Mss: **B**(10r), 399a-b[x]. — *Readings*: [1] Hvert: *so* 399a-b[x], B*Rydberg*, 'H[...]t' B, 'H[...]rt' B*FJ* [7] þo*sta: þorsta *all* [8] elskugi: *so* 399a-b[x], B*Rydberg*, B*FJ*, 'elsk[...]ge' B.

Editions: *Skj* Anonyme digte og vers [XIII], C. [3]. *Heilags anda vísur* 8: AII, 161, BII, 177, *Skald* II, 93, *NN* §1407; Sveinbjörn Egilsson 1844, 54, Rydberg 1907, 2, 46, Attwood 1996a, 56-7, 152.

Notes: [2] *sjúks hugar* 'of the sick mind': This phrase may also be construed with *hirtir* (l. 1), giving the kenning-like periphrasis *hirtir sjúks hugar* 'chastiser of the sick mind' for the Holy Spirit; cf. 14/2, 3 *lundgóðr hirtir böls* 'benevolent chastiser of sin'. This is however, a less preferable reading, as the Holy Spirit (and Christ) are usually represented as healers, not chastisers, of the sick mind. — [2] *liði mjúku*: This edn follows Finnur Jónsson (*Skj* B) in interpreting this phrase as describing the Spirit's aid, and is translated 'with gentle help'. This interpretation relies on taking *liði* as dat. sg. of *lið*, n. meaning 'help, assistance, care' (*Fritzner*: *lið* 2). It is also possible to interpret *lið*, n. in the sense 'people, folk' (*Fritzner*: *lið* 1), and to take the phrase as a reference to those cleansed by the Spirit (*pace* Kock, *NN* §1407). — [4] *glöðum* 'clear': *Skj* B emends to *glæps* gen. sg. of *glæpr* m. 'sin, wickedness', construing the kenning as *gegn hirtir glæps* 'gentle chastister of sin'. He takes *hvert mein sjúks hugar* 'every stain of the sick mind' as the object of the verb *þváið* 'you wash'. — [5-8]: There seems to be a curious reversal here of Christ's promise in John IV.13-14: *ei omnis qui bibit ex aqua hac sitiet iterum qui autem biberit ex aqua quam ego dabo ei non sitiet in aeternum sed aqua quam dabo ei fiet in eo fons aquae salientis in vitam aeternam* 'Whosoever drinketh of this water, shall thirst again; but he that shall drink of the water that I will give him, shall not thirst for ever: But the water that I will give him, shall become in him a fountain of water, springing up into life everlasting'. — [7] *brysti* : *þo*sta*: The rhyme remains imperfect, but B's *þorsta* must be normalised to the late form *þo*sta* to give a semblance of *skothending*.

9. Mærr vald*i* gefr mildi
meinlausum her beinan
guðs, þeim er grimmu niðra*r*
grandi hræzlu, anda.

Sú er prýðigjöf góðum
grundvöllr stöðugr undir
(náir gipt, e*r* krefr) kröptum
(Krist af hjarta tvistu).

Mærr vald*i* mildi gefr meinlausum her, þeim er niðra*r* grimmu grandi hræzlu, beinan anda guðs. Sú prýðigjöf er stöðugr grundvöllr undir góðum kröptum; náir gipt, e*r* krefr Krist af tvistu hjarta.

The great ruler of mercy [= God] gives the sinless army, which supresses terrible damage through fear, the helpful spirit of God. That magnificent gift is a secure foundation beneath good powers; he will obtain grace who calls on Christ from a repentant [*lit.* sorrowful*]* heart.

Mss: **B**(10r), 399a-b*ˣ*. — *Readings*: [1] vald*i*: valdr *all*   [3] niðra*r*: niðra *all*   [6] stöðugr: *so* 399a-b*ˣ*, B*Rydberg*, B*FJ,* 'stöðug[...]' B   [7] e*r*: en *all*.

Editions: *Skj* Anonyme digte og vers [XIII], C. [3]. *Heilags anda vísur* 9: AII, 161, BII, 177, *Skald* II, 93, *NN* §2339; Sveinbjörn Egilsson 1844, 54, Rydberg 1907, 2, 46, Attwood 1996a, 57, 153.

Notes: [1] *vald*i 'ruler': B has *valdr*, a m. noun with the same meaning as *valdi*. However, all eds (following Konráð Gíslason and Eiríkur Jónsson 1875-89, II, 27-9) emend to give a two-syllable word, as the l. would otherwise be too short. — [3] *þeim er niðrar* 'the one which supresses': The ms. reading 'þeim er ... nidra' gives a sg. subject with a pl. verb. *Skj* B emends to *niðrar*, 3rd pers. sg., but retains the pl. form *niðra* in the prose order (most likely a typographical error). *Hræzlu* 'through fear' (l. 4) is understood as an instrumental dat. referring to the fear of God, which the army of righteous Christians uses to suppress the damage caused by sin. Kock (*NN* §2339) sees the Holy Spirit, rather than Christian people, as the motive force. Kock's reading requires the emendation of *þeim* (dat.) to *þann* (acc.), construing *gefr meinlausum her beinan anda guðs, þann*s *niðra*r *grimmu grandi hræzlu* 'gives the sinless army the helpful spirit of God, which suppresses the terrible damage of fear'.

10. Rakkr dróttinn fremr rekka
ríkr ástgjöfum slíkum
(þeim er sigr ok sómi)
sólar fróns (at þjóna).

Syngr óskalof lengi
landherr spökum a*nda*
...

Ríkr rakkr dróttinn fróns sólar fremr rekka slíkum ástgjöfum, þeim er sigr ok sómi at þjóna. Landherr syngr lengi óskalof spökum a*nda* ...

The mighty, bold lord of the land of the sun [SKY/HEAVEN > = God] assists men with such love-gifts, which are a victory and an honour to gain. The army on earth [i.e. Christians] sings for a long time wished for-praise to the wise spirit ...

Mss: B(10r), 399a-b^x. — *Reading*: [6-8]: *abbrev. as* 'lannd herr spǫkum a. l.' B.

Editions: *Skj* Anonyme digte og vers [XIII], C. [3]. *Heilags anda vísur* 10: AII, 161-2, BII, 177, *Skald* II, 93; Sveinbjörn Egilsson 1844, 54, Rydberg 1907, 2, 46, Attwood 1996a, 57-8, 153.

Notes: [3] *þeim er*: Here interpreted as a rel. pron. referring back to *ástgjöfum* 'love-gifts' (l. 2). *Skj* B understands a separate cl. *er sigr ok sómi þeim* 'it is a victory and an honour to that one (i.e. God)'. — [4] *fróns sólar* 'of the land of the sun': Although the sky- or heaven-kenning *frón sólar* occurs elsewhere only in an anonymous *helmingr* on the Crucifixion quoted in Anon (*FoGT*) 6/2^III to illustrate the figure of *chronographia* (*SnE* 1848-87, II, 196; *TGT* 1884-6, 123), heaven-kennings on the same model occur very frequently in Christian verse. Cf. *land sólar* 'land of the sun' (*Leið* 26/1-2); *dags reitr* 'day's patch of land' (*Líkn* 32/6); *sólar reitr* 'sun's patch of land' (Anon *Lil* 11/4). — [5-8]: Repetition of a second *stef*, the two last ll. of which are not preserved, is indicated by the obelos symbol in the right-hand margin beside fol. 10r, l. 20. — [6] *a*nda 'spirit': B abbreviates this and the following words *a. l.* This edn follows Finnur Jónsson, Kock and Rydberg in adopting Sveinbjörn Egilsson's reconstruction to *anda*, acc. sing. of m. *andi* 'spirit', the recipient of the Christians' hymnsinging.

11. Kom nú, hreinskapaðr himna,
    hlutvandr föður andi;
    yðvarra frem, errinn,
    alsælan hug þræla.

    Himneskr*ar* fremr háska
    hjálp unnin* miskunnar
    gumna brjóst í grimmum
    guðs kraptr, *þau* er þú skaptir.

Kom nú, hreinskapaðr himna, hlutvandr andi föður; errinn, frem alsælan hug yðvarra þræla. Guðs kraptr, hjálp himneskr*ar* miskunnar, unnin* í grimmum háska, fremr brjóst gumna, *þau* er þú skaptir.

Come now, pure creator of the heavens, upright spirit of the father; powerful one, further the altogether-blessed minds [*lit*. mind] of your servants. God's power, help of heavenly mercy, won in terrible danger, strengthen the breasts [*lit*. breast] of men, which you created.

Mss: B(10r), 399a-b^x. — *Readings*: [1] hreinskapaðr ('hreinnskapadr'): *so* 399a-b^x, 'hreínn skapad[...]' B, B*Rydberg*, B*FJ* [5] Himneskr*ar*: himneskan *all* [6] unnin*: unninn *all* [8] guðs: *so* 399a-b^x, 'gu[...]' B, B*Rydberg*, B*FJ*; *þau*: 'þeim' *all*; er: *so* 399a-b^x, B*Rydberg*, B*FJ*, '[...]' B; skaptir: *so* 399a-b^x, spaktir B, B*Rydberg*, B*FJ*.

Editions: *Skj* Anonyme digte og vers [XIII], C. [3]. *Heilags anda vísur* 11: AII, 162, BII, 177-8, *Skald* II, 93, *NN* §1408; Sveinbjörn Egilsson 1844, 54-5, Rydberg 1907, 2, 46, Attwood 1996a, 58, 153.

Notes: [All]: Einar Ólafur Sveinsson (1942) pointed out that sts 11-16 are a direct and close translation of the C9th Lat. Pentecost hymn *Veni Creator Spiritus* (*AH* 50, 193, no. 144), which is sometimes attributed to Hrabanus Maurus. The Lat. text is often useful in interpreting B. The first *helmingr* of st. 11 corresponds to the first two ll. of the hymn:

Veni, creator spiritus, / mentes tuorum visita 'Come, creator spirit, visit the minds of your [people]'. Finnur Jónsson (*Skj* B) interprets what are presented here as two independent periphrases for the Holy Spirit as a single one, *hreinskapaðr, hlutvandr andi himna fǫður* 'purely-created, honest spirit of the father of the heavens', but this seems far from the Lat. original, as Einar Ólafur pointed out (1942, 143). — [1] *hreinskapaðr* 'pure creator': Cf. *LP*: *hreinskapaðr*; *-skapaðr* is a p.p., lit. 'created', but the sense of the agent noun seems required here, to judge from the Lat. *creator*. — [4] *alsælan hug yðvarra þræla* 'the altogether-blessed minds [*lit*. mind] of your servants': The *sæl* : *þræll* rhyme is also exploited in *Has* 58/8. — [5-8]: This *helmingr* corresponds loosely to ll. 3-4 of the first st. of the Lat. hymn: *imple superna gratia, / quae tu creasti, pectora* 'fill the breasts, which you created, with celestial grace'. It is difficult to make sense of B's text here, and considerable emendation has been necessary. B's 'spaktir' (l. 8) is clearly a scribal error, and 399a-b'''s *skaptir* is undoubtedly correct. Finnur Jónsson (*Skj* B) emends to *himneskum krapt** 'with heavenly power' (dat.) (ll. 5, 8), which he takes with *fremr*, 3rd pers. sg. pres. indic. of *fremja* 'to promote, further', translated as *styrker* '[he] strengthens'. Finnur construes the *helmingr*: *unnin hjálp miskunnar guðs fremr himneskum krapt, þeims þú skaptir, gumna brjóst í grimmum háska* 'the accomplished help of the mercy of God strengthens with heavenly power, which you created, men's hearts (*lit*. 'breasts') in cruel danger'. Rydberg (1907, 47) retains B's *kraptr* 'power' (nom.) (l. 8), but emends to *himneskra* (gen. pl.). He treats the *helmingr* as an apostrophe to God, the 'help of mercy': *Guðs unninn kraptr fremr brjóst himneskra gumna í grimmum háska, þeim er þú skaptir, hjálp miskunnar* 'God's accomplished power strengthens the breast of heavenly men (i.e. good men, or angels?) in cruel danger, which you created, help of mercy (i.e. God)'. Kock's arrangement (*NN* §1408) is essentially the same as Rydberg's, apart from the periphrasis for the Holy Spirit, which Kock renders *himneskrar miskunnar unnin hjálp* 'accomplished help of heavenly mercy', in apposition to *Guðs kraptr* 'God's power'. Although each of these arrangements makes grammatical sense, none of them is acceptable, since the Lat. text makes it clear that the rel. cl. *þau er þú skaptir* 'which you created' (l. 8) must refer neither to the might of heaven (*pace* Finnur Jónsson) nor worldly danger (Rydberg, Kock) but to the breasts (or hearts) of men. The present reading retains *brjóst* 'breast' (l. 7), assuming sg. for pl. 'breasts', corresponding to Lat. *pectora* in a learned style where the rel. pron., here emended *þau er*, does not agree with its antecedent (see *NS* §§260, 264). — [6] *unnin** 'won': In the present reading, all mss' *unninn* must be emended to agree with *miskunn*, f. 'mercy'.

12. Sanndyggra, mátt, seggja
    snjallr huggari, kallask
    harð*la* traust ins hæsta
    heiðgjöf konungs jöfra.

    Eldr ert elsku mildrar
    eilífr brunnr ok heilagr
    hinn er, andar sára
    einsmurning, vit hreinsar.

Snjallr huggari sanndyggra seggja, mátt kallask harð*la* traust heiðgjöf ins hæsta konungs jöfra. Ert eldr mildrar elsku, eilífr ok heilagr brunnr, hinn er hreinsar vit, einsmurning sára andar.

Wise comforter of truly faithful men, you can be called the very trusty honour-gift of the highest king of kings [= God]. You are the fire of gracious love, the everlasting and holy spring, which purifies the conscience, the unique unction of wounds of the soul.

Mss: **B**(10r), 399a-b˟. — *Reading*: [3] *harðla*: 'hard' B, 399a-b˟.

Editions: *Skj* Anonyme digte og vers [XIII], C. [3]. *Heilags anda vísur* 12: AII, 162, BII, 178, *Skald* II, 93, *NN* §1409; Sveinbjörn Egilsson 1844, 55, Rydberg 1907, 2-3, 46, Attwood 1996a, 58, 153.

Notes: [All]: The Lat. text of which this st. is a translation reads as follows: *Qui paraclitus diceris / donum Dei altissimi / fons vivus, ignis, caritas / et spiritalis unctio* 'You who are called Paraclete, gift of highest God, living spring, fire, love and spiritual unction'. — [2] *huggari* 'comforter': See Note to 4/2 above. Here the word is clearly a calque on the Lat. *paraclitus* lit. 'advocate, intercessor'. — [3] *harðla* 'very': The first part of the word, 'hard', is written at the end of 10r, l. 23 and may be incomplete. What is missing may be an adj. in the n. nom. sg., agreeing with n. *traust* 'trust, shelter' (l. 3), intensified by the prefix *harð-* 'very, greatly' etc. *Skj* B, *Skald* and Rydberg adopt Sveinbjörn Egilsson's reconstruction to n. *harðfengt* 'hardy, valiant'. They take the periphrasis for the Holy Spirit, *harðfengt traust seggja* 'valiant shelter of men' (ll. 3, 1) as parallel to *snjallr huggari* 'wise comforter' (l. 2). This edn follows the construction implied by Einar Ólafur Sveinsson (1942, 144), assuming that the missing element of l. 3 is an adv. like *harðla* or *harða* (both meaning 'very'). Einar (by implication) takes the addressee of the verse, the Holy Spirit, to be *snjallr huggari sanndyggra seggja* 'wise comforter of truly faithful men' and then construes *harð(l)a traust heiðgjöf ens hæsta konungs jöfra* 'you may be called the very trusty honour-gift of the highest king of kings', understanding *traust* as a strong adj. 'strong, trusty' in the f. sg. nom. This reading allows a much more straightforward w.o. to the *helmingr* and offers a direct translation of the Lat. *donum Dei altissimi*. — [6-8]: Finnur Jónsson (*Skj* B) construes *ertu ... eilífr ok heilagr brunnr, er hreinsar vit ens andar-sára einsmurning* 'you are ... an eternal and holy spring, which purifies the senses of the soul-sick with an excellent salve'. The Lat. text, however, lists four distinct attributes of the Spirit in apposition, confirming that *brunnr* 'spring' and *einsmurning* 'unique unction' must be treated as parallel: *fons vivus, ignis, caritas et spiritalis unctio*. — [7]: This l., as it stands in B, is unsatisfactory metrically and difficult in terms of sense; *hinn er* 'that which', referring to *brunnr* (l. 6), gives a l. in which alliteration falls on the unstressed rel. particle and the rhyme is imperfect. Kock (*NN* §1409) objects to this, and suggests emendation of *sára* to *undir* (acc. pl. of f. *und* 'wound'), also emending *vit* 'conscience' (l. 8) to *vítt* 'widely'. Finnur Jónsson, following Sveinbjörn Egilsson, deals with the problem by emending B's 'hin er' to *er ens* and taking the next two words as a cpd *andar-sára*, reading it with *vit ens andar-sára*, as detailed in the previous Note.

13. Þinn er, salkonungs sólar,
    sjauskiptr frami gipta,
    (vandask) hægri handar
    hreinn fingr (bragar greinir).

    Prýðir rausnar ræður,
    ríkr andi, þér líkaz;
    fyrirtígnari, fegra*,
    föður, kverkr meginverkum.

Hreinn fingr hægri handar sólar salkonungs, þinn frami gipta er sjauskiptr; bragar greinir vandask. Ríkr andi, prýðir ræður rausnar; fyrirtígnari föður, líkaz þér fegra* kverkr meginverkum.

Pure finger of the right hand of the king of the hall of the sun [(*lit.* 'the sun's hall-king') SKY/HEAVEN > = God], your distinction of grace [*lit.* good fortunes] is sevenfold; the poem's branches are elaborately crafted. Powerful spirit, you adorn speeches of magnificence; proclaiming messenger of the Father, it pleases you to beautify throats with mighty works.

Mss: **B**(10r), 399a-b˟. — *Reading*: [7] fegra*: fegnar B.

Editions: *Skj* Anonyme digte og vers [XIII], C. [3]. *Heilags anda vísur* 13: AII, 162, BII, 178, *Skald* II, 93, *NN* §2340; Sveinbjörn Egilsson 1844, 55, Rydberg 1907, 3, 46, Attwood 1996a, 58, 154.

Notes: [All]: The Lat. text, of which this st. is a rendition, reads as follows: *Tu septiformis munere, / dextrae Dei tu digitus, / tu rite promisso patris / sermone ditans guttura* 'You, with your sevenfold gift, you, finger of the right hand of God, you, duly according to the promise of the Father, enriching throats with speech'. — [1, 3, 4] *hreinn fingr hægri handar sólar salkonungs* 'pure finger of the right hand of the king of the hall of the sun [SKY/HEAVEN > = God]': Finnur Jónsson (*Skj* B) emends to *salkonungr* 'hall-king' (nom. sg.) (l. 1), taking the st. as an apostrophe to the first person of the Trinity. He construes *Sólar salkonungr, þinn hreinn fingr hægri handar er frami gipta sjauskiptr* 'King of the hall of the sun, the pure finger of your right hand is the sevenfold distinction of good fortunes'. The Lat. here, as elsewhere, is vocative, and B's text can be retained as a straightforward calque on *dextrae Dei tu digitus*. The God-kenning *salkonungr sólar* 'king of the hall of the sun' recurs in *Leið* 25/7, and is probably modelled on *salkonungr himna* 'king of the hall of the heavens' in *Geisl* 66/6 (see Note on *Leið* 13/5-8). — [3, 4] *bragar greinir vandask* 'the poem's branches are elaborately crafted': Finnur Jónsson (*Skj* B) interprets this cl. in a negative sense, as a reflection of the poet's concern about the difficulties of reconciling the skaldic medium to complex latinate poetic figures. Finnur glosses *digtet bliver nu vanskeligt* 'now the poem is becoming difficult'. This involves taking *vandask* as 3rd pers. pl. pres. sg. m.v. of *vanda*, used reflexively, meaning 'to become difficult, precarious' (*Fritzner: vandast* 5). *Vanda* can also mean 'to work elaborately, to take pains over' (*Fritzner: vanda* 3), however, so it is also possible to interpret the phrase as a boast about the poet's craftsmanship, and that is the sense adopted here. — [5-8]: This *helmingr* is difficult. Finnur Jónsson (*Skj* B), while indicating his uncertainty, interpreted the four ll. thus.: *rausnar-ríkr andi, fyrirtígnari föður kverkr, prýðir líkast ræður, fegnar þér, meginverkum* 'spirit powerful in magnificence, honourer of the Father's throat (speech), ornaments in the best way the speeches, you rejoice in, with mighty works'. Aside from the considerable syntactic fragmentation this involves, there are problems of sense. Taking *kverkr*, gen. sg. of *kverk*, f. 'throat' with *fǫður* gen., to form the epithet *fyrirtígnari fǫður kverkr* 'honourer of the father's throat' i.e. 'honourer of the father's word' for the Holy Spirit runs contrary to the Lat. text, which indicates that the *helmingr* should refer to the Holy Spirit's endowing the throats of human beings with speech. A reading that is much simpler syntactically, but which involves emending B's 'likaz' (l. 6) to *líkastr*, sup. adj. m. nom. sg., to agree with *andi*, is provided by Kock (*NN* §2340 and *Skald*): here ll. 5-6 and 7-8 form two separate main clauses. The present edn retains B's *líkaz* and emends *fegnar* (l. 7) to *fegra** 'to embellish, beautify'. This gives a close parallel to the Lat. *sermone ditans guttura* 'enriching throats with speech'.

14. Tendra ljós í leyndum, Hagr, efl, hallar fegrir,
     lundgóðr, vitum þjóðar, — hverr er leystr, er þér treystisk —
     böls hirtir (vek björtum) várn líkama veykan,
     björt (elskuga hjörtu).   vagns, eilífu magni.

Lundgóðr hirtir böls, tendra björt ljós í leyndum vitum þjóðar; vek hjörtu björtum elskuga. Hagr fegrir hallar vagns, efl várn veykan líkama eilífu magni; hverr er leystr, er treystisk þér.

Benevolent chastiser of sin, kindle bright lights in the secret consciousnesses of people; rouse hearts with bright love. Skilful beautifier of the hall of the wagon [SKY/HEAVEN], strengthen our weak body with everlasting strength; everyone is redeemed who trusts himself to you.

Mss: **B**(10r), 399a-b[x]. — *Readings*: [3] björtum: *so* 399a-b[x], B*Rydberg*, B*FJ*, 'bi[...]rtum' B [8] eilíf*u*: 'eilíf[...]' *all*.

Editions: *Skj* Anonyme digte og vers [XIII], C. [3]. *Heilags anda vísur* 14: AII, 162, BII, 178-9, *Skald* II, 93; Sveinbjörn Egilsson 1844, 55; Rydberg 1907, 46; Attwood 1996a, 154.

Notes: [All]: The Lat. text on which this st. is based is as follows: *Accende lumen sensibus / infunde amorem cordibus / infirma nostri corporis / virtute firmans perpeti* 'Kindle a flame in [our] senses, pour out love into [our] hearts, fortifying the weaknesses of our body, strengthening [it] with everlasting strength [*or* virtue]'. — [5, 8] *fegrir hallar vagns* 'beautifier of the hall of the wagon': The constellation formed by the seven brightest stars in Ursa Major is known in MIcel. as *karlsvagninn* 'Charles's wagon'; cf. OE *Carles wæn*, *OED*: 'Charles's Wain'. See Ník *Jóndr* 3/6 and Note; *Geisl* 71/7-8; Anon *Pét* 14/7-8, 21/4; *LP*: *vagn* 2.

15. Út rek óvin sleitinn,
    angrþverrir, veg langan,
    giptu framr, en gumnum
    gef traustan veg hraustum.

Ver þú, at vér megim forðask,
víss leiðtogi, píslir
lengr ok löst, á þröngum
lífs veg, siða fegrir.

Angrþverrir, framr giptu, rek sleitinn óvin út langan veg, en gef hraustum gumnum traustan veg. Ver þú, fegrir siða, víss leiðtogi á lífs þröngum veg, at vér megim lengr forðask píslir ok löst.

Harm-destroyer, outstanding in grace, drive the aggressive fiend a long way away, but give valiant men trustworthy honour. Beautifier of conduct [*lit.* conducts], be a true guide on life's narrow way, that we may for a long time escape torments and vice.

Mss: **B**(10r), 399a-b^x.

Editions: *Skj* Anonyme digte og vers [XIII], C. [3]. *Heilags anda vísur* 15: AII, 162, BII, 179, *Skald* II, 93, *NN* §§2341, 3280; Sveinbjörn Egilsson 1844, 55-6, Rydberg 1907, 3, 46, Attwood 1996a, 59, 154.

Notes: [All]: The Lat. text reads: *Hostem repellas longius / pacemque dones protinus / ductore sic te praevio / vitemus omne noxium* 'Drive the enemy further off and give peace continually; thus with you going before [us] as guide, we may avoid all evil'. — [4] *traustan veg* 'trustworthy honour': Kock (*NN* §2341) considers that, since the poet has spoken of driving the devil away *langan veg* 'a long way' (l. 2) and is about to speak of *lífs þrǫngum veg* 'life's narrow way' (ll. 7-8), *vegr* m. should also here be taken in the sense of 'way' (*LP*: 1. *vegr*), rather than 'honour, glory' (*LP*: 2. *vegr*). The Lat. *pacemque dones protinus* confirms that the interpretation offered here, which accords with those of Finnur Jónsson and Rydberg, is correct. The poet is, of course, exploiting the dual resonances of *vegr* throughout the st. The word-play is only fully resolved in the parallel characterisation of the Spirit as *fegrir siða* 'adorner of the faith' and *leiðtogi* 'guide'. The Spirit is able to guide men on the narrow path (*vegr*) to righteousness, which is marked by the gift of honour in the Christian sense of glory (*vegr*). — [7-8] *lífs þrǫngum veg* 'on life's narrow way': Compare Matt. VII.14, *quam angusta porta et arta via quae ducit ad vitam et pauci sunt qui inveniunt eam* 'How narrow is the gate, and strait is the way that leadeth to life: and few there are that find it'.

16. Veit, at vér megim réttan,
    vits brunnr, fyr þik kunna
    föður í fylking saðri,
    friðskýrðr, ok son dýrðar;

ok kæran þik þeira,
þrifa eggjandi, beggja
anda allar stundir,
alstyrkr, með trú dyrkim.

Friðskýrðr brunnr vits, veit, at vér megim fyr þik kunna réttan föður ok son í saðri fylking dýrðar; ok dyrkim þik, alstyrkr eggjandi þrifa, kæran anda beggja þeira allar stundir með trú.

Peace-glorified spring of wisdom, grant that we may, through you, come to know the true Father and the Son in the true crowd of glory; and [that] we may worship you, almighty encourager of well-being, dear spirit of both of them for all time with faith.

Mss: **B**(10r), 399a-b˟. — *Readings*: [2] vits brunnr: 'vizbrunnr' B   [4] friðskýrðr: *so* 399a-b˟, B*FJ*, 'fridsky[...]dr' B, 'friðsk(yr)ðr'(?) B*Rydberg*   [5] kæran: *so* 399a-b˟, B*Rydberg*, B*FJ*, 'kæ̅[...]' B   [7] allar: *so* 399a-b˟, B*Rydberg*, B*FJ*, 'all[...]' B.

Editions: *Skj* Anonyme digte og vers [XIII], C. [3]. *Heilags anda vísur* 16: AII, 163, BII, 179, *Skald* II, 94; Sveinbjörn Egilsson 1844, 56, Rydberg 1907, 3, 46, Attwood 1996a, 59, 154.

Notes: [All]: The Lat. text reads: *Per te sciamus da patrem / noscamus atque filium / te utriusque spiritum / credamus omni tempore* 'Grant that, through you, we may know the Father, and that we also become acquainted with the Son, and that we may believe in you, spirit of both of them, for all time'. — [1] *vér* (1st pers. pl. nom. pron.) 'we': *Skj* B has the 1st pers. dat. sg. pron., *mér*. This is an obvious mechanical error, and is corrected in the prose arrangement. — [2] *brunnr vits* 'spring of wisdom': Cf. *eilífr ok heilagr brunnr* 'eternal and holy spring' 12/6, a calque on *fons vivus*. B's reading, *vizbrunnr*, was understood as *brunnr vits* 'spring of wisdom' by Sveinbjörn Egilsson and has been adopted by all subsequent eds. — [3-4] *í saðri fylking dýrðar* 'in the true crowd of glory': Understood here to refer to the Trinity, though a case could be made for a reference to the angel host or the communion of saints.

17. Vegr sé feðr ok fögrum,   en salkonungs sólar
     fljótt, óskmegi dróttins;   sonr eingetinn hreinar
     lofi huggara hygginn   sendi oss með anda
     hirðprúðra kyn virða;   ört vingjafir björtum.

Vegr sé feðr ok fögrum óskmegi dróttins; kyn hirðprúðra virða lofi fljótt hygginn huggara, en eingetinn sonr sólar salkonungs sendi oss ört hreinar vingjafir með björtum anda.

Glory be to the Father and to the beautiful beloved Son of the Lord [= Christ]; may the kin of courtly men swiftly praise the thoughtful comforter, and may the only son of the king of the hall of the sun [(*lit.* 'son of the sun's hall-king') SKY/HEAVEN > = God > = Christ] graciously send us pure gifts of friendship along with the radiant spirit.

Mss: **B**(10r), 399a-b˟.

Editions: *Skj* Anonyme digte og vers [XIII], C. [3]. *Heilags anda vísur* 17: AII, 163, BII, 179, *Skald* II, 94, *NN* §§2832, 3281, 2386; Sveinbjörn Egilsson 1844, 56, Rydberg 1907, 3, 46, Attwood 1996a, 59, 155.

Notes: [All]: The Lat. doxology corresponding to *Heildr* 17 must have been known in some form to the Icel. poet. In the version given by Einar Ólafur, the Lat. reads: *Sit laus patri cum filio / sancto simul paraclito, / nobisque mittat filius / charisma sancti spiritus* 'Let there be praise to the Father with the Son, together with the Holy Paraclete, and may the Son send to us the gift of the Holy Spirit'. — [3] *hygginn huggara* 'the thoughtful comforter': That is, the Paraclete. — [6-8] *hreinar vingjafir* 'pure gifts of friendship': Lit. 'friendship-gifts'. Finnur Jónsson (*Skj* B) follows Rydberg in assuming that B's 'hreínnar' 'pure' (l. 6) qualifies f. gen. sing. *sólar* 'of the sun' (l. 5). They construe the Christ-kenning *sonr salkonungs hreinnar sólar* 'son of the king of the hall of the pure sun'. Kock (*NN* §3281) objects that, although kennings identical to, or on the same pattern as, *salkonungr sólar* occur frequently in Christian poetry (see Note to 13/1), none has an adj. qualifying *sól* (cf. *LP*: *sól*, kennings for God). This edn follows Kock in taking ms. 'hreínnar' (normalised to *hreinar*) as qualifying *vingjafir* f. acc. pl. (l. 8).

18. Fróns veitti sá sínum
    sauðum líf ept dauða
    hirðir framr, er himna
    heldr eilífu veldi.

    Greindr skínn orð ok andi
    ...

Sá framr hirðir fróns, er heldr eilífu veldi himna, veitti sínum sauðum líf ept dauða. Greindr andi skínn ok orð ...

May that outstanding shepherd of the earth [= God], who controls the eternal realm of the heavens, grant to his sheep life after death. The discerning spirit shines and the word ...

Mss: **B**(10r), 399a-b[x].

Editions: *Skj* Anonyme digte og vers [XIII], C. [3]. *Heilags anda vísur* 18: AII, 163, BII, 180, *Skald* II, 94; Sveinbjörn Egilsson 1844, 56, Rydberg 1907, 3-4, 46, Attwood 1996a, 59-60, 155.

Notes: [All]: In B, *Heildr* breaks off at the first l. of the *stef* previously cited in st. 2. The rest of the poem, which must have included the remainder of the *stefjabálkr* and the *slœmr*, or conclusion, is not present, and the scribe goes on immediately, at fol. 10r, l. 39, to the beginning of *Leið*.

- Number of stanza in a poem or group of stanzas

- Text of stanza: the second *helmingr* is placed next to the first in skaldic metres; italics indicate emended/conjectured text not found in any manuscript (not shown here) and an asterisk indicates that text has been removed (not shown here)

- Stanza text rearranged in prose order

- Translation of stanza; kennings are translated literally and *heiti* comprising personal names are glossed in angle brackets (e.g. Mist <valkyrie>; not shown here)

- Kenning referents, listed from innermost kenning to outermost kenning

- List of manuscripts in which the stanza occurs, followed by the folio or page on which it is recorded; the main manuscript is in bold; manuscripts are grouped by prose work where relevant (here, *Snorra Edda*)

- Readings from manuscripts which differ from the main text (may run on from the list of manuscripts); readings are grouped by line (in square brackets) and the word or words in the main text which have variants

- Categorisation and number of the stanza in Finnur Jónsson's *Skjaldedigtning*, followed by other editions of the stanza with page references; editions are grouped by prose work where relevant

- Description of the prose context in which the stanza occurs, where relevant

- Notes to the stanza (normally starting on a new line); line number(s) are given in square brackets followed by the word or words to be discussed